Greek Islands

Paul Hellander,
Kate Armstrong, Michael Clark, Chris Deliso, Des Hannigan,
Victoria Kyriakopoulos

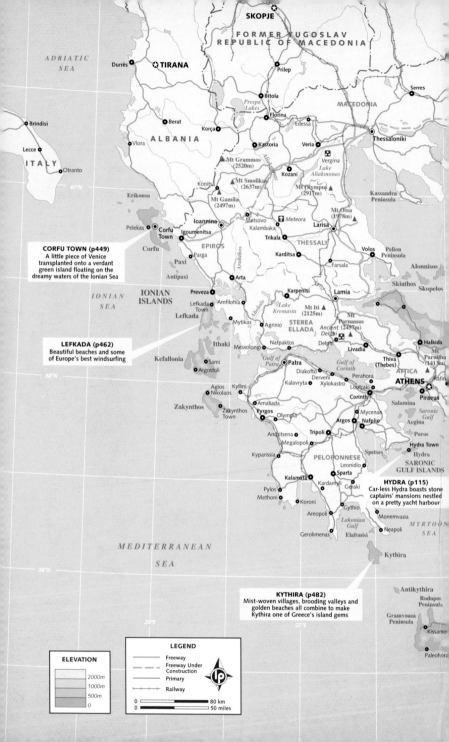

SKOPJE

FORMER YUGOSLAV
REPUBLIC OF MACEDONIA

*ADRIATIC
SEA*

Durrës

TIRANA

Brindisi

Lecce

ITALY

Otranto

Berat

Vlora

ALBANIA

Korça

Konitsa

Mt Grammos
(2520m)

Mt Smolikas
(2637m)

Mt Gamila
(2497m)

Erikousa

Pelekas

Corfu
Town

Corfu

Ioannina

Igoumenitsa

EPIROS

Paxi

Parga

Antipaxi

Metsovo

Kalambaka

Trikala

Prilep

Bitola

Florina

*Prespa
Lakes*

Edessa

Kastoria

Veria

Kozani

Vergina

*Lake
Aliakmonas*

Mt Olympus
(2911m)

MACEDONIA

Serres

Thessaloniki

Kassandra
Peninsula

Mt Ossa
(1978m)

Meteora

Larisa

THESSALY

Volos

Pelion
Peninsula

Alonnisos

Skiathos

Skopelos

CORFU TOWN (p449)
A little piece of Venice
transplanted onto a verdant
green island floating on the
dreamy waters of the Ionian Sea

Corfu

*IONIAN
SEA*

**IONIAN
ISLANDS**

Lefkada

LEFKADA (p462)
Beautiful beaches and some
of Europe's best windsurfing

Kefallonia

Ithaki

Sami

Argostoli

Preveza

Lefkada
Town

Mytikas

Amfilohia

Agrinio

Messolongi

Nafpaktos

Arta

Karpenisi

*Lake
Kremasta*

Mt Iti
(2125m)

Lamia

Mt
Parnassos
(2457m)

**STEREA
ELLADA**

Ancient
Delphi

Delphi

Livadia

Thiva
(Thebes)

Halkida

Mt
Parnitha
(1413m)

ATTICA

ATHENS

Rafina

Zakynthos

Agios
Nikolaos

Kyllini

Zakynthos
Town

Amaliada

Pyrgos

Olympia

Andritsena

Megalopoli

Kyparissia

Kalamata

Pylos

Methoni

Koroni

Areopoli

Gerolimenas

Diakofto

Derveni

Patra

*Gulf of
Patra*

*Gulf of
Corinth*

Perahora

Xylokastro

Loutraki

Corinth

Kalavryta

Tripoli

Argos

Mycenae

Nafplio

PELOPONNESE

Leonidio

Sparta

Kardamyli

Geraki

Gythio

*Lakonian
Gulf*

Elafonisi

Monemvasia

Neapoli

Kythira

Piraeus

Salamina

*Saronic
Gulf*

Aegina

Poros

Hydra Town

Hydra

**SARONIC
GULF ISLANDS**

Spetses

HYDRA (p115)
Car-less Hydra boasts stone
captains' mansions nestled
on a pretty yacht harbour

*MYRTOON
SEA*

KYTHIRA (p482)
Mist-woven villages, brooding valleys and
golden beaches all combine to make
Kythira one of Greece's island gems

*MEDITERRANEAN
SEA*

Antikythira

Rodopos
Peninsula

Gramvousa
Peninsula

Kissamo

Paleohora

LEGEND

Freeway

Freeway Under
Construction

Primary

Railway

ELEVATION

2000m

1000m

500m

0

0   80 km

0   50 miles

40°N

38°N

36°N

20°E

22°E

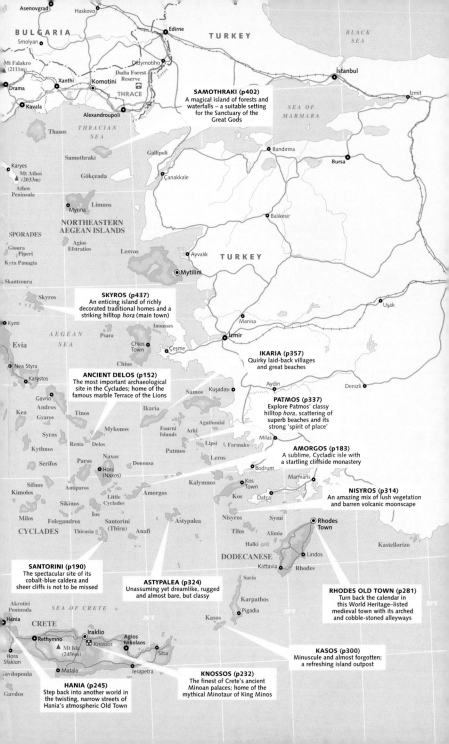

SAMOTHRAKI (p402)
A magical island of forests and waterfalls – a suitable setting for the Sanctuary of the Great Gods

SKYROS (p437)
An enticing island of richly decorated traditional homes and a striking hilltop *hora* (main town)

ANCIENT DELOS (p152)
The most important archaeological site in the Cyclades; home of the famous marble Terrace of the Lions

IKARIA (p357)
Quirky laid-back villages and great beaches

PATMOS (p337)
Explore Patmos' classy hilltop *hora*, scattering of superb beaches and its strong 'spirit of place'

AMORGOS (p183)
A sublime, Cycladic isle with a startling cliffside monastery

NISYROS (p314)
An amazing mix of lush vegetation and barren volcanic moonscape

SANTORINI (p190)
The spectacular site of its cobalt-blue caldera and sheer cliffs is not to be missed

ASTYPALEA (p324)
Unassuming yet dreamlike, rugged and almost bare, but classy

RHODES OLD TOWN (p281)
Turn back the calendar in this World Heritage–listed medieval town with its arched and cobble-stoned alleyways

KASOS (p300)
Minuscule and almost forgotten; a refreshing island outpost

HANIA (p245)
Step back into another world in the twisting, narrow streets of Hania's atmospheric Old Town

KNOSSOS (p232)
The finest of Crete's ancient Minoan palaces; home of the mythical Minotaur of King Minos

On the Road

PAUL HELLANDER

When I got to Leros (p334) and saw this wild-looking *gourouna* (sow) I just had to have it. It's a 50cc fun bike with fat tyres and lots of attitude. It was perfect to get around the lanes of Leros with all my gear. I have never had so much fun collecting information.

KATE ARMSTRONG

I'm in my favourite *kafeneio* (coffee house) in Greece, Kafeneio Burnaos (p461) on Paxi (p459). I was sitting next to a group of older local men who gather each afternoon to play cards and backgammon. The *kafeneio* hasn't changed since it opened in 1957 – the backgammon set and jars date from this time.

MICHAEL CLARK

Many of the bays on the west coast of Skiathos (p422) are perfect for snorkelling or a long morning swim. Of course, this part of the Aegean is subject to subtle tide and temperature changes. Clearly, someone had to test the water.

DES HANNIGAN
Glass of wine, hard copy, palmtop, foldaway keyboard and sun hat (though not necessarily in that order); I get my priorities right while catching up with the gruelling work of keying in the beta on rooftop Mykonos (p141). It rarely gets tougher than this…

CHRIS DELISO
The master sea-urchin hunter in Mesta (p382) was handier with the hoe than I, but nonetheless, I enjoyed a successful dive along the rocks in search of breakfast in beautiful southwestern Chios.

VICTORIA KYRIAKOPOULOS
My last days on the road in southwestern Crete, I drove south through the mountains to Sougia (p256). It's refreshingly undeveloped, the sea is clear, the long, pebble beach isn't overrun by umbrellas and loungers, and there are a couple of friendly tavernas and relaxed open-air clubs if you ever tire of staring at the stars.

See author bios p528

Greek Islands Highlights

From raucous parties to blissfully silent beaches, the Greek archipelago offers a huge diversity of experiences. Tiny, off-the-beaten-track islets, awe-inspiring ancient ruins, fresh local flavours, and simply the journey around the Aegean are some of our authors', staff and travellers' highlights. Share your own Greek islands highlights with us at lonelyplanet.com/bluelist.

IML IMAGE GROUP LTD / AL

1 MYRTOS, KEFALLONIA

Simply collapsing in the waves at the beach at Myrtos (p472).

Marina Kosmatos, Lonely Planet Oakland

SCOOTING ALL OVER SAMOS

Hiring a moped was a great way of getting around the villages of Samos (p366). We cruised from Vathy past the beach at Kokkari and then headed into the hills. We took a 'short cut' from the mountain village of Vourliotes to Manolates. It turned out to not be a short cut, and there were points where we had to climb off and push the moped up the unpaved road, but we got some great views across the countryside and saw a side of the island that we wouldn't have if we'd stayed on the main road.

Will Gourlay, Lonely Planet London

BLPHOTO / ALAMY

IOS

Ios (p186); early season; empty beaches. I called on an old friend, Petros Bournelis. He and his brother, Yiannis, were on the beach painting their little caïque. Petros threw a beer and a paintbrush at me. Greek poster colours – red, blue and yellow. This was so much better than working. The brothers run a great little hotel and taverna. 'Come out in the summer,' Petros said, 'Take the boat. We'll run the taverna. You catch the fish.' Just for one great big Greek moment, I nearly signed up...

Des Hannigan, Lonely Planet author

ANDRE JENNY / ALAMY

4 KNOSSOS

Exploring the stunning remains of the Palace of Knossos (p232) on Crete with my brother was my favourite experience in Greece. We picked our way through the ruins while we carried on a suitably philosophical discussion about people and time.

Fayette Fox, Lonely Planet London

5 ATHENS

Watching the sky turn pink over Athens (p71) in the late afternoon, the city mellows, the cafés over-flow, the Acropolis (p75) and ancient temples light up. On balmy summer nights, everyone seems to be out – the city comes alive, the atmosphere is relaxed and tinged with a sweet sense of anticipation. In Athens, you feel part of a living, human city.

Victoria Kyriakopoulos, Lonely Planet author

GREEK FERRIES

I never have epiphanies on Greek islands. No swooning over Santorini (Thira; p190) sunsets; no navel-gazing on deserted beaches. But I love hopping off ferries. All that rattle and crash of loosened anchors and the churn of big water under big props grinding astern. All those locals and fellow travellers amassed behind the ramp as it slowly descends into a burst of brilliant light to reveal yet another island quay, mirroring the same human excitement and anticipation. The lines snake ashore; the ramp clangs and grinds onto the quay. And then the two-way rush begins. Hello Syros (p135), Mykonos (p141), Paros (p152), Amorgos (p183), Folegandros (p203). Here we are again...

Des Hannigan, Lonely Planet author

IZZET KERIBAR

SARONIKOS FERRIES

SARONIKOS FERRIES

FILOXENIA

Ela! Come! An elderly man motions me to sit down. Eat! An old, chipped plate is put before me on which glistens *glyko tou koutaliou* (fruits poached in a thick syrup). This kind gesture – *filoxenia* (hospitality; see p39) – is integral to the Greek experience. The day continues with gifts from strangers: a handful of olives, chunks of freshly baked cake, steaming *spanakopita* (spinach pie). With my limited local lingo I struggle to chat, but gratefully consume their offerings. Love of Greek food is our common language; for the givers, this is thanks enough.

Kate Armstrong, Lonely Planet author

ALIKI SAPOUNTZI / ALIKI IMAGE LIBRARY / ALAMY

GEORGE TSAFOS

8 KASOS

There's a timeless almost unearthly feel to the south coast of Kasos (p300). Perhaps it's the silence, or maybe the dancing clouds as they scud across the rocky peaks of the island's ridge, or perhaps the occasional call of a circling hawk. Standing alone in the courtyard of Moni Agiou Mamma (p303) I can almost believe I am the only person in the world. Gazing out over the glistening Aegean that leads to Africa, I know I am at the end of Europe.

Paul Hellander, Lonely Planet author

COLINSPICS / A

9 SIPPING OUZO BESIDE THE HARBOUR AT MOLYVOS, LESVOS

Lesvos (Mytilini, p386) is one of the more traditional of the Greek islands. One of the highlights is sitting in the picturesque harbour of Molyvos (Mithymna, p392), dominated by the fortress above, at sunset tasting one of the many varieties of ouzo the island produces.

Frances J Summers, Bluelist contributor

SAMOTHRAKI

After exploring the winding stone streets of Hora (p404), the colourful mountain-side capital of Samothraki (p402) on that hot July afternoon, the peerless café's lemonade sweetened with honey and flecked with cinnamon was the most refreshing thing you could possibly imagine – a taste as fleeting and as fair as summer itself.

Chris Deliso, Lonely Planet author

10

TERRY HARRIS JUST GREECE PHOTO LIBRARY / ALAMY

CHRIS CHRISTO

11 **UNWINDING AT PREVELI BEACH**

Preveli Beach (p243) is a jewel: the palm tree–lined river valley offers one sparkling pool spilling into another, then another. There is something ancient and bewitching about the place, especially at night.

Steve Slattery, Lonely Planet Oakland

12 HEDONISM ON MYKONOS

The night on Mykonos (p141) always started with cocktails as we watched the sun set into the ocean. Then we'd make our way to one of the many bars in town for a bottle or two of Mythos, the local beer. The narrow, cobbled streets meant you sometimes lost your way, but all roads inevitably lead back to Pierro's (p148), for drag shows and dancing til the sun came back up.

James Taylor, traveller

13 RHODES

The real highlight of my visit to Rhodes (p276) was renting a jeep and heading out across the island. In little villages, old dames whipped up mouth-watering, traditional Greek salads and brewed coffee so strong you could stand a spoon in it. One restaurant proprietor (along with the clientele and locals hanging out around the doorway) directed us to quiet, sublime beaches and trailheads that allowed us to strut out across the arid interior. We felt like we'd experienced the 'real' Rhodes.

Korina Miller, Lonely Planet London

Contents

Regional Map Contents

Athens & the Mainland Ports p70

Northeastern Aegean Islands p358

Ionian Islands p444

Evia & the Sporades p416

Saronic Gulf Islands p107

Dodecanese p275

Cyclades p125

Crete pp222–3

Destination Greek Islands

The Greek islands are simply about location, location, location. There is no other island archipelago in the world quite like them. Imagine a compact geographical domain consisting of over 1400 islands and islets of which only 169 support a population. Most are within an hour's or less sail to the next one, and you can sometimes see another island or two from the one you're standing on. On some islands a vista of scattered rock and sky in a 360-degree circle dazzles visitors. It is simply magic. Not even Disney could have invented such a world.

Where you end up can be a matter of luck, convenience or deliberate planning. There is no argument over the majestic beauty of Santorini or the nightlife and beaches of hedonistic Mykonos. But if you want something a little more sedate or child-friendly you will find it. There is walking-a-plenty on all the islands, and for water babies a plethora of activities await including windsurfing and kitesurfing, or just plain lazing by azure waters. There is a great diversity of beaches, from sand and pebbles to rocks and even volcanic lava. You can sleep in a stone hut with a slate roof or a three-bedroom studio with Jacuzzi and pool. Eat bread, olives and crumbly cheese on a mountainside, or dine on oysters and caviar next to a plush yacht harbour. If you can't relax in the Greek islands, we'd suggest therapy.

The beauty about the islands is that no two are totally alike, yet they are inexorably bound by a shared history and culture that stretches back into the mists of time. For rugged individualism, hiking and a hospitality that is unparalleled, Crete is big in size and in heart. The wistful and languid Dodecanese are strung like a chain of emeralds beguilingly close to the Turkish mainland and proudly bear a personality that is distinct as it is unique. The northern Aegean is home to a cluster of islands, some havens for holidaymakers, others inhabited by birds and poets. The Cyclades are the jewel in an already dazzling crown.

The prosperity and insouciance apparent on the Greek islands though is a relatively new development. In the past many islanders forsook their homes as a result of diminishing returns from dying industries: wooden ship-building, sponge-fishing, even fishing itself. They left for the USA, Australia, and Europe; many resignedly relocated to the mainland leaving behind abandoned homes and fields.

Cruise ships in the 60s kicked off the turnaround – they brought well-heeled landlubbers to gaze upon some stunningly beautiful islands. Hippies and proto-island hoppers followed in the late 60s and 70s and set up camp on beaches and in caves. Mykonos and Matala were the buzzwords of the time. The trend continued through the 80s and 90s as charter jets began to bring northern Europeans who could vacation on a Greek island cheaper than at home. The renaissance was well under way. With Greece's accession to the EU in the early 80s, foreigners, too, began to be able to buy their stake in the Ionian and Aegean Seas sun at a fraction of the price that it would cost in their own country.

The islands have undoubtedly morphed in recent times from marginal agricultural land to prime real estate – and with a view at that. The influence of foreign residents has on the one hand driven up prices of land, yet on the other hand has upped the ante. Isolated, water short and transport restricted at the best of times, the Greek islands can be a challenge for the long-term investor, yet a boon for the short-term visitor seeking a unique experience.

FAST FACTS

Population: 10,706,290

Percentage of women: 50.5%

Tourists: 14.4 million annually

Number of inhabited Greek islands: 169

Smallest inhabited Greek island: Strongyli (9 inhabitants)

GDP: US$256.3 billion

Per capita income: US$26,920

Inflation: 3.3%

Unemployment: 9.6%

Number of islands with airports: 25

In the long hot summer of 2007 mainland Greeks awoke to find their country alight: literally. Forest fires had broken out across the Peloponnese and Epiros while the elongated island of Evia was the only non-mainland locale to be affected. Widely believed to have been deliberately lit by unscrupulous land developers the firestorm not only had an ecological fallout, but also severely dented the reputation of the conservative government of the New Democracy party of Konstandinos Karamanlis. Such was the anger directed at the government – accused by many of idly standing by while their country burned – that in the September 2007 national elections Karamanlis was returned with a majority of only two in the 300-seat parliament. It was a wake-up call, and he knew it.

The Greek islands have no doubt their issues and problems – fragmented infrastructures, water resources and seasonal isolation to name but a few, but they are unquestionably unique in the world as a traveller's destination. The islands' popularity as a place of recreation, sport and activity is unlikely to fade in the foreseeable future. Their unique geographic position and make-up ensure their passage well into this century as one of the world's premier destinations.

Getting Started

The Greek islands are easy to hop around, with good public transport and a range of accommodation to suit every budget, from the backpacker to the five-star traveller. For some, planning involves no more than heading out and buying a ticket; for others, planning the trip is half the fun – and there is certainly no shortage of information to help them on their way.

WHEN TO GO

Spring and autumn are the best times to visit the Greek islands. Most of the tourist infrastructure goes into hibernation in winter, particularly on the smaller islands, with islanders heading off to alternative homes in Athens. Many hotels, along with cafés and restaurants, close their doors from the end of November until the beginning of April; bus and ferry services are either drastically reduced or plain cancelled.

The cobwebs are dusted off in time for Easter, when the first tourists start to arrive. Conditions are perfect between Easter and mid-June, when the weather is pleasantly warm in most places; beaches and ancient sites are relatively uncrowded; public transport operates at close to full schedules; and accommodation is cheaper and easier to find.

From mid-June to the end of August is high season. It's party time on the islands and everything is in full swing. It's hot – in July and August the mercury can soar to 40°C in the shade just about anywhere. The beaches are crowded, the ancient sites are swarming with tour groups and in many places accommodation is booked solid. The season winds down in September, and conditions are ideal once more until the end of October.

By November, the endless blue skies of summer have disappeared. November to February are the wettest months. It can get surprisingly cold. Snow is common on the mainland and in the mountains of Evia and Crete; it also occasionally snows in Athens. There are plenty of sunny days though, and some visitors prefer the tranquillity that reigns.

See Climate Charts (p490) for more information.

COSTS & MONEY

The Greek islands are no longer cheap to travel around. Prices have increased dramatically since the adoption of the euro at the beginning of 2002. It's hard to believe that inflation is less than 4%, as claimed by the government, when prices have risen by a perceptibly higher margin since that time. Some dramatic price rises, particularly for accommodation options and restaurant meals, have been evident in recent years.

A rock-bottom daily budget would be €45. This means hitching, staying in hostels or camping, and rarely eating in restaurants or taking ferries. Allow at least €90 per day if you want your own room and plan to eat out as well as see the sights. If you want comfy rooms and restaurants all the way, you will need €130 per day. These budgets are for individuals travelling in high season. Couples sharing a room can get by on less.

Your money will go further if you travel outside high season – there are fewer tourists around and you're able to negotiate better deals. Accommodation, which often eats up a large part of the daily budget, is a lot cheaper outside the high season on the islands. You will also be able to negotiate much better deals if you stay a few days. Families can achieve big savings by looking for rooms with kitchen facilities.

All prices quoted in this guidebook are for the high season (notably during July and August).

HOW MUCH?

Local telephone call €0.30 per min

Minimum taxi fare €4

Litre of milk €1.60

International Herald Tribune €2.50

Coffee €3.50-5

Soft drink (can) €1.5

Cinema ticket €8

TRAVELLING RESPONSIBLY

Let's face it, the Greek islands are a hugely popular destination. While this may be sustainable in the quieter time of the year, from June to September the islands receive an enormous influx of travellers and tourists. Although it's a bonanza for the country, this annual influx puts great strains on the infrastructure, the environment, the often fragile flora and fauna and even the Greek people themselves.

Mega-destinations like Santorini, Mykonos, Rhodes and Corfu often struggle to house and feed visitors and manage their detritus. The building of new developments often clashes with eco-minded organisations (for more information, see p314). In a similar vein, champions of fauna often fight losing battles with this relentless push for expansion (see At Loggerheads, p480).

As a potential visitor to the Greek islands, with an understanding of what issues prevail upon them, you may be able to help alleviate some of the negative side effects of mass tourism and travel.

July and August is the time of the fabled European summer mass vacation. Outside this high season the Greek islands are cheaper, accommodation is easier to find and the weather is much more bearable.

Seriously consider a bicycle. Cycling the islands can be serious fun. You'll need good gears and a stout constitution at times – those mountains can be challenging on some islands – but the land is eminently suitable for cyclists.

Local transport is nonetheless well-developed and reasonably priced. You don't really need your own motorised transport: you just need a bit more time. There are lots of hiking options (for example Crete has the challenging Trans-European E4 Trail across the whole island, or the shorter yet still challenging Samaria Gorge hike, p253), or you may care to charter a yacht (see p69) with a few friends and use wind power to propel you from island to island in much the same way that Odysseus (Ulysses) did.

A growing number of hotels choose green options. Solar heating, the recycling of waste products, the use of energy efficient light bulbs and low impact architecture using local materials are all ways in which eco-savvy hotel and *pension* owners do their bit to keep green. Seek out such sleeping options and give them your mark of approval. An entire community in Crete has done away with electricity altogether (see p245).

DON'T LEAVE HOME WITHOUT...

Most travellers carry far too much gear, filling bags and backpacks with things that will never see the light of day. It's best to bring only the essentials; you can buy anything else you might need on the Greek islands. The essentials are:

- Sturdy shoes – ancient sites and historic towns and villages have rocky paths
- A shady hat and sunblock – indispensable in Greece's hot climate
- Your international driving licence – you can't drive without it
- Your mobile phone – buy a local SIM card and keep in touch with family and friends
- A few paperback novels – while away the hours spent riding ferries
- A mask, snorkel and flippers – the island water is so clear for snorkelling
- Your iPod – carry your photos of home and favourite music and video clips
- An inflatable neck pillow and sunglasses – for those long bus and ferry trips
- Lonely Planet's *Greek* phrasebook – talk like the locals

TOP 10

GREEK ISLANDS

Ionian Sea · Sea of Crete · Rhodes

Best Sights

With over 75 islands to choose from it's always going to be a hard task to decide what to visit and see. Every island has some attraction, but here is a list of the sights that Lonely Planet authors subjectively think are worthwhile heading out of your way to go and enjoy.

1 Moni Hozoviotissis (p185), Amorgos, Cyclades

2 Venetian streets (p449), Corfu, Ionian Islands

3 Samaria Gorge (p253), Crete

4 Cycladic architecture (p141), Mykonos, Cyclades

5 Rhodes' Old Town (p279), Rhodes, Dodecanese

6 Stone and slate villages (p357), Ikaria, Northeastern Aegean Islands

7 Caldera of Santorini (p190), Santorini (Thira), Cyclades

8 Crater of the Nisyros volcano (p316), Nisyros, Dodecanese

9 Hora of Patmos (p340), Patmos, Dodecanese

10 Traditionally furnished houses (p438), Skyros, Sporades

Must-See Movies

Pre-departure planning is definitely best done in a comfy lounge chair with a bowl of popcorn in one hand and a remote in the other. Head down to your local video store to pick up these flicks, from the best-known Greek films to the very cheesiest. For more information on Greek cinema see p49.

1 *A Touch of Spice* (2003) directed by Tasos Boulmetis

2 *My Big Fat Greek Wedding* (2002) directed by Joel Zwick

3 *Nyfes* (2004) directed by Pandelis Voulgaris

4 *Zorba the Greek* (1964) directed by Mihalis Cacoyannis

5 *Never on Sunday* (1960) directed by Jules Dassin

6 *Z* (1969) directed by Costa Gavras

7 *Eleni* (1985) directed by Peter Yates

8 *Eternity and a Day* (1998) directed by Theo Angelopoulos

9 *For Your Eyes Only* (1981) directed by John Glen

10 *Shirley Valentine* (1989) directed by Lewis Gilbert

Festivals & Events

Greeks love to celebrate, and there's almost always something, somewhere, that's worth the effort of having a celebration. The following list is our top 10 festivals and events in the Greek islands, but for a comprehensive list of all the main festivals and events throughout the year, go to p493.

1 Skyros Carnival (p440), Skyros, Sporades, February to March

2 Easter (p493), everywhere, March to April

3 Miaoulia Festival (p118), Hydra, Saronic Gulf Islands, June

4 Summer Arts Festival (p228), Iraklio, Crete, 23 June to 23 September

5 Folegandros Festival (p205), Folegandros, Cyclades, July

6 Milos Festival (p208), Milos, Cyclades, July

7 Santorini Jazz Festival (p198), Santorini, Cyclades, July

8 Renaissance Festival (p239), Rethymno, Crete, July to September

9 Diving Festival (p332), Kalymnos, Dodecanese, August

10 Panagia tou Harou (p352), Lipsi, Dodecanese, 24 August

'Organic' is a buzzword in the Greek islands, too. Greece has one of the healthiest dietary regimes around; couple that with local organic products and you are onto a culinary winner. Consider choosing your restaurants on the basis of their locally grown food products – and *tell* the owners – they will all get the message in good time. When you're thirsty, don't cart one of those dastardly plastic water bottles with you. Who will ultimately dispose if it? Drink from a water fountain or from a tap. (Although the water in Greece is generally fine, many islands have questionable, limited or no water supply, so it is best to check with the locals once you're there.) For more details on environmental issues, see p64.

Shop sensibly, too: look at labels and buy only locally made products. Don't just make a beeline for the most popular spots: everyone else will be doing the same thing. Select your destination with some inventiveness. You'll probably have a better time.

Above all, exercise common sense. Set the precedent yourself and travel responsibly, yet comfortably. It's not hard. The Greek islands and their people will be all the better off for it, and so will you.

TRAVEL LITERATURE

Travel writers can be a great source of inspiration for those planning to follow in their footsteps.

A Traveller's History of Athens (Richard Stoneman) A lively and compact look into Athens' complex and multifarious past.

Stars over Paxos (John Gill) Live the island life of a small Ionian island community through the seasons. It's a story with gossip, intrigue and social observations written with passion and insight.

Falling for Icarus: A Journey Among the Cretans (Rory MacLean) A light yet fascinating tale of a man obsessed with building an aeroplane on Crete.

My Family and Other Animals (Lawrence Durrell) Durrell offers an hilarious account of his family's chaotic and wonderful life on Corfu.

Prospero's Cell (Lawrence Durrell) This classic collection of tales records brother Laurence's experience on Corfu in the 1920s. Worth reading for the fire-engine story alone!

The Summer of My Greek Taverna (Tom Stone) Imagine yourself the owner of a Greek taverna on a rocky island then read how one American did it. Based on Patmos, this relaxed tale has a few twists and turns.

The Greek Islands (Lawrence Durrell) This coffee-table collection of stunning photos is one of the most popular books of its kind.

Still Life in Crete (Anthony Cox) Ever fancied migrating to a Greek island? Follow the exploits of an Englishman and his family as they struggle with the complexities of setting up home on Crete in this folksy, homespun tale.

INTERNET RESOURCES

There are a huge number of websites providing information about Greece and its islands.

Culture Guide (www.cultureguide.gr) Lots of information about contemporary culture and the arts.

Greek Ferries (www.greekferries.gr) One-stop site with access to all the latest international and domestic ferry information.

Greek National Tourist Organisation (www.gnto.gr) For concise tourist information.

Greek Search Engine (www.in.gr) The best starting point for those browsing the web.

Lonely Planet (www.lonelyplanet.com) Has postcards from other travellers and the Thorn Tree bulletin board, where you can ask questions before you go, or dispense advice when you get back.

Ministry of Culture (www.culture.gr) Information about ancient sites, art galleries and museums.

Itineraries

ISLAND-HOPPING

ONE WEEK TO SPARE
One Week / Piraeus to Spetses

You don't need to travel far from Athens to sample island life. This compact itinerary will allow you to sample several islands without straying too far from **Eleftherios Venizelos International Airport** (p83) for your flight home. First up take a local ferry from **Piraeus** (p87) to **Aegina** (p107), the Athenians' island playground. See the striking Temple of Aphaia and dine on fresh fish in the busy harbour. Detour to minuscule and cosy **Angistri** (p111) for a lazy day of swimming then head south for the mainland-hugging island of **Poros** (p112) where good water-skiing can be enjoyed. If you don't like cars, you'll love classy **Hydra** (p115) with its harbour for yachts and streets for donkeys and pedestrians. Painters love to hang out here, too. A final hop will take you across to the languid island of **Spetses** (p119), which is encircled by a serpentine road that guides you to quiet, pine-shaded beaches. Watch the sun go down over an ouzo on ice then enjoy the island's classy, yet refined nightlife before hopping on a fast ferry back to Piraeus.

This relaxed and close to home-port 130km-long trip is easily undertaken by visitors on a quick week's getaway from work. All islands are well connected and enjoy high standards of accommodation and dining.

THE CYCLADES

Two Weeks / Syros to Serifos

From Athens head first to **Syros** (p135) and spend a couple of days exploring its graceful capital, **Ermoupolis** (p137), once the busiest and largest port in the Aegean. The next port of call is **Mykonos** (p141), from where you can make the short excursion across to the island of **Delos** (p150) with its impressive antiquities. You can recover on **Naxos** (p161), the greenest and most fertile of the Cyclades and a great place for walkers.

If time permits, take a detour for a couple of days to either **Koufonisia** (p172) or **Schinousa** (p172), Greece's island outback where the tone is decidedly low-key, otherwise head straight on to spectacular **Santorini** (Thira; p190). Its white cubic, cliff-top houses defy gravity, while sunset from the village of Oia is perhaps the best in the Aegean Sea; divers can check out the activities of the new volcano that is developing underwater.

The journey back north starts with friendly **Folegandros** (p203), followed by **Milos** (p206), an underrated island that is often overlooked despite a wealth of attractions that range from its superior beaches to its unique Christian catacombs. The final port of call before returning to Athens is **Serifos** (p213), home to arguably the finest of all the Cycladic capitals.

For a classic Greek island-hopping holiday you can't do better than this looping 580km-long route around a cross-section of the most archetypically Aegean islands. Match glitter and splendour with coyness and history on this great trip.

NORTH TO SOUTH

Two Weeks / Thessaloniki to Crete

This unusual itinerary takes advantage of a weekly north-south link that binds the northern capital of **Thessaloniki** (p91) with the southern Cretan city of **Iraklio** (p224). Set off on your voyage with a summer hydrofoil to pine-scented and sand-fringed **Skiathos** (p422) in the Sporades. Unwind before taking the big weekly ferry south to **Syros** (p135), the main island of the Cyclades, which enjoys a deserved reputation as a cultured and busy island community. From the Cyclades' heartland now cut across to ebullient and traveller-friendly **Paros** (p152) – a good-sized island with a low-key atmosphere, but high quality lifestyle and abundant sandy beaches. Take your pick of ferry links to glitzy and spectacular **Santorini** (Thira; p190) where you can clamber on smouldering volcanic islets, shop 'til you drop or contemplate ouzo-enhanced sunsets. If you time it right, take the next north-south Thessaloniki-Iraklio ferry or, if you are in a hurry, slide across to Crete in style on a sleek catamaran that terminates in **Iraklio** (p224), the busy yet culture-endowed capital of the nation's largest island.

Fancy something really unusual and whacky? Go where few have ever thought to travel and traverse 685km of the Aegean from top to bottom. Start in the country's vibrant northern capital and end up on the buzzing mega-island of the south.

IONIAN EXPERIENCE   Two Weeks / Corfu to Zakynthos

Start with a few days on **Corfu** (p446) exploring the sights of the old town and savouring the island's distinctive cuisine. Include a day trip over to the west-coast resort of **Paleokastritsa** (p456), lingering long enough to enjoy the sunset. Next up is tiny **Paxi** (p459), where visitors can explore a lost world of ancient, gnarled olive groves and derelict farmhouses. In the absence of ferry connections, you'll need to return to Corfu to move on to the next island south, **Lefkada** (p462).

The beaches of the west coast are the finest beaches in the Ionians, while **Vasiliki Bay** (p466), in the south, is renowned as a prime windsurfing spot. It's also the departure point for ferries to **Kefallonia** (p467), which arrive at the charming port of **Fiskardo** (p472), the only Kefallonian town not devastated by the great earthquake of 1953. Hop across from Fiskardo to **Ithaki** (p473) and spend a couple of days exploring the homeland of Homer's Odysseus, and then return to Kefallonia.

Call in at the stunning west-coast village of **Assos** (p472) and magic beach of **Myrtos** (p272) on the journey south to Kefallonia's lively capital, **Argostoli** (p469), for connections to the final island in the group, **Zakynthos** (p476) – via the ports of Pesada (Kefallonia) and Agios Nikolaos (Zakynthos). Known to the Venetians as the 'Flower of the Orient', the island's capital, **Zakynthos Town** (p478), boasts some fine examples of Venetian and neoclassical architecture.

Done the Aegean and want to see the west? This 355km-long north–south route can be done just as easily south to north. See the best of the Ionians and their Italian-influenced culture. Mix Captain Corelli and Odysseus on this easy, island-hopping cruise.

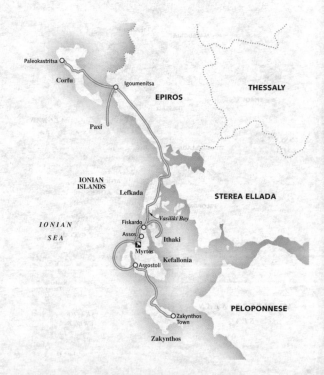

THE EASTERN ISLAND RUN   Three Weeks / Rhodes to Alexandroupoli

You'll need to spend a few days on **Rhodes** (p276), exploring the old city and visiting the **Acropolis of Lindos** (p288), before setting sail for **Tilos** (p310). Laid-back Tilos is a great place for walkers and one of the few islands in the Dodecanese to have escaped the ravages of development.

The next stop is **Nisyros** (p314), where the eruptions of Mt Polyvotis have created a bizarre volcanic landscape. You'll need to call briefly at **Kos** (p317) to pick up a ferry onward to **Patmos** (p337), an island that St John found sufficiently inspiring to pen his *Book of Revelations*. Patmos has good connections to ultra laid-back **Ikaria** (p357), where you can laze on some of the Aegean's best beaches before continuing to **Chios** (p375) and the fabulous villages of the island's south.

The next stop is **Lesvos** (Mytilini; p386), birthplace of the poet Sappho, and producer of Greece's finest olive oil and ouzo. **Limnos** (p398) is little more than a transit point on the journey north to **Samothraki** (p402) and the superbly named **Sanctuary of the Great Gods** (p405).

The final leg is to the Thracian port of **Alexandroupoli** (p103), where travellers will find several good transport connections to Athens and Thessaloniki.

Start this 735km-long trip in the busy resort island of Rhodes and work your way northwards through languid coastal islands. Take a slow boat and don't worry about the days. This longish trip can be undertaken with a mixture of slow boats, hydrofoils and catamarans.

THE GRAND TOUR

One Month / Athens to Kythira

From **Athens** (p71), head first to spectacular **Santorini** (Thira; p190), whose capital **Fira** (p193) perches precariously atop the sheer walls of a volcanic caldera created by one of the greatest eruptions ever recorded. Next up is fertile **Naxos** (p161), famous for its crops and fine wines, followed by party island **Mykonos** (p141), favoured by backpackers and socialites alike. Be sure to take a day trip to visit the temples and sanctuaries of sacred **Delos** (p150) before moving on to laid-back **Ikaria** (p357) – where Icarus crash-landed after he flew too close to the sun.

Next up is **Samos** (p366), where the unspoiled villages of the interior offer lots of opportunities for walkers. **Kos** (p317) need be no more than a stopover en route to **Rhodes Town** (p279), the amazing fortress city built by the Knights of St John.

The journey west from Rhodes offers the possibilities of stops at either **Karpathos** (p294) or **Kasos** (p300) on the way to the Cretan port of **Sitia** (p267). Travel along Crete's northern coast to **Iraklio** (p224) and **Knossos** (p232), the ancient capital of Minoan Crete, before moving west to the pretty twin ports of **Rethymno** (p236) and **Hania** (p245) with their harbourside restaurants and buzzing bars. The exit point from Crete is the northwestern port of **Kissamos** (p259) to **Kythira** (p482). From Kythira, there's a choice of catching a ferry or flight back to Athens, or travelling back through the Peloponnese.

With time on your hands and the Aegean as your horizon get into some serious island-hopping on this month-long (and 1350km-long) dawdle around the periphery of Greece's world of water and rock. Making use of scheduled ferries, this is a good trip if you want variety and the odd challenge.

TAILORED TRIPS

ISLAND-HOPPING WITH KIDS

Here are some ideas of places in the Greek islands that kids might enjoy.

Kids' imagination can run wild in the **Palace of Knossos** (p232) on Crete, a real palace with underground rooms and chambers. For beaches, try Koukounaries Beach on **Skiathos** (p422), where there are lots of trees, soft sand and gently sloping water; or Liendou Beach on **Lipsi** (p353), which has a little less shade, but very gentle sloping sand and shallow water. Boat trips are great fun and most islands will offer some kind of 'round the island' excursion. The trip round **Milos** (p206) is fun especially as it stops off at a few beaches for swimming and for lunch on neighbouring **Kimolos** (p210). Cycling might be one distraction that will keep more able children occupied and exercised. The picturesque and flat northern coastal road of **Kos** (p317) is fine for family riding and this activity can always be broken with a beach swim. Small islands lend themselves to walking and **Paxi** (p459) has lofts of leafy and shaded lanes and paths through olive groves that kids will enjoy. Finally, fast boat rides on catamarans are more fun than slow, boring rides on chug-a-lug old ferries. Getting around the **Cyclades** (p124) can be done almost exclusively on fun craft. The kids will have a happier time overall. You will be smiling, too.

WALK ON THE WILD SIDE

The islands offer wonderful opportunities for walkers. The best time to go is in spring (especially April and May) when the weather is pleasantly warm and wildflowers transform the countryside into a riot of colour.

Batsi (p128), on Andros, is an ideal base for exploring the countryside along ancient cobbled paths. **Naxos** (p161), the largest of the Cyclades, has a mountainous interior, especially the **Tragaea** (p167) region, that is a favourite walking destination.

The coastal resorts of **Samos** (p366) may be a tour-group fave, but the interior villages remain unspoiled. Travel through the Dodecanese to volcanic **Nisyros** (p314), where you can marvel at the landscape created by the eruptions from the crater **Polyvotis** (p316). Stop at **Tilos** (p310) for its picturesque **Potami Gorge** (p312), or **Symi** (p306) where you can pick up an excellent walking guide locally and criss-cross the islands' pine-covered hinterland on foot. Cross over to **Rhodes** (p291) and hike to the Mt Attavyros summit for the best views in the southern Aegean. Greece's most southerly island, **Crete** (p220) has many possibilities, starting with **Samaria Gorge** (p253), one of many excellent treks.

History

The Greek islands were the birthplace of two of Europe's earliest civilisations, the Cycladic and the Minoan.

Both can be traced to the introduction of Bronze Age smelting techniques in about 3000 BC by settlers from Phoenicia. The Cyclades were the first to blossom. The Cycladic civilisation is divided into three periods: Early (3000–2000 BC), Middle (2000–1500 BC) and Late (1500–1100 BC). The most impressive legacy of this civilisation is the statuettes carved from Parian marble – the famous Cycladic figurines. The finest were produced in the Early Cycladic period. Like statuettes from Neolithic times, they depicted images of the Great Mother (the earth goddess).

The people of the Cycladic civilisation were also accomplished sailors who developed prosperous maritime trade links. They exported their wares to Asia Minor, Europe and North Africa, as well as to Crete and continental Greece. The Minoans, named after the mythical King Minos, drew their inspiration from two great Middle Eastern civilisations: the Mesopotamian and the Egyptian. The civilisation reached its peak in the period between 2100 and 1500 BC.

The famous palaces at Knossos, Phaestos, Malia and Zakros were built at this time. They were destroyed by a violent earthquake in about 1700 BC, but were rebuilt to a more complex, almost labyrinthine architectural style. The interiors were decorated with the celebrated Minoan frescoes, now on display in the archaeological museum of Iraklio (p226).

After 1500 BC the civilisation began to decline, both commercially and militarily, against Mycenaean competition from the mainland. The Minoan civilisation came to an abrupt end around 1100 BC during a period of major upheaval throughout the eastern Mediterranean.

Some historians have suggested that the Minoans' demise was accelerated by the effects of the massive volcanic explosion on the Cycladic island of Santorini (Thira) in 1450 BC, an eruption vulcanologists believe was more cataclysmic than any on record.

The Mycenaeans' most impressive legacy is their magnificent gold jewellery and ornaments, the best of which can be seen in the National Archaeological Museum (p75) in Athens. The Mycenaeans wrote in what is called Linear B (an early form of Greek) and worshipped gods who were precursors of the later Greek gods.

> Greek is Europe's oldest written language, second only to Chinese in the world. It is traceable back to the Linear B script of Minoan Crete.

DORIAN GREECE

By the time life had settled down, it was the Dorians who had emerged as the new power on the Greek mainland, replacing the old order with new city-states, such as Sparta and Corinth. Thought to have arrived from northern

TIMELINE

3000 BC	3000–1100 BC	1700–1450 BC
The discovery of how to blend copper and tin into a strong alloy gives rise to the Bronze Age. Trade flourishes and increased prosperity sees the birth of the Cycladic, Minoan and Mycenaean civilisations.	For around 1900 years, two parallel civilisations, the Cycladic and the Minoan, prospered, developing sophisticated forms of manufacturing, governance and trade links.	During this period the island of Santorini erupts with a cataclysmic explosion, one of the largest volcanic events in recorded history, causing a Mediterranean-wide tsunami that probably contributed to the destruction of the Minoan civilisation.

Greece, the warlike Dorians brought a traumatic break with the past and the next 400 years are often referred to as Greece's 'dark age'. The Dorians worshipped male gods instead of fertility goddesses and adopted the Mycenaean gods of Poseidon, Zeus and Apollo, paving the way for the later Greek religious pantheon. They were also responsible for bringing the Iron Age to Greece, and for the development of a new style of pottery, decorated with striking geometrical designs.

The Dorians also spread their tentacles into the Greek islands, founding the cities of Kamiros, Ialysos and Lindos on the island of Rhodes in about 1000 BC, while Ionians fleeing to the Cyclades from the Peloponnese established a religious sanctuary on Delos.

By the 8th century BC, when Homer's *Odyssey* and *Iliad* were first written, the Greek city-states were powerful enough to start spreading their wings. Led by Athens and Corinth, which took over Corfu in 734 BC, the city-states created a Magna Graeca (Greater Greece) with southern Italy as an important component.

THE GOLDEN AGE

The next period of any historical consequence has become known as the classical (or golden) age. For Athens, it was a time of unparalleled growth and prosperity. In 477 BC it founded the Delian League, so called because the treasury was on Delos. Almost every state with a navy, including most of the Aegean islands, was forced to swear allegiance to Athens and to make an annual contribution of ships (and later money).

> 'The golden age ended with the Peloponnesian War'

When Pericles became leader of Athens in 461 BC, he moved the treasury from Delos to the Acropolis and used its contents to build the Parthenon and the other monuments of the Acropolis (p75). The golden age ended with the Peloponnesian War (431–404 BC) in which the militaristic Spartans defeated the Athenians.

So embroiled were they in this war that they failed to notice the expansion of Macedonia to the north under King Philip II, who easily conquered the war-weary city-states.

Philip's ambitions were surpassed by those of his son, Alexander the Great, who marched triumphantly into Asia Minor, Egypt, Persia and what are now parts of Afghanistan and India. After Alexander's untimely death in 323 BC at the age of 33, his generals divided his empire between themselves. The Dodecanese became part of the kingdom of Ptolemy I of Egypt, while the remainder of the Aegean islands became part of the League of Islands ruled by the Antigonids of Macedon.

ROMAN RULE & THE BYZANTINE EMPIRE

Roman incursions into Greece began in 205 BC. By 146 BC the mainland had become the Roman provinces of Greece and Macedonia. Crete fell in 67 BC, and the southern city of Gortyn became capital of the Roman province

1500–1200 BC	800–700 BC	800–650 BC
Mycenaean culture from the Peloponnese mainland usurps much of the Cretan and Cycladic cultures. Goldsmithing is a predominant feature of Mycenaean life, as is rigid authority.	Homer composes the *Iliad* and the *Odyssey* some time during this century. The two epic poems are Greece's earliest pieces of literary art and are still praised for their poetic genius.	Independent city-states begin to emerge in the so-called Archaic Age as the Dorians mature and develop. Aristocrats rule these mini-states while tyrants occasionally seize power by force. The Greek alphabet emerges from the Phoenician script.

of Cyrenaica, which included a large chunk of North Africa. Rhodes held out until AD 70.

In AD 330 Emperor Constantine chose Byzantium as the new capital of the Roman Empire and renamed the city Constantinople. After the subdivision of the Roman Empire into Eastern and Western empires in AD 395, Greece became part of the Eastern Roman Empire, leading to the illustrious Byzantine age.

'Greece became part of the Eastern Roman Empire'

In the centuries that followed, Venetians, Franks, Normans, Slavs, Persians, Arabs and, finally, Turks all took their turns to chip away at the Byzantine Empire. The Persians captured Rhodes in 620, but were replaced by the Saracens (Arabs) in 653. The Arabs also captured Crete in 824.

Other islands in the Aegean remained under Byzantine control until the sacking of Constantinople in 1204 by renegade Frankish crusaders in cahoots with Venice. The Venetians were rewarded with the Cyclades and they added Crete to their possessions in 1210.

THE CRUSADES

It is one of the ironies of history that the demise of the Byzantine Empire was accelerated not by invasions of infidels from the east, nor barbarians from the north, but by fellow Christians from the west – the Frankish crusaders.

The stated mission of the crusades was to liberate the Holy Land from the Muslims, but in reality they were driven as much by greed as by religious fervour. The first three crusades passed by without incident, but the leaders of the fourth crusade decided that Constantinople presented richer pickings than Jerusalem and struck a deal with Venice.

Constantinople was sacked in 1204 and much of the Byzantine Empire was partitioned into feudal states ruled by self-styled 'Latin' (mostly Frankish) princes. The Venetians, meanwhile, had also secured a foothold in Greece. Over the next few centuries they acquired all the key Greek ports, including the island of Crete, and became the wealthiest and most powerful traders in the Mediterranean.

Despite this sorry state of affairs, Byzantium was not yet dead. In 1259 the Byzantine emperor Michael VIII Palaeologos recaptured the Peloponnese and made the city of Mystras his headquarters. Michael VIII managed to reclaim Constantinople in 1261, but by this time Byzantium was a shadow of its former self.

THE OTTOMAN EMPIRE

The Byzantine Empire finally came to an end in 1453 when Constantinople fell to the Turks. Once more Greece became a battleground, this time fought over by the Turks and Venetians. Eventually, with the exception of Corfu, Greece became part of the Ottoman Empire.

Ottoman power reached its zenith under Sultan Süleyman the Magnificent (r 1520–66), who expanded the empire to the gates of Vienna. His successor

594 BC

Solon, a ruling aristocrat in Athens, introduces rules of fair play to his citizenry. His radical rule changing – in effect creating human and political rights – is believed to have been the first step to real democracy.

477 BC

Seeking security while building a de facto empire, the Athenians establish a political and military alliance called the Delian League. Many city-states and islands join the new club.

461 BC

New Athenian leader Pericles shifts power from Delos to Athens and sets about building a city with magnificent monuments using the treasury wealth of the Delian League to fund his massive works.

added Cyprus to their dominions in 1570, but his death in 1574 marked the end of serious territorial expansion.

Although they captured Crete in 1669 after a 25-year campaign and briefly threatened Vienna once more in 1683, the ineffectual sultans of the late 16th and 17th centuries saw the empire go into steady decline. They suffered a series of reversals on the battlefield, and Venice succeeded in recapturing the Peloponnese (1685–87) in a campaign that saw them advance as far as Athens.

Chaos and rebellion spread across Greece. Pirates terrorised coastal dwellers and islanders, while gangs of klephts (anti-Ottoman fugitives and brigands) roamed the mountains. There was an upsurge of opposition to Turkish rule by freedom fighters – who fought each other when they weren't fighting the Turks.

THE WAR OF INDEPENDENCE

The long-heralded War of Independence finally began on 25 March 1821, when Bishop Germanos of Patra hoisted the Greek flag at the monastery of Agia Lavra, near Patra in the Peloponnese. Fighting broke out almost simultaneously across most of Greece and the occupied islands. The fighting was savage, with atrocities committed on both sides. The islands weren't spared the horrors of war: in 1822, Turkish forces massacred 25,000 people on the island of Chios, while another 7000 died on Kasos in 1824.

Greece Before History, by Priscilla Murray and Curtis Neil Runnels, is a good introduction to Greece's earliest days.

Eventually, the Great Powers – Britain, France and Russia – intervened on the side of the Greeks, defeating the Turkish-Egyptian fleet at the Battle of Navarino in October 1827. Nafplio, in the Peloponnese, was eventually declared the first capital.

It was there that the country's first president, Ioannis Kapodistrias, a Corfiot who had been the foreign minister for Tsar Alexander I, was assassinated in 1831. Amid anarchy, the European powers stepped in again and declared that Greece should become a monarchy. In January 1833, 17-year-old Prince Otto of Bavaria was installed as king of the new nation.

King Otto (as his name became) displeased the Greek people from the start, arriving with a bunch of upper-class Bavarian cronies to whom he gave the most prestigious official posts. He moved the capital to Athens in 1834.

Patience with his rule ran out in 1843, when demonstrations in the capital, led by the War of Independence leaders, called for a constitution. Otto mustered a National Assembly, which drafted a constitution calling for parliamentary government consisting of a lower house and a senate.

By the end of the 1850s most of the original partisan leaders had been replaced by a group of university intellectuals. In 1862 they staged a bloodless revolution and deposed the king. But they weren't quite able to set their own agenda because, in 1863, Britain returned the Ionian Islands (a British protectorate since 1815) to Greece. Amid the general euphoria that followed, the British were able to push forward young Prince William of Denmark, who became King George I.

334–23 B C	1453	1814
Alexander the Great sets out to conquer the known world. Thebes was the first victim, followed by the Persians, the Egyptians and finally the peoples of today's central Asia. He dies in 323 BC.	Greece becomes a dominion of the Ottoman Turks after they seize control of Constantinople, sounding the death knell for the Byzantine Empire.	A chink in the Ottoman's armour is achieved with the establishment of a Hellenic Independence party known as the Filiki Eteria (Friendly Society). Its influence spreads throughout Greece.

His 50-year reign brought stability to the troubled country, beginning with a new constitution in 1864, which established the power of democratically elected representatives and pushed the king further towards a ceremonial role.

In 1897 there was an uprising in Crete against Turkish rule, as a consequence of which Prime Minister Theodoros Deligiannis declared a broader war on Turkey while sending help to the uprising in Crete. A Greek attempt to invade Turkey in the north proved disastrous – it was only through the intervention of the Great Powers that the Turkish army was prevented from taking Athens.

Crete was made a British protectorate in 1898, and the day-to-day government of the island was gradually handed over to the Greeks. In 1905 the president of the Cretan assembly, Eleftherios Venizelos, announced Crete's *enosis* (union) with Greece, although this was not recognised by international law until 1913. Venizelos went on to become prime minister of Greece in 1910 and was the country's leading politician until his republican sympathies brought about his downfall in 1935.

Although the Ottoman Empire was in its death throes at the beginning of the 20th century, it was still clinging onto Macedonia. It was a prize sought by the newly formed Balkan countries of Serbia and Bulgaria, as well as by Greece, leading to the Balkan Wars. The first, in 1912, pitted all three against the Turks; the second, in 1913, pitted Serbia and Greece against Bulgaria. The outcome was the Treaty of Bucharest (August 1913), which greatly expanded Greek territory by adding the southern part of Macedonia, part of Thrace, another chunk of Epiros and the Northeastern Aegean Islands, as well as recognising the union with Crete.

In March 1913, King George was assassinated by a lunatic and his son Constantine became king.

British influence in the Ionian Islands began in 1815 following the Treaty of Paris which henceforth regarded these islands as the United States of the Ionian Islands. The British greatly improved the islands' infrastructure and many British customs, such as afternoon tea, were adopted. Cricket is still played in Corfu. Greek independence put pressure on Britain to give sovereignty to the new Greek nation and in 1864 the British departed for good though they still retained the use of the port of Corfu.

'In 1905 Eleftherios Venizelos announced Crete's union with Greece'

IT'S NOT CRICKET!

Or is it? The stately British game was first played in Corfu Town (p449) on St George's Day in 1823 between the British Garrison and the Royal Navy. Locals soon adopted the game as their own and within two years had formed two sides to take on the British colonists. Today some 100 games are played annually both on the original Esplanade cricket ground and a new pitch at Kontakali Marina. With team names such as Feax, Byron, Ergatikos and Gymnastikos, it makes UK county team names look dull in comparison. So, pull up a deck chair, pour a G&T and howzat!

1821	1827–31	1833
The chink becomes a vast chasm when the movement for independence is officially launched on 25 March 1821. This is Greece's national day and is celebrated each year with much fanfare.	Ioannis Kapodistrias is appointed Prime Minister of a fledgling government with its capital in the Peloponnesian town of Nafplio. Discontent ensues and Kapodistrias is assassinated.	The powers of the Entente (Britain, France and Russia) decree that Greece should be a monarchy and dispatch Prince Otto of Bavaria to Greece to be the first appointed monarch in modern Greece.

WWI & SMYRNA

King Constantine, who was married to the sister of the German emperor, insisted that Greece remain neutral when WWI broke out in August 1914. As the war dragged on, the Allies (Britain, France and Russia) put increasing pressure on Greece to join forces with them against Germany and Turkey, and they made promises that they couldn't hope to fulfil, including offering land in Asia Minor.

Venizelos, the prime minister of Greece, favoured the Allied cause, placing him at loggerheads with the king. Tensions between the two came to a head in 1916 and Venizelos set up a rebel government, first in Crete and then in Thessaloniki, while the pressure from the Allies eventually persuaded Constantine to leave Greece in June 1917. He was replaced by his more amenable second son, Alexander.

Greek troops served with distinction on the Allied side, but when the war ended in 1918 the promised land in Asia Minor was not forthcoming. Venizelos took matters into his own hands and, with Allied acquiescence, landed troops in Smyrna (İzmir) in May 1919 under the guise of protecting the half a million Greeks living in that city (just under half its population). With a firm foothold in Asia Minor, Venizelos now planned to push home his advantage against a war-depleted Ottoman Empire. He ordered his troops to attack in October 1920 (just weeks before he was voted out of office). By September 1921 the Greeks had advanced as far as Ankara.

The Turkish forces were commanded by Mustafa Kemal (later to become Kemal Atatürk), a young general who also belonged to the Young Turks, a group of army officers pressing for Western-style political reforms. Kemal first halted the Greek advance outside Ankara in September 1921 and then routed them with a massive offensive the following spring. The Greeks were driven out of Smyrna and many of the Greek inhabitants were massacred. Mustafa Kemal was now a national hero, the sultanate was abolished and Turkey became a republic.

'King Constantine abdicated after the fall of Smyrna'

The outcome of the failed Greek invasion and the revolution in Turkey was the Treaty of Lausanne of July 1923. This gave eastern Thrace and the islands of Imvros (Gökçeada) and Tenedos (Bozcaada) to Turkey, while the Italians kept the Dodecanese (which they had temporarily acquired in 1912 and would hold until 1947).

The treaty also called for a population exchange between Greece and Turkey to prevent any future disputes. Almost 1.5 million Greeks left Turkey and almost 400,000 Turks left Greece. The exchange put a tremendous strain on the Greek economy and caused great hardship for the individuals concerned. Many Greeks abandoned a privileged life in Asia Minor for one of extreme poverty in shantytowns in Greece.

King Constantine, restored to the throne in 1920, identified himself too closely with the war against Turkey and abdicated after the fall of Smyrna.

1862	1914	1919–23
King Otto is deposed in a bloodless coup, yet the British manage to engineer the ascension to the Greek throne of Danish Prince William.	The outbreak of WWI sees Greece initially neutral but eventually siding with the Western allies against Germany and Turkey on the promise of land in Asia Minor.	With no redeemed land in sight Greece embarks on the 'Great Idea': a military campaign to liberate former Hellenic lands in Asia Minor. It ends in abject failure.

WWII & THE CIVIL WAR

In 1930 George II, Constantine's son, became king and appointed the dictator General Ioannis Metaxas as prime minister. Metaxas' grandiose ambition was to take the best from Greece's ancient and Byzantine past to create a Third Greek Civilisation. His chief claim to fame was his celebrated *ohi* (no) to Mussolini's request to allow Italian troops to traverse Greece in 1940. Despite Allied help, Greece fell to Germany in 1941, after which carnage and mass starvation followed. Resistance movements sprang up, eventually polarising into royalist and communist factions.

A bloody civil war resulted, lasting until 1949 and leaving the country in chaos. The sense of despair that followed became the trigger for a mass exodus. Almost a million Greeks headed off in search of a better life elsewhere, primarily to Australia, Canada and the USA.

For an insight into the 1967 colonels' coup read Andreas Papandreou's gripping account in *Democracy at Gunpoint*.

THE COLONELS

Continuing political instability led to the colonels' coup d'état in 1967, led by Georgos Papadopoulos and Stylianos Patakos. The colonels' junta distinguished itself by inflicting appalling brutality, repression and political incompetence upon the people.

In 1974 they attempted to assassinate Cyprus' leader, Archbishop Makarios. When Makarios escaped, the junta replaced him with the extremist Nikos Sampson, a convicted murderer. The Turks, who comprised 20% of the population, were alarmed at having Sampson as leader. Consequently, mainland Turkey sent in troops and occupied North Cyprus, the continued occupation of which is one of the most contentious issues in Greek politics today. The junta, by now in a shambles, had little choice but to hand power back to civilians.

In November 1974 a plebiscite voted 69% against restoration of the monarchy and Greece became a republic. An election brought the right-wing New Democracy (ND) party into power, led by Konstandinos Karamanlis. The ban on communist parties was then lifted, and Andreas Papandreou formed the Panhellenic Socialist Union (PASOK).

ND won again in 1977, but Konstandinos Karamanlis' personal popularity had already begun to decline.

THE ISLAND OF CYPRUS

While not part of the Hellenic Republic, the Republic of Cyprus is the only country apart from Greece where Greek is a majority language. While Turkish-speaking Cypriots also live on Cyprus they constitute only 17% of the total population. Cyprus is considered by many Greeks an extension of the Greek islands and in turn many Cypriots visit the Greek islands on cruise holidays from Cypriot ports. The island's history and future is of immediate interest and relevance to all islanders, and now that both countries are in the European Union and share the same currency and culture, that closeness has never been felt more intensely.

1924–34	1941–44	1944–49
The Great Depression counters a return to stability. Monarchists and Parliamentarians under Prime Minister Venizelos tussle for control of the country.	Germany invades and occupies Greece. Monarchists, republicans and communists form resistance groups that, despite infighting, drive out the Germans after three years.	The end of WWII sees Greece descend into Civil War, pitching Republicans against Communists. The monarchy is restored in 1946. Many Greeks migrate in search of a better life.

THE SOCIALIST 1980s

In 1981 Greece entered the EC (now the EU). Andreas Papandreou's PASOK won the next election, giving Greece its first socialist government. PASOK promised removal of US air bases and withdrawal from NATO, which Greece had joined in 1951.

Six years later these promises remained unfulfilled, unemployment was high and reforms in education and welfare had been limited. Women's issues had fared better, however – the dowry system was abolished, abortion legalised, and civil marriage and divorce were implemented. The crunch for the government came in 1988 when PASOK became embroiled in a financial scandal involving the Bank of Crete.

In July 1989 an unprecedented conservative and communist coalition took over to implement a *katharsis* (campaign of purification) to investigate the scandals. It then stepped down in October 1990, stating that the *katharsis* was complete.

'In 1981 Greece entered the EC (now the EU)'

THE 1990s

An election in 1990 brought the ND back to power with Konstantinos Mitsotakis as prime minister. Intent on redressing the country's economic problems – high inflation and high government spending – the government imposed austerity measures, including a wage freeze for civil servants and steep increases in utility costs and basic services.

By mid 1993 Mitsotakis' honeymoon with the voters was waning and he and his supporters abandoned the ND for the new Political Spring party. The ND lost its parliamentary majority and an early election was held in October, which returned Andreas Papandreou's PASOK party with a handsome majority.

Papandreou stepped down in early 1996 due to failing health and his death on 26 June marked the end of an era in Greek politics.

Papandreou's departure heralded the arrival of experienced economist and lawyer Costas Simitis as the new prime minister. Cashing in on his reputation as the Mr Clean of Greek politics, Simitis romped to a comfortable majority at a snap poll called in October 1996.

THE NEW MILLENNIUM

With the turn of the millennium the Simitis government focused on the push for further integration with Europe. This meant in general terms more tax reform and austerity measures. His success in the face of constant protest nonetheless earned him a mandate for another four years in April 2000. The goal of admission to the euro club was achieved at the beginning of 2001 and Greece adopted the euro as its currency in March 2002.

In April 2004 the Greek populace, perhaps tired of a long run of socialist policies, turned once more to the right and elected New Democracy leader Konstandinos Karamanlis as prime minister. This may have been a blessing in disguise for the socialists as they had been chiefly responsible for the

1959	1967–73	1974
Cyprus is declared an independent State amid pleas for union with Greece from Greeks and Greek Cypriots alike. Turkey maintains claims of sovereignty over the island.	Right and left continue to bicker provoking a right-wing military coup of army generals who impose martial law. Civil rights are abolished. Tanks storm the Athens Polytechnic in a bid to quash a student uprising.	A botched plan to unite Cyprus with Greece results in the fall of the military junta and the invasion of Cyprus by Turkish troops, paradoxically a catalyst for the restoration of parliamentary democracy in Greece.

preparations for the 2004 Olympic Games, which had for some time been dogged by delays and technical problems.

The August 2004 Olympic Games were a resounding success and the Greeks put on a well organised (if poorly attended) spectacle. The fiscal cost to Greece is yet to be counted as the eventual cost of the Games far exceeded the original budget.

Greece's relations with its neighbours – particularly Turkey – have become perceptibly warmer. Konstandinos Karamanlis made particular efforts to chip away at the occasional frost with Greece's eastern neighbour and the efforts seem to have paid off, with little to report on the brinkmanship front – a trend that all too often in the past had caused sabres to be rattled between the two military forces.

Greece by 2005 was a developed, yet still-maturing EU nation with a rising standard of living that was counterbalanced to some degree by a rising cost of living. A consumer credit squeeze began to take its toll as more and more middle- to low-income earners succumbed to a ballooning credit debt. Car and even house repossessions became common, a stark contrast to the previous years in which Greeks had traditionally shunned credit. Tourism grew unabated despite rising costs, and in the long hot summer of 2007, forest fires throughout the western Peloponnese, Epiros and Evia caused untold damage to the nation's flora and fauna.

The islands, despite the travails of the mainland during these times, posted a buoyant return on tourism visits and the prospects for ongoing future growth look as favourable as ever.

'The August 2004 Olympic Games were a resounding success'

1981	1981–90	2007
Greece joins the European Union (EU), effectively removing protective trade barriers and opening up the Greek economy to the wider world for the first time. Boosted by EU cohesion funds the economy grows smartly.	Greece acquires its first elected socialist government under the leadership of Andreas Papandreou. The honeymoon lasts nine years. The Conservatives ultimately reassume power.	General elections are held in September and the conservative government of Konstandinos Karamanlis is returned to power for a second consecutive term.

The Culture

REGIONAL IDENTITY

In a country where regional identities remain deep-rooted, it is not surprising that Greek islanders often identify with their island first (as Cretans, Ithakians or Kastellorizians etc) and as Greeks second. Even those who have left the islands to live on the mainland, or moved to bigger islands, or abroad invariably maintain a strong connection to their ancestral island. It is an important part of their identity and sense of community, with even the remotest island villages coming alive during summer, Easter, elections and other excuses for family reunions and homecomings.

With the Greek islands sprawling from the shores of Turkey to Italy, the regional distinctions and characteristics are apparent across the seven island groups. Individual histories and topography have influenced island customs and traditions, from their cuisine to architecture, music and dance, down to the characteristics of their people and the produce that gave them livelihoods.

In the Ionians, Corfu escaped Turkish rule and has a more Italian, French and British influence, and its people retain an aristocratic air. The Cretans are renowned for their independent (almost lawless) streak and hospitality, and have perhaps the most enduring and distinctive folk culture and traditions, as well as their own dialect. Mykonos' glamour and stylised island image is a far cry from traditional customs in villages such as Olymbos in far eastern Karpathos, where many women still wear traditional dress, including headscarves and goatskin boots. Sifnos is renowned for its unique pottery tradition, on Chios the mastic tree has spawned its own industry, while Kalymnos' sponge diving industry shaped the island's identity as much as fishing and agriculture have forged those of others.

While foreign invasions now take the form of tourists, these have nonetheless changed the fortunes and nature of many islands. Beneath the friendly and laid-back veneer of island life, the islands today are dealing with the rapid social and economic changes that have swept the country in the past 30 years.

In its fast-tracked quest for modernity, Greek society is facing a massive generational and technological divide, widening urban-rural disparities and all the while delicately balancing cultural and religious mores. The culture clash is most stark on the islands where many people continue to live in a time warp of traditional island life outside the bustling tourist resorts.

Greek islanders have by necessity been relatively autonomous, but they share a common history spanning centuries with the mainland, along with the peculiar traits of the Greek psyche.

Years of hardship and isolation has made islanders stoic and resourceful, generous yet shrewd and suspicious. Like most Greeks, they are fiercely independent, patriotic and proud of their heritage. They pride themselves on their *filotimo* (dignity and sense of honour), and their *filoxenia* (hospitality, welcome).

Personal freedom and democratic rights are almost sacrosanct and there is residual mistrust of authority and disrespect for the state. Rules and regulations are routinely ignored or seen as a challenge. Patronage and nepotism are rife, an enduring by-product of having to rely on personal networks to survive.

Greeks are forthright and argumentative and few subjects are off limits, from your private life and why you don't have children, to how much you paid for your house or shoes.

'Individual histories and topography have influenced island customs and traditions'

While some Greeks like to flaunt their newfound wealth with top-brand clothing and flashy cars and are prone to excess, as if making up for lost time, others continue to live frugal and traditional agrarian lives.

Stereotypes about Greek men being mummy's boys are not totally unfounded, while AIDS and the sexual liberation of Greek women has virtually killed off the Greek lover and the *kamaki* (a fishing trident, referring to the practice of fishing for foreign women) of the islands, ála *Shirley Valentine* (p50).

LIFESTYLE

Island life is completely seasonal. From May to September, the islands kick into summer mode, with visitors far outnumbering the local population. Traditional agrarian life on many islands has been replaced by tourism-related pursuits, though they often coexist, with families running hotels and beach tavernas in summer and engaging in other agricultural or business pursuits in the winter.

Winter can be especially tough for the people living on isolated smaller islands with short tourism seasons, especially those without airports. On larger islands such as Crete and Corfu, there is a winter population shift from the beach resorts back to mountain villages and larger towns with schools and infrastructure, while on some islands people move back to Athens after the season.

Overall, the lifestyle of the average Greek has changed beyond all recognition in the last 50 years. The tourism windfall has brought prosperity to many islands, while better transport, technology, telecommunication and infrastructure has made life a lot easier and far less isolated.

However, the sharp rise in the cost of living in recent years, particularly since the arrival of the euro, means many Greeks have been feeling the financial pinch, relying on credit and curtailing holidays and eating out (though Greeks still spend a higher percentage of their income on restaurants and holidays than their EU counterparts).

Island life has a more laid back and relaxed pace than the mainland, revolving largely around the tourism industries. The majority of people are self-employed and run family businesses. Most island stores and businesses close during the heat of the day and reopen in the evenings after the siesta until around 11pm, which is when locals generally head out to dinner.

Regardless of the long working hours, Greeks are inherently social animals and enjoy a rich communal life. Shopkeepers will sit outside their stores chatting to each other until a customer walks in, and in villages you will see people sitting outside their homes watching the goings-on. In the evenings, the seafront promenades and town squares are bustling with people of all ages, and at night the sophisticated bars and clubs are always lively.

PEOPLE & SOCIETY
Population

Greece's population exceeded 11.1 million in 2007, with nearly a third of the population (3.4 million) living in the Greater Athens area. Less than 15% live on the islands, the most populous being Crete, Evia and Corfu.

Regional development, decentralisation and the improved lot of many rural communities have largely stemmed the tide of people moving to Athens, especially in growth areas such as Iraklio in Crete, but many islands still lose their young people to the mainland or bigger islands for work and educational opportunities.

Greece has an ageing population and a declining birth rate, with large families a thing of the past. The main population growth has been the flood

Greeks have their own distinctive body language – 'yes' is a swing of the head and 'no' is a curt raising of the head (or eyebrows), often accompanied by a 'ts' click of the tongue sound.

Greeks are the biggest smokers in the EU: 42% of Greeks over 14 are heavy smokers and women smoke as much as men. Smoking is banned in public areas and on public transport but in restaurants it's widespread.

of migrants since 1991, with about one million migrants estimated to be living in Greece. Many migrants have moved to the islands with their families.

Family Life

Greek society remains dominated by the family. Extended family plays an important role, with grandparents often looking after grandchildren while parents work or socialise. Many working Athenians send their children to their grandparents on the islands for the summer.

It's still uncommon for young people to move out of home before marrying, unless they leave to study or work, which is inevitable on most islands where employment and education opportunities are limited. While this is also changing among professionals and people marrying later, low wages are also keeping young Greeks at home.

Parents strive to provide homes for their children when they get married, often building apartments for each child above their own (thus the number of unfinished buildings you see).

Greeks attach great importance to education, determined to provide their children the opportunities they lacked. English and other languages are widely spoken, while Greece has the highest number of students per capita studying at universities abroad.

Multiculturalism

Greece has been a largely homogenous society since independence. The disparate *xenoi* (foreigners) living in their midst were mostly the odd Hellenophile, and foreign women married to locals as a result of summer romances, especially on the islands.

But with the influx of economic migrants in the past 15 years, the islands are teeming with foreign labourers, who have become an economic necessity in the agriculture, construction and tourism sectors, doing the hard and menial labour Greeks no longer want to do.

Migration and multiculturalism are posing major challenges for both the community and the state, which were ill-prepared for dealing with the sudden wave of migrants. Economic migrants exist on the social fringe, but as they seek Greek citizenship and try to integrate into mainstream society, community tolerance and notions of Greek identity are also being tested.

Albanians, who make up roughly two-thirds the migrant population, remain stigmatised, as most Greeks initially reacted with xenophobia and resented their presence, blaming them for every crime committed. Mixed marriages are becoming increasingly common, particularly for men in rural communities and islands where local women leave to study or work.

First published in 1885, James Theodore Bent's *The Cyclades, or Life Among the Insular Greeks,* is a classic account of the islands, while John Freely's more recent *The Cyclades* is rich on history and insight.

ISLAND HOMECOMINGS

Every summer, the twang of Australian accents echoing around the tiny harbour of Kastellorizo has become a curious feature of the island. A large part of the island's population emigrated to Australia in the late 1920s, but their descendants (and a few of the oldies) return annually to what at times can seem like the furthermost Aussie outpost.

A similar phenomenon occurs on most islands, which see an annual procession of Greeks returning from America, Australia, Canada and other reaches of the Greek diaspora. Strong sentimental connections endure and many expat Greeks are involved in the political and cultural life of their ancestral islands, often retiring in Greece. A growing stream of young second- and third-generation Greeks are also repatriating.

More than five million people of Greek descent are said to be living in 140 countries around the world, having emigrated at various tumultuous times.

Media

Greece has a disproportionate number of newspapers and TV stations given its size – more than 20 national dailies (including 10 sports dailies) and seven national broadcasters. While coverage of island issues is patchy, many islands have their own newspapers, radio stations and some have small local TV stations.

Newspapers, like most Greeks, are openly partisan and represent the gamut of political views. Commercial TV news is highly sensationalist and dominated by domestic news and scandals.

The country's media owners have an extremely influential role in shaping public opinion, with media ownership spread around half a dozen major players. The often contentious entangled relationship between media owners, journalists, big business and the government is what the Greeks have coined *diaplekomena* (intertwined).

Religion & Identity

The Orthodox faith is the official religion of Greece and a key element of Greek identity and culture. While younger people aren't necessarily devout, nor attend church regularly, they observe the rituals and consider their faith part of their identity.

During foreign occupations, the church was principal upholder of Greek culture, language and traditions. Under Ottoman rule, religion was one of the most important criteria in defining a Greek. The church still exerts significant social, political and economic influence.

The Greek year is centred on the saints' days and festivals of the church calendar. Namedays (celebrating your namesake saint) are celebrated more than birthdays and baptisms are an important rite.

You will notice taxi drivers, motorcyclists and people on public transport making the sign of the cross when they pass a church, and many Greeks will go to a church when they have a problem to light a candle or leave a *tama* (votive offering) to the relevant saint. The tiny roadside iconostases you see everywhere are either shrines to people who died in road accidents or dedications to saints.

While religious freedom is part of the constitution, the only other officially recognised religions in Greece are Judaism and Islam.

There are more than 50,000 Roman Catholics, mostly of Genoese or Frankish origin living in the Cyclades, especially on Syros, where they make up 40% of the population. A small Jewish community lives in Rhodes (dating back to the Roman era).

If you wish to look around a church or monastery, you should always dress appropriately. Women should wear skirts that reach below the knees, men should wear long trousers, and arms (and cleavage) should be covered.

Time, Religion & Social Experience in Rural Greece, by Laurie Kain Hart, is a fascinating account of village traditions, many of which are alive and well, buried beneath the tourist veneer.

Women in Greece

Greek women have a curious place in Greek society and the male-female dynamic throws up some interesting paradoxes. Despite the machismo, it is very much a matriarchal society. Men love to give the impression that they rule the roost but, in reality, it's often the women who run the show, both at home and in family businesses.

While sexual liberation, education and greater participation in the workforce has given women a different sort of power, 'mother' and 'sex object' are still the dominant role models and stereotypes, which Greek women often play on with gusto.

Old attitudes towards the 'proper role' for women have changed dramatically since the 1980s, when dowry laws were abolished, legal equality of the sexes established and divorce made easier.

While there are many benefits for mothers in the public sector, Greek women generally do it tough in the male-dominated workplace. They are significantly under-represented and often earn less than men.

In provincial towns and villages, many women maintain traditional roles, though things are far more liberal in the cities.

On the domestic front, Greek women (at least the older generation) are famously house-proud and hone their culinary skills. It's still relatively rare for men to be involved in housework or cooking and boys are generally waited on hand and foot. While girls are involved in domestic chores from an early age, these days they are more likely to be found in a gym or beauty salon than in the kitchen.

ARTS
Architecture

The advanced Minoan palace complexes in Crete, including the famous palace at Knossos (p232), are among the earliest examples of ancient Greek architecture, along with the Akrotiri site (p199) on Santorini.

The Mycenaeans later built citadels on a compact, orderly plan, fortified by strong walls, while the next great architectural advance came with the monumental stone temples built in the Archaic and classical periods, characterised by the Doric, Ionic and Corinthian orders of columns.

The most famous Doric temple in Greece is the Parthenon (p75), but the Temple of Aphaia (p111) on Aegina and the small Doric temple of Isis (p152) on Delos, near Mykonos, are also fine examples.

Greek Art and Archaeology, by John Griffiths, Pedley is a super introduction to the development of Greek art and civilisation.

Theatre design was another hallmark of the classical period, with stone theatres built into hills providing excellent acoustics. On the islands, you will find the marble theatre at Delos (p152), the ancient theatre at Eretria (p418) on Evia, the Hellenistic theatre of Samothraki (p405), and theatres in Thassos, Rhodes, Crete, Santorini and Milos.

During the Byzantine period, churches usually featured a central dome supported by four arches on piers and flanked by vaults, with smaller domes at the four corners and three apses to the east. The external brickwork, which alternated with stone, was sometimes set in patterns. Fortified

---

THE BIG SPLIT

Greece was one of the first places in Europe where Christianity emerged, with St Paul reputedly first preaching the gospel in AD 49 in the Macedonian town of Philippi. After Constantine the Great officially recognised Christianity in AD 313, he transferred the capital of the Roman Empire to Byzantium (today's İstanbul) in AD 330.

By the 8th century, differences of opinion and increasing rivalry emerged between the pope in Rome and the patriarch of the Hellenised Eastern Roman Empire. One dispute was over the wording of the Creed, which stated that the Holy Spirit proceeds 'from the Father', but Rome added 'and the Son'. Other points of difference included Rome decreeing priests had to be celibate, while Orthodox priests could marry before becoming ordained, and the Orthodox Church forbidding wine and oil during Lent. Another big rift was the Western church using the Gregorian calendar and the Eastern church using the Julian calendar.

Their differences became irreconcilable, and in the great schism of 1054 the pope and the patriarch went their separate ways as the Orthodox Church (Orthodoxy means 'right belief'), and Roman Catholic Church.

Orthodox Easter is often held at different times to the western churches because of a continuing dispute about the calendars and complex formulas involving the full-moon cycles and dates of the Jewish Passover – it falls on the first Sunday after the first full moon after the vernal equinox (21 March on the Julian calendar), after the Jewish Passover. Every few years they coincide.

ISLAND STYLE

Stark white chapels juxtaposed against stunning blue Aegean skies and cubed houses with bright blue shutters are the most enchanting images of Greek island architecture. The distinctive blue-and-white Cycladic style was pragmatic more than aesthetic. Apart from reflecting the scarcity of construction materials, the labyrinthine narrow alleys with flat roofed-houses huddled together were designed to protect against the elements – strong winds and pirates – and the white-washed walls reflected the heat from the sun.

Mykonos is a superb example, with its unique asymmetrical buildings, exemplified by the church of Panagia Paraportiani (p145). On Santorini, the islanders protected themselves by building their cubed villages perched on the cliff tops, extending their homes into the rock, which provided insulation in winter and cooling in summer. A lack of water meant there were no gardens, just a few bright pots of hardy geraniums and bougainvillea. Blue-domed island chapels were built in this distinctive Cycladic style. One of the best preserved Cycladic settlements is Hora (p185), on Amorgos.

Apart from the iconic Cycladic style, Greek island architecture is diverse and reflects their wealth and turbulent and colourful history, giving each island a unique style.

Remnants of Ottoman times are evident in the Rhodes and Cretan towns of Hania (p245) and Rethymno (p236), where you will see old mosques and minarets, Turkish-style wooden balconies attached to Venetian mansions and *hammams* (Turkish baths) incorporated into hotels and restaurants. Hania and Rethymno are among Greece's most attractive towns.

The Venetian legacy of massive fortifications, grand squares, fountains and mansions is evident in Corfu Town (p449), which made it on to Unesco's World Heritage list in 2006, but even Mykonos has its famous Little Venice.

Gracious stone and white mansions dominate Hydra's stunning amphitheatrical port (p115), while the capital of Symi (p306) in the Dodecanese is a protected settlement of pastel- and ochre-coloured neoclassical mansions. Rhodes' Old Town, (p279) one of the largest inhabited medieval settlements in Europe, is also World Heritage–listed.

Byzantine monasteries include the imposing monastery of St John on Patmos (p340).

The Venetians left the greatest architectural legacies (see the boxed text, above), while little architecture of the Ottoman period survives. After the War of Independence, buildings took on the neoclassical style that had been dominant in Western European architecture and sculpture.

Architectural sensibilities took a back seat for most of the tumultuous 20th century, when many neoclassical buildings were destroyed in the untamed modernisation and sudden expansion that took place in the 1950s, '60s and '70s, during which most of the ugly concrete apartment blocks that characterise modern Athens (and most Greek towns) were built.

While there are some modern buildings of architectural note, it is only in recent times that modern architecture has come to the fore.

Theatre

Drama in Greece can be dated back to the contests staged at the Ancient Theatre of Dionysos in Athens during the 6th century BC for the annual Dionysia festival. During one of these competitions, Thespis left the ensemble and took centre stage for a solo performance. This is regarded as the first true dramatic performance – thus the term 'thespian'.

The so-called 'father of tragedy' was Aeschylus (c 525–456 BC), whose best-known work is the Oresteia trilogy. Sophocles (c 496–406 BC), regarded as the greatest tragedian, is thought to have written over 100 plays, of which only seven survive, including *Antigone, Electra* and his most famous play, *Oedipus Rex.*

Euripides (c 485–406 BC) was more popular than Aeschylus and Sophocles because his plots were considered more exciting. His most famous works are *Medea, Andromache, Orestes* and *Bacchae*.

Aristophanes (c 427–387 BC) wrote often ribald comedies dealing with topical issues, ridiculing Athenians who resorted to litigation over trivialities in *The Wasps* and poking fun at their gullibility in *The Birds*.

You can see plays by ancient Greek playwrights at the Hellenic Festivals (p77) in Athens and Epidavros, and festivals around the country.

The most distinguished modern Greek playwrights are Giorgos Skourtis, Pavlos Matessis and the father of postwar drama, Iakovos Kambanellis.

Literature

The first, and greatest, ancient Greek writer was Homer, author of the *Iliad* and *Odyssey,* which tell the story of the Trojan War and the subsequent wanderings of Odysseus.

Herodotus (5th century BC) was the author of the first historical work about Western civilisation. His highly subjective account of the Persian Wars, however, led some to regard him as the 'father of lies' as well as the 'father of history'. The historian Thucydides (5th century BC) was more objective, but took a high moral stance in his account of the Peloponnesian Wars.

Pindar (c 518–438 BC) is regarded as the pre-eminent lyric poet of ancient Greece. He was commissioned to recite his odes at the Olympic Games. The greatest writers of love poetry were Sappho (6th century BC) and Alcaeus (5th century BC), both of whom lived on Lesvos. Sappho's poetic descriptions of her affections for women gave rise to the term 'lesbian'.

Zakynthos-born Dionysios Solomos (1798–1857) and Andreas Kalvos (1796–1869) are regarded as the first modern Greek poets. Solomos' work was heavily nationalistic, and his *Hymn to Freedom* became the Greek national anthem.

The best-known 20th-century poets are Nobel prize–winners George Seferis (1900–71) and Odysseas Elytis (1911–96), while Stratis Myrivilis (1892–1969) is considered one of the great prose writers.

The most celebrated novelist of the early 20th century is Crete's Nikos Kazantzakis (1883–1957), whose widely-translated novels are full of drama and larger-than-life characters, such as the magnificent Alexis Zorbas of *Zorba the Greek* and the tortured Michalis of *Freedom and Death,* two of his finest works.

Leading contemporary Greek writers include Thanassis Valtinos, Ziranna Ziteli, Ersi Sotiropoulou and playwright Kostas Mourselas. Two award-winning writers from Crete are Rhea Galanaki and Ioanna Karystiani.

While not enough literature is translated into English, look out for Apostolos Doxiadis' *Uncle Petros and Goldbach's Conjecture,* Petros Markaris' excellent crime noir novels *The Late Night News* and *Zone Defence,* and the popular children's books by criminologist-cum-children's author Eugene Trivizas.

Young writers making inroads into foreign markets include Vangelis Hatziyannidis, Alexis Stamatis with the superb *Bar Flaubert* (2000), and Panos Karnezis *(The Birthday Party, The Maze).*

Fine Arts
PAINTING

Apart from drawings on vases, the few existing examples of early Greek painting are the famous frescoes unearthed on Santorini and now mostly housed in the National Archaeological Museum (p75) in Athens. Stylistically they are similar to the paintings of Minoan Crete found at Knossos.

Not your usual tale of idyllic island life, Vangelis Hatziyannidis' *Four Walls* – a compelling mystery of entangled lives, imprisonment, jealousy and the secret to making honey – was shortlisted for a British foreign literature award.

Acclaimed Greek writer Stratis Myrivilis' classic novel *The Mermaid Madonna* is set on his native Lesvos. He crafts a harsh yet poignant portrayal of life in a fishing village during the Greek expulsion from Anatolia.

Greek painting came into its own during the Byzantine period, when churches were usually decorated with frescoes on a dark blue background with a bust of Christ in the dome, the four Gospel writers in the pendentives supporting the dome and the Virgin and Child in the apse. They also featured scenes from the life of Christ and figures of the saints. In the later centuries, the scenes in churches and icons involved more detailed narratives.

With the fall of Constantinople in 1453 many Byzantine artists fled to Crete, while many Cretan artists studied in Italy, where the Renaissance was in full bloom. The result was the Cretan school of icon painting that combined technical brilliance and dramatic richness. In Iraklio alone there were over 200 painters working from the mid-16th to mid-17th centuries who were equally at ease in Venetian and Byzantine styles, and the technique spread through monasteries throughout Greece. The finest exponent of the Cretan school was Michael Damaskinos, whose work is in Iraklio's Museum of Religious Art (p227).

The Cretan School was a formative influence for arguably Greece's most famous artist, Cretan-born El Greco (meaning 'The Greek' in Spanish; his real name was Dominikos Theotokopoulos), who became one of the great Renaissance painters in Spain.

Painting after the Byzantine period became more secular. From the first decades of the 20th century, artists such as Konstantinos Parthenis drew on their heritage and assimilated various developments in modern art, a trend that continues among the new generation of artists.

Significant artists of the 'thirties generation' were cubist Nikos Hadjikyriakos-Ghikas and surrealists Nikos Engonopoulos, Yiannis Tsarouchis and Panayiotis Tetsis.

Other leading artists include Yannis Moralis, Giorgos Zongolopoulos (with his trademark umbrella sculptures), Dimitris Mytaras, Yannis Tsoclis, abstract artist Yannis Gaitis, Christos Caras and Alekos Fassianos.

In the past 25 years, modern Greek painting has attracted serious sums at leading art auctions, with Lytras' *The Naughty Grandchild* setting a record for a Greek artist when it sold for more than one million euros in London in 2006.

The World of the Ancient Greeks (2002), by archaeologists John Camp and Elizabeth Fisher, is a broad and in-depth look at how the Greeks have left their imprint on politics, philosophy, theatre, art, medicine and architecture.

SCULPTURE

The sculptures of ancient Greece are works of extraordinary visual power and beauty that hold pride of place in the collections of the great museums of the world.

ISLAND READING

The Greek islands have, not surprisingly, inspired many books from foreign writers, including the Durrell brothers and their classic novels. Lawrence Durrell wrote *Prospero's Cell* about Corfu, *Reflections of a Marine Venus* about Rhodes, *The Dark Labyrinth* about Crete and the travelogue, *The Greek Islands*. His brother Gerald penned the amusing *My Family and Other Animals* about their life on Corfu. Louis de Bernières novel *Captain Corelli's Mandolin* is based on Kefallonia during WWII, while John Fowles' bestselling novel *The Magus*, was inspired by his time on Spetses.

The most amusing recent book about Crete is Rory McClean's *Flying with Icarus*, while *The Island*, by Victoria Hislop, tells a darker tale of family secrets and life on the Spinalonga island leper colony. On Patmos, Peter France goes on a poignant spiritual journey in *Patmos: a Place of Healing for the Soul*, while Tom Stone gets caught up in running a taverna in *Summer of My Greek Taverna*. The classic foreigner's quest for a Greek island home is told with added wit by John Mole who finds his paradise on Evia in *It's All Greek to Me*.

Tales From A Greek Island is an insightful mix of romance and harsh reality from Roger Jinkinson's 20 years in a village on Karpathos. Michael Kalafatas weaves an intriguing family history into a novel about the sponge divers of Kalymnos in *The Bellstone: the Greek sponge Divers of the Aegean*.

> **SUMMER ARTS**
>
> In summer, the Athens arts scene winds down and exhibitions by local and international artists are held on the islands. One of the big annual arts events is held on Andros at the **Museum of Modern Art** (p130), which also has a permanent exhibition of Andriot sculptor Michael Tombros and the Goulandris' private collection.
>
> In Hydra artist Dimitris Antonitsis curates the annual Hydra School Project at the island's primary school, while in Crete major exhibitions are run by the **Rethymnon Centre for Contemporary Art** (☎ 28310 52530; www.rca.gr; Himaras 5; Rethymno; ☼ 9am-1pm & 7pm-10pm Tue-Fri; 11am-3pm Sat).
>
> In Rhodes Town the **Rhodes Modern Greek Art Museum** (admission €3) is a major gallery spread across three historic buildings; the main permanent collection of 20th-century Greek art is in the **New Art Gallery** (☎ 22410 43780; Nestoridio Melathron Bldg, Haritou Sq; ☼ 8am-2pm & 5-8pm Tue-Sat), the **Municipal Gallery of Rhodes** (☎ 22410 23766; Plateia Symis 2; Old Town) and there is a **Modern Art Centre** (Sokratous 179, Old Town; ☼ 8am-2pm Tue-Sat) – the gallery has the most extensive collection of 20th-century Greek art, after the National Art Gallery (p75) in Athens.

The prehistoric art of Greece has been discovered only recently, most notably the remarkable figurines produced in the Cyclades from the high-quality marble of Paros and Naxos in the middle of the 3rd millennium BC. Their primitive and powerful forms have inspired many artists since.

Displaying an obvious debt to Egyptian sculpture, the marble sculptures of the Archaic period are precursors of the famed Greek sculpture of the classical period. They began to represent figures that for the first time were true to nature, rather than flat and stylised. Seeking to master the depiction of both the naked body and of drapery, sculptors focused on *kouroi* (figures of naked youths), with their set symmetrical stance and enigmatic smiles. These can be admired at the National Archaeological Museum (p75) in Athens.

The quest for total naturalism continued in the Hellenistic period; works of this period were animated, almost theatrical, in contrast to their serene Archaic and classical predecessors. These were revered by later artists such as Michelangelo, who was at the forefront of the rediscovery of Greek works in the Renaissance. The end of the Hellenistic age signalled the decline of Greek sculpture's pre-eminent position in the art form. The torch was handed to the Romans, who proved worthy successors.

Two of the foremost modern sculptors, Dimitrios Filippotis and Yannoulis Halepas, were from Tinos, where marble sculpture tradition endures today. Contemporary Greek and international sculpture can be seen at the **National Glyptotheque** (off Map p72; ☎ 210 770 9855; Army Park, Katehaki; adult/concession €6/3; ☼ 9am-3pm Mon & Wed-Sat, 10am-3pm Sun) in Athens.

For a comprehensive rundown of arts exhibitions and events around Greece check out www.goculture.gr.

POTTERY

Pottery is one of the most ancient arts, and Greek pots can be seen in museums around the country. At first, vases were built with coils and wads of clay, but the art of throwing on the wheel was introduced in about 2000 BC and was then practised with great skill by Minoan and Mycenaean artists.

Minoan pottery is often characterised by a high centre of gravity and beak-like spouts, with flowing designs of spiral or marine and plant motifs.

Mycenaean pottery shapes include a long-stemmed goblet and a globular vase with handles resembling a pair of stirrups. Decorative motifs are similar to those on Minoan pottery but are less fluid.

The 10th century BC saw the introduction of the Protogeometric style, with its substantial pots decorated with blackish-brown horizontal lines around the circumference, hatched triangles and compass-drawn concentric circles. This was followed by the new vase shape and more crowded decoration of the Geometric period. By the early 8th century BC figures were introduced, marking the introduction of the most fundamental element in the later tradition of classical art – the representation of gods, men and animals.

Reproductions of these styles are found at souvenir shops throughout the country. Some contemporary ceramicists are still making pots using ancient firing and painting techniques. Minoan-style pottery is made in Crete, while the island of Sifnos (p210) continues its distinctive pottery tradition.

Music

Greece's musical tradition dates back to the Cycladic figurines found holding musical instruments resembling harps and flutes from 2000 BC.

These days most people associate Greek music with the distinctive sound of the bouzouki, the long-necked lute-like instrument, which is a relative newcomer to the scene. Other traditional instruments include the *baglamas*, a baby version of the bouzouki used in *rembetika* (known as the Greek blues), and the *tzoura*, which is half-way between the two. The Cretan *laouto* (lute), the *toumberleki* (lap drum), the *mandolino* (mandolin) and the *gaida* (bag pipe) share many characteristics with instruments all over the Middle East.

Regional folk music, like dance, reflect the local conditions and history. *Nisiotika*, the upbeat music of the islands is far lighter than the grounded and sombre *dimotika* of the mainland, while powerful Cretan music brings the lyra to the fore. Cretan music, embodied by the legendary Nikos Xylouris, remains the most enduring traditional folk music in Greece.

Greek music today encompasses a range of styles, from traditional folk music to the modern pop *tsifteteli* (a kind of bellydance) hybrid beats played in Greek clubs. The urban *rembetika* music that emerged in the 1920s is still popular and played in clubs around Greece, as is *laïka* (urban folk music), which emerged in the 50s and 60s with the popular Stelios Kazantzidis and Grigoris Bithikotsis.

'The urban *rembetika* music (known as the Greek blues) that emerged in the 1920s is still popular'

Entehno (artistic) music was first introduced by the outstanding composers Mikis Theodorakis and Manos Hatzidakis, who used traditional instruments such as the bouzouki in more symphonic arrangements. They also brought poetry to the masses by making hits using lyrics from Greece's great poets. Cretan Yiannis Markopoulos continued this new wave by introducing rural folk music and traditional instruments, such as the *lyra*, *santouri*, violin and *kanonaki* into the mainstream and bringing folk performers like Crete's legendary Nikos Xylouris to the fore. During the junta years, Theodorakis' and Markopoulos' music became a form of political expression and protest. Theodorakis is one of Greece's most prolific composers, though somewhat to his dismay, he is best known for the classic 'Zorba' tune.

Comparatively few Greek performers have made it big on the international scene – 1970s icons Nana Mouskouri and kaftan-wearing Demis Roussos remain the best known. Composer Vangelis Papathanasiou's celebrated film scores include the Oscar-winning *Chariots of Fire*.

Greek music veteran George Dalaras has covered the gamut of Greek music and collaborated with Latin and Balkan artists, as well as Sting, while the deep and dulcet voice of Haris Alexiou has made her Greece's most popular songstress.

Other distinguished artists include Dimitra Galani, Eleftheria Arvanitaki, Alkistis Protopsalti, Glykeria, Dionysis Savopoulos and Alkinoos Ioannides.

Talented singer-songwriters include Nikos Papazoglou, Socrates Malamas, Nikos Portokaloglou, Thanassis Papaconstantinou, Dimitris Zervoudakis and Miltiadis Pashalidis.

Contemporary Greek music can include elements of traditional folk music, folk rock, heavy metal, rap and electronic dance music. Vocal artist Savina

Yannatou, folk-jazz fusion artists Kristi Stasinopoulou and Mode Plagal are making a mark on the world music scene, while other notable musicians include Haïnides, Achilleas Persidis and pop-rock band Raining Pleasure.

During summer you can see Greece's leading acts in outdoor concerts around the islands.

The country's big pop and laïka stars include Anna Vissi, Notis Sfakianakis, Despina Vandi, Yiannis Ploutarhos, Antonis Remos, Mihalis Hatziyiannis, heartthrob Sakis Rouvas and Greek-Swedish singer Elena Paparizou, who won Greece the 2005 Eurovision song contest.

Dance

Dancing has been part of social life in Greece since the dawn of Hellenism. Some of today's folk dances derive from the ritual dances performed in ancient Greek temples. The *syrtos* (traditional Greek dance) is depicted on ancient vases and there are references to dances in Homer's works. Many folk dances are performed in a circular formation; in ancient times, dancers formed a circle in order to seal themselves off from evil influences or would dance around an altar, tree, figure or object. Dancing was also part of military education, while under occupation it was a way for men to keep fit under the noses of their enemies.

Regional dance styles often reflect the climate or disposition of the participants. The islands, with their bright and cheery atmosphere, give rise to light, springy dances such as the *ballos* and the *syrtos*, while the graceful and most widely known *kalamatianos*, originally from Kalamata, reflects years of proud Peloponnese tradition. In Crete you have the graceful and slow *syrtos*, the fast and triumphant *maleviziotikos* and the dynamic *pentozali*, which has a slow and fast version, in which the leader impresses with high kicks and leaps.

The so-called 'Zorba dance', or *syrtaki*, is a stylised dance for two or three men or women with arms linked on each other's shoulders, though the modern variation is danced in a long circle with an ever-quickening beat.

The often spectacular solo male *zeïmbekiko*, with its whirling improvisations, has its roots in *rembetika*, while women have their own sensuous *tsifteteli*, a svelte, sinewy show of femininity evolved from the Middle Eastern belly dance.

The *syrtaki* dance immortalised by Anthony Quinn in the final scene in *Zorba the Greek* was in fact a dance he improvised, as he had hurt his leg the day before the shoot and could not perform the traditional steps and leaps originally planned.

Cinema & TV

Greek cinema took off after the end of the Civil War and peaked in the 1950s and early '60s, when domestic audiences flocked to a flurry of comedies, melodramas and musicals being produced by the big Greek studios. Since those heydays, Greece's film industry has largely been in the doldrums – Greece has not had a major international hit since *Zorba the Greek* made its debut in the '50s. The demise of the studios with the advent of TV and inadequate funding was compounded by the slow-moving cerebral style of the 'new Greek cinema' of the '70s and '80s, which was generally too avant-garde to have mass appeal.

The leader of this school is award-winning 'auteur' director Theodoros Angelopoulos, who received the 1998 Golden Palm award at the Cannes Film Festival for *Eternity and a Day*.

A shift in cinematic style in the 1990s achieved moderate domestic commercial successes with lighter social satires and a more contemporary style and pace.

Two major films released internationally in recent years – the first in many years – were Tassos Boulmetis' *A Touch of Spice* (*Politiki Kouzina* 2003) and Pantelis Voulgaris' 2004 hit *Brides* (*Nyfes*), which follows the American odyssey of 700 Greek mail-order brides in the 1920s.

> **ON LOCATION**
>
> You've seen the movie but where in Greece was it shot?
> **Big Blue** (1988) Memorable black-and-white opening scenes of unspoilt Amorgos.
> **Bourne Identity** (2002) The final scenes were shot at the Sea Satin restaurant in Little Venice, Mykonos.
> **Captain Corelli's Mandolin** (2001) Shot largely in the port of Sami, Kefallonia.
> **For Your Eyes Only** (1981) James Bond explores Corfu's beaches, hotels and even the Turkish fort in Corfu Town.
> **Mediterraneo** (1991) Italian soldiers are garrisoned on tiny Kastellorizo in the Dodecanese.
> **Never on a Sunday** (1960) Greece's big star Melina Mercouri received an Oscar nomination for her role as a prostitute in Piraeus.
> **Pascali's Island** (1988) Ben Kingsley plays a Turkish spy on Symi during the dying days of Ottoman occupation.
> **Shirley Valentine** (1989) The classic foreign woman's Greek island romance fantasy was in Mykonos.
> **Summer Lovers** (1982) Darryl Hannah and Peter Gallagher got raunchy on Santorini, Mykonos and Crete.
> **Tomb Raider** (2001–2) Lara Croft went diving off Santorini.
> **Zorba the Greek** (1964) Where else but Crete? The famous beach dance scene was at Stavros, near Hania.

The latest wave of filmmakers is presenting a grittier, candid look at contemporary Greek life. Directors to watch include Konstantinos Giannaris, whose provocative documentary-style films seem to split audiences and critics alike, and Yannis Economidis, who has been likened to a younger Mike Leigh on speed.

Another internationally known veteran Greek director is Paris-based Costa-Gavras, who won an Oscar in 1969 for *Z*. His recent films include *Amen* (2003) and *The Axe* (2005).

Greek TV offers a jumble of local programmes from histrionic comedy series, talk shows and soap operas to Greek versions of reality TV, game shows and star-producing talent shows, though there have also been some excellent dramas of late tackling social themes, such as immigration, single mothers and life in rural Greece.

SPORT

Two unexpected sporting triumphs – the Athens 2004 Olympic Games and the Greek football (soccer) team's astounding victory in the European Cup brought Greece into the international spotlight in 2004. The national basketball team kept up the momentum when they became European Champions the following year, for a brief time making Greece the reigning European champions in both football and basketball. But since then, Greece has hardly made a ripple in the international sporting arena, though the national soccer team did make a surprise comeback and managed to qualify to defend their title for the Euro 2008 championship with a determined win against Turkey.

Football remains the country's most popular spectator sport and you will see large TV screens set up outside cafés and tavernas on big match nights. The big glamour clubs are Olympiakos of Piraeus and Panathinaikos of Athens, whose rivalry is occasionally interrupted by AEK Athens and PAOK from Thessaloniki.

Basketball is the other major sport, gaining popularity after the Greek team first won the European championship in 1987. Panathinaikos, Olympiakos and AEK are also the big clubs of Greek basketball.

No islands are large enough or have a big enough permanent population to field a team in national sports leagues, with the exception of Crete. Corfu is the only place in Greece where they play cricket, a quirky legacy of the British.

Food & Drink

Greek cuisine derives from rustic provincial cooking, which is rich in flavour and steeped in tradition. It relies on fresh seasonal produce and simplicity and draws from the cuisine of each region. Greek cooking reflects versatility and resourcefulness that evolved from years of subsistence living during hard times. The cuisine of the Greek islands, spread across the seas from Italy to Turkey, is heavily influenced by their history and topography. Arid landscapes and the limited availability of local produce on many islands meant making the most the fruits of the sea and whatever grew wild, from capers to artichokes. Although you'll find the usual Greek staples on most island taverna menus, local variations and specialities abound, along with subtle Eastern and Italian accents. Simple, pure and intense flavours dominate – olive oil, garlic, lemon, pungent wild oregano, mint, capers, dill and fennel.

Long lunches by the sea and dining alfresco on balmy summer nights have long been some of the highlights of the Greek island experience. Exploring traditional island cuisine on the busier islands can often require venturing beyond the 'tourist' tavernas: heading to the mountain villages for fresh local meat, seeking out local cheese and wine, or sampling the day's catch in a tiny fishing village.

The casual taverna is the mainstay of the Greek islands, and some of the best meals are in family-run places where simple home-style food is cooked with produce from the owner's garden or livestock. In the cities and on larger and more cosmopolitan islands you will find modern tavernas and upscale Greek restaurants serving refined neo-Greek cuisine cooked by new generation Greek chefs, as well as international-style restaurants and ethnic cuisine.

The Glorious Foods of Greece, by award-winning food writer Diane Kochilas, is a superb and passionate regional exploration of Greek cuisine, its history and culture.

THE GREEK KITCHEN

Greek provincial cuisine epitomise the healthy Mediterranean diet. Vegetables, pulses and legumes feature prominently, made tastier by plentiful use of olive oil (low in saturated fat). Fruit, bread, wheat and cereals, plenty of fish, wild greens and red wine also contributed to the nutritional benefits identified in scientific studies into the Greek diet.

These were the staples of lean times, but meat has become a more prominent part of the modern Greek diet, especially locally reared lamb, kid goat and pork (most beef is imported).

Each region has its variation of meat and fish dishes and *pites* (pies), the most common being the *tyropita* (cheese pie) and *spanakopita* (spinach pie).

Greece has some exceptional produce that makes simple meals remarkable, not least the abundance of fresh fruit and vegetables. Extra virgin olive oil is used exclusively in cooking and salads. Bread is a mandatory feature of every meal, the most popular being the white crusty *horiatiko* (village) loaf.

Greece's tangy, thick-strained sheep's milk yogurt is exceptionally flavourful and ideal for breakfast or dessert with thick aromatic thyme honey, walnuts and fruit.

More than 75% of Greece's entire annual production of oil is good enough to be labelled extra virgin. Compare that to 50% for Italy and 30% for Spain.

DINING OUT

Eating out is an integral part of Greek social life. The relaxed taverna style of dining, sharing a range of dishes, is the most popular.

The key to picking a restaurant is to find places where locals are eating, rather than bland 'tourist' tavernas (touts and big illuminated photos and signs are usually a giveaway). Try to adapt to local eating times – a restaurant

Acclaimed London chef Theodore Kyriakou goes back to his roots in search of recipes for *The Real Greek at Home*, the follow-up to his first book *Real Greek Food*; both are co-written by Charles Campion.

WHERE TO EAT & DRINK

The most common Greek eatery is the taverna, basic and casual, family-run (and child-friendly) places where the waiter usually arrives with bread and cutlery in a basket; they have barrel wine, paper tablecloths and standard menus. Other eateries include the following.

- **Bar restaurant** A more recent urban concept, they become incredibly loud after 11pm.

- **Estiatorio** A restaurant, where you pay more for essentially the same dishes as in a taverna or *mayireio*, but with a nicer setting and formal service. These days it also refers to an upmarket restaurant serving international cuisine.

- **Kafeneio** A traditional coffee house serving Greek coffee and spirits (in villages many also serve food); they remain largely the domain of men.

- **Mayireio** Specialises in traditional home-style one-pot dishes and oven-cooked meals (*mayirefta*).

- **Mezedhopoleio** Offers lots of small plates of mezedhes (appetisers).

- **Ouzerie** Traditionally serving tiny plates of mezedhes with each round of ouzo. The Cretan equivalent is a *rakadiko* (serving *raki*).

- **Psarotaverna** Taverna specialising in fish and seafood.

- **Psistaria** Taverna specialising in char-grilled or spit-roasted meat (sometimes may be called a *hasapotaverna*).

- **Zaharoplasteio** A cross between a patisserie and a café (though some only cater for take-away and gifts).

---

that was empty at 7pm might be heaving at 11pm (see Habits & Customs, p55). Don't be fooled by super-extensive menus, you may well be better off at a nondescript place with only a handful of fresh dishes.

Solo diners remain a curiosity but are looked after. Most island tavernas are family-run and open all day, but upmarket restaurants often open for dinner only.

By law, all eating establishments must display a written menu with prices.

Mezedhes & Starters

Sharing a range of mezedhes is a great way to sample various dishes, and it is quite acceptable to make a full meal of these. You can also order a *pikilia* (mixed meze plate).

Common mezedhes include dips, such as *taramasalata* (fish-roe), tzatziki (yogurt, cucumber and garlic), *melitzanosalata* (aubergine), *keftedhes* (meatballs), *loukaniko* (sausage) and *saganaki* (skillet-fried cheese).

In *Prospero's Kitchen*, Diana Farr Louis and June Marinos present rare and traditional recipes from the Ionian Islands.

Vegetarians will appreciate rice-filled vine-leaf *dolmadhes*, deep-fried zucchini or aubergine slices, tasty *gigantes* (lima beans in tomato and herb sauce), and tongue-twisting *kolokythokeftedhes* (zucchini balls).

You will often see locally caught *ohtapodi* (octopus) hung out to dry ready to be grilled as a mezes (it is also commonly pickled). Other typical seafood mezedhes are *lakerda* (cured fish), mussel or prawn *saganaki* (with tomato sauce and cheese) and crispy fried calamari or *maridha* (whitebait). *Gavros* (mild anchovy) is delicious marinated or grilled.

Soup is not normally eaten as a starter, but can be an economical and hearty meal with bread. On the islands, you'll most likely find a *psarosoupa* (fish soup) with vegetables. *Kakavia*, a bouillabaisse-style speciality laden with various fish and seafood, is made to order.

The main summer salad is the ubiquitous Greek salad (*horiatiki*, translated as 'village salad'), with tomato, cucumber, onion, feta and olives (occasionally purslane or capers in the Cyclades). Other seasonal salads include lettuce, cabbage and *roka* (rocket), while *horta* (wild greens) make a great warm salad, and *pantzaria* (beetroot) are divine with garlic, vinegar and oil.

Most Greeks can't go past a plate of *patates tiganites*, hand-cut potatoes cooked in olive oil (though frozen potatoes are taking over).

Mains

Most tavernas have a combination of oven-baked and one-pot dishes (commonly referred to as *mayirefta*) and food cooked to order *(tis oras)*. *Mayirefta* are usually prepared early in the day and left to cool, which enhances the flavour (they're often better served lukewarm, though many places microwave them).

A summer favourite is *yemista* (tomatoes and seasonal vegetables stuffed with rice and herbs), while almost every taverna will have *mousakas* (layers of eggplant, minced meat and potatoes topped with cheese sauce and baked). Other popular dishes include hearty *youvetsi*, meat baked in a tomato sauce with *kritharaki* (rice-shaped pasta), and mince- and rice-filled cabbage rolls filled with *avgolemono* (egg and lemon) sauce.

Ladhera are a particular type of *mayirefta*, often vegetable dishes such as beans and okra, cooked in plenty of olive oil.

Meat is baked with potatoes, with lemon and oregano, or cooked in tomato-based stews *(kokkinisto)*. Rabbit and beef are made into a sweet *stifadho* (braised with onions and tomato), while *kokoras* (rooster) *kokkinisto* is served with pasta.

Tasty charcoal-grilled meats – most commonly *païdakia* (lamb cutlets) and *brizoles* (pork chops) – are often ordered by the kilo. Restaurants tend to serve souvlaki – cubes of grilled meat on a skewer, rather than *gyros* (meat slithers cooked on a vertical rotisserie; usually eaten with pitta bread).

Fish is normally cooked with minimum fuss, usually grilled (see Fishy Business, p54) or baked *plaki* – baked with tomato, potatoes and herbs.

Seafood dishes include octopus in wine with macaroni, grilled or stewed *soupies* (cuttlefish), squid stuffed with cheese and herbs or rice, and fried salted cod served with *skordalia* (a lethal garlic and potato puree).

Sweet Treats

After a meal, Greeks traditionally serve fruit rather than dessert, so peruse local bakeries and *zaharoplasteia* (patisseries) for sweet specialities.

Syros makes delicious *loukoumia* ('Grecian delight'; gummy squares usually flavoured with rosewater) and *halvadopites* (nougat-like confectionery). The Cyclades are known for *amygdalota* (almond confectionery), particularly the marzipan-style sweets made on Andros. Zakynthos specialities include sesame-seed-and-almond *pasteli* and nougat-like *mandolato*.

Traditional sweets include baklava, *kataïfi* (nut-filled angel-hair pastry), fluffy *loukoumadhes* (ball-shaped doughnuts), *rizogalo* (rice pudding) and *galaktoboureko* (syrupy custard slice). Look out for sweet *myzithra*-cheese-filled pies such as Crete's *lihnarakia* and Santorini's *melitinia*.

Fruit preserves (syrupy sweets served on a tiny plate eaten with a spoon, commonly referred to as spoon sweets), traditionally a welcome offering to guests, are also delicious on yogurt or ice cream.

ISLAND SPECIALITIES

While there are staple Greek dishes you will find throughout the islands, each island group – and sometimes each island – has its own specialities and subtle variations.

The cuisine of the Ionian Islands, which were never under Turkish rule, has a distinct Italian influence, as seen in Corfu's spicy braised beef or rooster

There are at least 100 edible *horta* (wild greens), though even the most knowledgeable would not recognise more than a dozen.

Boasting the largest collection of Greek recipes on the web is www.greek-recipe.com, which also includes a Greek culinary dictionary and cookbook reviews.

FISHY BUSINESS

Fresh fish from the Mediterranean and Aegean are very tasty and normally simply grilled and served whole, with a *ladholemono* (lemon and oil) dressing. Fish is usually sold by weight and it is customary to go into the kitchen and choose the fish yourself. Make sure it's weighed (raw) so you don't get a shock when the bill arrives, as it is no longer cheap or plentiful.

Overfishing and high demand mean there are nowhere near enough local fish to cater for the millions of tourists who descend each summer. Most places will state if the fish and seafood is frozen, though sometimes only on the Greek menu (indicated by the abbreviated 'kat' or an asterisk). Smaller fish are often a safer bet – the odder the sizes, the more chance that they are local.

The choice fish for grilling are *tsipoura* (sea bream), *lavraki* (sea bass) and *fangri* (bream), while smaller fish like *barbounia* (red mullet) are delicious fried. See the glossary (p59) for other common fish names.

pastitsada, served with pasta and in a red sauce, and *sofrito* – a braised veal with garlic and wine sauce – is cooked in Corfu and across the Ionians. In Zakynthos, grilled *pancetta* (pork spare ribs) is popular.

The arid landscape, dry climate and isolation of the Cyclades meant many islanders relied on beans and pulses as the foundation of their winter diet. Sifnos' famous *revithadha* (chick-pea stew) is made in a specially shaped clay pot slow-cooked overnight, while *revythokeftedhes* (chick-pea fritters) are another speciality. Santorini is renowned for its tasty *fava* (yellow split-pea) puree, usually topped with finely chopped onion and lemon juice. See also Island Gourmet Trails, p56.

In Folegandros you will come across *matsata*, a pasta dish with rabbit or chicken in red sauce. Before imports became feasible, the drier islands were limited to hardy sheep and goats for their meat and cheese.

The sea remains the other major food source. Spaghetti with lobster is a decadent island speciality, particularly in the Cyclades. *Ahinosalata*, fresh sea urchin egg salad, gives you a powerful taste of the sea, while it is always wise to seek out taverns run by local fishing families.

The preservation of food using various methods was integral to survival during the winter. Isolated islands like Symi are renowned for their sun-dried preserved fish and seafood. Cured fish such as *kolios* (mackerel) is a popular mezes, while the sun-dried fish dish *liokafto* is a speciality of Folegandros. You'll also find some excellent cured meats such as the vinegar-cured pork *apaki* in Crete, spicy wine-marinated and smoked *louza* (pork) in Tinos and rare goat *pastourmas* in Ikaria and Karpathos.

Barley or whole wheat *paximadia* (hard rusks), double-baked to keep for years, are moistened with water and topped with tomato and olive oil (and feta or *myzithra* cheese) in the Cretan *dakos*.

Crete produces the richest bounty and has the most distinctive island cuisine. You'll find spiky wild artichokes, and herb-rich dishes such as cuttlefish with wild fennel, or wild greens with rabbit and the local delicacy, *hohlioi* (snails). Lamb or goat is often cooked *tsigariasto* (sautéed) or *ofto* (grilled upright around hot coals), or stewed with *stamnagathi* (wild greens) or artichokes. The Cretan *boureki* (a cheese, zucchini and potato bake) is a favourite, while *kalitsounia* are the tasty local version of the *pita* (filled with *myzithra* or wild greens, the former also eaten with honey).

Chios' claim to fame is *mastic*, the aromatic resin from the Mastic trees that grow almost exclusively on the island. Most people associate it with chewing gum, or the sticky white fondant sweet served in a glass of water (called *ypovryhio* or submarine), but it is also used to flavour pastries and other foods (as well as for medicinal purposes and skin products).

Foods of the Greek Islands, by Aglaïa Kremezi, explores the history, culture and cuisine of the islands and presents classic and new recipes from her travels and from New York's Molyvos restaurant.

The people of Crete probably eat more snails than the French, and Cretan snails are even exported to France.

TRAVEL YOUR TASTE BUDS

Look out for the following specialities on your island travels.

ahinosalata – sea urchin eggs with lemon juice (various islands)

amygdalota – almond sweets from Andros and Mykonos

anthi – zucchini flowers stuffed with rice and herbs from Crete

astakomakaronada – decadent lobster spaghetti (Cyclades, all islands)

dakos – rusks topped with tomato, olive oil and *myzithra* cheese from Crete

domatokeftedhes – tasty tomato fritters from Santorini

fava – yellow split-pea puree from Santorini

hohlioi Bourbouristoi – Crete's famous snail dish

kopanisti – spicy creamy cheese from Mykonos

loukoumi – Syros' renowned 'Turkish delight', also available throughout Greece

mastiha – mastic-flavoured *ypovryhio* or 'submarine' sugar confectionary from Chios, served on a spoon dipped in a glass of water or try the chilled liqueur

raki – you're unlikely to leave Crete without tasting the local firewater

Samos dessert wine – prized sweet wine from the local Muscat grape

soumada – non-alcoholic almond drink from the Cyclades

Quick Eats

Souvlaki is the favourite fast food of Greece, both the *gyros* and skewered versions wrapped in pitta bread, with tomato, onion and lashings of tzatziki. Cheese and spinach pies can be found in every bakery and food store.

There are plenty of Western-style *fastfoudadika* (as fast-food joints are called) in major cities and towns.

VEGETARIANS & VEGANS

Greece has few vegetarian restaurants, but a combination of lean times and the Orthodox faith's fasting traditions means there are plenty of vegetarian options. Look for dishes such as *yigandes* (giant white beans), *fasolakia yiahni* (green-bean stew), *bamies* (okra) and *briam* (mixed vegetables).

Of the wild greens *vlita* (amaranth) are the sweetest, but common varieties include wild radish, dandelion, stinging nettles and sorrel.

FEASTS & CELEBRATIONS

Food plays an integral part in Greek religious and cultural celebrations, with every morsel laced with symbolism. The Lenten fast before Easter involves special dishes without meat or dairy products – or even oil if you go strictly by the book. Come the resurrection, though, the celebrations begin with a supper that includes a bowl of *mayiritsa* (offal soup), while the highlight of the Easter Sunday feast is spit-roasted or baked lamb.

Red-dyed boiled eggs are part of the Easter festivities, for both cracking and decorating the *tsoureki*, a brioche-style bread flavoured with *mahlepi* (mahaleb cherry kernels).

Easter sweets include *koulourakia* (biscuits), *melomakarona* (honey biscuits) and *kourabiedes* (almond biscuits).

The New Year's *vasilopita* (golden-glazed cake) is baked with a lucky coin in the mix, giving the recipient good luck for the year.

> With as many anecdotes as recipes, Emma Tennant's *Corfu Banquet: A Seasonal Memoir with Recipes* is a delightfully evocative book.

HABITS & CUSTOMS

Hospitality is a key element of Greek culture, from the glass of water when you arrive at a café or restaurant to the customary complimentary fruit at the end of the meal. Dining is a drawn-out ritual, so if you are eating with locals pace yourself and don't gorge on the mezedhes, because there will be more to come.

Culinaria Greece is a superb weighty tome that explores Greek cuisine by region, recipes, history, a guide to Greek products and wine. Edited by Marianthi Milona, it's a glossy and useful reference with plenty of photos.

Greeks generally order way too much, and notoriously over-cater at home, as they would rather throw it out (or give it away) than not have enough.

Though you will find Western-style breakfasts and omelettes, breakfast is not a big Greek tradition.

Though changes in working hours are affecting traditional meal patterns, lunch is still usually the big meal of the day and does not start until after 2pm. Most Greeks wouldn't think of eating dinner before the sun goes down, which coincides with shop closing hours, so restaurants don't fill up until after 10pm. Cafés do a roaring trade after the siesta, between 6pm and 8pm.

The pace of service in tavernas can be slow by Western standards, but they are not in a rush to get you out of there either. Once you have your meals they are likely to leave you alone and often not clear the table until you ask for the bill.

Greeks don't drink coffee after a meal and many tavernas don't offer it.

EATING WITH KIDS

Greece is very child-friendly and families will feel very comfortable at tavernas and *psistaries*, where no-one is too fussed if children play between the tables. You will see families dining out late at night and packs of children

ISLAND GOURMET TRAILS

Greece has been slow to promote its culinary culture but some islands are slowly leading the way, placing more emphasis on local cuisine and moving beyond the classic staples.

Mousakas, souvlaki and *yemista* are great dishes, but cuisine has to evolve,' says Yiorgos Hatziyannakis, who has run Santorini's acclaimed Selene restaurant (p196) in Fira for more than 20 years. 'Everyone wants to sample local cuisine when they travel,' he says. 'We started with traditional dishes and developed new recipes based on a product of Santorini or the Cyclades.'

'It's something the French, Italians and Spanish have been doing for years', he says, 'where part of the travel experience is experiencing different cuisine from one region to another.' 'This has started happening in Greece, too. In Crete it's taken off in the past few years, it's starting in Rhodes and Corfu to a lesser extent,' explains Hatziyannakis, who also runs cooking seminars on Santorini's wine and cuisine.

Island cuisine evolved from people making the most of local conditions. Santorini's volcanic soil is renowned for producing unique wines (see p197), but it also reaps intensely flavoured cherry tomatoes, made into tangy tomato fritters. Its famous *fava* is made into a delicious creamy puree, while Santorini has its own white eggplant. The Cyclades' plump wild capers are the best in Greece.

With the easy availability of produce, Hatziyannakis says few people were still growing fave beans and cherry tomatoes and even fewer on the Cyclades were rearing sheep and goats for produding cheese (see the boxed text, opposite).

'We try to keep them going because no-one wants to be a farmer or shepherd these days. They have five rooms (for rent) in summer and they're fine.'

Crete is starting to tap into its potential as a gourmet tourism destination and preserve its culinary heritage. Traditional food is making a comeback and evolving, helped along by agrotourism ventures and programmes such as Concred (www.concred.gr), which accredits restaurants serving authentic Cretan cuisine.

One of Crete's gourmet trailblazers is Katerina Xekalou, who presides over the elegant Avli restaurant (p240) in Rethymno, one of the finest restaurants in Greece.

'We use only Cretan ingredients and traditional dishes, though sometimes we change the combinations and method,' explains Xekalou. Mushrooms and *apaki* (cured pork) were never used in the same dish but it works beautifully, while Avli's signature goat with thyme and honey dish evolved from her grandmother dipping boiled goat in honey.

'It's Cretan food with a twist. You don't have to replicate the past for it to be authentic.'

SAY CHEESE

Greeks are the world's biggest per capita consumers of cheese, eating something like 25kg per capita annually. Widely used in both savoury and sweet dishes, cheese is also a virtually mandatory accompaniment to any meal.

Greece probably produces as many different types of cheese as there are villages, with infinite variations in taste. Most are made from goat's and/or sheep's milk.

Feta, the national cheese made from sheep's and/or goat's milk, was the first Greek product to gain the same protected status as Parma ham and champagne, but several other Greek cheeses have gained similar appellation of origin status.

Graviera, a nutty, mild gruyere-like sheep's milk cheese is a speciality of Naxos and Crete, where it is often aged in special mountain caves and stone huts called *mitata*.

Anthotyro, a low-fat soft unsalted whey cheese similar to *myzithra* and the hardened sour *xinomyzithra* are also specialties of Crete.

Other island cheeses include *ladotiri*, a hard golden cheese from Lesvos preserved in olive oil, *mastelo* from Chios, the soft *chloro* in Santorini and *krasotyri* from Sifnos.

Tinos, Syros, Naxos and Corfu produce cow's milk cheese, a tradition from the Venetians.

playing outside while their parents indulge in a long dinner. Kids' menus are not common, but most places will accommodate requests (see p489).

COOKING COURSES

Several cooking courses and food tours are held on the islands.

Santorini's acclaimed **Selene** (www.selene.gr) restaurant runs one-day courses focusing on island specialities and wine.

Aglaïa Kremezi and her friends open their kitchens and gardens on Kea for five-day hands-on **cooking workshops** (www.keartisanal.com).

Award-winning Greek-American food writer Diane Kochilas runs the **Glorious Greek Kitchen** (www.gloriousgreekkitchen.com) summer cooking course on her ancestral island Ikaria.

Crete's Culinary Sanctuaries (www.cookingincrete.com) combines cooking classes, farm tours, hiking and cultural excursions around the island.

Zante Feast (www.zante-feast.org), a slow food, non-profit venture, organises foodie tours and cooking lessons on Zakynthos.

DRINKS
Wine

The Greeks invented wine, with the wine god Dionysus tramping the vintage even before the Bronze Age, yet until recently Greek wine was not associated all that favourably with the distinctive retsina (pine-resinated white wine) introduced to the world in the 1960s.

In the past 20 years a renaissance in the Greek wine industry has seen a new generation of progressive internationally trained winemakers reinventing Greek wine. Indigenous Greek grape varieties are being revived and brought to the fore, with some exquisite results.

Island vineyards produce some distinctive local wines from unique and rare grape varieties, including *robola* in Kefallonia and *assyrtiko*, *athiri* and *aidani* in the Cyclades, especially on Paros and Santorini. Wine tourism is popular in Santorini, where the volcanic soil produces unique wines, the vines are trained into a circle to protect the grapes from wind and the cellars are underground because of the heat. Crete's massive wine industry (producing about 20% of Greek wine) has become savvier and produces fine local varieties, including the white *vilana* and *thrapsathiri* grapes and the reds, *liatiko*, *kotsifali* and *mandilari*.

The Illustrated Greek Wine Book by Nico Manessis is the definitive reference for wine connoisseurs. It traces the history of Greek wine, profiles leading winemakers, wine regions and local varietals and reviews hundreds of wines.

Other Greek varieties include the white *moschofilero, roditis,* and *savatiano,* and red *xinomavro and agiorgitiko.* A rose *agiorgitiko* is the perfect summer wine. Greek wines are produced in relatively small quantities, however, and many are boutique wines (and priced accordingly).

Greek island sweet wines include muscats from Samos, Limnos and Rhodes and Santorini's Vinsanto (yes, the Greeks invented it).

For comprehensive details of the country's wine regions and producers, visit www.greekwine.gr.

As for retsina, nowadays it has taken on an almost folkloric significance with foreigners, some of whom confuse it with barrel wine (which is non-resinated). It goes well with strongly flavoured food, especially seafood, but it's an acquired taste.

Spirits

Apart from ouzo, Greece's main firewater is *tsipouro,* a highly potent distilled spirit produced from grape skins left over from winemaking. A similar but smoother variation called *raki* or *tsikoudia* is drunk in copious amounts in Crete.

Look out for sweet liquors like Kumquat from Corfu, Mastiha from Chios (best served chilled) and citrus-flavoured Kitro from Naxos.

Greek brandies tend to be sweet and flowery in the nose. The dominant brandy is Metaxa.

Beer

The most common beer is locally brewed Amstel and Heineken, though you can find a range of European beers. Major Greek brands include Mythos and Alfa.

A number of excellent smaller boutique breweries have sprouted in recent years. Look out for Vergina, the organic Piraïki beer and Hillas, while Craft beer is widely available in draught form.

The only island with its own beer is Crete, where the Rethymniaki brewery produces a selection of blonde and dark lagers that are making inroads throughout Greece.

Corfu produces a unique non-alcoholic ginger beer called Tsitsibira.

Hot Beverages

A legacy of Ottoman rule, Greek coffee is traditionally brewed in special copper *briki* (pots) on hot sand (a *hovoli*) and served in a small cup, where the grounds sink to the bottom (don't drink them). It is best drunk *metrio* (medium). Greek coffee is, however, struggling to maintain its place as the national drink against the ubiquitous frappé, the iced instant coffee concoction that you see everyone drinking. Espresso also comes in refreshing chilled form – *freddo*.

Herbal tea is quite popular, especially camomile tea and aromatic *tsai tou vounou* (mountain tea), which is nutritious and delicious. Crete's native Diktamo (Cretan dittany) is known for its healing properties, and the island's other reputedly medicinal warm tipple (found in many parts of Greece) is *rakomelo* – *raki*, honey and cloves.

EAT YOUR WORDS

Get behind the cuisine scene by getting to know the language. For pronunciation guidelines, see p519.

Useful Phrases

I want to make a reservation for this evening.
Θέλω να κλείσω ένα τραπέζι για απόψε.   *the·*lo na *kli·*so e·na tra·*pe·*zi ya a·*po·*pse
A table for... please.
Ένα τραπέζι για... παρακαλώ.   *e·*na tra·*pe·*zi ya . . ., pa·ra·ka·*lo*
I'd like the menu, please.
Το μενού, παρακαλώ.   to me·*nu*, pa·ra·ka·*lo*
Do you have a menu in English?
Έχετε το μενού στα αγγλικά?   *e·*hye·te to me·*nu* sta ang·li·*ka*?
I'd like...
Θα ήθελα...   tha *i·*the·la...
Please bring the bill.
Το λογαριασμό, παρακαλώ.   to lo·ghar·ya·*zmo*, pa·ra·ka·*lo*
I'm a vegetarian.
Είμαι χορτοφάγος.   *i·*me hor·to·*fa·*ghos
I don't eat meat or dairy products.
Δεν τρώω κρέας ή γαλακτοκομικά προϊόντα.   dhen *tro·*o *kre·*as i gha·la·kto·ko·mi·*ka* pro·i·*on·*da

Food Glossary

STAPLES

ψωμί	pso·*mi*	bread
βούτυρο	*vu·*ti·ro	butter
τυρί	ti·*ri*	cheese
αυγά	a·*vgha*	eggs
μέλι	*me·*li	honey
γάλα	*gha·*la	milk
ελαιόλαδο	e·le·o·la·dho	olive oil
ελιές	e·*lyes*	olives
πιπέρι	pi·*pe·*ri	pepper
αλάτι	a·*la·*ti	salt
ζάχαρη	*za·*ha·ri	sugar
ξύδι	*ksi·*dhi	vinegar

MEAT, FISH & SEAFOOD

βοδινό	vo·dhi·*no*	beef
ροφός	ro·*fos*	blackfish
κοτόπουλο	ko·*to·*pu·lo	chicken

σουπιές	sou·pi·es	cuttlefish
τσιπούρα	tsi·pou·ra	gilthead sea bream
κέφαλος	ke·fa·los	grey mullet
ζαμπόν	zam·bon	ham
λαγός	la·ghos	hare
κατοικάκι	ka·tsi·ka·ki	kid (goat)
αρνί	ar·ni	lamb
αστακός	a·sta·kos	lobster
κολιός	ko·li·os	mackerel
μύδια	mi·di·a	mussels
χταπόδι	ohta·po·dhi	octopus
χοιρινό	hyi·ri·no	pork
γαρίδες	gha·ri·dhes	prawns
κουνέλι	kou·ne·li	rabbit
μπαρμπούνι	bar·bou·ni	red mullet
σαρδέλες	sar·dhe·les	sardines
λαβράκι	la·vra·ki	sea bass
φαγρί/λιθρίνι/μελανούρι	fa·ghri/li·thri·ni/me·la·nu·ri	sea bream
καλαμάρι	ka·la·ma·ri	squid
ξιφίας	ksi·fi·as	swordfish
μοσχάρι	mos·ha·ri	veal
σφυρίδα	sfi·ri·dha	white grouper
μαρίδα	ma·ri·dha	whitebait

FRUIT & VEGETABLES

μήλο	mi·lo	apple
αγγινάρα	ang·gi·na·ra	artichoke
σπαράγγι	spa·rang·gi	asparagus
μελιτζάνα	me·li·dza·na	aubergine
λάχανο	la·ha·no	cabbage
καρότο	ka·ro·to	carrot
κεράσι	ke·ra·si	cherry
σύκα	sy·ka	figs
σκόρδο	skor·dho	garlic
σταφύλια	sta·fi·li·a	grapes
(άγρια) χόρτα	(a·ghri·a) hor·ta	greens, wild
λεμόνι	le·mo·ni	lemon
κρεμμύδια	kre·mi·dhi·a	onions
πορτοκάλι	por·to·ka·li	orange
ροδάκινο	ro·dha·ki·no	peach
αρακάς	a·ra·kas	peas
πιπεριές	pi·per·yes	peppers
πατάτες	pa·ta·tes	potatoes
γλυστρίδα	gli·stri·da	purslane
σπανάκι	spa·na·ki	spinach
φράουλα	fra·u·la	strawberry
ντομάτα	do·ma·ta	tomato
καρπούζι	kar·pou·zi	watermelon

DRINKS

μπύρα	bi·ra	beer
καφές	ka·fes	coffee
τσάι	tsa·i	tea
νερό	ne·ro	water
κρασί (κόκκινο/άσπρο)	kra·si (ko·ki·no/a·spro)	wine (red/white)

Environment

THE LAND

Greece lies at the southern tip of the rugged Balkan Peninsula. Most of the mainland is mountainous but the mainland is only a small part of Greece. It also has some 1400 islands, of which 169 are inhabited. They contribute only a small percentage of the nation's total landmass of 131,900 sq km, but are responsible for extending Greek territorial waters over more than 400,000 sq km.

The majority of islands are spread across the shallow waters of the Aegean Sea between Greece and Turkey. These are divided into four main groups: the Cyclades, the Dodecanese, the islands of the Northeastern Aegean and the Sporades. The two largest Aegean islands, Crete and Evia, do not belong to any group.

The other island groups are the Saronic Gulf Islands, which lie between Athens and the Peloponnese, and the Ionians, in the Ionian Sea between Greece and southern Italy, while Kythira stands alone below the southeastern tip of the Peloponnese.

Like the mainland, most of the terrain is extremely rugged. Crete has half a dozen peaks over 2000m, the highest of which is Mt Ida at 2456m. Evia, Karpathos, Kefallonia and Samothraki all boast peaks of more than 1500m.

Like the mainland, most of the ground is either too arid, too poor or too steep for intensive agriculture. There are several exceptions, such as Naxos and Crete, both of which are famous for the quality of their produce, and verdant Samothraki.

WILDLIFE
Animals

You're unlikely to encounter much in the way of wildlife on most of the islands. The exception is on larger islands like Crete and Evia, where squirrels, rabbits, hares, foxes and weasels are all fairly common. Reptiles are well represented, too: snakes include several viper species, which are poisonous; you're more likely to see lizards though, all of which are harmless.

One of the pleasures of island-hopping in Greece is watching the dolphins as they follow the boats. Although there are many dolphins in the Aegean, the striped dolphin has been the victim of murbilivirus – a sickness that affects the immune system.

Bird-watchers, however, have more chance of coming across something unusual in the Greek islands.

EARTHQUAKES – ISLAND TREMBLERS

The Greek islands lie in one of the most seismically active regions in the world, and unpredictable tremblers regularly shake, rattle and roll the tenants of this vast watery archipelago. Almost 3000 years ago a chain of massive volcanic eruptions and earthquakes all but destroyed Santorini (see Santorini's Unsettling Past, p192) and helped to reshape the landscape of the region. More than 20,000 quakes have been recorded in Greece in the last 40 years. Recent accounts across the islands include the 1953 quake that razed many of Zakynthos' neoclassical buildings, and the massive 1956 quake in Santorini that killed scores of people and destroyed many homes. In August 2003 an earthquake measuring 6.4 hit Lefkada and quakes were also recorded in the Ionians in 2006 and 2007, giving more than a few islanders the jitters. Fortunately, most quakes are very minor in nature – detectable only by sensitive seismic monitoring equipment stationed throughout the country.

Not surprisingly, seabirds are a major feature. Assorted gulls, petrels, shearwaters and shags are common throughout the Aegean. The islands are also home to a rich variety of birds of prey, particularly the mountains of larger islands like Crete and Evia. They include the spectacular griffon vulture and several species of eagle as well as peregrine falcons, harriers and hawks.

About 350 pairs (60% of the world's population) of the rare Eleonora's falcon nest on the island of Piperi, northeast of Alonissos in the Sporades. The Eleonora's falcon can also be spotted on a number of other islands, including Tilos, Naxos and Syros.

There are also a large number of migratory birds, most of which are merely passing by on their way from winter feeding sites in North Africa to summer nesting grounds in Eastern Europe.

The larger islands boast all the usual Mediterranean small birds – wagtails, tits, warblers, bee-eaters, larks, swallows, flycatchers, thrushes and chats – as well as some more distinctive species such as the hoopoe.

The Northeastern Aegean Islands are extremely popular with birdwatchers, particularly Lesvos where birding has become big business. Other rewarding destinations for birders are the islands of Naxos, Sifnos and Syros in the Cyclades, and Kos and Tilos in the Dodecanese.

ENDANGERED SPECIES

Europe's rarest mammal, the monk seal (*Monachus monachus*), was once common in the Mediterranean, but is now on the brink of extinction in Europe – it survives in slightly larger numbers in the Hawaiian islands. There are between 300 and 400 estimated to be living in Greece. There is a small colony in the Ionian Sea and the rest are found in the Aegean. These creatures are susceptible to human disturbance and now live in isolated coastal caves. Small colonies live on the islands of Alonnisos and there have been reported sightings on Tilos. The majority of reported seal deaths are the result of accidental trapping, but the main threat to their survival is the destruction of habitat. Tourist boats are major culprits. For more information visit the Hellenic Society for the Study and Protection of the Monk Seal at www.mom.gr.

The waters around Zakynthos are home to the last large sea-turtle colony in Europe, that of the loggerhead turtle (*Caretta caretta*). The loggerhead also nests in smaller numbers in the Peloponnese and on Crete.

The golden jackal (*Canis aureus*) is a strong candidate for Greece's most misunderstood mammal. Although its diet is 50% vegetarian, in the past it has shouldered much of the blame for attacks on stock carried out by wild dogs. It was hunted to the brink of extinction until it was declared a protected species in 1990, and now survives only in central Greece and on the island of Samos. It's strictly nocturnal. The other 50% of its diet is made up of carrion, reptiles and small mammals.

The Cretan wild goat, the kri-kri, survives in the wild only in the Samaria Gorge area and on the tiny islet of Kri Kri, off Agios Nikolaos on Crete.

Plants

Greece is endowed with a variety of flora unrivalled in Europe. There are over 6000 plant species (some of which occur nowhere else) and more than 100 varieties of orchid, which flower from late February to early June. They continue to thrive on the islands because most of the land is too poor for intensive agriculture and has escaped the ravages of chemical fertilisers.

The mountains of Crete boast some of the finest displays. Common species include anemones, white cyclamens, irises, lilies, poppies, gladioli, tulips

---

RESPONSIBLE TRAVEL

Visitors should travel responsibly at all times. Please follow these common-sense rules.

- Take care with your beach umbrella – you may be disturbing turtle eggs
- Don't disturb nesting birds – they may be endangered
- Don't toss garbage into the sea from ferry boats
- Take all refuse with you when vacating a beach
- Use water sparingly in your hotel room – it is a costly commodity on an island
- Do not discard items that could start a fire (cigarette butts, glass bottles etc) – forest fires are an annual torment, and were horrendous in 2007
- Stick to footpaths wherever possible
- Do not pick flowers or wilfully damage tree bark or roots – some of the species you see are protected
- Respect landowners' property and do not trespass
- Take care when walking near cliffs – they can be dangerously slippery and quick to crumble

---

and countless varieties of daisy. Look out for the blue-and-orange Cretan iris (*Iris cretica*), one of 120 wildflowers unique to Crete. Others are the pink Cretan ebony, the white-flowered symphyandra and the white-flowered *Cyclamen cretica*.

Other rare species found on the islands include the *Rhododendron luteum*, a yellow azalea that grows only on Lesvos.

Spectacular plants include the coastal giant reed – you may get lost among high, dense groves on your way to a beach – as well as the giant fennel, which grows to 3m, and the tall yellow-horned poppy, both of which grow by the sea. The white-flowered sea squill grows on hills above the coast. The perfumed sea daffodil grows along southern coasts, particularly on Crete and Corfu. The conspicuous snake's-head fritillary (*Fritillaria graeca*) has pink flowers shaped like snakes' heads, and the markings on the petals resemble a chequerboard – the Latin word *fritillus* means dice box.

Another common species is the Cyprus plane (*Platanus orientalis insularis*), which thrives wherever there is ample water. It seems as if every village on the mainland has a plane tree shading its central square – and a Taverna Platanos (Plane Tree Tavern).

Australian eucalypts were widely used in tree-planting programmes from the 1920s onwards, particularly on Crete.

NATIONAL PARKS

National Parks in Greece are not quite like what they are in modern Western societies. They tend to be protected reserves for the flora and fauna of the region first, rather than Disney-fied recreational grounds for socially conscious visitors. Facilities can be basic and yet there will be abundant walking trails, some quite rough and more often than not a clutch of basic refuges for guests that don't mind sparse conditions. Still, they serve their purpose and for the appreciative and unfussy visitor they will be an excellent alternative to the Yellowstones and Grand Canyons of this world. The only national parks on the islands are the Samaria Gorge (p253) on Crete and the Tilos Park on Tilos (p314). There are marine parks off the coast of Alonnisos (p434) in the Sporades, and at the Bay of Laganas (p481) on Zakynthos in the Ionians.

ENVIRONMENTAL ISSUES

Greece is belatedly becoming environmentally conscious. Deforestation and soil erosion, however, are problems that date back thousands of years. Olive cultivation and goats have been the main culprits, but firewood gathering, shipbuilding, housing and industry have all taken their toll.

Check out www.greece .gr/environment for more details on contemporary environmental issues.

Forest fires are also a major problem, with an estimated 25,000 hectares destroyed every year. The 2000 summer season was one of the worst on record, particularly on the island of Samos, while the disastrous fires of 2007 affected only the island of Evia.

Water shortages are a major problem on many islands, particularly smaller islands without a permanent water supply. These islands import their water by tanker, and visitors are urged to economise on water use wherever possible: small things, such as turning the tap off while you brush your teeth, can make a big difference.

General environmental awareness remains at a depressingly low level, especially where litter is concerned. Environmental education has begun in schools, but it will be a long time before community attitudes change. Sadly, many tourists seem to follow the local lead instead of setting a good example.

Marine Life

Surprisingly perhaps for a country with such an expanse of sea territory, the state of Greece's marine life is precarious. To their credit the Greeks have taken great pains to clean up their act in and around the water. Water clarity in the Saronic Gulf – once notoriously polluted – is almost on a par with the further reaches of the Aegean archipelago. Biological treatment of waste is largely responsible and has been very successful. Legislation aimed at preventing water pollution has been noticeably effective at keeping the quality of Greece's seawater at a respectable level of salinity. The problems here arise from foreign ships that illegally discharge their waste into the sea.

The more endemic problem, however, lies in overfishing – a problem that is admittedly Mediterranean-wide. While Greeks love their fresh-fish restaurants and will pay a premium to eat in them, finding the fresh fish is getting ever harder. More often than not it will come from fish-farmers or from further afield. Greece now produces more than 60,000 tons per annum of farmed fish and around 60% of the EU's sea bass and sea bream.

Greek Islands Outdoors

The Greek islands, while a great playground for relaxing and soaking up culture, offer a whole lot more things to do to keep your mind active and your body fit. Water-based activities prevail, naturally, with windsurfing, water-skiing, kitesurfing and diving dominating, but there's more. You can scale precipitous rocks, hike hidden gorges, cycle a bike or even hire a yacht. This widely scattered archipelago is just waiting for you to get active and explore it.

HIKING

The Greek islands are a veritable paradise for hikers, offering an extraordinary variety of landscapes ranging from remote coastal paths to dramatic mountain gorges.

Spring (April to May) is the best time. Walkers will find the countryside green and fresh from the winter rains, and carpeted with the spectacular array of wildflowers for which the islands are justly famous. Autumn (September to October) is another good time, but July and August, when the temperatures are constantly up around 40°C, are not much fun at all. Whatever time of year you opt to set out, you will need to come equipped with a good pair of walking boots to handle the rough, rocky terrain, a wide-brimmed hat and a high UV-factor sunscreen.

Some of the most popular hikes are detailed in this book, but there are possibilities just about everywhere. On small islands it's fun to discover pathways for yourself, and you are unlikely to get into danger as settlements or roads are never far away. You will encounter a variety of paths – *kalderimia* are cobbled or flagstone paths that link settlements and date back to Byzantine times – but sadly, many have been bulldozed to make way for roads.

If you're going to be venturing off the beaten track, a good map is essential. Unfortunately, most of the tourist maps sold around the islands are pitifully inadequate. The best hiking maps for the islands are produced by Athens company Anavasi (see p496 for details).

The following is a brief description of the best hiking possibilities around the islands.

The Gorge of Ha near Ierapetra is considered too challenging for most hikers. It is extremely narrow and precipitous and has only been traversed by a handful of people. See www .climbincrete.com for details.

Crete

The spectacular Samaria Gorge (p253) needs little introduction as it is one of Europe's most popular hikes and one of the island's main tourist attractions, drawing thousands of walkers every year.

The gorge begins at Xyloskalo high on the southern slopes of the lofty Lefka Ori (White Mountains) and finishes at the coastal settlement of Agia Roumeli (p254). Its width varies from 150m to 3.5m (the famous Iron Gates)

ORGANISED HIKES

There are a number of companies running organised hikes and one of the biggest is **Trekking Hellas** (☎ 210 323 4548; www.trekking.gr; Filellinon 7, Athens 105 57). Its programme includes a nine-day island-hopping hike through the Cyclades making stops at Tinos (p132), Mykonos (p141), Naxos (p161) and Santorini (Thira; p190); and an eight-day hike in western Crete that takes in the Samaria Gorge (p253). Both tours start and finish in Athens and cost about €160 per day, including transfers, full board and an English-speaking guide. Trekking Hellas also runs half-day weekend hikes in the Lake Korision area of southern Corfu for €60, including transfers from Corfu Town.

You'll find more information about organised hikes in Hania (p247) and Rethymno (p238).

and its vertical walls reach 500m at their highest points. The gorge has an incredible number of wildflowers, which are at their best in April and May. It is also home to a large number of endangered species, including the Cretan wild goat, the shy and elusive kri-kri.

Winter rains and conditions render the gorge impassable from mid-October until mid-April.

People who prefer a more solitary hike will enjoy the coastal path that links the southwest coastal villages of Agia Roumeli and Hora Sfakion (p255). Another favourite is the two-hour stroll from Zakros to the remote Minoan palace site of Kato Zakros (p269) in eastern Crete. The walk passes through the mysterious sounding Valley of the Dead, so named because of the cave tombs dotted along the rugged cliffs that line the valley. The island has a number of other gorge walks that are all accessible to hikers with solid shoes and a stout constitution.

Cyclades

Naxos (p161) has long been a favourite destination for walkers, particularly the beautiful Tragaea region (p167) – a broad central plain of olive groves dotted with unspoiled villages and ancient Byzantine churches. The more energetic will enjoy the short but strenuous climb from the village of Filoti to the Cave of Zeus. Andros (p128) is another good choice, particularly the hills around the small west-coast resort of Batsi.

Dodecanese

Tranquil Tilos (p310) is one of the few islands that has escaped the ravages of mass tourism. It's a terrific place for walkers, with dramatic cliff-top paths that lead to uncrowded beaches. For something completely different, there's nothing to rival the bizarre landscape of volcanic Nisyros (p314), where walkers can check the hissing craters that dot Mt Polyvotis for signs of activity.

Evia & the Sporades

Alonnisos (p432) enjoys a glowing reputation as the Aegean's cleanest and greenest island. In recent years it's been attracting growing numbers of walkers, who come to hike a network of established trails and swim at remote pristine beaches. Skopelos (p427) has a good set of trails and many organised walking tours are available, some of them ending conveniently at a restaurant or taverna.

THE ISLANDS BY BIKE

It's not the most obvious way to get around the Greek islands, but carting your own pedal-powered wheels from island to island is an ideal way to carry you and your baggage from place to place. Bicycles usually travel for free on the ferries so there is no extra outlay, nor do you have to pony up valuable cash to hire motorised wheels when you arrive. You can be last onto the ferry and first off – free to pedal off to the nearest beach or to look for accommodation. Islands do not have the frenzied traffic of the mainland and cycling is actually fun. While islands tend not to be so flat, a bike with a good set of gears will tackle most inclines with ease. While virtually any island will lend itself to some kind of cycling activity, the Dodecanese island of Kos (p317) is perhaps the best equipped and most cyclist-friendly. Bicycle-hire outfits are everywhere and a bicycle is almost *de rigueur* for many visitors. Peletons of pedlers can be encountered all over the flat and winding lanes of the north coast of Kos. It is better to burn fat than oil, so pedal on and see the islands the natural way – on a bike.

For guided cycling tours see the Greece-based outfits **BicycleGreece** (www.bicyclegreece.com) or **CycleGreece** (www.cyclegreece.gr); or the UK-based **2 Wheel Treks** (www.2wheeltreks.co.uk).

ROCK CLIMBING

The sheer rugged cliffs and gnarled mountainsides of many of the Greek islands offer the potential for some adrenaline-pumping scaling of vertical rock. Yet until 1996 virtually no-one had even thought about rock climbing on Kalymnos (p332). At that time renowned Italian climber Andrea di Bari took a holiday on Kalymnos – without climbing equipment – and discovered several potential climbing routes on the sheers cliffs of the island's west side. Returning in 1997 with a group of enthusiasts they tested and opened up some 43 climbing routes. Within three years they had opened a rock-climbing course in collaboration with the Municipality of Kalymnos and there was no looking back. Greek instructors took over the day-to-day management of the course while the Municipality took on the responsibility for the management and protection of the routes. Today rock climbing remains one of the island's more lucrative yet little-known businesses. For fuller details on the sport, see the website of the Municipality of Kalymnos, www.kalymnos_isl.gr.

Ionian Islands

Good things come in small packages, or so the saying goes. It's certainly the case on tiny Paxi (p459), the smallest of the main Ionian Islands. Its landscape of ancient, gnarled olive groves and snaking dry-stone walls is a great choice for walkers who really want to escape the crowds.

On Ithaki (p473), the long-lost island homeland of Trojan War–hero Odysseus, mythology fans will enjoy seeking out the handful of sites associated with the Homeric legend.

Northeastern Aegean Islands

The Northeastern Aegean Islands are a long-time favourite with walkers. Samos (p366) is one of the most-visited islands in Greece, but most visitors stick to the resorts of the south coast – leaving the interior almost unscathed. The best walking area is around the delightful mountain villages of Manolates and Vourliotes (p374), set on the forested northern slopes of Mt Ambelos. Walkers who are still out and about at dusk may be lucky enough to spot one of the country's most-endangered species, the golden jackal (p62), which lives only on Samos and in parts of central Greece. Lesvos (Mytilini; p386) is another good choice, especially for bird-watching.

Saronic Gulf Islands

Walking has always been the main form of transport on traffic-free Hydra (p115), where a well-maintained network of paths links the island's various beaches and monasteries.

DIVING & SNORKELLING

There are some excellent dive sites around the Greek islands, but diving is subject to strict regulations in order to protect the many antiquities in the depths of the Aegean.

Any kind of underwater activity using breathing apparatus is strictly forbidden unless under the supervision of a diving school. Diving is only permitted between sunrise and sunset, and only in specified locations. There are also strict controls on diving activities: underwater photography of archaeological finds is prohibited, as is spear fishing with diving equipment.

Don't be put off by all the red tape. Diving is rapidly growing in popularity, and there are diving schools on the islands of Corfu (p455), Crete (at Rethymno; p239), Evia (at Halkida; p418), Hydra (p117), Leros (at Xirokambos; p336), Milos (at Adamas; p208), Mykonos (p149), Paros (p159) and Antiparos (p160), Rhodes (p284), Santorini (at Kamari; p200) and Skiathos (p427). Most charge around €50 for a dive, and from €250 for courses; prices include all equipment.

Check out the **Internet Scuba Diving Club** (www.isdc.gr) for more information about diving. You'll also get useful information from the **Professional Association of Diving Instructors** (PADI; www.padi.com); its website has a list of all PADI-approved dive centres in Greece.

Snorkelling is enjoyable just about anywhere in the islands and has the advantage of being totally unencumbered by regulations. All the equipment you need – mask, fins and snorkel – are cheaply available everywhere.

Especially good places are Monastiri (p158) on Paros; Paleokastritsa (p456) on Corfu; Telendos Islet (near Kalymnos; p332); Ammoöpi (p297) in southern Karpathos; Xirokambos Bay (p336) on Leros; and anywhere off the coast of Kastellorizo (Megisti; p303). Many dive schools also use their boats to take groups of snorkellers to prime spots.

Organised Tours

Trekking Hellas (☎ 210 323 4548; www.trekking.gr; Filellinon 7, Athens 105 57) offers four-day diving holidays on Paros that include dives off the islands of Iraklia, Schinousa, Koufonisia and Naxos. It also offers dives off Corfu and Lesvos.

WINDSURFING

> The excellent website www.club-mistral .com provides details on windsurfing holidays in Afiartis Bay, Karpathos in the Dodecanese. Good information on accommodation options and surfing conditions.

Windsurfing is the most popular water sport in Greece. Many people reckon that Vasiliki Bay (p466), on the south coast of the Ionian island of Lefkada, is one of the best places in the world to learn the sport. Hrysi Akti (p159) on Paros is another favourite.

There are numerous other prime locations around the islands, including Afiartis Bay (p297) on Karpathos; Ormos Korthiou (p131) on Andros; Kalafatis beach (p149) on Mykonos; Agios Giorgios beach (p167) on Naxos; Milopotas beach (p188) on Ios; Prasonisi (p290) in southern Rhodes; around Tingaki (p323) on Kos; Kokkari (p374) on Samos; around Skala Sotira (p411) on Thasos; and Koukounaries Beach (p426) on Skiathos.

You'll find sailboards for hire almost everywhere. Hire charges range from €10 to €25, depending on the gear and the location. If you are a novice, most places that rent equipment also give lessons; reckon on about €200 to €250 for a 10-hour beginners' course.

Sailboards can be imported freely from other EU countries, but importing boards from other destinations, such as Australia and the USA, is subject to some quaint regulations. Theoretically, importers need a Greek national residing in Greece to guarantee that the board will be taken out again. Contact the **Hellenic Windsurfing Association** (☎ 210 323 0330; www.ghiolman.com; Filellinon 7, Athens 105 57) for more information.

KITESURFING

> One of the craziest new sports to hit the Greek islands is kitesurfing. This is a wild mix of windsurfing and paragliding – only the fit and agile need apply. Lefkada, Rhodes and Paros are among the new sport's centres.

This relatively new action sport that combines windsurfing, snowboarding, wakeboarding, traction kites and paragliding is considered one of the most extreme watersports. The beaches of Greece are beginning to be festooned with the sight of athletic young surfers alternately surfing and flying on short, but fat surfboards. The **Greek Wakeboard and Kite Surf Association** (☎ 69445 17963; www.gwa.gr) has all the details of popular locales in Greece for this growing action sport.

WATER-SKIING

There are three islands with water-ski centres: Kythira (p482), Paros (p152) and Skiathos (p422).

Given the relatively calm and flat waters of most island locations and the generally warm waters of the Aegean, water-skiing can be a very pleasant activity. August can be a tricky month when the *meltemi* (northeasterly wind) can make conditions difficult in the central Aegean. The island of Poros (p112) near Athens is a particularly well-organised locale, with an organisation called **Passage** (☎ 22980 42540; www.passage.gr; Neorion Bay) hosting a popular school and slalom centre.

YACHTING

Despite some disparaging remarks among backpackers, yachting is *the* way to see the Greek islands. Nothing beats the peace and serenity of sailing the open sea, and the freedom of being able to visit remote and uninhabited islands.

The free EOT (Greek National Tourist Organisation) booklet, *Sailing the Greek Seas*, contains lots of information about weather conditions, weather bulletins, entry and exit regulations, entry and exit ports and guidebooks for yachties. You can pick up the booklet at EOT/GNTO offices either abroad or in Greece. The internet is the place to look for the latest information – **Hellenic Yachting Server** (www.yachting.gr) has general information on sailing around the islands and lots of links.

The sailing season lasts from April until October, although the best time to go depends on where you are going. The most popular time is between July and September, which ties in with the high season for tourism in general. Unfortunately, it also happens to be the time of year when the *meltemi* is at its strongest (see p490 for details). The *meltemi* is not an issue in the Ionian Sea, where the main summer wind is the *maïstros*, a light to moderate northwesterly that rises in the afternoon and usually dies away at sunset.

Greek Waters Pilot (1998), by Rod Heikell, is the definitive sailing handbook to the Greek islands. If you plan to sail your way around the islands this complete guide will help you find your way without going astray.

Organised Tours

Individuals can consider joining a yachting cruise, which usually has a maximum of around eight people. **Ghiolman Yachts & Travel** (☎ 210 323 3696; www.ghiolman.com; Filellinon 7, Athens 105 57) has a range of seven-day island cruises, including an Ionian cruise leaving Corfu every Saturday, a Dodecanese cruise leaving Rhodes every Thursday and a Cycladic cruise leaving Piraeus every Friday. Berths on board these boats are priced from €670, and include half-board and the services of an English-speaking guide. All three cruises operate weekly from early May to the end of September.

Trekking Hellas (☎ 210 323 4548; www.trekking.gr; Filellinon 7, Athens 105 57) also offers a range of yachting and sailing holidays around the Cyclades and the Ionians by caïque or by yacht.

Yacht Hire

You can hire a bare boat (a yacht without a crew) if two crew members have a sailing certificate. Prices start at about €1000 per week for a 28-footer that will sleep six and it will cost an extra €840 per week to hire a skipper.

Most of the big hire companies are based in and around Athens. They include the following:

Aegean Cruises (☎ 210 964 9967; www.aegean-cruises.gr; cnr Poseidonos & Davaki, Alimos 174 55)

Alpha Yachting (☎ 210 968 0486; www.alphayachting.com; Poseidonos 67, Glyfada 166 75)

Ghiolman Yachts & Travel (☎ 210 323 3696; www.ghiolman.com; Filellinon 7, Athens 105 57)

Hellenic Charters (☎ 210 960 7174; www.hellenic-charters.gr; Arsitotelous 19-21, Glyfada 166 74)

Vernicos Yachts (☎ 210 989 6000; www.vernicos.gr; Poseidonos 11, Alimos 174 55)

You'll find details about yacht-charter companies on the islands of Milos (at Adamas; p208), Paros (at Naousa; p158) and Syros (at Ermoupolis; p139) in the Cyclades.

Athens & the Mainland Ports

For most visitors to Athens a magical moment is spotting the gleaming marble columns of the Parthenon perched atop the rocky hulk of the Acropolis – a moment like no other.

Often rushed through by travellers in search of their magical Greek island, Athens deserves much more than a brief dalliance. It is a city that never sleeps; it's a city of world-class museums, and where antiquities still dot street corners or may lie buried and undiscovered under a layer of marble, cement and asphalt. For cuisine Athens rivals, if not surpasses, other capitals. Its nightlife only begins when many of us may be considering taking to our beds and takes a brief pause only just before the sun comes up. When you do sleep you can do so in homey comfort or world-class luxury. Athens' traffic is incessant and can seem like a Grand Prix on a busy day it is true, but a smooth metro system, trolley buses and even a tram can take you around in air-conditioned comfort.

Athens can exhilarate, exasperate and yet be exonerated in equal doses. As a city it is unique. It sits with one eye on the East and the other to the West. It's part of Europe but has never forgotten its oriental roots. It is definitely worth a few days, though even a month would hardly suffice. Athens is a city with a glorious past and a burgeoning future.

HIGHLIGHTS

- **Magic Moment** Ascending the funicular railway at night to Lykavittos Hill (p76) and and being greeted by the sight of Athens' lights
- **Northern Delight** Enjoying the subtle comforts of Macedonia's seaside town and port of Kavala (p101)
- **Dining** Sitting down to a table of Cretan delicacies in Thessaloniki (p93) to the sound of the violin or bouzouki
- **Showtime** Watching your favourite rock star perform under the stars at the Lykavittos Theatre (p77) in Athens
- **Historical Experience** Walking along the marble pathways of Athens historic Parthenon (p75)
- **Panorama** Catching the stunning views from the walls of the Kastra (p91) in Thessaloniki

★ Kavala
★ Thessaloniki
★ Athens

POPULATION: ATHENS 3.4 MILLION, ATTICA 4 MILLION	AREA: 3808 SQ KM

ATHENS ΑΘΗΝΑ

HISTORY

The early history of Athens is so interwoven with mythology that it's hard to disentangle fact from fiction.

The Acropolis has been occupied since Neolithic times. It was an excellent vantage point and the steep slopes formed natural defences on three sides. By 1400 BC the Acropolis was a powerful Mycenaean city. Its power peaked during the so-called golden age of Athens in the 5th century BC, following the defeat of the Persians at the Battle of Salamis. The city fell into decline after its defeat by Sparta in the long-running Peloponnesian War, but rallied again in Roman times when it became a seat of learning. The Roman emperors, particularly Hadrian, graced Athens with many grand buildings.

After the Roman Empire split into east and west, the power shifted to Byzantium (modern day İstanbul) and Athens fell into obscurity. By the end of Ottoman rule, Athens was little more than a dilapidated village (the area now known as Plaka).

Then, in 1834, the newly crowned King Otto transferred his court from Nafplio in the Peloponnese and made Athens the capital of independent Greece. The city was rebuilt along neoclassical lines, featuring large squares and tree-lined boulevards with imposing public buildings. The city grew steadily and enjoyed a brief heyday as the 'Paris of the Mediterranean' in the late 19th and early 20th centuries.

This came to an abrupt end with the forced population exchange between Greece and Turkey, which followed the Treaty of Lausanne in 1923. The huge influx of refugees from Asia Minor virtually doubled the population overnight, forcing the hasty erection of the first of the many concrete apartment blocks that dominate the city today. The belated advent of Greece's industrial age in the 1950s brought another wave of migration, this time of rural folk looking for work.

The city's infrastructure, particularly road and transport, could not keep pace with such rapid and unplanned growth, and by the end of the '80s the city had developed a sorry reputation as one of the most traffic-clogged and polluted in Europe.

The 1990s appear to have been a turning point in the city's development. Jolted into action by the failed bid to stage the 1996 Olympics, authorities embarked on an ambitious programme to prepare the city for the 21st century. Two key elements have been the extension of the metro network and the construction of a new international airport.

These projects played an important role in the city's successful staging of the 2004 Olympics. The legacy of the games is that Athens today is a radically different city – a more attractive, cleaner, greener and efficient capital, though still a work in progress.

ORIENTATION

Although Athens is a huge, sprawling city, nearly everything of interest to short-term visitors lies within a small area bounded by Plateia Omonias (Omonia Sq) to the north, Plateia Monastirakiou (Monastiraki Sq) to the west, Plateia Syntagmatos (Syntagma Sq) to the east and the Plaka district to the south. The city's two major landmarks, the Acropolis and Lykavittos Hill, can be seen from just about everywhere in this area.

Plaka, the old Ottoman quarter that was all that existed when Athens was declared the capital of independent Greece, nestles on the northeastern slope of the Acropolis. It may be touristy, but it's the most attractive and interesting part of Athens and the majority of visitors make it their base.

INFORMATION
Bookshops

Compendium (Map p78; ☎ 210 322 1248; Navarhou Nikodemou 5 & Nikis, Plaka) Specialises in books in English, and has a popular secondhand section.

Eleftheroudakis Syntagma (Map p78; ☎ 210 331 4180; Panepistimiou 17); Plaka (Map p78; ☎ 210 322 9388; Nikis 20) The seven-floor Panepistimiou store is the biggest bookshop in Athens, with a level dedicated to English-language books.

Road Editions (Map p72; ☎ 210 361 3242; www.road .gr; Solonos 71, Exarhia) A wide range of travel literature and all the Road Editions maps.

Emergency

Athens Central Police Station (☎ 210 770 5711/17; Leoforos Alexandras 173, Ambelokipi)
ELPA Road Assistance (☎ 10400)
Police (☎ 100)
Tourist police (Map p72; 24hr ☎ 171, 210 920 0724; Veïkou 43-45, Koukaki; ⏱ 8am-10pm)
Visitor Emergency Assistance (☎ 112) Toll-free 24-hour service in English or French.

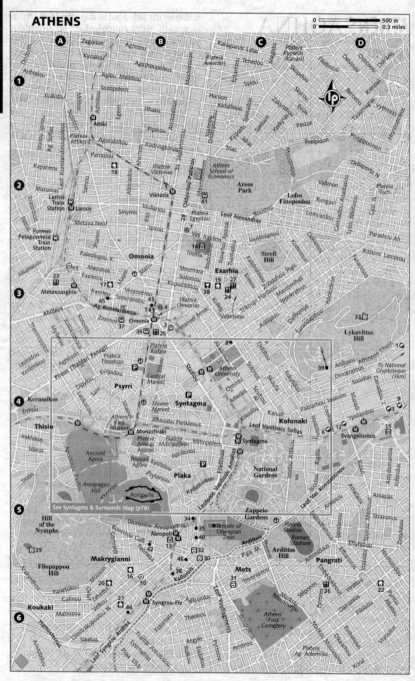

Internet Access

Most midrange and top-end hotels have in-room internet access. There are free wireless hotspots at Plateia Syntagmatos, at Starbucks cafés, some McDonald's stores and the port of Piraeus. Internet cafés around the city centre charge between €2 and €4 per hour.

Bits & Bytes Internet Café (Map p78; Kapnikareas 19; per hr €3; ☯ 24hr)

Cyberzone (Map p72; ☎ 210 520 3939; Satovrianidou 7, Omonia; per hr €2; ☯ 24hr) Cheaper rates of €1.50 per hour apply between midnight and 8am.

Ivis Internet (Map p78; Mitropoleos 3, Syntagma; per hr €3; ☯ 24hr)

Museum Internet Café (Map p72; ☎ 210 883 3418; 28 Oktovriou-Patision 46, Omonia; per hr €4.40; ☯ 10am-2am Mon-Fri, 11am-2am Sat & Sun) Next to the National Archaeological Museum.

Internet Resources

www.athenstourism.gr A handy site from the Athens Tourism and Economic Development Agency.

www.cityofathens.gr City of Athens site with walks, events and other useful information.

www.culture.gr The revamped Ministry of Culture guide to museums, archaeological sites and cultural events around Greece.

Laundry

Plaka Laundrette (Map p78; ☎ 210 321 3102; Angelou Geronta 10, Plaka; wash & dry 5kg €9; ☯ 8am-7pm Mon-Sat, 8am-1pm Sun)

Left Luggage

Many hotels will store luggage free for guests, although most do no more than pile the bags in a hallway. You'll find left-luggage facilities at the airport, at the metro stations of Omonia, Monastiraki and Piraeus, and at the Peloponnese train station next to Stathmos Larisis (p90).

Pacific Travel Luggage Storage (Map p78; ☎ 210 324 1007; Nikis 26, Syntagma; €2 per day; ☯ 8am-8pm Mon-Sat)

Medical Services

Ambulance/First-Aid Advice (☎ 166)

Duty Doctors & Hospitals (☎ 1434 in Greek) Published in *Kathimerini*.

Pharmacies (☎ 1434 in Greek) Check pharmacy windows for notice of nearest duty pharmacy. There is a 24-hour pharmacy at the airport.

SOS Doctors (☎ 1016, 210 821 1888; ☯ 24hr) Pay service with English-speaking doctors.

Money

Most major banks have branches around Syntagma and there are ATMs all over the city. Standard bank opening hours are 8am to 2.30pm Monday to Thursday and 8am to 2pm on Friday, though some private banks open certain branches until 8pm weekdays and on Saturdays.

Alpha Bank (Map p78; ☎ 210 324 1039 Panepistimiou 3; ☯ 8am-8pm Mon-Fri, 10am-4.30pm Sat)

American Express (Map p78; ☎ 210 324 4979; Ermou 7, Syntagma; ☯ 8.30am-4pm Mon-Fri)

Eurochange Syntagma (Map p78; ☎ 210 322 0155; Karageorgi Servias 2, Syntagma; ☯ 8am-9pm); Omonia (Map p72; ☎ 210 520 1371; Agiou Konstantinou 34) Exchanges Thomas Cook travellers cheques without commission.

National Bank of Greece (Map p78; ☎ 210 334 0500; cnr Karageorgi Servias & Stadiou, Syntagma) Has a 24-hour automated exchange machine.

Post

Athens Central post office (Map p72; www.elta.gr; Eolou 100, Omonia; ☟ 7.30am-8pm Mon-Fri, 7.30am-2pm Sat) Unless specified otherwise, all *poste restante* (general delivery) is sent here.

Parcel post office (Map p78; Nikis 33, Syntagma; ☟ 7.30am-2pm Mon-Fri) Parcels weighing over 2kg must be taken here, unwrapped, for inspection.

Syntagma post office (Map p78; Plateia Syntagmatos; ☟ 7.30am-8pm Mon-Fri, 7.30am-2pm Sat)

Telephone

Public phones all over Athens allow local, long-distance and international calls. They only take phone cards, which are widely available at kiosks. Use call cards, which like Hronokarta, are available from kiosks for much cheaper rates.

Toilets

Public toilets are relatively scarce in Athens and keep inconsistent hours, though there are 24-hour portable, self-cleaning pay toilets (€0.50) around the centre. Fast-food outlets are handy and cafés will normally let you use their facilities. Big hotels are also a safe bet.

Tourist Information

EOT Syntagma (Greek National Tourist Organisation; Map p78; ☎ 210 331 0392; www.gnto.gr; Amalias 26a, Syntagma; ☟ 9am-7pm Mon-Fri, 10am-4pm Sat & Sun); Airport (☎ 210 353 0445-7; Arrivals Hall; ☟ 9am-6pm Mon-Fri, 10am-3pm Sat & Sun) Has a handy free map of Athens, weekly ferry timetables and public transport information. You can also pick up a free copy of the glossy *Athens & Attica* booklet.

Tourist police (Map p72; 24hr ☎ 171, 210 920 0724; Veïkou 43-45, Koukaki; ☟ 8am-10pm) General tourist information and emergency help.

DANGERS & ANNOYANCES

Lonely Planet continues to hear from readers who have been taken in by one of the various bar scams that operate around central Athens. The scam runs something like this: friendly Greek approaches male traveller and discovers that the traveller knows little about Athens; friendly Greek then reveals that he, too, is from out of town. Why don't they go to this great bar that he's just discovered and have a beer? They order a drink and the friendly

owner then offers another drink. Women appear, more drinks are provided and the visitor relaxes as he realises that the women are not prostitutes, just friendly Greeks. The crunch comes at the end of the night when the traveller is presented with a huge bill and the smiles disappear. The con men who cruise the streets playing the role of the friendly Greek can be very convincing: some people have been taken in more than once.

Other bars don't bother with the acting. They target intoxicated males with talk of sex and present them with outrageous bills.

SIGHTS
Ancient Agora

The **agora** (Map p78; ☎ 210 321 0185; Adrianou; adult/concession €4/2; museum ☟ 8am-7.30pm Jun-Oct, 8am-5.30pm Nov-May) was the marketplace – and focal point – of civic life. The main monuments are the **Temple of Hephaestus**, the 11th-century **Church of the Holy Apostles** and the **Stoa of Attalos**, which houses the museum.

Roman Agora

The Romans built an **agora** (☎ 210 324 5220; cnr Pelopida Eolou & Markou Aureliou; adult/concession €2/1; ☟ 8am-7.30pm Jun-Oct, 8am-5.30pm Nov-May) east of the Ancient Agora. Visit the Tower of the Winds, built in the 1st century BC by Andronicus, a Syrian astronomer. This ingenious construction functioned as a sundial, weather vane, water clock and compass.

Changing of the Guard

Every Sunday at 11am a platoon of traditionally dressed *evzones* (guards) marches down Leoforos Vasilissis Sofias, accompanied by a band, to the Tomb of the Unknown Soldier in front of the **parliament building** (Map p78; Syntagma).

Keramikos

The city's cemetery from the 12th century BC to Roman times was the **Keramikos** ☎ 210 346 3552; Ermou 148, Keramikos; adult/concession €2/1 incl museum; ☟ 8am-7.30pm Apr-Oct, 8am-5.30pm Nov-Mar). It was discovered in 1861 during the construction of Pireos, the street that leads to Piraeus. It is one of the most green and tranquil of Athens' ancient sites. The Keramikos is a five-minute walk west of Thision metro station.

Temple of Olympian Zeus

This is the largest **temple** (Map p72; ☎ 210 922 6330; adult/concession €2/1; ☟ 8am-7.30pm Jun-Oct, 8am-

5.30pm Nov-May) in Greece and sits just east of the Acropolis. Construction was begun in the 6th century BC by Peisistratos, but was abandoned for lack of funds. Various other leaders had stabs at completing the temple, but it was left to Hadrian to complete the work in AD 131. It took over 700 years to build.

The temple is impressive for the sheer size of its 104 Corinthian columns (17m high with a base diameter of 1.7m), of which 15 remain – the fallen column was blown down in a gale in 1852. Hadrian put a colossal statue of Zeus in the cella and, in typically immodest fashion, placed an equally large one of himself next to it.

Museums & Galleries

One of the world's great museums, the **National Archaeological Museum** (Map p72; ☎ 210 821 7724; www.culture.gr; 28 Oktovriou-Patision 44, Athens; adult/concession €7/3; ☼ 10am-5pm Mon, 8am-7.30pm Tue-Sun Apr-Oct, 8.30am-3pm Nov-Mar) houses important finds from Greece's archaeological sites.

The museum, which was damaged in the 1999 earthquake, was totally overhauled and reopened in 2004 prior to the Olympic Games. The collection has been rearranged thematically and is beautifully presented, with information and labels in English and Greek. Hundreds of pieces held in storage are now on display, while galleries that were closed for many years have reopened. The final two galleries, with the Egyptian and Stathatos collections, were temporarily closed.

With 10,000 sq metres of exhibition space, it could take several visits to appreciate the museum's vast holdings, but it is possible to see the highlights in a half-day.

The crowd-pullers are the magnificent, exquisitely detailed gold artefacts from Mycenae and the spectacular Minoan frescoes from Santorini (Thira).

The long-awaited new **Acropolis Museum** (Map p72; ☎ 210 321 0219; Makrygianni 2-4; ☼ 8am-7pm Apr-Oct, 8am-5pm Nov-Mar) is set to open by 2008 on a massive site at the southern base of the Acropolis.

Construction of the museum was plagued by legal action and delays after the excavation uncovered the remains of an Athenian city dating back to prehistoric times. The impressive ruins have been incorporated into the design, with around 2000 sq metres of the old city on display in the basement through a series of elevated walkways and glass floors.

Designed by leading architect Bernard Tschumi, the museum will bring together all the surviving treasures of the Acropolis, including those transferred from the old museum up on the Acropolis, as well as pieces from other Athenian museums and storage facilities.

The **Benaki Museum** (Map p78; ☎ 210 367 1000; www.benaki.gr; Leoforos Vasilissis Sofias & Koumbari 1, Kolonaki; adult/concession €6/3, free Thu; ☼ 9am-5pm Mon, Wed, Fri & Sat, 9am-midnight Thu, 9am-3pm Sun) contains the collection of Antoine Benaki, accumulated during 35 years of avid collecting throughout Europe and Asia. The collection includes ancient sculpture, Bronze Age finds from Mycenae and Thessaly, two early works by El Greco and a stunning collection of Greek regional costumes.

The **Goulandris Museum of Cycladic & Ancient Greek Art** (Map p78; ☎ 210 722 8321; www.cycladic.gr; cnr Leoforos Vasilissis Sofias & Neofytou Douka, Kolonaki; adult/concession €5/2; ☼ 10am-4pm Mon & Wed-Fri, 10am-3pm Sat) houses a collection of Cycladic art second in importance only to that at the National Archaeological Museum. The museum was custom-built for the collection and the finds are beautifully displayed and labelled.

The emphasis in the **National Art Gallery** (Map p72; ☎ 210 723 5857; Leoforos Vasileos Konstantinou 50, Hilton; adult/concession €6/5; ☼ 9am-3pm Wed-Sat, 6-9pm Mon & Wed, 10am-2pm Sun), opposite the Hilton Hotel, is on Greek painting and sculpture from the 19th and 20th centuries. There are also 16th-century works, a few works by European masters, including paintings by Picasso, Marquet and Utrillo, and Magritte's sculpture *The Therapist*. Greek sculpture of the 19th and 20th centuries is displayed in the sculpture garden and sculpture hall, reached from the lower floor. In addition, there are works by Giannolis Halepas (1851–1937), one of Greece's foremost sculptors.

The Acropolis

Most of the buildings that grace the **Acropolis** (Map p76; ☎ 210 321 0219; adult/concession €12/6; ☼ 8am-7pm Apr-Oct, 8am-5pm Nov-Mar; ♿) were commissioned by Pericles during the golden age of Athens in the 5th century BC. The site had been cleared for him by the Persians, who destroyed an earlier temple complex on the eve of the Battle of Salamis.

The entrance to the Acropolis is through the **Beulé Gate**, a Roman arch that was added in the 3rd century AD. Beyond this is the

---

MORE FOR YOUR MONEY

The €12 admission charge to the Acropolis buys a collective ticket that gives entry to all the other significant ancient sites in Athens: the Ancient Agora, the Roman Agora, the Keramikos, the Temple of Olympian Zeus and the Theatre of Dionysos. The ticket is valid for 48 hours, otherwise individual site fees apply.

Propylaia, which was the ancient entrance. It was damaged by Venetian bombardment in the 17th century, but has been restored. To the south of the Propylaia is the small **Temple of Athena Nike** (not accessible to visitors).

Standing over the Acropolis is a monument that epitomises the glory of ancient Greece: the **Parthenon**. It was completed in 438 BC and is unsurpassed in grace and harmony. Its lines were ingeniously curved to counteract optical illusions. The base curves upwards slightly towards the ends, and the columns become narrower towards the top, with the overall effect of making it look straight.

Above the columns are the remains of a Doric frieze, which was partly destroyed by Venetian shelling in 1687. The best surviving pieces are the controversial Parthenon Marbles, which were carted off to Britain by Lord Thomas Elgin in 1801. The Parthenon, dedicated to Athena, contained an 11m-tall, gold-and-ivory statue of the goddess completed in 438 BC by Pheidias of Athens (only the statue's foundations survive today).

To the north is the **Erechtheion** with its popular Caryatids, the six maidens who support its southern portico. These are plaster casts. The originals (except for the one taken by Lord Elgin) are in the site's museum.

Lykavittos Hill

This striking rocky landmark (277m high) in central Athens rises out of a sea of concrete to offer the finest views in Athens. On clear days there are panoramic views of the city, the Attic basin, the surrounding mountains and the islands of Salamis and Aegina. A fairly steep path leads to the summit from the top of Loukianou. Alternatively, you can take the **funicular railway** (Map p72; ☎ 210 721 0701; return €5.50;

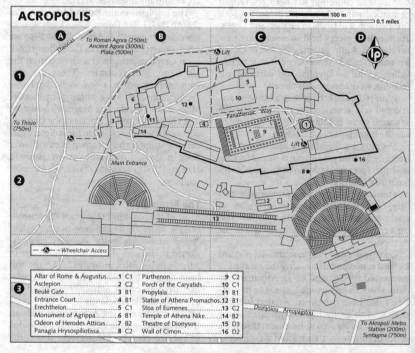

ACROPOLIS

| 0 | 100 m |
| 0 | 0.1 miles |

To Roman Agora (250m);
Ancient Agora (300m);
Plaka (500m)

To Thisio (750m)

Panathenaic Way

Main Entrance

Lift

Lift

— ♿ — Wheelchair Access

Dionysiou Areopagitou

To Akropoli Metro
Station (200m);
Syntagma (750m)

Altar of Rome & Augustus	1 C1	Parthenon	9	C2
Asclepion	2 C2	Porch of the Caryatids	10	C1
Beulé Gate	3 B1	Propylaia	11	B1
Entrance Court	4 B1	Statue of Athena Promachos	12	B1
Erechtheion	5 C1	Stoa of Eumenes	13	C2
Monument of Agrippa	6 B1	Temple of Athena Nike	14	B2
Odeon of Herodes Atticus	7 B2	Theatre of Dionysos	15	D3
Panagia Hrysospiliotissa	8 C2	Wall of Cimon	16	D2

9am-3am, half-hourly), referred to commonly as the 'teleferik' *(télépherique)*, from the top of Ploutarhou. At the top is the chapel of Agios Georgios and a rather expensive café-cum-restaurant.

The open-air Lykavittos Theatre, northeast of the summit, is used during the Summer on Lykavittos Hill festival programme (below).

FESTIVALS & EVENTS
Hellenic Festival
The annual **Hellenic Festival** is the city's most important cultural event, running from mid-June to late September. It features a line-up of international music, dance and theatre at the **Odeon of Herodes Atticus** (Map p78). The setting is quite stunning, backed by a floodlit Acropolis.

The festival has been going from strength to strength, and presents a diverse programme of international standing, ranging from ancient theatre and classical music to contemporary dance and world music. Events are held in venues around town.

Tickets can be bought at the **Hellenic Festival box office** (Map p78; ☎ 210 928 2900; www .hellenicfestival.gr; in arcade Panepistimiou 39, Syntagma; 8.30am-4pm Mon-Fri, 9am-2pm Sat). Tickets go on sale three weeks before a performance. There are student discounts for most performances on production of an International Student Identity Card (ISIC; see p492).

Summer on Lykavittos Hill
The **Lykavittos Theatre** (Map p72; ☎ 210 722 7233) on the Hill of Lykavittos makes a spectacular setting for a series of performances by Greek and international stars from June to the end of August. The theatre provides a spectacular setting for an eclectic annual programme that ranges from ancient Greek theatre to gospel choirs.

SLEEPING
Budget
HOSTELS
Athens International Youth Hostel (Map p72; ☎ 210 523 2540; www.aiyh-victorhugo.com; Victor Hugo 16; dm €10;) Under new management, this hostel was refurbished in 2006. As well as dorms, there are double and four-bed rooms with air-con.

Youth Hostel No 5 (Map p72; ☎ 210 751 9530; www .athens-yhostel.com; Damareos 75, Pangrati; dm €12) These dorms are very basic and dated, but it's a cheery

place in a quiet residential neighbourhood. Owner Yiannis is something of a philosopher, and visitors are encouraged to add their jokes and words of wisdom to the hostel notice-boards. Facilities include coin-operated hot showers (€0.50), communal kitchen, TV room and laundry. Take trolleybus 2 or 11 from Syntagma to the Filolaou stop on Frinis.

Hostel Aphrodite (Map p72; ☎ 210 881 0589; www .hostelaphrodite.com; Einardou 12, Stathmos Larisis; dm €13-15, d with bathroom €50, d/tr without bathroom €45/60;) If you are prepared to be less central, this well-run hostel is a good cheap option. It's a 10-minute walk from the Larisis train and metro stations or five minutes to Viktoria. It has clean, good-sized four- and eight-bed dorms, some with ensuite bathrooms, as well as double rooms with and without private bathrooms – many with balconies. Facilities include Internet access, laundry and a travel agency. Breakfast costs from €3.50.

Student & Travellers' Inn (Map p78; ☎ 210 324 4808; www.studenttravellersinn.com; Kydathineon 16, Plaka; dm €15-18, s/d/tr with bathroom €50/60/81, d/tr without bathroom €55/70;) This popular and well-run place in the heart of Plaka has a mixture of dorms and simple rooms for up to four people, with or without private bathroom and air-conditioning. It has a cheery, yellow-and-blue colour scheme and some rooms have fine, old timber floors. Facilities include a pleasant shady courtyard with large-screen TV, internet access and a travel service. Breakfast costs from €3.50 and rooms are heated in winter.

HOTELS
Plaka & Syntagma
John's Place (Map p78; ☎ 210 322 9719; Patroou 5; s/d/tr without bathroom €35/55/75;) This small, old-style, family-run place is ideally situated just west of Syntagma and the the timber staircase, old doors and high ceilings give it some charm. The furniture and bathrooms have been updated, each room has a hand basin, some have air-conditioning, but bathrooms are all shared.

Adonis Hotel (Map p78; ☎ 210 324 9737; fax 210 323 1602; Kodrou 3; s/d incl breakfast €55/89;) This comfortable, if bland, *pension* on a quiet street represents one of the best deals around. The rooms are neat and come with TV. There are great views of the Acropolis from the 4th-floor rooms and from the rooftop bar.

Adams Hotel (Map p78; ☎ 210 322 5381; adams@ otenet.gr; Herofontos 6, Plaka; s/d €65/80;) A decent

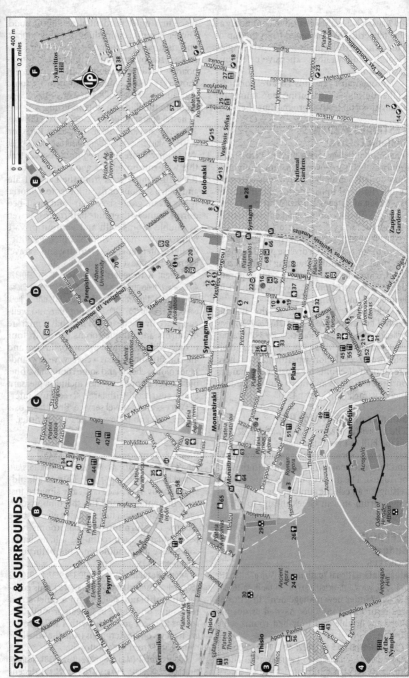

SYNTAGMA & SURROUNDS

budget option in Plaka, this place has simple, old-fashioned rooms with TV, as well as larger family rooms (from €140 to €150).

Monastiraki
Tempi Hotel (Map p78; ☎ 210 321 3175; www.tempi hotel.gr; Eolou 29, Monastiraki; d without bathroom €60, s/d/tr €40/50/70;) This friendly, family-run place on pedestrian Eolou has front rooms with balconies overlooking pretty Plateia Agia Irini, with its flower market and church, and views of the Acropolis. The popular bar next door may make it noisy at night. The rooms have satellite TV, but the bathrooms are still basic and the top-floor rooms are small and quite a hike. There is a communal kitchen.

Makrygianni & Koukaki
Marble House Pension (Map p72; ☎ 210 923 4058, 210 922 8294; www.marblehouse.gr; Zini 35a, Koukaki; s/d/tr with bathroom €44/50/57, d/tr without bathroom €44/51;) This *pension* in a quiet cul-de-sac is one of Athens' better budget hotels, though it is a fair way from the tourist areas. Rooms have been updated, with new pine beds and linen. All rooms have a fridge and ceiling fans and some have air-con (€9 extra). Breakfast costs €5.

Hotel Tony (Map p72; ☎ 210 923 0561; www.hotel tony.gr; Zaharitsa 26; s/d/tr €45/60/75;) This clean, well-maintained *pension* has been upgraded,

with all but one of the rooms having ensuite bathrooms. Air-con costs €9 extra. All have fridges. Hotel Tony also has roomy, well-equipped studio apartments nearby that are similarly priced and excellent for families or longer stays.

Omonia & Surrounds
Hotel Exarchion (Map p72; ☎ 210 380 0731; www.exar chion.com; Themistokleous 55, Exarhia; s/d/tr €40/50/60;) Right in the heart of bohemian Exarhia, this dated and rather bland 1960s high-rise hotel offers cheap and clean accommodation complete with washing facilities and an internet café in the foyer. There's a rooftop café-bar from which you can watch the action below.

CAMPING
Athens Camping (☎ 210 581 4114; www.campingathens .com.gr; Leoforos Athinon 198, Haidari; camping sites per adult/ tent €7/5; year-round) This unattractive place, 7km west of the city centre on the road to Corinth, is the nearest camping ground to Athens. It has reasonable facilities but little else going for it.

Midrange
PLAKA & SYNTAGMA
Niki Hotel (Map p78; ☎ 210 322 0913; www.nikihotel .gr; Nikis 27, Syntagma; s/d/q incl buffet breakfast €80/97/200;

☒) This small hotel bordering Plaka has undergone one of the more stylish makeovers in the area, with a contemporary design and furnishings. The rooms are well-appointed and there is a two-level suite for families with balconies offering Acropolis views.

Central Hotel (Map p78; ☎ 210 323 4357; www .centralhotel.gr; Apollonos 21, Plaka; s/d/tr incl buffet breakfast from €99/121/165; ☒) In a handy location between Syntagma and Plaka, this stylish hotel has been tastefully decorated in light, contemporary tones. It has comfortable rooms with all the mod cons and decent bathrooms. There is a lovely rooftop terrace, which has a small Jacuzzi, sun lounges and views of the Acropolis.

MONASTIRAKI
Hotel Attalos (Map p78; ☎ 210 321 2801; www.attalos hotel.com; Athinas 29, Psyrri; s/d/tr €72/89/106; ☒) Though décor has never been its strong point, this nonetheless comfortable hotel received an Olympic makeover. Its best features are the rooftop bar that offers wonderful views of the Acropolis by night, and the rooms at the back with Acropolis views from the balconies. All rooms have TV.

MAKRYGIANNI & KOUKAKI
Art Gallery Hotel (Map p72; ☎ 210 923 8376; Erehthiou 5, Koukaki; s/d €90/105; ☒) This small, family-run and friendly place is full of personal touches. Some rooms are a little small but all have been refurbished, with new bathrooms. Original furniture from the '60s has been retained in the communal areas. There is a balcony with Acropolis views where you can have a generous breakfast (€7).

OMONIA & SURROUNDS
Fresh Hotel (Map p78; ☎ 210 524 8511; www.fresh hotel.gr; Sofokleous 26 & Klisthenous, Omonia; d/ste incl buffet breakfast from €150/350; ☒ ☒) This designer hotel led the trend for hip hotels in the gritty Omonia area. Once inside, the seediness gives way to chic rooms and suites with individual colour schemes, clever lighting and all the mod cons. Plus, the fantastic rooftop with pool, bar and restaurant with Acropolis views couldn't be further from the world below.

Top End
There are some lovely luxury hotels in Athens but the upper end of the market is generally outrageously priced. Despite this, you can find the odd discount off season.

St George Lycabettus Hotel (Map p78; ☎ 210 729 0711/719; www.sglycabettus.gr; Kleomenous 2, Kolonaki; d from €180; ☒ ☒ ☒) It's a bit of a hike up to this boutique-style hotel at the foot of Lykavittos Hill, in chic Kolonaki. But you can look forward to cooling off in the rooftop pool and enjoying the spectacular views from the bar (and many of the rooms). The rooms are individually decorated and have been renovated in recent times.

EATING
For most people, Plaka is the place to be. It's hard to beat the atmosphere of an afternoon coffee break in its cobbled streets or dining out beneath the floodlit Acropolis.

Budget
PLAKA
Paradosiako (Map p78; ☎ 210 321 3121; Voulis 44a; mains €4-9) For great traditional fare at very fair prices you can't beat this inconspicuous, no-frills taverna on the periphery of Plaka, with a few tables on the footpath. There's a basic menu but it is best to choose from the daily specials, which include fresh and delicious seafood. Get there early before the locals arrive.

Taverna Vizantino (Map p78; ☎ 210 322 7368; Kydathineon 18; specials €4.80-16) This taverna is the best of the restaurants around Plateia Filomousou Eterias. Its menu is realistically priced and it's popular with locals year-round. The daily specials are good value, with dishes like stuffed tomatoes, *pastitsio* (a thick spaghetti and meat bake) and its excellent fish soup (with fish served on the side, €6.80).

Glykis (Map p78; ☎ 210 322 3925; Angelou Geronta 2; ☽ specials €4.80-16) In a quiet corner of Plaka, this casual *mezedhopoleio* (mezedhes restaurante) with a shady courtyard is mostly frequented by students and locals. It has a tasty selection of mezedhes, including traditional *mayirefta* (oven-cooked meals), such as *briam* (mixed vegetables) and cuttlefish in wine.

Platanos (Map p78; ☎ 210 321 8734; Diogenous 4; mayirefta €5-8; ☽ closed Sun) This age-old Plaka taverna is in a pleasant setting away from the main tourist drag, with tables outside in the courtyard under a giant plane tree. It is popular among locals and tourists for its reliable, delicious home-style fare, such as oven-baked potatoes with lemon and oregano.

SYNTAGMA

Ariston (Map p78; ☎ 210 322 7626; Voulis 10; pies €1-1.50; ☺ 10am-4pm Mon-Fri) If you are after a snack on the run, you can't go wrong with traditional *tyropites* (cheese pies) and their various permutations. This place has been around since 1910, serving the best range of tasty, freshly baked pies with all manner of fillings.

You can find **Vasilopoulos** (Map p78; Stadiou 19, Syntagma) here, one of many supermarkets in central Athens.

OMONIA & EXARHIA

Food Company (Map p72; ☎ 210 380 5004; Emmanuel 63-65; dishes €4.50-6.50; ☎ 10am-2am) This Kolonaki favourite has found a new cheery home in Exarhia. The good-value casual café-style eatery serves a range of healthy salads, wholesome dishes and hot and cold pasta and noodle dishes. The cheesecake is delicious.

Yiantes (Map p72; ☎ 210 330 1369; Valtetsiou 44, Exarhia; mains €5-7) This modern taverna is set in a lovely garden courtyard next to an open-air cinema. It is considered pricy for Exarhia, but the food is on the creative side and is made with organic produce.

Arheon Gefsis (Map p72; ☎ 210 523 9661; Kodratou 22, Metaxourgio; mains €10-21; ☺ Mon-Sat) This gimmicky but fun place turns the clock back 2500 years to ancient Greece. The staff dress in flowing robes and there are no glasses – the ancients used earthenware cups and spoons instead of forks – and the menu derives from ancient times. Roast meats and fish dishes dominate, served with purées of peas or chickpeas and vegetables.

The colourful **Athens central market** (Map p78; ☺ closed Sun) has the widest range of whatever's in season. The **fruit and vegetable market** (Map p78) is on the western side of Athinas, and the **meat market** (Map p78) is opposite on the eastern side. The meat market section might sound like a strange place to go for a meal but visiting the tavernas (such as the Epiros or Papandreou tavernas) inside it are an Athenian institution, turning out huge quantities of tasty, traditional fare. The clientele ranges from hungry market workers, to elegant couples emerging from nightclubs at 5am in search of a bowl of hangover-busting *patsas* (tripe soup).

The supermarket chain **Marinopoulos** (Map p72; Athinas 60, Omonia) offers convenient shopping in a couple of branches in the centre of town.

Midrange

PLAKA & SYNTAGMA

Palia Taverna tou Psara (Map p78; ☎ 210 321 8734; Erehtheos 16, Plaka; mezedhes €3.50-11.50) Hidden away from the main hustle and bustle of Plaka, this fish tavern is a cut above the rest. There is a choice of mezedhes – the *melitzanokeftedhes* (aubergine croquettes) are particularly good – but it is known as the best seafood tavern in Plaka.

AKROPOLI & THISIO

Filistron (Map p78; ☎ 210 346 7554; Apostolou Pavlou 23, Thisio; mezedhes €4.50-10; ☺ closed Mon) You may be hard pressed finding a table for dinner at this excellent *mezedhopoleio*, which serves an interesting range of reasonably priced, tasty mezedhes in a prized setting – a rooftop terrace overlooking the Acropolis. Try its baked potato with smoked cheese and pepper or the *mastelo* (a fried cheese from Chios) in a tomato sauce.

Kuzina (Map p78; ☎ 210 324 0133; Adrianou 9, Thisio; mezedhes €5-18) A classy newcomer on Adrianou, with tables outside next to the Temple of Haphaestus, Kuzina serves 'creative' Greek cuisine with largely successful results. The interior design is superb, as is the view from the terrace bar.

To Steki tou Ilia (Map p78; ☎ 210 345 8052; Eptahalkou 5, Thisio; chops per portion/kg €8/26; ☺ 8pm-late) This *psistaria* (tavern specialising in grills) – with its tasty, grilled lamb chops – has achieved celebrity status. There are tables outside on the pedestrian strip opposite the church. For those who don't eat lamb, there are pork chops and steaks, as well as dips, chips and salads.

PSYRRI

Oineas (Map p78; ☎ 210 321 5614; Esopou 9, Psyrri; 7; mezedhes €5-18) This cheery place on a pedestrian street in Psyrri stands out for the walls of kitsch Greek ads and retro paraphernalia. There are some creative dishes on the menu and excellent generous salads, best shared. Try the cheese pie made with *kataïfi* (angel-hair pastry).

Top End

Athens has a great variety of upmarket, blow-the-budget dining options in Athens. Reservations are essential.

Spondi (Map p72; ☎ 210 752 0658; Pironos 5, Pangrati; mains €37-55; ☺ 8pm-late) This superb restaurant has been consistently voted Athens best and the accolades are totally deserved. Spondi offers Mediterranean *haute cuisine*, with heavy French influences, in a relaxed, classy setting. There is a lovely garden terrace draped in bougainvillea in summer. This is definitely a special-occasion place.

DRINKING
Cafés
Athens seems to have more cafés per capita than virtually any other city and most of the time they are packed with Athenians sipping the ubiquitous frappé, prompting many a visitor to wonder if anyone ever works in this city. More recently, the burning question is why it has Europe's most expensive coffee (between €3.50 and €5). One unconvincing justification is that you actually hire the chair, not just pay for coffee, as people 'sit' on a coffee for hours.

Athinaion Politeia (Map p78; Akamandos 1, Thisio) There are great views from the tables outside this neoclassical building on the pedestrian walk.

Da Capo (Map p78; Tsakalof 1, Kolonaki) Has excellent coffee but is also a prime people-watching spot. It's self-serve if you can find a table.

Bars
Brettos (Map p78; ☎ 210 323 2110; Kydathineon 41, Plaka; ✆ 10am-midnight) This is a delightful old bar with a stunning wall of colourful bottles and huge barrels lining one wall. You can sample shots of Brettos' home brand of ouzo, brandy and other spirits, as well as the family wine.

Mike's Irish Bar (☎ 210 777 6797; www.mikesirishbar .gr; Sinopis 6, Ambelokipi; ✆ 8pm-4am) A long-time favourite of the city's expat community, who come to play darts and sip pints of Guinness or Murphy's stout. There's live music nightly from 11.30pm.

Craft (☎ 210 646 2350; Leoforos Alexandras 205, Ambelokipi) At Greece's first (and only) boutique brewery, drinkers can sample the various house brews safe in the knowledge that there's plenty more bubbling away in the giant stainless-steel vats in the background. It is also a restaurant.

Gay & Lesbian Venues
The greatest concentration of gay bars is around Makrygianni, south of the Temple of Olympian Zeus.

Most places open at 11pm, but you won't find much of a crowd until after midnight.

Popular spots include the long-running **Granazi** (Map p72; ☎ 210 924 4185; Lembesi 20, Makrygianni; admission €6 with free drink) and the **Lamda Club** (Map p72; ☎ 210 922 4202; Lembesi 15, Makrygianni; admission €6 with free drink).

ENTERTAINMENT
The best source of entertainment information is the weekly listings magazine *Athinorama*, but you'll need to be able to read some Greek to make much sense of it. It costs €1.50 and is available from *periptera* (street kiosks) all over the city.

English-language listings appear daily in the *Kathimerini* supplement that accompanies the *International Herald Tribune*, while the *Athens News* carries a weekly entertainment guide.

Greek Folk Dancing
Dora Stratou Dance Company (Map p72; ☎ 210 921 4650; www.grdance.org; Filopappou Hill; adult/concession €15/10; ✆ performances 9.30pm Tue-Sat, 8.15pm Sun May-Sep) Every summer the Dora Stratou company performs its repertoire of folk dances at its open-air theatre on the western side of Filopappou Hill. Formed to preserve the country's folk culture, it has gained an international reputation for authenticity and professionalism. The theatre is signposted from the western end of Dionysiou Areopagitou. Take trolleybus 22 from Syntagma and get off at Agios Ioannis.

Live Music
Athens has a healthy rock music scene and is on most European touring schedules. In summer check Rockwave and other festival schedules, as you may be able to see your favourite band perform in open-air theatres around town.

Gagarin 205 Club (off Map p72; Liosion 205) The Gagarin 205 Club is primarily a rock venue with gigs on Friday and Saturday nights featuring leading rock and underground music bands. Tickets are available for purchase from Ticket House (Map p78; ☎ 210 360 8366; Panepistimiou 42).

AN Club (Map p72; ☎ 210 330 5056; Solomou 13-15, Exarhia) The small AN Club hosts lesser-known international bands, as well as some interesting local bands.

Half Note Jazz Club (Map p72; ☎ 210 921 3310; Trivonianou 17, Mets) Jazz fans should head to this club opposite the Athens First Cemetery. It hosts an array of international names.

Top-name international acts play at a variety of venues, including the spectacular Lykavittos Theatre (p77) on Lykavittos Hill and the **Panathinaïkos Football Stadium** (Leoforos Alexandras).

Nightclubs

Admission to most places ranges from €5 (Monday to Thursday) to €10 (Friday and Saturday). The price often includes one free drink. Subsequently, expect to pay about €3 for soft drinks, €5 for a beer and €8 for spirits. Clubs don't start to get busy until around midnight.

Lava Bore (Map p78; ☎ 210 324 5335; Filellinon 25; ☻ 10pm-5am) The central Lava Bore is by no means one of the city's *in* clubs, but it stays open all year, and caters largely to tourists. The formula remains much the same: a mixture of mainstream rock and dance music and (relatively) cheap drinks. It's far more casual that most Athens clubs.

Envy (Map p78; ☎ 210 331 7801; Agias Eleousis & Kakourgodikiou, Psyrri; ☻ Wed-Sat) This popular club (the name changes but the venue seems to be fixed) plays the latest dance music in Psyrri during winter and in summer moves the partying to the massive Envy Mediterraneo club at Elliniko.

Kalua (Map p78; ☎ 210 360 8304; Amerikis 6, Syntagma) This established downtown club plays mainstream music and the odd Greek disco hit, and usually rocks till dawn. Don't bother getting there before midnight.

SHOPPING
Flea Market

This market is the first place to spring to people's minds when they think of shopping in Athens. It's the commercial area that stretches west of Plateia Monastirakiou and consists of shops selling goods running the whole gamut from high quality to trash.

These shops are open daily during normal business hours.

However, when most people speak of the Athens flea market, they are referring to the Sunday **flea market** (Map p78; ☻ 7am-2pm Sun), which spills over into Plateia Monastirakiou and onto Ermou. A visit to Athens isn't complete without a visit to the Sunday market. All manner of things – from new to fourth-hand – are on sale.

There's everything to be found from clocks to condoms, binoculars to bouzoukis, tyres to telephones, giant evil eyes to jelly babies, and wigs to welding kits.

Traditional Handicrafts

Stavros Melissinos (Map p78; ☎ 210 321 9247; www .melissinos-art.com; Agias Theklas 2, Psyrri; ☻ 10am-2pm & 4-7pm Mon-Sat, 10am-2pm Sun) Athens' famous septuagenarian sandalmaker and poet Stavros Melissinos names the Beatles, Rudolph Nureyev, Sophia Loren and Jackie Onassis among his past customers. But fame and fortune have not gone to his head. He still makes the best-value sandals based on ancient Greek styles in natural leather, a tradition continued by artist son Pantelis.

Centre of Hellenic Tradition (Map p78; ☎ 210 321 3023; Pandrosou 36, Plaka; ☻ 10am-7.30pm) Upstairs from the arcade are great examples of traditional ceramics, sculptures and handicrafts from around Greece. There is also a great *ouzerie* (place that serves ouzo and mezedhes) and a gallery on the 1st floor.

GETTING THERE & AWAY
Air

Athens is served by **Eleftherios Venizelos International Airport** (☎ 210 353 0000; www.aia.gr) at Spata, 27km east of the city. The state-of-the-art airport, named in honour of the country's leading 20th-century politician, has the standard facilities like cafés, restaurants and banks, great shopping and a transit hotel. If you've time, it's worth visiting the small archaeological museum on the 1st floor above the check-in hall. The airport website has real-time flight information. See Getting Around (p85) for public transport to/from the airport. For international flights to/from Athens, see p502.

DOMESTIC FLIGHTS

Most domestic flights are operated by **Olympic Airlines** (Map p72; ☎ 210 356 9111, 801 11 44 444; www .olympicairlines.com; Leoforos Syngrou 96), which also has branch offices at **Syntagma** (Map p78; ☎ 210 926 4444; Filellinon 15) and **Omonia** (Map p72; ☎ 210 926 7218; Marikas Kotopouli 1). For flight information call ☎ 210 966 6666. The tables overleaf give flight details from Athens to the islands and mainland ports in high season.

Aegean Airlines (reservations ☎ 801 11 20 000, 210 626 1000; www.aegeanair.com; Syntagma (Map p78; ☎ 210 331 5522; Othonos 15, Syntagma) competes with Olympic Airlines on the most popular domestic routes. Aegean has the best earlybird specials and bookings can be made online.

OLYMPIC AIRLINES FLIGHTS FROM ATHENS TO THE GREEK ISLANDS

Destination	Duration	Fare	Flights per week
Astypalea	1hr	€58	5
Chios	50min	€42	25
Corfu	1hr	€50	14
Crete (Hania)	50min	€90	35
Crete (Iraklio)	50min	€75	35
Crete (Sitia)	80min	€71	3
Ikaria	55min	€50	4
Kefallonia	65min	€75	14
Kos	55min	€75	21
Kythira	45min	€55	7
Leros	1hr	€54	7
Lesvos	50min	€76	28
Limnos	55min	€66	7
Milos	45min	€50	7
Mykonos	40min	€70	35
Naxos	45min	€56	8
Paros	40min	€57	8
Rhodes	1hr	€77	35
Samos	1hr	€73	28
Santorini	50min	€79	35
Skiathos	50min	€67	7
Skyros	35min	€35	2
Syros	35min	€38	7
Zakynthos	1hr	€76	7

OLYMPIC AIRLINES FLIGHTS FROM ATHENS TO OTHER MAINLAND PORTS

Destination	Duration	Fare	Flights per week
Alexandroupoli	65min	€75	28
Kavala	1hr	€76	14
Preveza	1hr	€65	5
Thessaloniki	55min	€45-105	49

Aegean Airlines has up to 12 flights per day to Thessaloniki, seven daily to Iraklio, six daily to Rhodes, at least four daily to Mykonos and Santorini, three daily to Hania and Lesvos, two daily to Alexandroupoli and Corfu, and one daily flight to Kavala.

Bus

There are two main intercity **KTEL** (www.ktel.gr) bus terminals in Athens.

The first of these stations is **Terminal A** (☎ 210 512 4910; Kifisou 100) about 7km northwest of Plateia Omonias. It has regular departures to the Peloponnese, the Ionian Islands, and western and northern Greece. City bus 051 (€0.45) runs between the terminal and the junction of Zinonos and Menandrou, near Omonia, every 15 minutes from 5am to midnight.

Terminal B (☎ 210 831 7181; Liosion 260, Kato Patisia) is about 5km north of Plateia Omonias off Liosion and has departures to central Greece and Evia. While the address is nominally Liosion 260 the terminal is actually one block further east on Agiou Dimitriou Oplon. To reach Terminal B you need to take bus 024 that travels from outside the main gate of the National Gardens (Map p78) on Leoforos Vasilissis Amalias and get off at Liosion 260 (ask for Praktoria KTEL).

From this stop you should turn right onto Gousiou and you'll then see Terminal B at the end of the street.

Buses for Rafina and Lavrio depart from the **SE Attiki Terminal** (Map p72; ☎ 210 821 0872; cnr Alexandras & Patision), which is commonly known as the Mavromateon Terminal. It is 250m north of the National Archaeological Museum.

For information on international bus services, see p505.

BUS DEPARTURES FROM ATHENS
Bus Terminal A

Destination	Duration	Fare	Frequency
Corfu*	9hr	€44.20	3 daily
Epidavros	2½hr	€10.40	2 daily
Igoumenitsa	7hr	€38.20	4 daily
Kalavryta	3hr	€14.40	daily
Lefkada	5hr	€29	4 daily
Nafplio	2½hr	€11.30	hourly
Olympia	5hr	€25.60	2 daily
Patra	3hr	€16.20	half-hourly
Zakynthos*	6hr	€28.50	6 daily

*includes ferry ticket

Bus Terminal B

Destination	Duration	Fare	Frequency
Agios Konstantinos	2½hr	€12.90	hourly
Delphi	3hr	€13	6 daily
Halkida	1hr	€5.90	half-hourly
Karpenisi	5hr	€21.50	3 daily
Trikala	4½hr	€22	8 daily
Volos	4¼hr	€23.50	10 daily

SE Attiki Terminal (Mavromateon)

Destination	Duration	Fare	Frequency
Cape Sounion via coast road	1½hr	€4.50	hourly
Lavrio port	1¼hr	€3.80	half-hourly
Marathon	1¼hr	€2.90	hourly
Rafina port	1hr	€1.90	half-hourly

Car & Motorcycle

The upgraded National Rd 1 (Ethniki Odos) is the main route north. It starts at Nea Kifisia. Take Vasilissis Sofias from Syntagma or the Ymittos ring road via Kaisariani, linking up with the new Attiki Odos, a toll motorway that links Elefsina with the airport and Central Attiki in the east. National Rd 8, begins beyond Dafni and goes to the Peloponnese and northwestern Greece. Take Agiou Konstantinou from Omonia.

Leoforos Syngrou, near the Temple of Olympian Zeus, is lined with rental firms. Local companies offer better deals than multinationals. An average price for a small car is €60 per day, less for three or more days.

Avis (Map p72; ☎ 210 322 4951; Leoforos Vasilissis Amalias 48)

Budget (Map p72; ☎ 210 921 4771; Leoforos Syngrou 8)

Europcar (Map p72; ☎ 210 924 8810; Leoforos Syngrou 36-38)

Hertz (Map p72; ☎ 210 922 0102; Leoforos Syngrou 12)

Sixt (Map p72; ☎ 210 922 0171; Leoforos Syngrou 23)

You can rent mopeds and motorcycles if you have the appropriate licence and the confidence to take on the traffic. **Motorent** (Map p72; ☎ 210 923 4939; www.motorent.gr; Rovertou Galli 1, Makrygianni) has a machines from 50cc to 250cc. High-season prices for a 50cc scooter start at €16 per day.

Train

Intercity trains to central and northern Greece and to the Peloponnese currently leave from **Larisis train station** (Map p72; ☎ 210 529 8837; cnr Deligianni & Filadelfias) located about 1km northeast of Plateia Omonias (metro Line 2).

For the Peloponnese, take the suburban rail to Kiato and change for other OSE services there. A new rail hub (SKA) is going to be located about 20km north of the city.

OSE (☎ 1110; www.ose.gr; ⏰ 24hr) has offices at **Omonia** (Map p72; ☎ 210 529 7516; Karolou 1; ⏰ 8am-3pm Mon-Fri) and **Syntagma** (Map p72; ☎ 210 362 4402; Sina 6; ⏰ 8am-3pm Mon-Sat), which handle advance bookings. See p505 for international trains.

GETTING AROUND
To/From the Airport

BUS

There are six special express bus services operating between the airport and the city, including a service between the airport and Piraeus. They leave from between Gates 4 and 5 outside the arrivals area.

Bus X92 runs between the airport and teh suburb of Kifisia. Bus X93 runs between the airport and the Terminal B (Kifisos) bus station. Bus X94 runs between the airport and the Ethniki Amyna metro station. Bus X95 operates between the airport and Plateia Syntagmatos and is the most convenient one for central Athens. This line operates 24 hours with services approximately every 30 minutes. The bus stop is outside the National Gardens on Leoforos Vasilissis Amalias on the eastern side of Plateia Syntagmatos.

Bus X96 operates between the airport and Plateia Karaïskaki in Piraeus (24 hours, about every 20 minutes). Bus X97 runs between the airport and the Dafni metro station (about 25 minutes).

Tickets for all these services cost €3.20 and are valid for one trip only, and are not valid for other forms of public transport. The journey from the airport to central Athens takes between an hour and 1½ hours, depending on traffic conditions.

Additionally, KTEL Attikis runs express buses from the airport to the port of Rafina (€3) roughly every one hour and 40 minutes; and to the port of Lavrio (€4, change at Markopoulo) roughly every two hours.

SUBURBAN RAIL & METRO

From the airport you can take the ultramodern, Finnish-built suburban rail train (Proastiakos) to the Larisis train station (€6 one way), the Doukissis Plakentias metro station or to Nerantziotissa, on the Piraeus Kifisia ISAP Metro Line. Suburban trains from the airport to Athens run from 5am to 1.20am (the trip takes 38 minutes and trains run every 15 minutes from Nerantziotissa until 9.30pm, then half-hourly; while trains to the airport from the Larisis train station run from 6.06am to 7.36pm.

In parallel, the metro network also runs to/from the airport by connecting with the metro network at Doukissis Plakentias. Take the metro if you wish to go directly to central Athens. The first metro leaves the airport at 5.30am and the last metro at 11.30pm. From Athens (Syntagma) the first metro leaves at 5.50am and the last one at 7.21pm. One-way tickets also cost €6.

TAXI

Taking a cab from or to the airport is a relatively easy business as long as the basic ground rules are understood and adhered to. Check that the meter is set to the correct tariff (day or night). You will be required to pay in addition to the fare a €3.20 surcharge on trips *from* the airport, a €2.70 toll for using the toll road connecting the airport to the city plus €0.32 for each piece of luggage over 10kg. In case of a dispute, take the taxi driver's permit number and car registration number, and report the details to the tourist police. Drivers can and will be prosecuted for overcharging.

The trip from the airport to the city centre – via the much faster Ymyttos ring road and the Katehaki exit – should take between 40 and 55 minutes depending on traffic. Taxis to Piraeus will take longer and cost more as drivers may prefer to take the longer, but less congested southern loop route via Vari, Voula and Glyfada. Expect to pay about €25 from the airport to the city, and €30 to Piraeus

Around Athens

BUS & TROLLEYBUS

The blue-and-white local express and regular buses operate every 15 minutes from 5am until midnight.

Buses run 24 hours between the centre and Piraeus – every 20 minutes from 6am until midnight – and hourly at other times. Trolleybuses operate from 5am until midnight. A free OASA map shows most of the routes.

Tickets for buses and trolleybuses (€0.50) must be purchased at a transport kiosk or at most *periptera* and validated on board. Plain-clothed inspectors make spot checks. The penalty for travelling without a validated ticket is 60 times the ticket price.

METRO

The gradually expanding **metro system** (www .ametro.gr) has transformed travel in central Athens. Journeys that once took an hour above ground can now be completed in much less time. The stations are an attraction in their own right, displaying finds from archaeological excavations. All have wheelchair access.

Ticket pricing still distinguishes between the old network (Line 1-ISAP) and the metro, and can be confusing. Travel on Lines 2 and 3 costs €0.80, while Line 1 is split into three sections: Piraeus–Monastiraki, Monastiraki– Attiki and Attiki–Kifisia (travel within one section costs €0.70; two or more sections costs €0.70.

Tickets must be validated at the machines at platform entrances. The penalty for travelling without a validated ticket is 60 times the ticket price.

Trains run between 5am and midnight, running every three minutes during peak periods, dropping to every 10 minutes at other times.

Line 1 (Green Line)

The old Kifisia–Piraeus line has transfer stations at Omonia and Attiki for Line 2; Monastiraki is the transfer station for Line 3. Nerantziotissa connects with the suburban rail.

There's also an hourly, all-night bus service (bus 500) along this route, with bus stops located outside the train stations.

Line 2 (Red Line)

Line 2 runs from Agios Antonios in the northwest to Agios Dimitrios in the southeast (check the boards so you don't confuse your saints). Attiki and Omonia are transfer stations for Line 1, while Syntagma is the transfer station for Line 3.

Line 3 (Blue Line)

Line 3 runs northeast from Egaleo to Doukissis Plakentias, with the airport train continuing from there. Syntagma is the transfer station for Line 2.

TAXI

Taxis are yellow. To hail a taxi, stand on the pavement and shout your destination as they pass. If a taxi is going your way the driver may stop even if there are passengers inside. This does not mean the fare will be shared: each person will be charged the fare shown on the meter. If you get in one that does not have passengers, make sure the meter is on.

The flag fall is €1, with a €1 surcharge from ports and train and bus stations, and a €3.20 surcharge from the airport. After that, the day rate (tariff 1 on the meter) is €0.30 per km.

The night tariff (tariff 2 on the meter) increases to €0.60 between midnight and 5am. Baggage is charged at the rate of €0.30 per item over 10kg. The minimum fare is approximately €3.

TRAM

Athens single **tram service** (www.tramsa.gr) makes for a scenic coastal trip to Faliro and Glyfada, but it is not the fastest means of transport.

It has services running from Syntagma to Faliro, Syntagma to Glyfada and Faliro to Glyfada. The tram operates from 5am to 1am Monday to Thursday, then 24 hours from Friday night to Sunday, servicing revellers travelling to the city's beach bars.

The trip from Syntagma to Faliro takes about 45 minutes, while Syntagma to Glyfada takes around 55 minutes. The central terminus is on Amalias, opposite the National Gardens. Tickets (€0.60) are purchased at platform vending machines.

A tram extension to Piraeus and Voula is in the pipeline.

THE MAINLAND PORTS

This section is designed to provide all the information a traveller needs to get from the mainland to the islands. It begins with the ports that serve more than one island group: Piraeus, Rafina, Thessaloniki and Gythio. The remaining ports are grouped according to the island groups they serve.

PIRAEUS ΠΕΙΡΑΙΑΣ
pop 175,697

Apart from being a port for Athens, Piraeus is Greece's main port and one of the Mediterranean's major ports. It's the hub of the Aegean ferry network; centre for Greece's maritime export-import and transit trade; and base for its large merchant navy. Nowadays, Athens has expanded sufficiently to meld imperceptibly into Piraeus.

History
The histories of Athens and Piraeus are inextricably linked. Themistocles transferred his Athenian fleet from the exposed port of Phaleron (modern Faliro) to the security of Piraeus at the start of the 5th century BC.

Piraeus was a flourishing commercial centre during the classical age but, by Roman times, it had been overtaken by Rhodes, Delos and Alexandria. During medieval and Turkish times Piraeus shrank to a tiny fishing village and by the time Greece became independent it was home to fewer than 20 people.

Piraeus' resurgence began in 1834 when Athens became the capital of independent Greece. By the start of the 20th century, Piraeus had superseded Syros as Greece's principal port.

WHICH PORT?

The following list details the ports serving each island group:

- Crete – Piraeus, Thessaloniki, Gythio, Kalamata
- Cyclades – Piraeus, Rafina, Thessaloniki, Lavrio
- Dodecanese – Piraeus, Thessaloniki, Alexandroupoli
- Evia & the Sporades – Rafina (Evia only), Agios Konstantinos, Thessaloniki, Volos
- Ionians – Patra, Igoumenitsa, Kyllini, Piraeus (Kythira only), Gythio (Kythira and Antikythira only), Neapoli (Kythira only)
- Northeastern Aegean Islands – Piraeus, Thessaloniki, Kavala, Alexandroupoli
- Saronic Gulf Islands – Piraeus, Porto Heli, Ermioni, Galatas

---

Orientation
Piraeus is 10km southwest of Athens. The largest of its three harbours is the Main Harbour (Kentriko Limani), on the western side of the Piraeus peninsula, which is the departure point for all ferry, hydrofoil and catamaran services. Zea Marina (Limani Zeas) and the picturesque Mikrolimano (Small Harbour), on the eastern side, are for private yachts.

The metro and suburban train lines from Athens terminate at the northeastern corner of the Main Harbour on Akti Kalimassioti. The suburban train station is handier for Cretan ferries while the metro station is convenient for other island ferries.

Information
Emporiki Bank (cnr Antistaseos & Makras Stoas) Has a 24-hour automated exchange machine.
Internet Café (cnr Tsamadou & Filonos; 7.30am-8pm Mon-Fri, 7.30am-2pm Sat)
National Bank of Greece (cnr Antistaseos & Tsamadou) Near the Emporiki Bank.
Post office (cnr Tsamadou & Filonos; 7.30am-8pm Mon-Fri, 7.30am-2pm Sat)

Sleeping
There's no reason to stay at any of the shabby cheap hotels around the Main Harbour when Athens is so close. The cheap hotels are geared more towards accommodating

PIRAEUS

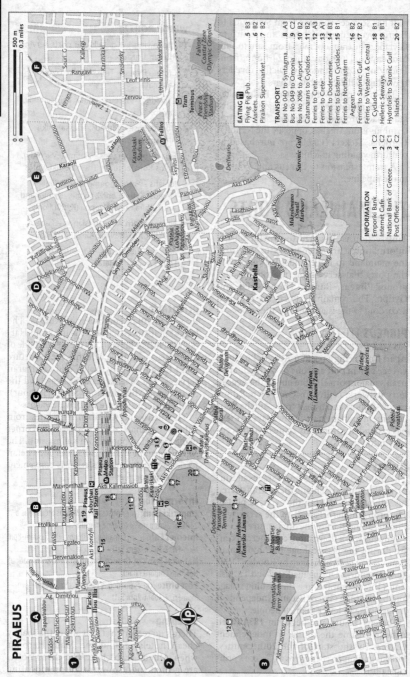

EATING		
Flying Pig Pub................	5	B3
Markets.........................	6	B2
Pirakion Supermarket....	7	B2

TRANSPORT		
Bus No 040 to Syntagma.....	8	A3
Bus No 049 to Omonia........	9	C2
Bus No X96 to Airport.........	10	B2
Catamarans to Cyclades.....	11	B2
Ferries to Crete..................	12	A3
Ferries to Crete..................	13	A1
Ferries to Dodecanese........	14	B3
Ferries to Eastern Cyclades..	15	B1
Ferries to Northeastern		
Aegean............................	16	B2
Ferries to Saronic Gulf.........	17	B2
Ferries to Western & Central		
Cyclades...........................	18	B1
Hellenic Seaways.................	19	B1
Hydrofoils to Saronic Gulf		
Islands..............................	20	B2

INFORMATION		
Emporiki Bank..................	1	C2
Internet Cafe..................	2	B2
National Bank of Greece..	3	C1
Post Office......................	4	C2

sailors than tourists. Whatever happens, don't attempt to sleep out – Piraeus is the most dangerous place in Greece to do so.

Eating

There are dozens of cafés and restaurants along the waterfront at the Great Harbour.

Flying Pig Pub (☎ 210 429 5344; Filonos 31; ⏰ 9am-1am) Run by a friendly Greek Australian, the Pig is a popular bar with a large range of beers. It also serves decent food, including a generous English breakfast.

You can stock up on supplies before a ferry trip in the area just inland from Akti Poseidonos. The **markets** (⏰ 6am-4pm Mon-Fri) are on Dimosthenous. **Piraikon supermarket** (☎ 210 417 5764; Ippokratous 1; ⏰ 8am-8pm Mon-Fri, 8am-4pm Sat) is opposite the markets.

Getting There & Away

BUS

Buses 040 and 049 operate 24 hours a day between Piraeus and central Athens; they run every 20 minutes from 6am until midnight and then hourly (€0.50). Bus 040 runs between Akti Xaveriou in Piraeus and Filellinon in Athens. Bus 049 runs between Plateia Themistokleous in Piraeus and Omonia in Athens.

The X96 Piraeus–Athens Airport Express buses leave from the southwestern corner of Plateia Karaïskaki.

METRO & SUBURBAN RAIL

The metro is the fastest and easiest way to get from Piraeus to central Athens. The station is at the northern end of Akti Kallimasioti. Travellers should take extra care as the section between Piraeus and Monastiraki is notorious for pickpockets. Piraeus is now connected to the suburban rail, whose terminus is opposite the metro station. To get to the airport or the Peloponnese you change trains at Nerantziotissa.

FERRY

Piraeus is the busiest port in Greece with a bewildering array of departures and destinations, including daily services to all the island groups except the Ionians and Sporades. The tables (right) list all the destinations that can be reached by ferry. The information is for the high season – from mid-June to September.

For the latest departure information, pick up a weekly ferry schedule from EOT in Athens (p74). See the Getting There & Away sections for each island for specific details, and p509 for general information about ferry travel. The departure points for ferry destinations are shown on the map of Piraeus. Note that there are two departure points for Crete. Ferries for Iraklio depart from the western end of Akti Kondyli, but the ferries for other ports in Crete occasionally dock there as well. The other departure point for Crete is on Akti Miaouli. It's a long way between the two, so check where to find your boat when you buy your ticket.

Ferries from Piraeus

Crete

Destination	Duration	Fare	Frequency
Agios Nikolaos	14hr	€34	3 weekly
Hania	10hr	€30	daily
Iraklio	10hr	€3	daily
Kastelli-Kissamos	12hr	€25	2 weekly
Sitia	14½hr	€34	3 weekly

Cyclades

Destination	Duration	Fare	Frequency
Anafi	11hr	€32.50	3 weekly
Folegandros	6-9hr	€23.50	3 weekly
Ios	7½hr	€32.50	4 daily
Kimolos	6hr	€28.60	2 weekly
Kythnos	2½hr	€12.10	2 weekly
Milos	7hr	€28.60	2 daily
Mykonos	5½hr	€28.50	2 daily
Naxos	6hr	€30	4 daily
Paros	5hr	€29.50	4 daily
Santorini	9hr	€34	4 daily
Serifos	4½hr	€15.20	2 daily
Sifnos	5½hr	€28.60	2 daily
Syros	4hr	€25	4 daily
Tinos	4½hr	€18	daily

Dodecanese

Destination	Duration	Fare	Frequency
Astypalea	12hr	€34.50	4 weekly
Halki	20hr	€34	4 weekly
Kalymnos	10-13hr	€36	daily
Karpathos	18½hr	€31.50	3 weekly
Kasos	17hr	€34	3 weekly
Kos	12-15hr	€39	2 daily
Leros	11hr	€25	daily
Lipsi	16hr	€38.40	weekly
Nisyros	13-15hr	€44.50	1 weekly
Patmos	9½hr	€25	daily
Rhodes	15-18hr	€47	2-3 daily
Symi	15-17hr	€44	2 weekly
Tilos	15hr	€44.50	2 weekly

Northeastern Aegean Islands

Destination	Duration	Fare	Frequency
Chios	8hr	€26	daily
Fourni	10hr	€30	3 weekly
Ikaria	9hr	€30	daily
Lesvos	12hr	€31.50	daily
Limnos	13hr	€27	1 weekly
Samos	13hr	€33	1-2 daily

Saronic Gulf Islands

Destination	Duration	Fare	Frequency
Aegina	1¼hr	€8	hourly
Hydra	3½hr	€13.20	1 daily
Poros	2½hr	€11.10	4 daily
Spetses	4½hr	€18.20	daily

HYDROFOIL & CATAMARAN

Hellenic Seaways (☎ 210 419 9000; www.hellenicseaways .gr; cnr Akti Kondyli & Elotikou, Great Harbour) has hydrofoil and catamaran services from Piraeus to the Saronic Gulf Islands and the Cyclades.

The information in the hydrofoil and catamarans timetable (below) is for the high season, from mid-June to September. For more information about these services, see the Transport chapter (p509) and the Getting There & Away sections for each island throughout this book.

Hydrofoils & Catamarans from Piraeus

Cyclades

Destination	Duration	Fare	Frequency
Ios	3¾hr	€47	1 daily
Kythnos	1¾hr	€27	5 weekly
Milos	4¼hr	€42	daily
Mykonos	3½hr	€46	2 daily
Naxos	3¼hr	€48.50	3 daily
Paros	3-5hr	€45.50	4 daily
Santorini	5¼hr	€52	daily
Serifos	2¼hr	€33	2 daily
Sifnos	2¾hr	€37	daily
Syros	2½hr	€39	2 daily
Tinos	3¾hr	€35	4 daily

Peloponnese

Destination	Duration	Fare	Frequency
Ermioni	2hr	€24.50	8 daily
Porto Heli	2hr	€30	4 daily

Saronic Gulf Islands

Destination	Duration	Fare	Frequency
Aegina	35min	€12	hourly
Hydra	1¼hr	€21	8 daily
Poros	1hr	€19	8 daily
Spetses	2hr	€29.50	4 daily

METRO

The metro is the fastest and easiest way of getting from the Great Harbour to central Athens (see p86). The station is at the northern end of Akti Kalimassioti. Travellers should take extra care of valuables on the metro; the section between Piraeus and Monastiraki is notorious for pickpockets.

TRAIN

The Piraeus train station is the terminus of the new suburban rail network. Suburban trains run from here to the new Central Station at Aharnon.

RAFINA ΡΑΦΗΝΑ

pop 11,909

Tucked into Attica's east coast, Rafina is Athens' main fishing port and second-most important port for passenger ferries. It is smaller than Piraeus and less confusing – and fares are about 20% cheaper, but you have to spend an hour on the bus and €1.90 to get there.

The **port police** (☎ 22940 22300) occupies a kiosk near the quay, which is lined with fish restaurants and ticket agents. The main square, Plateia Plastira, is at the top of the ramp leading to the port.

Getting There & Away

BUS

There are frequent buses from the SE Attiki (Mavromateon) terminal in Athens to Rafina (€2, one hour) between 5.45am and 10.30pm. The first bus leaves Rafina at 5.50am and the last at 10.15pm.

CATAMARAN

Blue Star Ferries operates high-speed catamarans to the Cyclades. There is a daily 7.40am service to Tinos (€30.10, 1¾ hours), Mykonos (€34, two hours 10 minutes) and Paros (€34.60, three hours), and a 4pm service to Tinos and Mykonos.

FERRY

Blue Star Ferries runs a daily service at 8.05am to Andros (€9.90, two hours), Tinos (€15, 3¾ hours) and Mykonos (€17, 4½ hours). Blue Star also has a 7.15pm daily ferry service to Andros.

Hellas Ferries sails to Andros and Tinos in the mornings for the same price and adds Mykonos to the route in the afternoons.

There are also five ferries daily to the port of Marmari on the island of Evia (€5.10, one hour).

THESSALONIKI ΘΕΣΣΑΛΟΝΙΚΗ
pop 363,987

It may be Greece's second-largest city, but being second does not mean Thessaloniki (thess-ah-lo-*nee*-kih) lies in the shadow of, or tries to emulate, the capital. It is a sophisticated city with its own distinct character.

Thessaloniki sits at the top of the Thermaic Gulf. The oldest part of the city is the Turkish quarter, with streets circling the Byzantine fortress on the slopes of Mt Hortiatis.

Orientation

Thessaloniki is laid out on a grid stretching back from Leoforos Nikis, which runs from the port in the west to the White Tower (Lefkos Pyrgos) in the east. The two main squares, both abutting the waterfront, are Plateia Eleftherias, which doubles as a local bus terminal, and Plateia Aristotelous. The other main streets of Mitropoleos, Tsimiski, Ermou and Egnatia run parallel to Leoforos Nikis. Egnatia is the main thoroughfare, running east from Plateia Dimokratias. Kastra, the old Turkish quarter, is north of Plateia Dimokratias.

Information
BOOKSHOPS
Travel Bookstore Traveller (☎ 2310 275 215; www .traveler.gr; Proxenou Koromila 41) This cosy shop outfits travellers with Road Editions maps and Lonely Planet guides.

EMERGENCY
First-Aid Centre (☎ 2310 530 530; Navarhou Koundourioti 10) Near the port.
Ippokration Hospital (☎ 2310 837 921; Papanastasiou 50) Two kilometres east of the city centre.
Tourist police (☎ 2310 554 871; 5th fl, Dodekanisou 4; ☯ 7.30am-11pm)

INTERNET ACCESS
Web (☎ 2310 237 031; S Gonata 4, Plateia Navarino; per hr €2.40; ☯ 24hr) Big, well-equipped café with fast internet and helpful staff.

LAUNDRY
Bianca Laundrette (Panagias Dexias 3; per 6kg load €7; ☯ 8am-8.30pm Tue, Thu & Fri, 8am-3pm Mon, Wed & Sat) In just two hours your clothes are washed, dried and folded at this no-nonsense laundromat powered by classic rock.

MONEY
National Bank of Greece (Tsimiski 11) Opens at the weekend for currency exchange.

POST
Post office Aristotelous (Aristotelous 26; ☯ 7.30am-8pm Mon-Fri, 7.30am-2.15pm Sat, 9am-1.30pm Sun); Koundouriotou (Koundouriotou 6; ☯ 7.30am-2pm) Next to the port.

TOURIST INFORMATION
Tourist information office (☎ 2310 500 310; ☯ 9am-2pm Mon-Fri, 8am-2pm Sat) In the port's passenger terminal.

Sights

The **Archaeological Museum** (☎ 2310 830 538; Manoli Andronikou 6; admission €4; ☯ 8.30am-3pm) houses finds from prehistoric Thessaloniki, including a well-preserved **Petralona hoard** – a collection of axes and chisels, and some filigree gold wreaths and jewellery from burial sites all over Macedonia.

The **Museum of Ancient Greek & Byzantine Instruments** (☎ 2310 555 263; Katouni 12-14; admission €4.40; ☯ 9am-3pm & 5-10pm Tue-Sun) houses a superb collection of instruments from antiquity to the 19th century.

The imposing **Arch of Galerius**, at the eastern end of Egnatia, is the finest of the city's Roman monuments. It was erected in AD 303 to celebrate the emperor's victories over the Persians in 297. The nearby **Rotunda** was built as a mausoleum for Galerius, but never fulfilled this function; Constantine the Great transformed it into a church.

The 15th-century **White Tower** (Lefkos Pyrgos; ☎ 2310 267 832; adult €2; ☯ 8am-7pm Tue-Sun, 12.30-7pm Mon) is both the city's symbol and most prominent landmark. During the 18th century the tower was used as a prison for insubordinate janissaries. In 1826 they were massacred there and it was known as the 'bloody tower'. After independence it was whitewashed as a gesture to expunge its Turkish function. You can climb to the top via a wide circular stairway – the views from the top are impressive and there is a small café.

In the northeast of the city, the Turkish quarter of **Kastra**, with its narrow steep streets flanked by timber-framed houses and tiny, whitewashed dwellings with shutters, is all

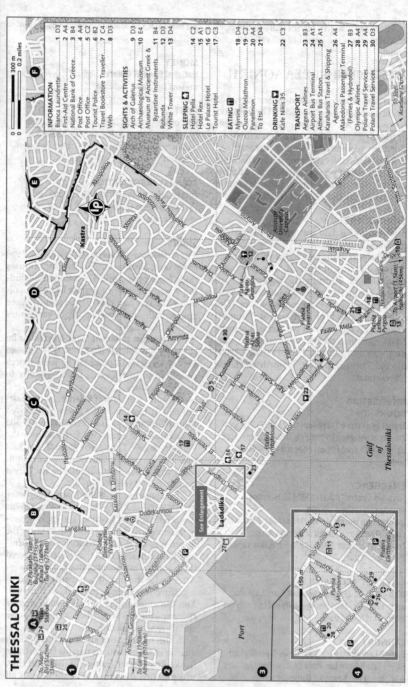

THESSALONIKI

0   300 m
0   0.2 miles

Kastra

Ladadika

See Enlargement

Gulf of Thessaloniki

Port

To Marmaras
Bus Station
(3km)

Train Station

To Perea (3km);
Bulgaria (3735km);
Turkey (377km)

To Larisa (150km);
Athens (510km)

To Airport (1.5km);
Halkidiki (45km)

To Bici
Academy (2km)

150 m

Plateia Eleftherias

Plateia Mborhevou

that is left of 19th-century Thessaloniki. The original ramparts of Kastra were built by Theodosius (379–475), but were rebuilt in the 14th century. From Kastra there are stunning views of modern Thessaloniki and the Thermaic Gulf.

Take bus 22 or 23 from Plateia Eleftherias, or walk north along Agias Sofias, which becomes Vlatadon then Dimadou Vlatadou after Athinas, and turn right into Eptapyrgiou at the top.

Sleeping

Hotel Pella (☎ 2310 524 221; Ionos Dragoumi 63; s/d €35/50) Decent for budget travellers, the Pella has small but clean rooms near the Ladadika/port district.

Hotel Rex (☎ 2310 517 051; Monastiriou 39; s/d €45/50) Ideal for those with early-morning trains or buses to catch, this unpretentious hotel near the train station has clean, though cramped rooms.

Tourist Hotel (☎ 2310 270 501; www.touristhotel .gr; Mitropoleos 21; s/d/tr €55/70/90; 🕸) This classic place (built 1925) has an old-school gated lift and ornate chandeliers. The clean, well-kept rooms have soundproof windows.

Le Palace Hotel (☎ 2310 257 400; www.lepalace.gr; Tsimiski 23; s/d €95/104; 🕸) Gaze down from your little balcony here at night, on twinkling Tsimiski roaring by below (there's soundproofing). Le Palace has spacious, modern rooms with all the mod cons.

Eating

To Etsi (☎ 2310 222 469; Nikoforos Fokas 2; pites €2.30) This bawdily decorated, iconic eatery near the White Tower offers refreshingly light souvlaki and *soutzoukakia* (spicy meatballs in tomato sauce) with vegetable dips, in Cypriot-style pitta bread. Look for the neon sign out front.

Ouzou Melathron (☎ 2310 275 016; Karypi 21; mezedhes €3-5.50, mains €5-11) Just from the sight of the scroll-like menu at this very popular sidestreet *ouzerie* you know you're in for something special. Occupy yourself with ouzo and mezedhes, then dig into heartier fare like lamb in sweet wine sauce.

Panellinion (☎ 2310 567 220; Salaminos 1; mains €6-8) This friendly taverna has traditional Ladadika décor, with its wooden floors and walls lined with olive-oil bottles and tins of produce. Panellinion has great variety, from ouzos and cheeses to delicious seafood mezedhes; only organic vegetables are used.

Myrsini (☎ 2310 228 300; Tsopela 2; mains €6-10) Myrsini serves up hearty portions of authentic Cretan dishes for Thessaloniki's boisterous young hedonists. The food is delicious and healthy, from rusks topped with tomato, Cretan olive oil and soft cheese (*dakos*) and flavourful *horta* (wild greens) to roast rabbit, pork and – crucially – flaky filo triangles with sweet *mizithra* cheese (*mizithropitakia*). Décor is simple, with worn, wooden floors and traditional accoutrements. Violin and bouzouki music from Crete plays on in the background.

Drinking

Kafe Nikis 35 (☎ 2310 230 449; Leoforos Nikis 35) A waterfront bar, but much more stylish than the generic ones around it, this snug, friendly café just under street level is perfect for a Sunday morning macchiato. Get a window table and feel the dappled sunlight dancing through the blinds.

Beer Academy (☎ 2310 449 606; Mihalakopoulou 2, Kalamaria) A metre of beer in Kalamaria is just what the doctor ordered on an unproductive Thessaloniki afternoon. It takes time, after all, to sample the very substantial offerings at Thessaloniki's trend-setting *biraria* (beer bar).

Getting There & Away

AIR

The **airport** (☎ 2310 473 212) is 16km southeast of town.

Olympic Airlines (☎ 2310 368 666; www.olympic airlines.com; Navarhou Koundourioti 1-3) is near the port, and **Aegean Airlines** (☎ 2310 280 050; www.aegeanair .com; Venizelou 2) is on Plateia Eleftherias.

Domestic

Olympic Airlines operates over 15 domestic routes. These are the more important ones: Athens (€45 to €105, 55 minutes, seven daily); Limnos (€65, 50 minutes, daily); and Mytilini (€87, one hour 50 minutes, six weekly). It also has two to four flights weekly to Corfu (€75, 55 minutes), Iraklio (€100, 1½ hours), Mykonos (€95, one hour), Hania (€105, 2½ hours), Chios (€80, 2¾ hours), Skyros (€58, 40 minutes) and Samos (€90). Some flights are via intermediate airports.

Aegean Airlines has 12 daily flights to Athens (€66 to €93), and with less frequent services to Mytilini (€80), Rhodes (€110) and Santorini (€105).

International

Thessaloniki's **Macedonia International Airport** (www.hcaa-eleng.gr/thes.htm) serves numerous destinations throughout Europe.

BUS

Thessaloniki's main **KTEL Makedonias bus station** (☎ 2310 595 408; Monastiriou 319), situated 3km west of the city centre, has departures to Athens (€38.80, seven hours, 13 daily), Alexandroupoli (€5.30, six hours, eight daily) and Kavala (€12.90, 1½ hours, hourly). Athens buses also depart from a small terminal opposite the train station. Local bus 1 travels between the bus station and the train station every 10 minutes.

FERRY

Four weekly ferries serve the Sporadic islands of Skiathos (€17.70, seven hours) and Skopelos (€19.90, nine hours); three continue to Alonnisos (€23.20, 10 hours).

Boats serve Chios three times weekly (€34.20, 19 hours) via Limnos (€22.10, eight hours, five times weekly) and Lesvos (Mytilini; €34.40, 14 hours, five times weekly). One boat weekly continues to Samos (€39.20, 20 hours). The Dodecanese is also served once weekly, to Kalymnos (€41.90, 21 hours), then Kos (€43.80, 22 hours) and Rhodes (€52.40, 26 hours). In summer, two boats weekly serve Iraklio (€45.60, 26 hours) on Crete.

You can get tickets from port-area travel agencies, like the helpful **Polaris Travel Services** (☎ 2310 548 655; fax 2310 548 290; Navarhou Koundourioti 19; ☼ 8am-8.30pm), which also has a second, **central office** (☎ 2310 278 613; fax 2310 265 728; polaris@otenet.gr; Egnatia 81; ☼ 8am-8.30pm) near Agias Sofias on Egnatia.

HYDROFOIL

In summer hydrofoils reach the Sporades islands of Skiathos (3¼ hours), Skopelos (four hours) and Alonnisos (4½ hours). Tickets are €35.30. Try **Karaharisis Travel & Shipping Agency** (☎ 2310 524 544; fax 2310 532 289; Navarhou Koundourioti 8; ☼ 8am-8.30pm).

To contact the port police you need to dial ☎ 2310 531 504.

TRAIN

There are four regular trains daily to Athens (€15.20, 6¾ hours), three daily to Alexandroupoli (€10, six hours) and Larisa with connections to Volos (€7, 4½ hours).

There are seven express intercity services to Athens (€35.50, 5½ hours) and two to Alexandroupoli (€18, 5½ hours).

GYTHIO ΓΥΘΕΙΟ

pop 4489

Gythio (yee-thih-o), once the port of ancient Sparta, is now an attractive fishing port at the head of the Lakonian Gulf. It is a convenient departure point for the island of Kythira, and for Kissamos on Crete.

Orientation

Gythio is not too hard to figure out. Most restaurants and cafés are along the seafront on Akti Vasileos Pavlou. The bus station is at the northeastern end, next to the small triangular park known as the Perivolaki. Behind this is the main square, Plateia Panagiotou Venetzanaki.

The square at the southwestern end of Akti Vasileos Pavlou is Plateia Mavromihali, hub of the old quarter of Marathonisi. The ferry quay is opposite this square. Beyond it the waterfront road becomes Kranais, which leads south to the road to Areopoli. A causeway leads out to Marathonisi Islet at the southern edge of town.

Information

EOT (☎ /fax 27330 24484; Vasileos Georgiou 20; ☼ 8am-2.30pm Mon-Fri) This is the information equivalent of Monty Python's famous cheese-free cheese shop: remarkably information-free, even by EOT's lamentable standards.

Internet Jolly Café (cnr Dirou & Grigoraki; internet access per hr €2.50) One block from the bus station.

Hassanakos Bookstore (☎ 27330 22064; Akti Vasileos Pavlou 39)

Police (☎ 27330 22100; Akti Vasileos Pavlou)

Post office (cnr Ermou & Arheou Theatrou; ☼ 7.30am-2pm Mon-Fri)

Sights

Pine-shaded **Marathonisi Island** is linked to the mainland by a causeway at the southern edge of town. According to mythology, it was here that Paris (prince of Troy) and Helen (wife of Menelaus) consummated the affair that kicked off the Trojan Wars. The 18th-century Tzanetakis Grigorakis tower houses a small **Museum of Mani History** (☎ 27330 24484; admission €1.50; ☼ 8am-2pm) that relates Maniot history through the eyes of European travellers who visited the region between the 15th and

19th centuries. The architecturally minded will find an absorbing collection upstairs of plans of Maniot towers and castles.

Sleeping

Matina's (☎ 27330 22518; d/tr €50/60) A great location, right in the heart of town, this budget diamond is appropriately above the town's jewellery shop. Matina speaks no English, but is welcoming and runs a clean and comfortable abode.

Saga Pension (☎ 27330 23220; d €50; ✖) This is a good-value (saga-free!), comfortable place with balconies. It's 150m from the port, on Kranai, overlooking Marathonisi Islet. The upmarket Saga Restaurant is below.

Eating

Saga Pension (☎ 27330 21358; mains €6-9, fish per kg €40-60; ⏰ lunch & dinner; ✖) Large, stylish with white cloths and fancy chairs, this serves top notch eating options. It's on Kranais.

Taverna Petakou (☎ 27330 22889; mains €3-7) This no-frills place is another favourite with locals. The day's menu is written down in an exercise book in Greek. It may include a hearty fish soup, which comes with a large chunk of bread on the side.

Taverna O Potis (☎ 27330 23245; mains €5.50-15, fish per kg €47) The model sea-craft hanging from the ceiling of this new place reflect its ship-shape condition. The locals flock aboard for its spotless kitchen, clean interior and generous helpings. The house red is a bit like a massive ocean swell, but it's well worth the walk to the far end of the promenade, opposite Marathonisi Islet.

Getting There & Away

BUS

The **KTEL Lakonias bus station** (☎ 27330 22228; cnr Vasileos Georgiou & Evrikleos) has buses north to Athens (€22.70, four hours, four daily) via Sparta (€3.70, one hour).

FERRY

ANEN Lines (www.anen.gr) has three weekly ferries to Kissamos-Kastelli on Crete (€21.40, seven hours), via Kythira (€9.90, 2½ hours) and Antikythira (€15.80, four hours) from July to early September, with two services weekly in winter. Check the ever-changing schedule with **Rozakis Travel** (☎ 27330 22207; rosakigy@otenet.gr), on the waterfront near Plateia Mavromihali.

PORTS TO THE SARONIC GULF ISLANDS

There are connections to the Saronic Gulf Islands from several ports around the Argolis Peninsula of the eastern Peloponnese.

Porto Heli, at the southwestern tip of the peninsula, has at least four hydrofoils a day to Spetses (€5, 10 minutes) and Hydra (€11.50, 50 minutes), while nearby **Ermioni** has four a day to Hydra (€7.50, 20 minutes).

Galatas, on the east coast, is a stone's throw from Poros. Small boats (€0.70, five minutes) shuttle back and forth across the adjoining Poros Strait from 6am to 10pm.

All three ports can be reached by bus from **Nafplio**, the main town/transport hub of the Argolis. There are two buses daily from Nafplio to Galatas (€7, two hours), but travelling to Ermioni and Porto Heli involves changing at Kranidi (€6.60, two hours, three daily except Sunday). There are hourly buses to Nafplio (€11.30, 2½ hours) from Terminal A in Athens.

PORTS TO THE CYCLADES

Lavrio Λαύριο

pop 8558

An unattractive industrial town on the east coast of Attica, 43km southeast of Athens, Lavrio, is the departure point for ferries to the islands of Kea and Kythnos, and for high-season catamaran services to the western Cyclades.

Getting There & Away

BUS

Buses run every 30 minutes to Lavrio departing from the Mavromateon terminal in Athens (€3.80, 1½ hours).

CATAMARAN

Hellenic Seaways (☎ 210 419 9000; www.hellenicseaways.gr) operates from Lavrio between mid-June and September. There are departures daily except Wednesday to Kythnos (€14.50, 40 minutes), Syros (€25.50, 1¾ hours) and Mykonos (€30, 2¾ hours).

FERRY

Goutos Lines (☎ 210 985 2992) runs the F/B *Myrina Express* from Lavrio to Kea (€6, 1¼ hours) and Kythnos (€9, 3½ hours).

From mid-June there are ferries to Kea every morning and evening Monday to Friday, and up to six daily at weekends. Six ferries weekly continue to Kythnos. In winter there are ferries to Kea every day except Monday, returning every day except Wednesday. One service a week continues to Kythnos. EOT in Athens gives out a timetable for this route. The ticket office at Lavrio is opposite the quay.

PORTS TO THE IONIANS
Patra Πάτρα
pop 167,600

Named after King Patreas, who ruled the Peloponnese prefecture of Achaïa in about 1100 BC, Patra is Greece's third-largest city and the principal port for boats travelling to and from Italy and the Ionian Islands. Despite a history stretching back 3000 years, Patra is not wildly exciting. Few travellers stay around any longer than it takes to catch the next boat, bus or train.

The city was destroyed during the War of Independence and rebuilt on a modern grid plan of wide, arcaded streets, large squares and ornate neoclassical buildings.

Many of these old buildings, such as the Apollon Theatre, were restored in preparation for the city's role as Europe's City of Culture in 2006.

ORIENTATION
Patra's grid system means easy walking. The waterfront is known as Iroön Polytehniou at the northeastern end, Othonos Amalias in the middle and Akti Dimeon to the south.

Customs is at the Iroön Polytehniou end, and the main bus and train stations are on Othonos Amalias.

Most of the agencies selling ferry tickets are on Iroön Polytehniou and Othonos Amalias.

INFORMATION
Bookshops
Newsstand (☎ 2610 273 092; Agiou Andrea 77) A small selection of novels, as well as international newspapers and magazines.

Emergency
First Aid Centre (☎ 2610 277 386; cnr Karolou & Agiou Dionysiou; ⏱ 8am-8pm)
Port police (☎ 2610 341 002; Iroön Polytehniou end of the waterfront)
Tourist police (☎ 2610 695 191; Gounari 52 & Ipsilandou, 4th fl; ⏱ 7am-9pm)

Internet Access
Netp@rk (Gerokostopoulou 36a; per hr €2; ⏱ 24hr)
Netrino Internet Cafe (Karaïskaki 133; per hr €3; ⏱ 24hr)

Laundry
Skafi Laundrette (Zaïmi 49; wash & dry per load €7.50; ⏱ 9am-3pm Mon-Sat, 5-8.30pm Tue, Thu & Fri)

Left Luggage
Train station (⏱ 6am-11pm) Charges €3.20 per item per day, or €1.60 if you have a train ticket.

Money
National Bank of Greece (Plateia Trion Symahon; ⏱ 8am-2.30pm Mon-Thu, 8am-2pm Fri) Opposite the train station.

Post
Post office (cnr Zaïmi & Mezonos; ⏱ 7.30am-8pm Mon-Fri, 7.30am-2pm Sat & Sun)

Tourist Information
Info Centre (☎ 2610 461 740/1; www.infocenter patras.gr; Othonos Amalias 6; ⏱ 8am-10pm) This is the best-organised information office in Greece, run by the city of Patra (rather than the EOT). It's stocked with maps and brochures on local points of interest plus information on everything including transport and hotels. The delightful English-speaking staff is eager to please. There's even free 20-minute internet access and free bikes.

SIGHTS
Kastro's wonderful old **fortress** (admission free; ⏱ 8am-7pm Tue-Sun Apr-Oct, 8.30am-5pm Tue-Fri, 8.30am-3pm Sat & Sun Nov-Mar) stands on the site of the Acropolis of Ancient Patrai. The structure is of Frankish origin, remodelled many times over the centuries by the Byzantines, Venetians and Turks. It was in use as a defensive position until WWII and remains in good condition.

Set in an attractive park, it's reached by climbing the steps at the end of Agiou Nikolaou.

FESTIVALS & EVENTS
Patra is noted for the exuberance with which its citizens celebrate the city's annual **carnival**. The carnival programme begins in mid-January, and features a host of minor events leading up to a wild weekend of costume parades, colourful floats and celebrations at the end of February or early March.

The event draws big crowds, so hotel reservations are essential if you want to stay overnight. Contact EOT (p74) for dates and details.

SLEEPING & EATING
Spyros Rooms (☎ 2610 427 278; www.patrasrooms.gr; Tofalou 2; s/d €30/40; ⌘) At the western end of the

port and handy to the ferries are these clean and basic rooms with TV.

Hotel Mediterraneé (☎ 2610 279 602; mediterran@ otenet.gr; Nikolaou 18; s/d €50/70) This place looks like it's seen a little too much of Patra's nightlife itself – despite the plush lobby, the rooms are on the verge of being a little worn, and the bathrooms are in a cupboard. It's pleasant and good value nonetheless and very central. Breakfast costs €5.

Olympic Star Hotel (☎ 2610 622 939; www.olym picstar.gr; Nikolaou 46; s/d inc breakfast €60/90; 🔲) A shining star indeed; Patra needed a place like this. The hotel has had a funky new overhaul and its contemporary rooms feature hydro showers and personal internet. Reduced prices without breakfast.

Europa Centre (☎ 2610 437 006; Othonos Amalias 10; mains €4-8; 7am-midnight) This convenient, cafeteria-style place is close to the international ferry dock and it is a good place to hang out en route. The helpful staff serves standard, but filling fare. There's free (short-term) luggage storage, TV, internet and pinball machines.

Dia Discount supermarket (Agiou Andreou 29) Ideally located for travellers planning to buy provisions and keep moving.

GETTING THERE & AWAY
Bus
The **KTEL Achaia bus station** (☎ 2610 623 888; Othonos Amalias) has buses to Athens (€16.20, three hours, half-hourly) via Corinth (€10.80,

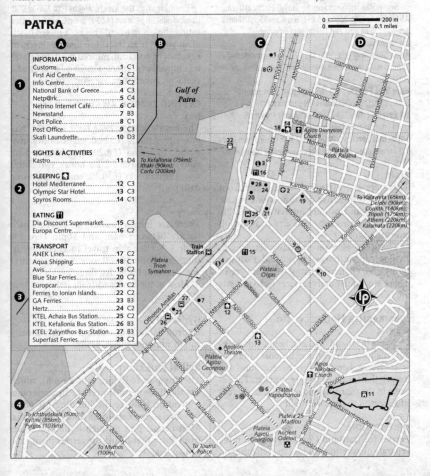

1½ hours). It also has buses to Thessaloniki (€37.90, seven hours, four daily) and Kalamata (€19.30, four hours, two daily).

The **KTEL Kefallonia bus station** (☎ 2610 274 938; cnr Othonos Amalias & Gerokostopoulou) has five buses a day to Kyllini (€6.50, 1¼ hours), timed to meet ferries to Argostoli and Poros.

Buses to Zakynthos (€13 including ferry, 3½ hours, five daily) leave from the **KTEL Zakynthos bus station** (☎ 2610 220 219; Othonos Amalias 58). They also travel via Kyllini.

Ferry

There are daily ferries to Kefallonia (€14.50, 2½ hours) and Ithaki (€14.50, 3¾ hours). Fares to Corfu (six to 7½ hours) cost €33 with ANEK Lines and Aqua Shipping.

See p506 for services to Italy. Ferry offices:

ANEK Lines (☎ 2610 226 053; www.anek.gr; Othonos Amalias 25) Ancona and Trieste via Corfu and Igoumenitsa.

Aqua Shipping (☎ 2610 455 622; Iroön Polytehniou 5) Ancona via Igoumenitsa; Venice via Igoumenitsa and Corfu.

Blue Star Ferries (☎ 2610 634 000; www.bluestar ferries.com; Othonos Amalias 12) Bari via Igoumenitsa.

GA Ferries (☎ 2610 276 059; Othonos Amalias & Gerokostopolou) Bari via Igoumenitsa.

Superfast Ferries (☎ 2610 622 500; Othonos Amalias 12) Ancona direct or via Igoumenitsa; Bari via Igoumenitsa.

Train

There are at least seven trains daily from Patra to Corinth; five are slow trains (€3.20, 2½ hours) and two are intercity (€6.40, 2½ hours). All trains between Patra and Corinth stop at Diakofto.

There are also several daily services to Pyrgos (express/normal €5.40/2.80, 1½/three hours). For Olympia, change trains at Pyrgos. There are regular daily services to Kyparissia and Kalamata.

Igoumenitsa Ηγουμενίτσα
pop 9104

Opposite the island of Corfu, Igoumenitsa (ih-goo-meh-*nit*-sah) is the main port of northwest Greece. Few travellers hang around any longer than it takes to buy a ticket. Ferries leave in the morning and evening, so there is little reason to stay overnight.

ORIENTATION

Ferries for Italy and Corfu leave from three separate quays situated close to each other on the waterfront at Ethnikis Andistasis. Ferries travelling to Ancona and Venice (in Italy) depart from the new port on the south side of town; those for Brindisi and Bari still use the old port situated in front of the main shipping offices; and ferries for Corfu (Kerkyra) and Paxi usually depart from just north of the new port.

The bus station is on Kyprou, two blocks back from the waterfront.

SLEEPING & EATING

Hotel Aktaion (☎ /fax 26650 22707; Agion Apostolon 17; s/d €40/50) and **Jolly Hotel** (☎ 26650 23971; jollyigm@otenet .gr; Ethnikis Andistasis 44; s/d €55/65) are both comfortable C-class hotels on the waterfront with uninspiring, yet quiet, rooms.

Popular with the locals, **Alekos** (☎ 26650 23708; Ethnikis Andistasis 84; mains €4.50-7) is one of the better eating choices in town. There is a mixed batch of *mayirefta* here, but the *mousakas* (layers of eggplant or zucchini, minced meat and potatoes topped with cheese sauce and baked), and veal with aubergines, are worth trying.

GETTING THERE & AWAY
Bus

The **bus station** (☎ 26650 22309; Kyprou 29) has buses to Athens (€32.60, eight hours, five daily), Ioannina (€8.20, two hours, nine daily), Preveza (€8.50, 2½ hours, two daily) and Thessaloniki (€30.20, eight hours, one daily).

Ferry

There are ferries heading to Corfu Town hourly between 5am and 10pm (€6, 1¾ hours). Ferries also travel to Lefkimmi in southern Corfu (€4.50, one hour, six daily) and Paxi (€7, 1¾ hours, three weekly).

Most of the ferries to/from Italy also stop at Corfu.

Hydrofoil

Hydrofoils to/from Corfu and Paxi usually run in summer; check locally.

Kyllini Κυλλήνη

The tiny port of Kyllini (kih-*lee*-nih), which sits about 78km southwest of Patra, warrants a mention only as the jumping-off point for ferries to Kefallonia and Zakynthos. Most people pass through Kyllini on buses from Patra that board the ferries plying the Ionian Sea.

GETTING THERE & AWAY
Bus
There are 10 buses daily to Kyllini (€6.50, 1¼ hours) from Patra, five from the KTEL Kefallonia bus station and five from the KTEL Zakynthos bus station.

Ferry
Boats travel to Zakynthos (€6.50, 1¼ hours, up to six daily), Poros (€8, 1½ hours, three daily) and Argostoli on Kefallonia (€12.50, 2½ hours, two daily).

PORTS TO KYTHIRA
Dangling from the tip of the southeastern tip of the Peloponnese, Kythira is the odd island out. It belongs in theory to the Ionian island group but in practice is administered from Athens. The best access is from the ports of Gythio and Neapoli.

Neapoli Νεάπολη
pop 2727
Lying close to the tip of the eastern finger of the Peloponnese, Neapoli (neh-ah-po-lih) is a fairly uninspiring town, in spite of its location on a huge horseshoe bay. Most travellers come to Neapoli only to catch a ferry to the island of Kythira, which is clearly visible across the bay.

SLEEPING & EATING
Hotel Aivali (☎ 27340 22287; Akti Voion 164; s/d €35/40; 🌐) is a small family hotel that is ideally located right on the seafront, close to the ferry dock for Kythira. Like all the hotels in town, it's booked out during August.

Numerous lively *ouzeries* line the waterfront, serving the local speciality: delicious grilled octopus.

GETTING THERE & AWAY
Bus
There are four buses daily from Neapoli to Sparta (€12.20, three hours), from where there are frequent buses to Athens.

Ferry
There are daily ferries travelling from Neapoli to Diakofti on Kythira (€8.20, one hour). Tickets are sold at **Dermatis Travel** (☎ 27340 24004), on the first road to your left on the waterfront. Frequency varies depending on the season; count on at least two per day in July and August.

PORTS TO THE SPORADES
Agios Konstantinos
Άγιος Κωνσταντίνος
pop 2657
The closest port serving the Sporades for travellers from Athens is Agios Konstantinos, 175km northwest of the capital.

SLEEPING & EATING
With judicious use of buses from Athens, you will not need to stay overnight. If you do stay, then look out for **Hotel Amfitryon** (☎ 22350 31702; fax 22350 32604; Eivoilou 10; s/d incl breakfast€45/65; 🌐), which is between the harbour and central square.

Several tavernas keep company with the ferry ticket offices, including the reliable **Taverna Kaitsas** (☎ 22350 33323; mains €4.50-8.50).

GETTING THERE & AWAY
Bus
There are hourly buses (starting from 6.15am) between Agios Konstantinos and Athens Terminal B bus station (€13, 2½ hours).

Ferry
Two **jet ferries** (☎ 22350 31614) make daily runs from Agios Konstantinos to Skiathos (€28, 2½ hours); Skopelos (€36, 3½ hours) and Alonnisos (€36, four hours).

Hydrofoil
There are three hydrofoils daily to Skiathos (€27, 1½ hours) and Skopelos Town (€36.50, 2½ hours) and Alonnisos (€36.50, 2¾ hours). **Bilalis Travel Agency** (☎ 22350 31614), near the quay, sells tickets.

Volos Βόλος
pop 85,394
A bustling city on the northern shores of the Pagasitic Gulf, Volos is the port for ferry and hydrofoil services to the Sporades.

According to mythology, Volos was ancient Iolkos, from where Jason and the Argonauts set sail on their quest for the Golden Fleece.

ORIENTATION
Volos is laid out on an easy grid system stretching inland parallel to the waterfront (called Argonafton), which is where most services for travellers are to be found. The main square, Plateia Riga Fereou, is at the northwestern end of Argonafton.

VOLOS

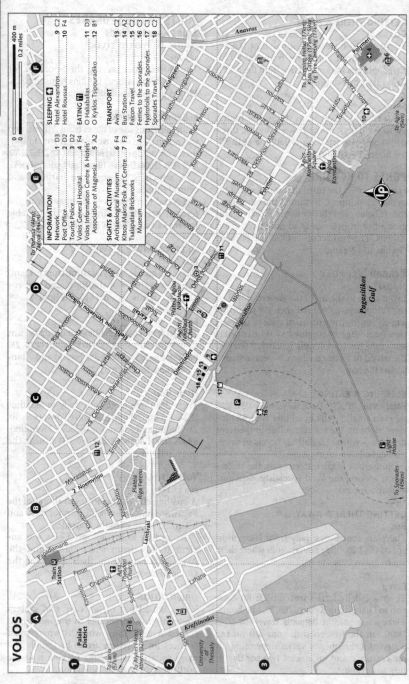

INFORMATION	
Network....................................	1 D3
Post Office..............................	2 D2
Tourist Police.........................	3 D2
Volos General Hospital.........	4 F4
Volos Information Centre & Hotels'	
Association of Magnesia........	5 A2

SIGHTS & ACTIVITIES	
Archaeological Museum..........	6 F4
Kitsos Makris Folk Art Centre...	7 F3
Tsalapatas Brickworks	
Museum.................................	8 A2

SLEEPING	
Hotel Alexandros..................	9 C2
Hotel Roussas.......................	10 F4

EATING	
O Haliabalias.......................	11 D3
O Kyklos Tsipouradiko........	12 B1

TRANSPORT	
Avis.......................................	13 C2
Bus Station...........................	14 A2
Falcon Travel........................	15 C2
Ferries to the Sporades........	16 C3
Hydrofoils to the Sporades...	17 C3
Sporades Travel....................	18 C2

0   400 m
0   0.2 miles

Pagasitikos Gulf

Palaia District

University of Thessaly

INFORMATION

National Bank of Greece (Argonafton)

Network (☎ 24210 30260; Iasonos 41; ⏰ 24hr) Volos' largest internet café.

Post office (cnr Dimitriados & Agios Nikolaou)

Tourist police (☎ 24210 76987; Alexandras 179)

Volos Information Centre & Hotels' Association of Magnesia (☎ 24210 20273; www.travel-pelion.gr; Gr Lambraki & Sekeri; ⏰ 8am-9pm mid-Apr–mid-Sep, 8am-8pm mid-Sep–mid-Apr; Ⓟ ▯) Gives out town maps, bus and ferry schedules and information about hotels.

SLEEPING & EATING

Hotel Roussas (☎ 24210 21732; fax 24210 22987; Iatrou Tzanou 1; s/d €29/35; ❄) This small and friendly, no-frills waterfront hotel near the Archaeological Museum has 15 spotless rooms with balcony. Street-side rooms, however, will catch weekend traffic noise.

Hotel Alexandros (☎ 24210 31221; fax 24210 31224; Topali 13; s/d/tr €45/65/80; ❄) The well-maintained Alexandros is one of the best values among several waterfront hotels. Large rooms feature wooden floors, desks and small bathtubs. The quietest rooms are toward the front, away from busy Iasonos.

O Haliabalias (☎ 24210 20872; Mikrasiaton 85; mezedhes €1.50-6) Flagstone floors and wood-beamed ceilings lend plenty of atmosphere to this popular student hangout. The speciality is potatoes baked in a traditional wood-fired oven.

O Kyklos Tsipouradiko (☎ 24210 20234; Orfezos 8; mains €4.50-10) Tucked away on a pedestrian side street near Agios Nikolaos church, O Haliabalias is known for good variations on traditional dishes like chicken with orzo pasta and *briam*.

GETTING THERE & AWAY

Bus

There are 10 buses daily to Athens (€23.50, 4½ hours) and nine buses to Thessaloniki (€15.80, 2½ hours).

Ferry

There are two ferries daily to Skiathos (€15, 2½ hours), Glossa (Skopelos; €16.50, 3½ hours), Skopelos Town (€19.50, four hours) and Alonnisos (€19.50, four hours). You can buy tickets from **Sporades Travel** (☎ /fax 24210 35846; Argonafton 33).

Hydrofoil

From the port of Volos four hydrofoils travel daily to the island of Skiathos (€25, 1¼ hours)

in the Sporades, and Skopelos Town (€32.50, 2¼ hours); and three travel to Glossa (Skopelos; €27.50, 1¾ hours) and Alonnisos (€32.50, 2½ hours).

Tickets are available from **Sporades Travel** (☎ /fax 24210 35846; Argonafton 33) or **Falcon Travel** (☎ 24210 39299; Argonafton 34; ⏰ 7am-10pm).

Train

There are three intercity trains daily to Athens (€23.90) and three daily to Thessaloniki (€20.20). There are also slower conventional trains.

PORTS TO THE NORTHEASTERN AEGEAN

Kavala Καβάλα
pop 60,802

It's hard not to admire Kavala, one of Greece's most attractive cities. The town spills gently down the foothills of Mt Symvolon to a large harbour. The old quarter of Panagia nestles under a big Byzantine fortress.

Kavala is an important ferry hub with sea connections to the northeast Aegean, the Dodecanese and Attica.

ORIENTATION

Kavala's focal point is Plateia Eleftherias. The two main streets, Eleftheriou Venizelou and Erythrou Stavrou, run west from here parallel with the waterfront Ethnikis Andistasis. The old quarter of Panagia occupies a promontory to the southeast of Plateia Eleftherias, reached by a steep signposted access road at the east side of the harbour.

INFORMATION

ATM-equipped banks line the strip Eleftheriou Venizelou.

Cybernet (☎ 25102 30102; Erythrou Stavrou 64; internet access per hr €2; ⏰ 6am-4am)

National Bank of Greece (cnr Megalou Alexandrou & Dragoumi) Has exchange machine and ATM.

Newsstand (Erythrou Stavrou 32) Sells foreign newspapers and magazines.

Papadogiannis Bookshop (Omonias 46) Stocks international newspapers and magazines.

Post office (cnr Hrysostomou Kavalas & Erythrou Stavrou)

Tourist information (☎ 25102 31011; Plateia Eleftherias; detaktic@otenet.gr; ⏰ 8am-2pm Mon-Fri) Helpful staff provides maps, plus accommodation, transport and events information.

Tourist police (☎ 25102 22905; Omonias 119)

KAVALA

INFORMATION
Cybernet	1 A2
National Bank of Greece	2 C2
Newsstand	3 A2
Papadogiannis Bookshop	4 C1
Port Police	5 B2
Post Office	6 B2
Tourist Information	7 C2
Tourist Police	8 D2

SIGHTS & ACTIVITIES
Archaeological Museum	9 A2
House of Mehmet Ali	10 D3
Imaret	11 D3
Municipal Museum of Kavala	12 A1
Statue of Mehmet Ali	13 D3

SLEEPING
Galaxy Hotel	14 C2
Giorgos Alvanos Rooms	15 D3

EATING
Ariko	16 C2
Tembelhanio	17 D3

TRANSPORT
Aegean Airlines	18 B2
Alkyon Travel Service	19 B2
Budget Rent a Car	20 B2
Bus Station	21 B2
Bus Stop for Alexandroupoli	22 B2
Europcar	(see 19)
Ferries for Aegean Islands	23 C3
Hydrofoils for Thasos	24 C3
Nikos Miliadis Shipping Agency	25 C3
Olympic Airlines	26 B2
SAOS Ferries	27 C3
Taxi Stand	28 B2

SIGHTS

If you've got time to spare, spend it exploring the streets of **Panagia**, the old Turkish quarter surrounding the massive Byzantine fortress on the promontory south of Plateia Eleftherias.

The pastel-hued houses in the narrow, tangled streets of the Panagia quarter are less dilapidated than those of Thessaloniki's Kastra and the area is less commercialised than Athens' Plaka. The most conspicuous building is the **Imaret**, a huge structure with 18 domes, which overlooks the harbour from Poulidou.

The **archaeological museum** (☎ 25102 22335; Erythrou Stavrou 17; adult €2, free Sun & public holidays; ☷ 8am-3pm Tue-Sun) houses well-displayed finds from ancient Amphipolis, between Thessaloniki and Kavala.

SLEEPING & EATING

Giorgos Alvanos Rooms (☎ 25102 21781; Anthemiou 35; s/d €20/30) Kavala's best budget option, marked by consistent prices, clean and comfortable rooms, these simple domatia are in a 300-year-old house up in Panagia. Rooms have refrigerators and sea views, but bathrooms are shared. It's a steep walk uphill to get here, so call Giorgos first to make sure there's a room.

Galaxy Hotel (☎ 25102 24521; fax 25102 26754; Eleftheriou Venizelou 27; s/d €40/55; ☒) This standby has good, if unremarkable rooms with all mod cons and a nice location above the waterfront, but there's street noise.

Tembelhanio (☎ 25102 32502; Poulidou 33b; mezedhes €3-5) A good spot for seafood mezedhes,

VOLOS OUZERIES

If you transit the busy port of Volos on your way to or from the Sporades be sure to linger for dinner at one of the town's famous *ouzeries*; Volos is reputed to have the best *ouzeries* in Greece. An *ouzerie* is an informal restaurant where you eat from small plates of mezedhes – or appetisers. Normally undertaken with a group of friends, you nibble on selections of anchovies, olives, cheese, spicy dips, octopus, fried courgettes or whatever the ouzerie's owner can imagine, and wash it down with a few stiff carafes of ouzo – taken neat or with water. You dine and imbibe until you are full, or fall over when you attempt to stand up. *'Stin iyia sas!'*

this has a relaxed setting in Panagia and a dedicated, ouzo-imbibing Greek clientele.

Ariko (☎ 25102 27173; Erythrou Stavrou 2; mains €5) Housed in the old fish-market building, this popular place with its inviting outdoor dining has a wide-ranging fish menu and other traditional specialities. The owner recommends the clam *saganaki* (usually skillet-fried with feta cheese).

Poulidou in Panagia has good tavernas, while lively café-bars are on the western waterfront.

GETTING THERE & AWAY

Air

Kavala shares the Alexander the Great airport near Hrysoupolis (29km), with Xanthi. **Olympic Airlines** (☎ 2510 223622; www.olympicairlines.com; Ethnikis Andistasis 8) does two daily Athens flights (€76), Aegean Airlines, once daily (€66).

Bus

The **bus station** (☎ 25102 23593) has departures to Athens (€45, 9½ hours, three daily), Keramoti (€4, one hour, hourly) and Thessaloniki (€12.90, two hours, hourly).

Buses for Alexandroupoli (€12.95, two hours, seven daily) depart from the **bus stop** (Hrysostomou Kavalas 1) outside the 7-Eleven Snack Bar and opposite the KTEL office. Get departure times and tickets from inside the store.

Ferry

There are ferries to Skala Prinou on Thasos (per person €3.30, 1¼ hours, hourly). There

is also an hourly service in summer from the small port of Keramoti, 46km east of Kavala, to Limenas (per person €2, 40 minutes).

In summer, ferries go to Samothraki (€14.50, four hours). Times and frequency vary month by month. Buy tickets and check the latest schedule at **SAOS Ferries** (☎ 25108 35671) near the entrance to the Aegean Islands ferry departure point.

There are ferries to Limnos (€15.30, four to five hours) and Lesvos (€26.50, 10 hours). Some services also go through to Rafina (in Attica) and Piraeus via Chios and Samos. Tickets and the latest schedules are available from **Nikos Miliadis Shipping Agency** (☎ 25102 26147; fax 25108 38767; Karaoli-Dimitriou 36).

Hydrofoil

There are about nine hydrofoils daily to Limenas (€8, 40 minutes). Purchase tickets at the departure point at the port.

Both hydrofoil and ferry schedules are posted in the window of the port police near the hydrofoil departure point.

Alexandroupoli Αλεξανδρούπολη
pop 49,176

The capital of the prefecture of Evros, Alexandroupoli (ah-lex-an-*droo*-po-lih) is a modern town with a lively student atmosphere supplemented by a population of young soldiers. Most travellers come here in transit heading east to Turkey, or to catch ferries to Samothraki or to the Dodecanese. The maritime ambience of this town, and its year-round liveliness, make it a pleasant stopover. The town was named Alexandroupoli (Alexander's City) in honour of King Alexander and has been part of the Greek state since 1920. There are few sights, except for the still-operating, 19th-century lighthouse parked conspicuously on the main promenade, to which crowds flock on warm summer evenings, to stroll and to relax in the many cafés and restaurants that stretch westwards from the port.

ORIENTATION

The town is laid out roughly on a grid system, with the main streets running east-west, parallel with the waterfront, where the lively evening *volta* (promenade) takes place. Karaoli Dimitriou is at the eastern end of the waterfront, with Megalou Alexandrou at the western end.

ATHENS & THE
MAINLAND PORTS

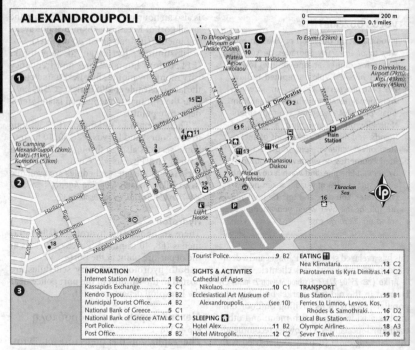

INFORMATION		SIGHTS & ACTIVITIES		EATING 🍴	
Internet Station Meganet.......1 B2		Cathedral of Agios		Nea Klimataria.....................13 C2	
Kassapidis Exchange............2 C1		Nikolaos.....................10 C1		Psarotaverna tis Kyra Dimitras.14 C2	
Kendro Typou.....................3 B2		Ecclesiastical Art Museum of			
Municipal Tourist Office.........4 B2		Alexandroupolis..............(see 10)		TRANSPORT	
National Bank of Greece.........5 C1				Bus Station.........................15 B1	
National Bank of Greece ATM.6 C1		SLEEPING 🛏		Ferries to Limnos, Lesvos, Kos,	
Port Police.........................7 C2		Hotel Alex.......................11 B2		Rhodes & Samothraki........16 D2	
Post Office.........................8 B2		Hotel Mitropolis...............12 C2		Local Bus Station.................17 C2	
Tourist Police.....................9 B2				Olympic Airlines...................18 A3	
				Sever Travel.......................19 B2	

The two main squares are Plateia Eleftherias and Plateia Polytehniou, both just one block north of Karaoli Dimitriou.

The train station is on the waterfront just south of Plateia Eleftherias and east of the port where boats leave for Samothraki and other ports south. The bus station (Eleftheriou Venizelou 36) is five blocks inland. The local bus station is on Plateia Eleftherias, just outside the train station.

INFORMATION

All major banks have ATMs along Leoforos Dimokratias.

Internet Station Meganet (☎ 25510 33639; Crnr Dikastirion & Psaron; internet access per hr €2.40; ✆ 24hr)

Kassapidis Exchange (☎ 25510 80910; Leoforos Dimokratias 209; ✆ 8am-9.30pm Mon-Sat, 10am-2pm Sun) Changes 87 kinds of currency, including all the Balkan ones; does Western Union money transfers.

Municipal tourist office (☎ 25510 64184; Leoforos Dimokratias 306; ✆ 7.30am-3pm) The helpful staff at the town hall gives out maps and accommodation and transport information.

Port police (☎ 25512 26468)

Post office (cnr Nikiforou Foka & Megalou Alexandrou)

Tourist police (☎ 25510 37424; Karaïskaki 6)

SIGHTS

The **Ethnological Museum of Thrace** (☎ 25510 36663; www.emthrace.com; 14 Maiou 63; adult €3; ✆ 10am-2pm Tue-Sun & 6-9pm Tue-Sat) houses a superb collection of traditional artefacts and tools.

The excellent **Ecclesiastical Art Museum of Alexandroupoli** (☎ 25510 82282; Plateia Agiou Nikolaou; adult €3; ✆ 9am-2pm Tue-Fri, 10am-2pm Sat) is one of the best in the country. It has a priceless collection of icons and ecclesiastical ornaments brought to Greek Thrace by refugees from Asia Minor. The museum is in the grounds of the Cathedral of Agios Nikolaos.

SLEEPING & EATING

Camping Alexandroupoli (☎ 25510 26055; fax 25510 28735; Leoforos Makris; camping sites per adult/tent €5/4.50) This large camping ground, 2km west of town is a clean, well-run site with good facilities. Take local bus 7 from Plateia Eleftherias.

Hotel Mitropolis (☎ 25510 26443; Athanasiou Dhiakou; s/d/t €30/40/50; ✦) Don't be put off by the dated sign out front – the Mitropolis is a clean, handsomely appointed hotel, not only the budget traveller's first choice but a good bet for anyone who wants to be close to the water and the town's best restaurants and cafés.

Hotel Alex (☎ 25510 26302; Leoforos Dimokratias 294; s/d/t €35/40/50; ☒) Up on the main road, this decent budget option has good rooms, though cramped, and the necessary amenities. Ask for a back room to minimise noise.

Nea Klimataria (☎ 25510 26288; Plateia Polytehniou; mains €5-8) This heavy-duty, popular place on the square is not setting records, but it does have tasty *mayirefta*, good roast chicken and big salads.

Psarotaverna tis Kyra Dimitras (☎ 25510 34434; Karaoli Dimitriou 104; fish €5.50-11) Choose from the daily fish catch, set out on ice at the front; golden *tsipoura* (sea bream) is tasty and only €20 per kilo, while a plateful of crunchy *koutsomoura* (striped mullet) makes for a scrumptious lunch.

GETTING THERE & AWAY
Alexandroupoli's Dimokritos Airport is 7km east of town near Loutra.

Olympic Airlines (☎ 25510 26361; www.olympic airlines.com; cnr Ellis 6 & Koletti) is downtown, **Aegean Airlines** (☎ 25510 89150; www.aegeanair.com) is at the airport. Both offer four daily flights to/from Athens (€75, 55 minutes). Olympic also has three weekly direct flights to Siteia, Crete (€80, 1¾ hours). A **taxi** (☎ 25510 28358) to the airport costs about €7.

Bus
The **bus station** (☎ 25510 26479; Eleftheriou Venizelou) has buses to Athens (€58, 12 hours, one daily) and Thessaloniki (€25.30, six hours, six daily) via Xanthi and Kavala.

Ferry
There are up to three boats daily to Samothraki (€11, two hours) in summer, which drops back to one daily in winter. Get tickets and departure details from the portside SAOS Ferries kiosk or from travel agencies like **Sever Travel** (☎ 25510 22555; fax 25510 88841; sever1@otenet.gr; M Alexandrou 24). SAOS also serves Limnos once weekly (€14.90, 5 hours).

There is also a weekly **Agoudimos Lines** (www .agoudimos-lines.com) ferry to Rhodes via Lesvos (€20.90, 11¼ hours), Chios (€27.20, 15¼ hours), Samos (€33.50, 18¾ hours), Kalymnos (€38.50, 23¼ hours), and Kos (€39, 24½ hours) to Rhodes (€44, 28¾ hours). It currently leaves on Monday at 11am.

Hydrofoil
Summer hydrofoils usually serve Samothraki, but are unpredictable; check locally.

Train
Trains run regularly to Thessaloniki (€10, seven hours, six daily), including one that continues on to Athens (€24, 14 hours) and intermediate stations. Intercity trains are about 40% more expensive.

SARONIC GULF ISLANDS

Saronic Gulf Islands
Νησιά του Σαρωνικού

The Saronic Gulf Islands pepper the great waterway south of Athens like colourful stepping stones to the wider Aegean world.

The most accessible islands of the group, Salamina, Aegina and Angistri, are just a short ferry-hop from the mainland. Salamina, the most accessible, is too easily dismissed as a mere suburb of Athens; yet this historic island boasts quiet rural areas and a few modest beaches to fit the island idyll. Next comes brash and cheerful Aegina, just an hour south from Piraeus by hydrofoil, while near-neighbour Angistri is a genuine holiday island, but with reassuring corners of tranquillity, even in high season.

Further south again is Poros, a popular weekend escape for Athenians, yet still within a few hundred metres of the Peloponnese and with a peaceful hinterland. Next comes the Saronic diva, Hydra, where tiers of pastel-hued houses rise majestically from a harbourside that is always bustling with life. Deepest south of all is pine-scented Spetses, nudged up against the mainland also, yet with an alluring sense of escape from the mainstream.

There are decent beaches on all of the Saronics, with Angistri and Spetses having the best of the bunch. The islands do not boast a great number of architectural glories, although Aegina's Temple of Aphaia is a premier site. If beaches and ancient sites are not your sole interests, then the Saronics offer authentic and rewarding Greek island experiences within easy reach of Athens.

HIGHLIGHTS

- **Ancient Awe** Exploring Aegina's glorious history at the superb Temple of Aphaia (p111)
- **Tasteful Taverna** Going the € distance for modern Greek cuisine in the top-end restaurants on Hydra (p118) or Spetses (p122)
- **Dolphin Encounter** Diving near Hydra on a non-intrusive dolphin safari (p117)
- **Walk on the Wild Side** Heading inland from Hydra Town (p116) or Spetses Town (p121) for a more rustic Greece experience
- **Fictional Feast** Curling up amid the pines of Spetses (p119) with John Fowles' erotically charged *The Magus*

Temple of Aphaia ★

Poros ★

Hydra Town ★

Spetses Town ★

■ POPULATION: 45,600 ■ AREA: 318 SQ KM

SARONIC GULF ISLANDS

Hydrofoil & Catamaran

Hellenic Seaways (☎ 210 419 9000; www.hellenic seaways.gr) operates a busy schedule to the islands and the nearby Peloponnesian ports with its Flying Dolphin hydrofoils and Flying Cat catamarans. See the destination sections for full details. **Euroseas** (☎ 210 413 2105/6) runs a daily service from Piraeus to Hydra, Poros and Spetses. Recent newcomer **Aegean Flying Dolphins** (☎ 210 422 1766), whose hydrofoils have a distinctive blue and yellow livery compared with the Hellenic Dolphins red, white and blue, runs a similar service to the same destinations as Hellenic Seaways. Prices are about €1 less. All services depart from the Great Harbour at Piraeus.

Tours

Cruise ships offer daily cruises from Piraeus to the islands of Aegina, Poros and Hydra.

The cruises leave Piraeus at 9am, returning at about 7pm, and allow for about one hour on shore at each island – long enough for snaps, snacks and souvenirs.

The official price is €93, including buffet lunch, but there are bargain-deal tickets if you book through your hotel.

Introduced in 2007, **easyCruise** (www.easy cruise.com) runs several Greek Island cruises, including three-night midweek minibreaks from Piraeus to Poros and Spetses and back. It costs from €51.50 per person (high season from €79.50). Longer cruises to the Cyclades and to a mix of the Saronics and Cyclades are also available.

AEGINA ΑΙΓΙΝΑ

pop 10,500

Aegina (eh-yi-nah) rocks with a rough-and-ready charm. It has less of a tourist sheen than most holiday islands, due in part to its substantial agricultural and commercial sectors and its proximity to the mainland. Athenian weekenders sharpen the mix.

By the 7th century BC, Aegina was the leading maritime power of the region and had amassed wealth through trade. The island made a major contribution towards the Greek victory over the Persian fleet at the Battle of Salamis in 480 BC. In spite of this generous support, Athens, grown jealous of Aegina's status and of its liaison with Sparta, invaded in 459 BC. Aegina never regained its

GETTING THERE & AWAY
Ferry

The Saronic Gulf Islands have one of the best ferry networks across Greece, with several fast hydrofoil and catamaran services racing to and from Piraeus at regular intervals every day. Slower conventional ferries operate several times a day to and from Aegina, Poros, Methana and Hydra in high season and less so in winter. There is currently one daily service to Spetses throughout the year. You should always check details close to the date of your planned trip. The following times and prices are for conventional ferries.

FERRIES FROM PIRAEUS' GREAT HARBOUR

Destination	Duration	Fare	Frequency
Aegina	1hr 10min	€8	8 daily
Angistri	2hr	€8.80	2 daily
Poros	2½hr	€11.60	5 daily
Hydra	3hr 10min	€13.20	daily
Spetses	4½hr	€15.30	daily

previous glories although in the early 19th century it played a bold part in the defeat of the Turks and was the temporary capital of a partly liberated Greece from 1827 to 1829. Today the island plays a more mundane role as Greece's main producer of pistachio nuts. The ghosts of greater days still invest Aegina with romance, however, not least at the splendid ruin of the Temple of Aphaia, built soon after the Battle of Salamis. There are modest beaches too and an enjoyable taverna and nightlife scene.

Getting There & Away
FERRY
There are several ferries a day between Piraeus and Aegina Town (€7.80, one hour 10 minutes). There are also services from June to September between Piraeus and Agia Marina (€8.50, one hour) and Souvala (€7.40, one hour 35 minutes). Schedules should always be checked in advance. There are at least four boats daily to Poros (€7.30, 50 minutes) via Methana (€4.90, 40 minutes), two daily to Hydra (€9.20, two hours) and one to Spetses (€12.80, three hours).

Tickets can be bought at the departure quays at Piraeus and at Aegina Town, where there are lists of daily sailings.

A small ferry makes several trips between Aegina and Angistri's main port of Skala (€5, 20 minutes, three daily). It leaves from midway along the harbour front and timetables are displayed there.

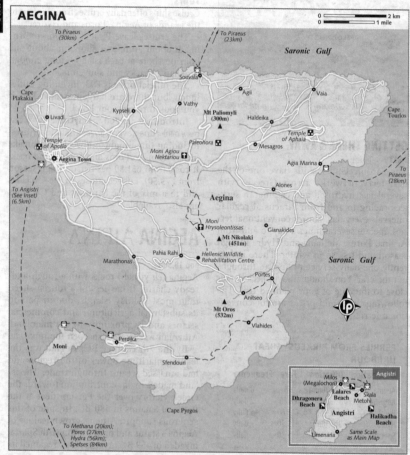

AEGINA

A SALAMINA SAGA

The famous sea battle of 480 BC between Greeks and Persians, in the murky channel that separates the Greek mainland and the island of Salamina, has been billed as the 'Greatest Battle of the Ancient World'. The odds were certainly great. A mere 371 Greek ships (triremes) routed a Persian fleet of 1207. Thus Salamina, one of the least touristed islands in Greece, can rest on its historic laurels.

If you have time to spare in Athens, it's worth making the trip to Salamina (population 23,000) by public transport, or by bike. The first part of the trip gives a vivid insight into how Athens triumphs over its urban gridlock. You begin the trail outside Monastiraki metro station by catching a Perama-bound bus (€0.50, 40 minutes). It's an entertaining dash along narrow roads jammed with traffic and overshadowed by buildings. Car ferries run all night from Perama to Paloukia, Salamina's port; but catch the smaller passenger ferry (€0.70, 15 minutes) across this historic strait for a mind's-eye view of ghostly triremes and the chaos of that ancient sea battle.

If you're biking, head off into Salamina's surprisingly green interior and quiet coastal areas with their handful of small beaches. Otherwise catch a short bus ride to the island's modest capital of Koulouri, or to the equally modest resort of Selinia, from where you can catch a ferry directly back to Piraeus. (Note, there were forest fires on Salamina during 2007. Areas affected were around Selinia – and around Batsi on the north coast.)

HYDROFOIL & CATAMARAN

There are no fast services south from Aegina to Poros, Hydra or Spetses.

Hellenic Seaways (☎ 22970 24456; www.hellenicseaways.gr) operates its Flying Dolphins (€12, 35 minutes) almost hourly from early morning to mid-evening between Piraeus and Aegina. Tickets can be bought at the departure quays at Piraeus and Aegina Town.

Aegean Flying Dolphins (☎ 210 422 1766) runs a similar schedule as Hellenic Seaways between Aegina and Piraeus, with prices being about €1 less. They continue to Angistri (€4.50, 10 minutes, two to four times daily).

Getting Around

Buses run frequently between Aegina Town and Agia Marina (€2, 30 minutes), via Paleohora and the Temple of Aphaia. Other buses go to Perdika (€1.20, 15 minutes) and Souvala (€1.40, 20 minutes). Departure times are displayed outside the ticket office on Plateia Ethnegersias and you must buy tickets at the booth.

There are numerous places in Aegina that hire cars and motorcycles. Advertised prices start at around €40 to €45 a day for a car and €15 to €20 a day for a 50cc machine. There is not much discounting, even out of season.

AEGINA TOWN

pop 7410

Aegina Town has a gritty engaging charm. Athenians visit regularly and many have holiday homes on the island. Foreign visitors are not too common. The town is the capital and main port, and its long harbour front fizzes with life. The two-lane road is a bit of a speedway, so take care when crossing.

Canopied cafés, packed with cheerfully voluble locals, line the inland promenade. Narrow lanes lead inland from here across streets that are more reminiscent of downtown Athens and are crammed with everyday shops. A few crumbling neoclassical buildings survive from the town's heyday as the Greek capital.

Orientation

The large outer quay, with its little church of St Nikolaos, is where the bigger ferries dock. The smaller inner quay is where hydrofoils come in. Crossing the road and heading left from the end of either quay leads to Plateia Ethnegersias, where the bus terminal and post office are located. This road then continues on to the Temple of Apollo and the north coast. Turning right from the end of the quays leads along the busy harbour front for about 500m to the Church of Panagytsa and then on to Perdika and Agia Marina.

Information

Aegina does not have an official tourist office, but you can find some useful information at www.aeginagreece.com.

Alpha Bank and the Bank of Piraeus are located opposite the end of the hydrofoil quay. The National Bank of Greece is about 300m to the right of the ferry quays. All the banks have ATMs.

Kalezis Bookshop (☎ 22970 25956) Midway along the harbour front; has a selection of foreign newspapers and books.

Port police (☎ 22970 22328) At the entrance to the ferry quay.

Post office (Plateia Ethnegersias; 7.30am-2pm Mon-Fri)

Surf and Play (☎ 22970 29096; Afeas 42; per 30min €2; 9am-late) Hot spot with fast connections, photo printing, burning. Located several blocks inland from Hotel Pavlou (below).

Tourist police (☎ 22970 27777; Leonardou Lada) Opposite the ferry quay.

Sights

The solitary surviving Doric column of the **Temple of Apollo** (☎ 22970 22637; adult/concession €3/2; 8.30am-3pm Tue-Sun) stands on the hill of Coloni, and is Aegina Town's significant ancient site. The column is all that's left of the 5th-century-BC temple, once part of an ancient acropolis. Just below is the **Sanctuary Museum** (admission €3; 8.30am-3pm Tue-Sun), which displays artefacts from the temple. There are plans to move the exhibition to an expanded collection at the Capodistrias House, a one-time orphanage and later prison, about 1km east of the ferry quays.

Sleeping

Aegina has a fair selection of hotels and rooms, but it's advisable to book ahead, especially at weekends.

Hotel Plaza (☎ 22970 25600; s/d/tr €35/40/60) A decent budget option, the Plaza is 100m north of Plateia Ethnegersias. Its young owner took over a few years ago and has worked hard at brightening things up. Rooms are clean and are a reasonable size.

Hotel Pavlou (☎ 22970 22795; Aiginitou 21; s/d/tr €35/50/60) Well run by a cheerful no-nonsense family, the Pavlou's rooms are clean, if plain. They may offer you cheaper rooms at a less salubrious place, the Hotel Athina, about 750m inland. The Pavlou is just behind the Church of Panagitsa about 500m along the main harbour front from the ferry quays.

Hotel Brown (☎ 22970 22271; www.hotelbrown.gr; s/d/tr €60/75/100; P) The name of this fine hotel relates to its owner, George Brown, a local who has an English grandfather. Rooms are comfortable and stylish and the bungalows are in a shaded garden. There's a generous

buffet breakfast. The hotel is right at the far end of the harbour front.

our pick Rastoni (☎ 22970 27039; www.rastoni.gr; Metriti 31; d/ste €80/110; P) Within easy walking distance of the harbour is this delightful hotel, styled with flair and with a relaxing atmosphere. Each room is themed with individual décor and there is a charming garden. There are discounts for several days' stay. Breakfast is €5.

Eating

The inland side of the harbour front is packed with cafés and restaurants that steal most of the promenade. They make for lazy world-watching, but are not particularly good value, unless you hit the local unvarnished *ouzeries* scattered throughout.

our pick Babis (☎ 22970 23594; mains €5-12) A few metres beyond Hotel Brown, Babis has a stylish menu and décor. Cool colours enhance the interior and there's a pleasant beachside terrace across the road. Friendly service goes with some innovative dishes such as melt-in-the-mouth chicken with pistachio and unsalted cheese.

Mezedopoleio To Steki (☎ 22970 23910; Pan Irioti 45; seafood mezedhes €6-12) Seafood with attitude. This cramped, noisy, sunless, yet somehow vivid place is right behind the fish market, midway along the harbour front. Like its immediate neighbour I Agora, it's always packed with people tucking into hell-fired octopus (€6) and sardines (€5) or other mezedhes (appetisers). Romantic moments are not on the menu.

Local pistachio nuts are on sale everywhere, priced from €6 for 500g.

Entertainment

Music bars and cafés along the harbour front vie with each other for the most luxurious seating.

Yes! (☎ 22970 28306; Dimokratias; 9am-3am) This modish place has easy-listening daytime sounds and sharper spins from local and visiting Athenian DJs at night and at weekends. There's a good selection of coffee, drinks, snacks and breakfasts.

Avli (☎ 22970 26438; Pan Irioti 17; 9am-3am) A favourite with a cooler, older crowd, Avli mixes '60s and Latin music and plays Greek sounds when weekenders hit town.

Aegina has three outdoor cinemas. Of these the **Akrogiali** (☎ 22970 53675; admission €8; mid-Jun–Aug) has the most attractive setting. It lies just outside town along the Perdika road and has a pretty garden setting.

AROUND AEGINA
Temple of Aphaia
The impressive **Temple of Aphaia** (☎ 22970 32398; adult/concession/under 18yr €4/2/free; ⏰ 8am-7.30pm Apr-Oct) celebrates a local deity of pre-Hellenic times and is the major ancient site of the Saronic Gulf Islands. It was built in 480 BC, soon after the Battle of Salamis.

The temple's pediments were decorated with splendid Trojan War sculptures, most of which were robbed in the 19th century and now decorate Munich's Glyptothek. The temple is a compelling site and stands on a pine-covered hill with views over the Saronic Gulf as far as Cape Sounion.

Aphaia is 10km east of Aegina Town. Buses to Agia Marina stop at the site (€1.60, 20 minutes). A taxi from Aegina Town costs about €11.

Paleohora Παλαιοχώρα
The ancient town of Paleohora was Aegina's capital from the 9th century and throughout the medieval period and was only abandoned in the 1820s. It originated as a refuge from pirates who attacked vulnerable coastal settlements. The ruins of the settlement lie on a hillside 6.5km east of Aegina Town near the road to the Temple of Aphaia and Agia Marina. A side road to the site leads in about 500m from a left-hand junction with the main road about 4km from Aegina Town.

There are extensive but vestigial ruins of Paleohora's domestic buildings, but numerous small chapels, most fairly intact, are dotted around the hillside. Remnants of frescoes can be seen in some and the Orthodox faithful still revere them – as we should all do.

Buses from Aegina Town to Agia Marina stop at the turn-off to Paleohora (€1.20, 10 minutes).

Perdika Πέρδικα
The likable fishing village of Perdika lies about 9km south of town on the southern tip of the west coast. Its long seafront terrace is crammed with tavernas and bars.

Perdika is also the caïque (little boat) departure point for the pleasant little island beach at Moni, a few minutes away.

Perdika's harbour inlet is very shallow and swimming is not much fun. Instead, catch one of the regular caïques (€3) from the harbour to Moni Islet. Once targeted as the site of an exclusive casino, it's now a nature reserve and has a magic tree-lined beach and summertime

café. Peacocks and deer wander about peacefully. Make sure to catch the last boat back – or you sleep with the peacocks.

There are a couple of hotels and a few rooms in Perdika. **Villa Rodanthos** (☎ 22970 61400; www.villarodanthos.gr; s/d €45/65) is a gem of a place, not least because of its charming and kindly owner. Each room has its own colourful décor and is equipped with a kitchen. There's a sunny roof patio balanced by an attractive basement lounge and bar. Villa Rodanthos is about 100m along the right-hand branch road opposite the bus stop at the edge of town.

Tavernas line the harbour-front terrace and dish up Greek staples for about €5.50 to €9. Some places are getting a touch careless about quality, especially in low season when they really need to look after occasional visitors as much as the weekend high fliers. It all buzzes with life and colour in summer all the same, and the tavernas mix it with some swaggering late-night music bars.

Buses run every couple of hours to Perdika from Aegina Town (€1.20, 30 minutes). A taxi is €10 one way.

Beaches
Beaches are not Aegina's strong point. The east-coast town of **Agia Marina** is the island's main package resort. It has a shallow-water beach that is ideal for families, but it's backed by a fairly chic-less main drag and there's some high-decibel revelling during the summer.

There are a couple of sandy beaches by the roadside between Aegina Town and Perdika, such as the pleasant Marathonas where the taverna **Ammos** (☎ 22970 28160; Marathonas; mains €5.50-12) offers excellent local dishes with an appealing international flair. Starters are imaginative, mains include specialities such as Chicken Marengo and fillet steaks in tasty sauces, and there's a great selection of seafood, and fish by the kilo.

ANGISTRI ΑΓΚΙΣΤΡΙ

pop 700

Angistri lies a tempting few kilometres off the west coast of Aegina. It's a rewarding day trip from the larger island, or a worthwhile longer escape from the mainstream, better so out of high season.

The port of **Skala** is a resort village these days, crammed with small hotels and apartment

SARONIC GULF ISLANDS

blocks, tavernas and cafés. Its beach, the best on the island, all but disappears beneath sun loungers and a tide of tanning oil in July and August; but life, in general, still ticks along gently.

Orientation & Information

A right turn from Skala's ferry quay leads westwards to the small harbour beach and then along a paved walkway to a church on a low headland. Beyond here lies the long, but narrow, main beach. A kilometre further west takes you to **Mylos** (Megalochori), an attractive, small settlement with rooms and tavernas, but no beach. Turning left from the ferry quay takes you south in about half an hour to the pebbly and clothing-optional **Halikadha Beach**.

Above Skala, and now absorbed by it, is the old settlement of **Metohi**.

Skala Tours (☎ 22970 91228; pannek@aig.forthnet .gr) has an office in the main street, just inland from the main beach. It can help with accommodation and other services. There is a branch of Emboriki Bank just up from Skala Tours. It has an ATM, although you should bring enough cash, since it may dry up over busy holiday weekends.

Sleeping & Eating

There are dozens of sleeping places in Skala and its surroundings, but most are booked up in advance in high season and on summer weekends. If you want to stay for a couple of nights it's best to book ahead; otherwise, ask around or check through Skala Tours.

Alkyoni Inn (☎ 22970 91378; s/d/tr €35/55/65; ☯ mid-Apr–Oct) The welcoming Alkyoni Inn is a 10-minute stroll east of the ferry quay. Its seafront rooms and apartments have great views. Other rooms back onto the road. The Alkyon has a popular taverna (mains €4.50 to €9) offering such delights as tuna salad, spaghetti with shrimps, and pork and chicken dishes in spicy sauces.

There are tavernas that offer reasonable Greek standards at similar prices in Skala and at the beaches.

Getting There & Away

Two ferries a day run from Piraeus (€8.80, two hours) via Aegina, and four fast ferries run during July and August (€12.50, one hour).

A small ferry makes several trips from Aegina to Angistri's main port of Skala (€3, 20 minutes) and then on to neighbouring Mylos

(€3.20, 25 minutes). It leaves from midway along the harbour front and timetables are displayed there.

Aegean Flying Dolphins (☎ 210 422 1766) has a Piraeus to Aegina service, which continues to Angistri two to four times a day (€4.50, 10 minutes).

Another option is the **water taxi service** (☎ 22970 91387, 6972229720; per trip €30) to Aegina.

Getting Around

About four buses a day run during the summer months from Skala and Mylos to the little village of Limenaria on the southeast coast. It's worth renting a moped (€15) or sturdy mountain bike (€9) to explore the island's coastline road. You can also follow tracks from Metohi overland through cool pine forest to reach the west coast beach of Dhragonera. Take a compass with you; the tracks divide often and route finding can be frustrating.

POROS ΠΟΡΟΣ

pop 4500

Unassuming Poros lies a few hundred metres from the village of Galatas on the shores of the mountainous Peloponnese, and its main settlement feels more like a lakeside resort than an island port. Poros is a rewarding holiday island with a refreshing sense of remoteness in its sparsely populated interior, although forest fires during 2007 took their toll on the southwestern coastal and inland area of Kalavria, the larger 'island' of Poros that is separated from the town of Poros by a canal. The areas of Neorion Beach and around Russian Beach have been affected.

Poros is made up of two islands: Kalavria and Sferia. An isthmus, cut by a narrow canal and spanned by a road bridge, connects them. Most people live on tiny Sferia, which is occupied mainly by the town of Poros. Sferia projects from the southern coast of Kalavria, a large, forested island, which has most of the bigger, seasonal hotels along its southern shore.

Getting There & Away
FERRY

There are at least five ferries daily in summer and about four daily in winter, to and from Piraeus (€11.60, 2½ hours), via Methana (€3.40, 30 minutes) and Aegina (€7.30, one hour 15 minutes), two daily to Hydra (€6, 50 minutes), and one to Spetses (€9.60, two hours). **Family Tours** (☎ 22980 25900; www.familytours .gr) handles tickets.

Small boats shuttle constantly between Poros and Galatas (€0.70, five minutes) on the mainland. They leave from the quay opposite Plateia Iroön in Poros Town. Car ferries to Galatas leave from the dock on the road to Kalavria.

HYDROFOIL & CATAMARAN

Hellenic Seaways (www.hellenicseaways.gr) has about eight services daily to and from Piraeus (€19.30, one hour). Most outgoing ferries continue to Hydra (€9.50, 30 minutes). These include the Flying Cat/Flying Dolphin that also continue to Spetses (€15.50, one hour). **Marinos Tours** (☎ 22980 23423; Plateia Iroön) sells tickets.

Aegean Flying Dolphins (☎ 210 422 1766) runs a similar service to the same destinations as Hellenic Seaways and prices are about €1 less. **Hellenic Sun Travel** (☎ 22980 25901; www.hellenic suntravel.com), opposite the ferry dock, is the local agent.

Getting Around

A bus operates almost constantly on a route that starts near the main ferry dock on Plateia Iroön in Poros Town. It crosses to Kalavria and goes east along the south coast as far as Moni Zoödohou Pigis (€1.10, 10 minutes), then turns around and heads west as far as Neorion Beach (€1.10, 15 minutes).

Some of the caïques operating between Poros and Galatas switch to ferrying tourists to beaches during summer. Operators stand on the harbour front and call out destinations.

There are several places on the road to Kalavria offering bikes for hire, both motorised and pedal-powered. Bikes start at €7 per day, and mopeds and scooters are €15 to €20.

POROS TOWN

pop 4102

Poros Town, with its whitewashed houses and red-tiled roofs, looks out towards the shapely mountains of the Peloponnese, a few kilometres across the water. Huge ferries glide through the channel to dock on the harbour front and smaller vessels scurry to and fro between the island and the mainland town of

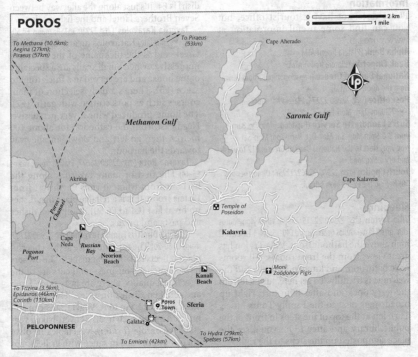

POROS

| 0 | 2 km |
| 0 | 1 mile |

To Methana (10.5km); Aegina (27km); Piraeus (57km)

To Piraeus (53km)

Cape Aherado

Methanon Gulf

Saronic Gulf

Akritsa

Cape Kalavria

Poros Channel

Temple of Poseidon

Kalavria

Cape Neda

Russian Bay

Neorion Beach

Pogonos Port

Kanali Beach

Moni Zoödohou Pigis

To Trizina (3.5km), Epidavros (46km), Corinth (110km)

Poros Town

Sferia

PELOPONNESE

Galatas

To Ermioni (42km)

To Hydra (29km); Spetses (57km)

Galatas. Behind the harbour front, lanes and steps lead up to a maze of other lanes that link small squares and the focal points of a prominent clock tower and the cathedral. The town is a useful base from which to explore the ancient sites of the adjacent Peloponnese.

Orientation

The main ferry dock is at the western end of the town's long harbour front.

A right turn from the ferry dock takes you across the road to the triangular open space of Plateia Iroön. To either side of the *plateia* (square) the road is lined with cafés, tavernas and tourist shops. The island bus leaves from next to the kiosk at the eastern end of Plateia Iroön. Steps lead up from the inner corner of the square to the attractive lanes and squares of the upper town and to the clock tower and cathedral. A short distance south of Plateia Iroön is Plateia Karamis, set back from the harbour-front road.

A left turn from the dock leads along the extended harbour front and on to the Kalavria road.

Information

Poros does not have a tourist office, but you can find some useful information at www.poros.gr.

Alpha Bank (Plateia Iroön) ATM.

Bank Emporiki (Plateia Iroön) ATM.

National Bank of Greece (Papadopoulou) About 100m from the dock; has ATM.

Post office (☎ 22980 22274; Plateia Karamis; ☙ 7.30am-2pm Mon-Fri)

Suzi's Laundrette Service (Papadopoulou; ☙ 8am-2pm & 6-9pm Mon-Sat May-Oct, 9am-2pm Mon-Sat Nov-Apr) Next to the National Bank of Greece; €12 to wash and dry a 5kg load.

Tourist police (☎ 22980 22462/22256; Dimosthenous 10) Behind the Poros high school.

Sleeping

Villa Tryfon (☎ 22980 22215/25854; villatryfon@poros .com.gr; off Plateia Agios Georgiou; s/d €40/55; ❑) Located high above the harbour front, Villa Tryfon has great views from the front rooms. All rooms have bathroom and kitchen facilities and the welcome is friendly. To get here, turn left from the ferry dock and after 80m turn right up broad steps next to the Family Tours office. Turn left at the top of the steps in front of the public library and after 150m you'll see the place signposted up the steps to the right.

Seven Brothers Hotel (☎ 22980 23412; www.7brothers .gr; Plateia Iroön; s/d/tr €55/65/75; ❑ ❑) A good option at the heart of the harbour front near the hydrofoil dock, this modern hotel has bright comfy rooms with small balconies and tea- and coffee-making facilities.

Hotel Dionysos (☎ 22980 23511/22530; www.hotel dionysos.com; Papadopoulou 78; s/d/tr €50/70/80; ❑ ❑) This restored mansion retains some of its character, although it can feel a touch gloomy. The rooms are comfortable and are a decent size. It's located a couple of hundred metres to the left of the ferry quays and opposite where the car ferry from Galatas docks. Breakfast starts at €8. There's a separate café-bar on the ground floor, which has internet access (per hour €3).

Eating

There's not much *haute cuisine* here, but there are some fine traditional tavernas with character to match the cooking.

Taverna Kyriakos (☎ 22980 22581; mains €2-6) Previously the Pantelis, this taverna is still a great calorie booster. Everything, including beer, is much cheaper than elsewhere. Greek salads are €4 and *pastitsio* (a macaroni and minced lamb dish) is €4. It's just along the alleyway between Seven Brothers Hotel and the fish market.

Taverna Karavolos (☎ 22980 26158; mains €4.50-7.40; ☙ 7pm-late) Karavolos means 'big snail' in Greek and is the nickname of the taverna's impressive owner. Small snails are a speciality of the house and are served in a thick tomato sauce (€5). There's a daily selection of main courses such as pork stuffed with garlic (€7). The home-produced wine is very persuasive. Head east from the cathedral for about 100 metres, then go left and down an alleyway towards the harbour.

Taverna Rota (☎ 22980 25627; Plateia Iroön; mains €5-14) The first of many tavernas along the harbour front where it runs northwest from Plateia Iroön, this is a reliable place that dishes up breakfast (€4 to €6.50), traditional dishes and pasta and pizzas.

our pick Dimitris Family Taverna (☎ 22980 23709; mains €4.50-20) The top-end price at this cheerful place reflects terrific meat dishes. The owners have a butcher's business, and cuts are of the very finest quality There are tasty pork, lamb and chicken dishes on offer. 'Honeymoon' steak costs €22. Go to it. Vegetarians can still mix and match such treats as oven-baked vegetable casserole *(briam)*, vegetables in olive oil, or butter beans in sauce with grilled pep-

ECO SARONICS

There are ups and downs to ecology and environmentalism in the Saronic Gulf Islands. The downs are often a genuine burning issue, as they are in many parts of Greece. Forest fires flare up accidentally, but in some parts of the country they have been caused by arsonists. Fires erupt especially in times of drought; remember the destruction of swathes of woodland on Salamina, Hydra and Poros in summer 2007 and in many other parts of Greece.

On the upside, there's the sterling work of groups such as the **Hellenic Wildlife Rehabilitation Centre** (Elliniko Kentro Perithalpsis Agrion Zoön; ☎ 22970 31338; www.ekpaz.gr; ⏰ 10am-7pm) on the island of Aegina. The centre tackles the damage caused to thousands of Greece's wild birds and animals by hunting and by pollution. Some of its current projects are the release of raptors into the wilds of Crete and Northern Greece. You can pay a visit to the centre, which is about 10km southeast of Aegina Town and 1km east of Pahia Rahi on the road to Mt Oros. Admission is free, but donations are appreciated. And if you want a more hands-on commitment, the centre welcomes volunteers. Accommodation is supplied.

pers. To get here, head west from the cathedral for a couple of hundred metres.

AROUND POROS

Poros has a few beaches. **Kanali Beach**, on Kalavria 1km east of the bridge, is pebbly. **Neorion Beach**, 3km west of the bridge, has water skiing and banana boat and air chair rides. The best beach is at **Russian Bay**, 1.5km past Neorion.

The 18th-century **Moni Zoödohou Pigis**, on Kalavria, has a beautiful gilded iconostasis from Asia Minor. The monastery is well signposted, 4km east of Poros Town.

From the road below the monastery you can head inland to the 6th-century **Temple of Poseidon**. There's very little left of this temple, but the walk is worthwhile and there are superb views of the Saronic Gulf and the Peloponnese.

From the ruins you can continue along the road and go back to the bridge onto Sferia. It's about 6km in total.

PELOPONNESIAN MAINLAND

The Peloponnesian mainland opposite Poros can be explored conveniently from the island.

The ruins of ancient **Troizen**, legendary birthplace of Theseus, lie in the hills near the modern village of Trizina, 7.5km west of Galatas. There are buses to Trizina (€1.20, 15 minutes) from Galatas, leaving a walk of about 1.5km to the site.

The inspiring ancient theatre of Epidavros can be reached from Galatas. A couple of buses depart daily from Galatas for Nafplio (€7, two hours) and can drop you off at the ancient site.

Getting There & Away

Small boats run constantly between Galatas and Poros (€0.70, five minutes).

HYDRA ΥΔΡΑ

pop 2900

Hydra (ee-dhr-ah) is the showcase of the Saronics and still wears its celebrity with style. The island's picturesque harbour attracts throngs of tourists, cruise passengers, yacht crews and the occasional celebrity on their way to hidden holiday homes among the tiers of picturesque buildings that rise above the harbour. You pay for the privilege of visiting, with inflated prices throughout, but the deal is still worthwhile.

An undoubted bonus, for modern Greece, is the absence of scooters and screeching motorbikes from Hydra Town. The island has no motorised transport, except for sanitation and construction vehicles. Donkeys and mules are the main means of transport.

Hydra suffered from devastating wildfires during the searingly hot summer of 2007. Most of the area to the east of Hydra Town was affected and there has been substantial tree loss. Hydra Town itself was untouched.

History

Hydra experienced only the light hand of an overstretched Ottoman influence. Consequently the island prospered. Enterprising Greeks from the Peloponnese settled here to escape Turkish repression and taxes on the mainland. Agriculture was difficult, so these new settlers began building boats and took

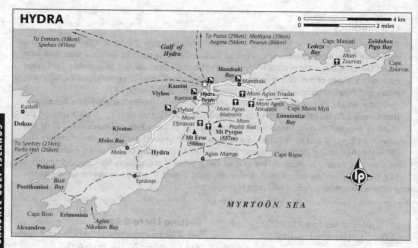

HYDRA

to the thin line between maritime commerce and piracy. By the 19th century, Hydra had become a substantial maritime power, earning itself the ambivalent sobriquet of 'Little England'. From considerable profits, wealthy shipping merchants built most of the town's grand old mansions. During the Greek War of Independence, Hydra supplied 130 ships for a blockade of the Turks. It also supplied leaders such as Georgios Koundouriotis, who was president of the emerging Greek nation's national assembly from 1822 to 1827, and Admiral Andreas Miaoulis, who commanded the Greek fleet. Streets and squares all over Greece are named after these two.

Getting There & Away
FERRY

There is a daily ferry to/from Piraeus (€12.50, three hours 10 minutes), which also sails to Poros (€4.10, one hour), Methana (€6.10, 1½ hours), Aegina (€6.50, two hours) and Spetses (€6, one hour).

You can buy tickets from **Idreoniki Travel** (☎ 22980 54007; www.hydreoniki.gr), opposite the ferry dock.

HYDROFOIL & CATAMARAN

Hellenic Seaways (☎ 21041 99000; www.hellenicseaways .gr) has about eight services daily to/from Piraeus (€22, 1½ hours). Direct services take 1½ hours, but most go via Poros (€9.50, one hour, 50 minutes). There are also frequent services to Poros (€9.50, 30 minutes) and Spetses (€11, 30 minutes), some of which call at Ermioni on

the mainland, adding 20 minutes to the trip. Many of the services to Spetses continue on to Porto Heli (€11.50, 50 minutes). Buy tickets from Idreoniki Travel.

Euroseas (☎ 22980 52184; www.euroseas.com) runs two boats a day to Piraeus (€21, one hour 20 minutes), Poros (€8.50, one hour) and Spetses (€10.70, 30 minutes). Tickets are bought from **Saitis Tours** (☎ 22980 52184; saitisllours@otenet.gr) on the harbour front.

Aegean Flying Dolphins (☎ 21042 21766) runs a similar service to Hellenic Seaways and prices are about €1 less. Saitis Tours sells tickets.

Getting Around

In summer, there are caïques from Hydra Town to the island's beaches. There are also **water taxis** (☎ 22980 53690), which will take you anywhere you like; examples are Kamini (€9) and Vlyhos (€12).

The donkey owners clustered around the port charge around €15 to transport your bags to the hotel of your choice.

HYDRA TOWN
pop 2526

Hydra Town's showpiece harbour is backed by an amphitheatre of red-tiled houses with whitewashed and pastel-painted walls. The harbour front is usually thronged with ambling crowds, donkeys and mules. Smart yachts line the harbour front. Behind the harbour front, narrow, stepped streets and alleyways lead to still corners and cool squares, with a tempting rise towards the rock-studded slopes beyond. The streets that lead in-land have numerous craft and clothes shops and galleries.

Information

There is no tourist office on Hydra but a very useful website is www.hydradirect.com.

There is an **ATM** at Saitis Tours, on the harbour front. The **post office** (☿ 7.30am-2pm Mon-Fri) is opposite the fish market on a small side street between the Bank Emporiki and the National Bank of Greece, both of which have

ATMs. The **tourist police** (☎ 22980 52205; Votsi; ☿ mid-May–end Sep) can be found sharing an office with the regular police.

There are toilets alongside the fishmarket.

You can check email at the **Flamingo Internet Café** (☎ 22980 53485; Tombazi; per 30 min €4; ☿ 8.30am-10pm).

Sights & Activities

The star attraction is the grand **Lazaros Koundouriotis Historical Mansion** (☎ 22980 52421; nhmuseum@tee.gr; adult/concession €4/2; ☿ 9am-4pm Tue-Sun), former home of one of the major players in the Greek Independence struggle. It's a fine example of late-18th-century traditional architecture. The main reception rooms of the 2nd floor have been restored to their full splendour, furnished with all the finery of the period.

The **Historical Archives Museum of Hydra** (☎ 22980 52355; museumhy@otenet.gr; adult/child €3/1.50; ☿ 9am-4.30pm & 7.30-9.30pm Jul-Oct, 9am-4.30pm Nov-Jun) is close to the ferry dock on the eastern side of the harbour. It houses a collection of portraits and naval oddments, with an emphasis on the island's role in the War of Independence.

The **Ecclesiastical Museum** (☎ 22980 54071; admission €2; ☿ 10am-5pm Tue-Sun Apr-Oct), upstairs at the Monastery of the Assumption of the Virgin Mary, houses a collection of icons and assorted religious paraphernalia. The entrance is through the archway beneath the clock tower on the harbour front. The monastery courtyard, cathedral and associated buildings offer a peaceful sanctuary.

Kallianos Diving Center (☎ 2754031095; www.kallianos divingcenter.gr) is based at the island of Kapari, south of Ermioni on the mainland. The centre offers a broad range of diving activities including a two-dive outing with full equipment supplied for €80, or €125 with instructor. Staff runs a once-monthly Diving with Dolphins

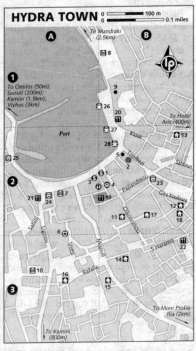

HYDRA TOWN

0 _____ 100 m
0 _____ 0.1 miles

trip starting at €200, with a 50% refund if the dolphins don't turn up. The centre does pick up and return to Hydra, and non-divers can also take the trip to Kapari (€15).

Festivals & Events

Hydriots celebrate their contribution to the War of Independence struggle by staging a mock battle in Hydra harbour during the **Miaoulia Festival**, held in honour of Admiral Miaoulis, in late June. Much carousing, feasting and fireworks accompany it. **Easter** is also celebrated in colourful fashion.

Sleeping

Accommodation in Hydra is of a generally high standard. You pay accordingly. These prices are for high season, which in Hydra means weekends as well as July and August. Most owners will meet you at the harbour if pre-arranged and will organise luggage transfer.

BUDGET

Pension Erofili (☎ /fax 22980 54049; www.pensionerofili .gr; Tombazi; s/d/tr €45/55/65; ⚡) Tucked away in the inner town, these pleasant, unassuming rooms are a decent budget deal for Hydra. The young family owners add a friendly sparkle. It also has a large family room with private kitchen.

Hotel Dina (☎ 22980 52248; Stavrou Tsipi; s/d/tr €45/60/78) An engagingly old-fashioned place, Hotel Dina has dated but reasonable rooms, several with views. It's tucked away up a steep, narrow alleyway off Sahtouri and is a Greek-speaking household.

Bahia (☎ 22980 52257, 6977462852; Oikonomou; s/d €50/60; ⚡) Located above an interesting clothes and jewellery shop called Alexander, this place has reasonable rooms with kitchen.

MIDRANGE

Pension Alkionides (☎ /fax 22980 54055; www.alkion ideshydra.com; off Oikonomou; s/d/tr €60/65/80; ⚡) The Alkionides is in a peaceful cul-de-sac and has a pretty courtyard. Rooms are smart, though some are quite small, and they have tea- and coffee-making facilities.

Hotel Aris (☎ 22980 53002, 6977248599; www.aris -hydra.com; s/d incl breakfast €60/80; ⚡) Close proximity to Hydra's rock-studded slopes adds to the peace and quiet of this charming hotel. Rooms are comfortable and a good size. There's a lovely roof terrace with great views over the town.

TOP END

Hotel Miranda (☎ 22980 52230/53953; www.miranda hotel.gr; Miaouli; s/d/tr incl breakfast €93/118/171; ⊙ Mar–mid-Oct; ⚡) Built in 1810 by a wealthy Hydriot sea captain, the Miranda was converted to a hotel in 1962. Wood beams and coved ceilings of the original construction survive and the ceilings retain the original motifs that were painted by Italian artists hired by many of Hydra's wealthy households. The mood is restrained and gracious and captures a flavour of old Hydriot life. Breakfast is enjoyed on a charming patio.

Hotel Leto (☎ 22980 53385; www.letohydra.gr; off Miaouli; s incl breakfast €109-125, d €140-160, tr from €188; ⚡ ▢) Smoothly modern and relaxing, this is one of Hydra's classiest hotels. Rooms are spacious and have subtle décor. Leto also has a fully equipped room for disabled use. The price ranges depend on such variables as room size, balconies and floor location. Buffet breakfast is included and there's a fitness studio, sauna and bar.

Hotel Orloff (☎ 22980 52564; www.orloff.gr; Rafalia; s/d incl breakfast €165/185; ⚡) Hydra history and tradition invest this beautiful old mansion with great taste and style. A Russian admiral of the 18th century gave his name to the original house. The comfortable rooms have elegant furnishings and there's a lovely garden in which buffet breakfast is served.

Hotel Bratsera (☎ 22980 53971; www.bratserahotel .com; Tombazi; d incl breakfast €154-215, ste incl breakfast €270-323; ⚡ ⚡) There's a pleasingly rustic feel to the décor of this spacious hotel, which merges the best of the new with decorative antiques and period details. There's a swimming pool for guests only, but you can take a dip if you eat at Bratsera's restaurant (opposite).

Eating

Some of the cafés along the harbour front push their luck with their high prices/low service; but if you want lively people-watching you pay the price. A good bet is the **Isalos Café** (☎ 22980 53845) right by the ferry dock, offering decent snacks and drinks at reasonable prices.

Taverna Gitoniko/Manolis & Christina (☎ 22980 53615; Spilios Haramis; mains €4-9) When a taverna is better known by the Christian names of its owners it says something about quality and family tradition. Classic Greek favourites are well prepared at Gitoniko and there's a pleasant roof garden. Try the delicious zucchini balls and spinach pies or fresh green beans in oil with fava and tomato sauce.

Bratsera (☎ 22980 52794; Tombazi; mains €8.50-20; ⏱ 1-4pm & 8-11pm Apr-Oct) There's fine Mediterranean cuisine by the pool at this restaurant, which is attached to the hotel of the same name. Starters include feta with sesame and honey, and the spinach salad, with bacon, pine nuts and olive oil and lemon dressing, is delicious. Mains include treats like veal fillet with rosemary sauce and fresh salmon, when available; there's also a selection of imaginative pasta dishes. Wine ranges from €20 for a decent Cabernet to €56 for Chardonnay.

Sunset (☎ 22980 52067; mains €9.50-22) An outstanding location on a huge terrace overlooking the sea makes this restaurant a great favourite. The food lives up to the view, with such starters as mackerel salad (€6.50) and mains such as grilled sea bream (*tsipoura*) marinated in herbs, or tagliatelli with wild porcini (mushrooms). The wine list matches the food with the likes of Boutaris white (€17) and Château Semeli red (€67).

There's a supermarket, fruit shop and fish market just inland, mid-harbour side. O Fournos is a good bakery next to the Pirate club across the alleyway.

Entertainment

Hydra's harbour front revs up at night, when daytime cafés become hot music bars. Most bars are at the far end of the harbour, where places like **Pirate** (☎ 22980 52711) and **Saronikos** (☎ 22980 52589) keep going until dawn. Most play lounge sounds by day; at night Pirate plays rock, while Saronikos goes more Greek pop.

A few blocks inland from the harbour front the cooler, celebrity-honed **Amalour** (☎ 6977461357; Tombazi) does a lively line in cocktails and smoothies to a Latin rhythm. About 100m beyond the western edge of the harbour is the waterside **Omilos** (☎ 22980 53800), the old Lagoudera Club, which has been transformed into a chic café, restaurant and night-time dance zone with eclectic DJs.

AROUND HYDRA

Hydra's stony, arid interior, now with some regenerating pine woods, makes a robust but peaceful contrast to the clamour of the quayside catwalk, although the eastern part of the island may take some time to recover from the fires of 2007. Heading up Miaouli and

onward, there's a strenuous but worthwhile 2km walk up to **Moni Profiti Ilia**. Monks still live in the monastery, from where there are grand views down to the port. It's a short walk from the monastery to the convent of **Moni Efpraxias**. Other paths and tracks lead over and down to the south coast, while you can stroll up to the top of Mt Eros (588m), the highest point in the Saronic islands.

Hydra's shortcoming – or blessing – is its lack of appealing beaches to draw the crowds. There are a few strands all the same. **Kamini**, about a 1.5km walk along the coastal path from the port, has rocks and a very small pebble beach. **Vlyhos**, a 1.5km walk further on from Kamini, is an attractive village offering a slightly larger pebble beach, two tavernas and a ruined 19th-century stone bridge.

A path leads east from the port to the reasonable pebble beach at **Mandraki**, 2.5km away. **Bisti Bay**, 8km away on the southwestern side of the island, has a decent pebble beach.

Water taxis from the port to various beaches cost about €12.

SPETSES ΣΠΕΤΣΕΣ

pop 4000

Open water runs far to the south of Spetses and, although the mainland Peloponnese is only a few kilometres away, there's a stronger sense of island Greece here than in other Saronic Gulf destinations. The novelist John Fowles used the island as the setting for his powerful book *The Magus* (1965). His portrayal of lascivious heat and pine-scented seduction probably sent many a northern European hotfooting it to the beautiful south on their first Greek island idyll.

Long before Fowles' day, Spetses, like Hydra, grew wealthy from shipbuilding. Island captains busted the British blockade during the Napoleonic Wars and refitted their ships to join the Greek fleet during the War of Independence. In the process they immortalised one local woman, albeit from a Hydriot family, the formidable Laskarina Bouboulina, ship's commander and fearless fighter (see p122).

The island's forests of Aleppo pine, a legacy of the far-sighted and wealthy philanthropist Sotirios Anargyrios, were devastated by fires in 1990 and 2001. Many trees survive, however, and the burnt areas are slowly recovering.

SARONIC GULF ISLANDS

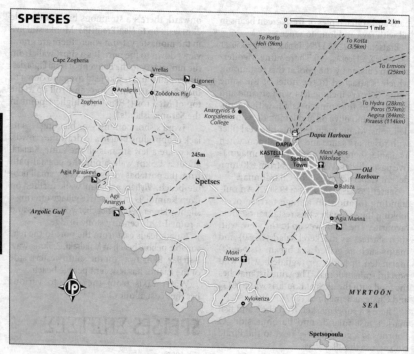

SPETSES

0 _____ 2 km
0 _____ 1 mile

Cape Zogheria

Vrellas
Ligoneri
Analipsis   Zoödohos Pigi
Zogheria

To Porto
Heli (9km)   To Kosta
                  (3.5km)

                  To Ermioni
                  (25km)

                  To Hydra (28km);
                  Poros (57km);
                  Aegina (84km);
                  Piraeus (114km)

Anargyrios &
Korgialenios
College

245m ▲

Agia Paraskevi

Agii
Anargyri

Argolic Gulf

Spetses

DAPIA ● Dapia Harbour
KASTELLI
        Spetses
        Town
        Moni Agios
        Nikolaos
                  *Old
                  Harbour*
        Baltiza

Agia Marina

Moni
Elonas

                  *MYRTOÖN
                  SEA*

Xylokeriza

Spetsopoula

Anargyrios was born on Spetses in 1848 and emigrated to the USA, returning in 1914 as a very rich man. He bought two-thirds of the then largely barren island and planted the pines that stand today. Anargyrios also financed the Spetses' road network and commissioned many of the town's grand buildings.

Getting There & Away
FERRY

From June to September there is one ferry a day to and from Piraeus (€15.30, four hours). The rest of the year one ferry runs on Friday, Saturday, Sunday and Monday. The ferry goes to and from Hydra (€6.50, one hour), Poros (€9.10, two hours) and Aegina (€12.10, three hours). You'll find departure times on the harbour front outside **Alasia Travel** (☎ 22980 74098; www.spetses-online/alasia.gr), which sells tickets. It's wise to check the situation regarding both summer and winter schedules for these ferries.

There are water taxis to Kosta (€16, 15 minutes), on the Peloponnese mainland. A larger ferry runs to Kosta about four times daily (€0.90, 10 minutes). There are three buses daily from Kosta to Nafplio (€6.30, 2¼ hours).

HYDROFOIL & CATAMARAN

Hellenic Seaways (☎ 21041 99000; www.hellenic seaways.gr) runs at least six services a day to and from Piraeus (€29.50, two hours 10 minutes). Most services travel via Hydra (€10, 30 minutes) and Poros (€14, 70 minutes). There are also daily connections to Ermioni (€7, one hour) and Porto Heli (€5, 10 minutes). Tickets are available from **Bardakos Tours** (☎ 22980 73141; Dapia Harbour), located opposite the water taxis.

Euroseas (☎ 21041 32105; www.euroseas.com) runs two boats to and from Piraeus (€30, two hours 10 minutes), via Hydra (€10.70, 30 minutes) and to Porto Heli (€5, 10 minutes). Tickets are bought from **Mimoza Travel** (☎ 22980 75170; mimoza-kent@aig.forthnet.gr), which is on the harbour front just past Plateia Limenarhiou.

Aegean Flying Dolphins (☎ 21042 21766) runs a similar service to the same destinations as Hellenic Seaways and prices are about €1 less. **Alasia Travel** (☎ 22980 74098; www.spetses-online/alasia .gr) sells tickets.

Getting Around

Spetses has two bus routes that start over the Easter period, then continue, depending on demand, until the end of May. From June to September there are three or four buses daily. The routes are from Plateia Agiou Mama in Spetses Town to Agii Anargyri (€2.70, 40 minutes), travelling via Agia Marina and Xylokeriza. All departure times are displayed on a board by the bus stop. There are also hourly buses in summer (every two hours in winter) to Ligoneri (€1.20). They leave from in front of the Hotel Possidonion, the monumental old building (being renovated at the time of writing) on the seafront just to the northwest of Dapia Harbour.

Only locally owned vehicles are allowed on Spetses. There are not too many of these, although the number is increasing. Hundreds of scooters and motorbikes making a racket more than make up for it. There are motorbike-rental shops everywhere; rental is around €15 to €20 per day.

For quieter pedal power, there are sturdy bikes (€7 per day) at **Mountain Bikes** (☎ 22980 74505), 100m beyond Plateia Agiou Mama. Bikes (€6 per 24 hours) to suit all ages, as well as baby seats, are also for hire from the **Bike Center** (☎ 22980 74143; ☺ 9.30am-9.30pm), behind the fish market.

Spetses' horse-drawn carriages are a more expensive way of getting around (€8 one way to Old Harbour). Prices should be displayed on a board on Plateia Limenarhiou by the port.

CAÏQUE

In summer, there are caïques from the harbour to Agioi Anargyri (€8 return), Zogheria (€6 return) and Kosta (€3 one way), per person.

WATER TAXI

Water taxis (☎ 22980 72072; Dapia Harbour) leave from the quay opposite the Bardakos Tours office. Fares are displayed on a board. Sample one-way fares include €25 to Agia Marina and €48 to Agii Anargyri, or €63 for a round trip of the island. Fares are per trip, not per person. Add 50% to the price from midnight to 6am.

SPETSES TOWN

pop 3550

Spetses Town occupies a long stretch of the northeast coast of the island and its houses rise steeply from behind the main Dapia Harbour and harbour-front area.

There's evidence of an early Helladic settlement near the Old Harbour (Palio Limani) and at Dapia. Roman and Byzantine remains have been found in the area behind Moni Agios Nikolaos, halfway between the two.

From the 10th century Spetses is thought to have been uninhabited for almost 600 years until the arrival of Albanian refugees fleeing the fighting between the Turks and the Venetians in the 16th century.

The Dapia district has a few impressive *arhontika* (old mansions). The main part of town is given over to chic tourist shops and cafés. There are some delicious ironies, not least the juxtaposition of the cheerfully whiffy fish market with fashion shops selling such fragrant lines as Danoff, Clink, Zulu and Trussardi.

A kilometre or so along the eastern harbour front takes you to the attractive Old Harbour (Palio Limani), the fine old church of Agios Nikolaos, and Baltiza yacht anchorage and boatbuilding area.

Orientation

At Dapia Harbour the quay serves both ferries and hydrofoils. A left turn at the end of the quay leads east through Plateia Limenarhiou, where the horse-drawn carriages wait, and along the harbour-front road of Sotiriou Anargyriou, past the town beach and Plateia Agiou Mama. Beyond here the seafront road continues to the Old Harbour and on to Baltiza.

From the inner, left-hand corner of Plateia Limenarhiou a narrow lane leads left to Plateia Orologiou (Clocktower Sq), which is enclosed by cafés, tavernas and shops and is overlooked by its namesake clock tower.

The narrow 'Main Street' climbs directly inland from the back of Plateia Limenarhiou.

Above Dapia Harbour is a café-crammed terrace from where the road drops down right and then bends sharply left along the harbour-front Kounoupitsa area to become the road to Ligoneri.

If you're on a day visit and fancy a swim, there's a concrete swimming platform and a little beach at the east end of the harbour front, just beyond Plateia Agiou Mama.

Information

There is no tourist office on Spetses. A useful website is www.spetsesdirect.com.

Alpha Bank at Dapia Harbour has an ATM, as does the Bank of Piraeus at the entrance to Plateia Orologiou, and there are ATMs just up to the right along the harbour terrace.

The **port police** (☎ 22980 72245), **tourist police** (☎ 22980 73100; ☺ mid-May–Sep) and OTE all share the same building. It's crowned by a conspicuous satellite dish and is just beyond the cafés on the Dapia Harbour terrace.

1800 Net Café (☎ 22980 29498; near Hotel Possidonion; per 30min €2.50; ☺ 9am-midnight) Not the world's zippiest click.

Mimoza Travel (☎ 22980 75170; mimoza-kent@aig .forthnet.gr) On the harbour front just past Plateia Limenarhiou; can help with accommodation and other services.

Newsagent (☎ 22980 73028; Main St) Impressive selection of newspapers and magazines in numerous languages.

Post office (☺ 7.30am-2pm Mon-Fri) On the street running behind the seafront hotels.

Sights

The **Spetses museum** (☎ 22980 72994; adult/concession €3/2; ☺ 8.30am-2.30pm Tue-Sun) is housed in the old mansion of Hatzigiannis Mexis (1754–1844), a shipowner who became the island's first governor. The collections on view are not extensive, but are fascinating. They include traditional costumes, folkloric items and portraits of the island's founding fathers, icons, coins and archaeological items. Most items have Greek and English annotations. To reach the museum, go straight up from the top left-hand corner of Plateia Orologiou, turn left at the junction and then right, then follow signposts.

The mansion of Spetses' famous daughter, the 19th-century seagoer Laskarina Bouboulina, has been converted into a **museum** (☎ 22980 72416; www.bouboulina-spetses.gr; adult/concession/child €5/3/1; ☺ 9am-9pm Tue-Sun Jun–mid-Sep, 10.30am-4.30pm mid-Sep–May). You can only take a 40-minute guided tour. These run every 45 minutes during the Easter period and from June to mid-September, but less frequently the rest of the year. Billboards around town advertise the starting times of tours. To reach the museum, turn left at the end of the line of cafés on the Dapia Harbour terrace. There's an impressive statue of Bouboulina on the harbour front opposite the Hotel Possidonion.

The **Old Harbour** (Palio Limani), which is about a 1.5km stroll from Dapia, is usually filled with a jumble of commercial vessels. A bit further on is **Baltiza**, a sheltered inlet crammed with all types of craft, from half-built caïques to working fishing boats, minor-league private cruisers and yachts.

Sleeping

BUDGET

Spetses has a number of pleasant sleeping options. Most places offer good discounts outside August.

our pick Hotel Kamelia (☎ 22980 72415; s/d/tr €45/50/65; ☺ Apr-Sep; ☒) There's excellent value and a charming welcome at these fresh, airy rooms in a fine old house tucked away from the busy seafront. Head along the lane to the right of the kiosk in Plateia Agiou Mama for 100m, then bear right before a little bridge. In another 100m or so, go right along a narrow lane to a quiet square, where the Kamelia lies drenched in bougainvillea.

Villa Marina (☎ 22980 72646; off Plateia Agiou Mama; s/d €45/64; ☒) A charming, unfussy place with friendly owners. It's just up to the right of Plateia Agiou Mama. Some rooms look out onto a little garden full of flowers, while others front a big balcony with views to the sea. All rooms have refrigerators and there is a well-equipped communal kitchen downstairs.

MIDRANGE & TOP END

Hotel Roumani (☎ 22980 72344; www.hotelroumani.gr; Dapia Harbour; s/d €70/85; ☒) Refurbished in recent years, the Roumani has an attractive and fresh décor. It's on the terrace above Dapia Harbour, right in the heart of things.

Kastro (☎ 22980 75319; www.kastrospetses.com; s/d/tr incl breakfast €90/100/120, apt €200; ☒ ☒) These fine studios and apartments are in a choice position close to the centre, yet within a private and quiet complex. Décor and furnishings combine traditional style with modern amenities and there are attractive public areas. There are good discounts in low season. Head west along the harbour front for several hundred metres and Kastro is along a short lane to the left.

Nissia (☎ 22980 75000; www.nissia.gr; apt incl breakfast €245-310; ☺ Apr-Oct; ☒ ☐ ☒) Nissia is an exclusive oasis of peace and quiet in stylish surroundings. Apartments are arranged around a spacious courtyard, complete with swimming pool and soothing greenery. It's about 300m northwest of Dapia Harbour. The hotel has a restaurant (mains €8 to €24).

Eating

The swathe of canopied cafés overlooking Dapia Harbour offer choke-on-your-coffee prices. For better food and better deals, veer off smartish.

Cockatoo (☎ 22980 74085; mains €1.20-14; ☺ noon-midnight) At this cheerful budget base, you can get a souvlaki for €1.80, a Greek salad for €4 or a takeaway chicken for €14. Head left from the top of Plateia Limenarhiou, and then right.

Taverna O Lazaros (☎ 22980 72600; mains €5-6.50; ☺ 8pm-midnight) A steady but pleasant hike of about 400m up Main St from Dapia earns you rewards at this popular taverna, where the homemade *taramasalata* (thick purée of fish roe, potato, oil and lemon juice; €3.80) is the real thing. Other treats include young goat in lemon sauce (€8.80) and chicken in tomato sauce with spices (€7.20). Vegetarians can create their own dish and the retsina is very persuasive.

O Roussos (☎ 22980 72212; Plateia Agiou Mama; mains €6-9) A local favourite with decent traditional food and pizzas and pasta at reasonable prices, this pleasant taverna has a great view across the water, albeit with the busy harbourside road in between.

ourpick Akrogialia (☎ 22980 74749; Kounoupitsa; mains €5-12; ☺ 9am-midnight) Winning itself a deserved reputation because of its great food, appealing décor and friendly service, this fine restaurant is on the Kounoupitsa harbour front. Starters such as shrimp and crab salad get things going well and there are other treats on a tempting menu, including steamed mussels in wine and lemon, chicken and mushroom risotto and delicious steaks. Wines include excellent Makedonikos white and red for about €12 or a pricier Lazaridi white at €20 and red at €29. Breakfast, coffee and lunch are also available.

Self-caterers will find everything they need at **Kritikos Supermarket** (☎ 22980 74361; Kentriki Agora), next to the fish market on the harbour front. The entrance is along a covered passageway. There's also a good fruit and vegetable shop next to the newsagents in Main St.

Entertainment

Bar Spetsa (☎ 22980 74131; ☺ 8pm-late) This is one of those wonderful island bars where there's still a tradition of discerning background music that also allows great conversation in good company. The bar is 50m beyond Plateia Agiou Mama on the road to the right of the kiosk.

Balconi Wine Bar (☎ 22980 72594; Sotiriou Anargyriou; ☺ 10.30am-3am May-Oct, 7pm-3am Nov-Apr) Sophistication swirls gently round this stylish homage to cocktails, wine and impressively sourced whisky. There's a background of mainly classical music by day and subtle jazz riffs in the evening. Mop up with fine cheeses and salami, or hand-cut smoked salmon (€17). It's next to the seafront Stelios Hotel.

Socrates Bar, between Plateies Limenarhiou and Orologiou is big on big-screen football. Music venues are concentrated at the Old Harbour–Baltiza area and include **Fortezza** and **Mourayo**, which play pop Greek, **Tsitsiano** for traditional Greek, and the big dance venue **Baltiza**. All are open from about midnight to the early hours, and venues like Baltiza charge about €10 for special theme nights.

AROUND SPETSES

Spetses' coastline is speckled with numerous coves with small, pine-shaded beaches. A 24km surfaced road skirts the entire coastline, so a scooter is the ideal way to explore.

The beach at **Ligoneri**, about 2.5km west of town, is easily reached by bus. The long, pebbly **Agia Paraskevi** and the more sandy **Agii Anargyri** on the southwest coast have good, albeit crowded beaches; both have water sports of every description. **Agia Marina**, about 2km southeast of Spetses Town, is a small resort with a beach that gets crowded.

The interior of the island is crisscrossed with woodland tracks, where a compass is useful.

Cyclades Κυκλάδες

The Cyclades (kih-*klah*-dez), are Greek islands to dream about; sun-kissed outliers of rock and dappled earth lying scattered across the glittering Aegean Sea. Their characteristic white cubist houses, golden beaches, olive groves, pine forests, herb-strewn mountain slopes and terraced valleys make for an irresistible mix. Throw in a dash of hedonism, and a culture that draws vividly on ancient and modern themes, and the Greek Island dream can become reality.

Other realities can be a touch more down to earth, at least for native islanders, who have often struggled for a living through centuries of deprivation. Beneath the tourism gloss, many still raise livestock and grow food on reluctant soil, or chase a diminishing supply of fish from seas that are regularly rough and dangerous. Winters are often grey, bleak and unforgiving.

The Cyclades range from big fertile Naxos, with its craggy mountains and landlocked valleys, to the tiny outliers of Donousa, Iraklia and Anafi, where the sea dominates, with attitude, on every side.

The beaches of Mykonos, Santorini and Ios are awash with sun-lounger society and raucous diversions; their main towns seethe with commercialism. All of this has its appeal, but other islands, such as Andros, Amorgos and Sifnos, have kept tourism to a more sedate scale.

The Cyclades are so named because they form a *kyklos* (circle) around the island of Delos, one of the world's most haunting ancient sites. Closing that circle is still one of the most rewarding experiences for the dedicated traveller.

HIGHLIGHTS

- **Timeless Greece** Exploring the historic old *kastros* (original settlements crowned by a ruined castle) of Sikinos (p201) and Serifos (p215)

- **Spectacular Sunsets** Viewing the best over Santorini's submerged volcano (p190)

- **Ancient & Sublime** Indulging in Delos' (p152) archaeological feast

- **Secluded Sand** Hiding away on the islands of the Little Cyclades (p170) and on the east coast of Andros (p128)

- **High Flying** Kiteboarding on Paros (p159)

- **Dawn Patrol** Clubbing on Mykonos (p141) and Ios (p186)

- POPULATION: 109,814
- AREA: 2429 SQ KM

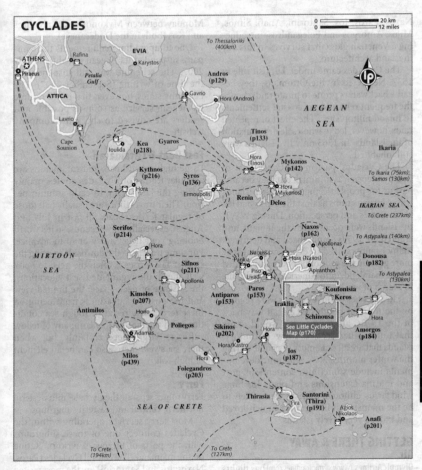

HISTORY

The Cyclades are said to have been inhabited since at least 7000 BC. Around 3000 BC there emerged a cohesive Cycladic civilisation that was bound together by seagoing commerce and exchange. During the Early Cycladic period (3000–2000 BC) the tiny but distinctive Cycladic marble figurines, mainly stylized representations of the naked female form, were sculpted.

In the Middle Cycladic period (2000–1500 BC) many of the islands were occupied by the Minoans – at Akrotiri, on Santorini, a Minoan town has been excavated. At the beginning of the Late Cycladic period (1500–1100 BC) the Cyclades passed to the Mycenaeans. The Dorians followed in the 8th century BC, bringing Archaic culture with them.

By the middle of the 5th century BC the islands were members of a fully fledged Athenian empire. In the Hellenistic era (323–146 BC) they were controlled by Egypt's Ptolemaic dynasties and then by the Macedonians. In 146 BC the islands became a Roman province, and lucrative trade links were established with many parts of the Mediterranean.

The division of the Roman Empire in AD 395 resulted in the Cyclades being ruled from Byzantium (Constantinople), but after the fall of Byzantium in 1204, they came under a Venetian governance that doled out the islands to opportunistic aristocrats. The most powerful of these was Marco Sanudo (self-styled Venetian Duke of Naxos), who acquired

Naxos, Paros, Ios, Santorini, Anafi, Sifnos, Milos, Amorgos and Folegandros, introducing a Venetian gloss that survives to this day in island architecture.

The Cyclades came under Turkish rule in 1537. Neglected by the Ottomans, they became backwaters prone to pirate raids, hence the frequent relocation of coastal settlements to inland hilltop sites. The effect of repeated raids, however, led to wholesale depopulation of the islands. In 1563 only five islands were still inhabited.

The Cyclades' part in the Greek War of Independence was minimal, but they became havens for people fleeing from other islands where insurrections against the Turks had led to massacres and persecution. During WWII the islands were occupied by the Italians, and entered the 1950s demoralised and deprived. Many islanders lived in deep poverty; many more gave up the economic battle and headed for the mainland, or to America and Australia, in search of work.

The fortunes of the Cyclades were revived by the tourism boom that began way back in the 1970s, although some would argue that tourism has created a few 'dormitory' islands that are all but empty of people during the winter months. New economic developments include sometimes contentious port and marina extensions and plans for huge wind farms, although tourism seems likely to be the mainstay of life on these much-loved and indeed very lovely islands.

GETTING THERE & AWAY
Air
Olympic Airlines (www.olympicairlines.com) has flights between Athens and Naxos, Syros, Santorini, Mykonos, Paros and Milos. From Mykonos there are flights to/from Thessaloniki, Santorini and Rhodes (see individual island sections for details).

Aegean Airlines (www.aegeanair.com) flies to Mykonos and Santorini from Athens and Thessaloniki.

Sky Express (☎ 28102 23500; www.skyexpress.gr) flies to Santorini from Athens and on from Santorini to Rhodes.

Until suspension of operations in July of 2007, the innovative **AirSea Lines** (www.airsealines.com) ran seaplane flights daily from Thursday to Monday between Lavrio (in southern Attica) and Mykonos, Paros, Ios and Santorini. It also ran flights daily from Thursday to Monday between Mykonos and Kalymnos and Kos (both in the Dodecanese).

Due to upgrading requirements the company suspended its Aegean schedule in July 2007. The schedule was still suspended at the time of writing (September 2007). The company states, however, that it will resume its Aegean service as soon as possible and readers are advised to check the company website.

Fast Boat & Catamaran
Large high-speed boats and catamarans are a regular feature on Cyclades' routes, mainly during the late spring to early autumn period. Their travel times are usually half those of regular ferries. Seats fill fast in July and August, especially on weekends, so it's worth booking your ticket a day or so in advance. For some travellers, the downside to using the smaller fast ferries is often the need to book well ahead; the regimented seat allocations; the absence of deck space; the limited view and the possible queasiness from being on these ferries, the result of rough sea conditions and the inescapable company of fellow sufferers. High speed certainly, but when there's a swell, there also can be an element of high roll.

Ferry
Ferry routes separate the Cyclades into western, northern, central and eastern subgroups.

Most ferry services operating within the Cyclades connect one of these subgroups with the ports of Piraeus, Lavrio or Rafina on the mainland. The central Cyclades (Paros, Naxos, Ios and Santorini) are the most visited and have the best ferry links with the mainland, usually to Piraeus.

The northern Cyclades (Andros, Tinos, Syros and Mykonos) have excellent connections with the mainland. The mainland port for Andros is Rafina, but it's possible to reach Andros from Piraeus by catching a ferry to Syros, Tinos or Mykonos and connecting from there.

Lavrio is the mainland port for ferries serving Kea, from where connections south to the other western Cyclades are not good. Kythnos has a reasonable number of connections to Piraeus and good connections south to other islands. Milos, Serifos and Sifnos have seen greatly improved ferry connections with Piraeus in recent years. Folegandros and

FERRY CONNECTIONS TO THE CYCLADES

Origin	Destination	Duration	Fare	Frequency
Agios Nikolaos (Crete)	Milos	7hr	€20.60	2 weekly
Iraklio (Crete)	Mykonos	9hr	€23.90	3 weekly
	Naxos	7½hr	€20.40	weekly
	Paros	7-8hr	€23.50	2 weekly
	Santorini	3¾hr	€15.10	3 weekly
Lavrio	Kea	1¼hr	€5.90	2 daily
	Kythnos	2½hr	€8.20	6 weekly
	Syros	3½hr	€14.30	2 weekly
Piraeus	Amorgos	10hr	€27.50	10 weekly
	Anafi	11hr	€27.10	3 weekly
	Donousa	7hr	€27.50	3 weekly
Piraeus	Folegandros	6-9hr	€26	4 weekly
	Ios	7hr	€27.10	4 daily
	Iraklia	6¾hr	€27.50	3 weekly
	Kimolos	6hr	€23	2 weekly
	Koufonisia	8hr	€27.30	5 weekly
	Kythnos	2½hr	€12.50	2 daily
	Milos	5-7hr	€25	2 daily
	Mykonos	6hr	€24.50	3 daily
	Naxos	6hr	€29	6 daily
	Paros	5hr	€28.80	6 daily
	Santorini	9hr	€31	4 daily
	Serifos	4½hr	€20	daily
	Sifnos	5hr	€24	daily
	Sikinos	10hr	€26.10	7 weekly
	Syros	4hr	€24	3 daily
	Tinos	5¼hr	€26	2 daily
Rafina	Andros	2hr	€10.90	3 daily
	Mykonos	4½hr	€19	2 daily
	Tinos	3½hr	€17.50	4 daily
Sitia (Crete)	Milos	10hr	€22	3 weekly
Thessaloniki	Mykonos	15hr	€37.30	3 weekly
	Naxos	18hr	€36.30	weekly
	Paros	16hr	€39.50	2 weekly
	Santorini	25hr	€41.10	3 weekly
	Syros	15hr	€35.20	weekly
	Tinos	18hr	€37.10	2 weekly

Sikinos have less frequent connections with the mainland.

The eastern Cyclades (Anafi, Amorgos, Iraklia, Schinousa, Koufonisia and Donousa) are the least visited and have the fewest ferry links with the mainland. However, for the foreseeable future Blue Star Ferries is running a regular service to Amorgos, Iraklia, Schinousa, Koufonisia and Donousa. These islands also have a daily service in summer to and from Naxos. Anafi is best reached from Santorini.

When planning your island-hopping it pays to bear this pattern of ferry routes in mind; however, Paros is the ferry hub of the Cyclades, and connections between different groups are usually possible via this port.

See the table (above) for an overview of high-season ferry services to the Cyclades from the mainland and Crete. The information relates to slower, traditional ferries.

GETTING AROUND

For information on travel within the Cyclades, see the individual island entries.

The Cyclades are more exposed to the summer *meltemi* (northeasterly wind) than other island groups. This is a fierce wind; it may be warm, but it can blast, and it often plays havoc with ferry schedules (especially for smaller vessels that ply the Little Cyclades routes, and for small hydrofoils). Keep this in mind if you're on a tight schedule.

ANDROS ΑΝΔΡΟΣ

pop 10,112

Big, beautiful Andros is a mere two hours by ferry from mainland Rafina and is a rewarding escape for those who want a less-tourist-logged Cycladic world. It's the most northerly island of the Cyclades and is the second largest after Naxos.

Satisfyingly remote in places, Andros boasts neoclassical mansions and Venetian tower-houses that contrast with the rough unpainted stonework of farm buildings and patterned dovecotes. Handsome stone walls, made up of a unique pattern of irregular slabs and smaller stones, lock the sometimes friable hill slopes in place. A network of footpaths, many of them stepped and cobbled, are also maintained, and the island has a fascinating archaeological and cultural heritage.

Andros has several beaches, many of them in out-of-the way locations. There are three main settlements: the unpretentious port of Gavrio, the cheerful resort of Batsi and the handsome main town of Hora, known also as Andros.

Getting There & Away
FERRY

At least three ferries daily leave Andros' main port of Gavrio for Rafina (€10.90 to 12.50, two hours). Daily ferries run to Tinos (€8, 1½ hours) and Mykonos (€10.50, 2½ hours), from where there are daily connections to Syros and Paros in high season. Services run direct to Syros, from May to October, three times a week (€9, two hours). On Saturday from May to September, a very slow ferry runs to Paros (€12.10, seven hours), Naxos (€12.20, eight hours and 20 minutes), Ios (€18.20, 12 hours) and Santorini (€20.80, 14¼ hours). This ferry continues to Anafi (€26.30, 16 hours), Sikinos (€18.20, 12 hours) and Folegandros (€18.20, 11 hours). On Thursday from May to September, a ferry runs to Kythnos (€11.70, six hours and 45 minutes) and Kea (€8, 8½ hours).

Getting Around

Nine buses daily (fewer on weekends) link Gavrio and Hora (€3.50, 55 minutes) via Batsi (€2, 15 minutes). Schedules are posted at the bus stops in Gavrio and Hora; otherwise, call ☎ 22820 22316 for information.

A **taxi** (☎ Gavrio 22820 71171, Batsi 22820 41081, Hora 22820 22171) from Gavrio to Batsi costs €8 and to Hora €25. Car hire is about €35 in August, and about €25 in the low season. **Euro Rent A Car** (☎ 22820 72440) is a friendly service with an office opposite the Gavrio ferry quay.

GAVRIO ΓΑΥΡΙΟ

Located on the west coast, Gavrio is the main port of Andros. Apart from the flurry of ferry arrivals it is very low key and a touch drab.

Orientation & Information

The ferry quay is situated midway along the waterfront and the bus stop is in front of it. The post office is 150m to the left as you leave the ferry quay. There's an ATM outside Kyklades Travel and there's a bank with ATM on the middle of the waterfront.

Kyklades Travel (☎ 22820 72363; lasia@otenet.gr)
A helpful office right opposite the ferry quay. It sells ferry tickets and can arrange accommodation.
Port police (☎ 22820 71213) On the waterfront.

Sleeping & Eating

Most visitors head for Batsi or Hora for accommodation. There are a couple of sleeping options on the Gavrio waterfront but these are essentially a last resort. A much better bet is **Ostria Studios** (☎ 22820 71551; www.ostria-studios .gr; s/d/apt €60/65/85; Ⓟ 🔀), about 300m along the Batsi road and with spacious rooms in a pleasant complex of rising terraces.

Peppering Gavrio's waterfront are several cafés and bars that are down-to-earth local places and weekend hang-outs for visiting mainlanders. **To Konaki** (☎ 22820 71733; mains €3.50-9) offers a healthy choice of fish, meat and vegetarian dishes with a local flavour. It's about 50m to the left of the ferry quay.

BATSI ΜΠΑΤΣΙ

Easy-going yet upbeat, Batsi is the island's main resort. Things are likely to liven up here with the completion of a yacht marina scheduled for 2008. The resort lies 7km south of Gavrio on the inner curve of a handsome bay. A sandy beach on the north side merges eventually with a harbour-side promenade backed by a colourful swath of cafés, tavernas and shops. There's a dusty car park across the road from the beach. **Greek Sun Holidays** (☎ 22820 41198; greeksun@travelling.gr), located towards the far end of the waterfront, is a good source of information and can help with accommodation, car rental and ferry tickets. Scooters can be hired for €16 to €22 per day from **Dino's Rent-a-Bike** (☎ 22820 42169) by the car park.

Well-maintained self-drive boats can be hired from **Riva Boats** (☎ 22820 24412, 6974460330; Hora). They carry four adults comfortably. A minimum rental of one day is about €90 (see Sights & Activities, p131).

The tiny post office is tucked away beside the taverna opposite the bus stop. The

taxi rank, and National and Alpha banks (with ATMs), are all on the middle of the waterfront.

Tours

From May to October **Greek Sun Holidays** (☎ 22820 41198; greeksun@travelling.gr) organises island tours (€22) that take in Paleopolis and some of the island's loveliest villages. There are also small-group half- or full-day guided walks (€18 to €28) following old paths through beautiful countryside.

Sleeping & Eating

It's wise to book accommodation well ahead for July and August and for weekends in June and September.

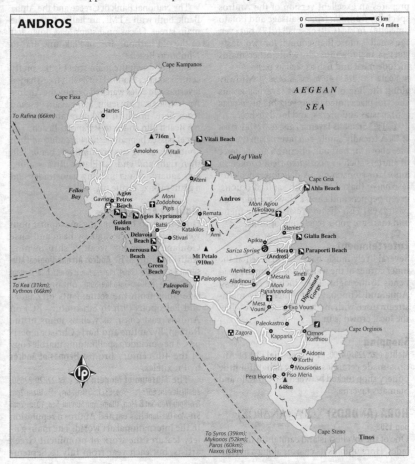

ANDROS

Cavo D'ora Pension (☎ 22820 41766; s/d €25/45) Located above a snack bar and pizzeria, the handful of pleasant rooms here offer outstanding value. You can get breakfast for €5.50 and tasty mezedhes and pizzas for €4.50 to €8. It's at the tree-shaded entrance to town, just across from the beach.

Likio Studios (☎ 22820 41050; www.likiostudios.gr; s/d/apt €60/75/120; P ⊠) Peaceful flower-filled surroundings and a friendly welcome make these family-run, spacious and well-equipped studios a great choice. The studios are open year round, have central heating and are located about 100m inland from Dino's Rent-a-Bike.

Oti Kalo (☎ 22820 41287; mains €4.50-9) The name means 'everything good', and it's no idle boast. Mother's in the kitchen and she prepares an excellent version of the Andros speciality *froutalia* (spicy sausage and potato omelette), in big (€20) or small (€17), but even the small is more than enough for two. Tasty starters include mussels, while other mains include meat and fish as well as pasta.

Koala (☎ 22820 41696; mains €4.90-9) Midway along the line of waterfront tavernas is this cheerful place noted for its very big breakfasts (€8), pastas and pizzas, and local dishes.

our pick Stamatis Taverna (☎ 22820 41283; mains €6-18) A friendly family-run taverna, on the terrace above the harbour, offering a great choice of starters such as *pikandiko* (feta cooked in a pot), or spinach pie. A delicious speciality is *exohiko* (baked lamb with sautéed onions, green peppers and cheese all wrapped in filo pastry; €9) Fish dishes are also on the menu and there are good vegetarian options.

Entertainment

Several lively music bars are clustered at the inner corner of the waterfront where the road bends to the right. They include Nameless, Aqua and Kimbo, all of which play mainstream disco with modern Greek music when the local crowd is in.

Shopping

Melita (☎ 22820 42005) For a special gift of Andros-made ceramics, try this delightful little pottery shop tucked between the Oti Kalo and Stamatis tavernas.

HORA (ANDROS) ΧΩΡΑ (ΑΝΔΡΟΣ)
pop 1508

One of the loveliest island capitals in the Cyclades, Hora unfolds its charms along a narrow rocky peninsula between two bays on the east coast of Andros, 35km southeast of Gavrio. The town reflects Venetian origins in its numerous neoclassical buildings, the elegance of which is underscored by Byzantine and Ottoman accents. Hora's cultural pedigree is even more distinguished by its Museum of Modern Art and an impressive archaeological museum.

Orientation & Information

The bus station is on Plateia Goulandri, from where a narrow lane leads past a taxi rank, beside the spacious town square, to a T-junction. The post office is to the left. The marble-paved and notionally pedestrianised main street leads down to the right.

The National Bank of Greece and the Alpha Bank, both with ATMs, are halfway down the main street. Occasional steps lead down left to the old harbour area of Plakoura, and to Nimborio Beach.

Further down the main street is the pretty central square, Plateia Kaïri, with tree-shaded tavernas and cafés watched over by the Andros Archaeological Museum. Steps again descend from here, north to Plakoura and Nimborio Beach and south to Paraporti Beach. The street passes beneath a short arcade and then continues along the promontory, bends left, then right and ends at Plateia Riva – a big, airy square with crumbling balustrades and a giant bronze statue of a sailor.

Sights & Activities

Hora has two outstanding museums; both were donated to the state by Basil and Elise Goulandris, of the wealthy ship-owning Andriot family. The **Andros Archaeological Museum** (☎ 22820 23664; Plateia Kaïri; adult/child/student €3/2/free; ☉ 8.30am-3pm Tue-Sun) contains impressive finds from the settlements of Zagora and Paleopolis (9th to 8th century BC) on Andros' east coast, as well as items of the Roman, Byzantine and Early Christian periods. They include a spellbinding marble copy of the 4th-century bronze **Hermes of Andros** by Praxiteles.

The **Museum of Modern Art** (☎ 22820 22650; adult/student €6/3 Jun-Sep, €3/1.50 Oct-May; ☉ 10am-2pm & 6-8pm Wed-Sat & Mon, 10am-2pm Sun Jul-Sep, 10am-2pm Sat-Mon Oct-Jun) has earned Andros a reputation in the international art world. The main gallery features the work of prominent Greek artists, but each year from July to September, the gallery stages an exhibition of the works by one of the world's great artists. To date there have been annual exhibitions featuring original works by Picasso, Matisse, Braque, Toulouse-Lautrec and Miro, a remarkable achievement for a modest Greek island. To reach the gallery, head down the steps from Plateia Kaïri towards the old harbour.

The huge **bronze statue** of a sailor that stands in Plateia Riva celebrates Hora's great seagoing traditions, although it looks more Russian triumphalist than Andriot in its scale and style. The ruins of a **Venetian fortress** stand on an island that is linked to the tip of the headland by the worn remnants of a steeply arched bridge.

A great option is to hire a self-drive boat and head out to some of the west and north coast's glorious beaches, most of which are difficult to reach by road. **Riva Boats** (☎ 22820 24412, 6974460330; Hora) has superb 4.5m Norwegian-built open boats with 20HP outboards. They are very seaworthy and come complete with life raft and anchor, and even a mobile phone. You do not need a licence to drive these boats. They can carry four adults comfortably. Hire per boat for a minimum of one day is about €90. The boats can be hired through Riva's shop and office, located in the narrow road leading to Nimboria Beach. Riva can also arrange for boats to be hired from Batsi.

Scooters and motorbikes can be hired from Riva down at Nimborio Beach, and through Karaoulanis Rooms (see below) for €12 to €18. Riva also sells fishing tackle and boat fittings.

Sleeping & Eating

Karaoulanis Rooms (☎ 22820 24412, 6974460330; www .androsrooms.gr; d/apt €50/100) Down by the old harbour area there's a friendly welcome at this tall old house, whose rooms and apartments have been refurbished in recent years to the highest standards. There are excellent discount prices in low season. Greek, English and French are spoken by family members. Check here also for scooter and boat hire.

Alcioni Inn (☎ 22820 24522, 6973403934; alcioni@ hellastourism.gr; Nimborio; d from €70 to €80) These self-catering rooms are very smart and comfortable. They are in the midst of the main waterfront, just across the road from the beach, but have a nicely secluded and relaxing atmosphere.

Niki (☎ /fax 22820 29155; xenonaw.nik@g.mail.com; s/d/tr €70/80/95) Imaginative restoration of this handsome old house has preserved beautiful timber ceilings and galleries. It's on the main street and there's a large veranda where you can relax and get breakfast for about €8, or a coffee.

Ermis (☎ 22820 22233; Plateia Kaïri) On the square is this pleasant little café and pastry shop.

Nonna's (☎ 22820 23577; Plakoura; mains €3.50-9) A small, family-run mezedhes place on the old harbour, next to Karaoulanis Rooms. Nonna's main dishes are fresh fish from the family's own boat. Monkfish and red mullet are two well-prepared dishes that are often available. Vegetarians have a decent choice, too, from salads to zucchini pie.

Palinorio (☎ 22820 22881; Nimborio; mains €8-15; ☻ 11am-2am) There's a great choice of traditional dishes, as well as good service and value at this popular taverna on the waterfront at the edge of Nimborio Beach. Shellfish dishes are more expensive, but are prepared with skill.

AROUND ANDROS

Between Gavrio and Paleopolis Bay are several pleasant beaches, including **Agios Kyprianos**, where there's a little church with a taverna close by, **Delavoia**, one half of which is naturist, **Anerousa** and **Green**.

Paleopolis, 7km south of Batsi on the coast road, is the site of Ancient Andros, where the Hermes of Andros was found. The small but intriguing **Archaeological Museum of Paleopolis** (☎ 22829 41985; admission free; ☻ 8.30am-3pm Tue-Sun) displays and interprets finds from the area.

If you have transport, a worthwhile trip is to head down the west coast of the island before turning northeast at Batsilianos through a charming landscape of fields and cypresses to reach **Ormos Korthiou**, a bayside village that lacks only a decent beach to give it full resort status. Head north from here along a lovely coastal road that climbs and turns through raw hills and wooded valleys for 20km to reach Hora.

North from Hora the road climbs into the mountains passing the pleasant village of **Stenies**, where **Taverna Barbarola** (☎ 22820 23111; mains €5-8) is a worthwhile stop for excellent traditional Andriot cooking, with a terrific view thrown in. Beyond Stenies the road heads over high hills before descending in twists and turns to Batsi.

ROMANCING THE STONES

The best structures made by humankind, from simple walls to cathedrals, often seem to grow naturally from the ground. On Andros and Tinos there are two compelling examples of this serendipity. Andros is famous for its network of stone walls that wriggle across the wild landscape of the island's hills. The walls are built of large flat slabs (often trapezium-shaped) that are interspersed with smaller clusters of boulders. Many older walls are in decay but there is now a programme of repair and of new wall building. The result adds a rich visual emphasis to the rugged landscape.

On Tinos, hundreds of white-painted dovecotes pepper the landscape. They are like tiny palaces, 'embroidered' with symbols of trees, wagon wheels, triangles, chevrons and sun symbols; all worked in slate and stone and then whitewashed, creating a rich interplay of light and shade. It's said that the Venetians first introduced dovecotes to the Cyclades, but most surviving structures date from the 18th and 19th centuries. The breeding of pigeons was an important island trade for many centuries. The birds supplied meat for the winter months, droppings for field manure and feathers for bedding.

TINOS ΤΗΝΟΣ

pop 8614

Hora, the port of Tinos, glows with religious fervour during Orthodox festivals at the splendid Church of Panagia Evangelistria, home to the sacred icon of the Megalochari, the Holy Virgin. A steady trickle of pilgrims continues throughout the year. The icon is one of Greece's most famous and is said to have been found in 1822 on land where the church now stands. Healing powers were accorded to the icon, thus leading to mass pilgrimage and a commercial future for Tinos.

Yet, beyond the overt religious life, Tinos survives as an island of great natural beauty. Its landscape of rugged hills is dotted with over 40 villages that protrude like marble outcrops from the brindled slopes. Scattered across the countryside are countless ornate dovecotes, legacy of Venetian influence (see boxed text, above). There is a strong artistic tradition on Tinos, not least in the sculptors' village of Pyrgos in the north of the island where the island's marble quarries are located. However, religion still takes centre stage in Hora, although the town rattles and hums around it all like a typical island port should.

Getting There & Away

FAST BOAT & CATAMARAN

There are at least three services daily to Mykonos (€9.50, 15 minutes) and Rafina (€34, 1¾ hours), plus daily services to Paros (€21.70, 1¼ hours), five weekly to Piraeus

(€43, three hours), four weekly to Naxos (€20, 1½ hours), Santorini (€33.20, 2¼ hours) and Ios (€28.50, two hours) and one daily to Syros (€9, two hours).

FERRY

At least six ferries daily go to Mykonos (€4.50, 30 minutes), and four daily to Rafina (€17.50, 3½ hours) and Andros (€9, 1½ hours). There are at least two daily to Syros (€5, 50 minutes) and Piraeus (€27, six hours).

Four weekly ferries go to Ikaria via connections through Mykonos (€16, 3½ hours) and Syros (€18, 3½ hours).

Three ferries weekly go to Thessaloniki (€37.10, 18 hours), and there are four ferries weekly to Paros (€8.80, five hours) and Santorini (€16.60, eight hours).

Two weekly services run to Naxos (€11, 4¼ hours) and Iraklio on Crete (€25, 10¼ hours).

Getting Around

From June to September there are frequent buses from Hora (Tinos) to Porto and Kionia (€1.20, 10 minutes) and several daily to Panormos (€3.30, one hour) via Kambos (€1.20, 15 minutes) and Pyrgos (€3, 50 minutes). Buses leave from the station on the waterfront, opposite the Blue Star Ferry Office, where there's a timetable in the window.

Motorcycles (per day €15 to €20) and cars (minimum per weekday €44; on weekends €60) can be hired from a number of outfits along the waterfront at Hora. Rates drop out of season. **Vidalis Rent a Car & Bike** (☎ 22830 25670; Trion Ierarhon 2) is a reliable firm.

HORA (TINOS) ΧΩΡΑ (ΤΗΝΟΣ)

Hora, also known as Tinos, is the island's capital and port. The harbourfront is lined with cafés and hotels and the narrow streets behind are full of restaurants and tavernas. The streets leading up to the Church of Panagia Evangelistria are full of numerous shops and stalls crammed with souvenirs and religious ware.

Orientation

There are two ferry departure quays, the locations of which visitors definitely need to know. Locals know them as 'ports'. The Outer Port is the dock for conventional ferries, including the bigger high-speed ones. It is about 300m to the north of the main harbour. The Middle Port, where smaller fast ferries such as Sea Jet and Flying Cats dock, is at the north end of the town's main waterfront.

When you buy a ferry ticket it's essential to check which of these two ports your ferry is leaving from. Allow at least 20 minutes to walk from the centre of town to the Outer Port.

The uphill street of Leoforos Megaloharis, straight ahead from the middle of the main waterfront, is the route pilgrims take to the church. The narrower Evangelistria, to its right, also leads to the Church of Panagia Evangelistria.

Information

The post office is at the southeastern end of the waterfront, just past the bus station, and the National Bank of Greece (with ATM) is 50m left of Hotel Posidonion.

Malliaris Travel (☎ 22830 24241; fax 22830 24243; malliaris@thn.forthnet.gr; Paralia) On the waterfront near Hotel Posidonion; sells ferry tickets.

Port police (☎ 22830 22348; Kionion) Just up from Windmills Travel.

Symposion (☎ 22830 24368; Evangelistria 13; internet access per 30min €3) A pleasant café-restaurant with internet access.

Windmills Travel & Tourism (☎ 22830 23398; www .windmillstravel.com; Kionion 2) Just across the way from

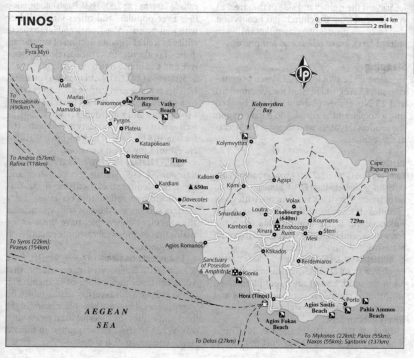

TINOS

the Outer Port ferry quay, this is very helpful, and staff can arrange accommodation, car hire and much more.

Sights

The neoclassical **Church of Panagia Evangelistria** (Church of the Annunciation; ⏲ 8am-8pm) is built of marble from the island's Panormos quarries. The complex lies within a pleasant courtyard flanked by cool arcades. Inside the main building the acclaimed icon of the Holy Virgin is draped with gold, silver, jewels and pearls, and is surrounded by gifts from supplicants. A hanging garden of fabulous chandeliers and lampholders fills the roof space.

Set into the surface of the street on one side of Leoforos Megaloharis is a rubberised strip, complete with side lights. This is used by pilgrims, who may be seen at any time of year heading for the church on their hands and knees, pushing long candles before them. The final approach is up carpeted steps.

Within the church complex, several **museums** house religious artefacts, icons and secular artworks.

The small **archaeological museum** (☎ 22830 22670; Leoforos Megaloharis; admission €2; ⏲ 8am-3pm Tue-Sun), on the right-hand side of the street as you descend from the church, has a collection that includes impressive clay *pithoi* (Minoan storage jars), grave reliefs and sculptures.

Sleeping

Hora should be avoided on 25 March (Annunciation), 15 August (Feast of the Assumption) and 15 November (Advent). If not booked into a hotel months ahead, you'll have to join the roofless devotees who sleep on the streets at these times.

BUDGET

Camping Tinos (☎ 22830 22344; www.camping.gr/tinos; camp sites per adult/child/tent €7/4/4, bungalows with/without bathroom €28/20) This is a fine site with good facilities. It's south of the town near Agios Fokas, about a five-minute walk from the ferry quay, and is clearly signposted from the waterfront. A minibus meets ferries.

Nikoleta (☎ 22830 24719; nikoleta@thn.forthnet.gr; Kapodistriou 11; s/d €25/35) Some distance inland from the south end of town, but its spotless, uncluttered rooms are exceptional value and come with a charming welcome. There is a lovely garden area.

Faros (☎ 22830 22712; s/d/tr €35/50/80; 🖳) This is a handy place for the Outer Port ferry quay.

The rooms are colourful and quite quirky, but vary in size. The small outside courtyard is filled with leafy colour.

MIDRANGE

Boreades (☎ 22830 23845; s €45-55, d €50-65, apt €160) A fairly ordinary location belies the style and comfort of this interesting place, which manages to convey an almost country-house ambience with its interior plan and creative décor. Breakfast in the sunny lounge is €7.

Oceanis (☎ 22830 22452; oceanis@mail.gr; Akti G Drosou; s/d/tr €45/75/97.50; 🖳) Rooms are not overly large at this modern, well-run hotel, but they are clean and well equipped. They even have some genuine, if very small, single rooms. There's a lift to all floors. Breakfast is €5.

Hotel Posidonion (☎ 22830 23123; fax 22830 25808; Paralia 4; s/d €60/75; 🖳) In a very convenient position, midwaterfront, Posidonian is a long-established, popular hotel. Communal lounges overlooking the harbour are an endearing feature. Most rooms are well appointed and comfortable.

Eating

Pallada Taverna (☎ 22830 23516; Plateia Palladas; mains €6-8) Ever popular, and offers Greek dishes with well-prepared veal, pork and lamb specialities as well as a good selection of vegetarian dishes. Local wines from the barrel are persuasive and the house retsina is brisk.

Symposion (☎ 22830 24368; Evangelistria 13; mains €6-17) This is an elegant café-restaurant reached by a pretty staircase. It does breakfasts (€4 to €16), crepes and sandwiches (€3 to €7.50), as well as pasta dishes and tasty mixed plates (€8 for one, €18 for two) of feta, anchovies, Tinian cheese and sun-dried tomatoes.

our pick **Metaxy Mas** (☎ 22830 25945; Plateia Palladas; mains €6.50-19) Stylish service, décor and modern Mediterranean cuisine make this one of the best restaurants on Tinos. Tasty starters such as giant beans with spinach, or the succulent cheese pie, pave the way for mains that include veal casserole or cuttlefish with spinach.

To Koutouki tis Elenis (☎ 22830 24857; G Gagou 5; mains €7-15) Gagou is a narrow lane that veers off from the bottom of Evangelistria. It's crammed with tavernas whose tables fill every corner. This cosy little place is one of the best and dishes up cheerful local treats such as chicken in lemon sauce, rabbit in tomato sauce and a tasty fish soup.

Drinking & Entertainment

Koursaros (☎ 22830 23963; ☒ 8am-3am) This long-established bar spins an engaging mix of rock, funk and jazz. It's at the far end of the line of cafés across from the Middle Port.

In the back lanes opposite the Middle Port there's a clutch of music and dance bars such as Volto and Sibylla, glowing with candy-coloured light and churning out clubby standards and Greek pop as a counterbalance to sacred song.

AROUND TINOS

Escaping from Hora's religious-commercial grip is essential if you want to make the most of Tinos and its numerous villages, beaches and dramatic countryside.

At **Porto**, 6km east of Hora, there's a fine, uncrowded beach facing Mykonos, while about 1km further on from Porto is the even lovelier **Pahia Ammos Beach**.

Kionia, 3km northwest of Hora, has several small beaches. Near the largest are the scant remains of the 4th-century-BC site of the **Sanctuary of Poseidon & Amphitrite**, a once enormous complex that drew pilgrims in much the same way as the present Church of Panagia Evangelistria does today.

About 12km north of Hora on the north coast is **Kolymvythra Bay**, where there are two pleasant sandy beaches, the smaller with sun loungers, umbrellas and a seasonal café, the larger backed by reed beds.

On the north coast, 28km northwest of Hora, is the seaside village of **Panormos**, from where the distinctive green marble, quarried in nearby **Marlas**, was once exported. The waterfront at Panormos is lined with tavernas.

Pyrgos, on the way to Panormos, is a handsome village where even the cemetery is a feast of carved marble. Many of the houses have attractive fanlights. During the late 19th century and early 20th century Pyrgos was the centre of a remarkable tradition of sculpture sustained by the supply of excellent local marble.

Just across the road from the car park at the entrance to Pyrgos is the **Museum House of Yannoulis Halepas** (adult/child €5/2.50; ☒ 10.30am-2.30pm & 5-8pm Apr–mid-Oct). It's a fascinating place, where the sculptor's humble rooms and workshop, with their striated plaster walls and slate floors, have been preserved. An adjoining gallery has splendid examples of the work of local sculptors. Outstanding are *Girl on a Rock* by Georgios Vamvakis; *Hamlet* by Loukas Doukas; and a copy of the superb *Fisherman* by Dimitrios Filippolis.

About 6km directly north of Hora is the tiny village of **Volax**, a scribble of white houses at the heart of an amphitheatre of low hills studded with thousands of dark-coloured boulders. Behind the doorways, Volax really is old Greece. There's a small **folklore museum** (ask at the nearest house for the key), an attractive Catholic chapel and a small outdoor theatre. There are a couple of tavernas at the entrance to Volax.

The ruins of the Venetian fortress of **Exobourgo** lie 2km south of Volax, on top of a mighty 640m rock outcrop.

SYROS ΣΥΡΟΣ

pop 20,220

Head for Syros if you want to witness authentic Greek island life and culture. This is one of the smallest islands of the Cyclades, yet it has the highest population. It is the legal and administrative centre of the entire archipelago, the ferry hub of the northern islands, and home to Ermoupolis, the largest and handsomest of all Cycladic towns. If you break the lightest of laws anywhere in the Cyclades, you may end up at court in Syros. Make your visit voluntary, instead; the rewards are substantial and include exposure to everyday island life, great eating and sleeping options and a handful of small but pleasant beaches.

History

Excavations of an Early Cycladic fortified settlement and burial ground at Kastri in the island's northeast date from the Neolithic period (2800–2300 BC).

During the medieval period Syros had an overwhelmingly Roman Catholic population. Capuchin monks and Jesuits settled on the island during the 17th and 18th centuries, and such was the Catholic influence that France was called upon by Syros to help it during Turkish rule. Later Turkish influence was benevolent and minimal and Syros busied itself with shipping and commerce. During the War of Independence thousands of refugees from islands ravaged by the Turks fled to Syros. They brought with them an infusion

CYCLADES

SYROS

0 ————— 2 km
0 ————— 1 mile

To Andros (57km); Rafina (63km);
Kythnos (74km); Kea (76km)

To Thessaloniki
(460km)

Cape Trimeson

Cape
Diapori

*AEGEAN
SEA*

Grammata
Beach

Kampos

Lia Beach

Kastri

To Tinos (22km);
Mykonos (35km);
Ikaria (75km);
Samos (150km)

Aetos
Beach

431m

Varvarousa

*AEGEAN
SEA*

Mytikas

Delfini
Beach

Pirgos
(440m)

Agios
Georgios

Kini

Ano Syros

Vrodado

Ermoupolis

Syros

Danakos

Mt Volakas
(312m)

To Paros (48km);
Naxos (55km);
Ios (102km);
Milos (115km);
Santorini (135km)

Cape
Katakefalos

*Galissas
Bay*
Armeos Beach

Galissas

Lazareto

Pagos

Mesaria

Manna

Parakopi

Ano
Manno

Vissa

Azolimnos
Beach

Finikas

Adiata

Hrousa

Atelio

*Finikas
Bay*
Posidonia
Beach

Mt Axachas
(319m)

Vari

Angathopes
Beach

Posidonia

Shinonisi

Megas
Gialos

Vari
Beach

Nisi

Strongylo

Megas Gialos
Beach

Cape Viglostasi

To Lavrio (102km); Piraeus
(154km); Crete (244km)

of Greek Orthodoxy and a fresh commercial drive that made Syros the commercial, naval and cultural centre of Greece during the 19th century. This position was lost to Piraeus in the 20th century. The island's industrial mainstay of shipbuilding has declined, but Syros still has textile manufacturing, a thriving horticultural sector, a sizable administrative and service sector and a small but healthy tourism industry.

Getting There & Away

AIR

Olympic Airlines (☎ 22810 88018; www.olympicairlines.com) operates at least one flight daily, except Thursday and Saturday, to and from Athens (€60, 35 minutes). The Olympic Airlines office is at the airport, but you can buy tickets at tourist agencies.

FAST BOAT & CATAMARAN

Services depart daily for Piraeus (€40, 2½ hours), Lavrio (€35, 1¾ hours), Paros (€16, 45 minutes), Naxos (€21, 1¼ hours), Mykonos (€15, 30 minutes), Tinos (€11, 30 minutes) and Santorini (€42.50, 3¾ hours).

FERRY

There are at least four ferries departing daily from Syros to Piraeus (€24, four hours), with two going to Tinos every day except Tuesday (€5.60, two hours), and four heading to Mykonos (€8, 1¼ hours).

There are two daily ferries to Paros (€8.50, 1¾ hours) and Naxos (€11.50, three hours). There are daily connections to Andros via Tinos (€11, 2¾ hours) and two direct connections weekly (€7.40, 4¼ hours).

At least four ferries weekly go to Amorgos (€19, 4½ hours), Ios (€19.50, 2¾ hours), Milos (€11.70, six hours) and Santorini (€23, 5¼ hours), and one weekly ferry serves Crete (€23.40, 8½ hours).

At least twice weekly there are boats to Andros (€7.40, 1¾ hours), Kea (€9.40, three hours), Kythnos (€7.50, two hours), Sifnos (€8.20, four hours), Serifos (€7.50, two to four hours), Kimolos (€11.70, five hours) and Anafi (€16.80, eight hours).

Five ferries weekly go to Patmos in the Dodecanese (€26, 4½ hours).

Each week, three ferries head to Sikinos (€11.10, five hours), Folegandros (€11.70, six hours), Lavrio (€14.30, 3½ hours), and Leros in the Dodecanese (€28, seven hours).

Two ferries a week go to Kos (in the Dodecanese; €32, nine hours) and Rhodes (€38.50, 15½ hours), and one goes to Thessaloniki (€35.20, 15 hours).

Getting Around

About nine buses per day run a circular route from Ermoupolis to Galissas (€1.30, 20 minutes), Vari (€1.30, 30 minutes) and Kini (€1.50, 35 minutes). They leave Ermoupolis every half-hour from June to September and every hour the rest of the year, alternating clockwise and anticlockwise routes. All of these buses will eventually get you to where you want to go, but it's always worth checking which route is quickest.

There is a bus from Ermoupolis bus station to Ano Syros at 10.30am every morning except Sunday (€1.20, 15 minutes). **Taxis** (☎ 22810 86222) charge €6 to Ano Syros from the port.

Cars can be hired per day from about €40 and scooters per day from €12 at numerous hire outlets on the waterfront.

ERMOUPOLIS ΕΡΜΟΥΠΟΛΗ

pop 13,000

Ermoupolis grew out of the refugee town that sprang up during the Greek War of Independence. The refugees were Greek Orthodox and, after initial resentments, lived in harmony with the original Catholic majority. In 1826 the town was named formally after Hermes, the god of commerce. Ermoupolis is a lively and likeable place, full of paved stairways, restored neoclassical mansions and handsome public buildings.

The Catholic settlement of Ano Syros and the Greek Orthodox settlement of Vrodado lie to the northwest and northeast, looking inland, and both spill down from high hilltops, with even taller hills rising behind.

Orientation

The main ferry quay is at the southwestern end of the port. The bus station is on the waterfront, just along from the main ferry quay.

To reach the central square, Plateia Miaouli, walk northeast from the ferry quay for about 200m, and then turn left into El Venizelou for another 100m. There are public toilets at the eastern end of the port, off Antiparou and on Akti Papagou near the ferry quay.

Information

There is an information booth run by the Syros Hotels' Association on the waterfront, about 100m northeast of the main ferry quay; opening times are not guaranteed. The website www.syros.com has a reasonable amount of information.

Alpha Bank (El Venizelou) Has an ATM.

Enjoy Your Holidays (☎ 22810 87070; Akti Papagou 2) Opposite the bus station. Sells ferry tickets and can advise on accommodation.

Eurobank (Akti Ethnikis Andistasis) Has an ATM.

Hospital (☎ 22810 96500; Papandreos)

Internet Café (☎ 22810 85330; Ground fl, Town Hall, Plateia Miaouli; per 20min €2) Not the fastest connection.

InSpot (☎ 22810 85330; Akti Papagou; per hr €3.40; ☒ 24hr) Faster connections but often monopolised by game fans.

Piraeus Bank (Akti Petrou Ralli) Has an ATM.

Police station (☎ 22810 82610; Plateia Vardaka) Beside the Apollon Theatre.

Port police (☎ 22810 82690/88888; Plateia Laïkis Kyriarchias) On the eastern side of the port.

Post office (Protopapadaki) Offers Western Union money transfer.

Teamwork Holidays (☎ 28810 83400; www .teamwork.gr; Akti Papagou 18) Just across from the main ferry quay; very helpful and friendly. Sells ferry tickets and can arrange accommodation, excursions and car rental.

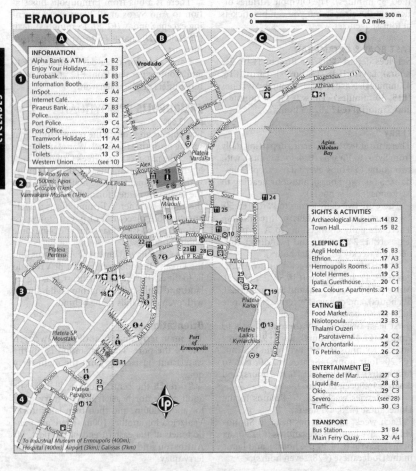

ERMOUPOLIS

0 _____ 300 m
0 _____ 0.2 miles

INFORMATION	
Alpha Bank & ATM	1 B2
Enjoy Your Holidays	2 B3
Eurobank	3 B3
Information Booth	4 B3
InSpot	5 A4
Internet Café	6 B2
Piraeus Bank	7 B3
Police	8 C2
Port Police	9 C4
Post Office	10 C2
Teamwork Holidays	11 A4
Toilets	12 A4
Toilets	13 C3
Western Union	(see 10)

SIGHTS & ACTIVITIES	
Archaeological Museum	14 B2
Town Hall	15 B2

SLEEPING	
Aegli Hotel	16 B3
Ethrion	17 A3
Hermoupolis Rooms	18 A3
Hotel Hermes	19 C3
Ipatia Guesthouse	20 C1
Sea Colours Apartments	21 D1

EATING	
Food Market	22 B3
Nisiotopoula	23 B3
Thalami Ouzeri Psarotaverna	24 C2
To Archontariki	25 C2
To Petrino	26 C2

ENTERTAINMENT	
Boheme del Mar	27 C3
Liquid Bar	28 B3
Okio	29 C3
Severo	(see 28)
Traffic	30 C3

TRANSPORT	
Bus Station	31 B4
Main Ferry Quay	32 A4

Sights

The great square of **Plateia Miaouli** is the finest urban space in the Cyclades and is worthy of Athens. Once the sea reached as far as here, but today the square is well inland and is flanked by palm trees and lined along its south side by cafés and bars. The north side of the square is dominated by the magnificent neoclassical **town hall**. The small **archaeological museum** (☎ 22810 88487; Benaki; admission €3; ☽ 8.30am-3pm Tue-Sun) at the rear, founded in 1834 and one of the oldest in Greece, houses a tiny collection of ceramic and marble vases, grave stelae and some very fine Cycladic figurines.

The **Industrial Museum of Ermoupolis** (☎ 22810 84764; Papandreos; adult/concession €3/2; ☽ 10am-2pm Wed-Mon, 6-9pm Thu-Sun Jun-Sep, 10am-2pm Mon, Thu & Fri, 10am-2pm & 6-9pm Wed, Sat & Sun Oct-May) is about 1km from the centre of town. It celebrates Syros' industrial and shipbuilding traditions and occupies old factory buildings. There are over 300 items on display.

Ano Syros, originally a medieval settlement, has narrow alleyways and whitewashed houses. It is a fascinating place to wander around and has views of neighbouring islands. Be wise and catch the bus up to the settlement. From its bus terminus, head into the steeply rising alleyways and search out the finest of the Catholic churches, the 13th-century **Agios Georgios** cathedral, with its star-fretted barrel roof and baroque capitals. Follow your nose down from the church, past stunning viewpoints to reach the main street, where you'll find the little **Vamvakaris museum** (☽ 10am-1pm Mon-Sat Jul & Aug), which celebrates the life of Markos Vamvakaris, a famous *rembetika* (blues) singer who was born in Ano Syros.

Activities

Cyclades Sailing (☎ 22810 82501; csail@otenet.gr) can organise yachting charters, as can **Nomikos Sailing** (☎ 22810 88527); call direct or book through **Teamwork Holidays** (☎ 28810 83400).

Tours

You can book a day coach trip (adult/child €20/7) round the island on Tuesday, Thursday and Saturday through **Teamwork Holidays** (☎ 28810 83400).

Sleeping

Ermoupolis has a reasonably broad selection of rooms, with most budget options clustered above the waterfront near where the ferry docks. Most places are open all year.

Ipatia Guesthouse (☎ 22810 83575; www.ipatiaguesthouse.com; Babagiotou 3; s/d with bathroom €40/65, without bathroom €30/40) Located in the Vaporia district, so called after the wealthy 19th-century *vaporia* (steamship) captains who built neoclassical mansions here. Ipatia is one such building. It overlooks Agios Nikolaos Bay and has been lovingly preserved. There's a comfy, lived-in atmosphere and the spacious rooms have antique furnishings and remnants of original ceiling frescoes. There's a warm welcome, in keeping with the house's family feel.

Hermoupolis Rooms (☎ 22810 87475; Naxou; s/d €35/50) A cheerful, family run place with clean, well-kept rooms tucked away in narrow Naxou, a short climb up from the waterfront. Front rooms open on to tiny, bougainvillea-cloaked balconies.

Sea Colours Apartments (☎ 22810 81181/83400; Athinas; s/d €50/66, apt €72) Facing Agios Nikolaos Bay, these pleasant apartments are ideally placed for the quieter end of town, yet are within a short stroll of the centre.

our pick **Ethrion** (☎ 22810 89066; www.ethrion.gr; Kosma 24; s €50, d €60-75; ☒ ☐) One of the best choices in town, these comfortable, relaxing rooms occupy a modern but traditionally designed building in a quiet location. There's a pleasant courtyard and the owner is friendly and helpful. The price range indicates rooms with or without balconies and sea views. The town centre and harbourfront are only a minute or two away.

Hotel Hermes (☎ 22810 83011; fax 22810 87412; Plateia Kanari; s/d/tr incl buffet breakfast €56/95/110) The Hermes is a long established hotel in a fine position on the eastern side of the waterfront. Public rooms are spacious and the bedrooms are smart, with bright interiors. There's a decent restaurant offering grills and pasta (mains €6.30 to €12).

Aegli Hotel (☎ 22810 79279; hotegli@otenet.gr; Klisthenous 14; s/d incl breakfast €83/100; ☒ ☐) Located in a quiet side street, this fine, peaceful hotel has an air of exclusivity. Rooms are comfortable, and upper-floor balconies at the front have great views over the port. There are good views over the town from a roof garden.

Eating

Standard restaurants and cafés throng the waterfront, especially along Akti Petrou Ralli

CYCLADES

and on the southern edge of Plateia Miaouli. However, dip into the quieter corners and you'll find places with character and good food.

Nisiotopoula (☎ 22810 81214; Antiparou 20; mains €3-7) You'll find Greek family cooking at its best at this down-to-earth taverna tucked behind the waterfront. On offer are delicious soups, pies and omelettes as well as chicken and pork dishes. A regular local clientele tells its own story.

To Archontariki (☎ 22810 81744; Emm Roidi 8; mains €5.50-12) An extensive menu of classic Greek dishes and a good selection of regional wines, including Santorini vintages, make this long-established restaurant a local favourite. Tasty starters include spinach with mushrooms, and leek pie, while lamb with artichoke and baked shrimps with tomato are typical of the appetising main dishes at the Archontariki.

To Petrino (☎ 22810 87427; Stefanou 9; mains €6-10) Swaths of bougainvillea bedeck the pleasant little enclave of Stefanou, and at its heart is the popular To Petrino. Cheerful service goes with delicious traditional dishes such as *kotopoula ala Spetsiota* (pieces of chicken fillet with peppers, tomatoes and melted cheese) and squid stuffed with feta.

our pick Thalami Ouzeri Psarotaverna (☎ 22810 85331; Kalomenopoulou 1; mains €6-18) You can eat on a balcony overlooking Agios Nikolaos Bay at this great restaurant, which occupies an old Vaporia mansion. Seafood is by the kilogram, but reasonably priced treats, such as a local *kakavia* (soup of fish, onions and tomatoes), or squid stuffed with feta cheese, green peppers and tomatoes, are only part of an excellent menu.

The best place to buy fresh produce is at the small, but well-stocked, morning **food market** (Hiou).

Entertainment

Music bars are clustered along the waterfront on Akti Petrou Ralli. They play mostly lounge music by day and a mix of house, funk and modern Greek music by night. They draw a great local crowd and rock into the early hours.

Boheme del Mar (☎ 22810 83354) Heads up the young scene.

Liquid Bar (☎ 22810 82284) About 60 metres north west of Boheme del Mar and also lively.

ELEFTHERIA *Michael Clark*

There is a distinctive type of young, modern Greek woman. Confident, wise, stylish, focused, thoughtful, fearless. And just a little bit scary. She has attitude, in the best sense of the word. On Syros there is Eleftheria Thymianou. She does not let me off with anything. 'That's a great name,' I say. 'Eleftheria equals "freedom". What do they call you for short?' I get the full weight of Greek history in my face. 'No-one shortens my name,' she says. 'That name means something...'

Severo (☎ 22810 88243) Next door to Liquid Bar, this has a great racy atmosphere and good DJs.

A couple of spirited little bars in the same area are **Traffic** (☎ 22810 86197) and **Okio** (☎ 22810 84133).

GALISSAS ΓΑΛΗΣΣΑΣ

When Ermoupolis becomes too metro for you, head west on a short bus ride to Galissas, a small resort with one of the best beaches on Syros, several cheerful bars and restaurants and some great places to stay. The main bus stop is at an intersection behind the beach.

Sleeping

Two Hearts Camping (☎ 22810 42052; www.twohearts-camping.com; camp sites per adult/child/tent €8/4/4) Set in a pistachio orchard about 400m from the village and beach, this popular camping ground has good facilities; from the main bus stop, cross the intersection and follow the signs. A minibus meets ferries in high season.

Oasis (☎ 22810 42357, 6948274933; freri_stefania@hotmail.com; s/d/studios €20/35/45) A genuine 'oasis', this lovely little farm has bright and airy rooms, and the welcome is charming. It's about 400m back from the village and is set amid olive trees and vines. Follow signs from the main bus stop intersection in the village.

Hotel Benois (☎ 22810 42833; www.benois.gr; s/d/tr incl breakfast €70/90/110, apt €150; 🅿 🖳 🌐) In recent years there's been a sparkling makeover at this family-run hotel, including the addition of a swimming pool. Courtesy and friendly service are backed up by pleasant, spick-and-span rooms. It's close to the beach at the northern entrance to the village.

Eating & Drinking

Iliovasilema (☎ 22810 43325; mains €4-12) Next door to Savvas, this is another good local eatery where fish is by the kilo, but where you can enjoy reasonably priced seafood starters and a delicious fish soup. Vegetarians can sidestep specials such as wild boar, venison and ostrich, and go for a pick'n'mix of nonmeat dishes.

Socrates (☎ 22810 43284; mains €4.50-9) Eat beneath a leafy canopy on the garden terrace at this well-run place that offers tasty dishes such as *giouvetsi* (choice pieces of lamb in a tomato sauce, baked with pasta). Turn right at the junction by the bus stop and it's about 100m on the left.

our pick **Savvas** (☎ 22810 42998; mains €6-10) Locally sourced ingredients and authentic Syran cuisine make Savvas one of the best tavernas around. Try the pork in honey and aniseed, or the chicken fillet stuffed with bacon, cheese and mushrooms. The taverna is just a few metres from the bus stop.

Also recommended is the Green Dollars Bar on the beach road, for daytime snacks and music while you drink. Rock and reggae are favourites from 10am to 4am.

AROUND SYROS

The beaches south of Galissas all have domatia (rooms, usually in a private home) and some have hotels. Some beaches are narrow roadside strips of dullish sand, but they're not too busy. They include **Finikas**, **Posidonia** and **Angathopes**. Back on the main road and on the south coast proper, the town of **Megas Gialos** has a couple of roadside beaches.

The pleasant **Vari Bay**, further east, has a sandy beach with some development, including a couple of hotels and a beachfront taverna.

Kini, out on its own on the west coast, north of Galissas, has a long stretch of beach and is developing into a popular resort with standard modern hotels, apartments, cafés and tavernas.

MYKONOS ΜΥΚΟΝΟΣ

pop 9660

Mykonos glitters happily under the sun and carries its glamorous and camp reputation with panache, but expensively so. Beneath the gloss this is a charming and hugely entertaining place where the sometimes frantic mix of good-time holidaymakers, cruise ship crowds, posturing fashionistas and preening celebrities is magically subdued by the cubist charms of Mykonos town, a traditional Cycladic maze. Local people have had 40 years to get a grip on tourism and have not lost their Greek identity in doing so.

Be prepared, however, for the oiled-up lounger lifestyle of the island's packed main beaches, the jostling street scenes and the relentless, yet sometimes forlorn, partying. That said, there's still a handful of off-track beaches worth fighting for. Plus, the stylish bars, restaurants and shops have great appeal, and you can still find a quieter pulse amid the labyrinthine old town. Add to all this the nearby sacred island of Delos, and Mykonos really does live up to its reputation as a fabulous destination.

Getting There & Away
AIR

Olympic Airlines (☎ 22890 22327; www.olympicairlines .com), based at the airport, runs two to three flights daily between Athens and Mykonos (€70, 40 minutes).

Aegean Airlines (☎ 22890 28720; www.aegeanair .com), also at the airport, has daily flights to Athens (€74, 40 minutes) and Thessaloniki (€88, one hour).

Sky Express (☎ 28102 23500; www.skyexpress.gr) has about four flights a week to Iraklio (€99, one hour and 30 minutes) via Santorini (€74, 35 minutes) and one flight a week direct to Iraklio (45 minutes). It also runs four flights a week to Rhodes (€119, two hours) via Santorini. You can book tickets through Mykonos Accommodation Centre (p145).

Until suspension of operations in July of 2007, **AirSea Lines** (☎ toll free 801 11 800 600; www .airsealines.com) ran one seaplane flight a day from Thursday to Monday between Lavrio and Mykonos. It also ran one flight daily, Thursday to Monday, between Mykonos and Kalymnos, and Kos. Due to upgrading requirements the company suspended its Aegean schedule in July 2007. The schedule was still suspended at the time of writing (September 2007). The company states, however, that it will resume its Aegean service as soon as possible and readers are advised to check the company website.

FAST BOAT & CATAMARAN

There are at least three daily services connecting Mykonos with Tinos (€9.50, 15 minutes).

CYCLADES

Four daily services go to Rafina (€39.90, two hours) and three go to Piraeus (€48, three hours) and Syros (€15, 30 minutes). There are three daily services to Paros (€17, one hour), which connect with services to Naxos (€19.50, 1½ hours), Santorini (€28, three to four hours) and Ios (€26.10, 2¾ hours). One service daily continues to Iraklio on Crete (€47.90, five hours).

FERRY

Mykonos has two ferry quays: the Old Port, 400m north of town, where some conventional ferries and smaller fast ferries dock; and the New Port, 2km north of town, where the bigger fast ferries and some conventional ferries dock. This is not a hard and fast rule, and when buying outgoing tickets you should always double-check which quay your ferry leaves from. There are bus connections to the New Port from the northern bus station (see Bus, right) and the Old Port (€1.20, 10 minutes); a taxi to the New Port is €4.

Mykonos has daily services to Rafina (€21.40, 4½ hours) via Tinos (€4.50, 30 minutes) and Andros (€11, 2½ hours), and to Piraeus (€24.50, six hours) via Tinos and Syros (€7, 1½ hours).

There are three ferries a week to Santorini (€15, six hours).

There is one ferry a week to Thessaloniki (€37.30, 18½ hours) and Crete (€23.90, 13 hours).

There are three ferries a week to Samos (€21.50, 4½ hours) and Ikaria (€15.50, 2¼ hours).

Getting Around
TO/FROM THE AIRPORT

Buses from the southern bus station serve Mykonos' airport (€1.20), which is 3km southeast of the town centre. Make sure you arrange an airport transfer with your accommodation (expect to pay around €6) or take a **taxi** (☎ 22890 22400, airport 22890 23700); there's a fixed fare of €5.90.

BUS

Hora (Mykonos) has two main bus stations and a pick-up point at the New Port. The **northern bus station** (☎ 22890 23360; Remezzo) is behind the OTE office and has frequent departures

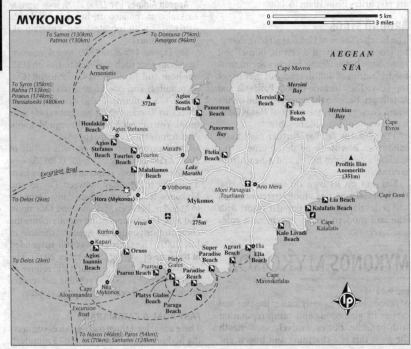

MYKONOS

0 — 5 km
0 — 3 miles

To Samos (130km);
Patmos (130km)

To Donousa (75km);
Amorgos (96km)

AEGEAN SEA

Cape Armenistis

Cape Mavros

To Syros (35km);
Rafina (133km);
Piraeus (174km);
Thessaloniki (480km)

372m

Agios Sostis Beach

Panormos Beach

Mersini Beach

Mersini Bay

Fokos Beach

Merchias Bay

Houlakia Beach

Agios Stefanos

Panormos Bay

Cape Evros

Agios Stefanos Beach

Tourlos Beach

Tourlos

Marathi

Ftelia Beach

Malaliamos Beach

Lake Marathi

Excursion Boat

Vothonas

Moni Panagias Tourlianis

Ano Mera

Profitis Ilias Anomeritis (351m)

To Delos (2km)

Hora (Mykonos)

Mykonos

Lia Beach

Kalafatis Beach

Cape Goni

Cape Kalalatis

Vrissi

275m

Korfos

Kalo Livadi Beach

Kapari

To Delos (2km)

Ornos

Agios Ioannis Beach

Psarou

Platys Gialos

Super Paradise Beach

Agrari Beach

Elia

Elia Beach

Psarou Beach

Paradise Beach

Cape Alogomandra

Nea Mykonos

Platys Gialos Beach

Paraga Beach

Cape Mavrokefalas

Excursion Boat

To Naxos (46km); Paros (54km);
Ios (70km); Santorini (128km)

CYCLADES

to Agios Stefanos via Tourlos (€1.20), and services to Ano Mera, (€1.20), Elia (€1.50), and Kalafatis Beach (€1.70). Trips range from 20 minutes to 40 minutes. There are two buses daily to Kalo Livadi Beach (€1.50). Buses for the New Port, Tourlos and Agios Stefanos stop at the Old Port. The **southern bus station** (☎ 22890 23360; Fabrika Sq [Plateias Yralos]) serves Agios Ioannis Beach (€1.20), Ornos, (€1.20), Platys Gialos (€1.20), Paraga (€1.20) and Paradise Beach (€1.50). Trips range from 15 minutes to 40 minutes.

Bus tickets are sold at street kiosks, minimarkets and tourist shops. You must buy a ticket before boarding (buy return tickets if required), validate the ticket on the bus and hang on to it. From 12.15am to 6am all prices are €1.50.

CAÏQUE
Caïque (little boat) services leave Hora (Mykonos) for Super Paradise, Agrari and Elia Beaches (June to September only) and from Platys Gialos to Paradise (€6), Super Paradise (€7), Agrari (€6) and Elia (€6) Beaches.

CAR & MOTORCYCLE
For cars, expect to pay (depending on model) about €40 to €98 per day in high season, or €31 to €80 in low season. For scooters it's about €15 to €30 in high season, €10 to €20 in low season. Reliable hire agencies are the **Mykonos Accommodation Centre** (p145) and **O.K. Rent A Car** (☎ 22890 23761; Agio Stefanos). There are several car and motorcycle rental firms around the southern bus station in Hora.

TAXI
If you're after a **taxi** (☎ 22400 23700/22400), you'll find them at Hora's Taxi Sq (Plateia Manto Mavrogenous) and by the bus stations and ports. The minimum fare is €2.85, but there's a charge of €0.30 for each item of luggage. Fares to beaches: Agios Stefanos €4, Ornos €4.40, Platys Gialos €5.90, Paradise €7.20 and Elia €11.40.

HORA (MYKONOS)
ΧΩΡΑ (ΜΥΚΟΝΟΣ)
pop 6467

Mykonos (also known as Hora), the island's port and capital, is a warren of narrow alleyways that wriggle between white-walled buildings, their stone surfaces webbed with

white paint. In the heart of the Little Venice area, tiny flower-bedecked churches jostle with trendy boutiques, and there's a deluge of bougainvillea round every corner. Without question, you will soon pass the same junction twice. It's entertaining at first, but can become frustrating as throngs of equally lost people and pushy Mykonos veterans add to the stress. For quick-fix navigation, familiarise yourself with main junctions and the three main streets of Matogianni, Enoplon Dynameon and Mitropoleos, which form a horseshoe behind the waterfront. The streets are crowded with chic fashion salons, cool galleries, jangling jewellers, languid and loud music bars, brightly painted houses and torrents of crimson flowers – plus a catwalk cast of thousands.

Orientation
The town proper is about 400m to the south of the Old Port ferry quay, beyond the tiny town beach. A busy square, Plateia Manto Mavrogenous (usually called Taxi Sq), is 100m beyond the beach and on the edge of Hora. East of Taxi Sq, the busy waterfront leads towards the Little Venice neighbourhood and the town's iconic hilltop row of windmills. South of Taxi Sq and the waterfront, the busy streets of Matogianni, Zouganelli and Mavrogenous lead into the heart of Hora.

The northern bus station is 200m south of the Old Port ferry quay, on the way into town. The southern bus station is on Fabrika Sq, on the southern edge of town. The quay from where boats leave for Delos is at the western end of the waterfront.

Information
BOOKSHOPS
International Press (☎ 22890 23316; Kambani 5) Numerous international newspapers, although editions are a day late. Also a very wide range of magazines and books.

EMERGENCY
Police station (☎ 22890 22716) On the road to the airport.
Port police (☎ 22890 22218; Akti Kambani) Midway along the waterfront.
Tourist police (☎ 22890 22482) At the airport.

INTERNET ACCESS
Angelo's Internet Café (☎ 22890 24106; Xenias; per hr €4.50) On the road between the southern bus station and the windmills.

HORA (MYKONOS)

0   200 m
0   0.1 miles

CYCLADES

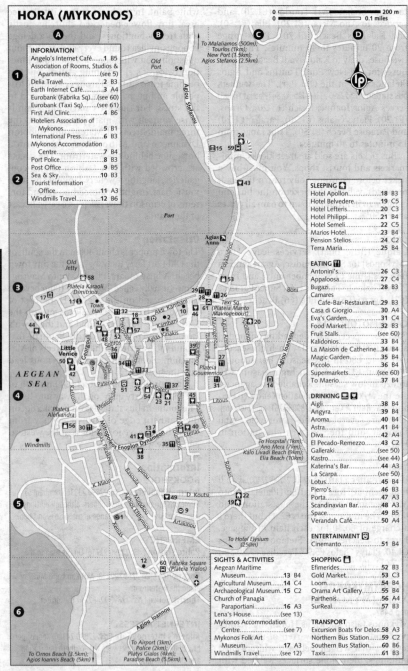

INFORMATION
Angelo's Internet Café......**1** B5
Association of Rooms, Studios &
  Apartments...............(see 5)
Delia Travel.....................**2** B3
Earth Internet Café...........**3** A4
Eurobank (Fabrika Sq)....(see 60)
Eurobank (Taxi Sq)........(see 61)
First Aid Clinic.................**4** B6
Hoteliers Association of
  Mykonos......................**5** B1
International Press............**6** B3
Mykonos Accommodation
  Centre........................**7** B4
Port Police......................**8** B3
Post Office......................**9** B5
Sea & Sky.....................**10** B3
Tourist Information
  Office.........................**11** A3
Windmills Travel.............**12** B6

SLEEPING 🛏
Hotel Apollon.................**18** B3
Hotel Belvedere..............**19** C5
Hotel Lefteris.................**20** C3
Hotel Philippi.................**21** B4
Hotel Semeli..................**22** C5
Marios Hotel..................**23** B4
Pension Stelios...............**24** C2
Terra Maria...................**25** B4

EATING 🍴
Antonini's......................**26** C3
Appaloosa......................**27** C4
Bugazi..........................**28** B3
Camares
  Cafe-Bar-Restaurant.....**29** B3
Casa di Giorgio...............**30** A4
Eva's Garden..................**31** B4
Food Market..................**32** B3
Fruit Stalls...................(see 60)
Kalidonios.....................**33** B4
La Maison de Catherine....**34** B4
Magic Garden..................**35** B4
Piccolo..........................**36** B4
Supermarkets................(see 60)
To Maerio......................**37** B4

DRINKING 🍷 🍸
Aigli.............................**38** B4
Angyra..........................**39** B4
Aroma...........................**40** B4
Astra.............................**41** B4
Diva..............................**42** A4
El Pecado-Remezzo..........**43** C2
Galleraki.....................(see 50)
Kastro.........................(see 44)
Katerina's Bar................**44** A3
La Scarpa.....................(see 50)
Lotus............................**45** B4
Pierro's.........................**46** B3
Porta............................**47** A3
Scandinavian Bar............**48** A3
Space............................**49** B5
Verandah Café................**50** A4

ENTERTAINMENT 📽
Cinemanto.....................**51** B4

SHOPPING 🛍
Efimerides.....................**52** B3
Gold Market...................**53** C3
Loom............................**54** B4
Orama Art Gallery...........**55** B4
Parthenis.......................**56** A4
SurReal.........................**57** B3

TRANSPORT
Excursion Boats for Delos.**58** A3
Northern Bus Station.......**59** C2
Southern Bus Station.......**60** B6
Taxis............................**61** B3

SIGHTS & ACTIVITIES
Aegean Maritime
  Museum......................**13** B4
Agricultural Museum.......**14** C4
Archaeological Museum..**15** C2
Church of Panagia
  Paraportiani................**16** A3
Lena's House.................(see 13)
Mykonos Accommodation
  Centre.......................(see 7)
Mykonos Folk Art
  Museum......................**17** A3
Windmills Travel............(see 12)

To Malaliamos (500m);
Tourlos (1km);
New Port (1.5km);
Agios Stefanos (2.5km)

Old Port

Old Jetty

Port

Agias Anna

Boni

Little Venice

AEGEAN SEA

Town Hall

Plateia Karaoli Dimitriou

Taxi Sq (Plateia Manto Mavrogenous)

Plateia Gourneniou

Plateia Alefkandra

Windmills

To Hospital (1km);
Ano Mera (7km);
Kalo Livadi Beach (9km);
Elia Beach (10km)

Fabrika Square (Plateia Yralos)

To Hotel Elysium (250m)

To Ornos Beach (3.5km);
Agios Ioannis Beach (5km)

To Airport (3km);
Police (2km);
Platys Gialos (4km);
Paradise Beach (5.5km)

Earth Internet Café (☎ 22890 22791; Zani Pitaraki 4; per 15min €1)

MEDICAL SERVICES
First Aid Clinic (☎ 22890 22274; Agiou Ioannou)
Hospital (☎ 22890 23994) Located about 1km along the road to Ano Mera.

MONEY
Several banks by the Old Port quay have ATMs. Eurobank has ATMs at Taxi Sq and Fabrika Sq.

POST
Post office (☎ 22890 22238; Laka) In the southern part of town.

TOURIST INFORMATION
Tourist Information Office (☎ 22890 25250; www .mykonos.gr; Plateia Karaoli Dimitriou; ✪ 9am-9pm Jul & Aug, 10am-5pm Easter-Jun, Sep & Oct) This is a new venture for Mykonos, introduced in 2007. It's run by the municipality and at the time of writing was just getting into gear with a few leaflets, maps and information printouts. Time will tell.

TRAVEL AGENCIES
Delia Travel (☎ 22890 22322; travel@delia.gr; Akti Kambani) Halfway along the inner waterfront. Sells ferry tickets and tickets for Delos. It's also the French Consulate.
Mykonos Accommodation Centre (☎ 22890 23408; www.mykonos-accommodation.com; 1st fl, Enoplon Dynameon 10) Well-organised and very helpful for a range of information, including gay related. Can also arrange midrange, top-end and gay-friendly accommodation.
Sea & Sky (☎ 22890 22853; Akti Kambani) Offers information and ferry tickets.
Windmills Travel (☎ 22890 23877; www.windmills travel.com; Fabrika Sq) By the southern bus station, this is another helpful office for all types of information, including gay related. Also sells ferry tickets.

Sights
MUSEUMS
Mykonos has five museums. The **archaeological museum** (☎ 22890 22325; adult/concession €2/1; ✪ 8.30am-3pm Tue-Sat, 10am-3pm Sun) houses pottery from Delos and some grave stelae and jewellery from the island of Renia (Delos' necropolis). Chief exhibits include a statue of Hercules in Parian marble.

The **Aegean Maritime Museum** (☎ 22890 22700; Tria Pigadia; adult/concession €3/1.50; ✪ 10.30am-1pm & 6-9pm Apr-Oct) has a fascinating collection of nautical paraphernalia, including ships' models.

Next door, **Lena's House** (☎ 22890 22390; Tria Pigadia; admission free, donations appreciated; ✪ 6.30-9.30pm Mon-Sat, 7-9pm Sun Apr-Oct) is a charming late-19th-century, middle-class Mykonian house (with furnishings intact). It takes its name from its last owner, Lena Skrivanou.

The **Mykonos Folk Art Museum** (☎ 6932178330; Paraportianis; admission free; ✪ 5.30-8.30pm Mon-Sat, 6.30-8.30pm Sun Apr-Oct), housed in an 18th-century sea captain's house, features a large collection of furnishings and other artefacts, including old musical instruments.

The **agricultural museum** (☎ 22890 22748; Agiou Ioannou; admission free; ✪ 4.30-7.30pm Mon-Sat, 5.30-7.30pm Sun Jun-Sep) has displays including a renovated windmill, a miller's house, a threshing floor, and a wine press and other artefacts.

CHURCH OF PANAGIA PARAPORTIANI
Mykonos' most famous church is the rocklike **Panagia Paraportiani** (beyond Delos ferry quay on the way to Little Venice; admission free, donations appreciated; ✪ variable, usually open mornings). It comprises four small chapels plus another on an upper storey that is reached by an outside staircase. Visitors should avoid entering during services, unless for genuine worship rather than sightseeing.

Tours
Mykonos Accommodation Centre (☎ 22890 23408; www.mykonos-accommodation.com; 1st fl, Enoplon Dynameon 10) Organises guided tours to Delos (see p150). The centre also offers tours to Tinos, as well as Mykonos bus tours and boat cruises, wine and culture tours, and exclusive gay boat cruises.
Windmills Travel (☎ 22890 23877; www.windmills travel.com; Fabrika Sq) The booking agent for snorkelling (€25 for 30 minutes) and island cruises (€35 to €55, four weekly).

Sleeping
There are scores of sleeping options in Mykonos, but if you arrive without a reservation between July and September and you find reasonably priced accommodation, grab it – 'budget' in Mykonos is relative, and this is reflected in the listings.

Otherwise, check out the local accommodation organisations – when you get off at the town ferry quay, you will see a low building with numbered offices. Number 1 is the **Hoteliers Association of Mykonos** (☎ 22890 24540; www .mha.gr; Old Port; ✪ 8am-midnight). The Association will book a room on the spot, but does not accept telephone bookings prior to your arrival.

CYCLADES

Number 2 is the **Association of Rooms, Studios & Apartments** (☎ 22890 24860; www.mykonosfamilyhotels .com; ☺ 9am-10pm May-Sep, 9am-4pm Oct-Apr). If you choose domatia from the owners who meet ferries – they rev up into one of the most raucous scrums in the Cyclades – check their exact location and ask if they charge for transport (some do).

If you plan to stay in Hora and want somewhere quiet, think carefully before settling for domatia on the main streets – bar noise until dawn is inevitable.

Some places only advertise doubles, but single occupancy may be negotiable. During late July and early August some hotels will only accept a minimum of three-night stays.

BUDGET

Hotel Philippi (☎ 22890 22294; chriko@otenet.gr; Kalogera 25; s €60-70, d €70-110; ☒) A pleasant garden full of trees, flowers and shrubs makes this a great choice in the heart of Hora. There's an appealing ambience in the bright, clean rooms that open onto a railed veranda overlooking the garden.

MIDRANGE

Pension Stelios (☎ 22890 24641, 6944273556; s/d/tr €85/100/130) A straightforward but well-equipped pension, Stelios has a hillside location halfway between the Old Port and town but is only a few minutes from the centre. There are great views over Hora from some of the small balconies. There are very good discounts in low season.

Hotel Apollon (☎ 22890 22223; fax 22890 24456; Akti Kambani; d with/without shower €90/65) An unashamed slice of traditional Mykonos in a prime position on the waterfront; the Apollon has old-fashioned furnishings to go with its well-kept rooms. The cheerful owner has survived the trendy gloss that has engulfed much of Hora.

Hotel Lefteris (☎ 22890 27117; lefterishot@yahoo.com; Apollonos 9; s/d €90/115, studios €180-230) A colourful entranceway sets the tone for this refuge from the mainstream hubbub of town. Tucked away just up from Taxi Sq, the Lefteris is something of an international meeting place for all ages. The conversation is always good, and the welcome is kind and friendly. Rooms are simple but comfy and bright, and the roof terrace is a great place to relax. Studios are well equipped and the hotel has other rooms nearby.

Terra Maria (☎ 22890 24212; www.terramariahotel .com; Kalogera; d €120; ☒ ▢) Sidestepping the busier streets, this cool, relaxing place has bright, clean rooms and friendly staff. There's a leafy garden to go with the bright décor. One room is equipped for disabled use. Low season prices drop substantially.

Marios Hotel (☎ 22890 24670; www.marioshotel -mykonos.com; Kalogera 31; s/d incl breakfast €120/135; ☒ ▢) Located right in the heart of town and all its action, gay friendly Marios has a pleasant central garden, an attractive breakfast room and bar, and a Jacuzzi. Rooms have wooden floors and furnishings are a pleasant mix of old and new.

TOP END

Hotel Elysium (☎ 22890 23952; www.elysiumhotel.com; s €210-280, d €230-300, tr €360; ☺ Apr-Oct; ▣ ☒ ▢ ▣) Located high above the main town in the School of Fine Arts area, this stylish gay hotel (although non-gays are also welcome) has cool décor and good-sized comfortable rooms. There are plenty of special trimmings, including personal computers in suites and deluxe rooms, and there's a spa and massage service.

Hotel Belvedere (☎ 22890 25122; www.belvedere hotel.com; Rohari; s €236-460, d €546-706; ▣ ☒ ▢ ▣) It's all billowing drapes and white linen amid the modernist landscape and furnishings of this leading Mykonos hotel, where sea and town views are panoramic in all but the cheapest rooms. There's also a restaurant with Japanese and South American influences. Jacuzzis, massage therapy, a fitness studio, a music and movie library and wi-fi seal the deal.

Hotel Semeli (☎ 22890 27466; www.semelihotel.gr; Rohari; s/d €286/310, studios €370-500; ▣ ☒ ▢ ▣) Adjacent to the Belvedere, the Semeli has the same level of luxury, but in a more traditional Cycladic style of white and pastel décor.

Eating

High prices don't necessarily reflect high quality in many Mykonos eateries. There are, however, excellent good-value restaurants of all kinds.

BUDGET

our pick Piccolo (☎ 22890 22208; Drakopoulou 18; snacks €3.70-7.50) There are no linen-draped tables at this impeccable little place, but the food is delicious, from crisp, fresh salads to a great selection of sandwich fillings that include Mykonian prosciutto, *manouri* (soft cheese), tomato and oregano, smoked eel or salmon.

Antonini's (☎ 22890 22319; Taxi Sq; dishes €5.50-9) A long-standing local hang-out with standard, but reliable, Greek food and a view of all of Mykonos passing by.

There's a cluster of cheap fast-food outlets and creperies around town:

Bugazi (☎ 22890 24066; snacks €2.50-5) Off the edge of Taxi Sq.

Taki's (☎ 22890 24848; Agion Saranta) A popular place with locals, Taki's dishes out kebabs and souvlaki for €2, and other budget fillers for €5 to €7.

There are also several supermarkets and fruit stalls, particularly around the southern bus station area, and there's a food market on the waterfront where Mykonos' famous pelicans hang out.

MIDRANGE & TOP END

Magic Garden (☎ 22890 26217; Tourlianis; dishes €8-15) There's a genuine garden ambience beyond the welcoming entrance bar of this long-standing and well-run restaurant. The food is prepared with a subtle touch to create delicious dishes such as shrimps in ouzo, and baked lamb with yogurt, garlic and nutmeg.

To Maerio (☎ 22890 28825; Kalogera 16; dishes €6.50-19) A simple, unpretentious menu of Mykonian favourites has earned this new eatery a good reputation. The mainly meat and poultry dishes include treats such as pieces of veal and pork in fresh tomato sauce, and beef fillet with parmesan in a wine sauce. Starters are just as tasty and there's a range of good salads.

our pick Kalidonios (☎ 22890 27606; cnr Dilou & Gerasimou; mains €8.90-20.50) The chef-owner and staff at this enjoyable restaurant put heart and soul into their work, and the results are outstanding. Try the savory *kolokythokeftedhes* (fried zucchini balls) or *imam baïldi* (baked eggplant stuffed with chopped onion, garlic, parsley, tomatoes and feta) – it's worth getting your tongue around the name, and then the food. Casseroles and *mousakas* (sliced eggplant and mincemeat arranged in layers and baked – made the way it should be) add to the feast. Desserts are delicious. House wines and a worthy wine list complement the food, while the surroundings are relaxing and the service enthusiastic and friendly.

Appaloosa (☎ 22890 27086; Mavrogenous 1, Plateia Goumeniou; mains €8-22) International cuisine with a Mexican influence sets the tone at this friendly, popular, stylish place. Starters have great taste, in every sense, and there are salads, grills and pasta dishes, too. A hot line

in tequila and cocktails goes with the cool background sounds.

Eva's Garden (☎ 22890 22160; Plateia Goumeniou; dishes €9-27) Family run for many years, this is one of Hora's most reliable bets for authentic Greek cooking. There's everything from simple dishes such as dolmades and spinach pie to generous meat treats.

La Maison de Catherine (☎ 22890 22169; cnr Gerasimou & Nikou; meals €22-40) Classic Greek cuisine of the highest order – with a magic touch of subtle, international influences – ensures 'Catrine's' remains Mykonos' top restaurant. Relax in stylish surroundings over home-marinaded anchovies with endives and tomato coulis, or lamb ribs in a delicious rosemary-flavoured sauce.

Also recommended:

Camares Cafe-Bar-Restaurant (☎ 22890 28570; Akti Kambani; dishes €5-15) On the waterfront just round from Taxi Sq. It offers decent helpings of meat dishes, salads and seafood.

Casa di Giorgio (☎ 6932561998; Mitropoleos; mains €5-22) Delicious pizzas and pastas, as well as good meat and seafood dishes, served on a big terrace.

Drinking

Halfway along Matogianni is the stylish **Lotus** (☎ 22890 22881; Matogianni 47), where you can sip drinks at the bar to the soothing strains of classical music. It also serves food.

Hora's Little Venice quarter (Venetia) is not exactly the Grand Canal, but it does offer the Mediterranean at your feet as well as rosy sunsets, windmill views, glowing candles and a swath of colourful bars. The music meanders through smooth soul and easy listening, but at quieter times bar staff play more esoteric and sharper sounds. A good spot is the friendly **Galleraki** (☎ 22890 27188; Little Venice), which turns out superb cocktails. Nearby, it's the sunset view at **Verandah Café** (☎ 22890 27400; Little Venice) while **La Scarpa** (☎ 22890 23294; Little Venice) lets you lean back from the sea on its cosy cushions. Further north, **Katerina's Bar** (☎ 22890 23084; Agion Anargyron) has a cool balcony and eases you into the evening's action with relaxing sounds.

Deeper into town, the relentlessly stylish **Aroma** (☎ 22890 27148; Enoplon Dynameon; ☼ breakfast-late) sits on a strategic corner, providing the evening catwalk view. It's open for breakfast and coffee as well.

Further down Enoplon Dynameon is **Astra** (☎ 22890 24767), where the décor is modernist Mykonos at its best, and where some of

CYCLADES

THERE BE PIRATES

Pirates push people about and in the Cyclades of old, the story is that they pushed coastal communities to build new towns inland, out of sight of the sea and high up, if possible.

The mazelike alleyways of Hora (Mykonos) and of a score of other Cycladic villages are said to have evolved as a way of confusing raiders, although the records show that pirates got their way eventually.

Seventeenth century writer George Wheler said of Mykonos, 'The greatest part of the inhabitants are Pyrats…' He went on to describe how the pirates kept their wives, children and mistresses on the island and that the women of Mykonos had 'a greater reputation for beauty than chastity.'

The Greek islands have certainly had their fair share of villains. In Greek hagiography it is usually Turkish or North African pirates who get the blame, yet even the Rhodes-based Knights of St John were lightly disguised freebooters as they sailed along the thin line between crime and enterprise.

Athens' top DJs feed the ambience with rock, funk, house and drum'n'bass. Just across from Astra, cocktail-cool **Aigli** (☎ 22890 27265) has another useful terrace for people-watching. Matogianni has a couple of music bars, including **Angyra** (☎ 22890 24273), which sticks with easy listening and mainstream.

Scandinavian Bar (☎ 22890 22669; Ioanni Voinovich 9) is mainstream mayhem with ground-floor bars and a space upstairs for close-quarters moving to dance and retro hits. The cocktail nomenclature is sometimes as cheap as the prices.

For big action into the dawn, **Space** (☎ 22890 24100; Laka) is the place. The night builds superbly through a mix of techno, house and progressive, and the bar-top dancing fires up the late-night action. **El Pecado-Remezzo** (☎ 22890 24100; Polykandrioti) is run by the Space team but features lounge and dance for a more relaxing scene. Entry is around €20 to each of the clubs.

GAY BARS
Stylish fashion and sun-seducing indulgence have made Mykonos one of the world's great gay-friendly destinations. Gay life is less overt here, but Hora has many gay-centric clubs and hang-outs from where the late night crowds spill out onto the streets.

Kastro (☎ 22890 23072; Agion Anargyron) With a leaning towards stylish classical sounds, this is a good place to start the night on cocktails as the sun sets on Little Venice.

Diva (☎ 22890 27271; K Georgouli) A great upbeat atmosphere makes this a Mykonos favourite with a mixed crowd and a loyal lesbian core.

Porta (☎ 22890 27807; Ioanni Voinovich) Head downstairs into Porta's cruisey ambience

where things get crowded and cosy towards midnight.

Pierro's (☎ 22890 22177; Agias Kyriakis) Longstanding last stop for the nightwatch, where things round off with a backdrop of heavy-beat house and superbly over-the-top drag action. Takes over the outdoors, also.

Entertainment
Cinemanto (☎ 22890 27190; Pitaraki; admission €9; ⌚ summer) Screenings are at 9pm and 11pm in the garden setting of this open-air cinema, which runs new films every few days. Most are English language films and any Greek films usually have English subtitles. There's a bar and you can get a tasty *souvlaki* (cubes of meat on skewers) for €2.50.

Shopping
The entire style scene vies for attention throughout Hora's streets and includes Lacoste, Dolce & Gabbana, Naf Naf, Diesel and Body Shop. But for something special, try **Parthenis** (☎ 22890 23089; Plateia Alefkandra), featuring the couture – in black-and-white only – of Athens designer and long-time Mykonos resident Dimitris Parthenis.

The **Orama Art Gallery** (☎ 22890 26339; Fournakia), off Enoplon Dynameon, shows the highly original work of Louis Orosko and Dorlies Schapitz. **Efimerides** (☎ 22890 79180; Drakopoulou 4) has an intriguing selection of *objets d'art*, and right opposite is **SurReal** (☎ 22890 28323; Drakopoulou 1), which specialises in leaflike leatherware. **Loom** (☎ 22890 27935; Kalogera 43) has a collection of beautiful rugs, wall hangings, throws and other pieces.

Jewellery shops are a Mykonos fixture but a good bet is **Gold Market** (☎ 22890 22770; Polykandrioti), right at the entrance to town.

CYCLADES

AROUND MYKONOS
Beaches

Mykonos' beaches are in good supply and most have golden sand and attractive locations. They're not big enough for you to escape the crowds, and they're extremely popular and busy. Do not expect seclusion, especially from June onwards, although there is often a sense of *exclusion* as various cliques commandeer the sun loungers; segregation zones for style and sheer snobbery dominate at some locations.

You need to be a party person for the likes of Paradise and Super Paradise. It can all get very claustrophobic, but it's heaven for the gregarious. Most beaches have a varied clientele, and attitudes to toplessness and nudity also vary, but what's accepted at each beach is obvious when you get there.

The nearest beaches to Hora (Mykonos), which are also the island's least glamorous beaches, are **Malaliamos**; the tiny and crowded **Tourlos**, 2km to the north; and **Agios Stefanos**, 2km beyond. About 3.5km south of Hora is the packed and noisy **Ornos**, from where you can hop onto boats for other beaches. Just west is **Agios Ioannis**. The sizable package-holiday resort of **Platys Gialos** is 4km from Hora on the southwest coast. All of the above beaches are family orientated.

Platys Gialos is the caïque jumping-off point for the glitzier beaches to the east, such as Paradise and Super Paradise.

Approximately 1km south of Platys Gialos you'll find the pleasant **Paraga Beach**, which has a small gay section. About 2km east of here is the famous **Paradise**, which is not a recognised gay beach, but has a lively younger scene. **Super Paradise** (aka **Plintri** or **Super P**) has a fully gay section. Mixed and gay-friendly **Elia** is the last caïque stop, and a few minutes' walk from here is the small and pleasant **Agrari**. Nudity is fairly commonplace on all of these beaches.

North-coast beaches can be exposed to the *meltemi* (northeasterly wind), but **Panormos** and **Agios Sostis** are fairly sheltered and becoming more popular. Both have a mix of gay and nongay devotees.

For out-of-the-way beaching you need to head for the likes of **Lia** on the southeast coast, or the smaller **Fokos** and **Mersini** on the east coast, but you'll need tough wheels and undercarriage to get there.

ACTIVITIES

Dive Adventures (☎ 22890 26539; www.diveadventures .gr; Paradise Beach) offers a full range of diving courses with multilingual instructors. Two introductory dives cost €110; snorkelling costs €30. There are various dive packages starting with a five-dive deal for €199.

On a great location at the delightful Kalafatis Beach, **Planet Windsailing** (☎ 22890 72345; www.pezi-huber.com; Kalafatis Beach) offers one-hour or one-day windsurfing for €22 or €55 respectively, or a three-hour beginner's course for €75.

Also at Kalafatis, the friendly **Kalafati Dive Center** (☎ 22890 71677; www.mykonos-diving.com; Kalafatis Beach) has the full range of diving courses including a 10-boat dive deal for €320. A single boat dive with tank and weights costs €35, or with all equipment €50. A 'discover scuba diving' session is €45.

SLEEPING
Budget

Mykonos Camping (☎ 22890 24578; www.mycamp .gr; camp sites per adult/child/tent €10/5/5, bungalows per person €15-30, apt €180-235) This is a decent budget option by the pleasant Paraga Beach (a 10-minute walk from Platys Gialos), and has reasonable facilities and bungalows and apartments that sleep two to six people.

Midrange & Top End

Princess of Mykonos (☎ 22890 23806; fax 22890 23031; s/d/tr incl breakfast €148/190/216; P ⊠ 🖳 🖭) Seaview rooms are the most expensive at this swish hotel, which merges traditional island style with Art Deco touches. The hotel is above the fairly oversubscribed Agios Stefanos beach.

Ornos Beach Hotel (☎ 22890 23216; fax 22890 22483; s or d incl breakfast €165-195; P ⊠ 🖭) Overlooking the busy beach, the traditional-style Ornos is right in the middle of the action and is handy for beach-hopping caïques.

EATING

our pick **Christos** (☎ 22890 26850; Agios Ioannis Beach; mains €6-15) Fisherman-chef and sculptor Christos runs his beachside eatery with unassuming style. It's right on the 'Shirley Valentine' shoreline, but Christos really is authentic Mykonos, where the best fish and seafood is prepared with skill. The mood is cool and relaxing around plates of superb *astakos* (lobster) plucked fresh from a huge sea water storage basin at the centre of the restaurant. Some of Christo's sculptures can be seen on the beach out front.

Tasos Trattoria (☎ 22890 23002; Paraga Beach; mains €9-19) Central to Paraga Beach, this popular taverna offers terrific fish, chicken, pork and veal dishes and a great mix of veggie options.

ENTERTAINMENT
Cavo Paradiso (☎ 22890 27205; www.cavoparadiso.gr) When dawn gleams just over the horizon, hard core bar-hoppers move from Hora (Mykonos) to Cavo Paradiso, the megaclub that's been blasting at Paradise Beach since 1993 and has featured top international DJs ever since.

Ano Mera Ανω Μέρα
The village of Ano Mera, 7km east of Hora, is the island's only inland settlement and is worth a passing visit as an antidote to Hora and the beaches. It's a fairly unassuming place with a big central square flanked on three sides by tavernas. There's a big car park adjoining the main square.

The 6th-century **Moni Panagias Tourlianis** (☎ 22890 71249; ☼ 9am-1pm & 2-7.30pm) has a fine multistage marble bell tower with elegant carvings and 16th-century icons painted by members of the Cretan School, but pride of place goes to an exquisite wooden iconostasis carved in Florence in the late 1700s.

The central square is surrounded by tavernas; popular **Vangelis** (☎ 22890 71577; dishes €4.50-12) offers tasty spit roasts and fish dishes including *kakavia*.

DELOS ΔΗΛΟΣ

The Cyclades fulfil their collective name *(kyklos)* by encircling the sacred island of **Delos** (☎ 22890 22259; museum & sites adult/concession €5/3; ☼ 8.30am-3pm Tue-Sun), but Mykonos clutches the island jealously to its heart. Delos has no permanent population and is a soothing contrast to the relentless liveliness of modern Mykonos, although in high summer you share it all with fellow visitors. The island is one of the most important archaeological sites in Greece and the most important in the Cyclades. It lies a few kilometres off the west coast of Mykonos.

History
Delos won early acclaim as the mythical birthplace of the twins Apollo and Artemis and was first inhabited in the 3rd millennium BC. From the 8th century BC it became a shrine to Apollo and the oldest temples on the island date from this era. The dominant Athenians had full control of Delos – and thus the Aegean – by the 5th century BC.

In 478 BC Athens established an alliance known as the Delian League, which kept its treasury on Delos. A cynical decree ensured that no-one could be born or die on Delos, thus strengthening Athens' control over the island by expelling the native population.

Delos reached the height of its power in Hellenistic times, becoming one of the three most important religious centres in Greece and a flourishing centre of commerce. Many of its inhabitants were wealthy merchants, mariners and bankers from as far away as Egypt and Syria. They built temples to their homeland gods, but Apollo remained the principal deity.

The Romans made Delos a free port in 167 BC. This brought even greater prosperity, due largely to a lucrative slave market that sold up to 10,000 people a day. During the following century, as ancient religions lost relevance and trade routes shifted, Delos began a long, painful decline. By the 3rd century AD there was only a small Christian settlement on the island, and in the following centuries the ancient site was looted of many of its antiquities. It was not until the Renaissance that its antiquarian value was recognised.

Getting There & Away
Boats for Delos (return €8, 30 minutes) leave Hora (Mykonos) at 9am, 9.50am, 10.15am, 11.10am, 11.40pm, 12.20pm and 12.50pm daily (except Monday, when the site is closed) from the Old Jetty at the western end of the harbour. The boats return between 11am and 3pm. Departure and return times are posted on the noticeboard at the Old Jetty, and you can buy tickets for the boat trip directly from the boat operators at the Old Jetty departure point. In Hora (Mykonos), **Delia Travel** (☎ 22890 22322; travel@delia.gr; Akti Kambani) and the **Mykonos Accommodation Centre** (☎ 22890 23408; www.mykonos-accommodation.com; 1st fl, Enoplon Dynameon 10) sell tickets.

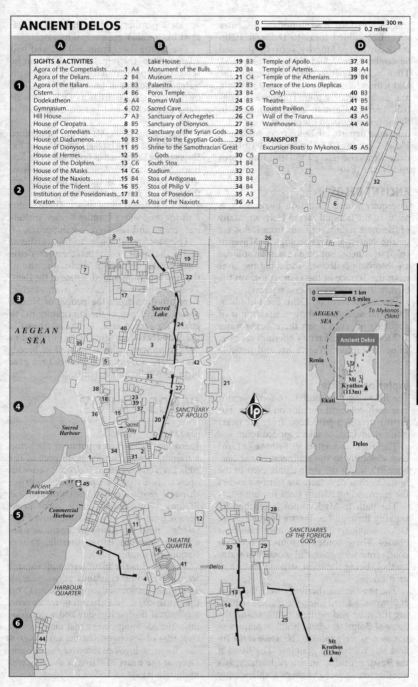

ANCIENT DELOS

0 — 300 m
0 — 0.2 miles

SIGHTS & ACTIVITIES

Agora of the Competialists	1	A4
Agora of the Delians	2	B4
Agora of the Italians	3	B3
Cistern	4	B6
Dodekatheon	5	A4
Gymnasium	6	D2
Hill House	7	A3
House of Cleopatra	8	B5
House of Comedians	9	B2
House of Diadumenos	10	B3
House of Dionysos	11	B5
House of Hermes	12	B5
House of the Dolphins	13	C6
House of the Masks	14	C6
House of the Naxiots	15	A4
House of the Trident	16	B5
Institution of the Poseidoniasts	17	B3
Keraton	18	A4
Lake House	19	B3
Monument of the Bulls	20	B4
Museum	21	C4
Palaestra	22	B3
Poros Temple	23	B4
Roman Wall	24	B3
Sacred Cave	25	C6
Sanctuary of Archegetes	26	C3
Sanctuary of Dionysos	27	B4
Sanctuary of the Syrian Gods	28	C5
Shrine to the Egyptian Gods	29	C5
Shrine to the Samothracian Great Gods	30	C5
South Stoa	31	B4
Stadium	32	D2
Stoa of Antigonas	33	B4
Stoa of Philip V	34	B4
Stoa of Poseidon	35	A3
Stoa of the Naxiots	36	A4
Temple of Apollo	37	B4
Temple of Artemis	38	A4
Temple of the Athenians	39	B4
Terrace of the Lions (Replicas Only)	40	B3
Theatre	41	B5
Tourist Pavilion	42	B4
Wall of the Triarus	43	A5
Warehouses	44	A6

TRANSPORT

Excursion Boats to Mykonos	45	A5

AEGEAN SEA

Sacred Lake

SANCTUARY OF APOLLO

Sacred Harbour

Sacred Way

Ancient Breakwater

Commercial Harbour

THEATRE QUARTER

HARBOUR QUARTER

Delos

SANCTUARIES OF THE FOREIGN GODS

Mt Kynthos (113m) ▲

0 — 1 km
0 — 0.5 miles

AEGEAN SEA

To Mykonos (5km)

Ancient Delos

Renia

Ekati

Mt Kynthos (113m) ▲

Delos

CYCLADES

The Mykonos Accommodation Centre organises guided tours to Delos at 10am every day except Monday, between May and September (adult/child €35/28, three hours). They include boat transfers from and to the Old Jetty, admission to the site and museum and an informative tour. Tours are in English, French, German and Italian, and in Spanish and Russian on request.

A boat departs for Delos from Mykonos' Platys Gialos (€10, 30 minutes) at 10.15am daily. Boats also operate to Delos from Paros and Naxos (€40).

ANCIENT DELOS

The quay where excursion boats dock is south of the tranquil Sacred Harbour. Many of the most significant finds from Delos are in the National Archaeological Museum (p75) in Athens, but the **site museum** still has an absorbing collection, including the lions from the Terrace of the Lions (those on the terrace itself are plaster-cast replicas).

Overnight stays on Delos are forbidden and boat schedules allow a maximum of about six or seven hours there. Bring water and food, as the cafeteria's offerings are poor value for money. Wear a hat and sensible shoes.

Exploring the Site

The following is an outline of some significant archaeological remains on the site. For further details, a guidebook from the ticket office is advised, or take a guided tour.

The rock-encrusted **Mt Kythnos** (113m) rises elegantly to the southeast of the harbour. It's worth the steep climb, even in the heat. On clear days there are terrific views of the surrounding islands from its summit.

The path to Mt Kythnos is reached by walking through the **Theatre Quarter**, where Delos' wealthiest inhabitants once built their houses. These houses surrounded peristyle courtyards, with colourful mosaics (a status symbol) being the most striking feature of each house.

The most lavish dwellings were the **House of Dionysos**, named after the mosaic depicting the wine god riding a panther, and the **House of Cleopatra**, where headless statues of the owners were found. The **House of the Trident** was one of the grandest. The **House of the Masks**, probably an actors' hostelry, has another mosaic of Dionysos resplendently

astride a panther, and the **House of the Dolphins** has another exceptional mosaic.

The **theatre** dates from 300 BC and had a large **cistern**, the remains of which can be seen. It supplied much of the town with water. The houses of the wealthy had their own cisterns – essential as Delos was almost as parched and barren then as it is today.

Descending from Mt Kythnos, explore the **Sanctuaries of the Foreign Gods**. Here, at the **Shrine to the Samothracian Great Gods**, the Kabeiroi (the twins Dardanos and Aeton) were worshipped. At the **Sanctuary of the Syrian Gods** there are the remains of a theatre where an audience watched ritual orgies. There is also a shrine area where **Egyptian** deities, including Serapis and Isis, were worshipped.

The **Sanctuary of Apollo**, to the northeast of the harbour, contains temples dedicated to the main man, and is the site of the much-photographed **Terrace of the Lions**. These proud beasts, carved from marble, were offerings from the people of Naxos, presented to Delos in the 7th century BC to guard the sacred area. To the northeast is the **Sacred Lake** (dry since it was drained in 1925 to prevent malarial mosquitoes breeding) where, according to legend, Leto gave birth to Apollo and Artemis.

PAROS ΠΑΡΟΣ

pop 12,853

Paros has a deserved reputation for being a friendly island, and the main port of Parikia certainly seems to welcome you with open arms. Beyond the port the island rises through gentle slopes to Mt Profitis Ilias (770m). White marble made Paros prosperous from the Early Cycladic period onwards – most famously, the *Venus de Milo* was carved from Parian marble, as was Napoleon's tomb.

The island is the main ferry hub for onward travel to other islands in the Aegean. The other major settlement, Naoussa, on the north coast, is a charming resort with a colourful fishing harbour and a developing waterside lounge scene that may one day rival that of Mykonos. On the east coast is the charming low-key resort of Piso Livadi. Deep at the heart of Paros is the peaceful mountain village of Lefkes.

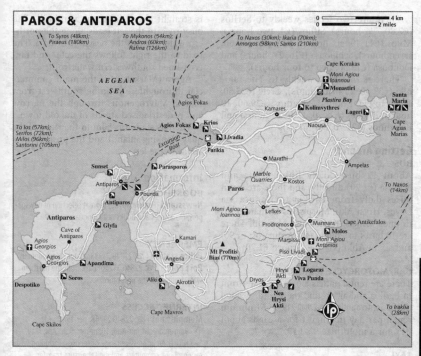

PAROS & ANTIPAROS

The smaller island of Antiparos, 1km southwest of Paros, is easily reached by car ferry or excursion boat.

Getting There & Away

AIR

Olympic Airlines (☎ 22840 91257; www.olympicairlines .com), at the airport, has daily flights to Athens (€57, 35 minutes).

Until suspension of operations in July of 2007, **AirSea Lines** (☎ toll free 801 11 800 600; www .airsealines.com) ran one seaplane flight a day from Thursday to Monday between Lavrio and Paros. Due to upgrading requirements the company suspended its Aegean schedule in July 2007. The schedule was still suspended at the time of writing (September 2007). The company states, however, that it will resume its Aegean service as soon as possible and readers are advised to check the company website

FAST BOAT & CATAMARAN

There are three services daily to Piraeus (€46, 2½ hours) and one a day to Rafina (€44.50, 2½ hours). There are also at least

two daily to Naxos (€13, 30 minutes), Tinos (€21.70, 1¼ hours), Syros (€16, 45 minutes), Mykonos (€16.50, one hour), Ios (€18.90, 1½ hours), Santorini (€30.50, 2¼ hours) and Amorgos (€22.50, 1½ to two hours). There is also one service daily to Iraklio on Crete (€46.90, four hours), and to Folegandros (€16, three hours and 50 minutes).

FERRY

There are around six boats daily to Piraeus (€28, five hours) and Naxos (€7, one hour), and three daily to Ios (€12.50, 2½ hours) and Santorini (€16.50, three to four hours). There are daily services to Mykonos (€6.80, 1¾ hours), Syros (€8.50, 1½ hours), Tinos (€8.80, 2½ hours) and Amorgos (€15, three to 4½ hours).

Six weekly go to Koufonisia (€15.50, 4½ hours); three weekly go to Sikinos (€7, three to four hours) and Anafi (€13.30, six hours), and four weekly go to Astypalea in the Dodecanese (€28.50, six hours).

There are three ferries weekly to Folegandros (€7.70, 5¾ hours).

There are two ferries weekly to Serifos (€7.80, 2½ hours), Sifnos (€4, two hours), Milos (€11.40, six hours), Kimolos (€9.60, seven hours), Schinousa (€10, 2¼ hours) and Donousa (€12.50, two to four hours).

There is one boat weekly to Thessaloniki (€37.50, 15 to 16 hours), Crete (€23.50, seven to eight hours), Skiathos (€29.60, 10 hours), Rhodes (€28.70, 12 to 15 hours) and Kalymnos (€22.70, 8¾ hours).

Getting Around
BUS
About 12 buses daily link Parikia and Naousa (€1.20) directly, and there are seven buses daily from Parikia to Naousa via Dryos, Hrysi Akti, Marpissa, Marmara, Prodromos, Lefkes, Kostos and Marathi. There are 10 buses to Pounta (for Antiparos; €1.90) and six to Aliki (via the airport; €1.20).

CAR, MOTORCYCLE & BICYCLE
There are rental outlets along the waterfront in Parikia and all around the island. A good outfit is **Acropolis** (☎ 22840 21830). Minimum rental per day in August for a car is about €45; for a motorbike it's €19.

TAXI
Taxis (☎ 22840 21500) gather beside the roundabout in Parikia. Fixed fares: airport €12, Naousa €10, Pounta €8, Lefkes €10 and Piso Livadi €13. There are extra charges of €1.50 for luggage and €2.50 if you book ahead.

WATER TAXI
Water taxis leave from the quay for beaches around Parikia. Tickets ranging from €7 to €12 are available on board.

PARIKIA ΠΑΡΟΙΚΙΑ
pop 4522

The harbourfront of Parikia is a busy, cheerful place compared with the town's Cycladic old quarter, where peaceful, narrow streets wriggle around the built-over shell of the 13th-century Venetian *kastro*. The fortification crowns a slight rise above the waterfront, southeast of the ferry quay.

Orientation
The busy hub of Parikia is the windmill roundabout, where you come off the ferry quay. The main square, Plateia Mavrogenous, which was being refurbished in 2007,

is straight ahead from the windmill. The busy road to the left leads along the northern waterfront to the beach at Livadia. The road to the right follows the café- and taverna-lined southwestern waterfront.

Agora (Market St) is the main commercial thoroughfare running southwest from Plateia Mavrogenous through the narrow and pedestrianised streets of the old town.

The bus station is 50m to the right of the quay (looking inland) and the post office is 400m to the left.

Information
BOOKSHOPS
Newsstand (Ekatondapylia) A great selection of newspapers, magazines and books in all languages.

EMERGENCY
Police station (☎ 22840 23333; Plateia Mavrogenous)
Port police (☎ 22840 21240) Back from the northern waterfront, near the post office.

INTERNET ACCESS
Memphis.net (☎ 22840 23768; per 15min €1; ☺ 9am-midnight Jun-Aug, 10am-midnight Apr, May, Sep & Oct) An impressive range of services, including wi-fi for notebook computers and digital picture transfer.
Wired Café (☎ 22840 22003; Agora; per hr €3.50; ☺ 10.30am-2pm & 6-11pm Mon-Sat, 6-11pm Sun) Reliable internet access in a relaxed atmosphere. Also has connections for laptop computers, and digital picture transfer.

INTERNET RESOURCES
Paros Life (www.paroslife.com)

LAUNDRY
Ostria Laundry (☎ 22840 21969, 6949079176; per wash & dry around €10; ☺ 9am-9pm Mon-Sat, 10am-2pm Sun Jun-Sep, 9am-2pm & 5.30-8.30pm Oct-May) The average load is ready in two hours at this friendly place.

MEDICAL SERVICES
Health Centre (☎ 22840 22500; Prombona; ☺ 9am-1.30pm Mon-Fri) Also has a dentist.

MONEY
All the following banks have ATMS.
Alpha Bank (Ekantondapylianis)
Commercial Bank of Greece (Plateia Mavrogenous)
Eurobank (Ekantondapylianis)
National Bank of Greece (Plateia Mavrogenous)

POST

Post office (☎ 22840 21236) Located 400m east of the ferry quay.

TOURIST INFORMATION

In high season, kiosks on the quay give out information on domatia and hotels (see Rooms Association, p156).

TRAVEL AGENCIES

Santorineos Travel Services (☎ 22840 24245) On the waterfront, just to the southwest of the windmill roundabout. Sells ferry tickets and can advise on accommodation and tours, and has a luggage store. Other services include bureau de change, FedEx and Moneygram (international money transfers).

Sights

The **Panagia Ekatondapyliani** (☎ 22840 21243; Plateia Ekatondapyliani; 7.30am-9.30pm Easter-Sep, 8am-1pm & 4-9pm Oct-Easter), which dates from AD 326, is one of the most splendid churches in the Cyclades. The building is three distinct churches: Agios Nikolaos, the largest, with superb columns of Parian marble and a carved iconostasis, is in the east of the compound; the others are the Church of Our Lady and the Baptistery. The name translates as Our Lady of the Hundred Gates, but this is a wishful rounding-up of a still-impressive number of doorways. The **Byzantine Museum** (admission €1.50; 9.30am-2pm & 6-9pm), within the compound, has a collection of icons and other artefacts.

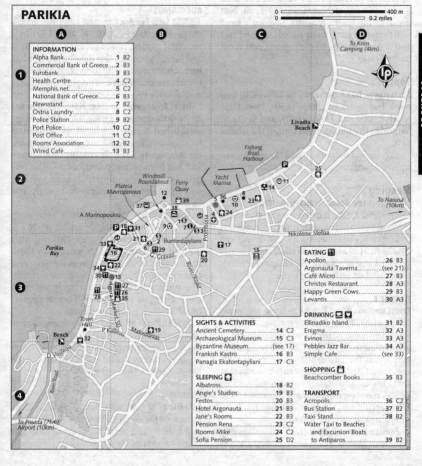

PARIKIA

0 ————— 400 m
0 ————— 0.2 miles

CYCLADES

INFORMATION	
Alpha Bank	1 B2
Commercial Bank of Greece	2 B3
Eurobank	3 B3
Health Centre	4 C2
Memphis.net	5 C2
National Bank of Greece	6 B3
Newsstand	7 B3
Ostria Laundry	8 C2
Police Station	9 B2
Port Police	10 C2
Post Office	11 C2
Rooms Association	12 B2
Wired Café	13 B3

SIGHTS & ACTIVITIES	
Ancient Cemetery	14 C2
Archaeological Museum	15 C3
Byzantine Museum	(see 17)
Frankish Kastro	16 B3
Panagia Ekatontapyliani	17 C3

SLEEPING	
Albatross	18 B2
Angie's Studios	19 B3
Festos	20 B3
Hotel Argonauta	21 B3
Jane's Rooms	22 B3
Pension Rena	23 C2
Rooms Mike	24 C2
Sofia Pension	25 D2

EATING	
Apollon	26 B3
Argonauta Taverna	(see 21)
Café Micro	27 B3
Christos Restaurant	28 A3
Happy Green Cows	29 B3
Levantis	30 A3

DRINKING	
Ellinadiko Island	31 B2
Enigma	32 A3
Evinos	33 A3
Pebbles Jazz Bar	34 A3
Simple Cafe	(see 33)

SHOPPING	
Beachcomber Books	35 B3

TRANSPORT	
Acropolis	36 C2
Bus Station	37 B2
Taxi Stand	38 B2
Water Taxi to Beaches and Excursion Boats to Antiparos	39 B2

To Krios Camping (4km)

Livadia Beach

Fishing Boat Harbour

Yacht Marina

Windmill Roundabout

Ferry Quay

Plateia Mavrogenous

A Marinopoulou

Parikia Bay

C. Gravari

Ekantondapylianis

Nikolaou Stellaa

To Naousa (10km)

Town Hall

Beach

P Kalliou

Makedonias

D Vasileou

Market St

Agora

River Road

To Pounta (7km); Airport (10km)

Next to a school behind the Panagia Ekatondapyliani, the **Archaeological Museum** (☎ 22840 21231; admission €2; ☺ 8.30am-3pm Tue-Sun) has some interesting reliefs and statues, including a Gorgon, but the most important exhibit is a fragment of the 4th-century Parian Chronicle, which lists the most outstanding artistic achievements of ancient Greece. It was discovered in the 17th century and most of it ended up in the Ashmolean Museum, in Oxford.

North along the waterfront there is a fenced **ancient cemetery** dating from the 7th century BC; it was excavated in 1983. Roman graves, burial pots and sarcophagi are floodlit at night.

The **Frankish Kastro** was built on the remains of a temple to Athena that was built by Marco Sanudo, Duke of Naxos, in AD 1260. Not much of the *kastro* remains, save for a large wall that is a jigsaw of unpainted column bases and dressed blocks, where pigeons now roost in the cracks.

Tours

Santorineos Travel Services (☎ 22840 24245) can book bus tours of Paros (€30), boat trips to Mykonos and Delos (€40), and boats to Santorini (including a bus tour of the island, €60).

Excursion boats also make the trip to Antiparos in summer.

Sleeping

In August the **Rooms Association** (☎ 22840 22722, after hrs 22840 22220), located on the quay, has information on domatia; otherwise, owners meet ferries. For Hotel Association details, call ☎ 22840 51207 for information about hotels on Paros and Antiparos. All camping grounds have minibuses that meet ferries.

BUDGET

Krios Camping (☎ 22840 21705; www.krios.page.tl; camp sites per adult/child/tent €7/4/4; ☺ Jun-Sep; 🖳) This fine site on the north shore of Parikia Bay is about 4km from the port, but there's a water taxi across the bay to Parikia every 10 minutes for €3 per person (return). You can rent tents for €8 and static tent 'bungalows' for €25. A new restaurant (dishes from €3.50 to €6) specialises in Greek and Italian food and offers breakfasts for €3.50 to €4.

Pension Rena (☎ 22840 22220; www.cycladesnet.gr /rena; s/d/tr €30/40/50; 🖳) One of the best choices

in town, these immaculate rooms are excellent value, and there's a charming welcome. The rooms are in a quiet but handy location just back from the waterfront. Air-conditioning is €5 extra. The owners also have good apartments to rent in Naousa.

Rooms Mike (☎ 22840 22856; roommike@otenet.gr; s/d/tr €30/40/50, studios €55; 🖳) A long-standing favourite in sight of the ferry quay, you'll never be short of a friendly chat and advice at Mike's place. There's a shared kitchen and a roof terrace. Studios are in another building, a block inland. Credit cards are accepted.

Festos (☎ 22840 21635; consolas@hol.gr; s/d incl breakfast €40/60; ☺ Apr-Oct) has a central location in a quiet street. Rooms are a touch cramped, but are well kept and clean.

MIDRANGE

our pick **Sofia Pension** (☎ 22840 22085; www.sofiapen sion-paros.com; s/d/tr €60/70/80; 🅿 🖳 🖳) Set in a beautiful garden, full of colour and greenery and lovingly tended, this delightful place has immaculate rooms with individual décor. The owners are charming and helpful. Breakfast is available for €6.

Hotel Argonauta (☎ 22840 21440; www.argonauta .gr; Plateia Mavrogenous; s/d/tr €60/71/85; 🖳) A long-established family-run hotel with a central location overlooking Plateia Mavrogenous, the Argonauta has a welcoming atmosphere and has been recently refurbished. The furnishings have charming traditional touches, and the rooms are spotless and comfy and have double-glazing.

Angie's Studios (☎ 22840 23909/6977; www.angies -studios.gr; Makedonias; d €65; ☺ Apr-Oct; 🅿 🖳) A delightful patio and garden glowing with bougainvillea and flowers surrounds these handsome studios. They're in a very quiet area that's a reasonable distance from the seafront. The studios are big and extremely well kept and each has its own kitchen. There are generous discounts in the low season.

Jane's Rooms (☎ 22840 21338; www.janesrooms.com; Kastro; s/d €50/65; 🖳) are pleasant rooms at the heart of the atmospheric Kastro area. There are also apartments on the north side of the bay at Krios, 1.5km out of town.

Eating

Café Micro (☎ 22840 24674; Agora) This great gathering spot for locals and visitors alike is bright and friendly and lies at the heart of Kastro. It offers breakfasts for €4, as well as coffee and snacks, fresh fruit and vegetarian juices. There are drinks and music into the early hours.

Albatross (☎ 22840 21848; D. Vasiliou; mains €5-14) A classic fish taverna, Albatross is a local favourite not least because of its excellent fish dishes. The fisherman's salad for €14 is a sure bet, or savour cuttlefish with spinach in an unfussy setting on the waterfront.

our pick **Levantis** (☎ 22840 23613; Kastro; dishes €9-15) A courtyard garden setting enhances the experience at this long-established restaurant at the heart of Kastro. There are subtle international touches to the imaginative cuisine in such dishes as Greek-style mussels with spicy sausage and ouzo. Other treats include rigatoni with spinach, wild mushrooms and roasted cherry tomatoes. Desserts such as white chocolate and amaretto mousse with sour cherries round things off. Excellent house wine is underpinned with a good choice of more-expensive wines.

Happy Green Cows (☎ 22840 24691; dishes €12-22; ☷ 7pm-midnight) Camp décor and cheerful service goes with the quirky name (inspired by a surreal dream, apparently) of this little eatery that is a vegetarian's delight. It's a touch pricey, but worth it for the often saucily named dishes. Meals include prawns in a vodka sauce, zucchini croquettes, crispy potatoes and yogurt sauce, or crispy pitta, peppers and creamy feta sauce.

Also recommended:

Christos Restaurant (☎ 22840 24666; Di Vasiliou; mains €4.50-8) Reliable Greek dishes and homemade pasta on the seafront.

Argonauta Taverna (☎ 22840 23303; mains €4.50-9) Attached to the hotel of the same name and offering sturdy Greek standards.

Apollon (☎ 22840 21875; Agora; mains €9-22) A long-established restaurant in Kastro. It exudes attention to detail, right down to the linen tablecloths and photo gallery of famous guests.

Drinking

Ellinadiko (☎ 22840 25046) Also known as 'Island', this popular local bar with foot-stomping Greek music and late-night dancing is in an alleyway between Plateia Mavrogenous and the seafront.

our pick **Pebbles Jazz Bar** (☎ 22840 22283) Heading down through Kastro in the late evening you'd think Pebbles' sunset backdrop was a vast painting. Perched above the seafront, this chilled, friendly place has classical music by day and jazz in the evenings, with

occasional live performers during July and August. Pebbles has an adjacent *mezedhopoleio* (restaurant specialising in mezedhes), open from 9am to 1am – it has breakfast from €4.50 to €7 and a great selection of mezedhes for €7 to €8, as well as omelettes and salads.

Enigma (☎ 22840 24664; D Vasileou) One of several music bars along the southern waterfront, Enigma goes hard into the early hours, when the sounds are a touch more Greek.

There are more bars along the southern waterfront, including some busy rooftop places like Evinos and Simple Cafe.

Shopping

Beachcomber Books (☎ 22840 28282, 6973620525; Agora) Everything from electrical goods to secondhand books are sold and bought for credit at this cheerful Aladdin's Cave.

NAOUSA ΝΑΟΥΣΑ

pop 2316

Fast stealing some of the glitz and glamour of Mykonos, Naousa has transformed itself from a quiet fishing village into a popular tourist resort. Found on the north coast of Paros, there are good beaches nearby, and the town has several excellent restaurants and a growing number of beachside eateries and bars. Behind the waterfront is a maze of narrow whitewashed streets, peppered with fish and flower motifs and with a mix of smart boutiques and souvenir shops.

Orientation & Information

The bus from Parikia terminates some way up from the main square just in from the waterfront, where a dried-up riverbed serves as a road leading south and inland. The main street of Naousa lies on the left of the riverbed. If arriving by car, be warned: parking in certain areas is banned from June to September. Signs may not be clear, but the €35 fines are painfully so.

Naousa Information (☎ 22840 52158; ☷ 10am-midnight Jul & Aug, 11am-1pm & 6-10pm mid-Jun–Jul) can find you accommodation and is based in a booth by the main square.

The post office is a tedious uphill walk from the main square. There are several banks with ATMs around the main square.

For internet access, try **Jamnet3** (☎ 22840 52203; per hour €2.50; ☷ 10am-1am), just by the entrance to the main square.

Sights & Activities

Naousa's **Byzantine museum** (admission €1.80; ⊙ 11am-1.30pm & 7-9pm Tue, Thu, Sat & Sun) is housed in the blue-domed church, about 200m uphill from the central square on the main road to Parikia. A small **folklore museum** (☎ 22840 52284; admission €1.80; ⊙ 9am-1pm & 6-9pm), which focuses on regional costumes, can be reached by heading inland from the main square to another blue-domed church. Turn right behind the church.

The best beaches in the area are **Kolymvithres**, which has interesting rock formations; and **Monastiri**, which has some good snorkelling and a clubbing venue. Low-key **Lageri** is also worth seeking out. **Santa Maria**, on the other side of the eastern headland, is good for windsurfing. They can all be reached by road, but caïques go from Naousa to each of them during July and August.

Kokou Riding Centre (☎ 22840 51818) has morning (€45), evening (€30) and one-hour (€25) horse rides, and can arrange pick-up from Naousa's main square for a small charge. The rides explore the surrounding countryside and coast of the area.

Tours

Naousa Paros Sailing Center (☎ 22840 52646; sailing@ par.forthnet.gr) offers sailing tours to Naxos, Delos or Iraklia. A full day is €90 per person and departs at 10am. Half-day tours and yacht charters are also available.

Sleeping

There are two camping grounds, both with minibuses that meet ferries. Visit the Naousa Information booth (p157) for help with finding accommodation.

Camping Naousa (☎ 22840 51595; camp sites per adult/child/tent €7/4/4) This pleasant camping ground is at Kolimvythres. It has a small taverna and lovely bays nearby.

Surfing Beach (☎ 22840 52491; fax 22840 51937; info@surfbeach.gr; camp sites per adult/tent €7.50/3.60) A fairly large site, but with reasonable facilities and a good location at Santa Maria. The site has a windsurfing and water-skiing school.

Young Inn (☎ 6976415232; www.young-inn.com; dm €15-20, d/tr €60/60; P ⊠ ▯) This cheerful, well-run place caters for a young, international clientele and organises events and outings. Scooter rental can be arranged. Breakfasts start at €3. It's located to the east of the harbour, behind Naousa's cathedral.

Hotel Galini (☎ 22840 51210; fax 22840 51949; s/d €50/60) Opposite the blue-domed local church (Byzantine museum), on the main road into town from Parikia, this charming and friendly little hotel has unfussy rooms that are being steadily updated.

Hotel Stella (☎ 22840 51317; www.hotelstella.gr; s/d €45/65) Deep in the heart of the old town and within a leafy, colourful garden, this friendly hotel has excellent rooms and good facilities. It's best reached by heading up the main street, turning left at the National Bank, going beneath an archway, and then turning right and up past a small church.

our pick Katerina's Rooms (☎ 22840 51642; www .katerinastudios.gr; s/d/tr €60/75/90, studio €120; ▧) Unbeatable views make these immaculate rooms (complete with tea- and coffee-making facilities) an excellent choice. You need to hike uphill a touch, but it's all worth it and the welcome is friendly. Prices drop substantially in low season.

Eating & Drinking

our pick Moshonas (☎ 22840 51623; dishes €4.50-9) Located alongside several harbourside tavernas is this long-standing favourite *ouzerie* (place that serves ouzo and light snacks). It's right on the edge of the harbour, and you're likely to see the family's own caïques tie up and deliver the fresh octopus that will soon be on your plate. Seafood is by the kilogram.

Glafkos (☎ 22840 52100; mains €6.50-12) There's a great beachside terrace at this little place, where you can enjoy some mouthwatering seafood dishes such as shrimps and *manouri*, and scallops in a tasty cream sauce.

Perivolaria (☎ 22840 51598; dishes €6.50-19) Relax in this long-established restaurant's garden and sample first-class Greek and international cuisine, including delicious pizzas and pastas. It is reached along the river road from the main square.

Christos (☎ 22840 51442; dishes €12-24; ⊙ 7pm-1am Apr-Oct) A leafy canopy of vines adds style to the lovely courtyard dining area of Christos', which is enhanced even more by the paintings that line the walls. The food matches the attentive service and is modern Mediterranean with exquisite touches, all backed by a superb wine list. To get here, head up the main street, and it's on the left after about 50m.

Along the beachfront beyond the harbour, there's a developing fringe of cafés and music bars with cool lounge décor worthy of

Mykonos. Places like **Fotis** (☎ 6938735017) and **Briki** (☎ 22840 52652) spill out onto little beaches and play a mix of classical strands by day and jazzier, funkier sounds by night.

AROUND PAROS

Lefkes Λεύκες

Lovely Lefkes clings to a natural amphitheatre amid hills whose summits are dotted with old windmills. Siesta is taken seriously here and the village has a general air of serenity. It lies 9km southeast of Parikia, high among the hills, and was capital of Paros during the Middle Ages. The village's main attractions are its pristine alleyways and buildings. The **Cathedral of Agia Triada** is an impressive building that's shaded by olive trees.

From the central square, a signpost points to a well-preserved Byzantine path, which leads in 3km to the village of **Prodromos**. At the edge of the village, keep left at a junction (signposted) with a wider track. Sections of the route retain their original paving.

Down on the coast is the attractive harbour and low-key resort of **Piso Livadi**, where there is a pleasant beach. **Perantinos Travel & Tourism** (☎ 22840 41135; perantin@otenet.gr) can arrange accommodation, car rental and boat trips to other islands. There is an ATM next to Perantinos.

Beaches

There is a fair scattering of beaches around the island's coastline, including a good one at **Krios**, accessible by water taxi (return €4) from Parikia. Paros' top beach, **Hrysi Akti** (Golden Beach), on the southeast coast, is hardly spectacular, but it has good sand and several tavernas, and is popular with windsurfers.

There is a decent enough beach at **Aliki** on the south coast.

SIGHTS & ACTIVITIES

The straits between Paros and Antiparos are especially suited to windsurfing and the spectacular sport of kiteboarding – effectively windsurfing in midair.

Down the coast at Pounda, **Eurodivers Club** (☎ 22840 92071; www.eurodivers.gr; Pounda) offers an impressive range of diving courses and dives for all levels and interests. A PADI open-water certification course costs €410, all inclusive.

Paros Kite Pro Centre (☎ 22840 92229; www .paroskite-procenter.com), well run by the same team as Eurodivers Club, offers a range of courses. These include an introductory one-hour kiteboarding session for €50, while more-intensive courses start at €220 for four to six hours.

Eurodivers and Paros Kite also run a useful mixed activities day that includes diving, kiteboarding, discovering scuba, snorkelling and a boat cruise, for €65.

At Golden Beach (Hrysi Akti), **Aegean Diving College** (☎ 22840 43347, 6932289649; www.aegeandiving .gr) offers a range of dives of archaeological and ecological interest led by scientists and experienced professional divers. A 'discover scuba' dive costs €75, and PADI open-water certification is €450.

Octopus Sea Trips (☎ 6932757123; www.octopu seatrips.com), based at Golden Beach and affiliated with Aegean Diving College, offers marine environmental courses and activities with snorkelling and diving for families and children.

Fanatic Fun Centre (☎ 6938307671; www.fanatic -paros.com; Hrysi Akti) offers catamaran sailing, water-skiing and windsurfing. One-hour windsurfing instruction costs €23 and a two-hour kiteboarding course is €75.

SLEEPING & EATING

Piso Livadi has a number of modern rooms and apartments and a few decent tavernas, and there's a camping ground on the outskirts of town.

our pick **Anna's Studios** (☎ 22840 41320; www .annasinn.com; Piso Livadi; s/d €50/65, studios €70-90; ❄ ▯) Located on the harbourfront at Piso Livadi, these rooms and studios are bright and immaculate and have tea- and coffee-making facilities. The family owners are charming. The studios are a little way out of the harbour area.

Halaris Taverna (☎ 22840 43257; mains €4.50-9) There are a number of tavernas and cafés on the waterfront at Piso Livadi, but Halaris is a great choice. There's fresh fish available from the family's own boat and a fish plate costs €8, while the shrimp pies are delicious. Other treats range from zucchini croquettes to homemade cheese and spinach pies.

Thea (☎ 22840 91220, 6945751015; dishes €9-14) With a waterside location near the Antiparos ferry quay at Pounta, echoes of old Greece and Asia Minor hang in the air at this great restaurant. Mains include Cappadocian lamb with apricots, or beef with quinces, rice and plums. There are over 450 different vintages

CYCLADES

kept in a wine room–cum-bar, which even has a glass floor with bottles nestling beneath your feet.

ENTERTAINMENT

Punda Beach Club (☎ 22840 41717; www.pundabeach.gr) This all-day clubbing venue, at Viva Punda, is a huge complex with swimming pools, bars, restaurants, a gym, live-music shows and a relentlessly crowded beach scene.

ANTIPAROS
ΑΝΤΙΠΑΡΟΣ

pop 1037

You'll feel you're escaping from the mainstream on this delightful island, which is rightly proud of its distinctiveness and of its independence from Paros; forget this at your peril in front of local people. The main village and port (also called Antiparos) is a bright and friendly place. There's a touristy gloss round the waterfront and main streets, but the village runs deep inland to quiet squares and alleyways that give way suddenly to open fields.

Getting There & Away

In summer, frequent excursion boats depart for Antiparos from Parikia.

There is also a half-hourly car ferry that runs from Pounta on the west coast of Paros to Antiparos (one way €0.70, per car €7, per scooter €1.80, 10 minutes); the first ferry departs for Antiparos at around 7.15am and the last boat returning leaves Antiparos at 12.30am.

Getting Around

The only bus service on Antiparos runs, in summer, to the cave in the centre of the island (€1.20). The bus continues to Soros and Agios Georgios.

Orientation & Information

Keep going straight ahead from the ferry quay and along the waterfront. Midway, the main street, Agora, strikes inland by Anargyros restaurant.

Halfway up the main street are an Emporiki Bank and National Bank of Greece, both with ATMs. The post office is also here. The central square is reached by turning left at the top of the main street and then right, behind Smiles Cafe.

To reach the *kastro,* another Venetian creation, go under the stone arch that leads north off the central square.

The rest of the island runs to the south of the main settlement through quiet countryside. There are several decent beaches, especially at Glyfa and Soros on the east coast.

There are several travel agencies, including **Antiparos Travel Agency** (☎ 22840 61300; ☯ Jun–mid-Oct) by the waterfront, which can help you with your accommodation needs. **Blue Island Divers** (☎ 22840 61493; www.blueisland-divers.gr) can also arrange accommodation and car hire.

Sights

Despite previous looting of stalactites and stalagmites, the **Cave of Antiparos** (admission €3.50; ☯ 10.45am-3.45pm summer) is still awe-inspiring. It is 8km south of the port. Follow the coast road south until you reach a signed turn-off into the hills. There are tours every hour.

From the port there are hourly buses to the cave (one way €1.20).

Activities

On the main pedestrian thoroughfare of town, with a gear and clothes shop attached, **Blue Island Divers** (☎ 22840 61493; www.blueisland-divers.gr) is friendly and helpful, and has a wide range of dive options. The owners have a great knowledge of the Antiparos scene. Accommodation and car rental can also be arranged. A four-day PADI open-water course is €380 and an advanced course is €320. A 'discover scuba diving' day session is €45. Trips can be tailored to suit individual wishes and there are advanced courses available.

Tours

MS Thiella (☎ 22840 61028) runs tours around the island daily, stopping at several beaches. The price (adults €40, children €20) covers barbeque and drinks; you can book at Antiparos Travel Agency (above).

Sleeping

Camping Antiparos (☎ 22840 61221; camp sites per adult/child/tent €6/4/4) This pleasant beachside camping ground is planted with bamboo and cedars and is 1.5km north of the port. It has a minimarket, bar and restaurant. A site bus picks up from the port.

Anarghyros (☎ 22840 61204; mak@par.forthnet.gr; s/d €35/50; ⊠) There's good value at this well-kept family-run hotel on the waterfront, where rooms are a decent size and come with tea- and coffee-making facilities. Attached to the hotel is a decent restaurant offering standard Greek dishes from €5 to €9.

Hotel Mantalena (☎ 22840 61206; www.hotelman talena.gr; s/d/tr €50/65/75; ⊠ ▢) The recently re-furbished Mantalena has bright, clean rooms and is located a short distance to the north of the main harbour quay. There's a pleasant terrace and the building is set back from the harbour road.

Eating & Drinking

The main street of Antiparos has several cafés and tavernas serving Greek staples and fish dishes.

Maki's (☎ 22840 61616; dishes €4.50-10) Seafood is the speciality at this harbourfront taverna. It's generally excellent, from the prawn *souvlaki* with calamari to lobster (when available).

Yam Bar Restaurant and Cocktail Bar (dishes €6-9; ⊗ 8pm-4am mid-Jun–mid-Sep) You can enjoy salads and delicious cold plates of chicken or pasta at this relaxing spot, with views of the sea. Sounds are a general mix that includes Latin and house and occasional jazz. It's signposted left off the top end of Market St.

Soul Sugar is along to the right from the top of the main street. It plays funk, disco and house into the small hours, and serves great cocktails.

NAXOS ΝΑΞΟΣ

pop 18,188

It was on Naxos that an ungrateful Theseus is said to have abandoned Ariadne after she helped him escape the Cretan labyrinth. In keeping with even mythic soap opera, she didn't pine long, and was soon entwined with Dionysos, the god of wine and ecstasy and the island's favourite deity. Naxian wine has long been considered a fine antidote for a broken heart.

The island was a cultural centre of classi-cal Greece and of Byzantium. Venetian and Frankish influences have left their mark.

Naxos is more fertile than most of the other islands and produces olives, grapes, figs, citrus fruit, corn and potatoes. Mt Zeus (1004m; also known as Mt Zas or Zefs) is the Cyclades' high-est peak and is the central focus of the island's mountainous interior, in which you find en-chanting villages such as Halki and Apiranthos. There are numerous fine beaches and the is-land is a wonderful place to explore on foot, as many old paths between villages, churches and other sights still survive. There are a number of walking guides and maps, including the useful *Central Naxos – A Guide with Map* (€8), avail-able from local bookshops.

Getting There & Away

AIR

There is at least one flight daily and two on Sunday to Athens (€58, 45 minutes). Olympic Airlines is represented by **Naxos Tours** (☎ 22850 22095; naxostours@naxos-island.com), on the water-front, which also sells ferry tickets.

FAST BOAT & CATAMARAN

There are at least two catamarans daily to Paros (€13.50, 45 minutes), Mykonos (€19.50, 1½ hours) and Piraeus (€51, four hours). There are also daily services to Ios (€20.20, 50 min-utes), Santorini (€23.60, 1½ hours) and Iraklio on Crete (€40.90, 3¼ hours), and four weekly to Tinos (€20, 1½ hours) and Syros (€21, 1¼ hours).

FERRY

There are price differences of about €1 to €3 between ferry companies whose vessels oper-ate on the same ferry route. The more-expen-sive price is given here.

Naxos has around six ferry connections daily with Piraeus (€29, five hours), Paros (€7, one hour), Ios (€11.50, 1¼ hours) and Santorini (€15.50, three hours), as well as four daily with Mykonos (€7.70, three hours).

There is one daily boat to Tinos (€7.80, 4¼ hours), Syros (€11.50, three hours), Iraklia (€7, one hour), Schinousa (€7.50, 1¼ hours), Koufonisia (€9, two hours), Amorgos (€14, 2½ hours), Donousa (€9, one to four hours) and Ikaria (€12.20, 1½ hours).

There are five ferries weekly to Anafi (€13.60, seven hours).

There are two boats weekly to Astypalea (€23, 5½ hours), Sikinos (€6.30, 3½ hours) and Folegandros (€9.30, 2½ hours).

One ferry goes weekly to Kythnos (€14.80, seven hours), Kea (€14.40, 8¾ hours), Lavrio (€18.50, 10 hours), Thessaloniki (€36.30, 15 hours), Rhodes (€23, 14 hours), Kos (€16, 8¼ hours) and Iraklio (€19.50, seven hours).

CYCLADES

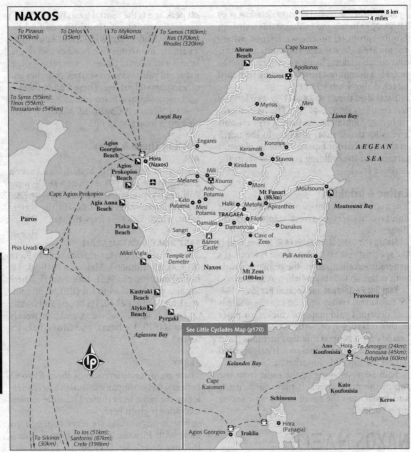

Getting Around

TO/FROM THE AIRPORT

The airport is 3km south of Hora. There is no shuttle bus, but buses to Agios Prokopios Beach and Agia Anna pass close by. A taxi costs €12 to €15 depending on the time of day and if booked.

BUS

Frequent buses run to Agia Anna (€1.40) from Hora. Five buses daily serve Filoti (€1.80) via Halki (€1.40); four serve Apiranthos (€2.60) via Filoti and Halki; and at least three serve Apollonas (€4.30), Pyrgaki (€2.20) and Melanes (€1.40). There are less-frequent departures to other villages.

Buses leave from the end of the ferry quay in Hora; timetables are posted outside the bus information office.

CAR & MOTORCYCLE

In August you can hire cars from about €45 to €55 per day, and motorcycles from about €20. **Rental Center** (☎ 22850 23395; Plateia Evripeou) is a good bet.

HORA (NAXOS) ΧΩΡΑ (ΝΑΞΟΣ)
pop 6533

Busy Hora, on the west coast of Naxos, is the island's port and capital. It's a large town, divided into two historic neighbourhoods – Bourgos, where the Greeks lived, and the hilltop Kastro, where the Venetian Catholics lived.

Orientation

The ferry quay is at the northern end of the waterfront, with the bus station at its inland end. The broad waterfront, Protopapadaki, known universally as Paralia, leads off to the south from the ferry quay and is lined with cafés, tavernas and shops on its inland side. Behind Paralia, narrow alleyways twist and turn beneath archways as they climb into the Kastro.

A northerly turn at the end of the ferry quay leads to a causeway over to Palatia Islet and the unfinished Temple of Apollo, Naxos' most famous landmark, known as the Portara. There is not much else to see at the temple other than the two columns and their crowning lintel surrounded by fallen masonry.

There are a few swimming spots along the waterfront promenade below the temple. Southwest of the town is the pleasant, but busy, beach of Agios Georgios.

Information

BOOKSHOPS
Zoom (☎ 22850 23675; Paralia) A large, well-stocked newsagent and bookshop that has most international newspapers and one of the biggest selections of books, in various languages, in the entire Cyclades.

EMERGENCY
Police station (☎ 22850 22100; Paparrigopoulou) Southeast of Plateia Protodikiou.
Port police (☎ 22850 22300) Just south of the quay.

INTERNET ACCESS
Rental Center (☎ 22850 23395; Plateia Evripeou; per hr €3)
Zas Travel (☎ 22850 23330; fax 22850 23419; Paralia; per hr €4)

LAUNDRY
To Ariston (☎ 22850 26750; 5kg wash & dry €10; ☻ 8am-2pm & 5.30-9pm Mon, Tue, Thu & Fri, 8am-2pm Wed & Sat)

MEDICAL SERVICES
Medical Centre (☎ 22850 23550; Prantouna)

MONEY
All the following banks have ATMs. There's also a National Bank of Greece ATM outside the Naxos Tourist Information Centre (see Tourist Information, below).
Agricultural Bank of Greece (Paralia)
Alpha Bank (cnr Paralia & Papavasiliou)
National Bank of Greece (Paralia)

POST
Post office (Agios Giorgiou) Go past the OTE, across Papavasiliou, and left at the forked road.

TELEPHONE
OTE (telecommunications office; Paralia) Has several phone kiosks in an alleyway.

TOURIST INFORMATION
Naxos Tourist Information Centre (NTIC; ☎ 22850 25201, emergency 22850 24525; apollon-hotel@naxos -island.com) There is no official tourist information centre on Naxos, but this privately owned office, directly opposite the main ferry quay, can arrange accommodation, excursions, rental cars and laundry service; luggage storage is also available (€1.50). The NTIC does not sell ferry tickets.

TRAVEL AGENCIES
Naxos Tours and Zas Travel both sell ferry tickets and organise accommodation, tours and rental cars.
Naxos Tours (☎ 22850 22095; www.naxostours.net; Paralia)
Zas Travel (☎ 22850 23330; zas-travel@nax.forthnet .gr; Paralia)

Sights

To see the Bourgos area, head into the winding backstreets behind the northern end of Paralia. The most alluring part of Hora is the residential **Kastro**. Marco Sanudo made the town the capital of his duchy in 1207, and several Venetian mansions survive. Take a stroll around the Kastro during siesta to experience its hushed, timeless atmosphere.

A short distance behind the northern end of the waterfront are several churches and chapels, and the **Mitropolis Museum** (☎ 22850 24151; Kondyli; admission free; ☻ 8.30am-3pm). The museum features fragments of a Mycenaean city of the 13th to 11th centuries BC that was abandoned because of the threat of flooding by the sea. It's a haunting place where glass panels underfoot reveal ancient foundations and larger areas of excavated buildings.

The **archaeological museum** (☎ 22850 22725; admission €3; ☻ 8.30am-3pm Tue-Sun) is in Kastro, housed in the former Jesuit school where novelist Nikos Kazantzakis was briefly a

CYCLADES

HORA (NAXOS)

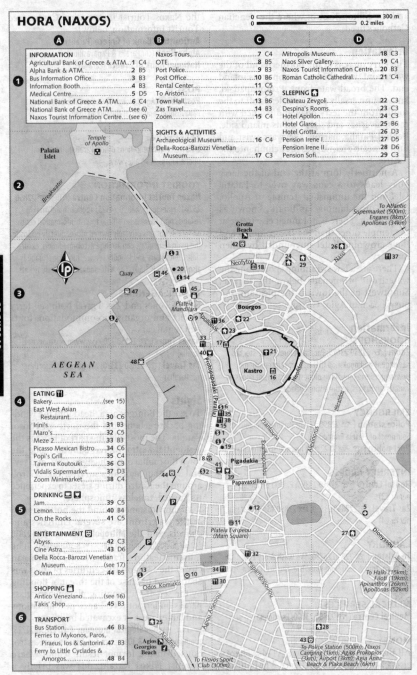

INFORMATION	
Agricultural Bank of Greece & ATM..1	C4
Alpha Bank & ATM....................................2	B5
Bus Information Office..............................3	B3
Information Booth....................................4	B3
Medical Centre...5	D5
National Bank of Greece & ATM...........6	C4
National Bank of Greece ATM........(see 6)	
Naxos Tourist Information Centre....(see 6)	

Naxos Tours..7	C4
OTE...8	B5
Port Police..9	B3
Post Office..10	B6
Rental Center.......................................11	C5
To Ariston...12	C5
Town Hall..13	B6
Zas Travel...14	B3
Zoom..15	C4

SIGHTS & ACTIVITIES	
Archaeological Museum.........................16	C4
Della-Rocca-Barozzi Venetian	
Museum...17	C3

Mitropolis Museum...............................18	C3
Naos Silver Gallery...............................19	C4
Naxos Tourist Information Centre.........20	B3
Roman Catholic Cathedral...................21	C4

SLEEPING	
Chateau Zevgoli...................................22	C3
Despina's Rooms...................................23	C3
Hotel Apollon......................................24	C3
Hotel Glaros..25	B6
Hotel Grotta..26	D3
Pension Irene I.....................................27	D5
Pension Irene II....................................28	D6
Pension Sofi...29	C3

EATING	
Bakery..(see 15)	
East West Asian	
Restaurant...30	C6
Irini's..31	B3
Maro's..32	C5
Meze 2...33	B3
Picasso Mexican Bistro.........................34	C6
Popi's Grill...35	C4
Taverna Koutouki.................................36	C3
Vidalis Supermarket.............................37	D3
Zoom Minimarket.................................38	C4

DRINKING	
Jam..39	C5
Lemon..40	B4
On the Rocks.......................................41	C5

ENTERTAINMENT	
Abyss..42	C3
Cine Astra...43	D6
Della Rocca-Barozzi Venetian	
Museum......................................(see 17)	
Ocean..44	B5

SHOPPING	
Antico Veneziano...........................(see 16)	
Takis' Shop...45	B3

TRANSPORT	
Bus Station...46	B3
Ferries to Mykonos, Paros,	
Piraeus, Ios & Santorini...................47	B3
Ferry to Little Cyclades &	
Amorgos..48	B4

pupil. The contents include Hellenistic and Roman terracotta figurines and some early Cycladic figurines.

Close by, the **Della Rocca-Barozzi Venetian Museum** (☎ 22850 22387; guided tours adult/student €5/3; ⏰ 10am-3pm & 7-10pm end May–mid-Sep), a handsome old tower house of the 13th century, is within the Kastro ramparts (by the northwest gate). A visit takes you into the fascinating world of the historic Kastro and its Frankish and Venetian past. There are changing art exhibitions in the vaults. Tours are multilingual. The museum also runs **tours** (adult/student €15/10) of the Kastro at 11am from Tuesday to Sunday; tours last just over two hours. Evening concerts and other events are staged in the grounds of the museum (see p167). The **Roman Catholic cathedral** (⏰ 6.30pm-8.30pm), also in the Kastro, is worth visiting.

Activities

Flisvos Sport Club (☎ 22850 24308; www.flisvos-sportclub .com; Agios Georgios) offers a range of windsurfing options, starting with a beginner's course of six hours for €160, or a four-hour Hobie Cat sailing course for €95. The club also organises walking trips and rents out mountain bikes for €6 to €8 a day.

Naxos Horse Riding (☎ 6948809142) organises daily horse rides (10am to 1pm and 5pm to 8pm), inland and on beaches (per person €45). You can book a ride up until 6pm the day before and can arrange pick-up and return, to and from the stables. Beginners, young children and advanced riders are catered for. Bookings can also be made at the **Naos Silver Gallery** (☎ 22850 24130) in Pigadakia.

Tours

There are frequent excursion boats to Mykonos (€40), Delos (€40) and Santorini (€55); book through travel agents.
Naxos Tourist Information Centre (☎ 22850 25201, emergency 22850 24525; apollon-hotel@naxos-island. com) Offers day tours of the island by bus (€20) or caïque (including barbecue, €40). One-day walking tours (per two people €46) are offered three times weekly.
Flisvos Sport Club (☎ 22850 24308; www.flisvos -sportclub.com; Agios Georgios) You can book a half-day guided mountain-bike tour for €20.

Sleeping

Naxos has a reputation for persistent domatia hawkers meeting ferries. Recently the authorities have cracked down hard, with talk

of heavy fines for badgering of tourists, and in 2007 there was certainly a reduction in the number of hawkers. If you're approached but aren't interested, be firm but polite and keep moving; Hora has plenty of good accommodation options. Booths on the quay have information about hotels and domatia.

BUDGET

Pension Irene II (☎ 22850 23169; www.irenepension -naxos.com; s/d €30/50; 🅿 🖵 ⚄) Another good choice, Irene II has been refurbished recently. Rooms are bright and comfortable with pleasant balconies. The swimming pool is an irresistible bonus. The same family runs Pension Irene I (☎ 22850 23169; www.irenepension -naxos.com), a peaceful, well-kept place in leafy surroundings, with air-con rooms for €25/35 a single/double.

Despina's Rooms (☎ 22850 22356; fax 22850 22179; Kastro; s/d €40/50) This cheerful family home is tucked away in the Kastro and has a selection of decent rooms, some with sea views. Rooms on the roof terrace are popular despite their small size. There's a communal kitchen.

There are several camping grounds near Hora, and all have good facilities. Minibuses meet the ferries. The grounds are all handy to good beaches and there's an approximate price per person of €8.
Camping Maragas (☎ 22850 24552) At Agia Anna Beach, south of Hora.
Naxos Camping (☎ 22850 23500; ⚄) About 1km south of Agios Georgios Beach. The camping ground closest to town.
Plaka Camping (☎ 22850 42700; fax 22850 42701) At Plaka Beach, 6km south of town.

MIDRANGE

Hotel Glaros (☎ 22850 23101; www.hotelglaros.com; Agios Georgios; s incl breakfast €55-60, d incl breakfast €75-80; 🅿 🖵) The attractive décor of Hotel Glaros captures the colours of sea and sky. Service is friendly and thoughtful and the rooms are bright and clean. Although not on the beachfront, the hotel is only a few steps away from the beach. The owners also have attractive apartments nearby (€65 to €95).

Pension Sofi (☎ 22850 25593; www.pensionsofi.gr; s/d/tw €65/70/90; 🅿) Great hospitality and kindness are the rule at this family-run place. It's just a short distance inland from the port and is framed by one of the biggest bougainvilleas you're likely to see. Rooms are clean and well equipped and include cooking facilities.

Hotel Apollon (☎ 22850 22468, 6976618384; www .apollonhotel-naxos.gr; Fontana; s/d incl breakfast €65/85; P ☒ ☐) Stylish décor and tasteful furnishings lend an atmosphere of Naxian good living to the Apollon's spacious, well-furnished rooms. The hotel is in a quiet area a few minutes from the waterfront.

Chateau Zevgoli (☎ 22850 26123; www.naxos townhotels.com; Kastro Bourgos; s/d €70/80, ste €120; ☒) The owner of Hotel Apollon also runs this long-established hotel, right in the heart of Kastro. It has a charming garden setting to go with the traditional Naxian style of rooms and furnishings.

ourpick Hotel Grotta (☎ 22850 22215; www.hotel grotta.gr; Grotta; s/d incl breakfast €70/85; P ☒ ☐) Located on high ground to the east of the ferry quay, this delightful modern hotel has comfortable and immaculate rooms, great sea views from the front, spacious public areas and a Jacuzzi. It's made even better by the friendly attentive service.

Eating

Naxian cuisine cherishes such local specialities as *kefalotyri* (a hard cheese made from sheep's milk), honey, *kitron* (a liqueur made from the leaves of the citron tree – see opposite), *raki* (Greek firewater, smoother than *tsipouro*), ouzo and fine white wine.

Maro's (☎ 22850 25113; Paparrigopoulou; mains €4-8) Maro's popularity with locals says everything, and there's a sense that good cooking is important here. Dishes such as cod in garlic sauce and roast pork with spaghetti are all the more tasty for it.

Meze 2 (☎ 22850 26401; Paralia; mains €3-9) The emphasis at this popular *mezedhopoleio* (restaurant specialising in mezedhes) is on fish, and even the local fishermen eat here. Superb seafood is prepared and served by family members in an atmosphere that is never less than sociable.

Irini's (☎ 22850 26780; Paralia; mains €5.50-9.50) The real deal at this pleasant taverna is the terrific selection of starters (€4 to €7.50) – such as delicious codfish croquettes – from which you can construct a delicious meal.

ourpick Picasso Mexican Bistro (☎ 22850 25408; Odos Komiakis; dishes €5.25-12.75; ☷ 7pm-late) The fajitas at this great Tex-Mex place are world class. Tables fill quickly with aficionados of tacos, nachos, burritos and fajitas. It also does great salads as well as hefty 'buffalo steaks'. There's a beach version, Picasso on

the Beach, at Plaka Beach, open mid-June to September.

East West Asian Restaurant (☎ 22850 24641; dishes €5.60-13) At this excellent eatery there's always a friendly welcome to go with the Thai, Chinese or Indian favourites, including green chicken coconut curry, made with chunks of tender chicken and vegetables. You'll find this place off Agiou Arseniou.

Also recommended (charging about €4 to €9 for a main dish):

Taverna Koutouki (Kastro) Famous for its outside tables in a narrow alleyway on the way up to Kastro.

Popi's Grill (Paralia) The best place for *souvlaki*.

Near the Zoom newsagent and bookshop is the town's best bakery. Next door is the Zoom Minimarket. The cheapest supermarkets are Atlantic and Vidalis, both a little way out of town on the ring road.

Drinking

BARS

ourpick On the Rocks (☎ 22850 29224; Pigadakia) The place to go for character and cocktails. Enjoy Havana cigars or a flavourful *sheesha* (water pipe) with Cuban-style daiquiris or tequila, or try the *karpouzi* bowl for two – fresh watermelon with a vodka base. It all goes well with sounds that vary between funk, house and electronic. Occasional live performances and karaoke stir the mix. There's also internet and wi-fi available.

Lemon (☎ 22850 24734; Paralia) A cool cocktail bar and café with relaxing décor, Lemon is one of the best places from which to watch the world go by.

Jam (Pigadakia) A huge playlist with rock and standard favourites is the background to this long-established music bar. There's also a great list of cocktails.

Entertainment

CINEMAS

Cine Astra (☎ 22850 25381; Andreas Papandreou; adult/ child €8/5) About a five-minute walk from the main square. It shows newly released mainstream films and has a bar. Sessions are from 9pm and 11pm.

NIGHTCLUBS

Abyss (Grotta; admission €10; ☷ 11.30pm-3am May–mid-Sep, 11.30pm-late Fri & Sat mid-Sep–Apr) Previously known as Super Island, this place has had something of a makeover inside and out, but offers much the same sounds with house and modern Greek at the fore.

Ocean (☎ 22850 26766; Seafront; admission €10; ☷ 11.30pm-3am May–mid-Sep, 11.30pm-late Fri & Sat mid-Sep–Apr) A sizable space features house and some modern Greek music, and runs special nights with guest DJs.

SUNSET CONCERTS

Della Rocca-Barozzi Venetian Museum (☎ 22850 22387; Kastro; events admission €15-20; ☷ 8pm Wed-Sun Apr-Oct) Special evening cultural events are held at the museum, and comprise traditional music and dance concerts, and classical and contemporary music recitals. Prices depend on seat position.

Shopping

Takis' Shop (☎ 22850 23045; Plateia Mandilara) Among the splendid wines here are such fine names as Lazaridis from Northern Greece, Tslepos from the Peloponnese and Manousakis from Crete – all masterful vintages. You can also find Vallindras *kitron* (see p168) and ouzo here. Adjoining is Takis' jewellery shop, where fine individual pieces from some of Greece's most famous designers often reflect ancient designs and the imagery of the sea.

Antico Veneziano (☎ 22850 26206; Kastro) Deep within Kastro is this upmarket antique store and gallery that makes for a fascinating visit.

In the streets heading up to the Kastro there are several shops selling fine embroidery and handmade silver jewellery.

AROUND NAXOS
Beaches

Conveniently located just south of the town's waterfront is **Agios Georgios**, Naxos' town beach. It's backed by hotels and tavernas at the town end and can get very crowded, but it runs for some way to the south and its shallow waters mean the beach is safe for youngsters.

The next beach south of Agios Georgios is **Agios Prokopios**, in a sheltered bay to the south of the headland of Cape Mougkri. It merges with **Agia Anna**, a stretch of shining white sand, quite narrow but long enough to feel uncrowded towards its southern end. Development is fairly solid at Prokopios and the northern end of Agia Anna.

Sandy beaches continue down as far as **Pyrgaki** and include **Plaka**, **Kastraki** and **Alyko**.

One of the best of the southern beaches is **Mikri Vigla** – its name translates as 'little look-out', a watching place for pirates, and reference to the rocky headland, all golden granite slabs and boulders, between superb beaches. The settlement here is a little scattered and is punctuated by half-finished buildings in places, but there's a sense of escapism and open space.

There are hotels, domatia and tavernas near most beaches. An excellent, out of the way option is **Oasis Studios** (☎ 22850 75494; www .oasisnaxos.gr; s/d €60/75; ☷ ☷ ☷ ☷) at Mikri Vigla. It is close to the beach and has lovely big rooms with kitchens. The owner and staff are friendly and helpful, and there's an outside terrace with a swimming pool and bar. The owner is a fount of local information and can help arrange horse riding, windsurfing and kiteboarding on the nearby beaches.

The beachside **Taverna Liofago** (☎ 22850 75214, 6937137737; dishes €3.50-7) has a dreamy beach location. It has been in business for decades and offers a terrific variety of dishes with special Naxian flavour. The *keftedhakia* (meatballs) are a delicious speciality.

Tragaea Τραγαία

The Tragaea region is a vast plain of olive groves and unspoilt villages, couched beneath the central mountains. **Filoti**, on the slopes of Mt Zeus, or Zas (1004m), is the region's largest village. It has an ATM booth, accessed with card, just down from the main bus stop. On the outskirts of the village (coming from Hora), an asphalt road leads off right to the isolated hamlets of **Damarionas** and **Damalas**.

From Filoti, you can also reach the **Cave of Zeus (Zas)**, a large natural cavern at the foot of a cliff on the slopes of Mt Zeus. There's a junction signposted Aria Spring and Zas Cave, about 800m south of Filoti. If travelling by bus, ask to be dropped off here. The side road ends in 1.2km. From the road-end parking, follow a walled path past the **Aria Spring**, a fountain and picnic area, and continue uphill to reach the cave. The path leads on from here to the summit of Zas. It's quite a stiff hike of about 3km. A good way to return to Filoti, taking another 4km, is to follow the path that leads north from the summit. This is not a mere stroll, so be fit and come equipped with good footwear, water and sunscreen.

HALKI ΧΑΛΚΕΙΟ

One of Naxos' finest experiences is a visit to the historic village of **Halki**, which lies at the

ART OF THE AEGEAN: L'OLIVIER, NAXOS *Des Hannigan*

The first time I walked into **L'Olivier** (☎ 22850 32829; www.fish-olive-creations.com), a ceramics gallery and shop in the little village of Halki on Naxos, it was late evening, early summer. The velvety dusk of the Tragaea, the mountain basin of Naxos, had settled like a veil on Halki's little village square. Young owls hooted from marble ledges on the façades of old Naxian mansions. The air was sweet with the scent of nearby olive groves and meadows. Inside L'Olivier it was as if the sunset glow had lingered. Even the artificial lighting was subtly deployed. Everywhere I looked were pieces of stoneware ceramics and jewellery that took my breath away.

Each piece of work seemed unique. Yet all reflected the ancient Mediterranean themes of fish and olive that are at the heart of the work of Naxian potter Katharina Bolesch and her partner, artist and craftsman Alexander Reichardt. Three-dimensional ceramic olives framed the edges of shining plates or tumbled down the side of elegant jugs and bowls. Grapes too, hung in little ceramic bunches. Painted shoals of fish darted across platters and swam around bowls and dishes. Ceramic and silver fish jewellery extended the theme. Those first impressions have never faded. Each time I walk into L'Olivier now, the world lights up.

Katharina Bolesch was partly brought up on Naxos and is rooted in the island's landscape and culture. Her major inspiration is the olive and its symbolism. Her work has been exhibited in major European galleries and in Athens' Goulandris Natural History Museum and the Academy of Athens and in New York. Her work will also feature as an official exhibit in Beijing during the 2008 Olympics. Reichardt is entirely of the Mediterranean. His life among islands and his long experience as a diver inspire his painted fish motifs, his ceramic and silver fish jewellery and his work in wood and marble.

L'Olivier has gathered many admirers worldwide. The president of the Goulandris Natural History Museum and a past European Woman of the Year, Mrs Niki Goulandris, is a longstanding patron. She speaks enthusiastically of the work of Bolesch and Reichardt and places it within the world of classical Greek and Cycladic art while recognising its modern context.

'Their work represents boldness and commitment to tradition,' she says. 'Their motifs are emphatically the symbols of the Greek land and sea.'

In spite of such a high profile and a developing international reputation, the work of Bolesch and Reichardt remains entirely accessible and affordable. L'Olivier is a cornucopia of beautiful yet functional work that includes tiny ceramic fish and silver jewellery, simple tiles and dishes, large jugs and bowls of luminous beauty, fine artefacts in olive wood, and olive products such as oil and soap.

In 2006 Bolesch and Reichardt opened a separate gallery and workshop just around the corner from their shop. Here they stage exhibitions by accomplished artists in a building that has been designed with great style and that fits perfectly amid Halki's traditional Naxian façades and the serene beauty of the Tragaea.

---

heart of the Tragaea, about 20 minutes' drive from Naxos town. Halki is a vivid reflection of historic Naxos and is full of the handsome façades of old villas and tower houses, legacy of a rich past as the one-time centre of Naxian commerce.

The main road skirts Halki. There is some roadside parking but you may find more at the schoolyard at the north end of the village and on a piece of rough ground just beyond the school. Lanes lead off the main road to the beautiful little square at the heart of the village.

Since the late 19th century Halki has had strong connections with the production of

kitron, a delicious liqueur. The citron (*Citrus medica*) was introduced to the Mediterranean area in about 300 BC and thrived on Naxos for centuries. The fruit is barely edible in its raw state, but its rind tastes delicious when preserved in syrup as a *ghlika kutalyu* (spoon sweet). *Kitroraki*, a *raki*, can be distilled from grape skins and citron leaves, and by the late 19th century the preserved fruit and a sweet version of *kitroraki*, known as *kitron*, were being exported in large amounts from Naxos.

The **Vallindras Distillery** (☎ 22850 31220; ☻ 10am-11pm Jul-Aug, 10am-6pm May-Jun & Sep-Oct) in Halki's main square, still distils *kitron* the old-fashioned way. There are free tours of the old distillery's atmospheric rooms, which still contain ancient jars and copper stills. *Kitron* tastings round off the trip and a selection of the distillery's products are on sale. To arrange a tour during the period November to April you need to phone ☎ 22850 22534 or ☎ 6942551161.

Another Halki treat is the ceramics shop **L'Olivier** and its nearby gallery (see boxed text, opposite), and the fascinating shop **Era** (☎ 22859 31009; eraproducts@mail.gr), where delicious marmalade, jam and spoon desserts are made and sold.

There are sleeping possibilities in Halki, but at present it's rather informal. Your best bet is to ask locally. Filoti has some decent, cheap rooms, but you're really best off asking at the village tavernas by the main bus stop.

In a classic location in the heart of Halki's central square, **Yianni's Taverna** (☎ 22850 31214; dishes €5.50-7.50) is well known for its good local meat dishes and delicious fresh salads with *myzithra* (sheep's-milk cheese).

The **Citron Café** (☎ 22850 31602) is next to the Vallindras Distillery and is a charming place that has retained the traditional style of old Halki.

An alternative scenic route from Hora to Halki is along the road that passes **Ano Potamia**. It's here that you'll find **Taverna Pigi** (☎ 22850 32292; mains €4.50-7), known for excellent local cooking, enjoyed with the serene music of the gurgling spring that the taverna is named after.

Panagia Drosiani Παναγία Δροσιανή

The **Panagia Drosiani** (⊙ 10am-7pm May–mid-Oct) just below **Moni**, 2.5km north of Halki, is one of the oldest and most revered churches in Greece. It has a warren of cavelike chapels, and several of the frescoes date back to the 7th century. Donations are appreciated.

Sangri Σαγκρί

The handsome towerlike building of **Bazeos Castle** (☎ 22850 31402; ⊙ 10am-5pm & 6-9pm) stands prominently in the landscape about 2km east of the village of Sangri. The castle was built in its original form as the Monastery of Timios Stavros (True Cross) during the 17th century, but monks abandoned the site in the early 19th century. It was later bought by the Bazeos family, whose modern descendants have refurbished the building and its fascinating late-

medieval rooms with great skill and imagination. The castle now functions as a cultural centre and stages art exhibitions and the annual **Naxos Festival** during July and August, when concerts, plays and literary readings are held. The price of admission to these varies.

About 1.5km south of Sangri is the impressive **Temple to Demeter** (Dimitra's Temple; ☎ 22850 22725; ⊙ 8.30am-3pm Tue-Sun). The ruins and reconstructions are not large, but they are historically fascinating, and the hilltop location is impressive. There is a site **museum** with some fine reconstructions of temple features. Signs point the way from Sangri.

Apiranthos Απείρανθος

Apiranthos is an atmospheric mountain village of unadorned stone houses, marble-paved streets and alleyways that scramble up the slopes of Mt Fanari. Its inhabitants are descendants of refugees who fled Crete to escape Turkish repression; they retain a strong individuality and a rich dialect, and the village has always been noted for its spirited politics and populism. The village has an impressive trio of museums.

On the main road, to the right of the start of the village's main street, is the **museum of natural history** (admission €3; ⊙ 8.30am-2pm Tue-Sun). The **geology museum** (admission €3; ⊙ 8.30am-2pm Tue-Sun) and the **archaeology museum** (admission free; ⊙ 8.30am-2pm Tue-Sun) are part-way along the main street. The latter has a marvellous collection of small Cycladian artefacts. The museums are notionally open from 7pm to 10pm in summer, but all the opening times stated here are 'flexible', in keeping with an admirable local spirit of independence.

Just before the main square, which is dominated by a huge plane tree, is **Stoy Lefteris** (☎ 22850 61333; dishes €8-15), with reliable local dishes in a peaceful terrace garden overlooking the valley.

There is parking at the entrance to Apiranthos, on the main Hora–Apollonas road.

Moutsouna Μουτσούνα

The road from Apiranthos to Moutsouna descends in an exhilarating series of S-bends through spectacular mountain scenery. Formerly a busy port that shipped out the emery mined in the region, Moutsouna is now a quiet place, although there is some development. Seven kilometres south of the village is a good beach at **Psili Ammos**.

There are a few pensions and tavernas, mainly in Moutsouna, but some are scattered along the coast road.

Apollonas Απόλλωνας

Tavernas line the waterfront adjoining a reasonable beach at Apollonas, on the north coast, but the main attraction here is a giant 7th-century BC **kouros**, which lies in an ancient quarry in the hillside above the village. It is signposted to the left as you approach Apollonas on the main inland road from Hora. This 10.5m statue may have been abandoned before being finished, because weaknesses in the stone caused cracking. Apollonas has several domatia and tavernas.

With your own transport you can return to Hora via the west-coast road, passing through wild and sparsely populated country with awe-inspiring sea views. Several tracks branch down to secluded beaches, such as **Abram**.

LITTLE CYCLADES
ΜΙΚΡΕΣ ΚΥΚΛΑΔΕΣ

Change down to Cycladic time and head for the chain of small islands between Naxos and Amorgos if you want an authentic island experience. Only four – Donousa, Ano Koufonisia, Iraklia and Schinousa – have permanent populations. All were densely populated in antiquity, as shown by the large number of ancient graves found on the is-

lands. During the Middle Ages, only wild goats and even wilder pirates inhabited the islands. Post-independence, intrepid souls from Naxos and Amorgos recolonised. Now, the islands welcome growing numbers of independent-minded tourists.

Donousa is the northernmost of the group and the furthest from Naxos. The others are clustered near the southeast coast of Naxos. Each has a public telephone and post agency and there are ATMs on all islands but Iraklia, although you should bring a decent amount of ready cash with you.

Getting There & Away

There are daily connections to and from Naxos to the Little Cyclades but the service can be disrupted when sea conditions are poor; make sure you have plenty of time before committing yourself – these islands are not meant for last-minute visits or for one-night tick lists.

Until about mid-2009, four times a week in summer and twice weekly in winter, Blue Star car ferries run from Piraeus via Naxos to all of the Little Cyclades islands and on to Amorgos and Astypalea. There's a standard price of €27.50 for one passenger to each of the Little Cyclades islands.

The sturdy little ferry **Express Skopelitis** (☎ 22850 71256/519; Katapola, Amorgos) provides a service (daily from mid-June to September, but on Monday, Wednesday, Thursday and Friday for the rest of the year, except January) between Naxos and Amorgos via all of

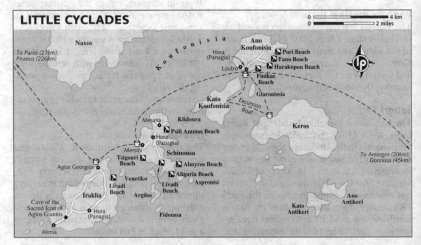

LITTLE CYCLADES

the smaller islands. It's a defining Cycladic experience. Bad weather can blow the schedule. Most seating is open deck, so when it's windy, brace yourself for some real rocking and rolling. In rough weather you'll know what's coming when the crew starts dishing out the *see-through* sick bags. If you're on deck, work out exactly which side of the boat is protected from wind and sea on each section between islands and stay there, or that bracing sea air may become a bracing Aegean Sea deluge. Regardless of sea conditions, locals, the crew and this writer head straight below for the comfy saloon and bar where they become engulfed in cigarette smoke and cheerful chatter. The choice is yours…

In high season the *Skopelitis* leaves Naxos at 3pm each day and calls at Iraklia (€8, 4½ hours), Schinousa (€7.50, four hours), Koufonisia (€7, 3½ hours), Donousa (€6.50, one hour and 20 minutes) and Amorgos (€10.50, six hours) where it docks overnight at Katapola.

There is also one weekly ferry from Donousa to Syros (€11, nine hours) and four weekly ferries to Paros (€12.50, two to four hours).

A useful weekly link from Donousa to Astypalea (€16, two hours 20 minutes) and the other Dodecanese islands is the rather lumbering *MV Dimitroula* (☎ 22410 87401) – you hear it before you see it. It calls at Donousa on its outward trip from Piraeus to Rhodes via Paros and Naxos on Tuesday, and calls in again on its return trip on Friday.

Four weekly ferries go from Schinousa to Paros (€10, 2½ hours).

Guaranteed until about mid-2009, the big **Blue Star** (☎ 21089 19800; www.bluestarferries.com) car ferry, *Blue Star Naxos*, will leave Piraeus for Paros, Naxos, all the Little Cyclades, and on to Amorgos, and Astypalea at 5.30pm on Monday and Wednesday all year and additionally on Saturdays from June 10 to September 20. The vessel will reverse the process on Tuesday and Thursday all year and additionally on Sunday from 10 June to 20 September.

A few other large, slow ferries stop at the islands during high season – 'ghost ships' – often in the dead of night.

IRAKLIA ΗΡΑΚΛΕΙΑ
pop 115

Iraklia (ir-a-*klee*-a) dozes in the Aegean sun and is one of the finest switch-off options anywhere in the world. Dump the party gear and spurn the nightlife, the 'sightseeing' and the dreary souvenirs. Instead, brace yourself for a serene and quiet life and Iraklia will not disappoint. Only in July and August will you have to share the idyll with like-minded others.

Iraklia measures only 19 sq km in area. The port and main village is Agios Georgios. It has an attractive covelike harbour, complete with a sandy beach. Turn right at the end of the ferry quay, and then go up left for a well-supplied general store, Perigiali Supermarket. Further uphill is a smaller store and *kafeneio* (coffee house) called Melissa's, which is also the ferry ticket office, postal agency and hub of island gossip. There are card phones outside Perigiali Supermarket and Melissa's. There is no ATM, but Perigiali Supermarket will cash cheques with card back-up. The island's website is www.iraklia.gr.

A surfaced road leads off to the left of the ferry quay, and after about 1km you'll reach **Livadi**, the island's best beach. A steep 2.5km further on is Hora (Panagia). Where the road forks at the village entrance, keep to the right for the main street.

The island's major 'sight' is the **Cave of the Sacred Icon of Agios Giannis**. The icon is said to have been discovered in the cave by a shepherd at the end of the 19th century, and is now kept in the little church in Hora village. A yearly **festival** celebrating the icon is held in Hora on the last weekend of August. The cave is above the sea on the island's northern side, and can be reached along a footpath from Hora in about three hours return. Coming uphill from the entrance to the village, the path starts just beyond the church at a signpost on the right. The path is very rocky and steep in places; boots or walking shoes are essential and you should take plenty of water. Beyond the cave the path leads to the beach at **Alimia**, which is also served by boat from Agios Georgios in summer.

During July and August, the *Anemos* ferries people to island beaches and also runs day trips (return €10) to nearby Schinousa. Enquire at Perigiali Supermarket.

Sleeping & Eating
Domatia and tavernas are concentrated in and around Agios Georgios, although a few open on the beach at Livadi in summer. Domatia owners meet the boats, but in high season it's advisable to book.

our pick Anna's Place (☎ 22850 71145; s/d €35/67; ⊠) Located on high ground above the port, these lovely, airy rooms have stylish furnishings and the front balconies have sweeping views. There's a friendly and helpful welcome that reflects Iraklia's overall style.

Alexandra (☎ 22850 71482; fax 22850 71545; d €45) Also on the hill above the port are these clean, unfussy rooms with pleasant patios.

Other options in the main village:

Melissa (☎ 22850 71539; fax 22850 71561; d €35) Has basic rooms.

Anthi & Angelo's (☎ 22850 71486; d €45) Has reasonable rooms, but is open in high season only.

There are only a few tavernas in Agios Georgios. All serve fresh fish dishes and other Greek standards. **Maïstrali** (☎ 22850 71807; dishes €3.80-7) has a pleasant terrace and also has rooms and fairly creaky internet access. **Perigiali** (☎ 22850 71118; dishes €4-7), a popular place, has a large marble table encircling an old pine tree.

In Hora, **Taverna to Steki** (☎ 22850 71579; dishes €3.30-6.50) is a classic village eatery and is well known for its locally sourced ingredients and traditional food.

SCHINOUSA ΣΧΙΝΟΥΣΑ
pop 206

Schinousa (skih-*noo*-sah) lies a mere 2km across the sea from Iraklia and is similar in nature – slow-paced, friendly and likeable. It has a number of beaches, although not all are attractive, and down-to-earth Hora (Panagia) on the breezy crest of the island has sweeping views of the sea.

Ferries dock at the fishing harbour of Mersini. Hora is a hot 1km uphill (domatia owners always meet ferries with transport).

There's a public telephone in the main square and a couple of general stores sell stamps. Tickets are sold at the port a few minutes before boats arrive. There is also a shop and tourist centre that sells ferry tickets at the entrance to Hora. In 2007 it was announced that Schinousa was to have an ATM installed in the near future. A reasonably useful website is www.schinousa.gr.

On the way down to Tsigouri beach is a little **folk museum** that features a reconstructed bread oven. Opening hours go with the flow of island life.

Dirt tracks lead from Hora to beaches around the coast. The nearest are **Tsigouri** and **Livadi**, both uncrowded outside August. Haul

a little further to decent beaches at **Almyros** and **Aligaria**. With the exception of Tsigouri, there are no shops or tavernas at the beaches, so take food and water.

Sleeping

There are a few rooms down at Mersini, but if you want to see the rest of the island you're much better off staying in Hora.

Anna Domatia (☎ 22850 71161; Hora; s/d €25/35) Just behind the main street on the west side of the village, these unfussy rooms are clean and comfortable and there's a friendly welcome.

Iliovasilema (☎ 22850 71948; iliovasilema@schinousa .gr; Hora; s/d €40/55) Ideally located on the western outskirts of the village, looking south over the island, this bright, clean place has good-sized rooms and most of the balconies have fine views.

Grispos Tsigouri Beach Villas (☎ 22850 71930; fax 22850 71176; www.grisposvillas.com; Hora; s/d/tr incl buffet breakfast €65/80/95, apt €150; ⊠) About 250m down the dusty track from Hora and located right on the edge of Tsigouri beach, these rooms are a good size and have bright décor and surroundings. There are also apartments and other rooms nearby.

Eating

Grispos (dishes €3.50-7) This beachside restaurant at Tsigouri is part of the Grispos accommodation complex and offers decent island standards.

Loza (☎ 22850 71864; dishes €4.50-8) Right on the main street of Hora, and a local rendezvous point, Loza offers breakfasts for €7.50 as well as salads and pizzas. It's also a bakery and produces delicious pastries, including baklava and walnut pie.

Margarita (☎ 22850 74278; dishes €5-12) The terrace at this charming place has dreamy views of the sea to go with the modern Greek cuisine, which includes pricier seafood options. It's all creatively prepared and backed by a good wine list. A great choice is the mixed plate. Margarita's is midway along the village street, down an alleyway.

KOUFONISIA ΚΟΥΦΟΝΗΣΙΑ
pop 366

The islands of Ano Koufonisia and Kato Koufinisia face each other across blue waters. It's Ano Koufonisia that's populated. Its

(Continued on page 181)

ISLANDS ADVENTURING

The Greek islands constitute a vast sprawling archipelago offering a wealth of activities and interest to the adventurous traveller. Yes, they are about beaches, white, cubed houses, bleached rocky landscapes and lingering dinners over ouzo and octopus mezedhes, but they are also about activities that can be enjoyed in the open air – on land or in the sea. Above all, the Greek islands are a diverse tapestry of culture and tastes. Some islands live life fast, others take it slow. We offer you a selection of activities that you can enjoy at your pace and on the island of your choice.

Watery Adventures

The abundance of water that surrounds and connects the Greek islands makes it a paradise for many water sports. Combine the warm weather with the clear blue seas and you have a formula made for both exhilaration as well as acceleration. Check out this water-based fun.

❷ Water-skiing
If you've got the skill and stamina, slap on a pair of skis and slide your way across the dark blue surf at any number of locations across the Greek islands. A good place to learn is on Poros (p112) in the Saronic Gulf Islands, a couple of hours' sail from Athens.

❸ Windsurfing
Where there's wind there's windsurfing and some of the best windsurfing beaches in the world can be found in Greece's sheltered yet windy waters, especially when the summer *meltemi* (northeasterly wind) blows in. It's fast action and you'll need good balance. Good surf spots (among many) are on Karpathos (p294), Kos (p317) and Lefkada (p462).

❶ Kitesurfing
Strap a surfboard to the feet and a thin kite to your waist and you have kitesurfing – a new water-sport craze for Greece. Not for the faint-hearted, it's fast and furious and you can fly it at Agios Ioannis (p462) on Lefkada or at Mikri Vigla (p167), Naxos.

❹ Beach Action
Fun and action on island beaches can range from the safe and slow water bikes to more splashy action, such as being towed at high speed on an inflatable 'banana'. For a gentle swim you'll find many protected bays that are generally wave free.

Land-based Adventures

Despite the predominance of water there's still lots to do on land on the islands. Rocky mountains, herb-laced valleys and gorges, and wide, open spaces all allow for recreation at your own pace and style throughout the scattered archipelago of the Greek islands. You can climb, walk, ride and hike on almost any island.

① Mountaineering

The Greek islands offer up some surprisingly rugged terrain and mountaineering is popular all year round. Crete (p220) dominates with its wide selection of sites for climbing and hiking, while Rhodes (p276) has at least one sizeable peak. In the north, Samothraki (p402) offers a less well-known option.

② Hiking

Almost every island has an existing network of traditional footpaths and byways crisscrossing the landscape. Some have been re-developed and are well marked, others are awaiting renovation. Throw on a pack, boots and a hat and get out there. Good islands to walk are Sifnos (p210), Skopelos (p427), Hydra (p115) and Amorgos (p183).

③ Rock Climbing

Generally a new sport in Greece, the vertiginous activity of scaling sheer rocks attracts climbers from all over the world. Where else can you scale cliffs with the startling view of blue seas before you? Kalymnos (p328) has been drawing in punters for a few years now, while Crete (p220), with its abundant mountains, also has its fans.

④ Cycling

Minimal pollution and traffic and clear open skies means cycling is ideal, and cycling an island is close to perfection: you get the wind in your hair, the smell of the flora and the chance to stop off at any beach you like at a moment's notice. Islands that lend themselves to a leisurely ride are Kos (p317) and Corfu (p446). Test yourself if you are fit enough on Crete's (p220) tortuous mountain roads.

Natural Paradise

Fauna and flora and water-based activities constitute the bulk of nature activities on the islands. A generally fertiliser-free terrain means that wildflowers and herbs abound, while fauna has, to date, had a rougher path thanks to uncontrolled hunting by trigger-addicted locals. The wheel is slowly turning and people now realise that nature is an industry in itself that both supports and encourages tourism.

③

① Birding

The Aegean islands are transit homes to millions of migratory birds that make the long trip from Africa to Europe and back each year. They're also home to rare and endangered species, such as the Eleonora's falcon and Bonelli's eagle. The island of Lesvos (Mytilini; p386) sees hundreds of birders descend each year while Tilos (p310) has declared a protection zone for its feathered fauna.

② Wildflowers & Herbs

Early spring to early summer is the time for the flowering of the hills, ridges and pastures of the islands. Poppies punctuate the landscape in a sea of red from April while the pathways and byways of all islands are redolent with the pungent aroma of acres of wild herbs such as sage, oregano and mountain tea. Crete (p220) is home to over 1500 species of wildflower, plus 20 species of orchid.

③ Eco-volunteering

Consider volunteering your time and energy to a number of organisations that work tirelessly to restore balance to flora and fauna. The Earth Sea & Sky volunteers on Zakynthos (p476) would like to hear from you, while the Sea Turtle Protection society on the same island is also a worthy cause (for details see At Loggerheads, p480).

④ Working the Land

A number of organisations are now offering aspiring hobby farmers the chance to grow mastic trees, pick olives, make wine or tend an organic vegetable plot. This is a great way to spend a holiday and learn how to put something back into nature. Chios (p375) is one island that offers such an option with a 'masticulture' operation that is very popular.

Underwater World

The Aegean waters are among the cleanest in the Mediterranean basin and the ambient water temperature for at least four months of the year means that wetsuits are not necessary. Diving to wrecks is a popular activity, while most beachgoers are content to float on the surface to watch fish and explore underwater seascapes.

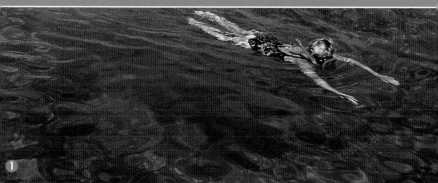

❶ Snorkelling & Underwater Fishing

It's easy to do and easy to find a perfect beach for this relaxing and accessible on- and under-water activity. Good snorkelling is best undertaken in protected south-facing bays. Karpathos (p294) is an ideal choice as are Milos (p206) and Kythira (p482).

❷ Diving

The Aegean and Ionian waters are without exception crystal clear and offer spectacular underwater rock formations and marine life to enjoy. Rhodes (p276) has a few diving schools, while you can visit wrecks on Leros (p334) through its one diving centre.

(Continued from page 172)

excellent beaches make it one of the most visited of the Little Cyclades islands, and modernisation has taken hold. New hotels and studios are springing up, a marina with capacity for 50 yachts is due to be completed in 2008, and a new sewage treatment plant was under construction in 2007. Koufinisia's substantial fishing fleet still sustains a thriving local community outside the fleeting summer season.

A caïque ride away, **Kato Koufonisi** has some beautiful beaches and a lovely church. Archaeological digs on **Keros**, the rocky, bull-backed mountain of an island that looms over Koufonisia to the south, have uncovered over 100 Early Cycladic figurines, including the famous harpist and flautist now on display in Athens' National Archaeological Museum (p75).

Orientation & Information

Koufonisia's only settlement spreads out behind the ferry quay. On the west side of the quay is the planned yacht marina and on its east side is a wide harbour filled with moored fishing boats. A large town beach of flat, hard sand gives a great sense of space to the waterfront. Its inner edge is used as a road and everyone uses it as a football pitch. The older part of town, the *hora*, sprawls along a low hill above the harbour and is one long main street.

There are a couple of supermarkets along the road that leads inland from the beach to link with the main street, and there's a ticket agency halfway along the main street. The post office is along the first road leading sharply left as you reach the beach and the road leading inland. There is an ATM alongside.

Sights

BEACHES

An easy walk along the sandy coast road to the east of the port leads in a couple of kilometres to **Finikas**, **Harakopou** and **Fano** beaches. All tend to become swamped with grilling bodies in July and August and nudity becomes more overt the further you go.

Beyond Fano a path leads to several rocky swimming places, then continues to the great bay at **Pori**, where a long crescent of sand slides effortlessly into the ultimate Greek-island dream sea. Pori can also be reached by an inland road from Hora.

Tours

Koufonisia Tours (☎ 22850 71671; www.koufonissiatours .gr), based at Villa Ostria hotel (see Sleeping, below), organises caïque trips to Keros, Kato Koufonisi and to other islands of the Little Cyclades. Bike hire is also available.

Sleeping

Wild camping is not permitted on Koufonisia. There is a good selection of domatia and hotels, and **Koufonisia Tours** (☎ 22850 71671; www .koufonissiatours.gr) organises accommodation on the island.

Koufonisia Camping (☎ 22850 71683) This camping ground has been behind the tree-lined beach at Harakopou to the east of Hora for many years. At the time of writing it was reported that the ground would not be opening in 2007. We advise checking ahead for 2008 and 2009.

Lefteris Rooms (☎ 22850 71458; d/tr €40/45) Right behind the town beach and above Lefteris restaurant are these simple but colourful rooms, with the ones at the back being the most peaceful.

Anna's Rooms (☎ 22850 71061, 6974527838; s/d/tr/q €50/60/70/80; 😂) In a quiet location at Loutro on the west side of the port, these big, bright rooms are a great choice and the welcome is charming. They overlook the old harbour and are set amid colourful gardens. Each room has tea- and coffee-making facilities.

Ermis (☎ 22850 71693; fax 22850 74214; s/d €55/70) Behind the post office in a quiet location are these spacious rooms with attractive décor and big generous balconies at the front.

Villa Ostria (☎ 22850 71671; www.koufonissiatours.gr; s/d incl breakfast €60/70) A stylish, small hotel, Villa Ostria stands on the high ground above the beach and has a charming garden area. Rooms are smart and comfortable and have fridges.

Eating

Melissa (☎ 22850 71454; mains €3.50-6) Easily identified by the front half of a little sailing boat protruding from its wall, and by its multicoloured tables and chairs, Melissa prepares excellent fish dishes. Meat eaters are catered for also and vegetarians can combine tasty eggplant and onions with *briam* (mixed vegetables).

Lefteris (☎ 22850 71458; dishes €3.50-9) The long-established Lefteris dishes up reasonably priced Greek standards to huge numbers of visitors in high summer. Its vast terrace looks out over the town beach and it's open for breakfast and lunch also.

Capetan Nikolas (☎ 22850 71690; dishes €4.50-8.50) Deservedly famous, especially for its seafood, this cheerful, family-run restaurant overlooks the little harbour at Loutro. Locally caught fish, such as red mullet and sea bream, are a speciality and are priced by the kilo – for your selection, you browse in the kitchen.

Drinking

Koufonisia caters to a fairly sophisticated music bar set and has a number of venues.

Scholeio (☎ 22850 71837; ⏲ 6pm-3.30am) A great little island bar and creperie that goes well with the island's laid-back ambience. Scholeio offers cocktails and plays jazz, blues and rock among other choice sounds. It's right at the western end of the village's main street above Loutro.

Sorokos (☎ 22850 71704; ⏲ 4pm-3am) Drinks and snacks and hot sounds that range from early-hours lounge music to harder vibes at night make this a popular hang-out beyond the town beach.

DONOUSA ΔΟΝΟΥΣΑ
pop 110

Cancel plans: Donousa is where you stop bothering about which day it might be. In late July and August the island can be swamped by holidaymaking Greeks and sun-seeking visitors, but out of season be prepared to linger – and be rewarded for it.

Agios Stavros is Donousa's main settlement and port, a cluster of functional buildings round a handsome church, overlooking a small bay. Little has changed over the years, but water shortage – on an island that was once always well supplied – has seen recent pipe-laying to houses from a new storage tank for imported water. The town also has a good **beach**, which also serves as a thoroughfare for infrequent vehicles and foot traffic to a clutch of homes, rental rooms and a taverna across the bay.

Roussos Travel (☎ 22850 51648) on the waterfront is the ticket agency for the local ferry *Express Skopelitis*.

Sigalis Travel (☎ 22850 51570, 6942269219) in the To Iliovasilema restaurant complex (see Sleeping & Eating, right) sells tickets for Blue Star ferries.

There is an ATM outside Roussos Travel (it's sometimes hidden behind a blue shutter for protection from blown sand, so don't miss it). But be sure to bring sufficient cash in high

season. There is a public telephone up a steep hill above the waterfront; it's hidden behind a tree. You can get telecards at the souvenir shop just up from the quay-end of the beach.

There is a **medical centre** (☎ 22850 51506) and postal agency just below the church.

Kendros, situated 1.25km to the southeast of Agios Stavros, along a rather ugly bulldozed track, is a sandy and secluded beach with a seasonal taverna. **Livadi**, a dusty 1km hike further east, sees even fewer visitors. Both Kendros and Livadi are popular with naturists and navel-/horizon-gazing dreamers. Bulldozed, unsurfaced roads have marred Donousa in places, but there are still delightful paths and tracks that lead into the hills to timeless little hamlets such as **Mersini**.

Sleeping & Eating

Most rooms on the island are fairly basic but are well kept, clean and in good locations. You should book ahead for stays in July and August, and even early September.

Prasinos Studios (☎ 22850 51579; d €35-50, apt €70) On the high ground on the far side of the beach is this pleasant complex with a mix of well-kept rooms.

To Iliovasilema (☎ 22850 51570; d/tr/studios €43/48/55; 🖳) Just below Prasinos Studios and overlooking the beach, some of these reasonable rooms have kitchens. There's a popular restaurant with a fine terrace and a good selection of food (dishes €3.50 to €20). New studios and apartments are planned for 2008.

DONOUSA

0 ——— 2 km
0 ——— 1 mile

To Mykonos (75km); Syros (105km)

Kalotaritissa

To Naxos (55km); Piraeus (250km)

Donousa

Mersini

Agios Stavros   Haravgi

Kendros Beach   Livadi Beach

To Naxos (45km); Paros (75km)

To Astypalea (116km); Rhodes (280km)

Capetan Giorgis (☎ 22850 51867; mains €3.50-7) Sturdy traditional food is on the menu at the Capetan's, where the terrace, just above the harbour, has good views across the bay.

There are a couple of food shops that have a reasonable selection of goods in July and August.

The hub of village life is Kafeneio To Kyma by the quay, where things liven up late into the night in summer.

AMORGOS ΑΜΟΡΓΟΣ

pop 1873

For many island lovers, Amorgos (ah-mor-ghoss) is the jewel in the Cycladic crown. Lying well to the southeast of the main group, this exquisite island rises from the sea in a long dragon's back of craggy mountains that is 30km from tip to toe and 800m at its highest point. The island's southeast coast is unrelentingly steep and boasts an extraordinary monastery embedded in a huge cliff. The northern half of the opposite coast is equally spectacular, but relents a little at the narrow inlet where the main port and town of Katapola lies.

Amorgos' other port town, Aegiali, lies at the island's northern end and is more appealing as a resort. It has a good beach and is encircled by rugged mountains. The enchanting Hora (also known as Amorgos) nestles high in the mountains above Katapola.

You need to work quite hard to get to Amorgos, although ferry connections in summer are good and at the time of writing there was talk of a seaplane service starting from the mainland in 2008. However, locals are determined to focus on sustainable tourism.

There's plenty of scope for beaching, but Amorgos is much more about compelling archaeology, Cycladic life and the outdoor world – there's great walking, scuba diving, and a burgeoning rock climbing scene, although currently the latter is for the very experienced rather than for the passing thrillseeker.

Getting There & Away

Until about mid-2009, four times a week in summer, twice a week in winter, Blue Star car ferries run a service from Piraeus via Naxos and the Little Cyclades to Amorgos

(€27.50, 9¼ hours). Arrival is in the early hours. Blue Star continues from Amorgos to Astypalea (€15.50, 1½ hours) and Kos (€22.50, 3¼ hours). One Blue Star ferry runs on Sunday from Amorgos to Rhodes (€25.50, 6½ hours).

There are several boats offering weekly services to Paros (€15, three hours) and Syros (€19, 4½hours).

The small ferry *Express Skopelitis* runs a circular route between Naxos and Amorgos and to the other islands in the Little Cyclades (see p170).

Most ferries stop at both Katapola and Aegiali, but well before your date of leaving be sure to check which town is the departure port for that day.

FAST BOAT & CATAMARAN

In July and August Hellenic Seaways runs a fast catamaran six days a week, except Wednesday, from Piraeus to Amorgos (€53, five hours) and on from Amorgos to Santorini (€18.50, 1¼ hours), Folegandros (€25, 2¼ hours), Sifnos (€32, three hours) and Syros (€28.50, 2½ hours).

Getting Around

Regular buses go from Katapola to Hora (€1.20, 15 minutes), Moni Hozoviotissis (€1.40, 15 minutes) and Agia Anna Beach (€1.30, 20 minutes), and less-frequent services go to Aegiali (€2.10, 30 minutes). However, there are fewer services on weekends. There are also buses from Aegiali to the picturesque village of Langada. Schedules are posted on bus windscreens.

Cars and motorcycles are available for rent from the travel agencies **N Synodinos** (☎ 22850 71201; synodinos@nax.forthnet.gr; Katapola; ☼ year-round) and **Aegialis Tours** (☎ 22850 73107; fax 22850 73394; www.amorgos-aegialis.com; Aegiali).

KATAPOLA ΚΑΤΑΠΟΛΑ

The island's principal port, Katapola, straggles round the curving shoreline of a dramatic bay in the most verdant part of the island. The fascinating and extensive remains of the ancient city of **Minoa**, as well as a **Mycenaean cemetery**, lie above the port and can be reached by a steep, surfaced road. Amorgos has also yielded many Cycladic finds; the largest figurine in the National Archaeological Museum (p75) in Athens was found in the vicinity of Katapola.

CYCLADES

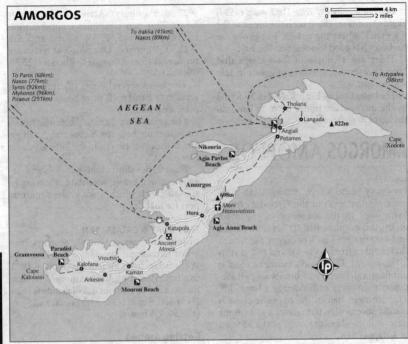

AMORGOS

0 —— 4 km
0 —— 2 miles

To Iraklia (41km);
Naxos (89km)

To Paros (68km);
Naxos (77km);
Syros (92km);
Mykonos (96km);
Piraeus (251km)

To Astypalea
(98km)

A E G E A N
S E A

Tholaria
Langada
Aegiali
Potamos
▲ 822m
Cape
Xodoto

Nikouria
Agia Pavlos
Beach

Amorgos

698m ▲
Moni
Hozoviotissis

Hora

Katapola
Ancient
Minoa

Agia Anna Beach

Gramvousa
Paradisi
Beach
Vroutsis
Kalofana
Kamari
Arkesini
Cape
Kalotassi

Mouron Beach

Orientation & Information

Boats dock right on the waterfront. The bus station is to the left along the main waterfront, on the eastern shore of the bay.

A bank (with ATM) is midwaterfront and there's an ATM next to N Synodinos. There is a postal agency next to the Hotel Minoa on the central square. The island's police station (☎ 22850 71210) is located in Hora.

Hotel Minoa (☎ 22850 71480; internet access per hr €2.50)

N Synodinos (☎ 22850 71201; synodinos@nax.forth net.gr; ☼ year-round) Sells ferry tickets and offers money exchange and car rental (per day in high season €50).

Port police (☎ 22850 71259) On the central square.

Sleeping & Eating

Domatia owners usually meet ferries and are among the most restrained and polite in the Cyclades.

Katapola Community Camping (☎ 22850 71802; camp sites per adult/child/tent €6/4/6) Set back from the eastern end of the bay, this shaded camping ground is a reasonable option.

ourpick Eleni's Rooms (☎ 22850 71628; rooms eleni@hack-box.net; s/d/tr/apt €50/60/70/100) An un-

beatable position to the west of the ferry quay makes these unfussy but bright and airy rooms an excellent choice, and the owner is friendly and kind. The rooms rise through several levels and offer unbeatable views. You can even hop down in seconds for a morning swim at an adjoining beach.

Diosmarini (☎ 22850 71636; diosmarini@yahoo.com; d/tr/apt €50/65/100) On the northern shores of the bay and about 1km from the ferry quay, Diosmarini is a delightful option with lovely big rooms in a handsome and modern Cycladic-style building. There are airy views from most balconies.

Pension Sofia (☎ 22850 71494; www.pension-sofia .com; d/apt €55/65; ⊠) The charming, family-run Sofia stands amid gardens and little meadows in a quiet area of town. Rooms are fresh and colourful.

Elichryson (☎ 22850 71517; €3-7; ☼ 8am-10pm) Ideal for breakfast (€3 to €6), this pleasant café is just back from the main waterfront.

Mouragio (☎ 22850 71011; dishes €4-7.50) A local favourite, not least for its expertise with fish dishes and seafood. This traditional taverna is on the main waterfront near the ferry quay.

Shellfish are by the kilo but reasonable dishes include delicious fish soup.

our pick **Vitsentzos** (☎ 22850 71518; dishes €5.50-9) Exposed stonework and a varnished wooden floor lend Vitsentzos an authentic old-worlde atmosphere. The waterfront terrace is also a delight and the food is satisfyingly traditional with an infusion of modern influences. Seafood is by the kilogram.

Kasbah (☎ 22850 71592) is a cheerful café next door to Vitsentzos and is run by the same family. Lip-smacking ice cream and delicious homemade cakes are the rule.

Drinking

Moon Bar (☎ 22850 71598) Set the world to rights in great company at this relaxing place on the northern waterfront, where the music ranges from classical through blues, rock and funk into the early hours. Breakfasts are €5.

Le Grand Bleu (☎ 22850 71633) Still flying on the name of the iconic film *The Big Blue,* this popular bar plays rock, reggae and modern Greek music on the northern waterfront.

HORA ΧΩΡΑ

The old capital of Hora sparkles like a snowdrift across its rocky ridge. It stands 400m above sea level and is capped by a 13th-century *kastro* atop a prominent rock pinnacle. Old windmills stand like sentinels on surrounding cliffs. However, there's a distinct veneer of sophistication, not least in the handful of trendy bars and shops that enhance Hora's appeal without eroding its timelessness.

The bus stop is on a small square at the edge of town. The post office is on the main square, reached by a pedestrian lane from the bus stop. The police station (☎ 22850 71210) is halfway along the main street.

Hora's **archaeology museum** (◷ 9am-1pm & 6-8.30pm Tue-Sun) is on the main pedestrian thoroughfare, near Café Bar Zygós.

Sleeping & Eating

Hora has a handful of pleasant pensions.

Pension Ilias (☎ 22850 71277; s/d/tr/apt €40/50/60/75) Tucked away amid a jumble of traditional houses just down from the bus stop is this unpretentious family-run place with decent rooms.

View To Big Blue (☎ 22850 71814/6932248867; s/d €45/60) At the top end of the village is this attractive place in its own little garden. Rooms are very bright and comfy.

Café Bar Zygós (☎ 22850 71350; snacks €3-10; ◷ 8am-3am) This café lies at the heart of Hora's main street. It's a charming place inside and out, and has a rooftop terrace. It offers breakfast, sandwiches, baguettes, salads and cold plates as well as coffee, delicious cakes, candied fruit and ice cream – all to Greek music by day, and '80s and '90s rock at night.

Keep heading up the winding main street to reach **Tsagaradiko** (☎ 6944872275; dishes €3-8), a great little mezedhes place with tables on a lovely small square.

MONI HOZOVIOTISSIS
ΜΟΝΗ ΧΟΖΟΒΙΩΤΙΣΣΗΣ

Amorgos is defined by the iconic **Moni Hozoviotissis** (◷ 8am-1pm & 5-7pm), a dazzling white building embedded in an awesome cliff face high above the sea. It lies on the precipitous east coast below Hora. A few monks still live here and short tours, which usually end with a pleasant chat with one of the monks, take place sporadically, usually when a reasonable number of visitors have gathered at the door of the monastery. The tour is free but donations are appreciated.

The monastery contains a miraculous icon that was found in the sea below the cliff. It got there (allegedly unaided) from Asia Minor, Cyprus or Jerusalem – depending on which legend you're told. Out of respect, modest dress is essential (long trousers for men, a long skirt or dress and covered shoulders for women).

A great round-trip is to catch the bus from Katapola to Hora, stroll the length of Hora's main street and on to an upper car park below a radio tower. Go down to the right of the car park viewpoint, through a gate and then follow a zigzag track with exhilarating views to reach the road. Turn left here to reach a junction, the left branch of which leads in 500m to the monastery. You can then catch the bus back to Katopola from the junction, or walk down to Agia Anna beach, which is 1.5km downhill, and catch the bus from the car park there after a dip.

AEGIALI ΑΙΓΙΑΛΗ

Aegiali is Amorgos' second port and has more of a resort style, not least because of the fine sweep of sand that lines the inner edge of the bay on which the village stands. Steep slopes and impressive crags lie above the main village.

CYCLADES

Efficient **Amorgos Travel** (☎ 22850 73401; www
.amorgostravel.gr), above the central supermarket
on the waterfront, can help with a host of
travel needs including ferry tickets, accommodation and island tours. Check it out for
diving and walking possibilities also. Long-
established **Aegialis Tours** (☎ 22850 73107; fax 22850
73394; www.aegialistours.com) sells ferry tickets,
and can organise accommodation, tours and
vehicle hire.

There's a postal agency about 100m uphill
from Aegialis Tours.

Tours
Ask at travel agencies about a daily bus outing
(€25) around the island that leaves at 9.30am
and returns at 4.30pm, with stops at Agia
Pavlos, Moni Hozoviotissa and Hora. Boat
trips around the island (€30) and to the little
Cyclades (€40) can also arranged.

Sleeping
As is the case in Katapola, domatia owners
meet the ferries.

Aegiali Camping (☎ 22850 73333; camp sites per
adult/child/tent €5.50/2.60/3.50) Good facilities and
a pleasantly shaded location on the road behind the beach makes this camping ground
an attractive proposition.

Pension Askas (☎ 22850 73333; www.askaspension
.gr; d/tr €60/70; ❄) Next to Aegiali Camping is
this decent pension in a garden setting, with
clean, attractive rooms.

Lakki Village (☎ 22850 73505; www.lakkivillage.gr;
s/d/tr incl breakfast €65/75/80, 2-/3-/4-person studios/apt
incl breakfast €85/100/115; ❄ 🖳 🖭) This attractive, well-kept complex ambles inland from
the beachfront through lovely gardens and
water features. Rooms are in Cycladic-style
buildings and have colourful traditional furnishings.

Eating
Restaurant Lakki (☎ 22850 73253; dishes €3.50-8) A
beach and garden setting makes the restaurant
of Lakki Village a relaxing place to enjoy well-
prepared Greek dishes.

To Koralli (☎ 22850 73217; dishes €4-7) Enviable
views enhance the good cuisine at this cheerful restaurant, which offers delicious fish and
mezes platters. It's reached by a flight of steps
at the eastern end of the waterfront.

ourpick To Limani (☎ 22850 73269; dishes €4-
9) Delicious traditional fare prepared with
home-grown produce makes Limani a

popular place. Local dishes include baked
goat and, for fish lovers, delicious fish soup,
while vegetarians can enjoy treats such as
black-eye beans with spinach. The downstairs walls exhibit works by local artists,
the big canvases by Wolfgang Mann being
particularly good. There's a hugely popular
Thai food night every Friday except during August. The owners also have beautiful
rooms, studios and apartments high above
the bay in the village of Potamos, starting
at €55 for a double.

AROUND AMORGOS
On the east coast, south of Moni Hozoviotissis, is **Agia Anna Beach**, the nearest beach to
both Katapola and Hora. Don't get excited;
the car park is bigger than any of the little
pebbly beaches strung out along the rocky
shoreline, and all the beaches fill up quickly.
Next to the car park on the cliff-top there's
a small cantina selling food and drinks.

The lovely villages of **Langada** and **Tholaria**
nestle amid the craggy slopes above Aegiali.
Their locations are magnificent and views
from both are worth the trip alone. The two
are linked to each other, and to Aegiali, by
a signposted circular path that takes about
four hours (Greek time). Regular buses run
between the villages and Aegiali.

IOS ΙΟΣ

pop 1838

Ios is slowly shedding its image as the party
capital of the Cyclades. It has always been as
traditional in landscape and cultural terms
as any other island in the group, and Greek
life goes on sturdily beyond the wall-to-wall
bars and nightclubs of Hora and the beach
scene. Families and older holidaymakers
are heading for Ios in increasing numbers.
There's still hard partying, however, and you
need some stamina to survive the late night
action in the centre of Hora.

Getting There & Away
AIR
Until suspension of operations in July of
2007, **AirSea Lines** (☎ 21094 02012; www.airsea
lines.com) ran one seaplane flight a day from
Thursday to Monday between Lavrio and
Ios. Due to upgrading requirements the
company suspended its Aegean schedule in

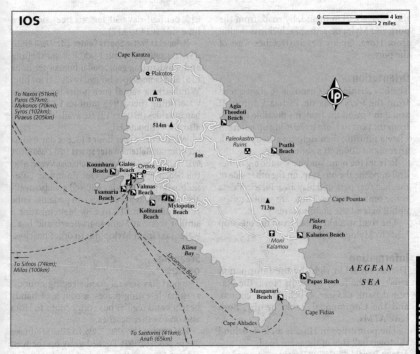

IOS

0   4 km
0   2 miles

Cape Karatza

Plakotos

417m

Agia
Theodoti
Beach

514m

Paleokastro
Ruins

Psathi
Beach

Ios

Koumbara   Gialos Ormos
Beach   Beach   Hora

Valmas
Beach

Tsamaria
Beach

Mylopotas
Beach

Kolitzani
Beach

713m

Plakes
Bay

Kalamos Beach

Moni
Kalamou

Klima
Bay

To Naxos (51km);
Paros (57km);
Mykonos (70km);
Syros (102km);
Piraeus (205km)

To Sifnos (74km);
Milos (100km)

AEGEAN

SEA

Cape Pountas

Papas Beach

Manganari
Beach

Cape Fidias

Cape Ahlades

To Santorini (41km);
Anafi (65km)

CYCLADES

July 2007. The schedule was still suspended at the time of writing (September 2007). The company states, however, that it will resume its Aegean service as soon as possible and readers are advised to check the company website.

FAST BOAT & CATAMARAN
There are daily catamarans to Piraeus (€49.50, 5½ hours), Santorini (€15.50, 40 minutes), Naxos (€20.20, one hour), Paros (€18.90, 1½ hours), Mykonos (€26.10, two hours) and Iraklio and Rethymno on Crete (€35.80, 2½ hours).

FERRY
There are at least four daily connections with Piraeus (€30.50, seven hours), Paros (€12.50, 2½ hours) and Naxos (€11.50, 1¼ hours). There are daily boats to Santorini (€8.50, 1¼ hours), five-weekly boats to Sikinos (€3.80, 30 minutes), Folegandros (€5.60, 1½ hours) and Anafi (€8.20, three hours) and four-weekly boats to Syros (€19.50, 2¾ hours).

There are three boats weekly to Milos (€14.10, 3½ hours) and Mykonos (€12.70, seven hours), two boats weekly to Kimolos (€9.40, 2½ hours), Sifnos (€11.10, five hours), Serifos (€12.20, six hours) and Kythnos (€16.20, 8½ hours).

One boat goes to Amorgos on Saturday (€9.70, 2½ hours).

Getting Around
In summer crowded buses run between Ormos, Hora (€1.20) and Mylopotas Beach (€1.20) about every 15 minutes. Private excursion buses go to Manganari Beach (€8, 10.30am and 12.30am) and Agia Theodoti Beach (€1.50, in July and August).

Caïques travelling from Ormos to Manganari cost €10 per person for a return trip (departing 11am daily). Ormos and Hora both have car and motorcycle rental that can be booked through the Plakiotis Travel Agency (p188) and Acteon Travel (p188).

HORA, ORMOS & MYLOPOTAS
ΧΩΡΑ, ΟΡΜΟΣ & ΜΥΛΟΠΟΤΑΣ
Ios has three population centres, all very close together on the west coast: the port, Ormos; the capital, Hora (also known as

the 'village'), 2km inland, by road, from the port; and Mylopotas, the beach 2km downhill from Hora. Gialos Beach stretches west of the port.

Orientation

The bus terminal in Ormos is straight ahead from the ferry quay on Plateia Emirou. If you don't mind the heat, it's possible to walk from the port to Hora by heading up left from Plateia Emirou, then right up a stepped path after about 100m. It's about 1.2km.

In Hora the main landmark is the big cathedral opposite the bus stop, on the other side of the dusty car park and play area. Plateia Valeta is the central square. There are public toilets uphill behind the main square.

The road straight ahead from the bus stop leads to Mylopotas Beach.

Information

There's an ATM right by the information kiosks at the ferry quay. In Hora, the National Bank of Greece, behind the church, and the Commercial Bank, nearby, both have ATMs.

The post office in Hora is a block behind the town hall side of the main road.

Acteon Travel (☎ 22860 91343; acteon@otenet.gr) On the square near the quay, and in Hora and Mylopotas.

Doubleclick Internet (☎ 22860 92155; Hora; per hr €4) A well-equipped place with good connection.

Hospital (☎ 22860 91227) On the way to Gialos, 250m northwest of the quay; there are several doctors in Hora.

Plakiotis Travel Agency (☎ 22860 91221; plaktr2@otenet.gr) On the Ormos waterfront.

Port police (☎ 22860 91264) At the southern end of the Ormos waterfront, just before Ios Camping.

Sights

Hora is a lovely Cycladic village with a labyrinth of narrow lanes and cubist houses. It's at its most charming during daylight hours when the bars are shut and it recaptures the atmosphere of other island towns.

The **archaeological museum** (admission free; ☼ 8.30am-3pm Tue-Sun) is in the town hall by the bus stop.

Activities

Banana rides (€10), canoe rental (per hour €8) and mountain-bike rental (per day €10) are all available at **Yialos Watersports** (☎ 22860 92463, 6944926625; ralfburgstahler@hotmail.com; Gialos Beach). Hire windsurfing equipment (per hour

€15, per half-day €30, lessons free), or take a tube ride (€14 to €17).

Mylopotas Water Sports Center (☎ 22860 91622; www.ios-sports.gr; Mylopotas Beach) has snorkelling and windsurfing gear, pedal boats (per hour €15) and canoes (per hour/day €8/24) for hire. Windsurfing rental (per hour/day €15/40), waterskiing (per 10/15 minutes €27/30) and banana rides (€10 to €15) are available. There's also a speedboat taxi.

Windsurfing (per hour €15, per day €40) is on offer at **Meltemi Water Sports** (☎ 22860 91680, 69321153912; www.meltemiwatersports.com; Mylopotas) at the beach opposite Far Out Camping. Laser sailboats (per hour/day €30/65) are also available for hire, as are canoes and pedalos. Tube rides cost from €15 to €30. Meltemi runs a similar scene at Manganari Beach and has a water taxi from Mylopotas to other beaches.

Sleeping

ORMOS

The port has several good sleeping options, reasonable eating places, a couple of handy beaches and regular bus connections to Hora and on to other beaches.

Ios Camping (☎ 22860 92035; fax 22860 92101; camp sites per person €8; ☻) Tucked away on the west side of Ormos, this site has good facilities, including a restaurant in high season. Head all the way round the waterfront.

Hotel Poseidon (☎ 22860 91091; www.poseidonhotel ios.gr; s/d/tr €71/85/102; ☒ ☻) A great choice: this family-run hotel stands high above the port and has terrific views from its front balconies. Rooms are immaculate and well equipped and there's a pleasant swimming pool.

GIALOS BEACH

Hotel Helena (☎ 22860 91276; www.hotelhelena.gr; s/d/tr €50/70/90, apt €120; ☒ 🖵) Set a short way back from the midpoint of the beach is this quiet and well-run place. It has a cool patio, bright, clean rooms and a friendly welcome.

To Corali (☎ 22860 91272; www.coralihotel.com; s/d incl breakfast €55/80; **P** ☒ 🖵) These sparkling rooms are in a good position right opposite the beach and are attached to the restaurant of the same name. There's a colourful garden at the rear and the owners create a happy atmosphere.

HORA

Francesco's (☎ 22860 91223; www.francescos.net; dm €15, s €35-40, d €45-50; 🖵) Long established and very well run, the famous Francesco's has clean dormitories and rooms and is in an enviable position with great views of the bay. It's away from the centre but is a lively meeting place for the younger international set. The party spirit rules supreme and there's a busy bar and terrace.

Skala Hotel (☎ 22860 92027; skalahtl@otenet.gr; d/tr €85/100, apt €90-160; ❄ 🖳 ▣) If you want to rise above the central hubbub, a short hike uphill from the centre takes you to this well-sited hotel with great views over Hora. Rooms are bright and a good size and have kitchenettes. There's a pool and a Jacuzzi.

MYLOPOTAS
Purple Pig Stars Camping & Bungalows (☎ 22860 91302; www.purplepigstars.com; Mylopotas Beach; camp sites per person €9, dm €20, d €44; ▣) This pleasant camping ground is right at the entrance to the beach and has a relaxing tempo while being close to the action. It's shaded by trees.

Far Out Camping And Beach Club (☎ 22860 91468; www.faroutclub.com; Mylopotas Beach; camp sites per adult/child €12/6, no charge for own tent, small/large bungalows €12/20, studio €90; 🖳 ▣) There's plenty of action here, backed by wall-to-wall facilities. Meltemi Water Sports (see opposite) is just across the road, and a diving centre has been established in recent years. There's a bar, restaurant and four swimming pools. The 'bungalows' range from small tent-sized affairs to neat little 'roundhouses' with double and single beds.

our pick Hotel Nissos Ios (☎ 22860 91610; www.nissosioshotel.com; Mylopotas Beach; s/d/tr €50/70/85; ❄ 🖳) This excellent place has bright and fresh rooms, and colourful wall murals add a cheerful touch. Each room has tea- and coffee-making facilities. The welcome is friendly and good-natured, and the beach is just across the road. There's an outdoor Jacuzzi. In front of the hotel is the Bamboo Restaurant & Pizzeria (p190).

Paradise Rooms (☎ 22860 91621; parios11@otenet.gr; Mylopotas Beach; s/d €55/65; ❄) The family-run rooms here are about half way along the beachfront, and the beautiful garden is looked after with love and skill. Breakfast costs from €3 to €4.

Paradise Apartments (☎ 22860 91621; Mylopotas Beach; apt €90-140; ❄ ▣) These apartments are located a short distance away from Paradise Rooms, and are run by a member of the same family. They're in a secluded setting and have a lovely pool and big patio. At both Paradise

accommodations, guests can get a 50% reduction at Mylopotas Water Sports Center (opposite).

Eating
ORMOS
Susannah (☎ 22860 51108; dishes €6.50-12) No-nonsense food, from Greek salads to pasta and pizza, keeps this harbour taverna popular with locals. It's set back from the street in a wide square, by Acteon Travel.

GIALOS BEACH
To Corali (☎ 22860 91272; dishes €5-9) Mouthwatering wood-fired pizzas are list-toppers at this friendly, well-run eatery that's right by the beach and in front of the hotel of the same name. You can sit out at tables on the beach. It does pastas and salads as well, and it's a great spot for coffee, drinks and ice cream.

HORA
Porky's (☎ 22860 91143; snacks €2-4.50) Fuel up with toasties, salads, crepes and hamburgers at this relentless Ios survivor just off the main square.

Old Byron (☎ 22860 92125; dishes €3.50-15; ⏲ 7pm-late) A little way up the main street from the cathedral is this wine bar and eatery (the previous location of Lord Byron – see below), offering an eclectic menu that includes pasta, mezedhes and even bangers and mash. There's background Greek and contemporary music.

our pick Pomodoro (☎ 22860 91387; dishes €5.50-12) Opened in recent years, this new Ios favourite spreads over two floors. There's a fabulous roof garden with panoramic views. It's just off the main square above Disco 69, and offers authentic wood-fired pizzas as just part of its excellent Italian and Mediterranean menu.

Ali Baba's (☎ 22860 91558; dishes €6-10) In the same venue as the restaurant of that name there's another great Ios favourite. This is the place for tasty Thai dishes, including *pad thai* (thin rice noodles stir-fried with dried shrimp, bean sprouts, tofu and egg) cooked by authentic Thai chefs. The service is very upbeat and there's entertainment. It's on the same street as the Emporiki bank.

Lord Byron (☎ 22860 92125; dishes €7-14) Near the main square, this long-standing favourite is relaxing and intimate, and the food is a great fusion of Greek and Italian. Dishes range from shrimp cooked in a tomato sauce with

CYCLADES

feta and ouzo to penne with a wild mushroom and cream sauce – and it all comes in generous helpings.

There are several *gyros* stands where you can get a cheap bite.

MYLOPOTAS

Drakos Taverna (☎ 22860 91281; dishes €3.50-9) Enjoy reasonably priced fish dishes (although some species are by the kilogram) at this popular taverna that overlooks the sea at the southern end of the beach. Whatever's on the dish, you get the feeling that it may well have hopped straight from the water into the kitchen and then onto your plate.

Harmony (☎ 22860 91613; dishes €3.50-12) Few places take chill-out to the honed level of this great bar. Hammocks, deckchairs and discerning sounds set the pace and kids are well looked after here. It's just along the northern arm of Mylopotas beach. There's live music too, and Tex-Mex food is the main attraction.

Bamboo Restaurant & Pizzeria (☎ 22860 91648; dishes €5-8.50) Run by a member of the same family that operates Hotel Nissos Ios (p189), this pleasant place offers traditional *mousakas* and tasty pizzas, plus a range of other Greek dishes.

Entertainment

Nightlife on Ios is a blitz. No-one signs up for an early night in Hora's tiny main square, where it gets so crowded by midnight that you won't be able to fall down, even if you want to. Be young and carefree – but (women especially) also be careful. For a marginally quieter life there are some less full-on venues around, including Ios Club, Ali Baba's and Orange Bar.

Slammer Bar (☎ 22860 92119; Main Sq, Hora) Hammers out house, rock and Latin. Multiple tequila shots, and head-banging in every sense.

Superfly (☎ 22860 92259; Main Sq, Hora) Plays funky house tunes.

Disco 69 (☎ 22860 91064; Main Sq, Hora) Offers hard-core drinking – and hard-core T-shirts – to a background of disco and current hits.

Sweet Irish Dream (☎ 22860 91141) It's Guinness on tap at this IOS (Ireland Over Seas) hang-out on the right-hand side of the road as you enter Hora.

Ios Club (☎ 22860 91410) Head here for a cocktail and watch the sun set to classical,

Latin and jazz music from a great terrace with sweeping views. It's along the pathway by Sweet Irish Dream.

Ali Baba's (☎ 22860 91558) Offers a mix of entertainment that includes the latest Hollywood films, mainstream music, and bands playing originals and covers.

Orange Bar (☎ 22860 91914) A more easy-paced music bar playing rock, indie and Brit-pop just outside the war zone.

Other popular late-night bars and clubs on the square:
Blue Note (☎ 22860 92271)
Flames Bar (☎ 22860 92448)
Red Bull (☎ 22860 91019)

Scorpion's is a late-night dance-to-trance and progressive venue with laser shows. Aftershock goes for sensation with raunchy dancers and house, trance and Greek hits as well as guest DJs.

AROUND IOS

Travellers are lured to Ios by its nightlife, but also by its beaches. Vying with Mylopotas as one of the best is **Manganari**, a long swath of fine white sand on the south coast, reached by bus or by caïque in summer (see Getting Around, p187).

From Ormos, it's a 10-minute walk past the little church of Agia Irini for **Valmas Beach**. A 1.3km walk northwest of Ormos, **Koumbara** is the official clothes-optional beach. **Tsamaria**, nearby, is nice and sheltered when it's windy elsewhere.

Agia Theodoti, **Psathi** and **Kalamos Beaches**, all on the northeast coast, are more remote. Psathi is a good windsurfing venue.

Moni Kalamou, on the way to Manganari and Kalamos Beaches, stages a huge **religious festival** in late August and a **festival of music and dance** in September.

SANTORINI (THIRA)
ΣΑΝΤΟΡΙΝΗ (ΘΗΡΑ)

pop 13,402

Fantastic, fabulous Santorini deserves all the superlatives. Even the most jaded traveller succumbs to the awesome drama of this surreal landscape, relic of what was probably the biggest eruption in recorded history. That you share the experience with hordes of other visitors is inevitable. Embrace it all.

The caldera and its vast curtain wall of multicoloured cliffs is truly awesome. If you want to experience the full dramatic impact it's worth arriving by a slower ferry with open decks, rather than by enclosed catamaran or hydrofoil.

Santorini is famous for its spectacular sunsets. The village of Oia on the northern tip of the island is a hugely popular sunset viewing site because there is an uninterrupted view of the sun as it finally sinks below the horizon. From farther south down the caldera edge, the last of the setting sun can be obscured by the islands of Nea Kameni and Thirasia. Take your pick, however. You can enjoy most of the sunset from almost anywhere along the rim of the caldera, especially if you want to avoid the sometimes feverish crush at Oia.

The main port, Athinios, stands on a cramped shelf of land at the base of Sphinx-like cliffs and is a scene of marvellous chaos that always seems to work itself out when ferries arrive. Buses (and taxis) meet all ferries and then cart passengers through an ever-rising series of S-bends to the capital, Fira, which fringes the edge of the cliffs like a snowy cornice.

History

Minor eruptions have been the norm in Greece's earthquake record, but Santorini has bucked the trend – and with attitude – throughout history. Eruptions here were genuinely earth-shattering, and so wrenching that they changed the shape of the island several times.

Dorians, Venetians and Turks occupied Santorini, as they did all other Cycladic islands, but its most influential early inhabitants were Minoans. They came from Crete some time between 2000 and 1600 BC, and the settlement at Akrotiri (p199) dates from the peak years of their great civilisation.

The island was circular then and was called Strongili (Round One). In about 1650 BC a colossal volcanic eruption caused the centre of Strongili to sink, leaving a caldera with high cliffs – now one of the world's most dramatic sights. Some archaeologists have speculated that this catastrophe destroyed not only

CYCLADES

SANTORINI (THIRA)

0   4 km
0   2 miles

To Sifnos (105km); Serifos (120km); Milos (131km)

To Ios (41km); Naxos (87km); Paros (105km); Mykonos (128km); Syros (135km); Piraeus (240km); Thessaloniki (627km)

Paradise Beach
Baxedes
Sigalas Winery
Oia
Finikia
Pori Beach
Cape Riva
Ammoudi
Armeni Beach
Potamos Beach
Potamos
Manolas
Agrilia
Thirasia
Santorini (Thira)
Imerovigli
Vourvoulos
Gialos Beach
Firostefani
Fira
Karterados Beach
Fira Skala
Monolithos
Monolithos Beach
Karterados
Cape Trypiti
Nea Kameni
Messaria
Hot Springs
Palia Kameni
Vothonas
AEGEAN SEA
Aspronisi
Exo Gonia
Mesa Gonia
Athinios
Pyrgos
Megalohori
Mt Profitis Ilias (567m)
Kamari
Kamari Beach
Cape Akrotiri
Akrotiri
Mони Profiti Ilia
Ancient Thira
Cape Mesa Vouno
Ancient Akrotiri
Emporio
Perissa
567m
Black Beach
White Beach
Red Beach
Perivolos Beach
Agios Georgios Beach
Vlyhada Beach
Cape Evo Mytis

To Crete (128km)
To Anafi (56km)

SANTORINI'S UNSETTLING PAST

Always unstable, Santorini was part of a series of volcanoes over a million years ago. The volcanoes became dormant, and around 3000 BC the first human settlers arrived to take advantage of the fertile soil. From evidence found at Akrotiri, it appears that they led civilised lives and fashioned a highly sophisticated culture.

But the peace and harmony didn't last, and around 1650 BC a chain of earthquakes and eruptions culminated in one of the largest explosions in the history of the planet. Thirty cubic kilometres of magma spewed forth and a column of ash 36km high jetted into the atmosphere. The centre of the island collapsed, producing a caldera that the sea quickly filled. The eruption also generated huge tsunamis that travelled with dangerous force all the way to Crete and Israel; nearby Anafi was engulfed by one such gigantic wave. It's widely held that the catastrophe was responsible for the demise of Crete's Minoan culture, one of the most powerful civilisations in the Aegean at that time.

After the Big One, Santorini settled down for a time and was even recolonised. In 236 BC volcanic activity separated Thirasia from the main island. Further changes continued intermittently. In 197 BC the islet now known as Palia Kameni appeared in the caldera, and in AD 726 there was a major eruption that catapulted pumice all the way to Asia Minor. The south coast of Santorini collapsed in 1570, taking the ancient port of Eleusis with it. An eruption in 1707 created Nea Kameni Islet next to Palia Kameni.

A major earthquake measuring 7.8 on the Richter scale savaged the island in 1956, killing scores of people and destroying most of the houses in Fira and Oia. The renaissance is remarkable; the resilience and insouciance of locals even more so. For lovers of impermanence, precariousness and drama, Santorini is beyond compare.

Akrotiri but the structure, and eventually the essence, of Minoan civilisation.

Getting There & Away

AIR

Olympic Airlines (☎ 22860 22493; www.olympicairlines .com), at the airport, operates five flights daily in high season between Athens and Santorini (€79, 45 minutes).

Aegean Airlines (☎ airport 22860 28500; www.aegean air.com) has five flights daily between Athens and Santorini (€56 to €75, 45 minutes), four flights daily to and from Mykonos (€99, 45 minutes) and two flights daily to and from Thessaloniki (€118, 45 minutes), via Athens.

From Easter to September, **Sky Express** (☎ 28102 23500; www.skyexpress.gr) has at least four flights a week to Iraklio, Crete (€74, 30 minutes), four flights a week to Mykonos (€74, 35 minutes) and daily flights to Rhodes (€84, 40 minutes). Book online or enquire at travel agencies.

From June to September, **AirSea Lines** (☎ 21094 02012; www.airsealines.com) runs one seaplane every day, except Tuesday and Wednesday, between Lavrio and Santorini (€112, 1¼ hours) via Ios.

Until suspension of operations in July of 2007, **AirSea Lines** (☎ 21094 02012; www.airsea lines.com) ran one seaplane flight a day from Thursday to Monday between Lavrio and Santorini via Ios. Due to upgrading requirements the company suspended its Aegean schedule in July 2007. The schedule was still suspended at the time of writing (September 2007). The company states, however, that it will resume its Aegean service as soon as possible and readers are advised to check the company website.

FAST BOAT & CATAMARAN

Daily services run to and from Ios (€16, 30 minutes), Naxos (€29, 1½ hours), Paros (€25.30, 2¼ hours), Mykonos (€28, three to four hours), Folegandros (€14, 45 minutes), Sifnos (€31, 1¾ hours), Iraklio (€30.90 1¾ hours) and Piraeus (€55.50, 5¼ hours).

FERRY

There are at least four boats daily to Naxos (€15.50, three hours), Paros (€16.50, three to four hours), Ios (€8.50, 1¼ hours) and Piraeus (€32.50, nine hours) and two boats a week to Tinos (€14, five hours), Kythnos (€19.70, eight hours) and Folegandros (€6.70, 1½ to 2½ hours). Change at Naxos for Amorgos.

Seven boats weekly go to Anafi (€6.90, one hour), Sifnos (€12.50, 7¾ hours), Sikinos

(€9.80, 2½ hours), Iraklio (€15.10, 4½ hours) and Skiathos (€33.50, 18½ hours).

There are two weekly ferries running to Mykonos (€14, six hours), Milos (€15.50, four hours), Kimolos (€16.20, 3½ hours), Syros (€23, 5¼ hours), Serifos (€16.20, nine hours) and Thessaloniki (€41.10, 25 hours).

Getting Around
TO/FROM THE AIRPORT
There are frequent bus connections in summer between Fira's bus station and the airport, located southwest of Monolithos Beach. Enthusiastic hotel and domatia staff meet flights, and some also return guests to the airport. A taxi to the airport costs €12.

BUS
In summer buses leave Fira every half-hour for Oia (€1.20), Monolithos (€1.20), Kamari (€1.20) and Perissa (€1.90). There are less-frequent buses to Exo Gonia (€1.20), Perivolos (€1.90) and Vlyhada (€2). In summer the last regular bus to Fira from Oia leaves at 11.20pm.

Buses leave Fira, Kamari and Perissa for the port of Athinios (€1.60, 30 minutes) 1½ hours before most ferry departures. Buses for Fira meet all ferries, even late at night. It is wise to check port departures well in advance.

CABLE CAR & DONKEY
A **cable car** (☎ 22860 22977; M Nomikou; ☼ every 20min 7am-10pm, to 9pm winter) hums smoothly between Fira and the small port below, known as Fira Skala. One-way tickets per adult cost €4, and €2 per child; luggage is €2. You can make a more leisurely upward trip by donkey (tickets cost €4).

CAR & MOTORCYCLE
A car is the best way to explore the island during high season, when buses are intolerably overcrowded and you're lucky to get on one at all. Be very patient and cautious when driving – the narrow roads, especially in Fira, can be a nightmare. Note that Oia has no petrol station, the nearest being just outside Fira.

Two very good local rental outfits are **Damigos Rent a Car** (☎ 22860 22048, 6979968192) and for scooters, **Zerbakis** (☎ 22860 33329, 6944531992).

TAXI
If you're after a **taxi** (☎ 22860 23951/2555), there's a stand in the main square. A taxi from the

port of Athinios to Fira costs €10, and a trip from Fira to Oia is also €10. Both cost €12 if you call ahead by telephone. If you miss the last bus from Oia to Fira, three or four people can bargain for a shared taxi for about €12.

FIRA ΦHPA
pop 2113
A multitude of fellow admirers cannot diminish the impact of Fira's stupendous landscape. Views from the edge of the caldera over the multicoloured cliffs are breathtaking, and at night the caldera edge is a frozen cascade of lights that eclipses the displays of the jewellery shops in the streets behind.

Orientation
The central square is Plateia Theotokopoulou. It's a fairly crowded, chaotic place; the main road, 25 Martiou, intersects the square as part of a one-way system that just manages to keep the nonstop traffic flow going. The **bus station** (25 Mitropoleos) is 150m south of Plateia Theotokopoulou. Between 25 Martiou and the caldera is the essence of Fira, a network of pedestrianised alleyways, the main ones running parallel to Martiou. Erythrou Stavrou is the main commercial thoroughfare.

A block west of Erythrou Stavrou is Ypapantis, whose southern section is known also as Gold St because of its many jewellers. It runs along the edge of the caldera and has superb panoramic views until the shops intrude. Below the edge of the caldera is the paved walkway of Agiou Mina, which heads north and merges eventually with the cliff-top walkway that continues north past the villages of Firostefani and Imerovigli. Keep going and you'll reach Oia; but it's a long, hot 8km.

Information
Fira doesn't have an EOT (Greek National Tourist Organisation) or tourist police. It's best to seek out the smaller travel agents in the town, where you'll receive helpful service.

There are toilets near the taxi rank. You may need to brace yourself (they're of squat vintage). Bring your own paper – but not to read.

EMERGENCY
Hospital (☎ 22860 22237) On the road to Kamari.
Police station (☎ 22860 22649; Karterados) About 2km from Fira.

CYCLADES

CYCLADES

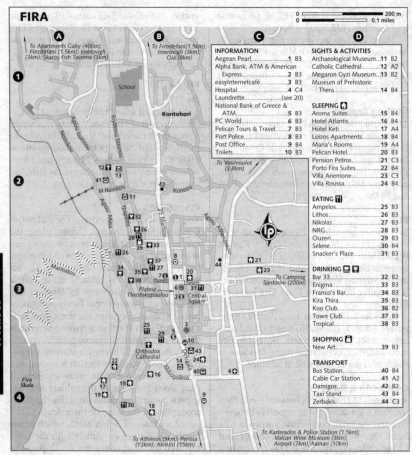

FIRA

0 ————————— 200 m
0 ————————— 0.1 miles

INFORMATION
Aegean Pearl.....................1 B3
Alpha Bank, ATM & American
  Express........................2 B3
easyInternetcafé................3 B3
Hospital........................4 C4
Laundrette...................(see 20)
National Bank of Greece &
  ATM.............................5 B3
PC World........................6 B3
Pelican Tours & Travel.......7 B3
Port Police.....................8 B3
Post Office.....................9 B4
Toilets........................10 B3

SIGHTS & ACTIVITIES
Archaeological Museum....11 B2
Catholic Cathedral.........12 A2
Megaron Gyzi Museum...13 B2
Museum of Prehistoric
  Thera.........................14 B4

SLEEPING
Aroma Suites..................15 B3
Hotel Atlantis................16 B4
Hotel Keti....................17 A4
Loizos Apartments.........18 B4
Maria's Rooms...............19 A4
Pelican Hotel.................20 B3
Pension Petros...............21 C3
Porto Fira Suites............22 B4
Villa Anemone...............23 C3
Villa Roussa..................24 B4

EATING
Ampelos........................25 B3
Lithos.........................26 B3
Nikolas........................27 B3
NRG............................28 B3
Ouzeri.........................29 B3
Selene.........................30 B4
Snacker's Place..............31 B3

DRINKING
Bar 33.........................32 B2
Enigma.........................33 B3
Franco's Bar..................34 B3
Kira Thira.....................35 B3
Koo Club......................36 B3
Town Club.....................37 B3
Tropical.......................38 B3

SHOPPING
New Art........................39 B3

TRANSPORT
Bus Station....................40 B4
Cable Car Station............41 A2
Damigos........................42 B3
Taxi Stand.....................43 B4
Zerbakis.......................44 C3

Port police (☎ 22860 22239; 25 Martiou) North of the square.

INTERNET ACCESS
PC World (☎ 22860 25551; Central Sq; per 30min €1.30; 🕙 10am-2am May-Oct, 10am-10pm Nov-Apr) A good range of services.
easyInternetcafé (25 Martiou; per hr €2.70) Self-service net connect, and wi-fi. Purchase a timed ticket from a coin machine – minimum charge is €1.

LAUNDRY
Laundrette (Danezi; average load wash & dry €6) Next to Pelican Hotel.

LEFT LUGGAGE
Laundrette (Danezi; locked luggage storage per 24hrs €1.50)

MONEY
There are numerous ATMs scattered around town.
Alpha Bank (Plateia Theotokopoulou) Represents American Express and has an ATM.
National Bank of Greece (Dekigala) Between the bus station and Plateia Theotokopoulou, on the caldera side of the road. Has an ATM.

POST
Post office (Dekigala)

TRAVEL AGENCIES
Aegean Pearl (☎ 22860 22170; www.aptravel.gr; Danezi) An excellent, helpful agency that sells all travel tickets and can help with accommodation, car rental and excursions.

Pelican Tours & Travel (☎ 22860 22220; fax 22860 22570; Plateia Theotokopoulou) Sells ferry tickets and books accommodation and excursions.

Sights & Activities
MUSEUMS

Near the bus station, the **Museum of Prehistoric Thera** (☎ 22860 23217; Mitropoleos; admission €3; ☒ 8.30am-3pm Tue-Sun) houses extraordinary finds that were excavated from Akrotiri (where, to date, only 5% of the area has been excavated). Most impressive is the glowing gold ibex figurine, measuring around 10cm in length and dating from the 17th century BC. Many of Akrotiri's fascinating wall paintings are on display.

The **Archaeological Museum** (☎ 22860 22217; M Nomikou; adult/student €3/free; ☒ 8.30am-3pm Tue-Sun), near the cable-car station, houses finds from Akrotiri and Ancient Thira, some Cycladic figurines, and Hellenistic and Roman sculptures.

Behind the Catholic cathedral, **Megaron Gyzi Museum** (☎ 22860 22244; Agiou Ioannou; adult/ concession €3.50/2; ☒ 10.30am-1pm & 5-8pm Mon-Sat, 10.30am-4.30pm Sun May-Oct) has local memorabilia, including fascinating photographs of Fira before and immediately after the 1956 earthquake.

If you fancy a great professional photography course, based on Santorini, contact **Greek Island Workshops** (www.glennsteiner.com). It's run by top professional Glenn Steiner.

Tours

Tour companies operate various trips including a bus-and-boat tour (€40), which lasts from four to eight hours depending on the itinerary and takes in Thirasia, the volcanic island of Nea Kameni, Palia Kameni's hot springs and Oia; book at travel agencies.

The *Bella Aurora*, an exact copy of an 18th-century schooner, scoots around the caldera every afternoon on a sunset buffet dinner tour (€42, from May to October), stopping for sightseeing on Nea Kameni and for ouzo on Thirasia. Most travel agencies sell tickets.

Sleeping
BUDGET

Few of Fira's sleeping options are cheap, and even budget places hike their prices in July and August. Domatia touts at the port reach impressive heights of hysteria in their bids for attention. Some claim their rooms are in town, when they're actually a long way out; be tough and ask to see a map showing the exact location. If you're looking for a caldera view, expect to pay at least double the prices of elsewhere. Many hotels in Fira, especially on the caldera rim, cannot be reached by vehicle. If you have heavy luggage, this is worth remembering.

Camping Santorini (☎ 22860 22944; www.santorinicamping.gr; camp sites per adult/child/tent €9/4/4; P ☐ ☒) Located on the eastern outskirts of town, this camping ground has some shade and decent facilities. There's a self-service restaurant, minimarket and pool. It's 400m east of Plateia Theotokopoulou. There are camping bungalows also; enquire about prices.

Also recommended:

Villa Roussa (☎ 22860 23220; Dekigala; s/d €50/60) Convenient and near the centre.

Pension Petros (☎ 22860 22573; www.astirthira.gr; s/d/tr €50/60/75; ☒) Decent rooms, though not much of a view. On the way to the campsite. Head down Danezi, turn left and then right.

MIDRANGE

Loizos Apartments (☎ 22860 24046; www.loizos.gr; s €60, d €65-80, apt €140; ☒ ☐ ☒) Unbeatable value and friendly, helpful management make this one of the best places in Fira. Loizos is in a quiet location and only minutes from the centre of town and the caldera edge. Rooms are bright, clean and comfortable and those on the front upper floor have a panoramic view towards Kamari and the sea. Breakfast is €5. The same owners have similar, but cheaper accommodation at Messaria, 2.5km southeast of Fira.

Apartments Gaby (☎ 22860 22057; Nomikou; d €65-85, tw €100, apt €120) The rooms on the series of roof terraces at this excellent place guarantee fantastic sunset views, and there's a reassuring local feel that transcends Fira's surface gloss. Gaby is just beyond the convention centre on the caldera-edge path where it reaches Firostefani.

Pelican Hotel (☎ 22860 23113; www.pelican.gr; Danezi; s/d/tr incl breakfast €68/84/100; ☒ ☐) A smart refurbishment in recent years has made Pelican a good value choice. There's no caldera view, but rooms are comfy and well appointed.

Maria's Rooms (☎ 22860 25143, 6973254461; Agiou Mina; d €70; ☒) A handful of charming rooms open onto a shared terrace that offers unbeatable caldera and sunset views. Rooms are small but immaculate, and are blissfully peaceful.

CYCLADES

Hotel Keti (☎ 22860 22324; www.hotelketi.gr; Agiou Mina; d €80-100, tr €105; 🖰) Recently refurbished, Hotel Keti is one of the smaller 'sunset view' hotels in a peaceful caldera niche. Its attractive traditional rooms are carved into the cliffs. Half of the rooms have Jacuzzis.

our pick Aroma Suites (☎ 22860 24112; www .aromasuites.gr; Agiou Mina; s €100, d €120-160) Opened in recent years at the quieter end of the caldera edge, this delightful boutique hotel has charming owners to match. Stylish modern facilities enhance traditional caldera interiors such as the honeymoon suite: a classic Fira cave chamber, complete with Jacuzzi. Rates are substantially reduced in low season.

Villa Anemone (☎ 22860 22573; www.astirthira.gr; s/d/tr €60/70/80) is run by the same family that operates nearby Pension Petros (see Budget, p195). On the way to the campsite. Head down Danezi, turn left and then right.

TOP END

Hotel Atlantis (☎ 22860 22232; www.atlantishotel.gr; Mitropoleos; s/d incl breakfast €200/284; **P** 🖰 🖳) The Atlantis is a handsome old building that overlooks the southern end of Ypapantis with a flourish. It's full of cool, relaxing lounges and terraces, and the bright and airy bedrooms in the front have caldera views.

Porto Fira Suites (☎ 22860 22849; www.portofira.gr; Agiou Mina; 2-4-person ste incl breakfast €297-439; 🖰 🖳) Luxury on the edge is the keynote of this top-rated Fira hotel that merges tradition with all the modern conveniences. Rooms are stylishly furnished and have huge stone-based beds and Jacuzzis. There's a bar and café.

Eating

Tourist-trap eateries, often with overpriced, indifferent food, are still an unfortunate feature of summertime Fira. In some places singles, and even families with young children, may find themselves unwelcome in the face of pushy owners desperate to keep tables full and their turnover brisk. However, there are excellent exceptions.

BUDGET

Snacker's Place (☎ 22860 22538; Danezi; snacks €1-2.30) A snack bar and takeaway that dishes out a terrific range of tasty sandwiches, wraps and other snacks as well as hot and cold drinks.

NRG (☎ 22860 24997; Erythrou Stavrou; dishes €2.20-6.20) This popular little creperie right at the heart of the action is a Fira institution. As well as delicious crepes, it also does sandwiches, tortillas, an ever-popular Indian curry (€4.80), ice cream, coffee and smoothies.

our pick Ouzeri (☎ 6945849921; Fabrika Shopping Centre; dishes €3-14.50) A complete refurbishment in 2007 reflected the popularity of this great *mezedhopoleio*. Its fish dishes are especially good, including prawn saganaki and a sea platter of mixed fish. Equally tasty meat dishes, including *tigania* (pork in wine with yogurt), will satisfy meat eaters while vegetarians can enjoy salads and a variety of nonmeat starters.

Nikolas (☎ 22860 24550; Erythrou Stavrou; dishes €6-10) A long-established restaurant at the heart of Fira offering traditional Greek cuisine such as stuffed zucchini and cuttlefish in wine.

Skaros Fish Taverna (☎ 22860 23616; dishes €8.50-16) You can escape Fira's seductive grip by heading north along the caldera edge to this long-established restaurant. Dishes such as seafood salad or pork fillet in Vinsanto are worth it – and so is the fantastic view.

There are several *gyros* stands in and around the main square.

MIDRANGE

Lithos (☎ 22860 24421; Agiou Mina; mains €7-19.50) Amid a swath of eateries on the caldera edge, Lithos stands out for its well-prepared dishes and friendly service. Choose from persuasive starters such as fava with cheese and cherry tomatoes; salads are crisp and fresh and mains cover poultry, meat, fish and shellfish dishes.

Ampelos (☎ 22860 25554; Fabrika Shopping Centre; mains €8-22) Dine with a view from the big upstairs space at this fine restaurant. Enjoy a flavourful chicken soup with egg and lemon, or the 'Ampelos Pie' with its mix of green onion, dill, pine nuts and Parmesan. Main dishes range across meat, poultry and fish and are all prepared with traditional (and a dash of Californian) style. The house wine is worthwhile at €7 per half-litre, while excellent Greek reds and whites are €16 to €45 per bottle.

Selene (☎ 22860 22249; Agiou Mina; dishes €23-26) There's fashionable, pricey cuisine at Selene, but if you're not into the prices or the sea urchin salad on artichoke heart, or fish and langoustine soup, you can at least gaze down at this top restaurant's sunset-aligned terrace from a public walkway on a higher level. Mains are a rich choice of meat and fish dishes such as cod in green pepper with saffron sauce.

SANTORINI WINES

Santorini's two lauded wines are its crisp, clear dry whites, and the amber-coloured, unfortified dessert wine Vinsanto. Most local vineyards hold tastings and tours.

The atmospheric **Volcan Wine Museum** (☎ 22860 31322; www.volcanwines.gr; admission €5; ☺ noon-8pm), housed in a traditional *canava* (winery) on the way to Kamari, has some interesting displays, including a 17th-century wooden winepress. Admission to the museum includes three tastings. On Sunday nights there's a traditional Greek night with a buffet, local dancers and the added spice of belly dancing.

There's also the Art Space gallery-winery outside Kamari – see p199.

The following should be contacted before visiting:

Boutari (☎ 22860 81011; www.boutari.gr; Megalohori)

Canava Roussos (☎ 22860 31349; www.canavaroussos.gr; Mesa Gonia)

Hatzidakis (☎ 22860 32552; www.hatzidakiswines.gr; Pyrgos Kallistis)

Santo Wines (☎ 22860 22596; www.santowines.gr; Pyrgos)

Sigalas (☎ 22860 71644; www.sigalas-wine.gr; Oia)

Drinking

Be ready to fork out some hefty prices, even for a beer, in the Fira clubs and bars (and check out the stellar cocktail prices). You're often paying for the view, so don't glaze over too early.

Kira Thira (☎ 22860 22770; Erythrou Stavrou) The oldest bar in Fira and one of the best. There are entrances from the streets on either side. Locals always use the same one. Guess which and you'll feel even more at home in this candle-lit bar with its smooth jazz, ethnic sounds and occasional live music.

Tropical (☎ 22860 23089; Marinatou) A seductive mix of rock, soul and occasional jazz, plus unbeatable balcony views, make this friendly bar a top Fira favourite. A stylish local crew and international crowd keep things going into the early hours.

Franco's Bar (☎ 22860 24428; Marinatou) Things move at a cooler pace at this ultimate sunset venue simply because of its sheer elegance and impeccable musical taste – it's always classical sounds here. Expensive cocktails with expensive names (Maria Callas, for starters) match the style.

Entertainment

After midnight Erythrou Stavrou fires up the clubbing caldera of Fira.

Koo Club (☎ 22860 22025; Erythrou Stavrou) Five bars with switching ambience through well-spaced levels make this a popular place with locals and visitors alike. Sounds are mainstream and Greek hits with a touch of hip-hop.

Town Club (☎ 22860 22820; Erythrou Stavrou) Modern Greek music and mainstream are just right for the charmingly kitsch landscape of this upbeat place.

Enigma (☎ 22860 22466; Erythrou Stavrou) Frontline fashionistas sashay round the cool white walls and muslin drapes to house and mainstream hits.

Bar 33 (☎ 22860 23065; Erythrou Stavrou) A lively bouzouki place in classic Thira barrel-roofed surroundings.

Shopping

So much shopping, so little time – this is the mantra of the hordes of cruise ship passengers who forage happily through Fira's glitzy retail zones. You can get everything from Armani and Versace to Timberland and Reef – at rather glitzy prices, too.

Fira's jewellery and gold shops are legion. The merchandise gleams and sparkles, and prices are high.

New Art (☎ 22860 23770; Erythrou Stavrou) If you want something different to sport back home, the quality T-shirts of designer Werner Hampel have real style.

Grapes thrive in Santorini's volcanic soil, and the island's wines are famous all over Greece and beyond. Local wines are widely available in Fira and elsewhere. **Sigalas Argyris** (La Cava; ☎ 22860 22802) in Firostefani has a good selection of wines and local delicacies, such as caper leaves and thyme honey.

AROUND SANTORINI

Oia Οία
pop 763

The village of Oia (*ee*-ah), known locally as Pano Meria, was so devastated by the 1956

CYCLADES

earthquake that it became something of a ghost town for a while. However, there is little evidence of that period because good restoration work and upmarket tourism have transformed Oia into an attractive place. Though quieter than tourist-frenzied Fira, its streets still have their share of trendy boutiques and expensive jewellery shops. Built on a steep slope of the caldera, many of its dwellings nestle in niches hewn into the volcanic rock. Oia, believe it or not, gets more sunset time than Fira, and its narrow passageways get crowded in the evenings.

ORIENTATION & INFORMATION

From the bus terminal, head left and uphill to reach the rather stark central square and the main street, Nikolaou Nomikou, which skirts the caldera. There is also an ATM by the bus terminal shelter.

Alpha Bank Branches on Main St, near the blue-domed church, and outside Karvounis Tours. With ATM.

Atlantis Books (☎ 22860 72346; www.atlantisbooks .org; Nikolaou Nomikou) A fascinating and well-stocked little bookshop run with flair and enthusiasm by an international group of young people. Cultural events, for a small number of people, are sometimes staged here.

Karvounis Tours (☎ 22860 71290; www.idogreece .com; Nikolaou Nomikou) For obtaining information, booking hotels, renting cars and bikes, and making international calls. It's also a wedding specialist.

SIGHTS & ACTIVITIES

The **maritime museum** (☎ 22860 71156; adult/student €3/1.50; ☽ 10am-2pm & 5-8pm Wed-Mon) is housed in an old mansion and has entertaining displays on Santorini's maritime history. It is located along a narrow lane that leads off right from Nikolaou Nomikou about 100m south of the Museum Hotel.

Ammoudi, a tiny port with good tavernas and colourful fishing boats, lies 300 steps below Oia. In summer, boats and tours go from Ammoudi to Thirasia daily; check with travel agencies in Fira (p194) for departure times.

SLEEPING

Oia Youth Hostel (☎ 22860 71465; www.santorinihostel .gr; dm incl breakfast €17; ☽ May–mid-Oct) Exceptionally clean and well run, this hostel has better facilities than some hotels. It has a small bar and a lovely rooftop terrace with great views. To find it, head on from the bus terminus for about 100m.

Chelidonia (☎ 22860 71287; www.chelidonia.com; Nikolaou Nomikou; studios €145 apt €170-205; ✷ ▯) Buried beneath the rubble of the 1956 earthquake, these cliff-side dwellings have been lovingly restored by the friendly and helpful owner, who was born here. Furnishings are a pleasant mix of traditional and modern, and each unit has a kitchenette.

Katikies (☎ 22860 71401; katikies@otenet.gr; Nikolaou Nomikou; d €245, studios incl champagne breakfast €290-750; ✷ ▯ ▣) One of Santorini's most beautiful hotels, Katikies is at the east end of the village, just below the main street. It revels in luxury and its cliff-edge pool is spectacular. Rooms here are traditional-chic and super swish.

EATING & DRINKING

1800 (☎ 22860 71485; Nikolaou Nomikou; dishes €13-29; ☽ 6.30-11.30pm) A former sea captain's house is now a temple to slow food. There's a magical use of herbs and subtle sauces to produce such gastro-delights as fillet of sea bream with cherry tomatoes, olives and baked fennel. The stylish dining room and terrace-patio add to the pleasure.

Edwin Polski Lokal (☎ 22860 71971; dishes €6.50-15) Popular and unreservedly nonglam, this little place does tasty salads, plates and home-cooked *gyros*. It has a sister establishment, Pizza Edwin, near the bus terminal.

Skala (☎ 22860 71362; Nikolaou Nomikou; dishes €8-14) A caldera-view terrace enhances Skala's fine traditional cuisine, which adds international touches to such treats as chicken fillet stuffed with mushrooms, or pork in honey and beer.

Kamari Καμάρι

pop 1351

Kamari is 10km from Fira and is Santorini's best-developed resort. It has a long beach of black sand, with the rugged limestone cliffs of Cape Mesa Vouno framing its southern end. The beachfront road is dense with restaurants and bars. Things get very busy in high season. Other less-appealing, but quieter, beaches lie to the north at Monolithos.

Lisos Tours (☎ 22860 33765; lisostours@san.forthnet .gr) is especially helpful – and knowledgeable about Santorini – and has an office on the main road into Kamari, and another just inland from the centre of the beach. Staff sell ferry tickets and can organise accommodation and car rental. All kinds of tours can be arranged through Lisos Tours, including fixed-wing flights over the caldera, horse riding and kayaking. There's internet access and a bureau de change.

The unmissable gallery and winery **Art Space** (☎ 22860 32774; Exo Gonia) is just outside Kamari. It is located in Argyro's Canava, one of the oldest wineries on the island. The atmospheric old wine caverns are hung with superb artworks while sculptures transform lost corners and niches. The collection is curated by the owner and features some of Greece's finest modern artists. Winemaking is still in the owner's blood, so a tasting of his Vinsanto greatly enhances the whole experience.

Kamari is fast becoming Santorini's Cine City with two movie venues. The long-established **Cinema Kamari** (☎ 22860 31974; www .cinekamari.gr), on the main road coming into Kamari, is a great open-air theatre that's set in a thicket of trees. It shows new releases at 9.30pm daily and midnight on Monday and Wednesday. In July it hosts the three-day **Santorini Jazz Festival** (☎ 22860 33452; www.jazzfestival .gr), featuring performances by Greek and foreign musicians. In Kamari Shopping Centre is the covered **Villaggio Cinema** (☎ 22860 32800; www .villaggiocinema.gr), showing films at 8.30pm.

SLEEPING

Anna's Rooms (☎ 22860 22765; s/d €25/35) Unbeatable budget deals can be had at these straightforward rooms. One group of rooms is behind Lisos Tours at the back of town; the other is behind Lisos' office in the village.

Boathouse Hotel (☎ 22860 33477; www.boathouse hotel.com; s/d/tr incl breakfast €60/80/96; P ⏼ ⏼) Located near the quieter north end of the beach, these bright, spacious and well-equipped rooms are in a handsome building just across from the beach.

[our pick] **Aegean View Hotel** (☎ 22860 32790; www.aegeanview-santorini.com; studios/apt €130/150; P ⏼ ⏼ ⏼) High on a hill, this outstanding place spreads over several levels below sculpted cliffs. It has terrific views out over Kamari to the sea and to distant Anafi. The spacious studios and apartments are superbly laid out and have 1st-class facilities, including small kitchen areas. Head up the steep road that leads to Ancient Thira and the hotel is easily located on the right, beneath steep cliffs.

Also recommended:

Hotel Selini (☎ /fax 22860 32625; s/d incl breakfast €35/45) Reliable, family-run hotel. Rooms are a good size and the hotel is just a few blocks in from Kamari beach.

Hotel Matina (☎ 22860 31491; www.hotel-matina .com; s/d incl breakfast €92/100; ⏼ ⏼ ⏼) Spacious, brightly decorated rooms and a convenient location make this year-round hotel a good choice.

EATING

Amalthia (☎ 22860 22780; dishes €3.50-12) A long-established local favourite. Amalthia is a couple of blocks inland at the southern end of town, and there's a lovely garden area and a terrace with barbecue. Friendly service goes with well-prepared Greek dishes; the lamb is particularly good. It also prepares very tasty pastas.

Eanos (☎ 22860 31161; dishes €4.50-14.80) Full of character – and characters – this long-running taverna, near the south end of the waterfront, does excellent Greek dishes, including terrific *mousakas*. Food is cooked on a wood-burning stove and pasta is also on offer.

Almira (☎ 22860 33477; mains €7-15.50) Adjacent to the Boathouse Hotel, the Almira offers an excellent range of fish, poultry and meat dishes, with lamb a speciality. Or you could try the 'drunken' chicken, in wine with tagliatelle.

[our pick] **Mario No 1** (☎ 22860 32000; Agia Paraskevi, Monolithos; dishes €5.50-12) Right on the beach at Monolithos, this big, well-run restaurant has a terrific take on fish cuisine. Fish is by the kilo and you can select shellfish from a display. There's a great selection of meat and vegetarian dishes as well.

Ancient Thira Αρχαία Θήρα

First settled by the Dorians in the 9th century BC, **Ancient Thira** (admission €4; ⏲ 8am-2.30pm) consists of Hellenistic, Roman and Byzantine ruins. The ruins include temples, houses with mosaics, an *agora* (market), a theatre and a gymnasium. There are splendid views from the site.

If you're driving, take the narrow, winding road from Kamari just over 1km. From Perissa, it takes about 45 minutes to walk to the site, along a path, on rocky, difficult ground.

Ancient Akrotiri Αρχαίο Ακρωτήρι

Excavations at **Akrotiri** (☎ 22860 81366), the Minoan outpost that was buried during the catastrophic eruption of 1650 BC, began in 1967 and have uncovered an ancient city beneath the volcanic ash. Buildings, some three storeys high, date back to the late 16th century BC. Outstanding finds are the stunning frescoes

CYCLADES

and ceramics, many of which are now on display at the Museum of Prehistoric Thera (p195) in Fira.

At the time of writing the site was closed indefinitely, pending completion of an official investigation – one visitor was killed and several others injured when a section of the roof collapsed during the summer of 2005. You may find that there is a degree of confusion locally about whether or not the site is open. Check the 'archaeological sites' section of www.culture.gr and check thoroughly on arrival at Santorini before making a bus or taxi journey to what may still be a closed site.

Beaches

At times Santorini's black-sand beaches become so hot that a sun lounger or mat is essential. The best beaches are on the east coast.

One of the main beaches is the long stretch at **Perissa**, a popular destination in summer. **Perivolos** and **Agios Georgios**, further south, are more relaxed. **Red Beach**, near Ancient Akrotiri, has high red cliffs and smooth, hand-sized pebbles submerged under clear water. **Vlyhada**, also on the south coast, is a pleasant venue. On the north coast near Oia, **Paradise** and **Pori** are both worth a stop.

Based at Perissa and Akrotiri Beach is the **Santorini Dive Centre** (☎ 22860 83190; www.divecenter .gr), offering a good range of courses including 'discover scuba diving' for €55, half-day snorkelling for €40 and a full open-water diving course for €380.

SLEEPING & EATING

The main concentration of rooms can be found in and around Perissa.

Hostel Anna (☎ 22860 81456; annayh@otenet.gr; dm €10, d €20; ⊙ Feb-Oct; 🖵) Recently renovated and under new management, Anna's is a friendly, popular hostel at the entrance to Perissa, and is a great place to meet fellow travellers. A minibus picks up guests from the ferry port.

Hotel Drossos (☎ 22860 81639; www.familydrossos .gr; s/d/tr incl breakfast €85/97/133; P 🖸 🖵 🕃) Behind the simple façade of this fine hotel lies a beautiful complex of rooms and studios. Rooms have stylish décor and furnishings and the service is courteous and friendly. Rates quoted rise by about 20% for the first three weeks of August and drop substantially outside summer.

Also recommended:

Stelio's Place (☎ 22860 81860; www.steliosplace.com; s/d/tr €50/60/75; P 🖸 🕃) Family-operated and close to the beach. A bright, well-run, friendly place.

Valvis (☎ 22860 81583; d/tr €67/73, ste €83-99; P 🖸 🕃) Modern hotel with decent-sized rooms and good facilities.

There's reliable Greek food on offer at **God's Garden** (☎ 22860 83027; dishes €3.50-9), a decent taverna with fish dishes starting at €6.

Most beaches have a range of tavernas and cafés.

THIRASIA & VOLCANIC ISLETS
ΘΗΡΑΣΙΑ & ΗΦΑΙΣΤΕΙΑΚΕΣ ΝΗΣΙΔΕΣ

Unspoilt Thirasia was separated from Santorini by an eruption in 236 BC. The cliff-top *hora*, **Manolas**, has tavernas and domatia. It's an attractive place, noticeably more relaxed and reflective than Fira could ever be.

The *Nisos Thira* leaves Athinios port for Thirasia on Monday and Friday, and on Wednesday mornings, but does not return to Santorini. Tickets are available only at the port. Take care of youngsters when on the upper deck near the rails (which have some child-sized gaps, especially on the port side). There are also morning and afternoon boats to Thirasia from Oia's port of Ammoudi.

The islets of **Palia Kameni** and **Nea Kameni** are still volcanically active and can be visited on half-day excursions from Fira Skala and Athinios. Two-hour trips to Nea Kameni are also possible. A day's excursion taking in Nea Kameni, the **hot springs** on Palia Kameni, Thirasia and Oia is about €28.

ANAFI ΑΝΑΦΗ

pop 272

Be ready to linger in this persuasive little island that lies well outside the mainstream and offers a perfect antidote to Santorini's fast-paced glitz. The rewards of Anafi include there being few other visitors (outside busy August, at least), a slow-paced traditional lifestyle and striking Cycladic landscapes.

The island's small port is **Agios Nikolaos**, where recent work has improved the quay. From here, the main village, **Hora**, is a 10-minute bus ride up a winding road, or a steep 1km hike up a less-winding walkway. In summer a bus runs every two hours from about

9am to 11pm and usually meets boats. Hora's main pedestrian thoroughfare leads uphill from the first bus stop and has most of the domatia, restaurants and minimarkets.

There is a postal agency that opens occasionally, next to Panorama rooms at the entrance to Hora. In 2007 it was announced that Anafi is to have an ATM installed in the near future.

Jeyzed Travel (☎ 22860 61253; jeyzed@san.forthnet .gr), halfway along Hora's main street, sells ferry tickets, exchanges money, can help with accommodation and rents out motorbikes. It also has internet access.

There are several lovely beaches near Agios Nikolaos. Palm-lined **Klissidi**, a 1½km walk to the port, is the closest and most popular.

Anafi's main sight is the monastery of **Moni Kalamiotissas**, a 6km walk from Hora in the extreme east of the island, near the meagre remains of a **sanctuary to Apollo**. At 470m, **Monastery Rock** is the highest rock formation in the Mediterranean, outstripping even Gibraltar. There is also a ruined Venetian *kastro* at **Kastelli**, east of Hora.

Sleeping & Eating

Camping is tolerated at Klissidi Beach, but the only facilities are at nearby tavernas. Domatia owners prefer long stays, so if you're only staying one night you should take whatever you can get. In high season, contact Jeyzed Travel in advance to be sure of a room; places at Klissidi fill fast.

Villa Apollon (☎ 22860 61348; www.apollonvilla.gr; s/ d/tr €45/58/68, studios €54-78; 🖭) At Klissidi Beach,

ANAFI
0 — 4 km
0 — 2 miles

AEGEAN SEA

Hora
Kastelli
Temple of Apollo
Monastery Rock (470m)
Agios Nikolaos
Klissidi Beach
Moni Kalamiotissas

To Santorini (56km);
Ios (65km);
Paros (130km);
Naxos (140km);
Piraeus (270km)

these pleasant rooms are a good size and have an authentic traditional style.

Rooms to Let Artemis (☎ 22860 61235; d €45) These are just above the sea at Klissidi, and there's a restaurant attached.

Rooms in Hora are all very similar. Many have good views across Anafi's rolling hills to the sea and to the great summit of Monastery Rock. The following recommended options are easily found on the main street, and all charge about €35 or €45 for a single or double:

Panorama (☎ 22860 61292)
Paradise (☎ 22860 61243)
Anafi Rooms (☎ 22860 61271)

There are several tavernas in Hora, all of which are in the main street. **Liotrivi** (☎ 22860 61209; mains €4-6) offers great fish dishes with the catch supplied from the family's boat. Cheerful, homely **Astrakhan** (☎ 22860 61249; mains €4.50-7), further along the street, serves up reliable Greek standards as if you're part of the family.

Klissidi has a few tavernas, with similar prices.

Getting There & Away

There are at least seven ferries weekly to Santorini (€6.90, 1¾ hours), six ferries weekly to Ios (€7.90, 3½ hours), Folegandros (€10.10, 4½ hours) and Sikinos (€9.30, 4¼ hours), three ferries weekly to Naxos (€11, seven hours), Paros (€13.80, nine hours) and Piraeus (€34, 17 hours), and two weekly to Syros (€16.80, 12 hours).

Getting Around

A small bus takes passengers from the port up to Hora. Caïques serve various beaches and nearby islands.

SIKINOS ΣΙΚΙΝΟΣ

pop 238
Out of the way Sikinos (*see-kee-noss*) is another wonderful escape from the clamour of Ios and Santorini, yet this lovely island is not much smaller than Santorini. It has a mainly empty landscape of terraced hills that sweep down to the sea. The main clusters of habitation are the port of **Alopronia**, and the inland villages of **Hora** and **Kastro**. The latter are reached by a 3.4km winding road that leads up from the port. There's a post office at the entrance

to Kastro, and a National Bank of Greece ATM with card-slot access in the central square. The medical centre is next door to the ATM. Ferry tickets can be bought in advance at **Koundouris Travel** (☎ 22860 51168, 6936621946) in Kastro and also down at the port before scheduled departures. There is a petrol station outside Alopronia on the road to Kastro. You can hire scooters here from about €15.

Sights

Kastro, so named from an original Venetian fortress of the 13th century of which little physical sign remains, is a charming place, with winding alleyways between brilliant white houses. At its heart is the main square with a central war memorial surrounded by peaceful old buildings, one with ornate stone window-frames and -sills long since whitewashed over. On one side is the **church of Pantanassa**. On the northern side of Kastro, the land falls sharply to the sea and the shells of old windmills punctuate the cliff edge. A flight of whitewashed steps leads up to the once-fortified church of **Moni Zoödohou Pigis** above the town.

To the west of Kastro, above steeply terraced fields and reached by an equally steep flight of steps, is the reclusive **Hora**, where numerous derelict houses are being renovated. If you continue past a telephone booth from the little main square you come to an olive press museum down flower-lined steps on the left. Opening times in summer are satisfyingly random.

From the saddle between Kastro and Hora, a surfaced road leads southwest to Episkopi. The remains here are believed to be those of a 3rd-century-AD Roman mausoleum that was transformed into a church in the 7th century and then became **Moni Episkopis** (admission free; 🕐 6.30pm-8.30pm) 10 centuries later. From here you can climb to a little **church** and **ancient ruins** perched on a precipice to the south, from where the views are spectacular.

Caïques (about €4) run to good beaches at **Agios Georgios**, **Malta** – with ancient ruins on the hill above – and **Karra**. **Katergo**, a swimming place with interesting rocks, and **Agios Nikolaos Beach** are both within easy walking distance of Alopronia.

At the time of writing, a surfaced road was being laid to Agios Georgios and beach. It is expected that buses will run to these beaches from Alopronia in summer.

Sleeping & Eating

In Hora and Kastro there are a few basic domatia that charge about €40 for a double. Ask at tavernas and the local shop. For a taste of old Greece, **Zagoreos Rooms** (☎ 22860 51263; d €40) on the little terrace square in Hora is worth a try. Otherwise, Alopronia has most of the accommodation.

Lucas Rooms (☎ 22860 51076; www.diakopes.gr; Alopronia; s/d/studios €35/50/70) Two good locations are on offer here and rooms are decent and clean; one set of rooms is on the hillside, 500m uphill from the port. The studios are on the far side of the bay from the ferry quay and have great views.

Porto Sikinos (☎ 22860 51220; www.portosikinos.gr; Alopronia; s/d/tr incl breakfast €80/99/115) Just up from the quay, the attractive rooms here rise in a series of terraces and have great balcony views. There's also a bar and restaurant.

Rock (☎ 22860 51186; Alopronia; dishes €2.60-7.50) High above the ferry quay is this cheerful seasonal café and pizza place, where you can also chill into the early hours (sometimes to live music). There are rooms here as well, with doubles priced at €40 to €45.

Lucas (☎ 22860 51076; Alopronia; dishes €3.50-7) Down at the port, this is the favourite taverna, offering Greek standards without frills.

To Steki tou Garbi (Kastro; dishes €4-8) A good traditional grill house just around the corner from Koundouris Travel in Kastro.

To Iliovasilema (☎ 22860 51173; mains €5-9) Outstanding views enhance a stop at this seasonal place, which dishes up standards as well as pizzas and pasta.

There's a minimarket next to Lucas and another in Kastro.

Getting There & Away

Seven ferries weekly go to Piraeus (€26.10, 11 hours) and six weekly go to Santorini (€6.50, 2½ hours). There are five weekly to Ios (€3.70, 30 minutes); two to Naxos (€6.30, 3½ hours) and Syros (€11.10, eight hours); six to Paros (€7.20 4½ hours); four to Folegandros (€4.30, 45 minutes), Kimolos (€8.20, four hours) and Anafi (€9.10, 4½ hours); three weekly to Milos (€10.90, 3½ hours); and two weekly to Sifnos (€9.50, five hours), Serifos (€11.60, six hours) and Kythnos (€15.20, 8½ hours).

Getting Around

The local bus meets all ferry arrivals and runs between Alopronia and Hora/Kastro (€1.10, 20 minutes) every half-hour in August, but less frequently at other times of the year. A timetable is sometimes posted near the minimarket. It's wise to be in good time at the departure point.

FOLEGANDROS
ΦΟΛΕΓΑΝΔΡΟΣ

pop 662

It's hard to leave Folegandros (fo-leh-gandross) and its beauty, its timelessness and its friendly local people. The island is a rocky ridge, barely 12km in length and just under 4km at its widest point. Much of the land is over 200m in height, the highest point being Agios Eleftherios at 414m.

The remoteness and ruggedness of Folegandros made it a place of exile for political prisoners from Roman times to the 20th century, and as late as the military dictatorship of 1967–74.

The capital is the concealed cliff-top Hora, one of the most appealing villages in the Cyclades. Boats dock at the little harbour of Karavostasis, on the east coast. The only other settlement is Ano Meria, 4km northwest of Hora. There are several good beaches, but be prepared for strenuous walking to reach some of them.

CYCLADES

FOLEGANDROS

0 ——— 2 km
0 ——— 1 mile

Agios Georgios Beach

To Sifnos (50km); Milos (64km); Serifos (73km); Piraeus (220km)

Cape Kiparissi

Zoödohous Pigis

312m

AEGEAN SEA

Agios Pantelemenos

Ampeli Beach

Merovigli

Agios Andreas

Ano Meria

To Syros (95km)

Livadaki Beach

Folegandros

Vorina Bay

Piakas Bay

Panagia

Agios Nikolaos Beach

Angali Beach

Vathi Bay

Hora

Vardia Beach

To Sikinos (19km)

Agios Eleftherios (414m)

Karavostasis

Karavostasis Bay

Vitsentzou

Petousis

Livadi

Livadi Beach

To Santorini (40km); Ios (45km); Naxos (57km); Paros (58km)

Katergo Beach

Cape Vigla

Getting There & Away
FAST BOAT & CATAMARAN
From about mid-June to mid-September there are six weekly ferries to Piraeus (€41.50, five hours), Sifnos (€16, 45 minutes), Santorini (€14, 45 minutes), Amorgos (€25, two hours), Naxos (€19, 3¼ hours) and Paros (€16, 3¾ hours).

FERRY
From May to October there are daily services to Piraeus (€26, 11 hours), Santorini (€6.90, 1½ to 2½ hours), Ios (€5.50, 1½ hours), Paros (€7.90, four hours), Naxos (€9.60, three hours) and Sikinos (€4.30, 45 minutes).

Three weekly services go to Syros (€12, five hours), Milos (€7, 2½ hours), Sifnos (€4.30, four hours) and Serifos (€10.30, five hours).

Two weekly ferries go to Kimolos (€5.50, 1½ hours) and Anafi (€12, five hours).

Once weekly there's a ferry to Kythnos (€15, six hours).

Getting Around
The local bus meets all ferry arrivals and takes passengers to Hora (€1.20). From Hora there are buses to the port one hour before all ferry departures, even for the late-night services. Buses from Hora run hourly to Ano Meria (€0.40), stopping at the road leading to Angali Beach. The bus stop for Ano Meria is located on the western edge of Hora, next to the Sottovento Tourism Office.

There is a **taxi service** (☎ 22860 41048, 69446 93957) on Folegandros. You can hire cars also for about €35 to €40 per day, and motorbikes from €15 to €20 per day, from a number of outlets.

KARAVOSTASIS ΚΑΡΑΒΟΣΤΑΣΙΣ
pop 55
Folegandros' port is a sunny little place serviced by a sprinkling of domatia and tavernas, and with a pleasant pebble beach. Within a kilometre north and south of Karavostasis lies a series of other beaches, all enjoyable and easily reached by short walks. In high season boats leave Karavostasis for beaches further afield.

Sleeping & Eating
Camping Livadi (☎ 22860 41204; www.folegandros .org; camp sites per adult/child/tent €6/4/4) This site is at Livadi Beach, 1.2km from Karavostasis. It has a bar-restaurant and laundry. To get

here turn south on the cement road skirting Karavostasis Beach.

Aeolos Beach Hotel (☎ 22860 41205; s/d/studios €45/65/90) Just across from the beach, this friendly hotel has a pretty garden and clean straightforward rooms.

Vrahos (☎ 22860 41450; www.hotel-vrahos.gr; s incl breakfast €68, d incl breakfast €85-98, studios & apt €145-170; 🅿 🖳) In a great location at the far end of the beach, Vrahos rises through a series of terraces, and the front balconies have great views of the bay. Rooms have cool décor and there's an outdoor Jacuzzi, a bar and a breakfast area. Breakfast is €12.50.

Restaurant Kati Allo (☎ 22860 41272; dishes €4.50-7) Reliable, traditional dishes are served up at this pleasant place right behind the beach. Seafood is by the kilogram.

Drinking
There are a couple of good beachside bars. For enduring character, Evangelos is right on the beach and is the place for relaxed drinks, snacks and great conversation.

HORA ΧΩΡΑ
pop 316
Hora's medieval *kastro*, with its attractive main street flanked by lovely traditional houses, is a major feature of Hora, but the rest of the village is a delight also. The meandering main street winds happily from leafy square to leafy square. On its north side, Hora stands on the edge of a formidable cliff.

Orientation
The port–Hora bus turnaround is in the square, called Plateia Pounta. From here follow a road to the left into Plateia Dounavi, from where an archway on the right, the Paraporti, leads into the *kastro*. Plateia Dounavi leads on to Plateia Kontarini, then to Plateia Piatsa and, finally, to Plateia Maraki. Keep on through Plateia Maraki to reach many of the music bars and the bus stop for Ano Meria and most beaches.

Information
There's no bank, but there is an ATM on the far side of Plateia Dounavi, next to the community offices. The post office is on the port road, 200m downhill from the bus turnaround.

Travel agencies can exchange travellers cheques.

Diaplous Travel (☎ 22860 41158; www.diaploustravel
.gr; Plateia Pounta) Helpful and efficient agency – sells
ferry tickets, exchanges money and arranges accommodation, car and bike rental and boat excursions. Internet
access per 15 minutes costs €1.

Maraki Travel (☎ 22860 41273; fax 22860 41149;
Plateia Dounavi; ⏲ 10.30am-noon & 5-9pm) Sells ferry
tickets and exchanges money.

Medical Centre (☎ 22860 41222; Plateia Pounta)

Police station (☎ 22860 41249) Straight on from
Plateia Maraki.

Sottovento Tourism Office (☎ 22860 41444; www
.folegandrosisland.com) At the west end of town; doubles
as the Italian consulate and is very helpful on all tourism
matters, including accommodation, international and
domestic flights and boat trips.

Sights

Hora is a pleasure to wander through. The
medieval **kastro**, a tangle of narrow streets
spanned by low archways, dates from when
Marco Sanudo ruled the island in the 13th
century. The houses' wooden balconies blaze
with bougainvillea and hibiscus.

The extended village, outside the *kastro*,
is just as attractive. From Plateia Pounta and
the bus turnaround, a steep path leads up to
the large church of the Virgin, **Panagia** (⏲ 6pm-
8pm), which sits perched on a dramatic cliff-
top above the town.

Tours

Boat trips around the island (per adult/child
including lunch €25/10) and to nearby Sikinos (per adult/child €22/11) can be booked
through Diaplous Travel and Sottovento
Tourism Office.

Festivals & Events

The annual **Folegandros Festival**, staged in late
July, features a series of concerts, exhibitions
and special meals, at venues around the
island.

Sleeping

In July and August most domatia and hotels
will be full, so book well in advance.

Hotel Polikandia (☎ 22860 41322; polikandia@yahoo
.gr; s/d €65/85; ✖ ▣) Just before the port–Hora
bus turnaround, this is a pleasant airy place
with good-sized rooms arranged around a
delightful reception and flower-filled garden
area. Breakfast is €7.50.

Aegeo (☎ 22860 41468; aegeofol@hol.gr; s/d/tr
€80/85/110; ✖ ▣) Located on the outskirts of

town, the beautiful rooms with immaculate
furnishings are in a peaceful complex here
at Aegeo that captures the classic Cycladean
style. This style is evident also in its central
courtyard area, all white and blue and draped
with crimson bougainvillea. The same family
has cheaper, but equally immaculate rooms,
at Evgenia Rooms on the approach to Plateia
Pounta.

our pick **Anemomylos Apartments** (☎ 22860 41309;
www.anemomilosapartments.com; d €130-180; ✖ ▣ ▣)
A prime position on top of a cliff ensures awesome views from the seaward-facing rooms of
this stylish complex. Rooms are the ultimate
in Cycladic cool, and fine antiques add to the
ambience. Anemomylos is just up from the
bus turnaround. One unit is equipped for
disabled use.

Eating

Melissa (☎ 22860 41067; Plateia Kontarini; mains €4-
7.50) A local favourite where good food is
matched by charming owners. The island
speciality of *matsata* (hand-made pasta) with
meat of your choice is always worthwhile and
vegetarians will relish the local ingredients
in dishes such as *briam*. Melissa also does
good breakfasts.

our pick **Pounta** (☎ 22860 41063; Plateia Pounta;
dishes €4.50-8) In Pounta's garden setting there's
an inescapable sense of old Greece, and the
courteous service enhances this. The traditional food is excellent, from tasty breakfasts
to evening meals of rabbit stew, lamb and
vegetarian dishes. It's all served on delightful crockery made by one of the owners,
Lisbet Giouri; you can buy examples of her
work.

Zefiros (☎ 22860 41556; dishes €5.50-9.50) A great
ouzerie and *mezedhopoleio* with a challenging
selection of ouzo varieties. There are mezedhes plates for two at €20, as well as mixed
small plates, all served up cheerfully. Keep
left past Plateia Kontarini.

Other recommended places:

Piatsa Restaurant (☎ 22860 41274; dishes €3-7.50)
Excellent Greek food such as *matsata*, usually with cockerel
or rabbit.

Chic (☎ 22860 41515; dishes €4-9.50) Classic Greek
cuisine as well as tasty vegetarian dishes, including spinach
pie with cheese, raisins and pine nuts.

Pizza Pazza (☎ 22860 41549; dishes €5.50-10) Above
the Greco Cafe-Bar.

To Mikro (☎ 22860 41550) Charming place for coffee,
crepes and tasty cakes.

CYCLADES

Entertainment

Folegandros has its own 'West End' – a clutch of great music bars at the western edge of Hora.

Greco Café-Bar (☎ 22860 41456) Near the Sottovento Tourism Office, and featuring vivid and appealing murals. The friendly ambience here is enhanced by a great mix of sounds from a stock of over 1000 CDs.

Avli Club (☎ 22860 41100) Near Greco, early evening lounge music gives way to rock, disco, Latin and Greek here, as things liven up into the night.

Apanemo (☎ 22860 41562) Further along the road from Avli Club is this pleasant bar that has a lovely garden.

Further on from Apanemo is a long-established and fine little bar, Laoumi, that plays jazz, ethnic, funk, soul, South American and Caribbean sounds, with style.

A Folegandros local treat is *rakomelo* – heated raki with honey and cloves. One of the best local bars where you can enjoy it and get into the spirit of things is Astarti, next to the Melissa taverna on Plateia Kontarini.

AROUND FOLEGANDROS

Ano Meria Ανω Μεριά

pop 291

The settlement of Ano Meria is a scattered community of small farms and dwellings that stretches for several kilometres. This is traditional island life where tourism makes no intrusive mark and life happily wanders off sideways.

The **folklore museum** (admission €1.50; ☼ 5pm-8pm) is on the eastern outskirts of the village. Ask the bus driver to drop you off nearby.

There are several good traditional tavernas in Ano Meria, including **I Synantisi** (☎ 22860 41208; dishes €4-8) and **Mimi's** (☎ 22860 41377; dishes €3.50-7), which specialise in *matsata*, the local hand-made pasta dish.

Beaches

For **Livadi Beach**, 1.2km southeast of Karavostasis, follow the signs for Camping Livadi. Further round the coast on the southeastern tip of the island is **Katergo Beach**, best reached by boat from Karavostasis.

The sandy and pebbled **Angali** beach, on the coast opposite to Hora, is a popular spot, but remember that while it's a 1km downhill walk from where the bus drops you off, it's a steep and sweaty hike back up. There are several domatia here and two reasonable tavernas.

About 750m over the hill by footpath west of Angali is **Agios Nikolaos**, a nudist beach. **Livadaki** beach is over 2km further west again. It is best reached by another 1.5km hike from the bus stop near the church of Agios Andreas at Ano Meria. Boats connect these west coast beaches in high season. **Agios Georgios** is north of Ano Meria and requires another demanding walk. Have tough footwear, sun protection and, because most beaches have no shops or tavernas, make sure you take food and water.

In July and August, weather permitting, excursion boats make separate trips from Karavostasis to Katergo, Angali and Agios Nikolaos and from Angali to Livadaki beach.

MILOS ΜΗΛΟΣ

pop 4771

Friendly, likeable Milos (*mee-loss*) has a surreal and dramatic coastal landscape with colourful and crazy rock formations that reflect the island's volcanic origins. Milos also has hot springs, the most beaches of any Cycladic island and some compelling ancient sites.

The island has a fascinating history of mineral extraction dating from the Neolithic period when obsidian was an important material. Over the years such materials as sulphur and kaolin have been mined and today Milos is the biggest bentonite and perlite production and processing centre in the EU.

Filakopi, an ancient Minoan city in the island's northeast, was one of the earliest settlements in the Cyclades. During the Peloponnesian Wars, Milos was the only Cycladic island not to join the Athenian alliance. It paid dearly in 416 BC, when avenging Athenians massacred the adult males and enslaved the women and children.

The island's most celebrated export, the beautiful *Venus de Milo* (a 4th-century-BC statue of Aphrodite, found in an olive grove in 1820) is far away in the Louvre (allegedly having lost its arms on the way to Paris in the 19th century).

Getting There & Away

AIR

There is a daily flight to/from Athens (one way €50, 40 minutes) with **Olympic Airlines** (☎ 22870 22380; fax 22870 21884; www.olympicairlines .com; airport), based at the airport. Flights are

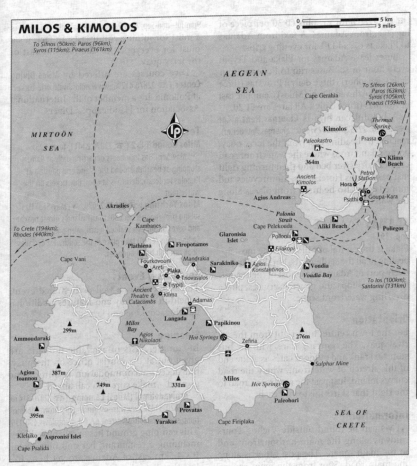

MILOS & KIMOLOS

To Sifnos (50km); Paros (96km); Syros (115km); Piraeus (161km)

AEGEAN SEA

MIRTOÖN SEA

To Crete (194km); Rhodes (440km)

Cape Gerahia

To Sifnos (26km); Paros (63km); Syros (105km); Piraeus (159km)

Thermal Spring

Kimolos

Paleokastro

364m

Prassa

Klima Beach

Ancient Kimolos

Petrol Station

Hora

Psathi

Goupa-Kara

Agios Andreas

Polonia Strait
Cape Pelekouda

Poliegos

Akradies

Cape Kambanes

Plathiena

Firopotamos

Glaronisia Islet

Pollonia

Aliki Beach

Filakopi

Cape Vani

Fourkovouni
Areti

Mandrakia

Sarakiniko

Agios Konstantinos

Voudia

Plaka

Triovasalos

Voudia Bay

Ancient Theatre & Catacombs

Trypiti

Klima

Adamas

To Ios (100km); Santorini (131km)

Milos Bay

Langada

Agios Nikolaos

Papikinou

Hot Springs

Zefiria

276m

299m

Ammoudaraki

Agiou Ioannou

387m

749m

331m

Milos

Hot Springs

Sulphur Mine

Paleohori

395m

Provatas

Yarakas

Cape Firiplaka

SEA OF CRETE

Klefiko

Aspronisi Islet

Cape Psalida

CYCLADES

often heavily booked by people in mining and related businesses.

FAST BOAT & CATAMARAN

One boat a day goes to Sifnos (€13.50, 1¾ hours) and Serifos (€14, 1¼ hours). At least one daily goes to Piraeus (€42, 3¾ hours).

FERRY

A car ferry departs five times daily from Pollonia for Kimolos at 9am, 11am, 2.15pm, 6.30pm and 10.40pm (per person €1.80, plus €1.50 for a moped, €3.20 for a motorbike and €8 for a car, 20 minutes).

From the main port of Adamas there are two ferries daily to Piraeus (€25, five to seven hours); Sifnos (€7, 1¼ hours, one daily), Serifos (€7.50,

two hours) and Kythnos (€11.50, 3½ hours); and six weekly to Kimolos (€4.50, one hour).

Three times weekly a ferry sails to the Cretan port of Sitia (€21.60, nine hours) and then on to Karpathos in the Dodecanese (€33.40, 15 hours) and Rhodes (€34, 21 hours).

There are three weekly ferries to Folegandros (€7.10, 2½ hours) and Sikinos (€10.90, three hours), and two weekly to Paros (€11.40, 4½ hours).

There is one weekly ferry to Santorini (€15.60, four hours), Ios (€13.70, 5½ hours) and Syros (€11.70, eight hours).

Getting Around

There are no buses to the airport (south of Papikinou), so you'll need to take a **taxi**

(☎ 22870 22219) for €7, plus €0.30 per piece of luggage, from Adamas. A taxi from Adamas to Plaka is €7; add €1 for evening trips.

Buses leave Adamas for Plaka and Trypiti every hour or so. Buses run to Pollonia (four daily), Paleohori (three daily), Provatas (three daily) and Arhivadolimni (Milos) Camping, east of Adamas (three daily). All fares are €1.20.

A helpful car hire is **Giourgas Rent a Car** (☎ 22870 22352, 6937577066; giourgas@otenet.gr), reached by heading east from the ferry quay, going inland from where the waterfront road crosses a dry river bed and then turning right just past Aeolis Hotel. Cars, motorcycles and mopeds can also be hired from places along the waterfront.

ADAMAS ΑΔΑΜΑΣ
pop 1391
Plaka is the capital of Milos and the most appealing of all the settlements, but the pleasant, lively port of Adamas has most of the accommodation, shops and general services, plus a diverting waterfront scene.

Orientation
For the town centre, turn right from the arrival quay. The central square, with the bus stop, taxi rank and outdoor cafés, is at the end of this stretch of waterfront, where the road curves inland. Just past the square is a road to the right that skirts the town beach.

Information
ATMs can be found outside Vichos Tours midway along the main harbourfront and in the main square. The post office is along the main road, 50m from the main square, on the right.

Municipal Tourist Office (☎ 22870 22445; www.milos -island.gr; ☼ 8am-midnight mid-Jun–mid-Sep) Opposite the quay; one of the most helpful offices in the Cyclades.

Terry's Travel Services (☎ 22870 22640; www .terrysmilostravel.com) Friendly, helpful service goes with a great love of the island here. Help with accommodation, car rental, kayaking and sailing trips, diving and much more. Head left from the ferry quay, and, just past the bend in the road, go right up a lane.

Police station (☎ 22870 21378) On the main square, next to the bus stop.

Port police (☎ 22870 22100) On the waterfront.

Sights & Activities
The **Milos Mining Museum** (☎ 22870 22481; www .milosminingmuseum.gr; admission free; ☼ 9am-2pm & 6-

9pm Jul–mid-Sep, 8am-2.30pm Tue-Sat mid-Sep–Jun) is a must for mining enthusiasts; in fact, it's a must for everyone. It's about 600m east of the ferry quay.

Dive courses are offered by **Milos Diving Center** (☎ 22870 41296; www.milosdiving.gr), based at Pollonia. It's a member of the International Association for Handicapped Divers.

Tours
Milos Round 1 & 2 (☎ 22870 23411; tours €25; ☼ May-Sep) Has tour boats departing daily at 9am, stopping at beaches around the island and pausing at Kimolos for lunch. Return is at 6pm. Buy tickets on the waterfront.

Milos Yachting (☎ 22870 22079; ☼ May-Sep) Has sailing trips (per person €60) to the island's nicest beaches and coves; includes a seafood lunch, ouzo and sweets. Sailing tours (€240) take place in the southwest Cyclades. Book through travel agencies.

Festivals & Events
The **Milos Festival**, a well-orchestrated event, is held in early July and features traditional dancing, cooking and jazz.

Sleeping
In summer, lists of available domatia are given out at the tourist office on the quay, but decent accommodation is thin on the ground – make sure you call ahead.

Arhivadolimni (Milos) Camping (☎ 22870 31410; fax 22870 31412; www.miloscamping.gr; Arhiva-dolimni; camp sites per adult/child/tent €7/4/4, bungalows €50-116) This camping ground has excellent facilities, including a restaurant, bar and bike rental. It's 4.5km east of Adamas; to get here, follow the signs along the waterfront from the central square or take the bus (see Getting Around, p207).

Hotel Delfini (☎ 22870 22001; fax 22870 22294; s/d €45/65; ☼ Apr-Oct; ❄) A pleasant, long-standing place with good rooms and facilities. Neighbouring hotels have rather stolen the view, but there's a lovely terrace. It's to the west of the ferry quay and is tucked in behind the Lagada Beach Hotel.

Aeolis Hotel (☎ 22870 23985; www.aeolis-hotel.com; d €85) An immaculate hotel with relaxing décor and fine furnishings, the Aeolis is a short distance inland from where the waterfront road crosses a dry river bed. Rates drop substantially outside August.

Villa Helios (☎ 22870 22258; fax 22870 23974; heaton .theologitis@utanet.at; apt €90-100; ☼ mid-May–mid-Oct;

) In an unbeatable location, high above the port, are these stylish, beautifully furnished apartments for two or four people.

Portiani Hotel (☎ 22870 22940; www.portianimilos.com; s/d incl buffet breakfast €120/150; P) The port's main waterfront hotel is right next to the square, but the fine rooms have a pleasant air of seclusion, and are worth the price, if you want all mod cons, and are including a lift for disabled access. The upper balconies have great views. The buffet breakfast features delicious local products.

Eating

Taverna Barko (☎ 22870 22660; dishes €2.30-9) A classic *mezedhopoleio*. On the road to Plaka, near the outskirts of town, Barko offers some real treats such as Milos cheese pie and octopus in wine. It also serves pasta.

I Milos (☎ 22870 22210; dishes €2.50-8) This likeable place is at the far end of the main square's line of waterfront cafés and tavernas. It offers breakfast (€4.10 to €6.20) and is great for coffee. Lunch dishes include pizzas and pastas. The sweet of tooth should try *loukoumadhes* – fried balls of dough flavoured with cinnamon and served with honey syrup.

Flisvos (☎ 22870 22275; dishes €4.50-7) Fish is by the kilogram at this busy waterfront taverna, to the east of the ferry quay. It serves good charcoal-grilled Greek specialities without fuss. Salads are crisp and fresh and the cheese and mushroom pies are delicious.

Entertainment

Halfway up the first staircase along from the ferry quay are a couple of popular music bars including Ilori and Vipera Lebetina, playing disco, pop and Greek music during July and August.

Akri (☎ 22870 22064) Further uphill, opposite Villa Helios, Akri is in a beautiful location with a fine terrace overlooking the port. Music favours ethnic, funk and easy listening. It's also open for breakfast (€5 to €8). Upstairs is an elegant gallery selling superb glass jewellery, paintings, pottery and sculpture, many by island artists.

PLAKA & TRYPITI
ΠΛΑΚΑ & ΤΡΥΠΗΤΗ

Plaka, 5km uphill from Adamas, is a typical Cycladic town with white houses and labyrinthine lanes. It merges with the settlement of Trypiti to the south and rises above a sprawl of converging settlements, yet has a distinctive and engaging character.

Plaka is built on the site of Ancient Milos, which was destroyed by the Athenians and rebuilt by the Romans.

Sights & Activities

The **archaeology museum** (☎ 22870 21629; admission €3; 8.30am-3pm Tue-Sun) is in Plaka, just downhill from the bus turnaround. It's in a handsome old building and contains some riveting exhibits, including a plaster cast of *Venus de Milo* that was made by Louvre craftsmen – as a sort of *Venus de Mea Culpa*, perhaps. Best of all is a perky little herd of tiny bull figurines from the Late Cycladic period.

The **Milos Folk & Arts Museum** (☎ 22870 21292; 10am-2pm & 6-9pm Tue-Sat, 10am-2pm Sun & Mon) has fascinating exhibits, including traditional costumes, woven goods and embroidery. It's signposted from the bus turnaround in Plaka.

At the bus turnaround, go east for the path that climbs to the **Frankish Kastro**, built on the ancient acropolis and offering panoramic views of most of the island. The 13th-century church, **Thalassitras**, is inside the walls.

There are some Roman ruins near Trypiti, including Greece's only Christian **catacombs** (☎ 22870 21625; admission free; 8am-7pm Tue-Sun). Stay on the bus towards Trypiti and get off at a T-junction by a big signpost indicating the way. Follow the road down for about 500m to where a track (signed) goes off to the right. This leads to the rather forlorn, but somehow thrilling, spot where a farmer found the *Venus de Milo* in 1820; you can't miss the huge sign. A short way further along the track is the well-preserved **ancient theatre**, which hosts the **Milos Festival** every July. Back on the surfaced road, head downhill to reach the 1st-century catacombs.

Sleeping & Eating

All of the following places are located in Plaka.

Betty's Rooms (☎ 22870 21538; d €70) Forget Santorini; these delightful rooms in a friendly family house are at the bottom end of Plaka and have fantastic views.

Archondoula Karamitsou Studios (☎ 22870 23820; www.archondoula-studios.gr; ste €130) More great views are enjoyed at these traditional rooms, which are full of local craftwork and island antiques. Prices drop substantially outside August.

CYCLADES

ourpick **Archondoula** (☎ 22870 21384; dishes €2.50–12) This cheerful, family-run *mezedhopoleio* is a delight. All the family is involved, and the food is classic traditional across a range of favourites from fresh salads to spicy grilled goat's cheese to shrimps with cream sauce. It's just along the main street from the bus turnaround in Plaka.

Utopia Café (☎ 22870 23678) One of best views in the Cyclades can be enjoyed from the cool terrace of Utopia. Head down the narrow alley opposite Archondoula and prepare to have your breath taken away. Mainly a cafe and drinks place, it's open until the early hours.

AROUND MILOS

The village of **Klima**, below Trypiti and the catacombs, was the port of ancient Milos. It's a picturesque fishing village with a lovely little harbour. Whitewashed buildings, with coloured doors and balconies, have boathouses on the ground floor and living quarters above.

Plathiena is a fine sandy beach below Plaka, to the north. On the way to Plathiena you can visit the fishing villages of **Areti** and **Fourkovouni**.

At **Sarakiniko** are snow-white rock formations and natural terraces. **Pollonia**, on the north coast, is a fishing village–cum–resort with a beach and domatia. The boat to Kimolos departs here.

The beaches of **Provatas** and **Paleohori**, on the south coast, are long and sandy, and Paleohori has hot springs.

KIMOLOS ΚΙΜΩΛΟΣ

pop 769

Perhaps because it is too often seen as an adjunct to its larger neighbour, Kimolos has hung on to a genuine otherworldliness. It lies just northeast of Milos and receives a steady trickle of visitors, especially day-trippers arriving from Pollonia. The boat docks at the port of **Psathi**, from where it's 1.5km to the pretty capital of **Hora**. The medieval *kastro*, embedded at the heart of Hora, is a joy. Albeit in ruins, there are surviving walls and restoration work is ongoing.

There's an ATM by the town hall in Hora.

Beaches can be reached by caïque from Psathi. At the centre of the island is the 364m-high cliff on which sits the fortress of **Paleokastro**.

There are domatia, tavernas, cafés and bars enough in Hora and Psathi. Domatia owners meet ferries. Expect to pay single/double rates of about €35/50.

The taverna **To Kyma** (☎ 22870 51001; dishes €3.50-9), on the beach at Psathi, is fine for Greek-standard meals.

There is one petrol station on Kimolos; it's about 200 metres to the north of Psathi.

Getting There & Away

Boats go daily to and from Pollonia on Milos, departing from Kimolos at 8am, 10am, 1.15pm, 5.30pm and 10pm (see p207 for details on boats to Kimolos).

There are six boats weekly to and from Piraeus (€17.50, eight hours) via Sifnos (€6.50, 1½ hours), Serifos (€5.90, 3¾ hours) and Kythnos (€11, three hours).

There are four ferries weekly to Adamas (€4.90, one hour) and Syros (€11.70, five hours) and two weekly to Folegandros (€5.50, three hours) and Sikinos (€8.20, four hours).

Two weekly ferries go to Paros (€9.60, 4½ hours) and Santorini (€12.80, 3½ hours).

SIFNOS ΣΙΦΝΟΣ

pop 2900

Sifnos (*see*-fnoss) masks it many charms behind a curtain of high barren hills. Beyond all this, however, is an abundant landscape of terraced olive groves and almond trees, with oleanders in the valleys and juniper and aromatic herbs covering the hillsides. It is a sizable island and has a number of villages. Plenty of old paths link these villages and walking on Sifnos is particularly satisfying. The Anavasi map series *Topo 25/10.25 Aegean Cyclades/Sifnos* is useful for footpath details.

During the Archaic period the island was very wealthy because of its gold and silver resources, but by the 5th century BC the mines were exhausted and Sifnos' fortunes were reversed. The island has a tradition of pottery making, basket weaving and cooking.

SIFNOS

0 _____ 4 km
0 _____ 2 miles

To Serifos (24km);
Kythnos (63km);
Paros (74km);
Piraeus (146km)

AEGEAN
SEA

Cape Heronisos

Heronisos

Agios Dimos

▲476m

Kamares
Bay

Kamares

Sifnos

Ano Petali

Artemonas

Kastro

Apollonia   Seralia
Katavati   Kato Petali

▲680m   Exambelas

To Milos (50km);
Santorini (105km)

Moni
Profiti Ilia

Moni
Hrysopigis   Faros
Fasolou
Beach

Vathy   Hrysopigis
Beach

Vathy   Platys Gialos
Bay

▲201m

Platys
Gialos Bay

Cape Kondou

Kitriani

Getting There & Away

FAST BOAT & CATAMARAN

In summer fast catamarans run daily except Wednesday between Serifos and Piraeus (€37.50, 2¾ hours), Milos (€12.50, 45 minutes), Folegandros (€16, 45 minutes), Santorini (€31, 1¾ hours), Serifos (€11.50, 20 minutes) and Syros (€21, 5¾ hours). Six weekly go to Paros (€10.50, five hours) and Naxos (€30, 4¼ hours) and one weekly heads to Kythnos (€12, 2¼ hours).

FERRY

There are daily ferries to Piraeus (€24, five hours) via Serifos (€6.50, one hour) and Kythnos (€8.50, 2½ hours). There are six ferries weekly to Milos (€7, two hours) and Kimolos (€6.50, 1½ hours), three ferries weekly to Folegandros (€4.30, four hours), Sikinos (€9.50, four hours) and Santorini (€12.50, eight hours), and four weekly to Paros (€4.20, two hours) and Syros (€8.20, five hours).

Getting Around

Frequent buses link the island's main town, Apollonia, with the following: Kamares

(€1.20), with some services continuing on to Artemonas (€1.20), Kastro (€1.20), Vathy (€1.70), Faros (€1.30) and Platys Gialos (€1.70).

Taxis (☎ 22840 31347) hover around the port and Apollonia's main square. Representative fares from Kamares are €6 to Apollonia, €8 to Platys Gialos and €9 to Vathy. Cars can be hired from **Stavros Hotel** (☎ 22840 31641) in Kamares, and from **Apollo Rent a Car** (☎ 22840 32237) in Apollonia, for €30 to €55.

KAMARES ΚΑΜΑΡΕΣ

The port of Kamares (kah-*mah*-rez) has a cheerful holiday atmosphere, not least because of its large beach. There are lots of waterfront cafés and tavernas and a good mix of shops, from food stores to craft shops. The bus stop is by the tamarisk trees just past the inland end of the ferry quay.

Information

There are toilets near the tourist office, plus an ATM booth.

Municipal tourist office (☎ 22840 31977/31975; www.sifnos.gr; 9.30am-11pm Jul & Aug, 9.30am-2.30pm & 5-11pm Easter-Oct, 10am-11pm Sun-Tue & Thu, 11am-5pm Wed, 10am-10pm Fri & Sat Sep-Easter) Opposite the bus stop is this very helpful and well-organised office. Opening times may vary depending on boat arrivals. The office opens for boats that arrive late into the night. It sells ferry tickets and can find accommodation anywhere on the island. There's luggage storage (per item €1) and you can buy a useful clutch of information sheets about the island. There's also information on walking trips, bus schedules and ferry times.

Yamas Café Bar Internet (☎ 22840 31202; per hr €4; 8.30am-early hrs) Half way along the waterfront and up some steps. It also serves light snacks and breakfasts (€5 to €8).

Sleeping & Eating

Domatia owners rarely meet boats and in high season it's best to book ahead.

Camping Makis (☎ 22840 32366; www.makiscamping.gr; camp sites per adult/child/tent €6.50/3.50/4, r from €50; Apr-Nov; P) Well-run, relaxing and friendly, this pleasant camping ground is just behind the beach. It has an outdoor café, a barbecue area, minimarket, a laundry and shaded sites.

Simeon (☎ 22840 31652; studios_simeon@hotmail.com; s/d/apt €40/55/120; Apr-Oct) From their little balconies, the small front rooms here have stunning views down across the port and along the beach to soaring mountains beyond. Other rooms are not so blessed, but are bigger. You get here by going up steepish steps from the waterfront.

Stavros Hotel (☎ 22840 31641/33383; www.sifnos travel.com; s/d/tr €55/70/75; ✖) Main street's Stavros has been refurbished in recent years. Rooms are comfy and bright and are a good size. Attached to the hotel is an information office that can arrange car hire and has a book exchange. The same family owns Hotel Kamari (☎ 22840 33383) on the outskirts of Kamares, on the road to Apollonia – rooms here are €40/50/55 per single/double/triple.

Hotel Afroditi (☎ 22840 31704; www.hotel-afroditi .gr; s/d incl breakfast €65/80; P ✖) The welcoming, family-run Afroditi is across the road from the beach. Rooms are a decent size and breakfast is a definite plus. There are sea views to the front and mountain views to the rear.

O Symos (☎ 22840 32353; dishes €2.50-8) Among a swath of waterfront tavernas, this popular place uses locally sourced ingredients in such appealing dishes as linguini and shrimps in saffron (€12) and a delicious *revithia* (chickpea) soup.

Another good eatery is the cheerful, family-run **Posidonia** (☎ 22840 32362; dishes €3-8), where you can get a full breakfast for €6.

APOLLONIA ΑΠΟΛΛΩΝΙΑ

The 'capital' of Sifnos is situated on the edge of a plateau 5km uphill from the port.

The stop for buses to and from Kamares is on Apollonia's busy central square, where the post office and Museum of Popular Art are located. Because of congestion, all other buses pick up passengers about 50m further on, at a T-junction where the road to the right goes to Vathy and Platys Gialos and the road to the left goes to Artemonas and Kastro. There is a big car park at the entrance to Apollonia. Constant traffic seems to be the norm, but step away from the main road onto the pedestrian thoroughfare behind the museum and Apollonia is transformed.

There is an Alpha Bank (with ATM), and the Piraeus Bank and National Bank of Greece (both with ATMs) are just round the corner from the Kamares stop on the road to Artemonas; the police station is another 50m beyond.

Internet Café 8 (☎ 22840 33734; per hour €4; ☾ 9am-1am) is about 150m along the road to Platys Gialos. **Bookshop** (☎ 22840 33523), just down from the bus stop, has newspapers and a good selection of books in various languages.

The quirky **Museum of Popular Art** (☎ 22840 31341; admission €1; ☾ 10am-2pm & 7.30-11.30pm Tue-Sun), on the central square and just opposite the post office, contains a splendid confusion of old costumes, pots, textiles and photographs that could keep you going for hours.

Sleeping & Eating

Mrs Dina Rooms (☎ 22840 31125, 6945513318; s/d/tr €40/55/65) There are flowers everywhere at this pleasant little complex of rooms, which are located a couple of hundred metres along the road south towards Vathy and Platys Gialos. The rooms are well above the road and have views towards Kastro.

Gerontios Rooms (☎ 22840 32316; s/d/tr €40/50/60) A fine choice, these flower-bedecked rooms are set high above the village centre with wide views to the village of Kastro. Head north towards Ano Petali from the centre of Apollonia.

Eftychia (☎ 22840 33274; d €55; ✖) These pleasant, well-kept rooms are in a garden setting along the road towards Vathy and Platys Gialos.

Taverna Sifnos (☎ 22840 31624; dishes €3-9) Beside an attractive little square at the heart of Apollonia's pedestrianised main street, this family-run taverna has a good menu of well-prepared island dishes. There are rooms here also, with singles/doubles for €50/70.

Apostoli to Koutouki (☎ 22840 31186; dishes €5-9) Fish is sold by the kilogram at this long-established place on the main street. It also serves meat and chicken specialities.

AROUND SIFNOS

Not to be missed is the walled cliff-top village of **Kastro**, 3km from Apollonia. The former capital, it is a magical place of buttressed alleyways and whitewashed houses. It has a small **archaeological museum** (☎ 22840 31022; admission free; ☾ 8.30am-3pm Tue-Sun).

Buses go to Kastro from Apollonia but you can walk there, mainly on old paved pathways. The start of the path is 20m to the right (Vathy road) from the T-junction in Apollonia. A pleasant path circumnavigates Kastro and is especially scenic on its northern side – midway round the northern side, above the glittering sea, is the wonderful little art workshop of **Maximos (Panagiotis Fanariotis)** (☎ 22840

33692), whose speciality is handmade jewellery in original gold and silver motifs. Prices for these lovely pieces start at about €6 and are far below the usual price charged for work of this high quality. There is also accommodation here (see Sleeping & Eating, below).

Platys Gialos, 6km south of Apollonia, has a big, generous beach, entirely backed by tavernas, domatia and shops. The bus terminates at the beach's southwestern end. **Vathy**, on the west coast, is an easy-going little village within the curved horns of an almost circular bay. **Faros** is a cosy little fishing hamlet with a couple of nice beaches nearby, such as the little beach of **Fasolou**, reached up steps and over the headland from the bus stop.

Sleeping & Eating
KASTRO
Maximos (☎ 22840 33692; r €50) A tiny terrace with unbeatable sea views comes with this quirky little room beside Maximos' workshop (see opposite), located on the northern side of Kastro.

Rafeletou Apartments (☎ 22840 31161, 69324 74001; d €60-77, tr €70-90, apt €105-120) For an authentic Kastro experience, these family-run apartments at the heart of the village are delightful.

ourpick To Astro (☎ 22840 31476; mains €5-9; ❤ mid-Apr–Oct) Kastro's genuine 'star', as the name translates, certainly lives up to its name. Lovingly run by the owner-cook, it offers delicious island dishes including eggplant and meatballs, octopus with olives, and lamb in traditional Sifniot style.

PLATYS GIALOS ΠΛΑΤΥΣ ΓΙΑΛΟΣ
Although there are plenty of sleeping places here, most cater for package tourists.

Camping Platys Gialos (☎ 22840 71286; camp sites per adult/child/tent €6/4/4) Located about 500m from the beach, this is a reasonable camping ground in an olive grove.

Platys Gialos Hotel (☎ 22840 71324; fax 22840 71325; s/d €150/170; P ⊠) This peaceful hotel overlooks the south end of the beach. It has lovely terraces and a garden area, and rooms have imaginative, old-fashioned fittings. There's a loyal clientele, so it's wise to book well in advance.

Angeliki Rooms (☎ 22840 71288; d/tr €48/57) A beachfront venue with pleasant rooms, near the quieter south end of the beach and just back from the bus terminus.

To Koutouki (☎ 22840 71330; dishes €5-9) Right on the beach and run by the family that has the same-name place in Apollonia (opposite), there are excellent fish dishes to be had here. Fish is by the kilogram but there's a reasonably priced choice.

VATHY ΒΑΘΥ
There are several sleeping options here, for ordinary mortals and for the mega-rich.

Areti Studios (☎ 22840 71191; d/apt €55/85; P ⊠) Lies a short distance back from the beach within its own lovely gardens. Rooms are clean and bright and the welcome is friendly. If you are driving, the approach is down a rough and at times very narrow track that goes off left just before the main road ends. Grit your teeth.

Elies Resort (☎ 22840 34000; www.eliesresorts.com; d €300-360, apt €480-950; ❤ May-Oct; P ⊠ 🖳 🖥) Inconspicuous, ultraprivate tourism, if you have the cash, is the story at this lush, luxury resort hotel. The huge complex, with gorgeous pool and gourmet restaurant, is subtly merged into the hillside above Vathy Bay and spills down to a beach. Rooms are sumptuous; suites and apartments are virtually houses, with the most expensive having their own terrace pool. All this and a champagne breakfast thrown in.

Vathy has a good choice of beachfront tavernas, such as Oceanida and Manolis, offering reliable Greek dishes.

SERIFOS ΣΕΡΙΦΟΣ

pop 1414
The traditional *hora* of Serifos (*seh*-ri-fohs) is a dramatic scribble of white houses that crowns a high and rocky peak, 2km to the north of the port of Livadi. It catches your eye the minute the ferry docks and transforms an otherwise everyday scene. Serifos is generally barren and rocky, but has a few pockets of greenery that are the result of tomato and vine cultivation. There are some pleasant paths linking various villages; the Anavasi map series *Topo 25/10.26 Aegean Cyclades/Serifos* is useful. Serifos is known for its windy mountain ridges, and there are plans afoot for a mega wind farm (see boxed text, p215) – however, there's fierce opposition from many.

CYCLADES

SERIFOS

AEGEAN SEA

Platys Gialos Bay
Sykamia Beach
Moni Taxiarhon
To Piraeus (135km)
Galani
Kendarhos
Panagia
Pirgos
Serifos
582m
Agios Ioannis Beach
Avessalos
Psili Ammos Beach
Hora
Lia Beach
502m
Koutalas
Livadi
Vodi
Ganema
Livadakia Beach
Megalo Livadi Beach
Vagia
Karavi Beach
To Paros (72km)
Ambeli Beach
Cape Katano

To Sifnos (24km); Kimolos (41km);
Milos (55km); Ios (83km); Santorini (120km)

Getting There & Away

FAST BOAT & CATAMARAN

In summer fast catamarans run daily except Wednesday between Serifos and Piraeus (€31.50, 2¼ hours), Sifnos (€11.50, 25 minutes), Milos (€14, 1¼ hours) and Folegandros (€20.50, 1½ hours).

FERRY

There is a daily ferry to Piraeus (€16, 4½ hours) and Sifnos (€6.50, one hour), and six ferries weekly to Milos (€7.50, two hours) and Kimolos (€8.50, 2½ hours).

Four times weekly a ferry goes to Kythnos (€8, 1½ hours), and twice weekly boats go to Paros (€7.60, three hours), Syros (€7.50, two to four hours) and Folegandros (€10.30, 5¼ hours).

There are weekly boats to Santorini (€16.20, seven hours), Ios (€12.20, six hours) and Sikinos (€11.60, five hours).

Getting Around

There are frequent buses between Livadi and Hora (€1.20, 15 minutes); a timetable is posted at the bus stop by the yacht quay. Vehicles can be hired from Krinas Travel in Livadi.

LIVADI ΛΙΒΑΔΙ

pop 537

The port town of Serifos is a fairly low-key place where, in spite of growing popularity, there's still a reassuring feeling that the modern world has not entirely taken over.

Just over the headland that rises from the ferry quay lies the fine, tamarisk-fringed beach at **Livadakia**. A walk further south over the next headland, **Karavi Beach** is the unofficial clothes-optional beach.

Information

There is an Alpha Bank (with ATM) on the waterfront and an ATM under the bakery sign opposite the yacht quay. There was once an official tourist information office that opened mid-July to August on the waterfront, but opening has been uncertain in recent years.

The post office is midway along the road that runs inland from opposite the bus stop and then bends sharply right.

Krinas Travel (☎ 22810 51488; sertrav@otenet.gr) Just where the ferry quay joins the waterfront road, this helpful agency sells ferry tickets and organises car (per day €45) and scooter (per day €19) hire. It also has internet access at €2 per half-hour.

Port police (☎ 22810 51470) Up steps just beside Krinas Travel.

Sleeping & Eating

Coralli Camping (☎ 22810 51500; fax 22810 51073; www.coralli.gr; camp sites per adult/child/tent €7/3/6, bungalows s/d €30/55; P ☐ ☒) This well-equipped camping ground, shaded by tall eucalypts, is just a step away from sandy Livadakia Beach. Bungalows have mountain or sea views. There's also a restaurant and a minimarket, and internet access for €2 per half-hour. A minibus meets all ferries.

Hotel Areti (☎ 22810 51479; fax 22810 51547; s/d/tr €50/65/75) With a great location on a hill above the ferry quay, and well-kept rooms with attractive décor, this is one of the better places in Serifos. There are also apartments nearby.

Alexandros-Vassilia (☎ 22810 51119; fax 22810 51903; s/d €50/70) Located right behind the beachfront of Livadakia. It's a complex of rooms in a rose-fragrant garden setting and is fronted by a taverna. Rooms and studios are a good size and are clean and well equipped (studios have cooking facilities). The taverna does sturdy Greek staples for €4.50 to €9.

Yacht Club Serifos (☎ 22810 51888; breakfast €2.50-11, snacks & sandwiches €2.80-€6; ☽ 7am-3am) There's a terrific ambience at this waterfront café-bar. Music ranges from lounge by day to mainstream, rock, disco and funk late into the night.

CYCLADES

Passaggio (☎ 22810 52212; mains €5.50-16)
Opened in recent years, this stylish waterfront restaurant brings some international touches to traditional cuisine. Starters such as cod dumplings are delicious, and other treats include steamed mussels or chicken pie with feta.

Also recommended for reliable Greek standards (both on the waterfront):

Stamatis (☎ 22810 51309; mains €3.50-7)
Taverna Takis (☎ 22810 51159; mains €5-11.50)

Entertainment

Metalleio (☎ 22810 51755; ☷ 9pm-early hrs) Tucked away on the road beyond the waterfront, Metalleio doubles as a decent restaurant and a very cool music venue featuring an eclectic array of sounds from around the world, including jazz, funk, Afro, Asian groove and Latin. The restaurant offers mainly poultry and meat dishes (mains €6 to €13.50).

There are a couple of fairly loud music bars on the central waterfront such as the Malabar Café and, in the same complex, the Captain Hook Club. The Yacht Club Serifos is one of the coolest venues.

HORA ΧΩΡΑ

The *hora* of Serifos spills across the summit of a rocky hill above Livadi and is one of the most striking of the Cycladic capitals. Ancient steps lead up from Livadi, though they are fragmented by the snaking road that links the two. You can walk up, but in the heat of summer, going up by bus is wiser. Just up from the bus terminus, steps climb into the wonderful maze of Hora proper, and lead to the charming main square, watched over by the imposing neoclassical town hall. From the square, narrow alleys and more steps lead ever upwards to the remnants of the ruined 15th-century **Venetian Kastro**. Low walls enclose the highest part of the kastro, from where the views are spectacular. A small church occupies part of the summit.

Back downhill, there's a post office just up from the bus turnaround.

Hora has a small **archaeological museum** (☎ 22810 51138; admission free; ☷ 8.30am-3pm Tue-Sun) displaying fragments of mainly Hellenic and Roman sculpture excavated from the *kastro*. Exhibits are sparse and the museum tiny, but it is a pleasure to visit. Panels in Greek and English spell out fascinating details, including the legend of Perseus.

CYCLADES

WIND & WATER: THE BIG GREEN ISSUES

The Cyclades have plenty of wind and water, and these two elements are at the forefront of current controversies among islanders. The big green issues in the Cyclades are projects such as the mega wind farm planned for Serifos where, at the time of writing, islanders were opposing a plan to site scores of wind generators along the windy crest of the island's mountainous interior. While acknowledging the 'green' credentials of wind power, many who love Serifos believe the number and size of the planned windmills makes for an intrusion too far, especially since most of the power generated would go to the mainland.

On several of the islands, yacht marinas are currently under construction, and these are projects that are seen as positive tourism ventures. But not all port extensions have been welcomed. In 2007 Naxos was gripped by controversy over plans that would have extended the port area substantially. A courageous handful of islanders believed that the plan was overwhelming in every way – in terms of its size and of its potential negative impact on the port's tourism appeal and general lifestyle. They took their case to the Council of State, Greece's highest administrative court, which ruled against the plan on the grounds that it was illegal. The matter caused sometimes bitter division on the island, and the future of the development remains unclear.

These are ground level 'green' issues that are capable of serious impact on the larger life of the Cyclades. They take the sheen off our often-rosy view of island life. They also resonate with many similar issues of our own countries. As visitors we can make a contribution to these debates by at least being aware of them, and perhaps by simply talking about them a general awareness may develop in Greece.

Meanwhile, on the remote island of Sikinos, locals are setting up imaginative ventures aimed at primary production such as livestock breeding, beekeeping and vine growing, and are staying with small-scale, sustainable tourism.

There is a pleasant walk on a fine cobbled pathway that starts just above the archaeological museum and leads up the mountain to the little church of **Agios Georgios**. The views are superb.

Sleeping & Eating

I Apanemia (☎ 22810 51717, 6942699762; s/d €30/35) You won't get better value than at this family-run place, where the decent, well-equipped rooms have front balcony views down towards the distant sea and side views up towards Hora.

ourpick Stou Stratou (☎ 22810 52566; plates €4-18) The tradition of the *mezedhopoleio* is alive and well at this bar-café in the pretty main square. There are tasty mezedhes (€3 to €4.50) and choices such as a vegetarian plate or a mixed plate of Cretan smoked pork, ham, cheese, salami, stuffed vine leaves, feta, potato, tomatoes and egg, which will keep two people more than happy. Also available are breakfasts, ice creams, delicious sweets and cocktails. The stylish menu (more of a booklet) provides added pleasure – it features the work of famous artists as well as excerpts from a number of writers.

Karavomylos (☎ 22810 51261; dishes €4.50-14) has a pleasant terrace. Delicious mezedhes and local dishes are a speciality and it serves an excellent choice of breakfasts (€3 to €9). There's music in the bar and occasional live sessions of Greek traditional music, including *rembetika*.

AROUND SERIFOS

About 1½ kilometres north of Livadi along a surfaced road is **Psili Ammos Beach**. A path from Hora heads north for about 4km to the pretty village of **Kendarhos** (also called Kallitsos), from where you can continue by a very windy road for another 3km to the 17th-century fortified **Moni Taxiarhon**, which has impressive 18th-century frescoes. The walk from the town to the monastery takes about two hours. You will need to take food and water, as there are no facilities in Kendarhos.

KYTHNOS ΚΥΘΝΟΣ

pop 1700

Kythnos is more of a weekend destination for mainlanders and glossy motor cruisers. The island doesn't attract too many foreign visitors. Yet this is a Greek island of some char-acter, and once you escape the rather dowdy port of Merihas, the island rewards, not least in its pleasantly relaxed way of life.

The main settlements are Merihas, the capital Hora and the very traditional village of Dryopida.

There's an Emboriki bank (with ATM) on the road above the Merihas waterfront, and an ATM just past the flight of steps as you come from the ferry quay. **Antonios Larentzakis Travel Agency** (☎ 22810 32104/32291) sells ferry tickets, can arrange accommodation and rents out cars and motorbikes. It's up the flight of steps near Ostria Taverna that leads to the main road. Hora has the island's post office and **police station** (☎ 22810 31201). The **port police** (☎ 22810 32290) are on the waterfront in Merihas.

Getting There & Away

FAST BOAT & CATAMARAN

There is one boat weekly to Piraeus (€27, 1½ hours) and Sifnos (€12, 2¼ hours).

FERRY

There are at least two ferries to Piraeus daily (€12.50, 2½ hours). Most services coming

KYTHNOS

0 ___ 4 km
0 ___ 2 miles

To Syros (74km);
Tinos (81km);
Mykonos (98km)

Cape Kefalos

AEGEAN SEA

To Lavrio (48km)

297m

Loutra

Kythnos

308m

Fikiado Beach
Apokrousi Beach
Hora (Kythnos)

Episkopi Beach

To Piraeus (96km)

Merihas

Dryopida

Cape Tzoulis

Flambouria Beach

302m

To Kimolos (41km);
Serifos (52km);
Sifnos (63km);
Milos (85km);
Santorini (155km)

Kanala

Dimitrios Beach

Cape Berou

from Piraeus continue to Serifos (€8, 1½ hours), Sifnos (€8.50, 2½ hours), Kimolos (€11, three hours) and Milos (€11.50, 3½ hours).

There are six weekly ferries to Lavrio (€8.20, 3½ hours), three weekly to Syros (€7.90, two hours) and two weekly to Kea (€5.90, 1¼ hours), Folegandros (€14.50, six hours), Sikinos (€15.20, seven hours) and Santorini (€19.70, eight hours).

A ferry runs once weekly to Andros (€11.70, five hours).

Getting Around

There are regular buses in high summer from Merihas to Dryopida (€1.20), continuing to Kanala (€2.20) or Hora (€1.30). Less-regular services run to Loutra (€2.20). The buses supposedly meet the ferries, but usually they leave from the turn-off to Hora in Merihas. Outside school holidays the only buses tend to be school buses.

Taxis (☎ 6944743791) are a better bet, except at siesta time. It's €12 to Hora and €7 to Dryopida. There are, however, only a few taxis on the island.

MERIHAS ΜΕΡΙΧΑΣ
pop 289

Merihas (*meh*-ree-hass) does not have a lot going for it other than a bit of waterfront life and a slightly grubby beach. But Merihas is a reasonable base and has most of the island's accommodation options. There are better beaches within walking distance north of the quay (turn left facing inland) at **Episkopi** and **Apokrousi**.

Sleeping & Eating

Domatia owners usually meet boats and there are a number of signs along the waterfront advertising rooms; alternatively enquire at Larentzakis Travel Agency (opposite). A lot of places block-book during the high season and there is some reluctance towards one-night stopovers. You should definitely book ahead for July and August.

Anna Gouma Rooms (☎ 22810 32105, 6949777884; s/d €40/50) These pleasant, good-sized rooms are right across the bay from the ferry quay, and are away from the hubbub.

Giannoulis Rooms (☎ 22810 32247; fax 22810 32092; d/tr €40/50) There are useful enough small rooms here, although they are rather faded. They're above the O Merihas café. It's es-

sential to book ahead here in high season and at weekends.

O Merihas (☎ 22810 32247, under €6 for coffee and cakes) A great local *zaharoplasteio* (patisserie) on the ground floor of Giannoulis Rooms, dishing up coffee, drinks, snacks and cakes.

Taverna to Kandouni (☎ 22810 32220; dishes €5-12) Near the port police on the waterfront, Kandouni is a popular family-run taverna specialising in fish dishes and grilled meats.

Ostria (☎ 22810 32263; dishes €6-13) On the waterfront near the quay, Ostria has reasonable Greek fare. Seafood is by the kilo.

AROUND KYTHNOS

The capital, **Hora** (also known as Kythnos or Messaria), is steadily taking on a distinctive charm, underpinned by its inherent Greek character. Small, colourful cafés and shops are growing in number. The long straggling main street makes for a pleasant stroll. The post office and police are at the entrance to town coming from Merihas.

The resort of **Loutra** is 3km north of Hora on a windy bay and hangs on to its status through its surviving thermal baths.

From Hora there's a pleasant 5km walk south to **Dryopida**, a picturesque town of red-tiled roofs and winding streets clustered steeply on either side of a ravine. It's home to a remarkable cave called Kataphyki that extends for 600m. Much work has been carried out to make the cave accessible, but things seem to have stalled at the time of writing. You're best to cover the 5km back by road to Merihas by bus or taxi.

There are good beaches at **Flambouria** about 2.5km south of Merihas, and near **Kanala** on the southeast coast.

Sleeping & Eating

There are plenty of rooms and apartments in Loutra although they tend to be block-booked for stays of more than two days. In Dryopida some private houses let rooms in summer. Ask at shops and tavernas.

Filoxenia (☎ 22810 31644; www.filoxenia-kythnos.gr; d/tr/q €65/75/90; P ✖) In Hora, these delightful, family-run studios are just at the entrance to the main village and overlook a garden. Rooms are immaculate and well appointed and there's a charming welcome.

There are several decent tavernas in Hora including Koursaros, To Steki and Mezzeria.

KEA ΚΕΑ (TZIA)

pop 2417

Kea is the most northerly island of the Cyclades and the island closest to Attica, and attracts more mainland locals than foreign visitors. It is an island that wears its many charms quietly and, between its bare hills, green valleys are filled with orchards, olive groves and almond and oak trees. The main settlements on the island are the port of Korissia, and the attractive capital, Ioulida, about 5km inland. There are several fine beaches and some excellent signposted footpaths. Local people use the name Tzia for their island.

Getting There & Away

Boats are usually packed on Fridays and you should avoid the Sunday night ferry to Lavrio, unless you enjoy controlled rioting. If you plan a Sunday departure, make sure you get your ticket before Friday – and have some rugby-playing experience.

Services connect Kea with Lavrio (€5.90, 1¼ hours) on the mainland at least twice daily

KEA

0 ————— 4 km
0 ————— 2 miles

To Lavrio (31km)
To Andros (31km)
Agia Irini
Otzias
To Kythnos (39km); Syros (76km)
Vourkari
Korissia
Moni Panagias Kastrianis
Gialiskari Beach
Ioulida
Flea
Pera Meria
Cape Spathi
570m ▲
Astra
Ellinika
Pisses Beach
Kea
Koundouros
▲ 450m
Havouna
AEGEAN SEA
Cape Tamelos

and as often as six times daily in summer. Three weekly ferries go to Kythnos (€5.90, 1¼ hours) and on to Syros (€9.40, four hours). One weekly boat goes to Tinos (€10.30, five hours) and Andros (€8, six hours). A slow ferry runs each Friday from Kea to Milos (€11.70, 15½ hours), Kimolos (€11.70, 14½ hours), Folegandros (€17.70, 13 hours), Sikinos (€19.20, 12 hours), Ios (€18.70, 11¼ hours), Naxos (€14.40, 9 hours) and Paros (€14.40, 8 hours).

Getting Around

In July and August there are, in theory, regular buses from Korissia to Vourkari, Otzias, Ioulida and Pisses although there may be irregularities in the schedules. A **taxi** (☎ 22880 21021/228) may be a better bet, to Ioulida (€6) especially. Motorcycle and car rental is well above the usual high-season prices on other islands. Expect to pay, per day, anything from €25 for a scooter and from €50 for a car.

KORISSIA ΚΟΡΗΣΣΙΑ

pop 555

The port of Korissia (koh-ree-see-ah) is a fairly bland place, but there are enough tavernas and cafés to pass the time. The north-facing port beach tends to catch the wind.

Information

There is an ATM next door to the Art Café and also near Hotel Karthea. The Piraeus Bank (with ATM) is behind the beach. There is a small ferry ticket office next to the car-rental agency on the waterfront.

Art Café (☎ 22880 21181; internet access per 30min €3.50; ☽ 8.30am-midnight) On the waterfront.

Tourist information office (☎ 22880 21500) The official tourist office, opposite the ferry quay, has lists of domatia in Greek, but not much more.

Sleeping & Eating

Domatia owners don't meet ferries. It's wise to book in high season and at weekends.

Hotel Tzia (☎ 22880 21305; fax 22880 21140; s/d/tr €50/57/60; ⊠) This is a functional beachfront building and is owned by the municipality of Kea; rooms are adequate and clean and it's a straight leap into the sea from the front.

Hotel Karthea (☎ 22880 21204; fax 22880 21417; s/d/tr €55/65/80) Architectural brutalism from a lost age defines the Karthea. And it's convenient for the port. Rooms are clean and comfortable and those at the rear overlook a quiet garden area. There's no lift to the several floors. In 1974, the deposed colonels of the Greek junta were said to have been imprisoned in the newly opened hotel for a short time.

Hotel Brillante Zoi (☎ 22880 22685; www.hotelbrill ante.gr; s/d incl breakfast €95/110, apt incl breakfast €135-160; P ✹) Individual décor in each room adds to the pleasant ambience of this boutique hotel. It has a charming garden setting and is midway along the beach road, about 300m from the ferry quay. The hotel is only robbed of sea views by the presence of Hotel Tzia, opposite.

There are several tavernas along the waterfront, all dishing up fairly standard fare for about €3.50 to €9, with **Akri** (☎ 22880 21196) being one of the best. The **Art Café** (☎ 22880 21181) has a pleasant ambience and is great for people-watching.

Kea has more supermarkets than most islands. On Friday nights they get very busy as the weekender influx stocks up.

IOULIDA ΙΟΥΛΙΔΑ
pop 700

Ioulida (ee-oo-*lee*-tha) is Kea's gem and has a distinctly metro feel at weekends. It's a delightful scramble of narrow alleyways and rising lanes that lies along the rim of a natural amphitheatre among the hills. It was once a substantial settlement of ancient Greece, but few relics remain and even the **Venetian kastro** has been incorporated into private houses. The houses have red-tiled roofs like those of Dryopida (p217) on Kythnos.

The bus turnaround is on a square just at the edge of town. From the turnaround, an archway leads into the village. Turning right and uphill takes you into the more interesting heart of Ioulida proper. The post office is part-way up on the right.

Sights

Ioulida's **archaeological museum** (☎ 22880 22079; admission free; ⏰ 8.30am-3pm Tue-Sun) is just before the post office on the main thoroughfare. It houses some intriguing artefacts, mostly from Agia Irini (below).

The famed **Kea Lion**, chiselled from slate in the 6th century BC, lies on the hillside beyond the last of the houses. Head uphill from the museum and keep going until abreast of the Kea Lion across a shallow valley. The path then curves round past a cemetery and the Lion, with its Mona Lisa smile, is ahead.

Sleeping & Eating

There are a few domatia in Ioulida, and several decent tavernas. Ask about rooms at tavernas.

Recommended eateries with good Greek dishes from about €4.50 to €10 (with lamb and fresh fish costing more):

Estiatorio I Piatsa (☎ 22880 22195) Just inside the archway.

Kalofagadon (☎ 22880 22118) On the main square.

AROUND KEA

The beach road from Korissia leads past **Gialiskari Beach** for 2.5km to where the waterfront quay at tiny **Vourkari** is lined with yachts and cafés. **Vourkariana Art Gallery** (☎ 22880 21458) is set back midwaterfront among the cafés and restaurants; it stages changing exhibitions of world-class art works over the summer.

Just across the bay from Vourkari are the truncated remains of the Minoan site of **Agia Irini**. Excavations during the 20th century indicated that there had been a settlement here since 3200BC and that it functioned for over 2000 years.

The road continues for another 3km to a fine sandy beach at **Otzias**. A dirt road continues beyond here for another 5km to the 18th-century **Moni Panagias Kastrianis** (☎ 22880 24348), which has terrific views.

Pisses is the island's best beach and is 8km southwest of Ioulida. It is long and sandy, and backed by a verdant valley of orchards and olive groves, with rugged hills rising above.

CYCLADES

Crete Κρήτη

Crete is more like a small country than another Greek island. It's not just Greece's largest island, but arguably the most fascinating and diverse.

Crete's remarkable history is evident across the island, from the ruins of Minoan palaces, Venetian fortresses, old mosques and Byzantine monasteries to the cave that is the legendary birthplace of Zeus. The Venetian ports of Hania and Rethymno are two of Greece's most evocative cities.

Crete is renowned for its natural beauty and diverse landscape. Spectacular mountain ranges dotted with caves are sliced by dramatic gorges that spill out to sea. The rugged interior is interspersed with vast plateaus and fertile plains. The east boasts Europe's only palm-tree forest beach and the south coast has some of the most stunning beaches and isolated coves.

Cretans are proud and hospitable people who maintain their culture and customs, particularly their strong musical tradition. Throughout the island you will come across traditional mountain villages and agricultural settlements unaffected by tourism. The young might drive four-wheel-drives but you will still pass shepherds tending their flocks and come across men in traditional dress.

An abundance of fresh produce and the distinct Cretan cuisine – renowned for its life-prolonging qualities – adds an interesting culinary dimension.

Crete has the dubious honour of hosting nearly a quarter of Greece's tourists. Much of the north coast has been commandeered and spoilt by hotels and cheap package tourism, but the island is big enough for independent travellers to venture off and find quiet beach settlements and mountain villages to explore.

HIGHLIGHTS

- **Evocative Towns** Discovering one of Greece's most beautiful cities, Hania's Old Town (p245)
- **Minoan Palaces** Opening a window into the magnificent Minoan civilisation at Knossos (p232)
- **History Explored** Inspecting the treasures in Iraklio's archaeological museum (p226)
- **Spectacular Gorges** Hiking through the Samaria Gorge (p253) – the longest in Europe
- **Southern beaches** Relaxing at Preveli (p243) and the spectacular south coast of Rethymno (p236)

- POPULATION: 540,045
- AREA: 8335 SQ KM

CRETE

HISTORY

Although Crete has been inhabited since Neolithic times (7000–3000 BC), for most people its history begins with the Minoan civilisation. The glories of Crete's Minoan past remained hidden until British archaeologist Sir Arthur Evans made his dramatic discoveries at Knossos in the early 1900s. The term 'Minoan' was coined by Evans and derived from the King Minos of Greek mythology. Nobody knows what the Minoans called themselves.

Among the ruins unearthed by Evans were the famous Knossos frescoes. Artistically, the frescoes are superlative; the figures that grace them have a naturalism lacking in contemporary Cycladic figurines, ancient Egyptian artwork (which they resemble in certain respects), and the Archaic sculpture that came later.

What is known is that early in the 3rd millennium BC, an advanced people migrated to Crete and brought with them the art of metallurgy. The Protopalatial period (3400–2100 BC) saw the emergence of a society of unprecedented artistic, engineering and cultural achievement. It was during this time that the famous palace complexes were built at Knossos, Phaestos, Malia and Zakros.

Also during this time, the Minoans began producing their exquisite Kamares pottery (see p227) and silverware, and became a maritime power trading with Egypt and Asia Minor.

Around 1700 BC the complexes were destroyed by an earthquake. Undeterred, the Minoans built bigger and better palaces on the sites of the originals, as well as new settlements in other parts of the island.

Around 1450 BC, when the Minoan civilisation was at its peak, the palaces were mysteriously destroyed again. While there is continued speculation as to the cause of this destruction, the latest theory suggests it was the result of a giant tsunami that followed the massive volcanic eruption on the island of Santorini (Thira). Knossos was the only palace to be salvaged. It was finally destroyed by fire around 1400 BC.

The Myceneans appeared in Crete during this time, but the Minoan civilisation was a hard act to follow. The war-orientated Dorians, who arrived in Greece around 1100 BC, were pedestrian by comparison. The 5th century BC found Crete, like the rest of the country, divided into city-states. The glorious classical age of mainland Greece had little impact on Crete, and the Persians bypassed the island. It was also ignored by Alexander the Great, so was never part of the Macedonian Empire.

By 67 BC, Crete had fallen to the Romans. The town of Gortyna in the south became the capital of Cyrenaica, a province that included large chunks of North Africa. Crete, along with the rest of Greece, became part of the Byzantine Empire in AD 395. In 1210 Crete was occupied by the Venetians,

THE MYSTERIOUS MINOANS

Of the many finds at Knossos and other Minoan sites, it is the celebrated frescoes that have captured the imagination of experts and amateurs alike, shedding light on a civilisation hitherto a mystery. They suggest a society that was powerful, wealthy, joyful and optimistic.

Gracing the frescoes are graceful white-skinned women with elaborately coiffured glossy black locks, dressed in stylish gowns that reveal perfectly shaped breasts. The bronze-skinned men are tall, with tiny waists, narrow hips, broad shoulders and muscular thighs and biceps; the children are slim and lithe. The Minoans seemed to know how to enjoy themselves. They played board games, boxed and wrestled, played leap-frog over bulls and over one another, and performed bold acrobatic feats.

As well as being literate, they were religious, as frescoes and models of people partaking in rituals testify. The Minoans' beliefs, like many other aspects of their society, remain an enigma, but there is sufficient evidence to confirm that they worshipped a nature goddess, often depicted with serpents and lions. Male deities were distinctly secondary.

Women enjoyed a respected position in society, leading religious rituals and participating in games, sports and hunting. Minoan society may have had its dark side, however, with evidence of human sacrifice being practised on at least one occasion, although probably in response to an extreme external threat.

CRETE

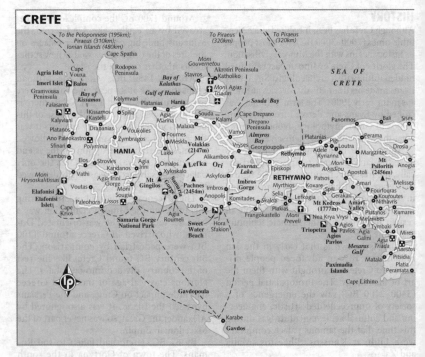

whose legacy is one of mighty fortresses, ornate public buildings and monuments, and handsome dwellings.

Despite the massive Venetian fortifications, which sprang up all over the island, by 1669 the whole of the mainland was under Turkish rule. The first uprising against the Turks was led by Ioannis Daskalogiannis in 1770. Many more insurrections followed, and in 1898 the Great Powers (Great Britain, France and Russia) intervened and made the island a British protectorate. It was not until the signing of the Treaty of Bucharest in 1913 that Crete officially became part of Greece, although the island's parliament had declared a de facto union in 1905.

Crete saw much heavy fighting during WWII. Germany wanted the island as an air base and on 20 May 1941 German parachutists landed on Crete. It was the start of 10 days of fierce fighting that became known as the Battle of Crete. For two whole days the battle hung in the balance until Germany won a bridgehead for its air force at Maleme, located near Hania. The Allied forces of Britain, Australia, New Zealand and Greece then fought a valiant rear-guard action which enabled the British Navy to evacuate 18,000 of the 32,000 Allied troops on the island. The German occupation of Crete lasted until the end of WWII.

During the war a large and active resistance movement was subject to heavy reprisals from the Germans. Many of Crete's mountain villages were bombed or burnt down and their occupants killed.

GETTING THERE & AWAY

This section provides an overview of air and boat options to and from the island of Crete. For more comprehensive information, see the relevant sections under specific town entries.

Air

Crete has two international airports. The main and biggest one is at Iraklio and there is a smaller one at Hania. Sitia's small domestic airport was expanded but has yet to start operating international charters. All three have flights to Athens and Thessaloniki; Iraklio also has flights to Rhodes.

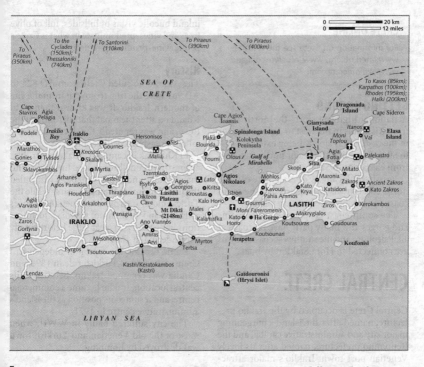

Ferry

Crete has ports at Iraklio, Souda (for Hania), Rethymno, Agios Nikolaos, Sitia and Kissamos. The car price for ferries from Crete to the mainland is about €86.

Ferries may stop at different islands en route and sailing times vary on some routes because of the type of craft used. The following are the main high-season schedules; services are reduced by about half during low season.

MAIN FERRY CONNECTIONS TO CRETE

Origin	Destination	Duration	Fare	Frequency
Gythio	Kissamos	7hr	€22.10	5 weekly
Kythira	Kissamos	4hr	€16.40	5 weekly
Piraeus	Agios Nikolaos	12hr	€34	2 weekly
Piraeus	Souda (Hania)	8½hr	€30	2 daily
Piraeus	Souda (Hania)*	4½hr	€51.50	daily
Piraeus	Iraklio	8hr	€32	2 daily
Piraeus	Iraklio	6½hr	€33.50	3 weekly
Piraeus	Rethymno	10hr	€28.70	2 daily
Piraeus	Rethymno*	6hr	€57	daily
Piraeus	Sitia	14½hr	€34	2 weekly
Rhodes	Iraklio	14½hr	€26.40	1 weekly
Rhodes	Agios Nikolaos	12hr	€27	2 weekly
Rhodes	Sitia	10hr	€27	2 weekly
Santorini	Iraklio	4½hr	€16	4 weekly
Santorini	Iraklio*	1¾hr	€31	daily
Thessaloniki	Iraklio	31hr	€46.50	4 weekly

*high speed services

> **CRETE ONLINE**
>
> For information on Crete see the websites www.interkriti.org, www.infocrete.com and www.explorecrete.com.

GETTING AROUND

A national highway skirts the north coast from Kissamos in the west to Agios Nikolaos in the east, and is slowly being extended east to Sitia. Buses link the major northern towns from Kissamos to Sitia.

Less-frequent buses operate between the north-coast towns and resorts and the south coast, via the inland mountain villages.

The south coast is spliced by mountains and gorges and many parts have no roads at all. Paleohora and the southwest coastal towns are connected to Hora Sfakion by boat.

CENTRAL CRETE

Central Crete is occupied by the Iraklio prefecture, named after the island's burgeoning major city and administrative capital, and the Rethymno prefecture, named after its lovely Venetian port town. Iraklio's major attractions are the Minoan sites of Knossos, Malia and Phaestos. The north coast east of Iraklio has been heavily exploited and, consequently, spoiled by package tourism, particularly around Hersonisos and Malia.

Rethymno has resorts spanning the coast to the east and one significant resort to the south, but much of the southern coast is still relatively unspoilt.

IRAKLIO ΗΡΑΚΛΕΙΟ
pop 130,914

Crete's capital Iraklio (ee-*rah*-klee-oh), also called Heraklion, is a bustling modern city and the fifth largest in Greece. Hectic, densely populated Iraklio lacks the architectural charm of Hania and Rethymno but is nonetheless a dynamic city. It has a lively city centre, chic boutiques, quality restaurants and buzzing cafés. Continuing redevelopment of the waterfront and new roads are helping to make the city more attractive. The port sees a constant procession of ferries, while charter jets bring thousands of visitors to Crete each year via Iraklio. Nearby the Minoan ruins of Knossos are the major drawcard, while further

inland bucolic vistas of hillsides, full of olive trees and vines, predominate in what is Crete's prime wine-producing region.

History

The Arabs who ruled Crete from AD 824 to AD 961 were the first to govern from the site of modern Iraklio. It was known then as El Khandak, after the moat that surrounded the town, and was reputedly the slave-trade capital of the eastern Mediterranean.

El Khandak became Khandakos after Byzantine troops finally dislodged the Arabs, and then Candia under the Venetians who ruled the island for more than 400 years. While the Turks quickly overran the Venetian defences at Hania and Rethymno, Candia's fortifications withstood a 21-year siege before finally surrendering in 1669.

Hania became the capital of independent Crete at the end of Turkish rule in 1898, and Candia was renamed Iraklio. Because of its central location, Iraklio became a commercial centre, and resumed its position as the island's administrative centre in 1971.

The city suffered badly in WWII, when most of the old Venetian and Turkish town was destroyed by bombing.

Orientation

Iraklio has two main squares. Plateia Venizelou, better known as the Lion Square because of its famous landmark Morosini Fountain, is in the heart of the city, while the sprawling Plateia Eleftherias overlooks the harbour.

The pedestrianised streets leading off the Lion Fountain, from Handakos and around Dedalou and Korai are the hub of the city's lively café scene. The ferry port is 500m to the east of the old port. Iraklio's airport is 5km east of the city centre.

Information
BOOKSHOPS

Planet International Bookshop (☎ 2810 289 605; Handakos 73) Excellent selection of literature, history and travel books, including most books recommended in this guide.

Road Editions (☎ 2810 344 610; Handakos 29) A specialist travel bookshop with a great selection of maps and guidebooks.

EMERGENCY

Tourist Police (☎ 28102 83190; Dikeosynis 10; ⏲ 7am-10pm)

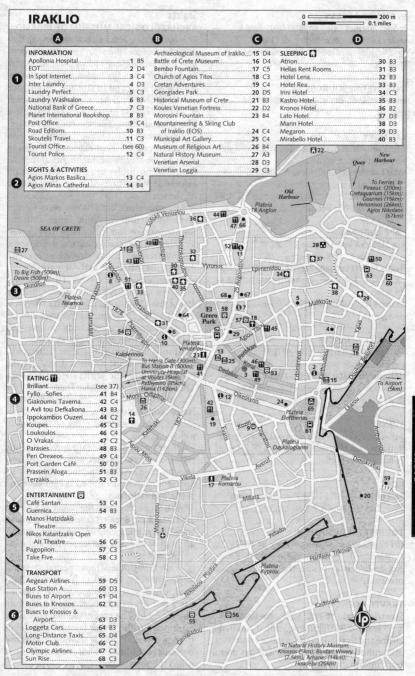

IRAKLIO

0 .... 200 m
0 .... 0.1 miles

INFORMATION	
Apollonia Hospital........................1	B5
EOT...2	D4
In Spot Internet...........................3	C4
Inter Laundry...............................4	D3
Laundry Perfect...........................5	C3
Laundry Washsalon......................6	B3
National Bank of Greece...............7	C3
Planet International Bookshop.......8	B3
Post Office...................................9	C4
Road Editions............................10	B3
Skoutelis Travel.........................11	C3
Tourist Office.......................(see 60)	
Tourist Police...........................12	C4

SIGHTS & ACTIVITIES	
Agios Markos Basilica.................13	C4
Agios Minas Cathedral................14	B4

Archaeological Museum of Iraklio..15	D4
Battle of Crete Museum..............16	D4
Bembo Fountain.........................17	C5
Church of Agios Titos.................18	C3
Cretan Adventures.....................19	C4
Georgiades Park.........................20	D5
Historical Museum of Crete.........21	B3
Koules Venetian Fortress............22	D2
Morosini Fountain......................23	B4
Mountaineering & Skiing Club	
of Iraklio (EOS)........................24	C4
Municipal Art Gallery..................25	C4
Museum of Religious Art.............26	B4
Natural History Museum.............27	A3
Venetian Arsenal......................28	D3
Venetian Loggia........................29	C3

SLEEPING	
Atrion......................................30	B3
Hellas Rent Rooms....................31	B3
Hotel Lena................................32	B3
Hotel Rea.................................33	B3
Irini Hotel.................................34	C3
Kastro Hotel..............................35	B3
Kronos Hotel.............................36	B2
Lato Hotel.................................37	D3
Marin Hotel...............................38	D3
Megaron...................................39	D3
Mirabello Hotel..........................40	B3

EATING	
Brilliant...............................(see 37)	
Fyllo...Sofies............................41	B4
Giakoumis Taverna....................42	C4
I Avli tou Defkaliona..................43	B3
Ippokambos Ouzeri....................44	C2
Koupes....................................45	C3
Loukoulos.................................46	C4
O Vrakas..................................47	C2
Parasies...................................48	B3
Peri Orexeos............................49	C4
Port Garden Café.......................50	D3
Prassein Aloga..........................51	B3
Terzakis...................................52	C3

ENTERTAINMENT	
Café Santan..............................53	C4
Guernica...................................54	B3
Manos Hatzidakis	
Theatre..................................55	B6
Nikos Katantzakis Open	
Air Theatre.............................56	C6
Pagopiion.................................57	C3
Take Five.................................58	C3

TRANSPORT	
Aegean Airlines.........................59	D5
Bus Station A............................60	D3
Buses to Airport........................61	D4
Buses to Knossos......................62	C3
Buses to Knossos &	
Airport...................................63	D3
Loggeta Cars............................64	B3
Long-Distance Taxis...................65	D4
Motor Club...............................66	C2
Olympic Airlines........................67	C3
Sun Rise..................................68	C3

CRETE

INTERNET ACCESS

In Spot Internet Cafe (☎ 28103 00225; Koraï 6; per hr €2.40; night rate midnight-noon €1.20; 24hr) High-speed access; printers, burners and PC games.

INTERNET RESOURCES

www.heraklion-city.gr Useful information and resources.

LAUNDRY

Most laundries charge €6 for wash and dry, and offer dry cleaning.

Inter Laundry (☎ 28103 43660; Mirabelou 25; 9am-9pm)

Laundry Perfect (☎ 28102 20969; Idomeneos & Malikouti 32; 9am-9pm Mon-Sat)

LEFT LUGGAGE

Bus Station A Left-Luggage Office (☎ 28102 46538; per day €2; 6.30am-8pm)

Iraklio Airport Luggage Service (☎ 28103 97349; per day from €2.50-5; 24hr) Near the local bus stop at the airport.

Laundry Washsalon (☎ 28102 80858; Handakos 18; per day €3)

MEDICAL SERVICES

Apollonia Hospital (☎ 28102 29713; Mousourou) Inside the old walls.

University Hospital (☎ 28103 92111) At Voutes, 5km south of Iraklio, it's the city's best-equipped medical facility.

MONEY

Most banks and ATMs are on 25 Avgoustou. **National Bank of Greece** (25 Avgoustou 35) Has a 24-hour exchange machine.

POST

Post office (☎ 28102 34468; Plateia Daskalogianni; 7.30am-8pm Mon-Fri, 7.30am-2pm Sat)

TOURIST INFORMATION

EOT (Greek National Tourism Organisation; ☎ 28102 46299; Xanthoudidou 1; 8.30am-8.30pm Apr-Oct, 8.30am-3pm Nov-Mar) is opposite the archaeological museum.

TRAVEL AGENCIES

Skoutelis Travel (☎ 28102 80808; www.skoutelistravel .gr; 25 Avgoustou 24) Helpful agent that can make airline and ferry bookings, arrange excursions, accommodation and car hire and has useful ferry information online.

Sights

ARCHAEOLOGICAL MUSEUM OF IRAKLIO

This outstanding **archaeological museum** (☎ 28102 79000; Xanthoudidou 2 (temp entry from Hatzidakis); admission €4, incl Knossos €10; 1-7.30pm Mon, 8am-7.30pm Tue-Sun Apr-Oct, 8am-3pm Tue-Sun, noon-3pm Mon late Oct–early Apr) is second in size and importance only to the National Archaeological Museum in Athens because of its unique and extensive Minoan collection. The museum was undergoing a major €21 million restoration, with the revamped museum expected to open in 2009. In the meantime, highlights of the collection are on display in a compact temporary exhibition being housed in another annexe on the site.

The musuem's collection covers Cretan civilization from Neolithic times until the Roman empire and includes pottery, jewellery, figurines and sarcophagi, as well as some famous frescoes, mostly from Knossos and Agia Triada. All testify to the remarkable imagination and advanced skills of the Minoans. While the temporary exhibition only includes 400 of the 15,000 artefacts that had been on display in the museum, it is presented to international museum standards and presents the key masterpieces of the collection.

Among the highlights are the famous Minoan frescoes from Knossos, including the **Procession fresco**, the **Griffin Fresco** (from the Throne Room), the **Dolphin Fresco** (from the Queen's Room) and the amazing **Bull-Leaping Fresco**, which depicts a seemingly double-jointed acrobat somersaulting on the back of a charging bull.

Other frescoes include the lovely, recently restored **Prince of the Lilies**, as well as two frescoes for the new Palace period – the priestess archaeologists have dubbed **La Parisienne** and the **Saffron Gatherer.**

Also on display from the palace at Knossos are **Linear A and B tablets** (the latter have been translated as household or business accounts), an ivory statue of a **bull leaper** and some exquisite **gold seals**.

From the Middle Minoan period, the most striking piece is the 20cm black-stone **Bull's Head**, which was a libation vessel. The bull has a fine head of curls, from which sprout horns of gold. The eyes of painted crystal are extremely lifelike. Other fascinating exhibits from this period include the tiny, glazed colour reliefs of Minoan houses from Knossos, called the '**town mosaic**'.

Finds from a shrine at Knossos include fine figurines of a bare-breasted **snake goddess**.

Among the treasures of Minoan jewellery is the beautiful, fine gold bee pendant found at Malia depicting two bees dropping honey into a comb.

The prized find from Phaestos is the fascinating **Phaestos Disk**, a 16cm circular clay tablet inscribed with pictographic symbols that have never been deciphered.

The famous elaborate **Kamares pottery**, named after the sacred cave of Kamares where the vases were first discovered is also on display, including a superbly decorated vase from Phaestos with white sculpted flowers.

Finds from the palace at Zakros include the gorgeous **crystal rhyton** vase that was found in over 300 pieces and which was painstakingly put back together again, as well as many vessels decorated with floral and marine designs.

The most famous and spectacular of the Minoan sarcophagi is the **sarcophagus from Agia Triada**. This stone coffin, painted with floral and abstract designs and ritual scenes, is regarded as one of the supreme examples of Minoan art.

Other significant pieces from Agia Triada include three celebrated vases. The **Harvester Vase**, of which only the top part remains, depicts a light-hearted scene of young farm workers returning from olive picking. The **Boxer Vase** shows Minoans indulging in two of their favourite pastimes – wrestling and bull-grappling. The **Chieftain Cup** depicts a more cryptic scene: a chief holding a staff and three men carrying animal skins.

Finds from Minoan cemeteries include two small clay models of groups of figures that were found in a *tholos* (tomb shaped like a beehive). One depicts four male dancers in a circle, their arms around each other's shoulders. The dancers may have been participating in a funeral ritual. The other shows two groups of three figures in a room flanked by two columns, with two large seated figures being offered libations by a smaller figure. It is not known whether the large figures represent gods or departed mortals.

Another highlight providing an insight into Minoan life is the elaborate **gaming board** decorated with ivory, crystal, glass, gold and silver, from the New Palace period at Knossos.

HISTORICAL MUSEUM OF CRETE

A fascinating collection from Crete's more recent past is presented at the excellent **Historical Museum** (☎ 2810 283 219; www.historical-museum .gr; Sofokli Venizelou; admission €5; ☽ 9am-5pm Mon-Fri, summer; 9am-3pm Mon-Sat winter). The ground floor covers the period from Byzantine to Turkish rule, displaying plans, charts, photographs, ceramics and maps. On the 1st floor are the only two El Greco paintings in Crete – *View of Mt Sinai and the Monastery of St Catherine* (1570) and the tiny recent addition, *Baptism of Christ*. Other rooms contain fragments of 13th- and 14th-century frescoes, coins, jewellery, liturgical ornaments and vestments, and medieval pottery.

Upstairs there is a reconstruction of the **library of author Nikos Kazantzakis**, a **Battle of Crete** section and an outstanding **folklore collection**.

NATURAL HISTORY MUSEUM

Established by the University of Crete, this leading **Natural History Museum** (☎ 2810 282 740; www.nhmc.uoc.gr; Leoforos Venizelou; adult/child €3, adults accompanying children free; ☽ 10am-2pm Mon-Sat, 10am-7pm Sun), has relocated to impressive new five-level premises in the restored former electricity building on the waterfront. Only two wings had opened at the time of research, including an impressive interactive discovery centre for kids, compete with labs and excavation projects. Apart from the broader evolution of humankind, it explores the flora and fauna of Crete, the island's ecosystem and habitats, and its caves, coastline and mountains, as well as Minoan life.

OTHER ATTRACTIONS

Iraklio burst out of its **city walls** long ago, but these massive fortifications, with seven bastions and four gates, are still very conspicuous, dwarfing the concrete structures of the 20th century. Venetians built the defences between 1462 and 1562. You can follow the walls around the heart of the city for views of Iraklio's neighbourhoods, although it is not a particularly scenic city.

The 16th-century **Koules Venetian fortress** (Iraklio Harbour; admission €2; ☽ 9am-6pm Tue-Sun), at the end of the Old Harbour's jetty, was called Rocca al Mare under the Venetians. It stopped the Turks for 22 years and then became a Turkish prison for Cretan rebels. The exterior is most impressive with reliefs of the Lion of St Mark. The interior has

CRETE

26 overly restored rooms and good views from the top. The ground-level rooms are used as art galleries, while music and theatrical events are held in the upper level.

The vaulted arcades of the **Venetian Arsenal** are opposite the fortress.

Several other notable vestiges from Venetian times survive. Most famous is **Morosini Fountain** (Lion Fountain) on Plateia Venizelou, which spurts water from four lions into eight ornate marble troughs. Built in 1628, the fountain was commissioned by Francesco Morosini while he was governor of Crete. Its centrepiece marble statue of Poseidon with his trident was destroyed during the Turkish occupation. Opposite is the three-aisled 13th-century **Agios Markos Basilica**. It has been reconstructed many times and is now the **Municipal Art Gallery** (☎ 28103 99228; 25 Avgoustou; admission free; 🕑 9am-1.30pm & 6-9pm Mon-Fri; 9am-1pm Sat). A little north is the attractively reconstructed 17th-century **Venetian Loggia**. It was a Venetian version of a gentleman's club; the male aristocracy came here to drink and gossip. It is now the Town Hall.

The delightful **Bembo Fountain**, at the southern end of 1866, was built by the Venetians in the 16th century. The ornate hexagonal edifice next to the fountain was a pump house added by the Turks, and now functions as a pleasant *kafeneio* (coffee house).

The **Museum of Religious Art** (☎ 28102 88825; Monis Odigitrias; admission €2; 🕑 9.30am-7.30pm Mon-Sat Apr-Oct; 9.30am-3.30pm winter), is housed in the former **Church of Agia Ekaterini** next to **Agios Minas Cathedral**. It has an impressive collection of icons, frescoes and elaborate ecclesiastical vestments, including six icons by Mihail Damaskinos, the mentor of El Greco.

The **Church of Agios Titos** (Agiou Titou) was constructed after the liberation of Crete in AD 961 and was converted to a Catholic church and then a mosque. It has been rebuilt twice after being destroyed by fire and then an earthquake.

The **Battle of Crete Museum** (☎ 28103 46554; cnr Doukos Beaufort & Hatzidaki; admission free; 🕑 8am-3pm) chronicles this historic battle.

Activities

Cretan Adventures (☎ 28103 32772; www.cretanadventures.gr; Evans 10, upstairs) is a well-regarded local company run by two intrepid brothers, who can organise hiking and trekking tours, mountain biking, and a range of specialist and extreme activities.

The **Mountaineering & Skiing Club of Iraklio** (EOS; ☎ 28102 27609; www.interkriti.org/orivatikos/orivat.html; Dikeosynis 53; 🕑 8.30-10.30pm) arranges mountain climbing, cross-country walking and skiing excursions across the island most weekends.

Iraklio for Children

The **Natural History Museum** (p227) is a safe bet for kids, as is an excursion to the **Cretaquarium** (see p231).

If the kids are museumed out, the waterfront **Port Garden Café** (☎ 28102 42411; Paraliaki Leoforo; 🕑 7am-late) opposite the Megaron hotel has indoor and shady outdoor play areas, including jumping castles and swings. You can also escape the heat and let the kids run around in **Georgiades Park**, where there is a pleasant shady café.

Tours

Iraklio's myriad travel agents run coach tours the length and breadth of Crete. Try the helpful **Skoutelis Travel** (☎ 28102 80808; www.skoutelis.gr; 25 Avgoustou 24).

Festivals & Events

Iraklio's **Summer Arts Festival** takes place at the **Nikos Kazantzakis Open Air Theatre** (☎ 28102 42977; Jesus Bastion; box office 🕑 9am-2.30pm & 6.30-9.30pm), near the moat of the Venetian walls, the nearby **Manos Hatzidakis theatre** and at the Koules fortress. Check www.heraklion-city.gr for the programme or ask at the **Municipal Cultural Office** (☎ 28103 99211; Androgeiou 2; 🕑 8am-4pm) behind the Youth Centre café.

Sleeping

Iraklio's central accommodation is weighted towards business travellers. Most hotels were upgraded in the lead up to the 2004 Olympics.

BUDGET

Hellas Rent Rooms (☎ 28102 88851; fax 28102 84442; Handakos 24; dm/d/tr without bathroom €10.50/30/42) This friendly and relaxed defacto youth hostel has a reception area and rooftop bar three flights up that's open all day. The rooms have fans and a wash basin and the shared bathrooms are basic but clean, and all rooms have balconies. You can have breakfast on the terrace from €2.50.

Mirabello Hotel (☎ 28102 85052; www.mirabello-hotel.gr; Theotokopoulou 20; s/d without bathroom €35/44, d with bathroom €65; 🞰) One of Iraklio's most pleasant budget hotels, the relaxed Mirabello is on a quiet street in the centre. The rooms are immaculate, though some are a little cramped, with TV, phones, balconies and upgraded bathrooms. Some rooms share single-sex bathrooms.

Hotel Rea (☎ 28102 23638; www.hotelrea.gr; Kalimeraki 1; d with/without bathroom €44/34) Popular with a wide range of backpackers, the family-run Rea has an easy, friendly atmosphere. Rooms all have fans and sinks, although some bathrooms are shared. There's a small, basic communal kitchen and it has family rooms (€60).

Hotel Lena (☎ 28102 23280; www.lena-hotel.gr; Lahana 10; s/d with bathroom €45/60, without bathroom €35/45; 🞰) On a quiet street, friendly Hotel Lena has 16 comfortable, airy rooms with phone, TV, fans and double-glazed windows. Most have private bathrooms but even the communal bathrooms are pleasant and upgraded.

MIDRANGE

Kronos Hotel (☎ 28102 82240; www.kronoshotel.gr; Sofokli Venizelou 2; s/d €48/60; 🞰 🖳) This well-maintained older waterfront hotel has comfortable rooms with double-glazed windows and balconies, phone and TV, and most have a fridge. It is one of the better-value two-star hotels in town. Ask for one of the rooms with sea views.

Kastro Hotel (☎ 28102 84185; www.kastro-hotel.gr; Theotokopoulou 22; s incl breakfast from €50, d & tr incl breakfast €75-90; 🞰 🖳) A refurbished, modern, cheery B-class hotel in the back streets, the Kastro is an excellent choice. The large rooms have fridges, TV, hairdryers, phones and ISDN internet connectivity.

Irini Hotel (☎ 28102 29703; www.irini-hotel.com; Idomeneos 4; s/d incl breakfast €71/100; 🞰) Close to the old harbour, Irini is a midsized establishment with 59 large, airy rooms with TV, radio and telephone, and plants and flowers on the balconies. You can get a lower rate if you skip breakfast.

Marin Hotel (☎ 28103 00018; www.marinhotel.gr; Doukos Beaufort 12; s incl breakfast €75, d incl breakfast €95-125; 🞰 🖳) The front rooms of this refurbished hotel have great views of the harbour and fortress and some have big balconies. Rooms are attractive and well-appointed, and staff are attentive.

Atrion (☎ 28102 46000; www.atrion.gr; Hronaki 9; s/d incl breakfast €95/110; 🞰) Fully refurbished in 2003, this is now one of the city's more pleasant hotels. Rooms are tastefully decked out in neutral tones, with TV, fridge, hairdryers and data ports. The top rooms have sea views and small balconies.

TOP END

Lato Hotel (☎ 28102 28103; www.lato.gr; Epimenidou 15; s/d €100/127, ste from €175; 🞰 🖳) This refurbished boutique hotel overlooking the fortress is one of Iraklio's prime hotels, with a smart contemporary design. Most rooms have spectacular views, especially the spacious suites, as does the rooftop restaurant and bar. There's a funky new fine-dining restaurant downstairs, **Brilliant** (☎ 28103 34959).

Megaron (☎ 28103 05300; www.gdmmegaron.gr; Doukos Beaufort 9; s/d €190/215, ste from €247; 🞰 🞰) This once-derelict historic building on the harbour has been stunningly transformed with top design and fittings throughout. There are comfortable beds, Jacuzzis in the VIP suites and plasma-screen TVs. The rooftop restaurant and bar have fine harbour views, along with a unique glass-sided pool.

Eating

Iraklio has some excellent restaurants to suit all tastes and pockets. Many restaurants are closed on Sunday.

BUDGET

Fyllo...Sofies (☎ 28102 84774; Plateia Venizelou 33; bougatsa €2.20; ⏲ 5am-late) Next to the Lion Fountain, this place does a roaring morning trade when both tourists off the early boats and the post-club crowd head straight for a delicious *bougatsa* pastry.

Giakoumis Taverna (☎ 28102 80277; Theodosaki 5-8; mayirefta €4-6; ⏲ closed Sun) There are tavernas clustered around the 1866 market side streets and this is one of the favourites. There's a full menu of Cretan specialities and vegetarian options. Turnover is heavy, which means that the dishes are fresh, while you can see the meat being prepared for the grill.

O Vrakas (☎ 69778 93973; Plateia 18 Anglon; seafood mezedhes €4.20-12) This small street-side *ouzerie* (place which serves ouzo and light snacks) grills fresh fish alfresco in front of diners. It's unassuming and the menu is limited, but still very popular with locals. Grilled octopus is a good choice.

CRETE

Ippokambos Ouzerie (☎ 28102 80240; Sofokli Venizelou 3; seafood mezedhes €4.50-9.50) Many locals come to this taverna at the edge of the tourist-driven waterfront dining strip. Take a peek inside at the fresh trays and pots of specialities such such as baked cuttlefish.

MIDRANGE

Koupes (☎ 69772 59038; Agiou Titou 22; mezedhes €2.50-6.50) One of a row of *rakadika* (Cretan *ouzeries*) along this pedestrian strip popular with students, this place opposite the school has a good range of mezedhes.

Terzakis (☎ 28102 21444; Marineli 17; mezedhes €3.60-10.20) On a small square opposite the Agios Dimitrios church, this excellent *ouzerie* has a good range of mezedhes, mayirefta and grills. Try the sea urchin salad or, if you are really game to try a local speciality, ask if they have 'unmentionables': *ameletita* (fried sheep testicles).

I Avli tou Defkaliona (☎ 28102 44215; Prevelaki 10; meat dishes €6-8.90; ☽ dinner) This traditional taverna with wicker chairs, checked tablecloths and plastic grapevines is known for its delicious food.

Peri Orexeos (☎ 28102 22679; Korai 10; mains €7-8) Right on the busy Koraï pedestrian strip, this restaurant offers excellent modern Greek food with creative takes like *kataïfi*-wrapped creamy chicken, huge salads, and solid Cretan cuisine. There's also a wicked chocolate dessert.

Also recommended is **Parasies** (☎ 28102 25009; Plateia Istorikou Mouseiou; grills €5-10) in the corner of the square next to the Historical Museum.

TOP END

Prassein Aloga (☎ 28102 83429; cnr Handakos & Kydonias 21; mains €12-18) This little rustic-style café/restaurant has excellent innovative Mediterranean food from an ever-changing menu, including dishes based on ancient Greek cuisine, such as pork medallions with dried fruit on wild rice.

Loukoulos (☎ 28102 24435; Korai 5; mains €15-32) Loukoulos offers fine dining in an elegant setting, with luscious Mediterranean specialities served on fine china and accompanied by soft classical music.

Entertainment

Pagopiion (☎ 28103 46028; Plateia Agiou Titou; ☽ 10am-late) This former ice factory is the most original café/bar/restaurant on the island.

Guernica (☎ 28102 82988; Apokoronou Kritis 2; ☽ 10am-late) A great combination of traditional décor and contemporary music makes this one of Iraklio's hippest bar/cafés. The rambling old building has a delightful terrace garden.

Take Five (☎ 28102 26564; Akroleondos 7; ☽ 10am-late) An old favourite on El Greco Park, this lively bar has been swamped by new louder arrivals on this recently pedestrianised strip.

Café Santan (☎ 69762 85869; Korai 13) This oriental café reflects the latest trend, with shishas, sofas and belly dancing from 11pm.

There are big dance clubs along Leoforos Ikarou, just down from Plateia Eleftherias and along Epimendou, though many close in summer. A new club and entertainment precinct has emerged along the revitalised waterfront to the west of the port, including some flashy open-air clubs. The most popular are **Big Fish** (☎ 28102 88011; Makariou 17 & Venizelou; ☽ all day), housed in a stunningly restored old stone building, and **Desire**, next door.

Getting There & Away

AIR

Aegean Airlines (www.aegeanair.com) City (☎ 2810 344 324; fax 2810 344 330; Leoforos Dimokratias 11); Airport office (☎ 2810 330 475)
Olympic Airlines (www.olympicairlines.com) City (☎ 2810 244 824; 25 Avgoustou 27; ☽ 8am-3pm Mon-Fri); Airport office (☎ 2810 337 203, 2810 397 129)

Domestic

Olympic and Aegean each have at least five flights daily to Athens (from €75) from Iraklio's Nikos Kazantzakis airport, as well as daily flights to Thessaloniki (from €106). Olympic also flies to Rhodes (from €89). Both airlines have regular special fare deals, although rarely in the summer peak season. Aegean's early-bird internet bookings are excellent value but dates cannot be changed. If you are flying last-minute, Olympic is normally cheaper.

The newcomer **Sky Express** (☎ 2810 223 500; www.skyexpress.gr) has daily flights from Iraklio to Rhodes and Santorini and up to three flights a week to Mytilini, Kos, Samos, Ikaria (from €79), though baggage is restricted to 12.5kg (they are small jets).

International

Iraklio has lots of charter flights from all over Europe, with flights to London available from €80 to €150. Skoutelis Travel (p226) is a good place to ask. **GB Airways** (www.gbairways.com) also has weekly scheduled flights from Gatwick to Iraklio.

Aegean Airlines has direct scheduled flights from Iraklio to Milan, Rome and other European cities.

BUS

Iraklio has two intercity bus stations. **Bus Station A** (☎ 28102 46534; www.ktel-heraklio-lassithi.gr), which serves eastern and western Crete (including Knossos), is on the waterfront near the quay, though there were plans to relocate it. **Bus Station B**, (☎ 28102 55965) just beyond Hania Gate, west of the city centre, serves Phaestos, Agia Galini and Matala.

Services reduce on weekends.

The airport bus stops in the centre of town at Plateia Eleftherias.

Buses from Bus Station A

Destination	Duration	Fare	Frequency
Agia Pelagia	45 min	€3.10	3 daily
Agios Nikolaos	1½ hr	€6.20	half-hourly
Arhanes	30 min	€1.60	hourly
Hania	3 hr	€10.50	18 daily
Hersonisos/Malia	45 min	€3.50	half-hourly
Ierapetra	2½ hr	€9.50	8 daily
Knossos	20 min	€1.15	3 hourly
Lasithi Plateau	2 hr	€4.70	1 daily
Milatos	1½ hr	€4.70	2 daily
Rethymno	1¾ hr	€6.50	18 daily
Sitia	3½ hr	€13.10	5 daily

Buses from Bus Station B

Destination	Duration	Fare	Frequency
Agia Galini	2 hr	€7.10	6 daily
Anogia	1 hr	€3.40	4 daily
Matala	2½ hr	€6.80	5 daily
Phaestos	1½ hr	€5.70	8 daily

FERRY

Minoan Lines (☎ 21041 45700, 28102 29624; www.minoan.gr) operates ferries each way between Iraklio and Piraeus (seven hours). The ferries depart from both Piraeus and Iraklio at 10pm. Fares start at €29 for deck class and €54 for cabins. The Minoan Lines' high-speed boats, the F/B *Festos Palace* and F/B *Knossos Palace*, are much more modern and comfortable than their ANEK rivals.

In summer, Minoan runs extra 6½-hour services (deck class €37) on weekends and some weekdays. This is the most convenient way to get to/from Iraklio.

GA Ferries (☎ 28102 22408; www.gaferries.gr) runs four ferries weekly from Iraklio to Thessaloniki (€46.50, 31 hours) via Santorini (€16, 4½ hours), Ios (€18.80, 6½ hours) and Paros (€24.30, 10 hours), stopping at several other islands en route. GA also has a weekly ferry from Iraklio (leaving Fri 5pm) to Rhodes (€26.40, cabin €39.20, 14½ hours,) via Kassos (€19.40, six hours,) and Karpathos (€17.40, eight hours).

Hellenic Seaways (www.hellenicseaways.gr) has a daily high-speed service to Santorini (€31, 1¾ hours), Ios (€36.70, 2½ hours), Paros €47.80, 3¼ hours), Naxos (€41.70, 4¼ hours) and Mykonos (€48.70, 4¾ hours).

ANEK Lines (☎ 28102 44912; www.anek.gr) has daily ferries between Iraklio and Piraeus (€32, cabin €58, eight hours) at 8.30pm.

LANE Lines (☎ 28103 46440; www.lane.gr) leaves Iraklio for Sitia, Kasos (€19.50, six hours), Karpathos (€19.50, eight hours), Diafani (€17.90, nine hours), Halki (€18.20, 11 hours) and Rhodes (€27, 14 hours).

Iraklio Port Authority (☎ 28102 44912) at the port has ferry schedule information.

Getting Around

Bus 1 goes to and from the airport every 15 minutes between 6am and 1am. The bus terminal is near the Astoria Capsis Hotel on Plateia Eleftherias. A taxi to the airport costs around €7 to €10. You can call **Ikarus Radio Taxi** (☎ 28102 11212) to arrange a ride.

Long-Distance Taxis (☎ 28102 10102) from Plateia Eleftherias, outside the Astoria Capsis Hotel and Bus Station B, can take you to all parts of Crete. Sample fares include Agios Nikolaos (€60), Rethymno (€70) and Hania (€120). The airport has a full range of car-rental companies but you'll likely get the best deal from local outlets. Try:

Sun Rise (☎ 28102 21609; 25 Avgoustou 46) Just off the pedestrian street.

Loggetta Cars (☎ 28102 89462; www.loggetta.gr; 25 Avgoustou 20)

Motor Club (☎ 28102 22408; www.motorclub.gr; Plateia 18 Anglon) Opposite the fortress, has the biggest selection of bikes.

AROUND IRAKLIO
Cretaquarium

The massive **Cretaquarium** (☎ 28103 37788; www.cretaquarium.gr; adult/child€8/6, free admission kids under 4; ☼ 9am-9pm May–mid-Oct, 10am-5.30pm Oct-Apr) at Gournes, 15km east of Iraklio, is the largest

WINE COUNTRY

Just south of Iraklio and Knossos is the wine-producing area of Peza, which produces about 70 percent of Crete's wine. The **Pezas Union of local producers** (☎ 2810 741 945; www.pezaunion.gr; admission free ☺ 9am-4pm Mon-Sat) have tastings and videos, as well as a mini-museum. The state-of-the-art **Boutari Winery** (☎ 28107 31617; www.boutari.gr; Skalani; tour & tasting €4.50; ☺ 10am-6pm), about 8km from Iraklio, is set on a hill in the middle of the Fantaxometoho estate and has a stunning tasting room and showroom overlooking the vineyard. Tours include a quirky futuristic video on Crete in an impressive cellar cinema where you watch the hi-tech show with headphones and a glass of wine.

aquarium in the Eastern Mediterranean region. There are several large tanks with an amazing display of marine life, though it is light on really big fish. There are some interactive multimedia features and displays in several languages.

The north-coast buses (€1.60, 30 mins) can drop you on the main road; from there it's a 10-minute walk. The turn-off to Kato Gouves is well signposted on the new national road.

Arhanes & Houdetsi

The village of Arhanes, 14km south of Iraklio, once boasted one of the island's great Minoan palaces. Today only scraps of the palace (signposted from the main road) remain, but Arhanes is a vibrant village with meticulously restored old houses and pleasant squares with excellent tavernas. It's considered a model of rural town revival.

The **Archaeological Museum of Arhanes** (☎ 28107 52712; admission free; ☺ 8.30am-3pm Wed-Mon) has several interesting finds from regional archaeological excavations. The exhibits include *larnakes* (coffins) and musical instruments from Fourni and an ornamental dagger from the Anemospilia temple.

You can find visitor information at www.arhanes.gr.

Neraidospilios (☎ 69727 20879; www.neraidospilios .gr; s/apt €40-70; ✹ ✺) These superbly-appointed spacious studios and apartments on the outskirts of the village overlooking the mountains are run by the brothers at the Diahroniko café in town.

South of Arhanes, in the otherwise unremarkable village of **Houdetsi**, the much-lauded musician Ross Daly has established a **museum of musical instruments** (☎ 28107 41027; www.labyrinth music.gr; admission €3; ☺ 10am-8pm Mar-Oct) displaying his extensive collection of mostly stringed instruments. The restored stone manor is the base for the Labyrinth Musical Work-

shop which each summer holds concerts with leading international musicians in the lovely grounds.

There are buses hourly from Iraklio to Arhanes (€1.40, ½ hour) and three buses daily to Houdetsi (€2.20, ¾ hour).

KNOSSOS ΚΝΩΣΟΣ

Knossos (k-nos-*os*), 5km from Iraklio, was the capital of Minoan Crete and the **Palace of Knossos** (☎ 28102 31940; admission €6; ☺ 8am-7pm Jun-Oct, 8am-3pm Nov-May) is the island's major tourist attraction.

The ruins of Knossos, home of the mythical Minotaur kept by King Minos, were uncovered in the early 1900s by the British archaeologist Sir Arthur Evans. Heinrich Schliemann, who had uncovered the ancient cities of Troy and Mycenae, had had his eye on the spot but was unable to strike a deal with the landowner.

Evans spent 35 years and £250,000 of his own money excavating and reconstructing parts of the palace. Some archaeologists have disparaged Evans' controversial reconstruction, believing he sacrificed accuracy to his overly vivid imagination. However, most nonexperts agree that Sir Arthur did a good job and the reconstructions allow you to visualise what a Minoan palace looked like.

You will need to spend some time at Knossos to explore it thoroughly.

History

The first palace at Knossos was built around 1900 BC. In 1700 BC it was destroyed by an earthquake and rebuilt to a grander and more sophisticated design. It is this palace that Evans reconstructed. It was partially destroyed again sometime between 1500 and 1450 BC. It was inhabited for another 50 years before it was devastated once and for all by fire.

The city of Knossos consisted of an immense palace, residences of officials and

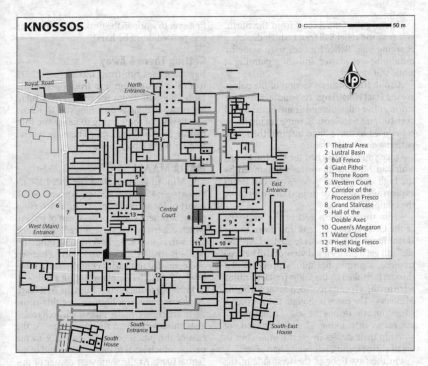

KNOSSOS

0 —————— 50 m

1 Theatral Area
2 Lustral Basin
3 Bull Fresco
4 Giant Pithoi
5 Throne Room
6 Western Court
7 Corridor of the Procession Fresco
8 Grand Staircase
9 Hall of the Double Axes
10 Queen's Megaron
11 Water Closet
12 Priest King Fresco
13 Piano Nobile

Royal Road
North Entrance
East Entrance
Central Court
West (Main) Entrance
South Entrance
South House
South-East House

priests, the homes of ordinary people, and burial grounds. The palace comprised royal domestic quarters, public reception rooms, shrines, workshops, treasuries and store-rooms, all built around a central court. Like all Minoan palaces, it also doubled as a city hall, accommodating all the bureaucracy.

Until 1997 it was possible to enter the royal apartments, but the area was cordoned off before it disappeared altogether under the continual pounding of tourists' feet. Extensive repairs are under way but it is unlikely to open to the public again.

Exploring the Site

Thanks to Evans' reconstruction, the most significant parts of the complex are instantly recognisable (if not instantly found), such as his reconstructed columns, most painted deep brown-red with gold-trimmed black capitals. Like all Minoan columns, they taper at the bottom.

It is not only the vibrant frescoes and mighty columns that impress at Knossos. Notice the little details which are evidence of a highly sophisticated society – the drainage system, the placement of light wells, and the relationship of rooms to passages, porches, light wells and verandas, which kept rooms cool in summer and warm in winter.

The usual entrance to the palace complex is across the **Western Court** and along the **Corridor of the Procession Fresco**. The fresco depicted a long line of people carrying gifts to present to the king; unfortunately only fragments remain. A copy of one of these fragments, called the **Priest King Fresco**, can be seen to the south of the Central Court.

If you leave the Corridor of the Procession Fresco and walk straight ahead to enter the site from the northern end, you will come to the **Theatral Area**, a series of steps that could have been a theatre or the place where people gathered to welcome important visitors arriving by the Royal Road.

The **Royal Road** leads off to the west. The road, Europe's first (Knossos has lots of firsts), was flanked by workshops and the houses of ordinary people. The **Lustral Basin** is also in this area. Evans speculated that this was where the Minoans performed a ritual cleansing before religious ceremonies.

CRETE

Entering the **Central Court** from the north, you pass the relief **Bull Fresco** which depicts a charging bull. Relief frescoes were made by moulding wet plaster and then painting it while still wet.

Also in the northern section of the palace are the **Giant Pithoi**, large ceramic jars used for storing olive oil, wine and grain. Evans found over 100 *pithoi* at Knossos, some 2m high. The ropes used to move them inspired the raised patterns decorating the jars.

Once you have reached the Central Court, which in Minoan times was surrounded by the high walls of the palace, you can begin exploring the most important rooms of the complex.

From the northern end of the west side of the Central Court, steps lead down to the **Throne Room**. This room is fenced off but you can still get a pretty good view of it. The centrepiece, a simple, beautifully proportioned throne, is flanked by the **Griffin Fresco**. (Griffins were mythical beasts regarded as sacred by the Minoans.) The room is thought to have been a shrine, and the throne the seat of a high priestess, rather than a king. The Minoans did not worship their deities in great temples but in small shrines, and each palace had several.

On the first floor of the west side of the palace is the section Evans called the **Piano Nobile**, for he believed the reception and state rooms were here. A room at the northern end of this floor displays copies of some of the frescoes found at Knossos.

Returning to the Central Court, the impressive **Grand Staircase** leads from the middle of the eastern side of the palace to the royal apartments, which Evans called the **Domestic Quarter**. This section of the site is now cordoned off and is off limits to visitors. Within the royal apartments is the **Hall of the Double Axes**. This was the king's megaron, a spacious double room in which the ruler both slept and carried out certain court duties. The room had a light well at one end and a balcony at the other to ensure air circulation. The room takes its name from the double axe marks on its light well, the sacred symbol of the Minoans.

A passage leads from the Hall of the Double Axes to the **Queen's Megaron**. Above the door is a copy of the **Dolphin Fresco**, one of the most exquisite Minoan artworks, and a blue floral design decorates the portal. Next to this room is the queen's bathroom, complete with terracotta bathtub and **water closet**, touted as the first ever to work on the flush principle; water was poured down by hand.

Getting There & Away

Regular buses run from Iraklio (see p231) from the bus station and from outside the Lion Fountain. From the coastal road there are occasional signs directing you to Knossos. Beware of touts trying to usher you into private paid-parking areas. There are several free car parks closer to the site.

MALIA ΜΑΛΙΑ

The Minoan **Palace of Malia** (☎ 28970 31597; admission €4; ⏰ 8.30am-3pm Tue-Sun), 3km east of the resort of Malia, is the only cultural diversion on the northern stretch of coast east of Iraklio, which otherwise has surrendered lock, stock and barrel to the package-tourist industry. Malia is smaller than Knossos and Phaestos and consisted of a palace complex and a town built on a flat, fertile plain, not on a hill.

Entrance to the ruins is from the **West Court**. At the extreme southern end of this court there are eight circular pits which archaeologists think were used to store grain. To the east of the pits is the main entrance to the palace, which leads to the southern end of the **Central Court**. At the southwest corner of this court you will find the **Kernos Stone**, a disc with 34 holes around its edge. Archaeologists still don't know what it was used for.

The **Central Staircase** is at the north end of the west side of the palace. The **Loggia**, just north of the staircase, is where religious ceremonies took place.

The exhibition hall has reconstructions of the site and interesting photos, including aerial shots. There is a good beach nearby.

There are buses to Malia from Iraklio every 30 minutes (€3.50, one hour).

ZAROS ΖΑΡΟΣ

pop 2215

About 46km southwest of Iraklio, Zaros is a refreshingly unspoilt village that's known for its spring water and bottling plant. Various excavations in the region indicate that the Minoans and the Romans settled here, lured by the abundant supply of fresh water.

If you have your own wheels, the Byzantine monasteries and traditional villages tucked away in the hills are worth exploring. **Moni Agiou Nikolaou**, which is at the mouth of the verdant **Rouvas Gorge**, contains some 14th-century paintings. A few kilometres later, the **Moni Agiou Andoniou Vrondisiou** is noteworthy for its 15th-century Venetian fountain and early 14th-century frescoes.

Just outside the village, the lovely shady park at **Votomos** makes a great picnic stop, with a small lake, excellent taverna and café **I Limni** (☎ 28940 31338; trout per kg €22; ☻ 9am-late) and a children's playground. From the lake, there is a walking path to Moni Agiou Nikolaou monastery (900m) and Rouvas Gorge (2.5km).

In the village, the charming **Studios Keramos** (☎/fax 28940 31352; s/d incl breakfast €30/35; ☻) is decorated with Cretan crafts, weaving and family heirlooms, antique beds and furniture. Owner Katerina is up early cooking up a copious traditional Cretan breakfast – don't miss it.

On the main street, the excellent taverna, **Vengera** (☎ 28940 31730), is run by vivacious Vivi and her mother Irini who cook honest traditional Cretan food.

There are two afternoon buses daily to Zaros from Iraklio (€4.10, one hour).

GORTYNA ΓΟΡΤΥΝΑ

Conveniently, Crete's three other major archaeological sites lie close to each other forming a rough triangle some 50km south of Iraklio. It's best to visit them all together.

Lying 46km southwest of Iraklio and 15km from Phaestos, on the plain of Mesara, is **Gortyna** (☎ 28920 31144; admission €4; ☻ 8am-7.30pm, to 5pm winter), pronounced *gor*-tih-nah. It's a vast and wonderfully intriguing site with bits and pieces from various ages. The site was a settlement from Minoan to Christian times. In Roman times, Gortyna was the capital of the province of Cyrenaica.

The most significant find at the site was the massive stone tablets inscribed with the **Laws of Gortyna**, dating from the 5th century BC and dealing with just about every imaginable offence. The tablets are on display at the site.

The 6th-century **Basilica** is dedicated to Agios Titos, a protégé of St Paul and the first bishop of Crete.

Other ruins at Gortyna include the 2nd-century-AD **Praetorium**, which was the residence of the governor of the province, a **Nymphaeum**, and the **Temple of Pythian Apollo**. The ruins are on both sides of the main Iraklio–Phaestos road.

PHAESTOS ΦΑΙΣΤΟΣ

The Minoan site of **Phaestos** (☎ 28920 42315; admission €4/2, incl Agia Triada €6; ☻ 8am-7.30pm Jun-Oct, 8am-5pm Nov-Apr), 63km from Iraklio, was the second-most-important palace-city in all of Minoan Crete. Of all the Minoan sites, Phaestos (fes-*tos*) has the most awe-inspiring location, with all-embracing views of the Mesara Plain and Mt Ida. The layout of the palace is identical to Knossos, with rooms arranged around a central court, though there has been no reconstruction.

In contrast to Knossos, the palace at Phaestos has very few frescoes. It seems the palace walls were mostly covered with a layer of white gypsum. Like the other palatial-period complexes, there was an old palace here that was destroyed at the end of the Middle Minoan period. Unlike the other sites, parts of this old palace have been excavated and its ruins are partially superimposed upon the new palace.

The entrance to the new palace is by the 15m-wide **Grand Staircase**. The stairs lead to the west side of the **Central Court**. The best-preserved parts of the palace complex are the reception rooms and private apartments to the north of the Central Court; excavations continue here. This section was entered by an imposing portal with half columns at either side, the lower parts of which are still *in situ*. Unlike the Minoan freestanding columns, these do not taper at the base. The celebrated Phaestos disc was found in a building to the north of the palace. The disc is now in Iraklio's archaeological museum (p226).

Getting There & Away

Eight buses a day head to Phaestos from Iraklio (€5.70, 1½ hours), also stopping at Gortyna. There are also buses from Agia Galini (€2.80 minutes, five daily) and Matala (€1.60, 30 minutes, five daily).

AGIA TRIADA ΑΓΙΑ ΤΡΙΑΔΑ

Pronounced ah-*yee*-ah trih-*ah*-dha, the small Minoan site of **Agia Triada** (☎ 28920 91564; admission €3, incl Phaestos €6; ☻ 10am-4.30pm summer, 8.30am-3pm winter), 3km west of Phaestos, was smaller than the other royal palaces but built to a similar design. This, and the opulence of the objects found at the site, indicate that it was a royal residence, possibly a summer palace of Phaestos' rulers. To the north of the palace is a small town where remains of a *stoa* (long, colonnaded building) have been unearthed.

Finds from the palace, now in Iraklio's archaeological museum, include a sarcophagus, two superlative frescoes and three vases: the Harvester Vase, Boxer Vase and Chieftain Cup.

The road to Agia Triada takes off to the right, about 500m from Phaestos on the road to Matala. There is no public transport to the site.

MATALA ΜΑΤΑΛΑ
pop 100

Matala (*ma*-ta-la), on the coast 11km southwest of Phaestos, was once one of Crete's best-known hippie hang-outs. When you see the dozens of eerie **caves** speckling the rock slab on the edge of the beach, you'll see why '60s hippies found them, like, groovy man, and turned them into a modern troglodyte city. The caves were originally Roman tombs cut out of the sandstone rock in the 1st century AD and have been used as dwellings for many centuries.

Matala expanded to the point where much of its original appeal was lost and these days it is a struggling resort, though it still has its loyal returnees and is a popular stop for day-trippers and tour buses every summer. The beautiful sandy **beach** below the caves is one of Crete's best and the resort is a convenient base to visit Phaestos and Agia Triada. The caves are normally fenced off at night but there was no guard or entry charge at research time.

Sleeping & Eating

Fantastic Rooms to Rent (☎ 28920 45362, fax 28920 45292; s/d/tr €20/25/25, d & tr with kitchen €30; 🐱) Has been here since the hippie heydays, and has added a newer block at the back. The rooms are plain but comfortable, many with kitchenette, phone, kettle and fridge.

Pension Andonios (☎ 28920 45123, fax 28920 45690; d/tr €25/30) Run by the genial Antonis, this comfortable pension has attractively furnished rooms set around a lovely courtyard, many with kitchenette, and the top rooms have balconies.

Hotel Zafiria (☎ 28920 45366, fax 28920 45725; d incl breakfast €40; 🅿 🐱 💻) The sprawling Zafiria has comfortable rooms with balconies, sea views and telephones and a new pool beneath the cliffs.

Eating in Matala is hardly an experience in *haute cuisine*. Overlooking the beach, **Lions** (☎ 28920 45108; specials €6-9) has been popular for many years and the food is better than average, with big trays of home-style dishes inside. It is also a good place for a drink, as it gets lively in the evening.

Gianni's Taverna (☎ 28920 45719; mains €5-7) is a no-frills place with good-value grills.

Getting There & Away

There are five buses daily between Iraklio and Matala (€6.80, 2½ hours), and between Matala and Phaestos (€1.60, 30 minutes).

VORI ΒΩΡΟΙ
pop 755

In the village of Vori, 4km east of Tymbaki past Phaestos, you will find the outstanding private **Museum of Cretan Ethnology** (☎ 28920 91112; admission €3; ⏰ 10am-6pm Apr-Oct, by appointment in winter ☎ 28920 91110). The modern museum provides a fascinating insight into traditional Cretan culture, with exhibits following themes such as rural life, war, customs, architecture, music, and the herbs, flora and fauna that form the basis of the Cretan diet. There are some beautiful weavings, furniture, wood-carvings and musical instruments. It's well signposted from the main road.

RETHYMNO ΡΕΘΥΜΝΟ
pop 27,868

Rethymno (*reth*-im-no) is Crete's third-largest town and one of the most picturesque, with a charming harbour and massive Venetian fortress. The delightful Venetian-Ottoman quarter is a maze of narrow streets, graceful wood-balconied houses and ornate Venetian monuments, with minarets adding a touch of the Orient. The city has a campus of the University of Crete, bringing a student population that keeps the town alive outside the tourist season. An added attraction is a beach right in town.

The approaches to the town couldn't be less inviting. The modern town has sprawled out along the coast, dotted with big package hotels along the stretch on the sandy beach to the east.

History
The site of Rethymno has been occupied since Late Minoan times. In the 3rd and 4th centuries BC, the town was called Rithymna, an

autonomous state of sufficient stature to issue its own coinage. A scarcity of references to the city in Roman and Byzantine times suggest it was of minor importance.

The town thrived under the Venetians, who ruled from 1210 until 1645, when the Turks took over. Turkish forces ruled until 1897, when it was taken by Russia as part of the Great Powers' occupation of Crete.

Rethymno became an artistic and intellectual centre after the arrival of a large number of refugees from Constantinople in 1923.

Orientation

Rethymno is a fairly compact town with most of the major sights and places to stay and eat near the old Venetian harbour. The beach is on the eastern side, around from the Venetian harbour.

If you arrive by bus, you will be dropped at the rather inconveniently located terminal at the western end of Igoumenou Gavriil, about 600m west of the Porto Guora (although this was due to relocate). If you arrive by ferry, the old quarter is at the end of the quay.

Information

BOOKSHOPS

Ilias Spondidakis bookshop (☎ 28310 54307; Souliou 43) Stocks novels in English, books about Greece, tapes of Greek music and has a small second-hand section.
Xenos Typos (☎ 28310 29405; Ethnikis Antistasls 21) Stocks foreign press, guide books and maps.

EMERGENCY

Tourist police (☎ 28310 28156; Delfini Bldg, Venizelou; 🕑 7am-2.30pm) In the same building as the municipal tourist office.

INTERNET ACCESS

Cybernet (Kallergi 44-46; per hr €3; 🕑 10am-5am)

LAUNDRY

Laundry Mat (☎ 28310 29722; Tombazi 45; wash & dry €9; 8.30am-2pm & 5.30-9pm Mon-Fri, 8.30am-2.15pm Sat) Next door to the youth hostel.

LEFT LUGGAGE

KTEL (☎ 28310 22659; cnr Kefalogiannidon & Igoumenou Gavriil) The bus station stores luggage for €1.50 per day.

MEDICAL SERVICES

Rethymno Hospital (☎ 28210 27491; Triandalydou 17; 🕑 24hr)

MONEY

Alpha Bank (Pavlou Koundouriotou 29)
National Bank of Greece (Dimokratias)

POST

Post office (☎ 28310 22302; Moatsou 21; 🕑 7am-7pm Mon-Fri)

TOURIST INFORMATION

Municipal tourist office (☎ 28310 29148; www .rethymno.gr; Delfini Bldg, Eleftheriou Venizelou; 🕑 8.30am-8.30pm Mon-Fri, 9am-8.30pm Sat & Sun Mar-Nov)

TRAVEL AGENCIES

Ellotia Tours (☎ 28310 24533; www.rethymnoatcrete .com; Arkadiou 155; 🕑 9am-9pm Mar-Nov) Helpful office that handles boat and plane tickets, changes money, rents cars and motorcycles, and books excursions.

Sights

Rethymno's 16th-century **fortress** (fortezza; ☎ 28310 28101; Paleokastro Hill; admission €3.10; 🕑 8am-8pm Jun-Oct) is the site of the city's ancient acropolis. Within its massive walls a great number of buildings once stood, of which only a church and a mosque survive intact. The ramparts offer good views, while the site has lots of ruins to explore.

The small **archaeological museum** (☎ 28310 54668; admission €3; 🕑 8.30am-3pm Tue-Sun), near the entrance to the fortress, was once a prison. The exhibits are well labelled in English and contain Neolithic tools, Minoan pottery excavated from nearby tombs, Mycenaean figurines and a 1st-century-AD relief of Aphrodite, as well as an important coin collection.

Rethymno's **Historical & Folk Art Museum** (☎ 28310 23398; Vernardou 28-30; admission €3; 🕑 9.30am-2.30pm Mon-Sat) gives an excellent overview of the area's rural lifestyle, with its collection of old clothes, baskets, weavings and farm tools whose purpose would remain obscure without the useful explanatory labels on the exhibits. It is in a lovely historic Venetian building.

Pride of place among the many vestiges of Venetian rule in the old quarter goes to the **Rimondi Fountain** with its spouting lion heads and Corinthian capitals; and the 16th-century **Loggia**, now a museum shop.

At the southern end of Ethnikis Antistaseos is the well-preserved **Porto Guora** (Great Gate), a remnant of the defensive wall.

The **Centre for Byzantine Art** (☎ 28210 50120; Ethnikis Antistaseos) is a great example of a restored

CRETE

Venetian/Turkish mansion and has a terrace café with great views of the old town. Other Turkish legacies in the old quarter include the **Kara Musa Pasha Mosque**, which has a vaulted fountain; and the **Nerantzes Mosque**, which was converted from a Franciscan church in 1657. The building's minaret, built in 1890, was being restored at the time of researching

this book. The building now houses the **Hellenic Conservatory** and makes a lovely venue for concerts and recitals.

Activities

The **Happy Walker** (☎ /fax 28310 52920; www.happywalker.com; Tombazi 56; ⏰ 5pm-8.30pm) runs various walks in the region.

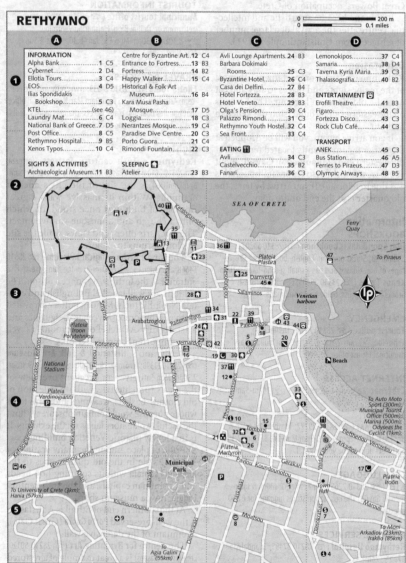

RETHYMNO

0 — 200 m
0 — 0.1 miles

Rethymno's chapter of the **EOS** (Greek Alpine Club; ☎ 28310 57766; eos.rethymnon.com; Dimokratias 12) can give advice on mountain climbing in the region.

The **Paradise Dive Centre** (☎ 28310 26317; www .diving-center.gr;) runs diving activities and PADI courses for all grades of divers from their dive base at Petres, about 15 minutes west of Rethymno.

Odyseas the Cyclist (☎ /fax 28310 58178; odyseasthe cyclist@hotmail.com; Velouhioti 31) runs guided rides in the area.

Festivals & Events

Rethymno's main cultural event is the annual **Renaissance Festival** (☎ 28310 51199; www .cultureguide.gr; ☾ Jul-Sep), primarily held in the Erofili Theatre at the fortress. Most years there's a **Wine Festival** in mid-July in the municipal park. There are lively carnival celebrations in February.

Sleeping
BUDGET
Rethymno Youth Hostel (☎ 28310 22848; www .yhrethymno.com; Tombazi 41; dm without bathroom €9; ▣) The hostel is friendly and well run with free hot showers. Breakfast is available from €2 and there's a bar in the evening. There is no curfew and it is open all year.

Olga's Pension (☎ 28310 28665; Souliou 57; s/d/tr €35/45/65; ⊠) Friendly Olga's is tucked away on touristy but colourful Souliou. It has a faded charm, with a quirky décor and a network of terraces connecting a range of basic but colourful rooms. Most have a fridge, TV, fan and basic bathrooms. Rates include breakfast at Stella's kitchen downstairs.

Atelier (☎ 28310 24440; atelier@ret.forthnet.gr; Himaras 27; r €35-45) Some of the best-value options are these clean and attractively refurbished rooms attached to Frosso Bora's pottery workshop. They have exposed stone walls and many Venetian architectural features, as well as small flat-screen TVs, new bathrooms and kitchenettes.

Sea Front (☎ 28310 51981; www.forthnet.gr/elo tia; Arkadiou 159; d €35-45; ⊠) This conveniently located pension on the beach has pleasant budget rooms with timber floors, fridge and air-con. It also has cheerful studio apartments with sea views and ceiling fans further towards the town beach, and rooms in another building nearby.

Byzantine Hotel (☎ 28310 55609; Vosporou 26; d incl breakfast €45) This excellent-value small hotel in a historic building near the Porta Guora maintains a traditional feel. The rooms are simply decorated with carved timber furniture and some have bathtubs. The back rooms overlook the old mosque and minaret. There's no air-con, though there were plans to install it.

MIDRANGE & TOP END
Casa dei Delfini (☎ 28310 55120; kzaxa@reth.gr; Niki-forou Foka 66-68; studio €45-70, ste €80-140; ⊠) Turkish and Venetian architectural features have been cleverly maintained in this elegant pension, including an old stone trough and the hammam ceiling in one of the studio bathrooms. There is a range of traditionally decorated rooms, all with kitchenettes, through the most impressive is the massive maisonette with a large private terrace.

Hotel Fortezza (☎ 28310 55551; www.fortezza.gr; Melissinou 16; s/d incl breakfast €57/69; ℗ ⊠ ⊠) Housed in a refurbished old building in the heart of the old town, the tasteful rooms have TVs, telephones and air-con. After a day of roaming through Rethymno, it's pleasant to relax by the swimming pool.

Hotel Veneto (☎ 28310 56634; www.veneto.gr; Epimenidou 4; studio/ste incl breakfast €112/127; ⊠) The oldest part of the hotel dates from the 14th century and many traditional features have been preserved without sacrificing modern comforts. There's a stunning pebble mosaic in the foyer and the eye-catching rooms of polished wood floors and ceilings have iron beds, satellite TV and kitchenettes. Rates drop significantly out of high season.

Palazzo Rimondi (☎ 28310 51289; www.palazzori mondi.com; Xanthoulidou 21 & Trikoupi 16; d studio/ste incl breakfast €160/190; ⊠) This charming Venetian mansion in the heart of the old city has exquisite individually decorated studios with kitchenettes. There's a small splash pool in the courtyard where breakfast is served.

Avli Lounge Apartments (☎ 28310 58250; www.avli.gr; cnr Xanthoudidou 22 & Radamanthyos; ste incl à la carte breakfast €199-239; ⊠) These decadent eclectic suites are spread over two beautifully restored Venetian buildings in Rethymno's historic old town. There are ornate iron or wooden beds, antiques, exquisite furnishings and objets d'art.

Eating
The waterfront and Venetian harbour are lined with similar tourist restaurants fronted by fast-talking touts. Rethymno's best restaurants are inland from the harbour.

CRETE

BUDGET

Taverna Kyria Maria (☎ 28310 29078; Moshovitou 20; Cretan dishes €2.50-6.50) For traditional atmosphere, head inland down the little side streets to Kyria Maria, behind the Rimondi Fountain. This taverna has outdoor seating with bird cages hanging from the leafy trellis.

Samaria (☎ 28310 24681; Eleftheriou Venizelou; mayirefta €4-6.50) Of the waterfront tavernas, this is one of the few where you'll see local families eating. There's a large range of casserole-style *mayirefta* (ready-cooked meals), the soups and grills are excellent and the fruit and *raki* (Greek fire water, smoother than *tsipouro*) are complimentary.

MIDRANGE

Fanari (☎ 28310 54849; Kefalogiannidon 15; mezedhes €2.50-10) West of the Venetian harbour, this welcoming waterfront taverna serves good mezedhes, fresh fish and Cretan cuisine. The *bekri mezes* (pork with wine and peppers) is excellent or try *apaki*, the local smoked pork speciality. The home-made wine is decent, too.

Thalassografia (☎ 28310 52569; Kefalogiannidon 33; mezedhes €3.80-7.30) This excellent *mezedhopoleio* (restaurant specialising in mezedhes), in a breathtaking setting under the *fortezza* with views out to sea, is the place to watch the sunset and try some fine mezedhes. The grilled sardines are excellent, as are the creamy mushrooms.

Lemonokipos (☎ 28310 57087; Ethnikis Antistasls 100; mains €5.80-9) Dine among the lemon trees in the lovely courtyard of this well-respected taverna in the old quarter. It's good typical Cretan fare, with a good range of vegetarian dishes and lots of tasty appetisers.

Castelvecchio (☎ 28310 55163; Himaras 29; mains €7-16; ☺ dinner only Jul-Aug, dinner & lunch Sep-Jun) The affable Valantis will make you really feel at home in the garden terrace of this family taverna located on the edge of the *fortezza*. Try the *kleftiko* (slow oven-baked lamb).

Avli (☎ 28310 26213; www.avli.com; cnr Xanthoudidou 22 & Radamanthyos; mains €13.50-30) This delightful former Venetian villa is the place for a special night out. The Nuevo-Cretan style food is superb, the wine list excellent and you dine in an idyllic garden courtyard bursting with pots of herbs, bougainvillea canopies, fruit trees and works of art.

Entertainment

Rethymno's livelier nightlife is concentrated in the cluster of bars, clubs and discos around Nearhou and Salaminos, near the Venetian harbour area as well as the waterfront bars off Plastira Square, which are popular with younger locals. Students frequent the lively *rakadika* on Vernadou.

Rock Club Cafe (☎ 28310 31047; Petihaki 8; ☺ 9pm-dawn) One of Rethymno's classic hang-outs, tourists fills the club nightly.

Fortezza Disco (Nearhou 20; ☺ 11pm-dawn) Big and flashy with three bars, a laser show and a well-groomed international crowd that starts drifting in around midnight.

Figaro (☎ 28310 29431; Vernardou 21; ☎ noon-late) Housed in an ingeniously restored old building, Figaro is an atmospheric 'art and music' all-day bar that attracts a subdued crowd for drinks, snacks and excellent music.

Getting There & Away
BUS

From the **bus station** (☎ 28310 22212; Igoumenou Gavriil) there are hourly summer services to both Hania (€6, one hour) and Iraklio (€6.50, 1½ hours). There are also seven buses a day to Plakias (€3.50, one hour), six to Agia Galini (€5.30, 1½ hours), three to Moni Arkadiou (€2.40, 30 minutes), two to Omalos (€11.90, two hours) and four to Preveli (€4). There are daily buses to Hora Sfakion via Vryses. Services are greatly reduced in the low season.

CATAMARAN & FERRY

ANEK (☎ 28310 29221; www.anek.gr; Arkadiou 250) operates a ferry three times a week between Rethymno and Piraeus (€29, 10 hours), leaving both ports at 8pm. Note that some ferries leave from the port and others from the marina further east.

NEL LINES (☎ 28310 24295; www.nel.gr) runs a high-speed service between Rethymno and Piraeus (€57, five hours) daily from July to September (four times a week May to June).

SeaJets (www.seajets.gr) runs the Superjet catamaran on Thursday and Saturday between Rethymno and Santorini (€37.90, two hours and 40 minutes), Ios, Naxos and Mykonos (€58).

Getting Around

Auto Moto Sport (☎ 28310 24858; www.automotosport .com.gr; Sofokli Venizelou 48) rents cars and has 300 motorbikes, from mopeds and 50cc bikes to a Harley 1200cc.

AROUND RETHYMNO
Moni Arkadiou Μονή Αρκαδίου

This historic 16th-century **monastery** (Arkadi; ☎ 28310 83136; admission €2; ☼ 9am-7pm Apr-Oct) stands in attractive hill country 23km southeast of Rethymno. The most impressive building is the Venetian baroque church. Its striking façade has eight slender Corinthian columns and is topped by an ornate triple-belled tower.

In November 1866 the Turks sent massive forces to quell insurrections that were gathering momentum throughout the island. Hundreds of men, women and children who had fled their villages used the monastery as a safe haven. When 2000 Turkish soldiers staged an attack on the building, rather than surrender, the Cretans set light to a store of gun powder. The explosion killed everyone, Turks included, except one small girl, who lived to a ripe old age in a village nearby. A bust of this woman, and the abbot who lit the gun powder, stand outside the monastery.

To the left of the Venetian church is a small **museum**. The ossuary in the former windmill outside the museum grounds has a macabre collection of skulls and bones of the 1866 fighters.

There are three daily buses from Rethymno to the monastery (€2.40, 30 minutes).

Margarites Μαργαρίτες
pop 331

Known for its pottery tradition, Margarites, 27km from Rethymno, is invaded by tour buses in the morning. There are more than 20 ceramic studios and among the garish pieces that line the main street there are some places with good-quality, authentic local designs. The traditional potters use local clay collected from the foot of Mt Psiloritis, which is of such fine quality it needs only one firing and no glazing – the outside is smoothed with a pebble. You will see many pieces bearing the flower motif of the area.

The most traditional place is the workshop of septuagenarian potter **Manolis Syragopoulos** (☎ 28340 92363) who is the only one still using manual wheels and a wood-fired kiln to make pottery the way his great-grandfather did. It's about 1km outside the town on your left.

Other stand-out places include Konstantinos Gallios' excellent studio **Ceramic Art** (☎ 28340 92304) and the friendly **Kerameion** (☎ 28340 92135) on the main street, which has many pieces based on Minoan designs.

There are wonderful views over the valley from the taverna terraces on the main square.

From Margarites, you can visit **Ancient Eleftherna** with its amazing Roman cisterns.

There are two buses daily Monday to Friday from Rethymno (€3, 30 minutes).

ANOGIA ΑΝΩΓΕΙΑ
pop 2454

If ever there was a village that embodies quintessential Crete, it is Anogia, a bucolic village perched on the flanks of **Mt Psiloritis** 37km southwest of Iraklio. Anogia is well known for its rebellious spirit and its determination to hang on to its undiluted Cretan character. Its famous 2000-guest **weddings** involve the entire village. It's also known for its stirring music and has spawned a disproportionate number of Crete's best-known musicians.

Anogia is a macho town where the *kafeneia* (coffee shops) on the main square are frequented by black-shirted moustachioed men, the older ones often wearing traditional dress. The women stay behind the scenes or flog traditional crafts that hang all over the shops in town.

During WWII Anogia was a centre of resistance to the Germans, who massacred all the men in the village in retaliation for their role in sheltering Allied troops and aiding in the kidnap of General Kreipe. Today, Anogia is the centre of a prosperous sheep-husbandry industry and a burgeoning tourist trade, bolstered as much by curious Greeks as by foreign travellers seeking a glimpse of real Crete.

The town is spread out on a hillside with the textile shops in the lower half and most accommodation and businesses in the upper half. There's an Agricultural Bank with an ATM, and post office in the upper village. You can check mail at **Infocost** (☎ 28340 31808; per hr €3; ☼ 5pm-late) in the upper village.

In the upper village, the friendly **Hotel Aristea** (☎ 28340 31459; d incl breakfast €40) has good views from the simple but well-outfitted rooms with TV, private bathrooms and balconies, and there's an excellent set of new studios next door.

CRETE

Ta Skalomata (☎ 28340 31316; grills €4-8) provides a wide variety of grills and Cretan dishes at very reasonable prices. Zucchini with cheese and aubergine is very tasty, as is its home-baked bread. The restaurant is on the eastern side of the upper village and enjoys great views.

There are four buses daily from Iraklio (€3.40, one hour), and two buses daily Monday to Friday from Rethymno (€4.70, 1¼ hours).

SPILI ΣΠΗΛΙ

pop 642

Spili (*spee*-lee), 30km southeast of Rethymno is a pretty mountain village with cobbled streets, rustic houses and plane trees. Its centrepiece is a unique Venetian fountain, which spurts water from 19 lion heads, though its recent refurbishment was ill-advised. Bring along your own containers and fill up with the best water on the island. Tourist buses regularly stop in the town during the day, but in the evening Spili belongs to the locals. It is a good spot for lunch and a great base for exploring the region, midway between the north and south coast.

The bus stop is just south of the square. There are two ATMs and the post office on the main street and you can check mail at Café Babis near the fountain.

Friendly **Heracles Rooms** (☎/fax 28320 22411; heraclespapadakis@hotmail.com; s/d €29/40; ✗) has spotless, nicely furnished rooms with insect screens, fridge and air-con and great mountain views.

Costas Inn (☎ 28320 22040; fax 28320 22043; d incl breakfast €40) has well-kept, pleasant rooms with a homey atmosphere, satellite TV, radio and ceiling fans. Some of the rooms have a fridge.

Yianni's (☎ 28320 22707; mains €4-7), past the fountain, is a good dining option with a big courtyard and excellent traditional cooking such as the delicious rabbit in wine, mountain snails and a decent house red.

Pantelis Vasilakis and his wife Calliope run a fine traditional taverna, **Panorama** (☎ 28320 22555), in a picturesque location on the outskirts of town towards Agia Galini. The bread is usually home-made, the mezedhes are excellent and the mains include Cretan specialities such as kid goat with wild greens.

PLAKIAS ΠΛΑΚΙΑΣ

pop 177

Plakias is one of the liveliest resort towns on the southern coast. The well-run youth hostel helps attract a younger crowd than many of the resorts nearby. The medium-size hotels in town attract independent travellers. Off-season it attracts many families and an older crowd.

Plakias has some decent eating options, good regional walks, a large sandy beach and enough activities and nightlife to keep you entertained. It is also a good base from which to explore the region, with a number of excellent beaches nearby.

Orientation & Information

It's easy to find your way around Plakias. One street skirts the beach and another runs parallel to it one block back. The bus stop is at the middle of the waterfront.

Plakias has two ATMs, while **Monza Travel Agency** (☎ 28320 31882), near the bus stop, arranges car and bike hire and excursions. The post office is on the street off Monza Travel. Check www.plakias-filoxenia.gr for hotel information.

You can check mail at **Ostraco Bar** (☎ 28320 31710; per hr €4; ⊗ 9am-late) on the main street or at the **Youth Hostel Plakias** (☎ 28320 32118; per hr €3.60).

Anso Travel (☎ 28320 31712; www.ansotravel.com) runs a range of **guided walking tours** in the area.

Sleeping

Youth Hostel Plakias (☎ 28320 32118; www.yhplakias .com; dm €9; 🖳) For independent travellers this is *the* place to stay in Plakias. Manager Chris from the UK has created a very friendly place with spotless dorms, green lawns, volleyball court and internet access. He also upgraded the toilets and showers and built a porch. It's a 10-minute signposted walk from the bus stop.

Castello (☎/fax 28320 31112; r/studio €30/33; ✗ P) It is the relaxed owner Christos and his well-tended garden that makes this place a happy haven. All rooms are cool, clean and fridge-equipped and most have cooking facilities and big shady balconies. There are also big two-bedroom apartments ideal for families (€45 to €55). Air-con is an extra €5.

Paligremnos Studios (☎ 28320 31835; www.palig remnos.com; r €35-40; ✗) At the far eastern end of the beach, these family-run studios are dated but are a decent budget option. They have kitchenettes and some have great sea views from the balconies. There is an attached shady taverna.

Pension Thetis (☎ 28320 31430; thetisstudios@gmail .com; studio €45-70; ☒) is a very pleasant and clean family-oriented set of studios. The rooms have fridge, basic cooking facilities, coffee maker and satellite TV. Relax in the cool and leafy garden where there is a small play park for kids.

Eating

Lisseos (☎ 28320 31479; meals €5.30-8.50; ☒ from 7pm) In an uninspiring location below the road near the bridge, Lisseos is nevertheless well-known for the best home-style cooking in town.

Taverna Christos (☎ 28320 31472; specials €5-11) An established waterfront taverna, Christos has a romantic tamarisk-shaded terrace overlooking the sea. It has a good choice of Cretan dishes and fresh fish, and an inviting daily specials board.

O Tasomanolis (☎ 28320 31129; mixed fish for 2 €16) This traditional fish taverna on the western end of the beach is run by a keen fisherman. You can sample his catch on a pleasant terrace overlooking the beach, grilled and accompanied with wild greens and wine. Top fish are €45. He also takes boat trips (€12 return) to Preveli.

Nikos Souvlaki (☎ 28320 31921) is a popular and cheap souvlaki place frequented by the hostel crowd, but locals reliably swear by **To Xehoristo** (☎ 28320 31214) on the main road.

It is worth the drive through the spectacular Kotsifou Gorge to eat hearty home-style Cretan food at **Iliomanolis** (☎ 28320 51053; mains €4-6) in the village of Kanevos. Maria is happy to show you the tempting array of pots in the kitchen (between 20-25 dishes each day).

Getting There & Away

In summer there are six buses a day from Rethymno (€3.50, one hour). It's possible to get to Agia Galini from Plakias by catching a Rethymno bus to the Koxare junction (referred to as Bale on timetables) and waiting for a bus to Agia Galini. The bus stop has a timetable.

Getting Around

Cars Alianthos (☎ 28320 31851; www.alianthos.com) is a reliable car-hire outlet.

Easy Ride (☎ 28320 20052; www.easyride.gr), close to the post office, rents out mountain bikes, bicycles, scooters and motorcycles.

AROUND PLAKIAS
Moni Preveli Μονή Πρέβελη

Standing in splendid isolation above the Libyan Sea, 14km east of Plakias and 35km from Rethymno, is the well-maintained **Moni Preveli** (☎ 28320 31246; www.preveli.org; admission €2.50; ☒ 8am-7.30pm Jun-Oct). Like most of Crete's monasteries, it played a significant role in the islanders' rebellion against Turkish rule. It became a centre of resistance during 1866, causing the Turks to set fire to it and destroy surrounding crops. After the Battle of Crete in 1941, many Allied soldiers were sheltered here before their evacuation to Egypt. In retaliation the Germans plundered the monastery. The monastery's **museum** contains a candelabra presented by grateful British soldiers after the war.

From June through August there are four buses daily from Rethymno to Moni Preveli (€3.90).

Preveli Beach

At the mouth of the Kourtaliotis Gorge, Preveli or Palm Beach (Paralia Finikodasous) is one of Crete's most photographed and popular beaches. The river Megalopotamos meets the back end of the beach before it conveniently loops around and empties into the Libyan Sea. The palm-lined banks of the river have freshwater pools ideal for a swim and there are also pedal boats for hire. The beach is fringed with oleander bushes and palm trees.

A steep path leads down to the beach from a car park about 1km before Moni Preveli. Alternatively, you can drive to within several hundred metres of the beach by following a signposted, 5km, drivable dirt road from a stone bridge just off the Moni Preveli main road. The road ends at Amoudi beach, from where you can walk west along a 500m access track over the headland and you're home.

You can also get there by boat from Plakias or Agia Galini from June through August.

AGIOS PAVLOS & TRIOPETRA
ΑΓΙΟΣ ΠΑΥΛΟΣ & ΤΡΙΟΠΕΤΡΑ

It's not surprising that the fabulous remote sandy beaches of Agios Pavlos and Triopetra have been chosen by yoga retreats. These unspoilt and peaceful beaches, about 53km

CRETE

from Rethymno, surrounded by sand dunes and rugged cliffs are arguably one of the most beautiful stretches of coastline in Crete.

Agios Pavlos is little more than a few rooms and tavernas around a small cove with a sandy beach, but the best beaches are on the subsequent sandy coves, which are about a 10-minute walk over the cliffs (though you'll get sandblasted on very windy days).

The coves stretch all the way to the three giant rocks rising from the sea that give Triopetra its name. The long stretch of beach beyond can be reached from Agios Pavlos (about 300m is drivable dirt road) or via a 12km-long windy asphalt road from the village of Akoumia, on the Rethymno–Agia Galini road.

Agios Pavlos Hotel & Taverna (☎ 28320 71104; www .agiospavloshotel.gr; d €30-40) is a family-run place with simple rooms in the main building with small balconies overlooking the sea, as well as rooms under the shady terrace below the taverna; it has good Cretan food (*mayirefta* €4.50 to €7). The café-bar next door has internet facilities. The same family also has large self-contained studios at the **Kavos Melissa complex** (r €45) further up on the cliff.

For real isolation, **Pavlos Taverna Pension** (☎ / fax 28310 25189; www.triopetra.com.gr; d/tr/q €30/35/40; 🖳), on the smaller eastern beach in Triopetra, has decent rooms with small kitchens and great sea view balconies. The taverna serves local meat, home-grown organic produce and fresh fish and lobster (which Pavlos normally catches).

There is no public transport to any of these beaches.

AGIA GALINI ΑΓΙΑ ΓΑΛΗΝΗ
pop 1260

Agia Galini (a-ya ga-*lee*-nee) is another erstwhile picturesque fishing village where package tourism and overdevelopment have spoilt much of its original charm. Hemmed in against the sea by large sandstone cliffs and phalanxes of hotels and domatia, Agia Galini can be rather claustrophobic.

It is probably the most touristy southern beach resort, though inoffensive compared to the north coast. While it still gets lively during peak season, and has a great atmosphere at night, it has become a more sedate resort attracting a middle-aged crowd and families.

It's a convenient base to visit Phaestos and Agia Triada, and although the town beach is crowded there are boats to better beaches.

Orientation & Information

You can get information at www.agia-galini .com. The bus station is at the top of the approach road. The post office is just past the bus stop. There are ATMs and travel agencies with currency exchange.

Many cafes have internet access, including **Hoi Polloi** (☎ 28320 91102; per hr €4; 🕑 9am-late).

Sleeping

Agia Galini Camping (☎ 28320 91386; camp sites per adult/tent €6/4; 🖳) Next to the beach, 2.5km east of the town, this well-run camping ground is shaded and has a pool, restaurant and mini-market.

Hotel Rea (☎ /fax 28320 91390; http://hoter-rea.mes sara.de; s/d €30/35; 🖳) On the main road near the port, this budget hotel is dated, but has clean, reasonably sized twin and double rooms with pine furniture. The bathrooms are basic but the front rooms have balconies with sea views.

Stohos Rooms & Taverna (☎ 28320 91433; d incl breakfast €40-45; 🖳) On the main beach, with apartments upstairs with kitchenettes and big balconies, and huge studios downstairs that are ideal for families or groups. Friendly Fanourios presides over the excellent taverna downstairs. Try the *kleftiko* or other clay-oven dishes (€8.50).

Adonis (☎ 28320 91333; www.agia-galini.com; r €50-120; 🖳 🖳) This pleasant hotel is spread over several buildings but the rooms, studios and apartments all have use of the large pool. Rooms are light and clean and most have been refurbished. Some have balconies with sea views.

Eating

Madame Hortense (☎ 28320 91351; Greek dishes €4.50-13) The most atmospheric and elegant restaurant in town is on the top floor of the three-level Zorbas complex, enjoying great views of the harbour. Cuisine is Greek Mediterranean and it does steaks (€12).

La Strada (☎ 28320 91053; pizzas €5.50-7.50, pastas €5-6) On the first street left of the bus station, this place has excellent pizzas, pastas and risottos.

Kostas (☎ 28320 91323; fish dishes €6-27) Right on the beach at the eastern end, this established fish taverna decked out in classic blue and white is always packed with locals. There's a big range of mezedhes and pricey but excellent seafood.

ALTERNATIVE TOURISM ON CRETE

Crete is far more than a sea-and-sun island destination, and a slow but steady shift towards alternative tourism is offering more responsible and appealing options than the cheap all-inclusive packages in the northern beach resorts. Formerly abandoned mountain villages are being restored to attract year-round rural tourism, agrotourism is quietly on the rise, along with cultural- and gourmet-travel-based programmes and well-run outdoor activities and extreme sports.

One of the ecotourism trailblazers is the isolated mountain settlement of **Milia** (☎ 28220 51569; www.milia.gr). The abandoned stone farmhouses were reconstructed into ecolodges with only solar energy for basic needs and promote a back-to-nature philosophy. You can visit Milia just to dine at the superb taverna, which uses organic produce from its farm (it's after the village of Vlatos via a drivable 3km dirt road), including its own oil, wine, milk and cheese.

Another fine example of classy rural developments is **Enagron** (☎ 28340 61611; www.enagron .gr) in the central mountain village of Axos, where guests are just as likely to be found in the kitchen as they are by the pool, and can participate in agricultural and productive life, from raki- or cheese-making with the local shepherds to picking wild greens.

Sustainable tourism and Cretan food is the theme of **Crete's Culinary Sanctuaries** (www .cookingincrete.com), which runs visits to organic farms, wineries and traditional cooking demonstrations in village homes.

Crete has long been a magnet for nature lovers, with endless opportunities for hiking and hard-core trekking, but you can also experience the thrill of parasailing with the griffon vultures and riding through the hills at Avdou (www.horseriding.gr), bungee jumping off the Aradena bridge (www.bungy.gr), climbing up Mt Kofinas (www.korifi.de) or participating in a raft of activities around the island organised by a new generation of local nature enthusiasts (www .cretanadventures.gr).

Faros (☎ 28320 91346; fish dishes €7-11) Inland from the harbour, this no-frills place is one of the oldest fish tavernas in town, dishing up reasonably priced fresh fish (per kilogram €45) as well as a range of grills and *mayirefta*.

Getting There & Away

In peak season there are six buses each day to Iraklio (€7.10, two hours), six to Rethymno (€5.30, 1½ hours) and five to Phaestos and Matala (€2.80, 40 to 45 minutes).

In summer there are daily boats from the harbour to the beaches of Agios Giorgios, Agiofarango and Preveli Beach (€1 to €20).

WESTERN CRETE

The westernmost part of Crete comprises the prefecture of Hania, named after the charming old Venetian city that is the region's capital. Its most famous attraction is the spectacular Samaria Gorge. The hinterland is fascinating to explore and the south-coast towns of Paleohora and Sougia are some of the island's most laid-back resorts.

HANIA XANIA
pop 53,373

Hania (hahn-*yah*; also spelt Chania) is unreservedly Crete's most evocative city. Its beautiful Venetian quarter is a web of atmospheric streets that tumble onto a magnificent harbour. Restored Venetian townhouses have been converted into chic restaurants and boutique hotels, while ruins house stunning tavernas. The prominent former mosque on the harbour and other remnants of the city's Turkish rulers add to Hania's exotic charm. Hania has a lively tradition of artisanship and boasts some of the island's finest restaurants. The Old Town is a great place to spend a few days.

The Hania Prefecture gets its fair share of package tourists, but most of them stick to the beach developments that stretch out to the west. It is a main transit point for trekkers heading for the Samaria Gorge.

History

Hania is the site of the Minoan settlement of Kydonia, which was centred on the hill to the east of the harbour. Excavation work continues, but the discovery of clay tablets

CRETE

with Linear B script has led archaeologists to believe that Kydonia was both a palace site and an important town.

Kydonia met the same fiery fate as most other Minoan settlements in 1450 BC, but soon re-emerged as a force. It was a flourishing city-state during Hellenistic times and continued to prosper under Roman and Byzantine rule.

The Venetians took over at the beginning of the 13th century, and changed the city's name to La Canea. They constructed massive fortifications to deter marauding pirates and invading Turks but they did not prove very effective against the Turks, who took Hania in 1645 after a two-month siege.

The Great Powers made Hania the island capital in 1898 and it remained so until 1971, when the administration was transferred to Iraklio.

Hania was heavily bombed during WWII, but enough of the Old Town survives for it to be regarded as Crete's most beautiful city.

Orientation

Hania's bus station is on Kydonias, two blocks southwest of Plateia 1866, from where the Old Harbour is a short walk north up Halidon.

Most accommodation is to the left as you face the harbour. The headland separates the Venetian port from the crowded town beach in the modern quarter, called Nea Hora. Koum Kapi is a rejuvenated precinct in the old Turkish quarter further east, lined with waterfront cafés.

Boats to Hania dock at Souda, about 7km southeast of town.

Information
BOOKSHOPS
Mediterraneo Bookstore (☎ 28210 86904; Akti Koundourioti 57) An extensive range of English language novels and books on Crete, as well as international press.
Pelekanakis (☎ 28210 92512; Halidon 98) Has maps, guidebooks and books in 11 languages.

EMERGENCY
Tourist police (☎ 28210 73333; Kydonias 29; ☼ 8am-2.30pm) At the Town Hall.

INTERNET ACCESS
Triple W (☎ 28210 93478; Valadinon & Halidon; per hr €2; ☼ 24hr)
Vranas Internet (☎ 28210 58618; Agion Deka 10; per hr €2; ☼ 9.30am-1am)

INTERNET RESOURCES
www.chania.gr The Municipality website has information on the city and cultural events.
www.chania-guide.gr Has good information on Hania city and prefecture.

LAUNDRY
Laundry (☎ 28210 57602; Agion Deka 18; wash & dry €6)

LEFT LUGGAGE
KTEL bus station (☎ 28210 93052; Kydonias 73-77; per day €1.50)

MEDICAL SERVICES
Hania Hospital (☎ 28210 22000; Mournies) Located south of town.

MONEY
Most banks are concentrated around the new city, but there are ATMs in the Old Town on Halidon, including **Alpha Bank** (cnr Halidon & Skalidi) and **Citibank**. The **National Bank of Greece** (cnr Tzanakaki & Giannari) has a 24-hour exchange machine.

POST
Post office (☎ 28210 28445; Peridou 10; ☼ 7.30am-8pm Mon-Fri, 7.30am-2pm Sat)

TOURIST INFORMATION
The **Municipal Tourist Information Office** (☎ 28210 36155; tourism@chania.gr; Kydonias 29; ☼ 8am-2.30pm) is located under the Town Hall and provides helpful practical information and maps. An information booth behind the mosque in Old Harbour also tends to be manned between noon and 2pm.

TRAVEL AGENCIES
Tellus Travel (☎ 28210 91500; Halidon 108; www.tellustravel.gr; ☼ 8am-11pm) Rents cars, changes money, arranges air and boat tickets, accommodation and excursions.

Sights
MUSEUMS
Hania's **Archaeological Museum** (☎ 28210 90334; Halidon 30; admission €2, incl Byzantine Collection €3; ☼ 8.30am-3pm Tue-Sun, closes later in summer but hr vary) is housed in the impressive 16th-century Venetian Church of San Francisco. The Turkish fountain in the grounds is a relic from the building's days as a mosque. The museum houses a well-displayed collection of finds

from western Crete dating from the Neolithic to the Roman era, including statues, vases, jewellery, three splendid floor mosaics and some impressive painted sarcophagi from the Late-Minoan cemetery of Armeni.

The **Naval Museum** (☎ 28210 91875; Akti Koundouri-oti; admission €3; ☼ 9am-4pm) has an interesting collection of model ships dating from the Bronze Age, naval instruments, paintings, photographs and memorabilia from the Battle of Crete. The museum is housed in the Firkas Fortress on the headland, once the old Turkish prison.

The **Byzantine and Post Byzantine Collection of Hania** (☎ 28210 96046; Theotokopoulou; admission €2, incl Archaeological Museum €3; ☼ 8.30am-3pm Tue-Sun) is in the impressively restored Church of San Salvatore, on the western side of the fortress. It has a small but fascinating collection of artefacts, icons, jewellery and coins, including a fine mosaic floor and a prized icon of St George slaying the dragon.

Hania's quaint and jam-packed **Cretan House Folklore Museum** (☎ 28210 90816; Halidon 46; admission €2; ☼ 9.30am-3pm & 6-9pm) contains a selection of crafts and implements including traditional weavings.

OTHER ATTRACTIONS

The massive fortifications built by the Venetians to provide a decent defence for their city remain impressive. The best-preserved section is the western wall, running from the **Firkas Fortress** to the **Siavo Bastion**. You can walk up to the top of the bastion for some good views of the Old Town (entry through the Naval Museum).

The Venetian **lighthouse** at the entrance to the harbour has been restored, though the new lighting along the sea wall could have been more subtle. It's a 1.5km walk around the sea wall to get there.

On the eastern side of Hania's inner harbour you will see the prominent **Mosque of Kioutsouk Hasan** (also commonly known as the Mosque of Janissaries), which houses regular art exhibitions.

The **Great Arsenal** has been stunningly restored and is now home to the Centre for Mediterranean Architecture, which hosts regular events and exhibitions.

The restored **Etz Hayyim Synagogue** (Paro-dos Kondylaki; ☎ 28210 86286; www.etz-hayyim-hania .org; ☼ 10am-8pm Tue-Fri, 5-8pm Sun, 10am-3pm & 5-8pm Mon) has a very moving memorial to the Jews of Hania who were extinguished by the Nazis.

Hania's **Municipal Art Gallery** (☎ 28210 92294; www.pinakothiki-chania.gr; Halidon 98; ☼ 10am-2pm & 7-10pm Mon-Fri, 10am-2pm Sat; €2; free admission Wed) hosts exhibitions of modern Greek art.

You can escape the crowds of the Venetian quarter by taking a stroll around the Turkish **Splantzia quarter** – a delightful tangle of narrow streets and little squares that is slowly being restored and the streets paved and cut off to traffic. It is attracting new boutique hotels, galleries and artistic or alternative pursuits. Along Daliani, you will see one of Hania's two remaining **minarets**.

You can see excavation works at the site of **Ancient Kydonia**, to the east of the old harbour at the junction of Kanevaro and Kandaloneou.

Activities

Alpine Travel (☎ 28210 50939; www.alpine.gr; Bo-niali 11-19) organises a range of trekking programmes.

EOS (☎ 28210 44647; www.eoshanion.gr; Tzanakaki 90), the Hania branch of the Greek Mountaineering Association, has information about serious climbing in the Lefka Ori, Greece's mountain refuges and the Trans-European E4 Trail. It runs regular weekend excursions.

Trekking Plan (☎ 28210 60861; www.cycling.gr), 8km west of town in Agia Marina, organises treks to the Agia Irini and Imbros gorges, climbs of Mt Gingilos, mountain-bike tours, canyoning, rappelling, rock-climbing and kayaking trips.

Blue Adventures Diving (☎ 28210 40608; www .blueadventuresdiving.gr; Arholeon 11) offers a PADI certification course (€370) and daily diving trips around Hania (two dives €75), including beginner dives. There are also snorkelling trips and cruise options.

Hania for Children

If your five-year-old has lost interest in Venetian architecture, head to the **public garden** between Tzanakaki and Dimokratias, where there's a playground, a small **zoo** with two resident kri-kri (Cretan goat) and a shady café. A few kilometres south of town the giant water park **Limnoupolis** (☎ 28210 33246; Varypetro; day pass adult/children 6-12 €17/12; afternoon pass €12/9; ☼ 10am-7pm) has enough slides and rides to keep kids amused.

Buses leave regularly from the KTEL bus station (€1.60).

CRETE

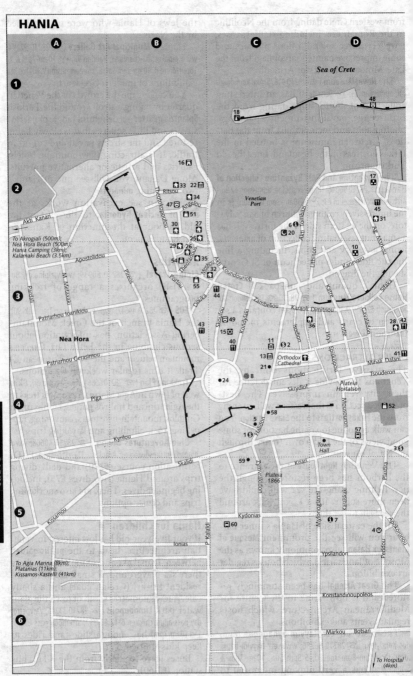

HANIA

Sea of Crete

Venetian Port

To Akrogiali (500m);
Nea Hora Beach (500m);
Hania Camping (3km);
Kalamaki Beach (3.5km)

Nea Hora

Akti Kanari

Apostolidou

Piros

Paidari

M. Mekaraki

Patriarhou Ioanikiou

Patriarhou Gerasimou

Piga

Kyrilou

Skalidi

Kissamou

To Agia Marina (8km);
Platanias (11km);
Kissamos-Kastelli (41km)

Ionias

Kydonias

P. Kalaidi

Theotokopoulou

Ritsou

Angelou

Theofanous

Portou

Douka

Moschon

Zambeliou

Akti Koundourioti

Akti Tombazi

Lithinon

Kanevaro

Sifaka

Kasre

Potie

Hrys. Episkopou

Cavaladon

Karaoli Dimitriou

Karaoli Dimitriou

Isodion

Betolo

Skrydlof

Halidon

Kondylaki

Sarpidona

Mylonogianni

Town Hall

Zimvrakidon

Plateia 1866

Knari

Kriari

Plateia Hortatson

Moussouron

Sfakianaki

Plastira

Tsouderon

Mihali Dafani

Peridou

Apokoronou

Ypsilandon

Konstandinoupoleos

Markou Botsari

Ionias

Plateia Hortatson

Orthodox Cathedral

To Hospital (4km)

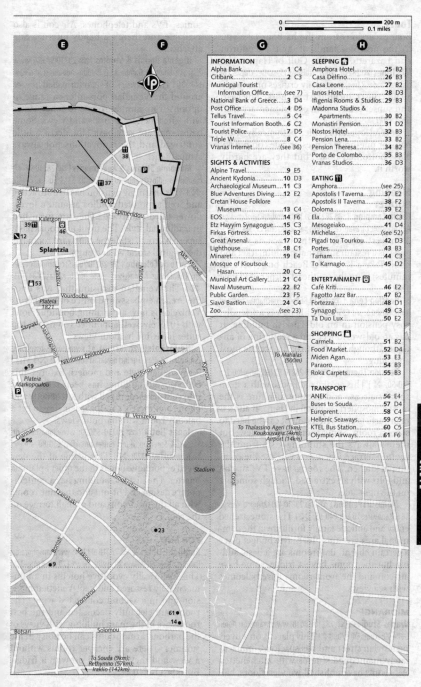

INFORMATION		
Alpha Bank	1	C4
Citibank	2	C3
Municipal Tourist		
Information Office	(see 7)	
National Bank of Greece	3	D4
Post Office	4	D5
Tellus Travel	5	C4
Tourist Information Booth	6	C2
Tourist Police	7	D5
Triple W	8	C4
Vranas Internet	(see 36)	

SIGHTS & ACTIVITIES		
Alpine Travel	9	E5
Ancient Kydonia	10	D3
Archaeological Museum	11	C3
Blue Adventures Diving	12	E2
Cretan House Folklore		
Museum	13	C4
EOS	14	F6
Etz Hayyim Synagogue	15	C3
Firkas Fortress	16	B2
Great Arsenal	17	D2
Lighthouse	18	C1
Minaret	19	E4
Mosque of Kioutsouk		
Hasan	20	C2
Municipal Art Gallery	21	C4
Naval Museum	22	B2
Public Garden	23	F5
Siavo Bastion	24	C4
Zoo	(see 23)	

SLEEPING		
Amphora Hotel	25	B2
Casa Delfino	26	B3
Casa Leone	27	B2
Ianos Hotel	28	D3
Ifigenia Rooms & Studios	29	B3
Madonna Studios &		
Apartments	30	B2
Monastiri Pension	31	D2
Nostos Hotel	32	B3
Pension Lena	33	B2
Pension Theresa	34	B2
Porto de Colombo	35	B3
Vranas Studios	36	D3

EATING		
Amphora	(see 25)	
Apostolis I Taverna	37	E2
Apostolis II Taverna	38	F2
Doloma	39	E2
Ela	40	C3
Mesogeiako	41	D4
Michelas	(see 52)	
Pigadi tou Tourkou	42	D3
Portes	43	B3
Tamam	44	C3
To Karnagio	45	D2

ENTERTAINMENT		
Café Kriti	46	E2
Fagotto Jazz Bar	47	B2
Fortezza	48	D1
Synagogi	49	C3
Ta Duo Lux	50	E2

SHOPPING		
Carmela	51	B2
Food Market	52	D4
Miden Agan	53	E3
Paraoro	54	B3
Roka Carpets	55	B3

TRANSPORT		
ANEK	56	E4
Buses to Souda	57	D4
Europrent	58	C4
Hellenic Seaways	59	C5
KTEL Bus Station	60	C5
Olympic Airways	61	F6

CRETE

Tours

Boat excursions from the harbour take you to the nearby islands of Agii Theodorou and Lazaretto and the Gulf of Hania. The **M/S Irini** (☎ 28210 52001; cruises €15, sunset cruises €8, children under 7 free) runs daily cruises on a lovely 1930s cruiser, including free snorkelling gear, and sunset cruises with complimentary fruit and *raki*.

Several operators offer pathetically short half- or one-hour cruises or rides on murky glass bottomed boats, but they are hardly worth it.

Sleeping

BUDGET

Hania Camping (☎ 28210 31138; camhania@otenet.gr; Agii Apostoli; caravan/camp sites per adult/tent €7/5/4; 🏊), 3km west of town on the beach, is shaded and has a restaurant, bar and minimarket and pool. Take a Kalamaki Beach bus (every 15 minutes) from the southeast corner of Plateia 1866.

Pension Lena (☎ 28210 86860; lenachania@hotmail .com; Ritsou 5; s/d €35/55; 🖳) Lena's is a friendly, cosy pension in an old Turkish building. It has an old-world feel and a scattering of antiques, though the front rooms are the most appealing.

Pension Theresa (☎ /fax 28210 92798; Angelou 2; r €40-50; 🖳) This creaky old house with a steep spiral staircase and antique furniture is the most atmospheric pension in Hania. It attracts many artists and writers and it can be hard to score a room. Some rooms have a view, but there's always the stunning vista from the rooftop terrace where you can use the communal kitchen. The rooms have TV, air-con and lofts with an extra bed, though some are on the tight side.

Monastiri Pension (☎ /fax 28210 41032; Agiou Markou 18 & Kanevarou; d & tr €40-55; 🖳) The stone arched entry and antique family furniture in the communal area give this older-style budget place a certain charm. Bathrooms are a basic add-on, but the rooms have a fridge, some have air-con and the front rooms have balconies with sea views.

MIDRANGE

Vranas Studios (☎ 28210 58618; www.vranas.gr; Agion Deka 10; studio €40-70; 🖳) This place is on a lively pedestrian street and has spacious, immaculately maintained studios with kitchenettes. All rooms have polished wooden floors, bal-

conies, TVs and telephones. Air-con is also available and there's a handy internet café attached.

Ifigenia Rooms & Studios (☎ 28210 94357; www .ifigeniastudios.gr; Gamba 23 & Parodos Agelou; studio €35-140; 🖳) This network of six refurbished houses around the Venetian port offers a range of options from simple rooms to fancy suites with kitchenettes, Jacuzzis and views. Some bathrooms are very basic, the décor a little contrived and the renovations not always sympathetic.

Madonna Studios & Apartments (☎ 28210 94747; madonnastudios@yahoo.co.uk; Gamba 33; studio €70-110; 🖳) This charming pension has five attractive and well-appointed studios around a lovely flower-filled courtyard. They are furnished in traditional style. The front top room has a superb balcony, while the courtyard room has the original stone wash trough.

Porto de Colombo (☎ 28210 70945; colompo@otenet .gr; Theofanous & Moschon; d/ste incl breakfast €84/103; 🖳) The Venetian mansion that was once the French embassy and office of Eleftherios Venizelos is now a charming boutique hotel with 10 lovely, well-appointed rooms; the top suites have fine harbour views.

Nostos Hotel (☎ 28210 94743; www.nostos-hotel.com; Zambeliou 42-46; s/d/tr incl breakfast €60/80/120; 🖳) Mixing Venetian style and modern fixtures, this 600-year-old building has been remodelled into split-level rooms all with kitchenette and phone and there's a roof garden. Try to get a balcony room with harbour views.

Ionas Hotel (☎ 28210 55090; www.ionashotel.gr; Sarpaki & Sorvolou; d incl buffet breakfast €50-80, ste incl buffet breakfast €120; 🖳) This is one of the new breed of boutique hotels in the quiet Splantzia quarter. The historic building has a contemporary design and fit-out and the nine rooms with all the mod-cons and a small terrace on the roof.

TOP END

Amphora Hotel (☎ 28210 93224; www.amphora.gr; Parodos Theotokopoulou 20; d with view €120, ste €145; 🖳) This historically evocative hotel is in an immaculately restored and kept Venetian mansion and in a second connected wing. The rooms are elegantly decorated and the best rooms are in the main building with views of the harbour. Front rooms can be noisy in the summer. There are cheaper rooms without a view and they could all do with a fridge. Breakfast is €10.

ourpick Casa Leone (☎ 28210 76762; www.casa -leone.com; Parodos Theotokopoulou 18; s & d incl breakfast €120-150; 🕸) This Venetian residence has been converted into a classy and romantic boutique hotel. The rooms are spacious and well appointed, with balconies overlooking the harbour.

Casa Delfino (☎ 28210 93098; www.casadelfino.com; Theofanous 7; d & apt incl buffet breakfast €186-316; 🕸) This elegant 17th-century mansion is the most luxurious hotel in the Old Town. Breakfast is in the splendid pebble-mosaic courtyard.

Eating

Hania has some of the finest restaurants in Crete. Most of the prime-position waterfront tavernas are predictably mediocre, overpriced and fronted by annoying touts. Head for the back streets, where some of the best tavernas are housed in roofless Venetian ruins.

BUDGET

Doloma (☎ 28210 51196; Kalergon 8; mayirefta €4.50-6; 🕑 Mon-Sat) This unpretentious taverna is half-hidden amid the vines and foliage that surround the outdoor terrace at the far end of the harbour. The traditional cooking is faultless.

Michelas (☎ 28210 90026; mains €5-7; 🕑 10am-4pm Mon-Sat) Near the meat section of the food market (see p252), Michelas has been serving great fresh, and cheap, traditional cuisine for 75 years.

Tamam (☎ 28210 96080; Zambeliou 49; mains €5.50-8.50) Housed in old Turkish baths, Tamam presents a superb selection of vegetarian specialities and eastern influenced dishes. The Tamam salad is excellent and the Beyendi chicken with creamy aubergine purée a favourite.

MIDRANGE

ourpick Portes (☎ 28210 76261; Portou 48; mains €6-8.50) Affable Susanna from Limerick cooks up Cretan treats with a difference at this superb restaurant in a quiet street in the Old Town. Try her divine *gavros* (marinated anchovies) or stuffed fish baked in paper or the tasty meatballs with leek and tomato.

To Karnagio (☎ 28210 53366; Plateia Katehaki 8; Cretan specials €5-10.50) is a popular place with outdoor tables near the Great Arsenal. There is a good range of seafood (try the grilled cuttlefish) and classic Cretan dishes, plus a fine wine list.

Mesogeiako (☎ 28210 59772; Daliani 36; mezedhes €3.20-5.60) This promising newcomer near the

minaret in the revitalised Spantzia quarter is a trendy *mezedhopoleio* serving an array of classic and more creative dishes. Try the pork meatballs and excellent *raki*.

Ela (☎ 28210 74128; Kondylaki 47; mains €6.50-18; 🕑 noon-1am) This 14th-century building was a soap factory, then a school, distillery and cheese-processing plant. Now Ela serves up a decent array of Cretan specialities, such as goat with artichokes, while musicians create a lively ambience. The tacky board outside tells you it's in every guidebook but the accolades are not undeserved.

Pigadi tou Tourkou (☎ 28210 54547; Sarpaki 1-3; mains €10-14.30; 🕑 dinner, closed Mon-Tue) Features from this former steam-bath, including the well it is named after (Well of the Turk), are incorporated into the design of this popular restaurant, which has tantalising dishes inspired by Crete, Morocco and the Middle East. The service can be patchy and prices have crept up.

Apostolis I & II Taverna (☎ 28210 43470; Akti Enoseos; fish per kg up to €55) In the quieter eastern harbour, this is a well-respected place for fresh fish and Cretan dishes in two separate buildings. Apostolis II is the more popular as the owner reigns there, but the original has the same menu at marginally cheaper prices. A seafood platter for two, including salad, is €30.

Also recommended is the excellent **Amphora** restaurant below the hotel (see opposite).

Entertainment

The harbour's lively waterfront bars and clubs are mostly patronised by tourists. Party animals head to the clubs in Platanias and Agia Marina, 11km west of Hania, but there are some lively bars in the Old Town.

Synagogi (☎ 28210 96797; Skoufou 15) Housed in a roofless Venetian building that was once a synagogue, this is the favourite haunt of young locals.

Fagotto Jazz Bar (☎ 28210 71877; Angelou 16; 🕑 7pm-2am Jul-May) A Hania institution housed in a restored Venetian building playing jazz and light rock and blues. Check out the saxophone beer tap.

Fortezza (☎ 28210 46546) This café, bar and restaurant, installed in the old Venetian ramparts across the harbour, is a good place for a sunset drink. A regular free barge will save you the walk.

The arty café/bar **Ta Duo Lux** (☎ 28210 52519; Sarpidona 8; 🕑 10am-late) remains a perennial

CRETE

favourite hangout for younger crowds and is popular day and night, while the rough-and-ready **Café Kriti** (☎ 28210 58661; Kalergon 22; ☽ 8pm-late) has live Cretan music.

Shopping

Hania offers the best combination of souvenir hunting and shopping for crafts on the island, with many local artisans at work in their stores. The best shops are along Zambeliou and Theotokopoulou. Skrydlof is 'leather lane', and the central market is well worth a look. Hania's magnificent covered **food market** is worth a visit even if you don't want to shop.

Carmela (☎ 28210 90487; Angelou 7) This exquisite store has a tempting array of original jewellery designs as well as Carmela's unique ceramics using ancient techniques. It also has jewellery and ceramics by leading Greek artists.

Paraoro (☎ 28210 88990; Theotokopoulou 16) Stamatis Fasoularis' distinctive series of metal boats are functional as well as decorative, like his nifty steamship oil-burner. This workshop also has unique ceramics by artist Yiorgos Vavatsis, including his trademark skewed drinkware. Their bigger gallery pieces are exhibited upstairs.

Roka Carpets (☎ 28210 74736; Zambeliou 61) You can watch the charming Mihalis Manousakis weave his wondrous rugs on a 400-year-old loom. This is one of the few places in Crete where you can buy genuine, hand-woven goods.

Miden Agan (☎ 28210 27068; www.midenaganshop.gr; Daskalogianni 70; ☽ 10am-3.30 Mon & Wed, 10am-2.15pm & 6.15-10pm Tue & Thu-Sat) Foodies and wine lovers will be delighted with the range at this excellent shop that sells its own wine and liquors, along with over 800 Greek wines. There is a wide variety of local gourmet delights.

Getting There & Away

AIR

Hania's airport (CHQ) is 14km east of town on the Akrotiri Peninsula.

Olympic Airlines (☎ 28210 58005; www.olympicair lines.com; Tzanakaki 88) operates five daily flights to/from Athens (€76 to €106) and four flights per week to/from Thessaloniki (€126 to €136).

Aegean Airlines (☎ 28210 63366; www.aegeanair.com) has four daily flights to Athens (€76 to €123) and one to Thessaloniki (€125 to €135).

Sky Express (☎ 28102 23500; www.skyexpress.gr) This newcomer operates daily flights from

Hania to Rhodes on 18-seater planes (from €104, one hour).

BUS

In summer, buses depart from Hania's **bus station** (☎ 28210 93052) during the week for the following destinations.

BUS SERVICES FROM HANIA

Destination	Duration	Fare	Frequency
Elafonisi	2½ hr	€9.60	1 daily
Falasarna	1½ hr	€6.50	3 daily
Hora Sfakion	1 hr 40min	€6.50	3 daily
Iraklio	2¾ hr	€10.70	half-hourly
Kissamos-Kastelli	1 hr	€4	13 daily
Moni Agias Triadas	30 min	€2	2 daily
Omalos (for Samaria Gorge)	1 hr	€5.90	3 daily
Paleohora	1 hr 50min	€6.50	4 daily
Rethymno	1 hr	€6	half-hourly
Sougia	1 hr 50min	€6.10	2 daily
Stavros	30 min	€1.80	3 daily

CATAMARAN & FERRY

Hania's main port is at Souda, about 7km southeast of town. There are frequent buses to Hania (€1.15), as well as taxis (€7).

ANEK (☎ 28210 27500; www.anek.gr; Plateia Sofokli Venizelou) has a daily boat at 9pm from Piraeus to Hania (€30, nine hours) and at 8pm from Hania to Piraeus. In July and August there is also a morning ferry from Piraeus (€30).

Hellenic Seaways (☎ 28210 75444; www.hellenicsea ways.gr; Plateia 1866 14) has a high-speed catamaran service that takes only 4½ hours (€53). It's a better option for getting to Hania as it arrives at 8.30pm, but it returns to Athens rather inconveniently at 2am.

Port Police (☎ 28210 89240) can provide ferry information.

Getting Around

There are three buses a day to the airport (€2, 20 mins). A taxi to the airport will cost about €18.

Local blue buses (☎ 28210 27044) meet the ferries at the port of Souda, just near the dock. In Hania, the bus to Souda (€1.15) leaves from outside the food market, and buses for the western beaches leave from the main bus station on Plateia 1866.

Most motorcycle-hire outlets are on Halidon, but the companies at Agia Marina are competitive and can bring cars to Hania. Most of the old town is pedestrian only. The best place to park is in the free parking area near the Firkas Fortress (turn right off Skalidi at the sign to the big supermarket car park and follow the road down to the waterfront).

Europrent (☎ 28210 27810; Halidon 87)

Tellus Travel (☎ 28210 91500; www.tellustravel.gr; Halidon 108)

AKROTIRI PENINSULA ΧΕΡΣΟΝΗΣΟΣ ΑΚΡΩΤΗΡΙ

The Akrotiri (ahk-ro-*tee*-rih) Peninsula, to the northeast of Hania, has a few places of fairly minor interest, Hania's airport, port and a military base. There is an immaculate **military cemetery** at Souda, where about 1500 British, Australian and New Zealand soldiers who lost their lives in the Battle of Crete are buried. The buses to Souda port from outside the Hania food market can drop you at the cemetery.

Almost at the northern tip of the peninsula is the lovely sandy beach of **Stavros**, famous as the dramatic backdrop for the final dancing scene in the classic film *Zorba the Greek*.

There are two working monasteries on the Akrotiri Peninsula. The more visitor-friendly is the impressive 17th-century **Moni Agias Triadas** (☎ 28210 63310; admission €2; ☻ 8am-7pm), which was founded by the Venetian monks Jeremiah and Laurentio Giancarolo, converts to the Orthodox faith. A small store sells the monastery's fine wine, oil and *raki*.

The 16th-century **Moni Gouvernetou** (☎ 28210 63319; ☻ 9am-midday & 5-7pm Mon, Tue & Thu, Sat & Sun 5am-11am & 5-8pm) is 4km north of Moni Agias Triada. The church inside the monastery has an ornate sculptured Venetian façade.

There are six buses daily to Stavros beach (€1.80) and two buses weekdays to Moni Agias Triadas (€2, 40 minutes). If you're driving, follow signs to the airport and branch off at the signposted turnoff.

HANIA TO XYLOSKALO ΧΑΝΙΑ ΠΡΟΣ ΞΥΛΟΣΚΑΛΟ

The road from Hania to the beginning of the Samaria Gorge is one of the most spectacular routes on Crete. It heads through orange groves to the village of **Fournes** where a left fork leads to **Meskla**. The main road continues to the village of **Lakki**, 24km from Hania. This unspoilt village in the Lefka Ori Mountains affords stunning views wherever you look. The village was a centre of resistance during the uprising against the Turks, and during WWII.

From Lakki, the road continues to **Omalos** and **Xyloskalo**, the start of the Samaria Gorge. A number of hikers choose to stay at Omalos in order to make the earliest start possible.

The big stone-built **Hotel Exari** (☎ 28210 67180; www.exari.gr; s/d €20/30) has pleasant, well-furnished rooms with TV, bathtub and balconies. The owner Yiorgos will give walkers lifts to the start of the Samaria Gorge and can deliver luggage to Sougia for groups. There is an attached taverna.

Rooms at the friendly **Hotel Gingilos** (☎ 28210 67181; s/d/tr €20/25/35) are rather sparse, but are large (the triples are huge), clean and have tasteful timber furniture. There is a communal balcony and a taverna downstairs.

The Hania EOS (Greek Mountaineering Club) maintains the **Kallergi Hut** (☎ 28210 33199; dm members/nonmembers €10/13), located in the hills between Omalos and the Samaria Gorge. It makes a good base for exploring Mt Gingilos and surrounding peaks.

SAMARIA GORGE ΦΑΡΑΓΓΙ ΤΗΣ ΣΑΜΑΡΙΑΣ

Despite the crowds who tramp through the **Samaria Gorge** (☎ 28210 67179; admission €5; ☻ 6am-3pm May–mid-Oct), a trek through this stupendous gorge is still an experience to remember.

At 16km, the Samaria (sah-mah-rih-*ah*) Gorge is supposedly the longest in Europe. It begins just below the Omalos Plateau, carved out by the river that flows between the peaks of Avlimanakou (1857m) and Volakias (2116m). Its width varies from 150m to 3m and its vertical walls reach 500m at their highest points. The gorge has an incredible number of wild flowers, which are at their best in April and May.

It is also home to a large number of endangered species, including the Cretan wild goat, the kri-kri, which survives in the wild only here and on the islet of Kri-Kri, off the coast of Agios Nikolaos. The gorge was made a national park in 1962 to save the kri-kri from extinction. You are unlikely to see too many of these shy animals, which show a marked aversion to trekkers.

An early start (before 8am) helps to avoid the worst of the crowds, but even the early bus from Hania to the top of the gorge can be packed. There's no spending the night in the gorge so you must complete the hike in the time allocated.

CRETE

The trek from **Xyloskalo**, the name of the steep stone pathway with wooden rails that gives access to the gorge, to **Agia Roumeli** takes from between 4½ hours for the sprinters to six hours for the strollers. Early in the season it's sometimes necessary to wade through the stream. Later, as the flow drops, it's possible to use rocks as stepping stones.

The gorge is wide and open for the first 6km, until you reach the abandoned settlement of **Samaria**. The inhabitants were relocated when the gorge became a national park. Just south of the village is a small church dedicated to **Saint Maria of Egypt**, after whom the gorge is named.

The gorge then narrows and becomes more dramatic until, at the 11km mark, the walls are only 3.5m apart – the famous **Iron Gates** (Sidiroportes). Here a rickety wooden pathway leads trekkers the 20m or so over the water and through to the other side.

The gorge ends at the 12.5km mark just north of the almost abandoned village of **Old Agia Roumeli**. From here it's a further uninteresting 2km hike to the welcoming seaside resort of Agia Roumeli, where most hikers end up taking a refreshing dip in the sea.

Getting There & Away

There are excursions to the Samaria Gorge from every sizable town and resort on Crete. 'Samaria Gorge Long Way' is the regular trek from Omalos and 'Samaria Gorge Easy Way' starts at Agia Roumeli and takes you up as far as the Iron Gates.

Obviously it's cheaper to trek the Samaria Gorge under your own steam. Hania is the most convenient base. There are buses to Xyloskalo (Omalos; €5.90, 1½ hours) at 6.15am, 7.30am, and 8.30am. There's also a direct bus to Xyloskalo from Paleohora (€5.50, 1½ hours) at 6.15am.

AGIA ROUMELI ΑΓΙΑ ΡΟΥΜΕΛΗ
pop 121

These days most travellers just pass through Agia Roumeli waiting to catch the boat to Hora Sfakion. It's pleasant enough for a stopover, although the surrounding mountains can make it very hot and stifling.

If you've just trekked through the gorge and you're in no hurry to leave, there are quite a few decent places to stay and eat.

Farangi Restaurant (☎ 28250 91225; mains €4.50-8.50) has excellent Cretan specials and there are some tidy rooms (d/tr €30/35; 🔁) above the restaurant.

Gigilos Taverna & Rooms (☎ 28250 91383; gigilos@mycosmos.gr; s/d/tr €25/35/40; 🔁) on the beach at the western end of the village are clean and nicely furnished, with decent new bathrooms and a communal fridge. The taverna has a huge shady deck on the beach. Meals cost €4 to €7 for mains.

There are two afternoon boats daily (3.45pm and 6pm) from Agia Roumeli to Hora Sfakion (€7.50, one hour) via Loutro (€5, 45 minutes) that connect with the bus back to Hania, as well as a morning boat from Paleohora to Hora Sfakion. You can also head west to Paleohora (€11, 1½ hours) at 4.45pm, via Sougia (€6.30, 45 minutes). The **ticket office** (☎ 28250 91251) is near the port.

LOUTRO ΛΟΥΤΡΟ

The former fishing village of **Loutro**, between Agia Roumeli and Hora Sfakion, is little more than a crescent of white-and-blue domatia around a tiny beach. It's a tiny, pleasant, lazy resort that is never overwhelmed with visitors, although it can get busy in July and August. Loutro is the only natural harbour on the south coast of Crete and is only accessible by boat or on foot. The absence of cars and bikes makes it quiet and peaceful.

A SHORT SURVIVAL GUIDE TO THE GORGE

The Samaria gorge is not a walk in the park and you should only attempt it if you have a reasonable level of fitness. If you find that the going is too tough within the first hour, there are park wardens with donkeys who will take you back to the beginning.

Rugged footwear is essential for walking on the uneven ground, which is covered by sharp stones. Don't attempt the walk in unsuitable footwear – you will regret it. Take a hat and sunscreen, plus a small bottle of water that can be refilled along the way in the many springs spurting cool water (it's inadvisable to drink water from the main stream). Bring energy food to snack on. Be wary of falling rocks, which have caused fatalities.

Given the captive market, the tavernas that line the waterfront in Loutro are surprisingly good.

The Blue House (☎ 28250 91127; bluehouseloutro@chania-cci.gr; d €40-45; ✗) has a mix of spacious, well-appointed rooms with big verandas overlooking the port. The nicer rooms are in the refurbished top floor section. The taverna downstairs serves excellent *mayirefta* (€5 to €7), including delicious garlicky spinach and a great *boureki* (zucchini, potato and goat's cheese bake).

HORA SFAKION ΧΩΡΑ ΣΦΑΚΙΩΝ
pop 351

Hora Sfakion (*ho-rah sfah-kee-on*) is a small coastal port where hordes of walkers from the Samaria Gorge spill off the boats from Agia Roumeli. Most people pause only long enough to catch the next bus out. Hora Sfakion does however have some decent sleeping and eating options, and is a convenient base for heading westwards to other resorts or taking a ferry to Gavdos.

Hora Sfakion played a prominent role during WWII when thousands of Allied troops were evacuated by sea from the town after the Battle of Crete.

The ferry quay is at the eastern side of the harbour. Buses leave from the square up the hill on the eastern side. There is one ATM. The post office is on the square.

Up the steps at the western end of the port, **Rooms Stavris** (☎ 28250 91220; stavris@sfakia-crete.com; s/d €21/24; ✗) has clean, basic rooms – some with kitchenettes and fridges – and there were plans to refurbish them.

The best value rooms in town are in **Xenia** (☎ 28250 91490; fax 28250 91491; d €33/38; ✗), a refurbished hotel well-positioned at the western edge of town. The rooms in the main building are a little cramped but those in the modern wing are spacious and enjoy a superb seafront position.

Getting There & Away
BUS

There are four buses a day from Hora Sfakion to Hania (€6.50, two hours) – the afternoon buses at 5.30pm and 7pm wait for the boats from Agia Roumeli. In summer there are two daily buses to Rethymno via Vryses (€6.50, 1 hour). There are two buses daily to Frangokastello (€1.50, 25 minutes).

FERRY

Boat tickets are sold in the **booth** (☎ 28250 91221) in the car park. From June through August there is a daily boat from Hora Sfakion to Paleohora (€11, three hours) via Loutro, Agia Roumeli and Sougia. There are four additional boats between Hora Sfakion and Agia Roumeli (€7.50, one hour) via Loutro (€4, 15 minutes). From 1 June there are boats (€12, 1½ hours) to Gavdos island (see p259) on Friday, Saturday and Sunday.

AROUND HORA SFAKION

The road from Vryses to Hora Sfakion cuts through the heart of the Sfakia region in the eastern Lefka Ori. The inhabitants of this region have long had a reputation for fearlessness and independence – characteristics they retain to this day.

One of Crete's most celebrated heroes, Ioannis Daskalogiannis, was from Sfakia. In 1770 Daskalogiannis led the first Cretan insurrection against Ottoman rule. When help promised by Russia failed to materialise, he gave himself up to the Turks to save his followers. The Turks skinned him alive in Iraklio.

The Turks never succeeded in controlling the Sfakiots, and this rugged mountainous region was the scene of fierce fighting.

The village of **Imbros**, 23km from Vryses, is at the head of the beautiful 8km **Imbros Gorge** (admission €2), which is far less visited than the Samaria Gorge. To get there, take any bus bound for Hora Sfakion from the north coast and get off at Imbros. Walk out of the village towards Hora Sfakion and a path to the left leads down to the gorge. The gorge path ends at the village of **Komitades**, from where you can walk 5km or take a taxi to Hora Sfakion (€17 to €20).

FRANGOKASTELLO
ΦΡΑΓΚΟΚΑΣΤΕΛΛΟ
pop 153

Frangokastello is a magnificent 14th-century fortress on the coast 15km east of Hora Sfakion. It was built by the Venetians as a defence against pirates and rebel Sfakiots, who resented the Venetian occupation as much as they did the Turkish.

On 17 May 1828 many Cretan rebels were killed here by the Turks. Legend has it that at dawn each anniversary their ghosts, the '*drosoulites*', can be seen marching along the beach.

The wide, packed white-sand beach beneath the fortress slopes gradually into shallow warm water, making it ideal for kids. Most accommodation is set back from the shore, leaving the area's natural beauty largely untouched. Frangokastello is popular with day-trippers, but it is a peaceful retreat.

Oasis (☎/fax 28250 92136; www.oasisrooms.com; mains €4.50-8), is an excellent family-run taverna and accommodation complex at the western end of Frangokastello, which has spacious rooms with full-size kitchens set in a lovely garden. You can walk to a quiet stretch of beach. The taverna has an extensive menu of well-executed Cretan dishes.

Two daily buses from Hora Sfakion stop at Frangokastello (€1.50).

SOUGIA ΣΟΥΓΙΑ

pop 109

Sougia (*soo*-yah), 67km from Hania, is a tiny laid-back beach resort with a wide curve of sand-and-pebble beach and a tree-lined coastal road. Sougia's tranquillity has been preserved largely because of archaeological remains at the eastern end of the beach which prohibit development. It lies at the foot of a narrow, twisting road that also deters most tour buses and passing traffic. There are a few small complexes of rooms, a few tavernas, a couple of lazy beach bars, two beach clubs and a small settlement of campers and nudists at the eastern end of the beach.

Information

There is an ATM next to Taverna Galini Sougia but no post office. The bus stop is outside the Santa Irene Hotel. Check out www.sougia .info for more accommodation options. **Internet Lotos** (☎ 28230 51191; per hr €3) is open from 7am until late.

Sleeping

Aretousa (☎ 28230 51178; fax 28230 51178; s/d/studio €35/40/42; 🕸) This lovely pension on the road to Hania has bright and comfortable refurbished rooms with new beds and linen, flat screen TVs, as well as studios with kitchenettes.

Rooms Ririka (☎ 28230 51167; s/d €35/40; 🕸) Has small but homey rooms right on the eastern side of the beach over a lovely garden courtyard.

Captain George (☎ 28230 51133; g-gentek@otenet .gr; r/studio/tr €35/40/48; 🕸) Attractive, good value rooms and studios in a lovely garden with a resident kri-kri. The owner runs taxiboat trips to nearby Lissos and other beaches.

Arhontiko (☎ 28230 51200; r €40-50; 🕸) Tucked behind the supermarket, Arhontiko has spacious, attractive new studios and apartments comfortable for longer stays.

Eating

Taverna Rembetiko (☎ 28230 51510; mezes €2.30-3.80) This popular taverna has an extensive menu including Cretan dishes such as *boureki* and stuffed zucchini flowers. It has a great atmosphere and is known for its good Greek music.

Polyfimos (☎ 28230 51343; mains €5.20-7.80; 🕭 dinner) Tucked off the Hania road behind the police station, ex-hippy Yianni makes his own oil, wine and *raki* and even makes dolmadhes (vine leaves stuffed with rice and sometimes meat) from the vines that cover the shady courtyard. The food is excellent and service from the affable Savvas delightful.

Kyma (☎ 28230 51670; meat dishes €5.50-7) On the beach, this has a good selection of *mayirefta* and fresh fish.

Also recommended are the international-style cuisine and French-run Omikron, towards the eastern end of the beach; and the Livykon taverna at the western end of the beach.

Getting There & Away

There's a daily bus travelling from Hania to Sougia (€6.10, one hour and 50 mins).

Sougia is also on the Paleohora–Hora Sfakion boat route. Boats leave in the morning for Agia Roumeli (€6.30, 1¾ hours), Loutro (€10, 1½ hours) and Hora Sfakion (€11, 1¾ hours). For Paleohora (€7, one hour) to the west there is a departure at 5.15pm.

PALEOHORA ΠΑΛΑΙΟΧΩΡΑ

pop 2213

Paleohora (pal-ee-o-*hor*-a) was discovered by hippies back in the 1960s and from then on its days as a tranquil fishing village were numbered. Despite the midsized hotels and package tourists, the place is still appealing and retains a certain laid-back feel. The number of backpackers is dwindling and it has become more of a family destination, though it gets livelier in the peak of summer. It is also the only beach resort on Crete that does not go into total hibernation in winter.

The little town lies on a narrow peninsula with a long, curving tamarisk-shaded sandy beach exposed to the wind on one side, and a sheltered pebbly beach on the other. On summer evenings the main street and beach road is closed to traffic and the tavernas move onto the road.

Orientation & Information

Paleohora's main street, Eleftheriou Venizelou, runs north–south. There are three ATMs and a laundry on the main drag. The post office is at the northern end of Pahia Ammos beach. Boats leave from the old harbour at the southern end of the beach.

Erato Internet (☎ 28230 83010; Eleftheriou Venizelou; per hr €2) Run by the town IT guru.

Notos Travel (per hr €2; ☼ 8am-10pm) You can also check mail here.

Tourist information office (☎ 28230 41507; ☼ 10am-1pm & 6-9pm Wed-Mon May-Oct) On the beach road near the harbour.

Sights & Activities

It's worth clambering up the ruins of the 13th-century **Venetian castle** for the splendid view of the sea and mountains. The castle was built so the Venetians could keep an eye on the southwestern coast from this commanding hill-top position. There's not much left of the fortress, however, as it was destroyed by the Venetians, the Turks, the pirate Barbarossa

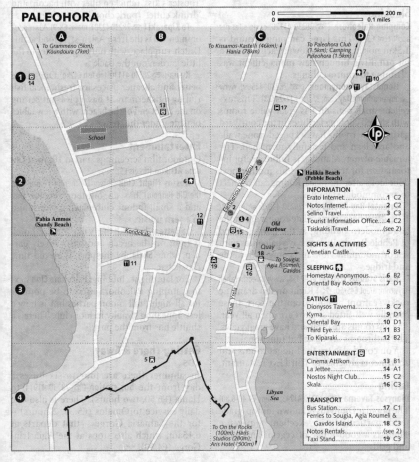

PALEOHORA

```
0        200 m
0        0.1 miles
```

INFORMATION
Erato Internet...................1 C2
Notos Internet...................2 C2
Selino Travel.....................3 C3
Tourist Information Office....4 C2
Tsiskakis Travel.............(see 2)

SIGHTS & ACTIVITIES
Venetian Castle.................5 B4

SLEEPING
Homestay Anonymous.........6 B2
Oriental Bay Rooms............7 D1

EATING
Dionysos Taverna................8 C2
Kyma...............................9 D1
Oriental Bay....................10 D1
Third Eye.........................11 B3
To Kiparaki.......................12 B2

ENTERTAINMENT
Cinema Attikon..................13 B1
La Jettee.........................14 A1
Nostos Night Club..............15 C2
Skala.............................16 C3

TRANSPORT
Bus Station......................17 C1
Ferries to Sougia, Agia Roumeli &
   Gavdos Island................18 C2
Notos Rentals...............(see 2)
Taxi Stand.......................19 C3

in the 16th century, and later the Germans during WWII.

From Paleohora, a six-hour walk along a scenic **coastal path** leads to Sougia, passing the ancient site of Lissos. You can trek the Samaria and Agia Irini Gorge from Paleohora, either through organised tours or the local KTEL bus service, returning by ferry.

Tours

Travel agents around town offer dolphin-watching trips (€16) and day trips to Elafonisi (€7, one hour).

Selino Travel (☎ 28230 42272; selino2@otenet.gr) Also sells boat tickets.

Tsiskakis Travel (☎ 28230 42110; www.notoscar.com; Eleftheriou Venizelou 53)

Sleeping

Camping Paleohora (☎ 28230 41120; camp sites per adult/tent €5/3) This large camping ground is 1.5km northeast of the town. Facilities are a bit primitive, though new management was planning to improve things.

Homestay Anonymous (☎ 28230 41509; www .anonymoushomestay.com; s/d/tr €17/24/28) This excellent small pension has great value rooms with shared cooking facilities in the courtyard garden. The rooms have exposed stone walls and are clean and tastefully furnished. The amiable owner, Manolis, is full of useful information for travellers and his mother next door looks after the place. Rooms can connect to accommodate families.

Oriental Bay Rooms (☎ 28230 41076; s/d/tr €30/35/38; 🐾) These immaculate rooms are in the large modern building at the northern end of Pebble Beach. Rooms have balconies with sea or mountain view and come with kettle and fridge.

Haris Studios (☎ 28230 42438; www.paleochoraholi days.com; d/apt €45/50; 🐾) Right on the dramatic rocky seafront around from the port, these friendly well-fitted studios are open all year. The top rooms are nicer and have great views. The bathrooms are basic but functional.

You could also try the budget rooms and apartments attached to Third Eye restaurant.

Eating

Dionysos Taverna (☎ 28230 41243; mains €4.40-6.80) The popular Dionysos is known for top-grade food, particularly its excellent *mayirefta*. There is a good range of vegetarian dishes and grills.

Grammeno (☎ 28230 41505; Cretan specials €4.50-9) For excellent traditional Cretan food it is worth the trip to this spot about 5km west of Paleohora. The menu includes specialities like braised rooster, various wild greens, lamb in vine leaves and tender roast goat.

ourpick Third Eye (☎ 28230 41234; mains €5) It's not just vegetarians who flock to Crete's only vegetarian restaurant, just inland from Pahia Ammos. It has an eclectic menu of curries, salads, pastas and Greek and Asian dishes, and there is live music weekly.

Oriental Bay (☎ 28230 41322; mains €5-8) This beachside taverna is one of the best options on this side of the village. In addition to a range of cheap vegetarian choices, such as green beans and potatoes, there are dishes such as 'rooster's kiss' (chicken fillet with bacon) and 'drunk cutlet' (pork chop in red wine).

To Kiparaki (☎ 28230 42281; mains €8-9) Also recommended is the fresh Asian-style food at this Dutch-run place, with only eight tables in the little garden out the back.

Kyma (☎ 28230 41110; top fish €42kg) One of the better and cheaper places for fresh, local fish run by a fisherman. It has a pleasant setting on the quiet end of the beach, with a few tables outside under the trees.

Entertainment

Outdoor film screenings start at 10pm at **Cinema Attikon** (tickets €5).

Nostos Night Club (btwn Eleftheriou Venizelou & the Old Harbour) has an outdoor terrace bar and a small indoor club playing Greek and Western music.

La Jettee, behind the Villa Marise hotel, is right on the beach and has a lovely garden, while **Skala**, by the port, is an old-time classic bar.

For late-night clubbing, **Paleohora Club** next to Camping Paleohora used to be popular for all-night, full-moon parties but is now a less-appealing swanky indoor club. There's a shuttle bus from the port.

Getting There & Away
BUS

In summer there are four to six buses a day from the **bus station** (☎ 28230 41914) to Hania (€6.50, two hours). There is also one daily service to Omalos (€5.50, 2 hours) – for the Samaria Gorge – that departs at 6.15am, which also stops at the Agia Irini Gorge (€4.50).

FERRY

Boat schedules change year to year so check with travel agents. In summer there is a daily morning ferry from Paleohora to Hora Sfakion (€14, three hours), via Sougia (€7, 50 minutes), Agia Roumeli (€11, 1½ hours) and Loutro (€13, 2½ hours). The same boat also continues three times a week in summer to Gavdos (€15, 2½ hours).

Getting Around

Notos Rentals (☎ 28230 42110; notosgr@yahoo.gr; Eleftheriou Venizelou) rents cars, motorcycles and bicycles.

GAVDOS ΓΑΥΔΟΣ
pop 98

Gavdos, in the Libyan Sea 65km from Paleohora, is the most southerly place in Europe and is the island for those craving total isolation and peace. The island has three tiny villages and lovely, unspoilt beaches, some of which are accessible only by foot or boat. Gavdos attracts a loyal following of campers, nudists and free spirits seeking natural beaches, long walks and laid-back holidays. There are no hotels but quite a few people rent rooms and tavernas.

Until the late 1960s Gavdos had little water, electricity or phone lines. While water is now plentiful, there can still be the odd electricity shortages and blackouts. It is wise to take a torch. Strong winds can leave you stranded for days on end, but you won't find too many people complaining.

Sarakiniko Studios (☎ 28230 42182; www.gavdostudios.gr; d/tr studio incl breakfast €50/60), above Sarakiniko beach, has comfortable studios and new villas sleeping up to five (€80 to €100). You can be picked up at the port or it is a 20-minute walk north of the port.

Services to Gavdos vary throughout the year and can take between 2½ to five hours depending on the boat and other stops, so it can be confusing. The most direct route to Gavdos is from Hora Sfakion on Friday, Saturday and Sunday (€15, 1½ hours). There are also two boats a week from Paleohora, increasing to three from mid-July to August (€15), though these services are going via the southern ports and Hora Sfakion making it a long trip.

Only some ferries take cars so check if you plan on taking one across.

You can rent a bike or car at the port or in Sarakiniko, though be wary that they may not be insured.

ELAFONISI ΕΛΑΦΟΝΗΣΙ

As one of the loveliest sand beaches in Crete it's easy to understand why people enthuse so much about Elafonisi, at the southern extremity of Crete's west coast. The beach is long and wide and is separated from Elafonisi Islet by about 50m of knee-deep turquoise water on its northern side. The islet is marked by low dunes and a string of semi-secluded coves. Unfortunately it is invaded by busloads of day trippers.

There is one boat daily from Paleohora to Elafonisi (€7, one hour) from mid-June through September that leaves at 10am and returns at 4pm. There are also two buses daily from Hania (€9.60, 2½ hours) and Kissamos (€5.90, 1¼ hours) that return in the afternoon.

KISSAMOS ΚΙΣΣΑΜΟΣ
pop 3821

The north-coast town of Kissamos is near the port that serves the ferry from the Peloponnese or Kythira. Kissamos is a rural working town that neither expects nor attracts much tourism, though many small family hotels have sprouted in recent years. While it is not immediately appealing, it is worth more than a passing glance. The huge Kissamos Bay has some fine pebble and sand beaches, and the almost bucolic feel of the region is a welcome antidote to the bustling Crete further east. There's a string of waterfront tavernas and bars lining the seafront promenade but the place only ever gets busy in August. Kissamos is a good base for walking, touring and unwinding. Cruises to the Gramvousa Peninsula (p261) leave from Kissamos port.

In antiquity, Kissamos was the main town of the province of the same name. When the Venetians came and built a castle here, it became known as Kastelli (the name persisted until 1966 when authorities decided that too many people were confusing it with Crete's other Kastelli, near Iraklio). Parts of the castle wall survive to the west of Plateia Tzanakaki.

Orientation & Information

The port is 3km west of town. From June through August a bus meets the boats; otherwise a taxi costs around €4. The

CRETE

bus station is on the main square, Plateia Tzanakaki; and the main commercial street, Skalidi, runs east from Plateia Tzanakaki.

Kissamos has a reasonably informative website, www.kissamos.net. The post office is on the main through-road, while there are banks with ATMs along Skalidi.

Sights & Activities

Archaeological Museum of Kissamos (☎ 28220 83308; Plateia Tzanakaki; ◷ 8.30am-3pm; free admission). This new museum in an imposing Venetian-Turkish building on the main square has a well-displayed collection of artefacts unearthed during archaeological digs in the area, including statues, jewellery, coins and a large mosaic floor from a Kissamos villa.

Strata Walking Tours (☎ 28220 24336; www.strata tours.com) offers a range of walking tours for small groups, from leisurely day-trips (€40 including lunch) to full-on 15-day round trips (€895) to the south coast. It also runs jeep safaris to interesting off-road destinations (€40).

Sleeping

Bikakis Family (☎ 28220 22105; www.familybikakis.gr; Iroön Polemiston 1941; s/d/studio €20/25/30; ⚇ 🖳) A great budget option, these rooms and studios sparkle and most have garden and sea views, kitchenettes and extras such as TV, hairdryers and free internet. It maintains a family environment and friendly owner Giannis is a font of local knowledge. There are adjoining rooms for families.

Thalassa (☎ 28220 31231; www.thalassa-apts.gr; Paralia Drapanias; studios €35-55; ⚇ 🖳) This isolated complex is an ideal spot to retreat to with a stack of books. The immaculate studios are airy and well-fitted out with irons, hairdryers and ADSL and wi-fi connections. There's a barbecue on the lawn, a small playground and it's just across from the beach, 100m east of Camping Mithymna.

Galini Beach (☎ 28220 23288; r €38-48) At the eastern end of the beach next to the soccer ground, this well-maintained, friendly, family-run hotel has spacious rooms decorated in cool tones, some with kitchenette, as well as adjoining family rooms.

Eating

Kellari (☎ 28220 23883; Cretan specials €3-7.50) This well-regarded taverna on the eastern end of the beach strip has an extensive range of

Cretan dishes, grills and fresh fish as well as a Greek tasting menu for two (€16). Owned by the same family that runs Strata Walking Tours, it uses its own meat, wine, oil and other produce.

Papadakis (☎ 28220 22340; mains €6-9.30) One of the oldest tavernas in town, this place is well patronised by local diners. The taverna has a very relaxing setting overlooking the beach and serves well-prepared fish dishes such as oven-baked fish (€6), or fish soup.

Also recommended for fine home cooking is **Violaki Estiatorio** on the main through road and **Akroyiali**, well signposted east of Kissamos, for excellent fresh fish on the beach.

Getting There & Away

BUS

From Kissamos' **bus station** (☎ 28220 22035), there are 14 buses a day to Hania (€4, 40 minutes), where you can change for Rethymno and Iraklio; two buses a day for Falasarna (€3, 20 minutes); and one bus a day to Paleohora (€6.50, 1¼ hours) and Elafonisi (€5.90, 1¼ hours).

FERRY

ANEN Ferries operates the F/B Myrtidiotissa on weekends on a route that takes in Antikythira (€9.40, two hours), Kythira (€16.40, four hours) and Gythio (€22.10, five hours). You can buy tickets from **Horeftakis Tours** (☎ 28220 23250) and the **ANEN Office** (☎ 28220 22009; Skalidi).

Getting Around

Moto Fun (☎ 28220 23440; www.motofun.info; Plateia Tzanakaki) rents cars, bikes and mountain bikes.

AROUND KISSAMOS

Falasarna Φαλάσαρνα

pop 21

Falasarna, 16km west of Kissamos, was a Cretan city-state in the 4th century BC but there's not much of the ancient city left to see. It attracts a mixed bunch of travellers due to its long, wide stretch of sandy beach, which is considered one of the best in Crete. It is split up into several coves by rocky spits and is known for its stunning sunsets and the pink hues reflecting from the fine coral in the sand. There is no village, just a scattering of widely spaced rooms and tavernas among the greenhouses that somewhat mar the approach to the beach.

Rooms Anastasia-Stathis (☎ 28220 41480; fax 28220 41069; d/apt €40/50; 🏠) Owner Anastasia makes her home the friendliest place to stay. The airy rooms with fridges and large balconies are perfect for stress relief, as Anastasia puts it. Her enormous breakfasts (€6) are open to all comers and are a sight to be savoured.

Galasia Thea (☎ 28220 41421; mayirefta €4.50-6) On the cliff overlooking the great expanse of beach, this place has spectacular views from its huge terrace. There's a big range of baked dishes and *mayirefta* such as the Sfakiano lemon lamb.

From June through August there are three buses daily from Kissamos to Falasarna (€3) as well as three buses from Hania (€6.50).

Gramvousa Peninsula Χερσόνησος Γραμβούσας

North of Falasarna is the wild and remote Gramvousa Peninsula and the stunning sandy beach of **Balos** on the west side of the peninsula's narrow tip. The idyllic beach is overlooked by the two islets of **Agria** (wild) and **Imeri** (tame).

The rough but drivable dirt road (best in a 4WD) to Balos begins at the end of the main street of **Kalyviani** village. The road ends at a car park (with a *kantina*) from where the path to the beach is a 30-minute walk down the sandy cliffs (45 minutes on the way back up).

West-bound buses from Kissamos will let you off at the turn-off for Kalyviani, from where it is a 2km walk to the beginning of the path at the far end of the main street. The shadeless walk to Balos is around 3km – wear a hat and take plenty of water. An easier way to get there is via one of the three daily **cruises** (☎ 28220 24344; www.gramvousa.com; adult/concession €22/12; ⏰ 55mins) The morning boats stop at Imeri Gramvousa, which is crowned with a **Venetian castle**. Departures are at 10am, 10.15am and 1pm and return trips at 5.45pm and 8pm. The trip can be rough if it is windy.

EASTERN CRETE

Lasithi, Crete's easternmost prefecture, may receive far fewer visitors than the rest of the island, but the exclusive resorts around Elounda and Agios Nikolaos are the strong-hold of Crete's high-end tourism. Agios Nikolaos is the region's contribution to the party scene. The fertile Lasithi Plateau, tucked in the Mt Dikti ranges, provides excellent cycling opportunities through quiet rural villages to the Dikteon Cave, where legend has it that Zeus was born. The east's other main attractions are the famous palm forest and beach at Vaï and the remote Minoan palace of Zakros.

LASITHI PLATEAU ΟΡΟΠΕΔΙΟ ΛΑΣΙΘΙΟΥ

The Lasithi Plateau, 900m above sea level, is a vast expanse of pear and apple orchards, almond trees and fields of crops. It would have been a stunning sight when it was dotted by some 20,000 metal windmills with white canvas sails. They were built in the 17th century to irrigate the rich farmland but there are less than 5000 still standing today and few of the original windmills are in service; most having been replaced by less attractive mechanical pumps.

The plateau's rich soil has been cultivated since Minoan times. The inaccessibility of the region made it a hotbed of insurrection during Venetian and Turkish rule. Following an uprising in the 13th century, the Venetians drove out the inhabitants of Lasithi and destroyed their orchards. The plateau lay abandoned for 200 years. Food shortages led the Venetians to cultivate the area and build the irrigation trenches and wells that still service the region.

There are 20 villages dotted around the periphery of the plateau, the largest of which is **Tzermiado** (population 747), with a couple of ATMs and a post office. The town sees a fair amount of tourism from the tour buses going to the Dikteon Cave.

The **Restaurant Kourites** (☎ 28440 22054; wood-oven specials €7-8; www.kourites.eu) serves excellent Cretan cuisine, including many vegetarian delights. Try some of the wood oven dishes – the suckling pig with baked potatoes is delicious. There are simple rooms (single/double including breakfast €25/40) above the taverna with small balconies and you have free use of the bicycles. The same family also runs the lovely **Argoulias** (☎ 28440 22754; www.argoulias .gr; d incl breakfast €60-80) complex of stone-built spacious apartments built into the hillside in the abandoned top part of the village, with panoramic views.

CRETE

In the relaxing village of **Agios Georgios** (pronounced *agh*-ios ye-*or*-gios; population 554), **Hotel Maria** (☎ 28440 31774; s/d €20/25) has nicely decorated rooms with weavings and traditional furnishings (although larger people should note that the beds are very narrow). Maria also does the cooking at **Taverna Rea** (☎ 28440 31209; mains €4.50-6.50) on the main street.

Psyhro is the closest village to the Dikteon Cave. Its main street has a few tavernas, and plenty of souvenir shops selling 'authentic' rugs and mats of non-Cretan origin. It is prettier and less dusty than Tzermiado and makes for a better rest stop. Buses to Psyhro drop you at the end of the town where it's about a kilometre walk uphill to the cave.

Petros Taverna (☎ 28440 31600; grills €6), opposite the entrance to the cave, is run by former cave guardian Petros Zarvakis. It has great views from the balcony. He also organises regular hikes up to Mt Dikti, camping out under the stars.

Dikteon Cave Δικταίον Αντρον

Lasithi's major sight is the **Dikteon Cave** (adult/child €4/2; ⏱ 8am-6pm Jun-Oct, 8am-2.30pm Nov-May), just outside Psyhro. Here, according to legend, Rhea hid the newborn Zeus from Cronos, his offspring-gobbling father.

The cave covers 2200 sq metres and features both stalactites and stalagmites. It was excavated in 1900 by the British archaeologist David Hogarth, who found numerous votives indicating it was a place of cult worship (on display in the archaeological museum in Iraklio; see p226 for more information).

It is a steep 15-minute (800m) walk up to the cave entrance. You can take the fairly rough but shaded track on the right with great views over the plateau or the unshaded paved trail on the left of the car park next to the Chalavro taverna. You can also let a donkey do the hard work (€10 or €15 return).

Getting There & Away

From Iraklio there are daily buses to Tzermiado (€3.50, two hours), Agios Georgios (€4.70, two hours) and Psyhro. There are also buses to the villages from Agios Nikolaos.

AGIOS NIKOLAOS ΑΓΙΟΣ ΝΙΚΟΛΑΟΣ

pop 10,080

Lasithi's capital, Agios Nikolaos (*ah*-yee-os nih-*ko*-laos), is an undeniably attractive former fishing village set around a pleasant harbour and a small, picturesque lake connected to the sea.

In the early 1960s it became a chic hideaway for the likes of Jules Dassin and Walt Disney, but by the end of the decade, package tourists were arriving in force and it became an overdeveloped tourist town. It's had its ups and downs ever since.

'Agios' remains popular, drawing people from nearby resorts at night when the ambience turns more vibrant and cosmopolitan. While there is superficially little to attract the independent traveller, there is reasonable accommodation, prices are not too horrendous and there is enough activity to cater for all tastes.

Orientation

The **bus station** (KTEL; ☎ 28410 22234) has been rather inconveniently relocated to the northwestern side of town, about 800m from the town's centre at Plateia Venizelou. The de facto town centre is around the Voulismeni Lake. Most banks, ATMs, travel agencies and shops are on Koundourou and the parallel 28 Oktovriou.

Information

Anna Karteri Bookshop (☎ 28410 22272; Koundourou 5) Well stocked with maps, guide books, literature in English and other languages.
General Hospital (☎ 28410 66000; Knosou 3) On the west side of town.
Municipal Tourist Office (☎ 28410 22357; www .agiosnikolaos.gr; ⏱ 8am-9pm Apr-Nov) Right by the bridge; changes money and assists with accommodation.
National Bank of Greece (Nikolaou Plastira) Has a 24-hour exchange machine.
PK's Internet Cafe (☎ 28410 28004; Akti Koundourou 1; per hr €2; ⏱ 9am-2am) Has full printing, burning, Skype and video cams set up.
Post office (☎ 28410 22062; 28 Oktovriou 9; ⏱ 7.30am-2pm Mon-Fri)
Tourist Police (☎ 28410 91408; Erythrou Stavrou 47; ⏱ 7.30am-2.30pm Mon-Fri)

Sights

It is well-worth the hike up the hill to the **Archaeological Museum** (☎ 28410 24943; Paleologou Konstantinou 74; admission €4; ⏱ 8.30am-3pm Tue-Sun; ♿), which has an extensive and well-displayed collection from eastern Crete. While it has no major showpiece, it is probably the second most significant Minoan collection and includes clay coffins, ceramic musical

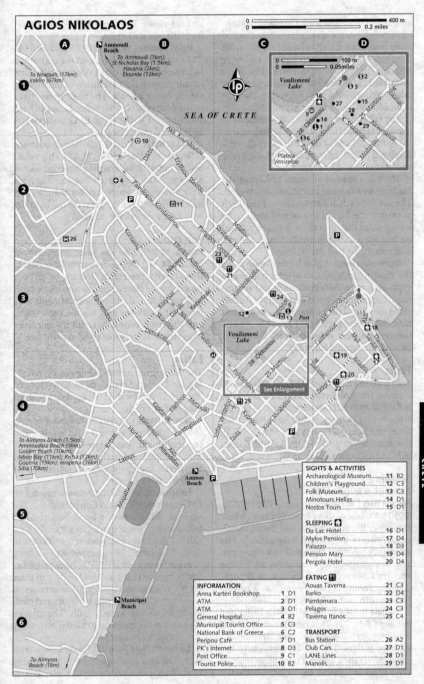

AGIOS NIKOLAOS

SEA OF CRETE

To Neapolis (17km);
Iraklio (67km)

Ammoudi
Beach

To Ammoudi (1km);
St Nicholas Bay (1.5km);
Havania (2km);
Elounda (12km)

Voulismeni
Lake

Plateia
Venizelou

Voulismeni
Lake

See Enlargement

Port

To Almyros Beach (1.5km);
Ammoudara Beach (3km);
Golden Beach (10km);
Istron Bay (11km); Kritsa (12km);
Gournia (19km); Ierapetra (36km);
Sitia (70km)

Ammos
Beach

Municipal
Beach

To Almyros
Beach (1km)

CRETE

INFORMATION	
Anna Karteri Bookshop...........1	D1
ATM...........2	D1
ATM...........3	D1
General Hospital...........4	B2
Municipal Tourist Office...........5	C3
National Bank of Greece...........6	C2
Peripou Café...........7	D1
PK's Internet...........8	D3
Post Office...........9	C1
Tourist Police...........10	B2

SIGHTS & ACTIVITIES	
Archaeological Museum...........11	B2
Children's Playground...........12	C3
Folk Museum...........13	C3
Minotours Hellas...........14	D1
Nostos Tours...........15	D1

SLEEPING	
Du Lac Hotel...........16	D1
Mylos Pension...........17	D4
Palazzo...........18	D3
Pension Mary...........19	D4
Pergola Hotel...........20	D4

EATING	
Aouas Taverna...........21	C3
Barko...........22	D4
Pamtomaca...........23	C3
Pelagos...........24	C3
Taverna Itanos...........25	C4

TRANSPORT	
Bus Station...........26	A2
Club Cars...........27	D1
LANE Lines...........28	D1
Manolis...........29	D1

instruments and gold from the island of Mohlos. The exhibits are arranged in chronological order beginning with Neolithic finds from Mt Tragistalos, north of Kato Zakros, and early Minoan finds from Agia Fotia, then finds from Malia and Mohlos. The highlight is the odd-looking *Goddess of Myrtos*, a clay jug from 2500 BC found near Myrtos.

The **folk museum** (☎ 28410 25093; Paleologou Konstantinou 4; admission €3; ⏰ 10am-2pm Tue-Sun), next to the municipal tourist office, has a small, well-displayed collection of traditional handicrafts and costumes.

The town beaches of **Ammos** and **Kytroplatia Beach** are smallish and can get rather crowded. The sandy beach at **Almyros** about 1km south of town is the best of the lot and tends to be less crowded than the others. It can be reached on foot via a coastal path starting at the end of the road just past the stadium.

Ammoudara Beach, 1.5km further south along the road to Ierapetra, is a little better and supports a fairly busy restaurant and accommodation scene. Or you can venture further along the coastal road towards Sitia to pleasant coves with long stretches of sandy beach and turquoise waters at **Golden Beach** (Voulisma Beach) and around **Istron Bay**.

Tours

Boat trips to Spinalonga (€17) include a swim stop on the Kolokytha Peninsula **Minotours Hellas** (☎ 28410 23222; www.minotours.gr; 28 Oktovriou 6) has a range of tours, including guided coach tours of Phaestos, Gortys and Matala (€33), the Samaria Gorge (€45), the Lasithi Plateau (€34) and Knossos (€30).

Sleeping
BUDGET & MIDRANGE

Pension Mary (☎ 28410 23760; Evans 13; s/d/tr €15/25/30; 🅿) This is one of those friendly places where the owner lives downstairs and bonus homemade sweets are almost guaranteed. The rooms are basic but clean and most have private bathrooms, fridge, balconies with some sea views and access to a communal kitchen. The top room is cramped but has a private terrace with barbecue. Breakfast is €5.

Pergola Hotel (☎ /fax 28410 28152; Sarolidi 20; d with view €20-40; 🅿) This family-run hotel has a homey feel. Rooms are comfortable and all have fridges, TV and air-con. There is a pleasant veranda under a pergola to relax or have breakfast. Front rooms have balconies

and sea views. The owners can pick you up from the bus station.

Mylos Pension (☎ 28410 23783; Sarolidi 24; d €40; 🅿) From the fake flowers on the bed to the family photos and icons on the walls, this quaint pension is an extension of the friendly elderly owner's home. The front rooms have sensational views (try for room 2) and all have a fridge and TV. The sprightly Georgia swears by the hard mattresses.

Du Lac Hotel (☎ 28410 22711; www.dulachotel.gr; 28 Oktovriou 17; s/d/studio €40/60/80; 🅿) This refurbished hotel on the lake has standard rooms and spacious, fully fitted-out studios; both have stylish contemporary furnishings and nice bathrooms. It's in a great central location, with lovely views over the lake.

TOP END

Palazzo (☎ 28410 25086; www.palazzo-apartments.gr; apt €90-110; 🅿 💻) Opposite Kytroplatia Beach, these classy apartments sleeping up to four people are the closest thing to a boutique hotel in town. It has 10 charming apartments with mosaic-tiled floors and marble bathrooms, and the front rooms have lovely balconies with views. There's free email downstairs.

Eating

The lakeside restaurants, while visually tempting, tend to serve bland and often overpriced 'tourist' Greek food. Head further afield for the genuine article.

Taverna Itanos (☎ 28410 25340; Kyprou 1; mayirefta €4-9) This place is popular with locals wanting traditional home-style Cretan cooking. You can pick from the trays of excellent *mayirefta*, such as goat with artichokes or lamb fricassée.

Pelagos (☎ 28410 25737; Katehaki 10; mezedhes €4-8.50) For an excellent selection of fresh fish and seafood, this place, in a beautifully restored house with ambient garden, is generally considered the best (and priciest) restaurant in Agios Nikolaos. The mezedhes are excellent.

Aouas Taverna (☎ 28410 23231; Paleologou Konstantinou 44; mezedhes €5.20-9.60) This family-run place on the road to the museum has a range of Cretan specialities such as herb pies and pickled bulbs, as well as tasty grills. The interior is plain but the enclosed garden is refreshing and the mezedhes are good.

Barko (☎ 28410 24610; Akti Pagalou 8; Cretan dishes €8.50-13.80) Has gone upmarket since moving to flashier premises on Kytroplatia Beach.

There are still excellent Cretan-style dishes but the menu includes more creative Mediterranean-style cuisine such as a light risotto with pumpkin and *anthotyro* (Cretan cream-cheese). There's a decent wine list.

Also recommended as a good budget option is the colourful Catalano-Mediterranean combo at **Pamtomaca** (☎ 28410 82394; Paleologou 52; 7pm-midnight).

Getting There & Away

BUS

Buses leave from Agios Nikolaos' **bus station** (☎ 28410 22234) for Elounda (€1.30, 16 daily), Ierapetra (€3.30, eight daily), Iraklio (€6.20, half-hourly), Kritsa (€1.30, 10 daily) Lasithi Plateau (€3.50, two daily) and Sitia (€5.90, seven daily).

FERRY

LANE Lines (☎ 28410 89150; www.lane.gr) has ferries two times a week from Agios Nikolaos to Piraeus (€34, cabin €46, 14 hours), via Santorini (five hours, €20.20) and Milos (nine hours, €20.60). There is also a service from Piraeus via Milos to Agios Nikolaos, Sitia, Kasos, Karpathos, Halki and Rhodes.

Getting Around

Club Cars (☎ 28410 25868; www.clubcars.net; 28 Oktovriou 30) rents cars from €32 per day and **Manolis** (☎ 28410 24940; 25 Martiou 12) has a huge range of scooters, motorcycles, quad bikes and top of the range mountain bikes.

ELOUNDA ΕΛΟΥΝΤΑ

pop 1655

There are magnificent mountain and sea views along the 11km road north from Agios Nikolaos to Elounda (el-*oon*-da). A cluster of luxury resorts occupy the lovely coves along the coast. The first elite hotel was built here in the mid-1960s, quickly establishing Elounda as the playground for Greece's glitterati and high flyers – soon after, the world's rich and famous followed suit. Elounda boasts some of the most exclusive resorts in Greece.

Past the resorts, the once-quiet fishing village of Elounda now bristles with package tourists, though it's quieter than neighbouring Agios Nikolaos. Busloads of day-trippers rock up on their way to Spinalonga Island. The pleasant but unremarkable sandy town beach, to the north of the port, can get very crowded. Elounda has limited appeal unless you are lucky enough to be staying in one of the posh resorts. While there are some nice places around, Elounda is not particularly good value in peak season and many hotels are booked out by tour operators.

Information

Municipal Tourist Office (☎ 28410 42464; 8am-11pm Jun-Oct), on the main square, helps with accommodation and information, and changes money.

Sleeping & Eating

Hotel Aristea (☎ 28410 41300; www.aristeahotel.com; s/d/tr incl breakfast €30/45/55; 🖾) In the town centre is this uninspiring but decent and clean budget option. Most rooms at least have a sea view, double-glazed windows, TV, fridge and hairdryers.

Corali Studios (☎ /fax 28410 41712; www.coralistudios.com; studio €60-70; 🖾) On the northern side, about 800m from the clock tower, these handy self-catering studios are set in lush lawns with a shaded patio. Next door and under the same management the spacious apartments at **Portobello Apartments** (2-/4-bed apt €65-75; 🖾) are a good option for two or three people.

Elounda Island Villas (☎ 28410 41274; www.elounda island.gr; d from €70; 4-person r €105; 🖾 P) are a secluded option on Kolokytha island, reached along a narrow peninsula. The apartments are set amid a pleasant garden and decorated with traditional furnishings. Kitchens are well-equipped, bathrooms functional and there are split-level living and sleeping areas. There is an attached tavern and it's a 20-minute walk into town.

Eating

Nikos (☎ 28410 41439; fish per kg €35-40) While it lacks the ambience of the seafront eateries, no-frills Nikos on the main street is a good choice for fish and lobster because they generally catch their own. Service can be erratic but the food is good value.

Ferryman (☎ 28410 41230; local fish platter for 2 €44) With a lovely setting on the waterfront, the Ferryman claims its moment of fame from being featured in the TV series *Who Pays the Ferryman*. The food and service is excellent (they even clean the fish for you), though it is on the pricey side. Its speciality is fish and lobster, but there's a broader menu of Cretan specialities.

CRETE

Megaro (☎ 28419 42220; top fish per kg €45; mains €4-8) This recently refurbished place on the corner of the square is popular with locals around the district. The owner is a fisherman and the menu also includes Cretan specials.

Getting There & Away

Boats go across to Spinalonga every half-hour (adult/child €10/5). There are 13 buses daily from Agios Nikolaos to Elounda (€1.30, 20 minutes).

SPINALONGA ISLAND
ΝΗΣΟΣ ΣΠΙΝΑΛΟΓΚΑΣ

Spinalonga Island lies just north of the Kolokytha Peninsula. The island's massive **fortress** (☎ 28410 41773; admission €2; ☟ 10am-6pm) was built by the Venetians in 1579 to protect Elounda Bay and the Gulf of Mirabello. It withstood Turkish sieges for longer than any other Cretan stronghold, finally surrendering in 1715, some 30 years after the rest of Crete. The Turks used the island as a base for smuggling. Following the reunion of Crete with Greece, Spinalonga Island became a leper colony. The last leper died here in 1953 and the island has been uninhabited ever since. It is still known among locals as 'the island of the living dead.' The island is a fascinating place to explore. It has an aura that is both macabre and poignant.

Regular excursion boats visit Spinalonga from Agios Nikolaos (€17) with Minotours Hellas (see p264); ferries leave from Elounda (€10) or you could also take a cheaper boat from Plaka (5km further north).

KRITSA ΚΡΙΤΣΑ
pop 1614

The village of Kritsa (krit-sah), perched 600m up the mountainside 11km from Agios Nikolaos, is a pretty mountain village renowned for its strong tradition of needlework and weaving. The village has morphed into a bit of a tourist attraction, with busloads of day trippers swarming through the streets all summer and villagers are eager to exploit these invasions to the full. It creates a colourful atmosphere but not much of the stuff on sale is handmade these days and few of the rug designs are authentic. It's still possible to find the traditional geometric designs of Crete and the odd finely crocheted blankets and tablecloths, but they are becoming a rarity.

On the way to Kritsa, about 1km before the village, it is worth stopping at the tiny, triple-aisled **Church of Panagia Kera** (☎ 28410 51525; admission €3; ☟ 8.30am-3pm Mon-Fri, 8.30am-2pm Sat). The frescoes that cover its interior walls are considered the most outstanding examples of Byzantine art in Crete.

The taverna/kafeneio **Platanos** (☎ 28410 51230; mains €4.80-6.50) retains a traditional feel and has a lovely setting under a giant plane tree and vine canopy. There's a standard menu but it's well regarded by locals.

There are hourly buses from Agios Nikolaos to Kritsa (€1.30, 15 minutes).

ANCIENT LATO ΑΡΧΑΙΑ ΛΑΤΩ

The ancient city of **Lato** (admission €2; ☟ 8.30am-3pm Tue-Sun), 4km north of Kritsa, is one of Crete's few non-Minoan ancient sites. Lato (lah-to) was founded in the 7th century BC by the Dorians and at its height was one of the most powerful cities in Crete. It sprawls over the slopes of two acropolises in a lonely mountain setting, commanding stunning views down to the Gulf of Mirabello.

The city's name derived from the goddess Leto whose union with Zeus produced Artemis and Apollo, both of whom were worshipped here.

In the centre of the site is a deep well, which is cordoned off. As you face the Gulf of Mirabello, to the left of the well are some steps which are the remains of a **theatre**.

Above the theatre was the **prytaneion**, where the city's governing body met. The circle of stones behind the well was a threshing floor. The columns next to it are the remains of a stoa which stood in the agora. There are remains of a pebble mosaic nearby. A path to the right leads up to the **Temple of Apollo**.

There are no buses to Lato. The road to the site is signposted to the right on the approach to Kritsa. If you don't have your own transport, it's a pleasant 4km walk through olive groves.

GOURNIA ΓΟΥΡΝΙΑ

The important Minoan site of **Gournia** (☎ 28410 24943; admission €2; ☟ 8.30am-3pm Tue-Sun), pronounced goor-nyah, lies just off the coast road, 19km southeast of Agios Nikolaos. The ruins, which date from 1550 to 1450 BC, consist of a town overlooked by a small palace. The palace was far less ostentatious than the ones at Knossos and Phaestos, because it was the residence of an overlord rather than a king. The town is a network of streets and stairways flanked by houses with walls up to 2m in height. Trade, domestic and agricultural implements found on the site indicate Gournia was a thriving little community.

Gournia is on the Sitia and Ierapetra bus routes from Agios Nikolaos and buses can drop you at the site.

MOHLOS ΜΟΧΛΟΣ
pop 91

Mohlos (*moh*-los) is a pretty fishing village reached by a 5km winding road from the Sitia–Agios Nikolaos highway. In antiquity, it was joined to the eponymous island that now sits 200m offshore and was once a thriving Early Minoan community dating from the period 3000–2000 BC. Excavations still continue sporadically on both Mohlos Island and at Mohlos village. A short description of the archaeology of the area is presented on an information board overlooking the tiny harbour.

Mohlos is a chill-out place with simple accommodation, plenty of good walks and interesting villages to explore nearby. There is a small pebble-and-grey-sand beach where swimming is reasonable. Beware of strong currents further out in the small strait between the island and the village.

The tavernas enjoy a good reputation for fresh local fish and seafood, and attract many Cretans on weekends.

There are few facilities other than a couple of gift shops and a minimarket. There was, however, at the time of researching this book, an ominous construction frenzy evident nearby that did not bode well for peaceful Mohlos.

Hotel Sofia (☎ /fax 28430 94554; r €35-45; ❄) The rooms above the taverna have been spruced up with new furniture and bedding, and all have TV and fridge, but are rather cramped. The front rooms have balconies with sea views. Try the excellent home cooking at the taverna.

Kyma (☎ 28430 94177; soik@in.gr; studio €30) Fairly well signposted on the village's western side near a supermarket, the self-contained studios are spotless and good value.

Ta Kochilia (☎ 28430 94432; Cretan specials €4.50-6.50) This excellent place has superb views and is known for its fresh fish and simple, good food. Seafood lovers should try the sea-urchin

salad – dip your bread in it or the cuttlefish in black ink.

Also recommended is **To Bogazi** (☎ 28430 94200; mezedhes €2.50-6.50).

There is no public transport to Mohlos. Buses between Sitia and Agios Nikolaos will drop you off at the Mohlos turn-off. From there you'll need to hitch or walk the 6km to Mohlos village.

SITIA ΣΗΤΕΙΑ
pop 8238

Sitia (si-*tee*-ah) is quieter than the prefecture capital Agios Nikolaos, though it can get busy in summer with a mainly domestic crowd. While the town is traveller-friendly, it exists for the locals, who live from agriculture and commerce rather than tourism.

A sandy beach skirts a wide bay to the east of town. The main town is terraced up a hillside, overlooking the port. It has a pleasing mixture of new and fading Venetian architecture, while its attractive harbour-side promenade lined with tavernas and cafés makes for a pleasant evening stroll. Even at the height of the season the town has a relatively laid-back feel compared with the commercialism further west. It also makes a good jumping-off point for the Dodecanese.

Orientation & Information

The town's main square is Plateia Iroon Polytehniou. There are ATMs and places to change money in town. The bus station is at the eastern end of Karamanli, which runs behind the bay. Ferries dock about 500m north of Plateia Agnostou.

Akasti Travel (☎ 28430 29444; www.akasti.gr; Kornarou & Metaxaki 4) Good source of information.

Java Internet Cafe (☎ 28430 22263; Kornarou 113; ❄ 9am-late).

National Bank of Greece (Plateia Iroon Polytehniou) Has a 24-hour exchange machine.

Post office (Dimokritou; ❄ 7.30am-3pm) To get here, follow El Venizelou inland and take the first left.

Tourist office (☎ 28430 28300; Karamanli; ❄ 9.30am-2.30pm & 5-8.30pm Mon-Fri, 9.30am-2.30pm Sat) On the promenade; has town maps.

Sights

Sitia's excellent **Archaeological Museum** (☎ 28430 23917; Piskokefalou; admission €2; ❄ 8.30am-3pm Tue-Sun) houses a well-displayed and important collection of local finds spanning Neolithic to Roman times, with emphasis on the Minoan civilisation. One of the most significant exhibits is the *Palekastro Kouros* – a figure pieced together from fragments made of hippopotamus tusks and adorned with gold. The finds from the palace at Zakros include a wine press, bronze saw, jars, cult objects and pots that are clearly scorched from the great fire that destroyed the palace. Among the most valuable objects in the museum are the Linear A tablets which reflect the palace's administrative function.

Towering over the town is the fort or **kazarma** (from 'casa di arma') which was a garrison under the Venetians. The only remains of the wall that once protected the town, the site is now used as an open-air venue. It's open 8.30am to 3pm.

The **folklore museum** (☎ 28430 22861; Kapetan Sifinos 28; admission €2; ☒ 10am-1pm Mon-Fri) displays a fine collection of local weavings.

Sleeping

Hotel Arhontiko (☎ 28430 28172; Kondylaki 16; d/studio without bathroom €30/33) This guesthouse, in a beautifully maintained neoclassical building uphill from the port, has a real old-world feel. It's spotless, with shared bathrooms and a lovely shady garden in the front; the top rooms have sea views.

Apostolis (☎ 28430 28172; Kazantzaki 27; d/tr €37/47) These domatia have ceiling fans and relatively modern bathrooms with handy touches such as shower curtains. There's a communal balcony and fridge.

El Greco Hotel (☎ 28430 23133; elgreco@sit.forth net.gr; Arkadiou 13; s/d with breakfast €35/50; ☒) The quaint El Greco has very clean and presentable rooms, and all have a fridge, phone and extras like hairdryers (some sleep up to four).

Hotel Flisvos (☎ 28430 27135; www.flisvos-sitia .com; Karamanli 4; s/d/tr from €40/50/60; ☒) Along the southern waterfront, Flisvos is a decent modern hotel. Rooms are neat and have air-con, TV, fridge, phone and balconies; there is a recently renovated back wing with more spacious rooms and a lift.

Also recommended are the more upmarket **Sitia Bay Hotel Apartments** (☎ 28430 24800; www.sitia bay.com; Tritis Septemvriou 8; apt/ste from €110/160; ☒).

Eating

Sitia Beach (☎ 28430 22104; Karamanli 28; specials €5.50-8) is an unassuming place on the beach that makes a decent pizza but it is more highly

recommended for home-style cooking that appears daily on the specials board.

Taverna O Mihos (☎ 28430 22416; Kornarou 117; mixed grill for 2 €20) This *psistaria* (restaurant serving grilled food) in a traditional stone house one block back from the waterfront has excellent charcoal-grilled meats as well as Cretan cooking. There are also tables on a terrace nearby on the beach.

Balcony (☎ 28430 25084; Foundalidou 19; mains €10.60-18.80) The finest dining in Sitia is on the 1st floor of this charmingly decorated neoclassical building. The Balcony has an eclectic menu of fusion cuisine, from Cretan to Mexican and Asian-inspired dishes from the charmingly feisty owner/chef Tonya's travels. Service can be patchy.

For a more classic local experience try the old **Houlis Rakadiko** (☎ 28430 28298; Venizelou 57) for a wide range of mezedhes accompanied by good *raki*. It has no signage, but it's second from the corner – by day you'll see it packed with men playing backgammon.

Getting There & Away

AIR

Sitia's **airport** (☎ 28430 24666) opened an expanded international-size runway in 2003, but international flights had yet to operate in 2007.

Olympic Airlines (☎ 28430 22270; www.olympicair lines.com; 4 Septemvriou 3) has four weekly flights to Athens (€71, one hour), Alexandroupolis (€80, two hours), three flights a week to Preveza (€80, two hours and 20 minutes) and daily flights to Kasos (20 minutes), Karpathos (one hour) and Rhodes (€47, two hours).

BUS

From Sitia's **bus station** (☎ 28430 22272) there are six buses a day to Ierapetra (€5.40, 1½ hours), seven buses a day to Iraklio (€13.10, three hours) via Agios Nikolaos (€6.90, 1½ hours), four to Vaï (€3, ½ hour), and two to Kato Zakros via Palekastro and Zakros (€4.50, one hour). Buses to Vaï and Kato Zakros run only between May and October.

FERRY

LANE Lines (☎ 28430 25555; www.lane.gr) has weekly ferries from Sitia to Rhodes via Kasos (€19.50, six hours), Karpathos (€19.50, eight hours), Diafani (€17.90, nine hours), Halki (€18.20, 11 hours) and Rhodes (€27, 14 hours).

Departure times change annually, so check locally for latest information.

AROUND SITIA

Moni Toplou Μονή Τοπλού

The imposing **Moni Toplou** (☎ 28430 61226; admission €2.50; ⏰ 9am-6pm Apr-Oct), 18km east of Sitia on the road to Vaï, looks more like a fortress than a monastery. It was often treated as such, being ravaged by both the Knights of St John and the Turks. Its star attraction is an 18th-century icon by Ioannis Kornaros, with 61 small beautiful scenes inspired by an Orthodox prayer.

An excellent **museum** has a fine collection of icons, engravings and books, as well as weapons and military souvenirs from the Resistance. The well-stocked shop sells ecclesiastical souvenirs and books on Crete, plus the monastery's award-winning organic olive oil and wine.

The monastery is a 3km walk from the Sitia–Palekastro road. Buses can drop you off at the junction.

Vaï Βάϊ

The beach at Vaï, on Crete's east coast 24km from Sitia, is famous for its palm forest. There are many stories about the origin of these palms, including the theory that they sprouted from date pits spread by Roman legionaries relaxing on their way back from conquering Egypt. While these palms are closely related to the date, they are a separate species unique to Crete.

In July and August you'll need to arrive early to appreciate the setting, because the place gets packed. It's possible to escape the worst of the ballyhoo – jet skis and all – by clambering over a rocky outcrop behind the taverna to a secluded beach.

About 3km north is the ancient Minoan site of **Itanos**. Below the site are several good swimming spots.

There are buses to Vaï from Sitia (€2.50, one hour, five daily) that stop at Palekastro. The car park charges €3, but there's free parking on the roadside 500m before Vaï.

PALEKASTRO ΠΑΛΑΙΚΑΣΤΡΟ

pop 1084

Palekastro (pah-*leh*-kas-tro) is a small farming town in the midst of a rocky, barren landscape, but within easy striking distance of the lovely Kouremenos Beach, Vaï Beach and Moni Toplou. About 1km from town is the small archaeological site of Ancient Palekastro, where archaeologists believe a major Minoan Palace is buried. Excavations continue on the site, which uncovered the *Palekastro Kouros* now residing in the Archaeological Museum in Sitia (p267).

The **tourist office** (☎ 28430 61546; ⏰ 9am-10pm May-Oct) is also a good source of information. There's an ATM next door.

Hotel Hellas (☎ 28430 61240; hellas_h@otenet.gr; s/d €30-45; ❄) has simple rooms with a fridge and updated bathrooms, while downstairs at the taverna you'll find hearty home-style cooking (specials €4 to €6.90).

The closest beaches to Palekastro are **Kouremenos**, a nearly deserted pebble beach with excellent windsurfing and **Hiona Beach**, which has some fine fish tavernas.

You can rent boards from **Freak Surf Station** (☎ 28430 61116; www.freak-surf.com) on the beach.

At Kouremenos Beach, **Casa di Mare** (☎ 28430 25304; casadimare@hotmail.com; studio €40-60; ❄ ⏰) has six spacious, comfortable studios with stone floors and rustic-style décor that sleep up to four. There's a small pool among the olive groves.

There are five buses a day from Sitia that stop at Palekastro on the way to Vaï. The are also two buses daily from Sitia to Palekastro (€2.20, 45 minutes) that continue to Kato Zakros (€4.50).

KATO ZAKROS ΚΑΤΩ ΖΑΚΡΟΣ

pop 793

The village of Zakros (*zah*-kros), 37km southeast of Sitia, is the nearest permanent settlement to the Minoan site of Zakros, a further 7km away next to the peaceful beach settlement Kato Zakros (*kah*-to *zah*-kros). Little more than a long stretch of pebbly beach shaded by pine trees with a string of welcoming tavernas, it is just about the most tranquil place to stay on Crete's southeastern coast.

The settlement is unlikely ever to expand thanks to restrictions imposed by the archaeological service. There are several great walks in the area, including a not-too-challenging 8km walk from Zakros through a gorge, known as the **Valley of the Dead** because of the cave tombs dotted along the cliffs. The gorge emerges close to the Minoan site.

CRETE

Sleeping

Stella's Apartments (☎ /fax 28430 23739; www.stelapts .com; studio €40-75) are charming studios in a verdant, pine-tinged setting 800m along the old road to Zakros. Decorated with wooden furniture made by the owner, they have barbecues and hammocks and are perfect for longer stays. The engaging owners can take guests on treks and walks.

Four good places are managed by Nikos at the **Akrogiali Taverna** (☎ 28430 26893; www.katozakros .cretefamilyhotels.com). The taverna is at the far end of the beach, as are all of the rooms except Katerina Apartments.

Athena & Coral Rooms (d €40-50; 🕄) Athena has pleasant rooms with stone walls, while Coral next door has small but spotless rooms with a fridge and sea views from the communal balcony.

Katerina Apartments (apt €40-60; 🕄) Comfortable, large, stone-built studios and maisonettes with superb views. Opposite Stella's.

Poseidon Rooms (d with/without bathroom €25/20) Basic budget rooms right on the beach.

Eating

There are a couple of good-quality rival tavernas along the beach.

Restaurant Nikos Platanakis (☎ 28430 26887; specials €4.50-7) This well-regarded restaurant has a wide range of Greek staples such as rabbit stew, as well as excellent grilled meat and fish. Most of the produce is from the massive vegetable garden out the back.

Akrogiali Taverna (☎ 28430 26893) Relaxed seaside dining and excellent service from the inimitable owner Nikos Perakis make this place a winner. The speciality is grilled swordfish steak (€9) and the *raki* is excellent.

Getting There & Away

There are buses to Zakros from Sitia via Palekastro (one hour, €4.50, two daily). From June to August, the buses continue to Kato Zakros.

ANCIENT ZAKROS ΑΡΧΑΙΑ ΖΑΚΡΟΣ

The smallest of Crete's four palatial complexes, the **Palace of Zakros** (☎ 28430 26897; Kato Zakros; admission €3; ⏱ 8am-7.30pm Jul-Oct, 8.30am-3pm Nov-Jun) was a major port in Minoan times, maintaining trade links with Egypt, Syria, Anatolia and Cyprus. The palace comprised royal apartments, storerooms and workshops flanking a central courtyard.

The town occupied a low plain close to the shore. Water levels have risen over the years so that some parts of the palace complex are submerged and are occupied by turtles. The ruins are not well preserved, but a visit to the site is worthwhile for its wild and remote setting.

XEROKAMBOS ΞΕΡΟΚΑΜΠΟΣ

pop 34

Xerokambos (kse-*ro*-kam-bos) is a quiet, unassuming agricultural settlement on the far southeastern flank of Crete. Its isolation has so far meant that tourism is pretty much low-key and most certainly of the unpackaged kind. There are a couple of splendid beaches, a few scattered tavernas and a smattering of studio accommodation that is ideal for people wanting peace and quiet.

The smallish but cosy **Ambelos Beach Studios** (☎ /fax 28430 26759; studio €30-40) have basic kitchenettes, fridges and flyscreens. There is a barbecue and outdoor wood oven for guests, and a tree-shaded garden courtyard that makes it well-suited to families. It's just across from the beach.

Villa Petrino (☎ 28430 26702; d €40; 🕄) has attractive, large, fully-equipped apartments, which are suitable for families, overlooking the garden. They have built-in beds, marble floors and the top rooms have beach views. The same management runs **Kostas Taverna** (specials €3-6), a well-regarded taverna that has a shady veranda with views out to sea. The multilingual owner Nikos is happy to show you the day's offering in the kitchen. Try the rabbit *rismarato* with rosemary and vinegar, served with hand-cut potatoes.

Akrogiali Taverna (☎ 28430 26777; mayirefta €4.50-8) is 50m from Ambelos Beach. Under new management, it does a range of mezedhes, grills and home-style specials like rabbit (in busy periods).

There are no buses to Xerokambos. From Zakros there's a signposted turn-off to Xerokambos, which becomes an 8km winding dirt road that is rough but drivable in a conventional vehicle (though it is slowly being asphalted). Otherwise there is a good paved road from Ziros.

IERAPETRA ΙΕΡΑΠΕΤΡΑ

pop 11,678

Ierapetra (yeh-*rah*-pet-rah) is Europe's most southerly major town that services the surrounding farming region. It was a major port of call for the Romans in their conquest of

Egypt. Ierapetra's main business continues to be agriculture, as the greenhouses that mar the landscape along the coast will attest, rather than tourism. Despite its wealth, it is a largely unremarkable place and it attracts relatively few tourists. There are tavernas and cafés along the waterfront, a small Venetian fort on the harbour and the odd remnant of a Turkish quarter.

The town beach and surrounding beaches are good, the nightlife busy enough to keep you entertained and the scene is still Cretan enough to give you a less touristy experience of the island.

From Ierapetra you can visit the offshore, low-lying, sandy island of Gaïdouronisi (also known as Hrysi).

Orientation & Information

The bus station is on the eastern side of town, one street back from the beachfront. There are ATMs around the main square.

City Netcafe (☎ 28420 23164; Kothri 6; per hr €2.50; ☺ 9am-late)

Post office (☎ 28420 22271; Vitsentzou Kornarou 7; ☺ 7.30am-2pm)

www.ierapetra.net Helpful website.

Sights & Activities

Ierapetra's one-room **archaeological museum** (☎ 28420 28721; Adrianou (Dimokratias) 2; admission €2; ☺ 8.30am-3pm Tue-Sun) is perfect for those with a short concentration span. It does have a good collection of headless classical statuary and a superb statue of the goddess Persephone that dates from the 2nd century AD. Also notable is a *larnax*, or clay coffin, dating from around 1300 BC. The chest is decorated with 12 painted panels showing hunting scenes, an octopus and a chariot procession, among others. The 1899 building was a school during Ottoman times.

South along the waterfront from the central square is the 'Kales' **medieval fortress** (admission free; ☺ 8.30am-3pm Tue-Sun), which was built in the early years of Venetian rule and strengthened by Francesco Morosini in 1626. It was in a pretty fragile condition and closed for restoration at the time of research.

The main **town beach** is near the harbour, while a second **beach** stretches east from the bottom of Patriarhou Metaxaki. Both have coarse, grey sand, but the main beach offers better shade.

Sleeping

Cretan Villa Hotel (☎ /fax 28420 28522; www.cretan-villa .com; Lakerda 16; d €40/50; ☒) This well-maintained 18th-century house is the most atmospheric hotel in town. The traditionally furnished rooms have a fridge and TV, and there is a peaceful courtyard. It's a five-minute walk from the bus station. Rooms are cheaper without air-con.

Ersi (☎ 28420 23208; Plateia Eleftherias 19; d €30; ☒) This refurbished central hotel has neat rooms with a fridge, TV and sea views, though some are rather compact. It is run by the same family as **Coral Hotel** (☎ 28420 22846; Katzonovatsi 12; d €30), another reasonable budget option in a quiet pocket of the old town, as well as the larger fully-equipped **Coral Apartments** (Lambraki; €45-60) on the other side of town for families or longer stays.

Eating

Portego (☎ 28420 27733; Foniadaki 8; mezedhes €3-5) This delightful restaurant serves excellent Cretan and Greek cuisine and has specials cooked in the wood-fired oven (so is its bread). Try the lamb in a clay pot with yogurt. It is housed in a historic 1900s house with a lovely courtyard for summer, and there is a cool bar and *kafeneio* attached if you just want a drink.

Oi Kalitehnes (☎ 28420 28547; Kyprou 26; mains €4-7) is a colourful little place in a backstreet among hardware stores and tyre shops. It offers great-value organic food, home-made bread and some spicier falafel and kebabs introduced by the Egyptian owner.

Napoleon (☎ 28420 22410; Stratigou Samouil 26; mains €4.50-9) This is one of the oldest and most respected establishments. It's on the waterfront on the south side of town. There is fresh fish and Greek and Cretan specialities, but whatever you order is of a high quality.

Ierapetra has some excellent *rakadika*, relaxed evening hang-outs where a carafe of *raki* or wine comes with half a dozen or more tasty tid-bits. You could also try **To Kafeneio** opposite the town hall, or the modern **Pavlis**, near the port.

Getting There & Away

There are nine buses a day from Ierapetra's **bus station** (☎ 28420 28237; Lasthenous) to Iraklio (€9.50, 2½ hours), via Agios Nikolaos (€3.30, one hour) and Gournia; seven to Sitia (€5.40,

CRETE

1½ hours) via Koutsounari (for camp sites); and seven to Myrtos (€1.80, 30 minutes).

GAÏDOURONISI (HRYSI)
ΓΑΪΔΟΥΡΟΝΗΣΙ (ΧΡΥΣΗ)

Just off the coast of Ierapetra, you will find greater tranquillity at Gaïdouronisi (Donkey Island) – universally marketed in Ierapetra as Hrysi or Hrysi (Golden Island) – where there are good, sandy beaches, a taverna (alarmingly rumoured to be taken over by an incongruous chain snack store), and a stand of Lebanon cedars, the only one in Europe. It can get very crowded when the tour boats are in, but you can always find a quiet spot.

In summer, **excursion boats** (€15) leave from the quay near the town centre for the islet every morning and return in the afternoon.

MYRTOS ΜΥΡΤΟΣ
pop 440

Myrtos (*myr*-tos), on the coast 17km west of Ierapetra, is popular with more mature European travellers who like the authentic village ambience. It is one of the few places with any character in this part of the south-eastern coast, which is marred by greenhouses and haphazard unattractive beach developments. Myrtos has no big hotels, and there's a reasonable patch of beach and some decently priced places to stay and eat.

Internet is available at **Prima Tours** (☎ 28420 51035; www.sunbudget.net; per hr €3.50).

Big Blue (☎ 28420 51094; www.big-blue.gr; d/studio/apt €35/60/75; 🔀) on the western edge of town, has a choice of more expensive, large airy studios with sea views, or cheaper, ground-floor rooms. All have cooking facilities.

Cretan Rooms (☎ 28420 51427; d €35) are excellent traditional-styled rooms with balconies, fridges and shared kitchens, popular with independent travellers.

The reliable eating option is **Myrtos Taverna** (☎ 28420 51227; mayirefta €5-8), attached to the Myrtos hotel, which is popular with both locals and tourists for its wide range of mezedhes as well as vegetarian dishes.

Platanos (☎ 28420 51363; mains €4.50-8) seems to be the heartbeat of the town for foreigners, with tables under a giant thatched umbrella below a plane tree.

There are seven buses daily from Ierapetra to Myrtos (€1.80, 30 minutes).

Dodecanese
Δωδεκάνησα

Strung out along the coast of western Turkey, like jewels upon an impossibly aquamarine sea, the Dodecanese both entrance and attract passers-by – many of whom return year after year to sample some of the most culturally and geographically diverse islands in the Aegean.

These 18 islands (including satellites) are an entity unto themselves. Under Italian rule until 1947, they maintain an air of slight separateness and, unsurprisingly, still attract large numbers of curious Italian visitors. The islands are a beguiling mix of sea, mountain and meadow and, because they are all close to one another, can easily be 'hopped'. They need that extra effort to get to, but the rewards far outweigh the investment.

The spiritually inclined will make a beeline for Patmos. The developed resorts of Rhodes and Kos have beaches and bars galore, while Lipsi and Tilos have seductive beaches, minus the crowds. The far-flung islands of Agathonisi, Arki, Kasos and Kastellorizo await Greek-island aficionados in pursuit of traditional island life, while everyone gapes at the extraordinary volcanic landscape that geological turbulence has created on Nisyros. The islands' chequered history has also endowed them with a wealth of diverse archaeological remains.

HIGHLIGHTS

- **Historical Experience** Viewing Lindos (p287), the most famous of the ancient cities of the Dodecanese
- **Getting Away from it All** Enjoying Kastel-lorizo (p303) with slow, laid-back life un-fussed by mainstream tourism
- **Chill-out Spot** Relaxing on Astypalea (p324), an island of tranquillity, spirituality and beautiful beaches
- **Green Haven** Viewing fertile, volcanic Nisyros (p314)
- **Wine Country** Indulging in Rhodes' wine country (p291) on the slopes of Mt Attavyros
- **Romantic Restaurants** Dining in Rhodes' Old Town (p285)
- **Adrenaline Rush** Cliff-diving around Kalymnos (p332)
- **Sporting Event** Windsurfing fast and furious at Afiartis Bay (p297) on Karpathos

- POPULATION: 190,071
- AREA: 2714 SQ KM

DODECANESE

HISTORY

The Dodecanese islands have been inhabited since pre-Minoan times, and by the Archaic period Rhodes and Kos had emerged as the dominant islands within the group. Distance from Athens gave the Dodecanese considerable autonomy and they were, for the most part, free to prosper unencumbered by subjugation to imperial Athens. Following Alexander the Great's death, Ptolemy I of Egypt ruled the Dodecanese.

The Dodecanese islanders were the first Greeks to become Christians. This was through the tireless efforts of St Paul, who made two journeys to the archipelago, and through St John, who was banished to Patmos, where he had his revelation.

The early Byzantine era saw the islands prosper, but by the 7th century AD they were plundered by a string of invaders. By the early 14th century it was the turn of the crusaders – the Knights of St John of Jerusalem, or Knights Hospitallers – who eventually became rulers of almost all the Dodecanese, building mighty fortifications, but not mighty enough to keep out the Turks in 1522.

The Turks were ousted by the Italians in 1912 during a tussle over possession of Libya. The Italians, inspired by Mussolini's vision of a vast Mediterranean empire, made Italian the official language and prohibited the practice of Orthodoxy. The Italians constructed grandiose public buildings in the Fascist style, which was the antithesis of archetypal Greek architecture. More beneficially, they excavated and restored many archaeological monuments.

After the Italian surrender of 1943, the islands became a battleground for British and German forces, with much suffering inflicted upon the population. The Dodecanese were formally returned to Greece in 1947.

GETTING THERE & AWAY
Air

Astypalea, Kalymnos, Karpathos, Kos, Leros and Rhodes all have direct flights to Athens. In addition, Rhodes has flights to Astypalea (via Kos and Leros), Iraklio, Kasos (via Karpathos), Thessaloniki, and in summer to Mykonos and Santorini (Thira) in the Cyclades. Additional seaplane service operates out of Kos and Kalymnos linking those islands with Lavrio on the mainland.

Ferry & Hydrofoil
DOMESTIC

Ferry schedules to the Dodecanese are fairly complex, but they do follow a predictable and rarely varying pattern. Departure times

FERRY CONNECTIONS TO THE DODECANESE				
Origin	Destination	Duration	Fare	Frequency
Alexandroupoli	Kalymnos	23hr	€38.50	weekly
	Kos	26hr	€39	weekly
	Rhodes	29hr	€44	weekly
Piraeus	Astypalea	10-12hr	€33.50	5 weekly
	Halki	22hr	€35	2 weekly
	Kalymnos	9-11hr	€42	daily
	Karpathos	18½hr	€33-49	3 weekly
	Kasos	17hr	€32.50	3 weekly
	Kos	10-15hr	€42-45	2 daily
	Leros	11hr	€32-36	daily
	Nisyros	17hr	€44	2 weekly
	Patmos	7-8hr	€32.50	daily
	Rhodes	15-18hr	€48-51.50	2 daily
	Symi	15-17hr	€44	2 weekly
	Tilos	15hr	€42	1 weekly
Sitia	Halki	7½hr	€20	3 weekly
	~Karpathos	4¼hr	€17	3 weekly
	Kasos	2½hr	€10.50	3 weekly
	Rhodes	10hr	€25	3 weekly
Thessaloniki	Kos	18hr	€44	1 weekly
	Rhodes	21hr	€53	1 weekly

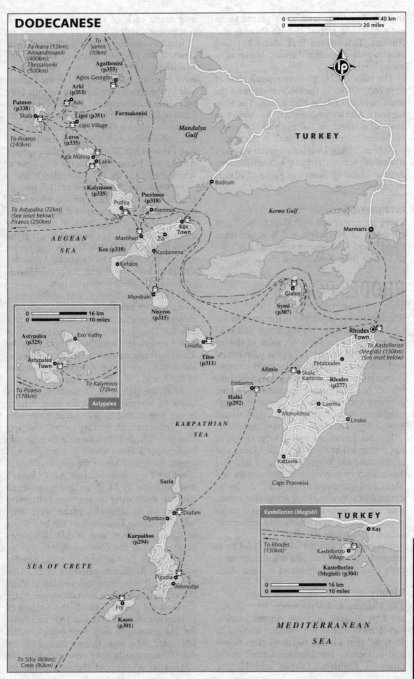

DODECANESE

0 _____ 40 km
0 _____ 20 miles

To Ikaria (12km);
Alexandroupoli
(400km);
Thessaloniki
(500km)

To
Samos
(10km)

Agathonisi
(p355)

Agios Georgios

Arki
(p353)

Arki

Patmos
(p338)
Skala

Lipsi (p351)

Lipsi Village

Farmakonisi

Leros
(p335)

To Piraeus
(240km)

Agia Marina

Lakki

Mandalya
Gulf

TURKEY

Kalymnos
(p329)

Pserimos
(p318)

Pothia

Bodrum

Pserimos

To Astypalea (72km)
(See inset below);
Piraeus (250km)

*AEGEAN
SEA*

Kerme Gulf

Mastihari

Zia

Kos
Town

Marmaris

Kos (p318)

Kardamena

Kefalos

Mandraki

Nisyros
(p315)

Gialos

Symi
(p307)

**Rhodes
Town**

0 _____ 16 km
0 _____ 10 miles

Astypalea
(p325)

Exo Vathy

Livadia

Tilos
(p311)

To Kastellorizo
(Megisti) (130km)
(See inset below)

Petaloudes

Astypalea
Town

Alimia

Skala
Kamirou

Rhodes
(p277)

To Piraeus
(178km)

To Kalymnos
(72km)

Embonos

Halki
(p292)

Laerma

Astypalea

Monolithos

Lindos

*KARPATHIAN
SEA*

Kattavia

Cape Prasonisi

Saria

Kastellorizo (Megisti)

TURKEY

Olymbos

Diafani

Karpathos
(p294)

To Rhodes
(130km)

Kaş

Kastellorizo
Village

Kastellorizo
(Megisti) (p304)

SEA OF CRETE

Pigadia

Ammoōpi

0 _____ 16 km
0 _____ 10 miles

Fry

Kasos
(p301)

*MEDITERRANEAN
SEA*

To Sitia (60km);
Crete (90km)

DODECANESE

in both directions tend to be geared to an early morning arrival at both Piraeus and Rhodes. This means that island-hopping southwards can often involve some anti-social hours.

The table (p274) gives an overall view of ferry connections to the Dodecanese from the mainland and Crete in high season. The service from Alexandroupoli may be subject to seasonal demand, so always check the schedule before committing yourself to the trip.

Aegean Flying Dolphins operates a daily hydrofoil service from the Northeastern Aegean island of Samos to Kos and islands in between.

INTERNATIONAL

There are ferries and hydrofoils to the Turkish ports of Marmaris and Bodrum from Rhodes and Kos, respectively, and day trips to Turkey from Kastellorizo and Symi.

RHODES ΡΟΔΟΣ

Rhodes (*ro*-dos in Greek) is the jewel in the Dodecanese crown. It's big, brash and bold and receives by far the lion's share of visitors to this island group. It's open year-round and enjoys an exceptionally mild climate. It combines all that is needed in a holiday island: beaches, nightlife, culture, scenery, greenery and comfort. Like Crete, its larger neighbour to the southwest, it could almost exist independently of the Greek mainland.

Rhodes grows on you slowly. If you're not captivated at once by its intriguing and almost magical World Heritage–listed Old Town with its labyrinthine back streets and Mediaeval fortifications, you will be by its dreamy beaches, snaking mountain roads, wild almost untouched interior and rocky mountains. The best dining and accommodation is found on Rhodes.

The island is also the focal point for most regional transport and you will almost inevitably pass through the island at some stage.

History

The Minoans and Mycenaeans were among the first to have outposts on the islands, but it wasn't until the Dorians arrived in 1100 BC that Rhodes began to exert power and influence. The Dorians settled in the cities of Kamiros, Ialysos and Lindos,

and made each of them prosperous and autonomous states.

Rhodes continued to prosper until Roman times. It was allied to Athens in the Battle of Marathon (490 BC), in which the Persians were defeated, but had shifted to the Persian side by the time of the Battle of Salamis (480 BC). After the unexpected Athenian victory at Salamis, Rhodes hastily became an ally of Athens again, joining the Delian League in 477 BC. Following the disastrous Sicilian Expedition (416–412 BC), Rhodes revolted against Athens and formed an alliance with Sparta, which it aided in the Peloponnesian Wars.

In 408 BC the cities of Kamiros, Ialysos and Lindos consolidated their powers for mutual protection and expansion by cofounding the city of Rhodes. Rhodes became Athens' ally again, and together they defeated Sparta at the Battle of Knidos (394 BC). Rhodes then joined forces with Persia in a battle against Alexander the Great, but when Alexander proved invincible, quickly allied itself with him.

In 305 BC Antigonus, one of Ptolemy's rivals, sent his son, the formidable Demetrius Poliorketes (the Besieger of Cities), to conquer Rhodes. The city managed to repel Demetrius after a long siege. To celebrate this victory, the 32m-high bronze statue of Helios Apollo (Colossus of Rhodes), one of the Seven Wonders of the Ancient World, was built.

After the defeat of Demetrius, Rhodes knew no bounds. It built the biggest navy in the Aegean and its port became a principal Mediterranean trading centre. The arts also flourished. When Greece became the battleground upon which Roman generals fought for leadership of the empire, Rhodes allied itself with Julius Caesar. After Caesar's assassination in 44 BC, Cassius besieged Rhodes, destroying its ships and stripping the city of its artworks, which were then taken to Rome. This marked the beginning of Rhodes' decline, and in AD 70 Rhodes became part of the Roman empire.

When the Roman empire split, Rhodes joined the Byzantine province of the Dodecanese. It was given independence when the crusaders seized Constantinople. Later the Genoese gained control. The Knights of St John arrived in Rhodes in 1309 and ruled for 213 years until they were ousted by the Ottomans, who were in turn kicked out by the Italians nearly four centuries later. In 1947, after 35 years of Italian occupation,

Rhodes became part of Greece along with the other Dodecanese islands.

Getting There & Away
AIR

Olympic Airlines has at least five flights daily to Athens (€77), two daily to Karpathos (€28) and Kasos (€34), one daily to Kastellorizo (€22) and Iraklio (€82), four weekly to Thessaloniki (€100), three weekly to Astypalea (€47) and two weekly to Samos (€37). Direct inquiries to **Olympic Airlines** (Map p280; ☎ 22410 24571; www.olympicairlines.com; Ierou Lohou 9).

Aegean Airlines (☎ 22410 98345; www.aegeanair. com; Diagoras airport) offers flights to Athens, Thessaloniki and Iraklio at similar rates,

plus a service to Rome (€152, three hours) via Athens.

CAÏQUE

There is a daily car-carrying caïque between Skala Kamirou, on Rhodes' west coast, and Halki (€8.50, 1¼ hours). From Skala Kamirou services depart at 2.30pm, and from Halki at 6am.

CATAMARAN

The *Dodekanisos Express* starts its daily run up the Dodecanese at around 8.30am from the Commercial Harbour (Kolona), stopping at Kos, Kalymnos and Leros daily, with stops at other times in Symi, Lipsi and Patmos. There is usually a seasonal weekly service to Kastellorizo

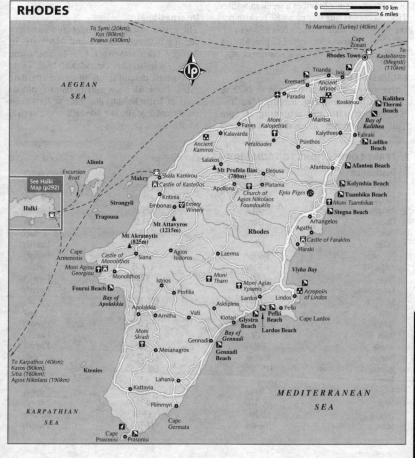

RHODES

as well. Its sister vessel the *Dodekanisos Pride* runs a similar schedule starting at around the same time from Patmos.

Tickets can be bought at **Skevos Travel** (Map p280; ☎ 22410 22461; skeyos@rho.forthnet.gr; Amerikis 11) or **Dodekanisos Seaways** (Map p282; ☎ 22410 70590; www.12ne.gr; Afstralias 3).

The Tilos-owned *Sea Star* links Rhodes with Tilos. Its schedules tend to fluctuate yearly, but there are generally at least six sailings weekly to Tilos. Check with **Triton Holidays** (Map p280; ☎ 22410 21690; www.tritondmc.gr; Plastira 9, Mandraki) for schedules and tickets, or the Sea Star ticket booth on Mandraki Harbour.

There are two daily catamarans from Rhodes' Commercial harbour to Marmaris (50 minutes) from June to September at 8am and 4.30pm, respectively, dropping back to maybe only three or four services a week in winter. Tickets cost €31 one way plus €19 Turkish port tax. Same-day return tickets cost €38 plus €19 tax. Open return tickets cost €42 plus €33 tax. Book online at rhodes.marmarisinfo.com.

EXCURSION BOAT

There are excursion boats to Symi (€22 return) daily in summer, leaving Mandraki Harbour at 9am and returning at 6pm. You can buy tickets at most travel agencies, but it's better to buy them at the harbour, where you can check out the boats personally. Look for shade and the size and condition of the boat, as these vary greatly. You can buy an open return ticket if you want to stay on Symi.

FERRY
Domestic

Rhodes is the main port of the Dodecanese and offers a complex array of departures. The table (below) lists scheduled domestic ferries from Rhodes to other islands in the Dodecanese and Piraeus in high season. The **EOT** (Greek National Tourist Organisation; Map p280; ☎ 22410 35226; cnr Makariou & Papagou; ☺ 8am-2.45pm Mon-Fri) in Rhodes Town can provide you with current schedules.

International

There is a weekly passenger and car ferry service between Rhodes and Marmaris in Turkey (car/passenger €95/49 including taxes, 1¼ hours) on Thursday at 1pm. There is a small discount on open return date rates. Book at www.marmarisinfo.com or contact **Triton Holidays** (Map p280; ☎ 22410 21690; www.tritondmc.gr; Plastira 9, Mandraki) upon arrival to arrange a crossing.

FERRY CONNECTIONS TO/FROM RHODES

Destination	Duration	Fare	Frequency
Agios Nikolaos	12hr	€25.50	2 weekly
Astypalea	8-10hr	€28.50	1 weekly
Amorgos	6hr	€25.50	1 weekly
Chios	13hr	€31.50	1 weekly
Halki	1½-2hr	€8	daily
Iraklio	14hr	€25.50	1 weekly
Kalymnos	3-5½hr	€18.50	6 weekly
Karpathos	3-5½hr	€18-22	5 weekly
Kasos	7-8hr	€22	4 weekly
Kastellorizo	4-5hr	€17	4 weekly
Kos	3½hr	€14-18.50	2 daily
Leros	4½hr	€20-25	daily
Limnos	23hr	€38	1 weekly
Milos	21hr	€34	1 weekly
Nisyros	4½hr	€12	2 weekly
Patmos	6-8½hr	€23-28.50	daily
Piraeus	11½-19hr	€48-51.50	2 daily
Samos	9½hr	€27	2 weekly
Sitia	10hr	€25	3 weekly
Syros	8½-11hr	€30-38.50	3 weekly
Symi	1-2hr	€7-14	2 daily
Tilos	1½-4hr	€12-18.50	5 weekly

DODECANESE

HYDROFOIL

South of Mandraki Harbour, **ANES** (☎ 22410 37769; www.anes.gr; Afstralias 88, Rhodes) operates a single hydrofoil, the *Aegli*, from Rhodes to Symi. Tickets are available at Mandraki Harbour, the main office or from travel agents around town.

Getting Around

TO/FROM THE AIRPORT

The Diagoras airport is 16km southwest of Rhodes Town, near Paradisi. There are 21 buses daily between the airport and Rhodes Town's west side bus station (€1.90, 25 minutes). The first leaves Rhodes Town at 5am and the last at 11pm; from the airport, the first leaves at 5.55am and the last at 11.45pm. Buses from the airport leave from the main road outside the airport perimeter.

BICYCLE

A range of bicycles is available for rent at **Bicycle Centre** (Map p280; ☎ 22410 28315; Griva 39; per day €5).

CAR & MOTORCYCLE

There are numerous car- and motorcycle-rental outlets in Rhodes Town. Shop around and bargain because the competition is fierce. A reliable agency is **Drive Rent a Car** (Map p280; ☎ 22410 68243; www.driverentacar.gr). Call ahead for an airport pick-up if required. Book through **Triton Holidays** (Map p280; ☎ 22410 21690; www.tritondmc.gr; Plastira 9, Mandraki) for even cheaper rates.

EXCURSION BOAT

There are excursion boats to Lindos (return €15) daily in summer, leaving Mandraki Harbour at 9am and returning at 6pm.

LOCAL TRANSPORT

Rhodes Town has two island bus terminals, which service one half of the island each. From the **east side bus terminal** (Map p280; Plateia Rimini) there are 18 buses daily to Faliraki (€1.80), 14 to Lindos (€4.70), three to Kolymbia (€2.40), nine to Gennadi (€4.40) via Lardos, and four to Psinthos (€1.90).

From the **west side bus terminal** (Map p280), next to the New Market, there are buses every half-hour to Kalithea Thermi (€1.80, 15 minutes), 10 daily to Koskinou (€1.80, 20 minutes), five to Salakos (€3.60, one hour), two to Ancient Kamiros (€4.60, 55 minutes), one to

Monolithos (€6, one hour 20 minutes) via Skala Kamirou (€4.60, one hour 10 minutes), and one to Embonas (€4.60, one hour 10 minutes). The EOT office (p281) gives out schedules.

Unlimited travel tickets are available for one/two/three days (€10/15/25).

Local buses around the city charge a flat €1. They depart from a stand on Mandraki Harbour.

TAXI

Rhodes Town's main taxi rank (Map p280) is east of Plateia Rimini. There are two zones on the island for taxi meters: Zone One is Rhodes Town and Zone Two (slightly higher) is everywhere else. Rates are a little higher between midnight and 6am.

Taxis tend not to use meters but prefer to use set fare rates. All drivers carry a booklet stating the current approved set fares. Request to see it if in doubt. Sample fares: airport €16, Filerimos €15, Petaloudes €25, Ancient Kamiros €32, Lindos €38 and Monolithos €65. Taxi company contact phone numbers include ☎ 22410 64712, ☎ 22410 64734 and ☎ 22410 64778.

RHODES TOWN

pop 56,128

The heart of Rhodes Town is the Old Town, enclosed within massive walls. Avoid the worst of the tourist crowds by beginning your exploration early in the morning. At any time, away from the main thoroughfares and squares, you will find deserted serpentine alleyways. Much of the New Town to the north is dominated by package tourism, but it does have a few places of interest for visitors and the advantage of being right next to the town's best beaches.

Orientation

The Old Town is nominally divided into three sectors: the Kollakio, or Knights' Quarter, the Hora and the Jewish Quarter. The Kollakio contains most of the mediaeval historical sights of the Old Town, while the Hora, often referred to as the Turkish Quarter, is primarily Rhodes Town's commercial sector and shows off most of the shops and restaurants. The Old Town is accessible by nine *pyles* (main gates) and two rampart-access portals. The whole town is a mesh of Byzantine, Turkish and Latin architecture, featuring quiet, twisting alleyways that are punctuated by lively squares.

RHODES TOWN

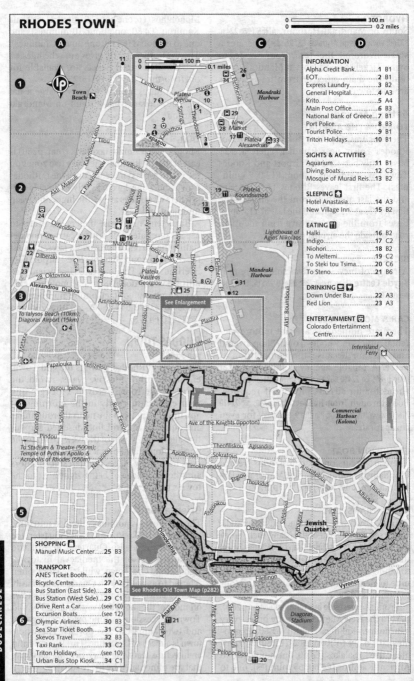

INFORMATION

Alpha Credit Bank	**1** B1
EOT	**2** B1
Express Laundry	**3** B2
General Hospital	**4** A3
Krito	**5** A4
Main Post Office	**6** B3
National Bank of Greece	**7** B1
Port Police	**8** B3
Tourist Police	**9** B1
Triton Holidays	**10** B1

SIGHTS & ACTIVITIES

Aquarium	**11** B1
Diving Boats	**12** C3
Mosque of Murad Reis	**13** B2

SLEEPING

Hotel Anastasia	**14** A3
New Village Inn	**15** B2

EATING

Halki	**16** B2
Indigo	**17** C2
Niohori	**18** B2
To Meltemi	**19** C2
To Steki tou Tsima	**20** C6
To Steno	**21** B6

DRINKING

Down Under Bar	**22** A3
Red Lion	**23** A3

ENTERTAINMENT

Colorado Entertainment Centre	**24** A2

SHOPPING

Manuel Music Center	**25** B3

TRANSPORT

ANES Ticket Booth	**26** C1
Bicycle Centre	**27** A2
Bus Station (East Side)	**28** C1
Bus Station (West Side)	**29** C1
Drive Rent a Car	(see 10)
Excursion Boats	(see 12)
Olympic Airlines	**30** B3
Sea Star Ticket Booth	**31** C3
Skevos Travel	**32** B3
Taxi Rank	**33** C2
Triton Holidays	(see 10)
Urban Bus Stop Kiosk	**34** C1

See Enlargement

See Rhodes Old Town Map (p282)

The commercial centre of the New Town lies north of the Old Town and is easily explored on foot. Most commercial activity is centred on two blocks surrounding Plateia Kyprou. The hotel district is centred on a large sector bordered by 28 Oktovriou and G Papanikolaou.

The Commercial Harbour (Kolona) is east of the Old Town. Excursion boats, small ferries, hydrofoils and private yachts use Mandraki Harbour, further north.

Information

EMERGENCY

Emergency first aid & ambulance (☎ 22410 25555, 22410 22222)

INTERNET ACCESS

Mango Cafe Bar (Map p282; ☎ 22410 24877; www.mango.gr; Plateia Dorieos 3; per hr €5; 9.30am-midnight) In the Old Town.

On The Spot Net (Map p282; ☎ 22410 34737; Perikleous 21; per hr €5; 8am-midnight) In the Hotel Spot.

INTERNET RESOURCES

www.rhodesguide.com A comprehensive guide to what's on in Rhodes.

www.rodos.gr A good cultural and historical background to Rhodes.

LAUNDRY

Express Laundry (Map p280; Kosti Palama 5) Machine washes for €3.

MEDICAL SERVICES

General Hospital (Map p280; ☎ 22410 80000; Papalouka El Venizelou) Just northwest of the Old Town.

Krito (Map p280; ☎ 22410 30020; krito@rho.forthnet.gr; Ioannou Metaxa 3; 24hr) Private medical provider.

MONEY

All the banks listed have ATMs.

Alpha Credit Bank (Map p282; Plateia Kyprou) In the New Town.

Commercial Bank of Greece (Map p282; Plateia Symis) In the Old Town, plus an ATM near where the boats leave for Turkey on the east side of Commercial Harbour.

National Bank of Greece New Town (Map p280; Plateia Kyprou); Old Town (Map p282; Plateia Mousiou)

POST

Main post office (Map p280) On Mandraki Harbour.

Post office branch (Map p282; Orfeos; daily) In the Old Town.

TOURIST INFORMATION

EOT (Map p280; ☎ 22410 35226; cnr Makariou & Papagou; 8am-2.45pm Mon-Fri) Supplies brochures and maps of the city. Has the *Rodos News,* a free English-language newspaper.

Port police (Map p280; ☎ 22410 22220; Mandrakiou)

Tourist police (Map p280; ☎ 22410 27423; 24hr) Next door to the EOT.

TRAVEL AGENCIES

Triton Holidays (Map p280; ☎ 22410 21690; www.tritondmc.gr; Plastira 9, Mandraki) Perhaps the best overall travel, tourist information and accommodation agency in Rhodes. The exceptionally helpful staff provide a wide range of services catering to individual needs, as well as air, sea and land tickets.

Sights

OLD TOWN

In medieval times the Knights of St John lived in the Knights' Quarter, while other inhabitants lived in the Hora. The 12m-thick city walls are closed to the public but you can take a pleasant walk around the imposing walls of the Old Town via the wide and pedestrianised moat walk.

Knights' Quarter

An appropriate place to begin an exploration of the Old Town is the imposing cobblestone **Avenue of the Knights** (Map p282; Ippoton), where the knights lived. The knights were divided into seven 'tongues' or languages, according to their place of origin – England, France, Germany, Italy, Aragon, Auvergne and Provence – and each was responsible for protecting a section of the bastion. The Grand Master, who was in charge, lived in the palace, and each tongue was under the auspices of a bailiff.

To this day the street exudes a noble and forbidding aura, despite modern offices now occupying most of the inns. Its lofty buildings stretch in a 600m-long unbroken wall of honey-coloured stone blocks, and its flat façade is punctuated by huge doorways and arched windows.

First on the right, if you begin at the eastern end of the Ave of the Knights, is the 1519 **Inn of the Order of the Tongue of Italy** (Map p282); next to it is the **Palace of Villiers de l'Isle Adam** (Map p282). After Sultan Süleyman had taken the city, it was Villiers de l'Isle who had the humiliating task of arranging the knights' departure from the island. Next along is the

RHODES OLD TOWN

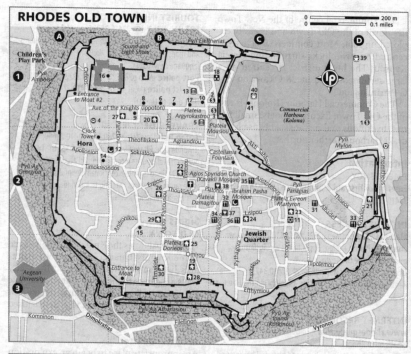

Inn of France (Map p282), the most ornate and distinctive of all the inns. On the opposite side of the street is a wrought-iron gate in front of a Turkish garden.

Back on the right side is the **Chapelle Française** (Chapel of the Tongue of France; Map p282), embellished with a statue of the Virgin and Child. Next door is the residence of the Chaplain of the Tongue of France. Across the alley-

way is the **Inn of Provence** (Map p282), with four coats of arms forming the shape of a cross, and opposite is the **Inn of Spain** (Map p282).

On the right is the truly magnificent 14th-century **Palace of the Grand Masters** (Map p282; ☎ 22410 23359; Ippoton; admission €6; ☒ 12.30-7pm Mon, 8.30am-7.30pm Tue-Sun). It was destroyed in the gunpowder explosion of 1856 and the Italians rebuilt it in a grandiose manner, with a lavish interior, intending it as a holiday home for Mussolini and King Emmanuel III. It is now a museum, containing sculpture, mosaics taken from Kos by the Italians and antique furniture.

Housed in the old 15th-century knights' hospital is the **archaeological museum** (Map p282; ☎ 22410 27657; Plateia Mousiou; admission €3; ☼ 8am-4pm Tue-Sun). Its most famous exhibit is the exquisite Parian marble statuette, the *Aphrodite of Rhodes*, a 1st-century-BC adaptation of a Hellenistic statue. Less impressive to most is the 4th-century-BC *Afroditi Thalassia* in the next room. The **Museum of the Decorative Arts** (Map p282; ☎ 22410 72674; Plateia Argyrokastrou; admission €2; ☼ 8.30am-3pm Tue-Sun), further north, houses a collection of artefacts from around the Dodecanese. A €10 inclusive ticket covers all three of the above sites.

On Plateia Symis, there are the remains of a 3rd-century-BC **Temple of Aphrodite** (Map p282), one of the few ancient ruins in the Old Town.

Hora

Bearing many legacies of its Ottoman past is the **Hora** (Map p282). During Turkish times churches were converted to mosques, and many more Muslim houses of worship were built from scratch, although most are now dilapidated. The most important is the pink-domed **Mosque of Süleyman** (Map p282), at the top of Sokratous. Built in 1522 to commemorate the Ottoman victory against the knights, it was renovated in 1808.

Opposite is the 18th-century **Muslim Library** (Map p282; Plateia Arionos; Sokratous; admission free; ☼ 9.30am-4pm Mon-Sat). Founded in 1794 by Turkish Rhodian Ahmed Hasuf, it houses a small number of Persian and Arabic manuscripts and a collection of Korans handwritten on parchment.

Jewish Quarter

The **Jewish Quarter** (Map p282) is an almost forgotten sector of Rhodes Old Town, where life continues at an unhurried pace and local residents live seemingly oblivious to the hub-bub of the Hora, no more than a few blocks away. This area of quiet streets and sometimes dilapidated houses was once home to a thriving Jewish community.

Kahal Shalom synagogue (Map p282; www.rhodes jewishmuseum.org; Dosiadou), built in 1577, has a commemorative plaque to the many members of Hora's Jewish population who were sent to Auschwitz during the Nazi occupation. Jews still worship here and it is usually open in the morning. Close by is **Plateia Evreon Martyron** (Sq of the Jewish Martyrs; Map p282).

NEW TOWN

The **Acropolis of Rhodes** (Map p280), southwest of the Old Town on Monte Smith, was the site of the ancient Hellenistic city of Rhodes. The hill is named after the English admiral Sir Sydney Smith, who watched for Napoleon's fleet from here in 1802. It has superb views.

The restored 2nd-century-AD **stadium** once staged competitions in preparation for the Olympic Games. The adjacent **theatre** is a reconstruction of one used for lectures by the Rhodes School of Rhetoric. Steps above here lead to the **Temple of Pythian Apollo**, with four re-erected columns. This unenclosed site can be reached on city bus 5.

North of Mandraki, at the eastern end of G Papanikolaou, is the graceful **Mosque of Murad**

THE KNIGHTS OF ST JOHN

The Knights of St John existed during their tenure in Rhodes within an organisation that is known today as the Sovereign Military Hospitaller Order of St John of Jerusalem, of Rhodes and of Malta. Its origins are from the Knights Hospitaller, an organisation founded in Jerusalem in 1080 as an Amalfitan hospital to provide care for poor and sick pilgrims on their way to the Holy Land. After the first Crusade in 1099 and the loss of Jerusalem, the knights relocated to Rhodes (via Cyprus) where after a three-year struggle in 1309 they managed to eject the incumbent tenants, the Genoese. The Knights of St John in Rhodes were ostensibly a chivalrous Christian organisation but soon established themselves as purveyors of legitimate and semilegitimate commercial activities – primarily piracy and antipiracy against Ottoman shipping and pilgrims. This naturally irked the Ottoman Sultan Süleyman the Magnificent who set about dislodging the knights from the stronghold. Rhodes capitulated in 1523, after which the remaining knights relocated to Malta and remain to this day.

Reis (Map p280). In its grounds are a Turkish cemetery and the Villa Cleobolus, where Lawrence Durrell lived in the 1940s, writing *Reflections on a Marine Venus*.

If you fancy a fishy experience, the **Aquarium** (Map p280; ☎ 22410 27308; info@hsr-ncmr.gr; Kos 1; admission €3.50; 9am-8.30pm) is worth a look. The Art Deco building was built during the 1930s by the Italians as a biological research station. Visitors can view anthozoa, molluscs, crabs, echinoderms, sea turtles and specimens from up to 12 types of fish family.

The town **beach** begins north of Mandraki and continues around the island's northernmost point and down the west side of the New Town. The best spots will depend on the prevailing winds but tend to be on the east side.

Activities

GREEK DANCING LESSONS

The **Nelly Dimoglou Dance Company** (Map p282; ☎ 22410 20157; deyappet@otenet.gr; Andronikou 7; admission per person/group €16/11) gives lessons and stages performances (9.15pm on Monday, Wednesday and Friday) in folk dance theatre.

SCUBA DIVING

Three diving schools operate out of Mandraki: **Waterhoppers Diving Centre** (☎ /fax 22410 38146, 6972500971; www.waterhoppers.com), **Diving Centres** (☎ 22410 23780) and **Scuba Diving Trident School** (☎ /fax 22410 29160). All offer a range of courses, including a 'One Day Try Dive', for €40 to €50. You can get information from their boats at Mandraki Harbour (Map p280). Kalithea Thermi is the only site around Rhodes where diving is permitted.

Sleeping

BUDGET

The Old Town has a wide selection of well-priced and relaxing accommodation. Seek out the following.

Hotel Isole (Map p282; ☎ 22410 20682; www.hotel isole.com; Evdoxou 35; s/d incl breakfast €38/48;) Sequestered away in the back streets, but helpfully signposted, is this cosy pension consisting of seven homely rooms in blue and white. There's a welcoming lobby lounge with a small bar.

Pension Olympos (Map p282; ☎ /fax 22410 33567; www.pension-olympos.com; Agiou Fanouriou 56; s/d €40/50;) This pension has pleasant rooms with fridge and TV, and an attractive little

courtyard. Dream away on its wrought-iron country-style beds with soft mattresses.

Mango Rooms (Map p282; ☎ 22410 24877; www.mango.gr; Plateia Dorieos 3; s/d €45/52; year-round;) This place has clean, nicely furnished rooms with bathroom, TV, ceiling fan, safety box and refrigerator. It has heating in winter.

Pink Elephant (Map p282; ☎ 22410 22469; www.pinkelephantpension.com; Timakida 9; s/d €36/60) The fan-equipped and very presentable rooms have large bathrooms, though there are some cheaper rooms with shared bathrooms. Owner Mari makes guests feel at home away from home.

Hotel Spot (Map p282; ☎ 22410 34737; www.spot hotelrhodes.gr; Perikleous 21; s/d incl breakfast €45/60;) The Spot has exceptionally clean, pleasant and tastefully decorated rooms, with fridge. Owner Ilias is a welcoming host. There is also a small book exchange and roof garden, and the hostel offers a wi-fi centre.

Most of the New Town's hotels are modern and characterless, but there are a couple of exceptions.

New Village Inn (Map p280; ☎ 22410 34937; www.newvillageinn.gr; Konstantopedos 10; s/d €24/35) This cosy inn has tastefully furnished rooms with fridge and fan, and a traditional stone-walled courtyard festooned with plants.

Hotel Anastasia (Map p280; ☎ 22410 28007; www.anastasia-hotel.com; 28 Oktovriou 46; s/d incl breakfast €35/51;) This old-style, renovated hotel, in a former Italian mansion, is a quiet getaway. The high-ceilinged rooms with tiled floors are spotless. The lush garden sports a tortoise and cat family. Italian and French is spoken.

MIDRANGE

Apollo Tourist House (Map p282; ☎ 22410 32003; www.apollo-touristhouse.com; Omirou 28c; s/d €50/60) This is a small, quality pension comprising six rooms, the best of which boasts a four-poster bed. Rooms all have good views and there is a cosy courtyard for breakfasts or the occasional barbecue.

Hotel Via Via (Map p282; ☎ /fax 22410 77027; www.hotel-via-via.com; Lisipou 2; d €42-75; year-round;) This pristine boutique hotel, in a discreet quarter of the Old Town, has tastefully furnished and individually named rooms. There's a spacious sun roof where breakfast is served by gregarious Belgian owner Bea.

ourpick Pension Andreas (Map p282; ☎ 22410 34156; fax 22410 74285; www.hotelandreas.com; Omirou 28d; s/d €50/75; ☼ year-round; ☒) In one of the quietest parts of the Old Town this exceptionally friendly small boutique hotel, with ever-helpful staff, has 11 tastefully decorated and individually named rooms. There is a very social breakfast bar with panoramic views across the Old Town.

TOP END

When it comes to top-class accommodation, Rhodes has it all. For the most atmospheric stay, stick to the Old Town. Getting in with bulky luggage can be a problem. Leaving can be even harder as you will have little incentive to do so.

Hotel Cava d'Oro (Map p282; ☎ 22410 36980; www.cavadoro.com; Kistiniou 15; s/d €100/110; P ☒) A handy choice for visitors with luggage as your taxi can come to the door. Constructed from an 800-year-old building, the rooms have solid walls and classy furnishings, including wrought-iron beds.

Nikos & Takis Hotel (Map p282; ☎ 22410 70773; www.nikostakishotel.com; Panetiou 29; s/d €140/160; P ☒ ☐) Housed in a former old mansion, the richly decorated rooms at this discreet and rather trendy establishment are pretty plush. Each of the seven rooms is individually named, from the smallish Marokino to the capacious Grand Master, where amenities are aplenty, including piped music in the bathroom. Breakfast is taken on a banana tree–shaded patio.

Marco Polo Mansion (Map p282; ☎ 22410 25562; www.marcopolomansion.gr; Agiou Fanouriou 40-42; s/d €90/170) Featured in glossy European magazines, this old-fashioned Anatolian inn is decorated in rich Ottoman-era colours. A cool and shady lodging, right in the heart of the Old Town, it's run by the effervescent Effie and gastronome husband Spyros.

ourpick Avalon (Map p282; ☎ 22410 31438; www .hotelavalon.gr; Ippoton; s/d €285-525; ☒ ☐) For the utmost in luxury and discretion you can't beat the Avalon. As Rhodes' newest boutique getaway, the whole establishment oozes class. Finding it can be a challenge as it is sequestered away in an alley off Ippoton. The furnishing and facilities are world-class and the atmosphere rarefied. From the plasma TV to the programmable shower – enjoy!

Eating
BUDGET
Old Town

Avoid the restaurant touts along Sokratous and around Plateia Ippokratous. Hit the backstreets to find less touristy places to eat.

O Meraklis (Map p282; Aristotelous 30; soup €4; ☼ 3am-8am) After a night out on the tiles a plate of belly-caressing tripe and entrails soup is what is needed – at least according to Greeks who swear by its hangover-curing properties. It's pretty much all it serves. It's rough, it's ready, it's an experience worth trying.

Laganis (Map p282; ☎ 22410 35571; Alhadef 16; mains €4-7) If you are looking for an unpretentious places with genuine food and uninflated prices, seek out this family-style taverna in the back streets. Two dishes worth sampling are the succulent fish souvlaki or the mussels filled with cheese and oven-baked.

Taverna Kostas (Map p282; ☎ 22410 26217; Pythagora 62; mains €5-7) For reliability, quality and sheer down-to-earth wholesomeness, Kostas will fit the bill. You can be sure of good grills and fish dishes relying less on flashiness than time-tested ingredients, served up without fuss in good portions.

New Town

The New Town has some surprisingly good places to eat, as long as you're prepared to look.

Halki (Map p280; ☎ 22410 33198; Kathopouli 30; mezedhes €2.50-5; ☼ dinner) Looking and feeling somewhat out of time, Halki is a thoroughly idiosyncratic eatery almost hidden away in the New Town. Forget about swish décor; choose instead from a wide range of mezedhes and dishes on display. Order the excellent draught house wine.

Niohori (Map p280; ☎ 22410 35116; I Kazouli 29; mains €3-6) Like Halki, this essentially non-touristy eatery makes little concession to appearance. Niohori serves up its own meat – the owner is a butcher – and prepares a mouth-watering array of low-cost ready-cooked meals daily.

To Steno (Map p280; ☎ 22410 35914; Agion Anargyron 29; mezedhes €4-7; ☼ dinner) It's a short walk out of the Old Town from the Agios Athanasios gate to To Steno and it's worth the effort for the old-style atmosphere and outdoor dining in summer. Dine ouzo-style with mezedhes such as chickpea patties, zucchini fritters or country sausages.

DODECANESE

Indigo (Map p280; ☎ 69726 63100; New Market 105-106; mains €8-16; ☾ dinner) You wouldn't expect to find quality in among the fast-food joints of the New Market. But there is Indigo. Salads feature strongly: the Indigo salad with croutons, rocket, walnut, lettuce oil and garlic entices, as does a 'playful chicken' salad made up of chicken strips in vegetables and a hazelnut salad with blue cheese. Subtle and scrumptious at the same time.

MIDRANGE & TOP END
Old Town

ourpick **Marco Polo** (Map p282; ☎ 22410 29115; Agiou Fanouriou 45-47; mains €8-10) You mightn't know about this seriously select dining locale if you didn't read it here. Original Graeco-Italian creations include pork with balsamic vinegar, rocket and sliced parmesan cheese, pork fillet with *manouri* cheese (a creamier and unsalted version of feta) and fig jam, or Santorini fava lentils with caramelised onions with a sweet wine sauce and mint. Select, but palate-pleasing wine list. Dining at its best in a palm tree caressed courtyard.

La Varka (Map p282; ☎ 22410 75688; Sofokleous 5; mains €6.50-11) Blink and you've missed this quietly satisfying café-restaurant tucked away among a myriad of establishments. The menu is small, but it's fair dinkum Greek. Tourists don't often find their way here, though it's easy to find. Symi shrimps excel.

Nireas (Map p282; ☎ 22410 31741; Sofokleous 45-47; mains €6.50-11) Another back-street beauty, Nireas is nominally a fish restaurant but still covers the full gamut of dishes. The *mydia ahnista* (steamed mussels) in a rich flavoursome broth are worth particular mention, as are the skillet-seared *mydia saganaki* (mussels with tomato and feta cheese). Eat mezes (appetiser) style if you can. The locale is quiet and relaxing.

Hatzikelis (Map p282; ☎ 22410 27215; Alhadef 9; mains €8.50-12) A former bakery turned fish restaurant, Hatzikelis shuns the mainstream tourist trade and sticks to noticeable quality. The shellfish excel. Look for mussels, scallops with garlic butter and *kefalotyri* cheese, fresh clams or sea urchin roe. Divine!

New Town

To Steki tou Tsima (Map p280; ☎ 22410 74390; Peloponisou 22; mezedhes €5-7) To Steki is an unpretentious and totally untouristy fish restaurant on the south side of Old Town. Sample from an imaginative, and occasionally unusual, array of fish such, as *yermanos* (leatherback) and shellfish-based mezedhes: try grooved *fouskes* (sea squirts) to be different!

To Meltemi (Map p280; ☎ 22410 30480; cnr Plateia Kountourioti & Rodou; mains €6-13) Unusual in that the New Town sports virtually no beachside tavernas, Meltemi occupies a prime spot just north of Mandraki harbour. Dishes run a predictable gamut of fish and grills, while the oven-baked feta and an original 'Meltemi salad' are worth sampling. Piped music and nautical memorabilia complete the scene.

Drinking & Entertainment
OLD TOWN

Feelings run strong from Old Town locals about noise pollution, so there is an ongoing campaign to move disco-style bars out of the walls. What will remain are quieter, talk-oriented venues like the following options.

Kafe Besara (Map p282; ☎ 22410 30363; Sofokleous 11-12) This Aussie-owned bar is one of the Old Town's liveliest, and a great place to hang out for gossip, coffee and cheer.

Mango Cafe Bar (Map p282; ☎ 22410 24877; Plateia Dorieos 3) This bar claims to have the cheapest drinks in the Old Town, as well as internet access (see p281), and is the preferred haunt of local expats, scuba divers and die-hard travellers.

Resalto Club (Map p282; ☎ 22410 20520; Plateia Damagitou; ☾ 11pm-late) This indoor Greek music centre features live music on weekends. The repertoire ranges from *entehna* (artistic compositional) to *laïka* (urban popular music) to the ever-present *rembetika* (Greek blues).

Sound & Light Show (Map p282; ☎ 22410 21922; www.hellenicfestival.gr; admission €7) This impressive show takes place from Monday to Saturday next to the walls of the Old Town, off Plateia Rimini and near the Amboise Gate. English-language sessions are staggered, but in general begin at either 9.15pm or 11.15pm. Other languages offered are French, German and Swedish.

NEW TOWN

There is a rash of discos and raucous bars in the New Town. The two main areas are Alexandrou Diakou and Orfanidou, where Western music blares from every establishment.

Down Under Bar (Map p280; ☎ 22410 32982; Orfanidou 37) For a wild night of dancing on the bar, make for this Aussie-influenced watering hole.

Red Lion (Map p280; Orfanidou 9) For something more subdued, this bar has the relaxed atmosphere of a British pub. Ron and Vasilis will gladly answer questions about Rhodes for the price of a drink.

Colorado Entertainment Centre (Map p280; ☎ 22410 75120; Orfanidou 57) The Colorado consists of six venues in one – Studio Fame, Heaven Club R&B, Colorado Live, Förfesten, Swedco Café and IN 4 U Music Bar – and is more fun than you can shake your rear end at.

Shopping

Look out for gold and silver jewellery, leather goods and ceramics in the Old Town. Shoes are also a good buy, with styles not always found back home.

Manuel Music Center (Map p280; ☎ 22410 28266; 25 Martiou 10-13) All the latest CDs and DVDs are on sale here, including good-quality Greek releases not normally heard or bought by tourists.

Getting Around

Local buses leave from the **urban bus stop** (Map p280; Mandraki). Bus 2 goes to Analipsi, bus 3 to Rodini, bus 4 to Agios Dimitrios and bus 5 to Monte Smith. You can buy tickets at the kiosk on Mandraki.

EASTERN RHODES

Rhodes' best beaches are along the east coast. There are frequent buses to Lindos, but some of the other beaches are a bit of a hike from the road. It's possible to find uncrowded stretches of coast even in high season.

Kalithea Thermi (admission €2.50), 10km from Rhodes Town, is a restored Italian-built spa. Within the complex are renovated colonnades, domed ceilings and mosaic floors. There is shaded and sheltered swimming available. Buses from Rhodes Town stop opposite the turn-off to the spa. The beach is used by Rhodes' diving schools (see p284). To the right there's a small sandy beach (with a snack bar); take the track that veers right from the turn-off to the spa.

Ladiko Beach, touted locally as 'Anthony Quinn Beach', is in fact two back-to-back coves with a pebbly beach on the north side and volcanic rock platforms on the south. The swimming is good, though the water is noticeably colder and development is relatively low-key.

At Kolymbia, further down the coast, a right turn leads to over 4km of pine-fringed road to the **Epta Piges** (Seven Springs), a beautiful cool, shady valley where a lake fed by springs can be reached either along a path or through a tunnel. This is a popular tourist attraction in its own right. There are no buses to Epta Piges, so take a Lindos bus and get off at the turn-off.

Back on the coast, **Kolymbia** and **Tsambika** are sandy but somewhat crowded beaches. A steep road (signposted) leads inland 1.5km to **Moni Tsambikas**, from where there are terrific views. The monastery is a place of pilgrimage for childless women. On 18 September, the monastery's festival day, women climb up to it on their knees and then pray to conceive.

Arhangelos, 4km further on and inland, is a large agricultural village with a tradition of carpet weaving and making goatskin boots by hand. Just before Arhangelos there is a turn-off to **Stegna Beach**, and just after to the idyllic sandy cove of **Agathi**, perhaps the best of the bunch along this coastline. Agathi has three beach restaurants to choose from. The 15th-century **Castle of Faraklos**, above Agathi, was a prison for recalcitrant knights and the island's last stronghold to fall to the Turks. The somnolent fishing port of **Haraki**, just south of the castle, has a pebble and sand beach – not the best for swimming. There are more beaches between here and Vlyha Bay, 2km north of Lindos.

Lindos Λίνδος
pop 1091

Lindos is unquestionably the next most popular tourist destination on Rhodes after the Old Town. Excursion boats set sail daily from Mandraki Harbour and buses from resort hotels to disgorge their willing charges an hour or two later at this once quiet and pretty village with its twin bays. Today Lindos is a pretty *and* busy village, or at least it is between 10am and 4pm when most of the day-trippers congregate. There are local moves afoot to restore some of the original dignity of Lindos, including a ban on rooftop evening dining – a practice that was considered until recently a *de rigueur* experience for visitors to the village.

The village is a showpiece of dazzling white **17th-century houses**, many boasting courtyards with *hohlakia* (black-and-white pebble mosaic

DODECANESE

floors). Once the dwellings of wealthy admirals, many have been bought and restored by foreign celebrities. The teeming main thoroughfares are lined with tourist shops and cafés, so you need to explore the labyrinthine alleyways on foot to fully appreciate the place.

Lindos is the most famous of the ancient cities of the Dodecanese, and was an important Doric settlement because of its excellent vantage point and good harbour. It was first established around 2000 BC and is overlaid with a conglomeration of Byzantine, Frankish and Turkish remains.

After the founding of the city of Rhodes, Lindos declined in commercial importance, but remained an important place of worship. The ubiquitous St Paul landed here en route to Rome. The Byzantine fortress was strengthened by the knights, and also used by the Turks.

The 15th-century Church of Agios Ioannis, in the Acropolis, is festooned with 18th-century frescoes.

ORIENTATION & INFORMATION

The village is totally pedestrianised. All vehicular traffic terminates on the central square of Plateia Eleftherias, from where the main drag, Acropolis, begins. The donkey terminus, for rides up to the Acropolis, is a little way along here. Turn right at the donkey terminus to reach the post office, after 50m.

By the donkey terminus is the Commercial Bank of Greece, with an ATM. The National Bank of Greece, located on the street opposite the Church of Agia Panagia, also has an ATM.

Lindianet (☎ 22440 32142; per hr €3.60; ⏰ 9am-9pm) Internet access plus ethernet cable connection for laptop owners. In lower village.

Lindos Laundry (☎ 22440 31333; Acropolis; per load €7.50) Laundry service and second-hand English books.

Lindos Sun Tours (☎ 22440 31333; Acropolis) Has room-letting services; also rents cars and motorcycles.

Municipal Tourist Office (☎ 22440 31900; Plateia Eleftherias; ⏰ 7.30am-9pm) Helpful, although too few staff, too many tourists. You may have to wait a while.

www.lindos-holiday.com A handy private website with a number of alternative villa accommodation options.

SIGHTS
Acropolis of Lindos

Spectacularly perched atop a 116m-high rock is the **Acropolis** (☎ 22440 31258; admission €6;

⏰ 8.30am-2.40pm Tue-Sun Sep-May, until 6pm Tue-Sun Jun-Aug). It's a strenuous 10-minute climb to the well-signposted entrance gate. Once inside, a flight of steps leads to a large square. On the left (facing the next flight of steps) is a trireme, hewn out of the rock by the sculptor Pythocretes; a statue of Hagesandros, priest of Poseidon, originally stood on the deck of the ship. At the top of the steps ahead you enter the Acropolis via a vaulted corridor. At the other end, turn sharp left through an enclosed room to reach a row of storerooms on the right. The stairway on the right leads to the remains of a 20-columned **Hellenistic stoa** (200 BC). The Byzantine **Church of Agios Ioannis** is to the right of this stairway. The wide stairway behind the stoa leads to a 5th-century-BC propylaeum, beyond which is the 4th-century **Temple to Athena**, the site's most important ancient ruin. Athena was worshipped on Lindos as early as the 10th century BC, and this temple has replaced earlier ones on the site. From its far side there are splendid views of Lindos village and its beach.

Donkey rides to the Acropolis cost €5 one way – be aware that the poor creatures should not be carrying anyone over 50kg (112lbs), though this stipulation is rarely enforced. Better still; exercise your legs.

SLEEPING

Accommodation can be expensive, hard to find or already reserved, as much is pre-booked. Budget accommodation is limited essentially to one remaining place.

Pension Electra (☎ 22440 31266; s/d €40/50;) Your only budget option. Electra has an expansive and popular roof terrace with superb views and a beautiful shady garden. Rooms all have fridges and there is a communal kitchen. Follow the donkey route to find it.

Filoxenia Guesthouse (☎ 22440 31266; www.lindos -filoxenia.com; d/ste incl breakfast €95/130;) Consisting of five double rooms and three suites, these exceptionally tastefully decorated rooms inside a traditional house make for a cosy midrange choice.

EATING

Kalypso (☎ 22440 31669; mains €7-7.50) Set in one of Lindos' historic buildings in the lower village, Kalypso is one of the better dining choices. Try either sausages in mustard, pork in a pot with oregano wine and spices (*hirino stam-*

nato), or rabbit stew in red wine with pearl onions.

Mavrikos (☎ 22440 31232; mains €7-10) Right by the bus and taxi terminal, Mavrikos is Lindos' longest established and most respected restaurant. The extensive menu contains all the classic Greek dishes. In addition you should look out for individual creations, such as the fillet of port in kumquat sauce, or the chicken with fenugreek, saffron and pickled lemons.

WESTERN RHODES

Western Rhodes is greener and more forested than the east coast, but it's more exposed to winds so the sea tends to be rough, and the beaches are mostly of pebbles or stones. Nevertheless, tourist development has made strong inroads in the suburb resorts of Ixia, Trianda and Kremasti. Paradisi, despite being next to the airport, has retained some of the feel of a traditional village.

Ancient Ialysos Αρχαία Ιαλυσός

Like Lindos, Ialysos, 10km south of Rhodes Town, is a hotchpotch of Doric, Byzantine and medieval remains. The Doric city was built on Filerimos Hill, an excellent vantage point, and attracted successive invaders over the years. The only ancient remains are the foundations of a 3rd-century-BC temple and a restored 4th-century-BC fountain. Also at the site are the **Monastery of Our Lady** and the **Chapel of Agios Georgios**.

The ruined **fortress** (adult €4; ☒ 8am-5pm Tue-Sun) was used by Süleyman the Magnificent during his siege of Rhodes Town. No buses go to ancient Ialysos. The airport bus stops at Trianda, on the coast, from where Ialysos is 5km inland.

Ancient Kamiros Αρχαία Κάμειρος

The extensive **ruins** (adult €4; ☒ 8am-5pm Tue-Sun) of the Doric city of Kamiros stand on a hillside above the west coast, 34km south of Rhodes Town. The ancient city, known for its figs, oil and wine, reached the height of its powers in the 6th century BC. By the 4th century BC it had been superseded by Rhodes. Most of the city was destroyed by earthquakes in 226 and 142 BC, but the layout is still easily discernible.

From the entrance walk straight ahead and down the steps. The semicircular rostrum on the right is where officials made speeches to the public. Opposite are the remains of a **Doric**

temple, with one column still standing. The area next to it, with a row of intact columns, was probably where the public watched priests performing rites in the temple. Ascend the wide stairway to the ancient city's main street. Opposite the top of the stairs is one of the best preserved of the **Hellenistic houses** that once lined the street. Walk along the street, ascend three flights of steps and continue ahead to the ruins of the 3rd-century **great stoa**, which had a 206m portico supported by two rows of Doric columns. It was built on top of a huge 6th-century cistern that supplied the houses with rainwater through an advanced drainage system. Behind the stoa, at the city's highest point, stood the **Temple to Athena**, with terrific views inland.

Buses from Rhodes Town to Kamiros stop on the coast road, 1km from the site.

Ancient Kamiros to Monolithos
Αρχαία Κάμειρος προς Μονόλιθο

Skala Kamirou, 13.5km south of ancient Kamiros, is a fairly unremarkable place sporting a few market gardens, a scattering of tavernas and a petrol station. More importantly, it serves as the access port for travellers heading to and from the island of Halki (p291). The road south from here to Monolithos has some of the island's most impressive scenery. From Skala Kamirou the road winds uphill, with great views across to Halki. This is just a taste of what's to come at the ruined 16th-century **Castle of Kastellos**, reached by taking a rough turn-off from the main road, 2km beyond Skala Kamirou. There is a left fork to the wine-making area of Embonas (p291) 8km further on. The main road continues for another 9km to **Siana**, a picturesque village below Mt Akramytis (825m), famed for its honey and *souma* – a brew made from seasonal fruit, similar to Cretan *raki* (distilled grape spirit).

The village of Monolithos, 5km beyond Siana, has the spectacularly sited 15th-century **Castle of Monolithos** perched on a sheer 240m-high rock and reached via a dirt track. To enter, climb through the hole in the wall. Continuing along this track, bear right at the fork for **Moni Agiou Georgiou**, or left for the very pleasant shingled **Fourni Beach**.

Most people come this way en route to Halki via the afternoon caïque, or on a round-island tour. While waiting for the ferry take a relaxed lunch at **O Loukas** (☎ 22460 31271; mains

€5-8), the closest taverna to the ferry jetty. The menu is limited but is excellent value. The daily lunch specials – including beer or wine – are €13.

SOUTHERN RHODES

South of Lindos, Rhodes becomes progressively less developed. Although **Pefki**, 2km south of Lindos, does attract package tourists, it's still possible to escape them, away from the main beach.

Lardos is a pleasant village 6km west of Lindos and 2km inland from Lardos Beach. From the far side of Lardos a right turn leads in 4km to **Moni Agias Ypsenis** (Monastery of Our Lady) through hilly, green countryside.

Heading south from Lardos, don't miss the almost hidden **Glystra Beach**, 4km south along the coast road. This diminutive bay is one of the best swimming spots along the whole eastern coastline.

The well-watered village of **Laerma** is 12km northwest of Lardos. From here it's another 5km to the beautifully sited 9th-century **Moni Tharri**, the island's first monastery, which has been re-established as a monastic community. It contains some fine 13th-century frescoes and is worth a visit.

Asklipieio, 8km north of Gennadi, is an unspoilt village with the ruins of yet another castle and the 11th-century **Church of Kimisis Theotokou**, which has fine Byzantine wall paintings.

Gennadi Γεννάδι

pop 655

Gennadi (ye-*nah*-dhi), 13km south of Lardos, is an attractive, largely untouched agricultural, seaside village masquerading as a holiday centre. For independent travellers it's probably the best base for a protracted stay in the south. The village itself, a patchwork of narrow streets and whitewashed houses, is set several hundred metres back from the beach.

There's a few sleeping and eating choices. **Effie's Dreams Apartments** (☎ 22440 43410; www .effiesdreams.com; d/tr €54/58; 🔀 💻) offers both. It is right by an enormous 800-year-old mulberry tree and has modern, spotlessly clean studios with lovely rural and sea vistas from the communal balcony. The friendly Greek-Australian owners will meet you if you call ahead. Below the apartments, **Effie's Dream Cafe Bar** (☎ 22440 43410; snacks €3-5) serves drinks

and filling snacks, such as country-style sausage with onions and peppers.

I Kouzina tis Mamas (☎ 22440 43547; pasta €5-6) on the main street specialises in pizza and pasta, as well as a wide range of Greek grills.

Gennadi to Prasonisi Γεννάδι προς Πρασονήσι

From Gennadi an almost uninterrupted beach of pebbles, shingle and sand dunes extends down to **Plimmyri**, 11km south. It's easy to find deserted stretches.

From Plimmyri the main road continues to **Kattavia**, Rhodes' most southerly village. The 11km dirt road north to Messanagros winds through terrific scenery. From Kattavia a 10km road leads south to remote **Cape Prasonisi**, the island's southernmost point, once joined to Rhodes by a narrow sandy isthmus but now split by encroaching seas. It's a popular spot for windsurfing.

A good place to sleep is at **Lahania**, signposted 2km off the main highway, in **Studios Alonia** (☎ 22440 46027; studios €42; 🔀), where each self-catering studio has a kitchenette and fridge. These are owned by the proprietors of **Taverna Platanos** (☎ 22440 46027; mains €3-5), a relaxed taverna in the main square of Lahania that underwent a recent major facelift.

Down on Prasonisi, **Faros Taverna** (☎ 22440 91030; mains €5-8) is one of two tavernas on the beach. The food is uncomplicated and features grills and fish, while the comfortable rooms (doubles €40) attract a mainly windsurfing crowd.

South of Monolithos

Lonely and exposed, Rhodes' southwest coast doesn't see as many visitors as other parts of the island. Forest fires in recent years have devastated many of the west-facing hillsides and there is a general end-of-the-world feeling about the whole region.

The beaches south of Monolithos are prone to strong winds. From the important crossroads village of **Apolakkia**, 10km south of Monolithos, a road crosses the island to Gennadi, passing through the unspoilt villages of **Arnitha** and **Vati** with an optional detour to **Istrios** and **Profilia**, where you can dine in rustic comfort at **To Limeri tou Listi** (☎ 22440 61578; mains €6-8) on dishes such as rooster in red-wine sauce or other solid country fare.

A turn-off to the left, 7km south of Apolakkia, leads to the 18th-century **Moni Skiadi**.

It's a serene place with terrific views down to the coast, and there is free basic accommodation for visitors.

THE INTERIOR

The east–west roads that cross the island have great scenery and very little traffic. If you have transport, they're well worth exploring. It's also good cycling territory if you have a suitably geared bicycle.

Petaloudes Πεταλούδες

Known as the Valley of the Butterflies, **Petaloudes** (adult €1-3; 8.30am-sunset 1 May-30 Sep) is one of the more popular 'sights' on the package-tour itinerary. It's reached along a 6km turn-off from the west-coast road, 2.5km south of Paradisi.

The so-called 'butterflies' are in fact strikingly coloured moths (*Callimorpha quadripunctarea*) that are lured to this gorge of rustic footbridges, streams and pools by the scent of the resin exuded by the storax trees. While the moths have undoubtedly benefited from having a reserve of their own, there is an inevitable trade-off as they become an object of human curiosity. So regardless of what you may see other people doing, do not clap your hands or make any noises to disturb the butterflies as their numbers are under threat due to such unwanted noise disturbance.

Around Petaloudes

From Petaloudes a winding cross-island road leads to the 18th-century **Moni Kalopetras**, built by Alexander Ypsilandis, the grandfather of the Greek freedom fighter. This same road leads north across the central mountain spine of roads through a rather dry landscape full of olive trees to the pretty village of **Psinthos**, which makes for a very pleasant lunch break.

From Psinthos you can choose to loop back to Rhodes Town (22km), via a fast but undistinguished direct route passing through **Kalythies**, or head further south and pick up the very pretty cross-island route from **Kolymbia** to **Salakos**.

Just off the main square in Psinthos you'll find the well-regarded **Pigi Fasouli Estiatorio** (22410 50071; mains €5-7), where you dine under cool plane trees next to running water – all to the sound of incessant cicadas. Good dishes on offer are goat and chickpeas, pork and lima beans, and small pies called *pitaroudia*.

Wine Country

From Salakos you may detour to **Embonas** on the slopes of Mt Attavyros (1215m), the island's highest mountain. Embonas is the wine capital of Rhodes and produces some of the island's best tipples. The red Cava Emery, or Zacosta and white Villare are good choices. You can taste and buy them at **Emery Winery** (22410 41208; www.emery.gr; admission free; 9.30am-3.30pm) in Embonas.

Embonas is no great shakes itself, despite being touted by the tourism authorities as a 'traditional village'. However, **Bakis** (22460 41442; mains €5-8) on the main square is a good spot to try some grills from local meat. The *païdakia* (spare-rib chops), or the chunky *kondosouvli* (Cypriot-style spit-roast kebabs) are particularly succulent.

You may nonetheless wish to detour around Mt Attavyros to **Agios Isidoros**, 14km south of Embonas, a prettier and still unspoilt wine-producing village that you can visit en route to Siana.

HALKI ΧΑΛΚΗ

pop 313

The dry rocky island of Halki (*hal-ki*) lies almost unnoticed, piggybacked off the western flank of its larger neighbour Rhodes. Out of reach of most day-trip excursions from Rhodes, Halki sees a steady flow of visitors who come for its relaxation value. Almost abandoned at the turn of the 20th century when the sponge-fishing industry took a nose dive, Halki existed in almost forgotten silence until the vacation boom of the 1970s and 1980s saw its fortunes rise once more.

Most people come to stay in restored stone villas that once belonged to sea captains. There's not a lot to do other than chill out, read, contemplate, eat, swim and socialise. There's little traffic on the island and most people walk to where they want to go. Admittedly, the palpable foreign element has sanitised the Greek element somewhat but Halki still has soul – and a Greek one at that.

If you are a bibliophile, a poet, a writer, spiritually motivated or incurably romantic, Halki is ideal for you.

DODECANESE

HALKI

0 — 3 km
0 — 2 miles

AEGEAN SEA

Areta Beach

Tarpon Springs Blvd

Halki

Horio

Kania Beach

Moni Agiou Ioanni

Knights of St John Castle

Emborios

Yiali Cove

Yiali Beach

Podamos Beach

Trahia Beach

Ftenagia Beach

To Rhodes (10km)

KARPATHIAN SEA

To Karpathos (50km);
Kasos (110km);
Crete (160km);
Piraeus (400km)

Getting There & Away

CAÏQUE & BUS

There is a daily local ferry to Halki at 2.30pm from Skala Kamirou (€8.50, 1½ hours) on Rhodes. From Halki to Skala Kamirou the ferry leaves at 6am Monday to Friday and Sunday, 7am on Saturday. A bus to Rhodes Town connects with the arriving ferry at 7.40am and at 9.30am on Saturday. There is no bus on Sunday.

Walk 150m from the Skala Kamirou ferry quay to the main road to find the bus stop. The two ferries operating the route are the **Nissos Halki** (☎ 6973460968) and the **Nikos Express** (☎ 6945743539).

FERRY

Ferries serves Halki three times weekly in either direction, with services to Rhodes (€8, two hours), Pigadia on Karpathos (€11.50, three hours), Sitia on Crete (€20, 7½ hours), Santorini (€27, 15 hours) and Piraeus (€34, 22 hours).

A Nisyros–Tilos–Rhodes–Halki service commenced at the time of writing with the small *Panagia Spiliani*. Tickets are available from Chalki Tours and Zifos Travel in Emborios (see right).

Getting Around

There is a minibus that runs hourly from Emborios to and from Moni Agiou Ioanni (€2) and stops in between. There is also an overpriced **taxi** (☎ 6944434429; Emborios), that charges

€4 to Pondamos Beach from Emborios, €6.50 to Ftenagia Beach and €33 return to Moni Agiou Ioanni.

There are no rental cars or motorcycles, but there is a water taxi to the main beaches and excursions to the island of Alimia (€30). Additionally, day excursions are run on Sundays in summer to Tilos (€23) by the two Skala Kamirou ferries (see left).

EMBORIOS ΕΜΠΟΡΕΙΟΣ

pop 52

The picturesque port village of Emborios resembles Gialos on Symi, but on a smaller scale. The port is draped around a narrow horseshoe bay, and surrounded by former sea captains' mansions – some renovated, some in a state of disrepair, yet slowly being renovated. They garland the petite, crystal-blue harbour waters in an almost externally voyeuristic display of blue- and brown-shuttered windows. Cars are banned from the harbour once the ferries have come and gone, so the waterside always enjoys a relaxing, vehicle-free setting.

Orientation & Information

Boats arrive at the middle of Emborios. Most commercial services and accommodation options are within 200m of the harbour. The free quarterly newspaper the *Halki Visitor*, available on the island from the two travel agencies – among other outlets – is a good source of local information.

There's a reliable DodecNet ATM in a stand-alone booth on the harbour itself.

Chalki Tours (☎ 22460 45281; fax 22460 45219) For assistance on accommodation, travel, excursions and currency exchange.

Diafora (☎ 22460 45061; per 30min €6) Internet access; behind the bakery in Emborios.

Doctor (☎ 22460 45206; ☒ 9am-noon & 6-8pm Mon-Fri) Can be contacted on call.

Port police (☎ 22460 45220) On the harbour.

Post office (☒ 9am-1.30pm Mon-Fri) On the harbour.

www.chalki.gr A helpful reference point.

www.halkivisitor.com A useful website hosted by the local newspaper.

Zifos Travel (☎ 22460 45028; zifos-travel@rho.forthnet .gr) For assistance on accommodation, travel, excursions and currency exchange.

Sights

Halki's main visual feature are the old **mansions** that festoon the harbour. Many have been, or are being, restored to their former glory, while others are in a complete state of disrepair, overgrown with weeds and decrepit. Either way they give Halki that picturesque look that visitors so appreciate.

The impressive stone **clock tower** at the southern side of the harbour is a gift from the Halkiots of Florida. While the clock tower may look resolutely impressive, don't rely on it for the time; each of the four faces is stuck on a different hour of the day.

The **Church of Agios Nikolaos** has the tallest belfry in the Dodecanese and boasts a particularly well-made and impressive pebbled courtyard on the east side. There is a small upstairs **museum** (adult €2; 6-7pm Mon & Fri, 11am-noon Sun) with ecclesiastical exhibits.

Sleeping

Most villa and studio accommodation is pre-booked by foreign tour companies. What little private accommodation there is can be in high demand, so bookings are best. There is no formal hotel as yet on the island, though the old sponge factory on the south side of the harbour was due to open by the time of this book's publication.

Avgi Rooms (22460 45045; s/d €30-40) Slap-bang in the middle of the harbour next to the minimarket are a clutch of simple rooms for travel-weary voyagers arriving from an afternoon or evening ferry. Call ahead to be sure of a bed.

Captain's House (/fax 22460 45201; captainshouse@ath.forthnet.gr; d €35-40) This homey 19th-century house, with period furniture and a tranquil tree-shaded garden, is perhaps the most comfortable place to stay for solo travellers. Bookings are always recommeded.

Mouthouria (22460 45071; halkifrances@yahoo .co.uk; house €65-95, minimum stay 2 nights) Rent a whole renovated captain's house that can accommodate up to six people. It's spacious, fully equipped, has superb south-side harbour views, and is ideal for longer stays and romantic getaways.

our pick **Villa Praxithea** (69724 27272; www.villapraxithea.com; apt €140-210) If you like to be close to the water, check out this set of fully furnished high-ceilinged and wooden-floored rooms. Available as individual rooms or as an apartment package, they are a 200m hike to the right of the port jetty. Owned by the same family as Villa Aristea, it's ideal for couples or families with up to two children.

Eating

Mavri Thalassa (22460 45021; mains €4-6) This restaurant at the south side of the harbour is generally well regarded and offers fresh seafood dishes. The whole grilled calamari, when available fresh, is delicate and soft, while the local, minuscule Halki shrimps – eaten whole – are initially crunchy and then beautifully succulent.

Maria's Taverna (22460 45300; mains €4-7) Dishes up solidly satisfying and reliable home-cooked fare, with Halki lamb stew being the house speciality and spaghetti bolognese well recommended. Its drawcard is its central location under the few shady trees left in the port village.

Avra (69451 48196; mains €4-7) Avra offers fast, efficient service and a comprehensive and tempting mezes and mains menu. The Georgian owners serve excellent chicken dishes, while Halki shrimps downed with draught white wine will assuage jaded travel taste buds.

Remezzo (22460 45010; mains €5-7) Touting itself as a pizza and pasta joint, its menu transcends Italian offerings. The Mexican bean and corn-charged salad gives respite from the omnipresent 'Greek salad' while the baked *halvas* and apple desert will caress post-prandial taste buds.

AROUND HALKI

Podamos Beach is the closest and the best beach, located 1km from Emborios in the direction of Horio. The narrowish beach is sandy and the water is shallow – ideal for kids. For food you can try the **Podamos Beach Taverna** (22460 45295; mains €5-7; lunch), which also offers four basic rooms. **Ftenagia Beach**, past the headland and 500m to the south of Emborios, is a mite short in the sand stakes, but there is excellent rock swimming and it offers good snorkelling. The **Ftenagia Beach Taverna** (6945998333; mains €5-7; lunch & dinner) is a cosy waterside eatery with friendly service and a range of satisfying lunch and dinner choices.

Horio, a 30-minute walk along Tarpon Springs Blvd from Emborios, was once a thriving community of 3000 people, but it's now almost completely derelict, bar a small church and a few renovated structures. A barely perceptible path leads from Horio's churchyard to a **Knights of St John castle**, with spectacular views.

Moni Agiou Ioanni is a two-hour, unshaded 8km walk along a broad concrete road from Horio. The church and courtyard, protected by the shade of an enormous cypress tree, is a quiet, tranquil place, but it comes alive each year on 28 and 29 August during the feast of the church's patron, St John.

KARPATHOS
ΚΑΡΠΑΘΟΣ

pop 6084

Like an elongated bridge between Rhodes and Crete, Karpathos (*kar*-pa-thos) offers a winning mix of size, scenery, beach scenes, food and culture, making a visit to this southern Dodecanese destination a winner. While off the beaten track somewhat, the island is well served by transport and even attracts a slow but steady trail of packaged visitors.

It's an island with an anonymous history and doesn't feature prominently in the chronicles of the region. Many of its inhabitants migrated to the USA, from where they slowly trickle back and invest their overseas earnings into their homeland. It's an island with a pleasant feel – a comfortable mix of mountain, sea and plains. It showcases some stunning beaches with excellent diving, while windsurfing devotees flock to its windy southern shores to engage in fast and furious water fun.

The north of the island is an almost separate destination. Isolated for years from the south by an atrocious and precipitous road, it stubbornly survives and proudly sports a village that is as culturally idiosyncratic as anywhere in the Aegean.

Getting There & Away
AIR

In summer there are 10 flights weekly to and from Athens (€73), seven weekly to Kasos (€25, five minutes) and Sitia (€47, one hour), and up to three daily to Rhodes (€28, 25 minutes). **Olympic Airlines** (☎ 22450 22150; www.olympic airlines.com) is on the central square in Pigadia. The airport is 13km southwest of Pigadia.

FERRY

LANE Lines of Crete provides three services weekly to Rhodes (€18.50, four hours) via Halki (€11.50, three hours), as well as to Piraeus

KARPATHOS

0   6 km
0   4 miles

Karpathos Strait

Cape Parasponi

Saria

Tristomo

Cape Vroukounda   Vroukounda

Moni Agiou Ioanni

Avlona   Vananda Beach

Moni Agiou Konstantinou   Diafani

To Halki (50km); Rhodes (60km)

Mt Profitis Ilias (716m)   Olymbos

SEA OF CRETE

Agios Minas

Spoa

Mesohori   Agios Nikolaos

Apella Beach   Excursion Boat

Karpathos

Kyra Panagia Beach

Roman Cistern   Mertonas   Kato Lakos Beach

Lefkos

Kali Limni (1215m)   Aperi   Ahata Beach

Volada

Adia   Othos

Cape Proni   Pyles

Vrondi Bay

Kamarakia Beach

Agios Georgios Beach   Menetes

Agios Nikolaos Beach   Finiki   Pigadia

Arkasa   Ammoopi   Cape Volakas

Cape Agios Theodoros

Afiartis Bay

Cape Akrotiri   Cape Lingi

Cape Kastello

To Kasos (10km); Crete (80km); Piraeus (420km)

DODECANESE

(€33, 18½ hours) via Kasos (€7.50, 1½ hours), Sitia (€17, 4¼ hours), Agios Nikolaos (€20, seven hours), Milos (€33, 13 hours) and Santorini (€26, 10 hours).

Tickets can be bought from **Possi Travel** (☎ 22450 22235; possitvl@hotmail.com; Apodimon Karpathion) in Pigadia.

Getting Around
TO/FROM THE AIRPORT
There is no airport bus. Travellers must take a taxi (€15) or seek independent transport.

BUS
Pigadia is the transport hub of the island; a schedule is posted at the **bus terminus** (☎ 22450 22338; M Mattheou). Buses (€1.50 to €2) serve most of the settlements in southern Karpathos, including the west-coast beaches. There is no bus between Pigadia and Olymbos or Diafani in the north, but in summer a bus meets the excursion boats from Pigadia at Diafani and connects to Olymbos.

CAR, MOTORCYCLE & BICYCLE
On the east side of Pigadia, **Rent a Car Circle** (☎ 22450 22690; 28 Oktovriou) rents cars and motorcycles. **Possi Travel** (☎ 22450 22148; possitvl@hotmail .com; Apodimon Karpathion) also arranges car rental.

The precipitous, and at times hairy, 19.5km stretch of road from Spoa to Olymbos is being slowly graded and will one day be sealed. You can drive it with care; do not tackle this road by motorcycle or scooter. If you rent a vehicle and plan to drive to Olymbos, opt for a small jeep and fill up your tank before you leave.

EXCURSION BOAT
In summer there is a daily excursion boat from Pigadia to Diafani (return including the bus to Olymbos €20, one way excluding the bus to Olymbos €8). There are also frequent boats to the beaches of Kyra Panagia and Apella (€10). Tickets can be bought at the quay.

From Diafani, excursion boats go to nearby beaches and occasionally to the uninhabited islet of Saria, where there are some Byzantine remains. See p299 for details.

TAXI
Pigadia's **taxi rank** (☎ 22450 22705; Dimokratias) is close to the centre of town. A price list is displayed. A taxi to Ammoöpi costs €8, the airport €15, Arkasa and Pyles €16, and Kyra Panagia €20.

PIGADIA ΠΗΓΑΔΙΑ
pop 1692
After being spoilt with the picturesque harbours of Symi, Chalki and Kastellorizo, Pigadia (pi-*gha*-dhi-ya), Karpathos' capital and main port, does not immediately grab your attention. It's a modern town and is attractive enough in its own way, but without any eminent buildings or sites. Much of the cement-based architecture was erected during a boom in the 1960s and '70s. Upon further investigation, however, Pigadia is a pleasant and busy town. It is built on the edge of **Vrondi Bay**, a 4km-long sandy beach where you can rent water-sports equipment. A 2km walk southwest along the beach are the remains of the early Christian **Basilica of Agia Fotini**.

Orientation & Information
The ferry quay is at the northern end of the wide harbour. It's a short walk to the centre of Pigadia, which is punctuated by the main street, Apodimon Karpathion. This in turn leads west to the central square of Plateia 5 Oktovriou.

Caffe Galileo Internet 2000 (☎ 22450 23606; Apodimon Karpathion; per hr €3; ☾ 9am-2pm & 6pm-1am) Offers internet access.

National Bank of Greece (Apodimon Karpathion) Has an ATM.

NewsStand (☎ 22450 22718; Dimokratias) Sells foreign newspapers and magazines.

Police (☎ 22450 22224) Near the hospital at the western end of town.

Possi Travel (☎ 22450 22148; possitvl@hotmail.com; Apodimon Karpathion) The main travel agency for ferry and air tickets.

Post office (Ethnikis Andistasis) Near the hospital.

Pot Pourri (☎ 22450 29073; Apodimon Karpathion; per hr €3; ☾ 7am-1am) Offers internet access.

Tourist information office (☎ 22450 23835; ☾ Jul-Aug) In a kiosk in the middle of the seafront.

www.inkarpathos.com Mainly local information – mixed Greek and English.

www.karpathos.com General travel and island information in English.

Sleeping
There's plenty of accommodation in Pigadia; a few enterprising owners meet the boats.

Avra Hotel (☎ 22450 22388; fax 22450 23486; 28 Oktovriou 50; s/d €20/25) This E-class hotel has small but comfortable rooms with ceiling fan, fridge and a small common kitchen.

DODECANESE

Elias Rooms (☎ 22450 22446; www.eliasrooms.com; s/d €20/25, s/d apt €25/35; 🖥️) Cosy Elias Rooms is located in a quiet part of town with great views and a lot of convenience. Choose a room or a larger traditional apartment. Owner Ilias Hatzigeorgiou is a mine of local information.

Hotel Karpathos (☎ 22450 22347; fax 22450 22248; s/d €30/35; ❄️) Where budget takes precedence over complete comfort you might just give this C-class hotel a look-in. Appearing a tad old and jaded from the outside, the rooms inside are well-lit, airy and comfortable enough. It also has a TV and fridge.

Amarylis Hotel (☎ /fax 22450 22375; www.amarylis.gr; s/d €35/50; ❄️) In a quiet part of Pigadia is this C-class hotel, offering a mixture of airy and exceptionally clean studios and apartments.

All have kitchenette and TV, and at least half of them enjoy sea views.

Hotel Titania (☎ 22450 22144; www.titaniakarpathos .gr; s/d €40/55; ❄️) Handy for out-of-season travellers, the Titania is open all year. While the lobby looks a bit gloomy with its heavy, dated furniture, the rooms are of standard comfort and do have a fridge and a TV. Request a sea-view room if you can.

Odyssey Hotel (☎ 22450 23240; www.odyssey-kar pathos.gr; studios €50/65 ❄️) When self-catering is your preferred option, look no further than this tidy and welcoming complex set back in a quiet part of Pigadia. Owner Helen Stamatiadis offers a choice of small to capacious studios that can cater for between four and six people. They are well equipped, very comfort-

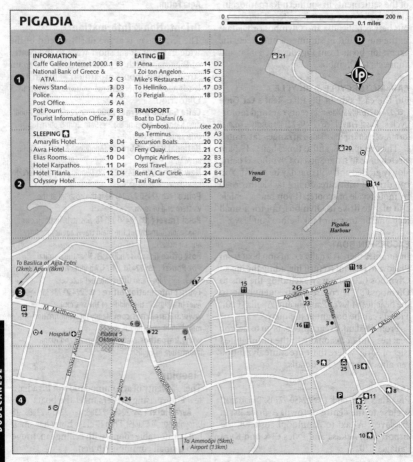

PIGADIA

0 — 200 m
0 — 0.1 miles

INFORMATION
Caffe Galileo Internet 2000..1 B3
National Bank of Greece &
    ATM.....................................2 C3
News Stand..............................3 D3
Police......................................4 A3
Post Office...............................5 A4
Pot Pourri................................6 B3
Tourist Information Office..7 B3

SLEEPING 🏠
Amaryllis Hotel........................8 D4
Avra Hotel................................9 D4
Elias Rooms............................10 D4
Hotel Karpathos.....................11 D4
Hotel Titania..........................12 D4
Odyssey Hotel........................13 D4

EATING 🍴
I Anna....................................14 D2
I Zoi ton Angelon.................15 C3
Mike's Restaurant................16 C3
To Helliniko..........................17 D3
To Perigiali...........................18 D3

TRANSPORT
Boat to Diafani (&
    Olymbos)..................(see 20)
Bus Terminus........................19 A3
Excursion Boats....................20 D2
Ferry Quay.............................21 C1
Olympic Airlines...................22 B3
Possi Travel...........................23 C3
Rent A Car Circle..................24 B4
Taxi Rank..............................25 D4

Vrondi Bay

Pigadia Harbour

To Basilica of Agia Fotni
(2km); Aperi (8km)

M. Mattheou

Hospital

Plateia 5
Oktovriou

Apodimon Karpathion

28 Oktovriou

To Ammoöpi (5km);
Airport (13km)

DODECANESE

able and, most importantly for a longer stay, have room to breathe.

Eating

There are plenty of choices when it comes to eating. The waterfront establishments tend to be hit and miss when it comes to quality, though there are some exceptions. *Makarounes* (home-made pasta cooked with cheese and onions) is the local speciality.

I Zoi ton Angelon (☎ 22450 22984; Apodimon Karpathion; mains €5-7.50) Overlooking the harbour and set around a balcony running along the building, this quirky little eatery does some top dishes. There's a vegetarian platter for meat avoiders. Then there's a rich and filling beef stew, runner beans in tomato sauce, sardines and an excellent spicy cheese salad.

To Perigiali (☎ 22450 22334; Apodimon Karpathion; mains €3-8) Lurking unobtrusively among its more commercial neighbours, this little *ouzerie* (place that serves ouzo and light snacks) is a cut above most. Fish mezedhes feature predominantly, though you might graze on the rich Karpathian salad with capers or sample some steamed snails.

Mike's Restaurant (☎ 22450 22727; grills €6-8) One of the longer-standing and more popular eateries, and now under the management of Manolis and Minas, Mike's serves consistently good, solid fare with bright service. Among the specials are chicken spaghetti and stuffed zucchini flowers.

I Anna (☎ 22450 22820; Apodimon Karpathion; mains €5.50-9) Ignore the fading picture menus and tacky restaurant sign and snap up Pigadia's freshest fish, caught daily off the owner's own boats. Other suggested dishes are fisherman's macaroni with octopus, shrimps and mussels, or the Karpathian sardines in oil.

our pick To Helliniko (☎ 22450 23932; Apodimon Karpathion; daily specials €5-11; 🕐 year-round) Boasting a pleasant outdoor terrace and a tasteful interior, the Helliniko is very popular. Check the daily specials board for the best deal. The Karpathian goat cooked in a tomato purée is particularly commendable, as is the hearty Karpathian salad, which includes egg and potato.

SOUTHERN KARPATHOS

Ammoöpi Αμμοöπή

If you are seeking sun and sand, and some of the best and clearest water for snorkelling in the whole of the Aegean, head for Ammoöpi

(amm-oh-oh-*pee*), 5km south of Pigadia. Ammoöpi is a scattered beach resort without any real centre or easily identifiable landmarks.

In addition to snorkelling, die-hard windsurfers in the know head for the broad **Afiartis Bay**, a further 8km south of Ammoöpi, to enjoy some world-class conditions. The bay supports windsurfing centres and caters for advanced surfers at the northern end and beginners in the sheltered Makrygialos Bay lagoon at the southern end. While most surfers come on package tours from Germany, casual 'blow-ins' are more than welcome. One particularly good outfit is **Pro Center** (☎ 22450 91062; www.chris-schill.com; Afiarti).

SLEEPING & EATING

All sleeping and eating recommendations are at the northern end of Ammoöpi. There is a pretty wide choice of options. The places to eat are rather scattered.

Hotel Sophia (☎ /fax 22450 81078; www.sophiahotel .gr; d/tr €40/47; 🅿 🏊) For starters, this is a quiet and comfortable midrange hotel at the northern end of the settlement.

Blue Sea Hotel (☎ /fax 22450 81097; huguette@rho .forthnet.gr; d/t incl breakfast €45/50) Just in front of Hotel Sophia and marginally better, this hotel has 27 comfortable double rooms, each with fridge and ceiling fan.

our pick Vardes (☎ /fax 22450 81111; www.hotel vardes.com; s/d €45/55; 🅿) For a really laid-back and relaxing choice try Vardes, a small block of tasteful, spacious and airy studios, set back against the hillside among a lush olive grove and a few banana palms. All have large, breezy rooms, shaded balcony, phone and TV.

Ammoöpi Taverna (☎ 22450 81138; mains €4-7) At the far northern end of Ammoöpi and right on the beach, the food here is uniformly good. Look for the daily specials – the clove-laced *mousakas* (sliced eggplant and mincemeat arranged in layers and baked) excels. There is a fairly genuine 'Greek music night' once a week.

Taverna Helios (☎ 22450 81148; mains €5-7) Just back from the main beach and handy for lunch after a swim, Helios offers Greek and international cuisine with large portions.

Menetes Μενετές
pop 450

Menetes (me-ne-*tes*) is perched precariously on top of a sheer cliff overlooking the rolling landscape leading to Pigadia, 8km distant.

DODECANESE

It's a picturesque, unspoilt village with pastel-coloured neoclassical houses lining its main street. Behind the main street are narrow, stepped alleyways that wind between more modest whitewashed dwellings. The village has a small but well-presented **museum** (admission free) on the right as you come in from Pigadia. Opening hours are upon request – the owner of Taverna Manolis will open it up for you.

There is only one place to stay and that's on the north side of Menetes; **Mike Rigas Domatia** (☎ 22450 81269; d/tr €20/25), signposted on the outside as 'Rigas Kato Nero'. Its eight rooms bask in a traditional flower-bedecked Karpathian house, caressed by a fruit and vegetable-filled garden and accompanied by a menagerie of languid dogs and cats.

Stop by **Taverna Manolis** (☎ 22450 81103; mains €5-7) for generous helpings of grilled meat, or take a break at **Dionysos Fiesta** (☎ 22450 81269; mains €5-7), specialising in local dishes, including an omelette made with artichokes and Karpathian sausages.

Top culinary marks go to **Pelagia Taverna** (☎ 22450 81135; mains €5-8), on the road down to (or up from) Ammoöpi, where free-range goat and lamb are on offer. Opt for the Karpathian salad, the local sheep's milk and white *manouri* cheese or the excellent mashed fava lentils served with raw onion.

Arkasa & Finiki Αρκάσα & Φοινίκι

The west coast is a little wilder than the Pigadia side, yet it has its own beauty. There are few settlements and only a few decent places to swim. Coming from Pigadia via Menetes you will come across the two main settlements. Arkasa (ar-*ka*-sa), 9km from Menetes, has morphed from being a traditional Karpathian village into a low-key resort of sorts. The village itself is set back from its beach annexe.

Follow a turn-off for 500m to the remains of the 5th-century **Basilica of Agia Sophia**, where two chapels stand amid mosaic fragments and columns. **Agios Nikolaos Beach** is just south across the headland from here.

The serene fishing village of Finiki (fi-*ni*-ki) lies 2km north of Arkasa. The best local swimming is at **Agios Georgios Beach** between Arkasa and Finiki, though the small, sandy and protected beach in Finiki itself is OK. **Kamarakia Beach**, signposted before Agios Georgios, is a narrow protected cove, but there are strong sea currents.

Sleeping is neat at **Glaros Studios** (☎ 22450 61015; fax 22450 61016; Agios Nikolaos; studios €55-60), right on Agios Nikolaos Beach. Done out in Karpathian style, the few studios have raised sofa-like beds and large terraces with sun beds that enjoy a cool sea breeze. There's a relaxed adjoining restaurant with a limited but satisfactory menu.

On the road to Finiki, **Eleni Studios** (☎ /fax 22450 61248; www.elenikarpathos.gr; Arkasa; apt €50; 🖳) has fully equipped and very tidy apartments built around a relaxing garden. There's an on-site bar, too, for sunset drinks.

In Finiki an obvious yet recommendable place to eat is the **Finiki View Taverna** (☎ 22450 61026; mains €5-7.50). Taking poll position on the location stakes overlooking the beach this place does look touristy, but it's Greek enough when it comes to the crunch. The whitebait, octopus salad or the caper salad are all excellent options.

Some 9km north of Finiki, just before the road winds uphill to Lefkos, are the secluded **Pine Tree Studios** (☎ 69773 69948; pinetree_adia@hotmail.com; Adia; d €35; 🖳). These comfortable studios with views over to Kasos make for a quiet rural retreat and include an excellent yet casual outdoor restaurant specialising in dishes cooked in a wood oven. Taste the *katsiki stifadho* (goat in red-wine sauce). The studios are equipped with fridge and kitchenette. Owner Nikos Papanikolaou will tell you about a therapeutic mineral water spring nearby. Don't miss it.

Walkers might want to hike up the **Flaskia Gorge**, or as an easier option hike to the happily named **Iliondas Beach**. Again Nikos Papanikolaou will provide details.

Lefkos Λευκός
pop 120

LeLefkosfkos (lef-*kos*), 13km north of Finiki and 2km down from the main coastal road, is a burgeoning resort centred on a series of attractive, sandy coves. In summer Lefkos can get crowded, but at other times it still has a rugged, all-mine feel about it.

Archaeology buffs may care to explore the underground remains of a **Roman cistern**, reached by heading up the approach road and looking for the brown-and-yellow sign on the left to the 'catacombs'.

Accommodation is often prebooked but you can almost always find a spot upon arrival. There are many options, among which a solid choice would have to be **Le Grand Bleu** (☎ /fax 22450 71400; www.legrandbleu-lefkos.gr; studio/apt €55/90; 🖵), a set of tastefully decorated studios and larger apartments fully equipped for easy self-catering; wi-fi should be available by the time you read this. It overlooks the curving Gialou Horafi middle beach.

Nearby and abutting the beach in the Frangolimnionas neighbourhood of Lefkos are the three separate blocks of **Aegean View Studios** (☎ /fax 22450 71462; studios €45), run by a Greek Australian. An uncomplicated and economical bet, all studios are airy and have modern kitchenettes.

Come dine time, head to the little harbour where, of the handful of tavernas, **Dramundana** (☎ 22450 71167; mains €5-8) is an unfussy, homey place with a dishes to look and pick. Fish cakes and fragrant chicken stand out. Better still, **Le Grand Bleu** (☎ /fax 22450 71400; mains €7.50-12) also boasts a commendable taverna. It offers a shady retreat from the beach, and is neat and flower-decked. Mezedhes include garlic mushrooms and a vegetarian-cooked *imam baïldi* (eggplant in oil with herbs), while the Karpathian mixed platter comprising sausages, cheese, capers and sardines will fill.

GETTING THERE & AROUND

There are daily buses to Lefkos and a taxi from Pigadia costs €24. Hitching can be slow as there is not much traffic.

Lefkos Rent A Car (☎ /fax 22450 71057; sissamis@hol .gr) is a reliable outlet with competitive prices: €30 a day in summer for a small car. Owner Nikos will deliver vehicles, free of charge, to anywhere in southern Karpathos.

NORTHERN KARPATHOS

Diafani Διαφάνι
pop 250

Diafani is Karpathos' small northern port, where scheduled ferries stop regularly and in summer an excursion boat arrives daily from Pigadia. It's a lazy indolent kind of place and is in stark contrast to its busy sister port, Pigadia, to the south. If you are visiting Olymbos by boat, you will pass through Diafani. In summer, buses meet the daily excursion boat and transport visitors to Olymbos. Otherwise, scheduled buses leave for Olymbos daily at 7.30am, 2.30pm and 5pm year-round.

There's no post office or ATM, so bring cash supplies with you. Currency-exchange facilities are available, however.

There's a fair smattering of accommodation choices. These include the comfortable **Balaskas Hotel** (☎ /fax 22450 51320; www.balaskashotel.com; s/d €30/40; 🔀), a pleasant option set back from the waterfront, where all rooms have fridge, TV and phone. On the waterfront itself, at the northern end, **Thalassa View Apartments** (☎ 6977620011; studios €35-45; 🔀) are modern and very comfortable, and handy for a quick swim off the pebbled harbour beach.

There are a number of places to dine along the waterfront. **Rahati** (☎ 22450 51200; mains €4-6.50) is a newish eatery with a line of organic dishes, such as green beans in tomato sauce, as well as octopus in red wine sauce and the more common fish options. **La Gorgona** (☎ 22450 51509; mains €4-7) is a casual, Italian-style café-restaurant with top-class coffee, snacks and a variety of pasta offerings.

You can take short excursion trips on the *Captain Manolis* out of Diafani to the remoter and otherwise inaccessible – other than on foot – reaches of Karpathos. The boat typically leaves for trips to the satellite island of **Saria** at around 10.30am.

Walkers may want to explore the region on foot. The Road Editions *1:60.000 Karpathos-Kasos* map (available in Pigadia) details several walking trails to the Hellenistic site of **Vrykounda** with its few remaining walls, via the agricultural village of **Avlona**, with a seasonal taverna, or to the sheltered bay and anchorage of **Tristomo**. Take all your food and water with you as there are no facilities up here. An alternative coastal track will bring you back via **Vananda Beach**, where there is a camping ground.

Olymbos Ολυμπος
pop 330

Clinging to the ridge of barren Mt Profitis Ilias (716m), and 4km inland from Diafani, Olymbos is ostensibly a living museum where, to this day, the inhabitants speak in a vernacular that contains some Doric words. Women are seen wearing bright, embroidered skirts, waistcoats, headscarves and goatskin boots, and still bake their bread in outdoor communal ovens. The interiors of the houses are decorated with embroidered cloth and their façades feature brightly painted, ornate plaster reliefs.

Olymbos, however, is no longer a pristine backwater caught in a time warp. Tourism has taken hold in a big way and is now a vital money spinner for the villagers. The 'traditional' village is finding it ever harder to remain genuine and is in danger of becoming a kind of kitsch eco-Disney for day-trippers from Pigadia. Olymbos is certainly fascinating and picturesque, but is sadly rather overrated for what it ultimately has to offer.

Accommodation in the village is pretty basic. At the far end of Olymbos and close to the central square, **Hotel Aphrodite** (☎ 22450 51307; filippasfilipakkis@yahoo.gr; d €40) is as good as it's going to get. It has simply furnished, airy rooms and impressive west-facing sea views. If you don't mind a shoebox-sized sleeping space reminiscent of Japanese cubicle hotels, the 'traditional' rooms of the **Olymbos Taverna** (☎ 22450 51252; s/d €30/35) might just suffice for a night's sleep.

Makarounes is served in Olymbos in most restaurants. The best place to eat would have to be the atmospherically endowed **Taverna O Mylos** (☎ 22450 51333; mains €4-7.50) on the north side of the village. Built around a restored and working windmill, the excellent food is cooked in a wood oven and features organic meat and vegetable produce, including goat in red-wine sauce, artichokes and filling *pites* (pies).

At the south side of the village, on the main street, **Olymbos Taverna** (☎ 22450 51252; mains €3-4) is a good place for *makarounes*, and there's a daily changing menu of oven-cooked specials that includes artichokes in oil, or *mizithropittes* (small *pites* made from a sweet cottage cheese).

KASOS ΚΑΣΟΣ

pop 980

Strung like a punctuation mark between Karpathos and Crete, Kasos (*ka*-sos) is one of the remotest outposts of the scattered Aegean islands. Most travellers don't even know of its existence. Few ever make it to the far southwest Dodecanese, where this speck of rock and people thrives almost unnoticed, yet welcomes its visitors with a broad smile and a warm embrace. There are no enticing beaches, throbbing nightlife or major archaeological sites, and on the face of it, little to entice a wayward traveller. Yet Kasos attracts in its own inimitable way.

It's an island of olive and fig trees, prickly pears, dry-stone walls, sheep, goats and birds. Its craggy peaks are often shrouded in mist and ferries are frequently diverted. The Kasiots are friendly, curious and open, yet not totally driven by the tourist euro. Come for a day or two and you may end up staying a week. It's that kind of place.

History

Despite being diminutive and remote, Kasos has an eventful history. During Turkish rule the island flourished, and by 1820 it had 11,000 inhabitants and a large mercantile fleet. Mohammad Ali, the Turkish governor of Egypt, regarded this fleet as an impediment to his plan to establish a base on Crete from which to attack the Peloponnese and quell the uprising. On 7 June 1824 Ali's men landed on Kasos and killed around 7000 inhabitants. This massacre is commemorated annually on the anniversary of the slaughter, and Kasiots return from around the world to participate. During the late 19th century, many Kasiots emigrated to Egypt and around 5000 of them helped build the Suez Canal. During the last century many emigrated to the USA.

Getting There & Away

AIR

There are up to eight flights weekly in summer to Rhodes (€38, 1¼ hours), Karpathos (€25, 10 minutes) and Sitia (€42, 40 minutes). **Olympic Airlines** (☎ 22450 41555; www.olympic airlines.com; Kritis) is at the airport.

EXCURSION BOAT

The **Athina excursion boat** (☎ 22450 41047, 6977911209) travels daily in summer, departing at 3pm and returning at 7pm from Fry to the uninhabited Armathia Islet (return €15), where there are some superb sandy beaches.

FERRY

LANE Lines of Crete includes Kasos on its long run to/from Rhodes and Piraeus via Karpathos, Crete and Milos. Destinations include Piraeus (€32.50, 17 hours), Rhodes (€22, 6½ hours) and Sitia (€10.50, 2½ hours). There are usually three departures weekly in each direction.

A small local caïque runs three times weekly between Fry and Finiki on Karpathos. Check locally for details.

Getting Around

The local bus serves all the villages of the island with a dozen or so scheduled runs; tickets are all €0.60. There are two **taxis** (☎ 6977944371, 6973244371) on the island. Scooters or cars can be rented from **Oasis – Renta-a-Car & Bikes** (☎ 22450 41746) in Fry.

FRY ΦΡΥ

pop 270

Fry *(free)* is the island's capital and port. It's a pleasant, ramshackle kind of place, with little tourism, though it attracts many returned Kasiot Americans. The sizable village can be thoroughly explored in under an hour. Its narrow whitewashed streets are usually busy with locals in animated discussion. The village's focal point is the cramped yet picturesque old fishing harbour of Bouka. The annexe settlement of Emborio is located 1km east of Fry.

THE SHORTEST FLIGHT

Forget inflight movies and meals when flying from Kasos to Karpathos or vice-versa. You barely have time to buckle your seatbelt before you're preparing for landing. At just five minutes, this Olympic Airlines Karpathos–Kasos sector is the shortest of the airline's routes. As you lift off in a Canadian-built de Havilland DHC-8 (Dash 8) prop aircraft, you'll barely have time to view the rugged coastline of Kasos slip away to your right as you skim across the waves to Karpathos airport at the southern tip of that island. 'Cabin crew prepare for landing.' You've arrived.

Orientation & Information

Fry's large harbour complex abuts the port village right next to its main square, Plateia Iroön Kasou. Turn left from the harbour to get to Emborio. The airport is 1km west along the coast road from Fry (not 8km as signposted from near Bouka harbour). Fry's main street is Kritis.

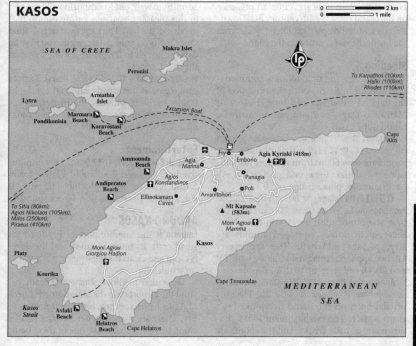

KASOS

SEA OF CRETE

Makra Islet
Peronisi
Armathia Islet
Lytra
Marmara Beach
Pondikonisia
Karavostasi Beach
Excursion Boat

To Karpathos (10km);
Halki (100km);
Rhodes (110km)

Cape Akti

Fry
Emborio
Agia Kyriaki (418m)
Ammounda Beach
Agia Marina
Andiperatos Beach
Agios Konstandinos
Panagia
Ellinokamara Caves
Arvanitohori
Poli

To Sitia (80km);
Agios Nikolaos (105km);
Milos (250km);
Piraeus (410km)

Mt Kapsalo (583m)
Moni Agiou Mamma

Kasos

Platy
Moni Agiou Giorgiou Hadion

Kourika

Kasos Strait
Avlaki Beach
Helatros Beach
Cape Helatros
Cape Trousoulas

MEDITERRANEAN SEA

0 — 2 km
0 — 1 mile

DODECANESE

A stand-alone Commercial Bank ATM is next to the port entrance, while there's a Co-Operative Bank of the Dodecanese branch, with ATM, on Plateia Iroön Kasou.

ACS Internet (☎ 22450 42751; zwankie@otenet.gr; per hr €3; ☼ 10am-2pm & 5pm-12am) Offers wi-fi.

Farmacy (☎ 22450 41164) For all medicinal needs.

Kasos Maritime & Travel Agency (☎ 22450 41495; www.kassos-island.gr; Plateia Iroön Kasou) For all travel tickets.

Police (☎ 22450 41222) On a narrow paved street running south from Kritis.

Port police (☎ 22450 41288) Behind the Agios Spyridon Church.

Post office (☎ 22450 41255; ☼ 7.30am-2pm Mon-Fri) Diagonally opposite the Police.

www.kasos.gr An informative website in Greek and English.

Sights

Fry's minuscule **Archaeological Museum** (☎ 22450 41865; admission free; ☼ 9am-3pm) won't turn heads, but it is a commendable effort to display some of the island's treasure. It includes a thematic display on the 'sea' – wine amphorae and other objects pulled from ancient shipwrecks – and 'lighting', a collection of ancient oil lamps. Finds from Polis indicate a human presence on the island since the 4th century BC. Downstairs a cultural display exhibits objects from the life of the last century on the island.

Sleeping

There is a growing number of accommodation options in Kasos. With the exception of the days on either side of 7 June (Holocaust Memorial Day) – a room can normally be found quite easily.

Fantasis (☎ 69779 05156; www.fantasishotel.gr; Fry; d/t incl breakfast €40/45; ⊠) These six airy and spruce rooms are only 600m from the port just outside Fry and make for a good quiet retreat. All have balconies plus a fridge and TV.

our pick Evita Village (☎ 22450 41731, 6972703950; evitavillage@mail.gr; Fry; s/d €40/50; ⊠) Currently the best accommodation option on the island, these meticulously equipped studios are airy, spacious and tasteful. They sport every kitchen appliance imaginable, along with TV and DVD, and sleep up to three people.

Anagennisis Hotel (☎ 22450 41495; www.kassos-island.gr; Plateia Iroön Kasou; s/d €40/50; ⊠) The only official hotel on the island overlooks Fry's main square. The establishment looks run-down and a shade creaky, and the rooms are on the small side. Nonetheless it's central and handy for most of Fry's facilities.

Galanou Viou Apartments (☎ 22450 41235; Fry; studios €50; ⊠) Opened mid-2007, these self-catering studios are located on a hillside on the southern side of Fry. They comprise six tastefully equipped and furnished units with modern equipment.

Eating & Drinking

Fry is not over endowed in the eating stakes, but there are at least one or two decent places to dine.

O Mylos (☎ 22450 41825; Plateia Iroön Kasou; mains €3.50-4.50) This cosy corner overlooking the west side of the port is the most reliable eatery. The food is wholesome, with fish, meat and casserole dishes on the menu, as well as the odd home-cooked special. Ask for roïkio – an unusual, locally produced green salad.

Apangio (☎ 22450 41880; Bouka; mezedhes €3-5; ☼ 9am until late) Enjoying a very atmospheric Bouka harbour location, the Apangio is a classy ouzerie-cum-café, serving select mezedhes, drinks, snacks, coffee and late breakfasts.

Taverna Emborios (☎ 22450 41586; mains €6-8) A 20-minute walk out to Emborio will lead you to this pleasant, spacious eating option that overlooks the bay. The local goat in red-wine sauce melts on your palate, while you may be daring enough to try bousti – stuffed goat or sheep intestines.

Cafe Zantana (☎ 22450 41912; Bouka) Kasiots congregate at this trendy café that overlooks Bouka harbour. Mihalis, the owner, makes excellent cappuccinos and cocktails and cooks up a fine breakfast omelette.

Entertainment

Perigiali Bar (☎ 22450 41767; Bouka) This diminutive bar, between Bouka and Plateia Iroön Kasou, is Kasos' only nightclub. The music is a mixture of Greek and non-Greek sounds.

AROUND KASOS

Emborio is the satellite port of Fry used for small craft. Its beach is sandy and the water is clean and clear. It's the nearest place to Fry for a quick dip.

The rather mediocre **Ammounda Beach**, beyond the airport near the blue-domed church of Agios Konstandinos, is the next nearest to Fry. There are slightly better beaches further along this stretch of coast, one of them being the fine-pebble **Andiperatos Beach** at the end of the road system. Neither Ammounda or Andiperatos has shade.

The island's best beach is the isolated pebbled cove of **Helatros**, near Moni Agiou Georgiou Hadion, 11km southwest from Fry along a paved road. The beach has no facilities or shade and you'll need your own transport to reach it. **Avlaki** is another decent yet small unshaded beach here, reached along a track from the monastery.

Agia Marina, 1km southwest of Fry, is a pretty village with a gleaming white-and-blue church. On 17 July the **Festival of Agia Marina** is celebrated here. Agia Marina is the starting point for the former rock shelter known as **Ellinokamara**, with its odd, stone-blocked entrance. Follow the Hrysoulas signpost at the southern end of Agia Marina. Proceed 500m to the end of the road then follow a path between stone walls for about seven minutes. Look for a badly signed and gated track upwards and to the left to reach the cave.

From Agia Marina the road continues to verdant **Arvanitohori**, with abundant fig and pomegranate trees. **Poli**, 3km southeast of Fry, is the former capital, built on the ancient acropolis. **Panagia**, between Fry and Poli, now has fewer than 50 inhabitants; its once-grand sea captains' and many ship owners' mansions are either standing derelict or under repair.

Monasteries

The island has two monasteries: **Moni Agiou Mamma** and **Moni Agiou Georgiou Hadion**. The uninhabited Moni Agiou Mamma, on the south coast, is a 1½-hour walk from Fry or a 20-minute scooter ride. The road winds uphill through a dramatic, eroded landscape of rock-strewn mountains, crumbling terraces and soaring cliffs. Occasionally clouds and mist swirl over the road as it crests the ridge high above Poli and dips dramatically down to the monastery at the end of the paved road. A lively *panigyri* (annual religious feast) takes place here on 2 September yearly. Detour to the chapel of **Agia Kyriaki** (no obvious sign) for aerie-like views over Fry and the basin villages.

Similarly, there are no monks at Moni Agiou Georgiou Hadion, but there is a resident caretaker for most of the year. Free accommodation may be available for visitors, but don't bank on it. The *panigyri* at Agiou Georgiou Hadion takes place during the week after Easter.

KASTELLORIZO (MEGISTI)
ΚΑΣΤΕΛΛΟΡΙΖΟ (ΜΕΓΙΣΤΗ)

pop 430

Leaping to unexpected fame thanks to the 1991 Italian film *Mediterraneo*, Kastellorizo (ka-stel-*o*-rizo) is truly the last outpost in the Greek islands. Omitted on many maps, this literal speck of Greek territory lies tucked beneath the underbelly of neighbour Turkey. It's nearest human inhabitants are in the Turkish port of Kaş, a mere 2.5km across the water and clearly visible. Kastellorizo is 130km east of Rhodes and is named after the Knights of St John castle, the ruins of which now overlook the port and main settlement. You'll probably come to Kastellorizo for one of three reasons: you're a third-generation Kastellorizian and it's your mission to see your grandparents' homeland; you're Italian and you just *have* to see where the movie was made; or you are truly curious and determined: perhaps even lost. Either way you have arrived – now go discover.

History

Kastellorizo has a tragic history. Once a thriving trade port serving Dorians, Romans, crusaders, Egyptians, Turks and Venetians, Kastellorizo came under Ottoman control in 1552. The island was permitted to preserve its language, religion and traditions, and its cargo fleet became the largest in the Dodecanese, allowing the islanders to achieve a high degree of culture and advanced levels of education.

Kastellorizo lost all strategic and economic importance after the 1923 Greece–Turkey population exchange. In 1928 it was ceded to the Italians, who severely oppressed the islanders. Many islanders chose to emigrate to Australia, where a disproportionate number still live.

During WWII Kastellorizo suffered bombardment, and English commanders ordered the few remaining inhabitants to abandon the island. Most fled to Cyprus, Palestine and Egypt. When they returned they found their houses in ruins and re-emigrated. The island has never fully recovered from its population

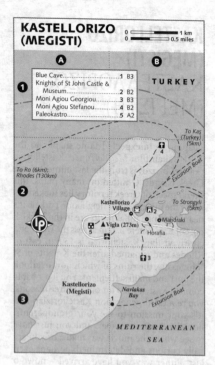

KASTELLORIZO (MEGISTI)

Blue Cave..............................1	B3
Knights of St John Castle & Museum..............................2	B2
Moni Agiou Georgiou..............3	B3
Moni Agiou Stefanou..............4	B2
Paleokastro..........................5	A2

Travel (☎ 22460 70630, 6937212530; www.kastelorizo.gr) in Kastellorizo Village sells tickets.

The *Dodekanisos Express* catamaran runs once a week to/from Rhodes (€33, 2½ hours), usually on Monday or Friday, but the scheduled day changes yearly. Contact **Dodekanisos Seaways** (Map p282; ☎ 22410 70590; www.12ne.gr; Afstralias 3) in Rhodes for the current schedules.

Getting Around
EXCURSION BOAT

Excursion boats go to the islets of Ro, Strongyli and the spectacular Blue Cave (Parasta), famous for its brilliant blue water, produced by refracted sunlight. Visitors are transferred from a larger caïque to a small motorised dingy in order to enter the very low cave entrance – claustrophobics be warned. Bring your bathing gear as the boatman usually allows visitors a quick dip in the cave itself. Captained by **Georgos Karagiannis** (☎ 6977855756), the *Varvara* and the *Agios Georgios* are the two most popular boats.

The trip to the cave costs €15, and the longer trip to Ro, Strongyli and around Kastellorizo costs €20. All leave at around 9am daily and return by 1pm.

Excursion Boat to Turkey
Islanders go on frequent shopping trips to Kaş in Turkey, and day trips (€20) are also offered to tourists. Passports are required by the police 24 hours beforehand. Look for the signs along the middle waterfront.

The status of Kastellorizo as a legal entry port to/from Greece has been the subject of heated debate in recent years. At the time of writing it looked as though the impasse had been resolved and that the island would become an official exit and entry port. Check with the Kastellorizo police to be on the safe side. Travellers from Turkey may have to take pot luck.

loss. In recent years returnees have been slowly restoring buildings and the island is now enjoying a tenuous but pleasant period of resurgence and resettlement.

Getting There & Away
AIR

During the summer months of July and August there are daily flights to and from Rhodes (€26, 20 minutes), dropping to three weekly at other times. Tickets are available from **Papoutsis Travel** (☎ 22460 70630, 6937212530; www.kastelorizo.gr) in Kastellorizo Village. You can either take the sole island **taxi** (☎ 6938739178) to get from the airport to the port (€5), or the local community bus (€1.50). The bus leaves the square by the port 1½ hours prior to each flight departure.

CATAMARAN & FERRY
Kastellorizo's links to the Dodecanese archipelago is limited to a ferry and catamaran service. Ferry links are subject to seasonal changes. **ANES** (☎ 22460 71444; www.anes.gr) runs between Kastellorizo and Rhodes (€23.50, 7½ hours) and beyond twice weekly. **Papoutsis**

KASTELLORIZO VILLAGE
pop 275

Besides Mandraki, its satellite neighbourhood over the hill and to the east, Kastellorizo Village is the only settlement on the island. Built around a U-shaped bay, the village's waterfront is skirted by imposing, spruced-up, three-storey mansions with wooden balconies and red-tiled roofs. It is undoubtedly pretty nowadays, but the alluring façade of today's waterfront contrasts starkly with backstreets of abandoned houses overgrown with ivy, crumbling stairways and winding stony pathways. Newer, brightly painted houses are emerging like gaudy mushrooms from among the ruins, while some of the older, ruined houses are slowly being restored to their former glory.

Orientation & Information

The quay is at the southern side of the bay. The central square, Plateia Ethelondon Kastellorizou, abuts the waterfront almost halfway round the bay, next to the yachting jetty. The settlements of Horafia and Mandraki are reached by ascending the wide steps at the east side of the bay.

There are a couple of cardphones, while mobile-phone users can pick up both Greek and Turkish networks. There is no wi-fi access on the island.

Health Centre (☎ 22460 49267) For basic heath needs.
National Bank of Greece (☎ 22460 49054) ATM equipped.
Papoutsis Travel (☎ 22460 70630; www .kastelorizo.gr) For air and sea tickets.
Police station (☎ 22460 49333) On the bay's western side.
Port police (☎ 22460 49333) At eastern tip of the bay.
Post office (☎ 22460 49298) Next to the police station.
Radio Café (☎ 22460 49029; per hr €3) For internet access.

Sights

The **Knights of St John Castle** stands above the quay. A rickety metal staircase leads to the top from where there are splendid views of Turkey. Lower down the castle grounds, a well-displayed collection is held at the **museum** (☎ 22460 49283; admission free; ☉ 7am-2pm Tue-Sun). Beyond the museum, steps lead down to a coastal pathway, from where more steps go up the cliff to a **Lycian tomb** with a Doric façade, which dates back as far as the 4th century BC. There are several along the Anatolian coast in Turkey, but this is the only known one in Greece.

Moni Agiou Georgiou is the largest of the monasteries that dot the island. Within its church is the subterranean Chapel of Agios Haralambos, reached by steep stone steps. Greek children were given religious instruction here during Turkish times. The church is kept locked; ask around the waterfront for the whereabouts of the caretaker. To reach the monastery, ascend the conspicuous zigzag-

ging white stone steps behind the village and at the top follow the prominent path.

Moni Agiou Stefanou, on the north coast, is the setting for one of the island's most important celebrations, the feast of Agios Stefanos on 1 August. The path to the little white monastery begins behind the post office. From the monastery, a path leads to a bay where you can swim.

Paleokastro was the island's ancient capital. Within the old city's Hellenistic walls are an ancient tower, a water cistern and three churches. Concrete steps, just beyond a soldier's sentry box on the airport road, mask the beginning of the pretty steep path to Paleokastro.

Sleeping

There is generally sufficient accommodation in Kastellorizo Village for most visitors, but it tends to be a little on the pricey side for the quality it offers. Book ahead in high season to be sure of a berth.

Villa Kaserma (☎ 22460 49370; fax 22460 49365; d/tr €35/43; ☒) Set back high on the western side of the harbour, this red-and-white coloured pension has oldish, fridge-equipped rooms with perhaps the best views of Kastellorizo harbour.

Pension Asimina (☎ 22460 49361; s/d €40/50; ☒) Equipped with optional ceiling fans as well as fridge and TV, most of these very tidy double and triple rooms have private bathrooms. It's behind the fish market and to the right.

Poseidon (☎ 22460 49257; www.kastelorizo -poseidon.gr; s/d €50/60) Comprising two yellow-, white- and blue-painted restored houses, the Poseidon offers large, well-furnished rooms, some with wrought-iron balconies. You'll find the establishment on the west side of the harbour, one block back from the waterfront.

Pension I Orea Palameria (☎ 22460 49282; fax 22460 49071; d/tr €45/65) This converted building on the small square at the northwest corner of the waterfront has spotless rooms with kitchen and dining areas. Inquire about them at To Mikro Parisi (p306).

Mediterraneo (☎ 22460 49007; www.mediterraneo -kastelorizo.com; s & d €60-80) At the far western tip of the harbour, these smallish but otherwise comfortable rooms offer a quiet accommodation choice, yet are very convenient for a quick harbour dip. There's a more expensive suite available.

DODECANESE

ourpick **Kastellorizo Hotel Apartments** (☎ 22460 49044; www.kastellorizohotel.gr; s/d €74/100; ﹡ ﹡) The best accommodation is on the west side of the harbour. All of these spacious, airy rooms have satellite TV, phone and fridge. The pint-sized pool is mainly for sitting in, but you can jump into the harbour's beckoning quartz-blue waters from directly in front of the hotel.

Eating

Eating in Kastellorizo is fun as a number of restaurants have tables that perch precariously over the harbour edge. One false move and you are in for a ducking. Food offerings are predictable, but generally of good and nonplasticised tourist quality.

ourpick **Radio Café** (☎ 22460 49029; breakfast & snacks €2-5) Other than internet access, this newish Dutch-Greek run café dishes up filling and moderately priced breakfasts – including the best coffee on the island – as well as light snacks, and pizzas and foccacias in the evening. It's also a hot spot to watch the sun sink low with a cooling white-wine spritzer in hand.

Akrothalassi (☎ 22460 49052; mains €3-5) Popular with visiting Greeks, this relaxed taverna on the southwest side of the harbour has the advantage of midday shade under grape vines. It also does exceptionally good *mayirefta* (ready-cooked meals), such as spring veal, with capsicum and onion served with basmati rice.

Kaz Bar (☎ 22460 49067; mezedhes €3-6; ﹡ 15 Jun-30 Sep) For an alternative take on mezedhes, drop by owner Colin Pavlidis' bar-cum-bistro on the middle waterfront. Pizza, chicken wings and spring rolls, as well as original salads, feature on the menu and there's a decent selection of Greek wines.

Sydney Restaurant (☎ 22460 49302; mains €4.50-6) Hearty home-cooked dishes and grilled fish feature at Sydney, a little further around from To Mikro Parisi. It's a popular low-key eatery, with its tables teetering precipitously on the edge of the harbour.

To Mikro Parisi (☎ 22460 49282; mains €5-7) Going strong since 1974, To Mikro Parisi still serves generous helpings of grilled fish and meat. Fish soup is the house speciality, but the rich *stifadho* (sweet stew cooked with tomato) is equally satisfying.

Entertainment

There are several easy-going cafés on the waterfront. **Kaz Bar** (☎ 22460 49067; mezedhes €3-6; ﹡ 15 Jun-30 Sep), when open, is a good place to kick off.

Next door, Meltemi has tempting waterside chairs and cold beers, while the Eolis on the east side of the harbour is a popular late-night hangout that commonly kicks on into the small hours.

SYMI ΣΥΜΗ

pop 2606

You can hardly miss Symi (*see*-me). It's one of the most popular day-trip destinations from Rhodes. It's also a popular holiday destination in its own right. Like other islands in the southern Dodecanese, it's rocky, mostly dry, postcard pretty, and a popular port of call for yachties and other sea-struck travellers. The island's past was once a different call. Shipbuilding, sponge diving and commerce were the island's mainstay economies; now it's tourism and more tourism.

You could perhaps be forgiven for believing that the island has been colonised by northern Europeans; so prevalent is their presence – there is even a local English-language newspaper – and the large crowds of day-trippers add to the image. It has a picturesque harbour with restored and tiered sea captains' houses. Most visitors congregate here, but there is also a surprisingly green interior, a sprinkling of scattered beaches and an enormous monastery that is one of the few religious sites that warrants its own ferry connection.

History

Symi has a long tradition of both sponge diving and shipbuilding. During Ottoman times it was granted the right to fish for sponges in Turkish waters. In return, Symi supplied the sultan with first-class boat builders and top-quality sponges scooped straight off the ocean floor.

These factors, and a lucrative shipbuilding industry, brought prosperity to the island. Gracious mansions were built and culture and education flourished. By the beginning of the 20th century the population was 22,500 and the island was launching some 500 ships a year. But the Italian occupation, the introduction of the steamship and Kalymnos' rise as the Aegean's principal sponge producer put an end to Symi's prosperity.

The treaty surrendering the Dodecanese islands to the Allies was signed in Symi's Hotel (now Pension) Catherinettes (p308) on 8 May 1945.

Getting There & Away
EXCURSION BOAT
There are daily excursion boats between Symi and Rhodes. The Symi-based *Symi I* and *Symi II*, operated by **ANES** (☎ 22460 71444; www.anes.gr), are the cheapest and usually go via Panormitis; tickets (return €12) can be bought on board.

Symi Tours (☎ 22460 71307; fax 22460 72292) has excursion trips from Gialos to Datça in Turkey (including Turkish port taxes €35).

FERRY, CATAMARAN & HYDROFOIL
Symi has only two long-haul ferries a week heading north to other Dodecanese islands and Piraeus (€44, 15 to 17 hours). **ANES** (☎ 22460 71444; www.anes.gr) transports cars and people between Symi and Rhodes (one way €7, one

hour and 10 minutes), while there is a twice-weekly link with Kastellorizo (€23.50, 7½ hours).

The *Dodekanisos Express* and *Dodekanisos Pride* catamarans service the island at least four times weekly with connections to Rhodes (€14, 50 minutes) and islands further north. One service calls in at Panormitis on the south side of the island.

The ANES-owned *Aigli* hydrofoil also connects Symi with Rhodes (€14, one hour).

Getting Around
BUS & TAXI
The bus stop and taxi rank are on the south side of the harbour in Gialos. The grey **minibus** (☎ 6945316284) makes frequent runs between

SYMI

0 ——— 5 km
0 ——— 3 miles

To Kos (60km);
Patmos (125km);
Piraeus (380km)

To Datça
(Turkey) (12km)

Cape Makria

Hondros

Nimos Islet

Platy

To Tilos (30km)

Diapori Straits

Nimborios
Gulf

Oxia

Cape Toli

Nimborios

Kokkinohoma
Bay

Nos
Harani

Cape
Koutsoumpos

Agia Marina

▲ 249m

Pedi Bay

Moni Agiou
Georgiou

Gialos

Pedi

Moni Agiou
Fanouriou

Symi

Horio

Agios
Nikolaos

Agios
Emilianos

Cape
Kefalaki

Ladi
Bay

▲ 471m

Agios
Georgios
Bay

Cape Koupi

Pidima

Ghi

Gulf
of Agios
Vasilios

▲ 594m

Symi

Nanou
Bay

Kefalos
Bay

Megalonisi

Cape Agios
Nikolaos Kefalis

▲ 528m

To Rhodes
(20km)

To Kos (60km);
Kalymnos (75km);
Patmos (125km)

Panormitis
Bay

Lopidia
Bay

Marathounda
Bay

Vathygialos
Bay

Cape Faneromeni

Panormitis

Faneromeni
Bay

Cape
Potos

Moni Taxiarhou
Mihail Panormiti

Cape
Parathyras

Sesklion
Islet

To Rhodes
(20km)

A E G E A N
S E A

Strongylos

DODECANESE

Gialos and Pedi beach (via Horio). The flat fare is €1. Another minibus runs twice daily between Gialos and Panormitis. Taxis depart from a rank 100m west of the bus stop.

EXCURSION BOAT

Several excursion boats do trips to Moni Taxiarhou Mihail Panormiti and Sesklion Islet, where there's a shady beach. Check the boards for the best-value tickets. There are also boats to Agios Emilianos beach, on the far west side of Symi.

WATER TAXI

The small **boats** (☎ 22460 71423) *Konstantinos* and *Irini* do trips (€10 to €15) to many of the island's beaches, leaving at 10.15am and 11.15am respectively.

GIALOS ΓΙΑΛΟΣ
pop 2200

Gialos, Symi's port, is by all accounts a visual treat. Neoclassical mansions in a harmonious medley of colours are heaped up the hills flanking its harbour. Behind their strikingly beautiful façades, however, many of the buildings are derelict. It is a slightly claustrophobic place and can get unbearably hot in summer.

Orientation & Information

The town is divided into two parts: Gialos, the harbour, and Horio above it, crowned by the *kastro* (castle). Arriving ferries, hydrofoils and catamarans dock just to the left of the quay's clock tower; excursion boats dock a little further along. The centre of activity in Gialos is the promenade at the centre of the harbour. Kali Strata, a broad stairway, leads from here to hill-top Horio.

There is no official tourist office in Symi Town. The *Symi Visitor* is a free English-and-Greek-language newspaper distributed by portside newspaper vendors and restaurants.

Kalodoukas Holidays (☎ 22460 71077; www.kalodoukas.gr) At the beginning of Kali Strata; rents houses and organises excursions.

Laundry (☎ 22460 70065) On the middle waterfront.

Police (☎ 22460 71111) By the ferry quay.

Port police (☎ 22460 71205) By the ferry quay.

Post office (☎ 22460 71315) By the ferry quay.

Roloï bar (☎ 22460 71595; per hr €4; 🕑 9am-3am) For internet access; a block back from the waterfront.

Symi Tours (☎ 22460 71307; fax 22460 72292) Does excursion trips, including to Datça in Turkey.

Symi Visitor Office (☎ 22460 72755)

www.symivisitor.com A useful source of island information and gossip.

Sights

Horio consists of narrow, labyrinthine streets crossed by crumbling archways. As you approach the **Knights of St John Kastro** dominating Horio, the once-grand 19th-century neoclassical mansions give way to the modest stone dwellings of the 18th century. The castle incorporates blocks from the ancient acropolis, and the **Church of Megali Panagia** is within its walls.

On the way to the *kastro*, Hellenistic, Byzantine and Roman exhibits, as well as some folkloric material, are kept in the **Archaeological and Folklore Museum** (admission €1.50; 🕑 10am-2pm Tue-Sun) in the Lieni suburb of Horio. In the port of Gialos the **Naval Museum** (admission €2; 🕑 10am-2pm Tue-Sun) has some noteworthy wooden models of ships and other naval memorabilia.

Activities

Symi Tours (☎ 22460 71307; fax 22460 72292) has multilingual guides who lead **guided walks** around the island. The publication *Walks in Symi* by Lance Chiltern list 20 walks on the island for novices and pros alike. Call into the **Symi Visitor Office** (☎ 22460 72755) to purchase a copy.

Sleeping

Most accommodation is in studios or a few private rooms. There are a couple of good hotels as well.

Pension Catherinettes (☎ 22460 71671; marina-epe@rho.forthnet.gr; Gialos; d €58; 🕮 🖳) The historic Catherinettes (see History, p306) is on the north side of the harbour. The pink-stuccoed pension has wrought-iron balconies and some of the rooms have magnificently painted high ceilings.

Hotel Fiona (☎ 22460 72755; www.symivisitor.com/fiona.htm; Horio; s/d €55/60) This hotel in Horio has lovely rooms, with wood-panelled ceilings and great views, and is a shade cooler than accommodation in Gialos as it catches welcome breezes. To reach it, turn left at the top of the stairs and walk for 50m.

Hotel Nireus (☎ 22460 72400; www.nireus-hotel.gr; Mouragio; s/d €47/80; 🕮) One of the two regular hotels in Gialos, the prominently sited Nireus, by the clock tower, has traditional rooms and suites with fridge, TV and phone.

Opera House Hotel (☎ 22460 72034; operasym@otenet.gr; Gialos; studios €85-100; 🕮) Named after Australia's Sydney Opera House, these spacious fully self-contained studios in a peaceful garden are well signposted 150m back from the harbour.

Eating

There are plenty of eating options. Many are mediocre, while a handful excel.

GIALOS

Taverna Neraïda (☎ 22460 71841; mains €4-5) Serving unpretentious and solid Greek dishes, Neraïda is an excellent, low-priced option, a block back from the waterfront and opposite the carpark. Fish *souvlaki* features on the menu, as does a range of vegetarian dishes. Walk into the kitchen and select from the dishes on display.

Tholos (☎ 22460 72033; mains €5-9) Out on the headland just before Nos beach, this little low-key taverna is a good choice to escape the crowds in Gialos and dine on good-quality fare, including grills, mezedhes and the ubiquitous fish dishes. Cabbage rolls with fava lentil purée or with mushrooms and dill are two good vegetarian options.

Estiatorio Mythos (☎ 22460 71488; mezedhes €4-10) Voted best restaurant in Greece by one of the UK dailies, this neat little harbour-side taverna serves up imaginative food. At lunch it's mainly pasta dishes, while mezedhes feature in the evening. For palate pleasing, consider calamari stuffed with pesto, or fish fillet parcels in a saffron cream sauce.

ourpick **Mylopetra** (☎ 22460 72333; mains €7-15; ☺ dinner) Considered locally to be one of the better restaurants on Symi, Mylopetra takes care with its ingredients and serves up Mediterranean-Greek creations, including home-made bread and pasta dishes. The menu changes yearly, but among the better creations have been lamb in a hollandaise sauce, or skate with mushrooms in a light peanut sauce.

HORIO

Restaurant Syllogos (☎ 22460 72148; mains €5-7) Similar in style to Giorgos, Syllogos offers imaginative fare such as chicken with prunes, pork with leek, fish with rosemary and tomato, plus vegetarian options like artichokes in egg and lemon sauce, or *spanakopita* (spinach pie).

Filos (☎ 22460 71007; mains €6-9) Decked out in terracotta and Grecian urns, this place is predisposed to relaxed dining with its Minoan-style mien. The menu is stock standard Greek but its *kleftiko* (oven-baked lamb) has been known to please diners. It's at the top of Kali Strata.

Giorgos (☎ 22460 71984; mains €6-9) There is an always-changing and enticing menu of oven-cooked dishes here, with such mouth-watering offerings as chicken stuffed with rice, herbs and pine nuts, lamb in vine leaves, or stuffed onions.

Entertainment

There are several lively bars in the streets behind the south side of the harbour.

Vapori Bar (☎ 22460 72082) Drop by here during the day to read the free papers and then in the evenings for schmoozing, drinks and cruising.

Roloï Bar (☎ 22460 71595) A busy, happening little watering hole one block inland from the south side of the port, Roloï is open most of the day and a large part of the night.

Jean and Tonic Bar (☎ 22460 71819; ☺ 9pm-late) In Horio, Barry White and Tina Turner still reign in this convivial home away from expat home, the self-styled 'late place'. Proprietor Jean welcomes Aston Villa fans. And you can have a soothing G&T or two, too.

ourpick **Kali Strata Bar** (☎ 69744 27948; ☺ all day) In Horio at the top of the Kali Strata is the perfect antidote to the maddening crowds of Gialos. Escape for a sunset cocktail with a Latin twist and some classy, sassy chill music.

AROUND SYMI

Pedi is a little fishing village and busy mini-holiday resort in a fertile valley 2km downhill from Horio. It has some sandy stretches on its narrow beach and there are rooms and studios to rent, as well as hotels and tavernas. Walking tracks down both sides of the bay lead to **Agia Marina** beach on the north side and **Agios Nikolaos** beach on the south side. Both are sandy, gently shelving beaches, suitable for children.

Nos is the closest beach to Gialos. It's a 500m walk north of the campanile at Panormitis Bay. There is a taverna, bar and sun beds (per person €4).

Nimborios is a long, pebbled beach 3km west of Gialos. It has some natural shade, as well as sun beds and umbrellas. You can walk there from Gialos along a scenic path – take the road by the east side of the central square and continue straight ahead; the way is fairly obvious, just bear left after the church and follow the stone trail. Over this way you can stay at **Niriides Apartments** (☎ 22460 71784; www.niriideshotel.com; apt €60-80) in one of eight capacious units on the hillside, in a very quiet location.

Water taxis are the only convenient way to get to **Agios Georgios Bay** and the more developed beach at **Nanou Bay**, which has sun beds, umbrellas and a taverna.

The more remote **Marathounda Bay** beach can be reached by road, while **Agios Emilianos** beach, on the far west side of Symi, is best reached by excursion boat.

Moni Taxiarhou Mihail Panormiti
Μονή Ταξιάρχου Μιχαήλ Πανορμίτη

An often winding but good sealed road leads you across the island, through scented pine forests, before dipping in spectacular zigzag fashion to the expansive but protected Panormitis Bay. This is the site of Symi's principal attraction – the large **Moni Taxiarhou Mihail Panormiti** (Monastery of Archangel Michael of Panormitis; ☾ dawn-sunset; admission free). The large monastery complex, with its ornate Italianate campanile, occupies most of the foreshore of the bay.

A monastery was first built here in the 5th or 6th century, but the present building dates from the 18th century. The principal church contains an intricately carved wooden iconostasis, frescoes, and an icon of St Michael that supposedly appeared miraculously where the monastery now stands. St Michael is the patron saint of Symi, and protector of sailors.

The monastery is also a magnet for hordes of day-trippers who commonly arrive at around 10.30am on excursion boats; it's a good idea to visit early or after they have left.

The monastery complex comprises a **Byzantine museum** and **folkloric museum** (admission for both €1.50), a bakery with excellent bread and apple pies, and a basic restaurant-café to the north side.

Accommodation is available at the fairly basic **guest house** (☎ 22460 72414; s/d €20/32), where bookings in July and August are mandatory. Some ferries call in to the monastery and there is a minibus from Gialos.

TILOS ΤΗΛΟΣ

pop 533

Basking in relative obscurity and often quietly ignored by the major transport companies, Tilos (*tee*-loss) is a small island that tends to be overshadowed by its more illustrious neighbours. Known in earlier years for its agricultural prowess rather than for its maritime eminence, Tilos today confounds common

commercial logic. It can be messy getting to the island, yet the effort is worth the reward. Lone among the Dodecanese, the island has embraced 'green' tourism with a vengeance. Walkers love the place, as will bird-watchers and conservationists once an ambitious ecological programme is fully in place. The island is blessed with just the right balance of hills, mountains, valleys, vistas, meadows and, of course, beaches to make a stay a gratifying experience. It's small enough to get around in a day, and the sleeping and eating options are excellent and getting better. Lost yachties take anchor here, as do travellers who have lost their compass; and that's not including a community of world-weary Brits who've swapped motorways for sanity. It's that kind of place.

History

Mastodon bones – midget elephants that became extinct around 4600 BC – were found in a cave on the island in 1974. The **Harkadio** cave (closed indefinitely) is signposted from the Livadia–Megalo Horio road and is brilliantly illuminated at night. Erinna, one of the least known of ancient Greece's female poets, lived on Tilos in the 4th century BC.

Elephants and poetry aside, Tilos' history shares the same catalogue of invasions and occupations as the rest of the archipelago.

Getting There & Away
CATAMARAN
The Tilos-owned **Sea Star** (☎ 22460 44000; fax 22460 44044) connects Tilos with Rhodes (€18.50). The timetable fluctuates wildly from year to year, but there is usually at least one connection a day with Rhodes. Departures from Rhodes are usually around 9am.

EXCURSION BOAT
There are a number of excursions advertised around Livadia. The **Duo Adelfia** (☎ 69391 06527) is a small caïque offering an all-inclusive beach barbecue excursion for €29 (food and wine included); another option is a multibeach island tour for a similar price. Look for posters around Livadia for details.

FERRY
Tilos is erratically served by mainline ferries. Blue Star Ferries provides one service a week to/from Piraeus (€42, 15 hours) and Rhodes (€12, 3½ hours), while **ANES** (☎ 22460 71444; www.anes.gr) ferries of Symi provides four connections

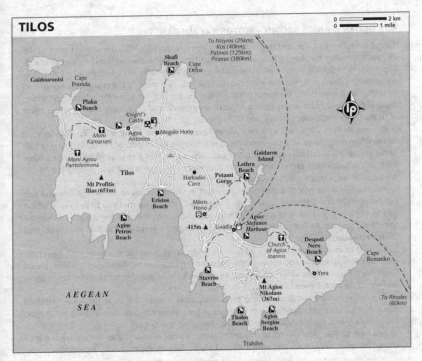

TILOS

To Nisyros (25km);
Kos (40km);
Patmos (125km);
Piraeus (380km)

Gaidouronisi

Cape Pounda

Skafi Beach

Cape Orfos

Plaka Beach

Knight's Castle

Moni Kamariani

Agios Antonios

Megalo Horio

Gaïdaros Island

Lethra Beach

Moni Agiou Panteleimona

Tilos

Harkadio Cave

Potami Gorge

Mt Profitis Ilias (651m)

Eristos Beach

Mikro Horio

Agios Petros Beach

415m

Livadia

Agios Stefanos Harbour

Church of Agios Ioannis

Despoti Nero Beach

Cape Rematiko

To Rhodes (60km)

Stavros Beach

Mt Agios Nikolaos (367m)

Yera

A E G E A N

S E A

Tholos Beach

Agios Sergios Beach

Trahilos

0 ———— 2 km
0 ———— 1 mile

a week north and south, including an onward connection to Kastellorizo. There are also services to Nisyros (€6.50, 1¼ hours) and Kos (€19, three hours). Tickets are sold at **Stefanakis Travel** (☎ 22460 44310; tilos11@otenet.gr) in Livadia.

Getting Around

Tilos' public transport consists of a bus that ploughs up and down the island's main road on a fairly regular basis. The timetable is posted at the bus stop in Livadia. The fares are €1 to Megalo Horio and €1.20 to Eristos Beach. On Sunday there is a special excursion bus to Moni Agiou Panteleimona (€4 return), which leaves Livadia at 11am and allows one hour at the monastery. Tilos currently has only two **taxis** Nikos (☎ 6944981727); Anna (☎ 6945200436).

LIVADIA ΛΙΒΑΔΕΙΑ
pop 470

Livadia is the main village and port, though not the principal village (capital): that honour belongs to Megalo Horio, situated 8km northwest of the port. Livadia is a sleepy, pleasant enough place, though it can get hot. In the village you will find most services and shops, as well as most of the island's accommodation.

Orientation & Information

All arrivals are at Livadia. The small port is 300m southeast of the village centre. Tilos has no official tourist bureau. The Bank of the Dodecanese has a branch and an ATM in Livadia. The post office is on the central square.

Kosmos (☎ 22460 44074; www.tilos-kosmos.com; per hr €5; 9.30am-1pm & 7-11.30pm) This gift shop has internet access. Its website is a useful source of information on Tilos. There is also a book exchange and new books for sale.

Police (☎ 22460 44222) In the white Italianate building at the quay.

Port police (☎ 22460 44350) On the harbour.

Sea Star (☎ 22460 44000; sea-star@otenet.gr) Sells tickets for the Sea Star catamaran.

Stefanakis Travel (☎ 22460 44310; stefanakis@rho .forthnet.gr) Between the port and Livadia village; sells ferry tickets.

Tilos Park Association (☎ 22460 70880; www .tilos-park.org) An umbrella group promoting ecological conservation on Tilos (see boxed text, p314).

Tilos Travel (☎ 22460 44294; www.tilostravel.co.uk) At the port; has helpful staff. Credit card withdrawals and

ROB OGDEN & ANNIE BROWN – MOTORWAY MIGRANTS

It's not everyone that ups and aways from their home, especially from the comfort zone of the UK, yet a growing number of Brits are doing just that. They're leaving the grey and drizzle of Blighty for a better life in the sun. Ex-Mancunians Rob and Annie smiled when asked why they emigrated to Greece. 'It was the motorways', said Rob, 'we were sick and tired racing up and down, wasting time doing the same old thing day in, day out. We knew there had to be something better. We'd much prefer driving to work with the view of Eristos Bay than have the worry of traffic lights and traffic that we had in England.'

Arriving in April 2007 to start a new life in Greece, Rob and Annie settled for Tilos as their home. When questioned why this anonymous island in the backblocks of the Dodecanese group, Annie explained, 'we always wanted to live out here, we wanted a change of lifestyle and some fresh air'. Rob rejoined enthusiastically, 'We had good jobs, but it was just getting too hectic. We decided we wanted a different way of life.'

When asked what practical difficulties they had in setting up home on Tilos, Annie and Rob sighed wistfully and admitted, 'You've got to get used to the idea that you have to take a boat ride to Rhodes if you want to get something essential done, like visit the dentist or shop for something specific. As long as you are patient and organise yourself, it will all work out', they confidently advised.

It's hard to imagine life in Greece without speaking Greek. How did this enterprising yet hitherto monolingual couple manage with the linguistic intricacies of modern Greek? 'Well, I studied Greek back home for six years', countered Annie, 'we have books and tapes and other material and we study a lot. I even did my GCSE in Greek!'

So what about the viability of living on a small rocky island? 'Ask us in two years!' laughed Rob, 'we might not get materially rich here and as long as we can pay the bills we'll be all right. But culturally and spiritually we'll do just fine. Those are our riches.'

You have to take your hat off to this bold couple. It's not everyone that can do it. But if it's a choice between motorways and meadows and life in the sun, there's hardly a contest.

currency exchange are available, as well as car, motorbike and mountain-bike rental.

Sights & Activities

WALKS

There are a number of popular walks that can easily be made from Livadia. The most popular is to **Lethra Beach**, an undeveloped pebble and sand cove with limited shade, 3km north of Livadia. The trail starts at the far north side of the port and is fairly easy. Return via the very picturesque, oleander-strewn and goat-inhabited **Potami Gorge**, which will bring you to the main island highway.

A second walk is a longer return track to the small abandoned settlement of **Yera** and its accompanying beach at **Despoti Nero**. From Livadia follow the road south, around Agios Stefanos Bay and past the Church of Agios Ioannis, on the east side of the bay, and keep walking. Allow half a day for this hike.

Iain and Lyn Fulton of **Tilos Trails** (☎ 69460 54593; fulton@otenet.gr) are licensed guides and run a number of walks (per person €20) around the island, graded from easy to challenging.

Sleeping

Accommodation on the island is generally of a high standard, though it may get block booked by low-key foreign tour operators.

Kosmos Studios (☎ 22460 44164; www.tilos-kosmos.com; d €45) These four cosy, self-catering units with private patios and fan are at the western end of the bay. A free supermarket delivery service with Giannis and Maria's Supermarket is available. Call into Kosmos to find the owners, Paul and Helen.

Irini Hotel (☎ 22460 44293; www.tilosholidays.gr; s/d incl breakfast €45/60; ☒) Catering mainly to package-tour travellers, the neat Irini also welcomes independents. The hotel is set back a little from the waterfront, in a citrus garden, and the rooms are very well appointed.

our pick **Olympus Apartments** (☎ 22460 44324; www.tilosisland.com; d/t €50/60; ☒) Recently renovated, these sparkling, stylishly designed and furnished apartments make for a very comfortable and pleasing stay. They have modern kitchenettes and screened windows.

Eleni Beach Hotel (☎ 22460 44062; www.eleni hoteltilos.gr; s/d incl breakfast €50/60) This airy blue- and white-painted hotel, 400m south along the beach road, has beautiful, tastefully equipped double rooms with refrigerator and telephone.

Livadia Beach Apartments (☎ 22460 44397; www .tilosisland.com; apt €70-85; 🕸 🖳) Right on the seafront on the bay side of Livadia these 16 apartments spread over their blue- and white-painted blocks are large and spacious and fully equipped for self-catering.

Eating

Restaurant Irina (☎ 22460 44206; mains €4-5) With its relaxing waterside location, Irina does great home-made food, including excellent *mousakas* and *papoutsaki* (stuffed baby eggplant), and a rich, beef *stifadho*.

Taverna Blue Sky (☎ 22460 44259; mezedhes €3-5.50) Blue Sky, on the harbour, is good for grilled fish and vegetarian mezedhes. Run by Italians, their culinary heritage is reflected in the food, with pasta featuring prominently on the menu.

Sofia's Taverna (☎ 22460 44340; mains €3-6) This family-run taverna, 100m along the beach road, serves wholesome, home-cooked food, as well as a good selection of entrées. Look for the daily oven-cooked specials.

Armenon (☎ 22460 44134; mains €3.50-7) For food with a somewhat international twist head for this warm, woody taverna with patterned slate floors and blue-painted rafters. Among the more original dishes are lamb and mixed vegetables in filo pastry, or turkey in orange sauce with almonds.

our pick **Croma Cafe Bar** (☎ 22460 44182; snacks €6.50-10) This café-bar is a popular breakfast, brunch and evening hang-out, serving excellent herb tea and vegetarian snacks such as baked potato and chilli, which go down satisfyingly well with an iced Irish Magners cider. Wi-fi is available.

Entertainment

Mikro Horio Music Bar (🕑 midnight-5am Jul & Aug) Determined clubbers head for the abandoned village of Mikro Horio, 3km from Livadia, where this place belts out music most of the night. A minibus ferries revellers to and from the port.

There are a few summer bars on Livadia's waterfront, such as Ino and Bozi.

MEGALO HORIO ΜΕΓΑΛΟ ΧΩΡΙΟ

pop 50

Megalo Horio, the island's capital, is a serene whitewashed village. Its alleyways are fun to explore, and the village makes a great alternative base if you are looking for a taste of rural life. There are places to sleep and at least one reliable restaurant to keep visitors suitably fed. From here you can visit the **Knight's Castle**, a taxing 40-minute upwards walk along a track starting at the north end of the village. Along the way you will pass the **ancient settlement** of Tilos, which in its time stood precariously on rocky ledges overlooking Megalo Horio. The remains of stone houses can be clearly seen here.

The little **museum** (admission free; 🕑 8.30am-2.30pm) on the main street houses mastodon bones from Harkadio Cave. It's locked, but if you ask at the town hall on the 1st floor someone will show you around.

When it comes to longer-term accommodation you might consider renting a secluded private villa with a swimming pool. **Eden Villas** (☎ 22460 44094, 6947065423; villa per week €1240; 🖳 🕸) accommodates up to eight people and is on the right (east) side of Megalo Horio. It's an ideal place to chill out with books and a wi-fi computer for a week or so. See Rob or Annie at Croma café for details.

In Megalo Horio itself are the cosy studios of **Miliou Rooms & Apartments** (☎ 22460 44204; d €40), sequestered in a tree-shaded garden that boasts a couple of banana palms.

To Kastro (☎ 22460 44232; mains €5-6.50), on the village's south side overlooking the Eristos plain below, is the best place to eat. The fare features charcoal-grilled meats, including organic goat and locally raised pork, as well as fresh fish and a range of daily oven-cooked specials.

AROUND MEGALO HORIO

Just before Megalo Horio, a turn-off to the left leads 2.5km to the pleasant, tamarisk-shaded **Eristos Beach**, a mixture of gritty sand and shingle. A signposted turn-off to the right from the junction leads to the quiet settlement of **Agios Antonios**, where the small Elpida Restaurant is the only reliable source of food and drink. The undeveloped **Plaka Beach**, 3km further west, is backed by shady trees and is clean and uncluttered.

The 18th-century **Moni Agiou Panteleimona** is 5km beyond here, along a scenic road. It is

---

THE TILOS PARK

There's a royal battle a-raging on Tilos between relatively newcomer conservationists and long-time local agriculturalists over a swath of land that is home to a few endangered birds. At stake is the welfare of the Eleonara's Falcon (*Falco eleonarae*), the Mediterranean Shag (*Phalacrocorax aristotelis desmarestii*) and the Bonelli's Eagle (*hHeraaetus fasciatus*), all of which make Tilos their nesting home. At stake also is any animal that moves and could be considered fair game by Tilos' would-be hunters and less conservation-minded residents.

Agriculturalists interested in making a fast euro or two want to open up their land to development, which would in turn threaten the equilibrium of the fauna and flora of the island. In response, the EU-sponsored Tilos Park Association has declared a Special Protected Area on the island that essentially stymies unfettered expansion and development. Tempers have been running hot and muttered threats have been made, so for now there is a resentful stand-off.

The admirable aims of the association are to be lauded and the frustrations of the locals are understandable, but the current winners are the animals and plants of Tilos that are enjoying a welcome breather in a cultural environment that has not always been so well disposed to conservation.

---

uninhabited but well maintained, with fine frescoes. The island's minibus driver takes groups of visitors here on Sunday. A well-attended and lively three-day annual **festival** takes place at the monastery, beginning on 25 July.

You can camp unofficially on Eristos Beach, but facilities are basic to nonexistent. The best place to stay is at the expansive plant-festooned grounds and studios of **Eristos Beach Hotel** (☎ /fax 22460 44024; d €32; ☒) abutting the northern end of the beach. Here you'll find excellent, airy studios for up to four people with fridge and kitchenette. There is also an on-site restaurant and bar.

An alternative eating option is **Tropicana Taverna** (☎ 22460 44020; mains €3.60-5.50) on the Eristos road, where the owner serves locally produced meat and vegetables and scrumptious *revithokeftedes* (chickpea rissoles).

NISYROS ΝΙΣΥΡΟΣ

pop 948

There are not many islands in the Aegean that sport their own dormant volcano. Nisyros (*ni-see-ross*) has one, though it's less active now than it was in its eruptive past. This almost round island of pumice, rock and lush vegetation is a bit of an anomaly because of its inherited geology. Other than that it's a thoroughly pleasant destination for individuals who want a quiet vacation on an island that still looks and feels totally Greek.

The beaches are not so hot – that's a fact – but you can visit the hissing floor of the volcano crater, which from high above on the rim looks like a nuclear bomb blast site. Hiking is good, too, with a number of route options usually involving the volcano rim and crater. Mandraki, the island's main port, is pretty and pleasing and lends to lingering sunset ouzos on ice.

Getting There & Away

Nisyros is linked by regular ferries to Rhodes (€12, three to five hours), Kos (€9, 1¾ hours) and Piraeus (€44, 17 hours). The *Dodekanisos Pride* catamaran calls in on Saturday and Sunday with connections to Kalymnos (€34, 1½ hours) and Rhodes (€43, 2¼ hours).

The small local ferry *Agios Konstantinos* links Mandraki with Kardamena on Kos (€7, two hours, 7am daily), while the larger *Panagia Spyliani* link Nisyros with Kos Town (€10, daily).

Getting Around

BUS

Bus companies run up to 10 excursion buses daily between 9.30am and 3pm to the volcano (€7.50 return), with around 40 minutes allowed to visit the volcano. These are in addition to the three daily buses that travel to Nikea (€2) via Pali. The bus stop is located at the port.

CAR & MOTORCYCLE

There are three motocycle-rental outlets on Mandraki's main street. **Manos Rentals** (☎ 22420 31029) right on the quay is the most handy. Budget for €20 to €40 a day for a car.

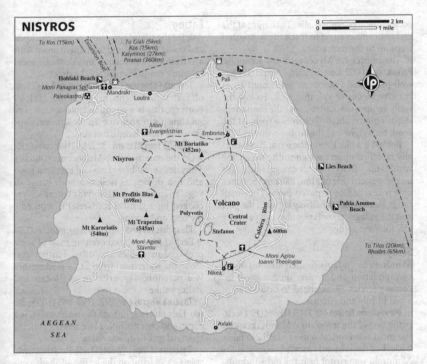

NISYROS

0 ___ 2 km
0 ___ 1 mile

To Kos (15km)

To Giali (5km);
Kos (15km);
Kalymnos (27km);
Piraeus (360km)

Excursion Boat

Hohlaki Beach
Moni Panagias Spilianis
Paleokastro

Mandraki

Pali

Loutra

Moni
Evangelistrias

Emborios

Mt Boriatiko
(452m)

Nisyros

Lies Beach

Mt Profitis Ilias
(698m)

Volcano

Polyvotis

Central
Crater

Caldera Rim

Pahia Ammos
Beach

Mt Trapezina
(545m)

Mt Karariatis
(540m)

Stefanos

600m

Moni Agiou
Stavrou

Moni Agiou
Ioanni Theologou

To Tilos (20km);
Rhodes (65km)

Nikea

AEGEAN
SEA

Avlaki

EXCURSION BOAT

In July and August there are excursion boats (return €10) to the pumice-stone islet of Giali, where there is a relaxing sandy beach.

TAXI

There are two taxis on Nisyros: **Babis Taxi** (☎ 69456 39723) and **Irene's Taxi** (☎ 69733 71281). A taxi from Mandraki to the volcano costs €20 return, to Nikea €11 and to Pali €5.

MANDRAKI ΜΑΝΔΡΑΚΙ

pop 661

Mandraki is the sleepy port and main village of Nisyros and it has just the right amount of somnolence to make the place perfect for a spot of aimless wandering. Two-storey houses sport brightly painted wooden balconies – predominantly ochre and turquoise – while others are whitewashed. The streets meander in an almost maze-like manner and it's easy to get lost. Ultimately you will end up in one of the two squares or back on the waterfront. Mandraki is the kind of settlement that feels right and cosy the moment you set foot upon it.

Orientation & Information

The port is 500m northeast of the centre of Mandraki. Take the road right from the port and you will hit the town centre. A shoreline road and an inner street both lead eventually to the tree-shaded Plateia Ilikiomenis, Mandraki's focal point.

The Co-Operative Bank of the Dodecanese has an ATM at the harbour and a branch in Mandraki.

Diakomihalis (☎ 22420 31015; diakimihalis@kos .forthnet.gr) In Mandraki. Sells ferry tickets.

Enetikon Travel (☎ 22420 31180; agiosnis@otenet.gr) Provides tourist information; 100m from the quay towards Mandraki.

Police (☎ 22420 31201) Opposite the quay.

Port police (☎ 22420 31222) Opposite the quay.

Post office (☎ 22420 31249) Opposite the quay.

Proveza Internet Cafe (☎ 22420 31618; www .proveza.net) For wi-fi and freshly ground coffee.

Sights

Mandraki's main tourist attraction is the cliff-top 14th-century **Moni Panagias Spilianis** (Virgin of the Cave; ☎ 22420 31125; admission by donation; 10.30am-3pm), which is crammed with ecclesiastical paraphernalia. Turn right at the end of the main street to reach the signposted steps up to the monastery.

The impressive Mycenaean-era acropolis, **Paleokastro** (Old Kastro) above Mandraki has well-preserved Cyclopean walls built from massive blocks of volcanic rock. Follow the route signposted '*kastro*', near the monastery steps. This eventually becomes a path. At the road, turn right and the *kastro* is on the left.

Hohlaki is a black-stone beach and can usually be relied upon for swimming unless the wind is up, when the water can get rough. It's on the western side of Moni Panagias Spilianis and is reached by a paved path. The small sandy **Mandraki beach** halfway between the port and the village centre is popular and perfectly OK for swimming.

Sleeping

Mandraki has a fairly limited amount of accommodation and owners do not meet incoming ferries. Book ahead to be assured of a bed in July and August.

Iliovasilema Rooms (☎ 22420 31159; d €25) Occupying one of the few central Mandraki spots, the most economical option are these fairly basic, but conveniently located rooms on the Mandraki waterfront near the old windmill.

Three Brothers Hotel (☎ 22420 31344; iiibrother@kos .forthnet.gr; s/d €36/36; ⚡) Handy for the port and overlooking the harbour, rooms are presentable, though rather small, and come with TV and fridge.

Hotel Porfyris (☎ 22420 31376; diethnes@otenet.gr; s/d €35/40; ⚡) Set at the back end of Mandraki, this hotel, with its now rather tired-looking early-1990s (solid, dull, rather chunky) décor is nonetheless a cool oasis. There is a large reception area, while the rooms, with fridge, TV and phone, tend to be on the cramped side.

Haritos Hotel (☎ 22420 31322; www.haritoshotel.gr; d/tr €40/50; ⚡ ⚡) A better choice, the Haritos is located 200m along the Pali road. The rooms are well appointed and have fridge, TV and telephone, and there's a welcome swimming pool fed by seawater.

our pick **Ta Liotridia** (☎ 22420 31580; ste €150; ⚡) For a classy and romantic place to sleep in Mandraki, book one of the two suites above two converted oil presses. Decorated in classic Nisyriot style, with raised beds, solid furnishings, TV and a little stove top, the suites are not cheap but they're worth it for the sea views alone.

Eating

Ask for the island speciality, *pitties* (chickpea and onion patties), and wash them down with a refreshing *soumada*, a nonalcoholic local beverage made from almond extract.

Taverna Panorama (☎ 22420 31185; grills €3-5) Just off Plateia Ilikiomenis, heading towards Hotel Porfyris, this is a commendable option. Try suckling pig or goat, or even the *seftelies* (Cypriot-style herb-laced sausages).

our pick **Tony's Tavern** (☎ 22420 31460; mains €3.50-5) On the waterfront, ex-Melbournian butcher Tony does great breakfasts and excellent meat and fish dishes, as well as a wide range of vegetarian choices. His *gyros* (meat slivers cooked on a vertical rotisserie) is reputedly the best on Nisyros.

Kleanthes Taverna (☎ 22420 31484; mezedhes €3.50-5) Perfect for a relaxed evening meal of well-prepared mezedhes and ouzo. Further east along the waterfront from Tony's, Kleanthes is a perennial favourite among locals and visitors alike.

Taverna Nisyros (☎ 22420 31460; grills €4-5; ☾ dinner) This taverna, just off the main street, is a cheap and cheerful little place serving enticing charcoal grills and *souvlakia*.

Restaurant Irini (☎ 22420 31365; Plateia Ilikiomenis; mains €3-5.50) Irini, on the leafy and shady central square, is recommended for its low-priced, no-nonsense and very good quality home cooking. Go inside and select your meal.

AROUND NISYROS
The Volcano Το Ηφαίστειο

Nisyros is on a volcanic line that passes through the islands of Aegina, Paros, Milos, Santorini, Nisyros, Giali and Kos. The island originally culminated in a mountain of 850m, but the centre collapsed 30,000 to 40,000 years ago after three violent eruptions. Their legacy are the white-and-orange pumice stones that can still be seen on the northern, eastern and southern flanks of the island, and the large lava flow that covers the whole southwest, around Nikea village. The first eruption partially blew off the top of the ancestral cone, but the majority of the sinking of the central part of the island came about as a result of the removal of magma from within the reservoir underground.

Another violent eruption occurred in 1422 on the western side of the caldera depression (called Lakki); this, like all others since, emitted steam, gases and mud, but no lava.

The islanders call the volcano Polyvotis because, during the Great War between the gods and the Titans, the Titan Polyvotis annoyed Poseidon so much that the god tore off a chunk of Kos and threw it at him. This rock pinned Polyvotis under it and became the island of Nisyros. The hapless Polyvotis from that day forth has been groaning and sighing while trying to escape – hence the volcano's name.

There are five craters in the **caldera** (admission €2.50; ☺ 9am-8pm). A not-so-obvious and unsignposted path descends into the largest one, **Stefanos**, where you can examine the multicoloured fumaroles, listen to their hissing and smell their sulphurous vapours. The surface is soft and hot, making sturdy footwear essential. Be careful you don't step into a fumarole, as the steam can cause severe burns. Another unsignposted but more obvious track leads you in six to seven minutes to **Polyvotis**, which is smaller and wilder looking, but doesn't allow access to the caldera itself.

The easiest way to visit the volcano is by tourist bus, but you will share your experience with hordes of day-trippers. Better still, scooter in from Mandraki or walk down from Nikia. Get there before 11am and you may have the volcano entirely to yourself.

Emborios & Nikea Εμπορειός & Νίκαια

Emborios and Nikea perch on the volcano's rim. From each, there are stunning views down into the caldera. Only a handful of inhabitants linger on in Emborios. You may encounter a few elderly women sitting on their doorsteps crocheting, and their husbands at the *kafeneio* (coffee house). But generally, the winding, stepped streets are empty, the silence broken only by the occasional braying of a donkey or the grunting of pigs. There's just one place to eat, the seasonal **To Balkoni tou Emboriou** (☎ 22420 31607; mains €3-5), where you can enjoy the view of the crater over a relaxed lunch.

In contrast to Emborios, picturesque Nikea, with 35 inhabitants, buzzes with life. It has dazzling white houses with vibrant gardens and a central square with a lovely pebble mosaic. The bus terminates on Plateia Nikolaou Hartofyli. Nikea's main street links the two squares.

The steep path down to the volcano begins from Plateia Nikolaou Hartofyli. It takes about 40 minutes to walk it one way. Near the beginning you can detour to the signposted **Moni Agiou Ioanni Theologou**, where there is an annual **feast** on 25 to 26 September.

Pali Πάλοι

Pali is a small yacht anchorage with limited accommodation, yet a number of places to eat. The island's better beaches start here. Pali's own narrow beach is shaded by tamarisk trees and the water is shallow and suitable for children. Further along at **Lies**, 5.5km around the coast, is another unshaded beach, but you are better off walking an extra kilometre along an occasionally precarious coastal track to **Pahia Ammos**, a broad expanse of gravelly, volcanic sand. Bring your own shade.

If you decide to stick around Pali, head for one of the 12 comfy, self-contained studios at **Mammis' Apartments** (☎ 22420 31453; www.mammis .com; d €50), on the last bend before you enter Pali proper. Thousands of butterflies may swarm here in June.

The most reputable of Pali's eating options is the **Captain's House** (☎ 22420 31016; grills €5-7), where you have a choice of home cooking or fish and meat grills, and where you can sit at lunch and watch the fishermen unravel their nets next to your table.

KOS ΚΩΣ

pop 17,890

Second only to Rhodes in popularity and population, Kos *(koss)* is a mellowed-down version of its big sister to the south. Beyond the resort hotels that welcome arrivals, Kos offers another less commercial face once you let the island get under your skin. Elongated and running almost west to east, Kos offers a spread of things to see and do – from beaches and bars to cycling and cars with which to tour verdant hills, remote coves, and high-energy beach resorts.

Archaeology buffs will find their niche in the home of western medicine. Hippocrates, the father of medicine, lived and practised here. The island has a good balance of amenities and attractions, and oodles of room to spread out. Kos certainly grows on you, but it needs a little more time than you might at first believe.

History

Kos' fertile land attracted settlers from the earliest days. So many people lived here by

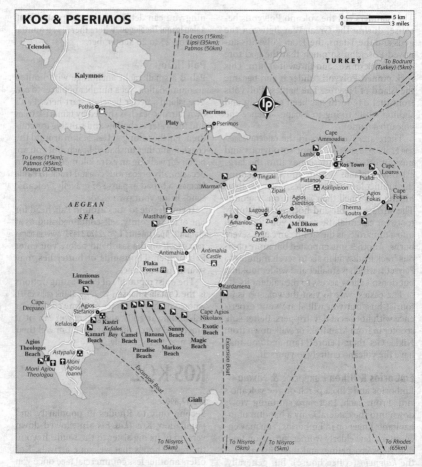

KOS & PSERIMOS

Mycenaean times that it sent 30 ships to the Trojan War. During the 7th and 6th centuries BC Kos prospered as an ally of the powerful Rhodian cities of Ialysos, Kamiros and Lindos. In 477 BC, after suffering an earthquake and subjugation to the Persians, it joined the Delian League and again flourished.

Hippocrates (460–377 BC), the ancient-Greek physician known as the founder of medicine, was born and lived on the island. After Hippocrates' death, the Sanctuary of Asclepius and a medical school were built, which perpetuated his teachings and made Kos famous throughout the Greek world.

Ptolemy II of Egypt was born on Kos, thus securing it the protection of Egypt, under

which it became a prosperous trading centre. In 130 BC Kos came under Roman domination, and in the 1st century AD it was administered by Rhodes, with which it came to share the same vicissitudes, right up to the tourist deluge of the present day.

Getting There & Away
AIR

There are three flights daily to Athens (€75, 55 minutes), and three flights a week to Rhodes (€45, 20 minutes), Leros (€45, 15 minutes) and Astypalea (€51, one hour). **Olympic Airlines** (☎ 22420 28330; www.olympicairlines.com; Vasileos Pavlou 22) is in Kos Town. The **airport** (☎ 22420 51229) is 24km from Kos Town near the village of Antimahia.

AirSea Lines (☎ 801 11 800 600; www.airsealines.com) also offers flights to Kalymnos (€30, 15 minutes), Mykonos (€92, 1½ hours) and Lavrio (€132, three hours), on the mainland. Flights leave from Kos airport.

FERRY
Domestic
Kos is well connected to Piraeus (€42 to €45, 10 to 15 hours) and with all the islands in the Dodecanese, such as Rhodes (€14.20, 3½ hours) and Patmos (€11.50, four hours), as well as additional connections to the Cyclades. In summer there is a weekly ferry service from Kos Town to Samos and Thessaloniki. Services are offered by three ferry companies: **Blue Star Ferries** (☎ 22420 28914), **G&A Ferries** (☎ 22420 28545) and the **ANE Kalymnou** (☎ 22420 29900).

Local car ferries run to Pothia on Kalymnos from Mastihari (€3.50, one hour, four daily). In addition there are faster, passenger-only small ferries run by ANE Kalymnou, namely the *Kalymnos Star* and *Kalymnos Dolphin* from Mastihari to Pothia running up to five times daily.

International
There are daily excursion boats in summer travelling from Kos Town to Bodrum in Turkey (€34 return, one hour). Boats leave at 8.30am and return at 4.30pm.

HYDROFOIL & CATAMARAN
Kos is served by Aegean Hydrofoils and the *Dodekanisos Express* and *Dodekanisos Pride* catamarans. In high season there are daily services to and from Rhodes (€28, two hours), with good connections to all the major islands in the group, as well as Samos (€25, four hours) in the Northeastern Aegean.

Information and tickets are available from the many travel agents in Kos Town, though in addition to **Exas Travel** (☎ 22420 28545; www .exas.gr), **Hermes Shipping Agency** (☎ 22420 26607; hermes@kos.forthnet.gr) is another reliable agency.

Getting Around
TO/FROM THE AIRPORT
An Aegean Airlines bus (€4) leaves the airline's office two hours before the Athens departure flights. The airport is 24km southwest of Kos Town. Kefalos buses stop at the big roundabout near the airport entrance. A taxi to/from the airport from Kos Town will cost around €22.

BUS
The **bus station** (☎ 22420 22292; Kleopatras 7) is just west of the Olympic Airlines office. Buses regularly serve all parts of the island, as well as the all-important beaches on the south side of Kos. A bus to the beaches will cost around €3.60.

Urban buses have two ticket prices: zone A (€0.80) and zone B (€1). An automatic ticket vending machine is in front of the Blue Star Ferries office on the harbour.

CAR, MOTORCYCLE & BICYCLE
There are numerous car, motorcycle and moped-rental outlets. You'll be tripping over bicycles to rent; prices range from €5 for a bone shaker to €10 for a half-decent mountain bike. Cycling is very popular in Kos, so make the best of the opportunity.

EXCURSION BOAT
From Kos Town there are many boat excursions around the island and to other islands. Examples of return fares: Kalymnos €10; Pserimos, Kalymnos and Platy €20; and Nisyros €20. There is also a daily excursion boat from Kardamena to Nisyros (€14 return) and from Mastihari to Pserimos and Kalymnos. In Kos Town these boats line the southern arm of Akti Koundourioti.

TAXIS
Taxis congregate at a stand on the south side of the port.

TOURIST TRAIN
You can take a guided tour of Kos in the city's (vehicular) Tourist Train (€4, 20 minutes), which runs from 10am to 2pm and 6pm to 10pm starting from the **Municipality Building** (Vasileos Georgiou 1). Or take a train to the Asklipieion and back (return €4), departing on the hour from 10am to 5pm Tuesday to Sunday, from the Municipal Tourist Office (p320).

KOS TOWN
pop 14,750
Kos Town, on the northeast coast, is the island's capital and main port. The New Town, although modern, is picturesque and lush, with an abundance of palms, pines, oleander and hibiscus. The Castle of the Knights dominates the port, and Hellenistic and Roman ruins are strewn everywhere. It's a pleasant

DODECANESE

enough place and can easily be covered on foot in half a day. The Old Town was destroyed by an earthquake in 1933 and only part of it exists intact today.

Orientation

The ferry quay is north of the castle. The central square of Plateia Eleftherias is south of the harbour-side street, Akti Koundourioti, along Vasileos Pavlou. What's left of Kos' Old Town is a smallish area bounded by Akti Koundourioti, Kolokotroni, Eleftheriou Venizelou and Vasileos Pavlou. It's now full of souvenir shops, jewellers and boutiques.

Southeast of the castle, the waterfront is called Akti Miaouli. It continues as Vasileos Georgiou and then Georgiou Papandreou, which leads to the beaches of Psalidi, Agios Fokas and Therma Loutra.

Information

BOOKSHOPS
News Stand (☎ 22420 30110; Riga Fereou 2) Sells foreign-language newspapers and publications.

EMERGENCY
Police (☎ 22420 22222) Shares the Municipality Building with the tourist police.
Port police (cnr Akti Koundourioti & Megalou Alexandrou)
Tourist police (☎ 22420 22444)

INTERNET ACCESS
Cafe Del Mare (☎ 22420 24244; www.cybercafe.gr; Megalou Alexandrou 4; per hr €2; ☷ 9am-1am) A regular café, too.

INTERNET RESOURCES
www.travel-to-kos.com Comprehensive guide to most of Kos' attractions.

LAUNDRY
Laundromat Center (Alikarnassou 124; wash & dry €7)

MEDICAL SERVICES
Hospital (☎ 22420 22300; Ippokratous 32) In the centre of town.

MONEY
Alpha Bank (Akti Koundourioti) Has a 24-hour automatic exchange machine and an ATM. There is another branch at El Venizelou, also with an ATM.
National Bank of Greece (Riga Fereou) With ATM.

POST
Post office (El Venizelou)

TOURIST INFORMATION
Municipal Tourist Office (☎ 22420 24460; www.kos info.gr; Vasileos Georgiou 1; ☷ 8am-2.30pm & 3-10pm Mon-Fri, 9am-2pm Sat May-Oct) Has general information on Kos Town.

Sights

ARCHAEOLOGICAL MUSEUM
There's a fine 3rd-century-AD mosaic in the vestibule of the archaeological museum (☎ 22420 28326; Plateia Eleftherias; adult/student €3/2; ☷ 8am-2.30pm Tue-Sun). The most renowned statue is that of Hippocrates.

ARCHAEOLOGICAL SITES
The ancient agora (admission free) is an open site south of the castle. A massive 3rd-century-BC stoa, with some reconstructed columns, stands on its western side. On the north side are the ruins of a Shrine of Aphrodite, Temple of Hercules and a 5th-century Christian basilica.

North of the agora is the lovely cobblestone Plateia Platanou, where you can pay your respects to the Hippocrates Plane Tree, under which Hippocrates is said to have taught his pupils. Plane trees don't usually live for more than 200 years, though in all fairness this is certainly one of Europe's oldest. This once-magnificent tree is held up with scaffolding, and looks to be in its death throes. Beneath it is an old sarcophagus converted by the Turks into a fountain. Opposite the tree is the well-preserved 18th-century Mosque of Gazi Hassan Pasha, its ground-floor loggia now converted into souvenir shops.

From Plateia Platanou a bridge leads across Finikon (called the Ave of Palms) to the Castle of the Knights (☎ 22420 27927; Leoforos Finikon; admission €4; ☷ 8am-2.30pm Tue-Sun). Along with the castles of Rhodes Town and Bodrum, this impregnable fortress was the knights' most stalwart defence against the encroaching Ottomans. The castle, which had massive outer walls and an inner keep, was built in the 14th century. Damaged by an earthquake in 1495, it was restored by the Grand Masters d'Aubuisson and d'Amboise (each a master of a 'tongue' of knights – see p281 for details) in the 16th century. The keep was originally separated from the town by a moat (now Finikon).

On the west of the town, facing Grigoriou, turn right to reach the western excavation site. Two wooden shelters at the back of the site protect the 3rd-century mosaics of the House of Europa. The best-preserved mosaic depicts

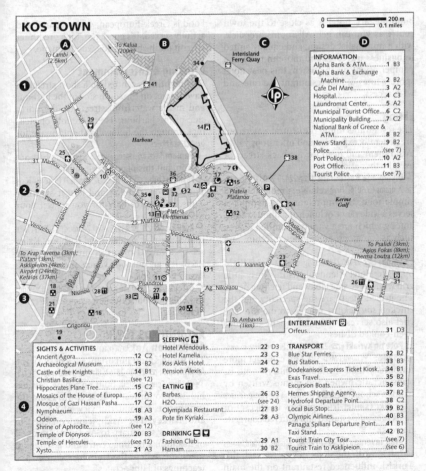

KOS TOWN

0	200 m
0	0.1 miles

INFORMATION
Alpha Bank & ATM	1 B3
Alpha Bank & Exchange Machine	2 B2
Cafe Del Mare	3 A2
Hospital	4 C3
Laundromat Center	5 A2
Municipal Tourist Office	6 C2
Municipality Building	7 C2
National Bank of Greece & ATM	8 B2
News Stand	9 B2
Police	(see 7)
Port Police	10 A2
Post Office	11 B3
Tourist Police	(see 7)

SIGHTS & ACTIVITIES
Ancient Agora	12 C2
Archaeological Museum	13 B2
Castle of the Knights	14 B1
Christian Basilica	(see 12)
Hippocrates Plane Tree	15 C2
Mosaics of the House of Europa	16 A3
Mosque of Gazi Hassan Pasha	17 C2
Nymphaeum	18 A3
Odeion	19 A3
Shrine of Aphrodite	(see 12)
Temple of Dionysos	20 B3
Temple of Hercules	(see 12)
Xysto	21 A3

SLEEPING
Hotel Afendoulis	22 D3
Hotel Kamelia	23 C3
Kos Aktis Hotel	24 C2
Pension Alexis	25 A2

EATING
Barbas	26 D3
H2O	(see 24)
Olympiada Restaurant	27 B3
Pote tin Kyriaki	28 A3

DRINKING
Fashion Club	29 A1
Hamam	30 B2

ENTERTAINMENT
Orfeus	31 D3

TRANSPORT
Blue Star Ferries	32 B2
Bus Station	33 B3
Dodekanisos Express Ticket Kiosk	34 B1
Exas Travel	35 B2
Excursion Boats	36 B2
Hermes Shipping Agency	37 B2
Hydrofoil Departure Point	38 C2
Local Bus Stop	39 B2
Olympic Airlines	40 B3
Panagia Spiliani Departure Point	41 B1
Taxi Stand	42 B2
Tourist Train City Tour	(see 7)
Tourist Train to Asklipieion	(see 6)

Europa's abduction by Zeus in the guise of a bull. In front of here is an exposed section of the **Decumanus Maximus** (the Roman city's main thoroughfare), which runs parallel to the modern road then turns right towards the **nymphaeum**, which consisted of once-lavish latrines, and the **xysto**, a large Hellenistic gymnasium with restored columns. On the opposite side of Grigoriou is the restored 3rd-century **odeion**. The **Temple of Dionysos** consists of a few scant ruins and is located a short distance from the main site.

Sleeping

Pension Alexis (☎ 22420 28798; fax 22420 25797; Irodotou 9; s/d €25/30;) This convivial travellers' pension has long been a budget favourite with visitors to the island. It has very clean rooms, a communal kitchen, and a large relaxing veranda and garden.

Hotel Kamelia (☎ 22420 28983; www.camelia-hotel.com; Artemisias; s/d €25/45; Jun-Oct;) On a quiet tree-lined street, the Kamelia is a pleasant C-class hotel with simple but comfortable rooms with satellite TV and video.

our pick Hotel Afendoulis (☎ 22420 25321; www.afendoulishotel.com; Evripilou 1; s/d €35/50;) The ebullient, English-speaking Alexis Zikas runs this very relaxed, traveller-friendly family-style establishment. The rooms are tastefully decorated and wi-fi is available in the hotel. Breakfast is optional and is offered until late.

Kos Aktis Hotel (☎ 22420 47200; www.kos.aktis.gr; Vasileos Georgiou 7; s/d €120/150;) Kos' newest

DODECANESE

boutique 'art' hotel is as close to the town centre as you can get. All rooms are slick, with a minimalist design, and equally suited to business travellers and those in need of a pamper. Right on the beach, this neat hotel sports a fine outdoor restaurant and café, and wi-fi access.

Eating

The restaurants lining the central waterfront are generally expensive and offer poor value; avoid them and head for the back streets or even further afield.

Olympiada Restaurant (☎ 22420 23031; Kleopatras 2; mains €3.50-4) For reliable, predictable and simple food, the unpretentious Olympiada serves a wide range of lunch and dinner meals, among which are a variety of stuffed dishes, such as tomatoes, aubergines, zucchini and vine leaves.

Barbas (☎ 22400 27856; Evripilou 6; mains €3-5) Right opposite Hotel Afendoulis is this busy little grill with street-side tables and fetching décor. The grilled meats are the speciality and the chicken *souvlaki* or fillet is to die for. The chef also serves a range of equally delicious oven-cooked dishes.

Pote tin Kyriaki (☎ 22420 27872; Pisandrou 9; mezedhes €3.50-5; ⏲ dinner Mon-Sat) You can't get more untouristy than this quirky *ouzerie* with its idiosyncratic owner and menus written by hand in school exercise books. Try the *garides saganaki* (skillet-fried prawns in cheese) or *kolokythoanthi* (stuffed and battered courgette flowers).

Arap Taverna (☎ 22420 28442; Memis, Platani; mains €4-7) It's worth the slight detour to reach this Turkish-influenced restaurant on the main square in Platani, 3km southwest from Kos town. Check out the yogurt-flavoured dishes like *yiaourtoglou* (fried aubergines and courgette slices in yogurt), or *kavourma* (pork cubes with hot green chillies in a tomato sauce).

our pick **Ambavris** (☎ 22420 25696; mains €4-8) For sheer ambience as well as excellent food, walk 15 minutes south out of town to this relaxed and totally nontouristy taverna. Unassuming, quality dishes are all served with a smile and friendly attitude. Try the *strapatsada* (vegetarian egg and tomato mix).

H2O (☎ 22420 47200; Vasileos Georgiou 7; mains €6-12) Part of the Kos Aktis Hotel complex, this cool, suave diner on the beach is almost totally overlooked by foreign travellers. It enjoys an almost exclusively discerning Greek clientele.

Food is Greek-European, well prepared and artfully served. It's good, too, for a predinner aperitif on the beach-side wooden patio.

Drinking & Entertainment

Kos' nightlife is centred on a short stretch of paved street on the south side of the harbour and in the waterfront streets on the north side of the harbour. There are lots of pickings, though the following should make for good starters.

Hamam (Akti Koundourioti 1) Most bars belt out techno, but this plays Greek music.

Fashion Club (☎ 22420 22592; Kanari 2) One of Kos Town's more popular and longer-standing clubs, with three bars for you to wet your whistle.

Kalua (☎ 22420 24938; Akti Zouroudi 3) Further round the north side of the harbour, Kalua serves a mixed menu of music, including R&B. It's an outdoor venue and also has a swimming pool.

Orfeus (☎ 22420 25036; Fenaretis 3; adult €6; ⏲ summer) This outdoor cinema screens a wide range of movies.

AROUND KOS TOWN
Asklipieion Ασκληπιείον

The island's most important ancient site is the **Asklipieion** (☎ 22420 28763; Platani; adult/student €4/3; ⏲ 8.30am-6pm Tue-Sun), built on a pine-covered hill 3km southwest of Kos Town. From the top there is a wonderful view of Kos Town and Turkey. The Asklipieion consisted of a religious sanctuary to Asclepius (the god of healing), a healing centre and a school of medicine, where the training followed the teachings of Hippocrates.

Hippocrates was the first-known doctor to have a rational approach to diagnosing and treating illnesses. Until AD 554, when an earthquake destroyed the Asklipieion, people came from far and wide to be treated here, as well as for medical training.

The ruins occupy three levels. The **propylaea** (approach to the main gate), Roman-era public **baths** and remains of guest rooms are on the first level. On the second level is a 4th-century-BC **altar of Kyparissios Apollo**. West of this is the **first Temple of Asclepius**, built in the 4th century BC. To the east is the 1st-century-BC **Temple to Apollo**; seven of its columns have been re-erected. On the third level are the remains of the once-magnificent 2nd-century-BC **Temple of Asclepius**.

Frequent buses and the Tourist Train (p319) go to the site, but it is pleasant to cycle or walk there.

AROUND KOS

Kos' main road runs southwest from Kos Town, with turn-offs for the mountain villages and the resorts of Tingaki and Marmari. Between the main road and the coast is a quiet road, ideal for cycling, which winds through flat agricultural land as far as Marmari.

The nearest decent beach to Kos Town is the crowded **Lambi Beach**, 4km to the northwest. Further round the coast, **Tingaki**, 10km from Kos Town, has an excellent, long pale-sand beach. **Marmari Beach**, 4km west of Tingaki, is slightly less crowded. You can easily ride your bike to these beaches via the quiet coastal road. Windsurfing is popular at all three beaches. In summer there are boats from Marmari to the island of Pserimos.

Vasileos Georgiou (later G Papandreou) in Kos Town leads to the three busy beaches of **Psalidi**, 3km from Kos Town, **Agios Fokas** (8km) and **Therma Loutra** (12km). The latter has hot mineral springs that warm the sea.

Mastihari Μαστιχάρι

Escapist travellers who seek to avoid the crowds of Kos Town head to Mastihari, 30km away. It's a resort destination of sorts, but also an arrival/departure point for ferries to Pothia on Kalymnos. It's better equipped to cater for independent travellers, with a wide range of rooms and studios to rent. The beach is wide and sandy, though it does get the summer winds, and it's an open, relaxed village that feels just a little more Greek than its neighbours. Excursion boats run from here to the island of Pserimos, where you can escape for a day to its protected sandy beach and convenient tavernas.

The back streets and seafront of Mastihari are full of rental options. Among these are **Athina Studios** (☎ 22420 59030; www.athinas-studios .gr; s/d €30-40), a block of bougainvillea-strewn apartments decorated in vivid blue and white, one street from the beach. Spacious and clean, they have full kitchen facilities. On the same street, **To Kyma** (☎ 22420 59045; kyma@kosweb .com; s/d €30/35) is a pleasant, small, family-run hotel with smallish but presentable rooms that enjoy a good sea breeze. There is a clean and homey communal kitchen for guests' use. Overlooking the west beach, **Rooms Panorama**

(☎ /fax 22420 59145; studios €35; ⚡) has tidy, fully equipped studios, most with a kitchenette.

Right on the harbour, the busy **Kali Kardia Restaurant** (☎ 22420 59289; fish €7-11) is commendable – the fish is particularly good. Ignore the kitsch name and sign, the **Tasty Palace** (☎ 22420 59019; mains €4-6.50) is right on the beach. Look for the daily specials board featuring 'mum's fish soup' (rabbit in red wine sauce or chicken in lemon sauce). It also serves as an internet access point.

For drinks, the **Saloon Bar** (☎ 22420 59318) at the beginning of the beach boardwalk serves ice-cold beer, ouzo and mezedhes and is a great spot to watch the sun go down. Come here for breakfast, too.

Mountain Villages

Several attractive villages are scattered on the northern slopes of the green and wooded alpine-like Dikeos mountain range. At **Zipari**, 10km from the capital, a road to the southeast leads to **Asfendiou**. Along the way, 3km past Zipari, you will pass **Taverna Panorama** (☎ 22420 69367; mezedhes €3-5; ⚡ lunch and dinner), which enjoys a splendid night-time view with barely a tourist in sight, as most head for Zia. Enjoy good mezedhes and excellent service in the company of a primarily Greek clientele.

From Asfendiou, a turn-off to the left leads to the pristine hamlet of **Agios Dimitrios**. The road straight ahead leads to the village of **Zia**, which pulls in coachloads of tourists, but is still worth a visit for the surrounding countryside, honey, herbs and spices, and some spectacular sunsets.

For eating choices in Zia, **Kefalovrysi** (☎ 22420 69605; mains €5-8), a six-minute walk from the square to the upper end of the village, takes top marks for its well-priced, high-quality dishes. Among the more original choices are tomato balls, *salamoura* (pork cubes with onions) and Florina peppers stuffed with cheese. Back along the main drag in Zia, **Taverna Olympia** (☎ 22420 69121; mains €5-8) is a less obvious choice – as it doesn't have the views down to the plains – but it earns its good reputation based on solid, reliable local cuisine and its repeat clientele.

Lagoudi is a small, unspoilt village to the northwest of Zia. From here you can continue to **Amaniou** (just before modern Pyli), where there is a left turn to the ruins of the medieval village of **Pyli**, overlooked by an interesting ruined **castle**. The village of Pyli has a pleasant eating venue, **Palia Pygi** (☎ 22420 41510; mains €5-7.50), a little taverna overlooking a lion-headed fountain just off the central square. It serves sizzling grills and filling home-cooked dishes from the oven.

Kamari & Kefalos Bay Καμάρι & Κέφαλος

From Antimahia the main road continues southwest to the huge Kefalos Bay, fringed by a 12km stretch of sand, which is divided into roughly seven 'name' beaches, forming the soft sandy, underbelly of Kos. Each is signposted from the main road. The most popular is **Paradise Beach**, while the most undeveloped is **Exotic Beach**; **Banana Beach** (also known as Langada Beach) is a good compromise.

Agios Stefanos Beach at the far western end is dominated by a vast Club Med complex. The beach, reached along a short turn-off from the main road, is still worth a visit to see the island of **Agios Stefanos** (named after its church), which is within swimming distance, and the ruins of two 5th-century basilicas to the left of the beach as you face the sea.

Kefalos, 43km southwest of Kos Town, is a sprawling village perched high above **Kamari Beach**. It's an animated village with few concessions to tourism. The central square, where the bus terminates, is at the top of the 2km road from the coast. There is a post office and a bank with an ATM here.

Kamari Beach, on the other hand, is an elongated holiday resort strip, some 2km from tip to toe and packed with restaurants, accommodation, shops and tourist facilities, including a handy ATM on the main road at the southern end. Water sports are big business here. Despite the clutter, the bay is quite alluring and the best overall stretch is at the southern end, where the beach is more easily accessible. Excursion boats leave from here for Nisyros (€16) two or three times weekly.

There is a good choice of sleeping options, mostly consisting of studios and rooms. About 150m south of the Kamari seafront bus stop you'll find **Anthoula Studios** (☎ 22420 71904; studios €40), a spotless set of airy and roomy studios surrounded by a flourishing vegetable garden. Also nearby, **Rooms to Let Katerina** (☎ 22420 71397; studios €40) is a similar choice, although studios are a bit smaller. For eating, **Stamatia** (☎ 22420 71245; mains €4-7.50) has a good range of well-prepared fish and meat dishes, plus some imaginative

vegetarian choices like onion balls, garlic mushrooms or fried zucchini.

The southern peninsula has the island's most wild and rugged scenery. **Agios Theologos Beach** is on the east coast, 7km from Kefalos at the end of a winding sealed road. The beach is often surf-battered and the waters tempestuous. The only place to eat is **Restaurant Agios Theologos** (☎ 69727 45691; mains €6.70-12.50), which enjoys the best sunsets in Kos, as well as serving up tasty fish dishes, such as white snapper, plus home-made goat's cheese and crusty home-baked bread.

ASTYPALEA
ΑΣΤΥΠΑΛΑΙΑ

pop 1238

If ever there was an island looking for an identity, it is Astypalea (ah-stih-*pah*-lia). Looking to all intents and purposes like an archetypically Cycladic island with its mandatory and picture-pretty hill-top *hora* (main town), yet belonging administratively to the Dodecanese, this butterfly-shaped gem of an island is a stunner and offers instant appeal. People come to Astypalea and never leave. It has that pull. Outside of the bustling port and cubist *hora*, the land is bare and eroded with nary a tree in sight. Its beaches are scattered, but most are excellent. Adventurers can seek off-road thrills in some rough and empty terrain, while gastronomes will dine well on fresh fish and lobster. Mass foreign tourism is never seen here, yet in July and August Athenians descend in force and generate controlled chaos. If you want that alternative holiday experience, look no further.

Getting There & Away

AIR

There are five flights weekly from Astypalea to Athens (€58, 50 minutes), plus three flights weekly to Leros (€45, 20 minutes), Kos (€51, one hour) and Rhodes (€51, 1½ hours). **Astypalea Tours** (☎ 22430 61571), in Skala, is the agent for Olympic Airlines.

FERRY

Astypalea has up to five services a week in summer to Piraeus (€33.50, 10 to 12 hours) via Naxos (€23, 3¾ hours) and Paros (€28.50, 4¾ hours), and two a week to Rhodes (€28,

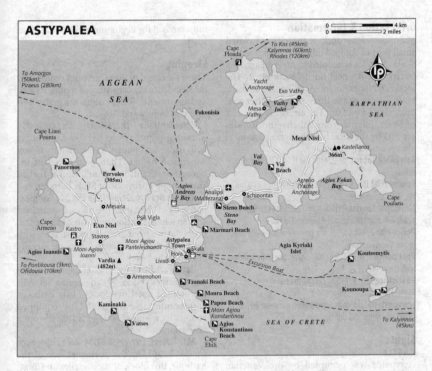

ASTYPALEA

seven to nine hours) via Kalymnos and Kos. The Kalymnos-based ferry *F/B Nissos Kalymnos* calls in three times weekly, linking the island with Kalymnos and islands further north in the Dodecanese. Ferry tickets are available from **Paradisos Ferries Agency** (☎ 22430 61224; fax 22430 61450) or from **Astypalea Tours** (☎ 22430 61571), both in Skala.

Getting Around

From Skala a bus travels every 30 minutes in July and August (four times daily other months) to Hora and Livadi (€1), and from Hora and Skala hourly in July and August (three times daily other months) to Analipsi (Maltezana; €1.50) via Marmari Beach. The 12pm departure terminates at the airport to connect with the Athens and Rhodes flights. There are only three taxis on the island. There are at least three car- and scooter-rental agencies on the island. **Vergoulis** (☎ 22430 61351) in Skala is a reputable agency.

EXCURSION BOAT

From June right through the summer to August there is a daily excursion boat, **Thalas-**

sopouli (☎ 6974436338), that owner Yiannis takes to the more remote western beaches of Agios Ioannis, Kaminakia and Vatses, or to the islets of Koutsomytis or Kounoupa. When the weather is good, he runs longer round-island excursions. Tickets (€10 to €15) can be bought on the boat.

SKALA & HORA ΣΚΑΛΑ & ΧΩΡΑ

The main settlement of Astypalea consists of the port of Skala (known officially as Pera Yialos) and the picturesque hill-top village of Hora, crowned by an imposing 15th-century castle. Skala can get hot and noisy in July and August, but offers a fairly popular and handy sand and pebble beach for a cooling dip. Most visitors head uphill to the usually much cooler Hora, where you can catch a hill-top breeze and enjoy a stunning view of the port and surrounds. The main square in Hora is backed by several restored windmills and is the main focal point of activity. Leading upwards from here to the castle is a series of narrow streets with dazzling-white cubic houses sporting brightly painted balconies, doors and banisters.

Orientation & Information

Mainline ferries dock at the rather isolated small port of Agios Andreas, 6.5km north of Skala. A bus is scheduled to meet all arriving ferries, but it's best not to bank on it. The local *F/B Nissos Kalymnos* still docks at Skala. Look for one of the three taxis or better still, prearrange a pickup. The airport is 8km east of Skala. Flights from Athens and Rhodes are met by the local bus, though a pick-up is always a better option.

Astypalea Tours (☎ 22430 61571) In Skala. For air tickets.

Commercial Bank (☎ 22430 61402) Has an ATM; on the Skala waterfront.

Municipal Tourist Office (☎ 22430 61412; ☒ 10am-12pm & 6-9pm) In a restored windmill in Hora.

Police (☎ 22430 61207) In a prominent Italianate building on the waterfront.

Port police (☎ 22430 61208) Shares the same building with the police.

Post office (☎ 22430 61223) At the top of the Skala–Hora road.

www.astypalaia.com Gives a good rundown on the island's facilities and sights.

Sights

CASTLE

Astypalea was occupied by the Venetian Quirini family, one of whom, Giovanni, built the imposing **castle** (admission free; ☒ dawn to dusk) starting in 1413. In the Middle Ages the population lived within its walls in order to escape the depredations of piracy that was rife in the Aegean Sea, but gradually the settlement outgrew them. The last inhabitants left in 1953, following a devastating earthquake, as a result of which the stone houses collapsed. Above the tunnel-like entrance is the **Church of The Virgin of the Castle** and within the walls is the **Church of Agios Giorgios**. The castle is currently undergoing a prolonged restorative facelift.

ARCHAEOLOGICAL MUSEUM

Skala is home to a small **archaeological museum** (☎ 22430 61206; admission free; ☒ 11am-1pm Tue-Sun). The whole island of Astypalea is, in fact, a rich trove of archaeological treasure, and many of the finds are on display here. The collection runs from the prehistoric Mycenaean period through to the Middle Ages. Look out for a fine selection of grave offerings from two Mycenaean chamber tombs excavated at Armenohori, and the little bronze Roman statue of Aphrodite found at Trito Marmari. The museum is at the beginning of the Skala–Hora road.

Sleeping

There's a range of good sleeping options on the island, usually consisting of rooms, studios and apartments. Reservations are pretty well essential in July and August.

Hotel Australia (☎ 22430 61275; d/tr €45/50; ☒) This long-popular hotel has well-kept rooms with fridge and phone, and a friendly Greek Australian owner. There's an excellent in-house restaurant, too. You'll find it tucked away on the north side of Skala harbour.

Avra Studios (☎ 22430 61363; d €50; ☒) For location you can't beat these five fully self-contained and spacious studios right on Skala beach. From the two front ground-floor studios, with their own shaded balconies, you are literally 5m from the beach.

Hotel Paradissos (☎ 22430 61224; www.astypalea-paradissos.com; s/d €45/55; ☒) This ageing but well-maintained hotel overlooks Skala harbour, with comfortable fridge and TV-equipped rooms. Its main advantage is that it's open year-round.

Akti Rooms (☎ 22430 61114; www.aktirooms.gr; d/tr €65/70; ☒) On the northeast side of the harbour, this block of rooms, all with fridge, phone and TV, enjoys some superb harbour views from its balconies. Restaurant Akti, a popular restaurant-café, is handily located here, too.

ourpick Thalassa Hotel (☎ 22430 59840; www.stampalia.gr; d/t incl breakfast €100/120; ☒ ☐) The newest and unquestionably most enticing place to stay on the island is this relaxing hotel apartment complex in Skala. Rooms are spacious and airy and come with all facilities, including a bar fridge equipped with French champagne. Breakfast is made from organic local products.

Eating

There are not a lot of eating options in Astypalea, though the food tends to be of good quality. *Astakomakaronadha* (lobster in pasta) is the island's traditional (though pricey) dish.

Agoni Grammi (☎ 22430 61730; snacks €3-6) Australians take note: sit under a gum tree with ouzo on the rocks at sunset and a small platter of mezedhes and you'll almost feel at home. On the main square in Hora, this cosy café-cum-snack bar is a neat place to chill out at the end of a long day.

Jolly Café (☎ 22430 22430; breakfast €5-6) The best place to grab some breakfast is slap-bang on the Skala waterfront under the shade of a tamarisk tree. Grab some waffles and coffee early and later in the day a cold Corona and snack.

Maïstrali (☎ 22430 61691; mains €5-8) Tucked away in the little street behind the harbour is this yachtie-popular eatery that has a predictably fish-based menu, but occasional oven-baked specials such as succulent lemon goat. Service is brisk and friendly, and dining is alfresco on the shaded, stepped balcony.

Restaurant Akti (☎ 22430 61114; mains €8-8.50) For the best harbour-side dining in Astypalea give Akti a whirl. Perched high up on a cliff on the north side of Skala, the few tables overlooking the harbour are enormously popular. So, too, is the food, which includes fisherman's pasta or *poungia* (cheese foldovers).

our pick **To Akrogiali** (☎ 22430 61863; mains €5.50-9.50) Dine on the beach, literally, or on a pleasant slate-paved patio punctuated by a huge tamarisk tree. The smell of freshly cooked food from the busy kitchen complements the friendly service and good-quality mezedhes at this cosy taverna. Try the *tigania* (pork cubes) or soft local cheeses, such as *hlori* or *ladotyri*.

LIVADI ΛΕΙΒΑΔΙ

The little resort of Livadi lies in the heart of a fertile valley 2km from Hora. Its wide pebble and fine-gravel beach is one of the best on the island, but can get fairly crowded in summer. There are at least a couple of recommendable sleeping options. First up are the smallish but well-equipped **Venetos Studios** (☎ 22430 61490; fax 22430 61423; studios €50-60; ❄), set around a shady orange-tree grove. On the seafront itself are the neat studios of **Manganas** (☎ 22430 61468; astyroom@otenet.gr; studios €50-60; ❄), some 20m from the beach and each with kitchenette and fridge.

There are a handful of places to eat at Livadi – all strung out along the tree-shaded waterfront. **Trapezakia Exo** (☎ 22430 61083; mains €4-6.50) is a neat little snack-bar-cum-restaurant at the western end of the beach strip. Snap up a fast sandwich, enjoy the cuttlefish speciality or check out the daily specials menu – **Astropelos** (☎ 22430 61473; mains €6-9) serves a small but imaginative range of dishes. There is the pricey pasta with lobster or grilled giant prawns and a cheaper fried calamari option. It's worth it

for its shaded beach-front patio as much as for its cuisine.

WEST OF SKALA

Heading west of Skala you hit the big Astypalea outback. Here is a land of gnarled, bare and rolling hills with scarcely a sealed road to speak of. It's all driveable (just), but you'll need a solid 4WD or off-road motorcycle. An access road peels upwards northwesterly from Skala and follows the hill ridges past Psili Vigla to a road junction at Stavros after 6km. Head north and follow the sign to the so-called **Kastro** (Castle) near the **Moni Agiou Ioanni**, which is reached via a detour after another 2km. The strictly fit may venture downwards from here on foot to **Agios Ioannis beach**. If you keep driving or biking, you'll struggle up and down along an abominably rough road with nevertheless stunning views of the uninhabited islets of **Pontikousa** and **Ofidousa** off-shore to the lonely, yet very swimmable, **Panormos Beach**. Chances are that the beach will be yours alone as few people venture up here.

From the Stavros junction another rough track winds upwards to the shepherd's hut on the mountain spine and then an *extremely* rough track (take care) winds downwards to **Kaminakia beach**, where there is a good seasonal restaurant, **Sti Linda** (☎ 6932610050; mains €4-7; ❄ Jul-Sep), which rustles up hearty fish soups, oven-baked goat and home-made bread. The road back to **Livadi** is still unsealed but appreciably better. Detour, if time or energy allows, to the pretty, tree-shaded **Agios Konstantinos beach** on the south side of Livadi Bay.

EAST OF SKALA

To the east of Skala is the easterly wing of the 'butterfly' – the waist being marked by a narrow isthmus that barely joins the two halves of the island. **Marmari**, 2km northeast of Skala, has three bays with pebble and sand beaches and is home to Astypalea's **Camping Astypalea** (☎ 22430 61900; camp sites per adult/tent €6/4). Though it only operates from June to September, this tamarisk tree–shaded and bamboo-protected camping ground is right next to the beach and has a café and a minimarket. **Steno Beach**, 2km further along, is one of the better but least frequented beaches on the island. It's sandy, has shade and is well protected. This is the point where the island is just 105m wide.

Analipsi (also known as Maltezana) is 7km beyond Marmari in a fertile valley on the isthmus. A former Maltese pirates' lair, it's a scattered, pleasantly laid-back settlement with a long sand and pebble beach, shaded by more ever-welcoming tamarisk trees. The water is clean and shallow. There are the remains of the **Tallaras Roman baths** with mosaics on the settlement's outskirts.

Accommodation is concentrated in Maltezana. **Maltezana Rooms** (☎ 22430 61446; fax 22430 61370; d €35) is a pretty reasonable option, just east of the quay set back 50m from the beach. **Villa Varvara** (☎ /fax 22430 61448; studios €45/54; ✷) has 12 blue-and-white painted studios overlooking a vegetable garden and is just 100m from the beach; all have TV and fridge. The most expensive accommodation here, and on the island overall, is **Hotel Maltezana Beach** (☎ 22430 61558; www.maltezanabeach.gr; s/d €75/110; P ✷) on the middle section of the foreshore. The cubed, white studios are all spacious and tastefully furnished, though feel a little lonely in their isolation.

Eating choices in Maltezana are strictly limited. **Astakos** (☎ 22430 61865; mains €3-5), just over the headland at Schinontas, is perhaps the best choice of very few options. Try the *strapatsada* (wild-greens mélange mixed with egg yolk) or the *bourloto* (spicy oven-baked cheese).

Drive or ride an additional 11km as far as **Mesa Vathy** if curiosity gets the better of you. Perhaps detour to the unsheltered **Vaï beach** if you want to swim, or duck down to the small yacht haven at **Agrelidi**. Remote Mesa Vathy hamlet is an indolent yacht harbour in a sheltered bay. The swimming is mediocre at best, but you can fish for your lunch or dine at the laid-back **Galini Café** (☎ 22430 61201; mains €3-5; ◷ Jun-Oct), which offers meat and fish grills and the odd oven-baked special.

KALYMNOS
ΚΑΛΥΜΝΟΣ

pop 16,441

Kalymnos (*kah*-lim-nos) was once renowned as the 'sponge-fishing island', whose islanders travelled far and wide in search of this strange marine animal to equip our bathrooms. Today sponge fishing is all but gone and the island is working hard to reinvent itself as a tourist destination. It has a challenging task ahead of it, but it's making progress. Kalymnos is a largish, arid island, dotted with fertile valleys and punctuated by rocky mountains. It's

to the perpendicular cliffs of some of these mountains that climbers flock to test their mettle, as rock-climbing is big on Kalymnos. Its resorts cater mainly to individuals, and walkers will find a network of ready-to-walk trails and paths that criss-cross the landscape. While the main town can be busy and brash, and the islanders may seem a little preoccupied with business, Kalymnos offers a holiday lifestyle that will suit many.

Getting There & Away
AIR

Kalymnos is linked by a daily Olympic Airways flight to and from Athens (€75, 20 minutes). Olympic Airlines is represented by **Kapellas Travel** (☎ 22430 29265; kapellastravel@gallileo .gr; Patriarhou Maximou 12) in Pothia. The airport is some 3.5km northwest of Pothia, perched high up on a mountain top.

The island is also linked to Kos (€30, 15 minutes), Mykonos (€80, 45 minutes) and Lavrio (€120, two hours) on the Attica mainland via a seaplane run by **AirSea Lines** (☎ 801 11 800 600; www.airsealines.com). The seaplane terminal is 1.5km east of Pothia.

FERRY

Kalymnos is linked to Rhodes (€18, five hours) and Piraeus (€42, nine to 11 hours) and islands in between, including useful links to Astypalea (€11, three hours) and Alexandroupoli (€38.50, 23¼ hours). Services are provided by **Blue Star Ferries** (☎ 22430 26000), **G&A Ferries** (☎ 22430 23700) and **ANE Kalymnou** (☎ 22430 29612). In high season there is usually at least one ferry daily.

Car and passenger ferries leave four times daily between 7am and 8pm from Kalymnos' main town Pothia to Mastihari on Kos (€3, 50 minutes). ANE Kalymnou also runs two high-speed, passenger-only vessels, the *Kalymnos Star* and the smaller *Kalymnos Dolphin,* between Pothia and Mastihari. On Friday and weekends it also includes Pserimos on the route.

The high-speed, passenger-only Lipsi-based **Anna Express** (☎ 22470 41215) links Pothia with Leros and Lipsi five times weekly. Tickets can be bought on board.

There is a daily caïque (€7) from Myrties to Xirokambos on Leros at 1pm and half-hourly services to Telendos Islet.

HYDROFOIL & CATAMARAN

One daily hydrofoil links Kalymnos with islands to the north such as Patmos (€20, 1½

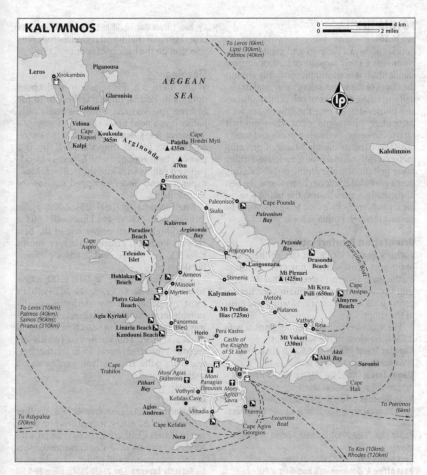

KALYMNOS

0 ———— 4 km
0 ———— 2 miles

AEGEAN SEA

To Leros (6km);
Lipsi (30km);
Patmos (40km)

Leros
Xirokambos

Piganousa

Glaronisia

Gabiani

Velona
Cape
Diapori
Kalpi

Koukoula
365m

Arginonda

Patella
435m

Cape
Hondri Myti

470m

Kalolimnos

Emborios

Paleonisos
Skalia

Cape Pounda

*Paleonisos
Bay*

Kalavros

*Arginonda
Bay*

Paradise
Beach

Cape
Aspro

Telendos
Islet

Arginonda

*Pezonda
Bay*

Drasonda
Beach

Excursion Boat

Hohlakas
Beach

Armeos

Masouri

Myrties

Platys Gialos
Beach

Agia Kyriaki

Linaria Beach
Kandouni Beach

Stimenia

Langounara

Mt Pirnari
(425m)

Mt Kyra
Psili (650m)

Cape
Atsipas

Almyres
Beach

Kalymnos

Metohi

Platanos

Mt Profitis
Ilias (725m)

Vathys
Rina

To Leros (10km);
Patmos (40km);
Samos (90km);
Piraeus (310km)

Panormos
(Elies)

Horio

Pera Kastro

Castle of
the Knights
of St John

Mt Vokari
(330m)

Akti
Akti Bay

Saronisi

Argos

Cape
Trahilos

Moni Agias
Ekaterinis

*Pithari
Bay*

Vothyni
Kefalas Cave

Agios
Andreas

Moni
Panagias
Eleoussis

Pothia

Moni
Agiou
Savra

Vlihadia

Therma

Cape
Hali

To Pserimos
(6km)

To Astypalea
(70km)

Cape Kefalas

Nera

Cape Agios
Georgios

Excursion
Boat

To Kos (10km);
Rhodes (120km)

hours), and Samos (€26, 2½ hours) and Kos (€12.50, one hour) to the south. Tickets can be bought from **Magos Travel** (☎ 22430 28777; magos@klm.forthnet.gr) in Pothia.

The *Dodekanisos Express* and *Dodekanisos Pride* catamarans call in four times daily during summer on their runs up and down the Dodecanese chain. Fares are similar to those of the hydrofoil. Tickets are issued by **G&A Ferries** (☎ 22430 23700).

Getting Around
BUS
In summer there is a bus departing hourly from opposite the cathedral to Masouri (€1.50) via Myrties, Emborios (€2) and Vathys (€2), four times daily. Buy tickets from the

Municipality of Kalymnos ticket office by the bus stop in Pothia.

EXCURSION BOAT
From Myrties there is a daily excursion boat to Emborios (€8), leaving at 10am and returning at 4pm. Day trips to the Kefalas Cave (€20), impressive for its stalactites and stalagmites, run from both Pothia and Myrties.

TAXI
Shared taxi services cost a little more than buses and run from the Pothia **taxi stand** (☎ 22430 50300; Plateia Kyprou) to Masouri. The taxis can also be flagged down en route. A regular taxi to Myrties costs €10 and to Vathys it costs €15.

DODECANESE

POTHIA ΠΟΘΙΑ
pop 10,500

Pothia (*poth*-ya), the port and capital of Kalymnos, is a fairly large town by Dodecanese standards. It is built amphitheatrically around the slopes of the surrounding valley, and its visually arresting melange of colourful mansions and houses draped over the hills makes for a particularly photogenic sight when you first arrive. However, Pothia is a brash and overly busy town and its nightly parade of preening motorcyclists can make for some nerve-rattling noise pollution, while dining out or relaxing over a port-side drink can be testing at the best of times. It is nonetheless the island's social focal point and – love it or leave it – you'll be passing through Pothia at some point.

Orientation & Information

Pothia's quay is located at the southern side of the port. Most activity, however, is centred on the main square, Plateia Eleftherias, abutting the waterfront. The main commercial centre is on Venizelou, along which are most of the shops.

The Commercial and Ionian Banks, with ATMs, are close to the waterfront.

Kapellas Travel (☎ 22430 29265; fax 22430 51800; Patriarhou Maximou 12) For air tickets.

Magos Travel (☎ 22430 28777; magos@klm.forthnet .gr) Hydrofoil and catamaran tickets.

Neon Internet Cafe (☎ 22430 48318; per hr €3; ☼ 9.30am-midnight) Modern large internet and gaming café.

Police (☎ 22430 29301; Venizelou) Before the post office.

Port police (☎ 22430 29304; 25 Martiou)

Post office A 10-minute walk northwest of Plateia Eleftherias. There is a more covenient agency south of Plateia Ethnikis Andistasis

Tourist Information (☎ 22430 59056; 25 Martiou)

www.kalymnos-isl.gr An informative website hosted by the Municipality of Kalymnos.

Sights

North of Plateia Kyprou, housed in a neoclassical mansion that once belonged to a wealthy sponge merchant, is the **Archaeological Museum** (☎ 22430 23113; adult/student €2/1; ☼ 8.30am-2pm Tue-Sun). In one room there are some Neolithic and Bronze-Age objects. Other rooms are reconstructed as they were when the Vouvalis family lived here.

In the centre of the waterfront is the **Nautical & Folklore Museum** (☎ 22430 51361; adult/student €2/1;

☼ 8am-1.30pm Mon-Fri, 10am-12.30pm Sat & Sun). Its collection is of traditional regional dress, plus a section on the history of sponge diving.

Sleeping

While there is a fair selection of sleeping options in Pothia, most travellers head for Myrties and Masouri. Pothia is really only handy if you need to take an early ferry.

Pension Greek House (☎ 22430 23752; s/d/studios €25/35/40) Inland from the port, this is a pleasant budget option with four cosy wood-panelled rooms with kitchen facilities. More expensive and better-equipped studios are also available.

Hotel Panorama (☎ 22430 23138; smiksis2003@yahoo .gr; s/d incl breakfast €25/45; ⚡) This small hotel is situated high up and enjoys one of the best views in Pothia. It's clean and breezy, rooms have TV and fridge, and it has a pleasant breakfast area.

our pick **Villa Melina** (☎ 22430 22682; antono santonoglu@yahoo.de; s/d €50/60; ⚡ ⚡) Pothia's most appealing accommodation is equally suitable for romantic couples seeking a hideaway, or for travellers in search of old-world peace and quiet. This stately villa (which was recently renovated) harks from another age, featuring palm trees, a lush garden and a swimming pool.

Eating

To Tholami (☎ 22430 51900; mains €3.50-5) Another well-established eatery, tucked away on a corner in Plateia Eleftherias, that is popular with locals and visitors alike. Recommended dishes are octopus patties and grilled tuna steaks.

Xefteris Taverna (☎ 22430 28642; mains €3-5.50) This long-standing (founded 1915) yet recently spruced up and expanded taverna serves solid quality food, confirming its good reputation. The meal-sized dolmadhes and the beef *stifadho* are recommended.

Pandelis Restaurant (☎ 22430 51508; mains €4.50-6) The specialities at this homey eatery favoured by locals are goat in red-wine sauce and home-made dolmades. Worth a mention also are the prawns in pasta and the charcoal-grilled meat cuts. Good wine selection and family atmosphere.

O Barba Stoukas (☎ 22430 24546; mains €6-8) Of the handful of waterside *ouzeries*, this one is about the closest you can get to the sea. Dishes are solid and well cooked, and the service is friendly. The Kalymnian, crouton-

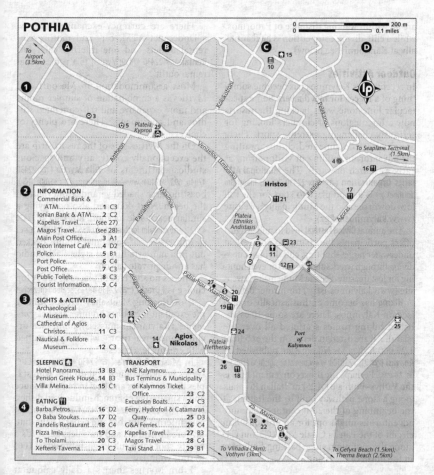

POTHIA

0   200 m
0   0.1 miles

To Airport (3.5km)

To Seaplane Terminal (1.5km)

Plateia Kyprou

Venizelou (Emboriou)

Hristos

Plateia Ethnikis Andistasis

Agios Nikolaos

Plateia Eleftherias

Port of Kalymnos

25 Martiou

To Vlihadia (3km); Vothyni (3km)

To Gefyra Beach (1.5km); Therma Beach (2.5km)

INFORMATION
Commercial Bank & ATM..................1 C3
Ionian Bank & ATM..................2 C2
Kapellas Travel..........(see 27)
Magos Travel..........(see 28)
Main Post Office..........3 A1
Neon Internet Café..........4 D2
Police..................5 B1
Port Police..................6 C4
Post Office..................7 C3
Public Toilets..................8 C3
Tourist Information..........9 C4

SIGHTS & ACTIVITIES
Archaeological Museum..................10 C1
Cathedral of Agios Christos..................11 C3
Nautical & Folklore Museum..................12 C3

SLEEPING
Hotel Panorama..........13 B3
Pension Greek House....14 B3
Villa Melina..................15 C1

EATING
Barba Petros..................16 D2
O Baba Stoukas..........17 D2
Pandelis Restaurant.....18 C4
Pizza Imia..................19 C3
To Tholami..................20 C4
Xefteris Taverna..........21 C2

TRANSPORT
ANE Kalymnou..........22 C4
Bus Terminus & Municipality of Kalymnos Ticket Office..................23 C2
Excursion Boats..........24 C3
Ferry, Hydrofoil & Catamaran Quay..................25 D3
G&A Ferries..................26 C4
Kapellas Travel..........27 B3
Magos Travel..................28 C4
Taxi Stand..................29 B1

loaded salad *mermizeli* features here, as does a rich skillet-cooked prawn and tomato sauce worth sampling.

Pizza Imia (☎ 22430 24809; pizza €7-12) If you don't mind the waterfront motorcycle racket, the imaginatively constructed and filling pizzas from the wood-fired oven make a great change from stock Greek fare. The wine list is impressive and the service brisk and cheery.

AROUND POTHIA

Running northwards from the port is a busy, densely populated valley with a series of almost contiguous settlements. The ruined **Castle of the Knights of St John** (Kastro Hrysoherias) looms to the left of the Pothia–Horio road. There is a small **church** inside the battlements.

On the east side of the valley **Pera Kastro** was a pirate-proof village inhabited until the 18th century. Within the crumbling walls are the ruins of stone houses and six tiny, well-kept churches. Steps lead up to Pera Kastro from **Horio**; it's a strenuous climb but the splendid views make it worthwhile.

A tree-lined road continues from Horio to **Panormos** (also called Elies), a pretty village 5km from Pothia. Its prewar name of Elies (olive trees) derived from its abundant olive groves, which were destroyed in WWII. An enterprising postwar mayor planted many trees and flowers to create beautiful panoramas wherever one looked – hence its present name, meaning 'panorama'. The sandy beaches of **Kandouni**, **Linaria** and **Platys Gialos**

DODECANESE

are all within walking distance of Panormos, while a cliff-diving competition is held annually at Kandouni (see below).

Outdoor Activities

In recent years Kalymnos has become something of a mecca for **rock climbers**. Some spectacular limestone walls backing the resorts now attract legions of climbers looking for seriously challenging extreme sport. There are about 21 documented climbs awaiting the adventurous, pulling in visitors from as early as March onwards. The **Municipal Athletics Organisation** (☎ /fax 22430 29612; mao@klm .forthnet.gr) is a good place to start for the full low-down; see also the Municipality's website (www.kalymnos-isl.gr).

The annual **Diving Festival** held in mid-August offers participants the chance to compete at underwater target shooting, cliff diving, scubadiving through wrecks and caverns or even hunting for lost treasure. See the Municipality's website (www.kalymnos-isl.gr) for further details.

Hiking has become enthusiastically organised on Kalymnos. There are some 10 established hiking routes scattered all over the island. All are listed in detail on the excellent 1:25,000 *Kalymnos Hiking Map* published by **Anavasi** (☎ 21032 18104; www.mountains.gr; Stoa Arsakiou 6a, Athens). Perhaps the most convenient hike is the Vathys–Pothia B1 4.25km 'Italian Rd' walk along a stone pathway built by the Italians at the beginning of the 20th century; the more adventurous might opt for an arduous 9km circuit of the Patella Castle loop (C3 and C4) along the mountain ridge backing Emborios in the north of the island.

MYRTIES, MASOURI & ARMEOS
ΜΥΡΤΙΕΣ, ΜΑΣΟΥΡΙ & ΑΡΜΕΟΣ

From Panormos the road continues to the west coast, with stunning views of Telendos Islet, until it winds down into **Myrties** (myr-*tyez*), **Masouri** (mah-*soo*-ri) and **Armeos** (ar-me-*os*). These contiguous and busy resort centres host the lion's share of Kalymnos' modest resort industry. The three centres are essentially one long street, packed head to tail with restaurants, bars, souvenir shops and minimarkets. Towards land, apartments and studios fill the hillside, while on the sea side an extinct volcano plug separates the dark sand beach into two distinct sections – Myrties beach, with Melitsahas harbour, and the marginally better Masouri and Armeos beaches to the north.

There are currency-exchange bureaus, a Dodecanet ATM, car- and motorcyclerental outlets and one internet café. **Avis Rental** (☎ 22430 47430; Myrties) is a professional rental outfit.

Most accommodation in Masouri and Myrties is a combination of simpler rooms and more expansive and self-contained studios and apartments. There are plenty of choices.

On the Myrties side of the resort strip are the exceptionally comfy, airy and spacious studios/apartments of **Villa Myrtia** (☎ 22430 47046, 6937942404; www.villamyrtia.gr; d/t €35/60; 🖳), boasting large shaded verandas and right on the beach. Next door and also occupying a similar beach-side location, **Acroyali** (☎ 22430 47521; acroyali@klm.forthnet.gr; d/t €35/45; 🖳) is a set of impressive self-contained studios decked out in a more traditional style. Each studio has a wide private balcony.

There's no shortage of places to eat. A top choice is **I Drosia** (☎ 22430 48745; seafood mezedhes €5-12) overlooking Melitsahas harbour. Among the excellent mezedhes on offer are *kalognomones* (Kalymnian mussels), *ahini* (sea urchins) and a real treat – whole squid stuffed with creamy feta cheese.

In Masouri, **Kelly's** (☎ 22430 48390; mains €3-6) serves breakfast, lunch and dinner, with staples like *mousakas* and beef in red wine sauce and a smattering of French-influenced dishes. In Myrties, **Babis Bar** (☎ 22430 47864) is a mix of café, internet joint, bar and general hang-out, favoured by expats and travellers alike. It's a hearty spot for a full English breakfast (€6) to start your day.

From Myrties there's a daily caïque at 12.30pm to Xirokambos on Leros (€7), and Emborios (€7) in the north of Kalymnos, as well as half-hourly boats to Telendos Islet (€1.50).

TELENDOS ISLET ΝΗΣΟΣ ΤΕΛΕΝΔΟΣ

The low-key, tranquil and (almost) traffic-free islet of Telendos, with a little quayside hamlet, was part of Kalymnos until separated by an earthquake in AD 554. It's now a super escape from the busy resort strip opposite.

Turn right from Telendos' quay and you will pass the ruins of the early Christian **basilica** of Agios Vasilios. Further on, there are several pebble and sand beaches, including a locally acceptable nudist beach. To reach the far superior, 100m-long and fine-pebbled **Hohlakas**

Beach, turn left from the quay and then right at the sign to the beach. Follow the paved path up and over the hill for 10 minutes. **Paradise Beach** on the northern side of Telendos is the beach for the unclads. Walk for five minutes past On the Rocks Cafe Rooms.

Telendos accommodation consists of a number of rooms and one hotel. Opposite the quay is **George's** (☎ 22430 47502; d €30), while adjoining the café of the same name is **On the Rocks Cafe Rooms** (☎ 22430 48260; www.otr.tel endos.com; studios €45; ✂) offering four studios equipped with every convenience imaginable, including fridge, satellite TV, double glazing and mosquito nets. Guests can also access the internet and will be picked up for free at Melitsahas harbour on Kalymnos or even in Pothia.

Telendos' only hotel as such is **Hotel Porto Potha** (☎ 22430 47321; portopotha@klm.forthnet.gr; s/d €30/35; ⌖), 100m beyond On the Rocks Cafe. Rooms are airy and bright, and there's a large lobby where guests come to relax and watch TV over a drink.

The best place to eat 'n' schmooze is **On the Rocks Cafe** (☎ 22430 48260; mains €5-8), where Greek Australian owner Georgos serves well-prepared meat and fish dishes as well as vegetarian *mousakas*, and baked or grilled tuna and swordfish. It turns into a lively music bar at night – with over 300 cocktails to choose from – and on two evenings a week it hosts lively 'Greek Nights'.

Up on the hill overlooking Hohlakas Beach is the **Sunset Restaurant** (☎ 6972792482; mains €5-6), which is a great spot to watch the sunset (naturally), as well as sample an international, yet Dutch-influenced, menu of mains and snacks.

Caïques for Telendos depart half-hourly from the Myrties quay between 8am and 1am (one way €1.50).

EMBORIOS ΕΜΠΟΡΕΙΟΣ

The scenic west-coast road winds a further 11.5km from Masouri to Emborios, where there's a pleasant, shaded sand and pebble beach, as well as a minimarket and **Artis-tico Café** (☎ 22430 40115) for evening entertainment, sometimes featuring live guitar renditions.

One of the best places to stay on Kalymnos for a full relax-out experience is **Harry's Apartments** (☎ 22430 40062; www.harrys-paradise.gr; d/tr €27/33; ✂ ⌨). Stressed-out executives from

Milano, lovers from London and poets from Poznań all find a piece of paradise in this quiet, relaxing corner of Kalymnos. The capacious rooms are tastefully decorated – each one coloured and decorated individually – and enjoy sea-view balconies. Choose the Kalymnian Traditional House (€45 to €55), with a raised bed for a spot of extra space and style.

A stay here is made all the more attractive by the lush flower garden and adjoining **Paradise Restaurant** (☎ 22430 40062; mains €4.50-7), run by the charming Evdokia. She rustles up a good line in vegetarian dishes, such as *revithokeftedes* (chickpea rissoles) and filo-pastry turnovers with fillings such as aubergine, vegetables and onion. Stuffed mushrooms or zucchini flowers is another one of her specialities.

VATHYS & RINA ΒΑΘΥΣ & PINA

Vathys, 13km northeast of Pothia, and its long fertile valley are one of the most beautiful and peaceful parts of the island. Vathys means 'deep' in Greek and refers to the slender fjord that cuts through high cliffs into the fertile valley, where narrow roads wind between citrus orchards. You can hardly miss the high stone walls called *koumoula* that ribbon along the narrow access roads. These mark the property extents of the landowners.

There is no beach at Vathys' harbour, Rina, but you can swim off the jetty at the south side of the harbour. **Water taxis** (☎ 22430 31316) take tourists to quiet coves, such as **Almyres** and **Drasonda** bays, nearby. An annual cliff-diving competition takes place at Vathys as part of the international Diving Festival (see opposite).

While there are at least a couple of accommodation and eating options, there is little incentive to stay as the proprietors do little to convince visitors to linger. It has all become a bit tired recently and after dark things can be a little too quiet. It's still worth the excursion out here, if only for a swim and a cold beer.

Visitors can now cut across the island from Vathys on a partially sealed road to Arginonda and then back to Masouri. By the time of writing the road was sealed as far as the ridge-top spur at Langounara (8.5km from Vathys). When finally complete by this book's publication, the road will be a much quicker way to get to the north of the island from Vathys.

LEROS ΛΕΡΟΣ

pop 8207

Almost completely overlooked by foreign travellers, languid Leros (*leh*-ros) lies lightly between Kalymnos and Lipsi, self-reliant, introspective and almost content to let mainstream tourism pass it by. But Leros has plenty on offer – an attractive mix of sun, sea, rest and recreation, a stunning medieval castle and some excellent dining. A popular Greek song wistfully remembers its hills, but there are the bays and beaches, the laid-back lifestyle and the pervading sense that this island has not yet given up its Greekness. Leros is popular with domestic travellers and always enjoys a busy summer season. The Italians loved Leros, too, having left their legacy in a set of prewar Art Deco buildings that are incongruous in their Aegean island setting. It is hard to pigeonhole Leros. Travellers need to savour the island themselves.

Getting There & Away

AIR

There is a flight daily to Athens (€54, one hour), as well as three flights a week to Rhodes (€45, two hours 10 minutes) via Kos (€38, 20 minutes). There are also three flights a week to Astypalea (€45, 15 minutes). **Olympic Airlines** (☎ 22470 22844; www.olympicairlines.com) is in Platanos, before the turn-off for Pandeli. The **airport** (☎ 22470 22777) is near Partheni in the north. There is no airport bus and the local bus does not accommodate arriving or departing flights. A taxi from the airport to Alinda will cost €8.

EXCURSION BOAT

The caïque *Katerina* leaves Xirokambos at 7.30am daily for Myrties on Kalymnos (one way €7) and returns at 1.30pm.

FERRY

Leros is on the main north–south route for ferries between Rhodes and Piraeus. There are daily departures from Lakki to Piraeus (€32 to €36, 11 hours), Kos (€11, 3¼ hours) and Rhodes (€23, 7¼ hours). Buy tickets at **Leros Travel** (☎ in Lakki 22470 24000, in Agia Marina 22470 22154).

The Lipsi-based **Anna Express** (☎ 22470 41215) links Leros with Kalymnos and Lipsi five times weekly, while once a week it detours to Arki, Marathi and Agathonisi. It departs from and arrives at the port of Agia Marina.

HYDROFOIL & CATAMARAN

In summer a hydrofoil and two catamarans depart daily from both Agia Marina and Lakki to Patmos (€16.50, 45 minutes), Lipsi (€11.50, 20 minutes), Samos (€20, two hours), Kos (€16.50, one hour) and Rhodes (€38, 3¼ hours).

Getting Around

The hub for Leros' buses is Platanos. There are three buses daily to Partheni via Alinda and four buses to Xirokambos via Lakki (€1 flat fare).

Car-, motorcycle- and bicycle-rental outlets tend to be centered on the Alinda tourist strip. **Motoland** (☎ 22470 24584) offers newer bikes and scooters as well as *gourounes* (four-wheeled bikes), which are hot fun to drive. Taxis can be hailed on (☎ 22470 23340, 22470 23070 or 22470 22550).

LAKKI ΛΑΚΚΙ

pop 2366

Arriving at Lakki (lah-*kee*) by boat is akin to stepping into a long-abandoned Federico Fellini film set. The grandiose buildings and wide tree-lined boulevards dotted around the Dodecanese are best (or worst) shown here, for Lakki was built as a Fascist showpiece during the Italian occupation. Few linger in Lakki, though it has decent accommodation and restaurants, and there are some secluded swimming opportunities on the road past the port. The port has internet access at the quayside Kinezos Café.

Worth detouring to is the historically relevant **War Museum & Merikia Bunker** (☎ 22470 22244; admission €3; ⏱ 9.30am-1.30pm), a short drive west beyond the Lakki Port to Merikia. Here you can escape the stifling Leros heat to seek cool solace in the hill-puncturing bunkers of former provisions and armament warehouses built by the Italians during WWII. They are now home to an eclectic and widely varied collection of memorabilia dating from the time of the Battle of Leros when the Germans captured Leros from the Italians and the British from September to November 1943.

XIROKAMBOS ΞΗΡΟΚΑΜΠΟΣ

Xirokambos Bay, on the south of the island, is a low-key resort with a gravel and sand

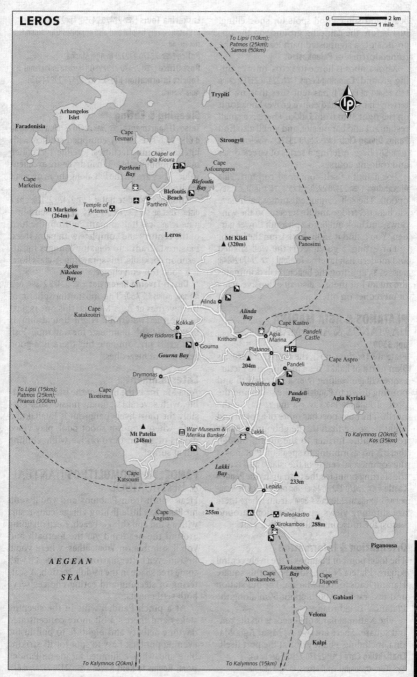

LEROS

0   2 km
0   1 mile

To Lipsi (10km);
Patmos (25km);
Samos (50km)

Trypiti

Arhangelos
Islet

Faradonisia

Cape
Tesmari

Strongyli

Chapel of
Agia Kioura

Cape
Markelos

Partheni
Bay

Cape
Asfoungaros

Blefoutis
Bay

Blefoutis
Beach

Temple of
Artemis

Mt Markelos
(264m)

Partheni

Leros

Mt Klidi
(320m)

Cape
Panosimi

Agios
Nikolaos
Bay

Cape
Katakrotiri

Alinda

Alinda
Bay

Cape Kastro

Kokkali

Pandeli
Castle

Agios Isidoros

Krithoni

Agia
Marina

Gourna

Platanos

Cape Aspro

Gourna Bay

204m

Pandeli

To Lipsi (15km);
Patmos (25km);
Piraeus (300km)

Cape
Ikonisma

Drymonas

Vromolithos

Pandeli
Bay

Agia Kyriaki

Mt Patelia
(248m)

War Museum &
Merikia Bunker

Lakki

To Kalymnos (20km);
Kos (35km)

Lakki
Bay

Cape
Katsouni

Lepida

233m

255m

Paleokastro

Cape
Angistro

Xirokambos

288m

Piganousa

AEGEAN

SEA

Xirokambos
Bay

Cape
Xirokambos

Cape
Diapori

Gabiani

Velona

Kalpi

To Kalymnos (20km)

To Kalymnos (15km)

beach and some good spots for snorkelling. Just before the camping ground, on the opposite side, a signposted path leads up to the ruined fortress of **Paleokastro**.

Xirokambos is home to Leros' only camping ground. **Camping Leros** (☎ 22470 23372; camp sites adult/tent €6.50/4) has tent sites that are interwoven into a shady olive grove. Look for it on the right 3km from Lakki. There is a small restaurant and bar on site, and you'll also find **Panos Diving Club** (☎ 22470 23372; www.lerosdiving .com; 🖳) here, offering a series of wreck dives and training courses.

For a spot of self-contained comfort, **Villa Alexandros** (☎ 22470 22202; d €55; 🗱) is a classy option. The self-contained studios each have kitchenette, fridge and fly screens on the windows, and look out onto a pleasant flower garden. You'll find it 150m back from the beach.

For eating, a good bet is the well-shaded and modern fish taverna **To Aloni** (☎ 22470 26048; mains €4-8), abutting the beach. Fish dominates the menu but there is also an extensive array of mezedhes on offer.

PLATANOS & AGIA MARINA
ΠΛΑΤΑΝΟΣ & ΑΓΙΑ ΜΑΡΙΝΑ
pop 3500

Platanos (*plah*-ta-nos), the capital of Leros, is 3km north of Lakki. It's a bustling and picturesque village spilling over a narrow hill and pouring down to **Pandeli** to the south and the port of **Agia Marina** (ay-*i*-a ma-*ri*-na) to the north. The busy port has more of a social and nightlife scene than the neighbouring **Alinda** resort a little further to the north, though there is no swimming to speak of. Platanos is the commercial centre of the island and is also the starting point for the path up to the **Pandeli Castle** (☎ 22470 23211; admission castle €2, castle & museum €3; 🕑 8am-12.30pm & 4-8pm), from where there are stunning views in all directions around Leros; the museum is also worth a visit.

Orientation & Information
The focal point of Platanos is the lively central square, Plateia N Roussou. From this square Harami leads to Agia Marina. The bus station and taxi rank are both about 50m along the Platanos–Lakki road.

The National Bank of Greece is on the central square. There are two ATMs at Agia Marina, including a handy one at the port itself.
Enallaktiko Café (☎ 22470 23500; per hr €4; 🕑 10am-midnight) Wi-fi access; in Agia Marina.

Laskarina Tours (☎ 22470 24550; fax 22470 24551) In Platanos; very helpful and also organises trips around the island.
Police (☎ 22470 22222) In Agia Marina.
Post Office (☎ 22470 22929) On Harami in Platanos.
Tourist Information Kiosk (☎ 22470 222244) In Agia Marina.

Sleeping & Eating
Tassos II Apartments (☎ /fax 22470 23769; Agia Marina; d €45; 🗱) These fully equipped studios with kitchen, ironing facilities, satellite TV, coffee maker, money safe and hairdryer are excellent value. They are on the left along the main road leading to Alinda.

Crithoni's Paradise Hotel (☎ 22470 25120; c.para dise@12net.gr; s/d €90/140; 🅿 🗱 🖳) Resembling a neoclassical Italian mansion from the turn of the century and complete with palm trees, bars, restaurant and relaxing lounges for afternoon cocktails, this sprawling A-class hotel is a good top-end choice.

Ouzeri-Taverna Neromylos (☎ 22470 24894; Agia Marina; mains €5-7.50) The most atmospheric of the tavernas at Agia Marina, this one is next to a former watermill. Night-time dining is best when lights illuminate the watermill. Fish and grills predominate but there is a good selection of mezedhes.

Entertainment
Agia Marina is the heart of the island's nightlife, with several late-night music bars. Possibly the most lively hang-out is Enallaktiko Cafe, where you can shoot pool, play video games or sip an ouzo on ice while chilling out at sunset.

PANDELI & VROMOLITHOS ΠΑΝΤΕΛΙ
& ΒΡΩΜΟΛΙΘΟΣ
Head south from Platanos and you'll soon hit **Pandeli**, a little fishing village-cum-resort with a sand and shingle beach. Keep on going around the headland via the footpath and you'll stumble on **Vromolithos**, where you'll find an even better, narrow shingly beach with some tree shade in the middle section. A scattering of sleeping and eating choices serve both settlements.

At a pinch Pandeli wins in the sleeping stakes and there's a bit more concentrated daytime activity and nightlife to pull in the evening punters. Easy to spot for its striking blue-and-white columned façade on Pandeli port, **Rooms to Rent Kavos** (☎ 22470 23247; d €35) is a sensible choice. Rooms are largish, sport balconies and have fan and fridge. Grab a front room if you want a harbour view. Up on the hill is the always popular **Pension Rodon** (☎ 22470 22075; d €30; ☼ year-round), a reliable and welcoming choice with comfortable rooms.

For an innovative culinary experience like you will find on few other islands, head on up to the aerie-like establishment of **Dimitris o Karaflas** (Dimitris the Bald; ☎ 22470 25626; mezedhes €3-7), with stunning views overlooking Vromolithos beach. Owner Dimitris combines fresh food elements in tantalising ways to make dining a refreshing change. His hallmark chicken in retsina, or pork in wine sauce, satisfy solidly, while his mezedhes options include *batiris* (a kind of dip), or *pita kaisarias*, a savoury pie featuring *pastourmas* (spicy cured beef).

At Pandeli, **Psaropoula** (☎ 22470 25200; mains €5-8) is right on the beach and is as good as any of the several tavernas plying their trade here. Psaropoula has a wide-ranging menu featuring fish; the prawn *souvlaki* with bacon is recommended.

KRITHONI & ALINDA ΚΡΙΘΩΝΙ & ΑΛΙΝΤΑ

Krithoni and Alinda are contiguous resorts on the wide Alinda Bay, running about 3km northwest from Agia Marina. Most of the action is concentrated at the Alinda end, where the only real danger is from the parades of kamikaze motorcyclists who roar indiscriminately up and down the narrow beachside road. The beach is pebbled and the water is very clean. Further to the north around the bay are some quieter coves and beaches.

On Krithoni's waterfront there is a poignant, well-kept **war cemetery**. After the Italian surrender in WWII, Leros saw fierce fighting between German and British forces; the cemetery contains the graves of 179 British, two Canadian and two South African soldiers.

Not surprisingly for the island's main resort area there are plenty of sleeping choices.

Hotel Alinda (☎ 22470 23266; fax 22470 23383; s/d €30/40; ☼) is an older-style but spick-and-span hotel, with 41 small, comfortable rooms offering good value. The highly regarded in-house restaurant does a fine line in home-made cooking.

Hotel Gianna (☎ /fax 22470 24135; s/d €35/45) is just behind the war cemetery and far enough away from the 'strip' to be quiet. All rooms are pleasantly furnished.

For comfortable self-catering, **Tassos Studios I** (☎ 22470 22769; fax 22470 23769; studios €42; ☼) has beautiful, fully equipped mini-apartments close to Krithoni beach, run by the same owners as Tassos II in Agia Marina.

Set amid a lush garden of flowers, shrubs and shady trees and backed by a small vineyard, the old-style mansion **To Arhontiko tou Angelou** (☎ 22470 22749; www.hotel-angelou-leros.com; s/d incl breakfast €90/155; ☼) is an ideal retreat for a few days. The capacious rooms are high ceilinged, have wooden floors and the wrought-iron beds are so comfortable: for once you can sleep in Greece on pillows that allow interrupted dreaming.

Lambros (☎ 22470 2154; mains €4-6.50) offers you tables no more than 2m from the lapping waters of Alinda Bay. Flavour-ridden home cooking characterises this friendly lunch or dinner taverna. The rich *mousakas* is worthy of an honourable mention.

Right next door and also on the beach, **Fanari** (☎ 22470 2169; mains €4-7) serves enticing mezedhes such as *bekri mezes* (meat chunks in a piquant sauce), or *spanakopitakia* (mini spinach turnovers).

PATMOS ΠΑΤΜΟΣ

pop 3044

If ever the sense of 'spirit of place' was a tangible entity, it's certainly true of Patmos (*paht-moss*). When you step off the ferry on Patmos (the northernmost Dodecanese island) you sense its appeal. The island has that quality like no other. Could it be that it was for that same reason that John the Divine ensconced himself in a cave and wrote the Apocalypse here? Patmos is a place of pilgrimage for both Orthodox and Western Christians and is, without doubt, the best place to come and experience Orthodox Easter. Spirituality aside, the beaches are many and magnificent; accommodation is top quality and in abundance (you can even get married in one hotel's church), and dining is a recommendable activity. The translucence of the light is remarkable and the landscape gives an inescapable sense of harmony and balance.

History

In AD 95 St John the Divine was banished to Patmos from Ephesus by the pagan Roman Emperor Domitian. While residing in a cave on the island, St John wrote the Book of

DODECANESE

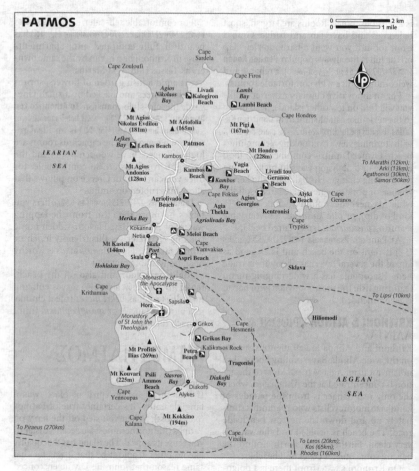

PATMOS

Revelations. In 1088 the Blessed Christodou-los, an abbot who came from Asia Minor to Patmos, obtained permission from the Byzantine Emperor Alexis I Komninos to build a monastery to commemorate St John. Pirate raids necessitated powerful fortifications, so the monastery looks like a mighty castle.

Under the Duke of Naxos, Patmos became a semi-autonomous monastic state, and achieved such wealth and influence that it was able to resist Turkish oppression. In the early 18th century a school of theology and philosophy was founded by Makarios and it flourished until the 19th century.

Gradually the island's wealth became polarised into secular and monastic entities. The secular wealth was acquired through ship-building, an industry that diminished with the arrival of the steam ship.

Getting There & Away
EXCURSION BOAT

The local **Patmos Star** (☎ 6977601633) leaves Patmos daily for Lipsi and Leros at 10am (return €8) and returns from Lipsi at 3.30pm.

The **Delfini** (☎ 22470 31995) goes to Marathi daily at 10.10am in high season and Monday and Thursday at other times (return €15). Twice a week it also calls in at Arki. From Marathi a local caïque will take you across to Arki (1¼ hours).

The *Lambi II* goes to Arki, Marathi and Lipsi on Wednesday and Saturday at 9am and returns at 2pm

FERRY

Patmos is connected with between four and five ferry services weekly to/from Piraeus (€32.50, seven to eight hours), Rhodes (€28.50, six to 7½ hours) and a number of islands in between. Mainline services are provided by the faster and sleeker Blue Star Ferries and the slower and less glamorous G&A Ferries.

The slow F/B *Nissos Kalymnos* provides additional links to Arki, Agathonisi and Samos, as well as to Leros and Kalymnos. Tickets are sold by **Apollon Travel** (☎ 22470 31324; apollontravel@stratas.gr) in Skala. Additionally the Lipsi-based and very fast *Anna Express* connects Patmos with Lipsi, Leros and Kalymnos. Tickets are bought onboard.

HYDROFOIL & CATAMARAN

There is a daily hydrofoil to Kos (€43, three hours) and destinations in between. This same hydrofoil also links Patmos with neighbouring Samos (€14.50, one hour).

The *Dodekanisos Express* and *Dodekanisos Pride* catamarans link Patmos twice daily during summer with islands to the south. Tickets can be bought at **Apollon Travel** (☎ 22470 31324; apollontravel@stratas.gr) in Skala.

Getting Around

BUS

From Skala there are 11 buses daily in July and August to Hora, eight to Grikos and four to Kambos. The frequency drops off during the rest of the year. Fares all cost a standard €1.

CAR & MOTORCYCLE

There are a number of car- and motorcycle-rental outlets in Skala. Competition is fierce, so shop around. **Moto Rent Express** (☎ 22470 32088) in the street behind the post office is a reliable outfit for car and scooter rentals.

EXCURSION BOAT

Boats go to Psili Ammos Beach from Skala, departing about 10.15am and returning about 4pm.

TAXI

You can catch a **taxi** (☎ 22470 31225) from Skala's taxi rank. Fares include Meloï Beach €3.50, Hora €4.50, Grikos €4.55 and Lambi €7.

SKALA ΣΚΑΛΑ

Patmos' port town is Skala (*ska*-la), a bright and glitzy place, draped around a curving bay and only visible from arriving ships once the protective headland has been rounded. The port bustles and large cruise ships are often anchored offshore, while smaller ones heave to at Skala's harbour. Once the cruise ships and ferries depart, Skala reverts to being a fairly normal, liveable port town. It has a wide range of excellent accommodation and restaurants, and all the island's major facilities are located here.

Orientation & Information

All transport arrives at the centre of the long quay, smack bang in the middle of Skala. To the right the road leads to the yacht port at Netia and on to the north of the island. To the left the road leads to the south side of the island. From near the ferry terminal a road leads inland and up to Hora. The bus terminal and taxi rank are at the quay. All main services are within 100m of the ferry quay.

There are two ATM-equipped banks in Skala: the National Bank of Greece and the Commercial Bank.

AB Food Market (☎ 22470 34023) There's a well-stocked AB (Vasilopoulos) Food Market 100m along the Hora road in Skala.

Apollon Travel (☎ 22470 31324; apollontravel@stratas .gr) Ticketing for flights, Blue Star Ferries, and hydrofoil and catamaran services.

Blue Bay Internet Café (☎ 22470 31165; per hr €4; ☼ 9am-2pm & 4-8pm) At the Blue Bay Hotel; offers wi-fi .

Dodoni Gelateria (☎ 22470 32202; per hr €4; ☼ 9am-9pm) Connect to the internet and eat ice-cream at the same time.

Hospital (☎ 22470 31211) Two kilometres along the road to Hora.

Laundry (☎ 22470 33170) On the bend between Skala and Netia. Dry cleaning and laundry services.

Municipal Tourist Office (☎ 22470 31666; ☼ summer) Shares the same building as the post office and police station.

Police (☎ 22470 31303) On the main waterfront.

Port police (☎ 22470 31231) Behind the quay's passenger-transit building.

www.patmos-island.com A useful website with information on Patmos.

Sleeping

BUDGET

Hotel and studio owners usually meet all arrivals at the port, but it's best to call ahead and arrange a pick-up, as mainline ferries often arrive at unsocial hours.

DODECANESE

Pension Maria Pascalidis (☎ 22470 32152; s/d €20/30) One of the better budget options is this long-standing traveller-friendly place, on the road leading to Hora. The simple but quite presentable rooms are set amid a leafy citrus-tree garden.

Domatia Katina (☎ /fax 22470 31327; s/d €35/50; 🌊) These four tidy rooms are out on the northern edge of Skala, each with good views, fridge, kitchenette, TV and four-poster bed. The ever-hospitable and smiling Katina will pick you up from the port if you call ahead.

Pension Avgerinos (☎ /fax 22470 32118; d €50) In a slightly quieter, elevated part of Netia, affording good views over the bay, this homey choice is run by a welcoming Greek Australian couple. All rooms are cosy and comfortable and have fridge and fan.

ourpick Yvonni Studios (☎ 22470 33066; www.12net .gr/yvonni; s/d €30/55; 🖳) These four exceptionally well-appointed, clean and pleasant studios are on the hillside in a verdant garden in Hohlakas Bay. Each is fully self-contained and has a balcony that faces the Monastery of St John in Hora. Call into Yvonni's gift shop in Skala and ask for Theologos.

MIDRANGE

ourpick Doriza Bay Hotel (☎ 22470 33123; www .dorizabay.com; d/maisonettes €40/70; 🌊) High above the south side of Hohlakas Bay is this newer room and apartment complex. Opt for a spacious two-storey maisonette with internal spiral staircase, or a very comfortable double room.

Captain's House (☎ 22470 31793; www.captains -house.gr; s/d incl breakfast €55/75; 🌊 🌊) A cool, open, split-level interior welcomes guests upon arrival. Each comfortable, stucco-walled room has TV, fridge and phone. The front rooms have the best views, but can get the noise from the sometimes rowdy nightlife nearby.

Blue Bay Hotel (☎ 22470 31165; www.bluebaypatmos .gr; s/d incl breakfast €70/100; 🖳 🌊) This Australian-Greek–owned waterfront hotel has very clean, pleasantly furnished rooms and is at the quieter far southern end of Skala, just round the last bend. The wi-fi is handy for laptop-equipped travellers.

Eating

Pandelis Taverna (☎ 22470 31230; mains €4-6.50) One of the more picturesque diners, this busy little taverna has been in business for over 50 years. Lunch in the street over a newspaper and a beer

can't be beaten. The service is efficient and the dining at night is very atmospheric. The best bets are the daily home-cooked specials.

Tzivaeri (☎ 22470 31170; mains €4-7) Solid, unsurprising menu choices but excellent quality – especially the squid – either stuffed or fried. The service is fast and courteous. Dine upstairs on the covered balcony and observe the active street life below. The owner Yiannis may bring out his lute for a round of island or Cretan music if the mood takes him.

Hiliomodi Ouzeri (☎ 22470 34080; mezedhes platter €10.50; 🕑 year-round) For the freshest fish on the island head to this *ouzerie* for its excellent seafood dishes and very reasonably priced seafood-based mezedhes. The Hiliomodi is patronised as much by locals as by visitors.

ourpick Vegghera (☎ 22470 32988; mains €8-14) Yachties and high-society diners head for this swish, air-conditioned establishment opposite the yacht marina. The cuisine is a mélange of French and Greek. Worth sampling is the calamari with pesto, or maybe *linguini* in a tangy tomato, orange and ginger sauce.

Entertainment

Skala's musical nightlife revolves around a scattering of bars and the odd club or two.

Arion (☎ 22470 31595) Café life and street gossip reach their zenith at this busy little meeting place, café, breakfast joint and general social hotspot at all times of the day.

Anemos (☎ 22470 33008; 🕑 9pm-late Thu-Sun) Just outside Skala and within walking distance on the hill heading up to Kambos is this trendy beer house and music bar in an old stone house.

Aman (☎ 22470 32323) On the south side of Skala, Aman predisposes people to sitting outside on its tree-shaded patio and listening to music to the feel of a cold beer or inventive cocktail.

HORA ΧΩΡΑ

Huddled around the Monastery of St John are the immaculate whitewashed houses of Hora. These houses are a legacy of the island's great wealth in the 17th and 18th centuries. Some of them have been bought and renovated by wealthy Greeks and foreigners. A stroll through the maze-like, whitewashed streets is an experience in itself. Walk randomly around the monastery and lose yourself in a timeless atmosphere.

(Continued on page 349)

OFF THE BEATEN TRACK

The Greek islands are an archipelago of glistening gems with many treasures: historical, natural and cultural. As a consequence, they have been receiving visitors for a long time. But while certain islands loom large in the popular imagination and are visited by hordes of tourists, there are countless other islands that go almost unnoticed. The Greek islands are, above all, about diversity. They offer much more than just the postcard clichés. They are a tapestry of landscapes, lifestyles and experiences, some of which we have pinpointed here. We'd suggest that if you have the time, the inclination and the energy then you should get off the beaten track and seek them out.

Central Aegean Islands

Archetypical Greek islands make up the bulk of this long swathe of islands from the green and forested Sporades group to the sun-bleached and rocky Cyclades. Tourism ranges from highly developed to oh-so low-key. There are islands for every pocket and taste. You'll get well away on these oft-overlooked destinations.

❶ Alonnisos
Green and lean Alonnisos (p432) has the cleanest water in the Aegean, but is out of the way for most travellers. Boasting a rustic hilltop *hora* (main town) the island is also home to monk seals, dolphins and endangered falcons.

❷ Anafi
Diminutive Anafi (p200) may be a little overshadowed by neighbouring Santorini, but the locals aren't bothered. They get on with life at their own languid pace, quietly welcoming visitors and directing them to south-facing beaches.

❸ Angistri
It's small, it's petite and inevitably almost easily overlooked, but Angistri (p111) is right next to Athens and makes for an easy and relaxing day trip from the mainland. Hire a motorbike, have a swim and enjoy a relaxing fish lunch.

❹ Kimolos
Normally only visited by day trippers from neighbouring Milos, overshadowed Kimolos (p210) is a perfect getaway in its own right. Get off the beaten track and unwind on your own Cycladic hideaway.

❺ Antiparos
Tucked away in the lee of its larger and better-known brother Paros, introspective Antiparos (p160) is a great antidote to the fast pace of its neighbour. Only twenty minutes by ferry from Paros, the island is homely, unpretentious and welcoming.

❻ Donousa
The harbourmaster is not often troubled by ferries in Donousa (p182); and therein lies its charm. A few adventurous campers and naturists come and go, but this is as remote as you can get in the Cyclades.

❼ Kea
It's hard to imagine that the Cyclades is on Attica's doorstep, but shy Kea (Tzia; p218) is an easy trip out from the Attica port of Lavrio. Ideal for a weekend getaway without the travel and the crowds.

❽ Sikinos
Dazzled by Santorini? Jump on a boat to recuperate at nearby Sikinos (p201). With sweeping terraced hills and scattered settlements, it makes for the perfect antidote to hype and hubris.

Eastern Aegean Islands

Ask any traveller about the Eastern Aegean islands and they'll be able to rattle off the big names. But beyond the well-known there are manifold other islands basking under the Hellenic sun. All have their own distinctive identity, and all offer different things to the visitor. Here are a few of our favourites.

① Kasos

Remote, rocky and sometimes shrouded in mist, Kasos (p300) is the last stop south before the African mainland. Come here to mix it with hospitable locals who fiercely preserve their culture and are unconcerned with the modern world.

② Tilos

Demure, unassuming and ecofriendly Tilos (p310) is often overlooked by passers-by. Stay a while and you will be surprised. Enjoy walks, wining and dining and maybe spot an odd rare bird or two.

③ Kastellorizo

Not exactly undiscovered – expat 'Kassies' will tell you that, but Kastellorizo (Megisti; p303) is as far as you can get from the beaten track. You'll know all your neighbours within 24 hours on this remote rock way east of Rhodes.

④ Fourni Islands

Think fish and you've found the Fourni Islands (p365). A pair of rocky islands dangling south of Ikaria, this unlikely getaway provides fish for Athenians and lulls its foreign visitors into a quiet cocoon of relaxation and rest.

⑤ Agios Efstratios

Arguably the remotest island in the Aegean and the hardest to get to, Agios Efstratios (p402) doesn't boast its wares, but is quietly happy in its self-sufficiency and isolation. Beaches, walking, sleeping and eating are about all you will need.

⑥ Arki & Marathi

With no cars, police or post office, there's little to trouble you on the little islands of Arki (p354) and Marathi (p354) in the north Dodecanese. Yachties may drop in occasionally, but visitors are few and low key.

⑦ Inousses

Home to shipping barons and quiet discreet sorts who are well-heeled, Inousses (p384) is alternative with a capital A. Swim, eat and sleep and do little else. You'll be in opulent company at least.

⑧ Psara

A pristine speck in the sea well out of the way, Psara (p385) is for latter-day Robinson Crusoes. It's remote, it's basic but it's essential island-hopping if you really want that well-away-from-the-mainstream feel.

Crete

The biggest of the Greek islands, Crete (p220) blends the modernity of the West with the spirit of the East in a beguiling package of mountains, plains, sea, sky, tradition and progress. It's big enough for you to find your own secluded corner and to have your own individual Cretan experience.

1 Elafonisi

The islet of Elafonisi (p259) hangs off the western end of Crete like an afterthought. The lagoon, 50m across and knee-deep – a gentle wade – separates the low dunes of the islet from the mainland.

2 Gavdos

Europe's southernmost island takes an effort to get to. Gavdos (p259) boasts an almost African climate – it's 65km south of Crete, in the Libyan Sea – and is the ultimate chill-out spot for campers, nudists and free spirits.

3 Myrtos

It's getting popular but it may still feel like you alone know about Myrtos (p272). Not featured in glossy mags, it's a small Cretan seaside village that still has a cosy, lived-in ambience, as well as providing creature comforts.

4 Sougia

The dizzying, spiralling drive into the small port of Sougia (p256) means that its wide sand-and-pebble beach is largely unvisited. There's little to do here but rest up for nearby walks at Samaria Gorge and Agia Irini.

5 Anogia

A bastion of Cretan culture – think black-clad, moustachioed shepherds who drink, sing and dance with abandon – Anogia (p241) is famous for its rebellious spirit, its musicians and its all-night come-one come-all weddings.

6 Kissamos Bay

With beaches, bars and – best of all – no tourists, the bay of Kissamos (p259) is tucked into Crete's northwestern corner. A great base for walking, it is close to the wild and remote Gramvousa Peninsula (p261).

7 Kato Zakros

Tranquillity resides on Crete's southeastern coast. Kato Zakros (p269) has a long, pebbly beach, a smattering of tavernas and a gentle walking path through the Valley of the Dead to an ancient Minoan site.

8 Mohlos

There's no bank or post office in Mohlos (p267), but there are good walks, good swimming and tavernas serving up locally caught fish. Put off your errands for a while and chill in this village bedecked with bougainvillea and hibiscus.

Ionian Islands

This westernmost group of islands wears a European air with grace and panache. Once belonging to the Venetians, French and British, the Ionian Islands offer a mild climate, rich green vegetation, bustling resorts and hideaway villages. Most easily visited as a distinct group, the Ionian Islands are popular with Greeks and Europeans alike, but there are still a few places where you can get away from the popular beats.

1 Ithaki

Allegedly the home of Homer's mythical Odysseus (Ulysses), discrete Ithaki (p473) is an ideal place to make your own Odyssey. Olive groves tumble down rocky hills to emerald-blue waters under a golden sun.

2 Antikythira

For the ultimate get-off-the-beaten-track experience you can't beat remote Antikythira (p486) – for die-hards only. Forget your worries and chill out in glorious solitude on a rock in the sea with a few smiling souls.

3 Meganisi

Blink and you've missed demure and subtle Meganisi (p467), hanging off the east coast of Lefkada. It is little more than three bougainvillea-fringed settlements amid ebullient greenery, all ringed by turquoise bays.

4 Paxi

Yachties and travellers with wanderlust love to amble along the tangled lanes and walled olive groves of tiny Paxi (p459). Windmills and olive presses punctuate lush green hills, while boats bob at three pretty harbours.

(Continued from page 340)

The immense **Monastery of St John the Theologian** (☎ 22470 31398; admission free; ☷ 8am-1.30pm daily, 4-6pm Tue, Thu & Sun), with its buttressed grey walls, crowns the island of Patmos. A 4km vehicular road winds up from Skala, but many people prefer to walk up the Byzantine path, which starts from a signposted spot along the Skala–Hora road.

Some 200m along, a dirt path to the left leads through pine trees to the **Monastery of the Apocalypse** (☎ 22470 31234; admission free; treasury €6; ☷ 8am-1.30pm daily, 4-6pm Tue, Thu & Sun), built around the cave where St John received his divine revelation. In the cave you can see the rock that the saint used as a pillow, and the triple fissure in the roof, from where the voice of God issued and which is said to symbolise the Holy Trinity.

The finest frescoes of this monastery are those in the outer narthex. The priceless contents in the monastery's **treasury**, billing itself as 'the Grandest Museum in the Aegean', include icons, ecclesiastical ornaments, embroideries and pendants made of precious stones.

Dine alfresco in the square or in the secluded garden at **Vangelis Taverna** (☎ 22470 31967; mains €5.50-8) and enjoy its cosy, intimate ambience. Good menu choices include *bekri mezes* and the similar *spetsofaï* – rich and spicy cubed-meat concoctions. **Loza** (☎ 22470 32405) on the northwest corner of Hora is the best spot for a sunset drink and snack with stunning views over Skala, while the **Stoa Cafe** (☎ 22470 32226) opposite Vangelis Taverna is an internet wi-fi hotspot.

NORTH OF SKALA

The relaxing, tree-shaded **Meloï Beach** is just 2km northeast of Skala. It's home to **Stefanos Camping** (☎ 22470 31821; camp sites per person/tent €7/2), the island's only camping ground. It offers bamboo-shaded sites, a minimarket, café-bar and motorcycle-rental facilities. Between Skala and Meloï, and set back alone abutting a verdant vegetable plot, is **Stefanos Studios** (☎ 22470 32415; stefstud@12net.gr; studios €25-35 ☒). Tastefully furnished in pine they are airy, spacious and have full kitchenette facilities. Feel free to help yourself to the fresh vegetables in the garden. **To Meloï** (☎ 22470 31888; grills €4-6), at pretty Meloï Beach, is a well-regarded and inexpensive fish taverna with a predictable menu mix of home-cooked dishes, fish and grills.

Heading north, just out of Skala on the hill enjoying stunning views, is the plush **Porto Scoutari Hotel** (☎ 22470 33123; www.portoscoutari.com; d/tr incl breakfast €70-160; P ☒ ☒ ☒). This is the classiest and most romantic place to sleep on Patmos. Each self-contained and individually named studio is impeccably decorated, and comes with a large personal balcony. There's even an on-site church, should you wish to get married and honeymoon in the same location.

ST JOHN THE DIVINE & THE APOCALYPSE

The island of Patmos is home to the Cave of the Apocalypse where St John the Divine was allegedly visited by God and instructed to write the tell-all Book of Revelations, more commonly known as the Book of the Apocalypse. He is often believed to be John the Apostle of Jesus or John the Evangelist, though many would dispute this. His AD 95 exile to Patmos by the pagan Roman Emperor Domitian would tend to rule out the first two options. In the Book of Revelations John wrote to the seven Christian churches of Asia about two apocalyptic visions he had received. Those churches were Ephesus, Smyrna, Pergamos, Thyatira, Sardis, Philadelphia and Laodicea. The first vision (1:11–3:22), relates *one like unto the Son of man, clothed with a garment down to the foot, and girt about the paps with a golden girdle', speaking with 'a great voice, as of a trumpet'*. The second vision comprises the remainder of the book (4–22) and begins with *'a door…opened in the sky'*. It goes on to describe the end of the world – involving the final rebellion by Satan at Armageddon, God's final defeat of Satan, and the restoration of peace to the world. 'Revelation' is considered to be open to interpretation at best and is not afforded the serious scholarly study that it would seem to merit – perhaps because of the obscure and essentially hard-to-interpret symbolism of the work. Some critics have even suggested that it was the work of a deranged man. Notwithstanding, what is clear is that a certain John did write an important spiritual work – perhaps divinely inspired – and most likely in the very cave close to the monastery that now bears his name.

A turn-off right from the main road leads to the relatively quiet and shaded **Agriolivado Beach**. Further along you'll quickly reach the inland village of **Kambos**, from where the road descends to the shaded and shingle **Kambos Beach**, perhaps the most popular and easily accessible beach on the island. Dining choices include **To Agnanti** (☎ 22470 32733; mezedhes €3.50-7), a neat little *ouzerie* with a range of reasonably priced mezedhes. At the northern end of the beach is the cool **George's Place** (☎ 22470 31881; snacks €3-5), where you can play backgammon to laid-back music, graze on a light lunch-time snack and knock back ice-cold beers or colas.

The main road soon forks left to **Lambi**, 9km from Skala, where you wind down to an impressive beach of multicoloured pebbles. High up above the beach on the approach road, the locally revered **Psistaria Leonidas** (☎ 22470 31490; mains €4.50-8) rustles up a wide range of homemade, home-cooked specials, various fish-of-the-day plates and highly recommended *saganaki* dishes.

Under the protected lee of the north arm of the island are several more beaches, including the shaded **Livadi tou Geranou Beach**, with a small church-crowned island opposite replete with the minichapel of **Agios Georgios**. For lunch, you can do no better than the excellent **Livadi Geranou Taverna** (☎ 22470 32046; mains €3-5) overlooking the sea and pulling in the main share of the local beach drifters. The food is home style, honest and relatively inexpensive.

SOUTH OF SKALA

A quiet little corner 3km south of Skala, **Sapsila** is ideal for book lovers who want space, peace and quiet, and a couple of under-used beaches to read on.

The best down-time spot for a week or more with a stack of novels is the immaculate, self-contained **Mathios Studios** (☎/fax 22470 32583; www.mathiosapartments.gr; d/tr studios €40/50; ❄ ▯). These eight fully equipped and tastefully decorated studios are set in a quiet, leafy garden 200m from Sapsila Beach. The upstairs units are the best as they catch the breeze and enjoy the finest views. Owners Giakoumina and Theologos make all guests feel very welcome.

For eating locally don't miss **Benetos** (☎ 22470 33089; Sapsila; mains €7-14; ☽ dinner Tue-Sun), perhaps the most enticing place to dine on Patmos. It's a working boutique farm-

house and specialises in Mediterranean fusion dishes with an occasional Japanese kick. Entrées could include sea urchin roe with a mayonnaise sauce – a fine match for ouzo on the rocks. Suggested mains might mean the hallmark zucchini blossoms stuffed with mushrooms and cheese, or the herb-crusted, pan-seared tuna served rare with a Mediterranean sashimi twist. Finish up with a fresh, vodka-laced *sgroppino*, a lemon sorbet, frozen dessert drink.

Grikos, 1km further along over the hill, is a relaxed low-key resort with a narrow sandy beach and shallow, clean water. Dining is best enjoyed at a couple of tavernas on the southwest side of Grikos Bay. **Flisvos Restaurant** (☎ 22470 31764; mains €4-7) is a well-shaded, modern establishment dishing up filling grills and *mayirefta* with particularly good oven-baked *revithia* (chickpeas), while 100m further along is **Ktima Petra** (☎ 22470 33207; mains €4-7), emphasising organic and home-grown produce. The stuffed and wood-oven baked goat just melts in your mouth and the organic cheese and vegetables simply ooze flavour. The menu selection is small, but there's a good wine list representative of Greece's best vines.

Diakofti, the last settlement in the south, is reached by a round-about sealed road, or a rougher and shorter coastal track passing the startling **Kalikatsos Rock**, abutting pebbly **Petra Beach**. The long, sandy, tree-shaded **Psili Ammos Beach** can be reached by excursion boat or walking track; here you'll find a popular, seasonal beach taverna.

LIPSI ΛΕΙΨΟΙ

pop 698

Blink on the deck of your ferry or catamaran and you might miss Lipsi (lip-*see*). Almost unheard of outside a slowly growing circle of island cognoscenti, Lipsi lives out a somewhat isolated yet palpably quality existence among a scattering of lesser-known northern Dodecanese islands. Long discovered by Italians and latterly by French travellers who jealously guard their discovery to themselves, this dry, rocky island boasts no major attractions. Its drawcard is its relative anonymity, its fine beaches, its undemanding treatment of visitors – no clubs or pubs to speak of – and a sense that you have the island to yourself, apart from two or three days in August when pilgrims and revellers descend upon Lipsi for its main religious festival.

Getting There & Away
FERRY
Connections with Lipsi are tenuous at best. There is currently only one long-haul G&A ferry per week linking the island directly with Piraeus (€40, 12 hours). Lipsi is better connected with its neighbouring islands. ANE Kalymnou's F/B *Nissos Kalymnos* calls eight times weekly in summer, linking Lipsi with Samos, Agathonisi, Leros and Kalymnos. The small local, but very fast ferry **Anna Express** (☎ 22479 41215) links Lipsi five times weekly with Kalymnos and Leros, competing in speed at least with the hydrofoil and catamarans. At other times it serves Patmos, Arki, Marathi and Agathonisi. The larger *Patmos Star* arrives from Patmos three days a week and links Lipsi with Leros and Patmos.

HYDROFOIL & CATAMARAN
In summer one Samos-based hydrofoil calls at Lipsi twice daily on its route between Samos and Kos and return. The *Dodekanisos Express* and *Dodekanisos Pride* catamarans call in up to six times weekly in summer on their route between Patmos (€9.50, 30 minutes) and Rhodes (€42, 4½ hours) and islands in between.

Getting Around
Lipsi has a minibus departing hourly to the beaches of Platys Gialos, Katsadia and Hohlakoura (each €1) between 10.30am and 6pm. Two **taxis** (☎ 6942409677, 6942409679) also operate on the island. There are one or two motorcycle-rental outlets.

LIPSI VILLAGE
pop 600
Hugging the deep harbour, Lipsi village is a cosy community of white-painted and blue-shuttered homes that have an immediately good feel to them.

Orientation & Information
All boats dock at Lipsi Port, where there are two quays. The ferries, hydrofoil and catamarans all dock at the larger, outer jetty, while excursion boats dock at a smaller jetty nearer the centre of Lipsi village. The *Anna Express*

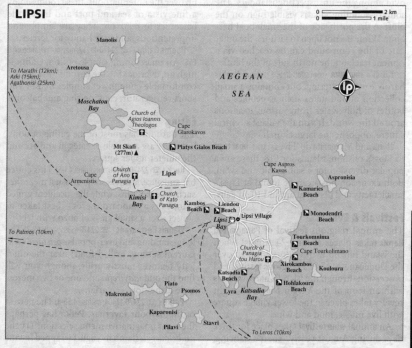

docks close to the large main church in the inner port. It's a 500m walk from the outer jetty to the church.

The post office is on the upper, central square (that is a little quieter than the lower, and busier, harbourside square).

The Cooperative bank of the Dodecanese on the port changes money and has an ATM.

Café Kavos (☎ 22470 44328) Towards the outer jetty; offers internet access which costs per hour €4.

Lipsos Travel (☎ 22470 44125) In Lipsi village; issues tickets for the *Anna Express* and organises excursions.

Police (☎ 22470 41222) In the port.

Port police (☎ 22470 41133) In the port.

Tourist office (☎ 22470 41250; 30min prior to ferry, hydrofoil & catamaran departures) This small office is at the outer jetty and issues ferry, hydrofoil and catamaran tickets.

www.lipsi-island.gr A fairly useful but limited resource about the island

Sights & Activities

Of macabre political interest is the **pink villa**, once occupied by the leader of the ultrasecretive November 17 terrorist group, who lived for a number of years under a pseudonym among the unsuspecting islanders. The solitary-standing villa is visible high on the bluff to the north side of the small boat harbour. While it's not open to visitors, the outer gate of the compound can be reached via a cement track on the north side of the bluff.

Lipsi's **museum** (admission free; 11am-1pm) is hardly earth shattering, but contains a small collection of odd items such as pebbles and bottles of holy water from various locations around the world. It's on the village's central square, opposite the large church.

Rena and Margarita do 'Five Island' **boat trips** to Lipsi's offshore islands for €18; these are a popular diversion for a sail, picnic and swim. Both excursion boats can be found at Lipsi's smaller jetty and depart at around 10am daily.

Festivals & Events

The annual religious festival of **Panagia tou Harou** takes places around 24 August when the island fills up with visitors from all over the Dodecanese. After a religious festival and procession through the island's narrow roads with an icon of the Virgin Mary, all-night revelry takes place in the lower village square with live music, food and wine.

An annual **wine festival** takes place for three days during August yearly. There's dancing,

free wine and festive fun. Check locally for the exact dates as they are not fixed.

Sleeping

O Glaros (☎ 22470 41360; d €30) Set back high up on the hill, about 100m from the village's small boat harbour, these smallish but airy and comfortable rooms have a wide communal balcony and a well-equipped shared kitchen.

Rizos Studios (☎ 69762 44125; fax 22470 44225; d/tr €44/50) These exceptionally well-presented studios are crafted onto the hillside inland from Liendou Bay. With immaculately decorated, cool, stone-paved floors and cushion-strewn rooms plus every kitchen utensil imaginable, they would have to be the best retreat on Lipsi for a self-contained getaway. Canadian-born but Nottingham-raised hostess Anna welcomes guests with an inimitable flashing smile.

Michalis Studios (☎ 22470 41266; mkramvousanos@ yahoo.gr; d €50;) Spacious open-plan studios sleeping two to three people, with fridge, TV and kitchenette. These are a good choice for a longer stay on the island.

Panorama (☎ 22470 41235; d/tr €50/55;) High up over the outer harbour, these rooms enjoy a fine vista of sea and port and have little balconies to relax on. They are simple and unpretentious, and very handy for ferries.

Rooms Galini (☎ 22470 41212; matsouri@yahoo.gr; d €55) An unassuming simple option, Galini is high up, overlooking the harbour. Rooms are comfortable enough yet simple, well lit and sport refrigerator, cooking ring and balcony.

Eating

The harbour has most of the eating options, but there are a couple of cafés in and around the quieter upper square.

Rock (☎ 22470 41180; mezedhes €3-5) This coffee bar and *ouzerie* offers some unusual mezedhes such as sea urchins, while the succulent grilled octopus is a standard mezes – best taken at sunset over a small glass of ouzo with ice.

Yiannis Restaurant (☎ 22470 45395; grills €5-7) The long-standing and ever-popular *psistaria* (restaurant serving grilled food) near the outer jetty features mostly grills, though you will find the odd *mayirefta* and one or two mezes-style dishes for vegetarians.

Pefko (☎ 22470 41404; mains €4.50-8) The newest of the harbour tavernas, Pefko has perhaps the most imaginative menu selection. Try the *ambelourgou* (lamb in yogurt wrapped in vine leaves), or the Pefkos special – oven-baked beef with eggplant.

Theologos (☎ 22470 41248; price upon request) Dine on the freshest fish on the island while seated on a pebble-covered ledge overlooking the harbour. Theologos specialises in fish, which is caught by the owner's boat moored right next to its tables. Non-fish dishes are also available.

Tholari (☎ 22470 41060; mains €4.50-8) Run by a Tasmanian-Greek family, this low-key but tidy taverna in the middle of the harbour rustles up popular dishes like prawn *saganaki* or a rich rabbit stew. Check the daily specials board for hearty *mayirefta*.

Karnagio (☎ 22470 41422; mains €8-13) One of the more innovative eating options is at this rather imposing restaurant at the far side of the harbour. Fish and pasta dishes dominate the menu but there is a wide selection of meat and *mayirefta* dishes.

AROUND THE ISLAND

Lipsi has quite a few beaches, all within walking distance of Lipsi village. Some are shaded, some are not; some are sandy, others gravely and at least one is for nudists. Getting to them makes for pleasant walks through countryside dotted with smallholdings, olive groves and cypress trees. The minibus services the main ones.

Liendou Beach is the most accessible and naturally the most popular beach. The water is very shallow and calm; the best beach for children. It's 500m from Lipsi village, just north of the ferry port over a small headland.

Next along is sandy **Kambos Beach**, a 1km walk along the same road that leads to Platys Gialos. Take the dirt road off to the left. There is some shade available.

Beyond Kambos Beach the road takes you after a further 2.5km to **Platys Gialos**, a lovely but narrow sandy beach. The water here is turquoise-coloured Caribbean, shallow and perfect for children. Nearby is the decent **Kostas Restaurant** (☎ 6944963303; grills €4.50-6.50; ⏰ 8am-6pm Jul-Aug, later on Wed & Sat), which dishes up excellent fish and grill dishes, as well as a smattering of daily *mayirefta*.

South, 2km from Lipsi village, is the sand-and-pebble **Katsadia Beach**, shaded with tamarisk trees and easily reached on foot, or by the hourly minibus.

There is one distinguished place to eat, the **Dilaila Cafe Restaurant** (☎ 22470 41041; mains

€5-8), which is right on the beach. The shady restaurant-cum-bar is caressed by an eclectic range of musical selections during the day and evening. Make sure to ask for 'mad feta', a spicy, baked feta cheese melange or the fried-rice specials. Accommodation can be found at the airy and tastefully furnished **Katsadia Studios** (☎ 22470 41317; d €55), which overlooks the beach.

The pebble **Hohlakoura Beach**, to the east of Katsadia, offers neither shade nor facilities. Further north, **Monodendri** is the island's unofficial nudist beach. It stands on a rocky peninsula, and there are no facilities. It's a 3km walk to get there, though it is reachable by motorcycle.

ARKI & MARATHI
ΑΡΚΟΙ & ΜΑΡΑΘΙ

These two satellite islands flung to the near east of Patmos may look down at heel upon first glance, but the yachts in the harbours belie the fact that they have been 'discovered' by voyageurs of the floating kind. Serious solace seekers chill out here: often for a week or more. Media personalities and computer geeks mingle with yachties, artists, politicians and the occasional backpacker on the courtyard-sized harbour front. There are neither cars nor motorbikes. Just pack your bathers, books and iPod and forget the world exists for a while.

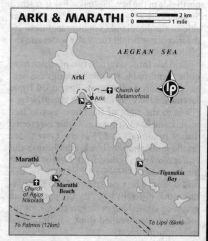

ARKI & MARATHI

AEGEAN SEA

Arki

Arki — Church of Metamorfosis

Marathi

Church of Agios Nikolaos — Marathi Beach

Tiganakia Bay

To Patmos (12km)   To Lipsi (6km)

Getting There & Away

The F/B *Nissos Kalymnos* calls in up to four times weekly as it shuttles between Patmos and Samos on its vital milk run. In summer the Lipsi-based excursion boats visit Arki and Marathi, and a number of Patmos-based caïques do frequent day trips (return €15).

ARKI ΑΡΚΟΙ
pop 50

Tiny Arki, 5km north of Lipsi, is hilly, with shrubs but few trees. Its only settlement, the little west-coast port, is also called Arki. Islanders make a living from fishing and tourism.

There is no post office or police on the island, but there is one cardphone. Away from its little settlement, the island seems almost mystical in its peace and stillness.

The **Church of Metamorfosis** stands on a hill behind the settlement. From its terrace are superb views of Arki and its surrounding islets. The cement road between Taverna Trypas and Taverna Nikolaos leads to the path up to the church. The church is locked, but ask a local if it's possible to look inside.

Several secluded **sandy coves** can be reached along a path skirting the right side of the bay. To reach the path, walk around the last house at the far right of the bay, go through a little wooden gate in the stone wall, just near the sea, and continue ahead.

Tiganakia Bay on the southeast coast has a good sandy beach. To walk there from Arki village, take the cement road that skirts the north side of the bay. Tiganakia Bay is reached by a network of goat tracks and lies at the far side of the headland. You'll recognise it by the incredibly bright turquoise water and the offshore islets.

Arki has three tavernas, two of which have quite comfortable rooms; bookings are necessary in July and August. First up, **O Trypas Taverna & Rooms** (☎ 22470 32230; tripas@12net.gr; d €35) is to the right of the quay, as you face inland, and has 16 rooms available. Suggested dishes (mains €5 to €7) at the taverna are *fasolia mavromatika* (black-eyed beans) and *pastos tou Trypa* (salted fish). Nearby **Taverna Nikolaos Rooms** (☎ 22470 32477; d €35) is the second option. The food (mains €5 to €7.50) is not much different here; try the potatoes au gratin or stuffed peppers with cheese, or the local goat cheese called *sfina*, which is like a milder form of feta.

MARATHI ΜΑΡΑΘΙ

Marathi is the largest of Arki's satellite islets. Before WWII it had a dozen or so inhabitants, but now has only one family. The old settlement, with an immaculate little church, stands on a hill above the harbour. The island has a superb sandy beach. There are two tavernas on the island, both of which rent rooms and are owned by the island's only permanent inhabitants, who speak English. **Taverna Mihalis** (☎ 22470 31580; mains €4-6) is the more laid-back and cheaper of the two places to eat and sleep (doubles €30), while **Taverna Pandelis** (☎ 22470 32609; mains €4-6) at the top end of the beach is a tad more upmarket (doubles €40) and not as traveller oriented as the former.

AGATHONISI
ΑΓΑΘΟΝΗΣΙ

pop 158

You could be forgiven for not knowing the existence of Agathonisi (agh-atho-*ni*-see). It barely shows up on any traveller's radar. Yet it's a smugly reserved and quiet little getaway isle, where latter-day Robinson Crusoes, serious island hoppers or north–south transients might just turn up. Agathonisi is predictably rocky and dry, has minimal settlements and little organised entertainment, yet pulls in a determined procession of travellers who really do want that left-of-centre holiday time out. Accommodation is fine yet simple, food is unfussy yet good quality, and there's little to do other than reflect, read and get ready for that next swim.

Getting There & Away

Agathonisi is linked to Samos (€5, one hour) and Patmos (€7, two hours) about four days a week by the F/B *Nissos Kalymnos*. A hydrofoil also links the island with Samos and destinations further south on the other three days. Ferry agent **Savvas Kamitsis** (☎ 22470 29003) sells tickets at the harbour prior to departures.

Getting Around

There is no local transport, and it's a steep and sweaty 1.5km uphill walk from Agios Giorgios to the main settlement of Megalo Horio; somewhat less to Mikro Horio. From

AGATHONISI

AEGEAN
SEA

Neronisi

Katholiko

Agathonisi

Agios
Giorgios

Poros
Beach

Church
of Agios
Nikolaos

Hohlia
Bay

Mikro
Horio

Tholos
Beach

Megalo
Horio

Spilia
Beach

Tholos (Agios
Nikolaos) Beach

Tsangari
Beach

Gaïdouravlakos
Beach

To Samos
(35km)

To Lipsi (20km);
Patmos (30km)

Kounelonisi

0 — 2 km
0 — 1 mile

Megalo Horio the island's eastern beach
coves are all within a 2km to 3km walk.

AGIOS GIORGIOS ΑΓΙΟΣ ΓΕΩΡΓΙΟΣ

The village of Agios Giorgios (*agh*-ios ye-*or*-
yi-os) is a languid settlement at the end of a
protected fjord-like bay. It has a 100m-long
curved, pebbled beach, where you can comfortably swim, but **Spilia Beach**, 900m southwest around the headland, is quieter; a track
around the far side of the bay will take you
there. A further 1km walk will bring you to
Gaïdouravlakos, a small bay and beach where
water from one of the island's few springs
meets the sea.

Orientation & Information

Boats dock at Agios Giorgios, from where
roads ascend right to Megalo Horio and left to
Mikro Horio. There is no tourist information,
post office, bank, ATM or internet access.

The police are in a prominently marked
white building at the beginning of the Megalo
Horio road.

Sleeping & Eating

Pension Maria Kamitsi (☎ 22470 29003; fax 22470
29004; d €35) In the middle of the waterfront,
the 13 comfortable rooms of Maria Kamitsi
are the easiest to find and more likely to have
vacancies in high season. There is a communal
fridge for every three rooms.

Domatia Giannis (☎ 22470 29062; d/tr €40/50;
❄ ▯) Above and just behind Glaros Restaurant, these five airy rooms offer the best
accommodation on the island. Most have harbour views, are well constructed and enjoy
modern furnishings.

Glaros Restaurant (☎ 22470 29062; mains €4.50-7)
Of the few harbour-side eateries, Glaros is
probably the best place to dine. Owners Voula
and Giannis are very engaging and serve
markakia (feta cheese fingers in vine leaves
with a special sauce), among other standard
oven-cooked meals, grills and fish dishes, all
made from predominantly organic produce.

George's Taverna (☎ 22470 29101; fish €7-15)
Closer to the ferry quay is the taverna of the
affable George and his German staff. Food
is predictably reasonable, though limited to
meat and fish grills and the occasional goat
in lemon sauce.

AROUND AGATHONISI

Megalo Horio is the only village of any size
on the island. Somnolent and unhurried
for most of the time, it comes to life yearly
with religious festivals **Agiou Panteleimonos**
(26 July), **Sotiros** (6 August) and **Panagias** (22
August), when, after church services, the village celebrates with abundant food, music
and dancing.

There are a series of accessible beaches to
the east of Megalo Horio: pebbled **Tsangari
Beach**, pebbled **Tholos Beach**, sandy **Poros
Beach** and pebbled **Tholos (Agios Nikolaos) Beach**, close
to the eponymous church. All are within
easy walking distance.

Further out at the end of the line is the
small fishing harbour of **Katholiko**, with the
uninhabited and inaccessible islet of **Neronisi**
just offshore.

If you prefer an even quieter stay than at
the port, **Studios Ageliki** (☎ 22470 29085; s/d €30/35)
in Megalo Horio will serve you very well.
The four basic but quite comfortable studios
all have stunning views over a small vineyard
and down to the port, and come equipped
with kitchenette, fridge and bathroom. Eating in the village is unfortunately limited to
the reliable **Restaurant I Irini** (☎ 22470 29054; mains
€5-6) on the central square, or the **Kafeneio Ta 13
Adelfia** (mains €3-4) on the south side of the central square, serving budget snacks and meals.

Northeastern Aegean Islands

Τα Νησιά του Βορειοανατολικού Αιγαίου

Diverse, mysterious and achingly beautiful, the islands of the northeastern Aegean offer endless rewards for those intrepid enough to seek them out. Hidden sandy coves, lush mountain waterfalls and ancient sites of divine power are only a few of the attractions in this far-flung archipelago – also known for its wild celebration of saints' feasts, delicious cuisine and good-natured sybaritism.

While exasperating ferry schedules make island-hopping here a challenge, the individual character of each island more than makes up for the effort. Ikaria, with its bizarre rock formations and laid-back, leftist lifestyle is unique, as is Lesvos, with its 11 million olive trees and idyllic mountain villages. Semitropical Samos and pine-scented Thasos boast great beaches, while the almost unvisited Inousses, Fourni and Psara offer total serenity.

These lesser-visited islands also have an importance entirely disproportionate to their size. Over one-third of Greece's ship-owning dynasties hail from Chios and nearby Inousses; and 70% of the national firewater, ouzo, comes from Lesvos – also famous for its olive oil, rare fossils and the only petrified forest outside the USA. One of Europe's most important ancient spiritual sites lies on distant Samothraki, and only in the villages of southern Chios is the renowned gum-producing mastic tree cultivated. And Little Thasos contains the world's second-whitest marble.

HIGHLIGHTS

- **Dining** Checking out Mytilini Town's gourmet *ouzeries* on Lesvos (p389)

- **Chill-out Spot** Relaxing on sultry Livadaki Beach on Samos (p370)

- **Adrenaline Rush** Mountain biking the mountains of Thasos (p412)

- **Magic Moment** Unwinding in the tranquil mediaeval town of Mesta on Chios (p382)

- **Getting Away From it All** Lounging in crystal-clear waters at Ikaria's Seychelles Beach (p363)

- **Historical Experience** Visiting the ancestral home of Greece's great shipping barons in Inousses (p384)

- **Green Haven** Hiking the lush waterfalls and rock pools of Samothraki (p407)

★ Thasos

★ Samothraki

★ Mytilini Town

★ Inousses

Mesta ★

Livadaki Beach ★

Seychelles Beach ★

- **POPULATION: 204,161**
- **AREA: 3842 SQ KM**

GETTING THERE & AWAY
Air
Samos, Chios, Lesvos, Limnos and Ikaria have flights to Athens and Thessaloniki. Interisland flights go between Lesvos, Limnos, Samos and Chios. Thasos and Samothraki don't have airports.

Ferry
Grand wars of one-upmanship between Greece's shipping barons continue to wreak havoc with ferry schedules in the eastern Aegean islands. If you're planning to hit them all, budget extra time and patience, and don't do it in low season, when voyages are reduced. In any season mutually unconnected Samothraki and Thasos are particularly difficult to reach, and require a link from the mainland port of Kavala or else transit via Limnos.

The table (p359) outlines scheduled high-season domestic ferries to the islands from mainland ports. These islands are also on various popular interisland routes; the Dodecanese and Mykonos are two popular destinations. Interisland links are covered in the sections on individual islands.

There are also international connections with the Turkish Aegean coast. In summer daily boats go between Samos and Kuşadası (for Ephesus), and between Chios and Çeşme. Ferries from Lesvos to Ayvalık run four times weekly.

Hydrofoil
Regular hydrofoils in summer go between Kavala and Thasos' two port towns, and between Alexandroupoli and Samothraki. Hydrofoils also operate from Samos west to Ikaria and Fourni, south towards the Dodecanese, and north towards Chios and Lesvos.

IKARIA & THE FOURNI ISLANDS
ΙΚΑΡΙΑ & ΟΙ ΦΟΥΡΝΟΙ

area 255 sq km
It will be a long time before Ikaria is paved over and packaged, and the locals seem to like it that way. Yet with therapeutic hot springs as radioactive as the communist sympathisers once exiled here, this laid-back island of stark ravines, windswept desert trees and shimmering waters lapping on white-pebbled beaches is starting to be discovered. Not to worry: most of the roads are still made of dirt, the bus service is almost nonexistent and no one wakes before noon.

Ikaria (pronounced ih-kah-*ree*-ah) is shrouded in myth. It was named after Icarus, the son of Daedalus, the mythical architect of the Cretan labyrinth of King Minos. When the two tried to escape from Minos' prison on wings of wax, Icarus ignored his father's warning, flew too close to the sun and crashed down into the sea, creating Ikaria – a rocky reminder of the dangers of overweening ambition, which the dozing locals appear to have taken to heart.

More happily, the island was also celebrated by the ancients as the birthplace of Dionysos, the god of wine, fruitfulness and foliage; the poetry of Homer attests that the Ikarians were the first wine-makers. Unfortunately, a phylloxera outbreak in the mid-1960s decimated Ikaria's wine industry, but visitors can still sample the island's signature cloudy red locally.

History records little about Ikaria between ancient times, when it was an ally of Athens, and the Byzantine period, when it was a safe haven for pirates and a place of exile. The latter function was reprised during the three-year Greek Civil War that raged following WWII, when the right-wing government exiled some 15,000 suspected communists to Ikaria. Today the comrades from Greece's Communist Party are still in power; travellers seeking refuge from a typical island's package tourism can thank them and their ambivalence to enterprise for Ikaria's timeless air.

Ikaria is full of pristine beaches, healing hot springs and bohemian attitude, and much more, too. *Panigyria* (festivals; the ritual annual celebrations of saints' days) are veritable events involving copious amounts of food, drink, music and dance that would do Dionysos proud. In spring Ikaria's meadows are ablaze with wildflowers, their range of colour complemented by an endlessly varied interplay of light and shadow on the island's boulder-strewn scrub-land interior – making it a perfect place for photographers and painters. Sculptors, too, are impressed by Ikaria's unusual abundance of different types of stone.

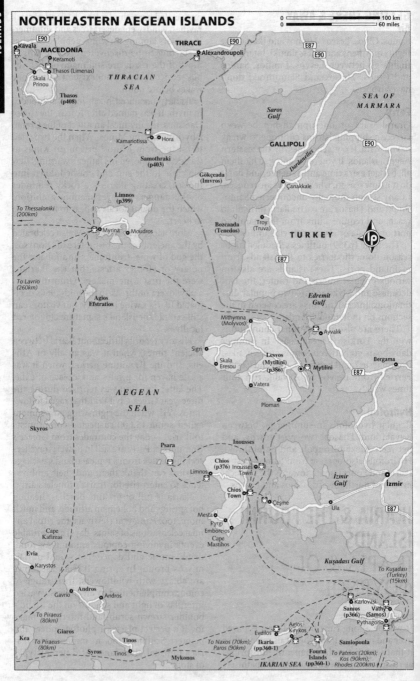

NORTHEASTERN AEGEAN ISLANDS

FERRY CONNECTIONS TO THE NORTHEASTERN AEGEAN ISLANDS

Origin	Destination	Duration	Fare	Freq
Alexandroupoli	Chios	15¼hr	€27.20	weekly
	Lesvos (Mytilini)	11¼hr	€20.90	weekly
	Limnos	5hr	€17.90	2 weekly
	Samos	18¾hr	€33.50	weekly
	Samothraki	2hr	€11	daily
Kavala	Chios	hr	€24.50	weekly
	Lesvos (Mytilini)	10hr	€24.70	2 weekly
	Limnos	5hr	€15.30	4 weekly
	Thasos (Skala Prinou)	1¼hr	€3.80	hourly
Keramoti	Thasos	40min	€2	hourly
Piraeus	Chios	8hr	€22.50	daily
	Ikaria	9hr	€25	daily
	Lesvos (Mytilini)	12hr	€27.90	daily
	Limnos	13hr	€55.50	3 weekly
	Samos	13hr	€26	2 daily
Lavrio	Limnos	13hr	€21.20	4 weekly
Thessaloniki	Chios	18hr	€34.20	weekly
	Lesvos	13hr	€30.20	2 weekly
	Limnos	7hr	€22.10	2 weekly

Getting There & Away

AIR

In summer there are six flights weekly from Athens (€50, 50 minutes), most departing after 1pm. There are also twice-weekly flights to Heraklion in Crete, leaving at 8am.

Olympic Airlines (☎ 22750 22214; www.olympicair lines.com) is in Agios Kirykos; **Nas Travel** (☎ 22750 31947) in Evdilos also sells tickets. There's no airport bus; taxis from Agios Kirykos cost around €10.

CAÏQUE

A caïque leaves Agios Kirykos at 1pm on Monday, Wednesday and Friday for the nearby Fourni archipelago (€4). The caïque calls at Fourni town and usually at Hrysomilia or Thymena; all have domatia (a cheap accommodation option) and tavernas. Day-trip excursion boats to Fourni also go from Agios Kirykos and Evdilos (€20).

FERRY

Most of Ikaria's ferries are on the Piraeus–Samos route. Two weekly ferries go to Piraeus (€32, nine hours) and three to Samos (€10, three hours). Five boats weekly serve Fourni (€8, two hours). Additionally, in summer **Kallisti Ferries** (☎ 801 117 7700; www.kallistiferries.gr) operates the high-speed *Corsica Express* four times weekly between Vathy (Samos), Karlovasi (Samos), Agios Kirykos/Evdilos (Ikaria)

and Piraeus (4¼ hours), with a once-weekly diversion to Fourni on Saturday.

The Cyclades are served by twice-weekly ferries to Paros (€14.30) and Naxos (€12.50), as well as five weekly ferries to Mykonos (€13.10, 2½ hours) and Syros (€14.50, 3½ hours).

Get tickets at **Icariada Holidays** (☎ 22750 22277; icariada@hol.gr) or **G&A Ferries** (☎ 22750 22426) in Agios Kirykos, or from **Nas Travel** (☎ 22750 71396; fax 22750 71397) in Evdilos and Armenistis.

HYDROFOIL

Ikaria's hydrofoil service is usually in July and August only. Common destinations are Piraeus, Samos, and some Dodecannesian and Cycladic islands. Check with **Dolihi Tours Travel Agency** (☎ 22750 23230; fax 22750 22346) in Agios Kirykos or **Nas Travel** (☎ 22750 71396; fax 22750 71397) in Evdilos and Armenistis.

Getting Around

BUS & TAXI

Ikaria's bus situation is not auspicious. Theoretically, in summer a bus leaves Evdilos for Agios Kirykos daily at 8am, returning at noon. However, since the bus system exists to transport school children, not tourists, don't depend on it.

The whims of individual drivers can determine the schedules from Agios Kirykos to Hristos Rahes (near Moni Evangelistrias),

NORTHEASTERN AEGEAN ISLANDS

IKARIA & THE FOURNI ISLANDS

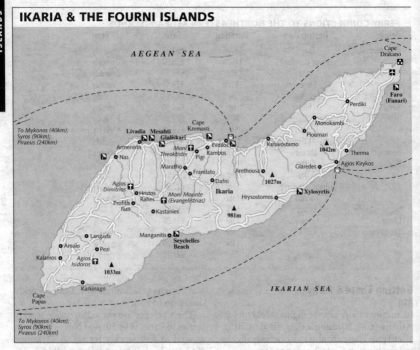

Xylosyrtis and Hrysostomos. If you don't rent a car, share a taxi; from Agios Kirykos to Evdilos costs around €35.

CAR & MOTORCYCLE

Given Ikaria's public transport limitations, renting a car or scooter is a wise idea if you want to see anything beyond the main towns. **Dolihi Tours Travel Agency** (☎ 22750 23230; fax 22750 22346) in Agios Kirykos, **Nas Travel** (☎ 22750 71396; fax 22750 71397) in Evdilos and Armenistis, and **Aventura Car & Bike Rental** (☎ 22750 31140; aventura@otenet.gr) in Evdilos and Armenistis can outfit you.

WATER TAXI

Water taxis are helpful for nondrivers, or anyone up for a good boat ride. In summer daily water taxis go from Agios Kirykos to Therma and to the sandy beach at Faro (also known as Fanari) on Ikaria's northern tip (€12 return). Heading the other way, there's also a caïque every Monday, Wednesday and Friday in summer from Agios Kirykos to the fishing village of Karkinagri on the southwestern coast, stopping at Maganitis and its celebrated

Seychelles Beach on the way. This boat is the only realistic way for nondrivers to get to this remote corner of Ikaria.

AGIOS KIRYKOS ΑΓΙΟΣ ΚΗΡΥΚΟΣ
pop 1879

Honorary capital of Ikaria, Agios Kirykos is a dependable Greek port with clustered old streets, tasty restaurants, unique nearby attractions and the services that will get you deeper into the island. Radioactive springs and a little nightlife are other pluses, as is Xylosyrtis Beach (4km southwest), the best of several local pebble beaches.

Orientation

The ferry quay is 150m south of the town centre; to reach the central *plateia* (square), turn right onto the main road. Leaving the quay, turn left on the central *plateia;* the bus stop is just west. Excursion boats and hydrofoils dock near Dolihi Tours Travel Agency.

Information

Alpha Bank, next to Dolihi Tours Travel Agency, and the National Bank of Greece,

on the *plateia*, have ATMs. The police station is above Dolihi Tours Travel Agency, and the post office is left of the *plateia*.

Dolihi Tours Travel Agency (☎ 22750 23230; fax 22750 22346) Helpful agency that can arrange accommodation; located below the police station.

Icariada Holidays (☎ 22750 23322; icariada@hol.gr) Helpful staff sell ferry and plane tickets, and can arrange accommodation in Fourni. On the waterfront.

Police (☎ 22750 22222)

Port police (☎ 22750 22207)

Tourist police (☎ 22750 22222)

Sights & Activities

Opposite the police station are the **radioactive springs** (admission €5; ☼ 7am-2.30pm & 5-9pm Jun-Oct). Their salutary effects include curing arthritis and infertility.

Agios Kirykos' small **archaeological museum** (☎ 22750 31300; admission free; ☼ 10am-3pm Tue & Wed, Fri-Sun Jul & Aug) boasts local finds, highlighting the large, well-preserved stele (500 BC) depicting a seated mother and family. The signposted museum is near the hospital.

Sleeping

Hotel Akti (☎ 22750 23905; fax 22750 22694; s/d €35/50; ❄) A good budget choice, the Akti has small but attractive rooms with fridge, TV and mosquito netting, with a nice location on the rocks overlooking the sea and port, and friendly, English-speaking owners. Follow the steps to the right of Alpha Bank.

Hotel Kastro (☎ 22750 23480; www.island-ikaria.com /hotels/kastro.asp; d €50; ❄ 🖥) This well-appointed hotel has handsome rooms with balconies and all mod cons. The bar is complemented by an appealing rooftop pool. At the top of the stairs leading from Dolihi Tours Travel Agency, go left 20m to the hotel.

Eating & Drinking

Taverna Klimataria (☎ 22750 22686; mains €6-9; ☼ year-round) This back-street taverna, strong on grilled meats, has a lovely summer courtyard.

Restaurant Dedalos (☎ 22750 22473; mains €7-10) This busy eatery on the central *plateia* is known for its tasty fresh fish.

AROUND AGIOS KIRYKOS

Some 2km northeast of town are the popular **hot springs of Therma** (☎ 69771 47014; admission €5; ☼ 7am-2.30pm & 5-9pm Jun-Oct), believed to cure many ailments. Along with the airport, Ikaria's eastern tip boasts the 2km-long **Faro Beach**, 10km north along the coast road, and the 3rd-century BC **fortress of Drakanos** (currently being excavated), which sponsored religious rites dedicated to Eilythia, a minor pregnancy-promoting deity.

While a few tavernas hug the beach, it remains blissfully quiet compared to the major northwest-coast beaches. Just up from it, on the main access road, the friendly Greek-Australian Evon Plakidis at **Rooms Evon** (☎ 22750 32580; www.evonsrooms.com; ste €50-110) rents clean, high-quality suites, some with spiral stairs, and all with kitchenettes. The studios can hold up to six people. There's also internet access for guests.

EVDILOS ΕΥΔΗΛΟΣ
pop 461

Evdilos, the island's second port, is 41km northwest of Agios Kirykos. The road connecting them is Ikaria's main road. If you don't have a car, a taxi costs around €35 for the memorable trip, which takes in high mountain ridges, striking sea views and slate-roof villages. Evdilos itself is sleepy, though

RELIGIOUS REVELRY ON THE ISLAND OF WINE

Pagan god Dionysos may no longer reign over the vineyards of Ikaria, but his legacy lives on in Christianised form in the summertime *panigyria* (festivals; all-night celebrations held on saints' days across the island). There's no better way to dive headfirst into Greek island culture than drinking, dancing and feasting in honour of a village's patron saint. Bring your wallet, however: *panigyria* are important fundraisers for the local community. Use this fact to explain any overindulgences as well-intended philanthropy.

Western Ikaria *panigyria* take place on the following dates:

- **Kambos** 5 May
- **Agios Isidoros** 14 May
- **Armenistis** 40 days after Orthodox Easter
- **Pezi** 14 May
- **Agios Kirykos & Ikarian Independence Day** 17 July
- **Hristos Rahes & Dafne** 6 August
- **Langada** 15 August
- **Evdilos** 14-17 August
- **Agios Sofia** 17 September

its narrow streets are chronically congested with cars, and fishing is strong. It also has a few stately old houses and winding streets (follow Kalliopis Katsouli, the cobbled street leading uphill from the waterfront square). Walk 100m uphill from the *plateia*, then take the path down past the last house on the left to reach the local beach.

Information

The waterfront's eastern and western ends have ATMs. The latter also hosts the ticket agencies for **NEL Lines** (☎ 22750 31572) and **Hellas Ferries** (☎ 22750 31990). **Aventura** (☎ 22750 31140), in a side street off the central waterfront, rents cars and bikes, sells tickets and offers information.

Sleeping

Hotel Atheras (☎ 22750 31434; www.atheras-kerame.gr; s/d €52/62; ❄ ☢) There's an almost Cycladic feel to the Atheras, marked by bright white décor contrasting with the blue Aegean beyond. This friendly and modern hotel also has a pool bar. Find it in the backstreets, about 200m from the port.

Kerame Studios (☎ 22750 31434; www.atheras-kerame.gr; studio/apt from €70; ❄ ☢) These diverse studios, apartments and rooms 1km before Evdilos have close beach access. Prices are as variable as the quarters, which include simple but well-maintained studios and apartments

for four people, with separate kitchen. Rooms have spacious decks with good views; the on-site restaurant is built into a windmill.

Hotel Evdoxia (☎ 22750 31502; www.evdoxia.gr; d €70; ❄) Although it's a bit of a climb, this B-class hotel has attractive modern rooms and many facilities, like a minimarket, laundry service, currency exchange and traditional restaurant. If you reserve in advance for several days, pick-up can be arranged free from the ferry.

Eating

Tsakonitis (☎ 22750 31684; Plateia Evdilou; mezedhes €3.50-5) This *ouzerie* (place that serves ouzo and light snacks) down on the water is a local favourite known for its home-made Greek yogurt.

To Steki (☎ 22750 31723; Plateia Evdilou; mains €5-7) This harbour-side dining 'hang-out' (as its name implies in Greek) is a dependable year-round option for taverna fare, such as cheese pies and *soufiko* (an Ikarian speciality, like a Greek ratatouille).

WEST OF EVDILOS

Kambos Κάμπος

pop 94

Little Kambos, 3km west of Evdilos, was once mighty Oinoe (derived from the Greek word for wine), Ikaria's capital. Traces of this ancient glory don't remain, though the village does have ruins of a Byzantine palace, Ikaria's oldest church and a small museum. Kambos' other main attractions are its sand-and-pebble beach and scenic hill-walking opportunities.

INFORMATION

If he's not cooking for the guests at his little hotel, charismatic local Vasilis Kambouris can be found at his village shop (it's on the right as you arrive from Evdilos), which also hosts Kambos' post box and a telephone. Vasilis, who has been assisting travellers for over 30 years, can help with anything you need in Kambos, and in Ikaria in general.

SIGHTS & ACTIVITIES

On the right-hand side when entering Kambos from Evdilos stand the modest ruins of a **Byzantine palace**. Kambos' centre has a small **museum** (☎ 22750 31300; admission free), with Neolithic tools, geometric vases, classical sculpture fragments, figurines and ivory trinkets. If it's not open, ask Vasilis Kambouris. Adjacent stands Ikaria's oldest surviving church, the 12th-century Byzantine **Agia Irini**. As is common in Greece, it was built on the site of an earlier church, in this case a 4th-century basilica: some columns come from this original. Alas, Agia Irini's frescoes remain covered with whitewash because of no funds to pay for its removal.

SLEEPING & EATING

our pick Rooms Dionysos (☎ 22750 31300; dionisos@hol .gr; d €35) The undisputed heavyweight champ of Ikarian tourism, ebullient Vasilis Kambouris, runs this wonderful *pension* with his Australian wife Dimitra and brother Yiannis. The fact that almost 50% of his guests are return visitors says it all about this welcoming little hotel with simple but well-maintained rooms and a lovely shaded patio overlooking

nearby Kambos Beach. Big breakfasts are the jovial Vasilis' hallmark; more intangibly, there is the sense of community and openness he fosters by bringing together people from all countries (a few unexpected marriages have even come from walking in and out of Rooms Dionysos!), who cherish the relaxed atmosphere and unique, friendly service. To find it, ask at Vasilis' village shop or look out for the blue-painted trees.

Balcony (☎ 22750 31604; d/tr €35/50) This family-friendly collection of six apartments requires a hike to get to, but rewards visitors with fantastic views. Classic wrought-iron furniture distinguishes the studios, which have a kitchen and a loft-sleeping area with twin mattresses. French-style doors lead to a private sitting area with coastal views.

Pashalia (☎ 22750 31346; mains €6-8) A family-run *ouzerie* with tradition, the Pashalia is a great place to meet engaging local characters and try delectable home-made *mezedhes* (appetisers), such as wild mushrooms, fresh mountain asparagus and goats cheese.

Kambos to the Southwest Coast

From Kambos, two roads head west: the main road, which hugs the northern coast until the resort of Armenistis, and then becomes a secondary road for the duration of the trip down the northwestern coast; and another secondary road, mostly dirt but doable with a good car, which ribbons slightly southwest through the stunning moonscapes of central Ikaria to the remote coastal village of Karkinagri. The latter is ideal for those who want to get off the beaten track, while the former is the obvious choice for beach lovers.

The southwest coast road through central Ikaria brings you to **Moni Theoktistis** and the tiny **Chapel of Theoskepasti** (see boxed text,

---

MOUNTAIN WALKS & MONKS' SKULLS

With its solitude and wild nature, Ikaria is perfect for mountain walks. One that is invigorating, but not too hard on the bones, is the one-day circular walk along dirt roads from **Kambos** south through the village of **Dafni**, the remains of the 10th-century Byzantine **Castle of Koskinas**, and the villages of **Frandato** and **Maratho**.

When you reach the village of **Pigi**, keep an eye out for the Frandato sign; continue past it to reach the unusual little Byzantine **Chapel of Theoskepasti**, tucked into overhanging granite. You have to clamber upwards to get to it, and duck to get inside. Provided the old monks' skulls on display don't creep you out, the chapel makes for a wonderfully peaceful visit and is near **Moni Theoktistis**, some of whose frescoes date from 1686. The kindly Maria runs the nearby *kafeneio* (coffee house), where you can stop in for a coffee or juice and chat with the locals.

p363), just northwest of the village of Pigi. From Pigi, continue south to Maratho, then follow the road west to reach **Moni Mounte**, also known as Moni Evangelistrias. Some 500m after it, on a duck pond with giant goldfish and croaking frogs, is the very unusual **I Kantina tou Papa** (☎ 22750 41133; mezedhes €3-5; ☺ 11am-9pm), a retro-fitted campervan, founded and operated by a priest, that serves mezedhes like *bourekaki* (cheese pies), fried zucchini flowers, and refreshing sweets made of cherry and lemon. You're seated at slate tables in the shade to eat and drink; the pond and its colourful inhabitants are a favourite with kids.

After the Kantina, the road forks either northwest or southwest: follow the signs and either will take you to **Hristos Rahes**, an eclectic village in the hills that is a good base for local hiking and was once known for its late-night shopping. Along with various traditional products, you can buy a useful walking map called *The Round of Rahes on Foot* (€3) at most tourist shops and markets.

After Hristos Rahes, follow the road south through rustic **Profitis Ilias**. Keep heading south when the road forks; after 1km take the left towards **Pezi**. The landscape now becomes even more rugged and extreme, with wind-whipped thick green trees clinging to bleak boulders, and rows of old agriculturalists' stone walls snaking across the terrain. It is a bouncy, dusty ride, but worth it for the views of the hard interior and, after you turn left at Kalamos, of the sea far below. The road finally terminates in the tiny and isolated fishing village of **Karkinagri**, which has a few tavernas, rooms and a nearby beach.

In summer Karkinagri also has a thrice-weekly boat service to Agios Kirykos. This highly recommended voyage brings you along Ikaria's rugged and partially inaccessible southern coast. The boat calls in at the village of **Manganitis**; nearby is a gorgeous, secluded stretch of white pebbles and crystal-clear waters – the appropriately named **Seychelles Beach** tucked within a protected cove and flanked by a cave.

SLEEPING & EATING

Hotel Raches (☎ 22750 91222; Hristos Rahes; s/d €25/35) Upstairs from Taverna Katoi these simple but clean and inexpensive domatia have balconies with views, a communal area and friendly owners – no wonder it's fully booked in high season.

Kaza Papas (☎ 22750 91222; www.karkinagri.gr; Karkinagri; d/apt €40/50; ☒) These simple but new air-conditioned domatia and apartments in Karkinagri have great views of the sea. Facing the water, you can turn right behind the tavernas and walk 100m along the waterfront to reach them, though it's better to call in advance.

Taverna Katoi (☎ 22750 41269; Hristos Rahes; mains €6-8) Hopefully the talk of this Hristos Rahes taverna not reopening will be proven false, as it's a wonderful, eclectic place filled with unusual bric-a-brac and with a relaxing garden. It also serves great Ikarian fare and local wine.

O Karakas (☎ 22750 91214; Karkinagri; mains €5-9) On a bamboo-roofed patio by the sea, this excellent family-run taverna does good fresh fish and salads. Especially tasty and unique is the Ikarian vegetable stew speciality, *soufiko*.

Armenistis to Nas Αρμενιστής προς Να

Armenistis, 15km west of Evdilos, is Ikaria's humble version of a resort. It boasts two long, sandy beaches separated by a narrow headland, a fishing harbour and a web of hilly streets to explore, but nothing particularly traditional. Moderate nightlife livens up the town in summer, but it's still light years away from the typical Greek island resort. **Dolihi Tours** (☎ 22750 71480; fax 22750 71340), by the sea, organises walking tours and jeep safaris. **Aventura** (☎ 22750 71117), by the patisserie before the bridge, rents cars and sells tickets.

Just 500m east of Armenistis is **Livadia Beach**, which will please surfers with its strong waves in summer – strong enough indeed to warrant a lifeguard service. Beyond Livadia are two other popular beaches, **Mesahti** and **Gialiskari**.

From Armenistis heading west, a road continues 3.5km to the pebbled beach of **Nas**, located far below the road and the handful of tavernas gathered nearby. The beach, which has an impressive location at the mouth of a forested river and behind the remnants of an ancient **Temple of Artemis**, is nudist friendly.

Nas itself has become a bit trendy, in a subdued way, and preserving this state of affairs has led the Greek police to vigorously break up impromptu beach hovels belonging to the hapless hippies the place attracts. They usually retreat into the river forest to camp, and are in any case benevolent, more so than the pushy Athenian anarchists who ruin the mood by slaughtering the occasional goat, perhaps as the ancient worshippers at the nearby Temple of Artemis once did.

SLEEPING

Rooms Fotinos (☎ 22750 71235; www.island-ikaria .com/hotels/PensionFotinos.asp; d €40; ☯ May-Oct; ❄) This family-run *pension* in Armenistis is 150m above the curving beach on which it looks down from the west. It has only seven rooms, all clean and modern, with a lovely, relaxing garden, and the owners are friendly and helpful.

Gallini (☎ 22750 71293; www.galinipension.gr; d €50; ☯ May-Oct) A good choice with fine views of the coast, these 12 domatia hover above Armenistis. They are small but beautifully furnished, with walls of inset stone and big windows. Studios are larger, with slanting, loft-style ceilings and kitchenettes.

Atsachas Rooms (☎ /fax 22750 71226; www.atsachas .gr; d €50) Right on Livadia Beach, the Atsachas has clean, well-furnished rooms, some with sophisticated kitchens. Most have breezy, seaview balconies. The café spills down to the lovely garden; the restaurant has also won plaudits.

Villa Dimitri (☎ /fax 22750 71310; www.villa-dimitri .de; 2-person studios & apt with private patio €50-65; ☯ Mar-Oct; ❄) This assortment of separate, secluded apartments set on a cliff amid colourful flowers and plants has a Cycladic feel. It's 800m west of Armenistis and not somewhere you just show up: advance bookings, for a minimum of one week, are essential.

Panorama (☎ 22750 71177; studios €80) This collection of five self-catering studios is located up a steep driveway right before the village. Rooms fit up to four people and feature handsome combinations of wood and marble, all with new fixtures and good sea views.

EATING

Pashalia Taverna (☎ 22750 71302; Armenistis; mains from €5; ☯ Jun-Nov) Meat dishes like *katsikaki* (kid goat) or veal in a clay pot are the speciality here, the first taverna along the Armenistis harbour road.

Kelari (☎ 22750 71227; Gialiskari; mains €6-13) Taking the fish straight off the boat, Kelari serves the best seafood available at this laid-back beach east of Armenistis.

Taverna Nas (☎ 22750 71486; Nas; mains €6-10) This simple taverna set on a high bluff over Nas beach has superb views of the coast and western sea at sunset. Although a bit touristy,

it serves hearty portions of Greek standbys and fresh fish.

FOURNI ISLANDS ΟΙ ΦΟΥΡΝΟΙ

pop 1469

The little archipelago of Fourni, once upon a time a pirate's lair, lies peacefully between Ikaria and Samos. With only three villages dotting an otherwise rugged and hilly landscape, Fourni is now a lair for travellers seeking total peace. The islands' far-flung, secluded beaches are immaculate, and its fishing fleet's reputation for supplying the best seafood is upheld as far away as Athens. Abundant in long sunsets and rocky old pirates' coves, Fourni will appeal to artistic types, hikers and swimmers.

The islands' port, Fourni (also called Kambos), has most of its accommodation, as well as a central beach and other close-by beaches. The much smaller Hrysomilia, 10km north, is connected to it by Fourni's only road. In the very south, the monastery of Agios Ioannis Prodromos gazes over several captivating beaches.

Given its relative isolation, Fourni is surprisingly well served. It has a **doctor** (☎ 22750 51202), **police** (☎ 22750 51222) and **port police** (☎ 22750 51207). The main road runs perpendicular with the water and continues 100m to the *plateia;* along it resides a National Bank of Greece with ATM, a post office, a **pharmacy** (☎ 22750 51188) and, adjacent to the latter, an **internet café** (per hr €3; ☯ 11am-midnight).

Accommodation can be found through Ikarian travel agencies or through Maria Kalfountzou at **Fournoi Island Tours** (☎ 22750 51546), located just up from the waterfront on the road to the *plateia.* There are a few signposted domatia as well, such as the well-maintained **Nectaria's Studios** (☎ 22750 51365; d/tr €35/45) on the habour's far side.

Fourni's exemplary fish tavernas are clustered along the waterfront; try the local speciality, grilled lobster at **Psarotaverna O Miltos** (☎ 22750 51407; mains from €8). For heavier fare, and to meet some animated local characters, follow the wafting Greek music and smell of roasting meat up to the main *plateia* and the **Taverna Kali Kardia** (☎ 22750 51217; mains €5.50-9) on the left.

Getting There & Away

FERRY

Fourni lies on the Piraeus–Samos ferry route. Besides daily boats to Ikaria (€3.20,

40 minutes), five boats go weekly to Samos (€8, two hours).

HYDROFOIL

Like Ikaria, Fourni's hydrofoils operate in summer only; check with a local travel agency.

Getting Around

Two weekly caïques serve Hrysomilia and three go to Thymena, year-round, departing at 7.30am. Group day trips to pristine, but far-flung Fourni beaches cost €15 per person; book through **Fournoi Island Tours** (☎ 22750 51546).

SAMOS ΣΑΜΟΣ

pop 32,814 / area 477 sq km

Lush forested mountains, sweet local wine, sacred ancient sites and almost tropical beaches all conspire to make Samos an immensely appealing island getaway. Since it's the busy ferry hub of the eastern Aegean islands and the jumping-off point for the nearby Turkish coastal resort of Kuşadası, however, visitors all too often just pass through without sampling the delights of what is, in fact, one of Greece's very best islands.

While high summer brings a plethora of package tourists to resorts around the pretty port towns of Vathy and Pythagorio, there is space aplenty for independent travellers seeking to get away from it all, too. Hiking the interior brings one into rolling mountains redolent of pine, wildflowers and jasmine, dotted by welcoming traditional villages. Samos' long and curving coastline is crowned by cliff-top churches offering stunning views of secret coves where temperate turquoise waters gently lap.

Samos also boasts a distinguished history. Its identity as the legendary birthplace of Hera, wife of Zeus, is attested by the ruins of the sanctuary in her honour, the Ireon – one of several architectural wonders on the island where both the great mathematician Pythagoras and the hedonistic father of atomic theory, the 4th-century BC philosopher Epicurus were born. The most illustrious Samian of modern times, Themistoklis Sofoulis (1860–1949), was a respected prime minister and a pioneer of Greek archaeology.

Getting There & Away

AIR

Olympic Airlines (www.olympicairlines.com) Vathy (☎ 22730 27237; cnr Kanari & Smyrnis); Pythagorio (☎ 22730 61213; Lykourgou Logotheti) has four flights daily from Samos to Athens (€73, 40 minutes) and two flights weekly to Thessaloniki (€149, one hour). The airport is 4km west of Pythagorio.

FERRY
Domestic

With its two northern ports of Vathy (Samos) and Karlovasi, and Pythagorio port on the southern coast, Samos is the eastern Aegean's maritime hub. Ferries link it with the Do-

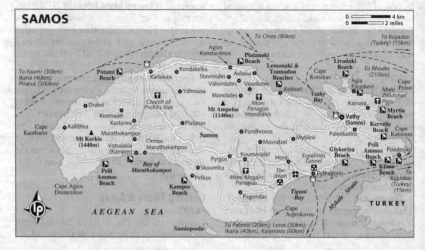

SAMOS

decanese and Cyclades, and with the other Northeastern Aegean Islands. The exceptionally helpful **ITSA Travel** (☎ 22730 23605; www.itsatravelsamos.com; Themistokleous Sofouli) directly opposite the ferry terminal in Vathy (Samos), offers free luggage storage without a catch. Considering that ITSA boss Dimitris Sarlas owns four ferries operating from Samos, it's no surprise that it has the most up-to-date information on schedule changes.

Two ferries go daily to Piraeus (€34, 13 hours), three to Ikaria (€10, three hours). Five boats go weekly to Fourni (€8, two hours), four weekly to Chios (€12, four hours), and two weekly to Lesvos (€17, 11 hours), Limnos (€27.50, 11 hours) and Alexandroupoli (€32, 16 hours). Three ferries a week go to Naxos (€21, seven hours) and Paros (€18.50, eight hours). Five weekly ferries serve Mykonos (€25, six hours). Three ferries weekly sail to Patmos (€8, 2½ hours), four to Leros (€7, 3½ hours) and Kalymnos (€10, four hours), and one to Kos (€15, 5½ hours) and Rhodes (€30, nine hours).

In summer **Kallisti Ferries** (☎ 801 117 7700; www.kallistiferries.gr) run the high-speed *Corsica Express* five times weekly between Vathy (Samos) and Piraeus (€49, 6¾ hours) via Ikaria.

International
In summer two ferries go daily from Vathy (Samos) to Kuşadası (for Ephesus) in Turkey. The *Samos Star* leaves at 8.30am, while a Turkish-flagged vessel departs at 5pm. From Pythagorio there is a once-weekly boat to Kuşadası. In low season there are two ferries weekly. Tickets cost around €47 open return and €37 one way (plus €10 port taxes). Daily excursions are also available from May through October; the Sunday trip is especially popular; for an extra €25, you can also see Ephesus. Again, **ITSA Travel** (☎ 22730 23605; www.itsatravelsamos.com; Themistokleous Sofouli), opposite the ferry terminal in Vathy (Samos), is the place to book.

The ticket office will take your passport in advance for port formalities, though Turkish visas, where required, are issued once in Turkey. Visas are not required for day trips.

HYDROFOIL
In summer hydrofoils link Pythagorio twice daily with Patmos (€15, one hour), Leros (€16, two hours), Kos (€25.50, 3½ hours) and Kalymnos (€21, 2½ hours). From Vathy (Samos) hydrofoils sail daily to Lipsi (€15, 1½ hours), once a week to Agathonisi (€11, 35 minutes) and twice weekly to Fourni (€14, 50 minutes).

Also from Vathy (Samos) one hydrofoil weekly serves Patmos (€20, one hour), Kos (€27), Leros (€24) and Paros (€32, four hours). Schedules are fluid, so double-check with the **tourist office** (☎ 22730 61389) or the **port police** (☎ 22730 61225) in Pythagorio. In Vathy (Samos), consult **ITSA Travel** (☎ 22730 23605; www.itsatravelsamos.com; Themistokleous Sofouli).

Getting Around
TO/FROM THE AIRPORT
There's no airport shuttle bus; a taxi from Vathy (Samos) costs €12. Alternatively, take a local bus to Pythagorio, from where a taxi to the airport costs €5.

BUS
From Vathy (Samos) **bus station** (☎ 22730 27262; Ioannou Lekati) there are six buses daily on weekdays to Kokkari (€1.30, 20 minutes), eight to Pythagorio (€1.50, 25 minutes), seven to Agios Konstantinos (€1.90, 40 minutes) and Karlovasi (via the north coast; €3.30, one hour), and five to the Ireon (€2, 25 minutes) and Mytilini (€1.20, 20 minutes).

In addition, from Pythagorio five buses go daily to the Ireon (€1.20, 15 minutes) and four to Mytilini (€1.20, 20 minutes). Buy tickets on the bus. Services are reduced on Saturday and nonexistent on Sunday.

CAR & MOTORCYCLE
The best rates on car, jeep and motorcycle rental are offered at **Pegasus Rent a Car** (☎ 22730 24470, 6972017092; pegasussamos@hotmail.com; Themistoklis Sofouli 5), directly opposite the port entrance and next to ITSA Travel. The big international car-rental outlets, like **Hertz** (☎ 22730 61730; Lykourgou Logotheti 77) and **Europcar** (☎ 22730 61522; Lykourgou Logotheti 65), tend to be more expensive and less understanding of extra sand in the car than Pegasus' Dutch manager Carolina, who gladly hands out free advice, maps and sun hats to renters.

EXCURSION BOAT
In summer excursion boats travel four times weekly from Pythagorio to the monasteries of St John in Hora on Patmos (return €35), leaving at 8am. Daily excursion boats go from Pythagorio to the islet of Samiopoula

(including lunch €25), and a round-island boat tour begins from Pythagorio's harbour twice weekly (€40).

TAXI

The **taxi rank** (☎ 22730 28404) in Vathy (Samos) is by the National Bank of Greece. In Pythagorio the **taxi rank** (☎ 22730 61450) is on the waterfront at Lykourgou Logotheti.

VATHY (SAMOS) ΒΑΘΥ (ΣΑΜΟΣ)
pop 2025

Lively Vathy (also called Samos) is the island's capital, and lies in the fold of a deep bay on the northeast coast. Its historic quarter of Ano Vathy features red-tiled 19th-century hill-side houses, while a fine archaeological museum houses ancient Samian treasures. Like most Greek port towns, Vathy's curving waterfront is lined with bars, cafés and restaurants; however, more atmospheric and equally lively nightspots cling to the town's northeastern cliff side, just before the Pythagoras Hotel. A bit further on past the hotel are two pebble beaches, the most popular being Gagou Beach (about 1km north of the town centre).

Orientation

Facing inland from the ferry terminal, turn right to reach the central square of Plateia Pythagorou on the waterfront, recognisable by its four palm trees and lion statue. A little further along, and a block inland, are the leafy municipal gardens. The waterfront road is named after local son and statesman Themistoklis Sofouli. The bus station is on Ioannou Lekati.

Information

ATMs available include Commercial Bank, on Plateia Pythagorou's east side, and the National Bank of Greece, on the waterfront; several others are located there, too.

Diavlos NetCafe (☎ 22730 22469; Themistokeous Sofouli 160; per hr €4; ☺ 8.30am-11.30pm) Offers internet access.

Municipal tourist office (☎ 22730 28582) This summer-only office north of Plateia Pythagorou in a little side street can find accommodation.

Port police (☎ 22730 27890) North of the quay, one block back from the waterfront.

Post office (Smyrnis) Four blocks from the waterfront.

Pythagoras Hotel (☎ 22730 28422; Kallistratou 12; per hr €3) Offers internet access.

Samos General Hospital (☎ 22730 27407) Up the hill from the port, opposite the Pythagoras Hotel.

Tourist police (☎ 22730 27980; Themistokleous Sofouli 129) On the waterfront's south side.

Sights

Along with the old quarter of **Ano Vathy**, the relaxing **municipal gardens**, and **Roditzes and Gagou Beaches**, the town's main attraction is its **archaeological museum** (☎ 22730 27469; adult/student €3/2, free admission Sun; ☺ 8.30am-3pm Tue-Sun, last entry 2.45pm), one of the best in the islands. Exhibits attest to the greatness of Samos during the rule of Polycrates (6th century BC), the most famous being the gargantuan (5.5m) *kouros* (male statue of the Archaic period), plucked from the Ireon (Sanctuary of Hera; p373) near Pythagorio and the largest standing *kouros* ever produced. Many other statues, most also from the Ireon, as well as bronze sculptures, stelae and pottery, round out the collection.

Sleeping

Pension Dreams (☎ 22730 24350; Areos 9; d with/without balcony €30/25; ☒) This small but central *pension* overlooks the harbour from a hill top. Pride of place goes to the expansive rooftop studio; if that's taken, try for a balcony room with garden views. The friendly owner speaks a bevy of languages.

our pick Pythagoras Hotel (☎ 22730 28422, 6944518690; www.pythagorashotel.com; Kallistratou 12; s/d €20/35; ☺ Feb-Nov; ℗ ▢) This friendly budget hotel run by Stelios Mihalakis and family offers the best of both worlds: the attentive service and serenity of a hotel, and the free-wheeling sociability of a hostel. Many rooms have sea-facing balconies. Meet like-minded independent travellers for a drink on the outdoor terrace, and enjoy good inexpensive home-cooked meals. It also has a shop and internet access, and a pebble beach just below. To arrange free pick-up from the ferry or bus station, ring Stelios, or inquire at ITSA Travel, opposite the port.

Hotel Aeolis (☎ 22730 28377; www.aeolis.gr; Themistokleous Sofouli 33; s/d incl breakfast €45/60; ☒ ☒) This grandiose and very central waterfront hotel that attracts a slick Greek crowd features two pools and a Jacuzzi, as well as a taverna and a frequently packed bar below. Rooms are ample and modern, though with less of a personal touch than at the smaller places in town. Light sleepers should factor in the nocturnal street noise from the café strip below.

Ino Village Hotel (☎ 22730 23241; www.inovillage.gr; Kalami; s/d/tr incl breakfast from €59/74/100; P 🍴 💻 🏊) With its central courtyard pool flanked by ivy-strewn, balconied white buildings, Ino Village is a citadel of subdued elegance. While this miniresort is sometimes booked out by tour groups, it never endangers the stylish quietude that also draws discerning independ-

ent travellers. The hotel's Elea Restaurant is patronised by nonguests also.

Eating

Kotopoula (☎ 22730 28415; Vlamaris; mezedhes around €4, mains around €6) While tourists have taken to this little restaurant in the backstreets, it remains a local favourite known for its spit-roasted

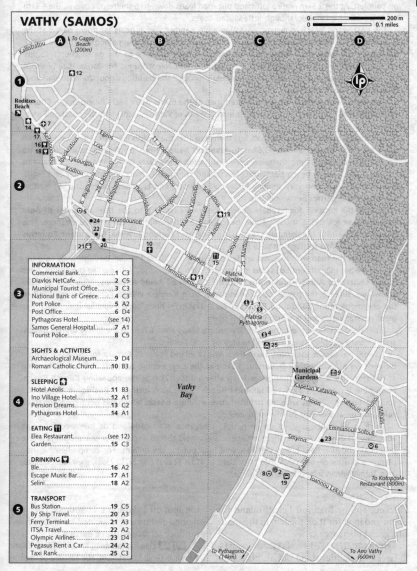

VATHY (SAMOS)

0 .... 200 m
0 .... 0.1 miles

To Gagou Beach (200m)

Vathy Bay

To Pythagorio (14km)

To Ano Vathy (600m)

To Kotopoula Restaurant (800m)

INFORMATION	
Commercial Bank.....................1	C3
Diavlos NetCafe.......................2	C5
Municipal Tourist Office...........3	C3
National Bank of Greece...........4	C3
Port Police..............................5	A2
Post Office..............................6	D4
Pythagoras Hotel..................(see 14)	
Samos General Hospital...........7	A1
Tourist Police.........................8	C5

SIGHTS & ACTIVITIES	
Archaeological Museum...........9	D4
Roman Catholic Church..........10	B3

SLEEPING 🛏	
Hotel Aeolis..........................11	B3
Ino Village Hotel...................12	A1
Pension Dreams......................13	C2
Pythagoras Hotel....................14	A1

EATING 🍴	
Elea Restaurant...................(see 12)	
Garden.................................15	C3

DRINKING 🍷	
Ble.......................................16	A2
Escape Music Bar...................17	A1
Selini...................................18	A2

TRANSPORT	
Bus Station...........................19	C5
By Ship Travel.......................20	A3
Ferry Terminal.......................21	A3
ITSA Travel............................22	A2
Olympic Airlines....................23	D4
Pegasus Rent a Car................24	A2
Taxi Rank.............................25	C3

HIDDEN BEACHES OF EASTERN SAMOS

Despite being only a few kilometres from Samos' capital, the jagged eastern coast is rarely visited by tourists, making it perfect for adventurous, off-roading swimmers and sun worshippers. The sultry beaches here are frequented only by locals and the tiny coves along the coast by very few.

A regular car or motorcycle will suffice for most of this route, though the complete day-tour requires a 4WD.

Set your odometer at Vathy (Samos) port and drive northwards, passing the Pythagoras Hotel on your left. At the 2.5km mark a left-hand dirt road leads down to a sheltered cove. At the 4.4km mark are other accessible, though little visited coves.

The best secret beach, however, an aquamarine, sandy cove, appears far down below at the 5.2km mark; to see it, pull over by the miniature model church standing alongside the road. Park here and walk backwards 500m, or drive back the same distance to the gated church facility reading (in Greek letters) *Paidikes Kataskinoseis Ieras Mitropoleos Samou kai Ikarias*. Park (without blocking the gate) and go down the grassy path through the bamboo about 200m to find your own private beach heaven.

Continuing along the coast, a signposted road at the 6.7km mark veers inland to the **Church of Profitis Ilias** (another 3km); it offers stunning views of Vathy (Samos) and the coast and islets sprawled below.

Continuing north on the main road, less than 1km after the Profitis Ilias turn-off, is a signposted dirt road leading, after another 2.6km, to **Livadaki Beach**. Here, tropical azure waters lap up against soft sand in a long sheltered cove with facing islets. Only Greeks in the know come to Livadaki, which has a beach bar with colourful and comfy soft chairs and music day and night. The water is warm and very shallow for a long way out, and Livadaki's hedonistic yet mellow summer beach parties easily spill into it.

Back at the turn-off for Livadaki Beach, continue east 5km to the fishing hamlet of **Agia Paraskevi**, which has a shady pebble beach and multicoloured boats moored offshore. This beach, popular with Greek families, also has a meat-and-seafood taverna, **Restaurant Aquarius** (☎ 22730 28282; Agia Paraskevi; mains €5-8).

After this, the road worsens on a white-knuckle course along the cliff through thick countryside. There are magnificent sea views and occasional unmarked revelations, like the cryptic ruins of the **Church of Agios Haralambos**, and the **Chapel of Agios Antonios**. After 3km of olive groves, you'll reach the paved road coming west from **Kamara** village. Follow the signs left to the enormous **Moni Zoödohou Pigis** (☎ 22730 27582; 🕑 10am-1pm & 6-8pm Sat-Thu), which has great coastal views and is worth visiting if open.

From the Kamara turn-off, the road downwards leads after 1.7km to the lovely **Myrtia Beach**, another long pebbled stretch visited mainly by local Greeks.

To continue down the coast, drive from Myrtia inland towards Kamara for 2.2km, and then turn left on a narrow, paved shortcut 3.5km; at the intersection, turn left and then left again at the stop sign 2.1km further on, arriving after another 2km at the appealing **Kerveli Beach**. From here it's another 3km to **Platanaki Beach**. Some 6km further is **Posidonio**, where the southeastern coast ends with the pebbled cove at **Klima Beach**, which has gentle waters, some cafés and great views of Turkey opposite.

To do it all in one day, fill up on petrol in advance, start early and be prepared for some adventurous driving. As elsewhere in Greece, swimmers should avoid rocky outcroppings where potentially hostile, hard-biting eels lurk, and look out for sea urchins. For comprehensive, free planning assistance, ask for Aussie Mick Daly, at **ITSA Travel** (☎ 22730 23605; www.itsatravelsamos .com; Themistokleous Sofouli) in Vathy (Samos).

chicken. Follow Ioannou Lekati inland for 800m and look for it on the left, in the shade of a grand plane tree.

Garden (☎ 22730 24033; Manolis Kalomiris; mains €4-9) Greek specialities stand out at this sooth-

ing spot off Lykourgou Logotheti. The aptly named restaurant is located on a tree-filled outdoor terrace within a garden.

our pick **Elea Restaurant** (☎ 22730 23241; Kalami; mains from €8-10) Located on the terrace of the Ino

Village Hotel, with contemplative views over Vathy and its harbour below, the Elea serves invigorated Greek cuisine and international dishes as well, while doing fine renditions of old classics like swordfish *souvlaki* (cubes of meat on skewers). Samian wines are well represented. Beware dedicated barman Dimitrios when he tries to whip you up one of his patented shots of tequila with lemon and ground coffee.

Drinking

Nightlife in Vathy (Samos) has a decidedly Greek flavour to it, especially when compared to the more Europeanised Pythagorio and the beach resorts. While the bulk of the bars congregate along the waterfront in the town centre, just as busy and more aesthetically pleasing are the hill-side bars over the water on Kefalopoulou, between La Calma restaurant and Pythagoras Hotel. These bars, which include **Escape Music Bar** (Kefalopoulou), **Ble** (Blue; Kefalopoulou) and **Selini** (Kefalopoulou), are distinguished not by their music (invariably, modern pop) but by their outside lighting, which shines on the gently rippling water below to dazzling, hypnotic effect.

PYTHAGORIO ΠΥΘΑΓΟΡΕΙΟ
pop 1327

Located on the sunny southeastern coast and the place of the island's ancient capital, World Heritage–listed Pythagorio boasts the bulk of Samos' archaeological sites. Its yacht-lined harbour flanked by touristy restaurants may make it seem twee, but Pythagorio is a place of real interest, for its sites, its flowering backstreets and for the fine nearby beaches. All boats travelling south of Samos dock at Pythagorio, from where day trips also depart to Samiopoula islet.

Orientation

From the ferry quay, turn right and follow the waterfront to the main street, Lykourgou Logotheti, a turn-off to the left. Most services are here. The central square (Plateia Irinis) is further along the waterfront. The bus stop is on the south side of Lykourgou Logotheti.

Information

Commercial Bank (Lykourgou Logotheti) Has ATM.
Digital World (☎ 22730 62722; Pythagora; per hr €4; 11am-10.30pm) Has internet access.
National Bank of Greece (Lykourgou Logotheti)

Port police (☎ 22730 61225)
Post office (Lykourgou Logotheti)
Tourist office (☎ 22730 61389; deap5@otenet.gr; Lykourgou Logotheti; 8am-9.30pm) The friendly and informative staff advise about the historical sites and sleeping options, provide maps, bus timetables and information about ferry schedules, and also exchange currency.
Tourist police (☎ 22730 61100; Lykourgou Logotheti) Left of the tourist office.

Sights

Samians took the lead locally in the 1821 War of Independence; the major relic of that turbulent time is the **Castle of Lykourgos Logothetis**, built in 1824 by resistance leader Logothetis on a hill at the southern end of Metamorfosis Sotiros, near the town car park. The **city walls** extend from here to the Evpalinos Tunnel, which can also be reached along this path.

The **Pythagorio Museum** (☎ 22730 61400; Town Hall, Plateia Irinis; admission free; 8.45am-2.30pm Tue-Sun) is not as good as the one in Vathy (Samos), but it does contain some nice finds from the Ireon.

Exiting Pythagorio towards the northeast, traces of an **ancient theatre** appear on a path to the left. The right fork past the theatre leads to **Moni Panagias Spilianis** (Monastery of the Virgin of the Grotto; ☎ 22730 61361; 9am-8pm), which, as the name might suggest, indeed has a lovely cool cave that makes for a welcome temporary respite from summer heat.

EVPALINOS TUNNEL ΕΥΠΑΛΙΝΕΟ ΟΡΥΓΜΑ

Back in 524 BC, when Pythagorio (then known as Samos) was a bustling metropolis of 80,000 people, securing reliable sources of drinking water became crucial. To solve the problem, ruler Polycrates put his dictatorial whims to good use, enlisting teams of labourers to dig into a mountainside according to the exacting plan of his ingenious engineer, Evpalinos. The result was the 1034m-long **Evpalinos Tunnel** (☎ 22730 61400; adult/student €4/2; 8.45am-2.45pm Tue-Sun), parts of which can be explored today. In mediaeval times locals used the tunnel as a hide-out during pirate raids.

The Evpalinos Tunnel is actually two tunnels: a service tunnel and a lower water tunnel visible from the walkway, deep below to the right. While the tunnel itself is wide enough, not everyone can get into it, as the entrance stairway is both low and has very narrow walls, with no grease provided.

PYTHAGORIO

If walking, reach the tunnel from the western end of Lykourgou Logotheti. If driving, a sign points to the tunnel's southern mouth after entering Pythagorio from Vathy (Samos).

Sleeping

In high summer, when foreign tour companies clamp down, book in advance.

Hotel Alexandra (☎ 22730 61429; Metamorfosis Sotiros 22; d €25) There are only eight rooms, but they are lovely and some have sea views. The enclosed garden is especially nice on hot summer days.

Pension Despina (☎ 22730 61677; pensiondespina@ yahoo.gr; A Nikolaou; s/d €30/40) A clean, quiet little *pension* on Plateia Irinis, the Despina offers simple studios and rooms with balconies; some have kitchenettes. It also has a relaxing back garden.

Hotel Evripili (☎ 22730 61096; fax 22730 61897; Konstantinou Kanari; s/d €45/60) A friendly and modern hotel with well-appointed, cosy rooms off the waterfront; some have balconies.

Polixeni Hotel (☎ 22730 61590; fax 22730 61359; d €65; 🖳) This homey place on the waterfront has nicely furnished, clean and comfortable

rooms with balconies and very amiable staff. A good bet.

Eating

Pythagorio's waterfront is lined with restaurants, their multilingual menus hinting at the target market; explore the backstreets for more homey fare.

Elia (☎ 22730 61436; mains €7-10) One of the newer restaurants in town, Elia gets high marks from locals for sophisticated Greek and international fare, though it's a bit on the pricey side. It's located at the waterfront's far end, before the town beach.

Restaurant Remataki (☎ 22730 61104; mezedhes €4-6, mains €7-10) Near Elia, the Remataki has a nice waterfront balcony and some splashy light meals; salad with rocket leaves, Cretan *dakos* (tomato and cheese on oil-softened rusks) and *dolmadhes* (rice wrapped in vine leaves) are all recommended. The almost unrecognisable *tyropitakia* (small fried cheese pies) should, however, be avoided.

Poseidonas (☎ 22730 62530; mains €6-12) Next door to Remataki, the Poseidonas specialises in seafood with an international flair.

AROUND PYTHAGORIO

The Ireon Το Ηραίον

To judge merely from the scattered ruins of the Ireon, Samos' ancient sanctuary of Hera located 8km west of Pythagorio, it would be impossible to imagine the magnificence of the rituals enacted along the Sacred Way. This path, once flanked by thousands of marble statues, led from the city to the World Heritage–listed **Ireon** (☎ 22730 95277; adult/student €4/3; ⏰ 8.30am-3pm Tue-Sun), built at the legendary birthplace of Hera. However, enough survives to provide a glimmer of insight into the divine sanctuary that was actually four times larger than the Parthenon.

Built in the 6th century BC on marshy ground, where the River Imbrasos enters the sea, the Ireon was constructed on the site of an earlier Mycenaean temple. Plundering and earthquakes since antiquity have left only one column standing, though extensive foundations remain. There is something deeply disconcerting about the headless statues of a family, the Geneleos Group, from whose number the giant *kouros* statue in the museum at Vathy (Samos) was taken (for more details, see p368). Other remains on the site include a stoa, more temples and a 5th-century Christian basilica.

Mytilinii Μυτιληνιοί

Skeletons of prehistoric animals, including forerunners of the giraffe and elephant, are displayed at this inland village's **palaeontology museum** (☎ 22730 52055; admission €2.50; ⏰ 10am-2pm), northwest of Pythagorio. For more (human) skeletal relics, **Agia Triada Monastery** (☎ 22730 51339; ⏰ 8am-1pm Mon-Sun) features an ossuary and a lovely rural setting. Hardy walkers can reach it from the museum.

Beaches

Sandy **Psili Ammos** (not to be confused with the beach near Votsalakia) is the finest beach near Pythagorio. Gazing across at Turkey, this lovely cove is bordered by shady trees and has shallow waters good for kids. If you fall in love with the place and want to be there at its quietest times, a few tavernas nearby rent rooms. To get there take the bus from Vathy (Samos) or an excursion boat (€15) from Pythagorio. If driving, you must take the Pythagorio–Vathy road north for a few kilometres and turn east where the beach is signposted. A unique pond on the left, 1km before the beach, comes to life in spring with the arrival of pink flamingos.

Glykoriza Beach, nearer Pythagorio, is a clean, pebble-and-sand beach that hosts a few hotels.

SOUTHWESTERN SAMOS

Pythagorio to Drakei Πυθαγόριο προς Δρακαίους

Driving west from Pythagorio brings you into spectacular mountain scenery with stunning views of the south coast, though the craggy forests are littered with charred trees from previous wildfires. This route also features many little signposted huts, where beekeepers sell the superlative but inexpensive Samian honey – stop in for a free sample and walk away with a jar.

The southwest coast of Samos held out against mass tourism for longer than the north, but the best beaches are starting to attract the inevitable resorts; tourism is still quite low-key, however, and you can find many secluded wild spots.

The drive from Pythagorio to the pebble beach at **Ormos Marathokampou** passes through

---

A MATTER OF MEASUREMENTS

While the obsession with getting the 'proper pint' may seem a modern one, the ancient Greeks, too, were fixated on measuring their alcohol. Pythagoras, that great Samian mathematician (and, presumably, drinker) came up with an ingenious invention that ensured party hosts and publicans could not be taken advantage of by guests aspiring to inebriation. What he came up with was dubbed the *dikiakoupa tou Pythagora* – 'The Just Cup of Pythagoras' – a mysterious multiholed drinking vessel that holds its contents perfectly well, unless one fills it past the engraved line, at which point the glass drains from the bottom and the naughty drinker is punished for gluttony.

Today faithful reproductions of the *dikiakoupa tou Pythagora*, usually made of colourful, glazed ceramic, are available in gift shops on Samos, a reminder of the Apollan Mean (the ancient Greek maxim of Apollo): 'Everything in moderation.'

wonderful mountains and the unvisited little villages of **Koumaradei** and **Pyrgos**. From the beach, it's a 6km drive inland to **Marathokamphos**, which has panoramic views of the immense **Bay of Marathokamphos**. Some 4km west of Ormos Marathokampou is **Votsalakia** (often called Kambos), which has a long, sandy beach. There's an even nicer one 2km further at **Psili Ammos**. Beach-side tavernas prepare fresh fish on the grill and in huge skillets, and there are many domatia around.

Forging on past Psili Ammos takes you on the rugged western route skirting **Mt Kerkis**. From here until the villages of **Kallithea**, and **Drakei** where the road abruptly terminates, the coast is almost totally undeveloped and isolated – a real treat for the adventurous.

NORTHERN SAMOS
Vathy to Karlovasi Βαθύ προς Καρλόβασι
From Vathy (Samos), the coastal road heading west passes many beaches and resorts, first among them **Kokkari**, 10km out of town. Once a little fishing village, Kokkari is now a popular holiday resort with a long, narrow pebble beach, a favourite with windsurfers for its strong summer winds. There are plenty of decent rooms, studios and tavernas available.

The popular nearby beaches of **Avlakia**, **Lemonaki** and **Tsamadou** are the most accessible for walkers staying in Kokkari. The latter two are clothing optional. Continuing west past the beaches brings you into increasingly leafy country, and a left-hand turn-off leads, after 5km, to the lovely mountain village of **Vourliotes**. From here it's a 3km hike to **Moni Panagias Vrondianis**, the island's oldest surviving monastery, built in the 1550s. Vourliotes is marked out by its multicoloured, shuttered houses clustered on a central square, and can also be reached by a footpath from Kokkari.

Retracing the route back to the coast road, continue west until the signposted left-hand turn-off for the enchanting village of **Manolates**, 5km further up the lower slopes of Mt Ampelos (known as the Balcony of Samos). Set amid thick forests of pine and deciduous trees, and made up of some truly gorgeous traditional houses, Manolates is nearly encircled by mountains and offers a cool alternative to the sweltering coast, impressive views of which can be had from the upper village. Manolates is also a paradise for hikers and bird lovers, who can count on being serenaded by nightingales, warblers

and thrushes. The villagers have shown a fondness for tourism, with numerous shops selling handmade ceramic art, icons and natural products. Despite the popularity of the place with organised groups, Manolates still makes a welcome refuge from the hectic summer scene down below, and is integral to the Samos experience.

Back on the coast heading west, the road continues through **Agios Konstantinos**, a pretty, flower-filled village before **Karlovasi**, Samos' third port. Karlovasi has a more quiet, workaday feel and sees most of its visitors only for ferry connections. The nearest beach is the sand-and-pebble **Potami**, 2km west of town.

Sleeping
In Kokkari, **EOT** (Greek National Tourist Organisation; ☎ 22730 92217) can find you accommodation. The office is next to the Greek Telecommunications Company (OTE; telephone office), about 100m after the large church by the bus stop.

Studio Angella (☎ 22730 94478, 21050 59708, in Athens 6972975722; Manolates; d €25; 🅿) The best place to stay in Manolates is this collection of five studios built into the side of a hill. The modern rooms have kitchenettes for self-caterers, and from the balconies there are sweeping views over the mountains to the sea.

Traditional Greek House (☎ 22730 94331, 22730 94174; Manolates; studio €30; 🅿) There is only one studio available in this large old house behind the Despina Taverna in central Manolates, so phone in advance. Otherwise ask at the taverna. The room is quiet, romantic and tastefully furnished – worth the trouble if you can get it.

Kokkari Beach Hotel (☎ 22730 92238; fax 22730 92381; Kokkari; d incl breakfast €68-73; 🅿 🖳) This classy establishment is about 1km west of the bus stop. It's set back from the road in a pretty yellow building, an oasis of calm from the busy village. Rooms are modern and comfortably furnished, and there is a café across the road.

Aidonokastro (☎ 22730 94686; fax 22730 94404; Valiondates; d/tr €60/75) Located in Valiondates, a tiny village on the road to Manolates, these renovated apartments set in five traditionally furnished houses make for a forested respite from the touristy coast. English-speaking manager Yiannis can assist hikers in plotting out routes. A large taverna is adjacent.

lonelyplanet.com CHIOS •• History 375

NORTHEASTERN AEGEAN ISLANDS

Eating

Kokkari is full of resort-type restaurants and the usual tavernas; for dining that is more atmospheric and guaranteed fresh, head for the mountain villages.

Grill Café (☎ 22730 93291; Vourliotes; mains from €5) This little taverna on the left of Vourliotes' main square specialises in mixed vegetarian mezedhes, though it does have some hearty meat fare; try traditional sausages in pitta.

Loukas Taverna (☎ 22730 94541; Manolates; mains €4-6) Since it's located at the tip-top of Manolates village, you work up an appetite just trying to get to this well-signposted taverna. While the magnificent views of mountains and sea from the outdoor balcony seem an ample enough reward for the effort, the fried zucchini flowers, hearty meat portions and local muscat wine really make it worthwhile. For dessert, Loukas also serves a tempting array of home-made cakes.

Despina Taverna (☎ 22730 94043; mains €5-7) This little taverna, halfway up the hill in Manolates, serves *mayirefta* (ready-cooked meals) and a good assortment of meats. It's almost as good as the Loukas Taverna, and a better bet if you're tired of walking.

CHIOS ΧΙΟΣ

pop 53,817 / area 859 sq km

Although Chios (*hee*-os) is one of Greece's largest and most unique islands, most of the 'foreigners' who visit it are diaspora Greeks with familial ties. Yet despite its low profile, Chios has much to offer, from sandy beaches, extraordinary caves and medieval stone villages, to remote mountains, unusual museums and a thoroughly Hellenic nightlife. Southern Chios is the only place where mastic (a kind of gum) trees can be fruitful, and the island as a whole has a history of maritime greatness.

Chios is one of those islands that grows on you slowly, but has a lasting effect. Its people are reserved, but friendly, very hospitable and surprisingly cosmopolitan; indeed, you will meet many whose shipping careers have taken them 'round the world. With its excellent home-style cooking, authentic villages and endless opportunities for solitude on a coastline largely untouched by organised tourism, Chios remains one of the great unknown Greek island getaways.

History

Chios is one of the big ones, not only in size, but also in historical and economic importance. Like Samos and Lesvos, its proximity to Asia Minor (Turkey's Karaburun peninsula lies just 8km away, across the Chios Straits) gave it a turbulent history of great successes and terrible tragedies. Many of Greece's grand old shipping dynasties hail from Chios and its dependencies, Inousses and Psara. Under the Ottomans, Chios' monopolistic production of mastic – the sultan's favourite gum – brought Chians wealth and special privileges.

At the same time, during the Greek War of Independence, thousands were slaughtered by the Turks. A century later the 'Great Idea' (Megali Idea) for the liberation of the Anatolian coast unfolded with a naval assault from Chios – and ended with the Greek armies being driven back into the sea, as waves of refugees from Asia Minor flooded Chios and neighbouring islands.

Some Greeks argue that Christopher Columbus was a Chian, an intriguing possibility that cannot be entirely proven or disproven (see boxed text, p381).

Getting There & Away
AIR

Between Aegean Airlines and Olympic Airlines, Chios has five flights daily to Athens (€42, 50 minutes), five weekly to Thessaloniki (€66, one hour 10 minutes) and two weekly to Lesvos (€32, 25 minutes). **Olympic Airlines** (☎ 22710 20359; www.olympicairlines.com; Leoforos Egeou) is in Chios Town. The airport is 4km from Chios Town. There's no shuttle bus; a taxi to/from the airport costs €6.

FERRY
Domestic

In summer there's at least one ferry daily to Piraeus (€29, eight hours) and Lesvos (€14, three hours). A weekly ferry serves Thessaloniki (€36, 18 hours) via Limnos (€23, 11 hours), while another serves Alexandroupoli (€27.20, 12½ hours) via Lesvos. Three boats go weekly to Samos (€12.50, four hours), and one weekly to Kos (€19.80, nine hours) and Rhodes (€31.40, 15 hours). Buy tickets from **NEL Lines** (☎ 22710 23971; fax 22710 41319; Leoforos Egeou 16) in Chios Town.

Miniotis Lines (☎ 22710 24670; www.miniotis.gr; Neorion 23) in Chios Town runs small boats twice weekly to Karlovasi (€10, four hours) and Vathy (€11, 4½ hours) on Samos. Three times weekly these boats also travel to Fourni (€12.40, 7½ hours) and Ikaria (€13, 8½ hours). Miniotis also has three boats weekly to Psara (€9.90, 3½ hours). Its boats occasionally dock at the harbour, near the corner of Leoforos Egeou and Kokali.

The little *Oinoussai III* serves the Inousses archipelago (€3.80 one way, 1¼ hours, daily). It mainly leaves Chios in the afternoon and Inousses in the morning, necessitating an overnight stay. Purchase tickets on board. **Sunrise Tours** (☎ 22710 41390; Kanari 28) in Chios Town also runs day trips to Inousses (€20) twice weekly in summer. Daily water taxis go

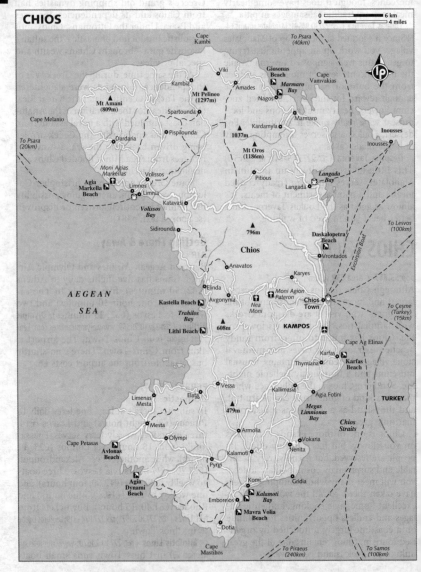

CHIOS

0 ———— 6 km
0 ———— 4 miles

To Psara (40km)

Cape Kambi

Cape Vamvakias

Viki

Giosonas Beach

Marmaro Bay

Kambia

Amades

Nagos

Mt Pelineo (1297m)

Spartounda

Marmaro

Mt Amani (809m)

Cape Melanio

1037m

Kardamyla

Inousses

Inousses

Dardaria

Pispilounda

To Psara (20km)

Mt Oros (1186m)

Moni Agias Markellas

Volissos

Pitious

Langada Bay

Agia Markella Beach

Limnos

Limnia

Langada

Katavasi

Volissos Bay

Sidirounda

796m

To Lesvos (100km)

Daskalopetra Beach

Chios

Vrontados

Anavatos

Karyes

AEGEAN SEA

Elinda

Moni Agion Pateron

Chios Town

Kastella Beach

Avgonyma

Nea Moni

To Çeşme (Turkey) (15km)

Trahilos Bay

Lithi Beach

608m

KAMPOS

Cape Ag Elinas

Karfas

Vessa

Kallimasia

Karfas Beach

Limenas Mesta

Elata

479m

Thymiana

Agia Fotini

Megas Limnionas Bay

TURKEY

Mesta

Armolia

Vokaria

Chios Straits

Cape Petasas

Olympi

Kalamoti

Nenita

Avlonas Beach

Pyrgi

Komi

Gridia

Agia Dynami Beach

Emboreios

Kalamoti Bay

Mavra Volia Beach

Dotia

Cape Mastihos

To Piraeus (240km)

To Samos (100km)

Excursion Boat

between Langada and Inousses (€35, shared between the passengers).

International

Boats to Turkey run year-round from Chios. From May to October daily ferries to Çeşme leave Chios at 8.30am and return at 6.30pm; on Sunday it returns at 5pm. The fare is €22 one way and €25 return. Get further information and tickets from **Miniotis Lines** (☎ 22710 24670; www.miniotis.gr; Neorion 23). **Sunrise Tours** (☎ 22710 41390; Kanari 28) does a day trip to İzmir via Çeşme for €40, which includes boat transport to Çeşme and then a bus to and from İzmir, one hour away. Turkish visas, where required, are issued upon arrival in Çeşme.

HYDROFOIL

From April to September three hydrofoils weekly serve Lesvos (€19.50, two hours) and Piraeus (€33, six hours).

Getting Around
BUS

From the **long-distance bus station** (☎ 22710 27507; www.ktelchios.gr; Leoforos Egeou) in Chios Town, there are four buses daily in summer to Pyrgi (€2.70), three to Mesta (€3.10) and four to Kardamyla (€3.10) via Langada (€1.70). Two weekly buses serve Volissos (€4.10). Buses also do the beaches of Kampia, Nagos and Lithi. Services are reduced on weekends. Up-to-date schedules for these and all other destinations, with prices, are listed on the KTEL-Chios website (www.ktelchios.gr).

Buses to Karfas Beach are serviced by the blue (city) bus company. Schedules are posted at both the **local bus station** (☎ 22710 22079), south of the public gardens, and the long-distance bus station.

CAR & MOTORCYCLE

Chios Town's car-rental outlets include **Aegean Travel** (☎ 22710 41277; aegeantr@otenet.gr; Leoforos Egeou 114), below Chios Rooms.

TAXI

Chios Town's **taxi rank** (☎ 22710 41111) is on Plateia Vounakiou.

CHIOS TOWN
pop 23,779

The island's port and capital, also called Chios, is on the central east coast, and home to almost half of the island's inhabitants. Like many island capitals, it features a long waterfront lined with cafés and a noisy large street hugging the water. Behind it, however, is a quieter, intriguing old quarter, where some lingering traditional Turkish houses stand around a Genoese castle and city walls. There's also a fun market area, and spacious public gardens where an open-air cinema operates on summer nights. The nearest decent beach is at Karfas, 6km south.

Orientation

Most ferries dock at the northern end of the waterfront; north of this is the old Turkish quarter, called Kastro. Getting off the ferry, turn left and follow the waterfront to reach the town centre. Turn right onto Kanari to reach the central square of Plateia Vounakiou. Northwest of it are the public gardens; southeast is the market area. Most shopping is found south of Plateia Vounakiou. Facing inland, the local bus station is to the right of the public gardens; the long-distance bus station to the left. Most hotels are near the waterfront, on the opposite end from the ferry berths.

Information

The National Bank of Greece and most other banks are between Kanari and Plateia Vounakiou. Several ATMs are also on the waterfront (Leoforos Egeou).

Aegean Travel (☎ 22710 41277; aegeantr@otenet.gr; Leoforos Egeou 114)

InSpot Internet Café (☎ 22710 83438; Leoforos Egeou 86; per hr €2.40; ⏰ 24hr)

Municipal Tourist Office (☎ 22710 44389; infochio@otenet.gr; Kanari 18; ⏰ 7am-10pm Apr-Oct, until 4pm Nov-Mar) Information on accommodation, car rental, bus and boat schedules, plus a useful free book, *Hiking Routes of Chios*.

News Stand (☎ 22710 43464; cnr Leoforos Egeou & Rodokanaki) Sells multilingual papers and books, like Lonely Planet guides *Greece* and *Turkey*.

OTE (Dimokratias Roidou) Public telephone.

Police (☎ 22710 44427; cnr Polemidi 1 & Koundouriotou)

Port police (☎ 22710 44432; Neorion)

Post office (☎ 22710 44350; Omirou 2) One block behind the waterfront.

Tourist police (☎ 22710 44427; Neorion)

Sights

The idiosyncratic **Filippos Argentis Museum** (☎ 22710 23463; Korais; admission €1.50; ⏰ museum & library 8am-2pm Mon-Fri, 5-7.30pm Fri, 8am-12.30pm Sat), in the same building as the impressive **Korais**

NORTHEASTERN AEGEAN ISLANDS

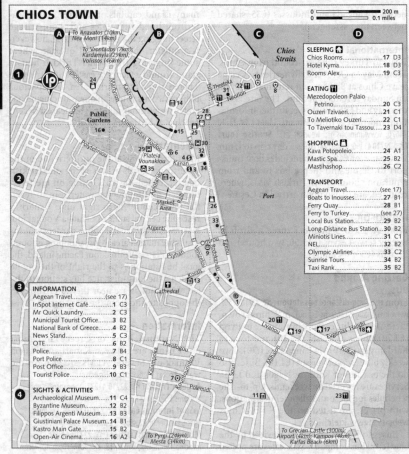

CHIOS TOWN

0 ———— 200 m
0 ———— 0.1 miles

Chios Straits

To Anavatos (10km);
Nea Moni (14km)

To Vrontados (7km);
Kardamyla (29km);
Volissos (46km)

Public Gardens

Port

Market Area

Argenti

Cathedral

To Grecian Castle (300m);
Airport (4km); Kampos (4km);
Karfas Beach (6km)

To Pyrgi (24km);
Mesta (34km)

Library, contains embroideries, traditional costumes and portraits of the wealthy Argentis family. Born in Marseilles in 1891, Argentis devoted his life to researching the history of Chios and wrote many significant works.

The **archaeological museum** (☎ 22710 44239; Mihalon 10; admission €2; ⏰ 8.30am-2.45pm Tue-Sun) contains sculptures, pottery and coins dating from the Neolithic period. Closed at the time of writing, the **Byzantine Museum** (☎ 22710 26866; Plateia Vounakiou) is housed in a former mosque, the Medjitie Djami. Its collection of sculptures dates from the 14th- to 15th-century Genoese occupation.

Within the Kastro's main gate is the tiny **Giustiniani Palace Museum** (☎ 22710 22819; admission €2 Mon-Sat, €1 Sun; ⏰ 9am-3pm Tue-Sun). Its restored

Byzantine wall paintings include important 13th-century frescoes of the prophets.

The **Public Gardens** make a nice spot for relaxing; in summer Hollywood hits are projected here in an enclosed **open-air cinema** (tickets €6). Shows start at 9pm.

Sleeping

Chios' municipal tourist office keeps a full list of domatia – useful for those wishing to avoid the waterfront accommodation's street noise.

Chios Rooms (☎ 22710 20198, 6972833841; www .chiosrooms.gr; Leoforos Egeou 110; s/d/tr €25/35/45) An eclectic, hostel-like neoclassical house on the waterfront, Chios Rooms is the inspiration of its owner, native New Zealander Don. Full of vintage furnishings, traditional rugs and lofty ceilings, the place has character, though bathrooms are separate. The rooftop 'penthouse' has its own terrace. Having spent over 30 years in Greece, owner Don has much wisdom to impart about Greek life, and life in general, and will readily do so over a beer; the dude abides.

Rooms Alex (☎ 22710 26054; Livanou 29; s/d €30/45) This friendly place is visible for its bright roof garden adorned with various flags. If the interior seems dark, imagine the dark of a ship's hull: kindly owner Alex Stoupas was a sea captain for 21 years, and his lovingly handmade model ships decorate each of the simple but clean rooms. The *kapetanios* will pick you up for free from the ferry, and speaks English, French and Spanish. Book ahead in summer.

Hotel Kyma (☎ 22710 44500; kyma@chi.forthnet.gr; Evgenias Handri 1; s/d/tr incl breakfast €61/78/97; 🖭) This century-old converted mansion impresses from the first sight of its central marble stairway (hewn in 1917). The rooms in the old wing live up to this promise, with stately décor, billowing curtains and sea-view balconies with red marble walls (ask for room 29). What makes the Kyma more than just another period hotel is its service; owner Theodoros Spordilis wants you to fall in love with Chios, and solves problems in English, Italian and German. There's free wi-fi, and transport and stays in the Kyma's sister hotel (p380) in Kardamyla can be arranged.

Eating & Drinking

There's good eating in Chios Town, especially near the waterfront; nightlife, too, primarily happens here, in a contiguous set of bars filled by the unworried heirs of shipping empires.

Ouzeri Tzivaeri (☎ 22710 43559; Neoreion 13; mains €3-6) The sort of food strong enough to soak up ouzo (the Tzivaeri serves 10 kinds) is dished out at this friendly portside eatery. You might need a cast-iron gut to lay into oil-drenched,sun-dried tomatoes, grilled cod strips and traditional Chios sausages – but then again, that's what a good *ouzerie* is all about.

Mezedopoleion Palaio Petrino (☎ 22710 29797; Leoforos Egeou; mains from €7) The only reason to lament Chios' wonderfully warm weather, perhaps, is that diners never have to sit indoors and enjoy the Palaio Petrino's splendidly painted interior. No matter, the food is good enough to enjoy inside or out. Try

the *tyrokafteri* (spicy cheese dip) and *ktapodi krasato* (octopus in wine sauce) with some hearty Northern Aegean wine.

To Meliotiko Ouzeri (☎ 22710 40407; Neoreion; mains around €4-7) Some Chians live in fear of the immense portions ladled out at the Meliotiko; this no-nonsense stronghold of the Greek culinary pantheon is where you fill your stomach while waiting for the ferry.

To Tavernaki tou Tassou (☎ 22710 27542; Livanou 8; mains €6-8) This family-friendly eatery near the sea offers standard taverna fare, Chios' own Kambos Lemonade and an adjoining kid's land that will help keep restless ones pacified during dinner.

Beer Academy (☎ 22710 27542; Livanou 8; 🕒 6pm-2am) This branch of the popular Thessaloniki watering hole is a welcome alternative to most bars' Greek holy trinity of Amstel, Heineken and Mythos, with over 30 brews representing Boston to Belgium and beyond.

Shopping

Mastihashop (☎ 22710 81600; Leoforos Egeou 36) Get mastic-based products such as lotions, toothpaste, soaps and condiments here.

Mastic Spa (☎ 22710 28643; Leoforos Egeou 12) The place for mastic cosmetics.

Kava Potopoleio (☎ 22710 23190; Inopionos 4) Fine wines and many kinds of European beer are sold in this little shop below the Public Gardens.

CENTRAL CHIOS

North of Chios Town, visit **Vrontados**, where you can sit on the legendary stone chair of Homer, the **Daskalopetra**. Immediately south of Chios Town is the **Kambos**, a lush area with citrus trees, where wealthy Genoese and Greek merchant families from the 14th century onwards kept summer homes. It's worth visiting to see the walled mansions, some restored, others crumbling, and elaborate gardens. The fairly extensive Kambos is best toured by bicycle, moped or car.

Chios' main beach resort, **Karfas**, lies nearby, 6km south of Chios Town. The sandy beach, with a few fancy hotels and development, can make it get crowded.

In Chios' centre is **Nea Moni** (admission free; 🕒 8am-1pm & 4-8pm), a grand 11th-century Byzantine monastery and a World Heritage–listed site. Since it's undergoing extensive renovations, some buildings may be closed. Nea Moni was built to commemorate a miraculous event: the appearance of an icon of the Virgin Mary before three shepherds. The monastery was once one of the richest in Greece, and the most pre-eminent artists of Byzantium were commissioned to create the mosaics in its *katholikon* (principal church of the monastic complex).

Disastrously, during the Greek War of Independence in 1822, the Turks torched the monastery and massacred its monks. Macabre monastic skulls are lined in the ossuary at the little chapel. Another catastrophe occurred with the earthquake of 1881, when the dome of the *katholikon* caved in, damaging the mosaics. Despite this, they still rank among the country's greatest surviving examples of Byzantine art. Nea Moni is now inhabited by nuns.

At the end of a silent road, 10km away, is spectral **Anavatos**, filled with abandoned greystone houses built on a precipitous cliff. In 1822, during the savage Turkish reprisals, the villagers hurled themselves over it rather than be taken alive. A place of great solemnity and significance to the Chians, Anavatos should be visited, though the narrow, stepped pathways leading between the houses to the summit can be dangerous, and the route is often closed.

More happily, the nearby 11th-century hilltop village of **Avgonyma** is currently undergoing a bit of a revival. **Spitakia** (☎ 22710 81200; www.spitakia.com; d from €90) offers unique studios in restored buildings.

The beaches on Chios' mid-west coast are quiet and good for solitude seekers, though they're not the island's most spectacular. **Lithi Beach**, the southernmost one, attracts the majority of sunbathers.

NORTHERN CHIOS

Lonesome northern Chios, its coastal towns once a stronghold of shipping barons, is full of craggy peaks (Mt Pelineo, Mt Oros and Mt Amani), deserted villages and barren hill sides. The drive north from Chios Town along the eastern coast is astonishing, and brings you through bizarre, boulder-strewn mountains like from some other planet.

After the small coastal settlements of **Vrontados** and **Langada**, you come to the area's main villages, **Kardamyla** and **Marmaro**, the ancestral homes of many wealthy ship-owning families, though you would never know it from the humble architecture. Streets are so narrow, in fact, that some buildings' walls feature painted lines so buses won't barge into them. There is an earthy sand beach at Marmaro, but better pebble ones exist 5km further at the fishing village of **Nagos**, and at **Giosonas**, 1km beyond. The beaches have very clear water and a few tavernas, but not much shade.

After Nagos, the coast road heads northwest and upwards, skirting craggy Mt Pelineo (1297m). This is one of Chios' most remote areas. **Amades** and **Viki** are two tiny villages you pass before **Kambia**, high up on a ridge overlooking bare hill sides and the sea. Here choose between turning south on the central road through the mountains, or continuing along the coast.

The latter option passes through wild, empty hills on a jagged road before reaching the pebbly **Agia Markella Beach** and the **monastery** above it, also named after Agia Markella, the island's patron saint. Some 8km southeast is **Volissos**, legendary birthplace of Homer, with its impressive Genoese fort. Volissos' port, **Limnia**, is not particularly striking but has a taverna. From Volissos the coastal road continues south until Elinda, where it returns eastwards to Chios Town.

Sleeping

Hotel Kardamyla (☎ 22720 23353; kyma@chi.forthnet.gr; Marmaro; s/d/tr €61/78/97; ﷯) Although the 1970s architecture is somewhat dated, the simple rooms are clean and well maintained at this quiet beachfront hotel in Marmaro. What keeps people coming back, however, is the warm hospitality of the joint Greek-Turkish Spordilis family, who invite their guests to join them for a patio lunch. Since this is the sister hotel of Chios Town's Hotel Kyma (p379), you can also arrange a stay from there.

SOUTHERN CHIOS

The evocative south of Chios is unique, not only in Greece but in the world: it's the only place where the gum-producing mastic tree can be cultivated, a blessing which for centuries made the area wealthy and self-reliant. The 20 villages comprising the Mastihohoria (Mastic villages) feature arid scrublands of rolling hills, criss-crossed with elaborate stone walls running throughout the placid olive and mastic groves.

Two of these villages, Pyrgi and Mesta, are particularly unique for their aesthetic appeal, the former filled with houses decorated in unusual colourful patterns, the latter a car-free, walled settlement inhabited since Genoese colonisers built it in the 14th century.

Mastic was a very valuable commodity, one prized for its medicinal powers since antiquity; as capital of the Mastihohoria, Mesta had to be especially well fortified. The town is well preserved today, and is a great, romantic place where children can run around safely. It's a good base for hill walks, exploring hidden southern beaches and caves, and getting back to nature by participating in mastic and olive cultivation with the locals.

Pyrgi Πυργί
pop 1044

Located 24km southwest of Chios, the striking village of Pyrgi (peer-*ghi*) is the Mastihohoria's largest, and truly an eye-opener. The vaulted, narrow streets of this fortified village pass through buildings with façades decorated in intricate grey and white patterns, some geometric and others based on flowers, leaves and animals. The technique used, called *xysta*, requires coating the walls with a mixture of cement and black volcanic sand, painting over it with white lime and then scraping off parts of the lime with the bent prong of a fork to reveal the matt grey beneath.

Pyrgi's central square, where the road passes through, is flanked by a few tavernas and shops and the little 12th-century **Church of Agios Apostolos** (☎ 10am-1pm Tue-Thu & Sat). The church's 17th-century frescoes are well preserved, and the façade of the larger church, on the square's opposite side, has the most impressive *xysta* designs in town.

On the main road, just east of the central square, is a house with a small plaque, attesting to its former Italian occupant, one Christopher Columbus (see boxed text, below).

While Pyrgi itself is a must-see, for sleeping Mesta is the place. However, if you do stay, there are signposted domatia and **Giannaki Rooms** (☎ 22710 25888, 6945959889; fax 22710 22846; d/quad €35/80; ⊠). Giannaki used to offer just simple rooms, but now offers a large house for up to eight people (€100).

Emboreios Εμπορειός

Six kilometres southeast of Pyrgi, Emboreios was the Mastihohoria's port back when the mastic producers were real high rollers. Today it's a quiet place known for the beautiful, though shadeless **Mavra Volia Beach**, named for its black volcanic pebbles. Ask around for domatia.

For eating, try the shady, atmospheric **Porto Emborios** (☎ 22710 70025; mains €5-7), decorated with fishing nets and hung chillies and garlic; they attest to its vegetable dishes (roast meats are well represented, too).

COLUMBUS OF THE RED EARTH

Despite being one of the world's greatest seafaring nations, Greece's Renaissance sea captains didn't get to the Americas – right?

According to a theory long propounded by some Greeks (and foreign philhellenes), great explorer Christopher Columbus was no Italian from the streets, as the conventional wisdom has it; rather, he was a Chios-born Greek, of noble Byzantine descent.

While the argument can't be proven, it is intriguing. Born at a time when the Ottomans were conquering Byzantium, the enigmatic Columbus identified himself simply as a citizen of the Genoese Republic, of which Chios was then a part. His unique signature involved Greek characters, and he called himself *Columbus de Terra Rubra* (Columbus of the Red Earth) – a reference, supporters believe, to the unique reddish soil of southern Chios.

In fact, the Columbus (Kolombos) surname is common in the Mastihohoria; some families date back to the explorer's time. Indeed, Spanish King Ferdinand could find no trace of Columbus' alleged family in Genoa. And Columbus' sea-captain log, the 'official' one in Latin, stated false information, whereas his 'secret' one, in Greek, gave true coordinates.

Why, then, did Columbus not come out of the Genoese closet? Being Greek Orthodox, one explanation goes, Columbus could never have convinced a Catholic king to fund his expeditions, which popular history records as being financially motivated. However, in his own writings, Columbus reveals that divine inspiration and a missionary fever fuelled his desire to explore new worlds. Indeed, at a bleak time when the expanding Ottoman Empire threatened to overrun Christian Europe, could a powerless Byzantine prince have done anything less?

Mesta Μεστά

Mesta (mest-*aah*) is the culmination of the southern Chios experience: indeed, it is one of the most unique experiences you can have anywhere in all of Greece. A miniature, car-free Rhodes, this mediaeval castle town features appealing stone alleyways that are intertwined with flowers and intricate balconies, and is completely enclosed by thick defensive walls.

The town was built in the 14th century by the island's Genoese overlords, to keep pirates and would-be invaders out. It's an ingenious example of mediaeval defensive architecture, featuring a double set of walls, four gates and a pentagonal structure. Since all of the rooftops are interconnected, with the right company you can actually walk across the entire town. Dastardly locals have been known to settle scores by dumping water on an adversary's head from the rooftops.

Although the streets are labyrinthine and narrow, you can't get lost in Mesta. The action is found around the central square, near the enormous church of the Taxiarhon; on the tranquil, secluded laneways, rooms for rent are indistinguishably attached to the residences of local elders, who sit outside, the occasional cat darting past and the laughter of running children filling the air.

Mesta is a very relaxing place to stay and the accommodation and eating offerings are some of the island's best. It's also a great base for outdoor activities, and has great nearby beaches and other attractions. Currently local leaders are trying to realise a vision for a low-key, sustainable tourism matching the town's aesthetic and the peaceful natural environment. In addition, newly built accommodation of unprecedented elegance has made Mesta an option for those who want serenity – and sophistication.

ORIENTATION

Buses stop on the main road, on the *plateia* known locally as Gyros. Facing the town from the bus shelter, turn right and then immediately left; a sign points to Mesta centre. The central square, with rooms, a taverna, café and church, is called Plateia Taxiarhon.

SIGHTS

Two **churches of the Taxiarhes** (Archangels) exist in Mesta, the older and smaller one dating from Byzantine times and featuring a magnificent 17th-century iconostasis. The larger church, just off Plateia Taxiarhon, was built in the 19th century, created entirely by the townspeople's donations and labour. It has an ornate outer patio, huge, glittering chandeliers and very fine frescoes.

ACTIVITIES

Aside from its historical attractions, Mesta and its neighbouring mastic fields, beaches and cave (opposite) offer great opportunities to participate in traditional Chian farming, cooking and cultural activities, as well as the full range of outdoor activities. The fun and well-informed folks at **Masticulture Ecotourism Activities** (☎ 6976113007; www.masticulture.com) can arrange all activities, as well as sell tickets, find accommodation and provide general travel information. Located on Plateia Taxiarhon closest to Mesaonas restaurant, Masticulture's office has a cool reading room for visitors, who can sink into cosy sofas and armchairs with organic gardening guides, maps and travel-related books in English.

SLEEPING & EATING

Rooms are plentiful in Mesta; head to Plateia Taxiarhan and the local travel agency, **Masticulture Ecotourism Activities** (☎ 6976113007; www.masti culture.com), or else ask in the adjacent Mesaonas restaurant for the proprietors listed following. Masticulture can also help find rooms in Limenas Mesta, Olympi and elsewhere.

Anna Floradis Rooms (☎ /fax 22710 76455; floradis@internet.gr; s/d €40/50; ✸) The friendly Anna Floradis, who speaks French and some English, has rooms, studios and self-catering suites in different but equally lovely parts of Mesta, all with TV and air-con.

Dhimitris Pipidhis Rooms (☎ 22710 76029; house €60; ☿ year-round; ✸) The friendly, English-speaking Dhimitris and Koula Pipidhis have two traditional houses for rent in Mesta. Each has two bedrooms, a *pounti* (the traditional small Mesta house atrium), kitchen and washing machine. Book in advance in summer.

Mesta Medieval Castle Suites (☎ 22710 76345; www.medievalcastlesuites.com; d/t incl breakfast €94/117; ✸) Discerning-yet-discreet luxury accommodation has finally come to Mesta with the new Medieval Castle Suites. The rooms are spread out throughout the village, blending in seamlessly with the neighbouring houses. Open the door, however, and you have ultrachic rooms with all modern amenities, including flat-screen laptops; the only thing lacking, perhaps, is a bathtub. Décor is minimalist and obeys the contours of the space. The staff is very professional and helpful, and can pick you up from the ferry or airport.

ourpick Mesaonas (☎ 22710 76050; Plateia Taxiarhon; mains €5-9) For years Kyria Dimitra has been serving excellent and hearty country food at this restaurant outside on the far end of the central square (the Mesaonas café for drinks and ice cream is opposite). Everything is great; try the roast chicken and Greek salad for a nourishing lunch. Everything is local, right down to the *souma* (mastic-flavoured firewater). You should order the mixed meat plate to share, but be sure to pounce on the incredibly delicious beef *keftedes* (fritters) before they're all gone.

Limani Meston (☎ 22710 76389; Limenas Mesta; mains €6-10) For excellent and unique seafood dishes, come to this little waterfront fish taverna of Limani Meston. The *astakomakaronada* (lobster pasta) and special *atherinopita* (small fried fish with onions) are both heartily recommended.

Around Mesta

Just north of Mesta on the coast is the village's small port of **Limenas Mesta**. It has a pretty harbour of colourful fishing boats and tavernas, and nearby pebble beaches. **Avlonia Beach**, 7.3km west of Mesta, is the best one around.

Some 3km southeast of Mesta is the small agricultural village of **Olympi**, like Mesta and Pyrgi, a mastic-producing village characterised by its defensive architecture. The road south towards the coast leads after 5km to the splendid **Cave of Sykia** (admission €4; ☼ 10am-8pm Tue-Sun), a 150-million-year-old cavern discovered accidently in 1985. Some 57m deep, the cave is filled with weird, multicoloured stalagtites and other rock formations, shaped like giant white organs and phantasmal figures. Selectively lit by floodlights and connected by a series of platforms with handrails, the cave is safe, though somewhat slippery. With its marvellous lighting and colours, the cave could be the set for some underground adventure movie. Guided tours are held every 30 minutes, the last at 7.30pm.

BACK TO MASTIC

One day, 32-year-old Vasilis Ballas and longtime girlfriend Roula had had enough: they decided, as one does, to quit their well-paying jobs in hectic Athens' IT sector and move to a small village in southern Chios, to cultivate mastic trees.

'Our friends thought we were crazy,' chuckles Vasilis, whose ancestors came from Mesta, the enchanting fortress town at the heart of Chios' Mastihohoria. 'But now many of them are saying, "I wish I was brave enough to do what you did!"'

Cultivating the trees was harder than the two had imagined. It consumed many of their summer mornings, involved 'hurting' the tree by making little gouges to encourage the mastic sap to drip out, and required endless hours of cleaning the sticky, pearly white substance before sending it off to the producers. The experience led the Ballas' to think bigger, and now they have created Masticulture Ecotourism Activities (opposite), an offbeat, environmentally friendly travel service that encourages visitors to get their hands dirty by participating in the traditional livelihood of southern Chios.

Masticulture's year-round activities include a 'mastic walking tour' through shady fields gleaming with the dark green, bushy trees, where travellers can learn how mastic cultivation is done first-hand. Along the way, they can pick tomatoes, cucumbers, melons and more from the Ballas' organic garden; at the end of the tour, a feast of traditional mezedhes follows. Other unusual activities arranged by Masticulture include olive gathering in winter, underwater sea urchin hunting in summer and grape-pressing (by foot, of course) in autumn.

Masticulture's other activities include trips to ouzo and olive-oil factories, hidden beaches and tours of mediaeval buildings, as well as seminars for professional photography, icon painting, traditional music and dance, and special activities for children.

For Vasilis and Roula, it was, in fact, the desire to have kids that influenced their decision to leave Athens. 'Mesta, and Chios in general, is a very safe and fun place for children,' says Vasilis. 'And there's so much to enjoy here. With Masticulture, our goal is to help visitors to Mesta enjoy the real Mastihohoria experience.'

After the cave, continue on the good-quality dirt road to the coast. The road goes through a little-used military range, as the signs (unhelpfully, Greek only) warn. Although there's no danger, this is not a place for random hiking; stick to the road. After 2km the road ends at a small church overlooking **Agia Dynami Beach**, a curving, sandy cove where the water is a stunning combination of blues and greens, flecked with white wavelets. The beach is completely pristine and undeveloped, and you're likely to have it all to yourself.

INOUSSES ΟΙΝΟΥΣΣΕΣ

pop 1050 / area 14 sq km

A little-visited group of islands off Chios' northeast coast, Inousses is nonetheless a place of huge significance: some one-third of Greece's shipping barons (the so-called *arhontes*) came from there. The descendents of ship-owning families from Kardamyla who first settled here in 1750, these Inoussans amassed huge fortunes in the 19th and early 20th centuries. Traces of Inousses' vital seafaring identity remain in its well-disciplined merchant marine academy, its nautical museum and its fishing fleet, and, of course, in the grand holiday homes of the Inousses shipping aristocracy, now ensconced in Athens, London or New York.

Inousses is deliberately kept tranquil and untouristed, some say, to keep it the private paradise of the locals and their illustrious relatives. This image has been overblown, however; Inousses is surprisingly lively in summer, with an open-air cinema, a couple of cafés and nighttime beach parties. You'll find rooms, a hotel and even whole houses for rent. Nevertheless, it has also retained its serenity and remains a soothing refuge from the outside world.

The islands' port and only town, also called Inousses, is a pleasing enough assortment of white stone houses crowned by two churches, with a waterfront lined by colourful boats where the plaintive cry of seagulls, and not domatia owners hawking rooms, greets travellers arriving from the ferry. Facing the port from the water is a small and green sculpted mermaid, the Mother of Inoussa (Mitera Inoussiotissa), who protects and watches over mariners.

Orientation & Information

Disembarking from the ferry, walk left along the waterfront and turn right to the central *plateia*, where the tavernas, museum and most of the town's services are found. Further along the waterfront are some cafés and, above them, a small church. A post office and National Bank of Greece stand side by side, around the corner from the Nautical Museum. However, there's no ATM, locals explain, because having one would mean unemploying one of the bank's two workers.

Doctor (☎ 22710 55300)

Dimarhio (Town Hall; ☎ 22710 55326)

Hotel Thalassoporos (☎ 22720 51475, 22710 55222) Just above Hotel Thalassoporos.

Police (☎

Post Office (☎ 22710 55398; ☒ 9.30am-2pm Mon-Fri)

Sights & Activities

Inousses has numerous hill-walking opportunities and untouched beaches. There's no tourist information, so ask for details at the *dimarhio* or the very helpful Hotel Thalassoporos. **Bilali Beach**, 2km from town, is the best nearby beach and in high summer has nightly parties. In summer an **open-air cinema** (tickets €4) near the central waterfront brings Hollywood hits to Inousses, nightly at 9.30pm.

Not only toy-boat aficionados will be impressed by Inousses' little **Nautical Museum** (☎ 22710 44139; Stefanou Tsouri 20; admission €1.50; ☒ 10am-1pm Mon-Fri), which celebrates the island's seafaring past. To create it, ship-owning *arhon* and museum founder Antonis Lemos donated his priceless collection of large model ships, which include early-20th-century commercial ships, whaling ships made of ivory and whalebone, and ivory models of French POW vessels from the Napoleonic Wars. However, the museum is more eclectic; along with these models (accompanied by vintage paintings of ships by eminent painter Aristeides Glykas), there's a swashbuckling collection of 18th-century muskets and sabres, a WWII-era US Navy diving helmet, a hand-cranking lighthouse made in 1864, antiquarian maps of Greece and, of course, the odd 6th-century-BC stone scarab seal and various Bronze Age antiquities.

In true Greek style, the museum is timed to close just before the afternoon ferry from Chios arrives and to open only after the morning boat back to Chios has left. Therefore you may have to stay over for two nights just to see it, unless you can get someone to intercede on your behalf (Eleni at Hotel Thalassoporos is particularly helpful) and get it opened out of hours.

To really feel the significance of Inousses and its heritage, take the 10-minute walk from the museum to the **Church of Agia Paraskevi** on the hill; in its leafy courtyard above the sea stands the **Mausoleum of Inousses** (Nekrotafion Inousson), where the island's shipowning dynasties have endowed the tombs of their greats with huge chambers, marble sculptures and miniature churches. It's a melancholy, moving place, and speaks volumes about the worldly achievements and self-perception of the extraordinary natives of these tiny islands.

Sleeping

There are allegedly 46 beds in private accommodation in Inousses town; ask at the *dimarhio*.

Hotel Thalassoporos (☎ 22720 51475; fax 22720 51476; s/d incl breakfast €40/50; ⚅) Friendly young Inoussan couple Eleni and Giorgos have breathed new life into this 30-year-old hotel. Although slightly dated, rooms are clean, all with TV, fridge and small balconies, with views of Inousses town's rooftops and the waterfront. Internet access is available. Eleni can also give general information, and help arrange house rental in more remote parts of the island. The hotel is a three-minute walk up a steep street on the ferry-dock side of the waterfront.

Eating & Drinking

Souvlaki Kostas (souvlaki €2.50) There's no name on this popular canteen above the central waterfront; you'll recognise it from the crowd happily munching outside, who know that cheerful Kostas, and his Brazilian sidekick Seline, serve the best *souvlaki* in Inousses.

Inomageireio To Pateroniso (☎ 22720 55586; mains €5-7) This whimsical taverna near the central *plateia* serves Greek standbys and whatever is the day's catch. Try a Greek salad with spongy feta and *kritamos* (rock samphire salad), along with a heads-and-all fry up of *atherinia* (minnows) and onions.

Naftikos Omilos Inousson (☎ 22720 55596; ⏰ 9am-3am) Walk along the quiet watefront long enough and you will reach this, the almost

chic bar of the Inousses Yacht Club. Its long bar and outdoor patio are filled mostly with young Greeks (and their vacationing diaspora relatives), and pop music plays till late.

Getting There & Away

The little *Oinoussai III* (€3.80 one way, 1¼ hours, daily) usually leaves in the afternoon and returns in the morning, meaning you'll be staying overnight. Purchase tickets on board, or from **Sunrise Tours** (☎ 22710 41390; Kanari 28) in Chios Town. There are also twice-weekly day excursions in summer (€20), again with Sunrise Tours.

Daily **water taxis** (☎ 6944168104) travel to/from Langada on Chios. The one-way fare is €35, which is split between the passengers. There are comparably priced water taxis to Chios Town, too.

Getting Around

Inousses has no buses or car rental; ask in one of the tavernas for its one taxi.

PSARA ΨΑΡΑ

pop 422 / area 45 sq km

Still more remote Psara (psah-*rah*) is a rocky, sparsely vegetated island off Chios' northwest coast. The island has been populated since Mycenaean times. Like Inousses and Chios itself, it prospered in Ottoman times because of its wealthy ship owners. However, after the Psariots aided the War of Independence, an Ottoman fleet landed on 21 June 1824, butchering over 15,000 people and taking others as slaves. Today the few inhabitants occupy one settlement, also called Psara.

Although few make it here, and the accommodation and eating scene is limited, intrepid, peace-seeking travellers will enjoy this pristine speck in the sea well off the beaten track (or any track).

Getting There & Away

From Chios, ferries go to Psara daily except Saturday in summer (€10, three hours). Contact **Miniotis Lines** (☎ 22710 24670; www.miniotis.gr; Neorion 23) in Chios Town, or check with a local **agent** (☎ 22710 25848). A direct ferry to Lavrio in Attica (€20.80, 5½ hours) sails once weekly.

Weekly local caïques also run from Limnos (€5, three hours) on Chios' west coast, but departure times depend on prevailing weather conditions.

LESVOS (MYTILINI)
ΛΕΣΒΟΣ
(ΜΥΤΙΛΗΝΗ)

pop 93,428 / area 1637 sq km

The third-largest island in Greece after Crete and Evia, Lesvos (Mytilini) is mountainous and fertile and prone, it seems, to always doing things in a big way. Some 11 million olive trees cling to Lesvos' rugged hills, yielding delectable, golden-hued oil by the tonne; the island also produces half of the world's ouzo, the aniseed-flavoured firewater revered as Greece's national spirit.

Culturally, too, Lesvos has gone above and beyond. From the musical composer Terpander and poet Arion of the 7th century BC, to 20th-century figures like Nobel Prize–winning poet Odysseus Elytis and primitive painter Theofilos, the island has given birth to artists of genius. Under the great ancient philosophers Aristotle and Epicurus, an exceptional philosophical academy flourished on the island. Most famous, however, is Sappho, one of ancient Greece's greatest poets. Her sensuous, passionate poetry, apparently created for a select group of female devotees, has fuelled a modern-day cult that draws lesbians from around the world to pay homage to the poet in Skala Eresou, the west Lesvos beach village where she was born around 630 BC.

Appropriately enough, the stark natural beauty that inspired all these artists and thinkers itself derived from a great event: a massive prehistoric volcanic eruption that buried and transformed its surroundings, making western Lesvos into a treasury of prehistoric fossils and gems, and the only place outside of the USA with a petrified forest.

Indeed, it is the natural abundance that primarily draws visitors. Hiking the idyllic southern olive groves as well as bird-watching –

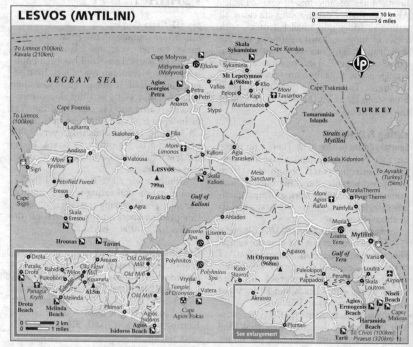

LESVOS (MYTILINI)

the island is the transit point and home to over 279 species of birds ranging from raptors to waders – are both very popular. Lesvos' long coastline, hardly touched by package tourism, is dotted with therapeutic hot springs and pristine beaches.

The island's festive nature, visible in the chic cafés and restaurants of the capital, Mytilini, comes to life with the midsummer *panigyria*, dating back distantly to Lesvos' passionate pagan past, with plenty of food, drink and music, as well as the racing of beautifully girded horses and the odd bull sacrifice.

Getting There & Away

AIR

Olympic Airlines (☎ 22510 28659; www.olympicairlines .com; Kavetsou 44), in Mytilini town, offers four flights daily to Athens (€76) and one daily to Thessaloniki (€87). There are two flights weekly to both Chios (€32) and Samos (€41), and five to Limnos (€46) and Rhodes (€58).

Aegean Airlines (☎ 22510 61120; www.aegeanair .com) has three daily flights to Athens (€68, one hour) and one to Thessaloniki (€84, one hour 10 minutes); its office is at the airport, which is 8km south of Mytilini town. An airport taxi costs €7 to €8.

To Heraklio in Crete, Sky Express has flights on Friday and Sunday (€119); buy tickets from **Picolo Travel Tourism** (☎ 22510 23720; Pavlou Kountourioti 73a).

FERRY
Domestic
In summer NEL Lines goes daily to Piraeus (€35.60, 12 hours) via Chios (€14.60, three hours). Hellenic Seaways has a faster daily ferry to Piraeus (€38.10, 8½ hours), again via Chios (€18, two hours). Two ferries weekly serve Kavala (€26.90, 10 hours), via Limnos (€18.40, six hours). One boat weekly goes to Thessaloniki (€37, 13 hours), also via Limnos, and one weekly ferry serves Alexandroupoli (€21.50, nine hours).

Ferry ticket offices on the eastern side of Pavlou Kountourioti include **Zoumboulis Tours** (☎ 22510 37755; www.zoumboulistours.gr; Pavlou Kountourioti 69) and **Samiotis Tours** (☎ 22510 42574; fax 22510 41808; Pavlou Kountourioti 43).

International
In summer two daily ferries go to Ayvalık, Turkey (€35, one hour 15 minutes).

Getting Around

BUS
From Mytilini's **long-distance bus station** (☎ 22510 28873; El Venizelou), near Agias Irinis Park, there are two daily buses to Skala Eresou (€8, 2½ hours) via Eresos, five to Mithymna (Molyvos; €5.90, 1¾ hours) via Petra (€5.50, 1½ hours), and one to Sigri (€8, 2½ hours). Five daily buses go to Plomari (€3.90, 1¼ hours) and four to Vatera (€5.30, 1½ hours), the latter via Polyhnitos. Travelling between these smaller places often requires changing buses in central Kalloni, which receives five daily buses from Mytilini (€3.90, one hour).

CAR & MOTORCYCLE
Mytilini's international rental chains include **Hertz** (☎ 22510 37355; Pavlou Kountourioti 87), though **Holiday Rent-a-Car** (☎ 22510 43311; Arhipelagous 21) is also good. Scooters and motorcycles are available along Pavlou Kountourioti.

FERRY
In summer there are half-hourly ferries across the Gulf of Yera (€1, five minutes), between Perama and Koundouroudia, near Loutra south of Mytilini town. Buses to Mytilini meet these ferries.

MYTILINI TOWN ΜΥΤΙΛΗΝΗ
pop 27,247
Easygoing Mytilini, the port of Lesvos, is kept lively year-round thanks to its capital status and irrepressible student population. The laid-back attitude to life in Mytilini reflects ingrained political preferences (Lesvos was long a bastion of the left), but even more so, perhaps, its love of food, drink and the arts on an island known eternally for its poets and painters, its olive oil and wine.

As with most Greek port towns, the action is centred on the waterfront; however, Mytilini boasts bigger attractions than the average island capital. It is interspersed with palm-fringed churches, grand 19th-century mansions and several museums, the most remarkable being the Teriade, boasting paintings by Picasso, Chagall and Matisse. Handmade ceramics, jewellery and traditional products are available on and around the main shopping street, Ermou, and epicureans will be delighted by the town's many fine *ouzeries*. Mytilini's student-fuelled nightlife, concentrated around the waterfront bars, carries on during summer and winter, too.

Orientation

Ferries dock on the northern end of Mytilini's long and curving waterfront thoroughfare, Pavlou Kountourioti. Further up and along the thoroughfare is Plateia Sapphou (where a statue of Sappho stands); many restaurants, cafés and hotels are nearby. The main shopping street, Ermou, links this southern harbour with the ancient, but now disused, northern port.

East of the harbours, a large mediaeval fortress stands surrounded by pines. Both bus stations are centrally located: the long-distance bus station is next to Agias Irinis Park and the local bus station is on Pavlou Kountourioti, near Plateia Sapphou. The airport is 8km south on the coast road.

Information

Numerous banks and ATMs line Pavlou Kountourioti.

Bostaneio General Hospital (☎ 22510 43777; E Bostani 48)

EOT (☎ 22510 42511; Aristarhou 6; ☿ 9am-1pm Mon-Fri)

InSpot (☎ 22510 45760; Hristougennon 1944 12; per hr €2.40) Internet access.

National Bank of Greece (Pavlou Kountourioti) Has an ATM.

Port police (☎ 22510 28827) Next to Picolo Travel Tourism.

Post office (Vournazon) West of the waterfront.

Sfetoudi Bookshop (☎ 22510 22287; Ermou 51) Sells good maps from Greece's leading Road Editions series; books on Lesvos include *39 Coffee Houses and a Barber's*

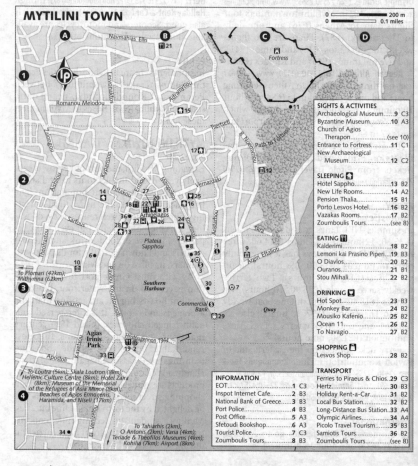

MYTILINI TOWN

SIGHTS & ACTIVITIES	
Archaeological Museum	9 C3
Byzantine Museum	10 A3
Church of Agios Therapon	(see 10)
Entrance to Fortress	11 C1
New Archaeological Museum	12 C2

SLEEPING	
Hotel Sappho	13 B2
New Life Rooms	14 A2
Pension Thalia	15 B1
Porto Lesvos Hotel	16 B2
Vazakas Rooms	17 B2
Zoumboulis Tours	(see 8)

EATING	
Kalderimi	18 B3
Lemoni kai Prasino Piperi	19 B3
O Diavlos	20 B2
Ouranos	21 B1
Stou Mihali	22 B2

DRINKING	
Hot Spot	23 B3
Monkey Bar	24 B2
Mousiko Kafenio	25 B2
Ocean 11	26 B2
To Navagio	27 B2

SHOPPING	
Lesvos Shop	28 B2

TRANSPORT	
Ferries to Piraeus & Chios	29 C3
Hertz	30 B3
Holiday Rent-a-Car	31 B2
Local Bus Station	32 B2
Long-Distance Bus Station	33 A4
Olympic Airlines	34 A4
Picolo Travel Tourism	35 B2
Samiotis Tours	36 B2
Zoumboulis Tours	(see 8)

INFORMATION	
EOT	1 C3
Inspot Internet Cafe	2 B3
National Bank of Greece	3 B3
Port Police	4 B3
Post Office	5 A3
Sfetoudi Bookshop	6 A3
Tourist Police	7 C3
Zoumboulis Tours	8 B3

Shop, a beautiful photo narrative by eminent local photographer Jelly Hadjidimitriou.

Tourist police (☎ 22510 22776) On the quay.

www.lesvos.com Information on Lesvos.

Zoumboulis Tours (☎ 22510 37755; Pavlou Kountourioti 69) Sells ferry and plane tickets, runs boat trips to Turkey and rents rooms.

Sights & Activities

Mytilini's imposing, early Byzantine **fortress** (adult/student €2/1; ☑ 8am-2.30pm Tue-Sun) was renovated in the 14th century by Genoese overlord Francisco Gatelouzo, and later the Turks enlarged it again. It's popular for a stroll and the surrounding pine forest is perfect for picnics.

The **archaeological museum** (☎ 22510 22087; adult/child €3/2; ☑ 8am-7.30pm), one block north of the quay, has impressive finds from Neolithic to Roman times, including ceramic, somersaulting female figurines and gold jewellery. The ticket grants entry to the **new archaeological museum** (8 Noemvriou; ☑ 8am-7.30pm), 400m away, which portrays island life from the 2nd century BC to the 3rd century AD. Spectacular floor mosaics under glass are among the highlights here.

The bulbous dome of the **Church of Agios Therapon** crowns Mytilini's skyline, and is visible from almost everywhere on the waterfront. The church's ornate interior boasts a huge chandelier, an intricately carved iconostasis, priest's throne and a frescoed dome. The **Byzantine Museum** (☎ 22510 28916; admission €2; ☑ 9am-1pm) in the church's courtyard has valuable icons.

TERIADE & THEOPHILOS MUSEUMS

From the northernmost section of Pavlou Kountourioti, take a local bus 4km south of Mytilini to the village of **Varia**, where an unexpected treasure awaits: the **Teriade Museum** (☎ 22510 23372; adult/student €2/1; ☑ 9am-5pm Tue-Sun), with its astonishing collection of paintings by world-renowned artists like Picasso, Chagall, Miro, Le Corbusier and Matisse.

The museum honours the Lesvos-born artist and critic Stratis Eleftheriadis, who Gallicised his name to Teriade in Paris. Teriade was instrumental in bringing the work of primitive painter and fellow Lesvos native Theophilos to international attention.

The **Theofilos Museum** (☎ 22510 41644; admission €2; ☑ 9am-2.30pm & 6-8pm Tue-Sun May-Sep, 9am-1pm & 4-6pm Tue-Sun Oct & Apr, 9am-2pm Tue-Sun Nov-Mar), lo-

cated next door, houses works commissioned by Teriade; several prestigious Greek museums and galleries display other more famous paintings of Theophilos, whose story followed the old pattern of many a great artist – living in abject poverty, painting coffee-house walls for his daily bread and eventually dying in the gutter.

Sleeping
BUDGET
Budget accommodation in Mytilini is scarce.

Zoumboulis Tours (☎ 22510 37755; Pavlou Kountourioti 69; r from €35) The travel agency rents simple, air-conditioned rooms.

Pension Thalia (☎ 22510 24640; Kinikiou 1; d €35) This friendly, family-run *pension* has cheery, clean rooms on a side street behind Ermou. There's not always someone at the door, so call in advance.

MIDRANGE
Hotel Sappho (☎ 22510 22888; sappho@microchip.gr; Pavlou Kountourioti 31; s/d/t €35/50/60; ⌘) The default option on the waterfront, the Sappho is a somewhat staid, older hotel with the necessary amenities and, fortunately for late-night ferry arrivees, 24-hour reception. The harbor-side location means it gets street noise.

Vazakas Rooms (☎ 22510 46571; Bizaniou 17; d/tr €50/60; ⌘) Once a budget choice, these domatia on the 2nd floor of a family house offer variety; some have balconies, others a kitchenette. All are clean and well maintained. It's just off Ermou, though it can be hard to find.

New Life Rooms (☎ 22510 42650; Ermou 68; s/d/t €30/50/70) Although the bristly green carpet out the front could come from a miniature-golf course, the recently redecorated rooms are bright and well furnished. The hotel, which also has a new outdoor bar, is central but quietly set on a side street.

Porto Lesvos Hotel (☎ 22510 22510; www.porto lesvos.gr; Komninaki 21; s/d €60/80; ⌘) Although the red carpets are a bit frumpy, and the rooms snug, some have panoramic views of Mytilini. The décor involves stone set in plaster. In its zeal to be a 'real' hotel, the Porto Lesvos offers toiletries, bathrobe and slippers.

Eating
The *ouzeries* listed in this section all have the seal of approval from local ouzo expert Leftheris Eleftheriadis (see boxed text, p390).

O Antonis (Tahiarhis; mezedhes €3-5; 🕒 Mon-Sat) An institution with the locals, this simple *ouzerie* is 2km from the town centre, on a breezy hill top offering sublime views of the sea and Mytilini town. Try the *koutavakia* (fried baby shark), sardines and *kolios* (mackerel). O Antonis has only a few tables, and fills up on weekends and after 8pm.

Stou Mihali (☎ 22510 43311; Ikarias 7, Plateia Sapphou; mains €3.50-5; 🕒 9am-9pm) It's getting hard to find a free table at lunch at this tasty and inexpensive place serving *mayirefta*. Unlike many other such eateries, here you can combine half-portions and thus enjoy more variety. Everything is good; try the *soutzoukakia* (tomato-soaked beef rissoles), *imam baïldi* (roast eggplant) and Greek salad.

our pick **O Diavlos** (☎ 22510 22020; Ladadika 30; mezedhes €3-6) What first attracts the eye in this unique *ouzerie* set in a lofty, wood-beamed building is the artwork lining the walls. Monthly exhibits show off local artists' works, which diners can purchase; might the next Theophilos be discovered here? However, aside from being an art lover, Diavlos owner Panayiotis Molyviatis crafts what might just be the most satisfying and nourishing mezedhes in all of Lesvos. Local specialities include *giouslemes* (a crunchy cheese pie) and *sfongatoa* (a sort of oven-baked cake made of zucchini, egg, onion and cheese). Also try the Turkish-flavoured beef kebabs on pitta bread with onions and *yiaourtlou kebab* (Greek yogurt). Music ranges from relaxed to *rembetika* (blues songs).

Ouranos (☎ 22510 47844; Navmahias Ellis; mezedhes €3-6) A popular *ouzerie* that looks across at Turkey from a breezy patio on the ancient northern port. Tempting mezedhes include *kolokythoanthi* (fried pumpkin flowers stuffed with rice), *ladotyri mytilinis* (the oil-drenched local cheese) and hefty servings of some of the most enormous calamari in the Mediterranean.

Kalderimi (☎ 22510 46577; Thasou 3; mezedhes €3.50-5, mains €7-10) Inconspicuously set on a shaded side lane, Kalderimi is another popular Mytilini *ouzerie;* try the tasty salted mackerel and sardines and fried zucchini flowers.

Lemoni kai Prasino Piperi (☎ 22510 42678; cnr Pavlou Kountourioti & Hristougennon 1944; mains €10-15; 🕒 7pm-1am) The poshest place in town, this

---

AN OUZO EDUCATION

A few years ago the young Mytilene cartographer Leftheris Eleftheriadis was looking for a book on Greece's great national aperitif, ouzo. A man of Hemingwayesque appetites, Eleftheriadis was disappointed to find there was none; and so, along with friend Stathiadis Georgiadis, he embarked on a three-year odyssey around Greece in which the two imbibed more than 500 kinds of the aniseed-flavoured firewater – all in the name of research.

In their well-illustrated new book, *Ouzo: The Greek Spirit* (ROAD Editions, 2007), the authors catalogue every conceivable detail about all of Greece's ouzo producers, the history behind the drink, and the peculiar, secretive genius of the ouzo makers, who combine some 25 different ingredients in various proportions to concoct their own distinctive blends.

Unsurprisingly, some of the most unique ouzos the authors discovered were from Lesvos, which produces approximately 70% of Greece's ouzo, and half of all ouzo sold in the world. One small distillery, Pitsiladi from Plomari – the southern Lesvos capital of ouzo – follows a unique method. Its anise seeds are stuffed in a sack and then stored in the sea for a few days before they are added to the ouzo; the result is a slightly salty and strengthened taste.

In general, says Eleftheriadis, the 'island ouzos' are slightly more full bodied than the mainland Greek ouzos. But they all have their own idiosyncratic tastes and special foods that go with them. The well-fed authors found this out while sampling local mezedhes all over Greece – and stealing the recipes from little old ladies.

The ouzo makers, on the other hand, 'weren't about to share their secret recipes with us,' jokes Leftheris. Nevertheless, he can disclose some Greek customs for the better enjoyment of ouzo. 'Before opening the bottle, you should slap it three times on the bottom – to hurt it so it won't hurt you,' he says. 'And then wave it in a circle three times, so it won't make you dizzy. Then it's ready to drink.'

The *ouzeries* listed in the Mytilini Eating section (p389) have all received the Leftheris Eleftheriadis seal of approval.

upstairs restaurant has great waterfront views and even better food, especially the Italian dishes. Try the simple yet exquisite tomato and mozzarella salad and tagliatelle amatriciana or tagliatelle alfredo with salmon. As expected, the wine list is deep; the Mexican offerings, however, remain somewhat of an unknown commodity.

Drinking

Most of Mytilini's cafés are strung together along the waterfront and double as bars at night, their blaring intermingled music creating a veritable cacophony for those sitting outdoors.

Mousiko Kafenio (cnr Mitropoleos & Vernardaki; ☺ 7.30am-2am) This relaxed, arty student café just in from the waterfront is full of colour, with eclectic paintings, mirrors and well-worn wooden fixtures.

To Navagio (☎ 22510 21310; Arhipelagous 23) A popular café-bar on Plateia Sapphou with comfy couches, perfect for a leisurely backgammon game and coffee.

Ocean 11 (☎ 22510 27030; cnr Arhipelogous & Pavlou Kountourioti; ☺ 7am-3am) This breezy patio café offers sweet frozen coffees by day, and becomes a slick and shiny bar by night.

Monkey Bar (☎ 22510 37717; Pavlou Kountourioti; ☺ 10am-3am) A big, thumping, packed nightspot on the water.

Hot Spot (☎ Pavlou Kountourioti; ☺ 10am-2am Mar-Oct) This intimate student bar has a warmer feel than its neighbours and plays more rock and roll.

Shopping

Lesvos Shop (☎ 22510 26088; Pavlou Kountourioti 33) This waterfront shop near the Hotel Sappho has all of Lesvos' distinctive natural products, from ouzos and olive oil and soap to jams, handmade ceramics, and local wine and cheese. Proceeds benefit the municipality.

Getting There & Away

Mytilini's **local bus station** (Pavlou Kountourioti), near Plateia Sapphou, serves destinations within the town and nearby Loutra, Skala Loutron and Tahiarhis. All other buses depart from the **long-distance bus station** (☎ 22510 28873; El Venizelou) near Agias Irinis Park.

SOUTH OF MYTILINI

Although it gets relatively few tourists, the small, olive-groved peninsula south of My-

tilini has several unique attractions. A long pebble beach 7km south on the coastal road opposite the airport hosts a decadent beach bar, **Kohilia** (☎ 6978773203; ☺ 8am-3am). Pulsating with house and techno music, and frequented by swimsuited students lounging on colourful couches and four-poster beds, Kohilia is a chilled-out hang-out on summer days; by night, however, it attracts several hundred young pleasure seekers who spill from the bar onto the beach, and sometimes into the water.

Somewhat quieter and more educational is the fishing village of **Skala Loutron**, 8km southwest of Mytilini on the Gulf of Yera. Here the **Hellenic Culture Center** (☎ 22510 91660, in Athens 21052 38149; www.hcc.edu.gr; 2-week courses €650) conducts intensive summer Greek-language courses, which attract students from the world over. Lessons are enhanced by cultural adventures, such as Greek singing and cooking classes, as well as by beach trips, olive-grove hikes and excursions to Turkey. Class sizes are deliberately small (25 students or less) and professional childcare is provided.

The course is held in a century-old olive-oil factory near the harbour, which has been restored quite splendidly into the **Hotel Zaira** (☎ 22510 91188; www.hotel-zaira.com; Skala Loutron; s/d €42/54), distinguished by lofty wood beams, nice stonework and home-cooked Greek food. Independent travellers can stay, too.

Also in Skala Loutron is the new **Museum of the Memorial of the Refugees of 1922** (☎ 22510 91086; admission free; ☺ 5-8pm), which commemorates the lost Greek culture of Anatolia, abruptly cut short by the population exchanges that occurred between Greece and Turkey in 1923 after the failed Greek offensive in Asia Minor. The museum features the photographs, documents, handmade clothes and silverwork of the refugees, as well as large wall maps showing over 2000 Anatolian villages that had been populated by Greeks until 1922 – and the places in Greece where the refugees were resettled. To arrange a special visit outside regular opening hours, ask at the Hotel Zaira.

Continuing 9km further south brings you to the peninsula's end, and the popular sand-and-pebble **Agios Ermogenis Beach** and **Haramida Beach**. The eastern stretch of the latter, **Niseli Beach**, is secluded under a bluff and separated by a headland from the main beach. What's more, the local community provides **camping** (camp sites free), with toilets and showers, under a quiet canopy of pines on the bluff above the beach. The camping ground is located near the lovably eccentric **Karpouzi Kantina** (☎ 6977946809), a drinks-and-snacks wagon named after its mascot – an old skiff, painted to look like a giant watermelon. Enthusiastic owner Fanis also oversees the camping ground.

NORTHERN LESVOS

With its rolling hills garbed in pine and olive trees, peaceful beaches and the aesthetically harmonious traditional town of Mithymna (usually called by its old name, Molyvos), northern Lesvos has only partially revealed its secrets. While its olive-rich heritage is now being commemorated in Agia Paraskevi's new museum, tourism remains largely limited to Mythimna (Molyvos) and its low-key beach resort of Petra, along with other attractive beaches like Skala Sykaminias and hot springs. There's plenty of bucolic authenticity in the villages surrounding Mt Lepetymnos, and off the northeast coast lie the enigmatic, unvisited Tomaronisia islands.

Mithymna (Molyvos)
Μήθυμνα (Μόλυβος)
pop 1497

While northern Lesvos' largest town has officially reverted to its ancient name of Mithymna, you're better off calling it Molyvos, as the locals do. This lovingly preserved town of narrow cobbled lanes and stone houses with jutting wooden balconies exemplifies traditional architecture of the Ottomans, under whose rule the town was politically and economically important. A relaxed stroll in the little streets of the upper town, crowned by a grand 14th-century Byzantine castle, gives a sense of those bygone times, while a dip in the invigorating north Lesvos waters down at the pebble-beached harbour at sunset is a perfect way to cap the day.

ORIENTATION

The bus stops on the main north–south road bisecting the town. Below this road is the waterfront, with a beach, several hotels and restaurants, and cafés on the northern end. Above the central road begins the upper town, consisting of narrow, winding streets, where some of the most atmospheric accommodation and restaurants are located. The so-called *agora* (market), clustered with tourist shops, is further up. Above this is the castle.

INFORMATION

The National Bank of Greece, with an ATM, stands by the municipal tourist office. The Commercial Bank booth opposite also has an ATM.

Central Internet Café (per hr €4.40) On the port road.
Medical Centre (☎ 22530 71702)
Municipal tourist office (☎ 22530 71347) A small office on the left of Kastrou, between the bus stop and the fork in the central road.
Post office (Kastrou) Along the left of the street.

SIGHTS & ACTIVITIES

Mithymna (Molyvos) is all about wandering, with its little streets in the upper town lined with bright-shuttered, traditional stone houses wreathed in flowers. The town's crowning achievement, the ruined 14th-century **Byzantine-Genoese castle** (☎ 22530 71803; admission €2; ☺ 8.30am-7pm Tue-Sun) stands guard over all from the top of the town; the steep climb is repaid by sweeping views of the town and the sea and Turkey shimmering on the horizon. Back in the 15th century, before Lesvos fell to the Turks, it was Genoese property and a feisty Italian woman called Onetta d'Oria, wife of the governor, repulsed an onslaught by the Turks by putting on her husband's armour and leading the people into battle from the castle. In summer a **drama festival** takes place here; ask the municipal tourist office for information.

Those seeking superlative beaches can take an **excursion boat** at 10.30am daily for Petra, Skala Sykaminias and Eftalou. Prices start at €20, and sunset cruises and boat 'safaris' are also available. Inquire with **Faonas Travel** (☎ 22530 71630; tekes@otenet.gr) at the port.

Eftalou beach also has the **baths of Eftalou** (old bathhouse/new bathhouse €3.50/5; ☺ old bathhouse 6am-8am & 6-10pm, new bathhouse 9am-6pm), with their clear, cathartic 46.5°C water. The old bathhouse has a pebbled floor; the new one offers private bathtubs. These springs treat rheumatism, arthritis, neuralgia, hypertension, gall stones, and gynaecological and skin problems.

SLEEPING
Budget

Over 50 registered, good-quality domatia exist in Mithymna (Molyvos). Look for signs, or arrange through the municipal tourist office.

Municipal Camping Mithymna (☎ 22530 71169; camp sites per adult/tent €5.50/3; ☒ Jun-Sep) This publicly run camping ground occupies an excellent shady site 1.5km from town and is signposted from near the municipal tourist office. If arriving before or after high season, call to ensure it's open.

Nassos Guest House (☎ 22530 71432, 6942046279; www.nassosguesthouse.com; Arionos; s/d €20/35) A fun, informal guesthouse with an international clientele and real personality, this refurbished Turkish mansion features brightly painted, though small, rooms with lovely little balconies overlooking the harbour. Bathrooms are separate. Tom, the affable Dutch manager, is unfailingly helpful, and also sells a useful book on local hiking routes for €8.

Captain's View (☎ 22530 71241; meltheo@otenet .gr; house €90-140; ☒) This restored old house is ideal for groups of friends or families, with its well-equipped kitchen, spacious balcony and lounge. The house has two bedrooms and a loft, and sleeps up to six people. There are no minimum-stay requirements, but book in advance in summer.

Midrange

Amfitriti Hotel (☎ 22530 71741; fax 22530 71744; s/d/tr incl breakfast €55/80/95; ☒ ☒) Just 50m from the beach, this snazzy traditional stone hotel has modern, tiled rooms and a refreshing garden pool. It fills up fast and deals with package tourists, but independent travellers are welcome.

Hotel Olive Press (☎ 22530 71205; www.olivepress -hotel.com; d with/without seaview €100/70; ☒ ☒) A converted olive-oil factory located on the beach, the Hotel Olive Press can get booked out by Northern European package tourists, though independent travellers are welcomed warmly, too. The rooms are very well done; especially evocative are those with balconies hanging out almost over the sea. With advance notice, pick-up can be arranged from Mytilini.

Hotel Sea Horse (☎ 22530 71630; www.seahorse -hotel.com; d incl breakfast €75; ☒) A good choice down on the harbour, the renovated Sea Horse is a friendly place with bright, breezy rooms and balconies overlooking the cafés and fishing boats. The hotel's small travel agency can arrange day trips and ferry tickets. Unlike other local hotels, it often has vacancies in August, since package groups arrive in September.

EATING & DRINKING

Betty's (☎ 22530 71421; 17 Noemvriou; mains €6-8) Look for the glossy-red overhanging balcony in this restored Turkish pasha's residence on the village's upper streets to find the best local cooking. Tasty *tyropitakia*, savoury lamb *souvlaki* and baked eggplant with cheese are recommended; what really stand out, however, are unusual seafood specialities, such as Betty's spaghetti shrimp.

Captain's Table (☎ 22530 71241; mezedhes €3-5, mains €7-10; ☒ dinner) It might seem a bit gimmicky, but this fish-and-mezedhes place at the far end of the harbour has great seafood and unusual mezedhes, like the Ukrainian-inspired *adjuka* (spicy eggplant).

Molly's Bar (☎ 22530 71209; ☒ 6pm-late) With its thick-painted walls and blue stars, beaded curtains and bottled Guinness, this whimsical, British-run bar is always in ship-shape condition. Molly's caters to an older and international crowd, and is located on the waterfront's far eastern side.

Petra Πέτρα
pop 1246

Petra, 5km south of Mithymna (Molyvos), has become a popular, though low-key, resort. While its sandy beach and seafront square are attractive enough, bland souvenir shops outnumber Petra's few remaining traditional stone houses. Nevertheless, Petra does have some unique sights, such as the enormous rock for which the village is named that looms behind it. Atop it is the 18th-century **Panagia Glykofilousa** (Church of the Sweet-Kissing Virgin), accessible on foot up 114 rock-hewn steps. The village of **Petri**, to the east, has characteristic old *kafeneia* and features excellent views of Petra and the sea.

Petra has a post office, an OTE, a bank, medical facilities and bus connections. The refurbished Turkish mansion known as **Vareltzidaina's House** (admission free; ☒ 8am-7pm Tue-Sun) is between the rock and the waterfront. Locals can provide directions.

For accommodation, excursions, boat and air tickets, visit the centrally located **Petra Tours** (☎ 22530 41390; petratours@otenet.gr).

Independent travellers should head straight to the **Women's Agricultural Tourism Cooperative** (☎ 22530 41238; womes@otenet.gr; s/d around €20), which works with Petra's 100 or so private rooms, ranging from studios to renovated farmhouses. The restaurant in which it's

COMRADES OF THE OLIVE

In the Lesvos of yesteryear there was no bachelor more eligible than an olive-soap purveyor; a woman working in an olive-oil factory, on the other hand, risked getting a 'reputation' for being in the company of strange men at a time when public appearances were meant to be restricted to the company of family.

These and other unexpected facts – such as that all of Lesvos' olive trees are of Turkish provenance, a great frost in 1850 having destroyed the trees existing until then – are presented with aplomb at the new **Museum of Industrial Olive Oil Production in Lesvos** (☎ 22530 32300; www .piop.gr; Agia Paraskevi; adult €3, student & child €1.50; ⏰ 10am-6pm Wed-Mon). This remarkable museum, housed in a restored communal oil mill and stocked with vintage machinery, tells the history of Lesvos' olive-oil production in Greek and English, showing the vital role of local cooperation and the gruelling physical labour involved with the olive trade.

The museum is located in the dusty agricultural village of Agia Paraskevi, until the Greek Civil War the economic centre of inland Lesvos. The villagers' communist sympathies, however, led the right-wing government to 'punish' the village by relocating major public services to previously insignificant Kalloni. The new museum, funded by the Bank of Piraeus, goes a small way towards rectifying Agia Paraskevi's loss.

To reach the museum from the main Mytilini–Kalloni road, take the Agia Paraskevi turn-off for 3.5km; the museum is on the left. It's not terribly well signposted, so if you reach the town centre, you've gone too far.

based, **Syneterismos** (☎ 22530 41238; fax 22530 41309; mains €4-7), features an ever-changing array of specials. Portions are hearty and home-cooked, with friendly service.

WESTERN LESVOS

Spectacular, lonesome western Lesvos is the afterthought of massive, primeval volcanic eruptions that fossilised trees and all other living things, making it one of the world's most intriguing sites for today's prehistoric treasure hunters. The striking, bare landscape, only broken by craggy boulders and the occasional olive tree, is very different from the rest of Lesvos.

Byzantine spiritualists in their high monastic refuges were inspired by the barren, burnt moonscapes of the west, and well before them, a certain Sappho, the 7th-century BC poet who was dubbed 'the tenth muse' by Plato, reflected on the powerful simplicity of this environment in her taut verse. Such was the power of her literary seduction that even the usually level-headed ancient ruler Solon despaired that he too must be taught Sappho's song, because he wanted 'to learn it and die'.

However, it is the sensuous, erotic nature of Sappho's surviving poems, and the fact that she probably taught them to an inner circle of female companions, that made Sappho into a latter-day lesbian icon. Today the southwestern coastal resort of Skala Eresou is a haven for lesbians from the world over, though its fine beaches and sunset cocktail bars have a more general clientele.

Although there are a few buses, it's best to rent a car to travel around Western Lesvos.

Kalloni to Sigri Καλλονή προς Σίγρι

After driving 34km west from Kalloni on the main road, the best place for a coffee or lunch break is **Andissa**, a jovial, rustic village kept cool by the two enormous plane trees that stand over its central stone *plateia*. Listen to the crickets and the banter of old-timers over a Greek coffee or frappe, while farmers hawk watermelons from the back of their trucks. Continue west for 9km and you'll find, at the top of a lone peak surrounded by volcanic plains, the Byzantine **Monastery of Ypsilou** (admission free; ⏰ 7.30am-10pm). Founded in the 8th century, this storied place includes a flowering arched courtyard, a sumptuously decorated church, and a small but spectacular museum with gold and silver reliquaries, antique liturgical vestments, centuries-old icons and Byzantine manuscripts dating back to the 10th century. From the top of the stairs, there are magnificent views of the desolate ochre plains stretching out against the sea.

After the monastery, continue on the main road west for 4km, and turn left at a signposted road for another 4.9km to reach Lesvos' celebrated **petrified forest** (☎ 22530 54434;

www.petrifiedforest.gr; admission €2; ⊗ 8am-5pm), which could be more honestly described as a petrified desert. The 20-million-year-old stumps that decorate this baking, shadeless valley are few and far between, though experts insist many more lurk under the ground, waiting to be dug up.

The best specimens have been relocated to the **Natural History Museum of the Lesvos Petrified Forest** (☎ 22530 54534; admission €5; ⊗ 8.30am-8pm Mon-Thu & Sat-Sun, until 10pm Fri) in Sigri, a coastal village 7km to the west of the forest. This engaging modern museum manages to make old rocks and dusty fossils interesting, helped by interactive displays and a veritable motherlode of glittering amethyst, quartz and other semiprecious stones.

Tucked below the museum in a sheltered cove is sleepy **Sigri**, a fishing port whose fortunes have waned with the discontinuation of ferries. The village has beautiful sea views, especially at sunset, and there are idyllic, rarely visited stretches of sand just southwest. A good-quality dirt coastal road pointing south out of the village passes these beaches and leads, after 45 minutes of magnificent scenery, to Skala Eresou, western Lesvos' most popular destination.

Skala Eresou Σκάλα Ερεσού
pop 1560
The key Lesvos experience for many is Skala Eresou, a bohemian beach town where the lesbian internationale meets to invoke the spirit of Sappho, much to the bemusement of local elders and much to the excitement of their teenaged grandsons. Its 2km-long beach is one of several exceptional nearby beaches, and is why (along with the fresh seafood and nightlife) the village is starting to attract a more mainstream clientele. Nevertheless, Skala Eresou remains a freespirited place, especially lively during the Women Together festival each September.

ORIENTATION & INFORMATION
The central square of Plateia Anthis and Evristhenous abuts the waterfront; the beach extends on both sides. Most restaurants and bars are found here, the latter on the eastern side of the *plateia*. Behind the *plateia* is the Church of Agias Andreas. Further west along Gyrinnis are the post office, the OTE, shops, an ATM and

Sappho Travel. The village now has a **doctor** (☎ 22530 53947; ⊗ 24hr).

The experienced **Sappho Travel** (☎ 22530 52140; www.sapphotravel.com) is Skala Eresou's main agency for travel information and tickets, accommodation, currency exchange and car rental. It organises sunset cruises for women and the increasingly popular **Women Together** festival. Held every September, this event has a worldwide reach, now attracting upwards of 400 women for two weeks of workshops, music, art, therapies and socialising. Book two months ahead if you want to stay in September.

SIGHTS
Eresos' **archaeological museum** contains Greek and Roman antiquities, but remained closed at the time of writing. It's near the exposed remains of the early Christian **Basilica of Agios Andreas**, which has partially intact 5th-century mosaics worthy of a peek.

SLEEPING
Skala Eresou has several reasonable domatia options, as well as some hotels that are steadily getting pricier. Some places that used to be women-only options have gone metrosexual, though two currently remain just for women.

Domatia Maria Pantermou (☎ 22530 53267; pantermou@in.gr; s/d/t €15/25/30; ❷) Dedicated budget travellers should find the lighthearted old couple Marianthi and Giorgios Pantermou, who operate these domatia on a back street across from the Mascot Hotel. While small and dated, rooms are clean and have balconies. The proprieters don't speak English, but their daughter (she who checketh the email) does.

Hotel Antiopi (☎ 22530 53311; s/d €30/50) A women-only hotel that benefitted when the Hotel Sappho went co-ed, the Antiopi has well-maintained but slightly cramped rooms that might strike one as either kitsch and cool or too cute.

Mascot Hotel (☎ 22530 52140; www.sapphotravel.com; s/d €30/60; ❷) The Mascot Hotel has taken up the mantle from the Hotel Sappho, fostering a bohemian air among its all-women clientele. A few blocks back from the beach, it features 10 snug modern rooms with balconies and a friendly staff. Book through Sappho Travel (☎ 22530 52140; www.sapphotravel.com).

Hotel Sappho (☎ 22530 53233; www.sapphohotel.com; s/d €40/60; ☼ 1 April 1-15 Oct; 🖳) The Sappho was the village's first women-only hotel, but under new management has taken a more staid and ecumenical approach, the wild girl-on-girl parties now a thing of the past. The hotel's once-famous restaurant has devolved into a bar. While it has thus lost some street credibility among the lesbian set, the Sappho still has a prime waterfront setting, smartly appointed rooms and free internet for guests.

Hotel Galini (☎ 22530 53137/74; fax 22530 53155; s/d/tr €35/45/60) This family-run hotel about 100m from the beach on the eastern side of town has rooms that are clean and modern but, price considered, a bit uninspiring. There is a flower garden outside and the staff is helpful.

EATING

Skala Eresou's best restaurants and liveliest bars are above the beach. The ambience is enhanced by the sound of lapping waves. On clear days Chios emerges on the horizon.

Soulatso (☎ 22530 52078; mains €6-10) After choosing a waterfront table on Soulatso's beachfront patio, walk in to inspect the day's catches. Among them are usually red mullet, lobster and sea bream, and all will be expertly cooked and presented. Also recommended are the crab salad, stuffed *kalamari* (calamari/squid) and mussels with wine.

Eressos Palace (☎ 22530 5385; mains €6-10) Another place known for seafood, like fisherman's *souvlaki* and oil-marinated tuna, this solid choice on the west end of town also does great meat and vegetable dishes and purveys local Eressos cheese.

DRINKING

Skala Eresou's nightlife consists of several bars strung along the eastern waterfront. First, along the main *plateia*, is the **Tenth Muse** (☎ 22530 53287), an old favourite of females strong on fruit drinks, Haagen-Dazs ice cream and conviviality. The orange-lanterned **Parasol** (☎ 22530 52050), further down on the waterfront, whips up tropical cocktails that match its South-Seas décor. A nightspot more popular with young Greeks is the ever-so-slick **Breez** (☎ 22530 537108; www .breez-lesvos.gr). Finally, furthest down on the eastern waterfront, **Zorba the Buddha** (☎ 22530 53777) is a colourful, easygoing watering hole above the water, where revellers sometimes head for a midnight swim.

SOUTHERN LESVOS

Endless groves of olive trees mixed with pine roll from the flanks of Mt Olympus (968m), southern Lesvos' highest peak, right down to the sea, where the island's premier beaches lie. This is a hot, intensely agricultural place where the vital olive-oil, wine and ouzo industries overshadow tourism. Southern Lesvos has thus retained authenticity in its villages and solitude on its beaches, a state of affairs that should prevail well into the future.

The first large southern village is **Agiasos**. On the northern side of Mt Olympus, Agiasos is a picturesque, popular day-trip destination known for its local artisanry. Everything from handcrafted furniture to pottery is sold here. Agiasos' **Church of the Panagia Vrefokratousa** hosts a **Byzantine Museum** and **Popular Museum**.

The road south to the coast leads to **Plomari**, the centre of Lesvos' ouzo industry and an attractive seaside village in its own right, with a large, palm-lined *plateia* and waterfront tavernas. Most visitors stay, however, at the beach settlement of **Agios Isidoros**, 3km east. This beach isn't bad but **Tarti**, a bit further east, is nicer and less crowded. Continuing west from Plomari along the coast, **Melinda** is a peaceful fishing village with a beach, tavernas and domatia.

Melinda to Vatera Μελίντα προς Βατερά

Most people going from Plomari further west to Vatera, a laid-back village with a wonderful 8km stretch of sand, err on the side of caution by going the long way around, heading back north and then west and then south on the main roads. There's no need for that, however. The much more direct route, which passes through tranquil mountain villages, is eminently doable for the average car, saving time and also crossing stunning terrain; rolling hills are richly forested with olive trees and pines, and between steep gorges there are innumerable breathtaking views down to the sea.

Driving north from Melinda, you pass first through tiny **Paleohori**. So authentic and untouristed that no one even took the time to make it look 'traditional', Paleohori has very small streets and gentle elders who will peer over their thick glasses curiously at you from *kafeneia* in the village's miniature *plateia*. It also boasts, in the upper part of town, an old church much grander and more ornate than Paleohori would seem to need. It's usually open and, if you speak

Greek, the priest can provide information about its history.

Continuing north from Paleohori, there are sweeping views of the sea behind you and glimpses of even tinier villages nestled in forested mountains opposite. Take the road west to Akrassio, and then north to Ambeliko; even though there is a more direct western route, locals say it is safer to go to Ambeliko first and then, just before reaching the village, turn left on the signposted, good-quality dirt road pointing downwards to Kato Stavros. This road lasts 9km before reverting to asphalt, and passes through serene forests of pine and olive trees. The total driving time from Melinda to Vatera on this route is little over an hour.

For hikers, there are even more options for experiencing the natural beauty of southern Lesvos' 'olive trails', as they are called, which fan out on trails and old local roads from Plomari and Melinda. Those close to the latter include the **Melinda–Paleohori trail** (1.2km, 30 minutes), which follows the Selandas River for 200m before ascending to Paleohori, passing a spring with potable water along the way. The trail ends at one of the village's two olive presses. You can continue southwest to **Panagia Kryfti**, a cave church near a hot spring and the nearby Drota Beach, or take the **Paleohori–Rahidi trail** (1km, 30 minutes), which is paved with white stone and passes springs and vineyards. Rahidi, which got electricity only in 2001, has several charming old houses and a *kafeneio* in summer.

There are several other trails heading northeast from Melinda, to shady **Kournela** (1.8km, 40 minutes), and from there to **Milos** (800m, 20 minutes), where there's an old flour mill. Milos can also be reached directly from Melinda (2km, one hour) on a trail that hugs the river and passes ruined olive mills, one spring and two bridges, as well as orange and mandarin trees. From Milos, follow the river northeast to **Amaxo** (1.75km, one hour) and be treated to refreshing mountain-spring water in plane, poplar and pine forests.

There are several other olive trails, and you could hike directly from Melinda to Vatera via some of them; consult the **EOT** (☎ 22510 42511; Aristarhou 6; ☯ 9am-1pm Mon-Fri) in Mytilini town or a travel agency to get precise details.

Vatera & Polyhnitos

Βατερά προς Πολυχνίτο

Lesvos' most celebrated beach, Vatera (vah-ter-*ah*), stretches for over 8km along the

tranquil southern coast. That said, one would immediately assume it to be long built up and packaged out; astonishingly, Vatera's tourism is very low-key, with only a few small hotels and domatia operating, and even fewer bars. Sandy, serene Vatera is thus a perfect destination for families, couples, or anyone looking to get away from it all.

Vatera has plenty of history. On its western edge, at Cape Agios Fokas, are the ruins of an ancient **Temple of Dionysos**, occupying a prime position near a headland overlooking the sea. In the cove between the beach and the cape, evidence has been found indicating ancient armies once camped there; indeed, historians believe this is the place Homer was referring to in the *Iliad* as the resting point for Greek armies besieging Troy. Legend also has it that the nearby village of Vrisa was named after a Trojan woman, Vrysseida, who died after being contested by two of the victorious Greek fighters. To this day old women and even the occasional baby girl with the name Vrysseida can be found here; the name is not given anywhere else.

Vatera's most remote history, however, is what has predominantly attracted international attention. Fossils dating back 5.5 million years have been found behind the village, including remains of a tortoise as big as a Volkswagen Bug and fossils of a gigantic horse and gazelle. A small **Museum of Natural History** (☎ 22520 61890; admission €1; ☯ 9.30am-7.30pm), located in Vryssa'a old schoolhouse houses these and other significant remains. Ongoing excavations carried out by the University of Athens and the University of Utrecht in the Netherlands mean that the most exciting finds may still be to come.

The agricultural village of **Polyhnitos**, about 10km north of Vatera on the main road leading back to Mytilini town, is unremarkable except for its nearby **hot springs**. There are two, one just to the southeast and the other 5km north, outside Lisvorio village. The former, known as the **Polyhnitos Spa** (☎ 22520 41449; fax 22520 42678; admission €3; ☯ 7am-12pm & 3-8pm) is in a pretty, renovated Byzantine building, and has some of the hottest temperatures of any baths in Europe, at 87.6°C. Rheumatism, arthritis, skin diseases and gynaecological problems are treated here.

The latter, the **Lisvorio Spa** (☎ 22530 71245; admission €3; ☯ 8am-1pm & 3-8pm) consists of two quaint little baths situated around a stream, surrounded by foliage. The baths are unmarked, so ask around for directions; the buildings are in a state of disrepair, but bathing is unaffected, and the temperature and water properties are similar to those at Polyhnitos.

Sleeping & Eating

ourpick **Hotel Vatera Beach** (☎ 22520 61212; www .vaterabeach.com; s/d €55/90; ✷ 🖳) While there are plenty of average domatia and a few overpriced hotels in southern Lesvos, there is only one Vatera Beach. This peaceful, family-run beachfront hotel regards its guests, many of whom come back year after year, as dear old friends. The congenial George and Barbara Ballis aim to ensure a relaxing holiday – whether for couples, families or single travellers – by providing for common needs; free newspapers in several languages, an 'internet corner' with computers and friendly service. The excellent Vatera Beach Restaurant, sought out by nonguests too, gets most of its ingredients from the owners' organic farm.

LIMNOS ΛΗΜΝΟΣ

pop 15,224 / area 482 sq km
A pleasant surprise awaits those who make the effort to reach balmy Limnos, seemingly all by itself in the north Aegean, accompanied only by its satellite island of Agios Efstratios. In successfully balancing tradition and tourism, Limnos has done the seemingly impossible. Its capital, Myrina, has a classic Greek fishing harbour feel, and is crowned by a grand Genoese castle. In summer the beautiful people fill Myrina's cozy streets, lined with sophisticated shops and stately neoclassical mansions, and flock to the sandy beaches that surround it, where happening café-bars open late into the night.

Limnos is not huge, but it does offer some variety. Spectacular flocks of flamingos visit its placid eastern lakes, while the austere central plain is filled with wildflowers in spring and autumn. Pristine sandy beaches, steep cliffs and sea caves line the coasts. Since package tourism is minimal, visitors are treated with friendly curiosity in the villages. Those who do arrive on an organised trip usually do so for windsurfing or adventure sports – thus providing some competition to the fearless

fellows in the Hellenic Air Force, which has its central command here.

Limnos is indeed in an ideal position for monitoring the Straits of the Dardanelles leading into İstanbul, and for this reason it played the key role in the failed Gallipoli campaign in WW1. Near the eastern port of Moudros, where the Allied ships were based, is a military cemetary for fallen Commonwealth soldiers, which you can visit today.

Getting There & Away

AIR
There is a daily flight to Limnos from Athens (from €66, one hour), six flights weekly from Thessaloniki (€65, 45 minutes) and three weekly to Lesvos (€41, 35 minutes). **Olympic Airlines** (☎ 22540 22214; www.olympicairlines .com; Nikolaou Garoufallidou) is opposite Hotel Paris in Myrina.

The airport is 22km east of Myrina; taxis cost about €16.

EXCURSION BOAT
Day trip to the nearby island of Agios Efstratios with the *Aeolis* ferry every Sunday, leaving at 8am and returning at 5pm. Tickets cost €6.60/15 one way/return and are sold at **Myrina Tourist & Travel Agency** (☎ 22540 22460; mirina@lim .forthnet.gr) on Myrina waterfront.

FERRY
SAOS Ferries (☎ 22540 29571; on the port) operates four ferries weekly to Lavrio (€27.70, 13 hours) and once weekly to Paralia Kymis on Evia (€22.50, six hours). There are six ferries weekly from Limnos to Kavala (€17, five hours).

SAOS also runs three to four boats weekly to Chios (€22, 10½ hours), Samos (€25, 13¼ hours) and Ikaria (€30, 15 hours) via Lesvos. There are three boats weekly to Thessaloniki (€25, eight hours) and one or two to Alexandroupoli (€20, five hours) via Samothraki (€15, three hours). Note some of these are faster boats and thus more expensive.

Two other companies, Agoudimos and NEL Lines, run ferries; buy tickets at **Pravlis Travel** (☎ 22540 22471; pravlis@lim.forthnet.gr; Parasidis 15). Cumulatively, they run one weekly boat to Piraeus (€30, nine hours), twice-weekly ferries to Thessaloniki (€22.10, 8½ hours), one weekly boat to Alexandroupoli (€14, 4½ hours) and two weekly boats to Chios (€21.60, 9½ hours) via Lesvos (€18.40, six hours);

one of these continues on to Samos (€27, 13 hours). One weekly ferry goes to Rhodes (€38, 24½ hours) via Kalymnos (€33.60, 17 hours) and Kos (€29.50, 18¼ hours).

Agios Efstratios is served five times weekly by the local ferry *Aiolis* (one way/return €6.60/15, two hours). Buy tickets at **Myrina Tourist & Travel Agency** (☎ 22540 22460; mirina@lim .forthnet.gr).

Getting Around
BUS
Limnos' bus service has one diabolical purpose: to bring villagers to town for their morning shopping and to get them home by lunch. Going and returning by bus in the same day is only possible to four destinations, by no means the most interesting ones either. Call or visit the **bus station** (☎ 22540 22464; Plateia Eleftheriou Venizelou), which displays schedules in the window and has printed copies you can take.

CAR & MOTORCYCLE
In Myrina cars and jeeps can be rented from **Myrina Rent-a-Car** (☎ 22540 24476; fax 22540 22484; Kyda-Karatza), near the waterfront. Prices cost €30

to €45 for a small car or jeep. There are several motorcycle-rental outlets on Kyda-Karatza.

TAXI
A **taxi rank** (☎ 22540 23033) is on Myrina's central square.

MYRINA ΜΥΡΙΝΑ
pop 5107
Limnos' striking capital is at once grandiose, with its volcanic-rock backrop and craggy Genoese castle, and serene, with its harbour full of colourful little fishing boats, and old fishermen sipping Greek coffee while unfolding their nets. Beyond the castle is a lovely sandy beach, while another, less windy one lies beyond that.

In summer especially, Myrina is a warm and lively town, full of shops selling traditional foods and local muscat, as well as clothing and trendy accoutrements for women in its bustling *agora*. Its whitewashed stone houses, old-fashioned barber shops and *kafeneia*, crumbling neoclassical mansions and wood-balconied homes all create a relaxed feel.

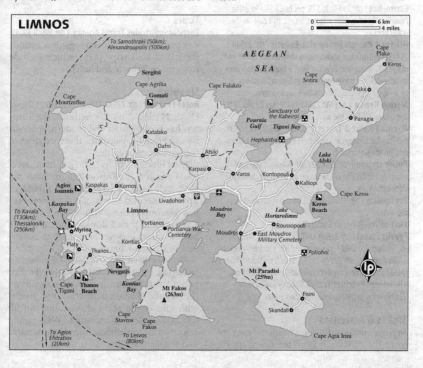

LIMNOS

NORTHEASTERN AEGEAN ISLANDS

At night the town is enlivened by garrulous Greeks at Myrina's tasty fish tavernas and the music from stylish beachfront bars. At the same time, however, the castle's overgrown hill is inhabited by scores of fleet-footed deer who dart around at night; in winter, locals say, the deer even come down to wander through the *agora* – presumably, to do their shopping.

Orientation

From the end of the quay turn right onto Plateia Ilia Iliou. Continue along the waterfront, passing Hotel Lemnos and the town hall. Turn left after the derelict Hotel Aktaion, then immediately veer half-left onto the main thoroughfare Kyda-Karatza to reach Myrina's central square. Continue and you will come to Plateia Eleftheriou Venizelou and the bus station.

Information

The National Bank of Greece, on the central square, has an ATM. There's a small tourist information kiosk on the quay during summer.

Excite-Net (☎ 22540 25525; per hr €1.50; ☼ 24hr) Prominently advertised internet access, in a café on the waterfront.

Hristos A Kazolis Fotografos-Ekdotis (☎ 22540 25445) Well-stocked photography shop on the upper end of Kyda-Karatza; sells *Deeds of Men*, a Greek-English book on now-defunct traditional crafts in Limnos, accompanied by a superb collection of evocative photographs.

Myrina Rent a Car (☎ 22540 24476; fax 22540 22484; Kyda-Karatza) Near the waterfront.

Myrina Tourist & Travel Agency (☎ 22540 22460; mirina@lim.forthnet.gr) Sells ferry tickets to Agios Efstratios; on the waterfront.

Police station (☎ 22540 22201; Nikolaou Garoufallidou) At the far end of the street, on the right coming from Kyda-Karatza.

Port police (☎ 22540 22225) On the waterfront near the quay.

Post office (Nikolaou Garoufallidou)

Pravlis Travel (☎ 22540 22471; pravlis@lim.forthnet .gr; Parasidi 15) Sells Agoudimos and NEL Lines ferry tickets.

SAOS Ferries (☎ 22540 29571) Sells ferry tickets from a small compartment on the castle side of the waterfront.

Theodoros Petrides Travel Agency (☎ 22540 22039; www.petridestravel.gr; Kyda-Karatza 116)

Sights & Activities

Myrina's **castle** stands on a headland over the town that divides it from the beach on the other side. Climb up for magnificent views over the sea to Mt Athos. As you walk from the harbour, take the first side street to the left by an old Turkish fountain. A sign here points you to the castle. At night, sitting in front of the church on the northeastern side of the castle combines great views of the café lights down below and, if you're lucky, quick glimpses of bounding deer in the darkness to the left.

Myrina has two good local beaches, the wide and sandy **Rea Maditos**, and a superior swath of sand, **Romeïkos Gialos**, which is beyond the harbour; it's accessible by taking any left from Kyda-Karatza as you're walking inland. Further on, it becomes **Riha Nera** (shallow water), named for its gently shelving, child-friendly beach. There is nightlife here, too.

Myrina's **archaeological museum** (admission €2; ☼ 9am-3pm Tue-Sun) is housed in a neoclassical mansion overlooking Romeïkos Gialos beach, and contains finds from all the three sites on Limnos – Poliohni, Sanctuary of the Kabeiroi and Hephaistia – exhibited in chronological order.

Tours

Theodoros Petrides Travel Agency (☎ 22540 22039; www.petridestravel.gr; ☼ Jun-Sep) organises round-the-island boat trips (€15), which include stops for swimming and lunch.

Sleeping

Hotel Lemnos (☎ 22540 22153; fax 22540 23329; s/d €35/45; ✦) Right on the harbour, the Lemnos has friendly staff and modern, spacious rooms. From the balconies, there are views of the waterfront or castle.

Hotel Filoktitis (☎ /fax 22540 23344; Ethnikis Andistasis 14; s/d €40/50; ✦) This welcoming hotel has airy, well-equipped rooms just inland of Myrina's second beach of Riha Nera. Follow Maroulas (the continuation of Kyda-Karatza) and then Ethnikis Andistasis; the hotel is located above the quite fine restaurant of the same name.

Apollo Pavillion (☎ /fax 22540 23712; www.apollo pavilion.com; d studios incl breakfast €50; ✦) Tucked behind the port in a neoclassical house, the Apollo Pavillion offers large rooms with kitchenette and balcony, and can fill up; book ahead in summer. Walk along Nikolaou Garoufallidou from Kyda-Karatza and the sign is 150m along on the right.

To Arhontiko (☎ 22540 29800; cnr Sahtouri & Filellinon; s/d/tr €50/60/70; ❄) This restored mansion, built originally in 1814, has lovely boutique rooms with simple charm, and helpful, friendly staff. It's located on a quiet alley around the corner from the main shopping street, and one street back from the beach.

Eating & Drinking

our pick **Ouzeri To 11** (☎ 22540 22635; Plateia KTEL; seafood mezedhes €4.50-6) This unassuming little *ouzerie* by the bus depot is actually Myrina's seafood emporium. From mussels with garlic and venus clams *(kydonia)* to limpets, sea urchins, crayfish and more, 'To En-dheka' (as it's pronounced) serves all the strange stuff, along with plenty of ouzo to make you forget what you're eating.

O Platanos Taverna (☎ 22540 22070; mains from €5) *Mayirefta* with an emphasis on meats are the order of business at this local institution under a giant plane tree, halfway along Kyda-Karatza. The menu is not particularly inventive, however.

Myrina's nightlife is centred around the bars above Romeïkos Gialos beach. A very popular one in summer, Karagiozis, on a leafy terrace near the sea, serves many kinds of cocktails and beers until late.

WESTERN LIMNOS

Driving north of Myrina, take the road left after **Kaspakas** village to the above-average beach at **Agios Ioannis**. The settlement has a few tavernas and beach houses, but the most unique thing here is at the end of the beach, where the aptly named **Rock Café** is set nicely beneath a large overhanging volcanic slab.

After Kaspakas, drive east and turn left at **Kornos**, and follow the road northwards to the remote beach at **Gomati** on the north coast; a good dirt road gets there from **Katalako**.

Alternatively, drive east from Kaspakas and keep going past Kornos, turning south only at **Livadohori**. This road passes barren, tawny hills as well as modest farmlands. Further south along the coast road is **Kontias**; this fairly prosaic, plastered old village has become a hot commodity for European property hunters, though it's not exactly clear why. Below Kontias the road swings southwest back to Myrina, on the way passing by two of Limnos' nicest and most popular beaches, **Nevgatis** and **Thanos**. Although they can get crowded, these beaches are truly idyllic and only a 10-minute drive from Myrina.

CENTRAL LIMNOS

The flat plateaus of central Limnos are dotted with wheat fields, small vineyards and sheep, as well as a major airbase of the Greek Air Force. Limnos' second-largest town, **Moudros**, is positioned on the eastern side of the muddy bay of the same name, famous for its role in WWI but, despite having a few hotels and tavernas, not for tourism. The **East Moudros Military Cemetery**, with the graves of Commonwealth soldiers from the Gallipoli campaign, is 1km east of Moudros on the road to Roussopouli. This cemetery, with its metal plaque that gives a short history of the Gallipoli campaign, and a second Commonwealth cemetery, **Portianos War Cemetery** (6km south of Livadohori on the road to Thanos beach and Myrina), are the sombre attractions here. Moudros, occupied by Royal Marines in February 1915, was the principal base for the ill-fated campaign.

EASTERN LIMNOS

Historical remnants and remote beaches are the drawcards for visitors to eastern Limnos. Its three **archaeological sites** (admission free; ❧ 8am-7pm) include four ancient settlements at **Poliohni** on the southeast coast, the most significant being a pre-Mycenaean city that predated Troy VI (1800–1275 BC). The site is well presented, but remains are few.

The second site, the **Sanctuary of the Kabeiroi** (Ta Kaviria), lies on remote Tigani Bay in northeastern Limnos. The worship of the Kabeiroi gods here actually predates that of Samothraki (see p405), more famous for this mystery cult. The major site, a **Hellenistic sanctuary**, has 11 columns. Nearby is the legendary **Cave of Philoctetes**, where that hero of the Trojan War was abandoned while his gangrenous, snake-bitten leg healed. A path from the site leads to the sea cave; there's also a hidden and narrow unmarked entrance to the left just past the main entrance.

To reach the sanctuary, take the left-hand turn-off after the village of **Kontopouli** for 5km; from Kontopouli, you can also follow a dirt road to the third site, **Hephaistia** (Ta Ifestia), once Limnos' most important city. It's where Hephaestus, god of fire and metallurgy, was hurled down from Mt Olympus by Zeus. Little remains, however, other than low walls and a partially excavated theatre.

Limnos' northeastern tip has some rustic, rarely visited villages, and a deserted beach at **Keros** popular with windsurfers. Flocks of flamingos sometimes strut on shallow **Lake Alyki**. From Cape Plaka, at the northeastern tip of Limnos, you can see the islands of Samothraki, and Imvros (Gökçeada) in Turkey. These three islands have historically been considered to form a strategic triangle for the defense of İstanbul (Constantinople); this was Turkey's case for clinging to Imvros in 1923, even after Greece had won back most of its other islands a decade earlier.

AGIOS EFSTRATIOS
ΑΓΙΟΣ ΕΥΣΤΡΑΤΙΟΣ

pop 371

Stranded on its own in the middle of the Aegean, Agios Efstratios is too big to be a dependency of Limnos but too small to be anything more. Nevertheless, though the island is sparsely populated and the architecture nothing spectacular – an effect of a 1968 earthquake that destroyed the island's old buildings – Aï-Stratis, as locals call it, does see a fair number of curious visitors. It has rooms, tavernas and modest nightlife, as well as some very fine beaches, some accessible only by boat.

Many dissidents and suspect communists were exiled here before and after WWII, among them the composer Mikis Theodorakis and poets Kostas Varnalis and Giannis Ritsos.

Sights & Activities
BEACHES

The **village beach** has dark volcanic sand and warm waters. A 90-minute walk northeast will bring you to **Alonitsi Beach**, a long, idyllic strand with intriguing facing islets offshore. To get there, take the little track from the northeast side of the village, starting by a small bridge, and when it splits, keep to the right. **Lidario**, a beach on the west side, can be reached on foot, but with difficulty. Try to arrange a boat trip locally to this and other hard-to-reach beaches, or else wander off for peaceful hill walks.

Sleeping & Eating

You can book rooms in Limnos through **Myrina Tourist & Travel Agency** (☎ 22540 22460;

mirina@lim.forthnet.gr) or **Theodoros Petrides Travel Agency** (☎ 22540 22039; www.petridestravel.gr; Kyda-Karatza 116), or else look out for domatia once you arrive; only in the height of summer might things ever be crowded.

There are a few tavernas, with generally reasonably priced fare and the seafood, of course, is excellent and fresh.

Getting There & Away

There are five services weekly to Limnos (€10, two hours) and one weekly to Kavala (€15.50, 6¾ hours). The local ferry *Aiolis* goes daily from Limnos in summer. Tickets cost €6.60/15 one way/return; buy at **Myrina Tourist & Travel Agency** (☎ 22540 22460; mirina@lim .forthnet.gr) in Myrina. Bad weather can cause unpredictable cancellations and delays to the schedule.

SAMOTHRAKI
ΣΑΜΟΘΡΑΚΗ

pop 2723 / area 176 sq km

For well over a thousand years, Samothraki's Sanctuary of the Great Gods was the site of a mystery religion respected and endowed by the Mediterranean world's greatest rulers. When you approach it on the ferry, the island does indeed seem to be holding many secrets within a hulking mass capped by mighty Mt Fengari (1611m), the Aegean's loftiest peak, from where Homer recounts that Poseidon, god of the sea, watched the Trojan War unfold.

Samothraki's greatness, however, does not just lie in the past. It offers some of the best – though still largely unexplored – hiking opportunities in Greece, with valleys filled with massive gnarled oak and plane trees, and forests redolent of olive and pine. There are barren and craggy peaks in the centre of the island, unvisited sandy beaches in the south and, in the northeast, a vertiginous series of lush waterfalls that plunge into deep, icy pools. The opposite kind of catharsis is found further west along the coast, with the therapeutic hot baths of Loutra (Therma).

Samothraki has always attracted an alternative, environmentally aware crowd, and in summer the proliferation of safari hats, dreadlocks and Hindu symbols add to the exotic, jungle vibe. The island's famous elec-

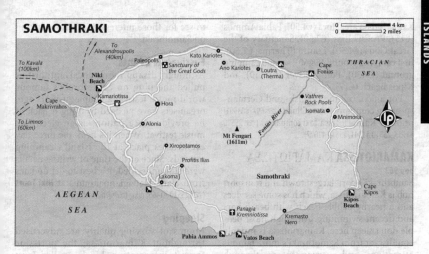

SAMOTHRAKI

tronic and world music festivals have also long drawn a hip young crowd for what is perhaps the modern equivalent of the ancient spiritual rites brought to the island by the Thracians around 1000 BC.

Historical sites of more recent creation, such as the Byzantine tower at Cape Fonias and the ruined Genoese castle that crowns the island's inland capital, Hora, will also appeal to the aesthetically inclined. Set amid stark cliffs, this very photogenic village is filled with narrow, flowering streets and boasts one of the best sweets shops in all of Greece.

Samothraki's remoteness and relatively poor transport links, however, mean that it's often left off the average island-hopping itinerary – a shame, considering that Samothraki is one of the coolest of all Greek islands, one reserved for the true initiates.

Getting There & Away
FERRY
Lacking an airport, Samothraki is accessible only by ferry, from Limnos and the mainland ports of Kavala and Alexandroupoli.

During the summer months the Samothraki-based SAOS Ferries goes twice daily to Alexandroupoli (€11, two hours). There are two weekly ferries to Kavala (€14.50, four hours) and two to Limnos (€10.50, three hours). The Kavala run is during summer only. Buy tickets at **Niki Tours** (☎ 25510 41465; niki_tours@hotmail.com) in Kamariotissa. Hydrofoils theoretically exist, but services change frequently.

Getting Around
BUS
In summer 10 buses daily go from Kamariotissa to Hora (€1) and eight to Loutra (Therma; €2) via Paleopolis (€1). Some of the Loutra buses continue to the two camping grounds. Five buses daily serve Profitis Ilias (€2) via Alonia and Lakoma.

CAR & MOTORCYCLE
On Kamariotissa's waterfront, opposite the buses, **X Rentals** (☎ 25510 42272) rents cars and small jeeps, as does **Kyrkos Rent a Car** (☎ 25510 41620, 6972839231). **Rent A Motor Bike** (☎ 25510 41057), opposite the quay, rents motorcycles and scooters.

EXCURSION BOAT
In summer the tour boat *Samothraki* circles the island (€17), departing from Loutra (Therma) at 11am and returning by 6.30pm. The boat hugs the coast, passing sites like the Byzantine castle of Fonias, the rock formations of Panias and Kremasto waterfall, before stopping at 1pm for four hours of swimming and sunbathing at Vatos Beach. A snack bar operates throughout the trip. For more information, ask at the taverna Petrinos Kipos in Kamariotissa or call the boat operator (☎ 25510 42266).

TAXI
Taxis on Samothraki are quick and, with three or more people, can be cheaper than the bus. The most popular destinations from

Kamariotissa are: Hora (€4.50), Pahia Ammos (€15), Profitis Ilias (€7.50), Sanctuary of the Great Gods (€4.50), Loutra (Therma; €7.50), first camping ground (€8.50), second camping ground (€9.50), Fonias River (€10.50), and Kipos Beach (€17).

For a taxi, call the English- and German-speaking company **Petros Glinias** (☎ 6972883501) or other Kamariotissa **taxi companies** (☎ 25510 41733, 25510 41341, 25510 41077).

KAMARIOTISSA ΚΑΜΑΡΙΩΤΙΣΣΑ

pop 963

Samothraki's port, largest town and transport hub is Kamariotissa, which has some services and a nearby pebble beach with beach bars and decent swimming. Although most people don't sleep here, Kamariotissa is roughly equidistant from Samothraki's more famous attractions, and everyone passes through it. While not the most exciting destination, Kamariotissa is hardly the least appealing of Greek island ports and is filled with flowers and good fish tavernas.

Orientation & Information

Turn left when disembarking from the ferry and you will see a tourist information kiosk after 50m, on the port side of the road running parallel to the water. Buses for the rest of the island are just behind this kiosk further east on the waterfront. Across the road are the majority of the town's tavernas, travel and car- and motorcycle-rental agencies, and two ATMs. Follow the waterfront further east and after 100m begins the town beach.

Café Aktaion (☎ 25510 41056; per hr €4) Internet café at the west end of the harbour.

Niki Tours (☎ 25510 41465; fax 25510 41304; niki_tours@hotmail.com) A very helpful starting point for any visit to Samothraki; across the street from the buses.

Port police (☎ 25510 41305) East along the waterfront.

www.samothraki.com General information about Samothraki, including boat schedules.

Activities

Haris Hatzigiannakoudis at **Niki Tours** (☎ 25510 41465; niki_tours@hotmail.com) runs a **Capoeira Camp** (a Brazilian martial art/dance) with Brazilian master Lua Rasta annually in late June, and can organise **hiking safaris** to Mt Fengari. As many of the hiking trails in Samothraki's lush interior are poorly marked or unmarked completely, and since the island has no official mountaineering guide, Haris is the man

to see for those interested in serious hiking on Samothraki.

Festivals & Events

Although disapproving local authorities pulled the plug on Samothraki's famous world music festival a couple of years ago, organisers have pledged to bring it back in its previous incarnation, as an electronic music festival. When it's held, the three-day event takes place at the island's camping grounds. Since at the time of writing details were still undecided, it's best to get updates from Haris Hatzigiannakoudis at **Niki Tours** (☎ 25510 41465; niki_tours@hotmail.com).

Sleeping

Rooms of varying quality are advertised throughout Kamariotissa; the port-side tourist information kiosk or **Niki Tours** (☎ 25510 41465; niki_tours@hotmail.com) can also arrange accommodation.

Niki Beach Hotel (☎ 25510 41545; fax 25510 41461; s/d €40/60) A good bet for those who want to stay in Kamariotissa, this spacious hotel with large, modern rooms has a lovely garden and is fronted by poplar trees. Just opposite is the town beach of the same name.

Hotel Aeolos (☎ 25510 41595; fax 25510 41810; s/d incl breakfast €60/70; 🖳 🌊) Up behind Niki Beach Hotel, the Aeolos stands on a hill overlooking the sea and has comfortable rooms. Front rooms overlook the large swimming pool and garden, while the back ones have views of Mt Fengari.

Eating

Klimataria Restaurant (☎ 25510 41535; mains from €5.50) This eatery at the eastern end of the waterfront serves an unusual speciality called *gianiotiko*, which is an oven-baked dish of diced pork, potatoes, egg and more, as well as the usual taverna fare.

I Synantisi (☎ 25510 41308; fish €4.50-10) For fresh fish at good prices, head to this hard-working outdoor *ouzerie* on the central waterfront. Check out the daily catch, preserved on ice inside. The *melanouri* (saddled bream), not as small as it looks, and a Greek salad make for a tasty lunch.

HORA ΧΩΡΑ

Set within a natural fortress of two sheer cliffs, and with a sweeping view of the sea, Hora (also called Samothraki) was the obvious choice for the island's capital. Indeed, its northwestern flank is watched over by a ruined Byzantine castle, thought to date from the 10th century but most often associated with Palamidi Gattilusi, a 15th-century Genoese lord who married into the Palaeologos family – the last imperial dynasty of Byzantium.

With its curving cobbled streets wreathed in flowers and colourful, crumbling traditional houses topped by terracotta roofs, Hora is a perfect place for ambling and enjoying a leisurely lunch or coffee. The village's great views and constant interplay of angles, shadows and colour make it great for photographers, and in summer there is eclectic nightlife to be found in Hora's small streets and roof bars.

Orientation & Information

Buses and taxis stop in a central square below the village. Walk straight upwards along the street, following the signs for the *kastro* (castle). This main street houses the OTE, Agricultural Bank and post office. The **police station** (☎ 25510 41203) is far up in Gattilusi's castle. Following the main street upwards brings you past several cafés and tavernas and, on the right, a small fountain with mountain water for filling your drink bottle.

Sleeping

There is no hotel in Hora; ask around for domatia. Midway up the main street, **Kyra Despina** (☎ 6974980263; s/d €40/50), who speaks some English, has fan-only self-catering studios with sweeping views, which sleep two to four people.

Eating & Drinking

ourpick O Lefkos Pyrgos (☎ 25510 41601; desserts €4-6; ☺ 9am-3am Jul-Aug) One of the best sweet shops anywhere, the summer-only Lefkos Pyrgos is the culinary laboratory of master desserts inventor Georgios Stergiou and wife Dafni. Georgios insists on only using all-natural ingredients, without preservatives or artificial flavourings. His concoctions are both extraordinarily refreshing (try the lemonade sweetened with honey and cinnamon on a hot summer's day) and unique, like Greek yogurt flavoured with bitter almond. Exotic teas, coffees and mixed drinks are also served. Some have amusing names like The Thief of The Louvre (vanilla ice cream and Grand Marnier), or the infamous Tar and Feather (Pissa kai Poupoula) – an indulgent, soufflé-

type cake oozing with liquid chocolate and topped with caramelised almond and vanilla ice cream. Occasional live music nights range from experimental jazz to classical.

Café-Ouzeri 1900 (☎ 25510 41224; mains €5-8) This relaxing taverna set under a shady trellis just before the fountain on the left offers friendly service and great views of the village's red rooftops, castle and sea – and even better food. Try the *spetsofaï* (stewed green peppers, tomatoes and sausage in an earthen pot), rice with seafood, or *tzigerosarmades* (goat flavoured with onion, dill and spearmint). The large, colourful menu, printed to look like a newspaper, is a take-home memento.

Meltemi (☎ 25510 41071; ☺ 8am-late) Continue higher up in Hora and take the side street to the left, opposite the fountain, to find this cool bar with great views; it has a popular roof garden that rocks in summer.

SANCTUARY OF THE GREAT GODS
ΤΟ ΙΕΡΟ ΤΩΝ ΜΕΓΑΛΩΝ ΘΕΩΝ

Beside the coastal village of Paleopolis, 6km northeast of Kamariotissa, is the **Sanctuary of the Great Gods** (admission €3, free Sun 1 Nov-31 Mar & public holidays; ☺ 8.30am-4pm Tue-Sun). The mysterious cult of the Great Gods, of even greater antiquity than the Olympian gods, was brought to Samothraki by the Thracians around 1000 BC. By the 5th century BC luminaries of the ancient world were coming for initiation into its rites, stilly largely unknown. The sanctuary was patronised by great rulers, such as Egyptian Queen Arsinou and Philip II of Macedon. Samothraki's sacred function remained until paganism was forbidden in the 4th century AD.

The principal Thracian deity, the Great Mother (Alceros Cybele), was worshipped as a fertility goddess and, when the original Thracian religion became integrated with the state religion, was merged with the Olympian female deities Demeter, Aphrodite and Hecate. The last of these was a mysterious goddess associated with darkness, the underworld and witchcraft. Other deities worshipped at Samothraki's temple were the Great Mother's consort, the virile young Kadmilos (god of the phallus), later integrated with the Olympian god Hermes and the demonic Kabeiroi twins, Dardanos and Aeton, later integrated with Castor and Pollux (the Dioscuri), the twin sons of Zeus and Leda. These twins were invoked by mariners to protect them against the perils of the sea. Samothraki's Great Gods were venerated for their immense power; in comparison, the bickering Olympian gods were frivolous and fickle, almost comic characters.

Today we know little about how the Great Gods were worshipped; initiates who revealed the rites were punished by death. The archaeological evidence, however, suggests that two initiations, a lower and a higher, were held. In the first, the Great Gods were invoked to grant the initiate a spiritual rebirth; in the second, the candidate was absolved of transgressions. All were allowed to participate.

The site's most celebrated relic, the *Winged Victory of Samothrace* (now in the Louvre in Paris), was found by Champoiseau, the French consul, at Adrianople (present-day Edirne in Turkey) in 1863. Subsequent excavations were sporadic until just before WWII, when Karl Lehmann and Phyllis Williams Lehmann of the Institute of Fine Arts, New York University, directed an organised dig.

Exploring the Site

The Sanctuary of the Great Gods' site is extensive but well labelled. After entering, take the left-hand path to the rectangular **anaktoron**. At its southern end was a **sacristy**, the antechamber where white-gowned candidates assembled before going to the *anaktoron's* main room for their first (lower) initiation. One by one, each initiate would then enter the small inner temple at the northern end of the building, where a priest would disclose the meanings of the ceremony's symbols. Afterwards the initiates received a sort of initiation certificate back in the sacristy.

Sacrifices took place in the **arsinoein**, southwest of the *anaktoron*. Once a grand cylindrical structure, it was built in 289 BC as a gift to the Great Gods from the Egyptian queen Arsinou. Southeast of it stands the **sacred rock**, the site's original altar.

Following the initiations, a celebratory feast was held, probably in the **temenos** to the south of the *arsinoein*, a gift from Philip II of Macedon. Adjacent is the prominent Doric **hieron**, the sanctuary's most photographed ruin, with five of its columns reassembled. Initiates received their second (higher) initiation here.

Opposite the *hieron* stand remnants of a **theatre**. Nearby, a path ascends to the **Nike monument** where once stood the magnificent

Winged Victory of Samothrace, a gift from Demetrius Poliorketes (the 'besieger of cities') to the Kabeiroi for helping him defeat Ptolemy II in battle. The ruins of a massive **stoa**, a two-aisled portico where pilgrims to the sanctuary sheltered, lie to the northwest. Initiates' names were recorded on its walls. Ruins of the **medieval fortress** lie to the north of the stoa.

A good site map is located on the path east from the Nike monument; the path continues to the southern **necropolis**, Samothraki's most important ancient cemetery, used from the Bronze Age to early Roman times. North of the cemetery once stood the sanctuary's elaborate Ionic entrance, the **propylon**, a gift from Ptolemy II.

MUSEUM

The admission cost includes the site's well-labelled **museum** (☎ 25510 41474; ⏱ 8.30am-3pm Tue-Sun). Exhibits include terracotta figurines, vases, jewellery and a plaster cast of the *Winged Victory of Samothrace.*

AROUND SAMOTHRAKI

Loutra (Therma) Λουτρά (Θερμά)

Loutra (interchangeably called Therma) is 14km east of Kamariotissa and near the coast. It's the most popular village for accommodation on Samothraki, a relaxing village of plane and horse chestnut trees, dense greenery and gurgling creeks. At night young people staying in local domatia or the nearby camping grounds congregate in its café and there is a laid-back feel to the place.

The village's synonymous names refer to its therapeutic, mineral-rich springs; a dip in the **thermal bath** (☎ 25510 98229; admission €3; ⏱ 7-10.45am & 4-7.45pm Jun-Sep) is said to cure everything from skin problems and liver ailments to infertility. The prominent white building by the bus stop houses the official bath; however, bathing for free can be done at another indoor bath, 50m up the road to the right of the main one, and at two small outdoor baths another 20m up the hill.

SLEEPING & EATING

Samothraki's two popular camping grounds are both on the beach east of Loutra. They are both called 'Multilary Camping' (no, they don't mean 'Military') and are quite similar. If you come before the camping grounds are officially open, you can usually stay for free.

Multilary Camping I (Camping Plateia; ☎ 25510 41784; sites per adult/tent €3/3; ✆ Jun-Aug) A shady, laid-back place on the left 2km beyond Loutra.

Multilary Camping II (☎ 25510 41491; sites per adult/ tent €3/3; ✆ Jun-Aug) A little further past Multi-lary Camping I, with a minimarket, restaurant and showers.

Studios Ktima Holovan (☎ 25510 98335; 6976695591; d/t €70/80) Located 16km east of Kamariotissa, before the Fonias River, this is a relaxing place for families or groups of friends. While the friendly owners would seem to offer enough with these very modern, two-room self-catering studios set on a grassy lawn 50m from the beach, and a mini-playground for kids, the price also includes a free rental car.

Mariva Bungalows (☎ 25510 98230; fax 25510 98374; d incl breakfast €80; ✆) These secluded bungalows, with breezy modern rooms, enjoy a great setting on a lush hill side near a waterfall. To reach the bungalows take the turning from the coast road, which leads inland towards Loutra, and then the first left. Follow the signs to the bungalows, which is 600m further.

Most of the food offerings in Loutra are *souvlaki* joints, though **Paradisos Restaurant** (☎ 25510 95267; mains €5-7) at the back of the village and **Fengari Restaurant** (☎ 25510 98321; mains €5.50-9) are two reasonable options, the latter slightly more adventurous; try its stuffed goat or *imam tourlou* (roast eggplant stuffed with potatoes and pumpkin).

Kafeneio Ta Therma (☎ 25510 98325) is also a very popular place in the town centre. This big open café near the baths is always full, whether for coffee in the morning, beer at night or home-made fruit sweets any time.

Fonias River

After Loutra on the northeast coast is the Fonias River, where the famous **Vathres rock pools** (admission €1) are located. The walk starts at the river bridge 4.7km east of Loutra, by the ticket booths. However, the site is unfenced and the ticket booths are only open in summer. The first 40 minutes of the walk are easy and on a well-marked track; you will then reach a large rock pool fed by a dramatic 12m-high waterfall. The cold water is very refreshing on a hot summer's day. The river is known as the 'Murderer', and in winter rains can transform the waters into a raging torrent. The real danger, however, is getting lost: though there are six waterfalls, marked paths only run to the first two; after that, the walk

becomes dangerously confusing. For serious hiking here and in the Mt Fengari area, first consult **Niki Tours** (☎ 25510 41465; niki_tours@hotmail .com) in Kamariotissa.

Beaches

Samothraki's best beach is the 800m-long **Pahia Ammos**, a superb stretch of sand along an 8km winding road from Lakoma on the south coast. In summer caïques from Kamariotissa may visit the beach, and the boat tour from Loutra stops around the headland at the equally superb, nudist-friendly **Vatos Beach**.

From Pahia Ammos, the former Greek island of Imvros (Gökçeada), ceded to the Turks under the Treaty of Lausanne in 1923, is sometimes visible.

Samothraki's other superlative beach, the pebbled **Kipos Beach** on the southeast coast, is accessible via the road skirting the north coast. The only facilities here are a shower and a freshwater fountain, and there is no shade; like the others, it can be reached in summer by caïque or excursion boat.

Other Villages

The small villages of **Profitis Ilias**, **Lakoma** and **Xiropotamos** in the southwest, and **Alonia** near Hora, are all serene and seldom visited, though they're linked on asphalt roads. The hill-side Profitis Ilias, with many trees and springs, has several tavernas, of which **Vrahos** (☎ 25510 95264) is famous for its roast goat.

THASOS ΘΑΣΟΣ

pop 13,530
Child friendly, lined with sandy beaches and very green, Thasos is one of the most popular Greek islands for families, though it does attract many 20-somethings, too. Indeed, if you're tired of meeting the same-old Euro/Anglo travellers, then Thasos, much-frequented by natives of ex-Yugoslav republics, Bulgaria and Romania, is the place to go. And, since it's just 10km from Kavala on the mainland, Thasos is an easy hop for independent travellers crossing northern Greece to or from Turkey.

While this proximity to the mainland has brought Thasos within the package-tour orbit, the island is only really crowded in July and August, and even then there are numerous empty beaches and hidden coves tucked away

THASOS

0 ——— 6 km
0 ——— 4 miles

To Kavala (10km)

Thasos Strait

To Keramoti (5km)

Glyfoneri

Pahys Beach
Cape Pahis
Skala Rahonis
Cape Vriokastro

Vasiliou
Cape Prinos
Skala Prinou
Agios Georgiou
Thasos (Limenas)
Makryammos

Prinos
Rahoni
Skala Sotira
Kasaviti (Megalos Prinos)
Hrysi Ammoudia (Golden Beach)
Cape Pyrgos

Kasaviti (Mikros Prinos)
Panagia
Potamia
Skala Potamia

Skala Kallirahis
Thasos
Maries
Mt Ypsario (1204m)

Kallirahi
Kastro
Kinira
Kinera Islet

Skala Marion
Kalyvia
Theologos
Paradise Beach

Limenaria
Pefkari
Alyki
Cape Stavros

Cape Kefalas
Potos

Moni Arhangelou
THRACIAN SEA

To Panagia Islet (10m)
Cape Salonikios

on its pine-ringed shores, connected by frequent buses plying the circular coastal road. Further inland, Thasos' traditional mountain villages, shaded by huge oaks and plane trees, feature old stone-and-slate architecture, crystal-clear mountain waterfalls, and great hiking and mountain biking opportunities.

The island of Thasos has a long and varied history, and the excellent little archaeological museum in the capital, Thasos (Limenas), tells some of the story. A few Greco-Roman remains in the town, a submerged ancient marble quarry, Byzantine monasteries and Neolithic tombs comprise the island's historical attractions.

In ancient times Thasos became wealthy enough to build a navy, due to its gold deposits. The Parians who founded the ancient city of Thasos (Limenas) in 700 BC struck gold at Mt Pangaion, and started a lucrative export trade. While the gold is long gone, Thasos' ancient gift of white marble – said to be the second whitest in the world – is still being exploited, much to the consternation of local environmentalists who decry the defacement of mountainsides this mining has caused. At the same time subdued exploration for offshore oil continues in the waters between Thasos and Kavala.

Thasos is part of the prefecture of Macedonia, and though an island, is considered more like an aquatic extension of northern Greece. This perception has resulted in a short high season; travellers coming before or after July and August, therefore, can have this, the so-

called 'emerald isle,' all to themselves. Indeed, some of the island's best activities happen in low season. In early spring Greece's largest sea cormorant colony, nesting on the islet of Panagia, hatches its young, and in late April there's the increasingly popular Thasos International Mountain Biking Race.

Getting There & Away
FERRY
Ferries go every two hours in summer between mainland Kavala and Skala Prinou (€3.30, 1¼ hours). Direct ferries to Thasos (Limenas), leave from Keramoti, 46km southeast of Kavala (€2, 40 minutes). The latter is best for those flying in to Kavala's airport, which is much closer to Keramoti than to Kavala. From the airport, take a taxi (€10, 15 minutes) to Keramoti.

On Thasos, get ferry schedules at the **ferry ticket booths** (☎ 25930 22318) and **port police** (☎ 25930 22106) in Thasos (Limenas) and Skala Prinou. The ferry dock for Keramoti is 150m west of Thasos town centre.

HYDROFOIL
Four daily hydrofoils connect Skala Prinou and Kavala (€7.50, 40 minutes); although the competition might tell you they don't, another four daily hydrofoils go directly from Thasos (Limenas) to Kavala (€10, 40 minutes). In Kavala, hydrofoils wait on the dock just behind the main intercity bus station, beside the small port police kiosk.

Getting Around
BICYCLE
While basic bikes are rented in Thasos (Limenas), serious mountain bikers should head to Potos on the west coast, where top-of-the-line models and detailed route information are available from the island's mountain biking expert, **Yiannis Raizis** (☎ 25930 52459; 6946955704; www.mtb-thassos.com).

BUS
At least for its buses, Thasos puts many other Greek islands to shame. Frequent buses circle the coast in both directions and service inland villages, too. Buses to various destinations meet all arriving ferries at Skala Prinou and Thasos (Limenas), the island's transport hub.

There are 10 daily buses from Thasos (Limenas) through the west-coast villages to

Limenaria (€3.80) and Potos (€4), with four continuing to the inland village of Theologos (€5.10). From Thasos (Limenas) four buses daily go further south to the beach village of Alyki (€3.20) and the nearby Moni Arhangelou. From Potos you can follow the same route to these places on to the east coast and Paradise Beach, Skala Potamia (€3.80) and nearby Hrysi Ammoudia (Golden Beach).

In summer 10 daily buses go the other way from Thasos (Limenas) to these east-coast villages, servicing Skala Potamia (€1.50) via Panagia (€1.20) and Potamia (€1.20). Doing a grand circular tour of the island (about 100km) is possible nine times daily (€9.10, 3½ hours), clockwise or counterclockwise. The **bus station** (☎ 25930 22162) on the waterfront in Thasos (Limenas) provides timetables, and sometimes the driver can, too.

CAR & MOTORCYCLE

Avis Rent a Car Thasos (Limenas) (☎ 25930 22535; fax 25930 23124); Potamia (☎ 25930 61735); Skala Prinou (☎ 25930 72075) has a big presence, though smaller, local companies may offer better rates. In Thasos (Limenas), **Billy's Bikes** (☎ 25930 22490), opposite the Newsagent, and **2 Wheels** (☎ 25930 23267), on the road to Prinos, specialise in bike and motorcycle rental.

EXCURSION BOAT

The **Eros 2 excursion boat** (☎ 6944945282) makes full-day trips (€25) around Thasos four times weekly, with stops for swimming and a barbecue. The boat leaves from the Old Harbour at 10am. Water taxis also run regularly to Hrysi Ammoudia (Golden Beach) and Makryammos beach from the Old Harbour. Excursion boats of varying sizes, nationalities and alcohol content set sail regularly from the coastal resort villages as well.

TAXI

The Thasos (Limenas) **taxi rank** (☎ 25930 223391) is on the central waterfront, next to the main bus stop. In Potos, a taxi rank with listed prices is besides the main road's bus stop.

THASOS (LIMENAS) ΘΑΣΟΣ (ΛΙΜΕΝΑΣ)

pop 2610 / area 375 sq km

The capital, Thasos (also called Limenas), has the island's most services and year-round life, as well as a picturesque fishing harbour, sandy beach, shopping, and moderately edifying ancient ruins and an archaeological museum. Still, considering the relatively expensive accommodation rates and lacklustre restaurant offerings, and the superior beaches, mountain forests and nightlife further on, lingering here isn't necessary.

Orientation & Information

Depending on your needs, the town's main shopping thoroughfare (18 Oktovriou) and its touristy shops will seem either an eyesore or an invaluable arsenal for equipping small children for the beach. Several ATMs are found along it near the central square. The National Bank of Greece, on the waterfront, has an ATM. The town beach, backed by waterfront tavernas and beach bars, is about 100m beyond the old harbour, a 10-minute walk from the town centre.

Billias Travel Service (☎ 25930 24003; www.billias -travel-service.gr; Gallikis Arheologikis Scholis 2) An all-services travel agency near the central square.

Children's Arcade (Opposite Hotel Angelica on waterfront) Has bumper cars, air hockey and other diversions.

Mood Café (☎ 25930 23419; cnr 18 Oktovriou & K Dimitriadi; per hr €3; ☺ 10am-2am) Internet café with fast connection.

Newsagent (Theogenous) Sells English-language newspapers.

Port police (☎ 25930 22106)

Tourist police (☎ 25930 23111)

www.gothassos.com Useful inside information and photos of Thasos.

Sights

Thasos' **archaeological museum** (☎ 25930 22180; ☺ 9am-3pm Tue-Sun), next to the ancient *agora* at the Old Harbour, caused a stir when it reopened after a lengthy hiatus. Moreover, it keeps expanding, with the most recent new additions being Neolithic utensils and other finds from a mysterious tomb in central Thasos. Exhibitions from the classic period spotlight Theagenes, an Olympic champion of the 5th century BC. However, the 5m-tall 6th-century BC *kouros* carrying a ram looms largest.

Next to the museum is the **ancient agora**, once the bustling centre of commerce for ancient and Roman Thasos. The foundations of stoas, shops and dwellings remain. Nearby, the **ancient theatre** stages performances of ancient dramas and comedies as part of the Kavala Festival of Drama (p410). The theatre is signposted from the small harbour.

THASOS (LIMENAS)

INFORMATION	
ATM	1 C2
Billias Travel Service	2 B2
Children's Arcade	3 C1
Mood Café	4 B2
National Bank of Greece	5 B2
Newsagent	6 C2

SIGHTS & ACTIVITIES	
Ancient Agora	7 D2
Archaeological Museum	8 C2

SLEEPING	
Amfipolis Hotel	9 C2
Hotel Akropolis	10 B3
Hotel Alkyon	11 B2
Hotel Angelica	12 C1
Hotel Mironi	13 A3
Hotel Possidon	14 C2
Hotel Timoleon	15 B2

EATING	
I Pigi Grill Room	16 B2
Simi	17 D1

DRINKING	
Grand Café	18 B3
To Karanti	19 D1

TRANSPORT	
Avis Rent a Car	20 B2
Babis Bikes	21 B2
Billy's Bikes	22 C2
Bus Station	23 B2
Ferries to Kavala	24 B2
Ferry Ticket Booths	25 B2
Taxi Rank	26 B2
Tickets for Eros 2 Excursion Boat	27 D1

From the theatre a path leads up to the **acropolis** of ancient Thasos, where substantial remains of a medieval fortress stand on the foundations of the town's ancient walls and where there are magnificent views of the coast. A carved rock staircase descends to the ancient wall's foundations. The Limenas–Panagia road is nearby.

Festivals & Events

In July and August performances of various ancient plays are held in the ancient theatre as part of the **Kavala Festival of Drama**. An annual **Full Moon concert** takes place each August; admission is free and singers come from all over Greece to participate. The **EOT** (☎ 2510 22425) in Kavala has information and tickets, or ask at the the **tourist police** (☎ 25930 23111) on Thasos. The **Thasos Festival** takes place almost every year during summer, featuring everything from classical drama and painting exhibitions to contemporary Greek rock. Programmes are widely available at hotels, cafés and tourist agencies.

Sleeping

Good budget accommodation in central Thasos (Limenas) is decidedly scarce, though nice midrange options exist and prices are sometimes lower for walk-in bookings, depending on season and occupancy.

BUDGET & MIDRANGE

Hotel Alkyon (☎ 25930 22148; fax 25930 23662; 18 Oktovriou; s/d €35/45) This almost budget option near the harbour has clean, though well-equipped, rooms that can get hot at night. Dynamic owner Persephone is famous for her home-made lemon meringue pie.

Hotel Akropolis (☎ /fax 25930 22488; M Alexandrou; s/d incl breakfast €45/55; ✿) This century-old mansion offers a classic touch, with eclectic antiques and a relaxing garden, though rooms are slightly cramped.

ourpick Hotel Possidon (☎ 25930 22739; www .thassos-possidon.com; Old Harbour; s/d €45/60; ✿) This friendly waterfront hotel's recently renovated lobby bar straddles both the harbour and main shopping street of 18 Oktovriou. It's one of the few hotels in town that doesn't work with package-tour companies. Rooms are modern and well maintained, many with comfortable balconies overlooking the water. Co-manager Nikos Stefanopoulos is proud to point out that the Possidon's rooftop bar, where he can sometimes be found playing reggae and world music, is the only one in town.

Hotel Angelica (☎ 25930 22387; www.hotel-angelica .gr; Old Harbour; s/d €50/60; ⊠) Another waterfront hotel, the Angelica is a dependable choice, though it does not overwhelm. Bathrooms are a bit dated but clean.

Hotel Mironi (☎ 25930 23256; fax 25930 22132; s/d/t €45/60/70; ⊠) On a hill near some of the capital's better bars, the Mironi has an unfailingly polite and helpful staff, though rooms are more adequate than inspirational.

TOP END
Hotel Timoleon (☎ 25930 22177; fax 25930 23277; Old Harbour; s/d €70/100; ⊠) Located next to the Hotel Possidon on the waterfront, the three-star Timoleon has 30 rooms (15 with sea view) characterised by smooth fixtures and spacious interiors; considering the price, though, perhaps not unique enough.

Amfipolis Hotel (☎ 25930 23101; www.hotelamfi polis.gr; cnr 18 Oktovriou & Theogenous; s/d/ste incl breakfast €80/120/200; ☑ Jun-Oct; ⊠ ⓢ) A grand recent renovation has brought wi-fi and a garden Jacuzzi seating five, among other innovations, to this national heritage–listed hotel with an imposing blue façade. Unquestionably the town's poshest place to stay, the Amfipolis, a hotel since 1938 and previous to that a tobacco warehouse, has elegant rooms with high, wood-panelled ceilings. Its well-known restaurant was closed at the time of writing, but was expected to reopen by this book's publication.

Makryammos Bungalows (☎ 25930 22101; www.makryammos-hotel.gr; s/d/tr incl breakfast & dinner €145/195/242; Ⓟ ⊠ ⓢ) This beach-front family resort 2km southeast of Thasos (Limenas) offers a small zoo, mini-club, tennis and basketball courts, and a pool for children, and for your inner child, yoga, tai chi and pottery classes. The hotel's unique layout means that its 200 or so bungalows are all but hidden in wooded groves behind the beach, guaranteeing privacy and serenity. Several on-site restaurants and bars add to the resort feel, as does the private boat running guests over to Thasos (Limenas) several times daily.

Eating & Drinking
Dining in Thasos (Limenas) has become both more bland and more expensive, as beach-front restaurants bank on location to save them from innovation. The drinking scene is more sedate than at the coastal beach resorts, though satisfactory watering holes do exist.

I Pigi Grill Room (☎ 25930 22941; Central Square; mains €5-7.50; ☑ dinner) This friendly, central restaurant next to a spring can seem to blend in with other nearby eateries, but is a cut above when it comes to Greek meats; seafood mezedhes and fresh salads are good, too.

Simi (☎ 25930 22517; Old Harbour; mains €7-10) At first glance, Simi looks like all the other Old Harbour tavernas with touting waiters; however, locals agree that it's the best place in town for fresh fish. A full menu of other food, including mezedhes and meat, is also offered.

Taverna Tarsanas (☎ 25930 23933; mezedhes €4, mains €10-15) Located 1km west of Thasos on the site of a former boatbuilder's, Tarsanas is known for its great fresh fish and unique seafood mezedhes.

To Karanti (☎ 25930 24014; Miaouli) An outdoor *ouzerie* on the Old Harbour frequented by locals as well as by tourists, To Karanti's picturesque setting opposite bobbing fishing boats is complemented by its traditional Greek music and tasty mezedhes.

Drift (Old Harbour) This chilled-out beach bar with wispy coloured curtains comes alive at night when its young international crowd trades in their frappes for cocktails.

Karnagio (☎ 25930 23170) Any long leisurely walk beyond the Old Harbour is made worthwhile when it ends at Karnagio, a nice open spot for a quiet sunset drink near the beach.

Grand Café (☎ 6948573947; cnr K Dimitriadi & Pavlou Melas; ☑ until late) Perhaps the best regular bar in Thasos (Limenas), the Grand Café has soft corner couches and caters to a mixed Greek/international crowd. In the same area as the town's few nightclubs, it's visible from its checkerboard pillars out the front. Friendly owner Dimitris Dimitriadis insists he was not named after the street on which his bar is located.

WEST COAST
Thasos' west coast consists of sandy beaches hidden by pines and seaside villages, which are accompanied by almost homonymous settlements further inland, the latter presaging the little-visited mountain wilds of central Thasos. There are ATMs in Skala Prinou, Limenaria and Potos.

Following the coast southwest from Thasos (Limenas), two sandy beaches emerge, first **Glyfoneri** and then **Pahys Beach**. The first real village, **Skala Rahonis**, is a package-tour destination, but has an excellent camping ground. The next coastal village, the port of **Skala Prinou**, is where you get on or off ferries to Kavala; though it has some services, accommodation and an ATM, there's little reason to linger. However, 1km south, the lovely beach of **Vasiliou** stands backed by trees, and the inland, hill-side villages of **Mikros Prinos** and **Megalos Prinos** (collectively known as **Kasaviti**) offer a refreshingly lush break from the touristed coast. Further down, two more small beaches appear at **Skala Sotira** and **Skala Kallirahis**. Some 2km inland from the latter, traditional **Kallirahi** features steep narrow streets and old stone houses.

Further on, **Maries** is another lovely inland village, accessible from its coastal companion, **Skala Marion**. The improbable turn-of-the-century capital of German industry on Thasos, Skala Marion is where long ago the Speidel Metal Company mined iron ore for export. Beaches line both sides of the village, and continue in long stretches between it and **Limenaria**, Thasos' second-largest town. Although it looks rather ungainly from the road, Limenaria has a nice, though small, sandy beach. The allure of the German industrialists accounts for its creation in 1903, and Speidel's ruined buildings, including a circular tower, still loom over the sea by the waterfront.

A few kilometres further south, the fishing-villages-turned-resorts of **Potos** and **Pefkari** have long sandy beaches, half of the former now lined with cafés and tavernas. Potos is a good base for explorating southwestern Thasos. A wooded 10km road leads inland from it to **Theologos**, Thasos' medieval and Ottoman capital. Theologos is a beautiful traditional village of whitewashed stone-and-slate houses set amid mountain foliage, and enjoys regular public bus service.

The drive southeast from Potos rounding the coast opens onto stunning, cliff-top views of southern bays, some with pristine sandy beaches that are usually almost empty and accessible by dirt roads. Continuing east on the main road, you will soon enough come upon **Moni Arhangelou** (admission free; ☉ 9am-5pm Mon Sun), an Athonite dependency and working nunnery, where those improperly attired will get shawled up for the tour of the monastery and its 400-year-old church; as at many Orthodox monasteries, pilgrims can stay overnight for free provided they attend services. Built on top of cliffs, the monastery has magnificent views of the sea, coast and far-off Mt Athos.

Activities
Nature lovers and outdoor-sports enthusiasts will be satiated on Thasos' west coast, where the range of activities includes scuba diving, mountain biking, bird-watching and more.

From Potos, bird-watching boat trips to little **Panagia Islet**, a rocky, uninhabited islet covered with wild olive trees, and home to Greece's largest colony of sea cormorants, can be arranged by local environmentalist Yiannis Markianos at Aldebaran Pension (opposite).

Also from Potos, the annual **Thasos International Mountain Biking Race** kicks off on the last Sunday in April. Fast becoming Greece's most popular amateur race, drawing over 200 contestants and counting, this 53km event follows a circular route from Potos east across the island's wooded interior, scales the 1204m Mt Ypsario and returns through the scenic village of Kastro. Incredibly, the entry fee is only €20, including three nights' hotel accommodation. To participate, contact **Yiannis Raizis** (☎ 25930 52459; 6946955704; www.mtb-thassos .com). Yiannis also rents high-quality mountain bikes year-round from his domatia in Potos, and runs guided biking and hiking tours of Thasos' hidden interior.

Further north, at the inland village of **Rahoni**, **Pine Tree Paddock** (☎ 6945118961; ☉ 10am-2pm & 5pm-sunset) rents mountain ponies and horses (per hour €20), and does guided trail rides (per hour €25); call 24 hours in advance to reserve.

Scuba-diving lessons for beginners and excursions for the experienced are both offered in Potos by Vasilis Vasiliadis of **Diving Club Vasiliadis** (☎ 6944542974; www.scuba-vas.gr); one of the most popular dives takes you to the underwater ancient marble quarry near Alyki on the south coast.

Sleeping
The seaside villages and coast are lined with signposted hotels and domatia. Inland villages sometimes have rooms, too.

Camping Pefkari (☎ 25930 51190; sites per adult/tent €3.60/4.30; ☉ Jun-Sep) Located on a wooded spot above Pefkari beach, this appealing camping ground is popular with families and has very clean bathrooms; a minimum three-night stay is required.

Camping Daedalos (☎ /fax 25930 58251; sites per adult/tent around €5/2.50) Camping north of Skala Sotira is made easy at Daedalos, where tents can be rented. This beach-front camping ground includes a minimarket and restaurant

Sailing, windsurfing and water-skiing lessons are offered, too.

our pick **Aldebaran Pension** (☎ 25930 52494, 6973209576; www.gothassos.com; Potos; d from €20; 🌐) One street back from Potos beach, and set in a relaxing, leafy courtyard, rooms at this great budget family-run hotel have satellite TV, refrigerator and generous balconies. Travellers can benefit from the vast local knowledge of friendly owner Yiannis Markianos, who also runs the informative Gothassos.com website. Yiannis rents boats and can arrange bird-watching boat trips to Panagia Islet.

MTB Yiannis Raizis Domatia (☎ 25930 52459, 6946955704; www.mtb-thassos.com; Potos; d/tr/q €45/50/55; 🌐) A good option for large groups, these spacious self-catering studios run by mountain biking enthusiast Yiannis Raizis fit two to eight people. The place is located on Potos' main road, 20m past the church and a five-minute walk from the beach. There are sea views from the roof garden, an adjacent pool and shaded lawn bar, and a weekly 'curry night' to placate British guests.

Alexandra Beach Hotel (☎ 25930 52391; www.alexandrabeach.gr; d incl full board from €150; P 🌐 🍴) One of Thasos' very few real resorts, the Alexandra Beach offers everything from total relaxation 'antistress programmes' to active activities such as tennis and volleyball, and it has two mini-soccer fields: nonguests can pay to play. Unfortunately, few rooms have sea views.

Eating

O Georgios (☎ 25930 52774; mains €4.50-7) This traditional Greek grillhouse set in a pebbled rose garden is a local favourite away from the tourist strip on Potos' main road, offering friendly service and big portions. Try the excellent, slow-roasted pork and chicken, or get adventurous with *sykoti* (liver), *kokoretsi* (lamb innards) or *kefalaki* (lamb brain) – all washed down, of course, with a cold beer.

Piatsa Michalis (☎ 25930 51574; mains €5.50-8) This 48-year-old beachfront taverna in Potos likes to start you off with a complementary ouzo and finish you with a complementary sweet Greek cake. In between, try the stewed rabbit or octopus in red-wine sauce, or choose from the day's fresh fish – which might just include the infamous sea scorpion.

Pefkospilia (☎ 25930 81051; mezedhes €3-6, mains €8-12) At Pahys Beach, in the shade of a large pine tree, this family-run taverna is strong on fish, such as the prized *mourmoura* (striped

seabream), crab salad, and octopus and squid dishes.

Psarotaverna To Limani (☎ 25930 52790; mains €8-13) The best spot for seafood in Limenaria, this waterfront restaurant opposite the National Bank of Greece has a good range of fresh fish, though prices can be steep.

Ciao Tropical Beach Bar (☎ 25930 81136) On Pahys Beach, this is the bar to kick back and feel Hawaiian. All the fixtures, from the umbrellas to the wood-carved lamps and furniture, have been crafted by the owner's own hand, and the drinks have a similarly South-Seas character.

EAST COAST

Thasos' east coast has the island's most famous long sandy beaches, and they do get packed in summer; nevertheless, it's less built up than the west coast and has a more relaxed feel. It also has some unique mountain villages and great natural attractions. The curious road signs on the main road near the inland mountain villages of **Panagia** and **Potamia**, referring to (Thasos) Limenas as Limin, date from a time when Panagia was the island's capital and Limenas just its harbour; the word Limin is the ancient Greek term for Limenas, and the old signs are residual reminders of the Katharevousa (linguistic 'cleansing') movement popular in the mid-20th century, which sought, unsuccessfully, to replace modern Greek with an archaising 'high' form of the language.

Despite being popular with tourists, these villages have retained their characteristic architecture, especially Panagia with its stone-and-slate rooftops and sumptuously decorated, blue-and-white domed **Church of the Kimisis tou Theotokou** (Church of the Dormition of the Virgin), which also has a valuable icon collection. To reach this peaceful quarter, follow the sound of rushing spring water upwards along a stone path heading inland. Potamia is less picturesque, but does boast a museum devoted to Greek-American artist Polygnotos Vagis, who was born here in 1894; the **Polygnotos Vagis Museum** (☎ 25930 61400; admission €3; ⏰ 8.30am-noon & 6-8pm Tue-Sat, until noon Sun & holidays) is beside the main church. (The Municipal Museum of Kavala also has a collection of Vagis' work – see p101.)

Potamia also makes a good jumping-off point for climbing Thasos' highest peak, **Mt Ypsario** (1204m), and for general hiking. A tractor trail west from Potamia continues to the valley's end, after which arrows and cairns point the way along a steep path upwards. The Ypsario hike is classified as being of 'moderate difficulty' and takes about three hours. You can sleep over at the **Ypsario Mountain Shelter** (☎ 6972198032; shelter €5), but first phone Leftheris of the Thasos Mountaineering Club (☎ 6972198032) in Thasos (Limenas) to book and pick up the key. The shelter has no electricity, but fireplaces and spring water are provided.

Both Panagia and Potamia are 4km west of the celebrated **Hrysi Ammoudia (Golden Beach)**, fine and sandy and tucked inside a long, curving bay. A short rocky stretch in the middle separates Hrysi Ammoudia from the equally sandy **Skala Potamia** on the southern end. The latter beach has very warm and gentle water, remaining shallow for a long way out, and so is especially good for small children. A bus between the two beaches (€1.20) runs every couple of hours. Both have accommodation, restaurants and some manner of nightlife. There is one Commercial Bank ATM in Skala Potamia, rather oddly set all by itself on the main road, 150m west of the village turn-off.

Further south of Skala Potamia is the nudist-friendly **Paradise Beach**, near the tiny village of **Kinira**; a similarly named islet lies just offshore. Accommodation and services are much more reduced both here and at **Alyki**, the last major beach on the southeast coast. Its two quiet stretches of sand lie back to back on a headland. A small **archaeological site** lies near the southern beach, where an ancient, now submerged **marble quarry** operated from the 6th century BC to the 6th century AD.

Sleeping & Eating

Domatia and small hotels run sporadically down the coast. There are much fewer at Kinira (Paradise Beach) and Alyki than at Hrysi Ammoudia (Golden Beach) and Skala Potamia. At the latter, you can find simple domatia on arrival during high season, even on the beach, especially in the rocky central section dividing Hrysi Amoudia from Skala Potamia beach.

Golden Beach Camping (☎ 25930 61472; fax 25930 61473; Hrysi Ammoudia; sites per adult/tent €3.80/4.20) A party feel pervades Golden Beach, the only camping ground in eastern Thasos. Boasting a minimarket, bar, beach volleyball, and a strong representation of young people from Greece, Serbia, Bulgaria and beyond, Golden Beach is a fun place to be on the best part of the beach.

Hotel Kamelia (☎ 25930 61463; www.hotel-kamelia.gr; Skala Potamia; s/d incl breakfast from €35/54) This recently renovated beach-front hotel has an understated, arty appeal, with flowery canvases, minimalist wall sculptures and cool jazz playing in the lawn-garden bar. The spacious, fresh-smelling rooms have large balconies and all mod cons.

Semeli Studios (☎ 25930 61612; www.semeli-studios.gr; Skala Potamia; d/t €50/60) The Kamelia's friendly owner Eleni Stoubou also has these larger, self-catering options just behind the hotel. From the bus stop, head towards Hryssi Ammoudia on the main road for 100m; both Hotel Kamelia and Semeli Studios are signposted on the right.

Studios Stefanos (☎ 25930 58160; www.thasos.info/stefanos; Hrysi Ammoudia; s/d €60/65) Located just across from Golden Beach Camping, these self-catering studios are kept in good order by the gracious owner, who also runs a well-stocked bar below.

Thassos Inn (☎ 25930 61612; www.thassosinn.gr; Panagia; s/d €50/70) Panagia's best accommodation has a perfect location near the church, with sweeping views of the village's clustered slate rooftops. It has all mod cons and good-sized rooms, though the simple floors are uninspiring. Even if you don't stay, drop in for a coffee on the inn's relaxing patio café – the only place in town serving frappé with ice cream. The inn is run by the welcoming Tasos Manolopoulos, who proudly shows off his vegetable patch and pool of gigantic goldfish.

Taverna Elena (☎ 25930 61709; Panagia; mains €4.50-8) Just next to the traditional products shop off Panagia's central square, this classic taverna has unexpected mezedhes like *bougloundi* (baked feta with tomatoes and chili), and excellent roast lamb and goat.

Restaurant Koralli (☎ 25930 62244; Skala Potamia; mains €6.50-9.50) A big, multilingual menu and waterfront setting often indicates more of the same, but some unique offerings make Koralli stand out. Tasty innovations at this Skala Potamia taverna include mushrooms stuffed with shrimp, eggplant baked with mozzarella and parmesan, zucchinis stuffed with crab, carpaccio and 330g sirloin steaks.

Restaurant Vigli (☎ 25930 61500; Hrysi Ammoudia; fish €8-10) Enjoying the excellent view of the Golden Beach/Skala Potamia bay is only half the experience at this fish taverna up on the northern edge of Hrysi Ammoudia; the fresh fish provides the rest.

Evia & the Sporades
Εύβοια & Οι Σποράδες

In a nation known for its magical islands, Evia and the Sporades are not exactly household names. Some would be surprised, in fact, that Evia is an island at all. Joined by a short bridge at Halkida, and separated from the mainland by a narrow gulf, it's one of those places that seem to be hidden in full view.

Only a couple of hours from Athens, Evia's busy gateway resorts get their car loads of weekend visitors. But across the island, the pace is slower and the landscape pristine for long stretches, dotted by hill-top monasteries, small farms and vineyards, and goats staring at you in the middle of the road. Small beaches dot the west and southeast coasts, many of them with no more than one or two tavernas, and crystal-clear bays that would be lined with matching umbrellas and beach bars elsewhere.

Skyros, the southernmost of the Sporades (in Greek, 'scattered ones'), retains a good deal of local character, and its unique cuisine gets a thumbs up from locals and visitors alike. Closest to the mainland is Skiathos; once a sleepy fishing port, it now sees charter flights from northern Europe, and claims the sandiest beaches in the Aegean, along with several prime diving spots. Low-key Skopelos kicks back with a postcard-worthy harbour and its share of fine bays, beaches and forest meadows laced with old walking trails. Alonnisos, the most remote of the group, anchors the National Marine Park of Alonnisos – established to protect the Mediterranean monk seal – and is a model for ecological awareness throughout Greece. Alonnisos, like much of Evia and the other Sporades, is certain to yield unexpected finds, some from the natural landscape, and others from the good-natured islanders you'll encounter at every turn.

EVIA & THE SPORADES

HIGHLIGHTS

- **Wine & Song** Sipping local wines at the Wine & Cultural Festival in Karystos (p421)
- **Fish Feast** Dining at the fish tavernas at Kalamakia (p436), Alonnisos
- **Wildlife Tours** Spotting young dolphins in the National Marine Park of Alonnisos (p434)
- **Guided Walks** Hiking the high meadows overlooking the neighbouring islands at Skopelos (p431)
- **Romantic Interlude** Enjoying sunset above Linaria Bay (p441) on Skyros
- **Authentic Music** Applauding the bouzouki players above the Kastro on Skopelos (p430)
- **Take the Plunge** Reef diving off Tsougria (p427), Skiathos

Alonnisos
Kastro ★ ★ Kalamakia
Tsougria ★ ★ ★
★ Skopelos
Linaria Bay ★

Karystos ★

■ POPULATION: 228,752	■ AREA: 4167 SQ KM

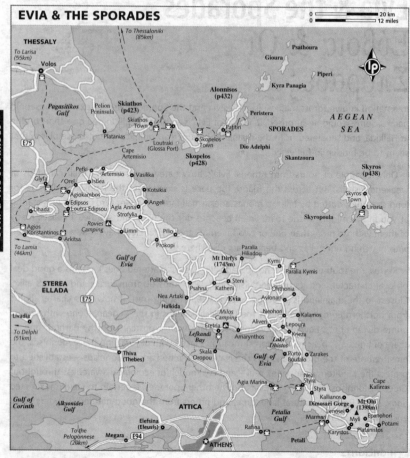

EVIA & THE SPORADES

GETTING THERE & AWAY
Air
Skiathos airport receives charter flights from northern Europe. There are also domestic flight services available from Athens (see p422). Skyros airport also handles domestic flights to and from Athens (see p437), as well as occasional charter flights from Oslo and Amsterdam.

Bus
From Athens' **Terminal B station** (☎ 210 831 7153; Liosion 260), there are buses departing to Halkida (€5.90, 1¼ hours, half-hourly); Paralia Kymis (€13.20, 3½ hours, two daily), for Skyros; and to Agios Konstantinos (€12.90, 2½ hours, hourly), for the Sporades. From

Athens' **Mavromateon terminal** (☎ 210 880 8080), opposite Areos Park, there are frequent buses to Rafina (€2, one hour, every 45 minutes), for Evia.

Ferry
There are daily ferries to the Sporades from both Agios Konstantinos and Volos, and weekly ferries from Thessaloniki to the Sporades, as well as five ferry routes connecting Evia to the mainland.

Updated summer ferry timetables are usually available in late April from the main ferry companies: **GA Ferries** (☎ 210 451 1720; www.ferries.gr/gaferries; Akti Miaouli & Kantharou 2, Piraeus) and **Minoan Lines** (☎ 281 033 0301; www.ferries.gr/minoan/domesticmain.htm; Thermopylon 6-10, Piraeus).

FERRY CONNECTIONS TO EVIA & THE SPORADES

Origin	Destination	Duration	Fare	Frequency
Agia Marina	Evia (Nea Styra)	45min	€2.10	4-6 daily
Agios Konstantinos	Alonnisos	4hr	€36.50	2 daily (jet ferry)
	Skiathos	2½hr	€18	daily
	Skopelos	3½hr	€31.60	1-2 daily
Arkitsa	Evia (Loutra Edipsou)	35min	€1.50	10-12 daily
Evia (Paralia Kymis)	Skyros	1¾hr	€8.30	1-2 daily
Rafina	Evia (Marmari)	1hr	€6	4-6 daily
Glyfa	Evia (Agiokambos)	25min	€1.50	8-12 daily
Skala Oropou	Evia (Eretria)	25min	€1.40	hourly
Thessaloniki	Skiathos	6hr	€17.70	weekly
Volos	Alonnisos	4½hr	€18.90	2 weekly
	Skiathos	2½hr	€14.70	2 daily
	Skopelos	3½hr	€18.90	1-2 daily

Car ferry prices are roughly three times the price for one person. Some one-way prices from the main ports:

Volos–Skiathos (€60)
Agios Konstantinos–Skiathos (€65)
Skiathos–Skopelos/Alonnissos (€18-22)
Evia (Paralia Kymis)–Skyros (€25)

Hydrofoil

There are frequent daily hydrofoil links from both Agios Konstantinos and Volos to the northern Sporades (Skiathos, Skopelos and Alonnisos only). Updated summer hydrofoil timetables are usually available in late April from **Hellenic Seaways** (☎ 210 419 9100; www.hellenicseaways.gr; Akti Kondyli & Etolikou 2, Piraeus GR-185 45). The timetable is also available from local hydrofoil booking offices located in Volos (p101) and Agios Konstantinos (p99).

HYDROFOIL CONNECTIONS TO EVIA & THE SPORADES

Origin	Destination	Duration	Fare	Frequency
Agios Konstantinos				
	Alonnisos	3hr	€36.50	2 daily
	Skiathos	1½hr	€26	2-3 daily
	Skopelos	2½hr	€35.40	2-3 daily
Volos				
	Alonnisos	2½hr	€31.50	3-4 daily
	Skiathos	1¼hr	€24.50	3-4 daily
	Skopelos	2¼hr	€31.50	3-4 daily
	Glossa	1¾hr	€25.50	2-3 daily

Train

There is an hourly train service from Athens' **Larisis station** (☎ 210 524 8829) to Halkida (€5.10, 1½ hours) via Ioni. To Volos, there are several normal trains (€11.30, 5½ hours) and one intercity train (€20.70, 4½ hours).

EVIA ΕΥΒΟΙΑ

Evia (*eh*-vih-ah), Greece's second-largest island after Crete and a prime holiday destination for Greeks, remains less charted by foreign tourists. Its attractions include scenic mountain roads, challenging treks, unusual archaeological finds and mostly uncrowded beaches. A mountainous spine runs north–south, dividing the island's precipitous eastern cliffs from the gentler and resort-friendly west coast. A number of ferry connections, as well as a short bridge over the narrow Evripous Channel to the island's capital, Halkida, connect the island to the mainland. The current in the channel reverses direction around seven times daily, an event whose full explanation has eluded observers since Aristotle.

CENTRAL EVIA

After crossing the bridge to Halkida, the road veers south, following the coastline to Eretria, a bustling resort and major archaeological site. Further on, a string of hamlets and fishing villages dot the route until the junction at Lepoura, where the road forks north towards Kymi. Several branch roads to the sea are worth exploring, and the beach at Kalamos is exceptional.

Along the coastal road south of Eretria you may still see scorched hillsides from the August 2007 forest fires, especially between the small towns of Amarinthos and Aliveri. Inland, in the direction of Steni and Mt Dryfys, several villages were devastated by the fires, resulting in tragic loss of life.

From the hillside town of Kymi, a rough but passable mountain road leads west above the north coastline to Paralia Hiliadou (opposite).

Halkida Χαλκίδα
pop 54,558
Halkida (also called Halkis) was an important city-state in ancient times, with several colonies dotted around the Mediterranean. The name derives from the bronze manufactured here in antiquity (*halkos* means 'bronze' in Greek). Today it's a lively industrial and agricultural town, but with nothing of sufficient note to warrant an overnight stay. However, if you have an hour or so to spare between buses, have a look at the **Archaeological Museum** (☎ 22210 60944; Leoforos Venizelou 13; admission €2; ☼ 8.30am-2.30pm Tue-Sun). It displays prehistoric, Roman and Hellenic finds from Evia's three ancient cities of Halkida, Eretria and Karystos, including the torso of Apollo from the Temple of Dafniforos at Eretria.

For emergencies, call the Halkida **tourist police** (☎ 22210 77777).

ACTIVITIES
The **Sport Apollon Scuba Diving Centre** (☎ 22210 86369; ☼ 9am-1.30pm & 5-9pm) in Halkida organises dives off the Alykes coast, led by dive team Nikos and Stavroula. A one-day dive costs about €40.

SLEEPING & EATING
Hara Hotel (☎ 22210 76305; www.harahotel.gr in Greek; Karoni 21; s/tr/ste €50/80/110, d 60-70; P ⚄) Should your connections require you to stay overnight in this transport hub, head for this smart place, set on the mainland side of town, overlooking the harbour.

GETTING THERE & AWAY
Bus
From **Halkida station** (☎ 22210 22640; cnr Papanastasiou & Venizelou), buses run to Athens (€5.90, 1¼ hours, half-hourly), Eretria (€1.80, 25 minutes, hourly) and Kymi Town (€7.30, two hours, hourly), one of which continues to Paralia Kymis to meet the Skyros ferry. There are also buses to Steni (€2.60, one hour, twice daily), Limni (€6.80, two hours, three daily), Loutra Edipsou (€9.20, 2½ hours, once daily) and Karystos (€10.10, three hours, three daily).

Train
The **Halkida train station** (☎ 22210 22386) is on the mainland side of the bridge. Frequent trains make the run to Athens, via Ioni (normal €5.10, 1½ hours, hourly; intercity €9.40, one hour, three daily) and to Thessaloniki, via Ioni (normal €12.90, 5½ hours, six daily; intercity €33.10, 4½ hours, three daily).

Eretria Ερέτρια
pop 3156
Heading southeast from Halkida, Eretria is the first place of interest, with a small harbour and a lively boardwalk filled with mainland families who pack its fish tavernas on holiday weekends. Ancient Eretria was a major maritime power and home to an eminent school of philosophy. The modern town was founded in the 1820s by islanders from Psara fleeing the Turkish.

INFORMATION
For emergencies, call the Halkida **tourist police** (☎ 22210 77777). For internet access, head to **Christos Internet Cafe-Bar** (☎ 22290 61604; per hr €2; ☼ 9am-1am) on the waterfront.

SIGHTS
From the top of the **ancient acropolis**, at the northern end of town, there are splendid views over to the mainland. West of the acropolis are the remains of a palace, temple and theatre with a subterranean passage once used by actors. Close by, the **Archaeological Museum of Eretria** (☎ 22290 62206; admission €2; ☼ 8.30am-3pm Tue-Sun) contains well-displayed finds from ancient Eretria. A 200m walk will bring you to the fascinating **House of Mosaics**, and ends 50m further at the **Sanctuary of Apollo**.

SLEEPING & EATING
Milos Camping (☎ /fax 22290 60420; www.camping-in -evia.gr/index_en.html; camp sites per adult/tent €6/4.50) This clean, shaded camping ground on the coast 1km northwest of Eretria has a small restaurant, bar and narrow pebble beach.

Island of Dreams Hotel (☎ 22290 61224; www.dream island.com.gr; s/d/f incl breakfast €50/60/95; P ⚄ ⚂) Tucked away on a nearby islet connected by a 20m causeway, the palm tree and bungalow setting is ideal for kids who can play Ping-Pong and minigolf while mum and dad sip a cool one at the beach bar.

Taverna Astra (☎ 22290 64111; Arheou Theatrou 48; mains €4-9) Just past the supermarket, this busy waterfront taverna is known for well-priced fresh fish, along with appetisers like *taramasalata* (purée of fish roe, potato, oil and lemon juice).

GETTING THERE & AWAY
Ferry

Ferries travel between Eretria and Skala Oropou (€1.40, 25 minutes, hourly).

Steni Στενή
pop 926

From Halkida, it's 31km to the lovely mountain village of Steni, with its gurgling springs and shady plane trees.

Steni is the starting point for a serious climb up **Mt Dirfys** (1743m), Evia's highest mountain. The **Dirfys Refuge**, at 1120m, can be reached along a 9km dirt road. From there, it's a steep 7km to the summit. Experienced trekkers should allow about six hours from Steni to the summit. For refuge reservations, contact **Stamatiou** (☎ weekdays 6972026862, weekends 22280 25655; per person €12). For more hiking information, contact the **Halkida Alpine Club** (☎ 22210 25230, 22280 24298; Angeli Gouviou 22, Halkida). An excellent topo/hiking map of *Mt Dirfys* is published by Anavasi (No 5.11).

A rough road continues from Steni to **Paralia Hiliadou** on the north coast, where a grove of maple and chestnut trees borders a fine pebble-and-sand beach, along with a few domatia and tavernas. Campers can find free shelter near the big rocks at either end of the beach.

SLEEPING & EATING
Hotel Dirfys (☎ 22280 51217; s/d incl breakfast €30/40) Conveniently located 50m uphill from the bus terminal, this is the best value of Steni's two hotels. It has comfortable carpeted rooms, pine furniture and balcony views of the forest and stream.

Taverna Orea Steni (☎ 22280 51262; mains €4-8) The best and most attractive among 10 brookside eateries, this taverna offers grills and traditional oven-ready dishes like the popular roast lamb with cheese, along with salads prepared from locally gathered greens.

Kymi & Paralia Kymis
Κύμη & Παραλία Κύμης
pop 3037

The untouristy, workaday town of Kymi is built on a cliff 250m above the sea. Things perk up at dusk when the town square comes to life. The port of Kymi (called Paralia Kymis), 4km downhill, is the only natural harbour on the precipitous east coast, and the departure point for ferries to Skyros.

The excellent **Folklore Museum** (☎ 22220 22011; 10am-1pm & 5-8pm Tue-Sun), 30m downhill from the main square, has an impressive collection of local costumes and historical photos, including a display commemorating Kymi-born Dr George Papanikolaou, inventor of the Pap smear test.

SLEEPING & EATING
Hotel Beis (☎ 22220 22604; fax 22220 29113; Paralia Kymis; s/d incl breakfast €40/60; P ☒) If you need to spend the night, try the reliable Hotel Beis, a cavernous white block with large and spotless rooms. It's conveniently opposite the ferry dock for Skyros.

In Paralia Kymis, a string of tavernas and *ouzeries* lines the waterfront. Try **Taverna Spanos** (☎ 22220 22641), near the port and popular for fresh fish and oven-ready dishes and salads.

Taverna To Balkoni (☎ 22220 24177; Kymi; mains €4-7.50) Head to this family-style eatery for good lamb grills and *pastitsio* (layers of buttery macaroni and seasoned minced lamb), just below the square in Kymi.

NORTHERN EVIA

From Halkida a road heads north to **Psahna**, the gateway to the highly scenic mountainous interior of northern Evia. The road climbs and twists through pine forests to the rambling and woodsy village of **Prokopi**, home of the pilgrimage church of **St John the Russian**. At Strofylia, 14km beyond Prokopi, a road heads southwest to picturesque **Limni**, then north to **Loutra Edipsou** and the ferry port at Agiokambos.

Loutra Edipsou Λουτρά Αιδηψού
pop 3600

The classic spa resort of **Loutra Edipsou** has therapeutic sulphur waters, which have been celebrated since antiquity. Famous skinny dippers have included Aristotle, Plutarch and Sylla. The town's gradual expansion over the years has been tied to the improving technology required to carry the water further and further away from its thermal source. Today the town has two of Greece's most up-to-date hydrotherapy and physiotherapy centres. There's also a good swimming beach (Paralia

Loutron), heated year-round thanks to the thermal waters, which spill into the sea.

INFORMATION

Dr Symeonides (☎ 22260 23220; Omirou 17) English-speaking Greek-Cypriot doctor.

Lan Arena (☎ 22260 22597; internet access per hr €3; ☽ 9am-midnight) Just opposite the ferry port, in a small arcade next to the police station.

Medical Centre (☎ 22260 53311; Istiea)

ACTIVITIES

The more relaxing (and affordable) of the resort's two best-known spas is the **EOT Hydrotherapy-Physiotherapy Centre** (☎ 22260 23501; 25 March St 37; ☽ 7am-1pm & 5-7pm 1 Jun–31 Oct), speckled with palm trees and with a large outdoor pool and terrace overlooking the sea. Whirlpool bath treatments start at a modest €7.

The other is the posh **Thermae Sylla Hotel & Spa** (☎ 22260 60100; www.thermaesylla.gr; Posidonos 2), with a somewhat late-Roman ambience befitting its name, and offering a wide range of health and beauty treatments, from mud baths to seaweed body wraps, from around €70.

SLEEPING & EATING

Prices here reflect the higher summer season, 15 July to 15 September; low-season rates drop about 20%.

our pick **Hotel Aegli** (☎ 22260 22215; fax 22260 22886; Paraliakis 18; s/d/tr from €25/35/45; ☒ ☐) For charm and value, you can't beat this neoclassic holdover from the 1930s. The high-ceilinged rooms are immense, and the lobby is decorated with framed autographs of luminaries who passed by, including Greta Garbo and Winston Churchill. The Aegli also offers 20-minute hydrotherapy baths.

Hotel Kentrikon (☎ /fax 22260 22502; www.kentrikonhotel.com; 25th Martiou 14; s/d/tr €42/60/70; ☒ ☒) The friendly Kentrikon is a combination hotel and spa with old-world charm, large tiled rooms, wood ceilings and balcony views of the sea.

Thermae Sylla Hotel & Spa (☎ 22260 60100; www.thermaesylla.gr; Posidonos 2; d/ste €280/500; ℗ ☒ ☐ ☒) This posh spa offers accommodation along with its beauty treatments. If you wish to stay, you'll find elegant designer rooms with high ceilings and clear views to the sea.

Captain Cook Self-Service Restaurant (☎ 22260 23852; mains €3.50-8) Fill up on oven-ready dishes like *yemista* (stuffed tomatoes and peppers), *psari plaki* (baked fish) or a hearty *psaro-*

soupa (fish soup) at this popular seaside eatery, 200m south from the port.

Taverna Aegli (☎ 22260 22215; Paraliakis 18; mains €4-8) This seaside extension of the Hotel Aegli puts together a few plates of grilled sardines, stuffed zucchini flowers and wine for about €10 per head.

GETTING THERE & AWAY

Bus

From the **bus station** (☎ 22260 22250; Thermopotamou), 250m up from the port, buses run to Halkida (€9.20, 2½ hours, daily at 4pm), Athens (€11.80, 3½ hours, three daily via Arkitsa) and Thessaloniki (€21.30, five hours, daily at 10am via Glyfa).

Ferry

The **ferry** (☎ 22260 31107) runs from mainland Glyfa to Agiokambos (€1.50, 25 minutes, eight to 12 daily) and from mainland Arkitsa to Loutra Edipsou (€2, 40 minutes, 10 to 12 daily).

Limni Λίμνη

pop 2072

One of Evia's most picturesque ports, little Limni faces seaward, its maze of whitewashed houses and narrow lanes spilling onto a busy waterfront of cafés and tavernas. The town's cultural **museum** (☎ 22270 31900; admission €2; ☽ 9am-1pm Mon-Sat, 10.30am-1pm Sun), just 50m up from the waterfront, features local archaeological finds along with antique looms, costumes and old coins. Seldom visited, Limni is well worth a stopover.

With your own transport or a penchant for walking, you can visit the splendid 16th-century **Convent of Galataki**, 8km southeast of Limni on a hillside above the road. The fine mosaics and frescoes in its *katholikon* (main church) merit a look, especially the *Entry of the Righteous into Paradise*. The convent is generally open from 9am to 6pm daily, with a good taverna under the trees nearby.

SLEEPING & EATING

Rovies Camping (☎ 22270 71120; www.campingevia .com/evia-holidays.html; camp sites per adult/tent €6/3.50; ℗) Attractive, shaded and well-tended Rovies sits just above a lovely sand-and-pebble beach, 12km northwest of Limni.

Zaniakos Domatia (☎ 6977936698; s/d €20/25; ☒) At these humble domatia, not much English is in evidence, but the rooms are spotless, quiet and overlook the village.

Ostria Apartments (☎ /fax 22270 32248; www.holi dayshop.gr/tapetrina; apt incl breakfast from €90; P ⊠ ⓡ) Olive trees and bougainvillea surround 10 handsome self-catering apartments across the road from a pool and good beach, 1km northwest of Limni.

Taverna Platanos (☎ 22270 31479; Plateia; mains €3.50-8) Pick an outside table at this inviting waterfront taverna and enjoy the passing parade of villagers, along with excellent Greek standards like souvlaki, *mousakas* and *gavros* (anchovies).

SOUTHERN EVIA

Continuing east from Eretria, the road branches at Lepoura: the left fork leads north to Kymi, the right south to Karystos. A turnoff at Krieza, 3km from the junction, leads to Lake Dhistos, a shallow lake bed favoured by egrets and other wetland birds. Continuing south, you'll pass high-tech windmills and catch views of both coasts as the island narrows until it reaches the sea at Karystos Bay, near the base of Mt Ohi (1398m).

Karystos Κάρυστος
pop 4960

Set on the wide Karystos Bay below Mt Ohi, and flanked by two sandy beaches, Karystos is the best of southern Evia's coastal resorts. The town's central square, Plateia Amalias, faces the bay and boat harbour. Karystos is the starting point for treks to Mt Ohi and the Dimosari Gorge.

INFORMATION
Polihoros Internet & Sports Cafe (☎ 22240 24421; Kriezotou 132; internet access per hr €4; ⏰ 9am-1am) Next to the Galaxy Hotel.

South Evia Tours (☎ 22240 25700; fax 22240 29011; set@eviatravel.gr; Plateia Amalias 7) Helps with local and island information, walking maps and excursions to Mt Ohi and Dimosari Gorge, plus bookings and accommodation.

SIGHTS
Karystos is mentioned in Homer's *Iliad*, and was a powerful city-state during the Peloponnesian Wars. The **Karystos Museum** (☎ 22240 25661; admission €2; ⏰ 8.30am-3pm Tue-Sun) documents the town's archaeological heritage, including tiny Neolithic clay lamps, a stone plaque written in the Halkidian alphabet, 5th-century-BC grave stelae depicting

Zeus and Athena, and an exhibit of the 6th-century *drakospita* (dragon houses) of Mt Ohi and Styra. The museum sits opposite a 14th-century Venetian castle, the **Bourtzi**.

TOURS
South Evia Tours (☎ 22240 25700; fax 22240 29091; set@eviatravel.gr) offers a range of services including car hire, accommodation, maps and excursions in the foothills of Mt Ohi, trips to the 6th-century-BC Roman-built *drakospita* near Skyra, and a cruise around the Petali Islands (€30). The owner, Nikos, can also arrange necessary taxi pick-up or drop-off for serious hikes to the summit of Mt Ohi and back, or guided walks to Dimosari Gorge (€20).

FESTIVALS
Karystos hosts a summer **Wine & Cultural Festival** from early July until the last weekend in August. Weekend happenings include theatre performances and plenty of traditional dancing to the tune of local musicians, along with painting, photo and sculpture exhibits by local artists. The summer merrymaking concludes with the Wine Festival, featuring every local wine imaginable, free for the tasting. Festival schedules are available at the Karystos Museum (left).

SLEEPING & EATING
Hotel Karystion (☎ 22240 22391; www.karystion.gr; Kriezotou 3; s/d incl breakfast €45/55; P ⊠) The Karystion's bright and well-appointed rooms with sea-view balconies are excellent value. A stairway off the courtyard leads to a sandy beach below.

our pick **Cavo d'Oro** (☎ 22240 22326; mains €3.50-7.50) Join the locals in this cheery alleyway restaurant, one block west of the main square, where tasty mains include lamb in lemon sauce along with generous plates of *garidha* (fried shrimp) and homemade *spanakopita* (spinach pie). The helpful and friendly owner, Kostas, is also a regular at the summer wine festival, bouzouki in hand.

Taverna Mesa-Exo (☎ 22240 23997; mains €3.50-8) The name of this boardwalk taverna means 'In-Out' in Greek. Locals love it for its grilled fresh fish, mezedhes (appetisers) and warm atmosphere.

DRINKING
Check out the late-night scene around the *plateia* (square) where **Bar Chroma** (☎ 22240 23085) delivers decent drinks and sounds, or

head to the swank **Club Kohili** (☎ 22240 24350), on the beach by the Apollon Suite Hotel.

GETTING THERE & AWAY
Bus
From the **Karystos bus station** (☎ 22240 26303), opposite Agios Nikolaos church, buses run to Halkida (€10.10, three hours, two daily), to Athens (€8, two hours, four daily) and to Marmari (€1.50, 25 minutes, for ferry to Rafina). A taxi to Marmari is about €11.

Ferry
There is a regular ferry service between Marmari, 10km west of Karystos, and mainland Rafina (€6, one hour, four to six daily). There is also a **ferry service** (☎ 22240 41533, 6944982879) from Nea Styra (35km north of Karystos) to Agia Marina (€2.10, 45 minutes, four to six daily).

Around Karystos
The ruins of **Castello Rosso** (Red Castle), a 13th-century Frankish fortress, are a short walk from **Myli**, a delightful, well-watered village 4km inland from Karystos. A little beyond Myli there is an **ancient quarry** scattered with green and black fragments of the once-prized Karystian *cippolino* marble.

With your own transport, or the help of a taxi, you can get to the base of **Mt Ohi** where a 1½-hour hike to the summit will bring you to the ancient *drakospita*, or dragon houses. The discovery of these Stonehenge-like dwellings hewn from rocks weighing up to several tons has spawned a number of theories regarding their origin, ranging from slave-built temples to UFO getaways.

Hikers can also head north by car from Karystos to the **Dimosari Gorge** and **Lenosei** village with views down to the coastal hamlet of **Kallianos**. A 10km trail to Kallianos can usually be covered in four to five hours (including time for a swim).

With a local map, you can easily explore the villages and chestnut forests nestling in the foothills between Mt Ohi and the coast. For other hikes, check with **South Evia Tours** (☎ 22240 25700; fax 22240 29091; set@eviatravel.gr) for trail conditions and maps.

The **Zarka Centre** (☎ 22230 53991; Zarakes; www .zarkacentre.com) is a residential health and creativity retreat with seminars in yoga, herbal medicine and environmental awareness, all tucked into a tranquil rural setting at Zarakes, between Kymi and Karystos.

SKIATHOS ΣΚΙΑΘΟΣ

pop 6160

The good news is that much of the pine-fringed coast of Skiathos is blessed with exquisite beaches. The bad news is that in July and August the island is overrun with package tourists and hotel prices soar. At the island's small airport, the arrival board is filled with incoming charter flights from northern Europe, not Athens. Despite the large presence of sun-starved Europeans, Skiathos remains one of Greece's premier resorts.

Skiathos Town, the island's major settlement and port, lies on the southeast coast. The rest of the south coast is a string of holiday villas and hotels, plus a number of sandy beaches with pine trees for a backdrop. The north coast is precipitous and less accessible; in the 14th century the Kastro Peninsula served as a natural fortress against invaders. Today, most people come to Skiathos for the sun and nightlife, but the truly curious will discover picturesque monasteries, hill-top tavernas and even secluded beaches.

Getting There & Away
AIR
As well as the numerous charter flights from northern Europe to Skiathos, during summer there is one flight daily to/from Athens (€67). **Olympic Airlines** (☎ 24270 22200) has an office at the airport, not in town.

FERRY
In summer there are ferries from Skiathos to Volos, Agios Konstantinos and Alonnisos via Skopelos. From June through September, there is a ferry service heading north to Thessaloniki, south to Crete and east to Limnos.

Tickets can be purchased from either **Hellenic Seaways** (☎ 24270 22209; fax 24270 22750) at the bottom of Papadiamantis, or from **GA Ferries** (☎ 24270 22204; fax 24270 22979), next to Alpha Bank.

HYDROFOIL
In summer, there are hydrofoils and jet ferries from Skiathos to Alonnisos, Skopelos

FERRY DESTINATIONS FROM SKIATHOS

Destination	Duration	Fare	Frequency
Volos	2½hr	€15	2 daily Jun-Sep
Agios Konstantinos	2½hr	€18	daily Jun-Sep
Alonnisos	2hr	€8.80	daily Jun-Sep
Skopelos	1¼hr	€7.50	daily Jun-Sep
Thessaloniki	6hr	€17.70	4 weekly Jun-Sep
Tinos	10hr	€22.30	2 weekly Jun-Sep
Mikonos	11hr	€21	2 weekly Jun-Sep
Paros	13hr	€29.60	2 weekly Jun-Sep
Naxos	14½hr	€29.90	2 weekly Jun-Sep
Ios	16hr	€32.10	2 weekly Jun-Sep
Santorini	18hr	€33.50	2 weekly Jun-Sep
Iraklio (Crete)	22hr	€38.10	2 weekly Jun-Sep
Limnos	7hr	€15	weekly

EVIA & THE SPORADES

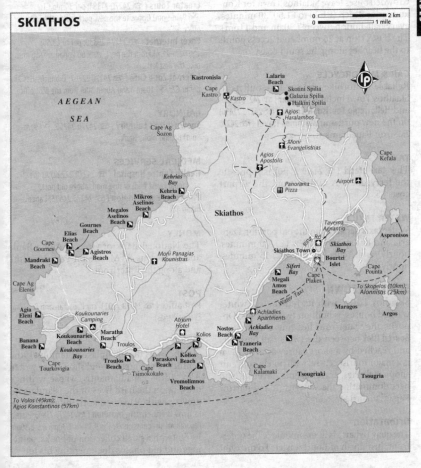

SKIATHOS

Town, Glossa, Volos, Agios Konstantinos and Thessaloniki. Hydrofoil tickets can be purchased from Hellenic Seaways.

Summer Hydrofoil & Jet Ferry Connections from Skiathos

Destination	Duration	Fare	Frequency
Volos	1¼hr	€25	3-4 daily
Agios Konstantinos	1½hr	€28	2-3 daily
Thessaloniki (Flying Cat hydrofoil)	3½hr	€35.30	daily
Alonnisos	1hr	€14.70	4-6 daily
Glossa	20min	€8	4-6 daily
Skopelos Town	35min	€12.50	4-6 daily

Getting Around
BUS
Crowded buses leave Skiathos Town for Koukounaries Beach (€1.20 to €1.50, 30 minutes, every half-hour between 7.30am and 11pm). The buses stop at 26 numbered access points to the beaches along the south coast.

CAR & MOTORCYCLE
Reliable motorbike and car-hire outlets in Skiathos Town include **Europcar** (☎ 24270 22385) and **Heliotropio Tourism & Travel** (☎ 24270 22430) on the new port; and **Mathinos Travel** (☎ 24270 23351) on Papadiamantis.

TAXI
The **taxi stand** (☎ 24270 21460) is opposite the ferry dock. A taxi to/from the airport costs €5.

WATER TAXI
Water taxis depart from the old port for Tzaneria and Kanapitsa beaches (€3, 20 minutes, hourly) and Achladies Bay (€2, 15 minutes, hourly).

SKIATHOS TOWN
Skiathos Town, with its red-roofed, white-washed houses, is built on two low hills. Opposite the waterfront lies tiny and inviting **Bourtzi Islet** between the two small harbours and reached by a short causeway. The town is a major tourist centre, with hotels, souvenir shops, galleries, travel agents, tavernas and bars dominating the waterfront and narrow Papadiamanti St.

Orientation
The quay (wharf) is in the middle of the waterfront, just north of Bourtzi Islet. To the right (as you face inland) is the newer small boat harbour; to the left is the curving old harbour used by local fishing and excursion boats. The main thoroughfare of Papadiamanti strikes inland from opposite the quay. Plateia Trion Ierarhon is above the old harbour, next to a large church. The bus terminus is at the northern end of the new harbour.

Information
EMERGENCY
Port police (☎ 24270 22017)
Tourist police (☎ 24270 23172; ☺ 8am-9pm) Opposite the regular police station about halfway along Papadiamanti; open daily during the summer season.

INTERNET ACCESS
Creator Tours (☎ 24270 21384; per 30min €1; ☺ 9am-9pm) Opposite the new port, inside the Europcar office.
Enter Internet (☎ 24270 29330; per hr €3.50; ☺ 9am-2am) From the port, walk up Papadiamanti and take the first left.
Internet Zone Café (☎ 24270 22767; Evangelistrias 28; per hr €2; ☺ 10am-1am) About 30m from the post office.

LAUNDRY
Snow White's Laundry (☎ 24270 24256; ☺ 9am-8pm) Behind Alpha Bank.

MEDICAL SERVICES
Health Centre Hospital (☎ 24270 22222) At the beginning (west end) of ring road, above old port.
Pharmacy Papantoniou (☎ 24270 24515; Papadiamanti 18)

MONEY
The National Bank of Greece, Alpha Bank and numerous ATMs are on Papadiamanti and along the waterfront.

POST
Post office (☎ 24270 22011; cnr Papadiamanti & Evangelistrias)

Sights
Skiathos was the birthplace of famous 19th-century Greek novelist and short story writer Alexandros Papadiamantis, whose writings draw upon the hard lives of the islanders he grew up with. Papadiamantis' humble house is now a charming **museum** (☎ 24270 23843; Plateia Papadiamanti; admission €1; ☺ 9.30am-1.30pm & 5-8.30pm Tue-Sun) with a small collection of books, paintings and old photos documenting his life.

Tours

Excursion boats make full- and half-day trips around the island (€9 to €20, approximately four to six hours), and usually include a visit to Cape Kastro, Lalaria Beach and the three *spilies* (caves) of Halkini, Skotini and Galazia, which are only accessible by boat. A few boats also visit the nearby islets of Tsougria and Tsougriaki for swimming and snorkelling. Check out the posted daily schedules at the old harbour, or contact **Mathinos Travel** (☎ 24270 23351; Papadiamantis 18) or **Heliotropio Tourism & Travel** (☎ 24270 22430; www.heliogtropio.gr) at the new port.

Sleeping

Most accommodation is booked from July to the end of August, when prices quoted here are nearly double those of low season. There's a quayside kiosk with information and pictures of rooms and domatia.

Hotel Meltemi (☎ 24270 22493; s/d/f incl breakfast €60/70/85; ❄) Set well back behind a shaded entry, the inviting Meltemi has balconied rooms with views of the harbour, large bathrooms and homey touches like antique ceramics and traditional wooden ceilings.

Villa Orsa (☎ 24270 22430; fax 24270 21952; s/d/f incl breakfast from €70/80/110; ❄) Perched above the old harbour, this classic cliffside mansion features very comfortable, traditionally styled rooms with balcony views. Breakfast is served on a garden terrace overlooking the sea.

Hotel Bourtzi (☎ 24270 21304; Moraitou 8; www.hotelbourtzi.gr/Bourtzi-Pothos/bhome.asp; s/d/tr incl breakfast €105/136/150; ❄ ▢ ▣) On upper Papadiamanti, the upmarket and family-friendly Bourtzi escapes much of the traffic noise of town, and features an inviting garden and two small pools (one for kids).

Also recommended:

Pension Lazou (☎ 24270 22324, 6946545713; s/d/apt-f €40/50/100; ❄) A clean and basic *pension*, a 50m walk up the steps, south of the old harbour.

Australia Hotel (☎ 24270 22488; fax 24270 22086; Evangelistrias; s/d €45/65; ❄) A clean and friendly budget option around the corner from the post office.

Hotel Pothos (☎ 24270 22694; www.hotelbourtzi.gr/Bourtzi-Pothos/phome.asp; s/d incl breakfast €80/90; ❄) A smart courtyard inn, 30m west of post office.

For last-minute accommodation in high season, try the resourceful **Georgia Asvesti** (☎ 6944137377), who often meets the boats on her motor scooter; or **Sotos & Maria** (☎ 24270 23219, 6974716408; sotos-2@otenet.gr), also helpful in a pinch.

Eating

Many eateries in Skiathos are geared to the tourist trade and are expensive. The places listed here offer better value, and food, than most.

Taverna Alexandros (☎ 24270 22341; Mavrogiali; mains €4-9) Excellent lamb grills, traditional oven-roasted chicken and potatoes, and live acoustic Greek music await at this friendly alleyway eatery under a canopy of mulberry trees.

Psaradiko Ouzeri (☎ 24270 23412; mains €4-10) Fresh fish at decent prices brings locals to this snappy taverna at the far end of the old port; favourites include a hearty fish soup, and grilled or fried calamari.

Taverna Anemos (☎ 24270 21003; mains €6-14) Locals know this fine fish taverna overlooking the harbour for its generous portions of fresh cod, lobster, mussels and *kritamos* (rock samphire salad), along with several outstanding Greek wines. The cook is a diver and fisherman, and more often than not is busy grilling the morning catch.

our pick **Maria's Pizza** (☎ 24270 22292; Syngrou 6; mains €8-15) You'll find superb handmade pizza (rolled out by Maria herself), stuffed garlic bread you cannot imagine, along with several pastas and dazzling salads, all in a flower-filled alleyway setting.

Also recommended:

Main Street (☎ 24270 21743; Papadiamantis; breakfasts €2-4) Next to the post office, with bargain breakfast, wraps and fresh juices.

Dinos (☎ 24270 23738; Papadiamantis; mains €4-8) Reliable café on the main drag, open from early morning till around 11pm.

Taverna Mouragio (☎ 24270 22216; mains €6-10) Waterfront Mouragio offers *tsipouro*-friendly mezedhes, grilled calamari.

Drinking

our pick **Kentavros Bar** (☎ 24270 22980) The long-established and handsome Kentavros, off Plateia Papadiamanti, promises rock, soul, jazz and blues, and gets the thumbs up from locals and expats alike for its mellow ambience and good drinks.

Bar Destiny (☎ 24270 24172; Polytechniou) Look for the soft blue light coming from this hip and gay-friendly side-street bar, with music videos, draught beer and a bit of dancing when the mood hits.

Ice Rooftop Bar (☎ 6949096465) This is a popular place to chill above the old port, with decent drinks and the longest happy hour on the waterfront.

Rock & Roll Bar (☎ 24270 22944) Huge beanbags have replaced many of the pillows outside this trendy but pricey bar by the old port, resulting in fewer customers rolling off.

The dancing and drinking scene amps up after midnight along the club strip past the new harbour. Best DJs are at **BBC** (☎ 24270 21190), followed by **Kahlua Bar** (☎ 24270 23205), both with dancing drinkers till dawn.

Entertainment

Cinema Attikon (☎ 24270 22352; Papadiamanti; admission €7; beer & snacks €2-4) Catch recent English-language movies at this open-air cinema, sip a beer and practise speed-reading your Greek subtitles at the same time. (Greece is one of the few countries in Europe to show films with original language, not dubbed.)

Shopping

Loupos & his Dolphins (☎ 24270 23777; Plateia Papadiamanti; ☒ 10am-1.30pm & 6-11.30pm) Look for hand-painted icons, fine ceramics by Greek artists, along with gold and silver jewellery at this high-end gallery shop, next to Papadiamantis Museum.

Archipelogos (☎ 24270 22163; Plateia Papadiamanti; ☒ 11am-1pm & 8-10pm) The work of contemporary Greek artists, along with elegant traditional weavings, stands out at this intimate shop.

Galerie Varsakis (☎ 24270 22255; Plateia Trion Ierarhon; ☒ 10am-2pm & 6-11pm) Browse for unusual antiques like 19th-century spinning sticks made by grooms for their intended brides, plus Greek and African textiles.

AROUND SKIATHOS
Beaches

With some 65 beaches to choose from, beach-hopping on Skiathos can become a full-time occupation. Buses ply the south coast, stopping at 26 numbered beach access points. **Megali Amos** is only 2km from town, but fills up quickly. The first long stretch of sand worth getting off the bus for is the pine-fringed **Vromolimnos Beach**. Further along, **Kolios Beach** and **Troulos Beach** are also good but both, alas, are very popular. The bus continues to **Koukounaries Beach**, backed by pine trees and touted as the best beach in Greece. But nowadays its crowded summer scene is best viewed at a distance, from where the 1200m long sweep of pale gold sand does indeed sparkle.

Banana Beach, known for its curving shape and soft white sand, lies at the other side of a narrow headland. It is nominally a nudist beach, though the skinny-dippers tend to abscond to **Little Banana Beach** (which also gets the big thumbs up from gay and lesbian sunbathers) around the rocky corner if things get too crowded.

West of Koukounaries, **Agia Eleni Beach** is a favourite with windsurfers. Sandy **Mandraki Beach**, a 1.5km walk along a pine-shaded path, is just far enough to keep it clear of the masses. The northwest coast's beaches are less crowded but are subject to the strong summer *meltemi* (northeasterly winds). From Troulos (look for bus stop 19), a road heads north to **Moni Panagias Kounistras**, from where a right fork continues 300m to **Mikros Aselinos Beach** and 5km further on to secluded **Kehria Beach**.

Lalaria Beach is a tranquil strand of pale-grey, egg-shaped pebbles on the northern coast. It is much featured in tourist brochures, but only reached by excursion boat from Skiathos Town (see Tours, p425).

Kastro Κάστρο

Kastro, perched dramatically on a rocky headland above the north coast, was the fortified pirate-proof capital of the island from 1540 to 1829; an old cannon remains at the northern end. Four of the crumbling town's old churches have been restored, and the views are magnificent. Excursion boats come to the beach below Kastro, from where it's an easy clamber up to the ruins.

Moni Evangelistrias Μονή Ευαγγελίστριας

The most appealing of the island's monasteries is the 18th-century **Moni Evangelistrias** (Annunciation; ☎ 24270 22012; ☒ 8am-8pm), poised above a gorge 450m above sea level, and surrounded by pine and cypress trees. The monastery was a refuge for freedom fighters during the War of Independence. Once home to 70 monks, it now has only two monks doing the chores, which include wine-making. You can sample the tasty results of their efforts in the museum shop. An adjacent shed of old presses and vintage barrels recalls an earlier era, long before the satellite dish was installed above the courtyard.

Also worth a visit is **Moni Panagias Kounistras** (Holy Virgin), with fine frescoes adorning its *katholikon*. It's 4km inland from Troulos.

Activities

DIVING

Octopus Diving Centre (☎ 24270 24549; www.odc-skiathos.com; new harbour) has a dive instructor team, Theofanis and Eva, who conduct half-day dives around Tsougria and Tsougriaki islets for beginners and experts alike (from €40 to €50, equipment included).

Dolphin Diving (☎ 24270 21599, 6944999181; www.ddiving.gr; Nostos Beach, bus stop 12) is the oldest diving school in the Sporades. It offers single dives in the €45 to €55 range (with equipment) including a morning beginners' dive off Tsougriaki Islet, which explores locations to 30m deep.

HIKING

A 6km-long hiking route begins at Moni Evangelistrias, eventually reaching **Cape Kastro**, before circling back through Agios Apostolis. Kastro is a spring mecca for bird-watchers, who may catch glimpses of long-necked Mediterranean shags and singing blue-rock thrushes on the nearby rocky islets.

Sleeping & Eating

Koukounaries Camping (☎ /fax 24270 49250; camp sites per adult/tent €8.50/4; **P**) Shaded by fig and mulberry trees, this excellent site near the eastern end of Koukounaries Beach features spotless toilets and showers, cooking facilities, laundry and a nearby minimarket and taverna.

our pick **Achladies Apartments** (☎ 24270 22486; http://achladies.apartments.googlepages.com; Achladies Bay; d/tr/f incl breakfast €50/65/87, 2-night min; **P**) Look for the hand-painted yellow sign to find this welcoming gem, 3km from Skiathos Town. It offers self-catering rooms with ceiling fans, an ecofriendly tortoise sanctuary and a succulent garden winding down to a taverna and sandy beach, from where a water taxi makes 20-minute runs to Skiathos Town.

Atrium Hotel (☎ 24270 49345; www.atriumhotel.gr; Paraskevi Beach; s/d/tr €98/130/170; **P** ✕ ▢ ▣) Traditional architecture and modern amenities make this handsome property the best in its class. Perched on a pine-covered hillside, it offers facilities such as satellite TV, a pool bar and a game lounge with Ping-Pong and billiards.

Panorama Pizza (☎ 6944192066; pizzas €7-10; ☾ noon-4pm, 7pm-late) Up the hill (2.5km) from the ring road, excellent Panorama overlooks Skiathos Bay below.

Taverna Agnantio (☎ 2427022016; mains €6-11) Family-run Agnantio attracts both locals and tourists, who come early to catch house specialities like slow-roasted lamb. It's 400m off the ring road, with superb terrace views down to the harbour. Reservations are a must from July to August.

SKOPELOS ΣΚΟΠΕΛΟΣ

pop 4700

Less commercialised than Skiathos, Skopelos is a beautiful island of pine forests, vineyards, olive groves and orchards of plums and almonds, which find their way into many local dishes.

Like Skiathos, the high cliffs of the northwest coast are exposed, while the sheltered southeast coast harbours several sand and pebble beaches. There are two large settlements: the capital and main port of Skopelos Town on the east coast; and the unspoilt west coast village of Glossa, 3km north of Loutraki, the island's second port.

In 1936 Skopelos yielded an exciting archaeological find, a royal tomb dating to ancient times, when the island was an important Minoan outpost ruled by Stafylos, the son of Ariadne and Dionysos in Greek mythology. The Minoan ruler Stafylos ('grape' in Greek) is said to have introduced wine-making here.

Getting There & Away

FERRY

In summer there are daily ferries between Skopelos and Alonnisos, Skiathos, Volos and Agios Konstantinos.

Tickets are available from **Hellenic Seaways** (☎ 24240 22767; fax 24240 23608) opposite the new quay; and **Lemonis Agency** (☎ 24240 22363) in Pension Lemonis towards the end of the new quay.

Summer Ferry Connections from Skopelos Town & Glossa

Origin	Destination	Duration	Fare	Frequency
Skopelos Town	Alonnisos	30min	€4.60	3-4 weekly
Skopelos Town	Skiathos	1hr	€7.50	daily
Skopelos Town	Volos	4hr	€19.50	1-2 daily
Skopelos Town	Agios Konstantinos	3½hr	€31.60	1-2 (jet ferries) daily
Glossa	Volos	3¼hr	€16.50	daily (morning)

HYDROFOIL

Skopelos has two hydrofoil ports, the main one at Skopelos Town and the other to the northwest at Glossa's port of Loutraki, both with service to Alonnisos and Skiathos.

There are also hydrofoils from Skopelos Town to Volos (€27.50, 1¾ hours, three daily) and to Agios Konstantinos (€30.50, two hours, two to three daily)

In Skopelos Town, purchase tickets from **Hellenic Seaways** (☎ 24240 22767; fax 24240 23608); in Glossa, from **Hellenic Seaways** (☎ 24240 33435; fax 24240 33042).

Summer Hydrofoil Connections from Skopelos Town & Glossa

Origin	Destination	Duration	Fare	Frequency
Skopelos Town	Alonnisos	20min	€7.70	5 daily
Skopelos Town	Skiathos	45min	€12.50	5 daily
Glossa	Skopelos Town	30min	€10.50	3-4 daily
Glossa	Skiathos	20min	€7.60	4-5 daily
Glossa	Alonnisos	55min	€12.20	3-4 daily

Getting Around

BUS

There are eight buses per day from Skopelos Town all the way to Glossa/Loutraki (€3.90, one hour), three that go only as far as Panormos (€1.90, 25 minutes) and Milia (€2.60, 35 minutes), and another two that go only as far as Agnontas (€1.20, 15 minutes) and Stafylos (€1.20, 15 minutes).

CAR & MOTORCYCLE

Several car- and motorcycle-rental outlets line the harbour in Skopelos Town, mostly located at the eastern end of the waterfront, including the friendly and efficient **Motor Tours** (☎ 24240 22986; fax 24240 22602) next to Hotel Eleni.

SKOPELOS

0 _____ 4 km
0 _____ 2 miles

To Skiathos (10km);
Volos (55km);
Agios Konstantinos (67km)

AEGEAN SEA

Cape Gourouni

Perivoliou Beach

Glossa
Mahalas
Pension Platanas
Church of Agios Ioannis
Loutraki

To Skiathos (10km)

Klima   383m

Kaloyeros

Glysteri Beach

Alonnisos Strait

Kalyves
Armenopetra Beach   690m
Elios

Kastani Beach

Milia Beach

Andrines Beach

Skopelos

Agios Georgios

Moni Prodromou
Moni Varvaras
Moni Metamorfosis Sotiros

Skopelos Bay

Skopelos Town
Ring Rd

Moni Evangelistrias   567m

Cape Kiourto

To Alonnisos (12km)

Skopelos Strait

Dasia

Moni Episkopis

Panormos Beach

258m
Limnonari Rooms

Ostria Hotel

Cape Myti

Limnonari Beach

Agnontas Beach

Stafylos Beach

Velanio Beach

Mando Rooms

AEGEAN SEA

Cape Velona

TAXI

The taxi stand is next to the bus stop along the waterfront. A taxi to Stafylos is €7, to Limnonari €12, to Glossa €25.

WATER TAXI

A regular water taxi departs late morning for Glysteri Beach (€5 one way), and returns at about 5pm.

SKOPELOS TOWN

Skopelos Town is one of the most captivating ports in the Sporades. It skirts a semicircular bay and clambers in tiers up a hillside, culminating in an old fortress and a cluster of four churches. Dozens of other churches are interspersed among dazzling white houses with brightly shuttered windows and flower-adorned balconies.

Orientation

Skopelos Town's waterfront is flanked by two quays. The old quay is at the western end of the harbour and the new quay is at the eastern end, used by all ferries and hydrofoils. From the dock, turn right to reach the bustling waterfront lined with cafés, souvenir shops and travel agencies; turn left (20m) for the bus stop. Less than 50m away is Plateia Platanos, also known as Souvlaki Sq.

Information

BOOKSHOPS

International newsstand (☎ 24240 22236; ✆ 8am-10pm) Twenty metres up from bus stop.

EMERGENCY

Police (☎ 24240 22235) Above the National Bank.
Port police (☎ 24240 22180)

INTERNET ACCESS

Blue Sea Internet Café (☎ 24240 23010; per hr €3; ✆ 8am-2am) End of the waterfront, beneath the Kastro steps.
Skopelos Internet Café (☎ 24240 23093; per hr €3; ✆ 9am-midnight) Next to the post office.

LAUNDRY

Blue Star Washing (☎ 24240 22844) Near the OTE office.

MEDICAL SERVICES

Health Centre (☎ 24240 22222) On the ring road, next to the fire station.

MONEY

There are three banks with ATMs along the waterfront.

POST

Post office South of Platanos Sq, 100m on the right.

TRAVEL AGENCIES

Madro Travel (☎ 24240 22300; www.madrotravel .com) At the end of the new port, Madro can provide help with booking accommodation and ticketing, and arrange walking trips, cooking lessons, even marriages.
Thalpos Holidays (☎ 24240 29036; www.holiday islands.com) The helpful staff at this waterfront agency offer a range of services including apartment and villa accommodation and tours around the island.

Sights

Strolling around town and sitting at the waterside cafés might be your chief occupations in Skopelos, but there is also a small **Folk Art Museum** (☎ 24240 23494; Hatzistamati; admission €2; ✆ 10am-10pm) with a Skopelean wedding room, complete with traditional costumes and bridal bed.

Tours

Day-long cruise boats (€20 to €45) depart from the new quay by 10am, and usually take in the Marine Park of Alonnisos (p434), pausing en route for lunch and a swim. There's a good chance of spotting dolphins along the way. For bookings, contact **Thalpos Holidays** (☎ 24240 22947) or **Madro Travel** (☎ 24240 22300) on the waterfront.

Sleeping

Hotel prices quoted are for the July to August high season, but are often reduced by 30% to 50% at other times. The **Rooms & Apartments Association** (☎ 24240 24567; ✆ 8.30am-2pm), next to the ferry dock, can help with accommodation.

BUDGET

ourpick **Sotos Pension** (☎ 24240 22549; www.skop elos.net/sotos; s/d €35/50; ✳) The traditional pine rooms at this charming waterfront *pension* are each a bit different; an old brick oven serves as a handy shelf in one. There's an interior courtyard, a whitewashed terrace overlooking the bay and a communal kitchen which is kept well stocked by the welcoming owner, Alexandra (Alex, for short).

Hotel Regina (☎ 24240 22138; www.skopelosweb
.gr/regina; s/d incl breakfast €40/55; ❄) Rooms at the
vaguely Victorian and very friendly Regina
have ceiling fans and small balconies. Breakfast is served on the rooftop veranda overlooking the nearby harbour.

MIDRANGE
Hotel Agnanti (☎ /fax 24240 22722; www.skopelos.net
/agnanti; s/d/tr incl breakfast from €45/65/90; P ❄ ▢)
Theo and Eleni run the show at this inviting
12-room hotel on the far bay, with ceiling
fans, traditional ceramic and wood decorations, plus a paperback lending library.

Perivoli Studios (☎ 24240 24480, 6974120450; www
.skopelos.net/perivoli; d/tr €60/70; P ❄) These stylish self-catering studios occupy a traditional
building just off the ring road, each with a
terrace overlooking an orchard of olive and
fruit trees.

Hotel Dionyssos (☎ 24240 23210; www.dionyssoshotel
.com; s/d/tr incl breakfast €100/120/130; P ❄ ⚲) The
low-key Dionyssos occupies a quiet street
between the ring road and the waterfront.
The upper rooms offer balcony views of the
harbour. Even in summer, the large lobby is
cool and inviting, and a pool bar awaits just
outside.

Eating
Just 100m up from the dock, Souvlaki Sq is
perfect for a quick bite of *gyros* or, not surprisingly, souvlaki. Skopelos is known for a
variety of plum-based recipes, and most tavernas will have one or two on the menu.

Taverna O Angelos (☎ 24240 22381; mains €5-8) The
oldest taverna on the island, O Angelos sits
at the end of the old quay. Ready-to-eat oven
dishes include hearty staples like lamb *stifadho*
and stuffed zucchini.

Taverna Englezos (☎ 24240 22230; mains €7-11) The
newest restaurant on the waterfront serves
great grills at good prices – half a chicken on
the spit for €7, tasty foil-wrapped and oven-
baked lamb (*kleftiko*) for €9. In true Greek
style, your meal usually ends with fresh fruit,
on the house.

our pick To Perivoli Restaurant (☎ 24240 23758;
mains €7-12) Just up from Souvlaki Sq, Perivoli
promises excellent Greek cuisine and snappy
service in an elegant and vine-covered courtyard setting. Specialities include rolled pork
with *koromila* (local plums) in wine sauce
and seafood risotto, plus a great selection of
Greek wines.

Anna's Restaurant (☎ 24240 24734; Gifthorema; mains
€7-12) On Wednesday, the menu at this handsome courtyard bistro is devoted to authentic
Skopelos dishes such as *tyropita* (cheese pie)
or lamb in plum sauce. Look for the palm tree
in the courtyard.

Also recommended:
Michalis (☎ 24240 23591; snacks & cakes €2-5;
☾ 9am-11pm) One of the best spots for traditional
tyropita, with several variations on the theme.

Nastas Ouzerie (☎ 24240 23441; mezedhes €2.50-5,
mains €6-10) Snappy *ouzerie* near the ring road, with
first-rate mezedhes.

DIA Discount Supermarket (☎ 24240 24340;
☾ 8.30am-9.30pm) Will appeal to self-caterers, with its
good prices and well-stocked aisles.

Drinking
Platanos Jazz Bar (☎ 24240 23661) Near the end of
the old quay, this leafy courtyard bar is open
for morning coffee and late-night drinks,
making it the ideal place to recover from a
hangover, or to prepare for one.

Oionos Blue Bar (☎ 6942406136) Cosy and cool,
little Oionos draws a local crowd to its traditional Skopelean digs, where it serves up blues
and soul along with 19 brands of beer and 25
malt whiskies at last count.

Le Bistro (☎ 24240 24741; Souvlaki Sq) Upmarket
Le Bistro's wine and cocktail bar often exhibits the work of local painters and photographers.

Anemos Espresso Bar (☎ 24240 23564; coffees &
snacks €2-4; ☾ 8am-1am) Count on excellent coffee and fresh juice at this shaded waterfront
café.

Shopping
Gray Gallery (☎ 24240 24266, 6974641597) Works by
island and visiting artists are featured in this
low-key fine art gallery.

Archipelogos (☎ 24240 23127; waterfront) Worth
a browse for the fine collection of antiques,
jewellery and old icons.

Entertainment
Ouzerie Anatoli (☎ 24240 22851; ☾ 7pm-2am, summer
only) For mezedhes and traditional music, head
to this breezy *ouzerie*, high above the Kastro.
From 11pm onwards you will hear traditional
rembetika (blues) music sung by Skopelos'
own exponent of the Greek blues, Georgos
Xindaris. Follow the path up the (steep) steps
past Agio Apostolis church at the northern end
of the quay, or take a taxi from the port (€5).

The summer club scene livens up late along Doulidi, near the post office and the small church of Panagia Eleftherotria. **Panselinos** (☎ 24240 24488; Doulidi; ☾ 10pm-3am) mixes Greek pop sounds with live performances on summer weekends. The nearby **Metro Club** (☎ 24240 24478; Doulidi; ☾ 9pm-3am) plays mostly high-volume Greek pop.

GLOSSA ΓΛΩΣΣΑ

Glossa, Skopelos' other major settlement, is considerably quieter than the capital. Another whitewashed delight, it has miraculously managed to retain the feel of a pristine Greek village.

The bus stops in front of a large church at a T-junction. One road winds down 3km to the port of Loutraki and a few domatia and tavernas; the other leads nearby to a bank, pharmacy, bakery and a few small stores.

Sleeping & Eating

Pension Platanas (☎ 24240 33188; Glossa; s/d €20/30) Close to nothing in particular, this friendly family *pension* with views to the sea is only 3km to the ferry port at Loutraki.

Kyra Lena Bakery (☎ 24240 33688; snacks €1.50-3.50) Check out the huge brick oven at Glossa's newest bakery, with *tyropita, piperopita* (sweet peppers and feta pie) and roasted almonds among the breads and little cakes.

Flisvos Taverna (☎ 24240 33856; Loutraki; mains €3-7) Perched above the rocks at the little port of Loutraki, this end-of-the-road family taverna offers fresh fish at decent prices, fresh chips, homemade *mousakas*, and traditional appetisers like *taramasalata*.

Agnanti Taverna & Bar (☎ 24240 33076; mains €7-12) Enjoy the views of Evia from swank Agnanti's rooftop terrace, along with Greek fusion dishes like grilled sardines on pita with sea fennel and sun-dried tomatoes, followed by simmered pork with plums. From July to August, book ahead.

AROUND SKOPELOS
Monasteries

Skopelos has several monasteries that can be visited on a beautiful scenic drive or day-long trek from Skopelos Town. Begin by following the road (Monastery Rd), which skirts the bay and then climbs inland. Continue beyond the signposted Hotel Aegeon until the road forks. Take the left fork, which ends at the 18th-century **Moni Evangelistrias**,

now a convent. The monastery's prize, aside from the superb views, is a gilded iconostasis containing an 11th-century icon of the Virgin Mary.

The right fork leads to the uninhabited 16th-century **Moni Metamorfosis Sotiros**, the island's oldest monastery. From here a decent track continues to the 17th-century **Moni Varvaras** with a view to the sea, and to the 18th-century **Moni Prodromou** (now a convent), 8km from Skopelos Town.

Moni Episkopis rests within the Venetian compound of a private Skopelian family, about 250m beyond the ring road. Ring **Apostolis** (☎ 6974120450) for details and an invitation. The small chapel within is a wonder of light and Byzantine icons.

Beaches

Skopelos' beaches are mostly pebbled, and almost all are on the sheltered southwest and west coasts. All bus services stop at the beginning of paths that lead down to the beaches. The first beach you come to is the sand-and-pebble **Stafylos Beach** (site of Stafylos' tomb), 4km southeast of Skopelos Town. From the eastern end of the beach a path leads over a small headland to the quieter **Velanio Beach**, the island's official nudist beach and a great snorkelling spot. **Agnontas**, 3km west of Stafylos, has a small pebble-and-sand beach and from here caïques sail to the superior and sandy **Limnonari Beach**, in a sheltered bay flanked by rocky outcrops. Limnonari is also a 1.5km walk or drive from Agnontas.

From Agnontas the road cuts inland through pine forests before re-emerging at the sheltered and popular **Panormos Beach**. One kilometre further, little **Andrines Beach** is sandy and less crowded. The next two beaches, **Milia** and **Kastani**, are considered to be two of the island's best for swimming.

Tours

If you can't tell a Cleopatra butterfly from a Madonna lily or Leopard orchid, join one of island resident Heather Parson's **guided walks** (☎ 6945249328; www.skopelos-walks.com; tours €15-20). Her three-hour walk above Skopelos Town follows an old path into the hills, and offers views to Alonnisos and Evia. Her book, *Skopelos Trails*, contains graded trail descriptions and illustrated maps, and is available in waterfront stores (€16).

Sleeping & Eating

There are small hotels, domatia, tavernas and beach canteens at Stafylos, Agnontas, Limnonari, Panormos, Andrines and Milia.

our pick **Mando Rooms** (☎ 24240 23917; www
.skopelos.net/mando; s/d/tr/f €80/90/110/150; P ✗)
Having its own cove on the bay at Stafylos
is a good start at this welcoming and family-
oriented *pension*. Other extras include free
coffee, a communal kitchen, satellite TV,
and a platform over the rocks to enter
the water.

Limnonari Rooms & Taverna (☎ 24240 23046;
www.skopelos.net/limnonari-rooms; Limnonari Beach; d/tr/
ste €60/80/120; P ✗) Set back on a beautiful
and sandy bay, this well-managed domatia

features self-catering ministudios, along with
a well-equipped communal kitchen and terrace, all about 30m from the water. The garden taverna (mains €6 to €8) serves a perfect
vegetarian *mousakas*, along with the owner's
homemade olives and feta.

ALONNISOS
ΑΛΟΝΝΗΣΟΣ

pop 2700

Alonnisos rises from the sea like a mountain
of greenery with thick stands of pine and
oak, along with mastic and arbutus bushes,
and fruit trees. The west coast is mostly pre-

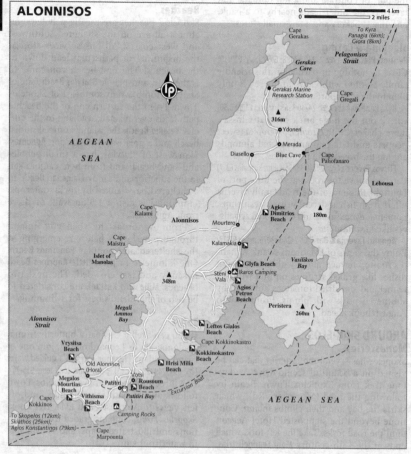

cipitous cliffs but the east coast is speckled with small bays and pebbly beaches. The water around Alonnisos has been declared a national marine park, and is the cleanest in the Aegean.

Lovely Alonnisos has had its share of bad luck. In 1952, the flourishing cottage wine industry came to a halt, when vines imported from California were struck with the disease phylloxera. Robbed of their livelihood, many islanders moved away. Then, in 1965, an earthquake destroyed the hill-top capital of Alonnisos Town. The inhabitants were subsequently rehoused in hastily assembled dwellings at Patitiri.

Getting There & Away
FERRY
From Alonnisos, there are ferries to Skopelos Town (€4.60, 30 minutes, three to four per week) and to Skiathos (€8.80, two hours, daily from June to September), to Volos (€18.90, 4½ hours, two weekly), to Agios Konstantinos (€36, four hours by jet ferry, daily), and to Thessaloniki (€23.20, seven hours, three per week). Outside of the summer season, service is less frequent. Check with ferry companies for current routes and schedules.

Tickets can be purchased from **Alonnisos Travel** (☎ 24240 65188) in Patitiri.

HYDROFOIL
In summer, hydrofoils connect Alonnisos to Skopelos Town (€7.70, 20 minutes, five daily), to Glossa (€12.20, one hour, four daily), to Skiathos (€14.70, 1½ hours, five daily), to Volos (€32.50, three hours, three daily) and to Agios Konstantinos (€36.50, three hours, two daily). Tickets may be purchased from **Alkyon Travel** (☎ 24240 65220) in Patitiri.

Getting Around
BOAT
Ionnisos Travel (☎ 24240 65188) rents out four-person 15HP to 25HP motorboats. The cost ranges from €48 to €60 per day in summer.

BUS
In summer, one bus plies the route between Patitiri (from opposite the quay) and Old Alonnisos (€1.20, hourly 9am to about 3pm). There is also a service to Steni Vala from Old Alonnisos via Patitiri (€1.30, twice daily).

CAR & MOTORCYCLE
Several motorcycle-hire outlets can be found on Pelasgon, in Patitiri, including reliable **I'm Bike** (☎ 24240 65010). Be wary when riding down to the beaches, as some of the sand-and-shale tracks are steep and slippery. Also try **Nefeli Bakery & Rent-A-Car** (☎ 24240 66497) and **Albedo Travel** (☎ 24240 65804).

TAXI
The four taxis on the island (Georgos, Periklis, Theodoros, Spyros) tend to congregate opposite the quay. It's €5 to Old Alonnisos, €8 to Megalos Mourtias and €12 to Steni Vala.

WATER TAXI
The easiest way during summer to get to and from the east-coast beaches is by taking the **water taxi** (☎ 24240 65461) that leaves from the quay at 11am and returns by about 5.30pm. The main stops are Kokkinokastro (€7), Steni Vala (€9) and Agios Dimitrios (€10).

PATITIRI ΠΑΤΗΤΗΡΙ
Patitiri sits between two sandstone cliffs at the southern end of the east coast. Despite its hasty origins following the devastating 1965 earthquake that levelled the old hilltop capital (Palia Alonnisos), Patitiri is gradually improving its homely looks. The town is small and relaxed, and makes a convenient base for exploring Alonnisos. Patitiri means 'wine press' and is where grapes were processed prior to the demise of the wine industry in the 1950s.

Orientation
Finding your way around Patitiri is easy. The quay is in the centre of the waterfront and two roads lead inland. With your back to the sea, turn left for Pelasgon, or right for Ikion Dolopon. In truth, there are no road signs and most locals simply refer to them as the left-hand road (Pelasgon) and right-hand road (Ikion Dolopon).

Information
EMERGENCY
Police (☎ 24240 65205) At the northern end of Ikion Dolopon; there is no tourist police office.
Port police (☎ 24240 65595) On the quay at Patitiri.

INTERNET ACCESS

Play Café (☎ 24240 66119; per hr €4; ☺ 9am-2pm & 6-9pm) Across the road from the National Bank.

Techno Plus (☎ 24240 29100; per hr €3; ☺ 9am-2pm & 5-9pm) On the right-hand road, opposite the school.

LAUNDRY

Lena's Gardenia (☎ 24240 65831; Pelasgon)

MONEY

National Bank of Greece Southern end of Ikion Dolopon, with an ATM.

POST

Post office (Ikion Dolopon) 100m from the bus stop.

Sights

The **Folklore Museum of the Northern Sporades** (☎ 24240 66250; admission €3; ☺ 11am-7pm) is largely a labour of love by the Mavrikis family, and includes an extensive display of pirates' weapons and tools, a horseshoe shop and antique nautical maps. A small café sits atop the museum with views of the harbour. Take the stone stairway at the far west end of the harbour.

NATIONAL MARINE PARK OF ALONNISOS

In a country not noted for ecological long-sightedness, the Alonnisos Marine Park is a welcome innovation. Started in 1992, its prime aim has been the protection of the endangered Mediterranean monk seal (*Monachus monachus*). See the boxed text (opposite).

The park is divided into two zones. The carefully restricted Zone A comprises a cluster of islets to the northeast, including Kyra Panagia. Zone B is home to Alonnisos itself and Peristera.

In summer, licensed boats from Alonnisos and Skopelos conduct excursions through the marine park. Though it's unlikely you'll find the shy monk seal, your chances of spotting dolphins (striped, bottlenose and common) are fairly good.

Activities

WALKING

Walking opportunities abound on Alonnisos, and the best ones are waymarked. At the bus stop in Old Alonnisos a blue notice board details several walks. From Patitiri, a 2km **donkey path** winds up through shrubbery and orchards before bringing you to Old Alonnisos.

The informative *Alonnisos on Foot: A Walking & Swimming Guide*, by Bente Keller and Elias Tsoukanas, is available at waterfront shops, along with *The Alonnisos Guide* by the same authors, detailing the history of the island.

Consider a **guided walk** (☎ 6974080039; www .alonnisoswalks.co.uk; walks €15-30) with island resident Chris Browne. A half-day walk above Patitiri winds through pine forest trails, past churches and olive groves overlooking the sea.

CYCLING

The best mountain-bike riding is over on the southwest coast around the bay of Megali Ammos. There are several bicycle- and motorcycle-hire outlets on Ikion Dolopon.

Tours

Three professional travel agencies on the waterfront provide maps and arrange popular marine park excursions. Inquire at **Ikos Travel** (☎ 24240 65320; www.ikostravel.com) for popular round-the-island guided excursions aboard the *Gorgona* (a classic Greek boat captained by island native, Pakis Athanasiou), which visit the **Blue Cave** on the northeast coast, and the islets of **Kyra Panagia** and **Peristera** in the marine park, with swimming breaks along the way. **Albedo Travel** (☎ 24240 65804; www.albedotravel.com) runs regular snorkelling and swimming excursions to Skantzoura and nearby islands, and even arranges island weddings. **Alonnisos Travel** (☎ 24240 66000; www.alonnisostravel.gr) also runs marine park excursions aboard the *Planitis*.

Sleeping

Prices here are for the higher July to August season; expect discounts of about 25% or more at other times. **Rooms to Let Service** (☎ 24240 66188; fax 24240 65577; ☺ 9.30am-2pm & 6.30-10pm), opposite the quay, offers a room-finder service in July and August only.

BUDGET

Camping Rocks (☎ 24240 65410; camp sites per adult/tent €6/3) Follow the signposts in town for Camping Rocks, a rough but shaded coastal spot 1km south of Patitiri.

Pension Pleiades (☎ 24240 65235; pleiadeshotel@yahoo .gr; s/d/tr from €25/35/50; ☼ ▢) This bright and cheerful budget option offers views of Patitiri Bay, along with nine immaculate, balconied rooms, plus four family-sized studios with kitchenette. Take the stairway behind the newsstand.

Ilias Rent Rooms (☎ 24240 65451; fax 24240 65972; Pelasgon 27; d €45, 2-/3-bed studios €50/55; ☼) Owners Ilias and Magdalini give their spotless domatia a warm and welcoming touch. Rooms and studios share a communal kitchen.

MIDRANGE

our pick Liadromia Hotel (☎ 24240 65521; fax 24240 65096; d/tr/ste incl breakfast €50/70/85; P 🔀 🖳) This welcoming and impeccably maintained hotel overlooking the harbour was Patitiri's first. All the rooms have a bit of character, from hand-embroidered curtains and old lamps to stone floors and traditional wood furnishings.

Nina Studios (☎ 24240 65242; www.ninna.gr; d/f €50/80; P 🔀) Take the stairs opposite the bank to these self-catering studios with stone floors, iron beds and large bathrooms, and vine-covered balcony views of Patitiri harbour.

Paradise Hotel (☎ 24240 65213; www.paradise -hotel.gr; s/d/tr €65/80/100; P 🔀) Wood ceilings and stone-tiled floors give a rustic feel to the balconied rooms, which overlook the bay or Patitiri harbour. Room prices include a buffet breakfast at the pool terrace.

Eating

Anais Restaurant & Pizzeria (☎ 24240 65243; mains €5-12; 🕥 breakfast, lunch & dinner) Patitiri's first restaurant, opposite the hydrofoil dock, is still going strong. You'll find tasty souvlakia, hefty Greek salads and a house favourite, *kleftiko* (slow-oven-baked lamb).

To Kamaki Ouzerie (☎ 24240 65245; Ikion Dolopon; mains €5-15) Start off with a sip of ouzo and mezedhes like fresh Alonnisos tuna salad at this traditional seafood eatery, then move on to the shrimp souvlaki or blow the budget on grilled local lobster.

Also recommended:

Taverna Archipelagos (☎ 24240 65031; mains €4-8) Opposite the hydrofoil dock, and a local favourite for Greek mezedhes and grills.

Café Flisvos (☎ 24240 65307; mains €5-8) Under the canopy opposite the dock, with excellent oven-ready dishes at decent prices.

OLD ALONNISOS ΠΑΛΙΑ ΑΛΟΝΝΙΣΟΣ

Old Alonnisos (also known as Palia Alonnisos, Hora, Palio Horio or Old Town), with its winding stepped alleys, is a tranquil, picturesque place with lovely views. From the main road just outside the village an old donkey path leads down to pebbled Megalos Mourtias Beach and other paths lead south to Vithisma and Marpounta Beaches.

Sleeping

Old Alonnisos has no hotels, but there are several well-managed domatia.

Fantasia House (☎ 24240 65186; Plateia Hristou; s/d €30/40) Tucked away between the church and square, these simple rooms are good value, and there is a snack bar in the courtyard.

Pension Hiliadromia (☎ /fax 24240 65814; Plateia Hristou; d/2-bed studio €35/55; 🔀) Several of the pine-and-stone-floor rooms at the Hiliadromia come with balcony views, and the studios have well-equipped kitchens.

our pick Konstantina Studios (☎ 24240 66165; www.konstantinastudios.gr; s/d €40/50; 🔀) Among the nicest accommodations on Alonnisos, these handsome and quiet self-catering studios with traditional styling come with balcony views of the southwest coast. The owner makes it a point to fetch her guests from the dock.

Eating

our pick Hayati (☎ 24240 66244; Old Alonnisos; snacks & mains €2-7; 🕥 9am-2am) Hayati is both a sweets shop at the upper entrance, and a late-night taverna and piano bar below, with sweeping views of the island from either level. Morning

---

THE MONK SEAL

Once populating hundreds of colonies in the Black Sea and the Mediterranean, as well as along the Atlantic coast of Africa, the Mediterranean monk seal has been reduced to about 400 individuals today. Half of these live in waters between Greece and Turkey.

One of the earth's rarest mammals, this seal is on the list of the 20 most endangered species worldwide. Major threats include deliberate killings by fishermen – who see the seal as a pest that tears holes in their nets and robs their catch – incidental capture in fishing gear, decreasing food supply as fisheries decline, habitat destruction and pollution.

Recognising that this seal may become extinct if not protected, Greece established the National Marine Park of Alonnisos in 1992 (see opposite), to both protect the seal and to promote recovery of fish stocks.

For more information, visit http://mofi.mom.gr/uk/fokia_alieia1.htm.

fare includes made-to-order Alonnisos *tyropita*. Later, you'll find homemade pastas and juicy souvlaki, along with the gracious hospitality of owner-cooks Meni and Angela. It's a five-minute walk from the village square.

Astrofengia (☎ 24240 65182; mains €5-12) This gracious courtyard taverna, near the bus stop, offers excellent cannelloni and fine mezedhes like *saganaki* (fried cheese) and dolmadhes. For dessert, find a way to squeeze in a slice of *galaktoboureko* (homemade custard pie).

Taverna Megalos Mourtias (☎ 24240 65737; mains €4-8; ☺ breakfast, lunch & dinner) A stone's throw from the surf, this laid-back taverna and beach bar prepares good salads and souvlakia, plus a hearty fish soup.

AROUND ALONNISOS

Alonnisos' main road reaches the northern tip of the island at Gerakas (19km), home to an EU-funded marine research station. Six kilometres north of Patitiri, another sealed road branches off to the small fishing port and yacht harbour of Steni Vala, and follows the shore past Kalamakia for 5km. A third road takes you from Patitiri to Megalos Mourtias.

The island's east coast is home to several small bays and beaches. The first one of note, tiny **Rousoum**, is tucked between Patitiri and Votsi and very popular with local families.

Next is the sandy and gently sloping **Hrysi Milia Beach**, another kid-friendly beach. Two kilometres on, **Cape Kokkinokastro** is the site of the ancient city of Ikos, with remains of city walls under the sea. Continuing north, the road branches off 2km to **Leftos Gialos**, with a lovely pebble beach and the superb **Taverna Eleonas** (☎ 24240 66066).

Steni Vala, a small fishing village and deep-water yacht port with a permanent population of no more than 40, has two small but decent beaches; pebbly **Glyfa** just above the village and sandy **Agios Petros** just below. Steni Vala is also home to the marine park's Rescue and Rehabilitation Centre for the Mediterranean monk seal. Four tavernas overlook the small marina, with **To Farnari** (☎ 24240 66013) claiming the best views of the harbour and open from morning till midnight.

There are 30-odd rooms in domatia, as well as modest **Ikaros Camping** (☎ 24240 65772), next to the beach and decently shaded by olive trees. Try **Ikaros Café & Market** (☎ 24240 65390) for reliable lodging information and more.

Kalamakia, 2km further north, is the last village of note, and has a few domatia and tavernas. The fishing boats usually tie up directly in front of **Margarita's Taverna** (☎ 24240 65738), where the morning catch of fish and lobster seems to jump from boat to plate.

THE ORIGINAL CHEESE PIE

Tyropita (cheese pie) is almost deified in the northern Sporades. The popular pie is made with goats cheese and delicate filo dough, the same flaky crust as in sweet baklava. The filled dough is rolled and coiled up, then fried quickly and served hot – a method that evolved in the wood-oven kitchens of Alonnisos. Of course, like anything with a place in folklore, the pie's origins are open to debate. One version, popular on neighbouring Skopelos, has it that when *spanikopita* (spinach pies) were slowly baking, resourceful mothers quieted hungry children by tearing off a piece of filo, throwing in a handful of cheese, and frying it quickly with a reprimand, 'Here, stop your screaming'.

Alonnisos residents tell another version and claim that history is on their side. In the 1950s, following the collapse of the cottage wine industry, many struggling Alonnisos farmers went to work on neighbouring Skopelos, picking plums. Their salty cheese pie lasted all day in the fields. Not surprisingly, it soon appeared in the country kitchens of Skopelos. In the 1990s, a popular daytime TV host touted the pie, but credited Skopelos with its origin. Predictably, frozen 'Skopelos Cheese Pie' soon showed up on mainland supermarket shelves. Today, you can even buy it in the Athens' airport departure lounge, 'the deterioration of an imitation', according to a longtime Alonnisos resident, Pakis. But don't count on the frozen pie resembling the original and superior island version. Of course, the tasty treat has evolved over the years, and you will find breakfast versions with sugar and cinnamon, and others using wild greens or lamb, especially popular in winter with red wine.

Stunned Alonnisos folk still can't get over what's happened to their simple and delicious recipe. As one Skopelos businesswoman, Mahi, confided, 'Basically, we stole it!'

Beyond Kalamakia, the sealed road continues 3km to a wetland marsh and **Agios Dimitrios Beach**, with a canteen and domatia opposite a graceful stretch of white pebbles. Beyond this, the road narrows to a footpath heading inland.

ISLETS AROUND ALONNISOS

Alonnisos is surrounded by eight uninhabited islets, all of which are rich in flora and fauna. **Piperi**, the furthest island northeast of Alonnisos, is a refuge for the monk seal and is strictly off-limits. **Gioura**, also off-limits, is home to an unusual species of wild goat known for the crucifix-shaped marking on its spine. Excursion boats can visit an old monastery and olive press on **Kyra Panagia**. The most remote of the group, **Psathoura**, boasts the submerged remains of an ancient city and the brightest lighthouse in the Aegean.

Peristera, just off Alonnisos' east coast, has several sandy beaches and the remains of a castle. Nearby **Lehousa** is known for its stalactite-filled sea caves. **Skantzoura**, to the southeast of Alonnisos, is the habitat of the Eleanora's falcon and the rare Audouin's seagull. The eighth island in the group, situated between Peristera and Skantzoura, is known as **Duo Adelphi** (Two Brothers); each 'brother' is actually a small island, both home to vipers, according to local fishermen who refuse to step foot on either.

SKYROS ΣΚΥΡΟΣ

pop 2602

Skyros is the largest of the Sporades group, though it can seem like two islands – the small bays, rolling farmland and pine forests of the north, and the barren hills and rocky shoreline of the south. A number of expats, particularly English and Dutch, have made Skyros their home.

In Byzantine times, rogues and criminals exiled here from the mainland entered into a mutually lucrative collaboration with invading pirates. The exiles became the elite of Skyrian society, decorating their houses with pirate booty looted from merchant ships: hand-carved furniture, plates and copper ornaments from Europe, the Middle East and East Asia. Today, similar items adorn almost every Skyrian house.

In Greek mythology, Skyros was the hiding place of young Achilles. See p440 for more information about the Skyros Lenten Carnival and its traditions, which allude to Achilles' heroic feats.

Skyros was also the last port of call for the English poet Rupert Brooke (1887–1915), who died of septicaemia on a French hospital ship off the coast of Skyros en route to the Battle of Gallipoli.

Getting There & Away
AIR

In summer there are three flights weekly (Wednesday, Saturday and Sunday) between Athens and Skyros (€38, 25 minutes). Between Thessaloniki and Skyros, there are three flights weekly on Monday, Tuesday and Saturday (€58, 35 minutes). For tickets, visit **Skyros Travel Agency** (☎ 22220 91600; www .skyrostravel.com; Agoras St).

FERRY

A regular ferry service is provided by *Achileas*, between the port of Kymi (Evia) and Skyros (€8.30, 1¾ hours). On Friday and Sunday, the ferry (usually) makes two crossings; on the remaining days, just one crossing. You can buy tickets from **Achileas ticket office** (☎ 22220 91789; fax 22220 91791; Agoras; ⊗ 9am-1pm & 7-10pm), near the bank on Agoras in Skyros Town. There is also a ferry ticket kiosk at the dock in Linaria, and another at the dock in Kymi (Evia).

Skyros Travel Agency also sells tickets for the Kymi–Athens bus (€13.20, 3½ hours), which always meets the ferry on arrival at Paralia Kymis (the port of Kymi).

Getting Around
BUS & TAXI

In high season there are daily buses departing from Skyros Town to Linaria (€1.20) and to Molos (via Magazia). Buses for both Skyros Town and Molos meet the ferry at Linaria. However, outside of high season there are only one or two buses to Linaria (to coincide with the ferry arrivals) and none to Molos. A taxi from Skyros Town to Linaria is €12; to the airport, it's €18.

CAR & MOTORCYCLE

Cars, motorbikes and mountain bikes can all be rented from **Martina's Rentals** (☎ 22220 92022; 6974752380) near the police station. The reasonable **Vayos Motorbikes** (☎ 22220 92957) is near the bus stop.

EVIA & THE SPORADES

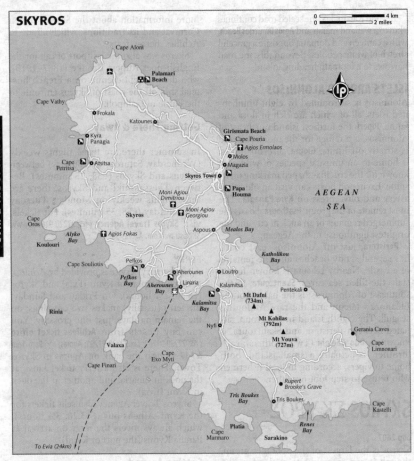

SKYROS

0 — 4 km
0 — 2 miles

Cape Aloni

Palamari Beach

Cape Vathy

Frokala

Katounes

Girismata Beach
Cape Pouria
Agios Ermolaos
Molos
Magazia

Kyra Panagia

Cape Petritsa   Atsitsa

Skyros Town

Papa Houma

AEGEAN
SEA

Moni Agiou Dimitriou

Skyros

Moni Agiou Georgiou

Cape Oros

Agios Fokas

Aspous   Mealos Bay

Alyko Bay

Koulouri

Katholikou Bay

Cape Souliotis   Pefkos

Pefkos Bay

Aherounes   Loutro
Aherounes Bay   Linaria   Kalamitsa   Pentekali
Kalamitsa Bay

Rinia

Mt Dafni (734m)

Nyfi   Mt Kohilas (792m)

Gerania Caves

Valaxa   Mt Vouva (727m)   Cape Limnonari

Cape Exo Myti
Cape Finari

Rupert Brooke's Grave

Cape Kastelli

Tris Boukes Bay   Tris Boukes

To Evia (24km)

Platia   Renes Bay

Cape Marmaro   Sarakino

SKYROS TOWN

Skyros' capital is a striking, dazzlingly white town of flat-roofed Cycladic-style houses draped over a high rocky bluff. It's topped by a 13th-century fortress and the monastery of Agios Georgios, and is laced with labyrinthine, smooth cobblestoned streets, which invite wandering.

Orientation

The bus stop is at the southern end of town on the main thoroughfare (Agoras) – an animated street lined with tavernas, bars and grocery stores and flanked by narrow winding alleyways. To reach the central *plateia*, you need to walk up the hill; the narrow road soon becomes even narrower, marking the begin-

ning of the town's pedestrian zone. Motorbikes still manage to squeeze through, but cars must park in the nearby car park.

About 100m beyond the *plateia*, the main drag of Agoras forks. The right fork leads up to the fortress and Moni Agiou Georgiou, with its fine frescoes and sweeping views. The left fork zigzags to two small museums adjacent to Plateia Rupert Brooke, where a simple bronze statue of a nude Rupert Brooke faces the sea. The frankness of the statue caused an outcry among the local islanders when it was first installed in the 1930s.

From Plateia Rupert Brooke the cobbled steps descend to Magazia Beach, located 1km away.

Information

EMERGENCY
Police (☎ 22220 91274) Take the first right after Skyros Travel Agency, and turn right at the T-junction. There is no tourist police office.

INTERNET ACCESS
Mano.com (☎ 22220 92473; Agoras St; per hr €3; ☒ 9am-1.30pm & 6.30-11.30pm)

Video Club Internet (☎ 22220 92802; Agoras St; per hr €3; ☒ 9am-1.30pm & 6-11pm)

MONEY
National Bank of Greece (Agoras St) Next to the central square.

POST
The post office is just west of the square.

TRAVEL AGENCIES
Skyros Travel Agency (☎ 22220 91600; www .skyrostravel.com; Agoras St; ☒ 9am-2pm & 6.30-11pm) It has island maps and can help with room bookings, travel reservations, car and motorbike rentals, diving and excursions around Skyros.

Sights & Activities
Skyros Town has two museums. The **Manos Faltaïts Folk Museum** (☎ 22220 91232; www.faltaits.gr; Plateia Rupert Brooke; admission €2; ☒ 10am-2pm & 6-9pm) is a one-of-a-kind private museum housing the outstanding collection of a Skyrian ethnologist, Manos Faltaïts, and detailing the mythology and folklore of Skyros. The 19th-century house is packed with Skyrian costumes, antique furniture and ceramics, vintage books, photographs and a small shop.

The **Archaeological Museum** (☎ 22220 91327; Plateia Rupert Brooke; admission €2; ☒ 8.30am-3pm Tue-Sun) features excellent examples of Mycenaean pottery found near Magazia. Interesting too is a traditional Skyrian house interior, transported in its entirety to the benefactor's home.

Every year around September, Skyros is host to a **half-marathon** (☎ 22220 92789), which starts in Atsitsa and ends on the *plateia* in Skyros Town, with drummers welcoming the first runners across the finish line. A minimarathon for the children sets the tone, followed by music and dancing on the square.

Courses
Reiki courses are offered by longtime island resident and reiki master **Janet Smith** (☎ 22220 93510; Skyros Town; www.simplelifeskyros.com). It's on the south edge of Skyros Town, 200m below Hotel Nefeli.

Atsitsa has the Skyros Centre (p441), which also runs courses.

Tours
A day-long boat excursion (€35) to the Gerania sea caves on the southeast coast or nearby Sarakino Islet includes lunch and a swim. Contact **Skyros Travel** (☎ 22220 91600) for details.

Sleeping
Accommodation in Skyros Town varies from conventional small hotels and domatia to individual rooms in traditional Skyrian houses. If you arrive by bus, you'll usually be met with offers on nearby domatia; prices should range from €25 to €40 for a single/double. Prices quoted here are for the summer season, mid-July to August.

BUDGET & MIDRANGE
Hotel Elena (☎ /fax 22220 91738; s/d/tr €30/45/60; ⓟ ☒ ⌨) The clean and renovated Elena is a good budget choice with comfortable beds, balcony and minifridge. It's just 50m past the bus stop, and easy to find after a night on the town.

ourpick Atherinis Rooms (☎ 22220 93510, 6979292976; d/apt from €45/60; ⓟ ☒) Managed by Dimitris Atherinis and English transplant Janet Smith, the self-catering apartments and double rooms feature hand-tiled baths and overlook a shaded garden. Breakfast (€5) includes fresh juice and homemade scones. Atherinis is located 300m below the bus stop, towards the sea.

Pension Nikolas (☎ 22220 91778; fax 22220 93400; s/d/tr €50/60/70; ⓟ ☒) Set back on a small quiet road, this comfortable and friendly *pension* is only a five-minute walk to busy Agoras. The upper rooms have air-conditioning and balconies; the lower rooms have fans and open onto a shady garden.

TOP END
Hotel Nefeli & Dimitrios Studios (☎ 22220 91964; www .skyros-nefeli.gr; d/studios/ste incl breakfast €125/190/300; ⓟ ☒ ⌨ ☒) This well-managed hotel on the edge of town has a minimalist-meets-Skyrian feel to it, with vintage photographs, handsome furnishings and large baths. The adjacent family-size studios are part of a remodelled

EVIA & THE SPORADES

EVIA & THE SPORADES

SKYROS CARNIVAL

In this wild pre-Lenten festival, which takes place on the last four weekends before Kathara Deftera (Clean Monday – the first Monday in Lent, 40 days before Easter), young men don goat masks, hairy jackets and dozens of copper goat bells. They then proceed to clank and dance around town, each with a partner (another man), dressed up as a Skyrian bride but also wearing a goat mask. During these revelries there is singing and dancing, performances of plays, recitations of satirical poems and much drinking and feasting. Women and children join in, wearing fancy dress as well. These strange goings-on are overtly pagan, with elements of Dionysian festivals, including goat worship. In ancient times, as today, Skyros was renowned for its goats meat and milk.

The transvestism evident in the carnival seems to derive from the cult of Achilles associated with Skyros in Greek mythology. According to legend, the island was the childhood hiding place for the boy Achilles, whose mother, Thetis, feared a prophecy requiring her son's skills in the Trojan War. The boy was given to the care of King Lykomides of Skyros, who raised him disguised as one of his own daughters. Young Achilles was outwitted, however, by Odysseus, who arrived with jewels and finery for the girls, along with a sword and shield. When the maiden Achilles alone showed interest in the weapons, Odysseus discovered his secret, then persuaded him to go to Troy where he distinguished himself in battle. This annual festival is the subject of Joy Koulentianou's book *The Goat Dance of Skyros*.

Skyrian house. Both properties share a beautiful saltwater swimming pool and bar.

Eating

Skyros welcomes a steady number of visiting Athenians, with the pleasant result that island cooks do not cater to touristy tongues. You can find a number of authentic Skyrian dishes in the smallest taverna, including several with goats milk or meat.

Maryetis Restaurant (☎ 22220 91311; Agoras St; mains €5-9) The local favourite for grilled fish and octopus *stifadho*, along with hearty soups and mezedhes like black-eyed beans and fava dip.

our pick O Pappous kai Ego (☎ 22220 93200; Agoras St; mains €6-9) The name of this small taverna means 'my grandfather and me', and it's easy to see how one generation followed another. Mezedhes are excellent, especially fava beans with wild aniseed and onions, along with Skyrian dolmadhes made with a touch of goats milk – and a very good washing-it-down house wine.

Liakos Café (☎ 22220 93509; mains €5-10) On summer evenings, head to the rooftop terrace at Liakos, where the fusion menu includes seafood risotto, cold octopus salad and fava beans with sun-dried tomatoes.

Taverna Lambros (☎ 22220 91388; mains €4.70-8) Family-run Lambros is just 3km south of Skyros Town in Aspous. Generous-sized dishes include lamb and pork grills, fresh fish gumbo and Skyrian cheese bread.

Drinking

Nightlife in Skyros Town centres mostly around the bars on Agoras; the further north you go away from the *plateia*, the more mellow the sounds.

Kalypso (☎ 22220 92696; Agoras St) Classy Kalypso plays lots of jazz and blues, and owner-bartender Hristos makes a killer margarita, along with homemade sangria. A side room sports an internet connection.

Rodon (☎ 22220 92168; Agoras St) This smart and comfortable late-night hang-out is a mellow spot to end the evening. Bonus points for big drinks and fresh juices.

Nostos Cafe & Bar (☎ 22220 91797; Agoras St) Above the National Bank, this swank bar overlooking the *plateia* serves a range of mixed drinks, coffees and appetisers.

Entertainment

Skyropoula Disco (☎ 22220 91180) Don't bother showing up before midnight at this ring road hang-out, where the DJs play a danceable mix of European and Greek pop sounds till dawn.

MAGAZIA & MOLOS
ΜΑΓΑΖΙΑ & ΜΩΛΟΣ

The resort of Magazia, a compact and attractive place of winding alleys, is at the southern end of a splendid, long sandy beach, situated a short distance north of Skyros Town. Skinny-dippers can leave it all behind at **Papa Houma** near the southern end of Magazia.

Quieter and more arid Molos is at the northern end of the beach. Until recently, there was little more than a windmill and the adjacent rock-hewn Church of Agios Ermolaos to mark it. Today, a number of tavernas and small domatia have opened up.

Sleeping

Georgia Tsakamis Rooms (☎ 22220 91357; gtsakamis@yahoo.gr; Magazia; d/tr €45/50; 🞪) You can't get much closer to the sand and sea than at these geranium-adorned domatia 20m from the beach, opposite a handy car park.

Deidamia Hotel (☎ 22220 92008; www.deidamia.com; d/f incl breakfast from €45/70; P 🞪 🖳) The spacious and tidy Deidamia is on the road entering Magazia, opposite a small market. Look for the bougainvillea garden and rooftop solar panels.

ourpick Perigiali Studios (☎ 22220 92075; www.perigiali.com; d/tr/f incl breakfast from €68/80/90; 🞪) Perigiali feels secluded despite being only 30m from the beach. The Skyrian-style rooms overlook a rambling garden anchored by a large fig tree, and English-speaking Ermelia is full of ideas for travellers.

Also recommended:

Studio Ireni (☎ 22220 91852, 6977167595; Molos; d/tr from €30/40; P 🞪) Welcoming bargain domatia.

Domatia & Studios Eleanna (☎ 22220 91863, 69725 22889; Molos; s/d/tr €50/70/80; P 🞪) Handsome Skyrian furnishings, balcony, kitchenette and large bath.

Eating & Drinking

Juicy Beach Bar (☎ 22220 933337; snacks €2-5; Magazia; ☻ 10am-1am) Escape the midday sun or chill out under the stars at busy Juicy's, with breakfasts throughout the day.

Taverna Stefanos (☎ 22220 91272; mains €4.50-8) Perch yourself on the terrace of this traditional eatery, overlooking the southern end of Magazia Beach, and choose from a range of ready-to-eat oven dishes, big portions of souvlakia and fresh fish by the kilo.

Oi Istories Tou Barba (My Uncle's Stories; ☎ 22220 91453; Molos; mains €4-10) Look for the light blue railing above the beach in Molos to find this excellent café and *tsipouradhiko* with well-prepared prawn and octopus mezedhes.

Shopping

Argo (☎ 22220 92158; Agoras St) Argo specialises in high-quality copies of ceramics from the Faltaïts Museum.

Andreou Woodcarving (☎ 22220 92926; Agoras St) Get a close look at the intricate designs that distinguish traditional Skyrian furniture at this handsome shop on the main drag.

Several pottery workshops spin their wheels in Magazia without bothering to put a sign out front, but they are happy to see visitors, and some of their exceptional work is for sale. English-speaking **Amanda** and **Stathis Katsarelias** (☎ 22220 92918) run a studio on the small lane between the main road and the beach; look for the yellow Kodak sign next door. The studios of **Efrossini Varsamou-Nikolaou** (☎ 22220 91142) are in the Deidamia Hotel.

AROUND SKYROS

Linaria Λιναριά

Linaria, the port of Skyros, is tucked into a small bay filled with bobbing fishing boats and lined with tavernas and *ouzeries*. Things perk up briefly whenever the *Achileas* ferry comes in, announcing its surreal arrival with the booming sound of Richard Strauss' *Also Sprach Zarathustra* blasting from the ship's huge speakers. The bus to Skyros Town lacks a similar sound system, but coincides perfectly with the ferry's arrival and departure.

SLEEPING & EATING

King Lykomides Rooms (☎ 22220 93249, 6972694434; soula@skyrosnet.gr; r incl breakfast €45-60; P 🞪 🖳) You can practically stumble off the ferry and into this efficient domatia, managed by the hospitable Soula Pappas. It has well-maintained rooms, each with balcony.

Ouzeri Maestros (☎ 22220 91995; drinks & snacks €2-4) Tasty ouzo-compatible mezedhes like grilled octopus and calamari are served up by Tasos, the welcoming owner of this port stand-by under the big plane tree.

Kavos Bar (☎ 22220 93213; drinks & snacks €2-5) This swank open-air bar, perched on the hill overlooking the port, pulls in Skyrians from across the island for drinks at sunset.

Taverna Filippeos (☎ 22220 93476; mains €4-9) This busy and friendly fish taverna near the ferry dock serves traditional ready-to-eat oven dishes such as *briam* (oven-baked vegetable casserole) and *pastitsio*.

Atsitsa Ατσίτσα

The sleepy and picturesque port village of Atsitsa on the island's west coast occupies a woodsy setting, shaded by pines that approach

---

WIND FARM DEBATE

Gauging which way the wind is blowing is becoming trickier on Skyros, where a controversy is heating up between vocal residents and the Greek Orthodox Church, which quietly began negotiations in 2005 with a mainland contractor and a government regulatory authority. At stake: whether to establish a massive wind farm (at an estimated cost of €500 million) on the southern half of the island to meet the EU's request that Greece utilise renewable energy to provide 20% of its needs by 2010.

If the plan is approved, Skyros would be home to the largest wind farm in Europe, and the island's delicate breeding grounds for the rare Skyrian pony and the Eleonora's falcon would be at the mercy of 150m-high wind turbines.

No-one on Skyros is opposed to sustainable solutions to Greece's energy needs. But as one resident said, 'It's a matter of scale'. The largest landowner in southern Skyros happens to be the Church and, with so much money at stake, there's not much trust in the wind these days.

---

the shore. Atsitsa is also home to the holistic and secluded **Skyros Centre** (☎ 22220 92842; Atsitsa; www.skyros.com), a New Age centre that runs residential courses on a range of subjects, from yoga and massage to sailing and windsurfing. Contact the centre for detailed information. **Taverna Antonis** (☎ 22220 92990; mains €4-8) is about 20m from the small pier where the family's fishing boat ties up. The menu has several excellent fish dishes.

Beaches

Beaches on the northwest coast are subject to strong winter currents and summer *meltemi* winds.

Atsitsa has a small pebble beach shaded by pines, good for freelance camping, but too rocky for swimming. Just to the north (1.5km) is the superior swimming beach of **Kyra Panagia**, named for the monastery on the hill above. Just 1.5km to the south, the tiny and protected north-facing bay at **Cape Petritsa** is also good for swimming.

At **Pefkos Bay**, 10km southeast of Atsitsa, there is a beautiful horseshoe-shaped beach with two tavernas and domatia at the southern end. Nearby, the beach at **Aherounes** has a gentle sandy bottom, and is very nice for

children. There are two tavernas and domatia opposite the road.

To the north and near the airport, **Palamari** is a graceful stretch of sandy beach that does not get crowded. Palamari is also the site of a well-marked **archaeological excavation** of a walled Bronze Age town dating from 2500 BC.

Rupert Brooke's Grave

Rupert Brooke's well-tended marble grave is in a quiet olive grove just inland from Tris Boukes Bay in the south of the island, and marked with a wooden sign in Greek on the roadside. The gravestone is inscribed with some of Brooke's verses, beginning with the following apt epitaph:

> If I should die think only this of me:
> That there's some corner of a foreign field
> That is forever England.

From coastal Kalamitsa, just east of Linaria, a road passes the village of Nyfi, and brings you to Brooke's simple tomb. No buses come here, and travel is restricted beyond this corner of the island, which is dominated by the Greek Naval station on Tris Boukes Bay.

Ionian Islands
Τα Ιόνια Νησιά

It's hard not to fall for the Ionian Islands, an archipelago that sweeps down the west coast of mainland Greece and includes Corfu, Paxi, Lefkada, Ithaki, Kefallonia and Zakynthos. Discovering these islands is a tantalising odyssey. Their natural beauty embraces the visitor – the vast olive groves, intriguing mountainscapes and iridescent waters of the Ionian Sea offer something for adventure seekers, culture vultures and beach bums alike.

Each island boasts a distinct tradition, cuisine and architecture – the remaining influences of former invading forces such as the Venetians, French and British. These influences are obvious in Corfu Town, where you can watch a cricket match on the Spianada, drink under Parisian-style arcades and wander through the town's Venetian-style alleyways. Elsewhere in the Ionians – in the traditional fishing or mountain villages – you can stroll through central plazas shaded by bougainvilleas and plane trees, or relax under a taverna's vine-covered canopy with the soporific scent of jasmine. Less-tasteful encounters exist, in the form of invasive, package-tourist beach developments, but these can be avoided. It's easy to get off the beaten track: find your own isolated swimming coves in a boat, wander through olive groves, or stumble across an authentic *kafeneio* (coffee house). Cultural adventurers can explore fortresses, Byzantine churches and Homeric sites. Adventure addicts can trek, cycle, windsurf and scuba dive, and anyone can try bird-watching or golf.

The culinary experience rounds off an Ionian journey: indulge in fresh, generous helpings of local dishes, served with a huge dollop of local *filoxenia* (hospitality).

IONIAN ISLANDS

HIGHLIGHTS

- ■ **Architecture** Wandering the narrow streets of Corfu's old town (p449), pausing for a frappé under one of many Venetian buildings

- ■ **Getting Away From It All** Walking through the ancient olive groves of Paxi (p459) and swimming in the crystal waters of nearby Antipaxi (p462)

- ■ **Scenic Splendour** Cruising along the lofty spine of Homeric Ithaki (p473)

- ■ **Beauty Spot** Exploring the pretty village of Assos (p472) and swimming in the iridescent blue waters of nearby Myrtos Beach (p472) on Kefallonia

- ■ **Food Frenzy** Following your taste buds around Zakynthos to discover local treats (p479)

Corfu Town
★ Paxi
★ Antipaxi
Assos ★ ★ Ithaki
Myrtos Beach ★
★ Zakynthos

| ■ POPULATION: 221,890 | ■ AREA: 2432 SQ KM |

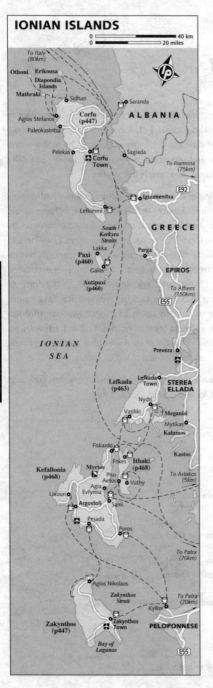

IONIAN ISLANDS

HISTORY

The origin of the name 'Ionian' is obscure, but it's thought to derive from the goddess Io. As yet another of Zeus' paramours, Io fled the wrath of a jealous Hera (in the shape of a heifer), and happened to pass through the waters now known as the Ionian Sea.

If we are to believe Homer, the islands were important during Mycenaean times; however, no magnificent palaces or even modest villages from that period have been revealed, though Mycenaean tombs have been unearthed. Ancient history lies buried beneath tonnes of earthquake rubble – seismic activity has been constant on all Ionian islands.

By the 8th century BC, the Ionian Islands were in the clutches of the mighty city-state of Corinth, which regarded them as stepping stones on the route to Sicily and Italy. A century later, Corfu staged a successful revolt against Corinth, which was allied to Sparta, and became an ally of Sparta's archenemy, Athens. This alliance provoked Sparta into challenging Athens, thus precipitating the Peloponnesian Wars (431–404 BC). The wars left Corfu depleted, as they did all participants, and Corfu became little more than a staging post for whoever happened to be holding sway in Greece. By the end of the 3rd century BC, Corfu, along with the other Ionian Islands, fell under Roman rule. Following the decline of the Roman Empire, the islands saw the usual waves of invaders suffered by Greece. After the fall of Constantinople, the islands became Venetian.

Corfu was never part of the Ottoman Empire. Paxi, Kefallonia, Zakynthos and Ithaki were variously occupied by the Turks, but the Venetians held them longest. The exception was Lefkada, which was Turkish for 200 years.

IONIAN KYTHIRA?

The island of Kythira (including its satellite, Antikythira) dangles off the southern tip of the Peloponnese between the Ionian and Aegean Seas. Historically, Kythira is considered part of the Ionian Islands (see p482 for full details), and today is administered from Piraeus. Though, due to its location and suitable ferry connections, visitors are most likely to visit Kythira from the Peloponnese.

Venice fell to Napoleon in 1797. Two years later, under the Treaty of Campo Formio, the Ionian Islands were allotted to France. In 1799 Russian forces wrested the islands from Napoleon, but by 1807 they were his again. The all-powerful British couldn't resist meddling, and in 1815, after Napoleon's downfall, the islands became a British protectorate under the jurisdiction of a series of Lord High Commissioners.

British rule was oppressive but, on a positive note, the British constructed roads, bridges, schools and hospitals, established trade links, and developed agriculture and industry. However, the nationalistic fervour throughout the rest of Greece soon reached the Ionian Islands, and a call for unity was realised in 1864 when Britain relinquished the islands to Greece.

In WWII the Italians invaded Corfu as part of Mussolini's plan to resurrect the mighty Roman Empire. Italy surrendered to the Allies in September 1943 and, in revenge, the Germans massacred thousands of Italians who had occupied the island. The Nazis also sent some 5000 Corfiot Jews to Auschwitz.

The islands saw a great deal of emigration after WWII, and again following the earthquakes of 1948 and 1953 that devastated the region. But while Greeks left the islands, the foreign invasion has never really stopped, and these days takes the form of package tourism from northern Europe.

GETTING THERE & AWAY
Air
Corfu, Kefallonia and Zakynthos have airports; Lefkada has no airport, but Aktion airport, near Preveza on the mainland, is about 20km away. These four airports have frequent flights to/from Athens. **Olympic Airlines** (www.olympicairlines.com) has introduced a useful service linking the Ionians: three times a week there are return flights from Corfu to Zakynthos, stopping en route at Kefallonia.

From May to September, many charter flights come from northern Europe and the UK to Corfu, Kefallonia, Zakynthos and Preveza.

AirSea Lines, a seaplane service, runs flights between changing destinations. At the time of research, these included Corfu, Paxi and Lefkada.

WWW.PLANNING YOUR TRIP.COM

There are loads of websites devoted to the Ionians – here are some of the best we've found:

Corfu www.kerkyra.gr, www.kerkyra.net
Kefallonia www.kefalonia.gr, www.kefalonia
.net.gr
Lefkada www.lefkada.gr, www.lefkas.net
Ionian Islands www.greeka.com/ionian
Ithaki www.ithacagreece.com
Paxi www.paxos-greece.com, www.paxos.tk
Zakynthos www.zakynthos-net.gr, www
.zanteweb.gr

Bus
KTEL (www.ktel.org) long-distance buses connect each major island with Athens and Thessaloniki, and usually also with Patra or Kyllini in the Peloponnese. Buses to Corfu, Lefkada, Kefallonia, Ithaki and Zakynthos depart from Athens' Terminal A bus station.

Ferry
DOMESTIC
The Peloponnese has two departure ports for the Ionian Islands: Patra for ferries to Corfu, Kefallonia and Ithaki; and Kyllini for ferries to Kefallonia and Zakynthos. Epiros has one port, Igoumenitsa, for Corfu (island) and Paxi; and Sterea Ellada has one, Astakos, for Ithaki and Kefallonia (although this service is limited to high season). A useful website is www.ferries.gr.

The following table gives an overall view of the scheduled domestic ferries to the Ionians from mainland ports in high season. Note: prices change regularly.

It is not possible to island hop directly between the northern and southern islands. Corfu and Paxi are connected by ferry and hydrofoil, but unfortunately there are no services from either Corfu or Paxi to Lefkada.

Within the southern Ionians, Lefkada, Kefallonia and Ithaki are well connected by ferry, and there's a twice-daily service between southern Kefallonia and northern Zakynthos (an alternative is to sail from Argostoli to Kyllini in the Peloponnese, and from there to Zakynthos Town).

Further details can be found under each island entry.

DOMESTIC FERRY CONNECTIONS TO THE IONIAN ISLANDS

Origin	Destination	Duration	Fare	Frequency
Astakos	Sami (Kefallonia)	3hr	€10	daily
	Piso Aetos (Ithaki)	2½hr	€8	daily
Igoumenitsa	Corfu Town	1¼hr	€6.50	16 daily
	Lefkimmi (Corfu)	1hr	€4.50	6 daily
Igoumenitsa	Gaïos (Paxi)	1½hr	€7.60	daily
Kyllini	Zakynthos Town	1hr	€6.50	5-7 daily
	Argostoli (Kefallonia)	2½hr	€12.50	daily
	Poros (Kefallonia)	1½hr	€8.10	2-5 daily
Patra	Corfu Town	6-7½hr	€33	1 daily
	Sami (Kefallonia)	2½hr	€14.50	daily
	Vathy/Piso Aetos (Ithaki)	4hr	€14.50	daily

INTERNATIONAL

Corfu has regular connections with three ports in Italy (Brindisi, Bari and Venice), operated by a handful of ferry companies sailing between Italy and Igoumenitsa and/or Patra. (Travellers can also sail between Ancona and Igoumenitsa, then transfer to a local ferry.) Crossings are most frequent in July and August, but there are year-round services at least weekly between Corfu and Brindisi, Bari and Venice.

From Corfu it's also possible to cross to Albania, or to visit on a day trip. Recommendations include the following:

Agoudimos Lines (www.agoudimos-lines.com) From Brindisi to Corfu and Igoumenitsa, and Bari to Kefallonia, Igoumenitsa and Patra.

ANEK Lines (www.anek.gr) From Venice to Corfu.

Blue Star Ferries (www.bluestarferries.com) From Bari to Corfu, Igoumenitsa and Patra.

Hellenic Mediterranean Lines (www.hml.it) From Brindisi to Corfu, Igoumenitsa, Kefallonia and Patra.

Minoan Lines (www.minoan.gr) From Venice to Igoumenitsa, Corfu and Patra.

SNAV (www.snav.it) High-season, high-speed catamaran services between Brindisi, Corfu and Paxi.

Superfast Ferries (www.superfast.com) From Bari to Corfu, Igoumenitsa and Patra.

Ventouris (www.ventouris.gr) From Bari to Corfu and Igoumenitsa.

Note: the only ferry companies that accept Eurail and Inter-rail passes are Bluestar, Superfast and Agoudimos. All international ferry companies also have special offers and concessions for seniors, families and last-minute tickets.

CORFU ΚΕΡΚΥΡΑ

pop 114,000

Corfu – or Kerkyra (ker-kih-rah) in Greek – is the second-largest and the greenest Ionian island. It is also the best known. It was Homer's 'beautiful and rich land', and Odysseus' last stop on his journey home to Ithaki. Shakespeare reputedly used it as a background for *The Tempest*. In the 20th century, writers the Durrell brothers – among others – extolled its virtues.

With the nation's highest rainfall, scores of vegetables and herbs thrive here, especially in spring. With its beguiling landscape of wildflowers, and cypress trees rising out of shimmering olive groves, Corfu hangs in there as one of Greece's most beautiful islands. Sadly, areas are suffering from blatant and unheeded over-development.

Getting There & Away

AIR

Olympic Airlines (☎ 26610 22962; www.olympicairlines .com) is based at the airport. The national airline has two flights to/from Athens daily (from €30 if booked extra early), and four flights a week to/from Thessaloniki (€70). You can also fly three times weekly to Preveza (€35), Kefallonia (€35) and Zakynthos (€47). Prices exclude changeable taxes.

Aegean Airlines (☎ 26610 27100; www.aegeanair .com) has two to three flights a day between Athens and Corfu (from €29). Its office is located at the airport and, if closed, calls will be diverted to its office in Athens.

AirSea Lines (Map p450; ☎ 26610 49800, 26610 99316; www.airsealines.com; Ethnikis Antistasis, Corfu Town) is a seaplane service that runs in high season to a schedule that seems to change annually. Check the website for the current permutations and combinations. At the time of research there were services between Corfu and Paxi (€40 to €50) and Corfu and Lefkada (€55 to €70). In Corfu, purchase tickets from the AirSea Lines office on Ethnikis Antistasis (near the new port). A minibus will take you from here to the departure point at Marina Gouvia, 8km away. Baggage weight allowances apply.

BUS
KTEL (☎ 26610 28898) runs buses three times daily (and another three per week via Lefkimmi in the island's south) between Corfu Town and Athens (€44.20, 8½ hours). There's also a daily service to/from Thessaloniki (€42, eight hours); for both destinations budget another €6.50 for the ferry between Corfu and the mainland. Long-distance tickets should be purchased in advance from Corfu Town's long-distance bus station (p448) on I Theotoki, between Plateia San Rocco and the new port.

FERRY
Domestic
Hourly ferries travel daily between Corfu and Igoumenitsa (per person/car €6.50/26, 1¼ to two hours). Car ferries go to Paxi (per person/car €7.60/55.60, three hours) two or three times weekly, and daily in high season (but the hydrofoil is a more frequent option). In high

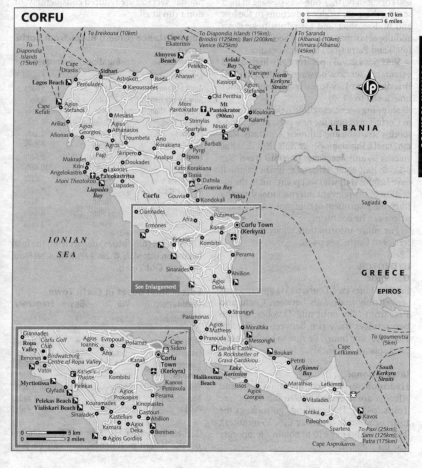

CORFU

0 — 10 km
0 — 6 miles

season you can travel to/from Patra on one of the international ferries that call at Corfu (€33, six to 7½ hours) en route to/from Italy.

There are also six ferries daily between Lefkimmi in the island's south and Igoumenitsa (€4.50, one hour).

International

Corfu is on the Patra–Igoumenitsa ferry route to Italy (Brindisi, Bari and Venice), although ferries to/from Ancona don't stop at Corfu (passengers need to disembark at Igoumenitsa and cross to Corfu on a local ferry).

Ferries go to Brindisi (€56, eight hours, two daily), and in summer usually once daily to Bari (€64, 10 to 12 hours) and Venice (€74, 24 to 26 hours). Fares listed here are for deck (not airline seats or cabin berths), one-way passage in high season; there are sizable reductions in the low and mid-seasons, and for return tickets. An additional tax may also apply. See Igoumenitsa (p98) and Patra (p98) for more details.

SNAV (www.snav.it) operates daily high-speed catamaran services between Corfu, Paxi and Brindisi from July to early September (four hours, €85 to €150).

Shipping agencies selling tickets are found in Corfu Town near the new port, along Xenofondos Stratigou and Ethnikis Antistasis. **Mancan Travel & Shipping** (p452; ☎ 26610 32664; Eleftheriou Venizelou 38) and **Agoudimos Lines/GLD Travel** (Map p450; ☎ 26610 80030; tickets@gld.gr; Ethnikis Antistasis 1) have helpful staff who will point you in the direction of the relevant international shipping lines; the assortment of companies, routes and prices can be confusing.

For more information regarding Italian ferries to Corfu, see p446.

HYDROFOIL
Domestic

Petrakis Lines (see Tours, p451) operates passenger-only hydrofoils between Corfu and Paxi from May until mid-October. One to two services daily run between Corfu and Paxi (€15, one hour). Be sure to book one day prior; places fill quickly.

International

Hydrofoil services connecting Corfu and Albania are operated by Petrakis Lines (see Tours, p451). Daily sailings go to/from the town of Saranda (one way €15, 25 minutes). Travellers also pay €10 to obtain a temporary visa for Albania.

Getting Around
TO/FROM THE AIRPORT

There is no bus service operating between Corfu Town and the airport. Buses 6 and 10 from Plateia San Rocco in Corfu Town stop on the main road 800m from the airport (en route to Benitses and Ahillion). A taxi between the airport and Corfu Town costs around €10.

BUS

Long-distance KTEL buses (known as green buses) travel from Corfu Town's **long-distance bus station** (Map p450; ☎ 26610 28927/30627; I Theotoki).

Fares cost €1.70 to €3.30. Printed timetables are available at the ticket kiosk. Sunday and holiday services are reduced considerably, or don't run at all.

Long-distance (Green) Buses from Corfu Town

Destination	Duration	Frequency
Agios Gordios	45min	7 daily
Agios Stefanos	1½hr	5 daily
Aharavi (via Roda)	1¼hr	6 daily
Arillas (via Afionas)	1¼hr	2 daily
Barbati	45min	4 daily
Ermones	30min	4 daily
Glyfada	30min	7 daily
Kassiopi	45min	6 daily
Kavos	1½hr	10 daily
Messonghi	45min	5 daily
Paleokastritsa	45min	6 daily
Pyrgi	30min	7 daily
Sidhari	1¼hr	8 daily
Spartera	45min	2 daily

Local buses (blue buses) depart from the **local bus station** (Map p452; ☎ 26610 28927; Plateia San Rocco) in Corfu Old Town.

Local (Blue) Buses in Corfu Town

Destination	Via	Bus	Frequency
Agios Ioannis	Afra	8	13 daily
Ahillion		10	7 daily
Benitses		6	12 daily
Evropouli	Potamas	4	11 daily
Kanoni		2	half-hourly
Kombitsi	Kanali	14	4 daily
Kondokali & Dasia	Gouvia	7	half-hourly
Kouramades	Kinopiastes	5	14 daily
Pelekas		11	7 daily

Tickets are either €0.75 or €1.10 depending on the length of journey, and can be purchased from the booth on Plateia San Rocco (although tickets for Ahillion, Benitses and Kouramades are bought on the bus). All trips are under 30 minutes.

CAR & MOTORCYCLE
Car- and motorbike-rental outlets are plentiful in Corfu Town and most of the resort towns on the island. Prices start at around €45 per day (less for longer-term rentals). Most international car-rental companies are represented in Corfu Town and at the airport. Most local companies have offices along the northern waterfront.

Recommended agencies:

Budget (Map p450; ☎ 26610 22062; Ioannou Theotoki 132)
Easy Rider (Map p450; ☎ 26610 43026) Opposite the new port; rents out scooters and motorbikes.
Ocean (Map p452; ☎ 26610 32351; Eleftheriou Venizelou 22)
Sixt (Map p452; ☎ 26610 35237; www.sixt.gr; Eleftheriou Venizelou 12)
Sunrise (Map p450; ☎ 26610 26511/44325; www.corfusunrise.com; Ethnikis Antistasis 6) A reliable choice along the waterfront near the new port.

CORFU TOWN
pop 28,200

Nicknamed 'Kastropolis' because of its position between two fortresses on a peninsula, Corfu Town can be summed up in three words: sophistication, beauty and charm. The town's architecture, culture and cuisine are a harmonious blend of Italian, French and British, with a contemporary Greek feel. Pink and ochre Venetian mansions dominate the old town, Parisian-style arcades line a majestic promenade – together known as the Liston, and an English-style cricket ground-cum-village green) graces the Spianada. The town's cosmopolitan old and new sections merge seamlessly. Linger over a frappé (Greek-style iced coffee) and crowd-watch from one of the many restaurants or bars found in historic plazas and near Byzantine churches and museums.

Orientation
The town is separated into northern and southern sections. The old town is in the northern section between the Spianada and the Neo Frourio (New Fortress). To the east, the Palaio Frourio (Old Fortress) projects out to sea, cut off from the town by a moat. The southern section is the new town where you'll find most services and shops.

The old port is north of the old town, and the new port is to the west, with the hulking New Fortress between them. The long-distance bus station is on I Theotoki (formerly known as Avramiou) between Plateia San Rocco and the new port. The local bus station is on Plateia San Rocco.

Information
BOOKSHOPS
Tourmoussoglou (☎ 26610 38451; Nikiforou Theotoki 47) This excellent bookshop has a wide range of guidebooks and paperbacks in English.

EMERGENCY
Tourist police (Map p452; ☎ 26610 30265; 3rd fl, Samartzi 4) Off Plateia San Rocco.

INTERNET ACCESS
The going rate for internet access is around €3 per hour.
Edenet (Map p452; Plateia San Rocco) In the basement of Café Eden.
Netoikos (Map p452; Kaloheretou 14) Good connection, near the Church of Agios Spyridon. Also has a bar on site.

MEDICAL SERVICES
Corfu General Hospital (Map p450; ☎ 26610 88200; Loulias Andreadi)

LAUNDRY
Laundry Self Service (Map p450; ☎ 26610 34857; Morpiki; per load €11; ☽ 8.30am-2pm Mon-Sat, plus 6-8pm Wed-Fri) Around the corner from Petrakis Lines.

MONEY
There are banks and ATMs around Plateia San Rocco, on Georgiou Theotoki and by both ports.
Alpha Bank (Map p452; Kapodistriou) Found behind the Liston.
National Bank of Greece (Map p452; Voulgareos)

POST
Post office (Map p450; Leoforos Alexandras)

TELEPHONE
Public telephones can be found on most major streets and squares. Prepaid telephone cards (from €6) are available from kiosks.

TOURIST INFORMATION
There is still no official tourist office in Corfu Town, despite past attempts to open one.

IONIAN ISLANDS

CORFU TOWN (KERKYRA)

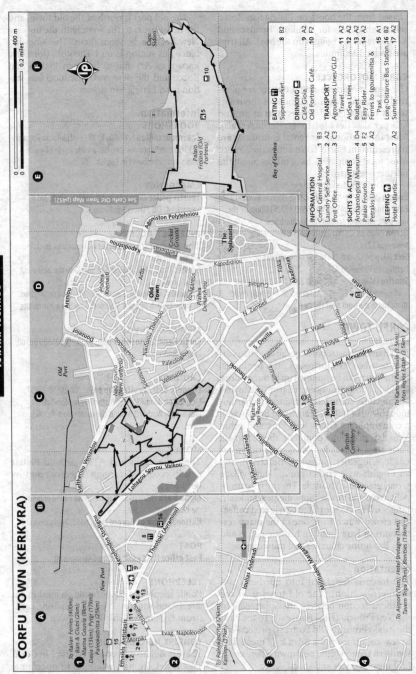

INFORMATION
Corfu General Hospital......**1** B3
Laundry Self Service..........**2** A2
Post Office.........................**3** C3

SIGHTS & ACTIVITIES
Archaeological Museum.....**4** D4
Palaio Frourio...................**5** F2
Petrakis Lines....................**6** A2

SLEEPING 🛏
Hotel Atlantis....................**7** A2

EATING 🍴
Supermarket.......................**8** B2

DRINKING 🍷
Café Gioia..........................**9** A2
Old Fortress Café...............**10** F2

TRANSPORT
Agoudimos Lines/GLD	
Travel............................**11** A2
AirSea Lines.......................**12** A2
Budget..............................**13** A2
Easy Rider.........................**14** A2
Ferries to Igoumenitsa &	
Paxi..............................**15** A1
Long-Distance Bus Station..**16** B2
Sunrise..............................**17** A2

During high season, a **tourist kiosk** (Map p452) may operate in Plateia San Rocco itself. At the very least you'll get a map of the town – produced mainly for day trippers from cruise ships – and information about what's on. English-speaking staff at **All Ways Travel** (Map p452; ☎ 26610 33955; www.corfuallwaystravel.com; Plateia San Rocco) happily receive disoriented tourists. Many hotels stock free Corfu maps. Definitely buy a copy of the *Corfiot* (€2), an English-language newspaper with listings, available from kiosks.

Sights & Activities

The **Archaeological Museum** (Map p450; ☎ 26610 30680; P Vraïla 5; adult/concession €3/2; ⏱ 8.30am-3pm Tue-Sun) displays a diverse collection of items from the island's archaeological heritage. The massive Gorgon Medusa sculpture, one of the best-preserved pieces of Archaic sculpture found in Greece, was part of the west pediment of the 6th-century BC Temple of Artemis at Corcyra (the ancient capital), a Doric temple that stood on the nearby Kanoni Peninsula. The fascinating coin collection reveals the circulation of foreign coins (and thus trade) on the island since ancient times.

Just north of the cricket ground is the **Museum of Asian Art** (Map p452; ☎ 26610 30443; adult/concession €3/2; ⏱ 8.30am-7pm Tue-Sun May-Oct, 8.30am-3pm Tue-Sun Nov-Apr), containing 10,000 objects donated from private collections. Items include Chinese and Japanese porcelain, bronzes, screens and sculptures. It's housed in the Palace of Sts Michael & George, built between 1818 and 1824 as the British Lord High Commissioner's residence.

At the eastern side of the building, up the staircase behind the Art Café (p453) is the **Municipal Art Gallery** (Map p452; admission €2; ⏱ 9am-5pm Tue-Sun). This lovely collection features Corfiot painters and 15th-century Byzantine icons. Of particular interest for their Italian influence are the paintings by the father and son Prossalendis, and Byzantine icons by the Cretan Damaskinas.

Inside the 15th-century Church of Our Lady of Antivouniotissa is the **Antivouniotissa Museum** (Byzantine Museum; Map p452; ☎ 26610 38313; admission €2; ⏱ 8am-7pm Tue-Sun Apr-Oct, 8.30am-2.30pm Tue-Sun Nov-Mar). This exquisite aisleless and timber-roofed basilica, located off Arseniou, has an outstanding collection of Byzantine and post-Byzantine icons and artefacts dating from the 13th to the 17th centuries. The collection extends into the restored sacristy.

Solomos Museum (Map p452; ☎ /fax 26610 30674; admission €1; ⏱ 9.30am-2pm Jun-Aug, 9.30am-1pm Sep-May) is housed in a charming building and is dedicated to Greece's famous poet Dionysios Solomos, who wrote Greece's national poem (see Museum of Solomos, p479) and lived in Corfu for 30 years. The display includes some of his poems and letters, his desk and old book editions.

It's worth wandering through the two fortresses, Corfu Town's most dominant landmarks. The hilltop on which the **Neo Frourio** (New Fortress; Map p452; admission €2; ⏱ 9am-9pm May-Oct) stands was first fortified in the 12th century. It's considered an engineering marvel. The views alone are worth the visit. The **Palaio Frourio** (Old Fortress; Map p450; ☎ 26610 48310; adult/concession €4/2; ⏱ 8.30am-3pm Nov-Mar, 8.30am-7pm May-Oct) was constructed by the Venetians on the remains of a 12th-century Byzantine castle on a natural headland. The moat later became notorious as the site of romantic suicides. Further alterations were made by the British but the buildings are now mainly ruins.

In Corfu, locals joke that if you call out 'Spyros', half the island's males will come running. Indeed, it seems that many lucky fellows are named after the island's saint, St Spyridon. The sacred relic of the town's patron saint lies in an elaborate silver coffin in the 16th-century **Church of Agios Spyridon** (Map p452; Agiou Spyridonos). The church is also important for its distinctive campanile.

On the southern outskirts of Corfu on the Kanoni Peninsula, the villa and garden at **Mon Repos Estate** (off Map p450; ⏱ 8am-7pm May-Oct, 8am-5pm Nov-Apr) are magical oases for an overheated traveller. The residence was commissioned by the second British Commissioner of the Ionians for his Corfiot wife. It was also the birthplace of the UK's current Duke of Edinburgh (Queen Elizabeth II's husband). The restored residence houses the recreational **Museum of Palaeopolis** (☎ 26610 41369; adult/concession €3/2; ⏱ 8am-7.30pm Tue-Sun May-Oct), with eclectic displays including archaeological finds and a Period Room. The sprawling gardens and grounds boast two **Doric temples**. Take a picnic and plenty of water – there's no nearby shop or kiosk.

Tours

Petrakis Lines (Map p450; ☎ 26610 31649; Ethnikis Antistasis 4) and **Sarris Cruises** (☎ 26610 25317;

IONIAN ISLANDS

Eleftheriou Venizelou 13) both organise day trips from Corfu Town, including an excursion to ancient ruins (Butrinti) in Albania; a boat trip taking in Paxi (and the Blue Caves) and Antipaxi. Prices for all tours range between €30 and €40 (including transfers, plus €10 for port taxes). Passports are required for trips to Albania.

Sleeping

Few real good-value budget options exist in the old town – these are found in the town's newer area. The nearest camping ground is Dionysus Camping Village (p456), 8km away. Book ahead in high season. If you can squeeze extra from your purse, the boutique hotels provide a great stay.

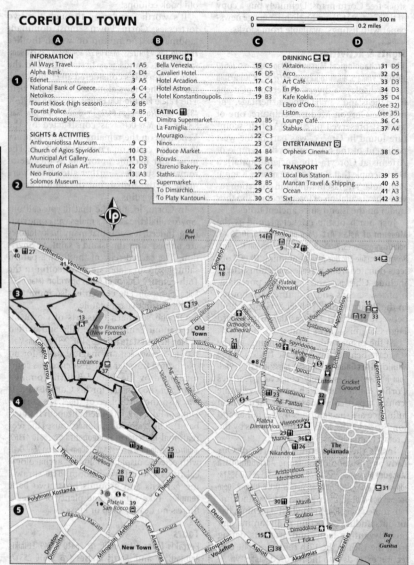

CORFU OLD TOWN

INFORMATION		
All Ways Travel	1	A5
Alpha Bank	2	D4
Edenet	3	A5
National Bank of Greece	4	C4
Netoikos	5	C4
Tourist Kiosk (high season)	6	B5
Tourist Police	7	B5
Tourmoussoglou	8	C4

SIGHTS & ACTIVITIES		
Antivouniotissa Museum	9	C3
Church of Agios Spyridon	10	C3
Municipal Art Gallery	11	D3
Museum of Asian Art	12	D3
Neo Frourio	13	C4
Solomos Museum	14	C2

SLEEPING		
Bella Venezia	15	C5
Cavalieri Hotel	16	D5
Hotel Arcadion	17	C4
Hotel Astron	18	C3
Hotel Konstantinoupolis	19	B3

EATING		
Dimitra Supermarket	20	B5
La Famiglia	21	C3
Mouragio	22	C3
Ninos	23	C4
Produce Market	24	B4
Rouvás	25	B4
Starenio Bakery	26	C4
Stathis	27	A3
Supermarket	28	B5
To Dimarchio	29	C4
To Platy Kantouni	30	C5

DRINKING		
Aktaion	31	D5
Arco	32	D4
Art Café	33	D3
En Plo	34	D3
Kafe Koklia	35	D4
Libro d'Oro	(see 32)
Liston	(see 35)
Lounge Café	36	C4
Stablus	37	A4

ENTERTAINMENT		
Orpheus Cinema	38	C5

TRANSPORT		
Local Bus Station	39	B5
Mancan Travel & Shipping	40	A3
Ocean	41	A3
Sixt	42	A3

0 — 300 m
0 — 0.2 miles

We list high-season prices here (July and August, and at Easter), but note that for most hotels, low- and mid-season prices (October to June) are *drastically reduced* and many hotel owners are willing to negotiate. Many hotels are open year-round.

BUDGET

Hotel Bretagne (off Map p450; ☎ 26610 30724; www.hotel bretagne.gr; K Georgaki 27; s/d/tr €50/70/80; 🖭) Don't overlook this because of its close proximity to the airport and its distance from the old town. It has adequate motel-style rooms; those at the back face onto a small grassy garden, which buffets air and street-noise pollution.

Hotel Astron (Map p452; ☎ 26610 39505; hotel_ astron@hol.gr; Donzelot 15; s €60-70, d €70-80, tr €80-90) The foyer and corridors have as much personality as a disused hospital, but don't let this (nor the kitsch paintings) deter you. The rooms are surprisingly light and pleasant and management is friendly and helpful.

MIDRANGE

Hotel Konstantinoupolis (Map p452; ☎ 26610 48716; www.konstantinoupolis.com.gr; K Zavitsianou 11; s/d/tr incl breakfast €88/98/117; 🖭) Former groupies of this old fave may be disappointed; it can be hard to get a booking here as groups occasionally block-book accommodation. Lucky guests will get light and breezy rooms, some with balcony and ye olde worlde Corfiot charm at better prices than other renovated hotels. Faithfuls should book ahead.

Hotel Atlantis (Map p450; ☎ 26610 35560; www .hotelatlantis.gr; Xenofondos Stratigou 48; s/d €86/100; 🖭) This nondescript monolith doesn't ooze personality, but is handily located opposite the new port, so it's useful for ferry access. It has friendly staff and adequate rooms.

TOP END

The following options are almost identical smartly refurbished boutique hotels, outfitted with tasteful Corfiot furniture (with the exception of Bella Venezia). Prices are for high season (reduced considerably at other times) and include breakfast.

Hotel Arcadion (Map p452; ☎ 26610 37670; www.arc adionhotel.com; Vlasopoulou 2; s/d/tr €105/130/160; 🖭) A charming hotel incongruously situated above a McDonalds, but right in the Liston's action.

Cavalieri Hotel (Map p452; ☎ 26610 39041; www .cavalieri-hotel.com; Kapodistriou 4; d €140-160; 🖭) Another good choice with tasteful old-world style. Features a fabulous rooftop bar that is also open to nonguests.

Bella Venezia (Map p452; ☎ 26610 46500; www .bellaveneziahotel.com; N Zambeli 4; d €170; 🗶 🖭 🖳) This recently renovated place has tasteful and contemporary rooms.

Eating

Corfu's cuisine has been influenced by the many cultures that have been part of its history, particularly Italian. Meat eaters mustn't go past local specialities like *sofrito* (veal with garlic, vinegar and parsley), *pastitsada* (meat in red sauce) or a *bourdeto* (fish casserole spiked with paprika). Vegetarians can enjoy selections of mezedhes (appetisers) and tasty morsels from bakeries. The *gelateria* (ice-cream shop) experience around the island shouldn't be missed, either.

CAFÉS

A true Corfu experience is to indulge in people-watching on the Liston – you'll pay around €3 to €5 for a coffee or fresh juice here. The locals partake in their *volta* (evening walk) at around eleven.

Other cafés are perfect for lingering over a frappé or snack, especially in the heat of the day and to rest weary sightseeing bones. The views, especially from waterside locations, are further sensual feasts. Good watering holes include the pretty Art Café (Map p452), in gardens to the east of the Museum of Asian Art; the Old Fortress Café (Map p450), inside the Old Fortress complex; En Plo (Map p452), at the corner of Arseniou and Kapodistriou (you need to go down a sloping road at St Nikolas Gate); **Aktaion** (Map p452; Agoniston Polytehniou); and Stablus (Map p452), in the New Fortress.

For a great coffee (at non-Liston prices) head to **Café Gioia** (Map p450; Xenofondos Stratigou 46) near the new port.

Whatever you do, don't miss the taste sensations at **Starenio Bakery** (Map p452; ☎ 26610 47370; Guilford 59; snacks under €2), including a huge selection of homemade gourmet pies, breads and the *best* of best cakes. Sweet indeed.

RESTAURANTS

Stroll around pretty Plateia Dimarchiou (Town Hall Sq; northeast of the Spianada) and along Guilford or Kapodistriou – and the latter's off-shoots – for traditional and contemporary eateries and mezedhes.

Mouragio (Map p452; ☎ 26610 33815; Arseniou 15; mains €6-14) The definite pick of this strip, despite the neighbouring (touristy) restaurants hogging the ocean view. This 'local's location' and good-value place serves massive portions of well-cooked grills and seafood.

Rouvás (Map p452; ☎ 26610 31182; S Desilla 13; mains €8-14; ☉ lunch) Just like Ma used to make. The Greek American chef here does magic with traditional dishes, so much so that he was recently filmed with UK celebrity chef Rick Stein for a TV cooking programme.

La Famiglia (Map p452; ☎ 26610 30270; Maniarizi Arlioti 16; mains €8-18; ☉ dinner) Check out the contemporary gingham tastes at this Greek-Italian eatery. A delectable range of pastas provides relief from the usual Greek square meal. Perfect for an Italian fix and faster than a ferry trip to Italy. It's a bit tricky to find – on a tiny laneway halfway along Nikiforou Theotoki.

our pick **Tavern Tripa** (off Map p450; ☎ 26610 56333; www.tripas.gr; set banquet €35) Calling all foodies, but with a warning: you'll need to fast for two days to make the most of this experience – 10 top-quality local dishes including cheese, antipasto, chicken and beef and everything in between. Oh, and they're just the appetisers. The main dishes (yes, plural), are yet to come. You can always burn off the calories on the dance floor, to the live music and dance performers. Not surprisingly, the tavern hosts hungry world presidents to (non-anorexic) film stars. In Kinopiastes, 7km from Corfu town. Book ahead.

Also recommended:

To Platy Kantouni (Map p452; ☎ 26610 32330; Guilford 16; plates €4-7) You can make a meal of these tasty traditional mezedhes plates – they add up in every sense.

Stathis (Map p452; ☎ 26610 25994; Elefteriou Venizelou 36; mains €6-12) Not the fanciest location in town (although handy for the ferry), but by far one of the best for price and taste – try the calamari.

Ninos (Krisi; Map p452; ☎ 26610 46175; Sevastianou 44; mains €8-14) Started in 1920, this family concern is as authentic as Zorba. Back-to-basics takeaways are available.

To Dimarchio (Map p452; ☎ 26610 39031; Plateia Dimarchiou; mains €9.50-25) Upmarket menu and a beautiful setting.

SELF-CATERING

North of Plateia San Rocco is the bustling **produce market** (Map p452; ☉ closed Sun), open morning to early afternoon and selling fresh fruit, vegetables and fish. For groceries try **Dimitra supermarket** (Map p452; G Markora), or try other supermarkets (Map p450) by the long-distance bus station, in the old town (Map p452), and on Theotoki I opposite the main plaza (Map p452).

Drinking

All the bars along the Liston are the places to be and be seen. The line-up includes (all on Map p452): Libro d'Oro, Arco, Liston and Kafe Koklia. Also recommended are Lounge Café (Map p452) and the classy rooftop bar at the Cavalieri Hotel (p453).

Entertainment

To hang out with the cool crowds in the high-tech – and very-late-night – scene, head to Corfu's bar-cum-disco strip, 2km northwest of the new port, along Ethnikis Antistasis (off Map p450; take a taxi). Recommended spots are the hip and classy Privilege and more local Au Bar (Ω in Greek), which caters to the locals. The €10 admission fee includes one freebie drink.

For visual entertainment, the old town's **Orpheus cinema** (Map p452; ☎ 26610 39768; G Aspioti) screens English-language films with Greek subtitles. Look around town for signs detailing music performances. Occasional folk festivals – music, dance and cultural – are held in Corfu. Check www.kerkyra.gr for further information.

Shopping

Numerous sweet shops and tourist haunts cram the streets of the tourist-oriented old town. Some reasonable fashion shops – for shoes, swimwear and dress items – are located in the new town, especially along G Theotoki.

NORTH OF CORFU TOWN

Much of the coast just north of Corfu Town is saturated by tourist mobs and tacky developments, though beyond **Pyrgi** the winding, scenic road reveals some of Corfu's delights.

However, before reaching Pyrgi, head to the quaint village of Kato Korakiana (near Dassia), to visit the **National Art Gallery – Alexandros Soutzos Museum, annex of Corfu** (☎ 26610 93333; ☉ 10am-2pm & 6-9pm Mon, Wed & Fri, 10am-2pm, Thu, Sat & Sun, closed Tue). This restored building, known as the Castellino Building, features permanent and temporary art exhibitions. Works are from the country's National Art Gallery, and include Greek masters and artists of the Ionian School. The village alone is worth visiting for its authenticity.

Just beyond Pyrgi, take a detour to **Mt Pantokrator** (906m), the island's highest peak. On your way, wind your way around the many hairpin bends and through the picturesque villages of **Spartylas** and **Strinylas**. At Strinylas, most pause under the greenery at **Taverna Oasis**, but **Taverna To Steki** opposite is renowned for its tasty good-value local cuisine (open evenings only). From here a road climbs through stark terrain with wonderful wildflowers, to the mountain's summit, the **Moni Pantokrator**. If you can ignore the presence of a massive telecommunications tower in the middle of its grounds, you can enjoy stupendous, if sometimes hazy, views.

Heading northeast from Pyrgi around the winding coastal road, the first decent place is **Nisaki**, little more than a tiny cove with a pebble beach, a couple of tavernas and some rooms. **Agni** is renowned for its three competing tavernas – **Taverna Toula** (☎ 26630 91350), **Taverna Nikolas** (☎ 26630 91243) and **Taverna Agni** (☎ 26630 91142), all of which serve excellent fare. The village of **Kalami** is famous for the White House, home to writer Lawrence Durrell and perched near water. The base of the building houses an inevitably touristy restau-

rant, while the house itself can be rented (see p456). Just round the next headland is the pretty fishing harbour and beach of **Kouloura**, which affords a good view of the neighbouring coast of Albania. **Agios Stefanos** is pretty in two respects – pretty upmarket (popular with British villa vultures) and with a beautiful harbour and small shingle beach. **Avlaki**, a bay further around the coast, reveals a lovely long beach and a couple of tavernas, including the atmospheric **Cavo Barbaro** (☎ 26630 81905; mains €7-15), and is a relaxing place surprisingly without touristy hordes (yet).

Kassiopi is worth considering for a night's stopover. Ignore the blow-up beach paraphernalia dominating the modern part of town and head to the attractive harbour. Opposite the church on the main street a small track leads to the town's castle ruins, and you can walk over the headland to the nearby Battaria and Kanoni Beaches. The main road continues inland to the overdeveloped and ultratouristy resorts of Aharavi, Roda and Sidhari.

Agios Stefanos in the island's west (not to be confused with the village of Agios Stefanos in the northeast) is pleasant, more for its long sandy beach and high sand-cliffs than for the rather plain and uninteresting village. Regular boat excursions and a local ferry service leave

IONIAN ISLANDS

CORFU ACTIVITIES

Naturally enough, the best activities in this part of the world relate to water. If you're not fortunate enough to be sailing in the region on a private yacht, several companies offer yacht charter services, flotilla holidays or sailing lessons, including **Corfu Sea School** (☎ 26610 99470; www .corfuseaschool.com; Marina Gouvia). For exploring coastal coves, renting a **motorboat** is the only way to go. Many places such as Marina Gouvia, Paleokastritsa and Kalami rent out boats.

You can **dive** in the crystal-clear waters off Corfu; diving operators are based in Kassiopi, Agios Gordios, Agios Giorgios, Ipsos, Gouvia and Paleokastritsa.

For landlubbers, **walking** here is superb. You can experience the countryside (with its wildflowers) and unspoilt villages. Keen walkers should tap into www.corfutrail.org. The Corfu Trail traverses the island and takes between eight and 12 days to complete. For help with coordinating accommodation along the trail, contact **Aperghi Travel** (☎ 26610 48713; www.travelling.gr/aperghi/). The book *In the Footsteps of Lawrence Durrell and Gerald Durrell in Corfu* (Hilary Whitton Paipeti, 1999) is great for lovers of the writing duo, and for keen explorers.

Given Corfu's hilly terrain, **mountain-biking** is popular. **Corfu Mountainbike Shop** (☎ 26610 93344; www.mountainbikecorfu.gr) is based in Dasia and rents out bikes for independent exploration, as well as organising day trips and cycling holidays.

Not far from Ermones on the island's west coast is the **Corfu Golf Club** (☎ 26610 94220; www .corfugolfclub.com), one of the few such courses in Greece. Or you can go horse riding through olive groves with **Trailriders** (☎ 26630 23090), based in the village of Ano Korakiana. Bird-watchers should pigeon the **Birdwatching Centre of Ropa Valley** (☎ 26610 94221), who meet regularly at the Golf Club. Wine-lovers can try a drop or three at **Triklino Vineyard** (☎ 6945890285; www .triklinovineyard.gr), on the Pelekas road near Karoubatika.

from its small harbour to the **Diapondia Islands**, a cluster of little-known satellite islands. For organised day excursions, contact **San Stefano Travel** (☎ 26630 51910; www.san-stefano.gr). Alternatively, contact the **Port Authority** (☎ 26610 32655) in Corfu Town for the ferry schedules to the islands.

Head inland to experience verdant landscapes plus hairpin bends that make the Monaco Grand Prix circuit seem like an airstrip. You'll pass through delightful hilltop villages including **Mesaria**, **Agios Athanasios** and **Agros**.

Sleeping & Eating

Dionysus Camping Village (☎ 26610 91417; www .dionysuscamping.gr; camp sites per adult/car/tent €5.40/ 3.30/3.80, huts per person €10; 🛋) The closest camping ground to Corfu Town, signposted between Tzavros and Dasia and well served by bus 7 and good facilities. Olive terraces serve as the camping area, or you can opt for simple pine-clad huts with straw roofs; tents can also be hired.

Bounias Apartments/Villa Alexandra (☎ 2660 24333; studio €45, 3-/4-person apt €47-95) Welcoming owner, Alexandra, enjoys hosting her guests as much as they enjoy their stay. The damp-smelling bottom-floor studios aren't as pleasant as the slightly dated, but clean and spacious apartments above. Located about 2km from Kassiopi, near Avlaki Beach.

Manessis Apartments (☎ 26610 34990; diana@otenet .gr; Kassiopi; 4-person apt €100) It's hard to pick what's more pleasant – the friendly Greek-Irish owner, or her homely bougainvillea- and vine-covered two-bedroom apartments. The location, at the end of Kassiopi's picturesque harbour, makes a lovely base.

White House (☎ 26630 91040; www.white-house -corfu.gr; Kalami; house per night €160) Lawrence Durrell fans can stay in the writer's former residence, which sleeps up to eight people. The interiors are nothing to write a book about, but the position, right on the water, and the wonderful outlook are novel. For meals, head below to the White House Taverna (☎ 26610 91251, mains €7 to €16.50).

Tassos Boat Hire & Accommodation (☎ 26630 91040; Kalami; apt per week from €500) If White House is full, Tassos can accommodate you in some pleasant studios near the waterfront. Rates can halve outside July and August.

Ice Dream Gelateria (☎ 26630 98200) Five minutes drive north of Kassiopi, opposite an EPKO petrol station, is this obligatory stop.

Authentic, creamy *gelati* (ice cream) made on the premises. Worth every lick.

SOUTH OF CORFU TOWN

The coast road continues south from Corfu Town with a turn-off to well-signposted **Ahillion Palace** (☎ 26610 56245; adult/concession €7/5; 🕑 8.30am-3pm Nov-Mar, 8am-7pm Apr-Oct), near the village of Gastouri. In the 1890s it was the summer palace of Austria's Empress Elizabeth (King Otho of Greece was her uncle). The beautifully landscaped garden is guarded by some elaborate statues of mythological heroes. Be sure to climb the stairs to the right of the villa to the marbled terrace for a view through the window of the fresco depicting Achilles, to whom she dedicated the villa.

The narrow winding streets of the old village are the only things that save the suburban-feel resort town of **Benitses**. That, and a decent taverna, **O Paxinos** (☎ 26610 72339), which, despite its multilingual menu and credit card stickers on the window, is popular with Greeks for its excellent fish (€46 to €56 per kilogram). Off the beaten track along the winding coastal road south of Messonghi is the spread-out **Boukari**. It ain't for the action-traveller, but it's tranquil and pretty. The non-intrusive tavernas under oleander trees on the edge of the water are a great place to unwind.

In Boukari you can stay at the **Golden Sunset Hotel** (☎ 26620 51853; www.korfusunset.de; d incl breakfast €55-60, tr incl breakfast €60). Although 'motel modern' in character, the rooms are bright and some have massive balconies with sea views. A restaurant is attached.

A stopover in the region's administrative town, **Lefkimmi**, just over 10km from Boukari in the southern part of the island, reveals one of the island's most authentic towns. Fascinating churches are dotted throughout the older section, and a rather quaint, but sometimes odorous, canal flows (or doesn't) through it. The best accommodation is the pleasant **Maria Madalena Apartments** (☎ 26620 22386; d €30). Eat at the **River Restaurant** (☎ 6972542153; mains €8-15), where UK celebrity chef Rick Stein reportedly filmed a segment for a TV cooking show. A basic alternative is **Taverna Maria** (dishes of the day around €6) on the canal.

WEST COAST

Some of Corfu's prettiest countryside, villages and beaches are situated on or around the west coast. The beautiful and popular town of **Pale-**

okastritsa, 26km from Corfu Town, is set along a 3km stretch of road. Small coves are hidden between tall cliffs, and cypresses and olive trees appear through the lush green mountain backdrop. You can venture to nearby grottoes or one of the 15 nearby beaches by small excursion boat (per person €8, 30 minutes), or water taxis can drop you off at a beach of your choice. There's a range of water-boat activities available. Cool sun-seekers can hang out at café-bar **La Grotta** (☎ 26630 41006; Paleokastritsa), which is set in a stunning rocky cove with café, sunbeds and diving board. To enter, descend the long flight of steps opposite the driveway up to Hotel Paleokastritsa on the main road.

Perched on the rocky promontory at the end of Paleokastritsa is the interesting and icon-filled **Moni Theotokou** (admission free; ☺ 7am-1pm & 3-8pm), a monastery founded in the 13th century (although the present building dates from the 18th century). Just off the monastery's garden – with ivy, vines, roses and pot plants – is a small **museum** (admission free; ☺ 9am-1pm & 3-6pm Apr-Oct). Most interesting is the olive mill exhibition under the museum, with a small shop selling oils and herbs.

From Paleokastritsa a path ascends to the unspoilt village of **Lakones**, 5km inland by road. Be sure to check out the town's only *kafeneio* (Kafeneio Olympia) and the village's growing photographic archive (see boxed text, p458). Quaint **Doukades** has a historic square and excellent tavernas. The 6km road west to **Krini** and **Makrades** meanders at elevated heights; many restaurant owners have capitalised on the vistas. Be sure to visit Krini's miniature town square and nearby Angelokastro, the ruins of a Byzantine castle and the most western bastion on Corfu. If you have time, tackle the winding mountain pass to **Pagi** and onto the resort of **Agios Georgios**

for an eating experience at the Fisherman's Taverna (see p459).

South of Paleokastritsa, the pebbly beach at **Ermones** is dominated by tasteless development, but is near the **Corfu Golf Club** (☎ /fax 26610 94220; Ropa Valley; per 18 holes €50), if you're craving a round. Hilltop **Pelekas**, 4km away, is a good base for beach bums. This friendly village has a reasonable infrastructure yet attracts more independent travellers than 'package people'.

The attractive, traditional mountain village of **Sinarades** has old buildings, narrow streets, a beautiful clock tower and several excellent tavernas. Its fascinating **Folkloric Museum** (adult/concession €1.50/0.60; ☺ 9am-2pm Mon-Sat) is housed in a former farmhouse. The curator, Tasa, can tell you more about Greek history than Homer himself.

Near Pelekas village are two sandy beaches, **Glyfada** and **Pelekas** (marked on some maps as Kontogialos, and also a resort in its own right), with water sports and sunbeds galore. These are quite developed, backed by large hotels and accommodation options. A free bus service runs from Pelekas village to these beaches. Further north is the popular, but dwindling (due to erosion) **Myrtiotissa** beach; the former unofficial nudist 'colony' has more or less merged with the happy families section, save for some giant boulders in between. Warning: it's a long slog down a steep, unsealed road before you see a bottom of any kind (drivers should park in the parking area on the hilltop).

Agios Gordios is a popular beach-bum hangout south of Glyfada. The long sandy beach can cope with the crowds. Its backdrop is a sparse and exposed flat landscape, appealing to travellers interested primarily in a serious sun scene.

IONIAN ISLANDS

A CUT ABOVE THE REST

Male travellers who may have 'let their hair down' during their vacation should razor on down to the small village of Kouramades, 5km southeast of Pelakas. This tiny place is home to a highly respected (and dare we say eccentric) barber, Mr Yiangos Hytiris (☎ 26610 54258). Since 1949 Mr Hytiris has been servicing hirsute clients who come not only from around the island, but as far away as Athens. He is well known for his quirky barber's shop, which is housed in a distinctive rust-coloured building with green shutters. It's a tribute to the bygone era of the barber's art – cut-throat razors and other manual and technical gadgets are mounted on the walls, along with a collection of hundreds of ornaments and mirrors. If you decide to pay him a visit, be respectful and dress appropriately – he's a proud and skilled artiste from the old world, and would not appreciate clients rocking up in beach gear.

While there's not much to see other than the cave itself, the ancient **Rockshelter of Grava Gardikiou** has a fascinating history: it dates from the Upper Palaeolithic period of 20,000 BC when Corfu was part of what is now mainland Epiros. Hunter-gatherers used such shelters during hunting trips – stone tools and animal bones have been found here. Turn off the main road to Halikounas Beach (and then to Gardiki Castle). Look for the faded roadside sign. The site is 400m uphill through olive groves (follow the orange arrows on the trees).

Sleeping & Eating

Paleokastritsa has many hotels, studios and a few domatia (rooms, usually in private homes) spread along the road.

Paleokastritsa Camping (☎ 26630 41204; Paleokastritsa; camp sites per adult/car/tent €4.80/2.90/3.40) On the right of the main approach road to town is this shady and well-organised camping ground, set on historic olive terraces.

Hotel Zefiros (☎ 26630 41088; www.hotel-zefiros.gr; Paleokastritsa; d incl breakfast €70-80, tr incl breakfast €80-100) It's hard to beat this perfect place. It's been recently refurbished, without losing its former friendly atmosphere or good prices. The 11 stylish rooms are contemporary yet comfortable, and some have a massive terrace. Hospitable owner Johnny clearly loves his job.

Rolling Stone (☎ 26610 94942; www.pelekasbeach.com; Pelekas Beach; r €30-40, apt €98) This atmospheric '70s throwback comes with laid-back hosts, clean and spacious apartments and double rooms, and the odd hippy touch – including that of its 'wellness' person (relaxation treatments €10 to €30). The terrace – with bar, funky bright stools and sofa – provides the perfect chill pad.

Jimmy's Restaurant & Rooms (☎ 26610 94284; jimmyspelekas@hotmail.com; d/tr €40/50; 🐾) No-nonsense rooms with rooftop views, plus restaurant (mains €6 to €11). Near the intersection of the roads to Pelekas Beach and Kaiser's Throne.

MR VASSILIS MICHALAS – SEPIA SNAPSHOT

As a local taxi driver, based out of Lakones, Vassilis Michalas ferries tourists and Corfiots around the island. That, he says, is a secondary focus: he's also part of a tourist accommodation association, is involved in local politics and sings in Lakones' choral group. Then, there's his role as a drummer in the village band and performer in the *barcarole* (the recreation of *Odyssey*, an annual event in Paleokastritsa).

More recently, however, he's zoomed in on a passion of a different kind – as the unofficial village archivist. He asked the people from his tiny village to donate photographs for safekeeping and display. The response was overwhelming and he has passionately set about the arduous task of photocopying and hand-framing hundreds of photos.

His reasons are simple. 'People are losing sense of our history!' he exclaims. 'The young people especially need to know their history. For example, why is our village called Lakones? Some older people know, but now the young people, they look after [are only concerned about] the football. I want to preserve old traditions. It's also good for outside people to know about the village.'

He points to a 1950 photograph of women in traditional dress, their hands on their hips and massive 100kg boulders on their head. 'This is very important. People need to *know* about this photo. These ladies built the first path between Paleokastritsa and Lakones. They received no money – nothing! – they had no machines. They alone decided to do this.'

Other photos reveal festivals and wedding groups, padres and floods. Then there are special events – the village's water connection in 1958 and (the irony isn't lost on him) a B&W photo of the very first tourists taking photos of local people in 1960.

As Vassilis points to the photo of the village's first choral group (the very same that he is currently a member of), he breaks into song. He smiles. 'I have been in a music group since I was 12 years old. Everybody goes to music groups – it's a natural part of our upbringing. Traditions are so important.'

It's well worth singing Vassilis' praises. Lakones' not-for-profit photographic archive is housed in the choral group's practice room in Lakones' municipal building. Interested visitors can phone ahead (☎ 26630 41771-3).

Yialiskari Beach Studios (☎ 26610 54901; d studio €50; Yialiskari Beach; ✖) Studios with great vistas, and perfect for those who want their own patch away from neighbouring Pelekas Beach. The studios are run by the owner of Yialiskari Beach's only taverna, 150m away.

Levant Hotel (☎ 26610 94230; www.levanthotel.com; s/d/f €50/95/160; ✖ ⍾) The oh-so-slightly shabby exterior of this neoclassical hotel hides luxury and elegance. Located near Kaiser's Throne lookout above Pelekas village, it has all the mod cons, a swimming pool set in gardens, and a restaurant (mains €6 to €12), plus a terrace with awesome views of the Adriatic and beyond.

Fisherman's Taverna (☎ 6942585550; Agios Georgios; mains per 2 people €25-30) A sign says, 'Dear Customer. We are sorry but we cannot serve you if you are in a hurry.' The eatery is tucked in to the right, 1.1km up a dirt road from the southern end of Agios Georgios Beach, northwest of Pagi. Ignore the first taverna visible from the road, whose sign also says 'Fish Taverna'. Go hungry and with time to spare.

Frequented by younger travellers for the all-in hostel experiences are **Pink Palace** (☎ 26610 53103; www.thepinkpalace.com; Agios Gordios Beach; r per person incl breakfast & dinner €18-25; ⍾). This huge, garish complex, south of Sinarades, is considered the must-do hassle-free activity and party palace by those on the backpacker circuit. **Sunrock** (☎ 26610 94637; www.geocities.com/sunrock_corfu; Pelekas Beach; r per person incl breakfast & dinner €18-24; ⍾ ✖) also offers the all-inclusive deal.

PAXI ΠΑΞΟΙ

pop 2500

Don't let the 10km by 4km size fool you: the tiny, alluring island package of Paxi offers a big – and possibly the best – Ionian experience. The smallest of the main islands, Paxi has three intimate harbour towns – Gaïos, Loggos and Lakka. All feature pretty waterfronts with Venetian-style pink-and-cream storeyed buildings, set against hilly backdrops of lush greenery. Their nearby coves can be reached by motorboat, if not by car or on foot. The dispersed inland villages sit by centuries-old olive groves, winding stone walls, ancient windmills and olive presses. On the less accessible west coast, sheer limestone cliffs plunge hundreds of metres and are punctuated by

grottoes. The old mule trails are a walker's delight. An obligatory purchase is the visually instructive and charming *Bleasdale Walking Map of Paxos* (€10 to €15), available from the island's travel agencies. Paxi has escaped the mass tourism of Corfu and caters to discriminating tour companies (mainly British) and Italians who arrive en masse in August. Its slow pace makes for a relaxing stay.

Accommodation mostly consists of pre-booked apartments and villas; all the island's agencies can help with bookings. For independent travellers, there are a few 'rooms for rent' signs around.

Getting There & Away

AIR

AirSea Lines (www.airsealines.com), a seaplane service, promotes several flights a day between Corfu and Paxi (one way €40 to €50). On Paxi, purchase tickets at **Bouas Tours** (☎ 26620 32245; www.bouastours.gr; Gaïos). Ask about the strict baggage weight allowance.

BUS

There's a twice-weekly direct bus service between Athens and Paxi (€45, plus €6.80 for ferry ticket between Paxi and Igoumenitsa, seven hours). On Paxi, tickets are available from Bouas Tours (above). The bus leaves from Plateia Karaiskaki in Athens (note: the terminal changes, so always check with Bouas beforehand).

FERRY

Domestic

Two car ferries operate daily services between Paxi, Igoumenitsa on the mainland, and Corfu. The Paxi–Igoumenitsa (per person/car €7/40) trip takes 1½ to two hours. Most island travel agents sell tickets. For connections to Corfu ring the information office in Igoumenitsa (☎ 26650 26280).

Ferries dock at Gaïos' new port, 1km east of the central square. Excursion boats dock along the waterfront.

International

You can reach Corfu and Igoumenitsa from the major ports in Italy, then transfer to a local ferry for Paxi.

SNAV (www.snav.it) operates a high-speed catamaran between Brindisi and Paxi (€90 or €140 depending on date of travel, 4¾ hours), via Corfu, daily from July to early September.

IONIAN ISLANDS

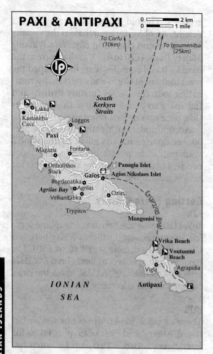

PAXI & ANTIPAXI

See Paxos Magic Holidays (right) in Gaïos for reservations.

HYDROFOIL

Popular passenger-only hydrofoils link Corfu and Paxi (and occasionally Igoumenitsa) from May until mid-October. There are one to two services daily (more on Mondays), between Corfu and Paxi (€15.10, 1¼ hours).

For information contact **Arvanitakis Travel** (☎ 26620 32007, Paxi), or Petrakis Lines (p451) in Corfu.

SEA TAXI

Sea taxis can be a fast and effective way of travel, especially if there are other people on board. The going rate between Corfu and Paxi is around €180 per boat, shared among the passengers. Try Nikos – from Gaïos – on ☎ 6932232072 (or try www.paxos seataxi.com); or Andreas – from Lakka – on ☎ 6977623033.

Getting Around

The island's bus links Gaïos and Lakka via Loggos up to four times daily in either direc-

tion (€1.80). Taxis between Gaïos and Lakka or Loggos cost around €10; at the time of research, the taxi rank in Gaïos was temporarily located at the bus stop (normally it's at the waterfront).

Daily car hire varies between €45 and €115 in high season. Reliable **Alfa Hire** (☎ 26620 32505) in Gaïos offers car rental, as does **Fougaros** (☎ 26620 32373; www.fougarostravel.com). **Rent a Scooter Vassilis** (☎ 26620 32598), opposite the bus stop in Gaïos, has a good range of scooters and mopeds, ideal for zipping around the island. Many travel agencies rent out small boats – this is a great way to access beach coves.

GAÏOS ΓΑΪΟΣ

pop 560

Gaïos, on a sweeping, east-coast bay, is the island's small and well-equipped capital. Its pink, cream and whitewashed buildings line the bay, and the town's main Venetian square, swamped with the inevitable bars and cafés, abuts the waterfront. The island is cosseted from the open sea by the nearby fortified islet of Agios Nikolaos. Panagia Islet, named after its monastery, lies at the northern entrance to the bay.

The main street (Panagioti Kanga) runs inland from the main square towards the back of town, where you'll find the bus stop. Banks and ATMs are near the square and you'll find an internet room on the waterfront **Bar Pío Pío** (per hr €6). There isn't a tourist office, but the helpful and efficient staff at **Paxos Magic Holidays** (☎ 26620 32269; www.paxosmagic.com) will happily direct you. They organise island excursions, including boating trips and wonderful walks. They can also arrange villa accommodation in advance.

The **Cultural Museum** (admission €2; 10am-2pm & 7-11pm), in a former school on the southern waterfront, has an eclectic collection of local historical artefacts, including a 17th-century sex aid.

Sleeping

Thekli Studios (Clara Studios; ☎ 26620 32313; d €70;) Thekli, the local fisher-diver and energetic personality about town, runs these immaculate and well-equipped studios. They're centrally located upstairs behind the museum, and overlook the village and sea. Thekli will meet you at the port – call ahead.

San Giorgio Apartments (☎ 26620 32223; d/tr €70/90) Pink, blue and white are the colours of these dated, but airy and clean, studios, and they boast the basic 'kitchen' facilities. Head towards town from the port by the lower (pedestrian) harbour road, and follow the signposted steps. Cheaper 'rooms only' are also available (€55).

Paxos Beach Hotel (☎ 26620 32211; www .paxosbeachhotel.gr; s/d/tr incl breakfast & dinner from €93/108/140; ⊠) The rather worn bungalows of this hillside complex, 1.5km south of Gaïos, are set a lobster claw apart, but they sprawl down to the sea, and have a range of rooms from standard to superior. There's a private jetty, tennis court, beach, bar and restaurant.

Eating

Capriccio Café Creperie (☎ 26620 32687; crepes €3-6; ☒ breakfast-late) For a cheap and filling sweet or savoury experience, head past the museum to this creperie. Tables are under large brollies near the seafront. Don't miss the Shepherd's Crepe, the fruit and yogurt choice (€5).

Taverna Vasilis (☎ 26620 32596; mains €6-14) The owner of this eatery is a former butcher, and this place makes the cut. Wrap your own chops around the tasty spit-roasts or other delicious meaty servings.

Karkaletzos (☎ 26620 32729; mains €7-10) This cheap and cheerful grill house is the overwhelming locals' choice, 1km behind town. The menu states (in English) that the proprietors will accept criticism or observations 'without any hysterical reaction'. As hospitable as this is, we suggest you just go with the flow.

Taka Taka (☎ 26620 32329; mains €8-20) This upmarket seafood experience behind the main square will leave you positively floating. As well as high-quality seafood (€40 to €75 per kilogram), the reputable Italian chef prepares pasta dishes. The *frutti di mare* (spaghetti marinara) will set you back €20.

The supermarket is west of the central square. Two excellent bakeries, one on the waterfront, the other near the main square, serve Paxiot delights.

LOGGOS ΛΟΓΓΟΣ

Loggos is 5km northwest of Gaïos. The hub of this small fishing village is the intimate quay, which is lined with chic bars and restaurants. At one end of the quay is an old, abandoned olive-soap factory. The town has a steep lush

backdrop and some wonderful coves and pebble beaches nearby. **Café Bar Four Seasons** (per hr €6) has internet facilities.

Sleeping & Eating

Studio (☎ 26620 31397, 26620 31030; d €55) This somewhat bohemian studio is owned by, and sits above, the gift shop Marbou, and it's a quaint bougainvillead option. Best to book in advance.

Arthur House (☎ 26620 31330; studio €75, apt €110) While the name implies an English-style villa, these modest but spotless studios are above the owner's house, a two-minute walk from the waterfront. Julia's boat and bike hire is part of the family deal.

O Gios (☎ 26620 31735; mains €6-14) The ugly duckling of the strip, with one of the best-value seafood and grill dishes.

Vasilis (☎ 26620 31587; mains €8-14) This classy terracotta-coloured family-run restaurant – running since 1956 – is headed by the quiet achiever and chef, Kostas. As well as the regular dishes, he conjures up daily specials – anything from octopus in red wine sauce to lamb casserole.

Drinking

Kafeneio Burnaos (Magaziá; ☒ no set hrs) Don't blink or you'll miss this delightful 60-year-old *kafeneio*, located in Magaziá, several kilometres southwest of Loggos. Locals gather here to play cards and backgammon (there's even a set from 1957). Third-generation owner Kosta has maintained its original feel; attractive jars and produce line the shelves. Well worth the stop – Kosta makes a great Greek coffee, too.

Chill out over one of Spyros' megafresh fruit cocktail sundowners with the bohemian crowd at To Taxidi, or try the friendly and upbeat Roxy Bar, with a crowd and music to match. You can move with your mood between the myriad of terraces.

LAKKA ΛΑΚΚΑ

The picturesque, tranquil and unspoiled harbour of Lakka lies at the end of an almost circular bay on the north coast. It's a yachties' haven, with many good bars and restaurants. There are small, but decent, beaches around the bay's headland, including Harami Beach, and pleasant walks nearby.

Routsis Holidays (☎ 26620 31807; www.forthnet.gr /routsis-holidays) and **Planos Holidays** (☎ 2662031744;

planos@otenet.gr) are helpful agencies responsible for well-appointed apartments and villas for all budgets.

Routsis will accommodate people for shorter-term stays at **Lefkothea** (d without bathroom €35), the nearest thing you'll find to a hostel here. Don't do the white glove test on the communal kitchen and bathroom, but the rooms themselves are clean and it's cheap and central.

The trendiest outlook for a drink, internet access (€7.50 per hour), or an upmarket meal is **Akis Bar** (☎ 26620 31665; snacks €3-11 & mains €9-17; 🖳). Try the 350g swordfish souvlaki (€17.50). The skewer itself cuts its own style; it hangs from a funky metal stand. An oldie but a goodie, **Nionios** (☎ 26620 31315) is the oldest taverna in Paxi (or so they claim – open since 1945), and it produces extra-tantalizing traditional dishes – and thankfully, not much has changed.

ANTIPAXI ΑΝΤΙΠΑΞΟΙ
pop 10
The stunning and diminutive island of Antipaxi, 2km south of Paxi, is covered with grape vines, olives and small hamlets. Caïques and tourist boats run daily from Gaïos and Lakka, and pull in at two beach coves, the small, sandy **Vrika Beach** and the pretty, pebbly **Voutoumi Beach**. Floating in the water here – with its dazzling clarity – is a sensational experience.

An inland path links the two beaches (a 30-minute walk), or if you are more of an energetic person you can walk up to the village of **Vigla**, or as far as the lighthouse at the southernmost tip (you should refer to the Bleasdale map and take plenty of water – allow 1½ hours minimum each way). Voutoumi Beach has two eateries – Bella Vista and a taverna on the beach. Vrika Beach also has two good competing tavernas – Spiros and Vrika. Main meals at both cost between €7 and €15. Check the price when offered the daily fish specials, or you could net a large catch in more ways than one. Both tavernas have designated areas with free use of beach umbrellas and sunbeds.

Accommodation is available through one or two of the beach tavernas. Ask the water-taxi drivers and taverna owners. Boats to Antipaxi (from €6 return) leave Gaïos at 10am and return around 5.30pm – there are more services in high season.

LEFKADA ΛΕΥΚΑΔΑ

pop 22,500
Lefkada (or Lefkas) is the fourth-largest island in the Ionians. Non-islanders tend to scorn its status as an island; it was once joined to the mainland by a narrow isthmus until the occupying Corinthians dug a canal in the 8th century BC. The 25m strait is now spanned by a causeway.

Lefkada's mountainous peaks exceed 1000m, and the island's fertile fields include olive groves, vineyards, and fir and pine forests. There are 10 satellite islets off the heavily developed east coast, and the less populated west coast boasts spectacular beaches.

Lefkada's beauty is also in its proud people. In the villages, look out for the older women in traditional dress.

Getting There & Away
AIR
Lefkada has no airport, but the airport near Preveza (Aktion) on the mainland is about 20km away. Flights operate daily between Athens and Preveza (€90 to €110), and three times a week between Corfu (€40) and Kefallonia (€35). Contact **Olympic Airlines** (☎ 26450 22881; Filippa Panagou 10, Lefkada Town) for bookings and information.

BUS
From Lefkada Town's **KTEL bus station** (☎ 26450 22364; Golemi) on the main waterfront road, buses head to Athens (€29, 5½ hours, four or five daily), Patra (€14, three hours, two to three weekly), Thessaloniki (€36, eight hours, one to two weekly and more in high season), Preveza (€2.60, 30 minutes, six to seven daily) and Igoumenitsa (two hours, daily).

FERRY
Four Islands Ferries runs a daily ferry service that sails to an ever-changing schedule (and with ever-changing prices) between Nydri (Lefkada), Frikes (Ithaki), Fiskardo (Kefallonia) and Vasiliki (Lefkada). Trips include Nydri to/from Frikes (per person/car €5.30/26.50, 1½ hours), Nydri to/from Fiskardo (via Frikes; €6.40/27.50, 2½ hours) and Vasiliki to/from Fiskardo (per person/car €6.40/27.50, one hour).

Information and tickets can be obtained from **Borsalino Travel** (☎ 26450 92528; borsalin@otenet.gr)

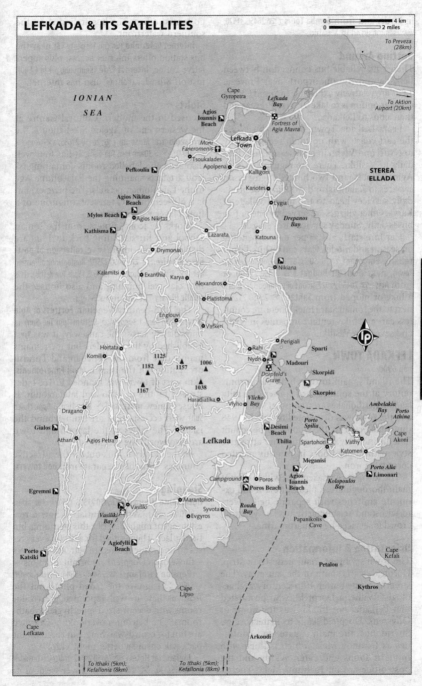

LEFKADA & ITS SATELLITES

0	4 km
0	2 miles

To Preveza (28km)

IONIAN SEA

Cape Gyropetra

Lefkada Bay

To Aktion Airport (20km)

Agios Ioannis Beach

Fortress of Agia Mavra

Moni Faneromenis

Lefkada Town

Tsoukalades

Apolpena

Kalligoni

STEREA ELLADA

Pefkoulia

Kariotes

Agios Nikitas Beach

Lygia

Drepanos Bay

Mylos Beach
Agios Nikitas

Kathisma

Lazarata

Katouna

Drymonas

Nikiana

Kalamitsi
Exanthia

Karya

Alexandros

Platistoma

Englouvi

Vafkeri

Hortata

Rahi
Perigiali

Sparti

Komili

▲ 1125

Nydri

Madouri

▲ 1182   ▲ 1157   ▲ 1006

Dorpfeld's Grave

Skorpidi

▲ 1167   ▲ 1038

Haradiatika

Vlicho Bay

Skorpios

Dragano

Vlyho

Ambelakia Bay

Porto Athina

Gialos

Syvros

Lefkada

Porto Spilia

Desimi Beach
Thilia

Spartohori

Vathy

Cape Akoni

Athani
Agios Petra

Katomeri

Meganisi

Porto Alia
Limonari

Egremni

Campground
Poros

Kolopoulos Bay

Poros Beach

Agios Ioannis Beach

Marantohori

Syvota

Rouda Bay

Vasiliki

Evgyros

Papanikolis Cave

Vasiliki Bay

Cape Kefali

Agiofylli Beach

Petalou

Porto Katsiki

Cape Lipso

Kythros

Cape Lefkatas

Arkoudi

To Ithaki (5km); Kefallonia (8km)

To Ithaki (5km); Kefallonia (8km)

IONIAN ISLANDS

in Nydri and from **Samba Tours** (☎ 26450 31520; www.sambatours.gr) in Vasiliki.

Getting Around

There's no reliable bus connection between Lefkada and Aktion airport, near Preveza. Taxis are relatively expensive (around €35); a cheaper option is to take a taxi to Preveza and then a bus to Lefkada

From Lefkada Town, frequent buses ply the east coast, with up to 20 services daily to Nydri and Vlyho in high season, and four daily to Vasiliki. There are regular buses to Agios Nikitas, and two limited high-season services to Kalamitsi and Athani. Around six daily services head to the inland village of Karya. Other villages are served by one or two buses daily. Sunday services are reduced.

Car hire starts at €35 per day, depending on season and model. Cars can be hired from reliable **Europcar** (☎ 26450 23581; Panagou 16, Lefkada Town), next door at **Budget** (☎ 26450 25274) or from **Aris** (☎ 26450 22027; Iroon Politechniou 32). Rent a bike or moped from **Santas** (☎ 26450 25250), next to the Ionian Star Hotel. There are countless car- and bike-rental companies in Nydri and several in Vasiliki.

LEFKADA TOWN

pop 6900

The island's main town is built on a promontory at the southeastern corner of a salty lagoon. Earthquakes are a constant threat here and the town was devastated by one in 1948 (but unaffected in 1953), only to be rebuilt in a distinctively quake-proof and attractive style with upper floors in brightly painted corrugated iron.

The town has a relaxed feel, with a vibrant main thoroughfare, a pleasant plaza and exquisite churches with separate bell towers to withstand seismic activity. The yachting crowd is serviced by a smart marina.

Orientation & Information

The town's vibrant main pedestrian strip, Dorpfeld, starts south of the causeway. The street is named after 19th-century archaeologist Wilhelm Dorpfeld, who postulated that Lefkada, not Ithaki, was the home of Odysseus. Dorpfeld leads to Plateia Agiou Spyridonos, the main square, and continues as Ioannou Mela, which is lined with modern shops and cafés. ATMs and the post office are on Ioannou Mela. There's

no tourist office. The bus station is on the southern waterfront.

Internet Cafezínho (Golemi 14; per hr €3) near the bus station offers internet access, plus superlative coffee. **Internet Café** (Koutroubi; per hr €2.40), just off 8th Merarchias, also has internet.

Sights

Housed in the modern Cultural Centre at the western end of Agelou Sikelianou is the **Archaeological Museum** (☎ 26450 21635; adult/concession €2/1; ☺ 8.30am-3pm Tue-Sun). It has four well displayed and labelled rooms containing island artefacts spanning the Palaeolithic Age to the Late Roman periods. The prize exhibit is a 6th-century-BC terracotta figurine of a flute player with nymphs.

Works by icon painters from the Ionian school and Russia dating back to 1500 are displayed in an impressive **collection of post-Byzantine icons** (☎ 26450 22502; Rontogianni; admission free; ☺ 8.30am-1.30pm Tue-Sun, 6-8.15pm Tue & Thu). It's in a classical building and also houses the **public library** off Ioannou Mela.

The 14th-century Venetian **Fortress of Agia Mavra** (☺ 9am-1.30pm Mon, 8.30am-1pm Tue-Sun) is immediately across the causeway. It was first established by the crusaders but the remains mainly date from the Venetian and Turkish occupations of the island. **Moni Faneromenis**, 3km west of town, was founded in 1634, destroyed by fire in 1886 and later rebuilt. It houses a new **museum** (☺ 9am-1pm, 6-8pm, closed Sun) with ecclesiastical art from around the island. The views of the lagoon and town are also worth the ascent.

In the old town, look out for the attractive churches, with their separate iron **bell towers**.

Sleeping

Hotel Santa Maura (☎ 26450 21308; s/d/tr incl breakfast €50/70/80; ☒) 'With potential' is how a real estate agent might describe this charming, but tired, place. There's need for a lift (in every respect) and some rooms are better than others – those onto Dorpfeld are bright, but noisy.

Pension Pirofani (☎ 26450 25844; Dorpfeld; d/tr €75/90; ☒) Ignore the faded photo out the front, as these are well-appointed, great-value rooms with decent-sized superhygienic bathrooms. The balconies overlooking Dorpfeld are fun for crowd-watching, but rooms at the back will ensure a better night's kip.

Ionian Star Hotel (☎ 26450 24762; s/d/tr incl breakfast €100/115/130; ☒ ☒ ☒) The foyer's elaborate

Greek statue promises special things. In reality, this pleasant five-star place has predictable offerings, but with enough trimmings to ensure a comfortable stay. There's even a good old '70s-style kidney-shaped pool. All the rooms are light and have good views.

Eating

Regantos (☎ 26450 22855; Vergioti 17; mains €5-12) The bright yellow and blue hues of this popular place seem a bit contrived – however, the food (such as fish, €35) at this family-run taverna is genuine and traditional. Everyone from Swedes to Greeks flocks here, but we found the service a bit surly.

Ey Zhn (Rontogianni 7; mains €8-17) 'Ease in', indeed. The food – a deliciously contemporary take on Greek food – isn't cheap, but the quality is outstanding.

Stylish bars and cafés line the western side of the waterfront; **Karma** (Dorpfeld), at the start of Dorpfeld, is the place to see and be seen. Plateia Agiou Spyridonos is crammed with cafés and crowds. The marina offers alternative options for a more-tranquil sundowner with the yachties.

Self-caterers can pick up supplies from the **supermarket** (Golemi) next to the bus station or from the well-stocked **bakery** (Ioannou Mela 182).

EAST COAST & SURROUNDS

To its detriment, the east coast is mainly associated with Nydri, once a fishing village but now an unattractive strip of tourist junk shops with a questionable beach. The coastal areas around Nydri have been affected by insensitive development, but it doesn't take much to avoid this; venture inland and you're in another world – scattered villages, local tavernas and good walks. Nydri is unavoidable if you want to access the islets of **Madouri**, **Sparti**, **Skorpidi** and **Skorpios**, plus **Meganisi**. Numerous **excursions** go to Meganisi and stop for a swim near Skorpios (€15 to €28), and some visit Ithaki and Kefallonia as well (€20). To go it alone, hire a motorboat from **Trident** (☎ 26450 92978) on the waterfront drag. Helpful **Borsalino Travel** (☎ 26450 92528; borsalin@otenet.gr) on the main street can organise the travel gamut.

The privately owned islet of Madouri, where Greek poet Aristotelis Valaoritis (1824–79) spent his last 10 years, is off limits. So too is Skorpios, where members of the Onassis family are buried in a cemetery, but cruise boats pause off a sandy beach

on the northern side of the island for a swim stop.

Amblers might enjoy the lovely walk to **waterfalls** 3km out of Nydri (and another 400m past the tavern). The walk follows a path through a ravine; be careful of the slippery rocks.

Yachties have caught wind of the small harbour of **Syvota**, 15km south of Nydri. Thankfully, it isn't to the detriment of the local fishermen, who anchor at harbour and fix their brightly coloured nets. It's a tranquil option for a base, although you'd need transport to explore, and there's no beach to speak of.

Sleeping & Eating

Ionian Paradise (☎ 26450 92268; ♿) At the time of research the Ioanian Paradise (formerly Gorgona Hotel), was being fully refurbished (prices unavailable), but judging from its former status, it should be a pleasant – if slighly pricier – option if you do stay in Nydri. It's down a side street diagonally opposite the Avis car-rental office.

Pinewood (☎ 26450 92075; mains €6-16.50) Okay, so Nydri does have something going for it. Locals highly recommend this efficiently run grill room, where meat is meat and they know how to cook it to perfection. It's signed to the right at the northern end of the main street.

Poros Beach Camping & Bungalows (☎ 26450 95452; www.porosbeach.com.gr; camp sites per adult/car/tent €8/4/5, studio €75-90; ♨) Twelve kilometres south of Nydri is this unpretentious complex overlooking pretty Poros Beach/Mikros Gialos. It has studio apartments and shady camping, plus restaurant, minimarket, bar and swimming pool.

Apartments Sivota (☎ 26450 31347; r €45, 2-person studio €55, 3-person apt €80-90), In Syvota, try these pleasant apartments. They're set slightly back from the beachfront, but have balconies and views, and there's a range of accommodation combinations.

Pavlos (☎ 26450 95296; mains €6.50-11; Haradiatika) 'Once upon a time, on the main square of a tiny village, stood a very special restaurant. It was basic, but it served food that all the people on the island spoke about...' This is no fairy tale; the reality is that it serves olde-style foods including *kokoretsi*, *frigadeli*, and *splinadero* (best you don't ask – think offal and innards). Eat here with the locals and you'll live happily ever after.

VASILIKI ΒΑΣΙΛΙΚΗ

Two types of people come to Vasiliki: the tanned and toned, and the sedate. Vasiliki is the centre of watersports and is considered *the* windsurfing location in Europe, due to distinct thermal winds. But it's not all fast sailing; the winding waterfront, with the eucalyptus and canopy-covered eateries, provides a tranquil environment in which to relax, unlike the unpleasant stony beach. Caïques take visitors to the island's better beaches and coves including Agiofylli Beach, south of Vasiliki.

Along the beach, windsurfing and sailing (catamaran) companies have staked their claims with flags, equipment and their own hotels for their package guests. If they have spare gear, some will willingly rent it to the independent enthusiast for a day or two.

Helpful **Samba Tours** (☎ 26450 31520; www .sambatours.gr) can organise car and bike hire, and answer most queries regarding the region. Other car rental places are **Christo's Alex's** (☎ 26450 31580) near the bus stop, and **GM Rentals** (☎ 26450 31650) in the main street.

Sleeping & Eating

Vassiliki Beach Camping (26450 31308; campkingk@otenet .gr; camp sites person/tent/car €7.50/5/6) A neat and compact camping option with easy access to the beach.

Pension Holidays (☎ 26450 31426; d €60; 🅿) Delightful Spiros offers Greek hospitality, breakfast on the balcony with harbour vista, and simply furnished but well-equipped rooms. Above the ferry dock. Prices vary according to length of stays.

Vasiliki Bay Hotel (☎ 26450 31077; www.hotel vassilikibay.gr; s/d incl breakfast €60/70; 🅿) If you don't mind being away from the water, you can't go too far wrong in this stylish and friendly place, up behind Alexander Restaurant. Prices enormously reduced outside August.

Delfini (Dolphin; ☎ 26450 31430; mains €6.50-13) The best of a ho-hum harbour haul; this eatery gets the most recommendations and it's open all year. Indeed, the food (including fish) is fresh and cooked to order.

WEST COAST & AROUND

Serious beach bods should skip Lefkada's east coast and head straight for the west. The sea here actually lives up to the clichéd brochure spiel; it's an incredible turquoise blue and most beaches are sandy. The best beaches include the long stretches of **Pefkoulia** and **Kathisma** in the north (the latter beach is becoming more developed and there are a few studios for rent here), and remote **Egremni** and breathtaking **Porto Katsiki** in the south. You'll pass by local stalls selling olive oil, honey and wine.

Word is out about the picturesque town of **Agios Nikitas**, and people flock to enjoy the holiday village's pleasant – if claustrophobic – atmosphere, plus the lovely **Mylos Beach** just around the headland (to walk, take the path by Taverna Poseidon. It's about 15 minutes up and over the peninsula, or for €2 you can take a water taxi from tiny Agios Nikitas beach).

The town's accommodation options are plentiful, and include **Camping Kathisma** (camp sites per person/tent/car €7/5/6), 1.5km south of town. Or try the modest, but very friendly, Greek Canadian-run **Olive Tree Hotel** (☎ 26450 97453; www.olivetreelefkada.com; Agios Nikitas; s/d incl breakfast €70/90) – ask a local for directions. **Hotel Agios Nikitas** (☎ 26450 97460; www.agiosnikitas.com; Agios Nikitas; d incl breakfast €120, 4-person apt €100; 🏊), a stylish hotel with tasteful rooms and apartments in a secluded complex, is bordered by jasmine and bougainvillea and is on the coastal road just north of the village. For the quintessential fish-by-the-turquoise-sea restaurant experience, don't swim past the terrace at **Sapfo** (☎ 26450 97497; Agios Nikitas; fish per kilo €40-60), Agios Nikitas' established fish tavern. It's right on the waterfront.

Beach bums can base themselves in the village of Athani in the no-frill rooms of **Panorama** (☎ 26450 33291; d/tr without bathroom €35/50), on top of hospitable Thomas' buzzing taverna of the same name. A beer or home-style meal (mains €5 to €9.50) on the taverna terrace are the perfect sunburn cure.

Further south near the turn-off to Porto Katsiki is **Taverna Oasis** (☎ 26450 33201; mains €6.50-9), a sprawling outdoor taverna set within an established pine grove. The taverna also offers free camping for those with campervans and tents.

CENTRAL LEFKADA

The spectacular central spine of Lefkada, with its traditional farming villages, lush green peaks, fragrant pine trees, olive groves and vines – plus occasional views of the islets – is well worth seeing if you have time and transport. The small village of **Karya** is a bit of a tourist haunt but it boasts a stunning square with plane trees, around which are tavernas and snack bars. Karya is famous for its special embroidery, introduced in the 19th century by one-handed local woman, Maria Koutsochero. Visit the **museum** (admission €2.50; ☉ hrs vary) for an interesting display of embroidery paraphernalia and local artefacts.

For food, **Taverna Karaboulias** (☎ 26450 41301; Karya main plaza; mains €6-13) is recommended for its meals, including *kokkinisto*, a beef, wine and tomato stew. For accommodation options ask British Brenda Sherry at **Café Pierros** (☎ 26450 41760; Karya) who can arrange all (as well as a cup of tea and signature toasted sandwich).

The island's highest village, **Englouvi**, is renowned for its honey and lentil production and is only a few kilometres south of Karya.

MEGANISI ΜΕΓΑΝΗΣΙ
pop 1090
Meganisi has the largest population of Lefkada's three inhabited satellite islets. The verdant landscape and deep bays of turquoise water, fringed by pebbled beaches, attract yachties and day visitors and, more increasingly, British 'villa fillers'. Try to spend a night; if not, a day trip is obligatory, either independently or on one of the excursion boats from Nydri (p465).

Meganisi has three settlements, including quiet and neat **Spartohori**, with narrow laneways and pretty, bougainvillea-bedecked houses, all perched on a plateau above Porto Spilia (where the ferry docks; follow the steep road or steps behind). **Vathy** is the island's second attractive harbour, and 800m behind it is the village of **Katomeri**. Those with more time up their sleeve can visit remote beaches such as **Limonari**.

Helpful **Asteria Holidays** (☎ 26450 51107), at Porto Spilia, is in the know for all things relating to the island, including trips, villas and real estate – just in case you get the urge to splurge.

Sleeping & Eating
Hotel Meganisi (☎ 26450 51240; Katomeri; d incl breakfast €100; ✱ ✱) This simple but modern hotel in Katomeri has sunny rooms with balconies and expansive outlooks to the country and sea, as does the generous-sized pool and terrace. Its restaurant also comes recommended. Follow the signs once you get to Katomeri.

Worthy dining options around the island include **Taverna Porto Vathy** (☎ 26450 51125; mains €7-14), the undisputed favourite fish taverna

(fish €30 to €55 per kilo) cast out on a small quay in Vathy; **Tropicana** (☎ 26450 51486), which serves excellent pizzas in Spartohori; or **Laki's** (☎ 26450 51228), your archetypal Greek taverna, also in Spartohori.

Getting There & Away
The Meganisi ferry boat runs about six times daily between Nydri and Meganisi (per person/car €2/14, 25 to 40 minutes). It calls at Porto Spilia before Vathy (the first ferry of the day stops at Vathy, then Porto Spilia).

A local bus runs five to seven times per day between Spartohori and Vathy (via Katomeri) but it's worth bringing your own transport, as there was no island car rental at the time of research.

KEFALLONIA
ΚΕΦΑΛΛΟΝΙΑ

pop 39,500
Kefallonia, the largest of the Ionian Islands, shouldn't be underestimated. It hides secrets and surprises below its rugged, towering mountain range: sprawling vineyards, stunning cliffs and beaches and unclassified Roman ruins. Kefallonia was devastated in the 1953 earthquake, so much of the island's architectural aesthetics are modern. Yet there's plenty for the traveller to discover, including beautiful harbours, walking trails and the local cuisine.

Kefallonia's capital is Argostoli, the main port is Sami, and ferry services also run from Fiskardo and Poros.

Getting There & Away
AIR
There are at least two daily flights between Kefallonia and Athens (€75), and connections to other Ionian Islands, including Zakynthos (€28) and Corfu (€35). **Olympic Airlines** (☎ 26710 28808; www.olympicairlines.com; Rokou Vergoti 1, Argostoli) can help with information and bookings.

BUS
Four daily buses connect Athens and Kefallonia (via Patra) using the various ferry services (to/from Argostoli, Sami and Poros) to the mainland. All cost around €35 and take about seven hours (prices include ferry tickets). For information contact the **KTEL bus**

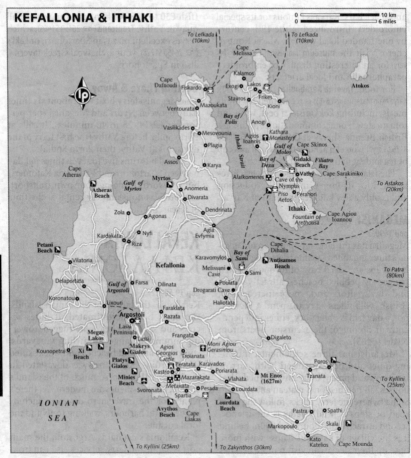

KEFALLONIA & ITHAKI

station (☎ 26710 22276/81; kefaloniakteltours@yahoo
.gr; A Tristi 5) on the southern waterfront in
Argostoli. The office produces an excellent
printed schedule.

FERRY
Domestic
There are frequent ferry services to Kyllini in
the Peloponnese from both Poros (per person/
car €8.10/38.10, 1½ hours, two to five daily)
and Argostoli (per person €12.50, three hours,
one daily). One ferry links Sami with Astakos
via Piso Aetos on Ithaki (€10, three hours). In
August there are direct ferries from Sami to
Astakos (€10, 2½ hours) on alternate days.

Strintzis Lines (www.ferries.gr/strintzis) has two
ferries daily connecting Sami with Patra (per

person/car €14.50/55, 2½ hours) and Vathy
(per person €5.10, one hour) or Piso Aetos
(per person/car €2.20/14.50, 30 minutes).

Sailing from Fiskardo to/from Frikes (per
person/car €3.40/14) takes just under an
hour; Fiskardo to/from Vasiliki (per person/
car €6.40/27.50) takes one hour. Information
and tickets for these routes can be obtained
from **Nautilus Travel** (☎ 26740 41440; Fiskardo), on
the waterfront.

From the remote port of Pesada in the
south there are two daily high-season services to Agios Nikolaos (€6, 1½ hours), on
the northern tip of Zakynthos. Getting to
and from both islands' ports without your
own transport can be difficult (and costly if
you rely on taxis). To get to the ferry point

in Pesada from Argostoli, you can catch one of two daily buses (in high season only and except Sundays). On Zakynthos, there are two buses per week to and from the port of Agios Nikolaos to Zante Town (via villages).

International
In high season there are regular ferries between Sami, Igoumenitsa, and Brindisi in Italy (Kefallonia–Brindisi including taxes €70, 14 hours). To get to other ports in Italy, take the ferry first from Sami to Patra.

Tickets and information can be obtained from **Vassilatos Shipping** (☎ 26710 22618; Antoni Tristi 54, Argostoli), opposite the port authority, and from **Blue Sea Travel** (☎ 26740 23007; Sami), on Sami's waterfront.

Getting Around
TO/FROM THE AIRPORT
The airport is 9km south of Argostoli. There isn't an airport bus service; a taxi costs around €15.

BUS
From Argostoli's **bus station** (☎ 26710 22281, 26710 25222) on the southern waterfront there are 11 buses daily heading to the Lassi Peninsula (€1), with four buses to Sami (€2.50), two to Poros (€4.50), two to Skala (€4.50) and two to Fiskardo (€5). There's a daily east-coast service linking Katelios with Skala, Poros, Sami, Agia Evfymia and Fiskardo. No buses operate on Sunday.

CAR & MOTORCYCLE
The major resorts have loads of car- and bike-rental companies. Lassi, a 20-minute walk up the hill from Argostoli, has the best choices around including **Avis/Liberatos** (☎ 26710 29112; www.liberatosrentacar.com; Lassi), which is also based at the airport. **Greekstones Rent a Car** (☎ 26710 42201; www.greekstones-rentacar .com) has a good reputation and will deliver to you within a 15km radius of Svoronata (7km from Argostoli, near the airport).

FERRY
Car ferries run hourly (more frequently in high season) from 7.30am to 10.30pm between Argostoli and Lixouri, on the island's western peninsula. The journey takes 30 minutes, and tickets cost €1.60/4/1 per person/car/motorbike.

ARGOSTOLI ΑΡΓΟΣΤΟΛΙ
pop 8900
Argostoli was not rebuilt to its former Venetian splendour after the 1953 earthquake, but it's an attractive and lively place with a pleasant, authentic Greek feel. It offers plentiful sleeping and eating options, plus shopping and nightlife. The whole town seems to gather in the evenings in the central plaza.

Orientation & Information
The main ferry quay is at the waterfront's northern end, and the bus station is on the southern waterfront. The centre of Argostoli's social and culinary activity is Plateia Valianou, the large palm-treed central square up from the waterfront off 21 Maïou, and its nearby surrounds. Other hubs are pedestrianised Lithostrotou, lined with smart shops, and the waterfront (Antoni Tristi, sections of which were formerly known as Ioannou Metaxa).

The **EOT** (Greek National Tourist Organisation; ☎ 26710 22248; ☼ 8am-2.30pm Mon-Fri) is on the northern waterfront beside the port police. There are banks with ATMs along the northern waterfront and on Lithostrotou. The post office is on Lithostrotou, and internet is available at **Excelixis** (cnr Minoos & Asklipiou; per hr €4).

Sights & Activities
The **Korgialenio History & Folklore Museum** (☎ 26710 28835; Ilia Zervou 12; admission €4; ☼ 9am-2pm Mon-Sat) and **Focas-Kosmetatos Foundation** (☎ 26710 26595; Vallianou; admission €3; ☼ 9.30am-1pm & 7-10pm Mon-Sat) provide interesting insights into Argostoli's cultural history – the former more general, the latter delving into the world of the nobility. The town's **Archaeological Museum** (☎ 26710 28300; Rokou Vergoti; admission €3; ☼ 8.30am-3pm Tue-Sun) has a collection of well displayed and labelled island relics, including Mycenaean finds. The one-room **Divisione Acqui Museum** (☎ 6945776294; Lithostratou; admission free; ☼ hrs vary), to the left of the Catholic church, details the disturbing history of the Italian 'Acqui Division' during their occupation of Kefallonia (and of their slaughter by the Germans).

Six kilometres from Argostoli in Davgata is the **Museum of Natural History** (☎ 26710 84400; admission €2.50; ☼ 9am-3pm), with fascinating exhibits on the geological and natural phenomena of the island, and an excellent topographical model of the island in relief.

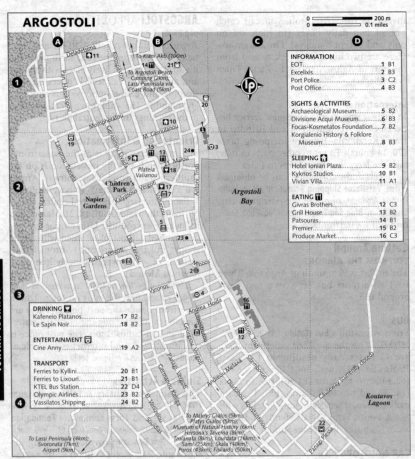

ARGOSTOLI

INFORMATION
EOT..1 B1
Excelixis.......................................2 B3
Port Police...................................3 C2
Post Office...................................4 B3

SIGHTS & ACTIVITIES
Archaeological Museum...............5 B2
Divisione Acqui Museum..............6 B3
Focas-Kosmetatos Foundation.....7 B2
Korgialenio History & Folklore
Museum...................................8 B3

SLEEPING
Hotel Ionian Plaza......................9 B2
Kyknos Studios..........................10 B1
Vivian Villa................................11 A1

EATING
Givras Brothers..........................12 C3
Grill House.................................13 B2
Patsouras...................................14 B1
Premier......................................15 B2
Produce Market..........................16 C3

DRINKING
Kafeneio Platanos......................17 B2
Le Sapin Noir............................18 B2

ENTERTAINMENT
Cine Anny..................................19 A2

TRANSPORT
Ferries to Kyllini........................20 B1
Ferries to Lixouri.......................21 B1
KTEL Bus Station.......................22 D4
Olympic Airlines........................23 B2
Vassilatos Shipping....................24 B2

The town's closest and largest sandy beaches are **Makrys Gialos** and **Platys Gialos**, 5km south. Regular buses serve the area.

Lourdata, 16km from Argostoli on the Argostoli–Poros road, has an attractive long beach set against a mountainous green backdrop.

Those wanting more physical exertion should contact **Monte Nero Activities** (☎ 6934010400, 6932904360; www.monte-nero-activities .com). Staff organise environmentally friendly sea kayaking (day tours €55 with lunch and snorkelling gear), cycling and hiking tours in the island's coastal regions.

Tours

KTEL (☎ 26710 25222/22281; kefaloniakteltours@yahoo.gr; tours €15-35) runs excellent-value day tours of Kefallonia, visiting several towns and villages around the island (including a folkloric tour to monasteries). It also takes tours to other islands (Ithaki and Zakynthos). Bookings can be made at the KTEL bus station building.

Sleeping

A string of shampoo-and-sewing-kit-style hotels line the waterfront and Plateia Valianou, with prices to suit most budgets. **KTEL Tours** (☎ 26710 23364; kefaloniakteltours@yahoo.gr) has a selection of apartments and hotel options available and will organise these via email.

Argostoli Beach Camping (☎ 26710 23487; www .argostolibeach.gr; camp sites per adult/car/tent €7.50/3.50/4) This pleasant camping spot is away from the humdrum, near the lighthouse on the northernmost point of the peninsula.

Kyknos Studios (☎ 26710 23398; P-Krousos@otenet.gr; M Geroulanou 4; d €50) An historic well sits in front of these seven bright, if a little faded, studios, each with small veranda. But you don't need to dig too deep to enjoy the surrounds and attractive, well-kept garden.

Vivian Villa (☎ 26710 23396; www.kefalonia-vivian villa.gr; Deladetsima 9; r/studio/apt €60/70/130; ☒) Highly recommended for its squeaky-clean bright rooms and bubbly owners. There are even tea-making facilities in each room, and prices are discounted for longer stays.

Hotel Ionian Plaza (☎ 26710 25581; www.ionian plaza.gr; Plateia Valianou; s/d/tr €82/119/155; ☒) Argostoli's smartest hotel has a marble-decorated lobby, stylish public areas and well-appointed rooms with balconies. Prices can be significantly reduced outside high season, as can (some of) the plaza noise, thanks to the window's double-glazing.

Eating

Grill House (gyros €2) This popular and cheap place is found among the pricey cafés on Plateia Valianou, next to Hotel Aeon.

Givras Brothers (☎ 26710 24259; Vasili Vandorou 1; mains €4-7) One of Argostoli's most traditional family-run restaurants and favourite old haunt of locals. Basic rooms (double with bathroom €30) can be found upstairs.

Patsuras (☎ 26710 22779; Antoni Tristi 32; mains €5-10) A great range of authentic dishes from which to choose. Locals think it's good value, and so should you.

Kiani Akti (☎ 26710 26680; mains €8-13) Posh and for those with dosh. This seafood restaurant serves top quality fish (€60 to €80 per kilo) in a nautical environment. It's located on the Argostoli quay opposite the merchant marine academy. The razor clams are sourced from secret locations by an Italian diver.

Premier (☎ 26710 23280; Plateia Valianou) The premier place to be seen, especially for mature locals with a bit of spare cash and a penchant for sweets and *gelati* that truly are *numero uno*.

Eight kilometres southeast from Argostoli, in the village of Troianata, **Hersona's Taverna** (☎ 26710 69940; mains €3-9) is a carnivore's dream. Fresh carcasses hang on display in the kitchen, a kitchen that produces superlative meaty delights.

You can pick up a range of self-catering supplies from the waterfront produce market and from bakeries and supermarkets nearby.

Drinking

Plateia Valianou is a barfly's delight, with both crowds and music upbeat until late. Cool cats chill at Le Sapin Noir or Kafeneio Platanos.

Entertainment

The outdoor cinema **Cine Anny** (☎ 26710 25880; Pan Harokopou 54; admission €8) shows films between June and August.

SAMI & SURROUNDS ΣAMH
pop 2200

Sami, 25km northeast of Argostoli and the main port of Kefallonia, was also flattened by the 1953 earthquake. Its exposed long strip is made up of tourist-oriented cafés, but beyond this it's an attractive place, nestled in a bay and flanked by steep hills. It promotes itself as the gateway to Kefallonia. Indeed, it provides an enjoyable introduction or stopover; it has several monasteries, ancient castle ruins, caves, walks and nearby beaches that reflect the region's ancient and rich history. All facilities, including a post office and banks, are in town. Buses for Argostoli usually meet ferries, and car hire is available through **Karavomilos** (☎ 26740 23769). Sami's **tourist office** (☒ 9am-8pm May-Oct) is at the northern end of town. An informative website is www.sami.com.

Sights & Activities

The Municipality of Sami has published a simple brochure called *Walking Trail*, which outlines wonderful walks through the local area. Trails encompass the acropolis of ancient Sami (around 500 BC), Roman ruins and churches, plus nature: pine forests, olive groves, streams and beaches. The brochures are available from the tourist office.

Don't miss **Antisamos Beach**, 4km northeast of Sami. The long, stony beach is in a lovely green setting backed by hills. The drive here is also a highlight, offering dramatic views from cliff edges.

The rather overrated **Melissani Cave** (admission incl boat trip €5; ☒ 8am-8pm), a subterranean sea-water lake that turns an extraordinary blue, is only worth visiting when the sun is overhead between noon and 2pm. It's 2.5km west of Sami. The extraordinary **Drogarati Cave** (☎ 26740 22950; admission €3.50; ☒ 8am-8pm) is a massive (natural) chamber with stalactites.

IONIAN ISLANDS

But be aware that tourism is taking its toll – hot lights, bodies and seasonal concerts within the area are increasing the temperatures in this two-million-year-old cave (stalactites grow at the rate of 1cm every 100 to 150 years), causing a speedy and ultimately detrimental meltdown.

Sleeping

Karavomilos Beach Camping (☎ 26740 22480; www .camping-karavomilos.gr; camp sites per adult/car/tent €7.50/3.50/5.50; 🖵) A large, green, award-winning camping ground in a glorious beachfront location, with all the facilities zipped up, too.

Hotel Melissani (☎ 26740 22464; d/tr €65/75) Sixties-cum-'70s, hip, hop and happenin'. Although built in the early '80s, a Maxwell Smart/Austin Powers morph would feel at home here, especially in the bar – an eclectic décor of swivelling vinyl bar stools, retro lights, marble floors and groovy tiles. Smallish rooms with balconies have good views of mountains or sea.

Hotel Kastro (☎ 26740 22656; www.kastrohotel.com; s/d/tr €67/96/115) If Hotel Melissani is full, try this place in the town centre, but expect it to be your average modern(ish) hotel experience.

Eating

Dining out in Sami tends to be a repetitive experience, with little to distinguish the menus or settings of the restaurants that line the waterfront. If you have your own wheels, you're better off following your tummy rumbles in the direction of village tavernas, or heading west to the tranquil Agia Evfymia.

Rombolis (☎ 0674023323; Poulata; 🕑 dinner) This is very much a local joint – the owner raises an animal herd for his eatery. While vegetarians might not appreciate the wholesome-beast-on-a-spit experience, this place is not to be missed by those who can gratefully stomach generous fillings and Greek hospitality. Located 5km from Sami, in Poulata village opposite the church.

Paradise Beach (☎ 26740 61392; mains €6.50-13, fish per kg €48-52; Agia Evfymia) Stavros, the charismatic owner of this place, is sentimental about serving Penelope Cruz and cast when they were on the island filming *Captain Corelli's Mandolin*. The movie cast may be long gone from the island, but his delicious dishes live on. Try the chocolate soufflé (€8.50). The location has a star-studded view of the natural kind.

ASSOS ΑΣΟΣ

Tiny Assos is an upmarket gem of whitewashed and pastel houses, straddling the isthmus of a peninsula on which stands a Venetian fortress. The fortress is a pleasant place to hike to and around, with superlative views and a great historical ambience.

For accommodation, try the **Pension Gerania** (☎ 26740 51526; www.pensiongerania.gr; d inc breakfast €80; ❉). True to its name, geraniums are the feature of this lush, shady garden, and the light and appealing rooms afford pleasant views. Follow the *pension* (and parking) sign as you enter town.

Cosi's Inn (☎ 26740 51420, 6936754330; www.cosisinn .gr; 2-/3-person studio €100/115; ❉) is not typically 'Greek' but has the marks of the young and hip interior designer owner: iron beds and sofas, frosted lights and white décor feature strongly.

Another favourite for quality and views is **Linardos Studios** (☎ 26740 51563; d €80, 4-person apt €95).

For eating, **Platanos** (☎ 6944671804; mains €6-13) is in an attractive shady setting near the waterfront. It has good vegetarian choices and even better meaty ones, including roast suckling pig.

AROUND ASSOS

One of Greece's most breathtaking and picture-perfect beaches is **Myrtos**, 8km south of Assos along the hair-raising stretch of road that goes north to Fiskardo. From the safety of a designated viewing area, you can admire and photograph the white sand and exquisite blue water set between tall limestone cliffs. The beach has minimal facilities – just a basic taverna and sunbed hire. Be aware that the beach drops off quickly and sharply, but once you are in the water it's a heavenly experience. Think clichéd turquoise and aqua water.

FISKARDO ΦΙΣΚΑΡΔΟ

pop 225

Fiskardo, 50km north of Argostoli, was the only Kefallonian village not devastated by the 1953 earthquake. Framed by cypress-mantled hills and with fine Venetian buildings, it has a delightful, if slightly sanitised, Disneyland-style feel. It's a favourite port-o'-call for yachties with attitude. Recently, ancient ruins have been uncovered in the village.

Prices in Fiskardo are as high as a mainsail. **Pama Travel** (☎ 26740 41033; www.pamatravel.com) on the harbour front can help with travel services including car and boat hire, plus it has internet access (per hour €4).

The **Fiskardo Nautical and Environmental Club** (☎ 26740 41081; www.fnec.gr; 🕙 10am-2pm, 5-7.30pm Mon-Sat May-Oct) is an excellent not-for-profit organisation that runs a small local museum and environmental information centre (up the stairs next to the church). It also takes scuba diving and runs dolphin-, turtle- and monk seal–spotting research activities. Volunteers are welcome for short- or long-term projects.

Sleeping & Eating

Regina's Rooms (☎ 26740 41125; d/r €50/70) Friendly Regina runs a popular place that has colourful rooms dotted with plastic flowers. Some rooms have kitchenettes and/or balconies enjoying views over the water. Enter from the main car park.

Stella Apartments (☎ 26740 41211; www.stella -apartments.gr; d €90, apt €190; 🗶) This Greek version of Fawlty Towers – in that it resembles an English-style guesthouse – has immaculate, spacious studios with kitchen, TV, phone, air-con and balcony, and a communal dining area. It's about 800m from the main car park.

Faros Suites (☎ 26740 41355; www.myrtoscorp.com; ste €105-160; 🗶 🗷) For your fluffy bathrobe–type experience, head to these apartments, where *Out of Africa* comes to Greece. With a luxury safari lodge feel (teak furniture and cotton linens) in a local setting (turquoise water views and bougainvillea), plus the hospitality of the Greek–South African owners, you'll have trouble moving from the tasteful rooms, relaxation areas, or swimming pool.

Café Tseleniti (☎ 26740 41344; mains €6.50-22) Housed in a 19th-century building that survived the 1953 earthquake, the international dishes here are sublime, as is the romantic outdoor setting, which features spotlighted brollies. Inside, be sure to view the fresco on the side wall, drawn by some wishful Greek patriots.

Also recommended:

Villa Romantza (☎ 26740 41322; www.villa-romantza .gr; r/studio €50/70, apt €80-110; 🗶) An excellent budget choice with simple and clean rooms. It's found next door to Regina's rooms on the car park. Cheaper out of season.

Emelisse Hotel (☎ 26740 41200; www.arthotel.gr; r/ste from €245/285; 🗶 🗷) Chic and luxurious (plus, we found, a little standoffish and snobby), this is the place for those who want the lot.

Uta & Toni's (☎ 26740 41022; utarose2@yahoo.gr; per week studio/apt/cottage €350/400/580) Regular guests may be miffed that the word's finally out. This old restored whitewashed Greek farmhouse – with a selection of rooms – provides isolation in a stunning setting. Not to mention the owners' personality on tap.

Getting There & Away

You can get to/from Fiskardo by ferry to/from Lefkada and Ithaki or by bus to/from Argostoli. The ferry is at one end of the waterfront; ask the bus to drop you at the turn-off, or it's a 10-minute walk from the car park to the ferry.

ITHAKI ΙΘΑΚΗ

pop 3700

Diminutive Ithaki is the diamond of the Ionians. It is believed to be the mythical home of Homer's Odysseus, where his loyal wife Penelope patiently awaited his homecoming. This tranquil island is two large peninsulas – joined by a narrow isthmus – with sheer cliffs, precipitous mountainous passages and pockets of cypresses and olive groves. Nestled around this compact gem are beautiful fishing hamlets (tastefully rebuilt after the 1953 earthquake) and discreet pebbly coves. Monasteries and churches offer Byzantine delights and splendid views. The locals here are rightfully proud of their island.

Getting There & Away

Strintzis Lines (www.ferries.gr/strintzis-ferries) has two ferries daily connecting Vathy or Piso Aetos with Patra (per person/car €14.50/55, four hours), via Sami on Kefallonia (per person €5.10 to/from Vathy, one hour, or to/from Piso Aetos €2.20, 30 minutes).

Ionian Pelagosruns a daily ferry (sometimes twice a day) in high season between Piso Aetos, Sami and Astakos on the mainland (per person/car €8/33, 2½ hours direct from Piso Aetos to Astakos, three hours from Astakos to Piso Aetos via Sami).

Other ferries run to ever-changing schedules from Vasiliki and Nydri (Lefkada) to Frikes (Ithaki) and Fiskardo (Kefallonia). The Frikes–Fiskardo trip takes just under an hour (per person/car €3.40/14) and Nydri–Frikes

IONIAN ISLANDS

takes 1½ hours (€5.30/26.50). Frikes–Vasiliki goes via Fiskardo and takes two hours.

Information and tickets for these routes can be obtained from Delas Tours (right) on the main square in Vathy.

Getting Around

Piso Aetos, on Ithaki's west coast, has no settlement; taxis often meet boats, as does the municipal bus in high season only. The island's one bus runs twice daily (weekdays only, more often in high season) between Kioni and Vathy via Stavros and Frikes (€3.50), and its limited schedule is not well suited to day-trippers. Taxis are relatively expensive (about €25 for the Vathy–Frikes trip), so your best bet is to hire a moped or car (or a motorboat) to get around. In Vathy, **Rent a Scooter** (☎ 26740 32840) is down the laneway opposite the port authority. For cars, try **Happy Cars** – contact Polyctor Tours (right) or **Alpha Bike & Car Hire** (☎ 26740 33243) behind Alpha Bank.

VATHY ΒΑΘΥ

pop 1820

Ithaki's pretty main town sprawls along its elongated seafront. Compact museums are situated in its twisting streets, while cafés and restaurants line the attractive central square, the centre's social hub.

The ferry quay is on the western side of the bay. To reach the central square (Plateia Efstathiou Drakouli), turn left and follow the waterfront.

Ithaki has no tourist office. Helpful Stavros at **Delas Tours** (☎ 26740 32104; www.ithaca.com.gr) and business-focused **Polyctor Tours** (☎ 26740 33120; www.ithakiholidays.com), both on the main square, can help with tourist information. The main square also has banks with ATMs; the post office; and internet access – try **Net** (per hr €4).

Sights & Activities

Behind Hotel Mentor is an excellent **archaeological museum** (☎ 26740 32200; admission free; ☽ 8.30am-3pm Tue-Sun). Of note are ancient coins depicting Odysseus. The informative **nautical & folklore museum** (admission €1; ☽ 10am-2pm & 5-9pm Tue-Sat) is housed in an old generating station one block behind the plaza. The interesting displays include traditional clothing, household items and shipping paraphernalia.

Boat excursions leave from Vathy harbour in the summer months and include day trips around Ithaki and to Fiskardo (€30); Lefkada (€35); and 'unknown islands' that include Atokos and Kalamos (€35). There's also a water taxi to **Gidaki Beach**. Note: the only way to access this beach on foot is to follow the walking track from Skinari Beach.

Sleeping

Grivas Gerasimos Rooms (☎ 26740 33328; d/tr €70/84) Pot plants, small balconies and a seaside vista are all pleasant features of this spacious studio budget option. Turn right at the Century Club on the waterfront and first left at the road parallel to the sea. The studios are 50m on

---

ODYSSEUS & ITHAKI

Ithaki has long been identified as the home of the mythical hero Odysseus (Ulysses); it was the island home he left so that he could fight in the Trojan War. According to Homer's The Iliad, and more specifically The Odyssey, the hero Odysseus took 10 long years to return home to Ithaki from Troy on the Asia Minor coast.

Odysseus survived tempestuous seas, sea monsters and a cunning siren, until finally he was helped by friendly Phaeacians and was returned to Ithaki. Here, disguised as a beggar, he – along with his son Telemachus and his old swineherd Eumaeus – slayed the conniving suitors who'd been trying to woo Penelope, Odysseus' long-suffering wife who'd waited 20 years for him to return.

No mention of Ithaki appears in writings of the Middle Ages. As late as 1504, the island was almost uninhabited following repeated depredations by pirates, so the Venetians convinced settlers from neighbouring islands to repopulate it. Yet – as enthusiasts point out – the island appears to be described in The Odyssey; it matches in many respects the physical nature of the island today. These sites include the 'Fountain of Arethousa' and the 'Cave of the Nymphs' (currently closed under controversial circumstances). However, many Homerists have been hard-pressed to ascribe other locales described in The Odyssey – particularly Odysseus' castle – to actual places on the islands, because of scant archaeological remains.

your right. Prices are negotiable depending on your length of stay.

Odyssey Apartments (☎ 26740 33400; www.ithaki-odyssey.com; apt €100-160; ⊠ ⓡ) It seems a bit of an odyssey to get here – 1.5km east of town – but those with a car or strong legs should consider this excellent option. There are light, breezy studios and apartments with balconies, and a magical view of the yacht harbour and beyond.

Hotel Perantzada (☎ 26740 33496; www.arthotel.gr/perantzada/; Odissea Androutsou; d €176-365, ste €260-585; ⊠ 🖵 ⓡ) Part of the Emelisse chain, this upmarket boutique hotel gets full marks for originality. Each room in this light-blue, neoclassical building (designed by 19th-century German architect Ernst Schiller) has been individually decorated with Italian-style flair and fabrics, including contemporary nautical and botanic themes. At the time of research the hotel was expanding; an adjoining building was being renovated, complete with breakfast area and infinity pool.

Eating & Drinking

Eating at the restaurants along the western waterfront is a *Groundhog Day* experience; identical menus in similar settings on the same patch. Distinct culinary sensations can be found within a 1km radius of the centre.

For a sweet experience, try *rovani*, the local speciality made with rice, honey and cloves, at one of the patisseries on or near the main square.

Café Karamela (☎ 26740 33580; snacks €2-6) The western quay is home to this welcoming place, where a massive window literally frames the bay view. Linger with the locals over the café's board games, books and TV, plus home-made snacks such as cake and pastries.

Drosia (☎ 26740 32959; mains €6-15) Ask a Vathy local where to eat, and the response is overwhelmingly consistent. This authentic taverna serves good hearty food at reasonable prices. The grilled meat includes chicken skewers (€6.50) and lamb chops (€8.50). You might catch the patrons spontaneously dancing to a bouzouki-playing friend. It's 1km up the hill on the road to Filiatro.

Also recommended:

Para thin'alos (☎ 26740 33567; snacks €7) A great bar serving French wines plus delicious light meals with an international twist. The owner-chef has savoir-faire.

Gregory's Taverna/Paliocaravo (☎ 26740 32573; www.paliocaravo.sphosting.com; mains €7-19) This long-standing family concern serves fish and tasty specialities to yachties and gourmands. It's 1km east of town on the waterfront.

Piccolo (☎ 26740 33626; meals €7-10) Head here for an Asian fix. It's nestled in behind the main square.

AROUND ITHAKI

Ithaki proudly claims several sites associated with Homer's tale, *The Odyssey* (see boxed text, opposite). Finding the hyped-up locations can be an epic journey – signage is a bit scant. Many seem to be myths themselves, so vague are their locations, but there's no questioning the spirit of this island. The **Fountain of Arethousa**, in the island's south, is where Odysseus' swineherd, Eumaeus, is believed to have brought his pigs to drink. The exposed and isolated hike – through unspoilt landscape with great sea views – takes 1½ to two hours (return) from the turn-off; this excludes the hilly 5km trudge up the road to the sign itself. Take a hat and water.

The **Bay of Dexa**, 1km west of Vathy, is thought to be ancient Phorkys, where the Phaeacians safely delivered Odysseus home. (Note: despite the sign, Cave of the Nymphs is closed and unsafe to visit).

The location of Odysseus' palace has been much disputed and archaeologists have been unable to find conclusive evidence; some present-day archaeologists speculate it was on **Pelikata Hill** near Stavros, while German archaeologist Heinrich Schliemann (p232) believed it to be at **Alalkomenes**, near Piso Aetos. Also in Stavros visit the small **archaeological museum** (☎ 26740 31305; admission free; ⏱ 9am-2.30pm Tue-Sun), where minder Fotini Couvaras is almost an exhibit herself, so committed is she to this site.

To move away from Homeric myths, head 14km north of Vathy to sleepy **Anogi**, the old capital. Its restored church of **Agia Panagia** (claimed to be from the 12th century) has incredible Byzantine frescoes and a Venetian bell tower. You can obtain the keys from Nikos, at the neighbouring *kafeneio*.

The tiny, understated village of **Frikes** is set in among windswept cliffs. It has several good accommodation options, a popular bar and a relaxed ambience. It's the ferry departure point for Lefkada.

Sleeping & Eating

Mrs Vasilopoulos' Rooms (☎ 26740 31027; Stavros; d/apt €50/70) These homely studios are in a lane

IONIAN ISLANDS

HOT HIKES IN ITHAKI

Walking is a great way to explore Ithaki and Homeric sites, and keen ramblers will not be disappointed. Ithaki's compact size allows walkers to experience dramatic scenery changes in relatively short walks, including 360-degree views of the ocean and surrounding islands. Thanks to the single-handed efforts of islander Denis Skinari and his band of helpers, around 10 cleared and marked trails exist around island. These include Kalamos to Exogi, Exogi to Stavros, Anogi to Kathara Monastery (Moni Katharon), and Aetos to Alalkomenae Castle. Mr Skinari has prepared brief notes and maps; if they are not available at the Town Hall, ring him direct on ☎ 26740 31080. Wear sturdy footwear, cover up against strong sun (as well as prickly bushes) and take plenty of water.

---

diagonally off to the right-hand side of Soris' Ways Café on the square, below the owner's house. The pretty garden overlooks olive and cypress groves. A great base from which to explore and visit the nearby Bay of Polis.

Fatouros Taverna (☎ 26740 31385; Stavros; mains €5-12) The faux-brick exterior of the building hides a homely interior and popular eatery; at the entrance there's a spit for roasting delicious meats. Not surprisingly, the house specialities include lamb on the spit (€7.50) and eggplant rolls (€5).

Kioni ΚΙΟΝΙ

Kioni is a small village draped around a verdant hillside and spilling down to a miniature harbour where yachties congregate. Lining the quay are tavernas, a bar or two and flower-covered buildings (some of the houses survived the 1953 earthquake). Swimmers can access a small beach at the cove's far-eastern end, or the bays between Kioni and Frikes.

Mrs Karatzis' Rooms (☎ 26740 31679; studio €50) Despite the white buildings' distinctive cherry-red shutters, you'll see blue before you – 'the sea, the beautiful sea' view from the balcony of these simple but pleasant studio rooms is stupendous. Situated on the hill-peak on the approach into Kioni, behind the village itself.

Captain's Apartments (☎ 26740 31481; www.captains-apartments.gr; d €65, 4-person apt €90) The Captain's studios and apartments are worth berthing at. Each well-maintained room is shipshape, with satellite TV and terrace or balcony. Good navigational signs show you the way.

Several tavernas are lined up like yachts along the harbour – each claims to serve better food than at the others, but in reality, most serve the same reasonable meals at the same reasonable(ish) prices (mains €7 to €13).

ZAKYNTHOS
ΖΑΚΥΝΘΟΣ

pop 38,600

Zakynthos (zakh-in-thos), also known as Zante, has a split personality. Its geography is mountainous and rocky in the west, with a fertile plain in the east. While the island's west remains largely unspoiled, its eastern coastal areas are the victim of the worst manifestations of package tourism. Tourism is also endangering the loggerhead turtle (see boxed text, p480). Yet the island has inspired many other descriptions. The Venetians called it Flower of the Orient; the poet Dionysios Solomos wrote that 'Zakynthos could make one forget the Elysian Fields'. Indeed, on the whole, Zakynthos has exceptional natural beauty, welcoming locals and great cuisine. To enjoy a relaxing holiday here avoid high season, especially in resorts such as Laganas.

Getting There & Away

AIR

There are at least one or two daily flights between Zakynthos and Athens (€76), and connections to other Ionian Islands including Kefallonia (€32) and Corfu (€51). **Olympic Airlines** (☎ 26950 28611/28322; Zakynthos Airport; ☎ 8am-10pm Mon-Fri) can help with information and bookings.

BUS

KTEL (☎ 26950 22255; Filita 42, Zakynthos Town) operates four buses daily between Zakynthos Town and Patra (€5.20, 3½ hours), and four daily connections to/from Athens (€22.10, six hours) via Corinth Canal (€15.80, five hours). There's also a twice-weekly service to Thessaloniki (€42.20). Budget an additional €6.50 for the ferry fare between Zakynthos and Kyllini.

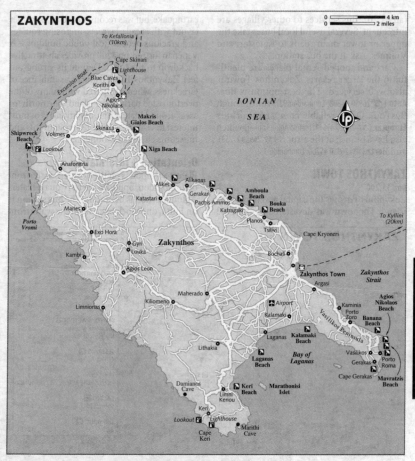

IONIAN ISLANDS

FERRY
Domestic
Depending on the season, between five and seven ferries operate daily between Zakynthos Town and Kyllini in the Peloponnese (per person/car €6.50/31.50, 1¼ hours). Tickets can be obtained from the **Zakynthos Shipping Cooperative** (☎ 26950 22083/49500; Lombardou 40) in Zakynthos Town.

From the northern port of Agios Nikolaos a ferry service shuttles across to Pesada in southern Kefallonia twice daily from May to October (€6, 1½hours). In high season, there are two daily buses from Pesada to Argostoli (Kefallonia), and two per week to Agios Nikolaos, making crossing without your own transport difficult. An alternative

is to cross to Kyllini and catch another ferry to Kefallonia.

International
Hellenic Mediterranean Lines (www.hml.gr) has July and August services once or twice a week between Brindisi and Zakynthos (one way €69 to €82, about 18 hours).

Getting Around
There's no bus service between Zakynthos Town and the airport, 6km to the southwest. A taxi costs around €10. Frequent buses go from Zakynthos Town's **bus station** (☎ 26950 22255; Filita 42), one block back from the waterfront, to the developed resorts of Alikes (€1.50), Tsilivi, Argasi, Laganas and Kalamaki

(all €1.20). Bus services to other villages are infrequent. Several useful local buses take the upper or lower main roads to Katastari and Volimes. Ask at the bus station.

Car- and moped-rental places are plentiful in the larger resorts. Zakynthos Town is also well serviced. The best option is **Hire-Auto** (☎ 26950 24808; Lombardou 92), run through BesTour. Other reliable companies include **Europcar** (☎ 26950 41541; Plateia Agiou Louka), which also has a branch at the airport (☎ 26950 22853), and **Hertz** (☎ 26950 45706; Lombardou 38).

ZAKYNTHOS TOWN
pop 11,200
Zakynthos Town is the capital and port of the island. The town was devastated by the 1953 earthquake, but was reconstructed to its former layout with arcaded streets, imposing squares and gracious neoclassical public buildings. A Venetian fortress on a hill provides an attractive backdrop to the town. Despite its strung-out feel, Zakynthos Town features a semblance of Greekness, when compared with many of the overtourised parts of the island. The northern area (around Plateia Agiou Markou) is of most interest to visitors, with hotels, restaurants and museums clustered around here.

Orientation & Information
Plateia Solomou is on the northern waterfront of Lombardou, opposite the ferry quay. Plateia Agiou Markou is behind it. The bus station is on Filita, one block back from the waterfront

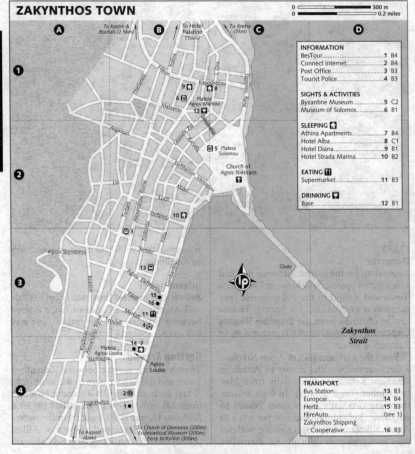

ZAKYNTHOS TOWN

0 — 300 m
0 — 0.2 miles

INFORMATION
BesTour.................................1 B4
Connect Internet....................2 B4
Post Office............................3 B3
Tourist Police........................4 B3

SIGHTS & ACTIVITIES
Byzantine Museum..................5 C2
Museum of Solomos................6 B1

SLEEPING
Athina Apartments..................7 B4
Hotel Alba.............................8 C1
Hotel Diana...........................9 B1
Hotel Strada Marina..............10 B2

EATING
Supermarket.........................11 B3

DRINKING
Base....................................12 B1

TRANSPORT
Bus Station...........................13 B3
Europcar..............................14 B4
Hertz...................................15 B3
HireAuto..........................(see 1)
Zakynthos Shipping
Cooperative.........................16 B3

and south of the quay. The main thoroughfare is Alexandrou Roma, running several blocks inland, parallel to the waterfront.

Zakynthos Town has no tourist office. The **tourist police** (☎ 26950 27367; Lombardou 62) has dated brochures for visitors – if the room is open, that is. Your best bet is to head to the 'nothing's-a-problem', professional staff at **BesTour** (☎ 26950 24808; www.bestour.gr; cnr Lombardou & Logotheton), who can answer queries and arrange accommodation and trips.

There are banks with ATMs along Lombardou and just west of Plateia Solomou. The **post office** (Tertseti 27; ✆ 7am-2pm) is one block west of Alexandrou Roma. **Connect Internet** (Lombardou 84; per hr €3; ✆ 9am-1am) offers good internet access.

Sights & Activities

The **Byzantine museum** (☎ 26950 42714; Plateia Solomou; admission €3; ✆ 8.30am-3pm Tue-Sun) houses two levels of fabulous ecclesiastical art, rescued from churches razed in the earthquake. It's all displayed in a beautiful setting overlooking the main plaza. Within, the St Andreas Monastery has been artfully 'replicated' to house its restored frescoes. The nearby **Museum of Solomos** (☎ 26950 28982; Plateia Agiou Markou; admission €3; ✆ 9am-2pm) is dedicated to Dionysios Solomos (1798–1857), who was born on Zakynthos and is regarded as the father of modern Greek poetry. His work *Hymn to*

Liberty became the stirring Greek national anthem. The museum houses his memorabilia and archives.

The peaceful, shady and pine tree–filled **kastro** (☎ 26950 48099; admission €3; ✆ 8.30am-6pm), a ruined Venetian fortress high above Zakynthos Town, makes a pleasant visit. It's 2.5km from town in the quaint village of Bochali (take Dionysiou Roma north and turn left at Kapodistriou; it's signed from here). Enjoy the bird's-eye view with an ice cream, or dine at one of Bochali's well-sited restaurants. The **Church of Dionysios**, the patron saint of the island, in Zakynthos Town's south has some amazing gilt work and notable frescoes. Behind the church is an **ecclesiastical museum** (admission €2; ✆ 9am-1pm & 5-9pm). It contains intriguing icons from the Monastery of Strofades, home to Dionysios, plus speech scrolls from the 13th and 14th centuries and a 12th-century book in Ancient Greek.

Sleeping

The newest sleeping options are netted by tour groups, but the following are safe bets for independent travellers.

Hotel Alba (☎ 26950 26641; www.albahotel.gr; L Ziva 38; s/d/tr incl breakfast €60/70/116; ❄) This friendly place, with a slightly old-fashioned feel, is a good budget option (the prices are slashed outside August). The views are a bit wire-ridden, but it's clean and adequate.

EXPLORING WITH YOUR TASTE BUDS

Gourmands may be surprised to know that Zakynthos boasts some excellent local cuisine, and any small village taverna serves a fine meal. Searching for the hidden eateries is a great way of discovering the island. Many are nondescript from the outside, but serve high-quality, delectable food to a mainly local clientele. Others are lovely for their location, in tiny villages or high above clifftops. Following are some popular places to get you exploring.

Dennis Taverna (☎ 26950 51387; mains €6-12; Lithakia; ✆ lunch & dinner) Meat-lovers mustn't miss this busy place, renowned for its quality meat cuts and grills. Half-serves might be adequate for a non-Greek – the servings are brontosaurus-size (there's even a kid's menu).

To Litrouvio (☎ 26950 55081; mains €6.50-14; Lithakia; ✆ lunch & dinner) You'll be impressed by this attractive option, which is built around an olive oil stone presser and features related oddments. It's a more touristy, yet extremely appealing, experience with out-of-this-world local fare. Go with an appetite; servings are plentiful.

Louha's Coffee Shop (☎ 26950 48426; mains €4-7; Louka; ✆ lunch & dinner) The type of place even a guidebook writer wants to keep secret: this is one of the most genuine experiences around. You sit in the host family's garden, enjoying their local specialities. This gem is hidden in the village, opposite the church. Ask here about the monastery walk.

To Pelagaki (☎ 6977633542; Xiga; ✆ breakfast, lunch & dinner) Situated on a sharp bend just before the odorous Xiga Beach (the waters have sulphuric properties, popular for health reasons), this serves basic, and OK, fare in a glorious cliff-top setting.

AT LOGGERHEADS

The Ionian Islands are home to the Mediterranean's loggerhead turtle (*Caretta caretta*), one of Europe's most endangered marine species. The turtles prefer large tracts of clean, flat and uninhabited sand, as do basking tourists, and this has led to the imminent extinction of the turtle.

Zakynthos hosts the largest density of turtle nests – around 1100 along the 5km Bay of Laganas. During hatching time (July to October), surviving hatchlings emerge after a 60-day incubation period in the sand. Many of the nests are destroyed by brollies and bikes, and the surviving young don't make it to the water – they are often disoriented by sunbeds, noise and lights.

Conservation lobbyists have clashed with local authorities, tourist operators and government, and in 1999, following pressure from the EU, the Greek Government declared the Bay of Laganas area a national marine park. Strict regulations were put in force regarding building, boating, mooring, fishing and watersports in designated zones.

All designated nesting beaches are completely off-limits between dusk and dawn during the breeding season (May to October). Despite this, dozens of illegal bars and tavernas operate in the area, illegal umbrellas and sunbeds are rented out to tourists, and boats cruise through protected waters.

The Greek Government is accused of having its head in the sand; it has been condemned by the European Court of Justice for failing to implement EU nature protection legislation. Meanwhile, WWF (Worldwide Fund for Nature), Archelon (the Sea Turtle Protection Society of Greece) and Medasset (Mediterranean Association to Save the Sea Turtles) continue their lobbying efforts. Volunteers from Archelon (www.archelon.gr) and National Marine Park provide informal beach wardens and run excellent education and volunteer programmes. For further information, visit the wildlife information centre at Gerakas Beach.

Visitors can also do the following:

- Avoid using umbrellas on dry sand (use the wet part of the beach).
- Do not enter nesting beaches between dusk and dawn, and avoid visiting Daphni beach.
- Be aware of boating trips – where they go and what's on offer.
- Seek information on the area's sea turtle conservation efforts and protective regulations.

Hotel Palatino (☎ 26950 27780; www.palatinohotel.gr; Kolokotroni 10; s/d €70/90; ✿ 🖳) The marble floors, arched windows and plants provide an overall '80s experience, and many businesspeople choose to stay in these well-appointed rooms; they have an eye for great value.

Hotel Strada Marina (☎ 26950 42761; hotel@strada marina.gr; Lombardou 14; s/d incl breakfast €85/130; ✿ 🖳) This is your no-surprises, standard-style hotel with well-equipped rooms including TV and fridge. The inviting rooftop area has a small pool.

Also recommended:

Athina Apartments (☎ 26950 26809; athina_apts@ yahoo.gr; 2 Agiou Louka; studio €50; ✿) Travellers have reported these basic, reasonably-priced studios, near the bus station.

Hotel Diana (☎ 26950 28547; Plateia Agiou Markou; s/d/tr incl breakfast €60/80/95; ✿ 🖳) Dated, but comfortable and well-appointed in a central location.

Eating & Drinking

Argostoli's sweet shop windows entice with their range of the tooth-dissolving local nougat, *mandolato*. This is especially good along Alexandrou Roma, home also to some good cafés and *gyros* (Greek version of döner kebab) places. Touristy – and overpriced – restaurants line Plateia Agiou Markou. If you have transport, you're better off heading to one of the nearby villages (see boxed text, p479).

Arekia (☎ 26950 26346; mains under €10) Munch to the melodies of live *kantades* (serenades) and *arekia* (folk songs) at this entertaining place, a 1km walk north of Plateia Solomou along the waterfront. The spritely 80-something-year-old band member dallies with ditties to aid digestion (Greek-speakers will get a kick). Gargantuan portions of traditional Greek fare hit the right note.

Base (☎ 26950 42409; Plateia Agiou Markou; cappuccino €3.50) This hip place just gets hipper; it's the alfresco hang-out among the younger Zantiot 'it' crowd.

There's a well-stocked supermarket on the corner of Filioti and Lombardou.

AROUND ZAKYNTHOS

Whether you're a culture vulture or sun-seeker, the best way to see the island is to hire a car and go exploring. Loggerhead turtles (see boxed text, opposite) come ashore to lay their eggs on the golden-sand beaches of the huge Bay of Laganas, a National Marine Park on Zakynthos' south coast, whereas party animals frequent Laganas, the highly developed, somewhat tacky resort. **Keri Beach** at Limni Keriou (not to be confused with Keri village further south) is a more attractive option, but the beach is narrow and stony. You'll find boat hire and a scuba diving centre here.

The **Vasilikos Peninsula** is the pretty green region southeast of Zakynthos Town, but it's being increasingly exploited by developers. It offers a number of ever-expanding settlements off the main road, with tavernas and accommodation. For beach bums, **Kaminia** is the first half-decent beach to consider. **Banana Beach**, a long and narrow strip of golden sand, offers plenty of action: crowds, watersports and umbrellas. Zakynthos' best beach is the long, sandy and much-coveted **Gerakas**. It's on the other side of the peninsula, facing Laganas Bay. This is one of the main turtle-nesting beaches, and access to the beach is forbidden between dusk and dawn during May and October (see boxed text, opposite).

With your own transport, you can semi-escape from the tourist hype by visiting the accessible west coast coves, such as **Limnionas** or **Kambi** (the latter has some popular, but tacky, tavernas ideally positioned for the sunsets). The most peaceful option is the quieter northeast coast around **Agios Nikolaos**, where development is proceeding slowly. Known primarily as the ferry point, this tiny place has a few food and drink dwellings, a small stretch of beach with clear water, free sunbeds and a pretty islet.

The inland areas in the island's north and west make for a fun and interesting visit, and provide a touch of rural tranquillity and great food (see boxed text, p479). Villages and settlements – some of which survived the 1953 earthquake – are scattered through the scrub and pines; here, the welcoming locals have maintained their cultural traditions and sell honey and other seasonal products. Churches and monasteries feature highly along this village route: **St Nikolaos** in **Kiliomeno** features an unusual roofless campanile; the bell tower of **Agios Leon** (in the village of the same name) was formerly a windmill. The small and charming hamlet of **Exo Hora** has a fascinating congregation of dried wells, and what is reputed to be the oldest olive tree on the island. **Volimes** is the unashamed sales centre for all traditional products.

Sleeping

Tartaruga Camping (☎ 26950 51967; www.tartaruga-camping.com; camp sites per adult/car/tent €5/3/3.60, r per person €20-45) A great place for happy campers – amid terraced olive groves, pines and plane trees that sprawl as far as the sea. It has a small store and a café, and rooms for rent. Well-signed on the road from Laganas to Keri.

Anna's Villas (☎ 6977236243, 6977236243; d €60-90; Limni Keriou) Two good-value studio apartments, in a garden setting. They're set a block or so back from Limni Keriou's main drag, but are close to the action.

SHIPWRECK BEACH & BLUE CAVES

The famous Shipwreck Beach (Navagio), whose photos grace virtually every tourist brochure about Zakynthos, is at the northwest tip of the island. It is a tad overhyped, if splendid, beach, and it's downright unappealing when round-the-island excursion boats from Zakynthos Town bring trippers en masse. Your best bet is to take a small-boat trip to see Shipwreck Beach and/or the Blue Caves (in the island's northeast). The northeastern coastal road is lined with hawkers offering the 'same-trip-better-boat' deals. **Potamitis Trips** (☎ 26950 31132) offers good glass-bottom boat trips at Cape Skinari, 3km beyond Agios Nikolaos (Blue Caves only, €7.50; Shipwreck Beach and Blue Caves, €15).

In any case, for a bungee-jump-style adrenalin rush, visit the precariously perched lookout platform over Shipwreck Beach on the west coast (signposted between Anafonitria and Volimes).

Seaside Apartments (☎ 26950 22827; www.seaside .net.gr; 2-/4-person studio €70/90) These excellent-value bright and artistic rooms are also in Limni Keriou.

Revera Villas (☎ 2695027524, 6974875171; www.revera -zante.com; d €75, studio €85, 4-/6-person villa €145/200; ✿ ➠) This delightful complex of Italian-feel villas is located 4km southwest of Limni Keriou village (and 500m southwest of Keri village), just off the road to the lighthouse. The individually decorated, luxury rooms incorporate old-style stone elements. There are Jacuzzi baths, a recently installed pool and a private patch of forest to amble in.

Earth Sea & Sky (through Ionian Eco Villagers – www.relaxing-holidays.com, ☎ 0871 711 5065 in the UK) can arrange short- or long-term stays in villas and cottages around the Vasilikos Peninsula. Alternatively, you could try your luck for a spontaneous booking with the same company at its wildlife information kiosk in Gerakas.

In the north, stop for a night at Cape Skinari, 3km north of Agios Nikolaos. Two **windmills** (☎ 26950 31132; 2-/4-person windmill €90/120; ✿) are an accommodation novelty, with great views. A nearby snack bar–café and a lovely swimming area (down steep steps) serve visitors. It's the departure point for boat trips to the Blue Caves and shipwreck beach (see boxed text, p481).

In Agios Nikolaos, near Cape Skinari, the friendly, English-speaking hosts at **Panorama Studios** (☎ 26950 31013; www.gozakynthos.gr/studios/pano rama; d €45) offer basic studio accommodation on the main road 600m uphill from the port.

KYTHIRA & ANTIKYTHIRA

KYTHIRA ΚΥΘΗΡΑ
pop 3334

The island of Kythira (*kee*-thih-rah), 12km south of Neapoli, is perfect for people who want to experience a genuine, functioning and unspoilt island.

Some 30km long and 18km wide, Kythira dangles off the tip of the Peloponnese's Lakonian peninsula, between the Aegean and Ionian Seas. The largely barren landscape is dominated by a rocky plateau that covers most of the island, and the population is spread among more than 40 villages that capitalise on small pockets of agriculturally viable land. The villages are linked by narrow, winding lanes, often flanked by ancient dry-stone walls.

Although Kythira is part of the Ionian Islands, some of the houses, especially those in the island's main town, Hora, are more Cycladic in looks, with whitewashed walls and blue shutters. Mythology suggests that Aphrodite was born in Kythira. She's meant to have risen from the foam where Zeus had thrown Cronos' sex organ after castrating him. The goddess of love then re-emerged near Pafos in Cyprus, so both islands haggle over her birthplace.

Tourism remains very low-key on Kythira for most of the year, until July and August, when the island goes mad. Descending visitors include the Kythiran diaspora returning from Australia to visit family and friends (who themselves have returned after leaving the island several decades ago). Accommodation is virtually impossible to find during this time, and restaurants are flat out catering for the crowds. For the remaining 10 months of the year, Kythira is a wonderfully peaceful island with some fine, uncrowded beaches. The best times to visit Kythira are in late spring and around September/October.

For information on the island, see www .kythira.com or www.kythera.gr.

GETTING THERE & AWAY
Air
In high season there are daily flights between Kythira and Athens (€47 to €60, 40 minutes). The airport is 10km east of Potamos, and **Olympic Airlines** (☎ 27360 33362) is on the central square in Potamos. Book also at **Kythira Travel** (☎ 27360 31390) in Hora.

Ferry
The island's main connection is between Diakofti and Neapoli (per person/car €8.30/40, one hour) in the Peloponnese. The frequency of the service ranges from four times daily in July and August, down to once a day in winter. Tickets are sold at the quay just before departure, or at **Kythira Travel** (☎ in Hora 27360 31390, in Potamos 27360 31848) in Hora and Potamos.

ANEN Lines (www.anen.gr) calls in at the southern port of Diakofti on its weekly schedule between Piraeus, Kythira, Antikythira, Gythio (Peloponnese) and Kissamos-Kastelli

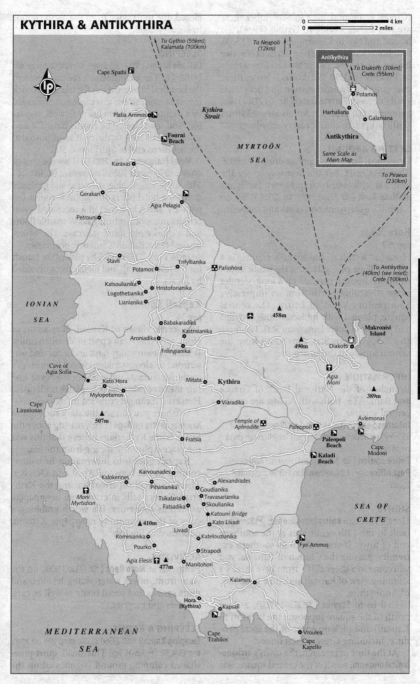

KYTHIRA & ANTIKYTHIRA

0 — 4 km
0 — 2 miles

To Gythio (55km);
Kalamata (100km)

To Neapoli
(12km)

Antikythira

To Diakofti (30km);
Crete (55km)

Potamos

Harhaliana

Galaniana

Antikythira

*Same Scale as
Main Map*

Cape Spathi

Platia Ammos

**Fourni
Beach**

*Kythira
Strait*

*MYRTOÖN
SEA*

To Piraeus
(230km)

Karavas

Gerakari

Agia Pelagia

Petrouni

Stavli

Trifyllianika

Potamos

Katsoulianika

Logothetianika

Hristoforianika

Lianianika

Paliohora

To Antikythira
(40km) (see inset);
Crete (100km)

*IONIAN
SEA*

Babakaradika

Kastrisianika

Aroniadika

Frilingianika

458m

490m

**Makronisi
Island**

Diakofti

Cave of
Agia Sofia

Kato Hora

Mylopotamos

Mitata

Kythira

Viaradika

*Agia
Moni*

389m

Cape
Limnionas

507m

Fratsia

*Temple of
Aphrodite*

Paleopoli

Avlemonas

**Paleopoli
Beach**

Cape
Modoni

**Kaladi
Beach**

Kalokerines

Karvounades

*Moni
Myrtidion*

Pitsinianika

Tsikalaria

Fatsadika

Alexandrades

Goudianika

Travasarianika

Skoulianika

Katouni Bridge

Kato Livadi

*SEA OF
CRETE*

410m

Livadi

Katelouzianika

Kominianika

Pourko

Agia Elesis

477m

Manitohori

Strapodi

Fyri Ammos

Kalamos

Hora
(Kythira)

Kapsali

*MEDITERRANEAN
SEA*

Cape
Trahilos

Vroulea

Cape
Kapello

IONIAN ISLANDS

(Crete). From mid-June to September there are two ferries weekly to Gythio (€9.90, 2½ hours) and two to Kissamos-Kastelli (€15.70, four hours), which call at Antikythira (€9, two hours). There are also three services weekly to Piraeus (€21.50, 6½ hours). Note: these change annually. Information and tickets are available from **Porfyra Travel** (☎ /fax 27360 31888; porfyra@otenet.gr) in Livadi. See also www.kythira -kithira-kythera.com for ferry schedules.

GETTING AROUND
Occasional buses may operate during August. There are taxis, but the best way to see the island is with your own transport. Panayotis at **Moto Rent** (☎ 27360 31600; fax 27360 31789) on Kapsali's waterfront rents cars and mopeds.

Hora Χώρα
pop 267
Hora (or Kythira), the island's capital, is a pretty village of Cycladic-style white, blue-shuttered houses, perched on a long, slender ridge stretching north from an impressive 13th-century Venetian *kastro*. The central square, planted with hibiscus, bougainvillea and palms, is Plateia Dimitriou Staï. The main street, Spyridonos Staï, runs south from the central square to the *kastro*.

INFORMATION
Branches of the National Bank of Greece and Bank ATE, both with ATMs, are on the central square.
Internet Service (Kodak shop, Spyridonos Staï; per hr €5; ☽ 9am-2pm & 6-9pm Mon-Sat) Travellers can check email here.
Police station (☎ 27360 31206) Near the *kastro*.
Post office (☽ 7.30am-2pm Mon-Fri) On the central square.

SIGHTS
Hora's Venetian **kastro** (admission free; ☽ 8am-7pm), built in the 13th century, is at the southern end of town. If you walk to its southern extremity, passing the Church of Panagia, you will come to a sheer cliff – from here there's a stunning view of Kapsali and, on a good day, of Antikythira.

Call in to **Stavros** (☎ 27360 31857), a shop north of the square (opposite the turn-off to Kapsali) and pick up some of the local produce, including Greece's best honey.

At the time of research, the town's **archaeological museum**, north of the central square, was closed due to damage from the earth tremor in January 2006.

SLEEPING
Castello Rooms (☎ 27360 31069; jfatseas@otenet.gr; d/tr €40/55; ☒) These comfortable rooms represent the best deal in town, if not the island. Set back from the main street, this place is surrounded by a well-tended garden full of flowers, vegetables and fruit trees. The rooms have TV and some have kitchen facilities. It's signposted at the southern end of Spiridonos Staï.

Hotel Margarita (☎ 27360 31711; www.hotel-margarita.com; off Spyridonos Staï; s/d incl breakfast €90/100; ☒) This white-walled, blue-shuttered and generally charming hotel offers atmospheric rooms (all with TV and telephone) in a renovated 19th-century mansion, featuring B&W marble floors and a quirky old spiral staircase. The whitewashed terrace affords fantastic port views.

Zorba's (☎ 27360 31655) The pick of the bunch for the town's meals and highly recommended by locals.

Kapsali Καψάλι
pop 34
The scenic village of Kapsali, 2km south of Hora, served as Hora's port in Venetian times. It features twin sandy bays and a curving waterfront; this looks striking viewed from Hora's castle. Restaurants and cafés line the beach, and safe **sheltered swimming** is Kapsali's trademark. However, it can get crowded in high season.

Offshore you can see the stark rock island known as **Itra** or **Avgo** (Egg), rearing above the water. Some Kytherians believe that this was the place Aphrodite sprang from the sea.

Kapsali goes into hibernation in winter, coming to life between April and October. There's a small supermarket, and the Kytherian Gallery sells international newspapers as well as souvenirs. It's worth grabbing a copy of the community newspaper *Kythera*, published in English.

ACTIVITIES
Panayotis at **Moto Rent** (☎ 27360 31600), on the waterfront, offers water-skiing lessons, and rents canoes and pedal boats as well as cars, mopeds and bicycles.

SLEEPING & EATING
Camping Kapsali (☎ 27360 31580; camp sites per adult/tent €5/4.50; ☽ Jun-15 Sep) This small, quiet pine-shaded camping ground (signposted on the

road from Hora) has minimum facilities. It's 400m from Kapsali's quay, behind the village.

Cengo Hotel (☎ 27360 31451; afrodite@aias.gr; s/d/tr €95/110/130; ❄) This modest place is located above and behind the Cengo Cafe Bar. The rooms are clean and adequate. Six rooms have balconies and a few have a view of the water. Only worth considering if you want to be close to the village action.

Spitia Vassilis (☎ 27360 33125; www.kythirabunga lowsvasili.gr; d €110, tr & q €120; ℗) This attractive green-and-white complex of studios has the perfect setting – away from the hordes and overlooking Kapsali Beach. The spacious rooms feature that rustic-painted-timber-floor look (one of the owner-artists has let loose with the brush) and good bay views. It is on the right as you approach Kapsali from Hora. Olga, the friendly manager, knows all there is to know.

Raikos Hotel (☎ 27360 31629; www.raikoshotel.gr; d/tr incl breakfast €160/192; ℗ ❄ ⌨) Signposted off the Hora–Kapsali road is this very smart, friendly hotel, offering spacious, pleasantly decorated rooms with terraces overlooking Kapsali and Hora's *kastro*. There's a lovely pool and bar area, too.

Hydragogio (☎ 27360 31065; mains €5-12, fish per kg €20-70) Occupying a great spot overlooking the beach at the far end by the rocks, and specialising in fresh fish and mezedhes (with a good vegetarian range), this is a good place to splurge on lobster (per kg €70) if your budget stretches that far.

Estiatorio Magos (☎ 27360 31407; mains €2.80-6) The *magos* (magician) in question is owner Antonis, who magically whips up lobster with spaghetti (lobster per kg €80) and a tasty fish soup (€4).

Potamos Ποταμός
pop 680

Potamos, 10km southwest of Agia Pelagia, is the island's commercial hub. Its **Sunday morning flea market** seems to attract just about everyone on the island.

INFORMATION
The National Bank of Greece (with ATM) is on the central square.

Kafe Selana (☎ 27360 33997; per hr €3) On the central square; has internet access.

Post office (⊙ 7.30am-2pm Mon-Fri) Just north of the central square.

SLEEPING & EATING
Taverna Panaretos (☎ 27360 34290; mains €6-10) This place is a natural – it's open year-round, popular with locals and uses home-grown everything, from oil to veggies and cheese. Want to try wild goat with olive oil and oregano (€8) or eggplant on coals (€3.50)? Naturally.

Mylopotamos Μυλοπόταμος
pop 70

Mylopotamos is a quaint village nestled in a small valley, 12km southwest of Potamos. Its central square is flanked by a charming church and authentically traditional **Kafeneio O Platanos** (☎ 27360 33397), which in summer becomes a restaurant with an outdoor setting in the square. It's worth a stroll to the **Neraïda** (water nymph) waterfall, with luxuriant greenery and mature, shady trees. As you reach the church, take the right fork and follow the signs to an unpaved road leading down to the falls. (Alternatively, you can head there on foot – follow the signs after the church.)

To reach the abandoned **kastro** of Mylopotamos, take the left fork after the *kafeneio* and follow the old faded sign for **Kato Hora** (Lower Village) and then the modern signs to the Cave of Agia Sofia. The road leads to the centre of Kato Hora, from where a portal leads into the spooky *kastro*, with derelict houses and well-preserved little churches (usually locked).

Further along the same road is the **Cave of Agia Sofia**, reached by a precipitous, unpaved 2km road. The staff at Kafeneio O Platanos can tell you when it's open (in summer only).

If you fall in love with the history of this place, stay at the comfortable, and newly converted **studio apartments** (☎ 27360 33439; d €65-75) of Pula Stratiga, or inquire at Kafeneio O Platanos about options.

Agia Pelagia Αγία Πελαγία
pop 280

Kythira's northern port of Agia Pelagia is a simple, friendly waterfront village, although sadly, this is on the verge of being ruined by modern buildings, as are the sand-and-pebble beaches either side of the quay. Nevertheless, it's pleasant for relaxing, and **Red Beach**, south of the headland, is a good swimming spot.

SLEEPING & EATING
Hotel Pelagia Aphrodite (☎ 27360 33926/7; pelagia@otenet.gr; s/d/tr €65/80/105; ⊙ Apr-Sep; ℗ ❄)

IONIAN ISLANDS

This Greek-Australian-run place is modern and spotless with large, airy rooms, most with balconies overlooking the sea. Its perfect location is a small headland on the southern edge of the village. Breakfast is €7.

Stellas (☎ 27360 33513; mains €6-11) You can't go wrong with any of the options along the waterfront; we like this for its unpretentious, family atmosphere. It serves reliable traditional Greek favourites from mezedhes to meats. Try Stella's veal (€7).

Around Kythira

If you have transport, a spin round the island is rewarding. The monasteries of **Agia Moni** and **Agia Elesis** are mountain refuges with superb views. **Moni Myrtidion** is a beautiful monastery surrounded by trees. From Hora, drive northeast to **Avlemonas**, via **Paleopoli** with its wide, pebbled beach. Archaeologists spent years searching for evidence of a temple at Aphrodite's birthplace at Avlemonas. Don't miss the spectacularly situated ruins of the Byzantine capital of **Paliohora**, in the island's northeast, fun for exploring.

Just north of the village of **Kato Livadi** make a detour to see the architecturally anomalous **Katouni Bridge**, a British-built legacy of Kythira's time as part of the British Protectorate in the 19th century. In the far north of the island the village of **Karavas** is verdant, very attractive and close to both Agia Pelagia and the reasonable beach at **Platia Ammos**. Beachcombers should seek out **Kaladi Beach**, near Paleopoli. **Fyri Ammos**, closer to Hora, is another good beach – but hard to access.

EATING

Varkoula (☎ 27360 34224; Platia Ammos; mains €5-7; ☉ lunch & dinner daily May-Oct, Fri & Sat Nov-Mar) Locals rave about this 'little boat' (varkoula). Where else can you enjoy freshly cooked fish to the tunes of the bouzouki-strumming owner and his cardiologist guitar-playing friend? Athena's famous fried bread with cheese is a real heart stopper. It's a beat away from Karavas, in the

island's north. As it's a decent drive north, ring ahead first to confirm opening hours.

Estiatorion Pierros (☎ 27360 31014; Livadi; mains €4-8; fish per kg €50) Since 1933 this family-run and long-standing favourite has served no-nonsense Greek staples. Visit the kitchen to view the daily offerings – there's no menu. On the main road through Livadi.

Sotiris (☎ 27360 33722; Avlemonas; ☉ lunch & dinner) This popular fish taverna in pretty Avlemonas has good lobster and fish soup (fish and lobster is priced per kilo).

Skandia (☎ 27360 33700; Paleopolis; mains €6-8; ☉ lunch & dinner) By all reports, it's currently the place to eat on the island, mainly because of its setting: near water, under shady elm trees, in a homey environment. Its fish is priced per kg.

Psarotaverna H Manolis (☎ 27360 33748; fish & lobster per kg €40-75; ☉ lunch & dinner) A star among Diakofti's uninspiring port setting. Locals head here for the excellent fresh fish and seasonal offerings.

ANTIKYTHIRA ΑΝΤΙΚΥΘΗΡΑ
pop 20

The tiny island of Antikythira, 38km southeast of Kythira, is the most remote island in the Ionians. It has only one settlement (Potamos), one doctor, one police officer, one telephone and a monastery. It has no post office or bank. The only accommodation option is 10 basic rooms in two purpose-built blocks, open in summer only. Potamos has a kafeneio-cum-taverna.

Getting There & Away

The ferry company **ANEN Lines** (www.anen.gr) calls at Antikythira on its route between Kythira and Kissamos-Kastelli on Crete, offering three services a week in each direction; single-leg tickets cost around €9.10 and take two hours, while the through journey, Kythira–Crete, is around €16.10. This is not an island for tourists on a tight schedule and will probably only appeal to those who really like isolation. For information and tickets, contact **Porfyra Travel** (☎ /fax 27360 31888; porfyra@otenet.gr) in Livadi on Kythira.

Directory

CONTENTS

ACCOMMODATION

The Greek islands boast accommodation to suit every taste and budget. All places to stay are subject to strict price controls set by the tourist police. By law, a notice must be displayed in every room that states the category of the room and the maximum price that can be charged. The price includes a 4.5% community tax and 8% VAT.

Accommodation owners may add a 10% surcharge for a stay of less than three nights, but this is not mandatory. A mandatory charge of 20% is levied if an extra bed is put into a room. During July and August, accom-

---

PRACTICALITIES

- Be aware that Greece belongs to region code 2 if you buy DVDs to watch back home, and uses the PAL TV system.

- Channel hop through a choice of nine free-to-air TV channels and an assortment of pay-TV channels.

- Find yourself a Greek radio station on the internet by searching through www.e-radio.gr.

- Greece is two hours ahead of GMT/UTC and three hours ahead during daylight-saving time.

- Greece uses the metric system for weights and measures.

- Keep up with Greek current affairs by reading the daily English-language edition of *Kathimerini* that comes with the *International Herald Tribune*.

- Plug your electrical appliances into a two-pin adaptor before plugging into the electricity supply (220V AC, 50Hz).

---

modation owners will charge the maximum price, but in spring and autumn, prices will drop by about 20%, and perhaps by even more in winter.

Rip-offs rarely occur, but if you do suspect that you have been exploited by an accommodation owner, make sure you report it to either the tourist police or to the regular police, and they will act swiftly.

Throughout this book we have divided accommodation into budget (up to €60), midrange (€60 to €150) and top-end categories

---

BOOK ACCOMMODATION ONLINE

For more accommodation reviews and recommendations by Lonely Planet authors, check out the online booking service at www.lonelyplanet.com. You'll find the true, insider lowdown on the best places to stay. Reviews are thorough and independent. Best of all, you can book online.

(€150+). This is a per-person rate in high season (July and August). Unless otherwise stated, all rooms have private bathroom facilities. It's difficult to generalise about accommodation prices in Greece as rates depend entirely on the season and location. Don't expect to pay the same price for a double on one of the islands as you would in central Greece or even Athens.

Camping

Camping is a good option, especially in summer. There are almost 200 camping grounds dotted around the islands, some of them in great locations. Standard facilities include hot showers, kitchens, restaurants and mini-markets – and often a swimming pool.

Most camping grounds are open only between April and October. The **Panhellenic Camping Association** (☎ /fax 210 362 1560; Solonos 102, www .panhellenic-camping-union.gr; Athens 106 80) publishes an annual booklet listing all camping grounds, its facilities and months of operation.

Camping fees are highest from 15 June to the end of August. Most camping grounds charge from €5 to €7 per adult and €3 to €4 for children aged four to 12. There's no charge for children aged under four. Tent sites cost from €4 per night for small tents, and from €5 per night for large tents. Caravan sites start at around €6.

Between May and mid-September the weather is warm enough to sleep out. Many camping grounds have covered areas where tourists who don't have tents can sleep in summer, so you can get by with a lightweight sleeping bag and foam bedroll. It's a good idea to have a foam pad to lie on and a waterproof cover for your sleeping bag. Pitching a tent in a nondesignated camping area is illegal, but the law is seldom enforced – to the irritation of camping-ground owners.

Domatia

Domatia are the Greek equivalent of the British B&B, minus the breakfast. Once upon a time domatia comprised little more than spare rooms in the family home that could be rented out to travellers in summer; nowadays, many are purpose-built appendages. Some come complete with fully equipped kitchens. Standards of cleanliness are generally high.

Domatia remain a popular option for budget travellers. They are classified A, B or C. Expect to pay from €25 to €40 for a single, and €35 to €55 for a double, depending on the class, whether bathrooms are shared or private, the season and how long you plan to stay. Domatia are found on almost every island that has a permanent population. Many are open only between April and October.

From June to September domatia owners are out in force, touting for customers. They meet buses and boats, shouting 'Room, room!' and often carrying photographs of their rooms. In peak season, it can prove a mistake not to take up an offer – but be wary of owners who are vague about the location of their accommodation.

Hostels

There is only one youth hostel in Greece affiliated to the International Youth Hostel Federation (IYHF), the **Athens International Youth Hostel** (Map p72; ☎ 210 523 4170; fax 210 523 4015; www.interland .gr/athenshostel; Victor Hugo 16). You don't need a membership card to stay there; temporary membership costs €1.80 per day.

Most other youth hostels in Greece are run by the **Greek Youth Hostel Organisation** (Map p72; ☎ 210 751 9530; www.athens-yhostel.com; Damareos 75, Pangrati, Athens 116 33). There are affiliated hostels in Athens, Olympia, Patra and Thessaloniki on the mainland, and on the islands of Crete and Santorini.

Hostel rates vary from €8 to €11 and you don't have to be a member to stay in any of them. Few have curfews.

Hotels

Hotels in Greece are divided into six categories: deluxe, A, B, C, D and E. Hotels are categorised according to the size of the room, whether or not they have a bar, and the ratio of bathrooms to beds, rather than standards of cleanliness, comfort of the beds and friendliness of staff – all elements that may be of greater relevance to guests.

As one would expect, deluxe, A- and B-class hotels have many amenities, private bathrooms and constant hot water. C-class hotels have a snack bar, rooms have private bathrooms, but hot water may only be available at certain times of the day. D-class hotels may or may not have snack bars, most rooms will share bathrooms, but there may be some with private bathrooms, and they may have solar-heated water, which means hot water is not guaranteed. E classes do not have a snack bar, bathrooms are shared and you may have to pay extra for hot water – if it exists at all.

Prices are controlled by the tourist police and the maximum rate that can be charged for a room must be displayed on a board behind the door of each room. The classification is not often much of a guide to price. Rates in D- and E-class hotels are generally comparable with domatia. You can pay from €35 to €60 for a single in high season in C class and €45 to €80 for a double. Prices in B class range from €50 to €80 for singles, and from €90 to €120 for doubles. A-class prices are not much higher.

Mountain Refuges

You are unlikely to need to stay at Greece's mountain refuges – unless of course you're going hiking in the mountains of Crete or Evia. The EOT (Ellinikos Organismos Tourismou; Greek National Tourist Organisation) publication *Greece: Mountain Refuges & Ski Centres* has details on all of the refuges in Greece; copies should be available at all EOT branches. See p499 for more information about EOT.

Pensions

Pensions in Greece are virtually indistinguishable from hotels. They are classed A, B or C. An A-class *pension* is equivalent in amenities and price to a B-class hotel, a B-class *pension* is equivalent to a C-class hotel and a C-class *pension* is equivalent to a D- or E-class hotel.

Rental Accommodation

There are plenty of places around the islands offering self-contained family apartments for either long- or short-term rent. Prices vary considerably according to the season and the amenities offered.

If you're looking for long-term accommodation, it's worth checking out the classified section of the *Athens News* – although most of the places are in Athens. On the islands, the local *kafeneio* (coffee house) is a good place to start asking about your options.

Villas & Apartments

A really practical way to save on money and maximise comfort is to rent a furnished apartment or villa. Many are purpose built for tourists while others, especially villas, may be homes that are not being used by their owners. The main advantage is that you can accommodate a larger number of people under one roof and also save money by self-catering.

This option is best for a stay of more than three days. In fact, some owners may insist on a minimum of a week's stay.

A good website to spot prospective villas is www.greekislands.com.

ACTIVITIES

For details on popular activities throughout the Greek islands, see Greek Islands Outdoors (p65).

BUSINESS HOURS

Banks are open 8am to 2pm Monday to Thursday, and 8am to 1.30pm Friday. Some banks in large towns and cities open between 3.30pm and 6.30pm in the afternoon on weekdays and 8am to 1.30pm Saturday.

Post offices are open from 7.30am to 2pm Monday to Friday. In the major cities they stay open until 8pm, and open 7.30am to 2pm Saturday.

In summer, the usual opening hours for shops are 8am to 1.30pm and 5.30pm to 8.30pm on Tuesday, Thursday and Friday, and 8am to 2.30pm on Monday, Wednesday and Saturday. Shops open 30 minutes later in winter.

These times are not always strictly adhered to. Many shops in tourist resorts are open seven days a week.

Department stores and supermarkets are open 8am to 8pm Monday to Friday, 8am to at least 3pm on Saturday and are closed Sunday.

Periptera (street kiosks) are open from early morning until late at night. They sell everything from bus tickets and cigarettes to hard-core pornography.

Restaurant opening hours vary enormously. They are normally open for lunch from 11am to 3pm, and for dinner between 7pm and 1am, while restaurants in tourist areas remain open all day. Cafés normally open at about 10am and stay open until midnight.

Bars open from 8pm until late, while nightclubs don't open until at least 10pm; it's rare to find much of a crowd before midnight. They close at about 4am, later on Friday and Saturday.

CHILDREN

The Greek islands are a safe and relatively easy place to travel with children. Greeks are well known for making a fuss of children, who will always be made the centre of attention.

DIRECTORY

Despite this, it's usually quite rare for younger children to have much success making friends with local children their own age, partly because Greek children tend to play at home and partly because of the language barrier. The language barrier starts to recede by about the age of 12, by which time many local children are sufficiently advanced in their studies to communicate in English.

Matt Barrett's website (www.greektravel .com) has lots of useful tips for parents, while daughter Amarandi has put together some tips for kids (www.greece4kids.com).

Practicalities

Travelling is especially easy if you're staying at a resort hotel by the beach, where everything is set up for families with children. As well as facilities like paddling pools and playgrounds, they also have cots and highchairs.

Best of all, there's a strong possibility of making friends with other kids.

Elsewhere, it's rare to find cots and highchairs, although most hotels and restaurants will do their best to help.

Mobility is an issue for parents with very small children. Strollers (pushchairs) aren't much use. They are hopeless on rough stone paths and up steps, and a curse when getting on/off buses and ferries. Backpacks or front pouches are best.

Fresh milk is available in large towns and tourist areas, but not on the smaller islands. Supermarkets are the best place to look. Formula is available everywhere, as is condensed and heat-treated milk.

Disposable nappies are an environmental curse, but they can be a godsend on the road. They are also available everywhere.

Travel on ferries, buses and trains is free for children under four. They pay half fare up to the age of 10 (ferries) or 12 (buses and trains). Full fares apply otherwise. On domestic flights, you'll pay 10% of the fare to have a child under two sitting on your knee; kids aged two to 12 pay half fare.

Sights & Activities

If you're travelling around, the shortage of decent playgrounds and other recreational facilities can be a problem, but it's impossible to be far from a beach anywhere on the islands.

Don't be afraid to take children to the ancient sites. Many parents are surprised by how much their children enjoy them. Young imaginations go into overdrive in a place like the 'labyrinth' at Knossos (p232).

CLIMATE CHARTS

Greece has a mild Mediterranean climate but can be very hot during summer – in July and August the mercury can soar to 40°C (over 100°F) in the shade, just about anywhere in the country. Crete stays warm the longest of all the islands – you can swim off its southern coast from mid-April to November.

Summer is also the time of year when the *meltemi*, a strong northerly wind that sweeps the Aegean (particularly the Cyclades), is at its strongest. The *meltemi* starts off as a mild wind in May and June, and strengthens as the weather hots up – often blowing from a clear blue sky. In July, August and September it can blow at gale force for days on end. The wind is a mixed blessing: it reduces humidity, but plays havoc with ferry schedules.

The Ionian Islands escape the *meltemi*, but here the main summer wind is the *maïstros*, a light to moderate northwesterly that rises in the afternoon – it usually dies away at sunset.

November to February are the wettest months, and it can also get surprisingly cold. Snow is common on the mainland and in the mountains of Evia and Crete.

For tips on the best times to visit the Greek islands, see When to Go (p19). See also the climate charts (right).

COURSES
Cooking

It is possible to do cooking courses on Santorini, Kea, Ikaria and Crete. See p57 for more information on cooking courses.

Dance

The **Dora Stratou Dance Company** (☎ 210 324 4395; fax 210 324 6921; www.grdance.org; Sholiou 8, Plaka, Athens 105 58) runs one-week courses for visitors at its headquarters in Plaka, Athens, during July and August.

Language

If you are serious about learning the Greek language, an intensive course at the start of your stay is a good way to go about it. Most of the courses are based in Athens, but there are also special courses on the islands in summer.

Athens Centre (☎ 210 701 2268; www.athenscentre.gr; Arhimidous 48, Mets, Athens) is in the suburb of Mets,

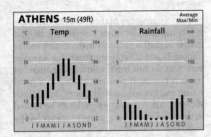

ATHENS 15m (49ft)

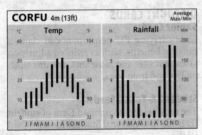

CORFU 4m (13ft)

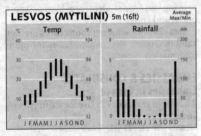

CRETE (IRAKLIO) 39m (128ft)

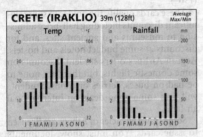

LESVOS (MYTILINI) 5m (16ft)

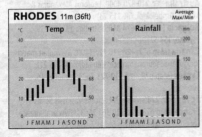

RHODES 11m (36ft)

and also runs courses on the island of Spetses in June and July. The three-week courses cost €1150, and involve 60 hours of classwork.

Hellenic Culture Centre (☎ 22750 61139/40; www .hcc.gr; ☺ May–Oct), in the village of Arethousa, 7km from Evdilos, offers courses in Greek language, culture and literature. All levels of language proficiency are catered for.

Painting

Painting courses are becoming increasingly popular, and British tour operators offer a range of possibilities.

Simply Travel (☎ 020-8541 2200; www.simply-travel .com) runs two-week tours to western Crete, while **Travelux** (☎ 01580 764344; www.travelux.co.uk) offers a week in the wonderful Zagorohoria region of Epiros, followed by a week on the island of Lefkada. Another operator, **Tapestry Holidays** (☎ 020-8235 7800; www.tapestryholidays .com), specialises in Crete and Kefallonia.

Photography

Hania-based British photographer **Steve Outram** (☎ 28210 32201; www.steveoutram.com) runs courses in Crete twice a year in May and October.

Photo-Tours Naxos (☎ 22850 22367; www.naxosphoto workshop.com) runs one-day photo outings for small groups (€35 per person) with on-the-spot advice (from professional Stuart Thorpe) on taking better pictures.

Pilates & Yoga

Looking for a healthy and relaxing holiday involving a bit of stretching and toning? The **NYSY Centre** (☎ 210 323 2004; www.nysystudios.com; Nikis 25, Athens) offers island retreats in both Pilates and yoga, including a comprehensive all-in package on Mykonos for around €1385 per person (double occupancy) for one week.

CUSTOMS

There are no longer duty-free restrictions in the EU. This does not mean, however, that customs checks have been dispensed with; random searches for drugs are still made.

Upon entering the country from outside the EU, inspection is usually cursory for tourists. There may be spot checks, but you may not have to open your bags. A verbal declaration is usually all that is required.

You may bring the following items duty-free: 200 cigarettes or 50 cigars; 1L of spirits or 2L of wine; 50g of perfume; 250mL of eau de cologne; one camera (still or video) and film; a pair of binoculars; a portable musical instrument; a portable radio or tape recorder; sports equipment; and dogs and cats (with a vet certificate).

Art and antiquities can be imported for free, but they must be declared, so that they can be re-exported. Import regulations for medicines are strict; if you are taking medication, make sure you get a statement from your doctor before you leave. It is illegal, for instance, to take codeine into Greece without an accompanying doctor's certificate (see also Warning, p517).

An unlimited amount of foreign currency and travellers cheques may be brought into Greece. If you intend to leave the country with foreign banknotes in excess of US$1000, you must declare the sum upon entry.

Restrictions apply to the importation of sailboards into Greece. See Greek Islands Outdoors (p65) for more details.

It is strictly forbidden to export antiquities (anything over 100 years old) without an export permit. This crime is second only to drug smuggling in the penalties imposed. It is an offence to remove even the smallest article from an archaeological site.

The place to apply for an export permit is the Antique Dealers & Private Collections Section at the **Athens Archaeological Service** (Map p78; Polygnotou 13, Plaka, Athens).

Vehicles

Cars can be brought into Greece for six months without a carnet; only a green card (international third-party insurance) is required. Your only proof of entry into the country will be your ferry ticket stub (if arriving from Italy) so don't lose it. Otherwise, and from other countries, a passport stamp will be ample evidence.

DANGERS & ANNOYANCES
Bar Scams
Bar scams continue to be an unfortunate fact of life in Athens and are particularly prevalent in the Syntagma area. See p74 for the full rundown on this scam.

Theft
Crime, especially theft, is low in Greece, but unfortunately it's on the increase. The area worst affected is around Omonia in central Athens – keep track of your valuables here, on the metro and at the Sunday flea market.

The vast majority of thefts from tourists are still committed by other tourists; the biggest danger of theft is probably in dormitory rooms in hostels and at camping grounds – so make sure you do not leave valuables unattended in such places. If you are staying in a hotel room, and the windows and door do not lock securely, ask for your valuables to be locked in the hotel safe – hotel proprietors are happy to do this.

DISCOUNT CARDS
Senior Cards
Card-carrying EU pensioners can claim a range of benefits, such as reduced admission at ancient sites and museums, and discounts on bus and train fares.

Student & Youth Cards
The most widely recognised form of student ID is the International Student Identity Card (ISIC).

These cards qualify the holder to some significant discounts including half-price admission to museums and ancient sites, and for discounts at some budget hotels and hostels. Aegean Airlines offers student discounts on some domestic flights, but there are none to be had on buses, ferries or trains. Students will find some good deals on international air fares.

Some travel agencies in Athens are licensed to issue cards. You must show documents proving you are a student, provide a passport photo and cough up €10.

Euro<26 (www.euro26.org) youth cards are not valid in Greece. Visit www.istc.org for more information.

EMBASSIES & CONSULATES
Embassies in Greece
All foreign embassies in Greece are in Athens and its suburbs.

Albania (☎ 210 723 4412; Karahristou 1, 115 21)

Australia ☎ 210 870 4000; Leoforos Alexandras & Kifisias, Ambelokipi, GR-115 23)

Bulgaria (☎ 210 674 8105; Stratigou Kalari 33a, Psyhiko, 154 52)

Canada (Map p72; ☎ 210 727 3400; www.dfait.maeci .gc.ca/canadaeuropa/greece; Gennadiou 4, 115 21)

Cyprus (Map p78; ☎ 210 723 7883; Irodotou 16, 106 75)

Egypt (☎ 210 361 8612; Leoforos Vasilissis Sofias 3)

France (Map p78; ☎ 210 361 1663; www.ambafrance -gr.org; Leoforos Vasilissis Sofias 7, 106 71)

Germany (Map p72; ☎ 210 728 5111; www.athen .diplo.de; Dimitriou 3 & Karaoli, Kolonaki, 106 75)
Hungary (☎ 210 672 5337; Kalvou 16, Psyhiko, 154 52)
Ireland (Map p72; ☎ 210 723 2771; Leoforos Vasilissis Sofias 60, 106 74)
Israel (☎ 210 671 9530; Marathonodromou 1, 154 52)
Italy (Map p72; ☎ 210 361 7260; Sekeri 2, 106 74)
Japan (☎ 210 775 8101; www.gr.emb-japan.go.jp; Athens Tower, Leoforos Mesogion 2-4, 115 27)
Netherlands (Map p78; ☎ 210 723 9701; www .dutchembassy.gr; Vasileos Konstantinou 5-7, 106 74)
New Zealand (Map p78; ☎ 210 687 4701; Kifisias 268, Halandri)
Serbia & Montenegro (☎ 210 777 4355; Leoforos Vasilissis Sofias 106, 115 21)
South Africa (Map p72; ☎ 210 680 6645; www .southafrica.gr; Kifisias 60, Marousi, 151 25)
Turkey (Map p78; ☎ 210 724 5915; Vasileos Georgiou 8, 106 74)
UK (Map p72; ☎ 210 723 6211; www.britishembassy .gr; Ploutarhou 1, 106 75)
USA (☎ 210 721 2951; http://athens.usembassy.gov; Leoforos Vasilissis Sofias 91, 115 21)

It's important to realise what your own embassy – the embassy of the country of which you are a citizen – can and can't do to help you if you get into trouble. Generally speaking, it won't be much help in emergencies if the trouble you're in is remotely your own fault. Remember that you are bound by the laws of the country you are in. Your embassy will not be sympathetic if you end up in jail after committing a crime locally, even if such actions are legal in your own country.

In genuine emergencies you might get some assistance, but only if other channels have been exhausted. For example, if you need to get home urgently, a free ticket home is exceedingly unlikely – the embassy would expect you to have insurance. If you have all your money and documents stolen, it might assist with getting a new passport, but a loan for onward travel is out of the question.

Some embassies used to keep letters for travellers or have a small reading room with home newspapers, but these days the mail-holding service has usually been stopped and even newspapers tend to be out of date.

FESTIVALS & EVENTS

The Greek year is a succession of festivals and events, some of which are religious, some cultural, others just an excuse for a good party, and some a combination of all three. The fol-

lowing is by no means an exhaustive list, but it covers the most important events, both national and regional. If you're in the right place at the right time, you'll certainly be invited to join the revelry.

More information about festivals and events can be found at www.cultureguide.gr.

January

Feast of Agios Vasilios (St Basil) The year kicks off with this festival on 1 January. A church ceremony is followed by the exchanging of gifts, singing, dancing and feasting; the New Year's *vasilopita* (golden-glazed cake) is cut and the person who gets the slice containing a coin will supposedly have a lucky year.

Epiphany (Blessing of the Waters) The day of Christ's baptism by St John is celebrated throughout Greece on 6 January. Seas, lakes and rivers are blessed and crosses immersed in them. The largest ceremony occurs at Piraeus.

February

Carnival Season The three-week period before the beginning of Lent (the 40-day period before Easter, which is traditionally a period of fasting) is carnival season. The carnivals are ostensibly Christian pre-Lenten celebrations, but many derive from pagan festivals. There are many regional variations, but fancy dress, feasting, traditional dancing and general merry-making prevail. The Patra carnival (p96) is the largest and most exuberant, with elaborately decorated chariots parading through the streets. The most bizarre carnival takes place on the island of Skyros (p440), where the men transform themselves into grotesque 'half-man, half-beast' creatures by donning goat-skin masks and hairy jackets.

Shrove Monday (Clean Monday) On the Monday before Ash Wednesday (the first day of Lent), people take to the hills throughout Greece to have picnics and fly kites.

March

Independence Day The anniversary of the hoisting of the Greek flag by Bishop Germanos at Moni Agias Lavras is celebrated on 25 March with parades and dancing. Germanos' act of revolt marked the start of the War of Independence. Independence Day coincides with the Feast of the Annunciation, so it is also a religious festival.

April

Easter This is the most important festival in the Greek Orthodox religion. Emphasis is placed on the Resurrection rather than on the Crucifixion, so it is a joyous occasion. The festival begins on the evening of Good Friday with the *perifora epitafiou*, when a shrouded bier (representing Christ's funeral bier) is carried through the streets to the local church. This moving candle-lit procession can be seen in towns and villages throughout the country. From an island-hopper's viewpoint, the most impressive of these processions can be witnessed on either Patmos or perhaps Corfu. The Resurrection Mass starts at 11pm on Saturday night. At midnight, packed churches are plunged into darkness to symbolise Christ's passing through the underworld. The ceremony of the lighting of candles, which follows, is the most significant moment in the Orthodox year, for it symbolises the Resurrection. Its poignancy and beauty are spellbinding. If you are in Greece at Easter you should endeavour to attend this ceremony, which ends with fireworks and candle-lit processions through the streets. The Lenten fast ends on Easter Sunday with the cracking of red-dyed Easter eggs and an outdoor feast of roast lamb followed by Greek dancing. The day's greeting is *Hristos anesti* (Christ is risen), to which the reply is *Alithos anesti* (Truly He is risen). On both Palm Sunday (the Sunday before Easter) and Easter Sunday, St Spyridon (the mummified patron saint of Corfu) is taken out for an airing and joyously paraded through Corfu Town. He is paraded again on 11 August.

Feast of Agios Georgos (St George) The feast day of St George, Greece's patron saint and patron saint of shepherds, takes place on 23 April or the Tuesday following Easter (whichever comes first).

May

May Day On the first day of May there is a mass exodus from towns to the country. During picnics, wildflowers are gathered and made into wreaths to decorate houses.

June

Navy Week The festival celebrates the long relationship between Greeks and the sea with events in fishing villages and ports throughout the country. Volos (p99) and Hydra (p115) each have unique versions of these celebrations. Volos re-enacts the departure of the *Argo*, for legend has it that Iolkos (from where Jason and the Argonauts set off in search of the Golden Fleece) was near the city. Hydra commemorates War of Independence–hero Admiral Andreas Miaoulis, who was born on the island, at its Miaoulia Festival, which includes a re-enactment of one of his naval victories, accompanied by feasting and fireworks.

Feast of St John the Baptist This feast day on 24 June is widely celebrated around Greece. Wreaths made on May Day are kept until this day, when they are burned on bonfires.

Hellenic Festival The Hellenic Festival is the most important of the many festivals staged throughout Greece during summer. It features performances of music, dance and drama at the Odeon of Herodes Atticus in Athens, and performances of ancient Greek drama at the world famous Theatre of Epidavros, near Nafplio in the Peloponnese.

July

Feast of Agia Marina (St Marina) This feast day is celebrated on 17 July in many parts of Greece and is a particularly important event on the Dodecanese island of Kasos (p300).

Feast of Profitis Ilias This feast day is celebrated on 20 July at the many hilltop churches and monasteries throughout Greece that are dedicated to the prophet Ilias.

Folegandros Festival The Folegandros Festival features a week-long programme of music and feasting at a range of locations around the island's beautiful old Hora (p205).

August

Feast of the Assumption Greeks celebrate Assumption Day (15 August) with family reunions. The whole population seems to be on the move either side of the big day, so it's a good time to avoid public transport. The island of Tinos (p132) gets particularly busy because of its miracle-working icon of Panagia Evangelistria. It becomes a place of pilgrimage for thousands, who come to be blessed, healed or baptised.

September

Genisis tis Panagias The birthday of the Virgin Mary is celebrated on 8 September throughout Greece with religious services and feasting.

Exaltation of the Cross This is celebrated on 14 September throughout Greece with processions and hymns.

October

Feast of Agios Dimitrios This feast day is celebrated in Thessaloniki (p91) on 26 October with wine-drinking and revelry.

Ohi (No) Day Metaxas' refusal to allow Mussolini's troops free passage through Greece in WWII is commemorated on 28 October with remembrance services, military parades, folk dancing and feasting.

December

Christmas Day Although not as important as Easter, Christmas is still celebrated with religious services and feasting. Nowadays much 'Western' influence is apparent, including Christmas trees, decorations and presents.

FOOD

For large cities and towns, restaurant listings in this book are given in the following order: budget (under €15), midrange (€15 to €40) and top end (over €40), and within each section the restaurants are listed in budget order. For information on the staples of Greek food, see p51.

GAY & LESBIAN TRAVELLERS

In a country where the church still plays a prominent role in shaping society's views on issues such as sexuality, it should come as no surprise that homosexuality is generally frowned upon – especially outside the major cities. While there is no legislation against homosexual activity, it pays to be discreet and to avoid open displays of togetherness.

This has not prevented Greece from becoming an extremely popular destination for gay and lesbian travellers. Athens has a busy gay scene – but most gay and lesbian travellers head for the islands. Mykonos (p141) has long been famous for its bars, beaches and general hedonism, while Paros (and Antiparos), Rhodes, Santorini and Skiathos all have their share of gay hang-outs.

The town of Skala Eresou (p395) on the island of Lesvos (Mytilini), birthplace of the lesbian poet Sappho, has become something of a place of pilgrimage for lesbians.

Information

The *Spartacus International Gay Guide*, published by Bruno Gmünder (Berlin), is widely regarded as the leading authority on the gay travel scene. The Greek section contains a wealth of information on gay venues throughout the country.

There's also stacks of information on the internet. For example, the website **Roz Mov** (www .geocities.com/WestHollywood/2225/index.html), is a good place to start. It has pages on travel information, gay health, the gay press, organisations, events and legal issues – and links to lots more sites.

Gayscape (www.gayscape.com/gayscape/menugreece.html) also has a useful website with lots of links.

HOLIDAYS
Public Holidays

All banks and shops and most museums and ancient sites close on public holidays. The following are national public holidays in Greece:

New Year's Day 1 January
Epiphany (Blessing of the Waters) 6 January
First Sunday in Lent February
Greek Independence Day 25 March
Good Friday March/April
(Orthodox) Easter Sunday March/April
Spring Festival/Labour Day 1 May
Feast of the Assumption 15 August
Ohi (No) Day 28 October
Christmas Day 25 December
St Stephen's Day 26 December

School Holidays

The Greek school year is divided into three terms. The main school holidays are in July and August.

INSURANCE

A travel insurance policy to cover theft, loss and medical problems is a good idea. Some of these policies offer lower and higher medical-expense options; the higher ones are chiefly for countries such as the USA, which have extremely high medical costs. There is a wide variety of policies available, so check the small print.

Some policies specifically exclude 'dangerous activities', eg scuba diving, motorcycling, even hiking. A locally acquired motorcycle licence is not valid under some policies.

You may prefer a policy that pays doctors or hospitals directly rather than you having to pay on the spot and claim later. If you have to claim later make sure you retain all documentation related to the claim. Some policies ask you to call back (reverse charges) to a centre in your home country where an immediate assessment of your problem is made.

Check that the policy covers ambulances or an emergency flight home. For more information on health insurance, see p516.

Buy travel insurance as early as possible. If you buy it just before you fly, you may find you're not covered for such problems as delays caused by industrial action. Paying for your ticket with a credit card sometimes provides limited travel insurance, and you may be able to reclaim the payment if the operator doesn't deliver.

INTERNET ACCESS

Greece has long since embraced the convenience of the internet big time. There has been a huge increase in the number of hotels and businesses using email, and these addresses have been listed here where available.

Internet cafés are everywhere, and are listed under the Information section for cities and islands where available. Some hotels also offer internet access. Many internet cafés and hotels now offer wi-fi access either for free or for a charge. In midrange hotels that will range from €6 for an hour to €20 for 24-hour access.

Travelling with a laptop computer is a great way to stay in touch with life back home. Today's machines are light and slip easily into a protected daypack. Your laptop becomes your portable office: internet access, a VoIP phone, your DVD and CD player, your photo archive and you can even create movies on the fly if you have a lightweight video camera with you, too. You simply need to be certain that the power supply of your machine is compatible with Greece's.

For travellers, dialling up to connect to the internet has become a thing of the past in Greece. As long as your laptop has a wireless card, or at least an Ethernet port, you can connect seamlessly at internet cafés or hotels or even hot spots in major towns. Major towns on all islands usually have hot spots. Many internet cafés will have an Ethernet cable, too, to connect your laptop if you do not have a wireless card. Wireless internet roaming is also a possible option. Greece has agreements with several countries' ISPs to provide wireless connectivity. Check with your local ISP.

Email

By far the easiest way to access your email is via the web-based email programme of your service provider. If you have your own laptop, dedicated email programmes, such as Outlook (Windows) or Entourage (Macintosh), will collect your mail for you via a wireless or Ethernet node, but you will most probably not be able to send mail using these programmes because of relay blocking by local ISPs.

If you don't have a laptop, or your service provider does not have an alternative web-based email page then use a service like Gmail, Yahoo! or Hotmail to send and read mail.

Finally, most current model mobile phones these days have the option to retrieve and send email, though configuring your phone to work in Greece may require some assistance, or the purchase of a local SIM card.

LEGAL MATTERS
Arrests

It is a good idea to have your passport with you at all times in case you are stopped by the police and questioned. Greek citizens are presumed to always have identification on

them; foreign visitors are similarly presumed to by the police. If you are arrested by police, insist on an interpreter (*the*-lo dhi-ermi-*nea*) and/or a lawyer (*the*-lo dhi-ki-*go*-ro).

Drugs

Drug laws in Greece are the strictest in Europe. Greek courts make no distinction between the possession of drugs and dealing them. Possession of even a small amount of marijuana is likely to land you in jail. See also p517 for the warning regarding codeine.

MAPS

Unless you are going to hike or drive, the free maps given out by the EOT will probably suffice, although they are not 100% accurate. On islands where there is no EOT office there are usually tourist maps for sale for around €1.50 but, again, these are not very accurate.

The best maps are published by the Greek company **Road Editions** (☎ 210 345 5575; www.road .gr; Kozanis 21 & Amfipoleos, Votanikos, Athens), whose maps are produced with the Hellenic Army Geographical Service. These maps are being updated using Global Positioning Satellite technology. There is a wide range of maps to suit various needs, starting with a 1:500,000 map of Greece. Crete is well covered by the company's maroon-covered 1:250,000 mainland series. Even the smallest roads and villages are clearly marked, and the distance indicators are spot-on – important when negotiating your way around the backblocks. Useful features include symbols to indicate the location of petrol stations and tyre shops. The company's blue-cover Greek island series includes all the main islands. The scale ranges from 1:100,000 for larger islands, like Corfu and Rhodes, to 1:30,000 for Syros.

Equally good if not better for the islands are the *Topo* series published by **Anavasi** (☎ 210 321 8104; www.mountains.gr; Stoa Arsakiou 6a, Athens). The durable plasticised paper is the main advantage, plus the detailed walking trails for many of the Aegean islands.

All maps can be bought online or at major bookstores in Greece.

MONEY

Greece dropped the drachma and adopted the euro at the beginning of 2002. There are eight euro coins, in denominations of two and one euros; 50, 20, 10, five, two and one cents, and six notes: €5, €10, €20, €50, €100 and €200.

COMING OF AGE

For the record:

- You can drive when you're 18.
- The legal age for voting in Greece is 18.
- The age of consent for homosexual/ heterosexual sex for girls is 15/15 and boys 16/17.
- The legal drinking age is 16.

See the inside front cover for currency exchange rates, and see p19 for information on costs in Greece.

ATMs

ATMs are to be found in every town large enough to support a bank – and certainly in all of the well-touristed areas. Automated foreign-exchange machines are common in major tourist areas. They take all the major European currencies, Australian and US dollars and Japanese yen.

Cash

Nothing beats cash for convenience – or for risk, but it's best to carry no more cash than you need for the next few days, which means working out your potential costs whenever you change travellers cheques or withdraw cash from an ATM.

Credit Cards

Credit cards are an accepted part of the commercial scene just about everywhere in Greece. They can be used to pay for a wide range of goods and services, such as meals accommodation, car hire and souvenirs. They can also be used as cash cards to draw cash from the ATMs of affiliated Greek banks in the same way as at home. The main credit cards are MasterCard, Visa (Access in the UK) and Eurocard, all of which are widely accepted in Greece.

Tipping

In restaurants a service charge is normally included in the bill and while a tip is not expected it is always appreciated and should be left if the service has been good. Taxi drivers expect you to round up the fare, while hotel porters (bellhops) who help you with your luggage to your room or stewards on ferries who take you to your cabin normally expect a small gratuity of between €1 and €3.

Travellers Cheques

Travellers cheques are losing popularity as more travellers opt to put their money in a bank at home and withdraw it from ATMs as they go along. Nonetheless they are still used and still popular among some travellers.

PHOTOGRAPHY & VIDEO

Digital photography has taken over in a big way in Greece and a range of memory cards can now be bought from camera shops. Film is still widely available, although it can be expensive in smaller towns. You'll find all the gear you need in the photography shops of Athens and major cities.

It is possible to obtain video cartridges easily in large towns and cities, but make sure you buy the correct format. It is usually worth buying at least a few cartridges duty-free to start off your trip.

As elsewhere in the world, developing film is a competitive business. Most places charge around €9 to develop a roll of 36 colour prints.

Lonely Planet's *Travel Photography: A Guide to Taking Better Pictures,* by well-known photographer Richard I'Anson, offers a comprehensive guide to technical and creative travel photography.

Restrictions & Etiquette

Never photograph a military installation or anything else that has a sign forbidding photography. Flash photography is not allowed inside churches and it's considered taboo to photograph the main altar.

Greeks love having their photos taken, but ask permission first. The same goes for video cameras, probably even more annoying and offensive for locals than a still camera.

POST

Tahydromia (post offices) are easily identifiable by the yellow signs outside. Regular post boxes are also yellow. The red boxes are for express mail only.

Postal Rates

The postal rate for postcards and airmail letters to all destinations outside Greece is €0.62 for up to 20g; for items up to 50g within the EU it is €0.90 and €1 outside the EU. Post within Europe takes between four and six days and to the USA, Australia and New Zealand, seven to 10 days. Some tourist shops also sell stamps, but with a 10% surcharge.

Registered mail costs an extra €2.50 and should ensure delivery in three days within the EU.

Sending Mail

Do not wrap a parcel until it has been inspected at a post office. In Athens, take your parcel to the **Parcel post office** (Map p78; ☎ 210 322 8940; Stadiou 4, Athens) in the arcade and elsewhere to the parcel counter of a regular post office.

Receiving Mail

While email has overtaken paper mail as the main form of communication for travellers on the move you can receive mail *poste restante* (general delivery) at any main post office. The service is free, but you are required to show your passport. Both Athens' **Central post office** (Map p72; Eolou 100, Omonia, 102 00; ⊙ 7.30am-8pm Mon-Fri, 7.30am-2pm Sat) and **Syntagma post office** (Map p78; cnr Mitropoleos & Plateia Syntagmatos 103 00; ⊙ 7.30am-8pm Mon-Fri, 7.30am-2pm Sat) hold *poste-restante* mail.

Parcels are not delivered in Greece; they must be collected from the parcel counter of a post office or, in Athens, from the Parcel post office (see p74).

SHOPPING

For Greeks and visitors alike, shopping in Greece is big business. At times, a tourist town can look like one big shop with all kinds of goods and trinkets on display. The trouble is a lot of it is overpriced and of inferior quality so the moral of the story is don't shop in tourist areas. That said, Athens' Flea Market (p83) has a bewildering array of items on sale and you can find some good bargains. Shoes and clothes are excellent buys, especially in the post-seasonal sales; and if you have room in your suitcase or backpack there are some really excellent quality artisanal works to be picked up from small boutiques and galleries including pottery, jewellery and metalworked objects.

Bargaining

Getting a bit extra off the deal through bargaining is sadly a thing of the past in Greece. You might be offered a 'special deal', but the art and sport of bargaining has gone the way of the drachma: out the window. Instead, know your goods and decide for yourself if the price you are being offered is worth it before accepting the deal.

SOLO TRAVELLERS

Greece is a great destination for solo travellers, especially in summer when the islands become an international meeting point. Hostels and other backpacker-friendly accommodation are good places to meet up with other solo travellers. See also Women Travellers (p500).

TELEPHONE

The telephone service in Greece is maintained by the public corporation known as OTE (pronounced o-*teh*; Organismos Tilepikoinonion Ellados).

The system is modern and reasonably well maintained. There are public telephones just about everywhere, including some unbelievably isolated spots. The phones are easy to operate and can be used for local, long-distance and international calls. The 'i' at the top left of the push-button dialling panel brings up the operating instructions in English.

Mobile Phones

The number of mobile (cell) phones in Greece now exceeds the number of landline phones. Mobile telephony is big business here.

If you have a compatible GSM mobile phone from a country with an overseas global roaming arrangement with Greece, you will be able to use your phone in Greece. You must inform your mobile phone service provider before you depart in order to have global roaming activated.

There are several mobile service providers in Greece – among which Panafon, CosmOTE and Wind are the best known. All offer 2G connectivity. Of these three, CosmOTE tends to have the best coverage in remote areas, so try re-tuning your phone to CosmOTE if you find mobile coverage is patchy. All three companies offer pay-as-you-talk services by which you can buy a rechargeable SIM card and have your own Greek mobile number. The Panafon system is called 'à la Carte', the Wind system 'F2G' and CosmOTE is 'Cosmokarta'.

USA and Canadian mobile-phone users won't be able to use their mobile phones, unless their handset is equipped with a dual or tri-band system.

Note: the use of a mobile phone while driving in Greece is prohibited, but the use of a Bluetooth headset is allowed.

Phonecards

All public phones use the OTE phonecards, known as *telekarta*, not coins. These cards (€3, €5 and €9) are widely available at *periptera*, corner shops and tourist shops. A local call costs €0.30 for three minutes.

It's also possible to use these phones using a growing range of discount-card schemes, which involve dialling an access code and then punching in your card number. The OTE version of this card is known as 'Hronokarta'. The cards come with instructions in Greek and English. The talk time is enormous compared to the standard phone card rates. Definitely consider.

TIME

Greece maintains one time zone throughout the whole country and is two hours ahead of GMT/UTC and three hours ahead on daylight-saving time, which begins on the last Sunday in March, when clocks are put forward one hour. For a run-down of current world times, see World Time Zones (Map pp546–7).

TOILETS

Most places in Greece have Western-style toilets. You'll occasionally come across Asian-style squat toilets in older houses, *kafeneia* and public toilets.

Public toilets are a rarity, except at airports and bus and train stations. Cafés are usually the best option if you happen to get caught short, but you'll most likely be expected to purchase something for the privilege.

One peculiarity of the Greek plumbing system is that it can't handle toilet paper; apparently the pipes are too narrow. Flushing away tampons and sanitary napkins is guaranteed to block the system.

Whatever the reason, anything larger than a postage stamp seems to cause a serious problem. Toilet paper etc should be placed in the small bin that is provided near every toilet.

TOURIST INFORMATION

All of the tourist information is handled by the Greek National Tourist Organisation, known by the initials GNTO abroad and EOT in Greece.

Local Tourist Offices

The EOT in Athens (p74) dispenses a variety of information, including a very useful timetable of the week's ferry departures from Piraeus. The office also provides details about public transport prices and schedules from Athens. Its free map of Athens is urgently in need of an update, although most places of interest are clearly marked. The office is about 500m from Ambelokipi metro station.

EOT offices are found in most major tourist locations, though these offices are increasingly being supplemented or sometimes even replaced by local municipality tourist offices.

Tourist Offices Abroad

GNTO offices abroad:

Australia (☎ 02-9241 1663/5; hto@tpg.com.au; 51-57 Pitt St, Sydney NSW 2000)

Austria (☎ 1-512 5317; grect@vienna.at; Opernring 8, Vienna A-10105)

Belgium (☎ 2-647 5770; fax 647 5142; 172 Ave Louise Louizalaan, B1050 Brussels)

Canada Montreal (☎ 514-871 1535; 1170 Place du Frère André, Montreal, Quebec H3B 3C6); Toronto (☎ 416-968 2220; gnto.tor@sympatico.ca; 91 Scollard St, Toronto, Ontario M5R 1G4)

Denmark (☎ 33-325 332; Vester Farimagsgade 1, 1606 Copenhagen)

France (☎ 01-42 60 65 75; eot@club-internet.fr; 3 Ave de l'Opéra, Paris 75001)

Germany Berlin (☎ 30-217 6262; Wittenbergplatz 3A, 10789 Berlin 30); Frankfurt (☎ 69-236 561; info@gzf-eot .de; Neue Mainzerstrasse 22, 60311 Frankfurt); Hamburg (☎ 40-454 498; info-hamburg@gzf-eot.de; Neurer Wall 18, 20254 Hamburg); Munich (☎ 89-222 035/036; Pacellistrasse 5, 2W 80333 Munich)

Israel (☎ 3-517 0501; hellenic@netvision.net.il; 5 Shalom Aleichem St, Tel Aviv 61262)

Italy (www.enteturismoellenico.com); Milan (☎ 02-860 470; Piazza Diaz 1, 20123 Milano); Rome (☎ 06-474 4249; Via L Bissolati 78-80, 00187 Roma)

Japan (☎ 03-350 55 917; gnto-jpn@t3.rim.or.jp; Fukuda Bldg West, 5F 2-11-3 Akasaka, Minato-ku, Tokyo 107)

Netherlands (☎ 20-625 4212; gnto@planet.nl; Kerkstraat 61, Amsterdam GC 1017)

Sweden (☎ 8-679 6480; grekiska.statens.turist byra@swipnet.se; Birger Jarlsgatan 30, Box 5298 S, 10246 Stockholm)

Switzerland (☎ 01-221 0105; eot@bluewin.ch; Loewenstrasse 25, 8001 Zürich)

UK (☎ 020-7734 5997; 4 Conduit St, London W1R 0DJ)

USA (www.greektourism.com); Chicago (☎ 312-782 1084; Suite 600, 168 North Michigan Ave, Chicago, Illinois 60601); Los Angeles (☎ 213-626 6696; Suite 2198, 611 West 6th St, Los Angeles, California 92668); New York (☎ 212-421 5777; Olympic Tower, 645 5th Ave, New York, NY 10022)

Tourist Police

The tourist police work in cooperation with the regular Greek police and EOT. Each tourist-police office has at least one member of staff who speaks English. Hotels, restaurants, travel agencies, tourist shops, tourist guides, waiters, taxi drivers and bus drivers all come under the jurisdiction of the tourist police. If you think that you have been ripped off by any of these, report it to the tourist police and they will investigate. If you need to report a theft or loss of passport, go to the tourist police first, and they will act as interpreters between you and the regular police. The tourist police also fulfil the same functions as the EOT and municipal tourist offices, dispensing maps and brochures, and giving information on transport. They can often help to find accommodation.

TRAVELLERS WITH DISABILITIES

If mobility is a problem and you wish to visit Greece, the hard fact is that most hotels, museums and ancient sites are not wheelchair accessible. This is partly due to the uneven terrain of much of the country, with its abundance of stones, rocks and marble, which presents a challenge even for able-bodied people.

If you are determined, then take heart in the knowledge that disabled people do come to Greece for holidays. But the trip needs careful planning, so get as much information as you can before you go. The British-based **Royal Association for Disability and Rehabilitation** (Radar; ☎ 020-7250 3222; fax 020-7250 0212; www.radar .org.uk; 12 City Forum, 250 City Rd, London EC1V 8AF) publishes a useful guide called *Holidays & Travel Abroad: A Guide for Disabled People*, which gives a good overview of facilities available to travellers with disabilities in Europe.

VISAS

The list of countries whose nationals can stay in Greece for up to three months without a visa includes Australia, Canada, all EU countries, Iceland, Israel, Japan, New Zealand, Norway, Switzerland and the USA. Other countries included are the European principalities of Monaco and San Marino and most South American countries. The list changes – contact Greek embassies for the full list (up-to-date visa information is also available on www .lonelyplanet.com). Those not included can expect to pay about US$20 for a three-month visa.

Visa Extensions

If you wish to stay in Greece for longer than three months, apply at a consulate abroad or at least 20 days in advance to the **Aliens Bureau** (☎ 210 770 5711/17; Leoforos Alexandras 173, Ambelokipi; ☉ 8am-1pm Mon-Fri) in the Athens Central Police Station. Take your passport and four passport photographs along. You may be asked for proof that you can support yourself financially, so keep all your bank exchange slips

(or the equivalent from a post office). These slips are not always automatically given – you may have to ask for them. Elsewhere in Greece apply to the local police authority. You will be given a permit that will authorise you to stay in the country for a period of up to six months.

Most travellers manage to get around this by visiting Bulgaria or Turkey briefly and then re-entering Greece.

WOMEN TRAVELLERS

Many women travel alone in Greece. The crime rate remains relatively low and solo travel is probably safer than in most European countries. This does not mean that you should be lulled into complacency; bag snatching and rapes do occur, although violent offences are rare.

The biggest nuisance to foreign women travelling alone are the guys the Greeks have nicknamed *kamaki*. The word means 'fishing trident' and refers to the *kamaki's* favourite pastime: 'fishing' for foreign women. You'll find them everywhere there are lots of tourists; young (for the most part), smooth-talking guys who aren't in the least bashful about sidling up to women in the street. They can be very persistent, but they are a hassle rather than a threat.

The majority of Greek men treat foreign women with respect, and are genuinely helpful.

WORK

EU nationals don't need a work permit, but they need a residency permit if they intend to stay longer than three months. Nationals of other countries are supposed to have a work permit.

Bar & Hostel Work

The bars of the Greek islands could not survive without foreign workers and there are thousands of summer jobs up for grabs every year. The pay is not fantastic, but you get to spend a summer in the islands. April and May is the time to go looking. Hostels and travellers hotels are other places that regularly employ foreign workers.

English Tutoring

If you're looking for a permanent job, the most widely available option is to teach English. A TEFL (Teaching English as a Foreign Language) certificate or a university degree is an advantage but not essential. In the UK, look through the *Times Educational Supplement* or Tuesday's edition of the *Guardian* newspaper for job opportunities – in other countries, contact the Greek embassy.

Another option is to find a job teaching English once you're in Greece. You will see language schools everywhere.

Strictly speaking, you need a licence to teach in these schools, but many will employ teachers without one. The best time to look is late summer.

Check out the notice board at the Compendium (p71) bookshop in Athens as it sometimes has advertisements looking for private English lessons.

Volunteer Work

The **Hellenic Society for the Study & Protection of the Monk Seal** (☎ 210 522 2888; fax 2105 222 450; www.mom .gr; Solomou 53, Athens 104 32) and **Sea Turtle Protection Society of Greece** (Archelon; ☎ /fax 210 523 1342; www .archelon.gr; Solomou 57, Athens 104 32) use volunteers

for the monitoring programmes they run on the Ionian Islands.

The **Hellenic Wildlife Rehabilitation Centre** (Elliniko Kentro Perithalpsis Agrion Zöon; ☎ 22970 28367; www.ekpaz.gr in Greek; ☼ 10am-11pm), in Aegina, welcomes volunteers, particularly during the winter months. The new centre has accommodation available for volunteer workers. For more information, see p115.

Other Work

There are often jobs advertised in the classifieds section of English-language newspapers, or you can place an advertisement yourself. EU nationals can also make use of the OAED (Organismos Apasholiseos Ergatikou Dynamikou), the Greek National Employment Service. The OAED has offices throughout Greece.

Seasonal harvest work is mainly handled by migrant workers from Albania and other Balkan nations, and is no longer a viable option for travellers.

Transport

CONTENTS

TRANSPORT (side tab)

GETTING THERE & AWAY

ENTERING THE COUNTRY

Entry into Greece from the EU is nominally free of any formalities. Spot checks for contraband may be made of individuals or vehicles at the entry ports. Authorities may pay you more attention if entering from non-EU countries.

Passport

All visitors must have a passport – or ID card if a resident of the EU – and depending on your nationality, a visa.

For more detailed information on visas, see p500.

THINGS CHANGE...

The information in this chapter is particularly vulnerable to change. Check directly with the airline or a travel agent to make sure you understand how a fare (and ticket you may buy) works and be aware of the security requirements for international travel. Shop carefully. The details given in this chapter should be regarded as pointers and are not a substitute for your own careful, up-to-date research.

AIR

Most travellers arrive in Greece by air, which is usually the cheapest and quickest way to get there.

Airports & Airlines

Greece has 16 international airports, but only those in Athens, Iraklio (Crete), Rhodes and Thessaloniki take scheduled flights.

Athens (Eleftherios Venizelos International Airport; code ATH; ☎ 210 353 0000; www.aia.gr)
Iraklio (Nikos Kazantzakis International Airport; code HER; ☎ 28102 28401)
Rhodes (Diagoras Airport; code RHO; ☎ 22410 83222)
Thessaloniki (Macedonia International Airport; code SKG; ☎ 2310 473 700)

Athens handles the vast majority of flights, including all intercontinental traffic. Thessaloniki has direct flights to Amsterdam, Belgrade, Berlin, Brussels, Cyprus, Düsseldorf, Frankfurt, İstanbul, London, Milan, Moscow, Munich, Paris, Stuttgart, Tirana, Vienna and Zürich. Most of these flights are with Greece's national airline, Olympic Airlines, or whichever flag carrier of the country concerned.

Iraklio has direct flights to Cyprus with Olympic, while Aegean Airlines flies direct to Paris, Germany and Italy.

Some airlines with offices in Athens:

Aeroflot (SU; ☎ 210 322 0986; www.aeroflot.org)
Air Berlin (AB; ☎ 210 353 5264; www.airberlin.com)
Air Canada (AC; ☎ 210 617 5321; www.aircanada.ca)
Air France (AF; ☎ 210 353 0380; www.airfrance.com)
Alitalia (AZ; ☎ 210 353 4284; www.alitalia.it)
American Airlines (AA; ☎ 210 331 1045; www.aa.com)
British Airways (BA; ☎ 210 890 6666; www.britishairways.com)
Cyprus Airways (CY; ☎ 210 372 2722; www.cyprusair.com.cy)
Delta Airlines (DL; ☎ 210 331 1660; www.delta.com)
easyJet (U2; ☎ 210 967 0000; www.easyjet.com)
EgyptAir (MS; ☎ 210 353 1272; www.egyptair.com.eg)
El Al (LY; ☎ 210 353 1003; www.elal.co.il)
Emirates Airlines (EK; ☎ 210 933 3400; www.emirates.com)
Gulf Air (GF; ☎ 210 322 0851; www.gulfairco.com)
Iberia (IB; ☎ 210 323 4523; www.iberia.com)

TRANSPORT

CLIMATE CHANGE & TRAVEL

Climate change is a serious threat to the ecosystems that humans rely upon, and air travel is the fastest-growing contributor to the problem. Lonely Planet regards travel, overall, as a global benefit, but believes we all have a responsibility to limit our personal impact on global warming.

Flying & Climate Change

Pretty much every form of motor travel generates CO_2 (the main cause of human-induced climate change) but planes are far and away the worst offenders, not just because of the sheer distances they allow us to travel, but because they release greenhouse gases high into the atmosphere. The statistics are frightening: two people taking a return flight between Europe and the US will contribute as much to climate change as an average household's gas and electricity consumption over a whole year.

Carbon Offset Schemes

Climatecare.org and other websites use 'carbon calculators' that allow jetsetters to offset the greenhouse gases they are responsible for with contributions to energy-saving projects and other climate-friendly initiatives in the developing world – including projects in India, Honduras, Kazakhstan and Uganda.

Lonely Planet, together with Rough Guides and other concerned partners in the travel industry, supports the carbon offset scheme run by climatecare.org. Lonely Planet offsets all of its staff and author travel.

For more information check out our website: lonelyplanet.com.

Japan Airlines (JL; ☎ 210 324 8211; www.jal.co.jp)
KLM (KL; ☎ 210 353 1295; www.klm.com)
Lufthansa (LH; ☎ 210 617 5200; www.lufthansa.com)
Qatar Airways (QR; ☎ 210 950 8700; www.qatar airways.com)
SAS (SK; ☎ 210 361 3910; www.sas.se)
Singapore Airlines (SQ; ☎ 210 372 8000, 210 353 1259; www.singaporeair.com)
Thai Airways (TG; ☎ 210 353 1237; www.thaiairways .com)
Turkish Airlines (TK; ☎ 210 322 1035; www.turkish airlines.com)
Virgin Express (TV; ☎ 210 949 0777; www.virgin -express.com)

Other international airports that service the islands are found on Mykonos, Hania (Crete), Kos, Karpathos, Limnos, Chios, Corfu, Samos, Skiathos, Aktion (for Lefkada), Karpathos, Kefallonia, Limnos, Santorini (Thira) and Zakynthos. These airports are used exclusively for charter flights, mostly from the UK, Germany and Scandinavia. Charter flights also fly to all of Greece's other international airports.

Olympic Airlines (OA; ☎ 2013 569 111; www.olympic airlines.com) is the country's national airline. Olympic is no longer Greece's only international airline. **Aegean Airlines** (A3; ☎ 8111 120 000; www .aegeanair.com) flies direct from Athens to Cairo, Larnaka, Milan, and Rome via Thessaloniki to Bucharest, Düsseldorf, Frankfurt, Munich, Sofia and Stuttgart.

Contact details for local Olympic and Aegean offices are listed in the appropriate sections throughout this book.

Asia

Most Asian countries offer fairly competitive deals, with Bangkok, Singapore and Hong Kong the best places to shop around for discount tickets.

Khao San Rd in Bangkok is the budget travellers' headquarters. Bangkok has a number of excellent travel agents, but there are also some suspect ones; ask the advice of other travellers before handing over your cash.

In Singapore you can find competitive discount fares for most destinations. Singapore, like Bangkok, has hundreds of travel agents, so it is possible to compare prices on flights. Chinatown Point shopping centre on New Bridge Rd has a good selection of travel agents.

Hong Kong has a number of excellent, reliable travel agencies and some that are not so reliable. A good way to check on a travel agent is to look it up in the phone book: fly-by-night operators don't usually stay around long enough to get listed.

TRANSPORT

Australia

There are plenty of well-established travel agencies in every city and town throughout the country. Visit your favourite one and book while you wait.

Qantas no longer flies direct to Athens, but you can use the Australian carrier to a European destination like London and fly with a partner airline, such as British Airways, back to Athens. Singapore Airlines has the best overall connections to Athens from Australian cities as well as a deserved reputation for good service.

Up and coming Middle Eastern airlines such as Qatar Airways or Emirates provide a handy link to Greece via Singapore with the option of a stopover in Doha or Dubai.

Canada

Canada has travel agencies galore in all major cities and towns. For online bookings you might like to check out www.expedia.ca or www.travelocity.ca.

Olympic Airlines has two flights weekly from Toronto to Athens via Montreal. There are no direct flights from Vancouver, but there are connecting flights via Toronto, Amsterdam, Frankfurt and London on Canadian Airlines, KLM, Lufthansa and British Airways.

Continental Europe

Athens is linked to every major city in Europe by either Olympic Airlines, Aegean Airlines or the flag carrier of each country. Commonly the cheapest way to get to Greece is via a charter flight, which may or may not have accommodation deals built in to the ticketed price.

Some handy websites:

Airfair (www.airfair.nl)
My Travel (www.mytravel.nl)
Nouvelles Frontières (www.nouvelles-frontieres.fr)
OTU Voyages (www.otu.fr)
STA Travel (www.statravel.de)
Voyageurs du Monde (www.vdm.com)

Cyprus

Olympic Airlines, Aegean Airlines and Cyprus Airways service the busy Cyprus-Greece routes. All airlines have flights daily from Larnaka to Athens, and there are five flights weekly to Thessaloniki. Cyprus Airways also flies from Pafos to Athens once a week in winter, and twice a week in summer, while Olympic has two flights weekly between Larnaka and Iraklio.

Turkey

Olympic Airlines and Turkish Airlines share the İstanbul–Athens route, with at least one flight a day each. There are no direct flights from Ankara to Athens; all flights go via İstanbul.

UK & Ireland

Discount air travel is big business in London. Advertisements for several travel agencies appear in the travel pages of the weekend broadsheet newspapers, such as the *Independent* on Saturday and the *Sunday Times*. Look out for the free magazines, such as *TNT*, which are widely available in London – start by looking outside the main train and underground stations.

For students or travellers under 26 discount 'student fares' may be available. Charter flights can work out as a cheaper alternative to scheduled flights, especially if you do not qualify for the under-26 and student discounts.

British Airways, Olympic Airlines and Virgin Atlantic operate daily flights between London and Athens. Pricing is very competitive. British Airways has flights from Edinburgh, Glasgow and Manchester.

The cheapest scheduled flights are with **easyJet** (☎ 087-1750 0100; www.easyjet.com), the no-frills specialist, which has flights from Luton and Gatwick to Athens. There are numerous charter flights between the UK and Greece.

Some websites to explore with online booking options:

ebookers (www.ebookers.com)
STA Travel (www.statravel.co.uk)
Trailfinders (www.trailfinders.co.uk)

USA

New York has the widest range of flight options to Athens. The route to Europe is very competitive and there are new deals almost every day. Both Olympic Airlines and Delta Airlines have direct flights but there are numerous other connecting flights.

There are no direct flights to Athens from the west coast. There are, however, connecting flights to Athens from many US cities, either linking with Olympic Airlines in New York or flying with one of the European national airlines to their home country, and then on to Athens.

LAND
Border Crossings
ALBANIA

There are four crossing points between Greece and Albania. The main one is at Kakavia, 60km northwest of Ioannina. The others are at Krystallopigi, 14km west of Kotas on the Florina–Kastoria road; at Mertziani, 17km west of Konitsa; and at Sagiada 28km north of Igoumenitsa.

BULGARIA

There are three Bulgarian border crossings: one at Promahonas, 109km northeast of Thessaloniki and 41km from Serres; one at Ormenio, in northeastern Thrace; and a new 448m-long tunnel border crossing at Exohi 50km north of Drama.

FORMER YUGOSLAV REPUBLIC OF MACEDONIA (FYROM)

There are three border crossings between Greece and FYROM. One is at Evzoni, 68km north of Thessaloniki. This is the main highway to Skopje, which continues to Belgrade. Another border crossing is at Niki, 16km north of Florina. This road leads to Bitola and continues to Ohrid. The third one is at Doïrani, 31km north of Kilkis.

TURKEY

Crossing points are at Kipi, 43km northeast of Alexandroupoli, and at Kastanies, 139km northeast of Alexandroupoli. Kipi is probably more convenient if you're heading for İstanbul, but the route through Kastanies goes via the fascinating towns of Soufli and Didymotiho, in Greece, and Edirne (ancient Adrianople) in Turkey.

Albania
BUS

The Greek Railways Organisation (OSE) operates a daily bus between Athens and Tirana (€35.20) via Ioannina and Gjirokastra. The bus departs Athens daily from Sidiridromou 1 near the Larisis train station, arriving in Tirana the following day.

Bulgaria
BUS

OSE runs a bus from Athens to Sofia (€45.50, 15 hours) at 7am daily, except Monday. It also runs Thessaloniki–Sofia buses (€19, 7½ hours, four daily). There is a private service to

Plovdiv (€29.50, six hours) and Sofia (€35.50, seven hours) from Alexandroupoli on Wednesday and Sunday at 8.30am.

TRAIN

There is a daily train to Sofia from Athens (€32, 18 hours) via Thessaloniki (€18, nine hours). From Sofia, there are connections to Budapest (€68) and Bucharest (€39).

Former Yugoslav Republic of Macedonia
TRAIN

There are two trains daily from Thessaloniki to Skopje (€12, five hours), crossing the border between Idomeni and Gevgelija. They continue from Skopje to the Serbian capital of Belgrade (€30, 13 hours).

There are no trains between Florina and FYROM, although there are one or two trains a day to Skopje from Bitola (€6, 4½ hours) on the FYROM side of the border.

Russia
TRAIN

There is one summer-only train service a week from Thessaloniki to Moscow. It departs Thessaloniki at 7.42am on Sunday and arrives in Moscow at 5.26am on Wednesday. It departs Moscow for the return trip at 11.32pm on the same day. The cost is €147.80 for a berth in a three-bed cabin.

Turkey
BUS

The OSE operates a bus from Athens to İstanbul (22 hours) daily except Wednesday, leaving the former Peloponnese train station in Athens at 7pm and travelling via Thessaloniki and Alexandroupoli.

One-way fares are €67.50 from Athens, €44 from Thessaloniki and €15 from Alexandroupoli. Students qualify for a 20% discount and children under 12 travel for half-fare. See the Getting There & Away sections for each city for information on where to buy tickets.

Buses from İstanbul to Athens leave the Anadolu Terminal (Anatolia Terminal) at the Topkapı *otogar* (bus station) at 10am daily except Sunday.

TRAIN

There are no direct trains between Athens and İstanbul. Travellers must take a train to Thessaloniki and connect with one of two daily services running to the Turkish city. The best option is the *Filia–Tostluk Express* service leaving Thessaloniki at 8pm (€48.25, 11½ hours) and arriving in İstanbul at 7.30am.

The other service is the indirect intercity IC90 service to Orestiada leaving Thessaloniki at 7am; passengers for İstanbul change at Pythio on the Greece–Turkey border.

Western Europe

Overland travel between Western Europe and Greece is nowadays usually confined to heading to an Italian port and picking up the most geographically convenient ferry. While quite feasible, the route through Croatia, Serbia and the Former Yugoslav Republic of Macedonia is outweighed by the convenience of a 'minicruise' from an Italian port to one of Greece's two main entry ports, and the avoidance of fuel and hotel costs on the trip down through the Balkan peninsula.

BUS

There are no bus services to Greece from the UK, nor from anywhere else in northern Europe. Bus companies can no longer compete with cheap air fares.

CAR & MOTORCYCLE

Most intending drivers these days drive to an Italian port and take a ferry to Greece. The most convenient port is Venice with Ancona coming a close second. The route through Croatia, Serbia and the Former Yugoslav Republic of Macedonia takes on average 2½ days from Venice to Athens, whereas a high-speed ferry from Venice to Patra can be completed in around 26 hours. From Patra to Athens is a further 3½ hours driving.

TRAIN

Unless you have a Eurail pass or are under the age of 26 and eligible for a discounted fare, travelling to Greece by train is prohibitively expensive. Indeed, the chances of anyone wanting to travel from London to Athens by train are considered so remote, it's no longer possible to buy a single ticket for this journey. The trip involves travelling from London to Paris on the *Eurostar*, followed by Paris to Brindisi, then a ferry from Brindisi to Patra – and finally a train from Patra to Athens.

Greece is a part of the Eurail network. Eurail passes can only be bought by residents of non-European countries and are supposed to be purchased before arriving in Europe. They can, however, be bought in Europe as long as your passport proves that you've been there for less than six months. In London, head for the **Rail Europe Travel Centre** (☎ 087-0584 8848; 179 Piccadilly). Check the Eurail website (www.eurail .com) for full details of passes and prices.

If you are starting your European travels in Greece, you can buy your Eurail pass from the OSE office (Karolou 1) in Athens (see p85), and at the stations in Patra and Thessaloniki.

Greece is also part of the **Inter-Rail** (www .interrailnet.com) pass system, available to residents in Europe for six months or more.

SEA
Albania

Corfu-based **Petrakis Lines** (☎ 26610 38690; www .ionian-cruises.com) has daily hydrofoils to the Albanian port of Saranda (€15, 25 minutes).

Cyprus & Israel

Passenger services from Greece to Cyprus and Israel have been suspended indefinitely. **Salamis Lines** (www.viamare.com/salamis) still operates the route, but carries only vehicles and freight.

Italy

There are ferries to Greece from the Italian ports of Ancona, Bari, Brindisi and Venice. For more information about these services, see the Patra, Igoumenitsa, Corfu and Kefallonia sections.

The ferries can get very crowded in summer. If you want to take a vehicle across it's necessary to make a reservation beforehand.

You'll find all the latest information about ferry routes, schedules and services on the internet. For an overview try logging on to www.greekferries.gr.

Most of the ferry companies have their own websites where you can make online bookings.

Agoudimos Lines (www.agoudimos-lines.com)
ANEK Lines (www.anek.gr)
Blue Star Ferries (www.bluestarferries.com)
Fragline (www.fragline.gr)
Hellenic Mediterranean Lines (www.hml.gr)
Italian Ferries (www.italianferries.it)
Minoan Lines (www.minoan.gr)
Superfast Ferries (www.superfast.com)
Ventouris Ferries (www.ventouris.gr)

The ferry services listed here are for high season (July and August), and prices are for one-way deck class. Deck class on these services means exactly that. If you want a reclining, aircraft-type seat, expect to pay 10% to 15% on top of the listed fares. All companies offer discounts for return travel. Prices are about 30% less in the low season.

ANCONA

The route to Igoumenitsa and Patra has become increasingly popular in recent years. There can be up to three boats daily in summer and at least one a day year round. All ferry operators in Ancona have booths at the *stazione marittima* (ferry terminal) off Piazza Candy, where you can pick up timetables and price lists and make bookings.

Blue Star Ferries and Superfast Ferries have two boats daily, taking 19 hours direct to Patra, or 21 hours via Igoumenitsa. Both charge €80 and sell tickets through **Morandi & Co** (☎ 071-20 20 33; Via XXIX Settembre 2/0). Superfast accepts Eurail passes. **ANEK Lines** (☎ 071-207 23 46; Via XXIX Settembre 2/0; €68) and **Minoan** (☎ 071-20 17 08; Via Astagno 3; €72) do the trip daily in 21 hours via Igoumenitsa.

BARI

Superfast Ferries (☎ 080-52 11 416; Corso de Tullio 6) has daily sailings to Patra via Corfu and Igoumenitsa, and also accepts Eurail passes.

Ventouris Ferries (☎ 080-521 7609) has daily boats to Corfu (10 hours) and Igoumenitsa (11½ hours) for €53.

BRINDISI

The trip from Brindisi was once the most popular crossing, but it now operates only between April and early October. **Med Link** (Discovery Shipping; ☎ 0831-54 81 16/7; Costa Morena) and **Hellenic Mediterranean Lines** (☎ 0831-54 80 01; Costa Morena) offer at least one boat a day to Patra between them.

Hellenic Mediterranean calls at Igoumenitsa on the way, and also has services that call at Corfu, Kefallonia, Paxi and Zakynthos, while Med Link calls at Kefallonia during July and August. All these services cost €50. Hellenic Mediterranean accepts Eurail passes, and issues vouchers for travel with Med Link on days when there is no Hellenic Mediterranean service.

Agoudimos Lines (☎ 0831-55 01 80; Via Provinciale per Lecce 29) and **Fragline** (☎ 0831-54 85 40; Via Spalato 31) sail only to Igoumenitsa.

Italian Ferries (www.italianferries.it) operates high-speed catamaran services to Corfu (€57 to €85, 3¼ hours) and Paxi (€73 to €110, 4¾ hours) daily from July to mid-September.

VENICE

Minoan Lines (☎ 041-24 07 177; Stazione Marittima 123) has boats to Patra (€74, 29 hours) four times weekly, calling at Corfu and Igoumenitsa. **Blue Star Ferries** (☎ 041-277 0559; Stazione Marittima 123) sails the route four times weekly for €64.

Turkey

There are five regular ferry services between Turkey's Aegean coast and the Greek islands. Tickets for all ferries to Turkey must be bought a day in advance. You'll be asked to turn in your passport the night before the trip but don't worry, you'll get it back the next day before you board the boat. Port tax for departures to Turkey is €9.

See the relevant sections under individual island entries for more information.

CHIOS

There are daily Chios-Çeşme boats from July to September, dropping back to two boats a week in winter. Tickets cost €22/25 one way/return. Port tax is extra.

KOS

There are daily ferries in summer from Kos to Bodrum (ancient Halicarnassus) in Turkey. Boats leave at 8.30am and return at 4.30pm. The one-hour journey costs €34. Port tax is extra.

LESVOS

There are up to four boats weekly from Lesvos to Turkey in high season. Tickets cost €35 one way or return, including port taxes.

In addition to these services, see the Kastellorizo (p304) and Symi (p307) sections of the Dodecanese chapter for information about excursion boats to Turkey.

RHODES

There are daily catamarans from Rhodes to Marmaris from June to September, dropping back to maybe only three or four services a week in winter. Tickets cost €31 one way, plus €19 Turkish arrival tax. In addition, there is a weekly passenger and car ferry service once a week on Friday at 4pm. The cost of ferrying a car to the Turkish mainland is €95 one way, while passengers pay €49 including taxes. Return rates usually work out cheaper.

SAMOS

There are two boats daily to Kuşadası (for Ephesus) from Samos in summer, dropping to one or two boats weekly in winter. Tickets cost €47 return, €37 one way. Port tax is €10.

GETTING AROUND

The Greek islands are an easy place to travel around thanks to a comprehensive maritime transport system.

Buses are a mainstay of island transport, with a network that reaches out to the smallest villages. To most visitors, though, travelling around the Greek islands means island-hopping on the multitude of ferries that criss-cross the Adriatic and the Aegean. If you're in a hurry, the islands also have an extensive domestic air network.

The information in this chapter was for the 2007 high season. You'll find lots of travel information on the internet. The website www.ellada.com has lots of useful links, including airline timetables.

AIR
Airlines in Greece

The vast majority of domestic flights are handled by the country's national carrier, **Olympic Airlines** (☎ 801 11 44 444; www.olympicairlines.com), together with its offshoot, Olympic Aviation. Olympic has offices wherever there are flights, as well as in other major towns.

Olympic also offers cheaper options between Athens and some of the more popular destinations such as Corfu, Iraklio, Lesvos, Rhodes and Thessaloniki. There are discounts for return tickets for travel between Monday and Thursday, and bigger discounts for trips that include a Saturday night away. You'll find full details on its website, as well as information on timetables.

The baggage allowance on all domestic flights is 15kg, or 20kg if the domestic flight is part of an international journey. Olympic offers a 25% student discount on domestic flights, but only if the flight is part of an international journey.

For more information on Olympic Airline's domestic routes, see p84.

Crete-based **Aegean Airlines** (☎ 801 11 20 000, 210 626 1000; www.aegeanair.com) offers flights from Athens to Corfu, Hania, Iraklio, Lesvos, Mykonos, Rhodes, and Santorini; from Thes-

saloniki to Iraklio, Lesvos, Mykonos, Rhodes and Santorini; and from Iraklio to Rhodes.

Full-fare economy costs much the same as Olympic, but Aegean often has special deals. It offers a 20% youth discount for travellers under 26, and a similar discount for the over-60s.

AirSea Lines (☎ 26610 49800; www.airsealines.com) is a seaplane service that runs flights between Corfu and Paxi, Lefkada, Ithaki and Patra. It also runs a service between Lavrio in Attica and Kos in the Dodecanese via Mykonos and Kalymnos.

Sky Express (☎ 28102 23500; www.skyexpress.gr) has daily flights from Iraklio to Rhodes and Santorini and up to three flights a week from Iraklio to Mytilini, Kos, Samos, Ikaria.

There is a comprehensive and useful website for Athens' Eleftherios Venizelos International Airport at www.aia.gr.

BICYCLE

Cycling is a cheap, healthy, environmentally sound and, above all, fun way of travelling around the Greek islands.

Crete is now a popular destination for cycling fans, but you'll find cyclists wherever the roads are good enough to get around. Most of them are foreigners; few locals show much enthusiasm for pedalling.

The time of year is an important consideration. It can get hot to cycle around in full summer and it can be very cold in winter, but for the rest of the year conditions are ideal. Frequent cooling winds on the Aegean Islands can bring some relief in summer.

If you want a decent touring bike, you should bring your own. Bicycles pose few problems for airlines unless you fly with one of the small carriers.

You can take it to pieces and put it in a bike bag or box, but it's much easier simply to wheel your bike to the check-in desk, where it should be treated as a piece of baggage. You may have to remove the pedals and turn the handlebars sideways so that it takes up less space in the aircraft's hold; check all this with the airline well in advance. Bikes are carried free of charge on ferries.

One note of caution: before you leave home, go over your bike with a fine-toothed comb and fill your repair kit with every imaginable spare part. As with cars and motorbikes, you won't necessarily be able to buy spares for your machine if it breaks down in the middle of nowhere.

For more information on cycling the Greek islands, see p66.

Hire
You can hire bicycles on only a few islands. Prices range from €6 to €12 per day, depending on the type and age of the bike. Only a few major islands sell bikes, eg Crete, Rhodes, Kos and Corfu, and prices are similar to the rest of EU Europe.

BOAT
Catamaran
High-speed catamarans have become an important part of the island travel scene. They are just as fast as hydrofoils – if not faster – and more comfortable. They are also less prone to cancellation in rough weather. Fares are the same as for hydrofoils.

Hellenic Seaways is the major player. It operates giant, vehicle-carrying cats from Piraeus and Rafina to the Cyclades, and smaller Flying Cats from Rafina to the central and northern Cyclades and on many routes around the Saronic Gulf.

Blue Star Ferries operates its Seajet catamarans on the run from Rafina to Tinos, Mykonos and Paros.

Dodekanisos Seaways (Map p282; ☎ 22410 70590; www.12ne.gr; Afstralias 3) operates two luxurious Norwegian-built passenger catamarans between Rhodes and Patmos in the Dodecanese.

Most services are very popular; book as far in advance as possible, especially if you want to travel on weekends.

Ferry
For most people, travel in Greece means island-hopping. Ferries are becoming more modern and comfortable and while class seating is more or less a thing of the past on older ferries, the closed catamaran-style ferries offer economy-, business- and even luxury-class seating.

Every island will have a ferry service of some sort or other, although in winter services to some of the smaller islands are fairly skeletal. The services start to pick up again from April onwards, and by July and August there are countless services crisscrossing the Aegean. Ferries come in all shapes and sizes, from the giant 'superferries' that work the major routes to the small, ageing, open ferries that chug around the backwaters.

The main ferry companies in Greece:
ANEK Lines (☎ 210 419 7420; www.anek.gr) Serving Italy and Crete.
Blue Star Ferries (☎ 210 891 9800; www.bluestar ferries.com) Serving Italy, Crete, Cyclades and the Dodecanese.
GA Ferries (☎ 210 419 9100; www.gaferries.com) Mainly serving the Cyclades.
Hellenic Seaways (☎ 210 419 9000; www.hellenic seaways.gr) Serving the Sporades and Cyclades.
Italian Ferries (www.italianferries.it) Serving Italy.

A SEA CHANGE
Following the sinking of the F/B *Express Samina* off Paros on 26 September 2000 and the subsequent tragic loss of 82 human lives, Greece's domestic ferry scene has undergone a radical transformation. Almost gone are the days of slow rust buckets that made Greek domestic ferry travel an experience to endure rather than enjoy. Sure, there are still a number of slow boats pounding the sea routes between islands and they are fun in an almost anachronistic way – especially if you have time – but you can now travel in serious comfort if you want to arrive at your island relaxed and rested. The sleek, fast ferries and catamarans are more like planes these days. They offer first-, business- and traveller-class seating, no-smoking sections (!), videos, cafeterias and bars. There is, however, a trade-off. You are essentially seat-bound for the duration of your trip as there are no decks to stroll on, no swimming pools to dip into or benches to park a sleeping bag on.

The high-speed ferries, such as those run by Minoan Lines and Blue Star Ferries, are a better option. They offer all of the above, but are more like conventional ferries. Not as fast as the former they are still very fast and make travel from one end of the Aegean to the other a breeze. The payback is that ferry travel can now be quite expensive, especially if you want a bed for the night in a cabin. The cost of a cabin bed from Piraeus to Rhodes can be noticeably more expensive than a discounted airline ticket. Still, if you long for the old days, you can still find the smoke-filled cafeterias with three TVs all showing different programmes, the insalubrious bathrooms and chug-a-lug voyages across the seas – just choose carefully. The sea change afoot in Greek waters means that those experiences will soon be limited to travellers' memories only.

TRANSPORT

FERRY ROUTES

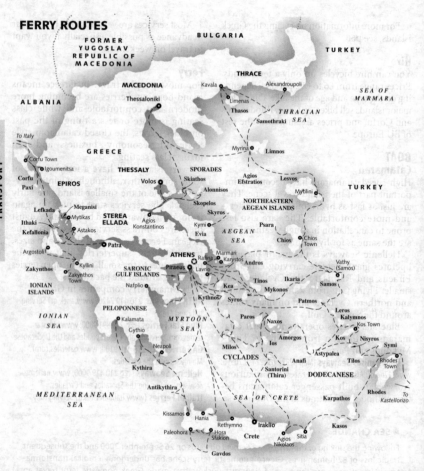

LANE Lines (☎ 210 427 4011; www.lane.gr) Serving Rhodes via Milos, Crete, Kasos, Karpathos and Halki.
Minoan Lines (☎ 210 414 5700; www.minoan.gr) Serving Italy and Crete.
NEL Lines (☎ 22510 26299; www.nel.gr) Serving the Northeastern Aegean Islands.

CLASSES

Classes are largely a thing of the past. The public spaces on the more modern ferries are generally open to all and sundry. What does differ is the level of accommodation. Your 'deck class' ticket typically gives you access to the deck and interior with no accommodation option. Next up, aeroplane-type seats give you a reclining seat in which to relax and hopefully sleep. Then come various shades of cabin

accommodation: four-berth, three-berth or two-berth interior cabins are cheaper than their equivalent outside cabins with a porthole. Then there are luxury cabins with a view to the front of the ship, and which resemble standard cruise-ship cabins.

Deck class remains an economical way to travel, while a luxury cabin ticket will inevitably cost more than an airline ticket to the same destination. On the deck you can usually pitch a sleeping bag and pillow; in a cabin you will sleep in comfort. Many modern high-speed ferries have limited outside deck space so you may find yourself juggling for floor or lounge seat space to sleep.

Children under four travel for free, while children between four and 10 pay half-fare.

Full fares apply for children over 10. Unless you state otherwise, you will automatically be given deck class when purchasing a ticket. Prices quoted in this book are for deck-class tickets.

COSTS

Prices are fixed by the government and are determined by the distance of the destination from the port of origin. The small differences in price you may find at ticket agencies are the results of some agents sacrificing part of their designated commission to qualify as a 'discount service'. The discount is seldom more than €0.50. Ticket prices include embarkation tax, a contribution to NAT (the seaperson's union) and 10% VAT.

ROUTES

Ferries for the Ionian Islands leave from the Peloponnese ports of Patra (p98; for Kefallonia, Ithaki, Paxi and Corfu) and Kyllini (p99; for Kefallonia and Zakynthos); and from Igoumenitsa (p98; for Corfu and Paxi) in Epiros.

Ferries heading for the Sporades leave from Volos (p101), Thessaloniki (p94), Agios Konstantinos (p99), and Kymi (p419) on Evia (for Skyros only). The latter two ports are easily reached by bus from Athens.

Some of the Northeastern Aegean Islands have connections with Thessaloniki and Piraeus. The odd ones out are Thasos (p407), which is reached from Kavala (p103), and occasionally from Samothraki, which can be reached from Alexandroupoli (p105) year-round and also from Kavala (p103) in summer.

SCHEDULES

Ferry timetables change from year to year and season to season, and can be subject to delays and cancellations at short notice due to bad weather, strikes or the boats simply conking out. No timetable is infallible, but the comprehensive weekly list of departures from Piraeus put out by the EOT (Greek National Tourist Office) in Athens is as accurate as is humanly possible. The people to go to for the most up-to-date ferry information are the local *limenarheio* (port police), whose offices are usually on or near the quay.

There's lots of information about ferry services available on the internet. Try www .greekferries.gr, which has a useful search programme and links, or www.gtp.gr. Many of the larger ferry companies have their own sites (see p509).

Throughout the year there is at least one ferry a day from a mainland port to the major island in each group, and during the high season (from June to mid-September) there are considerably more. Ferries sailing from one island group to another are not so frequent, and if you're going to travel in this way you'll need to plan carefully, otherwise you may end up having to backtrack to Piraeus.

Travelling time varies considerably from one ferry to another, depending on how many islands you decide to visit on the way to your destination. For example, the Piraeus–Rhodes trip can take between 15 and 18 hours depending on which route is taken. Before buying your ticket, check how many stops the boat is going to make and its estimated arrival time. It can make a big difference.

TICKET PURCHASE

Given that ferries are prone to delays and cancellations, it's best not to purchase a ticket until it has been confirmed that the ferry is leaving. If you need to reserve a car space, however, you may need to pay in advance. If the service is then cancelled you can transfer your ticket to the next available service with that company.

Agencies selling tickets line the waterfront of most ports, but rarely is there one that sells tickets for every boat, and often an agency is reluctant to give you information about a boat they do not sell tickets for. This means you have to check the timetables displayed outside each agency to find out which ferry is next to depart – or ask the port police.

High-Speed Ferries

These supermodern leviathans can slash travel times on some of the longer routes. **NEL Lines** (☎ 22510 26299; www.ferries.gr/nel) leads the way with its futuristic-looking F/B *Panagia Thalassini* and F/B *Aeolos Kenteris II*, which operate from Piraeus to Syros, Tinos, Mykonos, Paros, Naxos, Lavrio, Kythnos and Amorgos. There is, in addition, a high-speed service with the F/B *Aeolos Kenteris I* to Rethymo on Crete. These services cost roughly twice as much as standard ferries.

Blue Star Ferries (☎ 210 891 9800; www.bluestar ferries.com) is up there in almost the same league, and its fleet of modernistic boats serves many destinations in the Cycladic and Dodecanese islands cutting travelling time down considerably. It charges about 20% more than the regular ferries.

Hydrofoil

Hydrofoils used to be popular on the Greek transport scene but have seen their heyday come and go. They have been replaced in the main by more comfortable and just as fast catamarans and jet boats. They now exist in isolation in some of the more remoter parts of the Aegean archipelago.

Aegean Flying Dolphins (☎ 210 422 1766), based on Samos, links that island with Kos in the Dodecanese and islands in between. Other hydrofoil routes operate between Kavala and Thasos in the northeastern Aegean, and from Alexandroupoli to Samothraki and Limnos. **Hellenic Seaways** (☎ 210 419 9000; www.hellenicseaways.gr) operates hydrofoils on some of its Sporades services.

Tickets cannot be bought on board hydrofoils – you must buy them in advance from an agent.

Inter-island Boat

In addition to the large ferries that ply between the mainland ports and island groups, there are smaller boats that link islands within a group, and occasionally, an island in one group with an island in another.

In the past these boats were invariably caïques – sturdy old fishing boats – but gradually these are being replaced by new purpose-built boats, which are called express or excursion boats. Tickets tend to cost more than tickets for the large ferries, but the boats are useful if you're island-hopping.

Water Taxi

Most islands have water taxis – small speedboats that operate like taxis, transporting people to difficult-to-get-to places. Some owners charge a set price for each person, others charge a flat rate for the boat, and this cost is divided by the number of passengers. Either way, prices are usually quite reasonable.

BUS

All long-distance buses on the mainland and the islands are operated by regional collectives known as **KTEL** (Koino Tamio Eispraxeon Leoforion; www.ktel.org). Every prefecture on the mainland has

a KTEL, which operates local services within the prefecture and services to the main towns of other prefectures. Fares are fixed by the government.

Island Buses

Island services are less simple to summarise! There's an enormous difference in the level of services. Crete (which is split into three prefectures) is organised in the same way as the mainland – each prefecture has its own KTEL providing local services and services to the main towns of other prefectures. Most islands have just one bus company, some have just one bus.

On islands where the capital is inland, buses normally meet the boats. Some of the more remote islands have not yet acquired a bus, but most have some sort of motorised transport – even if it is only a bone-shaking, three-wheeled truck.

Mainland Buses

The network is comprehensive. All major ports on the mainland have daily connections to Athens. The islands of Corfu, Kefallonia and Zakynthos can also be reached directly from Athens by bus – the fares include the price of the ferry ticket. For details, see p84.

When you buy a ticket you will be allotted a seat number, which is noted on the ticket. The seat number is indicated on the back of each seat of the bus, not on the back of the seat in front; this can cause confusion among Greeks and tourists alike. You can board a bus without a ticket and pay on board, but this may mean that you have to stand. Keep your ticket for the duration of the journey; it will be checked en route.

Buses do not have toilets or refreshments on board, so make sure you are prepared on both counts. Buses stop about every three hours on long journeys. Smoking is prohibited on all buses in Greece.

Bus travel is reasonably priced. Following are fares and journey times on some of the major routes.

Route	Duration	Fare
Athens–Thessaloniki	7½hr	€31
Athens–Patra	3hr	€16
Athens–Volos	5hr	€20
Athens–Corfu*	5hr	€44
* including ferry		

CAR & MOTORCYCLE

Many of the islands are capacious enough to warrant having your own vehicle. Roads have improved enormously in recent years, particularly on the larger, more-visited islands, such as Crete.

Few people bother to bring their own vehicle from Europe; there are plenty of places to hire cars.

Almost all islands are served by car ferries. Some sample prices for small vehicles include Piraeus–Mykonos (€76); Piraeus–Crete (Hania and Iraklio; €79); and Piraeus–Samos (€81). The charge for a large motorbike is about the same as the price of a 3rd-class passenger ticket.

Petrol in Greece is cheaper than in most other European countries, but by American or Australian standards it is more expensive. Prices are generally set by the government but can vary from region to region. Leaded (*super*) and unleaded (*amolyvdi*) is always available, as is diesel (*petreleo kinisis*). Given the unprecedented rises in petrol costs of recent years it would be unwise to give a fixed figure, but by mid-2007 unleaded was hovering around the €1L mark. Diesel is usually cheaper.

Automobile Associations

ELPA (Elliniki Leschi Aftokinitou kai Periigiseon; www.elpa.gr) is Greece's domestic automobile association.

Bring Your Own Vehicle

EU-registered vehicles are allowed free entry into Greece, but may only stay six months without road taxes being due. Only a green card (international third-party insurance) is required. Your only proof of the date of entry – if requested by the police – is your ferry ticket (if coming from Italy), or your passport entry stamp if entering from elsewhere. Non-EU registered vehicles may be logged in your passport.

Driving Licence

Greece requires an International Driving Permit, which should be obtained before you leave home.

Insurance

Insurance is always included in any vehicle hire agreements, but you are advised to check whether it is fully comprehensive or third-party only. Otherwise, you may be up for hefty

---

> ### WARNING
>
> Greece is not the best place to initiate yourself into motorcycling. There are still a lot of gravel roads – particularly on the islands. Novices should be very careful; dozens of tourists have accidents every year. Scooters are particularly prone to sliding on gravelly bends. Choose a motorbike with thinner profile tyres. If you are planning to use a motorcycle or moped, check that your travel insurance covers you for injury resulting from a motorbike accident. Many insurance companies don't offer this cover, so check the fine print!

costs in the event of any damage caused to your vehicle if you are at fault.

Hire

CAR

Rental cars are available almost everywhere, but it's best to hire from major cities where competition lowers the prices. All the multinational companies are represented in Athens, and most have branches in other major towns and tourist destinations. Smaller islands often have only one outlet.

You can find better deals at local companies. Their advertised rates may be up to 50% cheaper, and they are normally more open to negotiation, especially if business is slow.

If you want to take a hire car to another country or onto a ferry, you will need advance written authorisation from the hire company. See the Getting Around sections of cities and islands for details of places to rent cars.

The minimum driving age in Greece is 18 years, but most car-hire firms require you to be at least 21 – or 23 for larger vehicles.

Some of the major car-hire players in Greece:

Avis (☎ 210 322 4951; www.avis.gr)
Budget (☎ 210 349 8800; www.budget.gr)
Europcar (☎ 210 960 2382; www.europcar.gr)
Hertz (☎ 210 626 4000; www.hertz.gr)

MOTORCYCLE

Mopeds and motorcycles are available for hire wherever there are tourists to rent them. In many cases their maintenance has been minimal, so check the machine thoroughly before you hire it – especially the brakes: you'll need them!

Greece has introduced regulations for hiring mopeds and motorcycles – to rent one you must produce a licence that shows proficiency in riding the category of bike you wish to rent; this applies to everything from 50cc up. Standard British driving licences are not sufficient – British citizens must obtain a Category A licence from the DVLA. In most other EU countries separate licences are automatically issued.

Motorbikes are a cheap way to travel around. Rates range from €10 to €15 per day for a moped or 50cc motorbike to €25 per day for a 250cc motorbike. Out of season these prices drop considerably, so use your bargaining skills. By October it is sometimes possible to hire a moped for as little as €5 per day. Most motorcycle hirers include third-party insurance in the price, but it's wise to check this. This insurance will not include medical expenses. Helmets are technically compulsory and rental agencies are obliged to offer one as part of the hire deal. Most riders ignore the regulation and go without.

Road Rules

In Greece, as in continental Europe, you drive on the right and overtake on the left. Outside built-up areas, main road traffic has right of way at intersections. In towns, vehicles coming from the right have right of way. Seat belts must be worn in front seats, and in back seats if the car is fitted with them. Children under 12 years of age are not allowed in the front seat. It's compulsory to carry a first-aid kit, fire extinguisher and warning triangle, and it's forbidden to carry cans of petrol. Helmets are compulsory for motorcyclists if the motorbike is 50cc or more.

Outside residential areas the speed limit is 120km/h on highways, 90km/h on other roads and 50km/h in built-up areas. The speed limit for motorbikes up to 100cc is 70km/h and for larger motorbikes, 90km/h. Drivers exceeding the speed limit by 20% are liable to receive a fine of €60; and by 40%, €150. In practice, most tourists escape with a warning.

The police have also cracked down on drink-driving laws. A blood-alcohol content of 0.05% is liable to incur a fine of €150, and over 0.08% is a criminal offence.

If you are involved in an accident and no-one is hurt, the police will not be required to write a report, but it is advisable to go to a nearby police station and explain what happened. A police report may be required for insurance purposes. If an accident involves injury, a driver who does not stop and does not inform the police may face a prison sentence.

HITCHING

Hitching is never entirely safe in any country in the world, and we don't recommend it. Travellers who decide to hitch should understand that they are taking a small but potentially serious risk. People who do choose to hitch will be safer if they travel in pairs and should let someone know where they are planning to go.

Hitching on the islands is not all that uncommon – even by the locals – as local transport may be poor to nonexistent. So be prepared to pick up, as well as be picked up, if you are using this method to get around. Local hitchers don't stick a thumb up, but rather they point a finger to the ground from an outstretched arm.

LOCAL TRANSPORT
Bus

Most Greek island towns are small enough to get around on foot. The only island towns where tourists are likely to use buses are Corfu Town, Iraklio, Kos Town and Rhodes Town. The procedure for buying tickets for local buses is covered in the Getting Around section for each city.

Metro

Athens is the only city in Greece large enough to warrant the building of an underground system. For information see p86.

Taxi

Taxis are widely available except on the very smallest islands. They are reasonably priced by European standards, especially if three or four people share costs.

Cabs in mainland ports are metered. Flag fall is €1, followed by €0.34 per kilometre (€0.64 per kilometre outside town). These rates double between midnight and 5am. Costs additional to the per-kilometre rate are €3.20 from an airport, €0.86 from a bus, port or train station and €0.32 for each piece of luggage over 10kg.

Island taxis generally do not have meters, so you should always settle on a price before you start off.

TRAIN

None of the islands have trains. On the mainland trains are run by the **Greek Railways Organisation** (Organismos Sidirodromon Ellados; www.ose .gr), referred to as OSE.

Trains are handy for getting to/from a number of mainland ports ie Patra, Piraeus, Volos, Thessaloniki and Alexandroupoli. The network is of a good standard and is being constantly upgraded.

There are two types of service: regular (slow) trains that stop at all stations, and faster intercity trains that link major cities.

Slow trains are the country's cheapest public transport: 2nd-class fares are absurdly cheap, and even 1st class is cheaper than bus travel. Sample journey times and 1st-/2nd-class fares include Athens–Thessaloniki (€24/15.20, 7½

hours) and Thessaloniki–Alexandroupoli (€15/10, seven hours).

Intercity trains linking the major ports are an excellent way to travel. Services aren't always express (Greece is too mountainous for that), but the trains are modern and comfortable.

Some sample intercity train journey times and the 1st-/2nd-class fares are Athens–Thessaloniki (€37.30/27.60, six hours) and Thessaloniki–Alexandroupoli (€21.90/16.20, 5½ hours).

Passes

Eurail and Inter-Rail passes are valid in Greece, but it's not worth buying one if Greece is the only place you plan to use it. The passes can be used for 2nd-class travel on intercity services.

TRANSPORT

Health

CONTENTS

BEFORE YOU GO

Prevention is the key to staying healthy while abroad. A little planning before departure, particularly for pre-existing illnesses, will save trouble later. Bring medications in their original, clearly labelled containers. A signed and dated letter from your physician describing your medical conditions and medications, including generic names, is also a good idea. If carrying syringes or needles, be sure to have a physician's letter documenting their medical necessity. If you are embarking on a long trip, make sure your teeth are OK and take your optical prescription with you.

INSURANCE

If you're an EU citizen, a European Health Insurance Card (EHIC; formerly the E111) covers you for most medical care but not emergency repatriation home or non-emergencies. It is available from health centres, and post offices in the UK. Citizens from other countries should find out if there is a reciprocal arrangement for free medical care between their country and Greece. If you do need health insurance, make sure you get a policy that covers you for the worst possible scenario, such as an accident requiring an emergency flight home. Find out in advance if your insurance plan will make payments directly to providers or reimburse you later for overseas health expenditures.

RECOMMENDED VACCINATIONS

No jabs are required to travel to Greece, but a yellow-fever vaccination certificate is required if you are coming from an infected area. The World Health Organization (WHO) recommends that all travellers should be covered for diphtheria, tetanus, measles, mumps, rubella and polio.

INTERNET RESOURCES

The WHO's publication *International Travel and Health* is revised annually and is available online at www.who.int/ith/. Other useful websites include www.mdtravelhealth.com (travel health recommendations for every country; updated daily), www.fitfortravel .scot.nhs.uk (general travel advice for the layperson), www.ageconcern.org.uk (advice on travel for the elderly) and www.mariestopes .org.uk (information on women's health and contraception).

IN TRANSIT

DEEP VEIN THROMBOSIS (DVT)

Blood clots may form in the legs during flights, chiefly because of prolonged immobility (the longer the flight, the greater the risk). The chief symptom of DVT is swelling or pain of the foot, ankle, or calf, usually but not always on just one side. When a blood clot travels to the lungs, it may cause chest pain and breathing difficulties. Travellers with any of these symptoms should immediately seek medical attention. To prevent the development of DVT on long flights you should walk about the cabin, contract the leg muscles while sitting, drink plenty of fluids and avoid alcohol and tobacco.

JET LAG

To avoid jet lag drink plenty of nonalcoholic fluids and eat light meals. Upon arrival, get exposure to natural sunlight and re-adjust your schedule (for meals, sleep etc) as soon as possible.

IN THE GREEK ISLANDS

AVAILABILITY & COST OF HEALTH CARE

If you need an ambulance in Greece call ☎ 166. There is at least one doctor on every island and larger islands have hospitals. Pharmacies can dispense medicines that are available only on prescription in most European countries, so you can consult a pharmacist for minor ailments.

All this sounds fine but, although medical training is of a high standard in Greece, the public health service is badly underfunded. Hospitals can be overcrowded, hygiene is not always what it should be and relatives are expected to bring in food for the patient – which could be a problem for a tourist. Conditions and treatment are much better in private hospitals, which are expensive. All this means that a good health-insurance policy is essential.

TRAVELLER'S DIARRHOEA

If you develop diarrhoea, be sure to drink plenty of fluids, preferably in the form of an oral rehydration solution, such as dioralyte. If diarrhoea is bloody, persists for more than 72 hours or is accompanied by fever, shaking, chills or severe abdominal pain you should seek medical attention.

ENVIRONMENTAL HAZARDS
Bites, Stings & Insect-Borne Diseases

Keep an eye out for sea urchins lurking around rocky beaches; if you get some of their needles embedded in your skin, olive oil should help to loosen them. If they are not removed they will become infected. You should also be wary of jellyfish, particularly during the months of September and October. Although jellyfish are not lethal in Greece, their stings can hurt. Dousing the affected area with vinegar will deactivate any stingers that have not 'fired'. Calamine lotion, antihistamines and analgesics may help reduce any reaction you experience and relieve the pain of any stings. Much more painful than either of these, but thankfully much rarer, is an encounter with the weever fish. The fish buries itself in the sand of the tidal zone with only its spines protruding, and injects a painful and powerful toxin if trodden on. Soaking your foot in very hot water (which breaks down the poison) should solve the problem.

> **WARNING**
>
> Codeine, which is commonly found in headache preparations, is banned in Greece; check labels carefully, or risk prosecution. There are strict regulations applying to the importation of medicines into Greece, so obtain a certificate from your doctor that outlines any medication you may have to carry into the country with you.

Weever-fish stings can cause permanent local paralysis in the worst case.

Greece's only dangerous snake is the adder. To minimise the possibilities of being bitten, always wear boots, socks and long trousers when walking through undergrowth where snakes may be present. Don't put your hands into holes and crevices, and be careful when collecting firewood. Snake bites do not cause instantaneous death and an antivenin is widely available. Keep the victim calm and still, wrap the bitten limb tightly, as you would for a sprained ankle, and attach a splint to immobilise it. Seek medical help, if possible with the dead snake for identification. Don't attempt to catch the snake if there is a possibility of being bitten again. Tourniquets and sucking out the poison are now comprehensively discredited.

Always check all over your body if you have been walking through a potentially tick-infested area as ticks can cause skin infections and other more serious diseases. If a tick is found attached, press down around the tick's head with tweezers, grab the head and gently pull upwards. Avoid pulling the rear of the tick's body as this may squeeze the tick's gut contents through the attached mouth parts into the skin, increasing the risk of infection and disease.

Greece is now officially rabies-free, however, even if the animal is not rabid, all animal bites should be treated seriously as they can become infected or can result in tetanus.

Mosquitoes can be an annoying problem in Greece so some precautions may be needed, though there is no danger of contracting malaria. The electric plug-in mosquito repellents are usually sufficient – and more bearable than coils – to keep the insects at bay at night. Nonetheless choose accommodation that has flyscreen window-protection wherever possible. Mosquito species can vary as can your reaction to their bites. Mosquitoes in northern Greece can provoke a severe reaction. The Asian tiger mosquito (aedes albopictus) may be encountered in mountainous areas and can be a voracious daytime biter. It is known to carry several viruses, including Eastern equine encephalitis, which can affect the central nervous system and cause severe complications and death. Use protective sprays or lotion if you suspect you are being bitten during the day.

Invisible bedbugs can be a major irritation if encountered. Symptoms are lots of pinprick bites that you may initially assign to mosquitoes – even if you are covered up. There is no protection other then to change to a non-infected bed. Airing the mattress thoroughly in the sun may alleviate the problem.

Heatstroke

Heatstroke occurs following excessive fluid loss with inadequate replacement of fluids and salt. Symptoms of heatstroke include headache, dizziness and tiredness. Dehydration is already happening by the time you feel thirsty – aim to drink sufficient water to produce pale, diluted urine. To treat heatstroke drink water and/or fruit juice, and cool the body with cold water and fans.

Hypothermia

Hypothermia occurs when the body loses heat faster than it can produce it. As ever, proper preparation will reduce the risks of getting it. Even on a hot day in the mountains, the weather can change rapidly so carry water-proof garments, warm layers and a hat, and inform others of your route. Hypothermia starts with shivering, loss of judgment and clumsiness. Unless rewarming occurs, the sufferer deteriorates into apathy, confusion and coma. Prevent further heat loss by seeking shelter, warm dry clothing, hot sweet drinks and shared bodily warmth.

TRAVELLING WITH CHILDREN

Make sure children are up to date with routine vaccinations and discuss possible travel vaccines well before departure as some vaccines are not suitable for children under a year old. Lonely Planet's *Travel with Children* includes travel health advice for younger children.

WOMEN'S HEALTH

Emotional stress, exhaustion and travelling through different time zones can all contribute to an upset in the menstrual pattern.

If using oral contraceptives, remember some antibiotics, diarrhoea and vomiting can stop the pill from working. Time zones, gastrointestinal upsets and antibiotics do not affect injectable contraception.

Travelling during pregnancy is usually possible but always consult your doctor before planning your trip. The most risky times for travel are during the first 12 weeks of pregnancy and after 30 weeks.

SEXUAL HEALTH

Condoms are readily available but emergency contraception may not be, so take the necessary precautions.

Language

CONTENTS

The Greek language is probably the oldest European language, with an oral tradition of 4000 years and a written tradition of approximately 3000 years. Its evolution over the four millennia was characterised by its strength during the golden age of Athens and the Democracy (mid-5th century BC); its use as a lingua franca throughout the Middle Eastern world, spread by Alexander the Great and his successors as far as India during the Hellenistic period (330 BC to AD 100); its adaptation as the language of the new religion, Christianity; its use as the official language of the Eastern Roman Empire; and its proclamation as the language of the Byzantine Empire (380–1453).

Greek maintained its status and prestige during the rise of the European Renaissance and was employed as the linguistic perspective for all contemporary sciences and terminologies during the period of Enlightenment. Today, Greek constitutes a large part of the vocabulary of any Indo-European language, and much of the lexicon of any scientific repertoire.

The modern Greek language is a southern Greek dialect which is now used by most Greek speakers both in Greece and abroad. It is the result of an intralinguistic influence and synthesis of the ancient vocabulary combined with words from Greek regional dialects, namely Cretan, Cypriot and Macedonian.

Greek is spoken throughout Greece by a population of around 10 million, and by some five million Greeks who live abroad.

PRONUNCIATION

All Greek words of two or more syllables have an acute accent which indicates where the stress falls. For instance, άγαλμα (statue) is pronounced *aghalma*, and αγάπη (love) is pronounced *aghapi*. In the following transliterations, italic lettering indicates where stress falls. Note also that **dh** is pronounced as 'th' in 'then' and **gh** is a softer, slightly guttural version of 'g'.

ACCOMMODATION

I'm looking for ...

psa-hno yi·a ...	Ψάχνω για ...
a room	
e·na dho·*ma*·ti·o	ένα δωμάτιο
a hotel	
e·na kse·no·dho·*chi*·o	ένα ξενοδοχείο
a youth hostel	
e·nan kse·*no*·na	έναν ξενώνα
ne·o·ti·tas	νεότητας

Where's a cheap hotel?
pou *i*·ne e·na fti·*no* xe·no·do·*hi*·o
Πού είναι ένα φτηνό ξενοδοχείο;
What's the address?
pya *i*·ne i dhi·*ef*·thin·si
Ποια είναι η διεύθυνση;
Could you write the address, please?
pa·ra·ka·*lo* bo·ri·te na *ghra*·pse·te ti· dhi·*ef*·thin·si
Παρακαλώ, μπορείτε να γράψετε τη διεύθυνση;
Are there any rooms available?
i·*par*·chun e·*lef*·the·ra dho·*ma*·ti·a
Υπάρχουν ελεύθερα δωμάτια;

I'd like to book ...

tha *i*·the·la na *kli*·so ...	Θα ήθελα να κλείσω ...
a bed	
e·na kre·*va*·ti	ένα κρεββάτι
a single room	
e·na mo·*no*·kli·no	ένα μονόκλινο
dho·*ma*·ti·o	δωμάτιο
a double room	
e·na *dhi*·kli·no	ένα δίκλινο
dho·*ma*·ti·o	δωμάτιο

THE GREEK ALPHABET & PRONUNCIATION

Greek	Pronunciation Guide		Example		
A α	a	as in 'father'	αγάπη	a-gha-pi	love
B β	v	as in 'vine'	βήμα	vi-ma	step
Γ γ	gh	like a rough 'g'	γάτα	gha-ta	cat
	y	as in 'yes'	για	ya	for
Δ δ	dh	as in 'there'	δέμα	dhe-ma	parcel
E ε	e	as in 'egg'	ένας	e-nas	one (m)
Z ζ	z	as in 'zoo'	ζώο	zo-o	animal
H η	i	as in 'feet'	ήταν	i-tan	was
Θ θ	th	as in 'throw'	θέμα	the-ma	theme
Ι ι	i	as in 'feet'	ίδιος	i-dhyos	same
Κ κ	k	as in 'kite'	καλά	ka-la	well
Λ λ	l	as in 'leg'	λάθος	la-thos	mistake
M μ	m	as in 'man'	μαμά	ma-ma	mother
N ν	n	as in 'net'	νερό	ne-ro	water
Ξ ξ	x	as in 'ox'	ξύδι	ksi-dhi	vinegar
O o	o	as in 'hot'	όλα	o-la	all
Π π	p	as in 'pup'	πάω	pa-o	I go
P ρ	r	as in 'road'	ρέμα	re-ma	stream
		a slightly trilled 'r'	ρόδα	ro-dha	tyre
Σ σ, ς	s	as in 'sand'	σημάδι	si-ma-dhi	mark
T τ	t	as in 'tap'	τόπος	to-pos	site
Y υ	i	as in 'feet'	ύστερα	is-tera	after
Φ φ	f	as in 'find'	φύλλο	fi-lo	leaf
X χ	kh	as the 'ch' in Scottish 'loch', or	χάνω	kha-no	I lose
		like a rough 'h'	χέρι	he-ri	hand
Ψ ψ	ps	as in 'lapse'	ψωμί	pso-mi	bread
Ω ω	o	as in 'hot'	ώρα	o-ra	time

Combinations of Letters

The combinations of letters shown here are pronounced as follows:

Greek	Pronunciation Guide		Example		
ει	i	as in 'feet'	είδα	i-dha	I saw
οι	i	as in 'feet'	οικόπεδο	i-ko-pe-dho	land
αι	e	as in 'bet'	αίμα	e-ma	blood
ου	u	as in 'mood'	πού	pou	who/what/where
μπ	b	as in 'beer'	μπάλα	ba-la	ball
	mb	as in 'amber'	κάμπος	kam-bos	forest
ντ	d	as in 'dot'	ντουλάπα	dou-la-pa	wardrobe
	nd	as in 'bend'	πέντε	pen-de	five
γκ	g	as in 'God'	γκάζι	ga-zi	gas
γγ	ng	as in 'angle'	αγγελία	an-ge-lia	announcement
γξ	ks	as in 'minks'	σφιγξ	sfinks	sphynx
τζ	dz	as in 'hands'	τζάκι	dza-ki	fireplace

The pairs of vowels shown above are pronounced separately if the first has an acute accent, or the second a dieresis, as in the examples below:

γαϊδουράκι	gai-dhou-ra-ki	little donkey
Κάιρο	kai-ro	Cairo

Some Greek consonant sounds have no English equivalent. The υ of the groups αυ, ευ and ηυ is generally pronounced 'v'. The Greek question mark is represented with the English equivalent of a semicolon ';'.

a room with a double bed
e·na dho·*ma*·ti·o me   ένα δωμάτιο με
dhy·o kre·*va*·ti·a   δυό κρεββάτια

a room with a bathroom
e·na dho·*ma*·ti·o me   ένα δωμάτιο με
ba·ni·o   μπάνιο

I'd like to share a dorm.
tha i·the·la na mi·*ra*·so e·na ki·*no* dho·*ma*·ti·o
me *al*·la a·to·ma
Θα ήθελα να μοιράσω ένα κοινό δωμάτιο
με άλλα άτομα

How much is it ...? *po*·so ka·ni ...   Πόσο κάνει ...;
per night   ti ·vra·*dhya*   τη βραδυά
per person   to a·to·mo   το άτομο

May I see it?
bo·*ro* na to dho   Μπορώ να το δω;
Where's the bathroom?
pou i·ne to·*ba*·ni·o   Πού είναι το μπάνιο;
I'm/We're leaving today.
fev·gho/fev·ghou·me   Φεύγω/φεύγουμε
si·me·ra   σήμερα

CONVERSATION & ESSENTIALS
Hello.
ya·sas (pol)   Γειά σας.
ya·su (inf)   Γειά σου.
Good morning.
ka·li·*me*·ra   Καλημέρα.
Good afternoon/evening.
ka·li·*spe*·ra   Καλησπέρα.
Good night.
ka·li·*nikh*·ta   Καληνύχτα.
Goodbye.
an·*di*·o   Αντίο.
Yes.
ne   Ναι.
No.
o·hi   Οχι.
Please.
pa·ra·ka·*lo*   Παρακαλώ.
Thank you.
ef·ha·ri·*sto*   Ευχαριστώ.
That's fine/You're welcome.
pa·ra·ka·*lo*   Παρακαλώ.
Sorry. (excuse me, forgive me)
sigh·*no*·mi   Συγγνώμη.
What's your name?
pos sas le·ne   Πώς σας λένε;
My name is ...
me le·ne ...   Με λένε ...
Where are you from?
a·po pou i·ste   Από πού είστε;

I'm from ...
i·me a·po ...   Είμαι από ...
I (don't) like ...
(dhen) ma·*re*·si ...   (Δεν) μ' αρέσει ...
Just a minute.
mi·*so* lep·to   Μισό λεπτό.

DIRECTIONS
Where is ...?
pou i·ne ...   Πού είναι...;
Straight ahead.
o·lo ef·*thi*·a   Ολο ευθεία.
Turn left.
strips·te a·ri·ste·ra   Στρίψτε αριστερά
Turn right.
strips·te dhe·ksi·a   Στρίψτε δεξιά
at the next corner
stin epo·me·ni gho·*ni*·a   στην επόμενη γωνία
at the traffic lights
sta fo·ta   στα φώτα

SIGNS
ΕΙΣΟΔΟΣ	Entry
ΕΞΟΔΟΣ	Exit
ΠΛΗΡΟΦΟΡΙΕΣ	Information
ΑΝΟΙΧΤΟ	Open
ΚΛΕΙΣΤΟ	Closed
ΑΠΑΓΟΡΕΥΕΤΑΙ	Prohibited
ΑΣΤΥΝΟΜΙΑ	Police
ΑΣΤΥΝΟΜΙΚΟΣ ΣΤΑΘΜΟΣ	Police Station
ΓΥΝΑΙΚΩΝ	Toilets (women)
ΑΝΔΡΩΝ	Toilets (men)

behind   pi·so   πίσω
in front of   bro·sta   μπροστά
far   ma·kri·a   μακριά
near (to)   kon·da   κοντά
opposite   a·*pe*·nan·di   απέναντι

acropolis   a·*kro*·po·li   ακρόπολη
beach   pa·ra·li·a   παραλία
bridge   yefira   γέφυρα
castle   ka·stro   κάστρο
island   ni·si   νησί
main square   ken·dri·ki· pla·*ti*·a   κεντρική πλατεία
market   a·gho·ra   αγορά
museum   mu·si·o   μουσείο
old quarter   pa·li·a po·li   παλιά πόλη
ruins   ar·he·a   αρχαία
sea   tha·las·sa   θάλασσα
square   pla·ti·a   πλατεία
temple   na·os   ναός

TRANSLITERATION & VARIANT SPELLINGS: AN EXPLANATION

The issue of correctly transliterating Greek into the Latin alphabet is a vexed one, fraught with inconsistencies and pitfalls. The Greeks themselves are not very consistent in this respect, though things are gradually improving. The word 'Piraeus', for example, has been variously represented by the following transliterations: *Pireas*, *Piraievs* and *Pireefs*; and when appearing as a street name (eg Piraeus St) you will also find *Pireos*!

This has been compounded by the linguistic minefield of diglossy, or the two forms of the Greek language. The purist form is called *Katharevousa* and the popular form is *Dimotiki* (Demotic). The Katharevousa form was never more than an artificiality and Dimotiki has always been spoken as the mainstream language, but this linguistic schizophrenia means there are often two Greek words for each English word. Thus, the word for 'baker' in everyday language is *fournos*, but the shop sign will more often than not say *artopoieion*. The baker's product will be known in the street as *psomi*, but in church as *artos*.

A further complication is the issue of anglicised vs hellenised forms of place names: Athina vs Athens, Patra vs Patras, Thiva vs Thebes, Evia vs Euboia – the list goes on and on! Toponymic diglossy (the existence of both an official and everyday name for a place) is responsible for Kerkyra/Corfu, Zante/Zakynthos, and Santorini/Thira. In this guide we usually provide modern Greek equivalents for town names, with one well known exception, Athens. For ancient sites, settlements or people from antiquity, we have tried to stick to the more familiar classical names; so we have Thucydides instead of Thoukididis, Mycenae instead of Mykines.

Problems in transliteration have particular implications for vowels, especially given that Greek has six ways of rendering the vowel sound 'ee', two ways of rendering the 'o' sound and two ways of rendering the 'e' sound. In most instances in this book, **y** has been used for the 'ee' sound when a Greek *upsilon* (υ, Υ) has been used, and **i** for Greek *ita* (η, Η) and *iota* (ι, Ι). In the case of the Greek vowel combinations that make the 'ee' sound, that is οι, ει and υι, an **i** has been used. For the two Greek 'e' sounds αι and ε, an **e** has been employed.

As far as consonants are concerned, the Greek letter *gamma* (γ, Γ) appears as **g** rather than **y** throughout this book. This means that *agios* (Greek for male saint) is used rather than *ayios*, and *agia* (female saint) rather than *ayia*. The letter *fi* (φ, Φ) can be transliterated as either **f** or **ph**. Here, a general rule of thumb is that classical names are spelt with a **ph** and modern names with an **f**. So Phaistos is used rather than Festos, and Folegandros is used rather than Pholegandros. The Greek *chi* (χ, Χ) has usually been represented as **h** in order to approximate the Greek pronunciation as closely as possible. Thus, we have Haralambos instead of Charalambos and Polytehniou instead of Polytechniou. Bear in mind that the **h** is to be pronounced as an aspirated 'h', much like the 'ch' in 'loch'. The letter *kapa* (κ, Κ) has been used to represent that sound, except where well known names from antiquity have adopted by convention the letter **c**, eg Polycrates, Acropolis.

Wherever reference to a street name is made, we have omitted the Greek word *odos*, but words for avenue (*leoforos*, abbreviated *leof*) and square (*plateia*) have been included.

HEALTH

| I'm ill. | *i*-me *a*-ro-stos | Είμαι άρρωστος. |
| It hurts here. | po-*nai*- e-*dho* | Πονάει εδώ. |

I have ...		
e-ho ...	Έχω ...	
asthma		
asth-ma	άσθμα	
diabetes		
za-ha-ro-dhi-a-*vi*-ti	ζαχαροδιαβήτη	
diarrhoea		
dhi-a-ri-a	διάρροια	
epilepsy		
e-pi-lip-*si*-a	επιληψία	

I'm allergic to ...		
i-me a-ler-yi-*kos*/	Είμαι αλλεργικός/	
a-ler-yi-*ki* ... (m/f)	αλλεργική ...	
antibiotics		
sta an-di-vi-o-ti-*ka*	στα αντιβιωτικά	
aspirin		
stin a-spi-*ri*-ni	στην ασπιρίνη	
penicillin		
stin pe-ni-ki-*li*-ni	στην πενικιλλίνη	
bees		
stis *me*-li-ses	στις μέλισσες	
nuts		
sta fi-*sti*-ki-a	στα φυστίκια	

condoms	pro·fi·la·kti·*ka* (ka·*po*·tez)	προφυλακτικά (καπότες)
contraceptive medicine	pro·fi·lak·ti·*ko* *farm*·a·ko	προφυλακτικό φάρμακο
sunblock cream	*kre*·ma i·*li*·u	κρέμα ηλίου
tampons	tam·*bon*	ταμπόν

LANGUAGE DIFFICULTIES

Do you speak English?
mi·*la*·te an·gli·*ka*   Μιλάτε αγγλικά;
Does anyone speak English?
mi·*lai* ka·*nis* an·gli·*ka*   Μιλάει κανείς αγγλικά;
How do you say ... in Greek?
ps *le*·ghe·te ... sta   Πώς λέγεται ... στα
el·li·ni·*ka*   ελληνικά;
I understand.
ka·ta·la·*ve*·no   Καταλαβαίνω.
I don't understand.
dhen ka·ta·la·*ve*·no   Δεν καταλαβαίνω.
Please write it down.
ghrap·ste to pa·ra·ka·*lo*   Γράψτε το, παρακαλώ.
Can you show me on the map?
bo·*ri*·te na mo·u to   Μπορείτε να μου το
dhi·xe·te sto *har*·ti   δείξετε στο χάρτη;

NUMBERS

0	mi·*dhen*	μηδέν
1	*e*·nas	ένας (m)
	mi·a	μία (f)
	e·na	ένα (n)
2	*dhi*·o	δύο
3	tris	τρεις (m&f)
	tri·a	τρία (n)
4	te·se·ris	τέσσερεις (m&f)
	te·se·ra	τέσσερα (n)
5	*pen*·de	πέντε
6	e·xi	έξη
7	ep·*ta*	επτά
8	oh·*to*	οχτώ
9	e·*ne*·a	εννέα
10	*dhe*·ka	δέκα
20	*ik*·o·si	είκοσι
30	tri·*an*·da	τριάντα
40	sa·*ran*·da	σαράντα
50	pe·*nin*·da	πενήντα
60	e·*xin*·da	εξήντα
70	ev·dho·*min*·da	εβδομήντα
80	oh·*dhon*·da	ογδόντα
90	e·*nen*·in·da	ενενήντα
100	e·ka·*to*	εκατό
1000	*hi*·li·i	χίλιοι (m)
	hi·li·ez	χίλιες (f)
	hi·li·a	χίλια (n)
2000	*dhi*·o chi·*li*·a·dhez	δύο χιλιάδες

PAPERWORK

name
o·no·ma·te·*po*·ni·mo   ονοματεπώνυμο
nationality
i·pi·ko·o·ti·ta   υπηκοότητα
date of birth
i·me·ro·mi·*ni*·a   ημερομηνία
yen·*ni*·se·os   γεννήσεως

EMERGENCIES

Help!
vo·*i*·thya   Βοήθεια!
There's been an accident.
ey·*i*·ne a·ti·hi·ma   Εγινε ατύχημα.
Go away!
fi·ye   Φύγε!

Call ...!   fo·*nak*·ste ...   Φωνάξτε ...!
   a doctor   e·na yi·a·*tro*   ένα γιατρό
   the police   tin a·sti·no·*mi*·a   την αστυνομία

---

place of birth
to·pos yen·*ni*·se·os   τόπος γεννήσεως
sex (gender)
fil·lon   φύλον
passport
dhia·va·*ti*·ri·o   διαβατήριο
visa
vi·za   βίζα

QUESTION WORDS

Who/Which?
pi·os/pi·a/pi·o (sg m/f/n)   Ποιος/Ποια/Ποιο;
pi·*i*/pi·es/pi·a (pl m/f/n)   Ποιοι/Ποιες/Ποια;
Who's there?
pi·os *i*·ne e·*ki*   Ποιος είναι εκεί;
Which street is this?
pi·a o·*dhos i*·ne af·*ti*   Ποια οδός είναι αυτή;
What?
ti   Τι;
What's this?
ti *i*·ne af·*to*   Τι είναι αυτό;
Where?
pu   Πού;
When?
po·te   Πότε;
Why?
yi·a·*ti*   Γιατί;
How?
pos   Πώς;
How much?
po·so   Πόσο;
How much does it cost?
po·so ka·ni   Πόσο κάνει;

LANGUAGE

SHOPPING & SERVICES

I'd like to buy ...
the·lo n'a·gho·ra·so ... Θέλω ν' αγοράσω ...
How much is it?
po·so *ka*·ni Πόσο κάνει;
I don't like it.
dhen mu a·*re*·si Δεν μου αρέσει.
May I see it?
bo·*ro* na to dho Μπορώ να το δω;
I'm just looking.
ap·*los* ki·*ta*·zo Απλώς κοιτάζω.
It's cheap.
i·ne fti·*no* Είναι φτηνό.
It's too expensive.
i·ne po·*li* a·kri·*vo* Είναι πολύ ακριβό.
I'll take it.
tha to *pa*·ro Θα το πάρω.

Do you accept ...? *dhe*·che·ste ... Δέχεστε ...;
  credit cards pi·sto·ti·*ki kar*·ta πιστωτική κάρτα
  travellers tak·si·dhi·o·ti·*kes* ταξιδιωτικές
  cheques e·pi·ta·*ghes* επιταγές

more pe·ri·*so*·te·ro περισσότερο
less li·*gho*·te·ro λιγότερο
smaller mi·*kro*·te·ro μικρότερο
bigger me·gha·*li*·te·ro μεγαλύτερο

I'm looking for ... *psach*·no ya ... Ψάχνω για ...
  a bank mya *tra*·pe·za μια τράπεζα
  the church tin ek·kli·*si*·a την εκκλησία
  the city centre to *ken*·dro tis *po*·lis το κέντρο της πόλης
  the ... embassy tin ... pres·*vi*·a την ... πρεσβεία
  the market ti· *lai*·ki· a·gho·*ra* τη λαϊκή αγορά
  the museum to mu·*si*·o το μουσείο
  the post office to ta·chi·dhro·*mi*·o το ταχυδρομείο
  a public toilet mya dhi·*mo*·sia tu·a·*let*·ta μια δημόσια τουαλέττα
  the telephone centre to ti·le·fo·ni·*ko ken*·dro το τηλεφωνικό κέντρο
  the tourist office to tu·ri·st·*iko* ghra·*fi*·o το τουριστικό γραφείο

TIME & DATES

What time is it? ti o·*ra i*·ne Τι ώρα είναι;
It's (2 o'clock). *i*·ne (*dhi*·o i· o·ra) είναι (δύο η ώρα).
in the morning to pro·*i* το πρωί
in the afternoon to a·*po*·yev·ma το απόγευμα
in the evening to *vra*·dhi το βράδυ
When? *po*·te Πότε;
today *si*·me·ra σήμερα
tomorrow av·ri·o αύριο
yesterday hthes χθες

Monday dhef·*te*·ra Δευτέρα
Tuesday *tri*·ti Τρίτη
Wednesday te·*tar*·ti Τετάρτη
Thursday *pemp*·ti Πέμπτη
Friday pa·ras·ke·*vi* Παρασκευή
Saturday *sa*·va·to Σάββατο
Sunday kyri·a·*ki* Κυριακή

January ia·nou·ar·*i*·os Ιανουάριος
February fev·rou·ar·*i*·os Φεβρουάριος
March *mar*·ti·os Μάρτιος
April a·*pri*·li·os Απρίλιος
May *mai*·os Μάιος
June i·*ou*·ni·os Ιούνιος
July i·*ou*·li·os Ιούλιος
August *av*·ghous·tos Αύγουστος
September sep·*tem*·vri·os Σεπτέμβριος
October ok·*to*·vri·os Οκτώβριος
November no·*em*·vri·os Νοέμβριος
December dhe·*kem*·vri·os Δεκέμβριος

TRANSPORT

Public Transport

What time does the ... leave/ arrive? ti o·ra fev·*yi*/ *fta*·ni to ... Τι ώρα φεύγει/ φτάνει το ...;
  boat *pli*·o πλοίο
  (city) bus a·sti·*ko* αστικό
  (intercity) bus le·o·fo·*ri*·o λεωφορείο
  plane ae·ro·*pla*·no αεροπλάνο
  train *tre*·no τραίνο

I'd like (a) ... tha *i*·the·la (*e*·na) ... Θα ήθελα (ένα) ...
  one way ticket a·*plo* isi·*ti*·ri·o απλό εισιτήριο
  return ticket i·si·*ti*·ri·o me e·pi·stro·*fi* εισιτήριο με επιστροφή
  1st class *pro*·ti· *the*·si πρώτη θέση
  2nd class *def*·te·ri *the*·si δεύτερη θέση

I want to go to ...
the·lo na *pao* sto/sti ...
Θέλω να πάω στο/στη ...
The train has been cancelled/delayed.
to *tre*·no a·ki·rothi·ke/ka·thi·ste·ri·se
Το τραίνο ακυρώθηκε/καθυστέρησε

the first to *pro*·to το πρώτο
the last to te·lef·*te*·o το τελευταίο
platform number a·rith*mos* a·po·*va*·thras αριθμός αποβάθρας
ticket office ek·dho·*ti*·ri·o i·si·ti·ri·on εκδοτήριο εισιτηρίων

timetable

dhro·mo·lo·gio   δρομολόγιο

train station

si·dhi·ro·dhro·mi·kos   σιδηροδρομικός

stath·mos   σταθμός

Private Transport

I'd like to hire	tha i·the·la na	θα ήθελα να
a ...	ni·ki·a·so ...	νοικιάσω ...
car	e·na af·ti·ki·ni·to	ένα αυτοκίνητο
4WD	e·na tes·se·ra	ένα τέσσερα
	e·pi tes·se·ra	επί τέσσερα
(a jeep)	(e·na tzip)	(ένα τζιπ)
motorbike	mya mo·to·si·	μια μοτοσυ·
	klet·ta	κλέττα
bicycle	e·na po·dhi·la·to	ένα ποδήλατο

Is this the road to ...?

af·tos i·ne o dhro·mos ya ...

Αυτός είναι ο δρόμος για ...

Where's the next service station?

pu i·ne to e·po·me·no ven·zi·na·dhi·ko

Πού είναι το επόμενο βενζινάδικο;

Please fill it up.

ye·mi·ste to pa·ra·ka·lo

Γεμίστε το, παρακαλώ.

I'd like (30) euros worth.

tha i·the·la (30) ev·ro

Θα ήθελα (30) ευρώ.

diesel	pet·re·le·o ki·ni·sis	πετρέλαιο κίνησης
leaded petrol	su·per	σούπερ
unleaded petrol	a·mo·liv·dhi	αμόλυβδη

Can I park here?

bo·ro na par·ka·ro e·dho

Μπορώ να παρκάρω εδώ;

Where do I pay?

pu pli·ro·no

Πού πληρώνω;

ROAD SIGNS

ΠΑΡΑΚΑΜΨΗ	Detour
ΑΠΑΓΟΡΕΥΕΤΕΑΙ Η ΕΙΣΟΔΟΣ	No Entry
ΑΠΑΓΟΡΕΥΕΤΑΙ Η ΠΡΟΣΠΕΡΑΣΗ	No Overtaking
ΑΠΑΓΟΡΕΥΕΤΑΙ ΗΣΤΑΘΜΕΥΣΗ	No Parking
ΕΙΣΟΔΟΣ	Entrance
ΜΗΝ ΠΑΡΚΑΡΕΤΕ ΕΔΩ	Keep Clear
ΔΙΟΔΙΑ	Toll
ΚΙΝΔΥΝΟΣ	Danger
ΑΡΓΑ	Slow Down
ΕΞΟΔΟΣ	Exit

The car/motorbike has broken down (at ...)

to af·to·ki·ni·to/mo·to·si·klet·ta cha·la·se sto ...

Το αυτοκίνητο/η μοτοσυκλέττα χάλασε στο ...

The car/motorbike won't start.

to af·to·ki·ni·to/mo·to·si·klet·ta dhen per·ni· bros

Το αυτοκίνητο/η μοτοσυκλέττα δεν παίρνει μπρος.

I have a flat tyre.

e·pa·tha la·sti·cho

Έπαθα λάστιχο.

I've run out of petrol.

e·mi·na a·po ven·zi·ni

Έμεινα από βενζίνη.

I've had an accident.

e·pa·tha a·ti·chi·ma

Έπαθα ατύχημα.

TRAVEL WITH CHILDREN

Is there a/an ...?	i·par·chi ...	Υπάρχει ...;
I need a/an ...	chri·a·zo·me ...	Χρειάζομαι ...
baby change	me·ros nal·lak·so	μέρος ν'αλλάξω
room	to mo·ro	το μωρό
car baby seat	ka·this·ma ya	κάθισμα για
	mo·ro	μωρό
child-minding	ba·bi sit·ter	μπέιμπι σίττερ
service		
children's menu	me·nu ya pe·dhya	μενού για παιδία
(disposable)	pan·nez Pam·pers	πάννες Pampers
nappies/diapers		
(English-	ba·bi sit·ter	μπέιμπι σίττερ
speaking)	pu mi·la	που μιλά
babysitter	an·ghl·ika	αγγλικά
highchair	pe·dhi·ki ka·rek·la	παιδική καρέκλα
potty	yo·yo	γιογιό
stroller	ka·rot·sa·ki	καροτσάκι

Do you mind if I breastfeed here?

bo·ro na thi·la·so e·dho

Μπορώ να θηλάσω εδώ;

Are children allowed?

e·pi·tre·pon·de ta pe·dhya

Επιτρέπονται τα παιδιά;

LANGUAGE

Glossary

For culinary terms see Food Glossary (p59), and also see Where to Eat & Drink (p52).

Achaean civilisation – see *Mycenaean civilisation*
acropolis – citadel; highest point of an ancient city
agia (f), agios (m) – saint
agora – commercial area of an ancient city; shopping precinct in modern Greece
Archaic period – also known as the *Middle Age* (800–480 BC); period in which the city-states emerged from the *'dark age'* and traded their way to wealth and power; the city-states were unified by a Greek alphabet and common cultural pursuits, engendering a sense of national identity
arhon – leading citizen of a town, often a wealthy bourgeois merchant; chief magistrate

basilica – early Christian church
bouzouki – long-necked, stringed lutelike instrument associated with *rembetika* music
Byzantine Empire – characterised by the merging of Hellenistic culture and Christianity and named after Byzantium, the city on the Bosphorus that became the capital of the Roman Empire; when the Roman Empire was formally divided in AD 395, Rome went into decline and the eastern capital, renamed Constantinople, flourished; the Byzantine Empire (324 BC–AD 1453) dissolved after the fall of Constantinople to the Turks in 1453

caïque – small, sturdy fishing boat often used to carry passengers
Classical period – era in which the city-states reached the height of their wealth and power after the defeat of the Persians in the 5th century BC; the Classical period (480–323 BC) ended with the decline of the city-states as a result of the Peloponnesian Wars, and the expansionist aspirations of Philip II, King of Macedon (r 359–336 BC), and his son, Alexander the Great (r 336–323 BC)
Corinthian – order of Greek architecture recognisable by columns with bell-shaped capitals that have sculpted, elaborate ornaments based on acanthus leaves; see also *Doric* and *Ionic*
Cycladic civilisation – the civilisation (3000–1100 BC) that emerged following the settlement of Phoenician colonists on the Cycladic islands

dark age – period (1200–800 BC) in which Greece was under *Dorian* rule
delfini – dolphin; common name for a hydrofoil
domatio (s), domatia (pl) – room, usually in a private home; cheap accommodation option

Dorians – Hellenic warriors who invaded Greece around 1200 BC, demolishing the city-states and destroying the *Mycenaean civilisation;* heralded Greece's *'dark age'*, when the artistic and cultural advancements of the Mycenaean and the *Minoan civilisations* were abandoned; the Dorians later developed into land-holding aristocrats, which encouraged the resurgence of independent city-states led by wealthy aristocrats
Doric – order of Greek architecture characterised by a column that has no base, a fluted shaft and a relatively plain capital, when compared with the flourishes evident on *Ionic* and *Corinthian* capitals

Ellada or Ellas – see *Hellas*
ELTA – Ellinika Tahydromia; the Greek post office organisation
EOT – Ellinikos Organismos Tourismou; main tourist office (has offices in most major towns), known abroad as *GNTO*

Filiki Eteria – Friendly Society; a group of Greeks in exile; formed during Ottoman rule to organise an uprising against the Turks
filoxenia – hospitality
frourio – fortress; sometimes also referred to as a *kastro*

Geometric period – period (1200–800 BC) characterised by pottery decorated with geometric designs; sometimes referred to as Greece's *'dark age'*
GNTO – Greek National Tourist Organisation; see also *EOT*

Hellas – the Greek name for Greece; also known as *Ellada* or *Ellas*
Hellenistic period – prosperous, influential period (323–146 BC) of Greek civilisation ushered in by Alexander the Great's empire building
hora – main town (usually on an island)
horio – village

Ionic – order of Greek architecture characterised by a column with truncated flutes and capitals with ornaments resembling scrolls; see also *Doric* and *Corinthian*

kastro – walled-in town; also describes a fort or castle
katholikon – principal church of a monastic complex
kouros – male statue of the *Archaic period*, characterised by a stiff body posture and enigmatic smile; female statue referred to as *kore*
KTEL – Koino Tamio Eispraxeon Leoforion; national bus cooperative; runs all long-distance bus services

laïka – literally 'popular (songs)'; mainstream songs that have either been around for years or are of recent origin; also referred to as urban folk music

leoforos – avenue; commonly shortened to 'leof'

meltemi – northeasterly wind that blows throughout much of Greece during the summer

Minoan civilisation – Bronze Age (3000–1100 BC) culture of Crete named after the mythical King Minos, and characterised by pottery and metalwork of great artisanship

moni – monastery or convent

Mycenaean civilisation – the first great civilisation (1900–1100 BC) of the Greek mainland, characterised by powerful independent city-states ruled by kings; also known as the *Achaean civilisation*

nisi – island

odos – street

OSE – Organismos Sidirodromon Ellados; Greek railways organisation

OTE – Organismos Tilepikoinonion Ellados; Greece's major telecommunications carrier

Panagia – Mother of God or Virgin Mary; name frequently used for churches

panigyri (s), panigyria (p) – festival; the most common festivals celebrate annual saints' days

Pantokrator – painting or mosaic of Christ in the centre of the dome of a Byzantine church

periptero (s), periptera (pl) – street kiosk

plateia – square

rembetika – blues songs commonly associated with the underworld of the 1920s

spilia – cave

stele (s), stelae (pl) – upright stone (or pillar) decorated with inscriptions or figures

stoa – long colonnaded building, usually in an *agora*; often used as a meeting place and shelter in ancient Greece

The Authors

PAUL HELLANDER
Coordinating Author

Paul is an incurable traveller with a passionate sense of belonging to his spiritual home Greece. Fluent in the Greek language, he's been in and out of the Greek islands countless times over the last 35 years. Heaven to Paul would be a hi-tech stone cottage on a sun-bleached Aegean island with books and music for company, a vine-dressed courtyard for relaxation and the endless vista of sea and rocks for thought. Home for now is Adelaide, South Australia. Paul wrote Destination Greek Islands, Getting Started, Itineraries, History, Environment, Greek Islands Outdoors, Islands Adventuring, Off the Beaten Track, Athens & Mainland Ports, Dodecanese, Directory, Transport and Glossary.

My Greek Islands

One of my favourite trips took me on a fast ferry from Piraeus (p87) to Paros (p152), where I swam at all the best beaches. I always wanted to visit slender Amorgos (p183) – an inspired choice and easy to get to with a daily ferry from Paros. Breezy Kos (p317) was next for a spot of cycling. I love Rhodes' Old Town (p276) to which I sped on a comfortable catamaran. A slow ferry then brought me to rugged, yet appealing, Karpathos (p294) for superb snorkelling and walking. I am a sucker for small islands and a five-minute plane ride lifted me to demure and distant Kasos (p300), where time means little. I finally sailed on to Crete (p220) for wining and dining under the stars.

KATE ARMSTRONG
Ionian Islands

Having studied history and fine arts, Kate headed to Greece aeons ago to view her first (non-celluloid) *kouros* (male statue), and fell in love with the country. This was her second Lonely Planet visit to retrace Odysseus' voyage in the Ionian Islands. She devoured honey and olives (delighting locals), several sheep (to the dismay of her vegetarian partner) and was treated to more hospitality than Aphrodite herself. When not wandering in mountainous terrains, Kate sets her itchy feet in Australia. She contributes to Lonely Planet's African and South American titles and is the author of travel articles and children's books.

LONELY PLANET AUTHORS

Why is our travel information the best in the world? It's simple: our authors are independent, dedicated travellers. They don't research using just the internet or phone, and they don't take freebies in exchange for positive coverage. They travel widely, to all the popular spots and off the beaten track. They personally visit thousands of hotels, restaurants, cafés, bars, galleries, palaces, museums and more – and they take pride in getting all the details right, and telling it how it is. Think you can do it? Find out how at lonelyplanet.com.

MICHAEL CLARK
Evia & Sporades

Born into a Greek-American community in Cambridge, Ohio, Michael's Greek roots go back to the village of Karavostamo on the Aegean island of Ikaria, home of his maternal grandparents. He first worked his way to Greece aboard a Greek freighter, trading English lessons for Greek over wine and backgammon. When not travelling to Greece, Michael teaches English to international students in Berkeley, California, listens to Greek *rembetika* (blues) music after midnight and tries to convert friends to the subtle pleasures of retsina wine.

CHRIS DELISO
Northeastern Aegean Islands

Chris was drawing maps of the Aegean by the age of five, and 20 years later he ended up in Greece while labouring away on an MPhil in Byzantine Studies at Oxford. Ever since studying the Greek language in Thessaloniki in 1998, he has travelled frequently in Greece, including a year spent on Crete and a long sojourn on Mt Athos. He now lives next door in Skopje, capital of the Former Yugoslav Republic of Macedonia, and visits Greece often. Chris' adventures researching this book included everything from inebriated priests to goat-hoisting Pomaks, while his dining responsibilities involved skewered swordfish, Ottoman sweets, too many cheese pies and squishy raw sea urchins.

DES HANNIGAN
Saronic Gulf Islands, Cyclades

Des first surfaced (literally) in Greece many years ago in Aegina harbour, having stepped off a boat into several feet of water. He's been drifting around the country whenever he can ever since, although home is on the edge of the cold Atlantic in sunny Cornwall, England. In a previous life Des worked at sea, valuable experience for coping with the Greek ferry system that always somehow gets him to the more remote corners of the Cyclades. One day he'd really like to hop the Cyclades in a very fast yacht with all sails set. Des worked on the previous Lonely Planet editions of *Greece* and the *Greek Islands* and has written guidebooks to Corfu and Rhodes for other publishers.

VICTORIA KYRIAKOPOULOS
The Culture, Food & Drink, Crete

Victoria is a freelance journalist in Melbourne, Australia – when she's not doing research and living her 'other life' in Greece. A regular visitor to Greece since 1988, she lived in Athens between 2000 and 2004, covering the Olympics preparations. She is the author of Lonely Planet's *Best of Athens,* a former editor of the Athens-based Greek diaspora magazine *Odyssey* and has been a researcher for a number of television programmes about Greece. She is also the author of the last two editions of Lonely Planet's *Crete*. A regular contributor to the *Age* and other Australian and international publications, she was formerly a staff writer with the *Bulletin* and a media relations consultant.

Behind the Scenes

THIS BOOK

This 4th edition of *Greek Islands* was updated by Paul Hellander, Kate Armstrong, Michael Clark, Chris Deliso, Des Hannigan and Victoria Kyriakopoulos. David Willett, Miriam Raphael and Andrew Stone authored on previous editions. This guidebook was commissioned in Lonely Planet's London office and produced by the following:

Commissioning Editors Stefanie Di Trocchio, Michala Green, Sally Schafer

Coordinating Editor Gina Tsarouhas

Coordinating Cartographer Andy Rojas

Coordinating Layout Designer Jacqui Saunders

Managing Editor Katie Lynch

Managing Cartographer Mark Griffiths

Managing Layout Designer Celia Wood

Assisting Editors Susie Ashworth, Nigel Chin, Gennifer Ciavarra, Alan Murphy, Joanne Newell, Kristin Odijk, Tom Smallman, Louisa Syme, Jeanette Wall, Simon Williamson

Assisting Cartographers Alissa Baker, Anita Banh, Fatima Basic, Anna Clarkson, Indra Kilfoyle, Tadhgh Knaggs, Wayne Murphy, Sophie Richards, Andrew Smith

Cover Designer Pepi Bluck

Project Managers Eoin Dunlevy, Fabrice Rocher, Sarah Sloane

Language Content Coordinator Quentin Frayne

Thanks to Imogen Bannister, David Burnett, Janine Eberle, Mark Germanchis, Lisa Knights, Rebecca Lalor, Alison Lyall, John Mazzocchi, Suzannah Shwer, Bob Topping.

THANKS
PAUL HELLANDER

Ευχαριστώ (thank you) to my band of fellow-authors and the Lonely Planet editorial production team for putting this convoluted research into print. On the Greek islands I would like to thank in south–north order the following persons who for various reasons made my island-hopping that much easier: Elias Hatzigeorgiou (Karpathos); Manolis Gryllis (Halki); Kim Sjögren (Rhodes); Nikos and Takis (Rhodes); Giannis, Despina and Dimitris Brokou (Rhodes); Giannis and Nikos Voulgaroglou (Kastellorizo); Paul and Helen Nuttall (Tilos); Alexis Zikos (Kos); Marianna Angelou (Leros); Anna Rizos (Lipsi); Theologos and Giakoumina Mathios (Patmos). In addition a million thanks to my wife Stella for holding the fort once more and my sons Marcus and Byron for making me come back to Greece again and again. Στη μνήμη του αείμνηστου Ηλία Αρχοντούλη (to the memory of Ilias who shall never be forgotten).

THE LONELY PLANET STORY

Fresh from an epic journey across Europe, Asia and Australia in 1972, Tony and Maureen Wheeler sat at their kitchen table stapling together notes. The first Lonely Planet guidebook, *Across Asia on the Cheap*, was born.

Travellers snapped up the guides. Inspired by their success, the Wheelers began publishing books to Southeast Asia, India and beyond. Demand was prodigious, and the Wheelers expanded the business rapidly to keep up. Over the years, Lonely Planet extended its coverage to every country and into the virtual world via lonelyplanet.com and the Thorn Tree message board.

As Lonely Planet became a globally loved brand, Tony and Maureen received several offers for the company. But it wasn't until 2007 that they found a partner whom they trusted to remain true to the company's principles of travelling widely, treading lightly and giving sustainably. In October of that year, BBC Worldwide acquired a 75% share in the company, pledging to uphold Lonely Planet's commitment to independent travel, trustworthy advice and editorial independence.

Today, Lonely Planet has offices in Melbourne, London and Oakland, with over 500 staff members and 300 authors. Tony and Maureen are still actively involved with Lonely Planet. They're travelling more often than ever, and they're devoting their spare time to charitable projects. And the company is still driven by the philosophy of *Across Asia on the Cheap*: 'All you've got to do is decide to go and the hardest part is over. So go!'

KATE ARMSTRONG

Special thanks to the Zotos Brothers and helpful Greekophiles and travellers. In the Pelops, efharisto: Claudia and Marcello, Nikki and Sotiris; Panagiotis and Kara of Staikos Tours; Gillian Bouras; Suzanne and Alki at Hotel Pelops; and Maria Dometiou, information-sharer extraordinaire. On the Ionian Islands: Diana and Vincent; Marilena Tombrou; Jenny Lewis; Carol at Paxos Magic; Katerina and Manthos; Manu and Christos Raftopolous; Stavros and Joannah. Thanks to: Nick Konstantatos for his enthusiasm and Malaysia Airlines for the extra kilos; Susanne Magonezos, Iren at Hotel Zefiros and my very own 'Kristos'; my fellow authors, especially Des, Victoria and co-ordinator Paul. For their support, Stef Di Trocchio, Imogen Hall, Michala Green (we'll miss you) and Sally Schafer, and to Gina and cartos. Finally, to Prue McKeown (aka Bridget J), for living the emotions and sharing her sense of adventure.

MICHAEL CLARK

My contribution to this book was made possible by the help of good friends, kind strangers, relatives and acquaintances, among them: my Athenian host Tolis and company; in Delphi, the ever-helpful Efi Tsiropoulou at the Municipal Office, Yannis Christopoulos at Sybilla, and Dr Elena Partida, Curator of Antiquities. Arthur and Mara in Kalambaka; in Volos, Anastasia; in the Pelion, Jill Sleeman; in Skiathos, Keyrillos Sinioris and Matt; in Skopelos, Makis at Thalpos; in Alonnisos, Bessie and Kostas. Nana and Kostas Vatsis provided invaluable help, not to mention sunglasses. To fellow author Paul Hellander, I promise to hook up the camera. And very best wishes to my long-time editor Michala Green at Lonely Planet as she hits a new road. And to my patient, splendiferous and loving family – Janet White and kids Melina and Alexander – Greek hugs and kisses all around. I wish to dedicate this work to the memory of my mother, Mary Efimedia Raptis Kent, who taught me to appreciate all things Greek, especially the voyage.

CHRIS DELISO

As always, the heroic George Karamanolis tops the list. I should also thank: Neni, Vasilis, Myrto and Maria (Thessaloniki); Ioannis Michaletos (Athens); Ismini Diamanti and Kyria Dalakoglou (Orestiada, Didymoteihon); Areti (Komotini); Hussein and family (Thermes); Byron Hellander and Giorgios Kontaxis (Ioannina); Yiannis and Katerina, and the Exarhou family (Konitsa); Dimitrios Boumbas (Metsovo); Leftheris Zygouris and family (Parga); Vasilis and Dimitra (Ikaria); Mick, Dimitrios and Stelios (Samos); Theodoros, Don, Anna, Vasilis and Roula (Chios); Eleni (Inousses); Ifigenia, Leftheris, Barbara and George (Lesvos); Giorgos and Haris (Samothraki); Nikos, Yiannis Markianos and Yiannis Raizis (Thasos), and finally Will Gourlay, Stef Di Trocchio and Paul Hellander (Lonely Planet).

DES HANNIGAN

Warmest thanks to the many friends and acquaintances who helped and advised me, with good humour, wit and patience, during my work in Greece. Thanks especially to those who know the business best of all; to Petros Koloventzos on Andros, Sharon Turner on Tinos, John van Lerberghe on Mykonos, Lisos Zilelides and Wiebke Godau on Santorini, Theresa Pirpinias-Ninou (and many friends) on Milos, and Christos Agioutantis on Sifnos. Special thanks as always to Kostas Karabetsos on Mykonos for the nightlife run among good friends, including Kevin and Dot Kavanaugh; and to Demetra Karakosti and Steve Brown on Aegina for their great company and conversation. Thanks, as always to my fellow authors for entertaining e-conferences and to Stefanie Di Trocchio and Michala Green at Lonely Planet's London office and coordinating author Paul Hellander, for holding it all together.

VICTORIA KYRIAKOPOULOS

Many thanks to Eleni Bertes, Maria Zygourakis, Antonis Bekiaris and Yiorgos Xylouris in Athens. Heartfelt thanks to all everyone who steered me through Crete. Thanks to Sonia Panagiotidou, Lefteris Karatarakis, Dimitris Skoutelis and Maya, Dimitris Kornaros, Yiannis Genetzakis in Iraklio, the Patramani family in Episkopi, Manolis Klironomakis in Paleohora, Vasilis Karamanlis in Makriyialos, Iakovos Sourgoutsidis in Hania, George Motakis and Sifis Papadakis in Agios Nikolaos, Pavlos and Renata Myssor in Sitia, Nikos Perakis and Elias Pagianidis in Zakros, Manolis Tambakos in Ierapetra and Nikki Rose. In Melbourne, thanks to Stathis Gauntlett, Bill Kyriakopoulos and Chris, Sam and Nikolas Anastassiades.

OUR READERS

Many thanks to the travellers who used the last edition and wrote to us with helpful hints, useful advice and interesting anecdotes:

Carolyn and Panos Alevizakis, Michael Baker, George Bakogiannis, Tomer Baram, Hugues Baudon, Rodger Berkley, Line Bliemeister, Chris Bolshaw, Michelle Bonavia, Lucas Chambers, Barbora Chochulova, Pamela Crosby, Christine Foden Davies, Michael Davies, Patrick Doyle, Christopher Ellis, Magdalena

BEHIND THE SCENES

Fedorowicz, Gary and Tamara Fine, Tobias Fog-Moeller, Richard Fong, Helen Georghiou, Dawn Gretton, Paul Gretton, Richard Griffiths, Amy Hackmann, John Haywood, R Michael Heerdegen, Christy Herman, Meredith Hobik, Darren Holland, Phivos Ioannides, Kieron Jenkins, Bob Kerr, Mary Kerr, Dejan and Elena Kolevski, Philippa Lane, Geoff and Robyn Lewis, Richard Lilly, Julian Lord, Per-Arne Lybekk, Maria Macdougall, Sophie Marquand, Keith McBride, Lesley McLeod, Aimee Meuchel, Eugene Moran, Steven Oxley, Janette Robinson, John Robinson, Marcel Sauer, Charlie Smith, Cathryn Spence, Stephanie Thorne, Francesca Traversa, Ivan Marshall, Simon Walsh, Laura Weight, Kristina West and Cathy White.

ACKNOWLEDGMENTS

Many thanks to the following for the use of their content:

Globe on title page ©Mountain High Maps 1993 Digital Wisdom, Inc.

Internal photographs p173 by Charles Stirling (Diving)/Alamy; p174 Paul Springett/Alamy; p175 (#2) IML Image Group Ltd/Alamy; p175 (#3) George Blonsky/Alamy; p176 (#2) FAN travelstock/Alamy; p177 Grega Rozac/Alamy; p179 David Boag/Alamy; p341 IML Image Group Ltd/Alamy; p342 (#1) Catriona Bass/Alamy; p342 (#2) IML Image Group Ltd/Alamy; p343 (#3) Rob Whitworth/Alamy; p343 (#4) IML Image Group Ltd/Alamy; p344 (#1) IML Image Group Ltd/Alamy; p346 (#1) LOOK Die Bildagentur der Fotografen GmbH/Alamy; p346 (#2) IML Image Group Ltd/Alamy; p347 imagebroker/Alamy. All other photographs by Lonely Planet Images, and p176 (#1), p178 (#2), p345 Stella Hellander; p178

(#1) David Tipling; p180 Wayne Walton; p344 (#2) Chris Christo; p348 George Tsafos.

All images are the copyright of the photographers unless otherwise indicated. Many of the images in this guide are available for licensing from Lonely Planet Images: www.lonelyplanetimages.com.

Index

Index

INDEX

000 Map pages
000 Photograph pages

000 Map pages
000 Photograph pages

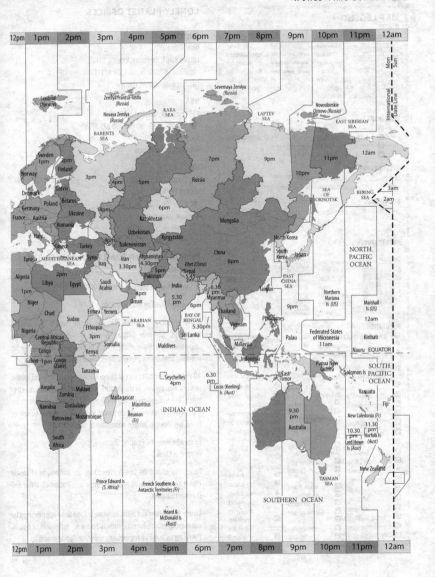

548

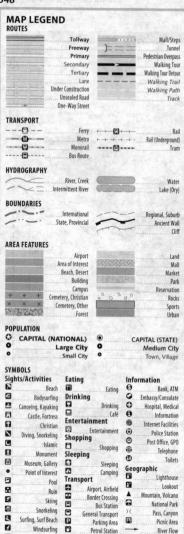

MAP LEGEND
ROUTES

Tollway
Freeway
Primary
Secondary
Tertiary
Lane
Under Construction
Unsealed Road
One-Way Street

Mall/Steps
Tunnel
Pedestrian Overpass
Walking Tour
Walking Tour Detour
Walking Trail
Walking Path
Track

TRANSPORT

Ferry
Metro
Monorail
Bus Route

Rail
Rail (Underground)
Tram

HYDROGRAPHY

River, Creek
Intermittent River

Water
Lake (Dry)

BOUNDARIES

International
State, Provincial

Regional, Suburb
Ancient Wall
Cliff

AREA FEATURES

Airport
Area of Interest
Beach, Desert
Building
Campus
Cemetery, Christian
Cemetery, Other
Forest

Land
Mall
Market
Park
Reservation
Rocks
Sports
Urban

POPULATION

○ CAPITAL (NATIONAL)
● Large City
○ Small City

◉ CAPITAL (STATE)
◎ Medium City
○ Town, Village

SYMBOLS

Sights/Activities
Beach
Bodysurfing
Canoeing, Kayaking
Castle, Fortress
Christian
Diving, Snorkeling
Islamic
Monument
Museum, Gallery
Point of Interest
Pool
Ruin
Skiing
Snorkeling
Surfing, Surf Beach
Windsurfing
Zoo, Bird Sanctuary

Eating
Eating
Drinking
Drinking
Café
Entertainment
Entertainment
Shopping
Shopping
Sleeping
Sleeping
Camping
Transport
Airport, Airfield
Border Crossing
Bus Station
General Transport
Parking Area
Petrol Station
Taxi Rank

Information
Bank, ATM
Embassy/Consulate
Hospital, Medical
Information
Internet Facilities
Police Station
Post Office, GPO
Telephone
Toilets
Geographic
Lighthouse
Lookout
Mountain, Volcano
National Park
Pass, Canyon
Picnic Area
River Flow
Waterfall

LONELY PLANET OFFICES

Australia
Head Office
Locked Bag 1, Footscray, Victoria 3011
☎ 03 8379 8000, fax 03 8379 8111
talk2us@lonelyplanet.com.au

USA
150 Linden St, Oakland, CA 94607
☎ 510 893 8555, toll free 800 275 8555
fax 510 893 8572
info@lonelyplanet.com

UK
2nd Floor, 186 City Road,
London ECV1 2NT
☎ 020 7106 2100, fax 020 7106 2101
go@lonelyplanet.co.uk

Published by Lonely Planet Publications Pty Ltd
ABN 36 005 607 983

© Lonely Planet Publications Pty Ltd 2008

© photographers as indicated 2008

Cover photograph: Clothes flapping in the Aegean Sea breeze, Imerovigli, Santorini (Thira), Greece © Robert Leon / www .robertleon.com. Many of the images in this guide are available for licensing from Lonely Planet Images: www.lonelyplanetimages.com.